Priscilla Anderson
1649 W. Juneway Ter. Apt. G
Chicago, IL 60626

The Complete Guide
To Special Interest Videos

1993 - 1994 Edition

More Than 9,000 Videos
You've Never Seen Before

By
James R. Spencer

Second edition, completely revised

JR | **JAMES-ROBERT**
P | **PUBLISHING**

SCOTTSDALE, ARIZONA

The Complete Guide To Special Interest Videos
More Than 9,000 Videos You've Never Seen Before

By James R. Spencer

Acknowledgment is due to the following:

Karen Carey, David Dotson, Kathy Haukkala, Sam Mongeau, Brent Moseley, Margaret Schmidt and Arlene Spencer.

With Special Thanks To: Marjie Marengo and Lynn Abbott.

All rights reserved. No part of this book may be reproduced or transmitted in any form or by any means, electronic or mechanical, including photocopying, recording or by any information storage and retrieval system without written permission from the author.

Copyright © 1990, 1992 and 1993 by James R. Spencer
First Printing 1990
Second Printing 1992
Third Printing 1993, completely revised
Printed in the United States of America

Publisher's Cataloging in Publication

Spencer, James R.
     The Complete Guide To Special Interest Videos: More Than 9,000
Videos You've Never Seen Before / James R. Spencer. — 2nd ed.
     p. cm
     Includes index.
     Preassigned LCCN: 90-92008.
     ISBN 0-9627836-1-7
     1. Video recordings — United States — Catalogs. 2. Video
recordings — United States — Reviews. I. Spencer, James R. II.
Title.

PN1992.95.S54 1993   016.79143

Knowledge is of two kinds.
We know a subject ourselves,
or we know where we can find information upon it.

Dr. Samuel Johnson
(1709 - 1784) English Author

About This Guide

The first edition of this **Guide** was printed in 1991. In just two years, more than 3,000 new how-to and special interest video titles have been added. Unfortunately, about 1,000 titles have been deleted because they are no longer available from the producer or distributor. We have attempted to list those titles which are currently available to the general public and those which are affordably priced.

We believe this **Guide** to be an objective listing of videos which, at the time of this printing, are available from your local video store retailer, various mail order catalogs and through local specialty retail outlets. Should one of your selections become unavailable ask your video retailer or supplier to recommend a suitable alternative title.

If you have any difficulty locating the titles listed in this **Guide**, you may write to the publisher for assistance.

Pricing and availability on all video tapes are subject to change without notice.

Notice to Producers

We have made every effort to include the many special interest videos in general distribution as of the publication date. We apologize for any error or omission we may have made. If you are a producer or distributor and your titles are not included, please forgive our oversight. To be listed in the next edition of **The Complete Guide To Special Interest Videos**, please send pertinent information to the publisher.

JR | **JAMES-ROBERT**
P | **PUBLISHING**

15838 N. 62ND STREET, SUITE 107
SCOTTSDALE, ARIZONA 85254-1988
(602) 483-7007

Table of Contents

Academic Studies

- ✓ *Math Skills*
- ✓ *Science*
- ✓ *Verbal Skills*
- ✓ *Miscellaneous*

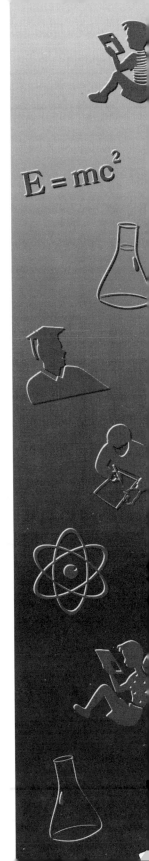

Math Skills

Algebra Basics for Beginners
Paves the way through the roadblocks to learning Algebra 1. Includes positive and negative integers, absolute value, order of operations, algebraic expressions and balancing equations.
01-154 60 min. $39.95

ACT Math Review
American College Testing Assessment.
01-095 110 min. $39.95

Basic Word Problems
Computer graphics and the unique electronic chalkboard complement instructor John Hall's lively and clear-cut explanations of basic mathematics.
01-8030 63 min. $29.95

Fractions Made Easy
An in-depth lesson about fractions. Includes equal fractions, addition, multiplication and division of fractions.
01-160 60 min. $39.95

GMAT Math Review
01-165 120 min. $39.95

GRE Math Review
01-167 120 min. $39.95

MATH TUTOR
These live action videos present comprehensive review lectures accompanied by colorful computer graphics, for grades 8-12 and college level.

- **Algebraic Terms and Operations**
01-145 42 min. $49.95

- **Factoring and Solving Quadratic Equations**
01-147 18 min. $49.95

- **Geometric Terms, Angles and Triangles, Circles**
01-150 24 min. $49.95

- **Introduction to Logic**
01-152 25 min. $49.95

- **Parallel Lines, Geometric Figures, the Parallelogram**
01-151 25 min. $49.95

- **Probability and Statistics**
01-153 27 min. $49.95

- **Solving Algebraic Equations of the First Degree and Inequalities**
01-146 42 min. $49.95

- **Solving Simultaneous Equations and Inequalities Geometrically**
01-148 23 min. $49.95

- **Verbal Problems and Trigonometry**
01-149 38 min. $49.95

MATHEMATICS FOR PRIMARY SERIES
Animated objects appear and disappear, mix and divide up, scurry about the screen, and line up in orderly rows to graphically illustrate the basic concepts of mathematics. This program is by Lawrence Levy and Alma Keating.

- **Addition**
01-8005 9 min. $49.95

- **Subtraction**
01-8006 8 min. $49.95

- **Multiplication**
01-8002 7 min. $49.95

- **Division**
01-8008 8 min. $49.95

INTERMEDIATE ALGEBRA SERIES

- **Properties of Real Numbers and Equations**
01-2913 100 min. $39.95

- **Graphing Equations and Linear Equations**
01-2914 100 min. $39.95

- **Systems of Equations and Quadratic Equations**
01-2915 100 min. $39.95

- **Polynomials, Functions and their Graphs**
01-2916 100 min. $39.95

• **Algebraic Fractions, Integer Exponents and Radicals**
01-2917 100 min. $39.95

• **Rational Exponents, Logarithms and Inequalities**
01-2918 100 min. $39.95

Metric Film
The metric film gives the history of metrics and the background of why the system is both logical and productive. The film is designed to lay to rest any fears students and teachers might have about the metric change over.
01-8062 15 min. $49.95

PRE-CALCULUS VIDEOTAPE SERIES

• **Volume 1**
The number system; inequalities and intervals; absolute value; exponents and radicals.
01-6716 60 min. $49.95

• **Volume 2**
Graphs in the coordinate plane; the distance formula; graphs and equations and circles in the plane.
01-6717 60 min. $49.95

• **Volume 3**
Functions; domain, range and graph of a function; graphic techniques; linear functions and graphs.
01-6718 60 min. $49.95

• **Volume 4**
The algebra of functions and composition; one-to-one functions and inverses.
01-6719 60 min. $49.95

• **Volume 5**
Quadratic functions; polynomial functions and graphs and graphing rational functions.
01-6720 60 min. $49.95

REAL LIFE MATH SERIES
This in depth review of fractions, decimals and percents includes charming skits that will make students learn and laugh.

Fractions

• **Introduction, definitions and illustrations.**
01-9942 20 min. $29.99

• **Equivalent fractions, comparing fractions and real-life examples.**
01-9943 20 min. $29.99

• **Addition and subtraction of fractions.**
01-9944 20 min. $29.99

• **Multiplication and division of fractions.**
01-9945 20 min. $29.99

Decimals

• **Introduction to decimals and operations.**
01-9946 20 min. $29.99

• **Decimals and fractions, conversions, ratios and proportions.**
01-9947 20 min. $29.99

• **Decimals in daily life, calculator and checkbook skills.**
01-9948 20 min. $29.99

Percents

• **Understanding and computing percents.**
01-9949 20 min. $29.99

• **Percents at home: budgets and rents**
01-9950 20 min. $29.99

• **Percents in home finance: interest and finance charges.**
01-9951 20 min. $29.99

• **Percents in taxes, auto leases and home mortgages.**
01-9952 20 min. $29.99

• **Percents in business: discounts, mark-ups and profits.**
01-9953 20 min. $29.99

Review of Arithmetic
01-163 120 min. $39.95

Review of Decimals
Intensive review of decimals, geared to elementary and middle school students.
01-2866 120 min. $39.95

Review of Differential Calculus
High school and college students, who may not be

math majors, will benefit from this intensive review of calculus. Two tape set.
01-2860 240 min. $79.95

Review of Elementary Algebra
(Four Tape Set)
Students will learn from this comprehensive review in ten easy lessons.
01-2859 440 min. $159.90

Review of Fractions
Elementary and middle school students who need a brush-up in fractions will benefit from this intensive review. Two Tape Set.
01-2865 240 min. $79.95

Review of Integral Calculus (Two Tape Set)
01-2861 240 min. $79.95

Review of Percent
Intensive review of percents, geared to elementary and middle school students.
01-2867 120 min. $39.95

Review of Probability
This review covers the standard topics of probability, designed for high school and college students. (Two tape set).
01-2862 240 min. $79.95

Review of Statistics
This review covers the major areas in statistics, designed for high school and college students. (Three tape set).
01-2863 240 min. $119.95

S.A.T. Score High (Math)
A practical in-depth seminar strategically designed to strip the SAT of its mystique. This video covers the necessary skills, methods, techniques, strategies and knowledge to prepare you for the SAT. The lessons are presented by an experienced SAT instructor.
01-161 60 min. $39.95

S.A.T.-P.S.A.T. Math Review
01-099 120 min. $39.95

Video Tutor: Decimals
Involves detailed explanation of addition, subtraction, multiplication, and division of decimals, including a variety of decimal word problems.
01-2137 63 min. $29.95

Video Tutor: Fractions
Color graphics introduce a thorough understanding of fractions. Student participation is required by use

of the companion workbook.
01-2138 98 min. $29.95

Video Tutor: Percents
A full program, using color graphics and an electronic chalkboard. Includes a companion student workbook.
01-2136 98 min. $29.95

Video Tutor: Pre-Algebra
The student is introduced to the basic concepts of algebra using non-threatening terminology, includes a companion workbook.
01-2139 95 min. $29.95

Vidisco: SAT - Math
This entertaining video uses humor to help ease students apprehension about taking the math portion of the SAT.
01-2972 113 min. $29.95

CALCULUS - SEMESTER I
At last--an easy effective way to study and master calculus. This series incorporates a variety of innovative techniques for helping students grasp the complexities of differential calculus.

• **Limits and Their Properties**
01-9961 35 min. $29.95

• **Differentiation, Part I**
01-9962 35 min. $29.95

• **Differentiation, Part II**
01-9963 35 min. $29.95

• **Application of Differentiation, Part I**
01-9964 35 min. $29.95

• **Application of Differentiation, Part II**
01-9965 35 min. $29.95

• **Application of Differentiation, Part III**
01-9966 35 min. $29.95

CALCULUS - SEMESTER II
Employing state of the art computer graphics and real life applications, this series is ideal for review of integrad calculus.

• **Integration, Part I**
01-9967 30 min. $29.99

• **Integration, Part II**
01-9968 30 min. $29.99

• **Transcendental Functions, Part I**
01-9969 30 min. $29.99

VIDEO TITLES LISTED IN THIS GUIDE ARE AVAILABLE FOR PURCHASE OR RENTAL. CONTACT YOUR LOCAL VIDEO STORE OR TELEPHONE (800) 383-8811

• **Transcendental Functions, Part II**
01-9970 30 min. $29.99

• **Applications of Integration**
01-9971 30 min. $29.99

• **Integration Techniques**
01-9972 30 min. $29.99

• **More Integration Techniques,
L'Hopital's Rule**
01-9973 30 min. $29.99

WELCOME TO ALGEBRA

Jack Wayne, an award winning teacher, provides a
unique and exciting approach to learning Algebra.
The viewer becomes a member of a study group
focusing on those specific areas of Algebra that
cause students the most difficulty. Real world
problems are used to motivate the discussion, and
over one hundred graphics allow the students to
"see" the concepts. Explanations are concise and to
the point, without using complicated vocabulary. A
workbook accompanies the program to provide
additional examples and explanations. The product
can be used to supplement the teacher in the
classroom, to provide independent study for the
student, or privately tutor the student at home.

• **Graphing Linear and Quadratic
Functions**
01-6238 40 min. $79.95

• **Solving Systems of Equations and
Equations**
01-6239 40 min. $79.95

Science

Adventures in Caves

Imagine walking into a cave which is 14 acres big.
That is the size of just one of the rooms in the
Carlsbad caverns. This program shows the
spectacular size and beauty that nature has
provided.
14-9448 30 min. $39.95

Alternative Energy Sources -
Geothermal, Wind and Water

Presented are methods for the derivation of energy
from the use of windmills, water power, the energy
to be derived from kelp farms and finally,

geothermal sources to harness our planet's energy.
01-001 30 min. $29.95

Ancient Man: Created or Evolved

The subject of the origin and history of mankind
has been a controversial issue that has triggered
heated debate between supporters of the two
opposing views--Creation and Evolution.
Join Roger Oakland as he examines both theories.
01-8094   61 min. $24.95

ANIMAL CONTRACT SERIES

Desmond Morris, author of The Naked Ape, takes
a timely look at the relationship between all the
animals that walk the earth. The Animal Contract is
a major science documentary.

• **Company of Animals**
01-8131 60 min. $99.95

• **Fair Game**
01-8132 60 min. $99.95

• **Man's Best Slaves**
01-8133 60 min. $99.95

Building Blocks of Life

Cell Structure I and II offer and exciting package
which anticipates tomorrow's headlines as it
examines the basic unit of life, the cell of which
there are an estimated 60 trillion in the human
body.
01-013 120 min. $74.95

Common Fossils of the United States

An introduction to the wide variety of fossils found
in the U.S. This program explores the age,
geologic range and environment for foraminifera,
corals, crinoids, bryozoans, sponges, brachiopods,
trilobites and vertebrates. Includes footage of the
famous dinosaur quarry at Dinosaur National
Monument. Grades 7-12.
01-6398 20 min. $53.95

Creation of the Universe

This is the ultimate detective story--the creation of
the universe. Award-winning journalist Timothy
Ferris takes viewers on a cosmic ride, from the Big
Bang 15 billion years ago, to the frontiers of
science today. Accompanied by an entertaining
musical score from popular composer Brian Eno.
Dazzling special effects and colorful computer
graphics make the mysteries of the universe highly
visual and understandable.
01-9989 92 min. $19.95

Death of the Dinosaur

Dinosaur extinction is a subject that seems to
fascinate just about everyone. This program
examines the mystery of dinosaur extinction by

VIDEO TITLES LISTED IN THIS GUIDE ARE AVAILABLE FOR PURCHASE
OR RENTAL. CONTACT YOUR LOCAL VIDEO STORE OR TELEPHONE (800) 383-8811

evaluating the observable evidence and comparing it with two opposite world views--creation or evolution.
01-8091 30 min. $29.95

Dinosaurs and Strange Creatures
An overview of dinosaurs, early mammals, and how some of the most unusual present day animals have evolved over millions of years. For ages 5-12.
01-2309 33 min. $16.95

Dinosaur, Dinosaurs, Dinosaurs
An exciting and fascinating journey into the world of dinosaurs. Mission: find the healing waters that will stop Gary from turning into a dinosaur!
01-1815 30 min. $14.95

Discovering Our Earth's Atmosphere
This program looks at the dynamic processes at work in the earth's atmosphere. Examples of meteorologic phenomena and rare footage of severe weather are combined with computer graphics that clearly explain the earth's fluid atmosphere, global climate winds, clouds, fronts and severe weather. Particular attention is paid to current topics in meteorology including interviews with weather experts that focus on the latest technology in forecasting and on man's impact on our changing global climate. Full motion.
01-6293 30 min. $87.95

Discovering Our Planet Earth
This program offers an exciting introduction to any earth science course. Four separate segments provide overviews to the introductory units found in leading earth science texts. The segments include Plate Tectonics, Locating Places on the Earth, Rocks and Minerals and Earth History. Grades 7-12.
01-6390 35 min. $87.95

Discovering Our Rivers, Lakes and Oceans
This program combines an introduction to oceanography with an overview of earth's fresh water and a tour through the hydrologic cycle. In the oceanography segment, topics explored include ocean basins, seamounts, trenches, tides and currents. The fresh water segment examines water resources contained in rivers, glaciers, lakes and reservoirs. The segment on the hydrologic cycle utilizes computer graphics and actual footage to portray each step in this critical process. Throughout the program, interviews with scientists underscore the need for humans to use all of their water resources wisely. Grades 7-12.
01-6392 30 min. $87.95

Discovering Our Universe
This program provides a comprehensive overview of the science of astronomy. Colorful computer graphics are utilized to demonstrate information about the earth, the moon, our solar system and the universe. Exciting photographs and film footage from NASA highlights segments on man's achievements in space shuttle missions. The program also focuses on ground based explorers-the men and women astronomers that are charting the heavens and fulfilling the quest to find life in the universe. Grades 7-12.
01-6394 30 min. $87.95

Discovering The Changing Surface of our Earth
This program combines exciting on-location footage of the geologic processes that change the earth's surface with computer graphics that clearly explain the forces at work. The program is divided into two segments: Building Up the Land and Wearing Down the Land. In Building Up the Land, topics include faulting, folding, earthquakes and volcanoes. The Wearing Down the Land segment explores physical and chemical weathering and erosion by rivers, glaciers and the wind. This program also includes information on how we are learning to predict and control the natural disasters that result from building up and wearing down forces. Grades 7-12.
01-6391 30 min. $87.95

Earthquakes
This program focuses on the causes and effects of movement within the earth. Faults, fractures, epicenters and primary and secondary waves are all discussed and illustrated. The use of seismographic equipment is also explored. Grades 7-12
01-6395 20 min. $53.95

Earth Science: Continents Adrift
Through animation and live action, the film examines paleomagnetism, sea-floor spreading, magnetism in rock and the drifting magnetic poles to illustrate the continental drift. Tomorrow's quake through live-action and animation, the film explores: continental drift, dilatency, plate tectonics, earthquake waves, seismic velocity changes, tiltmeters...and much more. The exciting conclusion shows motion pictures of an actual earthquake-one that was predicted.
01-107 30 min. $39.95

Evolution - Fact or Fiction
Roger Oakland examines the theory of evolution.
01-8094 61 min. $24.95

Evidence for Creation
The subject of origins has been a controversial issue that has triggered heated debate between supporters of the two opposing views...Creation and Evolution. Roger Oakland examines these two

theories in an attempt to understand which model is correct.
01-8092 60 min. $24.95

Expansion of Life

This videotape starts with the basics of single-cell life and moves on to invertebrates, fishes, amphibians and reptiles, and then takes the viewer up the evolutionary ladder to primates and the emergence of mankind. Here is a fascinating study encompassing most of the zoological sciences.
01-014 120 min. $74.95

Faulting and Folding

This program explores the processes that result in the faulting and folding of the Earth's crust. Recent footage from the California Earthquake of 1989 is used to illustrate one of the ways that faults and folds affect humans. The combination of full-motion footage and computer graphics provides vivid explanations for the often difficult concepts of faulting and folding. The Teacher's Guide includes a glossary, discussion questions and class activities. Grades 7-12.
01-6399 15 min. $53.95

Forces of Life

A four-part study of the essential properties which make up our physical universe. Considered tn turn are the origin of the elements, chemical change, origin of rocks and mountains and the dynamics of magnetism and electricity. This videotape represents a primer for physical science studies.
01-016 120 min. $74.95

Forces That Shape Our Earth

This program looks at the major causes of landforms on the earth. This looks at the various forces which shape our land--namely glaciers, volcanoes, wind, gravity, lakes and oceans.
14-9449 30 min. $69.95

GEOGRAPHY TUTOR SERIES

This series addresses critical areas of geographic knowledge that have been defined as problem areas for students. Written and designed by Beth Kirk, designated the State of Florida Geography Teacher of the year.

• **Map & Globe Terms**
01-8056 18 min. $49.95

• **Types of Maps & Map Projections**
01-8057 18 min. $49.95

• **Map Skills**
01-8058 18 min. $49.95

• **Earth's Physical Features**
01-8059 18 min. $49.95

• **Weather and Climate**
01-8060 18 min. $49.95

• **Global Problems and Issues**
01-8061 18 min. $49.95

Geomorphology: A Study of the Shape of the Land

An illustrated introduction to the landforms that make up our earth. The landforms have been created by one or more of the following processes: wind, running water, glaciation, volcanism, gravity, ocean action, faulting and folding. Examples of landforms created by each of these processes are shown and explained. Grades 7-12.
01-6402 28 min. $53.95

Geysers and Hot Springs

Filmed at Yellowstone National Park, this program examines the processes that form geysers and hot springs. Animation explains the physics of geysers including the relationship of ground water and a heat source to the regularity of eruptions. Grades 7-12.
01-6396 20 min. $53.95

Greenhouse Effect

This program looks at the debate now concerning scientists all over the world: Are humans beginning to turn up the global thermostat through the combustion of fossil fuels, deforestation of rain forests and inefficient agricultural practices? The causes and effects of global warming are explored as well as the use of computer modeling to predict earth's changing climate. A Teacher's Guide includes a glossary, discussion questions and class activities.
01-6406 17 min. $59.95

How to Start a Rock Collection

Filmed as a semi-documentary, the video follows a scientist as he takes a youngster on a rock and mineral hunt in such common places as a crushed rock, walkway, pond shoreline, city construction site and roadside cliff. The student is shown how to use a pick hammer, goggles, a magnifying glass and other rock-collecting tools. After the field trip, the geologist and child study the rocks and the specimens are numbered, identified and properly recorded.
13-448 51 min. $69.95

INFINITE VOYAGE SERIES

• **Champion Within**
Using athletes as living laboratories, scientists

---

reveal important discoveries about the amazing adaptive abilities of the human body.
01-8064 60 min. $29.98

• **Life in the Balance**
Conservationists study the looming environmental crisis and reveal how twentieth-century man is altering evolution on our planet.
01-8065 60 min. $29.98

• **To the Edge of the Earth**
From the frozen Arctic to a Costa Rican jungle, a globe-spanning expedition to places seldom if ever seen by human eyes.
01-8066 60 min. $29.98

Introduction To Rocks and Minerals
Look at the characteristics used to identify common rocks and minerals. The physical properties of minerals including hardness, luster and color are discussed, as well as the chemical compositions of important rock-forming minerals. Grades 7-12.
01-6404 20 min. $53.95

Invention
Investigate the great innovations that have altered our world, from sophisticated devices like the computer chip to simple gadgets like the mouse trap. Share the behind-the-scenes stories of enterprising individuals whose tenacity and ingenuity stimulate creativity in all of us.
A three volume set.
01-8093 300 min. $59.95

Journey to the Desert
All major deserts are located on the globe and an explanation is given as to why they exist. The desert insects and reptiles are studied as well as the large amount of different plant life.
14-9447 30 min. $29.95

LEARNING ABOUT SCIENCE SERIES
The basic principles of physical science are introduced in this series of seven programs. Experiments and demonstrations performed by kids give form to concepts and stimulate further investigation. Key words are superimposed on screen, serving to emphasize important concepts and expand youngster's reading vocabularies.

• **Learning About Air**
01-8021 11 min. $49.95

• **Learning About Light**
01-8022 11 min. $49.95

• **Learning About Liquids, Solids and Gasses**
01-8023 11 min. $49.95

• **Learning About Sound**
01-8024 8 min. $49.95

• **Learning About Water**
01-8025 12 min. $49.95

• **Learning About Solar Energy**
01-8026 12 min. $49.95

• **Learning About Electricity**
01-8027 16 min. $49.95

Life on Earth
A natural history written and hosted by David Attenborough, this is a magnificent, comprehensive video encyclopedia of the marvels of nature and the secrets of evolution. Based on the acclaimed television series and its best-selling companion book.
01-171 233 min. $39.95

MAKING OF MANKIND SERIES
Richard Leakey traces the origin of the species in this yet-to-be-equalled BBC production. From the fossil beds in East Africa, where Leakey himself made breakthrough discoveries, to toolmakers who walked upright. The aggression of the killer apes and the sensitivity of the caveman placing flowers beside a grave come together to form our legacy as a species.

• **In the Beginning**
01-8135 55 min. $99.95

• **One Small Step**
01-8136 55 min. $99.95

• **Human Way of Life**
01-8137 55 min. $99.95

• **Beyond Africa**
01-8138 55 min. $99.95

• **New Era**
01-8139 55 min. $99.95

• **Settling Down**
01-8140 55 min. $99.95

• **Survival of the Species**
01-8141 55 min. $99.95

• **Complete Set**
01-8142 420 min. $395.00

Miracle of Life
One of the most lauded, spectacularly successful shows in the PBS Nova series now on

videocassette. This program presents a fascinating look at the microscopic beginnings of human reproduction, and culminates in the birth of a baby. An extraordinary film and an excellent way to present the facts of reproduction to children and adolescents, as well as providing relevant information for pregnant women and their families.
01-104   60 min. $24.95

MIRACLE PLANET SERIES
This landmark PBS series is unique, combining American scientific theory with a Japanese sense of look and vision. Narrated by Bill Kurtis.

• **Third World**
01-8123   60 min. $99.95

• **Heat Within**
01-8124   60 min. $99.95

• **Life From the Sea**
01-8125   60 min. $99.95

• **Patterns in the Air**
01-8126   60 min. $99.95

• **Riddles of Sand and Ice**
01-8127   60 min. $99.95

• **Home Planet**
01-8128   60 min. $99.95

More Dinosaurs
The entire family is invited to journey back millions of years to help find those mysterious and incredible giants of the past dinosaurs. Travel the globe on this magical tour and discover how these fascinating creatures lived, what they were really like and ideas about why they vanished.
10-493   30 min. $14.95

Mount St. Helens; What Geologists Learned
This program incorporates excellent footage of the eruption of Mt. St. Helens and subsequent eruptions in exploring the causes of volcanism. Also featured are interviews with geologists who explain what new knowledge has been gained from the studies of the Mt. St. Helens eruption. Grades 9-12.
01-6405   40 min. $74.95

National Geographic: Born Of Fire
Travel to Iceland, Africa, Japan, California and Greece to record how the huge plates of the earth's crust crash together pull apart and override each other causing ground-shattering earthquakes and volcanic eruptions. Follow scientists on their search for clues as to the causes of these powerful geologic events.
13-460   60 min. $29.95

National Geographic: The Incredible Human Machine
Explore the fascinating, microscopic universe that exists within us all as National Geographic takes viewers on a truly fantastic journey through the internal world of the human body.
13-256   60 min. $29.95

Nature's Systems
With narration by Leonard Nimoy, Margaret O'Brien and William Shatner, this program examines the delicate balance of plant and animal life with their environments. For ages 5-12.
01-2310   30 min. $14.95

NEWTON'S APPLE SERIES
You may not have all the answers, but this delightful Emmy award-winning PBS series does. It's a funny, fastpaced, magazine-style kid's eye view of the world of science that children find irresistible.

• **Artificial Hearts, Penguins, Fire, Lie Detectors, Golf Balls, Hiccups, Cold Remedies**
01-8047   20 min. $16.95

• **Plastic Surgery, Tornadoes, Hi-Speed Bicycles, Beaches, Laryngitis, Vision, Sick Whales**
01-8048   20 min. $16.95

• **Boomerangs, Muscles & Bones, Cooking Chemistry, Stars, Einstein, Bears**
01-8049   20 min. $16.95

• **Dinosaurs, Bullet-Proof Glass, Whales, Sharks, Comets, Warts, Heartburn**
01-8050   20 min. $16.95

• **Skiing, Blimps, Beavers, Falcons, Dreams, Polarized Light, Baseball Bats, Inventor's Fair**
01-8051   20 min. $16.95

• **Mummies, Bicycles, Tigers, Helium, Owls, Sports Clinic, Radioactivity, Acne**
01-8052   20 min. $16.95

NOVA: ADVENTURE AND DISCOVERY SERIES

VIDEO TITLES LISTED IN THIS GUIDE ARE AVAILABLE FOR PURCHASE OR RENTAL. CONTACT YOUR LOCAL VIDEO STORE OR TELEPHONE (800) 383-8811

• **Ancient Treasures From the Deep**
This tape presents the incredible story of a
centuries old shipwreck.
01-8079 35 min. $19.98

• **Bermuda Triangle**
Uncovering the mystery of a watery graveyard.
01-8080 35 min. $19.98

• **UFO's: Are We Alone?**
The truth behind UFO sightings.
01-8081 35 min. $19.98

• **One Small Step**
Man's awe-inspiring voyage to the "last frontier",
the moon.
01-8082 35 min. $19.98

• **Hitler's Secret Weapon**
A frightning look at the deadliest weapon in
Hitler's arsenal.
01-8085 35 min. $19.98

• **Wonders of Plastic Surgery**
The "life-saving" techniques of medicine's miracle
workers.
01-8084 35 min. $19.98

Nova: Case of the Flying Dinosaur
Explores the contradictory findings of scientists
whose theories lead to the determination that birds
are desendants of dinosaurs.
01-8078 35 min. $19.98

NOVA: DISASTERS

• **Earthquake**
An in-depth account of possible future predictions
of the world's most frightning natural occurence.
14-8070 40 min. $19.98

• **Predictable Disaster**
The shaky science of predicting earthquakes is
explored in this program.
14-8071 40 min. $19.98

• **Yellowstone's Burning Question**
Explore the most extensive forest fire in human
history.
14-8072 40 min. $19.98

• **Back to Chernobyl**
A shocking account of the world's worst nuclear
accident.
14-8073 40 min. $19.98

NOVA: HUMAN NATURE SERIES

• **Fat Chance in a Thin World**
A look at why your diet doesn't work.
01-8085 35 min. $19.98

• **Secret of the Sexes**
A look at the sex roles we teach our children.
01-8086 35 min. $19.98

• **Einstein**
The private thoughts of a public genius.
01-8087 35 min. $19.98

• **Baby Talk**
The remarkable journey from infant cries to adult
speech.
01-8088 35 min. $19.98

NOVA: SCIENCE AND INDUSTRY

• **Science of Murder**
Death is their jobs--met America's medical
detectives.
01-8071 35 min. $19.98

• **Shape of Things**
A fascinating look at nature's perfect designs.
01-8072 35 min. $19.98

• **War From the Air**
Bombs: The creation--and destruction--of the
ultimate weapon.
01-8073 35 min. $19.98

• **Echoes of War**
The revealing inside story of World War II's top
secret technology: radar.
01-8074 35 min. $19.98

• **Will Venice Survive Its Rescue?**
Witness the controversial effort to save the
romantic "City of Canals".
01-8075 35 min. $19.98

• **Saving the Sistine Chapel**
The controversial restoration of a masterpiece.
01-8076 35 min. $19.98

• **Disguises of War**
The art of deception and the science of stealth.
01-8077 35 min. $19.98

Origins of Life
Evolution and the beginning of life, starting with
Darwinian theory and illustrating the different
stages of animal and human development from the
beginnings of fossil history on earth. As
background for the continuing controversy over
how to teach evolutionary theory, see actual

footage of the famous Scopes trial with Clarence Darrow and William Jennings Bryant.
01-023 120 min. $64.95

Physical Science: Anti-Matter

Fun...animation...imagination...reversed time...creation of the universe...strange phenomena...Is there an anti-earth existing somewhere in space? Scientists have pondered the existence of whole anti-galaxies...This exciting animated film discusses the possibility that large quantities of anti-matter are existing in space, the significance of the Tunguska Meter in relation to the annihilation process (the result of matter and anti-matter colliding)and explores the possibility of constructive use of energy released from annihilation. Gravity Waves This film is a study of the men, techniques and scientific methods used in searching for gravity waves. In many ways the theory and resulting equipment is analogous to the beginnings of astronomy...Through animation live-action, and interviews with Drs. Weber, Ruffini and Fairbanks, and with clear descriptions and views of their laboratory settings, the audience will learn more about this century's most exciting search.
01-108   27 min. $39.95

Planets of the Sun with Leonard Nimoy

This program is an exciting and up-to-date treatment of the basic concepts regarding our solar system for all ages.
01-024 26 min. $16.95

Plate Tectonics: The Puzzle of the Continents

This program explores the fundamentals of the Plate Tectonics Theory for Alfred Wegener's observations on continental drift the latest computer analysis of movements at plate boundaries. The different types of crustal motions and plate boundaries are illustrated through exciting on-location footage and computer generated graphics. The Teacher's Guide includes a glossary, discussion questions and class activities.
01-6407 15 min. $59.95

PORTRAIT OF AMERICA SERIES

• Northern California

This covers the various cultures and the history of the gold rush era.
01-8145 60 min. $99.95

• South Dakota

In this program you will visit the Sioux reservations and observe their values, as well as see the activities of farm families.
01-8146 60 min. $99.95

• New Hampshire

You'll explore the freedom, responsibility, home rule, and the lifestyle of the people whose motto is "Live Free or Die!"
01-8147 60 min. $99.95

• Oklahoma

This video covers the land rush of 1889 and the ranching and lure of Oklahoma country.
01-8148 60 min. $99.95

• North Carolina
01-8149 60 min. $99.95

Raining Water: From Rain to River to Ocean

An introduction to the hydrologic process including laminar, turbulent and shooting flow; waterfalls and floods. Also includes the relationship between velocity, gradient, discharge and the type of stream that occurs. Grades 7-12.
01-6397 20 min. $53.95

Running Water: Erosion, Deposition and Transportation

This program explores the relationship of running water to the land. Concepts investigated include suspension, solution, load, rapids, meanders and deltas. Also illustrated are the characteristics of youthful, mature and old streams. Grades 7-12.
01-6401 20 min. $53.95

Science and Technology: Lasers

Twenty years ago, scientists invented a new sort of light lasers. Now, as its breathtaking potential for visual entertainment is being realized, the laser is rapidly establishing itself as the world's most versatile industrial tool. As lasers develop their uses become more sophisticated; this program explores the widening world of the laser...holograms. Imagine a three-dimensional picture emerging from a two-dimensional glass plate. An optical illusion, yet utterly real...hologram. This beautiful new type of imagery is a form of photography which makes use of the very special nature of laser light. But holograms are much more than photographs with an extra dimension: their extraordinary properties will make them the basis of a completely new art form, and lead to a series of powerful new industrial techniques.
01-109 30 min. $39.95

Science Discovery for Children

Simple and fascinating science projects that can be done at home using materials readily available around the house. Designed to stimulate interest and excitement about science.
01-058 42 min. $29.95

SHAPE OF THE WORLD SERIES

This major production from PBS and IBM provides an interdisciplinary series, aimed at science and social studies instruction. Beginning with ancient European, African, Egyptian and Asian civilizations, the story moves through time to today, and the minute mapping of the DNA in our bodies.

• **Heaven & Earth**
01-8104 60 min. $99.95

• **Secrets of the Sea**
01-8105 60 min. $99.95

• **Staking a Claim**
01-8106 60 min. $99.95

• **Empire**
01-8107 60 min. $99.95

• **Pictures of the Invisible**
01-8108 60 min. $99.95

• **Writing on the Screen**
01-8109 60 min. $99.95

Solar Energy-Hope for the Future

A comprehensive look at how mankind's perception and use of the sun's energy has developed and matured. The program guides the viewer from the history of solar use to the possible political and environmental implications. Observe a solar-powered office in operation.
01-028 30 min. $29.95

Space

A chronicle of pre-20th century rocketry and visions of space travel showing that rockets date from the 13th century, when a Chinese scholar tied them to a chair, hoping to ride to the moon. For ages 5-12.
04-2313 30 min. $14.95

Story of America's: Great Volcanoes

Always threatening...always on the horizon...Native Americans called them "fire mountains"; we call them volcanoes. The amazing exploration of the awesome power that looms within these brooding mountains. Included are: Mt. St. Helens, Mt. Rainer, Sunset Crater, Craters of the Moon and many others that make up America's great volcanoes.
01-8045 56 min. $29.95

Under the Sea

Underwater cameras reveal the colorful and a variety of life amidst shallow reefs. For ages 5-12.
01-2312 30 min. $14.95

Universe with William Shatner

An incredible journey through our solar system, outward to the Milky Way Galaxy and beyond, narrated by Star Trek Captain William Shatner. Includes theories about the evolution of the universe, black holes, pulsars and more.
04-070 30 min. $29.95

Universe

A comprehensive survey of what we know today about our solar system and the seemingly infinite number of other systems and galaxies in universal space and time.
01-030 55 min. $64.95

Missions To: Jupiter, Uranus, Saturn, and Neptune

This is a world whose features exceeded our wildest expectations. Ancient moons with 16-mile high cliffs and surface temperatures 300 degrees below zero. A world with a watery core, tipped on its side. The geology, the weather, the moons the magnetic fields-even the operation of Voyager 2 are all explored by your host, Jet propulsion Laboratory scientist, Dr. Albert Hibbs.
01-1707 29 min. $39.95

VOLCANO SCAPES SERIES

This award winning series is photographed and written by Emmy Award Winner Mick Kalber. The series is narrated by Floyd Kalber and was scored by Bob Kindler.

• **Volume I**
This documentary captures the splendor of Hawaii's Kilauea, the world's most active volcano!
01-8035 40 min. $29.95

• **Volume II**
Go underwater and witness ocean explosions and boiling lava lakes.
01-8036 39 min. $29.95

• **Volume III**
Witness the slavation and the destruction of those who live near the Kilauea volcano.
01-8037 50 min. $29.95

Volcanoes of The United States

This comprehensive program takes the students to the regions of the United States where volcanic activity has been most concentrated. Footage includes Kilauea and Mauna Loa in Hawaii, Mt. St. Helens, Mt Shasta, Mt. Mazama and Katmai in Alaska. Grades 7-12.
01-6403 20 min. $53.95

Waves, Shorelines and Beaches

This live-action program deals with geological processes which take place where ocean meets land.

In addition, graphics and animation takes you below the water's surface to show you what is taking place just offshore, under water.
14-9450 30 min. $39.95

Weather
How the forces of nature interact to create our weather is discussed. Exciting insight into the forces at work in our atmosphere. For ages 5-12
01-2311 30 min. $14.95

WEATHER: AIR IN ACTION SERIES
These three programs give facts and information about weather that are vital to an understanding of our planet. Produced in collaboration with the U.S. Weather Bureau. For Intermediate-Junior High.

• **Temperature and Wind**
01-8009 8 min. $49.95

• **Pressure and Humidity**
01-8010 10 min. $49.95

• **Fronts and Storms**
01-8011 11 min. $49.95

Weathering and Erosion
This program explores how the surface of the earth is in constant struggle with the elements of nature. Wind, water, gravity, temperature and chemical reactions all break down rock formations to form soils, river deposits and dunes. Examples of each processes and landforms they produce are depicted. Grades 8-12.
01-6400 20 min. $54.95

What is Geology?
An overview of the science of geology, the study of the earth.
04-9446 30 min. $29.95

WORLD GEOGRAPHY SERIES
Understanding geography brings us to better understanding of the Earth's past, present and future. This series will help the viewer learn more about Continents, Countries, States, Provinces and more.

• **Understanding World Geography Using Maps and Globes**
01-8038 30 min. $24.95

• **Northeastern United States**
01-8039 30 min. $24.95

• **Southern United States**
01-8040 30 min. $24.95

• **North Central United States**
01-8041 30 min. $24.95

• **Western United States**
01-8042 30 min. $24.95

• **Australia/New Zealand**
01-8043 30 min. $24.95

Verbal Skills

ACT Verbal Review
American College Testing Assessment.
01-096 105 min. $39.95

Basic English Grammar by Video
A two-phased approach to human communication. Begins with a psychological review based on research on language acquisition. The second tape (Language in Life) provides an entertaining and stimulating study of the basic units of speech using a Buster Keaton-type actor.
01-038 60 min. $74.95

English Grammar I
Sentence types, parts of speech and punctuation. Ideal for those who need the basics of sentence writing.
01-156 60 min. $39.95

English: Basic Composition
Focuses on improving writing skills through practical and creative application of grammar of organization. It begins with the development of a single idea using the topic sentence and supporting sentence to make up one paragraph.
01-157 60 min. $39.95

FOREIGN LANGUAGE VIDEO DIALOGUES:

• **Spanish 5-part Set**
These videos were taped in and around Zaragosa in Aragon, Spain. Sequences are arranged by topic, with no progression in the level of difficulty.
01-8100 100 min. $295.00

• **French 10-part Set**
For beginners, these videos were recorded in and around Normandy and Caen, where the local inhabitants are seen at home, at work and out in their natural surroundings.
01-8101 200 min. $495.00

VIDEO TITLES LISTED IN THIS GUIDE ARE AVAILABLE FOR PURCHASE OR RENTAL. CONTACT YOUR LOCAL VIDEO STORE OR TELEPHONE (800) 383-8811

• French Advanced 10-part Set
This is aimed at third year French students.
01-8102 200 min. $495.00

• German 5-part Set
Each scene in this series has been chosen to provide practice in topics useful to travelers. Participants are various West German people, engaged in conversation.
01-8103 100 min. $295.00

GMAT Verbal Review
01-166 120 min. $39.95

GRE Verbal Review
01-168 120 min. $39.95

Language in Life
This videotape is a two-phased approach to the problems of human communications. Part I, (Basic English Grammar by Video) starts with a psychological approach based on recent studies in language acquisition patterns. Part II provides an entertaining and stimulating study of the basic units of speech: nouns and adjectives, verbs and adverbs, using Buster Keaton-type actors.
01-020 120 min. $64.95

Romance of Promise: Modern Poetry
This video showcases the poetry of Jean and Veryl Rosenbaum against a background of original music and the great outdoors. The poets recite their own works, and viewers are able to appreciate the sounds of the words while feasting their eyes on beautiful scenery. Includes booklet of written poetry.
01-8130 20 min. $24.95

S.A.T. Score High (Verbal)
A practical in-depth seminar strategically designed to strip the SAT mystique. This video covers the skills, methods, techniques strategies and knowledge to prepare you for the SAT. Lessons are presented by an experienced SAT instructor.
01-162 60 min. $29.95

Speak to Me
This is a fast and easy way to learn English. The combination of seeing the live image, hearing the spoken word, reading the written word, and, most importantly, speaking to your video instructor powerfully locks the language into memory.
01-8032 90 min. $199.00

SPEED READING SERIES
With the surprisingly simple techniques in this video program (and a little practice), you can get through your daily reading in a fraction of the time it used to take. This program also includes a 48-page workbook and a 90-minute audiocassette

"drill" tape. Anyone can learn to increase their reading skills with Steve Moidel's speed-reading techniques.

• Volume I
Learn the mechanics of speed reading and the drills that make higher speeds seem normal.
01-8004 88 min. $99.95

• Volume II
Learn advanced methods of speed reading and learn how to take in whole pages at a time.
01-8005 88 min. $99.95

Speed Reading Hand
Turn your hand into a super speed reading machine and read two to five times faster with better concentration, comprehension and recall after only a few short hours. Includes an informative instruction booklet.
01-068 60 min. $19.95

Super Speller Strategy
This program was designed with families in mind--the emphasis is on stress free learning. Created by Pat Mavredakis, M.A., a highly successful reading and learning specialist, this program makes learning to spell faster, easier and more fun!
01-8034 30 min. $29.95

SAT-PSAT Verbal Review
01-100 105 min. $39.95

Vidisco: SAT-Verbal
This entertaining video helps students overcome uncertainty about test questions on the verbal portion of the SAT.
01-2971 116 min. $39.95

Miscellaneous

Citizenship: U.S. History and Government
Ideal for learning basic U.S. history necessary to pass the U.S. citizenship test. Covers exploration, the Colonies, American Revolution, Declaration of Independence and the Constitution.
01-155 90 min. $39.95

Civil Service Exams
Federal, state, city and private employment.
01-097 120 min. $39.95

College Admission & Financial Aid Video

This fact-filled video is essential to any student or parent needing information on being admitted to or paying for college. This video features the on-camera expertise of admissions officers and counselors from Columbia University, University of California/Berkeley, University of Arizona, Loyola Marymount University, San Diego State University and Iowa State University. Viewers are informed on the admissions process, how to take entrance exams and what goes into choosing the right college and major. Also how to gain acceptance at the college of one's choice and everything you need to know about where to seek financial aid.

01-5349 60 min. $29.95

Complete College Admissions Financial Aid Kit

This deluxe kit contains it all-the College Admissions & Financial Aid Video, the College Admissions Planner & Organizer System, the Financial Aid Planner & Organizer System plus the specially designed College Admissions & Financial Aid Binder. Application preparation, entrance exams, college selection, letters of recommendation, essays, scholarships, grants and loans are all covered in this handsome boxed set of invaluable organizational tools.

01-5354 60 min. $49.95

College Success Video

This innovative program is designed to give you the insight and skills necessary to excel in college and get a "head start" on success in life. Features tips on time management, study habits, note taking, planning your schedule, preparing for and taking test, and much more.

01-1919 70 min. $39.95

Effective Study Strategies

Students in grades 7-12 will learn how to take notes from a lecture and written material, how to pre-read non-fiction and fiction, and how to improve comprehension and retention. Book included.

01-2213 58 min. $39.95

Elements of Style with Book

Host Charles Osgood presents an extensive amount of practical information in his own distinctive relaxed style. Utilizing the latest technology, this program gives you the basic elements of good writing in a clear and contemporary way.

01-9479 112 min. $29.99

Everything You Always Wanted To Know About Being The Perfect Student (But Were Afraid to Ask)

Comic quizmaster Ken Ober and student guides Joe and Jenny College lead you on the fantastic and sometimes funny voyage otherwise known as college life. Your fearless leaders will inform and entertain as they tell you everything you want to know about being the perfect college student. Plus they'll give special emphasis to those aspects involving the transition from high school to the university campus. This tape will tell you about: registration, safe sex, deciding on a major, time management, doing laundry and computers.

01-5317 33 min. $29.95

Four Advanced Study Skills

You will learn how to: quickly get the main ideas from any chapter in minutes. Learn effective reading and remember paragraphs. Charge your mind so that important information appears to fly off the page. And learn to use your four powerful memory tools to enable you to remember facts, concepts and numbers quickly.

01-8000 25 min. $29.95

GED

High school equivalency exam.

01-098 120 min. $39.95

How to Choose the Best College For You

This video provides you with tips on choosing the college that best suits your academic needs.

01-2875 30 min. $39.95

Learn How to Learn

These are the building blocks of better grades that most kids have to pick up on their own: organization, time mangement, note-taking and many others. Join the five thousands schools and colleges throughout the country who use this program to give students the tools of school success.

01-8046 110 min. $89.95

Legal Research Made Easy: A Roadmap Through the Law Library Maze

Robert C. Berring, a noted professor and author of textbooks on legal research, successfully presents in this video the subject of legal research, and does so in a manner easily understood by a layman and nonprofessionals. Bob explains in his famous entertaining way how to understand and navigate through a law library. Includes a 40 page handbook.

01-9569 150 min. $89.95

MOVEABLE FEAST SERIES: PROFILES OF AMERICAN CONTEMPORARY AUTHORS

Seen on Public Television stations, this program profiles contemporary American authors and their work in their environments that most influenced them. From the beaches of Hawaii to the streets of

VIDEO TITLES LISTED IN THIS GUIDE ARE AVAILABLE FOR PURCHASE OR RENTAL. CONTACT YOUR LOCAL VIDEO STORE OR TELEPHONE (800) 383-8811

New York, this unique collection presents interviews with, readings by, and documentary segments about some of the most vibrant voices in modern American literature. Hosted by Tom Vitale.

• **T. Corraghessan Boyle, "World's End"**
01-9071   30 min. $19.95

• **Trey Ellis with "Platitudes"**
01-9072   30 min. $19.95

• **Allen Ginsberg, "When the Muse Calls, Answer"**
01-9073   30 min. $19.95

• **Li-Young Lee, "Always A Rose"**
01-9074   30 min. $19.95

• **W.S. Merwin, "The Rain in the Trees"**
01-9075   30 min. $19.95

• **Joyce Carol Oats, "American Appetites"**
01-9076   30 min. $19.95

• **T.R. Pearson, "A Short History of a Small Place"**
01-9077   30 min. $19.95

• **Sonia Sanchez, "Wear the New Day Well"**
01-9078   30 min. $19.95

Rapid Review of the S.A.T.
Provides a quick review of a combination of math and verbal skills.
01-2874   90 min. $39.95

Reading Efficiency
Bill Cosby hosts this extremely motivating series designed for adults with a minimum eighth grade reading level. An excellent teacher, Cosby knows how to keep the viewer's interest while helping them achieve a noticeable improvement in their ability to read. A three tape set.
01-8095   96 min. $275.00

Review for the TOEFL (Test of English as a Foreign Language)
Preparation for foreign students taking the Test of English as a Foreign Language exam.
01-2031   120 min. $39.95

Review for Police Officer Exams
01-164   120 min. $39.95

S.A.T. Prep Video
This program helps you increase your test scores. Includes videotape, 70-page workbook and home viewing guide.
01-2212   120 min. $79.95

S.A.T. Prep Video: Math Edition
This video will help you overcome "freezing on the S.A.T.". Learn how to approach each question, use the study guide to schedule study time and then do the practice exercises.
01-2775   60 min. $19.95

S.A.T. Review
Improve your test-taking skills and confidence for those all-important, college entrance S.A.T. tests with this videotape. Sample tests and study packets are included. Review the verbal and math parts of the test, and conclude with ways to relieve anxiety and tension in order to excel on all aspects of the S.A.T.
01-027   120 min. $79.95

SCHOLASTIC APTITUDE TEST
A practical in depth seminar that is strategically designed to strip the S.A.T. of its mystique. Learn skills, methods, techniques, strategies and knowledge to score high and enter the University of your choice. Seminar teacher is an expert in this field. This video seminar also valuable for taking other type tests requiring similar preparation.

• **Verbal Part 1**
01-2776   60 min. $29.95

• **Verbal Part 2**
01-6635   60 min. $29.95

Secrets of Writing the College Admission Essay
A written essay is an important part of the college admission process. In this video, you will learn tips for s successful essay.
01-2868   60 min. $29.95

SUPERCAMP SUCCESS SERIES

• **Success Through Communications: Volume 1**
01-2738   30 min. $24.95

• **Success Through Communications: Volume 2**
01-2739   30 min. $24.95

• **Success Through Confidence**
This video shows how a group of teens learned how to reach their full potential by tackling one of the biggest challenges of their lives, a high ropes

course staged 60 feet in the air.
01-2741 30 min. $24.95

• **Success Through Motivation**
Learn why you are such a powerful person and
how you can be in charge of making it happen.
Discover how to boost you motivation to earn
better grades and learn more by acquiring the self-
confidence to succeed. For high school level.
01-2740 30 min. $24.95

• **Success Through Notetaking**
Learn how to take notes the way the brain stores
information through the art of mindmapping, a
visual method of recording data which is designed
to use the brain's natural way of thinking and
organizing thoughts.
01-2743 30 min. $24.95

• **Success Through Super Memory**
In this tape you'll learn three specific success
secrets used by top students to cut study time,
remember facts with ease, and get top grades. For
high school level.
01-2745 30 min. $24.95

• **Success Through Super Reading**
Improve reading performance by altering your
mental state through better posture, breathing,
concentration, and attitude. Reluctant readers will
find out how to make reading more fun. For high
school level.
01-2744 30 min. $24.95

• **Success Through Test Prep**
This video reveals a 15-step program designed to
help make big gains in test scores and confidence.
Discover methods for approaching and taking
different kinds of tests, from quizzes to mid-terms
and finals.
01-2742 30 min. $24.95

THERE'S AN "A" IN YOUR DAY
This program has been used by thousands of grade
school, high school, junior college, and universtiy
students across the country. Created by Professor
Darrel Montero of Arizona State University and
recommended by educators around the country.
You'll discover how to write an "A" term paper.
Get rid of math anxiety, cut your homework time,
improve your self-esteem and more!

• **Grade School Edition**
01-9566 122 min. $89.95

• **High School Edition**
01-9567 122 min. $89.95

• **College Edition**
01-9568 122 min. $89.95

Tour of the Library of Congress
Of the millions of visitors to the Library of
Congress each year, only a small number have the
opportunity to see the treasures in its enormous
collections and the many activities that take place
behind the scenes. Now everyone can have a close
up look at such things as the Gutenberg Bible, rare
photographs, maps, movies and prints. A short
history tells the story of how this grand institution
began in 1800.
01-8028 20 min. $24.95

**U.S. News College Guide: America's
Best Colleges**
An indispensable resource for parents and
prospective students. Features ranking of America's
top colleges, how to choose a college and pay for
it.
01-8070 45 min. $24.95

Using Your Library
Students will benefit from this refresher course in
learning to utilize resources available in a library.
01-2869 60 min. $39.95

Does Studying Make You a

Little Testy?

These Videos Can Help!

Video Titles Listed In This Guide Are Available For Purchase
Or Rental. Contact Your Local Video Store Or Telephone (800) 383-8811

New

Special Interest Video Titles

Become Available

Often.

Please Inquire

If A Title Or Subject

You Are Looking For

Is Not Listed.

Automotive

- ✓ *Auto Racing*
- ✓ *History & Collecting*
- ✓ *Maintenance*
- ✓ *Motorcycles & Off Road*
- ✓ *Miscellaneous*

Auto Racing

All American Crashes
What happens when Stock Car, Indy Car, Sprint Cars, and Oval Track Dirt Bike racers push themselves and their machines too fast, too far, and too ferociously? Watch as the best American driver's crash and burn in the most awesome racing action video ever!
30-5464 60 min. $39.95

Behind the Wheel with Jackie Stewart
Three-time world champion driver Jackie Stewart will teach you braking skills, proper acceleration techniques, quality cornering, driving finesse, safe and expert maneuvering, how to get into racing, and more.
30-636 60 min. $29.95

Bill Elliott: Racing Into History
Experience NASCAR racer Bill Elliott's exciting career from his burst onto the circuit in 1976 to his stunning 1988 Winston Cup Championship season. Host Benny Parsons gives you an intimate look at what makes this racer a champion, with behind the scenes conversation with Bill, his crew and his family, along with action footage of his incredible racing career.
30-5519 45 min. $14.95

Blast from the Past
Relive the heyday of drag racing with this modern day meet of dragsters, Hot Rods and muscle cars.
02-8001 30 min. $16.95

Crash Course in Racing
Hosted by A.J. Foyt, learn first hand how to be a more informed racing fan. See fourteen of the most dramatic crashes in NASCAR history.
30-8160 48 min. $16.95

Crash Fever
In the fever of determination to win, race car drivers and cyclists push themselves to the limit! At such times, accidents can--and often do--happen! This video assembles the most dramatic footage of crashes and smash-ups on one dramatic tape. You'll feel like you've got a front row seat for every gut-wrenching spill, wreck and crash! For thrills galore, Crash Fever is the ultimate video.
30-5443 36 min. $14.95

Crushers: Big Wheels
Born of the exhibition genre of the motorsports world, the Super Truck has emerged as the most popular of recreational vehicle extravagance. Based on the "bigger is badder" theory of motorivity, these colossal monster trucks stop at nothing to please a crowd. Standing anywhere from 7 to 20 feet tall, and sounding like thunder, the fire belching Crusher's favorite escapade is the thorough destruction of any vehicle fool enough to lay in its path! Wild entertainment for the entire family!
30-5440 60 min. $19.95

Danny Sullivan: A Man Apart
Get behind the wheel and experience the tension before the start of a race, then settle in the cockpit and endure the demands of speed. Hosted by Sam Posey.
02-8019 30 min. $16.95

Drag Racing
Funny Cars, Top Fuel Dragster and Super Gas class racers are highlighted on this program.
02-1982 30 min. $19.95

Driven by a Dream
In May 1983, Phil Parsons was almost killed after 14 flips, at 200 m.p.h. In 1988 he won at that very same track. Learn the triumphs one faces when breaking into the big time.
30-8161 28 min. $16.95

ESPN Presents Racing Tough
What does it take to become an auto-racing winner? ESPN's Benny Parsons knows. And Quaker State King Racing Buick driver Brett Bodine knows, too. But do YOU know? Benny and Brett take you on auto racing's toughest driving test as this interactive video challenges your knowledge of what drivers and crews do to make their machines faster than the competition.
30-5521 40 min. $14.95

Fantasy Cars
Now you can "test drive" four of the fastest, most expensive exotic sports cars ever made: Lamborghini Countach, 308 GTS Ferrari, Lotus Turbo Esprit, and Porsche 911 Turbo.
02-2241 30 min. $29.95

Indy Adventure
The joy and festivities of the 1964 Indianapolis 500 came to a screeching, fiery end when driver Dave MacDonald careened off a retaining wall. This video shows that horrifying moment, along with other vintage footage of what its like to be an Indy driver.
02-3059 30 min. $14.95

Legend of Big Daddy Don Garlits
Made-for-video documentary profiling the legendary three-time world champion of drag

racing. In interviews and film clips, Garlits relives his successes and the accidents that nearly cost him his life.
02-1949 60 min. $19.95

Legends at Speed: Ferrari
Shot on location at Nelson Ledges Road Course near Warren, Ohio, you'll see nine street Ferraris at their finest: being driven at speed!
02-2282 30 min. $39.95

Mastery of Motion
Get a feel for what motivates men to pursue a relentless quest for speed. Hosted by Sam Posey.
02-8018 30 min. $16.95

Meeting The Challenge
Five competitors in pursuit of the auto racing legacy of Carol Shelby. They come from different professions, yet they all share the desire to meet the challenge. The competitors are: John Crawford, marketing consultant; Graham Mcrae, professional auto racer; and Kal Showket, heating and air-conditioning contractor.
02-093 30 min. $29.95

Mud Warriors In Action
Top pro mudracers get down and dirty in heat after heat of mud racing competition. In the mud bog, success is measured differently according to vehicle classification. In the stock 4 x 4 class, the winner is determined by forward progress in the mud pit before "bogging" to a halt. The Hot Rod classes, which boast greater horsepower and creative design innovations, can usually succeed in crossing the 250 feet of murky obstacle and are thus judged by the time it takes to do so. Pitting man and machine against adversity, the Mud Bog is fast becoming one of America's most popular motorsports. A guaranteed crowd pleaser
30-5445 60 min. $19.95

Once Upon a Wheel
Superstar Paul Newman hosts this fast-paced, exciting program from trackside and shows his own skill on the track in his race car.
30-654 60 min. $39.95

Power Basics of Auto Racing
A step-by-step guide to road racing, street stock racing, and off-road racing, featuring Parnelli Jones. You will find a wealth of information on setting up your car to race and on driving to success.
02-032 78 min. $29.95

Quick and the Dead
Stacy Keach is joined by veteran drivers. Niki Lauda and Jackie Stewart in an exciting look at the world's most dangerous sport. You'll experience

the thrill and danger of driver and machine seconds away from victory and inches away from violent, fiery death. This critically acclaimed film presents, an inside look at both the sport and the drivers, revealing the intensity of competition, victory and defeat.
30-635 107 min. $39.95

Racers Of A Distant Dream
Promoted as the most dangerous and daring off-road race ever to be attempted, the first Trans-Amazon road rally lives up to its billing and beyond! Starting in Cartegena, Columbia, the grueling course winds its way south for 9,000 miles through South America's most treacherous jungles and searing deserts-and goes from seal-level to 15,000 feet above sea level. The eighty drivers who begin the race must face brutal roads, intense fluctuations in temperature and sheer exhaustion without the aid of accurate road books or maps. By the end of the first Trans-Amazon, several of the drivers have died, and only thirteen of the entrants can boast of successfully completing this unbelievable course.
30-5461 60 min. $19.95

Racing Experience
Paul Newman takes you on an exciting exploration of Formula One race car driving. Here, in all its glory is the dangerous, adventuresome world of hot asphalt, checkered flags, burning rubber and speed.
02-3058 48 min. $14.95

Roddin' Video Magazine
Join us for a cruise in some of the hottest street rods to hit the pavement. You'll visit car shows to get a better look at these hot cars.
02-8000 35 min. $16.95

Super-Pull World Champions
"Live from the Cow Palace" driver skill, gear ratios, proper weight distribution, and mega-horsepower are but a few of the necessitates to succeed as a winning Tractor-Puller! Although pulling a weighted sled 440 feet on a dirt track with machine might at first appear to be a simple task, rest assured that there's more to it than meets the eye! The machines themselves have become so sophisticated that the word "tractor' no longer seems to apply. These monsters of mechanical wizardry are as awe inspiring as any muscle car you've ever laid eyes on! If exhibition of raw power and torque are what turn you on, tune into the Super Pull Championships live from the Cow Palace, San Francisco. It'll blow you mind!
30-5442 60 min. $19.95

Turning The Power On
Give kids of all ages a full hour of championship monster truck action! This video brings together exciting events from all over the U.S., like the

---

Video Titles Listed In This Guide Are Available For Purchase Or Rental. Contact Your Local Video Store Or Telephone (800) 383-8811

Renegades Monster Truck Challenge, and star drivers like Jim Lyons and Ken Lamont.
30-5520 60 min. $14.95

Vintage Racing in the Rockies
Virtually every famous race car and timeless classic run head to head in traditional races through the mile-high streets of Steamboat Springs, Colorado.
02-8003 53 min. $16.95

History & Collecting

America's Favorite Sports Cars
Interviews and news footage document the history of the great 50's and 60's sports cars.
02-8024 60 min. $19.95

Best of Classic Wheels
A variety of classic and unique vehicles from the 1900's to the present day. This video gives you a personal guided tour through the International Motorsports Hall of Fame & Museum.
02-8017 60 min. $29.95

Cadillac
The evolution of the plush American Cadillac is visually told in this fascinating program. Once low-priced autos, the car was transformed in the 1920s after a revolutionary design change. Their most famous customers were gangsters.
02-5832 30 min. $14.95

Cars of the Future
Car and Driver magazine gives you an exclusive look at the world's most advanced cars from all the major car companies.
02-9828 35 min. $19.99

CLASSIC CAR SERIES
All of the programs demonstrate the step-by-step restoration of a 1966 Ford Mustang. Based on the television series, "Classic Car Shop".

• Finding The Car And Fixing It Up: Part I
02-8027 30 min. $24.95

• Paint Stripping, Metal Cutting, Panel: Part II
02-8028 30 min. $24.95

• Welding, Filling, Priming/Sanding: Part III
02-8029 30 min. $24.95

• Painting, Buff/Touch Up, Assembly: Part IV
02-8030 30 min. $24.95

Close Up Classics: A Look at Auto Elegance
Get close to the millions of dollars worth of exotic vintage racers and roadsters which competed for top honors in the annual Concours d' Elegance in Steamboat Springs, Colorado.
02-8002 41 min. $16.95

Collector Cars for Fun and Profit
Small investment, big return! Race car legend Big Daddy Don Garlitz, auction king Mitchell Kruse, and other industry leaders share years of knowledge in this highly informative program. They reveal the hot selling cars for the 90's, how to price cars, where to find hidden buyers, the pitfalls and benefits of restoration, costly projects to avoid, how to buy and sell at auction, insurance, transportation and dozens of more tips for those looking to invest in cars and have fun doing it.
02-8062 59 min. $29.95

Complete Mustang
A salute to the Ford Mustang, "America's Sports car".
02-8025 60 min. $19.95

Concours d'Elegance
From the 1898 Winton to the 1982 Ferrari experience the thrill and adventure that was so much a part of the "horseless carriage age". You'll visit Cleveland's Frederick C. Crawford Auto Aviation Museum and listen to Mr. Crawford, the museum's founder, discuss the history of the auto industry and the museum. You'll see the museum's restoration shop and attend one of the finest car shows in the country--the Pebble Beach "Concours d'Elegance". You will see over 100 of America's finest antique and classic automobiles.
02-091 39 min. $39.95

Corvette
Clean, slick, and efficient looking, the first Corvette debuted on June 30, 1953. The program shows the successful evolution of this car, and includes exciting racing footage.
02-5831 30 min. $19.95

Early Birds
A look at the 1955, 1956 and 1957 Ford Thunderbird.
02-2028 40 min. $16.95

Fabulous Fords
A nostalgic and entertaining look at a high point in automotive styling from the design stage to finished product.
02-8022 60 min. $19.95

Golden Age of the Automobile
You will see many of the automobiles that are long gone from the scene, but still manage to excite and stimulate people wherever they are. Covering a period from the late 1920's to the 1940's, this program answers many questions regarding the demise of marquees such as La Salle, Auburn, and Pierce Arrow and the development of many of today's engineering advances.
02-018 55 min. $29.95

Home of the Classics
Journey back in history to a time when individuals with spirit and ingenuity were building machines that could take man higher, farther and faster than ever before. Visit the Auburn Cord-Deusenberg Museum and listen as Director Skip Marketti talks about the museum, then hop aboard and tour the town in a 1911 Auburn Touring Car and race a 1930 Auburn speedster down a back country road.
02-090 40 min. $39.95

Jaguar
Sleek, beautiful, and powerful, the Jaguar was created in the 1920s by a small British manufacturer of motorcycle sidecars. This program will show you how the car developed into the ultimate in sporty luxury.
02-5830 30 min. $19.95

Johnson Manor Car Show
Take a behind-the-scenes look at a cavalcade of automotive history as the Ohio Region's Northern Chapter of the Antique Automobile Club of America celebrates the AACA's Golden Anniversary. Attend their news conference at Johnson Manor, a turn-of-the-century estate and sight of the Johnson Manor Carshow. At the show you will see over 440 antique, classic, milestone, and special-interest automobiles, including a 1935 Duesenberg once owned by Clark Gable.
02-092 26 min. $19.95

Low Rider Magazine
Features the best low-rider cars and trucks. See it all from cruising LA to the exciting car and truck hopping championship. Experience the outrageous Bikini and Macho-Man contests.
02-5052 90 min. $29.95

Marque of a Legend
An outstanding motorsports documentary, paying tribute to man's quest for the ultimate sports car. Some of the most important models of Alfa-Romeo, Aston Martin, Bentley, Bugatti, Ferrari, Jaguar, Maserati, Mercedes-Benz and Porsche are featured.
02-180 60 min. $59.95

Mustang
This is a comprehensive review of America's fun demon. Beginning with Lee Iacocca's concept for an affordable sports car, this program will take you back to the days of Mustangs.
02-5829 30 min. $19.95

Powered by Ford
The fascinating history of the development of motor racing is presented in this look at America's first major auto manufacturer.
02-2513 30 min. $19.95

Thunderbird
This is the true story of Ford's mythical American sports car and it's packed with rare facts and thrilling footage. Radically revolutionary, these fun cars were an experiment in engineering.
02-5828 30 min. $19.95

VISUAL HISTORY OF CARS SERIES:

• Volume 1
Includes the history of the Jeep, the Volkswagen, the Firebird and the Thunderbird.
02-5825 115 min. $59.95

• Volume 2
Includes the history of the Lincoln, the Cadillac, the Mercedes Benz, and the Jaguar.
02-5826 115 min. $59.95

• Volume 3
Includes the history of the Aston Martin, the Corvette, the BMW, and the Mustang.
02-5827 115 min. $59.95

Maintenance

Auto Dimensions
Takes you on an amazing trip through the inner working systems of your car, giving you a new look at your automobile.
02-2080 47 min. $19.95

Auto Repair for Dummies
Based on the best-selling book, this video teaches basic car maintenance, including how to help a car live linger, save fuel and money, and prevent 70% of all breakdowns. Everything car owners need to keep their cars driving well, running safely, and

Video Titles Listed In This Guide Are Available For Purchase Or Rental. Contact Your Local Video Store Or Telephone (800) 383-8811

looking great.
02-1525 30 min. $19.95

Body & Fender Repair

Automotive technician Mike Dann takes you through the full procedures for repairing simple dents and rust perforations on a steel body car.
02-169 80 min. $24.95

Bodyworks

Highly recommended as a basic course in dent repair for jobs that can be done with simple hand tools in our own back yard. You'll learn how to analyze damage and plan the repair, and tools and technique are discussed in full detail. Every step of the repair process, from prepping to primer, is simplified with explicit camera angles and editing. Avoid exorbitant repair bills...and learn to do it yourself.
02-5472 60 min. $49.95

Consumer Reports: Cars

This tape features all necessary information on selecting a new or used car and keeping it running. It teaches visual inspection, price shopping, what safety equipment to look for, how to attain the best purchase loans and insurance and how to keep your car in shape once you have found the "best bet".
02-166 50 min. $19.95

Detailing

This video leads you through each of the steps necessary to fully rejuvenate and maintain car interiors, exterior surfaces and trim and engine compartments.
02-168 22 min. $24.95

Fiberglass

One of the most versatile materials around today is fiberglass-but many uninformed bodymen and customizers are reluctant to use it. You'll find that working with glass is, in many ways, easier and less costly than metal. This video teaches basic fiberglass techniques that can be applied to almost any kind of repair: exotic cars, boats, spas, motorcycles, jet skis. You'll learn common examples of auto repair with fiberglass, and how to modify and scratch build parts.
02-5476 60 min. $49.95

FIX-IT SERIES WITH RAY HILL

• Get The Basics

Ray Hill guides you step-by-step through basic automobile maintenance and repair procedures. Includes jump starting a dead battery; tire care; how to change a flat tire; checking and changing fuses; headlight and taillight replacement; checking fluid levels; care of air filters, breather filters and PVC valves and changing engine oil, all in language that is easy to understand in close-up detail.
02-045 58 min. $24.95

• Keep Your Car Cool: Care/Cooling System

Ray Hill teaches you the proper way to service your car's cooling system. He will demonstrate how and when to replace the belts, hoses and thermostat, and show you how to drain, flush and replenish the radiator.
02-046 60 min. $24.95

• Running & Riding

Ray Hill shows you the step-by-step method to change spark plugs, points and condensers; service you car's PVC system; and use the proper meters and gauges for timing the engine.
02-047 60 min. $24.95

Flame Painting

This colorful trend was first ignited back in the '40's and has never really died out! The fad's been rekindled of late, and flame jobs appear on everything from Hot Rods to airplanes to boats. While you may not want to set your own car ablaze with flames, you can easily learn how to paint them on just about anything your customers bring in.
02-5474 60 min. $49.95

How the Automobile Works: It's Really Not Your Enemy

To overcome being intimidated by your auto-mobile is simply a matter of understanding how it works and the basics of automobile design. This program takes you in easy steps through the engine, fuel system, brakes, transmission and the electrical system.
02-020 28 min. $29.95

Know Your Car Course

This program was developed for all car owners, but especially the female driver, for they are often the victims of unscrupulous auto service and repair professionals.
02-2974 60 min. $29.95

Last Chance Garage

The ultimate, low-priced car repair home video features host Brad Sears teaching home viewers how to repair his or her car in easy, step-by-step instructions. Many projects can be completed on one's own; certain others are to be undertaken in conjunction with a local mechanic.
02-028 60 min. $24.95

Leadwork

Auto body soldering is a skill that few professionals still possess, due to the discovery of convenient plastic fillers used by most body shops today.

Leadwork is making a popular comeback, though, as more car owners demand quality work on their vehicles. This video is a one-of-a-kind guide through the repair of a '52 Rolls Royce, and acquaints you with lead repair tools. Master this time consuming but preferred repair method.
02-5473 60 min. $49.95

MUSTANG INTERIOR RESTORATION VIDEOS

• **Dash Area**
Covers dash pad, instrument panel, instrument bezel and lens, radio and speaker upgrade, glove box liner, defroster hoses, air conditioning registers, and sun visors.
02-6611 20 min. $29.95

• **Convertible Top**
Covers convertible top, folding glass, window, well liner, top and quarter pads and roof rail.
02-6612 20 min. $29.95

• **Upholstery and Interior Trim**
Covers upholstery, seat buns, carpet, under carpet insulation, kick panels, door panels, water shields, arm rest pads, quarter trim upholstery, interior paint and sill moldings.
02-6610 20 min. $29.95

Oil Change, Filters & Lube
A professional discusses the benefits of frequent oil changes, the need for filter changes, and other simple jobs you can perform on your car at the same time.
02-172 21 min. $19.95

Painting
The "How To" video that picks up where "Bodywork" and "Leadwork" leave off. If you're thinking about having your car repainted, save yourself a bundle-simply by doing the prep work yourself. "Painting" begins with small dent repair, guide coating, block sanding, priming and masking. Then, follow a pro into the booth and discover the secrets for achieving that custom look. In addition to full paint jobs, you'll learn spot painting of repaired panels and touch up.
02-5477 60 min. $49.95

Pinstriping
"Pinstriping" deals with all aspects of this lucrative skill: selection and maintenance of brushes and materials, developing your practice techniques, planning a design and, of course, how to correct mistakes. Includes invaluable tips on finding clients, and how to set yourself up in business, whether it's Pontiacs or popcorn carts.
02-5471 60 min. $49.95

Steel Flares
Recommended for the more experienced customizer, this video contains valuable advice for beginners, too! Although flare fabrication doesn't require a shop full of fancy equipment, it follow some basic procedures. Pattern making, layout and sheet metal forming are covered in depth, along with welding techniques for light gauge metal. Whether your flares are mild or wild, you'll love the superior results of fabricating with steel.
02-5475 60 min. $49.95

Replacing Exhaust Systems
This cassette fully covers the inspection, repair and replacement of exhaust-system components, from mufflers to pipes and resonators.
02-171 22 min. $19.95

Replacing Shocks & Struts
Replacement of front struts and typical tubular shock absorbers is the subject of this video. A factory engineer takes you through the process from initial checking the complete replacement and the final test drive.
02-170 40 min. $19.95

Restoration Game
Car-care experts reveal their secrets for acquiring, restoring and maintaining either classic or not-so-classic automobiles.
02-1977 43 min. $14.95

ROY'S AUTOBODY VIDEO SERIES
Do your own body repair and paint work at home. This series presents step-by-step instructions that are easy to follow, will save you money and give you the satisfaction of doing it yourself.

• **Basic Body Work**
02-074 28 min, $39.95

• **Basic Customizing**
02-077 54 min. $39.95

• **Complete Acrylic Enamel Refinishing**
02-076 63 min. $39.95

• **Fiberglass Body Repair**
02-078 62 min. $39.95

• **Spot Painting Repairs**
02-075 43 min. $39.95

Tune-Up & Maintenance
Carburetor, points, plugs, fluid levels, ignition wires and filters are but a few of the topics covered in depth.
02-173 60 min. $19.95

Under The Hood And Around Your Car
No need to fear having to perform easy services on your car. Use this video like a reference book. The subjects covered are reference by numbers that appear in the corner of the screen to help you find the service you wish to perform. Checking and servicing your car could not be easier.
02-7063 27 min. $14.95

Woman's Guide to Auto Maintenance with Janet Guthrie
Declare your freedom from auto aggravation. Top race driver Janet Guthrie shows you how to stay in control of auto maintenance.
02-2712 65 min. $19.95

Motorcycles & Off Road

4-WD Trail Riding
Whether you like a quiet drive off-road through the woods, or roaring up a 40 degree rock pile, this video will get you into the greatest sport on four wheels...off-road trail riding.
02-6453 30 min. $16.95

Beat the Baja
It's been called the "Superbowl of Off-Road Racing". Trace the history of the Baja and the racing legends-including Parnelli Jones and Ark Miller-who made if famous.
02-2294 48 min. $24.95

Desert Racers
Veteran motorcycle and off-road film-maker Norm Johnson has captured the sights and sounds of the world's fastest off-road racers as they tear across the California and Nevada deserts.
02-2532 60 min. $19.95

Dirt Bike: Stars
Thrilling motocross highlights featuring the top bike riders in the world.
02-058 30 min. $24.95

Easyriders Video Magazine
Harley-riding, modern-day legends. From the Great North to the Deep South, from the East Coast to the West...freedom-loving Americans daring to be themselves. This video will keep you glued to the tube!
02-5017 55 min. $39.95

Great Mountain Biking Video
Learn from the best how to select, ride, race,
maintain and become one with your mountain bike. Challenge yourself to the agony of the uphill climb and the ecstasy of downhill free-flight. Feast your senses on spectacular footage of California outback and intrepid "hammer-heads". See exciting Racing and Trials clips from the notorious Mammoth Kamikaze Downhill and Rockhopper South Races. For anyone who ever wanted to know what mountain biking is all about. Don't get left in the dust. A bold adventure awaits you.
30-6370 50 min. $29.95

Last of the Gladiators: Evil Knievel
All the jumps, all the crashes, plus incredible new footage. This is the story of the rise and fall of the world's greatest dare-devil. From Butte, Montana to international wealth and fame, he competed against death to become an American hero.
02-081 105 min. $39.95

Motorcycle Maintenance
Steve Kimball, managing editor of Cycle World Magazine, shows you how to service your own bike and take care of the common repairs necessary to keep it running safely and well. Includes instruction on tools, chain care and replacement, cable adjustments, oil changes, the electrical system, brakes, points, plugs, timing checks, filters, fork maintenance, and troubleshooting, with each procedure shown in detail.
02-050 59 min. $24.95

Off-Road Survival Tactics
This fast-moving video reveals the valuable secrets and hard-earned lessons of handling your dirt bike on killer hills, riding rocks and ruts, tips for water crossing, and much more.
02-2165 30 min. $29.95

Off Road Warriors
From Monster Trucks to spectacular death-defying crashes, this is spine-tingling motor mania at its best. "Off Road Warriors" brings you all the high-speed thrills and excitement of America's most popular spectator sport.
02-083 60 min. $39.95

On Any Sunday II
The cinematic "Bible" for motorcyclists shows action in the desert, on the road, and on the tracks around the world. Features interviews and races with World Champions Bruce Penhall, Brad Lackey, Bob Hannah and Kenny Roberts, plus old-time racing film footage.
02-031 89 min. $39.95

Superbikes
The super street bikes are a handful for all but the most experienced riders. Find out what it takes to stay on the most exciting two wheeled bikes ever built for the street. The latest "Micro Cam" on-

board camera lets you ride with all the action at Laguna Seca and Willow Springs Race Tracks... like you have never seen before.
02-6464 30 min. $16.95

Ultimate Mountain Biking
Experience all the thrills, spills, and non-stop action that have made mountain bikes the hottest selling sports equipment in America. Blaze down awesome off-road terrain with champion-class riders who share their skills and know-how in a way that will benefit every rider, from pro to novice.
30-5580 30 min. $14.95

Miscellaneous

Havoc 7
Top international drivers smashing their cars to pieces, world champion riders unceremoniously skating along on their backsides and complete unknowns doing the most extraordinary things with vehicles of all kinds. It's all the same for viewers of Havoc 7 which unashamedly sets out to do nothing other than bring together the dramatic scenes of what happens when things go wrong in motor sport. Total of 172 Incidents.
02-5133 60 min. $39.95

How to Beat a Speeding Ticket
Teaches the viewer courtroom tactics, featuring interviews with judges, police officers, lawyers and offenders.
02-174 30 min. $14.95

How To Negotiate A Car Deal
Do you dread your next "battle" with a care salesperson to get a good deal on a new or used car? Are you wary of the many mind games professional salespeople play to get you to pay too much? This video will help you turn their sales

tactics to your advantage.
02-5159 40 min. $29.95

Insiders Guide to Buying a New Car
Get all the facts and save thousands of dollars on your next car purchase. An informed consumer is the salesman's worst enemy.
02-8064 38 min. $24.95

Monster Mania
Witness incredible destruction as massive monster trucks smash anything and everything in their paths. Spectacular daredevil stunt driving, head-on collisions, mud-spattering war.
02-082 30 min. $16.95

Pat Boone Hits The Road (The RV Video Guide)
This exciting and informative video program, filmed in full color with stereo, will be an introduction to the world of recreational vehicles and how to get the most enjoyment out of the RV lifestyle. Pat's warmth, enthusiasm and personality sparkles throughout this memorable production. It's the perfect gift for anyone interested in RVing-from first-timers to life-timers! The producers worked closely with the Recreation Vehicle Industry Association to ensure addressing topics of interest to RV'ers of all ages and pocketbooks.
02-6309 53 min. $29.95

Smart Buyer's Guide to Purchasing A New Car
Nearly an hour of the most valuable information anyone could ask for when purchasing a new car! Tips, suggestions and insights on: how to choose the right car, how to negotiate, the do's and don't's of financing, the truth about rebates and incentives, how to keep it simple. "How to beat the salesman and dealer at their own game."
02-6552 51 min. $29.95

Stunt Mania
Two men, two vehicles and two of the most dangerous obstacles any stuntman ever tried to jump. Be part of history and join our heroes in their super jumps.
02-3064 30 min. $14.95

Changing Out An Engine?

Painting Your Own Detail?

These Videos Can Help.

VIDEO TITLES LISTED IN THIS GUIDE ARE AVAILABLE FOR PURCHASE OR RENTAL. CONTACT YOUR LOCAL VIDEO STORE OR TELEPHONE (800) 383-8811

Searching For

A Unique Gift That is

Informative and Appreciated?

The Video Titles

In This Guide

Make Wonderful Gifts.

Aviation

- ✓ *Combat*
- ✓ *Demonstration*
- ✓ *Flight Instruction/Aircraft Contruction*
- ✓ *Helicopters*
- ✓ *History*
- ✓ *Space Exploration*
- ✓ *Miscellaneous*

Combat

17th Airborne - The Bulge to the Rhine
This is the personal account of five soldiers, young men who went to war because there was a job to do. Enhanced by dramatic film footage and personal photos, their very real tale will be understood by fighting men everywhere.
04-8004 48 min. $29.95

Aces of the I.A.F.
This is a two-part action program about today's world class fighter aces of the Israeli Air Force. The best of East and West meet head on over Mid-East battlegrounds. Dog fights and air strikes by top-gun jocks at supersonic speeds where the odds are usually 12 to 1.
04-146 46 min. $39.95

Airborne
The continuation of the saga of our Paratroopers. From the South Pacific to Vietnam, American airborne forces in the Far East have fought and died in three wars, and developed weapons and tactics to fight the battles of the future. "Airborne" tells the story of what they did, how they did it, and what they are today.
04-6159 50 min. $29.95

Aircraft of the Soviet Union
Come explore with us, the exciting and often secret world of Soviet aircraft. See a wide variety of Soviet Airpower.
04-8022 60 min. $29.95

Air Power
Includes: 1) Air Powers and Armies: An in-depth study of how modern air strategy and tactics are implemented, as seen over Europe and North Africa in WWII. 2) Target Germany-8th Air Force: Gun camera free-for-all aboard the legendary 8th's array of medium and heavy bombers that took the fight to the enemy's home ground.
04-156 70 min. $39.95

Air Strike
A series of savage aerial combat with recently discovered rare footage. Includes: 1) A Day with the A-36: How about a fighter-bomber version of the legendary P-51? They called it the "Invader" and it played hell with the Luftwaffe in Sicily. 2) Pacific Step Up: Riding with the 5th, 10th AF and the RAF hitting enemy strongholds in China, plus a ringside seat as navy dive-bombers hit Wake Island. 3) Japs Over China: A look at the beginnings of Japanese military air power, tactics and strategy on a raid over Chungking.
04-158 71 min. $49.95

Air War in the Pacific: WWII
Return to World War II and the air war in the Pacific with this timeless air force black and white film. From 1941 through 1945, you will witness the war's most important and devastating air battles and raids, viewed from the bombardier's seat! Includes dogfights over China, raids on Japanese and, finally, the dropping of the atomic bomb on Hiroshima.
13-322 55 min. $29.95

Air War Over Europe: WWII
Return to World War II and the air war over Europe with this 1946 black and white air force film. You'll witness some of the most spectacular air battles ever fought against the German Luftwaffe, including D-Day, Patton's "Dash Across France," and the capture of Berlin. This is Flying Fortress vs. Messerschmidt, P-51 Mustangs, B-26 Marauders and more.
13-321 55 min. $29.95

Attack Carrier
From the Langley to the Enterprise, here are the legendary Yorktown, Ranger, Wasp, Hornet, Saratoga, Lexington and the challenge and battles of our naval air arm. They changed the role of fleet warfare forever. From the Marshalls to the Mariannas, they swept the seas. Included is "A Point intime," tribute to the Navy combat artist which presents a blend of live action combat with the skills of pen and brush, You will see warfare from WWII to Vietnam in a way you've never seen before. Rare footage of the four Seawolves in Vietnam included.
04-005 50 min. $39.95

Bombers
High-stakes strategic bombing missions. With first-person accounts and incredible live action footage.
04-8017 50 min. $19.95

Carriers
This is the story of naval aviation. It covers the early experiments with aircraft carriers by both British and American visionaries. Also included are tales of the Doolittle Raiders, of Midway and Leyte Gulf, the "Great Marianas Turkey Shoot," and the Kamikaze attacks off Okinawa. And as the grand finale, "Carriers" brings you Navy jet action off the coast of Korea, the Vietnam War and a thrilling account of the British conflict in the Falkland Islands.
04-6155 50 min. $29.95

Choppers
From medical evacuation carriers to attack chopper

in Vietnam combat, the saviours from the sky.
04-8018 50 min. $19.95

Confederate Air Force: Wings of Victory

These are the machines that won World War II, and the men and women that flew them. Come aboard the B-24, B-17 and PBY for a pilot's-eye view.
04-2953 120 min. $39.95

D-Z Normandy

Witness this epic of planes, gliders, and the men of the 82nd and 101st Airborne supported by waves of angry B-26 Marauders and P-47s as they land behind enemy lines on D-Day. And, experience "The Air Plan," the official RAF combat film of the Normandy battle from the air. Tree-Top gun cameras take you wing-level against German Panzers. See the Mustangs, Spitfires, Hurricanes and Typhoons at their flying, fighting best.
13-031 90 min. $39.95

Flight For The Sky

In this exciting black and white program, you will experience the lifestyle and heroism of the American Fighter Pilots who flew missions over Germany in World War II. See the various types of fighters used to escort the bombers deep into enemy territory, including the P-38 Lightning, P-51 Mustang and the P-47 Thunderbolt. Includes the raid on Emden, Germany.
04-6080 54 min. $29.95

Fighters

The evolution of the modern fighter/attack aircraft. This fascinating story that blazed the way to create the most sophisticated fighting weapons ever conceived. The F/A-18 the F-16, the F-15, the F-14, and the venerable F-4 are all here to demonstrate their capabilities. Included is a look at the development programs for the F-111 and the YF-12.
04-6157 50 min. $29.95

Fighting 5th AF: Mission to Rabaul

September/October 1943, the hellish triangle of blood-soaked mud, jungle and sky bore witness to one of history's most savage battles on October 12. Angry warbirds sweep Cape Gloucester, Hansa Bay, Lae and Salamanaua leaving a wake of devastation unequaled in the Pacific campaign. Imperial Japan lost 1,000 planes, hundreds of ships and barges, plus a brutal body count.
04-126 90 min. $39.95

Fighting 17: The Jolly Rogers

As related by the squadron's skipper, Tom Blackburn, and four of his men, the events of 1943-44 are enhanced by splendid film footage, personal photographs, and the memories of those

who were there. The true story of Navy squadron VF-17.
04-8005   52 min. $29.95

Flak, Jugs and Cobras

Uncensored footage of combat aircraft of World War II. Includes: 1) Flak: Evasive action and maneuvers on bombings missions. All shown against actual footage of enemy barrage and concentrated "flak" anti-aircraft fire. 2) Mission accomplished-The Flying Fortress Story: 25 tons of aerial fury at 30,000 feet, together with the story of the first operational raid of the immortal B-17 Fortress. 3) P-47 Pilot Familiarization: Examination of the legendary "jug"-eight guns, seven tons of flying hell made this aircraft one of the deadliest high-altitude fighters of WWII. 4) P-47 Ground Handling, Takeoff, and Normal Flight landings: Fascinating evaluation of the skills needed to fly this fabled fighting plane, originally "classified." 5) Report of Enemy Information by Fighter Pilots: P-39 Aircobras of the 181st take us on a mission, with special attention to briefing, debriefing, enemy positions and raid effectiveness.
04-025 96 min. $39.95

Golden Birds

It is 1985, the 50th Anniversary of two great "Golden Birds"-the venerable DC-3 and that great warbird, the Flying Fortress B-17. Included are two great award-winning programs, "Sentimental Journey," with James Stewart, and Memphis Belle with the fighting airmen of the 8th Air Force.
04-161 66 min. $39.95

Hell Over Korea

The definitive and bloody record of Korea's savage conflict. Watch as five North Korea divisions sweep across the 38th parallel; Pusan and Hungnam; Yalu and Seoul; Sabrejets and B-29s in action; the "human wave" of Chinese regulars; "Bloody Ridge"; "T-Bone"; "Heartbreak Ridge"; "Punch Bowl"; "Sniper Ridge"; the first 40 days, including the battling 24th, 25th Infantry, and 1st Cavalry.
13-043 100 min. $39.95

Kill That Zero! F6 Hellcat at War

See the Hellcats use machine guns, rockets and superior maneuvering to send Zeros flaming into the ocean. Included is rare footage from the Japanese military archives--the Zero being built, Japanese naval aviators in training, Admiral Yamamoto personally plotting attacks aboard his flagship.
04-8021 40 min. $16.95

Korean Jet Aces

These are the pilots who were the first Jet Aces. They made history as our F-80's an F-86's engaged in the first Jet to Jet combat in the Korean skies

with the Russian built MIG 17's. See our pilots with their actual gun camera footage engage in never before experienced speed. Watch as the pilots of the 4th fighter group tell you their stories as only they can tell it.
04-6455 30 min. $16.95

Hell's Aces High
This four-part videotape includes: 1) Fight for the Sky: Jugs P-51s, P-38s sweeping the skies of Fortress Europe. 100-mile-long air armadas. FW 190s ME 109s against our best. 2) USAF-50 Years: World War I ragwing scrape to Mig Alley and our 10-1 kills. Flying the Hump; Inchon; F-100s; F-4 Phantoms and more. 3) The Last Bomb: Mustangs ride shotgun on the longest bombing raids in history. Travel 1,500 miles from Tinian to Tokyo and watch P-51s against the enemy's finest. 4) Air Force Tribute to the Combat Cameraman: The most nerve shattering gun-camera stuff ever. Fore and aft camera pods low over Vietnam pick up graphic strike footage.
04-031 120 min. $39.95

Mig Alley
Unforgettable actual footage of Sabre/MIG dogfights is combined with true stories of bravery and heroism against incredible odds as America meets the Red Challenge on its own ground; "Mig Alley, Korea."
13-5713 30 min. $14.95

Mig Killers of the U.S. Navy
From the first engagement over the death filled skies of Vietnam to the most recent dogfight between F-14 Tomcats on patrol in the Mediterranean and Col. Kadaffi's Libyan Mig 23. "The Mig Killers" is a harrowing account of the dawn of modern jet air combat.
04-5066 50 min. $24.95

Paratroopers
The story of America's first paratroop and glider outfits in World War Two. They got their baptism by fire in the North African invasion, and then refined their daring trade in Sicily, Italy, and the jungles of Burma. They cried "Geronimo" on D-Day over Normandy and throughout the south of France. A thrilling program about the men who created a legend.
04-6158 50 min. $29.95

Road to Rome/Thunderbolt
Return to World War II and the crucial air war over Italy. Join the 12th Air Force and the 57th Fighter Group as they take control of the skies over Italy during 1943 and 1944 with the versatile P-47 Thunderbolt. Fly with them on their strafing/bombing missions to halt the German

Forces and disrupt their supply routes and ammunition supplies.
04-6083 57 min. $29.95

Second Home
This exciting video is set aboard the carrier John F. Kennedy. This provides an emotional and human portrait of three Navy men and their families, focusing on their last days ashore and their first days at sea.
04-8010 60 min. $29.95

Target for Today
From pre-flight to the blistering hell that was the skies over Fortress Europe, this in-depth story of the air armada that knocked out the Luftwaffe in aerial combat will thrill the viewer. You'll see no actors or staged scenes in this film; it's all the real thing. This is the closest look at the men themselves, battling men of the air taking their Flying Forts and Liberator B-24s to the homeland of the enemy. Full-length feature film, now on video, for WWII air combat buffs. Also included is R.A.F. Action, a WWII newsreel depicting the participation of British pilots in the Battle for Britain. Rare look at great warbirds: Hurricanes, Wellingtons, Sterlings, Halifax Bombers, Spitfires and more.
04-066 120 min. $39.95

Vietnam: A Mission
In Vietnam, as never before, the cooperation of air and ground forces proved to be essential to victory on the battlefield. The stories of three men, a staff sergeant, a chopper pilot, and the pilot of an F-4 Phantom jet are combined to retell a story of taut action and courage under fire.
04-6160 50 min. $29.95

War Aces
The exciting story of the men who flew pursuit/fighter aircraft from World War One through Vietnam. This exciting collection of dogfights highlights the exploits of men like Rickenbacker, Richthofen, Gabreski, Smith, Yeager, Jabara, and others.
04-6154 50 min. $29.95

War Hawks
According to the producer,"We have assembled the definitive air strike footage of the Vietnam war and put together an altogether disturbing, savage aerial display. This is the most awesome and unrelenting air rocketry and bombing you probably have ever seen. It is both beautiful to observe and terrible to contemplate".
13-458 35 min. $39.95

Warbird Film Festival: Volume 1
An expanded triple bill of great WW II aviation action, including: 1) "The Memphis Belle": On-the-

spot story of the legendary B-17 daylight raids over Germany, followed by the flight crew of the gallant Memphis Belle as they become part of the 1st bomber command on Saipan. 2) "Target Tokyo": Giant B-29 Super Forts flatten Nakajima aircraft plant. Narrated by Ronald Reagan. Rare footage of "Dauntless Dottie", last of the WW II giant bombers. Enemy flak and fighters couldn't stop them. 3) "Thunder-bolt": Outstanding gun camera coverage of the fabled P-47 "jugs" as they race up the boot of Italy. Deadly air to air and ground action-aerial combat footage at its best.

04-072 113 min. $39.95

Warbird Film Festival: Volume 2

Two more rare WW II classics with combat history from both sides of the globe. Witness the stark drama of war from the skies through award-winning film, now on video. Includes: 1) December 7th: The definitive record of the Japanese attack film documentary, it won an Academy award for Director John Ford. 2) Battle of Britain: The all-time WW II great, a documentary masterpiece dedicated to the iron will of the British as personified in the immortal Spitfire. Here are pilots who wrote a new meaning to "dogfight"-a handful of RAF Fliers who helped turn the tide of history.

04-073 90 min. $39.95

Warbirds Immortals

A super double bill, includes: 1) Spitfire: Starring Leslie Howard, David Niven and the R.A.F. This rare motion picture is the film biography of R.J. Mitchell, the engineering genius behind the creation of the immortal Spitfire. It is also Leslie Howard's last film; he died, ironically, under attack from a squadron of ME-109s. 2) Sentimental Journey: starring James Stewart, this AWA Award Winner has been widely acclaimed as the definitive salute to the venerable DC-3.

04-165 108 min. $39.95

Wild Aces

The "Wild Weasels"-Air Force Mach 2 jocks at their flying, fighting best. F-105 "Thuds" over Vietnam in a wild-turkey shoot you'll never forget. Go along as they take over SAM sites, convoys, bridges, MIGs missiles and much more. Nerve-jolting action beyond anything you've ever seen-a definitive aerial action of the Vietnam War. Strap yourself to the seat of a F-105 Thunderchief over the Vietnam battlefields.

04-074 58 min. $39.95

World War II Fighter Aces

Interviews with ten of the most famous Fighter Aces of World War II, discussing their planes, missions and adventures.

04-8023 60 min. $29.95

Demonstration

Airshow!

Amazing performances by the most aerobiotic acts. Fascinating one-hour program features the Blue Angels Canadian Snow-birds, Art Scholl, The Eagles Eddie, "Wingwalker" Green, and a look at the modern sport of air racing. Filmed at the world famous Reno Air Races.

04-114 60 min. $49.95

Airshow: The Ultimate Power Surge!

"Airshow" puts you in the pilot's seat of the world's fastest and sexiest aircraft. Gazing skyward from ground level, or experiencing the action from a nearby cockpit, you will thrill to the soaring, swooping and spinning motion of such legendary precision flying teams as the United States Navy's Blue Angels and Canada's Snowbirds. Spectacular photography of spine tingling flight formation accompanies the roar of raw firepower as warplanes zoom at and alongside one another inches away from certain disaster. But these greatest of flying aces are in complete command-down to landing and emerging together in unison. Truly magnificent men, in magnificent machines.

04-2433 60 min. $19.95

Blue Angels: A Backstage Pass

This exciting music video has fascinating Blue Angel team member pilot interviews, fantastic footage of the early piston engine F8F Bearcats as well as in-cockpit footage of the modern F18 jets. Featuring music by: Tom Petty, Georgia Satellites, Van Halen and more.

04-8012 30 min. $19.95

Burner: Once A Blue Angel

You will view some of the newest military aircraft and witness performances demonstrating some of the most famous and daring aerobiotic stunts currently executed. Burner will show you the amazing flying feats of the Green Machine; Wayne Handley in his astounding agrobatics bi-plane performance; the Ray Ban Gold team; Bob Hoover as he forces a 16 passenger Saberliner to fly like a Glasair; and aerobatics performances from the Air 18 Hornets. Within this unique airshow environment, you will see Bill putting his Bud Lite BD 5J through its paces and hear his personal recollections of the most challenging, frightening and exhilarating time in his life, his tour with the Blues.

04-6499 60 min. $39.95

VIDEO TITLES LISTED IN THIS GUIDE ARE AVAILABLE FOR PURCHASE OR RENTAL. CONTACT YOUR LOCAL VIDEO STORE OR TELEPHONE (800) 383-8811

California International Air Show
Bob Hoover's Strike Commander performance is the best-loved air show act ever, now you can see it from the cockpit!
04-2955 90 min. $39.95

Combat Teams
Three-part videotape on U.S. combat teams in action. 1) Super-sonic Thunderbirds: F-100 Sabrejets overfly the Grand Canyon and Death Valley. Symphony of aerial teamwork at super-sonic speeds including: Playing the Deck, Bomb Bursts Loops, Diamond Formation Rolls, Cloverleafs, Vertical 360 turns and more. 2) Talons for the Thunderbirds: USAF demonstrates; team straps on a brace of T-38 Talons. 3) The Golden Knights: 52 men of the U.S. Army parachute team put on a brilliant display of teamwork in the air: Free Fall Baton Pass, Diamond Track, X-Over, Star Burst and much more as they race earthward.
04-019 60 min. $39.95

Daredevil Flyers
Astounding aerobiotic excitement featuring General Chuck Yeager and his sound barrier-breaking Tiger Shark jet, plus the best in hang gliding and much more.
04-096 30 min. $14.95

Duxford Air Museum
Tour England's famed Duxford Air Museum.
04-2960 90 min. $29.95

Fiftieth Anniversary DC-3 Fly-In
Witness the most historic gathering of DC-3's ever.
04-2954 60 min. $39.95

Find Your Way Back
Hosted by the Discovery astronauts. This is a stirring music video tribute to the past, present and future of America's Space program. Featuring music by: Starship, Steve Winwood and Pat Benatar.
04-8014 30 min. $19.95

Fury of Eagles
One hour of exciting jet fighters, including: 1) The F-4 Phantom: A complete Air Force: Montage of Phantoms in action, Air Force, Navy, Marines, plus those of our allies. Tight formation demos plus Vietnam combat. 2) The Challenge: Jimmy Doolittle takes us from WWI and WWII to the present jet age demands. "Seek, meet and destroy" are the key words: from Ragwings to F-15 Eagles. 3) The Eagle at Farnborough: The biggest military airshow and the F-15 is the star. Includes 6-G turns, vertical climbs, low and high speed maneuvers. 4) Our Modern Air Force: Without a spoken word you are taken on a jet ride through our combat jet arsenal. See the F-15s, F-16s, F-

18s, Blackbird SR 71, A-10s, B-1 Bomber, and many more. For the pro and aviation buff alike.
04-028 60 min. $39.95

Ghosts of the Sky
An aviation adventure, this is the story of five men who chose to fly a B-25 Mitchel Bomber across the Pacific in 1983-a plane used in World War II. Glenn Ford narrates this unique flying adventure.
04-029 50 min. $39.95

Paris Air Museum
This tour of the Continent's most famous air museum is not to be missed.
04-2961 90 min. $29.95

Pima Air Museum
Pima Museum features one hundred planes on display.
04-2957 90 min. $29.95

Red Arrows: Smoke On-Go!
This is the story of England's Red Arrows jet demonstration team-the story of the planes and the men that fly them.
04-055 42 min. $39.95

Reno Air Show
The best-known air show in the United States comes home in this two hour collector's edition.
04-2952 120 min. $39.95

Sea Hawks
Todays fighting sea birds of the navy and their daily encounters with their adversaries, the Soviet fleet. Battle group commanders with a strike force second to none in today's air navy. Includes: 1) The Cutting Edge: The S3 Viking, a sea bird that can strap on missiles, bombs and homing torpedoes. With onboard computers and infra-red sensors, it locks onto Red subs and never lets go. 2) Orion-Guardian of the Seas: Able to range out for 14 hour and patrol thousands of miles, the P3C Orion scrambles fleet attack fighters to pin-point the enemy. Like the Viking she can haul a big bag of weapons plus six tons of mines. 3) The Marine Machine: A VTOL Brute, the AV-8B Harrier can hustle five tons of "stuff" including laser-guided missiles, bombs, and a 25mm high velocity gatling gun.
04-059 73 min. $39.95

Shuttleworth Collection
All aircraft are in flying condition at this famous British Air Museum. A must for collectors!
04-2958 60 min. $39.95

Skyhawk to Hornet, The Blue Angels Transition
Featuring the U.S. Navy Flight Demonstration

Squadron - The Blue Angels, provides the viewer with exclusive behind-the-scenes footage of the Blue Angels, including spectacular air-to-air footage and a 7-minute interview with the Flight Leader and Commanding Officer of the Blue Angels, Commander Gill "Boss" Rud.
04-6498 39 min. $49.95

Thunderbirds Music Video
Experience the most spectacular aerial artistry and teamwork of wing-tip aerobatics seen through a special on-board camera.
04-8013 30 min. $19.95

Top Gun: Story Behind the Story
See America's real Top Gun pilots in action over Libya, the Indian Ocean and off the Soviet Union. Hosted by Commander Randy " Duke" Cunningham, Top Gun instructor and adversary squadron commander.
04-2694 35 min. $16.95

Touch the Sky
Put on your helmet and strap yourself in, and get ready for the ride of your life. Christopher Reeve takes you inside the cockpit, and into the sky with the world's fastest and most spectacular stunt flying team, the navy's Blue Angels. From precision formation to high-speed maneuvers, you'll experience the ultimate flying thrill: man and machine as one.
04-124 60 min. $39.95

War Birds of Chino
More war birds are based at Chino than anywhere west of Texas. Each year, even more fly in for this show.
04-2956 120 min. $39.95

Flight Instruction/ Aircraft Construction

Air Force Academy: A Commitment To Excellence
This video program lets you tour the prestigious Air Force Academy in Colorado Springs, one of nation's finest institutions for higher learning. From basic cadet training to graduation you will experience the rigorous physical and mental training through which our future Air Force Officers must go.
04-6075 30 min. $29.95

Aviation Weather
A meteorological video library for convenient home playback. Five segments about the kinds of weather which concern every pilot: advection fog and ground fog; upslope fog and frontal fog; the cold front; ice formation on aircraft; and the warm front.
04-010 90 min. $39.95

Building the Rutan Composites
A step-by-step instructional program featuring Burt Rutan and Mike Melvill showing you the procedures for using fiberglass composite construction established by Burt Rutan and his associates. An absolute must for builders, certain to save many hours and help you avoid needless errors. Climaxed by a formation flight by the Long-Ex, Defiant and Vari-Viggen.
04-130 91 min. $39.95

King - The Right Stuff Flying Tips
All you wanted to know about flying and navigation.
04-8020 50 min. $29.95

KING SCHOOL "TAKE-OFF" LIBRARY

• Weather Wise
Learn how to make real-world use of weather information. You'll understand the dynamics of fog, thunderstorms, and frontal systems, and be able to predict local weather conditions. Know when to trust the forecast-and especially, when not to.
04-6682 54 min. $29.95

• Complete Airspace Review
Completely covers the alphabet soup of airspace requirements-TCA's, TRSA's, ARSA's, MOA's, MTR's.Know how to use the airspace system to your advantage.
04-6683 79 min. $29.95

• Rules To Fly By
Learn the hidden secrets of your pilot's operating handbook, how to prevent mechanical problems, and how to avoid being deceived by the optical illusions of flight. Includes a review of FAR's that every pilot should know.
04-6684 79 min. $29.95

• Communications
Actual inflight sequences give a real-life look at how to get the cooperation from ATC you deserve-even in a TCA or ARSA. Learn frequencies, radio call-up procedures, how to use your radio for increased safety and utility.
04-6685 77 min. $29.95

VIDEO TITLES LISTED IN THIS GUIDE ARE AVAILABLE FOR PURCHASE OR RENTAL. CONTACT YOUR LOCAL VIDEO STORE OR TELEPHONE (800) 383-8811

• **Practical Piloting**
Useful everyday information on how to get the most out of your aircraft. You'll learn "tricks of the trade" and "rules of thumb" that will help you get maximum performance and efficiency along with enhanced safety.
04-6687 56 min. $29.95

• **VFR With Confidence**
Learn how to plan a safe trip even in marginal weather conditions. Get the information you need from the briefer without ending up in a verbal wrestling match. Also includes a useful review of FAR's, runway markings, lighting aids, and aircraft operations.
04-6688 115 min. $29.95

• **IFR With Confidence**
Learn how to plan a safe trip even in difficult IFR weather conditions. Get and analyze the information you need from the briefer with ease. Also covers FAR's for IFR flight, new IFR procedures, and advanced navigation using HSI's RMI's and more.
04-6689 114 min. $29.95

• **Night Flying**
In-the-air video lets you experience the beauty and smoothness of flight at night. You get the tools you need for the added utility and enjoyment of safe night flying.
04-6690 42 min. $29.95

• **Maneuvers For The COM/CFI**
Pilot's point of view video, expert instruction, 3-D graphics, and animation combine to teach you lazy eights, chandelles, eithts-on-pylons and other advanced maneuvers.
04-6691 78 min. $29.95

• **Complete Jeppesen Chart Review**
Really understand Jeppesen Approach Charts, Enroute Charts, SID's and STAR's. Reveals little-known but important information about flying LDA's, SDF's and other unusual approaches.
04-6692 118 min. $29.95

• **Takeoffs and Landings Made Easy**
Impress your passengers with flawless takeoffs and landings. In-flight instruction ensures you really understand the keys to consistently good landings in any conditions.
04-6693 67 min. $29.95

• **Hangar Flying With A Point**
Learn valuable life-saving lessons in a fascinating hangar-flying session with John and Martha King, who share with you personally how they learned to avoid unwanted adventure through good planning.
04-6694 29 min. $29.95

KING VIDEO EXAM COURSE SERIES
Only King Video has the personal warmth and enthusiasm of John and Martha King, the most popular and highly-acclaimed aviation video instructors. You get the fun of flying along with the facts.

• **Recreational Pilot**
Five Tape Set. (2 Hrs. EA.)
04-6666 600 min. $199.95

• **Private Pilot**
Six Tape Set. (2 Hrs. Ea.)
04-6667 720 min. $169.95

• **Commercial Pilot**
Five Tape Set. (2 Hrs. Ea)
04-6668 600 min. $199.95

• **Instructor/FOI**
Seven Tape Set. (2 Hrs. Ea)
04-6669 840 min. $199.95

• **Instrument**
Six Tape Set. (2 Hrs. Ea.)
04-6670 720 min. $169.95

• **Instrument Instructor**
Seven Tape Set. (2 Hrs. Ea.)
04-6671 840 min. $169.95

• **ATP(121)/Dispatcher**
Six Tape Set. (2 Hrs. Ea.)
04-6672 720 min. $199.95

• **Flight Engineer**
Six Tape Set. (2 Hrs. Ea.)
04-6673 720 min. $199.95

• **Mechanics/General**
Five Tape Set. (2 Hrs. Ea.)
04-6674 600 min. $199.95

• **Mechanics/Airframe**
Five Tape Set. (2 Hrs. Ea.)
04-6675 600 min. $199.95

• **Mechanics/Powerplant**
Five Tape Set. (2 Hrs. Ea.)
04-6676 600 min. $199.95

KING FLIGHT TEST COURSES
An actual FAA examiner tells you what is expected for every task on your Flight Test and Oral, and gives you each question you will be asked. Your instructor shows you how to demonstrate your knowledge in the cockpit and on the ground. You'll

be expertly prepared to avoid errors that could lead to a costly retest.

• Recreational Pilot
Two Tape Set. (2 Hrs. Ea.)
04-6677 120 min. $59.95

• Private Pilot
Two Tape Set. (3 Hrs. Ea.)
04-6678 180 min. $59.95

• Instrument
Two Tape Set. (2 Hrs. Ea.)
04-6679 120 min. $59.95

• Commercial
Two Tape Set. (2 Hrs. Ea.)
04-6680 120 min. $59.95

• Instructor
Two Tape Set.
04-6681 120 min. $59.95

Let's Go Flying
If you've ever dreamed of soaring with the eagles...ever imagined yourself enjoying the absolute freedom of flying-then the time to take the air is now. The world's foremost flight instructors take you from zero time through absolutely everything you need to know for an exciting beginning in flying. How to get your license. The surprisingly low cost of learning. How to insure quality instruction, and priceless do's and don'ts.
04-5018 80 min. $29.95

NASA: Airmen & the Weather
Discover the ways in which NASA's space programs are helping us control the risks from natural disasters and better understand our flying environment. Includes: 1) Hurricane Below: Disaster phenomena and NASA's contribution of providing data to reduce casualties through observations from space. 2) Tornado Below: A young female student pilot on her first solo encounters a tornado. All about tornadoes with lab and satellite studies which improve our understanding. 3) The Weather Watchers: Dramatic explanations of how satellite information relates to severe storms. Unusual footage of tornado formation and its force. 4) Aeronautical Life Sciences at Ames: Exploring mans physical and psychological actions that are influencing factors in flight. 5) Flying Machines: Documenting our love affair with flight, plus a world challenge to U. S. aviation leadership.
04-042 92 min. $39.95

OFFICIAL FIXED WING PRIMARY FLIGHT TRAINING
A great training program for the general aviation

pilot, featuring the army's high wing light plane, the L-19. Study the military way for real proficiency. An outstanding series on videotape for the very first time.

• Volume 1
Includes Introduction to Aircraft Instruments; Four Basic Maneuvers; Basic Ground Track Maneuvers; Confidence Maneuvers-Steep Turns, Stalls and Spins.
04-047 75 min. $39.95

• Volume 2
Includes Take-Offs, Landings and Traffic Patterns; Forced Landings; Directional Control; Knowing Your Commands.
04-048 75 min. $39.95

Pilots Prescription for Flight
Four timely aviation medical subjects are presented to increase your knowledge and understanding of physical conditions critical to safe flying. Includes disorientation, hypoxia, medical facts for pilots and RX for flight.
04-164 75 min. $39.95

PILOT'S VIDEO SERIES

• Pilot's Video Seminar: Stall/Spin Awareness
Certified Flight Instructor and FAA Accident Prevention Counselor, Rich Stowell presents valuable information required by the F.A.R'.s. Everything you wanted to know about stalls and spins plus flight footage demonstrations and computer graphics. Stowell is well known for his easy to understand, well organized stall/spin presentations made at Oshkosh and other fly-ins. US Aviator named this the best new aviation video at Sun 'N Fun '92.
04-8000 83 min. $39.95

• Pilot's Video Guide: Getting Ready For Spins
Wondering if you have the right stuff to pursue spin or aerobatics training? CFI Rich Stowell answers all the questions you may have about spin and unusual attitude training: how to find the best school and instructor, emergency parachute requirements, tips on combatting motion sickness, and a pilot's eye view of what to expect, so you can be prepared before you spend the money to train.
04-8001 33 min. $29.95

• Pilot's Video Ground School: Emergency Maneuver Training
This video contains the ground school for the famed EMT flight training program taught at CP Aviation in Santa Paula, CA. The original

Emergency Maneuvers program pioneered by test pilots Tony LeVier and Sammy Mason was refined by CFI Rich Stowell into this current course. The complete ground school is included, as well as original video demonstrating maneuvers and graphics. Includes stalls, spins, off-airport landings, power plant failures and much more. This is the video to get to prepare for, or review emergency maneuver flight training.
04-8002 90 min. $89.95

• **Pilot's Video Guide: Basic Aerobatics**
This video is a must for pilots planning on taking aerobatics flight training or looking for a review of aerobatics skills. Hosted by Rich Stowell, Chief Aerobatics Pilot at CP Aviation in Santa Paula, CA, this program covers everything a good introductory aerobatics course will teach. From the building blocks of spins, loops, and rolls, to compound maneuvers like the Immelman, Barrel Roll, and the Hammerhead, all maneuvers are demonstrated from various views - pilot's, ground, and air, as well as being illustrated with computer graphics.
04-8003 54 min. $59.95

SAFE PILOT SERIES
Two volumes of FAA films custom-transferred to videotape. Provides a great refresher course or excellent initial training. Outstanding for student or experienced pilot. Cost is hundreds of dollars less than what you would pay to buy each of the films separately from the FAA.

• **Volume 1**
Stalling for safety; start-up; caution; wake turbulence; take-off and landing.
04-056 90 min. $39.95

• **Volume 2**
Overwater flying; mountain flying; take-off landing.
04-057 60 min. $39.95

Helicopters

Attack Copter
Five great helicopter programs for the "pros." 1) Evolution of the Attack Helicopter: concepts of deployment. Huey gunships in Vietnam; combat techniques; the Cobra and Cheyenne, artilery and anti-tank roles. 2) Tactical Formation Flying: "V" form staggered trail formation, diamond, trail, echelon, tactical heavy, defensive, offensive. 3) Helicopter Aero-Dynamics: Rotor blade actions, rotation, feathering, flapping and hunting. 4)

Helicopter Aerodynamics: The stabilizer bar, control pitch, roll, gyro properties stability. 5) Helicopter Aerodynamics: Dosimetry of lift, study of blades exerting lift in advanced half of rotation. 6) Rotor Blade Angles: Use of lift forces, pitch angle, angle of attack, and wind.
04-006 86 min. $39.95

Chopper War
The aircraft and the men. Beginning with the development of military helicopters, this program moves on to Vietnam and tales of "Mad Man" Kelly, Medal of Honor winner Stephen Pless, and the emergence of the Attach Helicopter. "Chopper War" combines the stories of these events with some of the most exciting action footage of helicopters ever filmed. A must-see for chopper lovers everywhere.
04-6156 50 min. $29.95

Chopper Pilot
Four great helicopter programs in one videotape: 1) Chopper pilot: From Ft. Wolter to Ft. Rucker, from Basic Training to advanced skills aboard Huey Gunships with combat veterans. 2) Helicopters: Advanced maneuvers and field operations. Maximum performance take-off and steep approach procedures aboard an Army Hughes OH-6. Perfecting ridgeline and pinnacle landings. 3) Helicopter Icing: Identifying ice producing situations. Preflight procedures and warning signs of ice buildup. Escape from icing areas. 4) Basic Cross-Country Helicopter Flights: In-depth course on special applications of navigation pertinent to helicopter flying: map reading pilotage, DED reckoning and much more.
04-013 90 min. $39.95

Helicopter-Safe Pilot
A "must" for any pro, includes four outstanding U.S. Army programs highlighting vital safety information for all pilots: 1) Helicopter Wake Turbulence: Slick combination of humorous animation and serious live action photography. Demonstrates the nature of helicopter wake turbulence and proper close formation techniques. 2) Power Off Landings-The Safe Approach: Showing the correct autorotation maneuvers. Methods of practice touch down. 3) Ground Safety Training: Entering and departing helicopters. Safety procedures for crew and passengers. Main and tail rotor hazards, rough terrain precaution, refueling, parking and moving. 4) Helicopter Orientation: Basic history of rotary flight. Sikorsky, Hiller and Bell. Fixed and rotary wing theory. Cockpit familiarization, controls.
04-030 90 min. $39.95

N.O.E.-Nap of the Earth
Six official U.S. Army helicopter programs designed for the "pro" and the serious aviation

enthusiast. Includes: 1) Introduction to N.O.E...Overview of N.O.E. close terrain flight techniques. 2) Flight and Down-Wind Flight Maneuvers: Pre-flight, high threat, OGE, hover check, quick stop, masking-unmasking coordination with friendly forces. 3) Survivability: Crash anticipation, clothing protection, boots, gloves, helmet. 4) High-Threat Environment: Soviet surface-to-air missiles, identifying Soviet systems, varying threats at altitude. 5) Visual Problems-Night Vision: How to avoid blind spots, visual scanning, fix of altitude on peripheral vision. 6) Cardinal Rules-Attack Helicopters: Heroism and courage not enough for a Huey Gun-Ship pilot in Nam. Details tactics and 12 cardinal rules for Attack Helicopters in battle environment.
04-045 90 min. $39.95

Vietnam Choppers
This is the story of that war and the men and machines who fought it. From Operation Junction City to the Tet Offensive to the Viet Cong's strong hold in the Iron Triangle, they were there. Here is stunning footage of ground battles together with hundreds of UH-1 Hueys and Cobras in action. Just as it happened, the "Chopper War."
13-5712 30 min. $14.95

History

Airmail Story
This features the aviation pioneers who established airmail postage and laid the groundwork for modern aviation in the process.
04-9819 45 min. $19.95

Flight of the Eagle
The fantastic, true story of the brave men of the eagle, a hydrogen balloon that vanished in 1897 en route to the North Pole. Photos, diaries and skeletons discovered 30 years later serve as the basis of this heroic survival adventure set in the vast arctic wasteland. Max von Sydow stars as the leader of the doomed expedition. Academy Award Nominee for Best Foreign Film.
04-103 115 min. $29.95

Greatest Story In Aviation History-Burnelli
Learn the fascinating story behind the conspiracy to keep the safest airplane ever designed from being placed into airline service. "The use of Burnelli airliners world reduce air crash fatalities by 85 %". Burnelli designs allow slower, thus safer takeoffs and landings without sacrifice of cruising speed,

use less fuel, can be built for half the cost, need half the runway, and have more capacity of people and cargo.
04-6412 30 min. $29.95

Hinkler: The Lone Eagle
Bert Hinkler was Australia's most famous aviator who flew for the RAF during World War II. Relive his adventurous life and daredevil flying against the Nazis.
04-032 50 min. $39.95

History of Aviation
Actual footage of man's early attempts at flight are included on this fascinating videocassette which chronicles aviation's progress from the prop planes and World War I fighters to modern-day jets and bombers.
04-035 50 min. $59.95

History of Flight
Examine man's unending quest to fly farther, faster, and higher with footage of the flying contraptions of the late 1800's, the Wright Brothers, Charles Lindbergh, and many others. Explore the creative role of research and technology in attaining our lofty goals.
04-036 24 min. $29.95

Queen Mary and the Spruce Goose
This video features the brilliant aviation career of the legendary Howard Hughes, his struggle to build the enormous Spruce Goose, including the amazing first flight, Senate hearings, and a detailed tour of the aircraft as it sits today.
04-038 24 min. $29.95

Howard Hughes and His Aircraft
A capsule history of Hughes and his aircraft, including color footage of the Spruce Goose.
04-2951 60 min. $39.95

History of Naval Aviation
Fifty years of Naval Aviation is brilliantly covered in this rousing program. You'll meet some of aviation's pioneers and learn the history of fight through the eyes of the brave men who lived and made it! Includes actual footage of the Wright Brothers' first public test fights at Ft. Meyers in 1908 and rare filmed accounts of World War I and World War II air battles fought over the Atlantic and South Pacific.
04-5779 84 min. $29.95

Kitty Hawk
Before the Wright Brothers flew for their first time at Kitty Hawk in 1903, man struggled to invent a machine that would stay up in the air. See how these early inventors competed to be the first in

flight, and how the needs of the early war machines brought about the first engine-powered flights.
04-5781 60 min. $19.95

Medal of Honor

The complete Air Force tribute to the flying Medal of Honor recipients from Eddie Rickenbacker and Charles Lindbergh to the aces of WW II and Vietnam. Kane, Johnson, Bong, Howard, Wilbanks over Ploesti, Guadalcanal and the Mekong Delta in everything from L-19s to Flying Forts, Mustangs, Lightnings and Thunderbolts. Above and beyond the call of duty, they laid their courage and their lives on the line. Exciting combat footage included in the 17 video segments.
04-041 90 min. $39.95

Naval Air Power

Four-part video series, includes: 1) Wings of Eagles, Wings of Gold: The evolution of naval aviation from its first days on the decks of the U.S.S. Langley to WW II, through Korea and Vietnam-nerve-shattering action including carriers in combat. 2) Down to the Wire: Five naval aviation cadets prepare as carrier pilots. Unusual insight into the flying techniques which train and qualify them to touch down on 10 feet of deck space. 3) Flight to the South Pole; Our naval airmen in a peacetime conquest of the pole, where cold runs at 100 degrees below zero, and a day lasts six months. You land atop solid ice at 9,000 feet above sea level. A contrast of rare footage of the original Byrd expedition with current flight operations. Includes U.S. Naval Fighters (1922-1980's), by Lloyd S. Jones, a full 352 pages of Navy and Marine Corps fighters with exciting photos.
04-044 83 min. $39.95

On Wings of Courage

A fascinating two-part program and historical review of the early years of aviation, featuring rare film coverage of events and planes. See Charles Lindergh, Wiley Post, Amelia Earhart and Kingsford Smith. Also included is a rare interview with Glen "Odi" Odekirk, a close associate of Howard Hughes. You'll see some rare footage of Howard Hughes, his daring feats, and wild escapades as an aviation pioneer.
04-093 55 min. $39.95

Those Magnificent Men in Their Flying Machines

The Wright Brothers signed a government contract in 1909 to produce fighter planes, and the idea of the airplane as a combat weapon was born. This thrilling history of the fighter plane includes fascinating footage of aerial dogfights and will thoroughly entertain anyone with an interest in combat or aviation.
04-5785 60 min. $39.95

Wings of Glory

A triple bill of memorable aviation greats: 1) 35th Anniversary of the Air Force: Official Air Force programs commemorating its founding. High adventure including such moments as the P-38 attack on Yamamoto, the Berlin Blockade, Mig Alley, Flying the Hump and much more. 2) General "Hap" Arnold: Narrated by Walter Matthau, here is the official Army Air Force biography of a founding father of our Air Force. Rare footage from the early days, WW I dogfights, and on to the daring daylight precision bombing raids over Germany in WW II. 3) Pacific Ace: Medal of Honor winner Richard Bong takes his P-38 to 40 official "kills."
04-076 70 min. $39.95

Space Exploration

America In Space: The First 25 Years

This is NASA's best, with 25 years of history-making space exploration compressed into one dynamic program. It features the most memorable achievements of America's exploration of space. From the 1958 Explorer 1 launch, to the Shuttle Challenger STS-7 flight-and everything in between-it's all here for you to enjoy.
04-105 50 min. $29.95

Apollo 11: The Eagle Has Landed

A documentary that captures all the drama and excitement of America's first lunar landing mission. The viewer experiences what a space mission is like, accompanying Neil Armstrong, Buzz Aldrin and Michael Collins from takeoff to final splashdown.
04-080 30 min. $16.95

Apollo 11: Man's First Moon Landing

The epic flight of Apollo 11 is regarded as a milestone in the accomplishments of mankind. Relive man's first steps on the moon-imagine the feeling of viewing earth from another planet. Complete coverage of the entire flight: launch, moon orbit, walking on the moon, recovery and more. Breathtaking scenes.
04-107 30 min. $29.95

Billion Dollar Image

Jet Propulsion Laboratory, 1976. The Viking spacecraft has landed on Mars. Capture the joy and excitement of those who watched as the spacecraft sent back its first revealing photographs of the Martian landscape. Includes interviews with famous

---

visionaries including Ray Bradbury, Carl Sagan and others.
13-309 30 min. $29.95

Blueprint for Space
Hosted by Astronaut Alan Shepard, the evolution of spaceflight is covered in a remarkable combination of rare paintings, footage, and the very latest computer animation.
04-8006 58 min. $24.95

Conquest
A thrilling look at man's shining achievements in space. A definitive work on the history of space exploration, from the rockets of Von Braun to the shuttle success of the eighties.
04-095 180 min. $59.95

Dream Is Alive
Narrated by Walter Cronkite, The Dream Is Alive gives you a window seat on the shuttle. Share the astronauts' experience of working, eating, and sleeping in zero gravity. Look back at our magnificent earth; witness an exciting satellite repair-proof that we can work in space, and the historic walk in space by an American woman.
04-5856 37 min. $29.95

Find Your Way Back
Find Your Way Back...is a rock salute to America's Space Program. Strap in for the most exciting ride on video tape...Now Discovery's STS-26 Astronauts host this soul stirring music video tribute to the past, present and future of America's Space program. These exclusive interviews reveal the human side of high tech space exploration. When combined with stunning NASA footage and high energy music, the result is an epic journey for all time. Music artists include: Starship, Steve Winwood, Bryan Ferry, Pat Benatar, Ronnie Montrose, and David Crosby.
04-6214 30 min. $19.95

First Flight of the Space Shuttle
From the incredible launch sequence at Cape Canaveral to the joyous landing at Edwards Air Force Base, this documentary lets you relive the historic maiden voyage of Shuttle Columbia. Includes a comprehensive overview of the shuttle program and its technology.
04-106 30 min. $19.95

Flight and Space
From Kitty Hawk to the moon and stars, this is the heroic history of America's race to space. It covers a technological revolution that saw mankind progress from horse and buggy to the moon in little more than two generations.
13-158 60 min. $24.95

Footsteps of Giants
This video chronicles 25 years of America's adventure in space, from Alan B. Shepard's historic flight in 1961, to the Space Shuttle Challenger's tragic explosion in 1986.
13-489 46 min. $24.95

Friendship In Quest of The Universe
Code named "Friendship 7" This space mission piloted by John Glenn was Americas official entry into the Global Space Race with the Soviet Union. Already in second place the success of the mission was of paramount importance to the president John F. Kennedy and to America as a whole dramatic, Friendship 7 to orbit the earth's atmosphere and safely splash down. The mission proved instrumental in America's successful attempt at beating the Soviets to the moon.
04-5459 59 min. $19.95

From Disaster To Discovery: The Challenger Explosion And The Rebirth Of America's Space Shuttle
On July 19, 1985, Vice President George Bush announced that our national search was over-after reviewing thousands of applications, a schoolteacher had been chosen to ride in the Challenger Space Shuttle. Her name was Crista McCullough. So begins the happy news broadcasts that would ironically lead into one of our key national disasters: the explosion of the Challenger Space Shuttle. The original news reports are here-the disbelief, the sadness, the search for meaning.
13-5753 60 min $24.95

History of the Apollo Program
From the early flight test to the historic landings on the moon, this documentary recounts each of the Apollo flights, examining the efforts and accomplishments of the Apollo Space Program. The best footage from all the flights of Apollo.
04-034 46 min. $29.95

INFINITY SERIES
Take a tour of the solar system through the latest moving pictures and photographs from NASA and observatories from around the world.

• **Solar System**
04-9421 60 min. $19.95

• **Deep Space**
04-9422 60 min. $19.95

• **Light, Beyond the Light of Life**
04-9423 60 min. $19.95

• **Crystal Space/Time Ship**
04-9424 60 min. $19.95

VIDEO TITLES LISTED IN THIS GUIDE ARE AVAILABLE FOR PURCHASE OR RENTAL. CONTACT YOUR LOCAL VIDEO STORE OR TELEPHONE (800) 383-8811

Journey Into Space

Journey Into Space documents a shuttle mission from launch to landing with segments showing the payload dropping off, astronauts walking in space and circling the globe. Computer graphics enhance footage of the earth to show particular states. There is no narration. It's all set to Craig Jackson's synthesized music.

04-128 30 min. $29.95

Jupiter & Saturn

Produced by Jet Propulsion Laboratory for NASA, this video film takes you on a billion-mile journey to the giant plants, Jupiter and Saturn. Through the eyes of Voyager 1 and 2, you will explore the planets and their rings and moons, learning of the most significant and surprising Voyager discoveries.

04-109 28 min. $29.95

Jupiter, Saturn, Uranus & Neptune

The Voyager Missions! Explore the planets, their rings, moon magnetic fields, geology and weather.

04-8007 52 min. $24.95

Kennedy Space Center: Window To The Universe

The Kennedy Space Center at Cape Canaveral is America's space program. From this dynamic facility, man has voyaged into the unknown, time and time again. Come with us on a tour of NASA's awesome launch facilities and exhibits and re-live many of the history-making missions which blasted-off here.

04-6085 35 min. $29.95

Lift Off: An Astronaut's Journey

With exclusive interviews and official NASA footage, this program gives a complete history of the fierce rivalry that existed between Russia and the United States to get to the moon first, utilizing spectacular footage of such milestones as John Glenn's historic orbit and Neil Armstrong's first steps on the moon.

04-5784 60 min. $19.95

Mars: The Red Planet

Through the eyes of the Mariner and Viking robot satellites explore Mars, its mysterious past, enormous mountains and canyons which dwarf anything found on earth.

04-040 30 min. $29.95

Mercury Spacecraft Missions

Relive the exciting first years of America's space program with Alan Shepard, John Glenn and President John F. Kennedy. The Mercury missions gave us our first manned flight, the first orbital flight and the determination to reach the moon and beyond. Captures the nervous moments of man's first expeditions into space.

04-110 30 min. $29.95

Moonwalk Man On The Moon

July 16, 1969. On a cloudless clear Cape Kennedy, Florida morning Apollo 11, codenamed Columbia lifted off for its far flung destination-The Moon. The three astronauts, making this historical trip were Neil Armstrong, Edwin "Buzz" Aldrin and Michael Collins. Armstrong and Aldrin would break away from lunar orbiting mother ship Columbia, and descend to the Moon's surface in the Lunar Lander named "Eagle". They would be the first men to ever walk on the moon. You are there as NASA footage records this heroic adventure.

04-5488 54 min. $19.95

NASA: The 25th Year

America's reach into space has been one of the most exciting chapters in our nation's recent history. Relive the triumphs in this retrospective look at the accomplishments of the National Aeronautic and Space Administration. Orbit the earth with John Glenn; walk on the moon with the Apollo astronauts; count down for take-off in the space shuttle; and much more.

13-5550 $19.95

NASA: The Quest for Mars

Includes: 1) Mars-The search Begins: Mariner 9 explores from orbit the mystery and splendor of this fascinating planet. Over 7,000 photos attest to the marvel of volcanoes 15 miles high and 100 miles across, plus rift valleys thousands of mile long. 2) The Planet Mars: The success of Viking 1 & 2 lead to Lander's touchdown on the Martian surface and the first opportunity to see the surface of Mars up close.

04-162 90 min. $39.95

NASA: The Space Series

Here, for the first time, a special combined program of official NASA films on video: America's high adventure in space, from Mercury to the moon, plus the historic U.S.-Soviet space link-up. Includes: 1) The World Was There (Mercury): World media coverage of Project Mercury, detailing the flights of Shepard, Grissom, Glenn, Carpenter, Schirra and Cooper from preparation through launch and recovery.) Legacy of Gemini: two-man space flights with outstanding photography of the earth and man in space. 3) Flight of Apollo 11 The Eagle Has Landed: Historic first landing of men on the moon, and the recovery of Armstrong, Aldrin and Collins. 4) Apollo/Soyuz: Yul Brynner narrates the U.S.-Soviet space rendezvous and docking. Astronauts and cosmonauts working together.

04-043 111 min. $39.95

NASA: Universe-Friend or Foe?

Four remarkable films: 1) Man's Reach Should Exceed His Grasp: Story of flight and man's search for freedom through aviation and space exploration. 2) America's Wings: Some of the ideas in aviation since Kitty Hawk: Sikorsky's helicopter, Osborne's jet transport theories, wind tunnels, swept wings winglets and other flying innovations. 3) Blue Planet: Narrated by Burgess Meredith, here is an important overview of our space program. 4) Who's Out There?: Orson Welles as host and star, from his 1938 "War of the Worlds" broadcast through scientific conclusions that there are indeed inhabitants in space.

04-163 90 min. $39.95

One Small Step for Man

A fascinating look at the story of the Apollo missions, culminating with Armstrong's historic walk on the moon.

04-050 60 min. $39.95

Planet Mars And Mercury

Two of NASA's best! First, trace man's evolving and sometimes imaginative theories about Mars from its discovery in 1669 to the historic Viking landing on its surface. The second program reveals the planet Mercury in startling detail with photographs and finding from the Mariner 45 10 mission. Excellent animation, high-resolution photographs, and geological comparisons of both planets.

04-6084 60 min. $29.95

Racing For The Moon: America's Glory Days In Space

We remember it well: the Soviets send up Sputnik and Yuri Gagarin; the U.S. retaliates with John Glenn and more-Mercury Missions, Apollo Missions, Neil Armstrong and The Moon. But no matter how many times these glory days have been rethought and reviewed, you can't beat the thrill and excitement of experiencing space flight for the first time. That's what is provided here, with the help of ABC News teams. As-it-is-happening coverage of truly heroic achievements.

13-5760 60 min. $24.95

Satellite Rescue in Space

A NASA-produced documentary of an actual space shuttle mission. The view joins the crew as they relive the excitement and tension of their mission. Experience the thrill of take-off. Float in zero gravity. Float in space outside the ship, tethered to the shuttle by just a thin cable. Repair a faulty circuit and rescue a dead satellite. Uses actual film footage taken by the astronauts and their commentary to capture all the breathtaking drama of a space shuttle mission.

04-104 20 min. $29.95

Space Conquerors The Final Frontier

An enthralling and illuminating panorama of man's upward struggle to the stars. From Robert Goodard and the birth of the rocket to Von Braun's infamous V-2 that devastated Europe. Mercury, Gemini, Apollo, the Moon landings, Skylab, Apollo-Soyuz and finally the Space Shuttle. It's all here! A grand, breathtaking, history marking spectacle that no science-fiction yarn could match.

04-5455 46 min. $19.95

Space Movie

A mind bending look at mankind's greatest adventure-the conquest of space! A stirring documentary record of the U.S. space program, assembled from spectacular NASA footage to a hypnotic soundtrack by Mike Oldfield (The Exorcist, The Killing Fields).

13-264 78 min. $49.95

Space Shuttle: Flights 1 through 8

Enjoy the triumphs of the first eight shuttle flights with this two-for-one video program. Features two NASA films - opening New Frontiers and We Deliver - summarizing the accomplishments of flights 1 thru 8. Includes spectacular views from space, satellite deployment, experiments and more.

04-112 60 min. $29.95

Space Shuttle: Mission to the Future

A comprehensive look at the U.S. Shuttle program, filled with exciting footage of the shuttle and her crews in action.

04-061 80 min $24.95

Space The Final Frontier

Here is the real story of man in space, the incredible highs extraordinary failure -- captured by the cameras and correspondents of the Independent Television News Network and rarely seen footage from the Soviet Union. Man's greatest adventure, The Space Race, begins as Yuri Gagarin blasts off on April 12, 1961, and Alan Shepard lifts off from Cape Canaveral three weeks later.

04-5173 60 min. $19.95

To Be an Astronaut

Experience the grueling training of the Mercury Astronauts, the Gemini teams' first walks in space, a drive on the moon with the crew of Apollo, and a stroll into space from the bay of the Shuttle.

04-8008 45 min. $24.95

We Remember: The Space Shuttle Pioneers, 1981-1986

Relive the tremendous accomplishments of the shuttle's pioneering missions, from Columbia's first launch to the Challengers's final mission, spanning 26 shuttle flights.

04-2676 58 min. $29.95

VIDEO TITLES LISTED IN THIS GUIDE ARE AVAILABLE FOR PURCHASE OR RENTAL. CONTACT YOUR LOCAL VIDEO STORE OR TELEPHONE (800) 383-8811

Women In Space "A Ride To Remember"
Women in Space gives an astonishing perspective on how women have impacted NASA's space program. featuring Sally Ride and her historic flight in June of 1982. Unique "You are There" footage and fascinating views on how it is determined just who has the "Right Stuff."
04-5456 60 min. $19.95

Miscellaneous

AIR FORCE STORY SERIES
The definitive history of the Air Force as only the Air Force can tell it. Contains 32 complete volumes from the original archives. A reference library of aerial greatness from the Wright Brothers through both World Wars to jet dogfights over Korea and the frontiers of space. This series is a rare and memorable treasure.

• **Volume 1**
Covers The Beginning, 1906-19; After the War, 1919-24; Struggle for Recognition, 1924-30; Between the Wars, 1930-35; Air Power Advances, 1935-37; Prelude to War, 1937-39; Air War Starts, 1939-41; and Drawing the Battle Lines: December 1941-April 1942.
04-014 108 min. $39.95

• **Volume 2**
Includes AAF Fights Back, April-June 1942; The Tide Turns, June-December 1942; North Africa, November 1942-may 1943; Expanding Air Power, June 1943; Schweinfurt and Regensburg, August 1943; Maximum Effort, October 1943; Road to Rome, September 1943 and June 1944; and Two Years At War, September-December 1943.
04-015 108 min. $39.95

• **Volume 3**
Includes Superfort, August 1943-June 1944; Prelude to Invasion, January 1944-June 1944; Ploesti Raid, March 1944-August 1944; Retreat and Advance, June 1944-March 1945; Victory in Europe, June 1944-May 1945; Air War Against Japan, 1944-1945; "D-Day", June 1944; and a New Air Force, 1945-47.
04-016 108 min. $39.95

• **Volume 4**
Includes Air Force Global Operations, 1946; The Cold War, 1948-50; Meeting the Red Challenge, Korea, June 1950; On to Yalu, Korea, June 1950; Final Phase, Korea, 1952; Our World-Wide Air

Force, 1953-59; Air Force and the "A Bomb", 1944-55; and Tactical Fire Power, 1950-60.
04-017 108 min. $39.95

Bombers
Ever since the first grenade was haphazardly thrown down and a battlefield below, the bomb and the plane have formed a pact that has changed the way wars are fought and won. See how balloons and zeppelins are used to drop bombs, how the first bombers were utilized in 1921, and how bombers have become increasingly more sophisticated with every war.
04-5782 60 min. $19.95

Dawn of The Jet Age: The First 25 years
This program traces the fascinating first 25 years of the jet plane. Beginning with the pilots and designers of the 1930's aircraft to the first breaking of the sound barrier, to the jets that fought during the Korean war.
04-5783 60 min. $19.95

FEEL THE "G" FORCE IN TODAY'S THREE HOTTEST PLANES
Ever dreamed of flying in the world's hottest fighter aircraft? Then get ready for three wild rides.

• **Advantage Hornet**
04-6119 62 min. $29.95

• **Eagle Country**
04-6120 85 min. $29.95

• **Falcon Domain**
04-6121 90 min. $29.95

Flying
Features flying-for-fun adventure segments from the popular 3-2-1-Contact series, including hot air ballooning, a ride in a blimp, kite flying in Japan, and soaring in a sailplane. Also includes all-new material with host David Quinn demonstrating some easy try-at-home activities.
04-6235 30 min. $19.95

Thunderbirds: A Team Portrait
Fly with the Thunderbirds, the United States Air Force Precision Flying Team, in this thrilling documentary profile that takes you up close and behind the scenes with the hottest jet jockeys in the air. Experience the power, the excitement, the sheer glory of flying with America's best!
13-5552 50 min. $19.95

Who's Out There
Narrated by Orson Wells, the man who brought the U.S. to it's knees with his "War of the Worlds"

broadcast, takes a probing look at mankind's search for extraterrestrial contact. The Mariner, Voyager and Viking programs are covered, as well as a panel of experts including Dr. Carl Sagan tackling "philosophical" questions like man's own superiority in the Universe.
04-5457 46 min. $19.95

Soaring In A Sailplane
Have you ever dreamt of flying? Find out what soaring in a fixed-wing glider is all about. You'll perform every aerobatics feat from take-off to landing. You'll drive, spiral, and loop the loop, "surf" the thermals and execute figure eights, rolls and wing-overs. Then you'll guide your wings up into altitude to start all over again! Shoot over the desert and mountains of gorgeous Southern California. If your spirit loves to fly, do it now in the comfort of your home!
04-6373 30 min. $29.95

STRANGE PLANES
The flights of fancy portrayed in this fascinating collection presents both the triumphs and the follies of pioneers taking aviation to-and sometimes beyond-the cutting edge of technical feasibility and imagination.

• Giants
From dirigibles to the Spruce Goose to the hugh jets of today, Giants captures the major milestones in mammoth aviation.
04-5942 60 min. $19.95

• Strange Shapes
Explore the most remarkable shapes ever sent into the air by humans including the Flying Pancake, the Tailless Fighter, and the Flying Wing-ancestor of the Stealth Bomber.
04-5943 60 min. $19.95

• Spyplanes
Examine delicate, exotic, high flying aircraft and the story of clandestine aviation.
04-5944 60 min. $19.95

• Vertical Take-Off
Investigates the planes that literally leap into the sky without a runway, and some that were supposed to, but didn't.
04-5945 60 min. $19.95

• Parasites
Focuses on craft that "piggyback" on a mother ship, from the German fighters designed to land on Zeppelins in World War I to today's Space shuttle.
04-5946 60 min. $19.95

• Drones, Mutants And Midgets
Recount the fascinating stories behind the most outlandish aviation designs ever conceived. An astounding wealth of true eccentricity.
04-5947 60 min. $19.95

Winter Training: A New Beginning
Containing fewer of the intricate details involved in the ground service of the F-4 Phantoms but all the thrills of riding in the skies behind master pilots.
04-6497 46 min. $19.95

Has Your Flyer Been Grounded?

Get Back in the Air

With One of These Videos!

New

Special Interest Video Titles

Become Available

Often.

Please Inquire

If A Title Or Subject

You Are Looking For

Is Not Listed.

Biography

✓ *Biography*

Biography

Abraham Lincoln By James McPherson

Fascinating archival images and contemporary photography of historic sites are woven together with James McPherson's eloquent commentary in this saga of the man who rose from obscurity to preserve the Union as our sixteenth President. From the frontier to the White House, Abraham Lincoln traces the life of one of history's greatest figures.
06-5187 35 min. $19.95

Adolf Hitler

You will never forget the incredible exclusive footage from all stages of Adolf Hitler's rise and fall, from this, the darkest period in human history.
06-1926 101 min. $59.95

Al Capone: Chicago's Scarface

No one man has done more for a city than Al Capone had for Chicago. This bootlegging, skull-breaking king of the gangsters ruled Chicago with brass knuckles for over a decade, and his ruthless power can still be felt in the streets of what was once America's most corrupt and dangerous city. This is a compelling, factual documentary about the man and his bloody business. Using rare footage of Capone that was shot in the Roaring '20s, this film provides a good idea of what it was like to live under his not-so-benevolent rule. Al Capone's vault may have been empty, but his legacy is as rich and provocative as ever.
06-047 110 min. $39.95

Amazing Howard Hughes

Millionaire, flyer, playboy, film mogul- Howard Hughes had it all. Now the story of a legendary eccentric comes alive with all the mystery that made him a modern American hero
13-470 119 min. $59.95

Ansel Adams; Photograp, Photographer

An Absorbing and warmhearted portrait of Ansel Adams, one of the greatest photographers of the 20th century. The film captures the spirit and artistry of the man as he talks about his life and demonstrates the techniques which have made his work legendary.
03-306 60 min. $24.95

BLACK HERITAGE SERIES

• Adam Clayton Powell Jr.

The most powerful black man in America's political history.
06-8013 57 min. $19.95

• Black Athlete

A chronicle on the rise of blacks in professional sports. Featuring: Jesse Owens, Kareem Abdul-Jabbar and O.J. Simpson.
06-8014 200 min. $19.95

• Black Like Me

A white reporter changes his skin color so he can experience life as a black man. Starring James Whitmore and Roscoe Lee Brown.
06-9087 107 min. $19.95

• Jackie Robinson Story

The first Black American to play major league baseball. Starring Jackie Robinson and Ruby Dee.
06-9089 60 min. $19.95

• Joe Lewis Story

The classic true life story of the first great black boxer.
06-9086 88 min. $19.95

• Lost, Stolen or Strayed

Bill Cosby examines how historians have failed to document achievements by Black Americans.
06-9088 60 min. $19.95

• Mahalia Jackson

Mahalia Jackson and Elizabeth Cotten are paired in a duo of filmed biographies, now on video. Returning to her origins in New Orleans, Mahalia sings such favorites as "Down by the Riverside" and "A Closer Walk With Thee'" while the over-80 incomparable Miss Cotten presents her original version of "Freight Train."
06-024 120 min. $64.95

• Malcolm X

This intense documentary examines the life and mysterious death of Malcolm X.
06-9090 60 min. $19.95

• Gordon Parks

Best selling author, award winning photographer, writer and director through his eyes.
06-9091 60 min. $19.95

• Medgar Evers

The incredible story of the Civil Rights activist. Staring Larry Fishburne and Howard Rollins Jr.
06-8012 90 min. $19.95

Bonnie and Clyde: Myth or Madness

This fascinating video explores the backgrounds of Bonnie and Clyde and documents their rise in the world of crime. It paints a bleak picture of two

undersized gunslingers who enjoyed killing people.
06-1925 69 min. $49.95

Churchill: The Finest Hours
Winston Churchill's memoirs of World War II, his
political setbacks and eventual leadership of Britain
(and the free world) against Hitler Germany make
up this fascinating tape. Narrated by Orson Welles,
this color videocassette is filled with actual footage
of the great man.
06-007 115 min. $39.95

Clifford Brycelea: Vision World
Artist and American Indian Clifford Brycelea
discusses his life in the two worlds of the White
and Red man. Famous for paintings of Louis
L'Amour's novels, the artist shows us his
reservation home and also life in his artist's world.
Many beautiful paintings.
13-284 30 min. $24.95

Eleanor Roosevelt Story
An inspired documentary on the life of one of the
greatest American women in history.
06-8028 90 min. $19.95

Elizabeth, The Royal Queen Mother
This program celebrates the life of the world's most
beloved dowager queen, who went from being just
another prince's wife to become a most elegant,
courageous queen.
06-8029 30 min $29.95

Elvis
The story of the most influential song stylist in
music history; a world-renowned phenomenon
whose concert performances, hit singles and chart-
topping albums made him the undisputed King of
Rock & Roll. The story of the legendary
performer's entire career; from the formative days
with Sun Records to his bold leap into television
and motion pictures, more than two decades of the
King's finest film roles are glimpsed.
04-6449 45 min. $16.95

Elvis 56
The debut of the King of Rock and Roll. His early
years, his concert and his music. An in depth look
at the man behind the legend and how it all began.
06-8024 61 min. $24.95

Elvis Files
Explore the curious circumstances of Elvis'
death...and his life since. Based on the best selling
book.
06-8023 50 min. $24.95

Elvis Presley's Graceland
Join Priscilla Beaulieu Presley as she fondly
remembers Elvis' live. Graceland was his

monument to the American Dream. Share in Elvis'
most meaningful moments, untold stories of his
generosity, his relationship with his friends and
family and his accomplishments. Highlights of the
tour include: the exotic Jungle Room, the Pool
Room, TV Room and the immaculately landscaped
grounds. Graceland was the center of Elvis
Presley's life, and remains a monument for those
who cared for him. Also included are interviews
and footage from his life and career.
13-157 60 min. $24.95

Elvis: The Echo Will Never Die
The King of Rock N' Roll's life, death and music
make up this intimate portrait of Elvis. From his
roots in gospel to his meteoric rise in film, Elvis
gave us his special talent that lives on, even today.
13-311 55 min. $29.95

Evel Knievel
George Hamilton stars in this stunning film on the
daredevil legend, and Evel himself performs many
of the stunts. Featuring some amazing footage of
his devastating crash at Caesar's Palace, this real-
life adventure story will leave you breathless.
06-069 90 min. $59.95

Evel Knievel's Greatest Hits
Breathtaking jumps and bone-jarring crashes with
America's most thrilling daredevil! Includes:
Malice at the Palace, Wounded at Wembley, the
Triumph at Toronto and many more.
06-1817 30 min. $19.95

FAMOUS AMERICANS SERIES
A look at the contributions that made these
Americans great.

• **Story of Babe Ruth**
06-8005 30 min. $29.95

• **Story of Charles A. Lindbergh**
06-8001 30 min. $29.95

• **Story of Douglas McArthur**
06-8002 30 min. $29.95

• **Story of Dwight D. Eisenhower**
06-8006 30 min. $29.95

• **Story of Franklin Delanor Roosevelt**
06-8004 30 min. $29.95

• **Story of G.I. Joe**
06-8011 30 min. $29.95

• **Story of Harry S. Truman**
06-8010 30 min. $29.95

• **Story of Helen Keller**
06-8003 30 min. $29.95

• **Story of Henry Ford**
06-8008 30 min. $29.95

• **Story of Knute Rockne**
06-8007 30 min. $29.95

• **Story of Thomas A. Edison**
06-8009 30 min. $29.95

Fergie, The Making of a Duchess
This comprehensive profile gives a full account of her childhood, courtship, marriage and lifestyle. In her way, she tells what it is like to be a member of the Royal family.
06-8025 55 min. $29.95

Godfathers: Crime in America
The true story of crime and the mob in America. Featured are: Al Capone, "Lucky" Luciano, and Murder Inc.
06-8022 65 min. $16.95

HALF SLAVE, HALF FREE SERIES

• **Volume I**
One man's struggle to regain freedom from slavery in pre-Civil War America.
Directed by Gordon Parks.
06-9092 113 min. $59.95

• **Volume II**
One woman's determination to prove to President Lincoln that the black man is equal.
06-8030 120 min. $59.95

Helen Keller: Separate Views
The Helen Keller story. A colorful dramatization of the life of this remarkable woman and her teacher, Annie Sullivan. Part II has Katherine Cornell, Marth Graham and President Dwight Eisenhower narrating her fascinating biography. The bonus film in this package is the 1974 Oscar-winning short, "One Eyed Men Are Kings".
06-013 60 min. $69.95

Houdini
Combining old photos, newsreel film, silent movie clips, and interviews with today's top illusionists, the enigmatic life of Harry Houdini is examined.
06-1851 30 min. $16.95

I Came as a Pilgrim: Pope Paul II, 1987
This collector's edition features an intimate portrait of the Holy Father and captures the spiritual moments as he talks to all Americans from every

ethnic background and homeland. Produced by the award-winning NBC News team and narrated by correspondent Maria Shriver.
06-2385 60 min. $19.95

James Dean
On September 30, 1955, James Dean died in an automobile accident, plunging an entire generation of Americans into deep mourning. He was 24 years old. Although he had starred in just three films, Dean generated tremendous adulation and became an idol to the youth of the 50's. A stunning documentary about this young leader without a program, spokesman with out a philosophy, a rebel without a cause.
06-051 90 min. $19.95

James Dean Story
This film is the ultimate portrait of James Dean, presented by producer/director Robert Altman. Recognizing Jimmy's worldwide fame, Altman explores his personal life, those moments between the films. This film contains never-before-seen footage from "East of Eden'" the famous Highway Public Safety Message made for television and rare film from the Hollywood premier of "Giant."
13-378 80 min. $24.95

JOHN F. KENNEDY: A CELEBRATION OF HIS LIFE & TIMES
Features three volumes beginning with: Man Who Would Be President, 1917-1956, Race for the White House, 1957-1961 and Presidency and the Legacy, 1961-1963. Sold only in three volume set.
06-8026 160 min. $69.95

Judy Garland Scrapbook
Born in Grand Rapids, Michigan in 1922, Francis Gumm (aka Judy Garland) was destined to become the shining star of her generation. This scrapbook pieces together odd aspects of her life, from family movies and behind-the-scenes footage and photographs to her great work in motion pictures. Captures the essence of her appeal and the power of her tragedy.
13-5797 50 min. $19.95

Kerouac
This is the critically acclaimed, award-winning biography of the King of the Best Generation. Jack Kerouac's life is examined through fascinating rare documentary footage and a masterful portrayal by Jack Coulter as the author. Featuring Allen Ginsberg, Lawrence Ferlinghetti and William Burroughs. Music by Charles Mingus, Duke Ellington, Thelonius Monk and Zoot Sims.
06-041 73 min. $39.95

VIDEO TITLES LISTED IN THIS GUIDE ARE AVAILABLE FOR PURCHASE OR RENTAL. CONTACT YOUR LOCAL VIDEO STORE OR TELEPHONE (800) 383-8811

Legend of Valentino
A brilliantly written and edited portrait following Rudolph Valentino through his triumphant career, his on-and off-screen romances, and his sudden and shocking death.
06-023 71 min. $24.95

Life and Times of Grizzly Adams
In a time when wild animals, especially the ferocious grizzly, were greatly feared and misunderstood by the early settlers of the American frontier, Adams emerged as a living legend who neither feared nor misunderstood any living thing-with the possible exception of man.
24-073 96 min. $29.95

Life And Times Of George Washington
This program tells the remarkable story of George Washington's life through original historical prints from the Willard-Budd Collection at Mount Vernon. The illustrations dramatically capture the highlights of Washington's career, including his early years as a surveyor of the western frontiers. Thrilling Revolutionary War scenes come to life: Victories at Trenton and Princeton, the desperate winter at Valley Forge and the climactic triumph at Yorktown. This video comes highly recommended for classroom use.
06-5192 30 min. $29.95

Life And Times Of John F. Kennedy
A warm and human portrait of one of America's best-loved presidents. Join Cliff Robertson as he explores the life of JFK, from prep school student to war hero, senator, and finally martyred president. Relive the triumph and the tragedy of this great American.
13-5547 60 min. $24.95

LIFE AND TIMES OF LORD MOUNTBATTEN
The Life and Times of Lord Mountbatten spans 70 years and brilliantly chronicles the career of this remarkable man through war and peace, triumph and revolution. Drawing from a wealth of archival footage, as well as revisiting several locations with Lord Mountbatten himself, this unique series is not only about but with the man widely recognized as the technical innovator of the Royal Navy.

• **1900-1922**
13-5555 96 min. $29.95

• **1922-1941**
13-5556 96 min. $29.95

• **1941-1945**
13-5557 96 min. $29.95

• **1945-1947**
13-5558 96 min. $29.95

• **1947-1955**
13-5559 96 min. $29.95

• **1955-1968**
13-5560 96 min. $29.95

LINCOLN SERIES:

• **Making of a President**
06-8015 60 min. $19.95

• **Pivotal Year--1863**
06-8016 60 min. $19.95

• **I Want to Finish the Job--1864**
06-8017 60 min. $19.95

• **Now He Belongs to the Ages--1865**
06-8018 60 min. $19.95

Man of Peace: Portrait of Pope John Paul II
Shows the unique beauty of Rome and St. Peter's Basilica and Square. Inside the Vatican you'll see private audiences between Pope John Paul II and Prince Charles and Princess Diana. Follow the Pope to India where he visits Mother Theresa-and much more.
06-2672 60 min. $29.95

Man Of The Trees (The Life Of Richard St. Barbe Baker)
Moved by his great love of life and a deep spiritual vision of a world made green again, Richard St. Barbe Baker dedicated most of his 93 years to preserving the world's forests. Scenes of his remarkable work from Africa, New Zealand, and North America make this an inspirational documentary for the whole family.
13-5098 25 min. $24.95

Man Who Saw Tomorrow
The rise of Napoleon, Hitler the Ayatollah; the slayings of Presidents Lincoln and Kennedy-one brilliant 16th century mind foretold it all and more. Orson Welles narrates this documentary about Nostradamus.
06-1921 88 min. $29.95

Manson
This chilling documentary examines the lives, actions and beliefs of convicted murderer Charles Manson and his "family." Previously banned in California, this documentary reveals, for the first time outside the courtroom, the staggering details of the most hideously bizarre murders in the annals

VIDEO TITLES LISTED IN THIS GUIDE ARE AVAILABLE FOR PURCHASE OR RENTAL. CONTACT YOUR LOCAL VIDEO STORE OR TELEPHONE (800) 383-8811

of crime-details not permitted on TV, radio or in family newspapers.
06-042 90 min $59.95

Marilyn And The Kennedys: Tragic Triangle

The product of a three year investigation by senior British and American journalists, reports for the first time on film the cover-up which followed: a cover-up which, incredibly, was kept in place for nearly 25 years.
13-5451 71 min. $29.95

Marlene

This film features off-screen commentary from Dietrich and numerous clips from her films, an award-winning documentary from Maximillian Schell.
06-2825 96 min. $19.95

McCarthy: Point of Order

Few men have inspired as much hatred and destroyed as many lives as the red-baiting senator from Wisconsin, Joseph McCarthy. "McCarthy" is his story- an emotional and frank documentary that vividly examines the man whose name has become synonymous with the blacklisting fever of the Cold War during the 1950's.
13-312 45 min. $29.95

Meet Babe Ruth

Incredible historic footage of the great Bambino-Babe Ruth. Featuring Highlights of his record-breaking career, rare personal interviews and "off the field" action plus much more.
06-2278 60 min. $19.95

Mussolini: Rise and Fall of a Dictator

From his humble origins to his ascent as the ultimate power in Italy, we are presented with the never-before-revealed facts about Italy's most controversial figure since Nero.
06-045 105 min. $29.95

Norman Rockwell: An American Portrait

America's most-loved artist, Norman Rockwell captured the spirit of our nation and its people. Host Mason Adams presents an authoritative and insightful overview of the man and his works, beginning with his first Saturday Evening Post cover in 1916. A must for anyone who has ever marveled at the humor, poetry and humanity of a Rockwell illustration.
13-5553 60 min. $24.95

Once at the Border: Aspects of Stravinsky

A musical biography of one of the most influential

and controversial composers of the 20th century.
06-2792 166 min. $59.95

Ozawa

A portrait of Seiji Ozawa, Boston Symphony Orchestra's musical director and conductor. Follow Ozawa to Europe and his native Japan, as he works, performs and remembers. Scenes of the maestro as teacher and student are interwoven with discussions, rehearsals and performances. A subtle, moving image of the individual and the musician, a man whose Eastern approach to Western music has been praised, criticized, and misunderstood.
06-1825 60 min. $24.95

Patton: Old Blood and Guts

He was much more than a general, he was a man who believed that war was the noblest human endeavor of man's begin. He believed that is was his destiny to lead desperate men in desperate battle. This film highlights the career of General George S. Patton from his early childhood to his great victories of World War II. Narrated by Ronald Reagan.
06-1591 25 min. $19.95

Princess Diana - A Portrait

Learn what it's like to be a Princess. You will see the daily tasks and what is expected of a member of Royalty in this in-depth program.
06-8019 50 min. $14.95

Princess Diana - A Model Princess

Learn about this new member of British Royalty and her new role.
06-8020 50 min. $14.95

Queen Elizabeth II: 60 Glorious Years

For anyone interested in royalty, this is a must, as the life of Queen Elizabeth II is brilliantly captured on video. You will see her childhood, her wedding, and her coronation. This is the story of her reign as the highly respected monarch of England in this production authorized by Buckingham Palace.
06-1592 55 min. $29.95

Reagan's Way: Pathway to the Presidency

Ronald Reagan is one of the most popular presidents in American history. His rise through the political ranks reads like a Hollywood script. Through the use of never before seen interviews and film clips, you will have an insightful look at the making of a President.
13-169 52 min. $39.95

Real Rainman

Richard Wawro is undoubtedly one of the most talented savants in the world. Born in Scotland, he suffered from severe childhood disabilities

including blindness, cancer and speech impediments. Yet his genius for drawing realistic pictures became evident at an early age, along with his inexplicable ability for rapid calculations and memory tricks. Find out why savants often have talents that surpass those of so-called "normal people".
06-6466 35 min. $16.95

Robert E. Lee
Deciphers the myth. From his birth in the Virginia aristocracy to the fiery battlefields of the Civil War this documentary chronicles the triumphs and defeats of the great Confederate general.
06-6549 30 min. $19.95

Rose Kennedy: A Mother's Story
Here is the heart-rending, soul-stirring story of the start of the Kennedys, told by Rose Kennedy herself and through Kennedy family home movies, rare documentary footage and interviews with major participants.
06-8027 46 min. $29.95

Rubinstein Remembered
Documentary on legendary pianist Arthur Rubinstein, tracing his career and featuring excerpts of the maestro performing Chopin.
06-2032 58 min. $39.95

Salvador Dali: A Soft Self-Portrait
Narrated by Orson Welles, this video is a surreal journey into the mind of Salvador Dali, one of the great artists of the 20th century, Filmed on location at Dali's beautiful villa in Spain this film visually explores Dali's outrageous world, his art and his philosophies.
03-331 60 min. $39.95

Shirley Temple Scrapbook
In 1935 she wasn't even ten years old-but she was the best-known celebrity in the world (with a bank balance to prove it). Includes rare early footage of Shirley Temple in the 1928 "Baby Burlesques," as well as the first "two-reelers" when she was paid $15/day to appear in a series of films called "The Frolics of Youth." Shirley Temple provided a unique release. Sit back and watch her spin her magic in War Babies, Kid in Africa, Polly Ticks, Baby Takes a Bow, and Suzannah of the Mountains. This video includes footage of her wedding.
06-5798 52 min. $19.95

Shirley Verrett
A film biography of this Black opera singer who struggled from the back rows of the chorus to the center of every opera stage in the world.
06-2793 60 min. $29.95

Stonewall Jackson
Tells the remarkable story of the legendary Confederate general, Thomas J. Jackson. From his orphaned youth in the Appalachian Mountains to his daring exploits on Civil War battlefields, this powerful documentary presents one of America's most brilliant-and eccentric-military leaders.
06-6550 30 min. $19.95

Story of Babe Ruth
The true story behind one of the greatest baseball players to ever live.
06-8021 55 min. $29.95

Thomas Jefferson
The viewer will feel like a part of early American times, having conversations with Thomas Jefferson and meeting the leading characters of the American Revolution. Experience the critical first years of the new nation through the wit and insights of one of the most important figures in history.
06-040 40 min. $19.95

Time There Was: A Profile of Benjamin Britten
A celebration of one man's work and life. Features excerpts from several more operas.
06-2791 120 min. $59.95

Toast to Lenny
A parade of renowned comedians pay tribute to Lenny Bruce, the comic whose irreverent humor revolutionized the art of stand-up comedy. Stars Bill Cosby, Steve Allen and George Carlin.
06-1849 60 min. $59.95

Toscanini: The Maestro and Verdi's Hymn of the Nations
Rare home movies, many in color, plus interviews with such luminaries as Bidu Sayao, Robert Merrill, Licia Albanese, and members of the NBC Symphony help make this a definitive statement on the legendary maestro. James Levine is your host. Also included is a performance of Verdi's patriotic "Hymn of the Nations" featuring Jan Peerce.
25-145 74 min. $39.95

Ulysses S. Grant
Recounts the life of the one-time shop clerk who became commander of the Civil War's victorious Union armies-and eighteenth President of the United States.
06-6551 30 min. $19.95

Up Close with Mackenzie Astin
Teen heartthrob Mackenzie hosts his own fan video that features glimpses of his home life and other aspects of his existence that are of vital importance to his fans.
06-1978 47 min. $19.95

VIDEO TITLES LISTED IN THIS GUIDE ARE AVAILABLE FOR PURCHASE OR RENTAL. CONTACT YOUR LOCAL VIDEO STORE OR TELEPHONE (800) 383-8811

W.C. Fields: On Stage, On Screen, On The Air
Born in Philadelphia in 1879, William Claude Duncanfield set at least two generations on fire with his chauvinistic, drunken, child-hating persona as W.C. Fields. It was an act, wasn't it? You can decide for yourself in these random clips from his life and times, including rare family movies, radio fights with Charlie McCarthy and appearances in Grade A and Grade Z films.
06-5796 52 min. $19.95

Yoko Ono: Then and Now
An intimate look at the life of Yoko Ono and John Lennon, highlighted by video clips of "Imagine", "Watching the Wheels Go Round" and their personal home movies.
06-032 56 min. $24.95

Searching For A Unique Gift

That Is Entertaining, Instructional

Or Amusing?

The Video Titles Described

In This Section and Throughout

The Guide Make Wonderful

Gifts.

VIDEO TITLES LISTED IN THIS GUIDE ARE AVAILABLE FOR PURCHASE OR RENTAL. CONTACT YOUR LOCAL VIDEO STORE OR TELEPHONE (800) 383-8811

Boating

- ✓ *Board Sailing*
- ✓ *Boat Building & Maintenance*
- ✓ *Instruction*
- ✓ *Power Boats & Yachts*
- ✓ *Racing & Regattas*
- ✓ *Sailboats*

Board Sailing

Beginning Boardsailing Technique
The basic techniques of boardsailing, with Anne Nelson and Rich Myers.
08-005 45 min. $39.95

Intermediate Boardsailing
A comprehensive break down of fundamental techniques of boardsailing, beach and water starts are discussed.
08-3118 15 min. $29.95

Thrillseekers
Thrillseekers blazes into your living room with supercharged sports action, propelled by a pounding rock soundtrack. Experience: Parasailing, repelling and snowboarding, barefoot water skiing, surfing, windsurfing, bmx, and skateboarding.
08-6181 60 min. $19.95

Water Sports: Windsurfing Part 1
This is the one you've been waiting for-a thorough explanation of the art and science of windsurfing. Learn the basics in fifty absorbing minutes of chat and demonstrations - even if you've never set foot on a board.
08-6170 60 min. $34.95

Water Sports: Windsurfing Part 2
State-of-the-art techniques and equipment are demonstrated in this video. The practical demonstrations will turn your windsufing competence into excellence.
08-6171 60 min. $34.95

Boat Building & Maintenance

COSMETIC GELCOAT & FIBERGLASS REPAIR

• Color Matching
08-8038 100 min. $39.95

• Air Voids and Stress Cracks.
08-8039 100 min. $39.95

Fiberglass Boat Repair
You will learn...the art of fiberglass repair, fabrication, gel-coating, techniques covering the application of non-skid decks, the proper handling of wood in fiberglass construction, what tools to use and how to use them, how to lay stringers and bulkheads, how to keep extensive wood rot from ever recurring, and much more. The most in-depth fiberglass boat repair video on the market today.
08-7059 120 min. $34.95

Fiberglass Repair With West System Epoxy
Take the frustration out of repairing fiberglass surfaces with the knowledge of the experts! The West System is one of the most trusted names in marine business. Step-by-step, you'll learn the about materials and procedures to make professional, long-lasting fiberglass repairs with epoxy.
08-6981 32 min. $24.95

How to Rig Your Boat for Fishing
The secret to bringing home a fish everytime is equipment. This program shows you all you need to know about professional rigging for your boat, from fighting chairs to rocket launchers.
08-3102 60 min. $39.95

Howie Diddit's Dream Boat: Hull Blister Repair
Learn all the important aspects of removing gelcoat, sealing the hull, moisture barriers and bottom painting by watching the restoration of a 26' cruiser. After you see "how he did it", you'll wonder why you've been putting it off!
08-6890 25 min. $39.95

Lines Plan
Master boatbuilder Arno Day explains the Lines Plan-the meaning and use of lines. Arno shows you the entire process of measuring a boat, drawing the sections, the body plan, the profile and half-breadth plans, and how to develop the waterlines and buttock lines.
08-083 120 min. $99.95

Marine Diesel Engine Maintenance
Save money, save time and enjoy your boat more with these integral insights on your marine diesel engine. Covered are specific features of trouble-shooting, diagnostics and maintenance on the electrical, cooling, fuel and exhaust systems of most major engine types in use today. Also, how to deal with an "on-the-water" breakdown.
08-6384 75 min. $39.95

Marine Gas Engine Maintenance
Periodic maintenance insures engine longevity and reliability. Included in this superb tape is a trouble-

shooting section, how to make your gas engine cooperate with your boating plans, details on ignition systems and how to deal with routine and not so routine maintenance.
08-6383 75 min. $39.95

Small Boat Engine Maintenance
Chief Warrant Officer and U.S. Coast Guard marine inspector Jim Storey, brings you his expertise on outboard and inboard marine engines. You will learn what to do if your motor quits while you are under way: how to gap a spark plug and good lube techniques.
08-032 56 min. $29.95

Varnishing Made Easy
Most people detest the chore of varnishing, usually because of the lack of knowledge needed to achieve that "professional look". This tape covers the right materials, tools and techniques along with "trade secrets" needed to transform you into a varnishing virtuoso and your boat...into a work of art.
08-6382 43 min. $24.95

Instruction

12 Volts Made Easy
Based on Miner Brotherton's best selling book "The 12 Volt Bible For Boats" this tape is a nuts and bolts primer on 12 volt electrical systems created for boat owners who are not skilled electricians.
08-8098 60 min. $39.95

Abandon Ship
Although we hope you'll never need this advice on this tape, it's indispensable if you plan to venture offshore. Produced for Avon, this tape details the necessary emergency procedures, and techniques proven to be effective indire straits. Most importantly, this tape will show you how to Survive!
08-6972 30 min. $24.95

ANNAPOLIS BOOK OF SEAMANSHIP

• Cruising Under Sail
John Rousmaniere demonstrates navigation, sailing and seamanship skills in a clear, easy-to-follow way. Includes basic navigation and planning a cruise, sailhandling and sail trim anchoring and docking, steering and boathandling, safety, attire, knots and more.
08-1832 72 min. $49.95

• Heavy Weather Sailing
John Rousmaniere demonstrates heavy weather techniques that every cruising sailor should know. Includes crew readiness, boat preparation shortening sail under difficult conditions heaving-to, use of a drogue, steering techniques and more.
08-1833 60 min. $49.95

• Safety at Sea
Organized around the four steps to safety at sea, this video is recommended viewing for every sailor. This tape features in-depth onboard safety inspections and demonstrations including emergency and rescue techniques. Additional demonstrations include flare firing, man overboard recovery, use of a drogue and a look inside a life raft.
08-1834 63 min. $49.95

• Sailboat & Racing
Step-by-step instruction of high-tech electronic navigation and classic piloting and dead-reckoning in good weather, in fog, by day and by night.
08-8065 70 min. $49.95

• Daysailers Sailing and Racing
For the novice/intermediate sailor of small keel boats, include hull design, rigging, boat handling, tacking and jibbing, crew overboard rescue, safety, spinnaker work, and an introduction to club racing.
08-8066 75 min. $49.95

Baja Passage
Join the "Hubba Hubba"' a Catalina 30, and her crew in their preparations and cruise down the 1000 mile long Baja peninsula on the tip of California.
08-3117 60 min. $39.95

Bareboat Chartering Checklist
A perfect tape for both first time charterers and old salts who need a little brushing up. Topics include: you and the charter operator, above and below inspections and daily maintenance.
08-8045 25 min. $24.95

Basic Navigation/Rules of the Road
Commander Dave Smith shows you the basic aids to navigation: buoys, light, ranges, structural charts, as well as where to purchase and how to read them. Also covered are symbols how to find out where you are by means of visual fix, line of position, dumb compass, triangulation and depth contours; and how to determine speed by chip log, and much more. For the beginning boater and a good refresher course for the intermediate and advanced boater.
08-029 60 min. $39.95

VIDEO TITLES LISTED IN THIS GUIDE ARE AVAILABLE FOR PURCHASE OR RENTAL. CONTACT YOUR LOCAL VIDEO STORE OR TELEPHONE (800) 383-8811

BETTER BOAT HANDLING SERIES
Learn how to handle and maintain your inboard and outboard motor.

- **Handling Your Twin I/O**
  08-8106 50 min. $29.95

- **Handling Your Single I/O**
  08-8107 50 min. $29.95

- **Handling Your Twin Outboard**
  08-8108 50 min. $29.95

- **Handling Your Single Outboard**
  08-8109 50 min. $29.95

Boat Handling Techniques For Fisherman
Become an expert boat handler and a better fisherperson, too. Learn to determine the best trolling speed for both natural baits and artificial lures and fuel management for safety and economy.
08-8001 40 min. $29.95

Boater's Video
An excellent refresher for the experienced boater or that new boater. Learn the basics of boating and maintaining your craft, rules of the water and more!
08-8001 50 min. $29.95

Boating Basics
This is an introduction to complete boating. Learn the basics and rules of boating. A great video for the first time boater or the captain's family.
08-8029 75 min. $24.95

Boating Techniques/Electronics that Perform
Commander Dave Smith, together with John Ford of Coastal Navigator, Inc. and Dan Aspoplund of Racal-Decca Marine, Inc., show you the newest electronics, including radios, CBs, autopilots, loran, loran chart plotter, radar, depth sounders, satellite navigation and fish finders.
08-031 60 min. $39.95

Coast Guard License Video With Book
This is the best tape to help you to obtain the internationally recognized U.S. Coast Guard License. Not only does it cover the essentials of the license test, but it's the definitive tape of the Complete Rules of the Road Advanced Piloting and much, much more. The tape comes with a special offer on our book "The Coast Guard License" by Budd Gonder.
08-6386 114 min. $69.95

Cold Water Survival
For every boater, whether inland or coastal, the fear of falling overboard and not being rescued is always on the skipper's mind. This program discusses cold water survival tips; types of flotation devices; and recognition, prevention of and treatment for hypothermia.
08-030 60 min. $39.95

Cruising Catalina and San Clemente Islands
An invaluable and entertaining guide to cruising California's Southern Channel Islands of Santa Catalina and San Clemente. Includes information on preparation and sailing conditions.
08-3116 60 min. $29.95

Every Boater Should Know
Learn why the Coast Guard can confiscate your boat, basic rules of the waterways, piloting procedures, and more.
08-8026 60 min. $24.95

Finding Fish with LCD Depthsounders
Learn how to interpret signals and the practice of sonar.
08-8102 30 min. $29.95

Finding Fish with Amber Video Depthsounder
Learn how the system works and how to use it.
08-8103 30 min. $29.95

GPS Navigation
Learn exactly what GPS is and how the system works.
08-8051 60 min. $39.95

Handling and Anchoring Your Boat
For single or twin screw, power or sail. This video shows you exactly how to put your boat where you want it and keep it there.
08-3100 75 min. $39.95

Improve Your Sailing Skills
Produced for the sailor with some sailing experience. Can help the novice become an expert. And each topic is presented by top California racers in an easy manner to understand.
08-8027 30 min. $29.95

Loran C: A Navigator's Approach
Very little has been done to help sailors new to electronic navigation to understand how to use the information generated by their Loran C receiver. This video will explain what the system is, how it works useful features and navigation plotting exercises and solutions.
08-084 104 min. $39.95

Modern Coastal Piloting
Here is a navigation tape that's easy to understand, interesting and packed full of vital information, from compass use to RADAR plots, and much more.
08-3103 75 min. $39.95

Navigation: Robin Knox-Johnston
This program provides a clear audio-visual tutor on the basic principles of navigation. Extremely useful for navigating in tidal areas.
08-3105 60 min. $39.95

New Boater's Video
A primer for the beginning boater and a great refresher course for experienced boaters. For power boats and sailboats under power.
08-3106 54 min. $39.95

Sailing for New Sailors
A hands-on introduction to the language, theory and excitement of sailing.
08-3107 30 min. $39.95

Sailing with Confidence
A comprehensive learn to sail program designed to give those with little or no sailing experience the knowledge and skills needed to sail with confidence.
08-8111 90 min. $29.95

Sailors' Knots and Splices
This video covers the basic knots and splices every sailor should know. Presented in a relaxed and informative context, the knots and splices are shown in close-up detail from the viewer's perspective, so that you can follow the steps with ease.
08-085 60 min. $39.95

Teach Yourself Knots & Splices
Proper knot tying skills are essential for every boater. Now you can learn to tie all the knots reliably and comfortably.
08-8099 60 min. $29.95

Top Gun - High Performance Boat Handling
Learn how to handle your high powered boat in this great instructional video for high performance boat owners. Covers docking, undocking, planing, trim tabs, high speed turns, safety and more.
08-8105 35 min. $29.95

U.S. Power Squadrons' Boating Course Video
U.S.P.S., the folks who produce over three million safer boaters have come to video. Rules of the Road, navigation aids, basic seamanship and much

more are contained in this exceptional video. 228 page companion book included.
08-6381 80 min. $39.95

Useful Knots for Boatmen
This Coast Guard produced film depicts clearly and concisely the most common and useful knots for boatmen. This will be a valuable addition to your boating video library.
08-8050 25 min. $16.95

Weather to go Boating
Become a better mariner by learning the weather basics that good seamanship demands. Subjects covered include: wind, waves, storms, weather maps, & symbols, clouds and more.
08-8110 90 min. $39.95

William F. Buckley's Celestial Navigation Simplified
One of the best navigation videos available. In 40 minutes Buckley simply and clearly explains the theory and practice of Celestial Navigation. Computer animated diagrams illustrate such topics as GP (Geographical Position), GHA, GMT, etc. Mr. Buckley's forceful lecture style keeps it all rolling on. Worth 12 weeks in night school!
08-011 48 min. $49.95

Power Boats & Yachts

Fast Boats and Beautiful Women
An extraordinary video featuring two of man's ultimate obsessions. It's high speed and heavenly bodies from start to finish.
08-8117 45 min. $24.95

How to Buy a Powerboat
For everyone looking to purchase a powerboat. It will guide through a maze of boat dealerships, yacht brokers, surveyors, insurance agents, bank financing, and much more.
08-3104 60 min. $39.95

Power Boating: Single Screw Boat Handling-Trailerable
Learn all the basics of safely trailering, launching, maneuvering, docking and retrieval. A reusable safety checklist is included with the tape which covers all the legally required safety equipment and step-by-step procedures of proper trailering.
08-081 76 min. $49.95

VIDEO TITLES LISTED IN THIS GUIDE ARE AVAILABLE FOR PURCHASE OR RENTAL. CONTACT YOUR LOCAL VIDEO STORE OR TELEPHONE (800) 383-8811

Power Boating: Twin Screw Boat Handling

This course was designed to take the viewer through the step-by-step basics of boat handling utilizing a "hands on" viewing system which allows you to get the feel of performing a variety of basic and complicated maneuvers. Areas of boat operation covered include: uses of the controls and their positions, basic maneuvers, docking, handling wind and currents, and emergencies. Excellent training for the power boat enthusiast.

08-051 50 min. $49.95

SAFE BOATING SERIES:

• **Boat Maintenance**
08-075 120 min. $49.95

• **Celestial Navigation**
08-079 120 min. $49.95

• **Coastal Piloting & Loran**
08-077 120 min. $49.95

• **Getting That Extra Knot**
08-076 120 min. $49.95

• **Offshore Cruising Guide**
08-080 120 min. $49.95

• **Using Marine Electronics**
08-078 120 min. $49.95

U.S. Powerboat Championships

Enter the pulse pounding world of muscle boat racing at its finest. Watch as America's top throttle jockeys push their high performance powerboats to their limits in heat after heat of the U.S. Powerboat Championships. To the thrillseeker, Powerboat racing boast 130 mph. speeds over water conditions that are ever-changing and unpredictable. At these speeds the victories are sweet, while the slightest driver error can prove disastrous. Strap on your life jackets and come along on the hottest ride in sports today...The U.S. Powerboat Championships.

30-5462 50 min. $19.95

Racing & Regattas

1986 Whitbred Round the World Race

Sir Anthony Quayle introduces this official film of the 4th Whitbred Around the World Race.

08-3110 52 min. $39.95

1987 America's Cup: The Official Film

Share in the excitement as the Americans avenge their 1983 loss to the Australians. Includes highlights of the qualifying races, opening ceremonies, an exclusive interview with Dennis Conner, and the spectacle and pageantry of the race.

08-2642 60 min. $19.95

1992 America's Cup

Narrated by three time veteran Gary Jobson. Here is exclusive footage of the inside story of the '92 America's Cup. See the American's beat the Italians.

08-8114 60 min. $29.95

Admiral's Cup 1987

This film captures all the highlights of the exciting 1987 series sailed by teams from 14 different nations. Join them as they sail a very exciting and stormy series of races off the Isle of Wight and in the Channel. Beautifully filmed by Colin Forbes, one of Britain's leading marine filmmakers.

08-6974 55 min. $29.95

America' Cup 1983

One of the most exciting races in yachting history show scenes not picked up by network. TV. Covers the seventh and final race of 1983.

08-003 60 min. $39.95

America's Cup '88

The most controversial Cup challenge ever! Gary Jobson narrates the race, with dramatic on-deck footage, never-before-seen film of the boats being built and exclusive interviews with Conner and Fay. The official America's Cup Video!

08-5503 64 min. $24.95

America's Cup: Yank it Back

The thrilling race for the America's cup.

08-1524 40 min. $19.95

Assault on the Record

Thrill to the setting of a new world outboard water speed record. Share the dream of shattering the existing record and establishing the new speed record.

08-8116 30 min. $24.95

Bermuda Overboard

This has been hailed as probably the best film made on ocean racing. Filmed on the Newport to Bermuda Race in 1982, it captures the atmosphere aboard an ocean racer during a long distance race. The excitement is intensified as one of the crew members is dragged overboard by a fouled spinnaker line and has to be rescued. There are also scenes above and below deck, both day and night.

Beautifully filmed and very entertaining.
08-036 30 min. $44.95

Big Bandicoot
An Australian sailing film, which provides an interesting and entertaining morale boost to demonstrate that men of "OZ" may indeed be formidable America's Cup adversaries, but are by no means invincible, as they attempt to shatter the worlds sailing speed record.
08-052 58 min. $39.95

Boc Challenge: Knockdown
World ocean racing at it's best. It's all here-- surfing at 30 knots, being washed overboard, colliding with a whale, the 360 degree rollover, hurricanes, icebergs and snow.
08-8100 105 min. $39.95

Drum: The Journey of a Lifetime
Simon LeBon, lead singer for "Duran Duran" experiences the heartaches, the happiness, the downfalls and the delights of racing with the best in the Whitebread Around The World Race.
08-8061 60 min. $29.95

Drag Boat Spectacular
Get ready for awesome action on the liquid quarter-mile! The best thrills and spills from the IHBA (International Hot Boats Association). Featuring highlights from the 1987 season's most electrifying races, this tape will take you on the ride of your life.
08-6973 82 min. $29.95

Chesapeake Bay Skipjacks and Racing on San Francisco Bay
Watch the last working sailboats in America dredge for oysters and clash in their famous annual race. And, if you think you've seen bad sailing weather before, view the wind tunnel racing through San Francisco Bay.
08-007 60 min. $39.95

Hot Boat
I.H.B.A. Drag Boat Racing at Firebird International Raceway. The liquid quarter mile... a 40' rooster tail... the thunderous roar of a top fuel hydro... this is drag boat racing at its finest!
08-6454 30 min. $16.95

J-WORLD SERIES
Some of the premier racing boats in the country: J-Boats are featured in this series.

• **Championship Sailing**
08-8033 50 min. $39.95

• **Downwind Sailing**
08-8034 40 min. $39.95

• **Upwind Sailing**
08-8035 30 min. $39.95

• **Starting Tactics**
08-8036 40 min. $39.95

• **1982 J-24 Worlds**
08-8037 50 min. $39.95

Let's Go Power Boating
Make boating a safe and enjoyable experience. Three sections prepare for the "before-you-go", all the "off-the-water" and all the vital "on-the-water" info. Great for the first time or seasonal boater!
08-6977 90 min. $29.95

Merit - Whitebread
Sail aboard the Merit on it's 33,000 mile, nine month, grueling bid against New Zealand's Steinlager to win the prestigious 89/90 Whitebread around the world race.
08-8119 65 min. $29.95

Ocean Racing Combination
This is a terrific video combination tape of ocean racing at its best. Learn technical information and see the onboard action.
08-3109 100 min. $49.95

Pleasure Boating Volume 1
From the creators of Twin & Single Screw Boat Handling comes this excellent video that will teach you, in depth, how to navigate a complete and safe cruise from harbor to harbor. This tape includes such needed aspects as pre-cruise preparations, knot tying, boating safety, basic navigation, rules of the road, getting under way, rough weather handling, anchoring and mooring, fire aboard and much more! A great trip planning and preparation video.
08-6979 60 min. $39.95

Powerboat Navigation
Produced in association with the US Coast Guard, this video provides complete coverage of all aspects of powerboat navigation by day and night, in good weather, fog and storms. The detailed section on use of electronic aids includes identification and plotting of objects on radar, use of loran and RDF, demonstrated at sea and on training simulators at the SCI professional mariners school in New York City.
08-6978 68 min. $49.95

Racing Rules Made Easy
Olympic sailor and founder of the Offshore Sailing School, Steve Colgate simplifies and illustrates the

VIDEO TITLES LISTED IN THIS GUIDE ARE AVAILABLE FOR PURCHASE OR RENTAL. CONTACT YOUR LOCAL VIDEO STORE OR TELEPHONE (800) 383-8811

current rules both graphically and on the water.
08-8113 52 min. $39.95

Racing to Win with Gary Jobson
Live action and new three dimensional computer animated tactical illustrations show you how Jobson performs and thinks. Learn Start, Windward and Downwind tactics with 3-D animation.
08-8112 60 min. $29.95

Sail to Glory
This feature film is the story of the first America's Cup in 1851, hosted by Robert Stack with music by Doc Severinson.
08-3113 54 min. $29.95

Shape of Speed
This film shows you just what fast looks like, from the boat crew's point of view. It is intended for serious sailors who want to get the most from their sails.
08-3108 50 min. $39.95

To Win at all Costs
This is a lively, informative, and often amusing look at the yacht race which found clubs, men and countries, challenging for the most prestigious trophy in yachting: the Americas Cup. This fascinating program traces the boats from schooners to 12 meter boats. Beginning with a reenactment of the first race at Cowes in 1851, it follows through to the lifting of the Cup from American grasp in 1983. Rare archival footage, paintings, stills and drawings illustrate the extraordinary men, yachts materials and effort that have surrounded this premiere and at times controversial yachting event!
08-045 56 min. $29.95

Sailboats

Airborne with William F. Buckley, Jr.
Sail with William F. Buckley, Jr. and his son on their journey across the Atlantic Ocean on their yacht, Cyrano. This video is based on a best-selling book. All the excitement and trials of a real transcontinental voyage are here, peppered with Buckley's unique dry style and wit. Learn how to weather storms, heave to, handle emergencies and more.
08-002 135 min. $39.95

AMERICA'S CUP YACHTING SERIES

• **America's Cup 1958, 1962**
08-8017 78 min. $29.95

• **America's Cup 1964, 1967**
08-8018 78 min. $29.95

• **America's Cup 1970, Duel in the Wind**
08-8019 78 min. $29.95

• **America's Cup 1974, The Grandest Prize**
08-8020 78 min. $29.95

• **America's Cup 1977, 1980**
08-8021 106 min. $29.95

• **25th Defense: End of an Era**
08-8022 30 min. $29.95

• **To Win at all Costs - Story of the America's Cup**
08-8023 56 min. $29.95

• **Yachting in the 30's**
08-8024 30 min $24.98

• **Sail to Glory**
The race to cross the finish line for the America's Cup.
08-8025 56 min. $29.95

Around Cape Horn
In 1929, the last great days of commercial sailing were passing. During that year Captain Irving Johnson sailed aboard the massive bark Peking. He narrates this program in the style that has made him a favorite on the lecture circuit around the world. He filmed the crew's daily activities, as the ship rounded the feared Cape Horn.
08-047 37 min. $24.95

Best Of Grand Prix Sailing
Host Gary Jobson takes an action packed look at today's high tech racing fleets, from the International 14 dinghies to the revived grandeur of the 130-foot J-Class, including 50-footers, 70-foot transpac "sleds", Maxi's and the Big Boat Series. This is the video every sailor should have...the best of the best!
08-5504 40 min. $24.95

Blue Water Odyssey
Join the Driscoll Family as they fulfill a dream and sail on a five-year circumnavigation of the globe. A delightful true life adventure.
08-3112 97 min. $49.95

Come Sail with Us
From Pearson Yachts, one of the largest sailboat manufactures in the U.S.., a new course to help you master the basics of sailing. Instruction is on board a 34-foot. Pearson, where you learn not only

fundamental skills but also the basics of anchoring, using a marine radio, knots, reading the weather and proper casting off and docking procedures.
08-072 35 min. $39.95

How to Buy a Sailboat
This is designed to help you through the process of buying your dream boat, whether a 15 foot daysailer or a 50 foot ocean racing yacht. Includes information on financing, insurance, new and used purchases, and much more.
08-3101 60 min. $39.95

Incredible Tristan Jones
A rare, intimate, wide-ranging discussion with sailing's most incredible author/adventurer. Tristan Jones has sailed over 350,000 miles in boats under 40 ft., 180,000 miles of which he was alone. Now with only one leg, he is sailing east around the world, a very difficult feat.
08-073 55 min. $39.95

Irving Johnson: High Seas Adventurer
This is a National Geographic Society tape which recounts seven of the round-the-world voyages of the Johnsons.
08-3114 43 min. $34.95

Kay Cotte - Australia's First Lady of Sailing
Kay Cotte is the first woman in history to sail, solo, non-stop and unassisted around the globe. Here is never before seen exclusive footage of this history making voyage.
08-8115 85 min. $29.95

Learn to Sail
Steve Colgate teaches you the step-by-step basics and intermediate sailing techniques that will make you a confident sailor. He is joined by Audrey Landers and Sam Jones on his sailboat, where he gives a comprehensive course in beginner's sailing.
08-017 106 min. $29.95

Michelob Sailing
Free your spirit on the high seas by watching this complete introduction to sailing. If you're a beginner or even if you've never sailed at all, this tape gives you the keys to unlock the doors to this enthralling sport and hobby.
08-2988 30 min. $16.95

MYSTIC SEAPORT SERIES
A look at the exciting and exotic locales of boat racing and the people who brave the seas to be part of it.

• **Mystic Seaport**
08-8002 30 min. $19.95

• **Around Cape Horn**
08-8003 37 min. $29.95

• **Irving Johnson - High Seas Adventure**
08-8004 43 min. $29.95

• **ARC: Across the Atlantic**
08-8006 52 min. $34.95

• **Transatlantic Rally**
08-8005 50 min. $34.95

• **Atlantic Circle**
08-8007 52 min. $24.95

• **Ways of Wallace and Sons**
08-8008 58 min. $29.95

• **Around the World in a Square Rigged Ship**
08-8009 22 min. $16.95

• **Offsounding Races**
08-8010 25 min. $19.95

• **Authentic - New York Thirties**
08-8011 28 min. $19.95

• **Sail to Win**
08-8012 83 min. $24.95

• **Sailing All Seas**
08-8013 60 min. $29.95

• **Life & Times Josh Gardner - Firstmate**
08-8014 55 min. $29.95

• **Record Passage to MoBay: Jamaica's Bluewater Challenge**
08-8015 60 min. $29.95

• **Cannonball Wins - Newport to Bermuda Yacht Race**
08-8016 30 min. $16.95

Multihull Fever
Primarily built in France, the boats featured in this video are huge catamarans and trimarans up to 85 feet in length that race across the open ocean at speeds of 35 to 40 knots. These sailboats are on the cutting edge of sailing speed and design, and not many people in the U.S. have had a chance to witness such spectacular sailing performance. Some of the scenes show racers sailing alone on wildly pitching gigantic craft. Other footage shows construction and launching, and also life glimpse at

a new kind of sailing.
08-037 30 min. $39.95

SET YOUR SAILS SERIES:

• Basic Sailing Skills
Shows you how much fun and how easy sailing can be. Discover the joy of small boat dinghy sailing, the attraction of cruising yachts, and the thrill of sailboat racing. This great three part tape is both educational and enjoyable to watch.
08-6975 75 min. $49.95

• Basic Cruising Skills
From weekend sailing to disappearing on an extended sail. Find your way from port to port, and squeeze in a week on a Caribbean charter boat. Live out a lifetime dream!
08-6976 75 min. $49.95

Sixty Minute Sailor
An excellent supplement to on-the-water instruction, this video is a visual guide to beginning sailing. The fundamentals of tacking and jibbing, beach, anchoring and docking are illustrated.
08-082 60 min. $39.95

Warren Miller's Sailing Film Festival
Enjoy Warren Miller's legendary filming of the joys of sailing from surfing the big waves in Hawaii, to trips on maxi racers and tall ships, to windsurfing in Florida and California. Learn match racing techniques and tuning tips from the experts.
08-026 60 min. $39.95

Water Sports: At One With The Wind
This is an instructional video for small craft sailors, starting with the basics and progressing onto more advanced sailing skills. Filmed on the Mediterranean, this video is a must for both beginner and advanced sailors.
08-6172 55 min. $39.95

Way of the Wind
This is the amazing personal story of successful businessman Charles Tobias five-year voyage with destiny on the high seas.
08-3111 125 min. $29.95

Miscellaneous

GREAT LAKES VIDEO CRUISING GUIDE SERIES
Take a ride down some of the old waterways and learn the history behind the old trading and travel routes of America's lakes.

• Straits of MacKinac
08-8075 48 min. $29.95

• Door Country and Green Bay
08-8076 48 min. $29.95

• Detroit Area & Port Huron To Lake Erie
08-8077 48 min. $29.95

• Toronto, The Wielland Canal & Western Lake Ontario
08-8078 48 min. $29.95

• Pentwater to MacKinac
08-8079 48 min. $29.95

Submarine: Steel Boats - Iron Men
This film explores the challenges faced by those select few who are qualified to serve aboard a submarine. You will visit a "wet trainer" at Sub School to see what these men can endure before they ever climb aboard on of these remarkable ships. Includes interviews with some of the most honored allied submarine commanders of both World Wars.
08-8000 60 min. $24.95

Sick of Sailing...

Knot!

Boating Videos Will Put

More Pleasure in Your Crews.

Business
&
Management

✓ *Entrepreneurship*
✓ *Management & Training*
✓ *Miscellaneous*

Entrepreneurship

Bulls, Bears and T. Boone Pickens, Jr.
One of the most successful businessmen of the decade shares invaluable insights into a special style of entrepreneurial management. Pickens reveals his three rules for success in business, describes techniques for developing loyalty and motivation in an organization, covers management style and stock market investment strategy.
07-1759 80 min. $79.95

Business Of Businesses
Describes the dynamic nature of the different types, sizes, and roles of business that comprise the American business system. It develops the concept of a private enterprise system and the role of profit and competition in the marketplace.
07-6838 45 min. $79.95

Business of Minor League Baseball
Bob Dres and Peter Heitman, president and owner of the Madison Muskies (a minor league baseball team) share their trade secrets about how they acquired a minor league franchise and why they are one of the few that know how to run such a business as a viable enterprise. They are having a good time and making money on a surprisingly low investment.
07-089 30 min. $89.95

Business of Off-Broadway
Art D'Lugoff, owner of the Village Gate and a highly successful off-broadway producer, talks about how he puts together projects and why they work.
07-101 30 min. $89.95

Business Mistakes I've Learned From
Three highly successful entrepreneurs-Len Mattioli, Sue Ling Gin, and Tom Holter-talk about some of their biggest mistakes the ones you'll want to avoid for sure and what they have learned from them.
07-095 30 min. $89.95

Business World of Art Linkletter
Art Linkletter has been an entrepreneur and wheeler-dealer since the age of 11. While entertaining has been a major career for Art, business has been just as significant a career in his life. Art reveals some of his business methods and many of his business experiences, including his current ventures.
07-086 30 min. $89.95

Buying and Running A Small Summer Resort
Paul and Joyce Crittenden, owners of the Griffin Inn in Ellison Bay, Wisconsin, join Cornell University School of Hotel Administration lecturer Malcolm Noden to talk about the common American fantasy of getting away from it all, buying and running that little summer resort. While Paul and Joyce share their experiences of doing just that, Malcolm Noden sheds some light on why so many others have not shared the success of the Crittendens.
07-088 30 min. $89.95

Can Anyone Publish Books?
A successful regional publisher and an author who has selfpublished eight books tells you the nitty-gritty of how to get your book published by someone else and how to do it yourself.
07-083 30 min. $89.95

Day Care Dollars: Making A Living In Child Care
Two day care center owners with different kinds of operations and the vice president of a day care chain with over 200 centers tell you about the opportunities and obstacles in starting a child care business and running it on a day-to-day basis.
07-084 30 min. $89.95

Financial Statement
This program shows how to prepare a financial statement. The program begins with a thorough and detailed explanation of how to perform a bank reconciliation as well as the reasons for performing this task monthly. Also this program shows you how to produce a revenue statement and a balance sheet.
07-8048 30 min. $98.00

Franchise Fever: How To Buy A Franchise
The exploding variety of franchise opportunities has made the dream of owning your own business much easier to attain. But it also makes it harder to find the one particular franchise that's right for you. In this 45-minute program, Robert Chesney (host of Window on Wall Street) takes you step-by-step through the franchise buying process: where to look for the hottest businesses, how to evaluate a franchise's potential, the pitfalls to avoid, and much more. He meets with franchise attorneys and consultants to get all the inside tips you'll need to make an intelligent franchise purchase.
07-5949 45 min. $39.95

From the Ground Up
Starting a new business might be compared with baking the perfect cake--you might assemble all the right ingredients and mix them together in the

proper way and in the right order before you can experience the sweet smell of success. Identifying personal strengths, operating on a shoestring budget and the progress of tracking your business is presented in this case study.
07-8049 30 min. $99.00

Growing A Business
Entrepreneurs. What makes them successful? What new ideas does the present generation of business founders have about products, people, management style? This series features a spirited group of company leaders from Ben & Jerry's Homemade Ice Cream to L.L. Bean, to Quad Graphics discussing their philosophies and the lessons they've learned in growing businesses today. Hosted by Paul Hawken, founder of Smith & Hawkin, who was chosen best of a generation by Esquire. The series consists of eighteen half-hour episodes.
07-9451 540 min. $149.95

HOW TO BUILD A PROFITABLE CONSULTING PRACTICE

• Volume 1
In the first tape of this two-part video series, consulting expert Howard Shenson concentrates on how to find consulting opportunities and marketing strategies for developing new business. Shenson explains the common mistakes beginning consultants make when trying to expand their business and offers practical steps consultants can use to market themselves and land lucrative consulting contracts. Also, learn how to maintain a constant flow of new consulting jobs. An ultimate source of advice for people in the business of giving advice.
07-5954 90 min. $49.95

• Volume 2
In this second volume, Howard Shenson reveals practical information on proposal writing, contracting strategies, fee setting, and collection techniques. His advice is directly applicable to the immediate problems faced by most consultants in the business world. An excellent insight into what it takes to achieve professional recognition and financial success as a consultant.
07-5955 90 min. $49.95

How To Buy A Business With Very Little Cash
An extensive four-hour course on how to realistically acquire a business through the technique of the leveraged buyout. Hosted by Joe Mancuso, founder of the Center for Entrepreneurial Management, the program packs in a wealth of information and can also be used as a "reverse guide" for learning how to sell a business. Find out all the latest creative financing strategies and alternatives and learn how to find business owners willing to sell on very workable terms. Two cassettes, four hours total running time.
07-5950 240 min. $99.95

How to Leave Your Job and Buy a Business of Your Own
The complete step-by-step guide that takes from employee to business owner. You'll learn how to decide what business is right for you, how to find it, how to price it and where to find the money to buy it. Based on the popular McGraw-Hill book.
07-9584 45 min. $29.95

How to Make $100,000 a Year With Your Own Export Management Company
This tape provides step-by-step directions to the exporting newcomer for starting a new Export Management Company from home or office with only a minimal investment. It shows the beginner how to find companies with products and services to export, how to locate overseas agents and necessary equipment and records.
07-8016 60 min. $89.95

How to Profit in the Computer Cleaning Business
Professional Computer Cleaning gets you into this multi-billion dollar business and requires no previous experience. This program is loaded with the information that makes you money, including marketing materials guaranteed to get you customers! Three video tapes show you how to make big money cleaning computers. You will also get a PC tool kit and all the supplies you need to clean 6 computers.
07-8000 300 min. $495.00

How to (Really) Start Your Own Business
From INC. magazine. This best-selling video tape covers: Getting the idea, trusting your gut, finding the money, the business plan and going for it.
07-207 90 min. $39.95

How to Run a Successful Family Business
The best minds in family business convene on this tape to address one of the biggest problems facing family business today -- succession.
07-8031 60 min. $99.95

HOW TO START YOUR BUSINESS

• Overview Of Small Business
A look at the recent surge in entrepreneurism and new business trends. Discusses the common

motives that lead people to start their own businesses and reveals many of the myths and misconceptions that plague first time business owners.
07-5956 45 min. $29.95

• **Market Research**
Market research is a crucial ingredient for success. Find out how you can uncover usable market data and determine the customer base for your new business.
07-5957 45 min. $29.95

• **Your Product Or Service**
Shows the different marketing approaches of selling a product versus a service.
07-5958 45 min. $29.95

• **Buying An Existing Business And Franchising**
Looks into the advantages and disadvantages of buying an on-going business or franchise instead of starting from scratch.
07-5959 45 min. $29.95

• **Legal Aspects: Laws You Should Know**
Covers the various forms of ownership, such as sole proprietorship, corporation, etc.., and also looks into the tax responsibilities of self employment.
07-5960 45 min. $29.95

• **Accounting**
All the basics of setting up your books and keeping the accurate financial records that will be needed if you ever want to raise money to expand your business in the future. Also covers record-keeping for tax purposes.
07-5961 45 min. $29.95

• **Advertising And Promotion**
A crucial aspect of all businesses. This in-depth program outlines the function of advertising and show how to set up an effective promotional program for a new venture.
07-5962 45 min. $29.95

• **Raising Money**
Everyone's primary concern when starting out. Find out all the potential sources of new business financing and how to approach each of the sources.
07-5963 45 min, $29.95

• **Pricing And Sales Strategy**
Put your new product or service out in the market at a price that beats out the competition and guarantees the most profit possible.
07-5964 45 min. $29.95

• **Preparing A Business Plan**
Don't even think about starting a business without learning how to prepare a solid and realistic business plan.
07-5965 45 min. $29.95

How to Start Your Video Business
Start your wedding and reunion video business now! Avoid costly mistakes and wasted time. Make the right equipment decisions on the front end. Economical plan covers equipment selection, purchase and operation for shooting, editing, and graphics.
07-8012 90 min. $29.95

INC. Magazine's Women Entrepreneurs
Woman in Business, from INC. Magazine, takes you to women executives who own companies in industries as diverse as real estate, construction, aerobics, and more. They offer excellent advice for other women planning to launch their own profitable company. The many topics in this 1-hour tape include: overcoming stereotypes; developing the entrepreneur within you; living with risk; seeking financing; building credibility; negotiating and selling, and balancing family and friends. An informative program.
07-5953 60 min. 19.95

Inside the Hotel Business
President of Marriott Hotels, Bill Marriott; and John Coleman, owner of the Ritz-Carlton in New York and Washington and the Tremont and Whitehall Hotels in Chicago, talk candidly about what it costs to build a hotel, how to choose a site, and how to staff and run it so that the guests are happy and the owner makes a profit. Bill Marriott has some surprising information to share about the responsibility he extends to workers at all levels.
07-085 30 min. $89.95

King of the B Movies Tells His Story
Roger Corman, maker of over 200 "B" films over the past 30 years talks about how it's done without the help of the major studios. Some of his better known films include "Easy Rider" and "Little Shop of Horrors."
07-104 30 min. $89.95

Lillian Vernon: Making It In Mail Order
America's mail order queen tells her story and gives tips to those considering entering the business of selling through the mail.
07-065 30 min. $89.95

Marketing Video Services
Finding customers for wedding, reunion and other event videos doesn't need to hinder your success. Discover effective ways to generate sales leads, promote and price your products, land new

VIDEO TITLES LISTED IN THIS GUIDE ARE AVAILABLE FOR PURCHASE OR RENTAL. CONTACT YOUR LOCAL VIDEO STORE OR TELEPHONE (800) 383-8811

business, and make more sales. Avoid customer procrastination, and find others who want to help sell your services.
07-8013 87 min. $29.95

Mary Kay Story
Mary Kay Ash, one of America's most successful businesswomen, discusses how she created her cosmetics empire, how her unique management philosophy motivates her salespeople and how being a woman has influenced her management style.
07-062 30 min. $89.95

One on One with Jerry Buchanan
The perfect primer and introduction to the home based business of gathering useful How-To information and selling the product directly to the consumer for up to a 400% mark-up profit on each mail order sale. He calls it "The World's Most Perfect Home-Based Business" and his 20 years experience doing it proves he's the one to learn from.
07-8135 60 min. $39.95

PROFILES OF ACHIEVEMENT SERIES:

• Curt Carlson
Born to poor Swedish-American immigrants, Curt Carlson is now the sole owner of the $3 billion-a-year Carlson Companies. His holdings include the Radisson Hotel Corporation, TGI Friday's and Ask Mr. Foster. Remarkably, Carlson's rise to riches started with a very simple idea-selling Gold Bond trading stamps to grocery store chains. He is a tribute to the American system of free enterprise.
07-1569 45 min. $49.95

• Henry A. Johnson
Henry Johnson started as an office boy, and worked his way up to the position of chairman of Spiegel Catalog. Johnson's biggest challenge was bringing the century-old catalog company into the 1980's by redesigning the catalog to appeal to upscale working women. The result-a remarkable increase in sales that revolutionized the entire catalog industry. His success illustrates how a creative, energetic approach to change can be the key to achievement.
07-1571 45 min. $49.95

• John Teets
John Teets quit school to build a fabulous restaurant business only to lose it all in a devastating fire. Undaunted, he changed direction and worked his way up the ladder at The Greyhound Corporation, reaching the position of Chairman. Teets admits it isn't easy getting to the top, or staying there. You've got to have drive and pay strict attention to the bottom line.
07-1573 45 min. $49.95

• Kemmon Wilson
Born a poor boy in Tennessee, Kemmon Wilson vowed to rise above his circumstances, and he did, by building his dream... Holiday Inn. Today, Holiday Inn is a multi-billion dollar enterprise and the world's largest hotel chain, with over 1750 hotels around the globe. Wilson's career is a case study in how to anticipate social trends and deliver good, standardized service to the consumer.
07-1570 45 min. $49.95

• Norman Brinker
Possessing only youth, enthusiasm, and $3000, Norman Brinker started Steak and Ale. Its success was established in one outstanding idea-the all-you-can-eat salad bar. Later, he sold out to Pillsbury for $100 million and became chairman of Pillsbury's Food Group and head of its Burger King Division. Now he runs Chili's restaurant, where he is applying his same formula for success.
07-1572 45 min. $49.95

• Oleg Cassini
Starting out as an immigrant in America, Oleg Cassini has become one of the world's foremost fashion leaders. But he is more than a trend-setting designer; he is also a marketing genius. Cassini was the first designer to realize the value of his own name and to license products for large volume distribution. Watch Cassini in action, and you'll realize that there's opportunity everywhere.
07-1574 45 min. $49.95

• Rocky Aoki
When he first arrived in America, Rocky Aoki was a stranger in a stranger land. Nonetheless, he opened his first restaurant a modest 28-seater paid for with $10,000 his own money and a $20,000 loan. Today Rocky and Benihana of Tokyo have 49 restaurants that gross $60 million annually.
07-1575 45 min. $49.95

Prosperity
"Prosperity" the definitive "how-to" video for success, is a visual & informational feast brimming with rich images and proven techniques that work! Psychologist Brenda Wade, PH.D, presents a powerful, multi-faceted system for achievement, and demonstrates how to apply it. It features: successful millionaires; ground-breaking interactive processes; financial experts and master teachers; dynamic, state-of-the-art visuals designed to reach and reprogram the superconscious.
07-6785 61 min. $39.95

Raising Capital: How to Finance Your Business
This will open your eyes to resources you never

knew were available for getting your business idea off the ground. Learn all of the do's and don'ts to attracting money.
07-8038 90 min. $99.00

Record Business: Not Just for the Big Guys
Recording artist and producer, Ben Sidran, and the owner of a small recording company, Stephen Powers, talk about the ins and outs of the recording business.
07-063 30 min. $89.95

Roger Corman on the Future of Independent Film Production
Mr. Corman, "King of the B Movies," looks at the present and future of independent film production, and covers some of the nitty gritty of his field: What would it take if he were to enter the business today? And how will independent film producing be different five years from now?
07-105 30 min. $89.95

Running a Movie Theatre
An owner of a small-town theatre and the owner of a large movie chain talk about how easy it is to enter this business and how hard it is to make a profit.
07-074 30 min. $89.95

Special Issues for Women
The discussion of internal and external barriers facing women starting and running their own business are discussed.
07-8055 30 min. $89.95

Starting and Running a Business
A dress shop owner, restaurant and business professor talk about the dos and don'ts of successfully starting a small business.
07-066 30 min. $89.95

Starting and Running a Restaurant
The owner of a highly rated gourmet restaurant and the co-owners of a family-type coffee shop tell you about the rewards and problems in starting and running a restaurant.
07-082 30 min. $89.95

Starting and Running Retail Stores
Carol Schroeder, gift store owner, Janice Durant, owner of a toy store and Russell Machus, owner of a men's clothing store, talk about how to successfully take an idea and convert it into a successful retail operation. They cover leasing your store, stocking, hiring employees and running the store for a profit.
07-094 30 min. $89.95

STRATEGIES FOR SMALL BUSINESS SUCCESS
Learn the all about starting a small business. Learn how to achieve you goal and be successful. This series covers all the essentials of running and maintaining a small business.

• **So You Want to be an Entrepreneur**
07-8138 28 min. $29.95

• **How to Finance Your Small Business**
07-8139 28 min. $29.95

• **Marketing Skills for Small Business**
07-8140 35 min. $29.95

Success Secrets Of Self-Made Millionaires
Discover the 21 qualities that rocketed self-made millionaires to the top, and that can take you there as well. With Brian Tracy, you'll learn to seize control of your financial destiny. What is the true starting point for all success? What is the major reason that people fail, and how can you avoid it? How can you "ask your way to success? The answers are here, and they can make you rich.
07-6823 60 min. $95.95

Ted Turner Looks Ahead
Ted Turner looks at the future of broadcasting, what cable TV will do to the face of entertainment in the 1980's and how he plans to position himself to be a winner in this transition.
07-099 30 min. $89.95

Ted Turner: How He Did It
WTBS, CNN 2 and Atlanta Braves owner, Ted Turner, talks in person about his career from the age of 24, when he inherited a billboard company, to his present status as the most powerful force in American broadcasting.
07-098 30 min. $89.95

Turning Your Job into a Business
Learn how a successful business consultant, once a secretary, turned her business skills into a secretarial service. Then hear as a former speech teacher describes the steps it took to become a speaking coach and his own boss.
07-064 30 min. $89.95

Two Good Business Ideas that Failed
Two entrepreneurs who had good ideas, ambition and energy talk with knowledge, humor and humility about why they still didn't make it.
07-067 30 min. $89.95

VIDEO TITLES LISTED IN THIS GUIDE ARE AVAILABLE FOR PURCHASE OR RENTAL. CONTACT YOUR LOCAL VIDEO STORE OR TELEPHONE (800) 383-8811

WALLSTREET WEEK WITH LOUIS RUKIESER
This popular PBS series includes specific information on handling stocks and bonds, with valuable insights to investing wisely.

* **Stocks, Bonds & Gold**
07-8145 60 min. $24.95

* **Mutual Funds, Options & Commodities**
07-8146 60 min. $24.95

Woman Entrepreneur: Do You Have What it Takes
Woman Entrepreneur is a video guide for women in business. Successful women provide experienced advice on how to start up and succeed as an entrepreneur.
07-1993 55 min. $24.95

Women in Business: Your Own Business (Risks, Rewards and Secrets)
Women entrepreneurs face different challenges than their male counterparts. In this program, you will get to know a variety of women who will share their experiences, as well as their insights to overcoming the challenges and obstacles of owning your own business. Learn about the risks they've taken, the rewards they've earned and their secret successes.
07-1618 60 min. $19.95

What They Still Don't Teach You At Harvard Business School
In this video Mark McCormack, founder and CEO of International Management Group, the world's leading sports marketing organization, will show you how "applied people sense" can turn you into a street-smart executive.
07-5882 60 min. $29.95

Young, Self-Made Millionaire
Lenny Mattioli reveals the hows, whys and costs of building his American TV empire.
07-108 30 min. $89.95

Zig Ziglar: Selling, A Great Way to Reach the Top
Zig Ziglar is the master motivator! He's been called the man who helped turn selling into a profession to be proud of. Zig tells you how to relate to your client, present your product and close the deal.
07-1837 50 min. $79.95

Management & Training

5 Steps To Successful Selling
In this video is your first exposure to Zig Ziglar and his brand of enthusiasm and logic, you will be overwhelmed by the experience. Ziglar has traveled more than 3,000,000 miles across the country over the past 20 years and has developed a loyal following by showing people clear-cut methods they can use to achieve their goals and dreams. In 5 Steps to Successful Selling, you'll learn the one fundamental principle that shapes the personalities of all top salespeople and see a clear-cut path you can follow to increase your sales ability almost overnight.
07-5967 45 min. $79.95

38 Proven Ways to Close That Sale
This program is packed with information that will help you read your prospects, pinpoint their needs and know when to close the transaction. You'll discover how to translate your product's features into "can't-do-without" benefits for your customers.
07-8113 87 min. $99.95

Achieving Excellence
This video gives you the "how-tos, why-tos and when-tos what-ifs" of excellence-oriented management. You'll learn how to handle details, handle mistakes and customer complaints the right way, get instant action on your ideas and more "excellence" techniques.
07-2248 88 min. $69.95

Art of Resolving Conflicts in the Workplace
Larry Schwimmer presents six easily learned techniques for smoothing office conflicts and dealing with hostile or uncooperative co-workers. These simple, direct, and usable techniques quickly ease tension, clear the air, and bring good business back into the forefront.
07-8065 37 min. $79.95

Basic Fundamentals...Selling Right
This instructional program brings you the foundations of selling together with some of the profession's most sophisticated techniques to help you close and sale.
07-6827 30 min. $95.00

Being Boss
Host Dick Goldberg talks about the advantages and disadvantages of "being boss" with Lenny Mattioli

(TV's Lenny), Severa Austin, and Bob Mohelnitzky.
07-111 30 min. $89.95

Beyond Success
Ram Dass reflects on the basic question of doing business in a conscious way. Discussion of success; personal power; stress, change and fear, competition and isolation; going beyond ego and roles. This offering is a useful and important tool for doing business.
07-6775 150 min. $49.95

Boss/Earl Nightingale
A compelling, informative lesson in basic economics for achieving and maintaining good customer relations. The "Boss" is always the customer! With graphic illustrations, this important session on personal and company success traces the development of our service-oriented society from prehistoric times to the present.
07-003 21 min. $59.95

Bringing Out The Leader In You
There's no magic to being a leader. In fact, you already have the keys to leadership inside you-vision, insight, energy, competence, and flexibility. Once you've learned the leadership basics, you can unlock your inner strength and use it to lead others. Whether you take charge of a project, head up a neighborhood group, chair a meeting, or coach a basketball team, you can develop the basic know-how and confidence to become a leader in your own right.
07-6833 30 min. $79.95

BUILDING A CUSTOMER DRIVEN ORGANIZATION - THE MANAGER'S ROLE
Learn how to manage your time and your employees productively. This series covers the right and the wrong way to handle customers and how to create better customer service.

• **Volume I**
07-8116 60 min. $99.95

• **Volume II**
07-8117 60 min. $99.95

• **Volume III**
07-8118 60 min. $99.95

BUSINESS WRITING SKILLS
Good writing is essential to get your ideas read and acted on. Business Writing Skills is chock-full of tips on how to write so your reports, memos and proposals get read. Learn why "less is best" in today's business writing. Organize your writing to get to the point quickly. Maintain your reader's interest, even on "boring" subjects. Debra Smith won't waste your time with tedious grammar rules and endless definitions. She'll give you tried-and-true skills to make your writing both accurate and appealing.

• **Volume 1**
07-6776 90 min. $69.95

• **Volume 2**
07-6777 90 min. $69.95

Closing the Deal
Make the most of all your preparation and hard work by learning how to wrap-up a sale for it's full potential. Top sales professionals share their techniques with you to help you achieve the best results in closing a deal.
07-8025 41 min. $99.00

Communicate And Win
Communicate and Win, shows you how to communicate with clout in every situation. You'll gain valuable insights into using the telephone effectively, persuading people to accept your ideas, listening better for clearer understanding, and conducting more productive meetings. You'll also learn techniques to improve your writing and speaking skills.
07-6809 48 min. $95.95

Effective Follow-up: Your Secret Weapon for Long-term Sales Success
Veteran sales professionals reveal their tips on how build better customer relationships.
07-8027 38 min. $99.00

Experts Guide To Business Negotiating
In preparing for business negotiations, most executives and managers gather facts and figures, try to anticipate the other person's position and prepare for it, and make the mistake of thinking they're ready. They're not! Because they haven't learned or reviewed basic negotiating strategies. Let negotiating pro Roger Dawson help you learn about the basic ploys, counter-ploys, and even counter-counter-ploys. Never again worry about giving away the "company store" in any negotiation. Be the star of the negotiating table as you get what you want and still keep your opposer as a friend.
07-5969 30 min. $79.95

HIGH IMPACT LEADERSHIP
Learn how you can be a better leader. This series covers basic steps of how to become more organized and be recognized for your effort.

• **Volume I**
07-8101 45 min. $99.95

VIDEO TITLES LISTED IN THIS GUIDE ARE AVAILABLE FOR PURCHASE OR RENTAL. CONTACT YOUR LOCAL VIDEO STORE OR TELEPHONE (800) 383-8811

• **Volume II**
07-8102 45 min. $99.95

• **Volume III**
07-8103 45 min. $99.95

How To Be A Winner
Make any day your day with these practical do's and don'ts of top achievers. Zig Ziglar's eight-point formula is easy to understand and simple to apply. Use it to identify and make changes in your present way of doing things, then view it whenever you need to revitalize or remind yourself of the important steps he talks about. It's the program that gives you your money's worth and then keeps on giving.
07-6822 67 min. $79.95

How to Deal With Buying Objections
Learn how to overcome one of your biggest obstacles in sales: "Buying objections", Master the art of overcoming objections and you'll master the art of salesmanship.
07-8089 42 min. $99.00

HOW TO DEAL WITH DIFFICULT PEOPLE
Everyone has difficult people in their life. The key to dealing with difficult people is to first understand them. In this two-part program, Drs. Brinkman and Kirschner first give you insights into why difficult people behave the way they do- through instructive "role plays" that help you lay the groundwork for communicating effectively with difficult people.

• **Volume 1**
07-6778 74 min. $99.95

• **Volume 2**
07-6779 116 min. $99.95

• **Volume 3**
07-8098 90 min. $99.95

How to Delegate Work and Ensure It's Done Right
Here's the truth: if you're going to move up in your job, you've got to delegate. How to Delegate work can help you do it right. It will teach you how to delegate the projects you should, and decide which projects only you should do. You'll delegate more intelligently and free up your time to initiate. You'll give your people an opportunity to grow. And, you'll be seen as a leader in your company.

• **Volume 1**
07-6780 90 min. $99.95

• **Volume 2**
07-6781 90 min. $99.95

How to Deliver Superior Customer Service
In this program you will learn the best techniques from the experts on customer service.
Learn all the do's and don'ts that will make your business a strong customer service oriented company.
07-8035 60 min. $99.00

HOW TO ENJOY FAILURE, BE AMUSED BY REJECTION AND THRIVE ON ANXIETY

• **"Becoming The Perfect Child"**
07-6761 60 min. $99.95

• **"Becoming Resilient"**
07-6762 60 min. $99.95

• **"Benefits Of Anxiety"**
07-6769 60 min. $99.95

• **"Positive Addictions"**
07-6771 60 min. $99.95

• **"Raising Your Self Image"**
07-6767 60 min. $99.95

• **"Staying In Balance"**
07-6770 60 min. $99.95

• **"Stepping Stones To Success"**
07-6764 60 min. $99.95

• **"Perceptions Of Reality"**
07-6765 60 min. $99.95

• **"Taking Rejection Personally"**
07-6766 60 min. $99.95

• **"Your Attitude Toward Failure"**
07-6763 60 min. $99.95

How to Find New Customers
LeRoy Leale, winner of 34 national sales awards, shows you how to visualize success and become a top salesman.
07-8030 20 min. $39.95

HOW TO GIVE EXCEPTIONAL CUSTOMER SERVICE

• **Volume 1**
This volume provides three sources you can draw

VIDEO TITLES LISTED IN THIS GUIDE ARE AVAILABLE FOR PURCHASE OR RENTAL. CONTACT YOUR LOCAL VIDEO STORE OR TELEPHONE (800) 383-8811

on to help serve customers better. You will find out the real reason behind most customer dissatis-faction, how to "cool off" an angry customer and five do's and don't's of exceptional customer satisfaction-and applying what you learn. An important lesson from Dr. Theodore Levitt and The Harvard Business Review.
07-6835 77 min. $99.95

• Volume 2
Specific phrases, vocal techniques and ways to save and build rapport with customers, 2 ways to save time on every phone call, specific techniques for dealing with customers who cannot speak English, what to do when an angry customer verbally attacks you or your people, how to enforce unpopular policies so customers understand and cooperate, emotional trigger words you must never use, what to do when you reach the "boiling point" with a customer.
07-6836 88 min. $99.95

• Volume 3
This tape shows you how to take inventory of your "Moments of Truth" and learn from them. When you should break the rules to serve a customer better, how to deliver bad news without alienating your customer, a 30-second stress reliever to help you cope with pressure and burnout, how to get recognized as a customer service star in your company, ways to make healthy thinking a habit (your customers will notice).
07-6837 80 min. $99.95

• Volume 4
Learn what to do if you don't know the answer to a customer's question. Here are the answers to the problems that arise when it comes to providing service to your customer.
07-8122 80 min. $99.95

How to Manage Your Sales Strategy for Greater Sales and Profits
Find out where you can, and should, improve your sales strategy. Seven sales experts will show you how.
07-8036 90 min. $99.00

How To Read People
Get the results you desire by reading individuals and actually "getting inside their head." Featuring Dr. Tony Alessandra, author of Non-Manipulative Selling, this one-hour program hand-carries you through the art of motivating others by the use of individual ideals. Use Dr. Alessandra's "Platinum Rule" to influence people positively by treating them as they want to be treated. Dr. Alessandra whos that every person is an open book if you know how to read them.
07-5968 55 min. $89.95

How To Really Create a Successful Business Plan
There's nothing like actually seeing how other successful companies accomplished what you want to do. Using real-life examples and interviews with key people at such companies as Ben & Jerry's and Pizza Hut, you get an overview of how to put together your own company's business plan.
07-8032 40 min. $59.95

How To Sell
The sales manager of America's largest hi-fi store, a highly successful realtor and a sales trainer all talk about how to sell almost anything.
07-081 30 min. $89.95

How to Sell Well - Brian Tracy
How to increase sales quickly. New model of selling; attitude and motivation, personal management, product analysis, competitive analysis and more.
07-8137 60 min. $95.00

HOW TO SET AND ACHIEVE GOALS
Take control of your life by setting and achieving your goals. With these skills, you and your team will be unstoppable.

• Volume I
07-8114 90 min. $99.95

• Volume II
07-8115 90 min. $99.95

How To Speak With Confidence
In literally every business or profession, the ability to speak with confidence and power is a must! Bert Decker reveals the keys to catching your listeners' attention, holding it, and making them hang on your every word. Whether you're speaking to one person or to a thousand, now you can be sure you'll be at the top of your form. You can't afford anything less.
07-6824 46 min. $79.95

How to Write & Conduct Effective Performance Appraisals (3-Volume set)
This video program gives you a step-by-step system for researching, writing and delivering a performance appraisal that will improve performance all year long.
07-8076 60 min. $199.95

I Love People... It's Customers I Can't Stand !!!
Welcome to the "Dimlit" zone. The place where few from Customer Service have ever returned to speak about their most horrible experiences with customers! Enter the world of messed-up orders, double billings, cranky customers, and burned-out

representatives. This fast-paced, humorous video explores six major problem customers types: emotional Eurice, handout Homer, Sally superiority, foul mouthed Franklin, Arthur authoritarian. Each of the five customer types is discussed in-depth including how to specifically respond to each. Viewers are encouraged to follow the six rules of good Customer Service: decision making, caring, warmth, thoughtfulness, responsibility, direct action. Six types of Customer Service representatives are portrayed, giving the customer service professional or the beginning student a hands-on feel for major mistakes that should be avoided.
07-6840 25 min. $99.95

Important Disciplines... Working Right
Better work-habits build competence, confidence, and peak efficiency! With Jack and Gary Kinder, you'll learn the key techniques of planning your day, prioritizing your activities, and setting goals for success.
07-6828 26 min. $95.00

Magic Word: Attitude
"The Dean of Self-Development" reveals the secrets to creating and maintaining a winner's frame of mind. Discover how to foster a positive attitude in yourself and your customers, how to profit from "intelligent objectivity" and what "being lucky" really means.
07-6829 43 min. $95.00

Making Effective Sales Calls
Interspersed with candid, unscripted sales calls, you get special tips and advice that boost your sales approach to expert level.
07-8026 47 min. $99.95

Management and Leadership Skills for Women
You'll learn how to handle "external challenges, such as people who don't support you or take you seriously. This is straight talk that gives you advice to help you advance in your management career. A three volume set.
07-8093 244 min. $299.95

Manager as Coach
Coaching skills have gained the attention of managers who are seeking new ways to boost performance. Why? Because the methods of coaching are proven in motivating people and changing problem behavior.
07-8075 45 min. $149.95

Managing People
People are your biggest asset. With competition so fierce in business, the companies with the best people will lead the field. This program contains the straight forward mechanics every team needs to succeed.
07-8039 120 min. $99.00

Million Dollar Sales Strategy
How do the million-dollar mega-stars of professional selling build their careers? First and foremost, they master the basics, and that's exactly what you learn to do in this exciting new video from renowned sales trainers Jim Cathcart and Tony Alessandra. With them, you'll discover the principles of time management, prospecting, closing techniques, and customer relations that lead straight to the pinnacle of the profession, What's more, you'll learn the refinements of organization and professional pride that are the real hallmarks of the top-earning pros.
07-6811 45 min. $79.95

Money Making Secrets
Hosted by self-made millionaire E. Joseph Cossman, this two-hour program shows you the first steps to take to start your own profitable business, regardless of your age, education, or background. It also shows you how Cossman built a $25 million financial empire, starting in his spare time with only postage and stationery. Loaded with practical, easy-to-follow advice, this video has helped thousands of people start money making businesses in their field of interest...It will help you too!
07-5951 35 min. $29.95

Mutual Respect Behavior Management I
William Meisterfeld, behavior management consultant, describes comprehensive, dramatic need analysis of true life, in-house management behavior. These valuable and practical principles improve efficiency, productivity and morale. The concepts of business culture, reprimand, attitude, management disloyalty and communication are demonstrated through live role-play and cartoons.
07-172 35 min. $79.95

Mutual Respect Behavior Management II
Continuance of true case histories. What causes management problems? Words or body-which speaks louder? These questions and other important principles of behavior are vividly expressed through role-play and cartoons. These concepts are easily applied any time, any place, by anyone in both office and home.
07-173 35 min. $79.95

Phone Power: Techniques To Communicate Better On The Telephone
You'll find no better coach then George Walther, one of the nation's leading experts on telephone communication and a noted writer on phone-related topics. George helps you see your telephone in a

new light. You'll want to make some big changes in the way you use your telephone-and on this video, you'll get the blueprint that will make those changes easy to implement.
07-6783 53 min. $79.95

Power Of Customer Service

As a manager in today's ultra-competitive economy, you simply cannot afford the staggering cost of customer dissatisfaction. The reason: attracting new customers costs five times more than keeping old ones. Now Paul Timm reveals the all-important keys to obtaining repeat business...and having the lowest price is not one of them. Find out what really motivates people to establish and maintain long-standing business relationships. With The Power Of Customer Service, you'll discover a wealth of practical, specific information that you can instantly put to use in doing your job more effectively and improving your customer relations.
07-6812 45 min. $95.00

Preparing for Successful Sales Relationships

If you want more than a one-shot sale, you need to build relationships with your customers. This video shows you how to strategically research your own product, your customers and your competition.
07-8029 40 min. $99.00

Professional Telephone Skills

Let's face it. The way you handle telephone calls makes a lasting impression on clients and customers. You'll learn: how to identify your caller's objections and objectives, the "7Cs" of winning and keeping new customers, building rapport by getting on the same "wavelength", specific words and phrases that sabotage your professional clout, the exact ring after which you should answer a call.
07-6784 90 min. $69.98

Psychology Of Winning In Action

Denis E. Waitley, PH.D., teaches principles of thought and behavior that you can use immediately in your organization, your career, and your personal life. Named the "Outstanding Speaker of the Year" by the Sales and Marketing Executives Association, Waitley tells how and why you should eliminate any self-limiting thoughts and put yourself on the road to positive self-awareness. Learn the importance of accepting responsibility for your actions and how to adjust your dominant thoughts toward reaching attainable goals.
07-5978 58 min. $79.95

PSYCHOLOGY OF WINNING LEARNING SYSTEM

Each volume of The Psychology of Winning Learning System comprises a full 60-minute video presentation by Denis Waitley himself; a 60-minute

audiocassette review of the video material; and an 80-page action guide which includes a test section worksheets, a reference guide, and a full transcript of the audio session.

* **Positive Self-Esteem**
07-6813 60 min. $95.00

* **Positive Self-Determination**
07-6814 60 min. $95.00

* **Positive Self-Expectancy**
07-6815 60 min. $95.00

* **Positive Self-Discipline**
07-6816 60 min. $95.00

* **Positive Self-Dimension**
07-6817 60 min. $95.00

Ross Perot: A Vision for Success in the 90's

This video brings you Perot at his best -- candid, passionate and full of humor. You'll hear his philosophy on what it really takes to build a great company. Perot's advice, experience, and honest wisdom will be an education you can't afford to miss.
07-8033 90 min. $99.00

Selling In The '90s

Simply comparing your product to the other guy's is a sales strategy long past its prime. To keep a competitive edge, the top sales professionals of the future will need the new techniques illustrated by major corporate executive and sales expert Larry Wilson in this practical, results-orientated videotape. You'll learn the three things that buyers really want, the keys to partnership selling, and why you deliver products buy selling dreams and solutions.
07-6818 61 min. $95.00

Selling With Service

You will acquire and maintain more customers with a commitment to marketing as a guiding philosophy, and not just as a department within your company. Most people don't know that the function of every company is to acquire and maintain customers and the goal is to make money. The confusion between these two concepts often leads to dissatisfied customers.
07-5966 55 min. $79.95

Setting Up a Telemarketing Program

Consultant Judy Lanier explains, by words and graphics,how one sets up an in-house business to business telemarketing operation. This video reviews telemarketing applications, prospecting,

and cost of outside calls.
07-8050 16 min. $74.95

PROJECT MANAGEMENT
Discover how to identify and manage the fine points and big picture of every project you manage. This program will help keep your projects on time and within budget.

* **Volume I**
07-8109 65 min. $99.95

* **Volume II**
07-8110 65 min. $99.95

SPEAKING OF SUCCESS: THE BUILDING BLOCKS FOR TOTAL ACHIEVEMENT
Now you can experience $55,000 worth of seminars from this extraordinary faculty of experts. These tapes will immediately improve your productivity, communication skills, problem-solving abilities, and help you create profitable opportunities.

* **How To Listen Effectively**
07-5970 55 min. $79.95

* **Achieving Personal Excellence**
07-5971 55 min. $79.95

* **The Psychology Of Self Management**
07-5972 55 min. $79.95

* **Maximizing People Potential**
07-5973 55 min. $79.95

* **Motivating Your American Generations**
07-5974 55 min. $79.95

* **Memory: What's In It For Me?**
07-5975 55 min. $79.95

Success And Prosperity
Your brain is a computer; it can be programmed to achieve specific results. This high-energy video gives you a step-by-step approach to using techniques like visualization, auto suggestion, and programming to overcome past negative programming and bring prosperity and success to all aspects of your personal and business life. Led by Lee Milteer, author of Reach Your Career Dreams and cable television host, this 90-minute program reveals a 21-day plan to bring about major change in your life.
07-5976 90 min. $79.95

SUCCESSFUL COLD CALL SELLING
Who can benefit from this program? This program is designed for the seasoned veteran, new salespeople, sales managers and sales trainers, and small business owners. This program will show you how to make selling easier and make it work.

* **Introduction**
07-9859 25 min. $99.95

* **Triumph Over Fear**
07-9590 25 min. $99.95

* **Planning the Opening Move**
07-9591 25 min. $99.95

* **Effective Opening Lines**
07-9592 25 min. $99.95

* **Magic Door Opener**
07-9593 25 min. $99.95

* **Getting Through to Decision Making**
07-9594 25 min. $99.95

* **Probing for Needs**
07-9598 25 min. $99.95

* **Getting Through Resistance**
07-9596 25 min. $99.95

Successful Self-Management
Prepare yourself for a completely interactive, multimedia experience in self-development. With Successful Self-Management, you no longer just watch a video, listen to a tape, or read a book-you do all three, and more! In the end, you'll have a practical methodology for determining your value system and putting it to work for a more positive and fulfilling life.
07-6810 45 min. $95.00

TIMELIFE TRAINING COURSES

* **Stress Management: A Positive Strategy**
This rational, down-to-earth course is proven throughout the business market. In its expanded form, the course has been used by nearly half the Fortune 500 companies, selling at prices of up to $4,450. This course includes five lessons, with video portions about 30 minutes each, plus workbook exercises.
07-8155 60 min. $99.95

* **Effective Writing for Executives**
This course uses Ed Asner in his best "Lou Grant" style to show executives, or would-be executives, how to get more from every memo, letter or

report. Designed for self-instruction, the course includes six lessons that take about one-hour each. Each lesson includes about 30 minutes of video instruction plus written exercises.
07-8156 60 min. $99.95

• Time Management
These techniques of time management have been proven to help people control their time, accomplish their goals and handle the workload required today. Six half-hour lessons introduce the process, and a workbook provides case studies which are relevant to any organization.
07-8157 60 min. $99.95

• Communication Skills for Managers
This is not a skill you can afford to do without ...no matter what budget cuts the 90's have brought. It is a skill you can learn from this well-designed video course, complete with realistic behavior models and an outstanding use of business examples.
07-8158 60 min. $99.95

• Writing for Work
Now you can train entry-level people to write well, without expensive seminars, using this highly rated self-instruction course. This program is set in a business environment and teaches real-world writing skills.
07-8159 60 min. $99.95

• Negotiating Successfully
Hosted by Chester Karrass, considered to be one of the foremost experts on negotiation. These programs are packed with content on how to master the art of deal making. The course includes six video lessons, about 30 minutes each and an interactive workbook.
07-8160 60 min. $99.95

Time Management
Let Mark McCormack show you: the time bombs that can blow up your business day, how to take control of transition times, how to use the biggest time bomb of all the phone, how to make the most of your leisure time, and the art of doing business on the road.
07-6541 30 min. $16.95

Time Management Ideas That Work
Discover how to eliminate your biggest time wasters by avoiding unexpected interruptions, running meetings more efficiently, and delegating to produce results and meet deadlines. Every minute of this videotape is crammed with specific ideas, tips, and hints you can put to use immediately!
07-6819 45 min. $79.95

TOASTMASTERS INTERNATIONAL COMMUNICATIONS SERIES
No one personality type, no one management style, and no single skill can guarantee leadership success. Every successful leader represents a unique blend of abilities, values, and personality. But all successful leaders share an essential trait: They understand themselves.

• Be Prepared to Lead
07-8077 27 min. $89.95

• Be Prepared to Sell
07-8078 27 min. $89.95

• Be Prepared for Meetings
07-8079 27 min $89.95

Tom Peters on Necessary Disorganization
Tom defined management style for the 80's. Now, he declares the 90's the decade of non-conformism and redefines the rules for success.
07-8034 40 min. $195.00

TOTAL QUALITY MANAGEMENT
The most flexible, economical way to train your team. Let Verne Harnish teach you the principles that will help ensure the long-term health of your organization and your career.

• Volume I
07-8090 60 min. $124.95

• Volume II
07-8091 60 min. $124.95

• Volume III
07-8092 60 min. $124.95

TRAINING SERIES FOR TARGETED SKILLS

• Selling Skills: A Thinking Person's Guide
This intelligent approach replaces pat closings and shot-in-the-arm speeches that are quickly forgotten. Aimed at experienced sellers who want to keep refining their skills, these videos are a perfect tool for sales meetings, take-home refreshers or discussion starters at staff gatherings.
07-8162 90 min. $375.00

• Basic Secretarial Skills
Many clericals hire in with little or no training in the parts of the job that are not measured in words per minute. This tape presents fundamental lessons that give new secretaries a chance to succeed before they become demotivated by confusion about how

to do their job.
07-8163 90 min. $275.00

• Performance Appraisal
The review process keeps employees on the right track, yet most managers dread the task. These videos teach a systematic approach that depends on objective results and not personality traits. Use the videos individually as refreshers before conducting reviews, or as a series to teach managers the entire process.
07-8164 90 min. $275.00

Twenty-Four Techniques For Closing The Sale
Now you need never again fail to close the sale. Brian Tracy unveils 24 of the finest, most effective closing techniques ever devised. This is the same seminar for which people pay hundreds of dollars and take several days out of their busy schedules to attend.
07-273 65 min. $79.95

Understanding Business Valuation
When you plan to buy or start a business, you must know how to establish its value and get the best possible price when it comes time to sell or retire. Hosted by Phillip Sabol of Management Alternatives, a business valuation consulting firm, this in-depth video looks at: how to establish a fair market value for a business: structuring the best price; identifying all the tangible and intangible elements of value; negotiating a win-win sale; packaging a business to sell and much more. A must for any serious entrepreneur.
07-5952 60 min. $39.95

Vocal Coach Public Speaker Video
Whether a professional speaker or someone who just wants to speak more confidently in group settings, this how to video will enhance your poise and presentation. Topics include: warm-up, breathing techniques, diction and over-coming nervousness.
07-5884 35 min. $69.95

Women and Corporations: Breaking In
Two female executives and Professor Alma Barron, an authority on women in management, examine whether breaking into corporate America is any different for a woman than for a man, and why.
07-071 30 min. $89.95

Women and Corporations: Moving Up
Three professionals talk candidly about what a woman should and must do after she lands a corporate position in order to reach the boardrooms.
07-072 30 min. $89.95

Miscellaneous

Alan Hirschfield on the Future of the Film Industry
Alan Hirschfield talks about how Hollywood will rise to meet the challenge of pay TV, cable TV and computer technology.
07-103 30 min. $89.95

ASSERTIVENESS TRAINING FOR PROFESSIONALS
Being too nice doesn't work in the professional world. Yet, we don't want to alienate others by coming on too strong. This video can help you and your people find a comfortable middle ground between aggressiveness and apathy. You'll learn how self-respect, honesty and self-control build an assertive style.

• Volume I
07-8132 60 min. $99.95

• Volume II
07-8133 60 min. $99.95

Black Monday And Beyond
An hour-by-hour account of the most dangerous event in financial history; the stock market crash of October, 1987. Although this tape comes loaded with revealing footage from those fateful two days on Wall Street, it also shoes the "miracle that saved the market" and offers a complete guide to survival in the new market environment after the Crash. Features top exchange officials, brokers, traders, money managers, and successful investors.
07-5980 60 min. $39.95

CONFIDENT PUBLIC SPEAKING
This program not only helps you shine in front of large audiences. You'll also be more effective in everyday interactions.You'll see the skills of public speaking come to life. By the end of this program you will finish with a new sense of confidence, eager for your next speaking opportunity.

• Volume I
07-8041 87 min. $99.95

• Volume II
07-8042 93 min. $99.95

DENIS WAITLEY ON WINNING
This program is based on breakthrough research by behavioral scientists. And it's presented by Denis

VIDEO TITLES LISTED IN THIS GUIDE ARE AVAILABLE FOR PURCHASE OR RENTAL. CONTACT YOUR LOCAL VIDEO STORE OR TELEPHONE (800) 383-8811

Waitley--one of the world's most accomplished personal growth teachers. You'll gain a new understanding of yourself and appreciate the difference as you become more confident, positive and effective in every situation.

• **Volume I**
07-8104 70 min. $74.95

• **Volume II**
07-8105 70 min. $74.95

• **Volume III**
07-8106 70 min. $74.95

• **Volume IV**
07-8107 70 min. $74.95

Don't Litigate...Mediate!
Court battles customarily are expensive, time-consuming, and bitter. Learn how mediation enables opponents to negotiate mutually beneficial agreements that can resolve disputes between them and save their relationship.
07-9157 23 min. $24.95

E Myth, Why Most Businesses Don't Work And What To Do About It
Small-business owners rave about this video (based upon the best-selling book of the same title). Hosted by author and entrepreneur Michael E. Gerber, America's leading authority on small business, viewers learn how solve business problems and turn any business into a money machine. Inspirational, compelling and packed with information.
07-7093 40 min. $79.95

Education For Competitiveness
Xerox CEO David Kearns highlights the need for education reform and explains how his company revitalized itself to win the prestigious Malcolm Baldrige Quality Award. Hosted by Morton Kondracke, moderator of the PBS foreign affairs series, American Interest.
07-6735 60 min. $199.95

Environment: Business And Labor
Focuses on the necessity for a business to recognize that labor impacts the environment. In addition to the principles of unionism, the basic strategies for labor and management to achieve their objectives as well as the actions necessary for them to successfully interact are discussed.
07-6839 30 min. $79.95

Film Industry After Television
Alan Hirchfield, chairman of the board of Twentieth Century Fox talks about how the business survived the onslaught of television,

conglomerates, and new technology, and how it got to where it is today.
07-102 30 min. $89.95

Guide to Everyday Negotiating
Buying a car or shopping for a new house doesn't have to be a terrible chore. Learn the basic how-to's of getting what you want - of feeling more confident and comfortable in your everyday negotiating. Meet the sharpest salespeople on even footing, and negotiate the terms you want!
07-1838 45 min. $79.95

HIGH IMPACT COMMUNICATION SKILLS
This program reveals the communication style of today's most powerful professionals--techniques you can use to get better results with bosses, co-workers and clients. You'll finish with renewed confidence. And you will have the communication skills you need to be seen as the competent professional you are.

• **Volume I**
07-8130 60 min. $99.95

• **Volume II**
07-8131 60 min. $99.95

How To Be A No-Limit Person
Based upon the personal experience of Dr. Wayne Dyer, this 57-minute motivational program deals in down-to-earth advice on: how people should seek serenity rather than acquisitions; to teach those you love to value knowledge more than material possessions, and; that quality of life is more important than outward appearance. Dr. Dyer shows you how to develop real personal authority and be a "no-limit" person.
07-5977 57 min. $79.95

How to Give a Good Deposition
A practical, step-by-step video guide to preparing yourself quickly and effectively for deposition.
07-8141 45 min. $29.95

How to Have a Moneymaking Garage Sale
07-274 24 min. $19.95

How to Succeed in a Home Business
Learn the secrets of starting a business at home and enjoy the freedom of "having it all" through a home-based business. Features interviews with successful entrepreneurs working from home.
07-1619 60 min. $19.95

Is Ethnic In?
Two black corporate executives and a St. Louis University professor who has helped minorities win

placement in American corporations disagree in their experience and viewpoint of corporate America.
07-073 30 min. $89.95

Inc. Magazine: Creating A Winner: Marketing
Inc. makes marketing simple by throwing out the jargon and buzz words and bringing you the essence of marketing: the key concepts that will enable you to market anything, the fundamental questions you must answer before entering the marketplace.
07-8063 70 min. $39.95

Love and Friendship at the Office
The President of an NBC TV affiliate married her newscaster and talks about the rewards and of difficulties of love and friendship within the office context.
07-070 30 min. $89.95

Marketing to Minorities
Tom Burrell, the most successful ad man in the county in marketing to Black Americans, explains his strategies and techniques in reaching that market, along with two of his best customers, Peter Sealey, Vice President of Coca-Cola, and William Youngclaus, Vice President of McDonald's Corporation.
07-096 30 min. $89.95

Marketing Successes of Coca-Cola-Why They Work
Peter Sealy, Vice President of Marketing Operations for Coca-Cola USA, reveals some thoughts behind the very successful marketing strategy of Coca-Cola. Included is a look at some of the company's best television commercials and an analysis of why they worked so well.
07-097 30 min. $89.95

Meeting the Foreign Challenge
Government help in warding off threats to U.S. business from unfair foreign competition is important, says textile industry leader Roger Milliken, CEO of Milliken Co. But's it's world beating quality and attention to detail that are the real weapons for winning battles against international rivals. Morton Kondracke of PBS's American Interests is host.
07-6731 35 min. $199.95

NIGHTLY BUSINESS REPORT VIDEO GUIDE

• **Guide to Buying Insurance**
07-8143 42 min. $24.95

• **How Wall Street Works**
07-8144 38 min. $24.95

• **Retirement Planning**
07-8142 47 min. $24.95

PROOFREADING AND EDITING SKILLS
Spotting and correcting mistakes can't be left to chance. Proofreading and editing require training-- and you'll find no better way to learn these skills than on this video. It features Debra Smith and Helen Sutton, two of CareerTrack's most popular trainers. They actually make proofreading and editing fun, and leave you with the skills that will make you more valuable.

• **Volume I**
07-8127 60 min. $99.95

• **Volume II**
07-8128 60 min. $99.95

• **Volume III**
07-8129 60 min. $99.95

Publish or Perish
The Sun Publication story illustrates how growth, transition and sound financial management go hand-in-hand. This program shows the demands and how a company deals with increasing complexity and the need for sophisticated capital management.
07-8051 30 min. $99.00

SELF DISCIPLINE AND EMOTIONAL CONTROL
This program can change your negative behaviors permanently. This powerful system is based on rational-emotive therapy, which uses some of the most effective tools in modern psychology. Put these tools to work in your toughest situations, and you'll see amazing results.

• **Volume I**
07-8099 100 min. $99.95

• **Volume II**
07-8100 100 min. $99.95

Strategy Lessons From The Harvard Business School Part 1
Professors Bruce Scott, Michael Porter, and Rosabeth Moss Kanter (editor of the Harvard Business Review) explain what American business must understand and do to retain global economic leadership. Morton Kondracke of The New Republic hosts this American Interests special.
07-6732 60 min. $199.95

VIDEO TITLES LISTED IN THIS GUIDE ARE AVAILABLE FOR PURCHASE OR RENTAL. CONTACT YOUR LOCAL VIDEO STORE OR TELEPHONE (800) 383-8811

Strategy Lessons From the Harvard Business School Part 2
The strategy sessions continue with HBS Professors Alfred Chandler, Robert Hayes, and Jay Lorsch.
07-6733 60 min. $199.95

STRESS MANAGEMENT FOR PROFESSIONALS
This is an upbeat program that helps you understand why you suffer from stress--and then shows you what to do about it. You'll gain simple, easy-to-implement strategies to help you deal with everything from conflict to overload to depression. If you're ready to feel better and perform at your peak, you owe it to yourself and your staff to invest in this program now.

• **Volume I**
07-8096 100 min. $99.95

• **Volume II**
07-8097 90 min. $99.95

Swann on Contracts
Professor Swann, a lawyer and teacher at UC Berkley and JF Kennedy School of Management has a step-by-step guide on how to make an enforceable contract.
07-8019 58 min. $59.95

TIME MANAGEMENT TODAY
Do you control your work day--or does it control you? This program shows you how to respond to other people's demands and accomplish your own.

You'll learn critical communication skills that establish a cooperative atmosphere. Plus you will find out how to delegate effectively and conduct meetings that stay on time and on track.

• **Volume I**
07-8111 105 min. $99.95

• **Volume II**
07-8112 105 min. $99.95

Turning Ideas Into Products--Is America Falling Behind
America has the best technology base in the world. But is the government paying enough attention to safeguarding it? And why are foreign competitors beating American companies to market with high-tech products? National Science Foundation director Erich Bloch and product development expert Gary Reiner of the Boston Consulting Group explain how American companies can regain the lead. Morton Kondracke of American Interests (PBS) hosts.
07-6736 60 min. $199.95

Yellow Page Insider
This video program will show you how to sort out the confusing and costly claims of Yellow Page directory publishers. No matter what size your ad budget, this video will show you how to maximize your total results and save you thousands of dollars.
07-8056 30 min. $79.95

Tired of

"Getting The Business?"

Learn to Negotiate Your Way to

Success With One of These

Videos.

Children

Entertainment

ADVENTURES OF BABAR
Follow the adventure of everyone's favorite elephant on his magical adventures. Children of all ages will enjoy this wonderful series.

- **Volume 1**
10-8091 60 min. $19.95

- **Volume 2**
10-8092 60 min. $19.95

- **Volume 3**
10-8093 60 min. $19.95

- **Volume 4**
10-8094 60 min. $19.95

- **Volume 5**
10-8095 60 min. $19.95

- **Volume 6**
10-8096 60 min. $19.95

- **Volume 7**
10-8097 60 min. $19.95

Adventures of Gallant Bess
Cameron Mitchell stars as a young wrangler and rodeo rider out to capture a magnificent, wild red horse for the rodeo stables. But a devious plot threatens to take away this horse. In a stirring climax Mitchell must confront the rodeo owner and his gang to save his horse known as Gallant Bess. Young and old will delight in this moving story of how love conquers all.
10-9117 73 min. $19.95

Amazing Children
From the creators of "The Amazing Book" comes a delightful tale of Rikki and Doc as they discover that being a kid is really one of the greatest (biggest) blessings of all. This animated feature is perfect for kids 2-10.
10-9116 30 min. $19.95

Animal Stories
Whether you're young in years or just young at heart, this unique collection of stories told by four of America's most accomplished storytellers offers an enchanting look at a tradition as old as the spoken word. Featured storytellers are Alice McGill, Joe Bruchac, Olga Loya and Jon Spelman.
10-8046 35 min. $16.95

Aesop and His Friends
A delightful cartoon film festival of family entertainment including most of Aesop's best-loved stories. Includes "The Fox and the Crow," "The Boy Who Called Wolf," plus the bonus cartoons "The Snowman's Dilemma" and "The Owl and the Pussy-cat," as told by Cyril Richard.
10-090 90 min. $64.95

Aladdin and His Magic Lamp
A delightful cartoon film festival of family entertainment including most of Aesop's best-loved stories "The Fox and the Crow," "The Boy Who Called Wolf," plus the bonus cartoons "The Snowman's Dilemma" and "The Owl and the Pussycat," as told by Cyril Richard.
10-407 90 min. $39.95

Arthur's Eyes
Bill Cosby narrates, Maya Angelou reads poetry. Includes selections from Arnold Adoff's "All the Color of the Race," Beau Gardner's "The Turnabout, Lookabout, Think "about Book" and Philip Newth's "Roly Goes Exploring.
10-450 30 min. $14.95

Baby Vision
A baby book that comes alive with movement and sound created for children between the ages of 9 and 36 months. There are six vignettes, beautifully filmed and scored, balancing action, sound and color into 32 scenes to interest, intrigue and pacify your child.
10-2494 75 min. $19.95

BARNEY & THE BACKYARD GANG
Features: live action with animation, traditional songs and rhymes, stories filled with excitement, fun and suspense. For children ages 2-8.

- **Backyard Show**
Features Sandy Duncan as Mom to Amy and Michael, who-along with their neighborhood friends and a dinosaur who magically comes to life-plan a lively surprise birthday show for their Dad.
10-5311 30 min. $29.95

- **Day At The Beach**
Features Sandy Duncan as Mom to Amy and Michael, who-along with their neighborhood friends and Barney, the dinosaur who magically comes to life-go on an adventure to the beach, discover a pirate ship, and meet the sea.
10-5310 30 min. $29.95

VIDEO TITLES LISTED IN THIS GUIDE ARE AVAILABLE FOR PURCHASE OR RENTAL. CONTACT YOUR LOCAL VIDEO STORE OR TELEPHONE (800) 383-8811

• **Three Wishes**
Features Sandy Duncan as Mom to Amy and
Michael, who-along with their neighborhood
friends and Barney, the dinosaur who magically
comes to life-enjoy three fun-filled wishes. There's
a great trip to a fun park, the moon, and to a
petting farm.
10-5309 30 min. $29.95

**Barry Louis Polisar Sings "My Brother
Threw Up on my Stuffed Toy Bunny"**
A guaranteed hit for older elementary school
children who really know what it's all about: "I've
Got a Teacher, She's So Mean, "When the House
is Dark and QUIET" and much more.
10-2746 40 min. $19.95

**Barry Louis Polisar: I'm a 3-Toed,
Triple-Eyed, Double-Jointed Dinosaur**
This intimate concert serves up Barry's unusual offbeat, zany humor, and crazy, fun-loving songs.
10-2718 40 min. $19.95

BEAR HUGS VIDEOS
Bear Hug Videos illustrate important Biblical
principles with cuddly bear characters at a level
children can appreciate. Each tape contains two
delightful animated stories.

• **Volume 1**
I Can Bearly Wait: A child learns patience and,
Bearing Burdens: A child learns to help.
10-5329 30 min. $19.95

• **Volume 2**
Bearing Fruit: A Child learns about the fruit of the
spirit, and Bear Buddies: A child learns to make
friends.
10-5330 30 min. $19.95

• **Volume 3**
Love Bears All Things: A child learns to love and,
Bear Up: A child learns to handle ups and downs.
10-5331 30 min. $19.95

Beaureguard's Bottle Buddies
Viewers learn to make simple puppets from plastic
bottles and other recyclable materials as they
watch puppeteer Bob Brown teach his canine friend
Beaureguard. The puppets are easy to make and
require minimal adult supervision. For ages 5 to
12.
10-9538 30 min. $24.95

Benny Bear
Fully animated half hour tape made up of 4-7
minute cartoon shorts about a loveable zoo bear
with an attitude.
10-8007 30 min. $12.99

Best of Spike Jones
This video features segments from Spike Jones'
Zany television show from the 1950's
10-2816 51 min. $29.95

Big Bird in Japan
Travel with Big Bird as he explores some of
Japan's famous sights, meets a Japanese family,
and learns some Japanese words and customs. Four
original songs make this a magical, musical trip.
10-8036 30 min. $16.95

Brave One
This moving story tells the tale of a Mexican boy
and his devotion to a beloved pet bull, and animal
he has cared for from birth. The two are
inseparable until the pet becomes a full-grown,
magnificent fighting bull and is taken to do battle at
the bullring in Mexico City.
10-412 100 min. $19.95

Brothers Grimm Fairy Tales
"Little Red Riding Hood" - Excitement builds as a
young girl skips through the woods to
grandmother's house. But is it grandmother? Or, is
it the trickery of the big bad wolf? "The Seven
Ravens" - A seven-year-old girl sets out to rescue
her seven brothers who have been turned into
ravens by a vengeful witch. She searches through
enchanted forests, over magic mountains, to the
sun, moon and stars. Will her determination be
rewarded inside the amazing glass hill?
10-437 35 min. $19.95

BUBBE'S BOARDING HOUSE SERIES
This series helps children understand the Jewish
religion and what holidays they celebrate.

• **Passover**
10-8098 60 min. $19.95

• **Chanuka**
10-8099 60 min. $19.95

CAPTAIN KANGAROO SERIES

• **Animal Alphabet**
Children learn the alphabet by using the beginning
letter of a type of animal.
10-8024 30 min. $16.95

• **Counting with the Captain**
Learn how to begin counting.
10-8027 30 min. $16.95

• **Fairy Tales and Funny Stories**
It's time to laugh and be enchanted as Captain
Kangaroo spins his magic with some classic and

not-so-classic fables. "Little Red Riding Hood","Sleeping Beauty","Rapunzel", and the tale of Cinderella's brother, "Cinderelliot."
10-487　60 min.　$39.95

• **Favorite Stories**
10-8028　30 min.　$16.95

• **Fun with Baby Animals**
Children learn about different baby animals and how they live and grow up.
10-8029　30 min.　$16.95

• **Going Places**
10-8026　30 min.　$16.95

• **His Friends**
Captain Kangaroo hobnobs with some of his celebrity pals in this gala, star-filled tape. You won't want to miss any of the fun.
10-485　60 min.　$39.95

• **Kids Like You**
10-8025　30 min.　$16.95

• **Let's Go to the Zoo**
Go on a field trip to the great zoos across the country with Captain Kangaroo as your guide. Meet the animals and their caretakers, and learn lots of interesting and fun facts about their life there.
10-486　60 min.　$39.95

• **Merry Christmas Stories**
Included are favorite stories of faith, heart, and good cheer for a glow as warm as a yule log on the fire.
10-489　60 min.　$39.95

• **Tales of Magic and Mystery**
This program will bewitch your children with this enchanting collection of stories and fables. They'll meet Wilbert the Wizard, Nilrim the Magician, the Great Wizard Inspector, Sam Charade, and even the Genie of the Banana.
10-490　60 min.　$39.95

Carnival of the Animals
An award-winning children's classic that combines poetry and classical music into a lighthearted romp through the animal world.
10-1816　30 min.　$14.95

Cartoons at War
Our animated heroes fight the enemy in a rare collection of 16 original wartime cartoons by America's foremost animation greats.
10-8059　90 min.　$16.95

Celebrity Storyteller Featuring Tina Yothers
Join Tina and her little friends as she tells the stories "Mouse In The House", "Monster On West 96th Street", "When An Elephant Spends The Night" and "A Magic Toy". The perfect way to entertain your child!
10-5724　30 min.　$14.95

Chocolate Princess and Other Children's Stories
Bill Cosby narrates this delightfully animated story that points out the valuable lesson of not judging a person by his appearance. Also included are "The Stolen Necklace," "A Little Girl and a Funny Wolf," "How Beaver Stole Fire." "The Smallest Elephant in the World," "Giants Come in Different Sizes," and "Gulliver's Travels."
10-035　55 min.　$16.95

Christopher Columbus
Fully animated and fun for the entire family.
10-8040　30 min.　$16.95

CHRISTOPHER COLUMBUS COMMEMORATIVE SERIES
This fully animated series chronicles the life of Christopher Columbus. From his humble beginnings to his triumphant discovery of the New World.

• **Sailor is Born**
10-8032　60 min.　$16.95

• **Setting Sail**
10-8030　60 min.　$16.95

• **Discovery of a New World**
10-8031　60 min.　$16.95

CHRONICLES OF NARNIA SERIES
Enter the magical world of C.S. Lewis. Children will enjoy this live action series.

• **Lion, The Witch, & The Wardrobe**
10-8105　165 min.　$24.95

• **Prince Caspian and the Voyage of the Dawn Treader**
10-8106　165 min.　$24.95

• **Silver Chair**
10-8107　165 min.　$24.95

Clever Jack
An all-new high-energy, magical musical version of the classic children's story, "Jack in the Beanstalk." Hosted by Lucie Arnaz and starring the critically acclaimed First All Children's Theatre, this film

VIDEO TITLES LISTED IN THIS GUIDE ARE AVAILABLE FOR PURCHASE OR RENTAL. CONTACT YOUR LOCAL VIDEO STORE OR TELEPHONE (800) 383-8811

includes a cast of more than 30 singing and dancing gifted young performers who will win the hearts of every family.
10-236 47 min. $19.95

Clifford's Sing Along Adventure
Come on a fun-filled adventure with Clifford, the Big Red Dog and his friends. Clifford leads the gang on a journey through his wonderful musical world. The songs are classics: "Old MacDonald" "Shoo Fly," "She'll Be Coming Around the Mountain," "Row, Row, Row Your Boat," and many others. Children are encouraged to get up and participate, to sing, dance and clap along. A delightful journey children will love and will want to return to again and again.
10-155 30 min. $14.95

COLORFORMS LEARN' N PLAY VCR ADVENTURES SERIES
This new series combines the best in video entertainment with Colorforms, the fun learning toys that kids know and love. This winning combination encourages creative play and hours of fun-filled activity. Designed by scholastic experts this series promotes reading-readiness and builds vocabulary. Kids at home will pay along as Max, Suzy and their friends journey through the Magic Jungle and take a voyage to Mermaid Island. Each adventure features original puppets, great music, and animation on a 30-minute videocassette. Plus, every package contains sixteen Colorforms pieces, a playboard, and a booklet containing advice for parents, written by a renowned reading expert.

- **Journey to the Magic Jungle**
10-262 30 min. $14.95

- **Voyage to Mermaid Island**
10-263 30 min. $14.95

Dance Along
Join Big Bird, Gina, Mike, and the kids as they show us "A New Way to Walk" with the Oinker sisters. All in all there are nine different dances sure to make every one wants to "Dance Along"!
10-8037 30 min. $16.95

FABLES AND LEGENDS: AESOP'S FABLES
The wit and wisdom of the great storyteller is revealed through Aesop's most famous fables.

- **Volume 1**
"The Lion and the Statue"; "The Lion and the Mouse"; "The Tortoise and The Hare"; "The Dog and His Shadow"; "The Boy Who Cried Wolf" and "The Fox and the Goat."
10-461 30 min. $14.95

- **Volume 2**
"The Milkmaid and Her Pail"; "Belling the Cat"; "The Wolf in Sheep's Clothing"; "The Goose and the Golden Eggs"; "The Dog in the Manger"; The Man, The Boy and the Donkey" and "The Hare with Many Friends."
10-462 30 min. $14.95

FABLES AND LEGENDS: HISTORY & VERSE
Stirring tales of America's first settlers and the struggle for independence as told by some of America's greatest poets such as William Makepeace Thackeray, Felicia Hemans, Kate Brownlee Sherwood, Frances Miles Finch, William Gilmore Simms, Margaret Junkins Preston, Stephen Vincent Benet, Henry Wadsworth Longfellow, Oliver Wendell Holmes and Will Carleton.

- **Volume 1**
"Paul Revere's Ride"; "Grandmother's Story of the Bunker Hill Battle" and "Casablanca."
10-470 30 min. $14.95

- **Volume 2**
"The Wreck of the Hesperus"; "Southern Ships and Settlers"; "The Ballad of William Sycamore"; "Pocahontas"; "Landing of the Pilgrim Fathers" and "The First Thanksgiving Day."
10-471 30 min. $14.95

- **Volume 3**
"The Little Black-Eyed Rebel"; "The Swamp Fox"; "Nathan Hale";"Molly Pitcher' and "Dunkirk."
10-472 30 min. $14.95

FABLES AND LEGENDS: ENGLISH FOLK HEROES

- **Volume 1**
"Arthur and the Sword" and "Ivanhoe."
10-476 30 min. $14.95

- **Volume 2**
"The Round Table" and "Beowulf."
10-477 30 min. $14.95

- **Volume 3**
"Sir George and the Dragon" and "Robin Hood."
10-478 30 min. $14.95

FABLES AND LEGENDS: HUMOROUS STORY POEMS - FOLK HEROES
Delightful and exciting stories of everyday Americans and their not-so-everyday adventures from some of America's greatest poets such as Oliver Wendell Holmes, Lewis Carroll and William Cowper.

VIDEO TITLES LISTED IN THIS GUIDE ARE AVAILABLE FOR PURCHASE OR RENTAL. CONTACT YOUR LOCAL VIDEO STORE OR TELEPHONE (800) 383-8811

• **Volume 1**
"The Cremation of Sam McGee"; "Darius Green and His Flying Machine" and "The Deacon's Masterpiece."
10-467 30 min. $14.95

• **Volume 2**
"John Gilpin - The Owl Critic"; "The Walrus and the Carpenter" and "Lady Clare."
10-468 30 min. $14.95

FABLES AND LEGENDS: THE TRAVELS OF ODYSSEUS
The hero of Homer's "The Iliad" and "The Odyssey" Battles monsters and gods in defense of his people in these mythical stories.

• **Volume 1**
"Circe and the Trojan War."
10-473 30 min. $14.95

• **Volume 2**
"The Cyclops" and "Odysseus and the Terrible Sea."
10-474 30 min. $14.95

• **Volume 3**
"Telemachus, Son of Odysseus" and "The Homecoming."
10-475 30 min. $14.95

Farm Animals
A video visit to a farm. The viewer will see cows, pigs and horses. Children who have never been to a farm or to the zoo will find a whole new world waiting for them.
10-8137 30 min. $16.95

Five Lionni Classics
These are big stories for little listeners. They celebrate the power of imagination, the joy of discovery and the importance of living together in harmony. Anyone who knows "Frederick," "Cornelius," "It's Mine!," "Fish is Fish" and "Swimmy" will readily understand why Leo Lionni's animal fables have become modern classics.
10-555 30 min. $14.95

GET ALONG GANG
Join The Get Along Gang-a bear, a fox, a beaver, two dogs and a lamb-in seven rousing animated stories that teach small fry about friendship.

• **Camp Get Along and The Bullies**
10-5672 23 min. $19.95

• **Engineer Rotary and Pick of the Litter**
10-5673 25 min. $19.95

• **The Get Along Gang**
10-5674 23 min. $19.95

• **Mischief Mania**
10-5675 23 min. $19.95

• **School's Out and Them's The Breaks**
10-5676 23 min. $19.95

• **Zipper's Millions**
10-5677 45 min. $19.95

• **Head In The Clouds**
10-5678 45 min. $19.95

GIGGLESNORT HOTEL SERIES
Check into the Emmy Award-winning Gigglesnort Hotel for seven treasurable volumes of puppet wizardry that delightfully entertain and educate.

• **Beauty Of Silence And Following Directions**
10-5680 50 min. $19.95

• **Being Afraid And Hope**
10-5683 50 min. $19.95

• **Fire Safety And Pulling Together**
10-5681 50 min. $19.95

• **Get Your Rest And Saving**
10-5684 50 min. $19.95

• **Gift For Granny And Billy Joe's Thanksgiving**
10-5682 50 min. $19.95

• **Is Winning Everything? And Littering Your Life Away**
10-5685 50 min. $19.95

• **Puppy Parenthood and Tender Is The Man**
10-5679 50 min. $19.95

Good Morning Sunshine
Spend the day with Patti and Laura and oodles of kids as they sing and dance their way through 15 favorite children's songs. This video captures the same gentle, wholesome feelings as the original award-winning audio cassette.
10-8163 35 min. $19.95

Great Circus Parade
The dazzling coverage of this parade intersperses the procession of wagons with documentary footage on the historical significance of the traveling circus.

VIDEO TITLES LISTED IN THIS GUIDE ARE AVAILABLE FOR PURCHASE OR RENTAL. CONTACT YOUR LOCAL VIDEO STORE OR TELEPHONE (800) 383-8811

Hosts Bob Keeshan and Joe Smith are your curbside guides, ready to bring you in for closer views of the powerful horses, antique wagons, exotic animals, and circus performers.
10-8111 60 min. $29.95

GREATEST STORIES EVER TOLD
This animated bible series is designed for children to be educational as well as entertaining. Narrated by some of Hollywood's finest actors.

• Savior is Born, Narrated by Morgan Freeman
10-8009 30 min. $16.95

• Noah & the Ark, Narrated by Kelly McGillis
10-8010 30 min. $16.95

• David & Goliath, Narrated by Mel Gibson
10-8011 30 min. $16.95

• Jonah & the Whale, Narrated by Jason Robards
10-8012 30 min. $16.95

Gulliver's Travels
This delightfully animated color film, based on the classic Jonathan Swift novel of these same name, is a brilliant example of the pinnacle of the Golden Age of Animation during the late 1930's and 1940's.
10-9114 88 min. $19.95

Hans Christian Andersen's Fairy Tales
Included are: The Steadfast Tin Soldier - one of Andersen's most famous tales tells of the tragic love of the one-legged tin soldier for a paper ballerina. Thumbelina - the adventures of the teeny-tiny girl who is stolen from her bed by an old toad. Together, they create for children a lasting fascination.
10-433 30 min. $24.95

Hawaii Adventure for Kids
Visit all of the islands and do other fun things like: ride in a helicopter, encounter whales, and learn the hula.
10-9170 30 min. $16.95

Here We Go: Volume 1
Five big-as-life rides just for kids to enjoy again and again. Featured here: construction equipment, a helicopter, a steam train, a hovercraft and a blimp.
10-2176 33 min. $19.95

Here We Go: Volume 2
Seven big-as-life rides to thrill kids over and over.

Featured here: a tramway, a double-decker bus, an ocean liner, a milk truck, a fire engine, bicycles and a hydrofoil.
10-2177 33 min. $19.95

HUMAN RACE CLUB SERIES

• Casey's Revenge
A story about Casey and a valuable lesson he learned about fights between brothers and sisters.
10-2154 25 min. $16.95

• Fair Weather Friend
A story about A.J. and an important lesson he learned about friendship.
10-2152 25 min. $16.95

• High Price to Play
A story about Teddy and an important lesson he learned about money and possessions.
10-2153 25 min. $16.95

• Lean Mean Machine
A story about Maggie and a valuable lesson she learned about handling uncomfortable feelings.
10-2150 25 min. $16.95

• Letter on Light Blue Stationery
A story about Pamela and an important lesson she learned about the value of each and every person.
10-2151 25 min. $16.95

• Unforgettable Pen Pal
A story about A.J. and a valuable lesson he learned about discrimination and prejudice.
10-2155 25 min. $16.95

Humpty
Fully animated, this video is perfect for teaching children why obedience is the real key to peace and contentment.
10-9121 30 min. $19.95

INTERACTIVE VIDEO FOR KIDS

• Look What I Made
10-8180 45 min. $16.95

• Look What I Found
10-8181 45 min. $16.95

• Look What I Grew
10-8182 45 min. $16.95

JENNIFER'S TRIP TO THE ZOO
Come along with Jennifer and her friends as she goes on fun filled visit to the zoo. Skip, dance, sing-a-long and learn while seeing all the exciting animals she meets along the way. Follow the

VIDEO TITLES LISTED IN THIS GUIDE ARE AVAILABLE FOR PURCHASE OR RENTAL. CONTACT YOUR LOCAL VIDEO STORE OR TELEPHONE (800) 383-8811

humorous misadventures of two lovable puppets: Cleeroy (an ape) and Jeradia (a frog) as they join Jennifer and her friends in this cheerful and entertaining video.

• **Jennifer's Trip To The Zoo: Visiting The Bears, Lions, And Elephants**
10-6468 30 min. $16.95

• **Jennifer's Trip To The Zoo: Visiting The Monkeys, Giraffes, And Petting Animals**
10-6467 30 min. $16.95

KIDPOWER SERIES:

• **Circus Power**
When the kids find they don't have enough money for the circus, they sneak in and get involved in a circus caper they'll never forget.
10-2410 30 min. $14.95

• **Don't Fake It**
The kids make a movie that'll make you laugh, but not until they learn you shouldn't lie - especially about what you don't know.
10-2409 30 min. $14.95

• **Pain, Pain Go Away**
The kids of kidpower will take the pain out of a scary trip to the dentist and show you that they can be your friends, too.
10-2412 30 min. $14.95

• **Polly and the General**
When the kids get new pets, they learn that they must treat them with as much respect as they give people.
10-2408 30 min. $14.95

• **Take a Hike**
The kids go on a hike and become friends with the animals of the forest, learning not to let the world go by, but to take part in it.
10-2411 30 min. $14.95

• **Teamwork**
Kids learn that when you're in a group, it's all for one and one for all.
10-2407 30 min. $14.95

Little David's Adventure
A rainbow-covered light beam streaks down form a unique L-O-V-E star constellation and magically transforms 6-year-old Mary Ann, her older brother Peter James and their friend Sauli from the All Nation's School into animated characters on a home computer screen.
10-281 55 min. $29.95

Lassie: The Painted Hills
Splendid family entertainment starring America's favorite collie.
10-9142 70 min. $16.95

Little Engine That Could
All aboard for a magical new milestone in children's entertainment! Featuring all the classic characters of the original book, with colorful new faces adding to the fun, it's the beloved story that has warmed the hearts of millions for over 60 years.
10-8177 30 min. $16.95

Little Duck Tale
This true-life story portrays the adventures of "Chibi," the little duckling, as he and his brothers and sisters struggle for survival in bustling downtown Tokyo. Children and parents alike will find joy in this tale of determination and triumph.
10-8183 50 min. $24.95

Little Match Girl
Introduced by Imogene Coca, this is a screen adaptation of Hans Christian Andersen's classic fairy tale, about a little girl, abused and finally abandoned by her parents, who seeks refuge from the cold by warming herself with the matches she sells.
10-2497 48 min. $19.95

Little Prince: Tales of the Sea
10-316 50 min. $29.95

McMillan's Amazing Adventures
Included in this volume: a short ride into space, a close look at a volcano, soap bubble magic, and kite flying.
10-9842 30 min. $19.99

McMillan's Dynamite Discoveries
Based on the top selling McMillan Illustrated Almanac for kids, inquiring young minds are treated to dazzling new worlds of fun, entertainment and imagination.
10-9841 30 min. $19.99

More Animal Bloopers
10-9174 30 min. $16.95

MOTHER GOOSE VIDEO TREASURY
Created by Frank Brandt, "The Mother Goose Video Treasury" includes 38 of the most cherished Mother Goose rhymes.

• **Volume 1**
10-2295 30 min. $14.95

• **Volume 2**
10-2296 32 min. $14.95

• **Volume 3**
10-2297 30 min. $14.95

• **Volume 4**
10-2298 28 min. $14.95

MOTHER NATURE - TALES OF DISCOVERY SERIES

• **Antlers Big & Small**
Explore the North American wilderness and meet almost a dozen different cousins of the deer family. Learn how antlers grow.
10-8176 25 min. $16.95

• **Babes in the Woods**
Visit baby animals in nursery habitats around the world and marvel at proud parents as they feed and teach their young.
10-8171 25 min. $16.95

• **Bringing Up Baby**
Watch as proud parents teach, protect and nurture their young in fascinating nursery habitats.
10-8173 25 min. $16.95

• **Business of Beavers**
Visit a beaver lodge and watch the busy antics of a growing beaver family in which siblings "baby-sit" for newborns.
10-8175 25 min. $16.95

• **Springtime Toddler Tales**
Witness the miracle of birth and watch baby animals explore, grow and learn in their cozy nursery habits.
10-8172 25 min. $16.95

• **When Bears Go Fishing**
Journey to the Alaskan wilderness and encounter great grizzly bears. Learn why they're such good fisherman.
10-8171 25 min. $16.95

Music Machine
Over a million copies of Music Machine book and cassette have enchanted listeners from age two to adult since it's release. Now you can too, in this beautifully animated, tale featuring the voices of Pat Boone and Stan Freberg.
10-9113 30 min. $19.95

MY FIRST ACTIVITY SERIES
These four programs focus on science experiments, nature projects, cooking recipes and craft activities.

• **My First Activity Video**
Learn how to do pasta jewelry, wrapping paper out of a potato and more.
10-8020 50 min. $16.95

• **My First Cooking Video**
Recipes are included on how to make bread animals, pizzas, quiches and decorated cookies.
10-8021 50 min. $16.95

• **My First Science Video**
Experiment include: chemistry, basics of light, magnetism and electricity.
10-8022 50 min. $16.95

• **My First Nature Video**
Learn how to start a garden in a bottle, plaster animal tracks and make a worm farm.
10-8023 40 min. $16.95

My Friend Liberty
A delightful clay animation feature by Oscar-winning film maker Jimmy Picker, starring the Statue of Liberty herself. Fun for the whole family.
10-261 30 min. $16.95

MY SESAME STREET HOME VIDEO SERIES

• **Big Bird's Story Time**
Favorite children's stories are told by familiar characters. Comes with activity book.
10-2796 30 min. $16.95

• **Getting Ready for School**
Offers children a preview of what they can expect on the first day of school.
10-2794 30 min. $16.95

• **Learning to Add and Subtract**
For children who have already learned to count, includes activity book.
10-2795 30 min. $16.95

• **Sing Along**
Familiar characters sing favorites such as "Rubber Duckie" and "Sing A Song," comes with songbook.
10-2797 30 min. $16.95

NEW ZOO REVUE SERIES

• **Spring**
10-6529 30 min. $14.95

VIDEO TITLES LISTED IN THIS GUIDE ARE AVAILABLE FOR PURCHASE OR RENTAL. CONTACT YOUR LOCAL VIDEO STORE OR TELEPHONE (800) 383-8811

• **Good Deeds**
10-6530 30 min. $14.95

• **Running Away**
10-6531 30 min. $14.95

• **Teachers**
10-6532 30 min. $14.95

• **Moving Away**
10-6533 30 min. $14.95

• **Shyness**
10-6534 30 min. $14.95

• **Getting Attention**
10-6535 30 min. $14.95

• **Being Thoughtless**
10-6536 30 min. $14.95

• **Rhythm**
10-6537 30 min. $14.95

• **Ocean**
10-6538 30 min. $14.95

On the High Seas
Co-stars Marlo, a young electronics genius and his talking computer, the Magic Movie Machine. They turn the TV screen into a children's delight above and below deck, taking the audience on a tour of the expected and the unexpected, You'll get a chance to steer the ship, fly in a helicopter and peer up the periscope, and even launch planes from the deck of the U.S.S. Eisenhower and meet the crew.
10-237 60 min. $19.95

PEPPERMINT PARK SERIES
Learn about letters, counting, stoplights, animals and more with the kids of Peppermint Park.

• **Magic Moments**
Learn about the letters "A" and "B".
10-8048 30 min. $16.95

• **Story Lady**
Learn about the letter "C".
10-8049 30 min. $16.95

• **Music Land**
Learn about the letters "M" and "W".
10-8050 30 min. $16.95

• **Musical Letters**
Learn about the letters "T" and "G".
10-8051 30 min. $16.95

• **Carnival Fun**
Learn about the letters "A" and "P".
10-8052 30 min. $16.95

• **Discover Feelings**
Learn about the letters "S" and "O".
10-8053 30 min. $16.95

Peter & the Magic Seeds
This moving story teaches children the basis for a healthy self-image and a valuable lesson in trust. Fully animated.
10-9120 24 min. $19.95

Pride of Jesse Hallum
Johnny Cash, Brenda Vaccaro and Eli Wallach star in this tale of man's determination to read. Held back by his inability to read or write, widower Jesse Hallum (Cash) reveals his secret with the help of a dedicated woman (Vaccaro) for the sake of his children.
10-422 105 min. $14.95

Reading With Mother Goose
In this video, children are taught to read 158 Dolch List words through Mother Goose cartoons and sing-along songs. They see, hear and sing the words all at once (The Neurological Impress Method) and soon children are able to read these words by themselves.
10-451 30 min. $14.95

Return of Rin Tin Tin
Escaping from a cruel kennel owner, Rinty pairs up with a young orphan boy.
Pursued and finally caught by his real owner, Rinty is forced to escape again and find his way back to his young master against incredible odds. Stars Robert Blake and Gaylord Pendleton.
10-9116 70 min. $19.95

Return of the King
This epic tale of Good vs. Evil in a world of wizards, dragons and magic, is the awesome conclusion to J.R.R. Tolkien's classic trilogy of Hobbit stories.
10-8033 96 min. $24.95

Rudyard Kipling's Classic Stories
This Rudyard Kipling collection will activate a child's most precious gift--curiosity! Episodes include: "How the First Letter Was Written," "How the Whale Got His Throat" and "How the Elephant Got His Trunk."
10-434 25 min. $14.95

Samantha and the Troll
This "live action" musical feature video for children tells the story of shy Samantha the puppy, who must endure the daily teasing of her three

puppy brothers until she reveals her cleverness and courage by saving them from the terrible troll.
10-9806 39 min. $19.95

SCHOLASTIC'S ANIMAL FRIENDS

• Animal Babies in the Wild
For ages 2-8. Stories, songs and baby animal bloopers.
10-549 30 min. $14.95

• Baby Animals Just Want to Have Fun
For ages 2-8.
10-548 30 min. $14.95

Scrabble People: A Pumpkin Full of Nonsense
Take a journey with Sir Scrabble, Tad and Terry to the Land of Nonsense, ruled by the nasty Muddler, who forbids his Scrabble People subjects to learn how to read or spell. The townspeople celebrate as Sir Scrabble overthrows the Muddler.
10-326 30 min. $16.95

Seabert: The Adventure Begins
In exciting stories filled with as much adventure as love, Seabert the baby seal, Tommy and Aura defend their animal friends and protect their environment from evil hunters and money-grubbing poachers.
10-2179 90 min. $29.95

Seabert: The Adventure Continues
The furry, fuzzy and fun Seabert is back with friends Tommy and Aura for more cold, icy adventures in Greenland.
10-2180 90 min. $29.95

Shari Lewis Bedtime Stories
Shari Lewis and her friends Lamb Chop, Charles Horse and Hush Puppy present a collection of favorite fairy tales. Book included.
10-396 30 min. $19.95

Shirley Temple: The Little Princess
Set in Victorian London, Shirley attends an exclusive boarding school run by a harsh headmistress. When rumors arrive that her father has been killed and his fortune lost, she is banished to an old basement and ordered to be a maid to the other girls in the school. In one of her most endearing roles, Shirley Temple shines as America's Favorite child star in this heartwarming feature film that will charm the entire family.
10-9115 93 min. $19.95

Show Off! A Kid's Guide to Being Cool
Join Malcolm-Jamal Warner, top-rated star of the award-winning "Cosby Show," and his zany friends for an unbelievable hour of no-holds-barred

hilarity. Kids can impress their friends and family and be the "life of the party" with instruction in the art of mouthsounds, facemaking, moonwalking, stunt fighting and more.
10-541 60 min. $59.95

Sing-A-Long/Read-A-Long "Johnny & The Giant"
This classic, exquisitely animated European fairy tale is a wonderful way for children to build a basic English vocabulary. Fast-paced and action-packed, this "Sing-a-Long/Read-a-Long" program will hold any child's attention and effortlessly improve his or her reading skills.
10-457 55 min. $16.95

Sing-A-Long/Read-A-Long "The Magic Pony"
This dramatically animated Russian version of "The Little Humpbacked Horse" is a delightful way for children to build a basic English vocabulary. Surreal and magical, this "Sing-a-Long/Read-a-Long" program will hold any child's attention and effortlessly improve his or her reading skills.
10-458 55 min. $16.95

Sometimes I Wonder
A story about a girl and boy who leave home because their new baby brother is getting all the attention. They run away to Grandma's ranch where their favorite mare is beginning to foal. Rare film footage captures the live birth of a colt. Stars Colleen Dewhurst.
10-2729 48 min. $14.95

Soviet Bedtime Stories - Films for Children
Includes "A Monkey Leads the Band", "The Wolf and the Tailor", "The Miracle Frost", "Little Cucumber's Adventure", "How the Donkey Sought Happiness". Each film is a fable with a wide range of animation techniques, from standard cartoon to silhouettes to puppets and clay.
10-8056 60 min. $19.98

Stanley, "I Like Myself"
An animated musical staring a Stanley, duck who's convinced he's "definitely not a duck." Traveling with his pal Nathan the Fox, Stanley tries to be a dog, a turkey, even a member of the rough and tough Hell's Eagles! Ultimately, Nathan teaches Stanley an important lesson in self-esteem - to be glad to be what he is, and stop trying to be what he isn't. In a touching, tender duet, Nathan gets Stanley to say the magic words, "I like myself."
10-225 30 min. $19.95

Steadfast Tin Soldier
Hans Christian Andersen's story of the tin soldier who would bravely endure any hardship for the

---

love of a ballerina has captured the imaginations of children ever since it was written more than 100 years ago. Features Jeremy Iron's elegant narration and Mark Isham's original music score.
10-248 30 min. $14.95

Story Of The Fattest Cat In The World
The delightful story of The Fattest Cat In The World, whose only love in life is eating, until he finds something other than food to dream about. When he does, he must then venture out into the world to find his dream...and in the process, discover himself as well.
10-5721 30 min. $14.95

Storybook Classics: How the Rhinoceros Got His Skin and How the Camel Got His Hump
In another of Kipling's "Just So Stories," a Parse man, though his special magic, seeks revenge on a nasty, piggish rhino, and we discover how the rhinoceros got his skin. The next tale involves an independent camel who refuses to work. A desert spirit teaches him a lesson about laziness and gives the camel his well-deserved "humph". Jack Nicholson, Bobby McFerrin and Tim Raglin are the trio of talents that joyfully capture the unique Kipling style.
10-1804 30 min. $14.95

Storybook Classics: Pecos Bill
Narrated by Robin Williams.
10-2939 30 min. $14.95

Storybook Classics: The Emperor and the Nightingale
The Emperor and his court of ancient China are illustrated vividly in this Hans Christian Andersen story. The Emperor is given a gift of a mechanical singing bird, only later to learn that the genuine song of the real nightingale is truly the best of all. This lovely tale is elegantly presented by Glenn Close, with music by Mark Isham and Robert Van Nutt's vivid illustration.
10-1805 40 min. $14.95

Storybook Classics: The Tailor of Gloucester
This delightful old favorite is narrated by Meryl Streep.
10-2940 30 min. $14.95

Storybook Classics: The Tale of Jeremy Fisher and The Tale of Peter Rabbit
In all of English literature, no characters are more famous to the young - and the not so young - readers than the curious and disobedient bunny, Peter Rabbit, and the angler frog, Mr. Jeremy Fisher. Beatrix Potter's beloved tales come to life through Meryl Streep's narration, Lyle Mays'

memorable music, and David Jorgenson's wonderful illustrations.
10-1803 30 min. $14.95

Sunshine Porcupine
The producer of the Beatles' Yellow Submarine puts his talents and energies behind this dazzling, animated, musical extravaganza. This lesson about the positive aspects of solar energy is told in a delightful, thrilling manner.
10-491 45 min. $19.95

Tales of Beatrix Potter
Generations of parents have chosen Beatrix Potter tales to introduce children to the wonders of literature. Tales of Beatrix Potter combines Miss Potter's original illustrations with a captivating narrative by master storyteller Sidney Walker, and a delightful musical score to create the perfect initiation for youngsters to this fairy tale world.
10-246 46 min. $19.95

Tales From Mother Goose and the World of Make Believe
These traditional favorites will suddenly spring to life again. Sure to be played over and over again are favorites such as "Little Miss Muffet," "Jack Be Nimble," "Jack and Jill" and "Little Bo Peep."
10-488 60 min. $19.95

TELL ME A STORY SERIES
This series features some of America's leading storytellers and is designed not only to entertain, but also to stimulate the creative and imaginative powers of its young viewers.

• Beauty and the Beast
In this video, a husband and wife storytelling duo present four folklore classics with a delivery that is a zesty balance of their individual talents.
10-2926 30 min. $14.95

• Chuck Larkin
Chuck Larkin crosses all age, ethnic and cultural barriers effortlessly with his down-home delivery of preposterously funny tales and original one-liners. He has performed as a professional storyteller since 1970 and has frequently been featured at the National Storytelling Festival.
10-497 30 min. $14.95

• Lynn Rubright
Lynn Rubright is an educator and a storyteller as well as a coordinator of special projects such as the Metro Theater Circus, a children's theater company, and Project Tell a program designed to teach English skills through storytelling. Here she tells several stories including: "How Woodpeckers Came To Be"' a story bout greed and what happens

VIDEO TITLES LISTED IN THIS GUIDE ARE AVAILABLE FOR PURCHASE OR RENTAL. CONTACT YOUR LOCAL VIDEO STORE OR TELEPHONE (800) 383-8811

to people who are granted wishes they don't deserve.
10-230 30 min. $14.95

• Mary Carter Smith
Mary Carter Smith is an educator, librarian, actress, singer poet, author, storyteller, folklorist and humanitarian. Here she tells the story of "John Henry," a classic tale of man versus machine, as well as several stories of African folklore and teaches her audience a memorable lesson on prejudice.
10-229 30 min. $14.95

• Michael "Badhair" Williams
Volume 1
Michael "Badhair" Williams has performed everywhere from the rural areas of Appalachia to the Smithsonian Institution in Washington, D.C., telling his tall tales and stories of American folklore. Here he tells the story "Muts-Mag" about a little orphan girl who joins her two older sisters on a fortune-seeking journey. He also takes his listeners on a journey to the mountains and sings a favorite Appalachian ditty.
10-232 30 min. $14.95

• Michael "Badhair" Williams
Volume 2
Mike is a natural storyteller with a unique ability to mesmerize his audience, no matter what age. He has performed in a variety of locations, from one-room schoolhouses in rural Appalachia to the Smithsonian Institution in Washington, D.C.
10-501 30 min. $14.95

• Nancy Schimmel
Teacher, author, recording artist and professional storyteller Nancy Schimmel performs a collection of folk tales and songs in a variety of traditions: American and international, modern and traditional. She is a regular member of the California based Plumb City Players, a renowned multilingual song and story troupe.
10-499 30 min. $14.95

• Ruthmarie Arguello-Sheehan
Ruthmarie Arguello-Sheehan has been a storyteller for over 30 years. She is founder and director of The American Storytelling Resource Center, and has a cable TV show called Ruthmarie's Room. Here she tells the story "Tommy Knocker and the Magic Fan", the tale of a lazy boy who makes a trade with Tommy Knocker for a magic fan and some other international and ethnic stories.
10-231 30 min. $14.95

Teeny Tiny Tune Ups
Are you looking for an exciting way to bring fun, action and purpose into your child's playtime?

Teeny Time Tune Ups combines the research of physical development specialist Holly Redding with music from the Grammy-nominated Agapeland record series, and is hosted by Olympic gymnast trainees Tamera and Tiffany Gerlack.
10-9119 30 min. $19.95

Treasure Island
In this colorful, animated version of Stevenson's masterpiece, kids get a taste of the excitement that comes from reading the book "Treasure Island." Also included are "The Emperor's Oblong Pancake," "The Naughty Owlette," and "The Dragon Over the Hill."
10-034 51 min. $16.95

Ugly Duckling
Hans Christian Andersen's well-loved tale of the lonely ugly duckling who finally discovers he is a swan is made even more memorable with Cher's distinctive narration and Patrick Ball's delightful musical score.
10-249 30 min. $14.95

Velveteen Rabbit
Narrated by Meryl Streep, this is Margery Williams' enchanting story about a toy rabbit, first published in 1922, that will live forever in the annals of children's literature.
10-206 30 min. $14.95

VISUAL TALES
Visual Tales is a series offered in three unique formats: signed English, American Sign Language and open captioned for the hearing impaired. There are five stores in all - a fable, three folk tales and a poem. These engaging stories open the world of imagination for all children, hearing and deaf alike.

• Father, the Son and the Donkey, American Sign Language
10-2197 15 min. $29.95

• Father, the Son and the Donkey, Signed English
10-2196 15 min. $29.95

• Father, the Son and the Donkey, Open captioned
10-2198 15 min. $29.95

• Greedy Cat, American Sign Language
10-2188 15 min. $29.95

• Greedy Cat, Signed English
10-2187 15 min. $29.95

VIDEO TITLES LISTED IN THIS GUIDE ARE AVAILABLE FOR PURCHASE OR RENTAL. CONTACT YOUR LOCAL VIDEO STORE OR TELEPHONE (800) 383-8811

• **Greedy Cat, Open captioned**
10-2189 15 min. $29.95

• **House that Jack Built, Open Captioned.**
10-2192 15 min. $29.95

• **House that Jack Built, Signed English**
10-2190 15 min. $29.95

• **House that Jack Built, American Sign Language**
10-2191 15 min. $29.95

• **Magic Pot, American Sign Language**
10-2185 15 min. $29.95

• **Magic Pot, Open captioned**
10-2186 15 min. $29.95

• **Magic Pot, Signed English**
10-2184 15 min. $29.95

• **Village Stew, Signed English**
10-2193 15 min. $29.95

• **Village Stew, Open Captioned**
10-2195 15 min. $29.95

• **Village Stew, American Sign Language**
10-2194 15 min. $29.95

WE ALL HAVE TALES SERIES
Kids will love this illustrated series of classic tales as told by well known actors and featuring music by well known artists. The stories featured are from all around the world.

• **Jack & the Beanstalk**
Told by Michael Palin and featuring music by Dave Stewart.
10-8139 20 min. $16.95

• **Anansi**
Told by Denzil Washington and featuring music by UB40.
10-8140 20 min. $16.95

• **East of the Sun West of the Moon**
Told by Max Von Sydow and featuring music by Lyle Mays.
10-8141 20 min. $16.95

• **Tiger & the Brahmin**
Told by Ben Kingsley and featuring music by Ravi Shankar.
10-8142 20 min. $16.95

• **King Midas & the Golden Touch**
Told by Michael Caine and featuring music by Ellis Marsalis and Yo-Yo Ma.
10-8143 20 min. $16.95

• **Boy Who Drew Cats**
Told by William Hurt and featuring music by Mark Isham.
10-8144 20 min. $16.95

• **Koi and the Kola Nuts**
Told by Whoopi Goldberg and featuring music by Herbie Hancock.
10-8144 20 min. $16.95

• **Rumpelstiltskin**
Told by Kathleen Turner and featuring music by Tangerine Dream.
10-8146 20 min. $16.95

• **Puss in Boots**
Told by Tracy Ullman and featuring music by Jean Luc Ponty.
10-8147 20 min. $16.95

• **Finn McCoul**
Told by Catherine O'Hara and featuring music by Boys of the Lough.
10-8148 20 min. $16.95

• **Monkey People**
Told by Raul Julia and featuring music by Lee Ritenour.
10-8149 20 min. $16.95

• **Fool & the Flying Ship**
Told by Robin Williams and featuring music by The Klezmer Conservatory Band.
10-8150 20 min. $16.95

• **Peachboy**
Told by Sigourney Weaver and featuring music by Ryuichi Sakamoto.
10-8151 20 min. $16.95

Wee Sing: King Cole's Party
This is the charming tale of your favorite nursery rhyme characters: Jack, Jill, Little Boy Blue and Mary (with her lamb), as they learn that gifts from the heart are the most special. Includes booklet.
10-2129 60 min. $19.95

Wee Sing Together
A delightful combination of completely orchestrated songs, live-action and special effects features 21 traditional children's songs taken from the best-selling book. Great entertainment for children and adults.
10-226 60 min. $19.95

WONDERFUL WORLD OF AESOP'S FABLES SERIES

• **Lion and his Cub/The Boy and the Eagle**
10-8060 30 min. $16.95

• **Two Woodcutters/The Greedy Dog**
10-8061 30 min. $16.95

• **Farmer and his Son/The White Crow**
10-8062 30 min. $16.95

World's Greatest Dinosaur Video
Hosted by Gary Owens and Eric Boardman, this award winning program combines live action, animation and incredible special effects. The ultimate dinosaur experience.
10-8110 80 min. $59.98

Instruction: Basic Learning Skills

3 R's
Ages 8-12. Features: "Larry, Mr. Jenkins, and the Antique Car" (develops creative writing skills), "Multiplication" (Chicago International Film Festival award-teaches how to multiply), "Division," "The Big Red Barn," and "The Dead Bird" (award-winning segments narrated by Margaret Wise Brown-teaches creative writing and reading skills).
10-164 54 min. $24.95

All About Animals
Ages 4-9. Features mammals, fish, amphibians, reptiles birds (teaches reading and the ways of animals).
10-162 53 min. $16.95

Alphabet and Numbers
Combined here are two award-winning programs in one fun video for ages 2 1/2 to 5. Visuals and songs provide an entertaining way for children to learn numbers and letters.
10-3005 30 min. $16.95

Alphabet Zoo
Teaching the art of mastering the ABC's and their sounds.
10-5659 30 min. $19.95

Alphabet Zoo: Reading With You
A program on how your child can improve their reading skills.
10-9173 30 min. $16.95

Animal Alphabet
A unique series for children that is both educational and entertaining for the whole family. "The Animal Alphabet" travels the globe with live-action film footage from National Geographic and colorful animated alphabet letters. There are 26 segments, in for each letter of the alphabet introduced by the character, Geoffrey. Each letter has an original song written by acclaimed Broadway composer and lyricist Elizabeth Swados that expresses the rhythm and movement of the animal as well as the sound of each letter. An innovative approach to learning the ABC's.
10-151 45 min. $14.95

Baby Animals
This program looks at different animals when they are small. In this feature you will follow a baby mouse, a baby elephant and baby chicks.
10-9171 42 min. $16.95

Basic Grammar
Ages 3-8. In a series of animated features, kids are taught the importance of reading from left to right, singular and plural word forms, descriptive phrases, sentence structure and punctuation and how to write sentences.
10-026 50 min. $15.95

Beezbo's Adventures: How to Behave Like a Human Being
This live action video is designed to teach manners to children. The adventures begin when Gilbert and Gracie Turner discover a disabled spaceship and its short, furry alien pilot, Beezbo, who suddenly transforms himself into a rather odd but cute human being. Through a series of enjoyable adventures, the children give Beezbo lessons in table and telephone manners, greeting and introductions, as well as basic courtesy.
10-291 48 min. $19.95

Beginning Reading & Sign Language
A way for children and some adults to learn sign language. This is for those who are not deaf as well as those who are.
10-8004 30 min. $19.95

Bubbly Baby Swim Video
Let Jim Booth show you how to start your baby in the water. Essential for families with infants and toddlers.
10-8178 45 min. $24.95

Colors and Ducks
Features colors, right and wrong, alphabet roll call, ducks (a seven-minute segment and winner of Chris Award, Columbus Film Festival, American Film Festival Award-teaches reading), The Chocolate Princes, an animated three minute segment narrated by Bill Cosby, and "America the beautiful"-learning to sing America's songs. Ages 3-8.
10-158 47 min. $24.95

Dragons and Sailboats
For ages 5-10, this video features: "Wind" (CINE Golden Eagle award - teaches reading, "Subtraction," "The Dragon over the Hill" (an eight-minute animated story and winner of American Film Festival award), "Stories in string" (an art lesson) and "God Bless America" (learning to sing America's songs).
10-161 45 min. $24.95

Good Housekeeping: Colors and Shapes
10-414 30 min. $14.95

Good Housekeeping: Cooking-Things Kids Can Do, Recipes and Menus
10-415 30 min. $14.95

GOOD NEWS FOR KIDS SERIES
An excellent series for kids to learn how to overcome selfishness, whining, lying and breaking things. Fully animated! Comes with parent's guide for family activities to help re-enforce these lessons.

• **Selfish Sally**
10-8101 25 min. $16.95

• **Destructive David**
10-8102 25 min $16.95

• **Wendy and the Whine**
10-8103 30 min. $16.95

• **Jimmy and the White Lie**
10-8104 22 min. $16.95

Grammar As Easy As ABC
Ages 8-12. Features nouns, verbs, modifiers.
10-163 38 min. $24.95

Have Fun Learning to Read
This video combines visual cues, spoken language prompts and phrase reading in a unique method. Tests indicate that children will watch the video over and over. Children learn to read while being entertained.
10-172 15 min. $19.95

How to Give Your Baby Encyclopedic Knowledge
Glen Dolman shows you how to give your baby large amounts of knowledge quickly, easily and pleasurable. He tells why you want to begin an early program of teaching, and how to do it.
10-040 60 min. $39.95

How to Teach Your Baby to Read
Nurture your baby's full potential. Your newborn doesn't have to know how to talk in order to begin learning to read. Glen Dolman, nationally recognized child development specialist, shows you how to prepare materials, how to use them with your baby, and how to expand the lessons as your baby learns. You'll be amazed at the results.
10-041 80 min. $49.95

I Like Animals
Ages 3 and up. In this video, kids observe animals performing, learning concepts and ideas, showing survival instincts and exploring the close relationship between wildlife and their habitats.
10-033 56 min. $15.95

I Like Science
In this program a child achieves a basic understanding of the scientific principles underlaying heat, energy, lights and electricity. The negative and positive effects of the sun are also presented.
10-029 58 min. $15.95

It's Potty Time
A great program for potty training your child. This video helps teach all the correct steps for kids learning how to use the toilet and the correct way to wash up through fun music and songs.
10-8058 25 min. $19.95

Kids Can Cook
This lively "kid" oriented presentation demonstrates a hands-on approach to cooking for children by children. Two youngsters actually do the food preparation under the supervision of an adult cooking professional, Mala Mendelssohn. This program also includes illustrated recipe cards.
10-8184 50 min. $19.95

Learn To Read
In Learn To Read, Barbara Phipps teaches letter recognition, correct writing instruction, the short vowel sound for each letter and how to slide sounds together to read words. The video is divided into five fifteen-minute learning segments, interspersed with songs, finger games and the antics of the children and "snoothy", a lovable furry snoothyguzzlesmort.
10-7060 75 min. $29.95

VIDEO TITLES LISTED IN THIS GUIDE ARE AVAILABLE FOR PURCHASE OR RENTAL. CONTACT YOUR LOCAL VIDEO STORE OR TELEPHONE (800) 383-8811

Learning As We Play
Ages 4-9. Features: "Addition," "In, Out, Up, Down, Under, Over, Upside-Down" (teaches reading); "Smallest Elephant in the World" (an animated story); "Stories in Clay" (art and counting); "Safety As We Play" (teaches safety and reading) - winner of American Film Festival Award); and "Battle Hymn of the Republic" (learning to sing America's songs).
10-160 49 min. $24.95

Learning Can Be Fun
Alaina Reed of TV's Sesame Street incorporates colorful Video graphics, cartoons, original songs and clever lyrics to teach some important lessons for younger children. Eight segments include the importance of good hygiene, the alphabet, colors, courtesy and counting from 1 to 10.
10-301 30 min. $14.95

Learning Letters, Numbers and Colors
In this video, children learn the numbers from one to ten by singing the "Number Song." They learn the letters of the alphabet by singing the "Alphabet Song" and the colors of the rainbow by singing the "Rainbow Song."
10-455 30 min. $14.95

LET'S LEARN ABOUT SERIES

• Manners
10-5728 60 min. $14.95

• School
10-5727 60 min. $14.95

• Temper Tantrums
10-5729 60 min. $14.95

LOOK AND LEARN SERIES

• Alphabet Soup
Professor Wise Old Owl teaches the alphabet through rhymes, lively music and pictures.
10-8084 20 min. $14.95

• Hello Numbers
Agent 007734 makes numbers fun with his count-a-long games.
10-8085 20 min. $14.95

• Soup Stories
Professor Wise Old Owl reviews the ABC's and tells six different stories that begin with the letters A, H, L, P and T.
10-8086 20 min. $14.95

• It's a Plus
Agent 07734 teaches kids the equal sign dance and sing about the plus sign.
10-8087 20 min. $14.95

• Bear Dreams
Kool Kat plays word recognition games to start his Video Pal on the road to reading.
10-8088 20 min. $14.95

• Bear Friends
Kool Kat introduces his pal to the world of reading and reads two stories about being friends.
10-8089 20 min. $14.95

MacDonald's Farm
Ages 3-8. Features: "Z is for Zoo" (reading); "One Turkey, Two Turkey" (reading and counting); "Tara the Stonecutter" (an animated folk story and Venice, London, and CINE award winner); "MacDonald's Farm Animals Go to School" and "America" (learning to sing America's songs).
10-159 47 min. $24.95

Mars: Red Planet
A lively and educational program on space for kids! Learn about mars as you travel through space to your destination via animation.
10-8185 28 min. $19.95

Mars: Red Planet
Includes an in-class room learning guide.
10-8186 28 min. $69.95

MATH CLASS: GRAMMAR SCHOOL & JUNIOR HIGH
Math can be one of the toughest subjects for students. This series gives you just what you need to excel. Experienced teachers explain the concepts of percents, decimals, fractions, and pre-algebra, using color graphics to make learning easier. Once you've mastered these concepts, you have the foundation you need to excel in high school math.

• Decimals
10-6128 63 min. $29.95

• Fractions
10-6129 93 min. $29.95

• Percents
10-6127 91 min. $29.95

• Pre-Algebra
10-6130 63 min. $29.95

Mommy, I Can Learn Myself-Experiences
Oopsey and her brother, Billy, talk about such new experiences as new additions to the family, getting

VIDEO TITLES LISTED IN THIS GUIDE ARE AVAILABLE FOR PURCHASE OR RENTAL. CONTACT YOUR LOCAL VIDEO STORE OR TELEPHONE (800) 383-8811

a new pet, going to school and trying new foods.
10-496 30 min. $16.95

Mommy, I Can Learn Myself-Feelings

Oopsey and Billy discuss different kinds of feelings, what to do when feelings are hurt, learning about responsibility, controlling emotions, respecting others and talking about sharing and honesty.
10-495 30 min. $16.95

Mommy, I Can Learn Myself-Manners

Oopsey and her brother, Billy, talk to kids about telephone etiquette, the difference between "May I?" and "Can I?," saying "Please," "Thank You," and "You're Welcome." Also covered are proper table manners, helping others, other common courtesies and good social behavior.
10-533 30 min. $16.95

Musical Multiplication

In this video, children learn the multiplication tables from one to 12 the new fun way! They will watch cartoons and see, hear and sing the times tables (The Neurological Impress Method). Soon they will know all the times tables and be able to recite them by themselves.
10-453 30 min. $14.95

Pom Pom's Day at School

Join Pom-Pom, a Panda bear and a new student, Adam, as they enjoy their first day at preschool. Show features live action with traditional and original songs and rhymes.
10-9042 35 min. $39.95

Primary Math

Ages 3-8. Different objects are used in an animated fantasy to show how to add, subtract, multiply and divide. Also included are the Bob Baker Marionettes showing a variety of measurement experiences.
10-028 45 min. $15.95

Read and Sing With America

In this video, children learn 282 Dolch list words by singing American songs and Watching cartoons. They see, hear and sing the words all at once (The Neurological Impress Method) and soon are able to read these words by themselves.
10-454 30 min. $14.95

READING PLANET SERIES

• Escape from Lethargia

Children are taught to derive meaning from context. Fluency and Comprehension are developed by reading units of thought rather than just words.
10-9655 20 min. $59.95

• Hope of the Future

Teaches the skill of understanding implied relationships in reading between and beyond the words. Excerpts from Mark Twain's Tom Sawyer and Charles Dickens' A Christmas Carol teach students to draw meaning from text to reach conclusions. Good for grades 2-6.
10-9657 20 min. $59.95

• Time Scrambler

Teaches children to use a time line and to recognize time signal words. Excerpts from Lewis Carolls' Alice in Wonderland help to illustrate the skill of recognizing sequence of events by bringing time order to their comprehension.
10-9656 20 min. $59.95

• Turn on the TV in Your Head

Demonstrates the importance of concentration and mental pictures in reading. Teaches a process for visualization. Grades K-6
10-9654 28 min. $59.95

RICHARD SCARRY SERIES

• Best Ever ABC Video

Join Huckle Cat, Lowly Worm, and all their friends for Alphabet Day at the Busytown School.
10-8038 20 min. $16.95

• Best Counting Video

Learn to count as easy as 1-2-3.
10-8039 20 min. $16.95

SCHOLASTIC LEARNING LIBRARY

Scholastic, one of the most trusted names in learning, presents this six-volume animated series designed to teach preschoolers and primary grade children the basic skills necessary to recognize and better understand letters, numbers, colors, shapes and sounds. Each tape features Scholastic's familiar storybook character, Clifford, the Big Red Dog.

• Clifford's Fun With Letters
10-6579 30 min. $19.95

• Clifford's Fun With Numbers
10-6680 30 min. $19.95

• Clifford's Fun With Opposites
10-6581 30 min. $19.95

• Clifford's Fun With Rhymes
10-6582 30 min. $19.95

• Clifford's Fun With Shapes
10-6583 30 min. $19.95

VIDEO TITLES LISTED IN THIS GUIDE ARE AVAILABLE FOR PURCHASE OR RENTAL. CONTACT YOUR LOCAL VIDEO STORE OR TELEPHONE (800) 383-8811

• **Clifford's Fun With Sounds**
10-6584 30 min. $19.95

SCHOOLHOUSE ROCK SERIES
This series uses animation and songs to help children learn and understand about math, reading, science, history and grammar.

• **Multiplication**
10-9366 32 min. $16.95

• **Science**
10-9440 32 min. $16.95

• **History**
10-9441 32 min. $16.95

• **Grammar**
10-9442 32 min. $16.95

• **Multiplication Rock**
10-8041 32 min. $16.95

• **Grammar Rock**
10-8042 32 min. $16.95

SCHOOLZONE EDUCATIONAL SERIES
This series helps educate children in all readiness areas: Language skills, number skills, perceptual skills, and general learning skills. Each program correlates with two "Get Ready!" workbooks, and includes a free "Start to Read!' book. The programs are new and use a variety of animation techniques, live action, puppets and original music. Program consists of seven or more educational segments per video.

• **Alphabet Uppercase**
Covers the uppercase letters of the alphabet and beginning sounds. Includes: "Beep, Beep", "Start to Read!" book and Parent Guide.
10-256 20 min. $14.95

• **Animal Antics**
Covers animals and what's missing. Includes: "I Want a Pet", "Start to Read!" book and Parent Guide.
10-260 20 min. $14.95

• **Crazy About Colors**
Covers colors and hidden pictures. Includes: "Sue Likes Blue", "Start to Read!: book and Parent Guide.
10-259 20 min. $14.95

• **Alphabet Lowercase**
Covers lowercase letters and experiencing feelings. Includes: "Get Lost, Becka!", "Start to Read!"

book and Parent Guide.
10-257 20 min. $14.95

• **Numbers 1-10**
Covers counting skills to ten. Includes: "Nine Men Chase a Hen" ("Start to Read!" book) and Parent Guide.
10-255 20 min. $14.95

• **Shipshape Shapes**
Covers shapes and following directions. Includes: "Elephant and Envelope" (Start to Read!" book) and Parent Guide.
10-258 20 min. $14.95

Starting to Read
This video presents five different segments dealing with an introduction to the alphabet, primary vocabulary words, letters and words, "high interest" words, and a visual-participatory learning experience for your child. Ages 3-8.
10-027 54 min. $15.95

STARTING TO READ SERIES
In these videos, Big Bird narrates three stories, on each tape, for beginning readers, accompanied by original music. The text of the stories appears on the bottom in large, easy-to-read print. A fun way to develop early reading skills.

• **Volume I**
10-3052 30 min. $14.95

• **Volume II**
10-3053 30 min. $14.95

SHALOM SESAME STREET SERIES
A fun and exciting introduction to the land, people, culture, traditions and language of Israel.

• **Land of Israel**
Take a fun-filled journey through Israel and meet some new Israeli friends.
10-8152 30 min. $24.95

• **Tel Aviv**
Join Itzhak Perlman for a tour of his hometown.
10-8153 30 min. $24.95

• **Kibbutz**
Discover life on an Israeli kibbutz filled with orchards, animals and kids.
10-8014 30 min. $24.95

• **People of Israel**
See how being different is something that everyone has in common.
10-8155 30 min. $24.95

• **Jerusalem**
It's an ancient capitol for Jews, Christians, Moslems and Armenians. A modern, bustling city with skyscrapers and street signs in three languages.
10-8156 30 min. $24.95

Teach Your Baby To Read
Dr. Glenn Dolman, an internationally respected pioneer in the field of child brain development, demonstrates methods and tools that can help gear your child toward faster development of reading skills.
10-5695 101 min. $39.95

TELL ME WHY

• **Americana**
10-1695 30 min. $19.95

• **Flowers, Plants and Trees**
10-1692 30 min. $19.95

• **Gems, Metals and Minerals**
10-1693 30 min. $19.95

• **Insects**
10-1694 30 min. $19.95

• **Space, Earth and Atmosphere**
10-1690 30 min. $19.95

• **Water and Weather**
10-1691 30 min. $19.95

• **Lifeforms, Animals & Oddities**
10-8112 30 min. $19.95

• **Birds & Rodents**
10-8113 30 min. $19.95

• **Mammals**
10-8114 30 min. $19.95

• **Animals & Arachnids**
10-8115 30 min. $19.95

• **Fish, Shellfish and Other Underwater Life**
10-8116 30 min. $19.95

• **Prehistoric Animals, Reptiles**
10-8117 30 min. $19.95

• **Healthy Body**
10-8118 30 min. $19.95

• **Anatomy and Genetics**
10-8119 30 min. $19.95

• **Medicine**
10-8120 30 min. $19.95

• **Sports & Games**
10-8121 30 min. $19.95

• **Science, Sound & Energy**
10-8122 30 min. $19.95

• **Beginnings**
10-8123 30 min. $19.95

• **Flight**
10-8124 30 min. $19.95

• **How Things Work**
10-8125 30 min. $19.95

• **Customs & Superstitions**
10-8126 30 min. $19.95

• **Electricity & Electrical Safety**
10-8127 30 min. $19.95

• **Time, Money & Measurement**
10-8128 30 min. $19.95

Think Big
Upbeat rock songs mix with baseball footage to teach children that winning at anything requires confidence, determination and teamwork.
10-1963 30 min. $19.95

VIDEO FLASH CARDS
This self-teaching series, designed by a certified educator, is a modern alternative to the cardboard flash cards methods of the past. This program can be used with or without parental supervision by one or more children. Two kids together can make a game!

• **Addition**
10-402 30 min. $14.95

• **Division**
10-405 30 min. $14.95

• **Multiplication**
10-404 30 min. $14.95

• **Subtraction**
10-403 30 min. $14.95

- **Spell Well: Part 1**
10-5152 30 min. $14.95

- **Spell Well: Part 2**
10-5153 30 min. $14.95

- **Spell Well: Part 3**
10-5154 30 min. $14.95

- **Spell Well: Part 4**
10-5155 30 min. $14.95

Writing The Alphabet
Children are taught to write the capital letters of the alphabet from A to Z, and then they get to pick out the letter they are learning in different words. Soon they will be writing the alphabet all by themselves.
10-452 30 min. $14.95

Instruction: Music & Crafts

Art of Creating Crafts: A Guide to Crafts Projects
The viewer is treated to an assortment of crafts that can be done at home. Kids will enjoy doing these many fun projects.
10-002 51 min. $29.95

Draw and Color a Cartoon-y Party
Uncle Fred Laswell, Artist-writer of the cartoon classic, uses Barney Google and Snuffy Smith to teach children how to create pictures from simple crayon squiggles.
10-309 61 min. $14.95

Draw and Color With Uncle Fred
If you can spell "cat" you can draw one! Plus, many more exciting cartoons, including five wild animals that will pose just for you
10-024 60 min. $19.95

DRAW SQUAD VIDEOS
An interactive three part series teaching kids to draw in 3-D and stimulate their imagination. Features Mark Kistler of National Public Television's "The Secret City" as he draws his way through three adventures and into the hearts of kids everywhere: Escape of the Twinkies, Pigusis Goes on a Diet and Moonbot's Birthday Party.

- **Adventure 1: Escape Of The Twinkies**
10-6189 40 min. $29.95

- **Adventure 2: Pigusis Goes On A Diet**
10-6190 40 min. $29.95

- **Adventure 3: Moonbot's Birthday Party**
10-6191 40 min. $29.95

ECO, You, And Simon, Too!
This video features Eco, an adorable sea otter puppet, and Simon, his inquisitive human friend. With a colorful computer graphic world as their playground, these two lovable characters set out on a wonderful adventure to the park. They teach children about friendship, nutrition, the environment, and skills such as counting and reciting the alphabet.
10-5701 40 min. $19.95

Good Housekeeping: Crafts and Activities For Kids
10-416 30 min. $14.95

Great Ape Activity Tape
Beat the rainy day blues for kids with great activities demonstrated by the Green Gorillas. Children learn a variety of crafts, tricks and games like Cootie Catchers, Newspaper Jungles, Paper Bag Puppets and lots more. You only need an assortment of everyday household items. Each category is color-coded so kids can find any activity easily. Zany entertainment, clear instructions and lots of fun.
10-156 30 min. $14.95

Greg & Steve Live: In Concert
Fantastic music for kids! Featuring: Simon Says, ABC Rock, and more. For ages 3-9.
10-8003 50 min. $29.95

Happy Birdy - Hey It's Your Birthday!
A music video birthday greeting. A sing-a-long that kids and friends will remember for years to come.
10-8090 60 min. $19.95

Infantastic Lullabies
This program presents basic shapes, primary colors, enchanting animals and easily recognizable objects in charming and imaginative animation set to familiar nursery songs, beautifully orchestrated.
10-8083 60 min. $19.95

I Like Music
Introduces children to an appreciation of music, various instruments and the traditions of different cultures though colorful, animated and live-action sequences set to classic and traditional tunes.
10-466 54 min. $15.95

VIDEO TITLES LISTED IN THIS GUIDE ARE AVAILABLE FOR PURCHASE OR RENTAL. CONTACT YOUR LOCAL VIDEO STORE OR TELEPHONE (800) 383-8811

Jessi Sings Just For Kids
International recording star Jessi Colter performs an
exciting hour of more than 25 international
favorites and original children's songs.
10-9436 60 min. $19.95

Joe Scruggs: Joe's First Video
This is a special blend of animation and live action
and irresistible enchanting songs. This is a musical
children's masterpiece in a class by itself.
10-8057 31 min. $16.95

KIDS' N' CRAFTS SERIES

• **Fun With Clay**
10-2807 30 min. $14.95

• **Make a Puppet**
10-2808 30 min. $14.95

• **New Ideas-Crayons and Paints**
10-2809 30 min. $14.95

• **Make a Point**
10-2810 30 min. $14.95

• **Easy Bread Dough Sculpture**
10-2811 30 min. $14.95

• **Paper Play**
10-2812 30 min. $14.95

• **Paint Without a Brush**
10-2813 30 min. $14.95

• **Egg Art**
10-2814 30 min. $14.95

• **Dip and Tie Dye**
10-2815 30 min. $14.95

Let's Sing & Dance
Finally, a music video designed especially for
children. Hit songs include: Don't Talk to
Strangers, Don't Do Drugs, and I Can Do It
Myself. This provides an entertaining outlet for
active children.
10-8138 30 min. $16.95

Making Playthings
For all ages. This informative and fun video shows
how to make playthings from boxes, containers and
common household items.
10-039 50 min. $15.95

Original Tales & Tunes
Presenting a sparkling new-collection of whimsical
stories and smile-making music especially for

young children! Recommended for ages 2-8.
10-8008 30 min. $16.95

**Pappy Lane: Learn To Draw With
Pappy Drew It**
From the moment you turn this tape on, you'll find
that Pappy Lane is one of the most unique
programs your children will ever experience. Never
has learning to draw been so creative and so much
fun. So get your kids and crayons ready, Pappy
Lane is about to begin. Ages 3-8.
10-6179 30 min. $14.95

Rainy Day Finger Play & Fun Songs
A classic "bouncing ball" sing-along videotape for
all kids to have fun and learn by. As they sing,
kids learn to read by following the old-time ball
over the song-words at the bottom of the screen.
The songs also get kids to participate with finger,
hand and body movements, like in "Eency Weency
Spider Climbed Up the Water Spout." Bring music
to life through bright graphics and fun sing-alongs.
10-076 30 min. $14.95

SEE AND SING SERIES

• **All-Time Favorites**
10-215 30 min. $14.95

• **Christmas Favorites**
10-214 30 min. $14.95

• **Songs of America**
10-215 30 min. $14.95

**Shari Lewis Presents 101 Things For
Kids To Do**
This film features magic tricks, riddles, quickie
puppets, novel games, silly stunts and instant crafts
that kids can do-along as they view-along with
Shari Lewis and her friends Lamb Chop, Charlie
Horse and Hush Puppy. Kids can share the fun as
they watch, because all of the activities are easy to
do and use everyday things found in the home.
10-554 60 min. $19.95

Silly Songs
All the fun family songs we remember from when
we were kids: "Mairzy Doats," "Johnny Jacob
Jinglemeyer Smith," "Pop Goes the Weasel" and
many more. Kids learn to read while following the
bouncing ball at the bottom of the screen.
10-077 30 min. $14.95

Sing-A-Long Fun For The Entire Family
The Sing-A-Long fun for the Entire Family video is
great entertainment and it's the perfect way to keep
children occupied while they learn, have fun and

participate. Great for parties!
10-5723 30 min. $14.95

Sing Along With Bob Schneider
An award-winning recording, television and concert artist, Bob is one of the most dynamic family entertainers around today. His live performances include a chorus line of children called "The Rainbow Kids". These singers and dancers, selected from schools in each city, go from classroom to stage to become stars of his show.
10-5726 30 min. $19.95

Sing And Play Songs That Tickle Your Funny Bone!
From the popular collection of Ruth Roberts' "Songs That Tickle Your Funny Bone", here is a rib-tickling children's sing-along to put a smile on your face and a happy tap in your toes. You'll meet Mr. Funny Bone, and the neighborhood kids as they fill the Funny Bone Clubhouse with fun and laughter, and learn the Funny Bone Handshake. Children will love the zany songs and activities, and the whole family can join right in.
10-5722 30 min. $14.95

Squiggles, Dots & Lines
In Squiggles, Dots & Lines, fourteen kids share their fun telling stories, making cards and books, creating a giant mural, getting ready for a party and singing original songs. You'll meet Ed Emberley, who uses computer graphics to teach you his drawing alphabet.
10-5047 25 min. $19.95

Toddler Treasury
From the creator of Nickelodeon and Pinwheel, a video album especially developed for children under the age of three. All these charming songs and stories were assembled under the supervision of Dr. Vivian M. Horner.
10-8109 20 min. $16.95

Toddler Tunes and Tales
This tape is the ideal gift for kids from two to six. This happy tape features musical numbers designed to teach even the youngest children how to hear the beat and rhythm in music and how to move to music. Using real children and teachers, viewers are encouraged to participate with the tape, using their minds and bodies in an educational and entertaining way. Like a favorite book, young viewers ask to see it repeatedly.
10-254 45 min. $29.95

Toys at Your Fingertips: Make Your Own Toys
Ages 6-12. Features: Boxes (award in Venice Film Festival), Cylinders, Play Clay, Sugar and Spice, Floats. Teaches how to make playthings out of everyday household materials.
10-165 53 min. $24.95

VITSIE VIDEO SITTER
Each video is a fun -filled, half-hour exploration into the world of Dinosaurs, Ocean life, and Space. This award-winning production invites children to play along, sing songs and learn crafts.

• **Vitsie Video Sitter: Dinosaurs**
10-6486 30 min. $16.95

• **Vitsie Video Sitter: Oceanlife**
10-6487 30 min. $16.95

• **Vitsie Video Sitter: Space**
10-6469 30 min. $16.95

Instruction: Physical Development

ABC Funfit: The Mary Lou Retton Workout For Kids
Olympic gold medalist Mary Lou Retton conducts an easy-to-follow exercise program for children designed to help them feel healthy, fit and good about themselves.
10-5671 33 min. $29.95

Adventurcize
Adventurcize is a great way for a child to exercise both body and imagination while having fun! Follow along with the imaginary adventure-- jumping through puddles, crawling through caves, and climbing mountain tops. Now your child or grandchild can be actively involved in front of the television.
10-9660 30 min. $14.95

Baby Body Works
A follow-along program of exercise, massage and family play for babies, ages four weeks to 12 months.
10-005 30 min. $34.95

Baby's First Workout
This video offers a systematic program for motor skills development in a child's first year, featuring different activities for each of four age groups: 0-3 months, 3-6 months, 6-9 months, and 9-12 months. Parents are shown the fun way to monitor their child's physical development through creative play.

VIDEO TITLES LISTED IN THIS GUIDE ARE AVAILABLE FOR PURCHASE OR RENTAL. CONTACT YOUR LOCAL VIDEO STORE OR TELEPHONE (800) 383-8811

Includes special chart to record progress.
10-6269 60 min. $29.95

Gymboree
Patterned after the Gymboree Developmental Play Centers for children of all ages and their parents. The program is designed to enhance learning, socialization, physical fitness and positive patenting in a non-competitive, supportive and most of all, a fun-filled environment which can be created in the home. Great for parent/child interaction.
10-244 50 min. $19.95

It's Not Always Easy Being A Kid
When young Charlie has to re-do his math lesson after school, he misses the show at The Judy Theatre. Arriving late, he meets two puppet friends, Mrs. Judy and the lovely Violet. They strike a deal: math whiz Violet will tutor Charlie, if he helps them put on a show... Aesop's famous fable, The Tortoise and the Hare with a "No Smoking" message. All is going according to plan, until smelly Mr. Skunky offers cigarettes to both runners. Soon the finish line in sight...for anyone who doesn't need to smoke and believes in himself.
10-9652 15 min. $19.95

Kid's Exercise Workout Tape
This is an exercise program designed for children aged 3 to 8 years old.
10-2818 30 min. $14.95

Kid Safe, The Video
They'll have fun watching Kathy, played by Andrea Martin of SCTV fame, while she encounters a houseful of scary sights, sounds, and smells. And they'll laugh along while she learns from Ernie the Policeman, Marty the Fireman, and Tina the Paramedic how to deal with emergency and non-emergency situations. But while your kids are having fun, they'll be learning some very important things like: calling 911, emergency first aid for kids, stop, drop, and roll, and more. An excellent safety program for home or classroom.
10-5377 30 min. $19.95

Kids For Safety
Award winning video educates school children about bicycle, fire, and personal safety, Highly entertaining and informational. Contains music, animation, flash quizzes, safety procedures, and activities.
10-6226 25 min. $19.95

Mr. Know-It-Owl's Health Tips
Ages 5-12. Features: Junk Food Man; Nutrition: Try it, You'll Like It; Magic Weapons for Healthy Teeth; and Ear Care. Teaches good eating habits and health care.
10-166 48 min. $24.95

Playtime with the Motion Potion Kids
Active parents want their kids to be physically fit too! Playtime is a unique play-along program currently featured at hundreds of nursery school, YMCA's, YWCA's and Head Start Programs. As seen on TV's Romper Room. Ages 2-7
10-2260 30 min. $19.95

PRESCHOOL POWER SERIES

• Preschool Power - Jacket Flips & Other Tips
This program is designed to help young children learn the basic skills of buttoning, buckling, zipping, washing their hands, putting on their jackets and pouring their drinks without spilling.
10-8013 30 min. $16.95

• More Preschool Power
This program covers children tying their shoes, brushing their teeth and making a fruit salad.
10-8014 30 min. $16.95

• Preschool Power 3
This program covers how to fold paper, put on gloves, sweep up spills and make french bread.
10-8015 30 min. $16.95

Rebound Aerobics for Kids
This designed to improve balance, coordination, rhythm, timing, dexterity, and kinetic awareness while building muscle bulk, speed and strength.
10-8100 45 min. $19.95

Suzy Prudden: Tip Top Volume 1
Exercise for kids 3-6. Suzy shows kids that everyday play can evolve into entertaining exercise that will help their growing bodies achieve maximum flexibility and strength.
10-187 53 min. $19.95

Suzy Prudden: Tip Top Volume 2
Exercise for kids 7-10.
10-188 48 min. $19.95

Swim Baby Swim!
Esther Williams created the ideal video for every parent-swimming lessons for kids of all ages! Swimming and water safety can be learned at a very early age-even at six months. Esther's program is easy to follow and fun for both you and your child. It works for kids of any age, teaching them not only how to swim, but how to feel comfortable and safe in the water.
10-080 60 min. $19.95

Swim Lessons For Kids
This highly acclaimed video and accompanying 30 page booklet is designed to inform parents how to teach their children to swim and to protect their

own life in an emergency situation. Parents will learn to teach their children to: float, swim the crawl stroke, breathe while swimming, do the back float, swim the back stroke, and master survival skills. For ages 3-12.

10-6523 40 min. $29.95

Water Fun!

In the process of teaching more than 30,000 children and their parents about the water, Maryalice Miner has developed a magical method of teaching swimming to the very young. She shares her secrets of this no-tears approach with you and brings her happy aquatic classroom to your pool in these step-by-step directions. She will show you how to introduce your baby to the water, how to teach skills to the toddlers, and how to turn the three-year-olds into swimmers. A workbook is included.

10-539 60 min. $39.95

Safety

All About Kids' Safety

How safe is your child when he rides his bicycle...or just walks down the street? If there were a fire in your home tomorrow, what world your child do? Put your mind at ease by teaching your child basic safety rules with this video.

10-558 40 min. $24.95

Baby-Safe Home with David Horowitz

Is your baby living in a danger zone? Each year, more infants and young children are injured, maimed or killed in accidents around the house than by all childhood diseases combined. Most of these accidents are predictable and preventable. This "Baby Safe Home" video contains potentially life-saving information you will want to review over and over. Award-winning consumer expert David Horowitz and his wife, Suzanne, take you on a guided tour through a typical home pointing out hazardous areas and offering suggestions and advice to keep your child safe.

26-009 45 min. $19.95

Gary Coleman For Safety's Sake: Home Safe Home

From accident prevention to common sense rules for being home alone, from first-aid to kitchen safety, this video provides entertaining and easily understood, step-by-step instructions. With its own "Be Prepared Guide" and techniques developed by the National Safety Council and the Red Cross, Home Safe Home supplies the foundation for any

home safety program.

10-435 40 min. $19.95

How to Raise a Street-Smart Child

Daniel J. Travanti gives parents practical advice on how to educate their children about the potential hazards of contemporary society.

10-1858 43 min. $19.95

It's O.K. to Say No!

The videotape which follows up the original book that sold over 1/4 million copies. The very best to help parents, guardians and teachers show kids how to avoid those situations we fear most. Teaches kids how to handle themselves in direct confrontation, learn to say "No" and mean it, and how to tell their parents, guardians or teachers when they know or feel that something is wrong.

10-069 30 min. $14.95

It's O.K. to Say No! to Drugs and Alcohol

With younger and younger children being pressured to use drugs and alcohol, specific resistance techniques must be taught to prevent future involvement. The simple, but powerful techniques are introduced and reinforced in this video.

10-242 30 min. $14.95

Mommy, I Can Learn Myself-Safety

Kids can learn about safety rules from friend Oopsey and Billy, including crossing the street, riding a bicycle, safety in the car, playing with animals, water safety, and safety, and safety at the playground.

10-494 30 min. $16.95

Mr. Baby Proofer

This is the first complete guide designed to create a baby-safe environment. Let Mr. Baby Proofer take you on a room-by-room inspection of a home, pointing out dangers and presenting practical solutions.

10-8002 45 min. $16.95

My Body is My Own

It is a child's right to decide who touches him or her and to have an understanding that parents and guardians will protect them from touches they don't want. These lessons are taught in an enjoyable and non-frightening way.

10-240 30 min. $14.95

Safe Schools: A Guide For Action

This fast moving video and accompanying book, shows you how parents, teachers, school administrators, students, business, law enforcement and communities can work together to give our

children truly Safe Schools. Hosted by Pat Morita.
10-9677 26 min. $49.95

Sometimes It's O.K. to Tell Secrets
Every child accepts the importance of "keeping a secret." This video helps children understand the difference between a good and bad secret, and also stresses, gently but firmly, that bad secrets need to be told.
10-241 30 min. $14.95

Strong Kids, Safe Kids
Henry Winkler and co-hosts are joined by Scooby-Doo, Yogi Bear and the Flintstones in this family guide to protecting kids against sexual abuse and other dangerous situations.
10-079 60 min. $24.95

Touch: What Your Child Needs to Know
An essential child rearing film on personal body safety. Created and performed by the Illusion Theater, Hosted by Lindsay Wagner. Positive in outlook, it focuses on the prevention of sexual abuse.
10-2728 45 min. $14.95

Miscellaneous

Big Bird in China
Join Big Bird and Barkley the Dog as they visit with Chinese schoolchildren, watch a Tai Chi demonstration, learn some Chinese words and songs, while learning about China's unique culture.
10-3055 75 min. $19.95

BLUE FRONTIER SERIES
Directed by award-winning director Fenton McHugh and hosted by celebrated actor Leslie Nielsen. This series explores the oceans of the world and some of the exotic creatures who inhabit it. Produced in association with Sea World U.S.A.. It brings home all of the majesty of the sea and shows man's effect on the oceans of the earth.

• Gigi's Legacy
The heartwarming story of a baby California grey whale who spent the first year of her life in captivity.
10-8070 30 min. $19.95

• Underseas Eden
The fragile marine life and the destruction of the coral reef of the waters of the Sulu Sea.
10-8071 30 min. $19.95

• To Save a Whale
This is about the methods used to rescue the "gentle giant" from total extinction.
10-8072 30 min. $19.95

• Sea of Many Moods
The sea of Cortez, will the miracles of civilization destroy this unique environment.
10-8073 30 min. $19.95

• King of the Sea
The killer whale is explored is this program.
10-8074 30 min. $19.95

• Natures Playground
The sea as a recreational area and an interview with Dennis Conner.
10-8075 30 min. $19.95

• Aquaspace Adventure
A look at undersea exploration.
10-8076 30 min. $19.95

• Shark, Shark, Shark
A close look at one of the most feared and least understood of all animal species.
10-8077 30 min. $19.95

• Clown or Criminal
A look at the sea otter.
10-8077 30 min. $19.95

• Antarctic Adventure
A venture into the Antarctic to obtain penguin eggs.
10-8079 30 min. $19.95

• Vanishing Mermaids
An account of the attempt to save the manatee(sea cow).
10-8080 30 min. $19.95

• Rescuers
A group of people who save beached animals.
10-8081 30 min. $19.95

• Tails from the Nursery
10-8082 30 min. $19.95

Bundle of Love: A Sibling Preparation Experience
This show is designed for the very young who are about to experience a new baby in the family. Featuring the Bonnie Blue Puppets. Includes guide.
10-8164 27 min. $19.95

Christmas Eve on Sesame Street
With the help of his Muppet and human Sesame

VIDEO TITLES LISTED IN THIS GUIDE ARE AVAILABLE FOR PURCHASE OR RENTAL. CONTACT YOUR LOCAL VIDEO STORE OR TELEPHONE (800) 383-8811

Street friends, Big Bird attempts to solve the Santa Claus riddle, and in the process discovers that the true miracle of Christmas is in the spirit of loving and sharing.
10-3057 60 min. $19.95

Dinosaurs
Everyone has an idea for a science project except for Phillip. Phillip decides to discover the truth about Dinosaurs. What follows will captivate the viewer just as it does Phillip's classmates. The Kingdom of the Dinosaurs comes to life through animation, live action, and special claymation.
10-9173 30 min. $19.95

Don't Eat the Pictures: Sesame Street at the Metropolitan Museum of Art
Follow the adventures of Big Bird, Snuffy, Cookie Monster and the rest of the gang as they find themselves accidentally locked in the Metropolitan Museum overnight.
10-3056 60 min. $19.95

Hey, What About Me?
Find out what to expect with a baby at home by watching three kids and their baby brothers and sisters in scenes you'll want to see again and again. Enjoy songs about your feelings written just for this tape. Learn games, lullabies, and bouncing rhymes to do with your brother or sister. Discover what you can do when you're angry or lonely.
10-5046 25 min. $19.95

Hysterical History
These funny, fascinating and informative rare documentaries show your child great cultural and historical moments in the first half of the 20th century.
10-459 50 min. $15.95

KIDS EXPLORE SERIES
Follow a group of kids as they travel to different countries and explore the life and culture of its people.

- **Kids Explore Mexico**
10-9079 30 min. $19.95

- **Kids Explore Alaska**
10-9080 30 min. $19.95

- **Kids Explore Kenya**
10-9081 30 min. $19.95

- **Kids Explore American National Parks**
10-9082 30 min. $19.95

Kids Get Cooking
A celebration of food and cooking. Endorsed by the National Education Association. 39 segments on the egg, including eggs in ethnic holidays and safety tips.
10-5061 30 min. $19.95

KIDSONGS SERIES
Live action videos that allow children to interact with music and dancing.

- **Circus**
10-1908 25 min. $14.95

- **Show Business**
10-1909 25 min. $14.95

- **Sports Fun**
10-1906 25 min. $14.95

- **When I Grow Up**
10-1907 25 min. $14.95

- **Cars, Boats, Trains and Planes**
10-222 25 min. $14.95

- **Day at Old MacDonald's Farm**
10-220 25 min. $14.95

- **Day with the Animals**
10-560 25 min. $14.95

- **Good Night, Sleep Tight**
10-221 25 min. $14.95

- **I'd Like to Teach the World to Sing**
10-223 25 min. $14.95

- **Sing Out America**
10-559 25 min. $14.95

Let's Get a Move On!
Millions of families move each year. This helps kids and parents survive the impact of changing places, saying goodbye and adjusting to new things. Enjoy all original songs from 60's rock to rap.
10-9168 25 min. $14.95

Let's Sing and Dance
This unique video addresses some of the problems and choices facing today's kids. Featured songs include: "Don't Do Drugs," "Don't Talk to Strangers," "Best Friends," and "Sing and Dance at the Fun Club."
10-1862 30 min. $14.95

Pee Wee's Playhouse Christmas Special
You're invited to the neatest Christmas part ever at

VIDEO TITLES LISTED IN THIS GUIDE ARE AVAILABLE FOR PURCHASE OR RENTAL. CONTACT YOUR LOCAL VIDEO STORE OR TELEPHONE (800) 383-8811

(where else?) Pee Wee's Playhouse! Featuring: Frankie Avalon, Charo, Magic Johnson, Grace Jones, Oprah, Santa Claus, and many more.
10-8047 49 min. $19.95

PRESCHOOL EXPRESS SERIES
The Preschool Express is an interactive educational experience combining a workbook and video. Designed by educators and child development specialists, the Preschool Express prepares the child for school and positive life experiences by developing confidence and ability. Each kit contains: a full-color videocassette, a workbook and 30 learning activities, large color illustrations for creative coloring, and colorful stickers for play value.

• **Life Skills**
10-172 30 min. $14.95

• **Making Friends**
10-169 30 min. $14.95

• **Motor Skills**
10-173 30 min. $14.95

• **My Own Feelings**
10-168 30 min. $14.95

• **Opposites**
10-170 30 min. $14.95

Rainy Day Sunday
Grab some paper bags, bowls, and crayons to create dragon puppets, paper dolls, bee costumes, and more! There's no limit to the fun-filled toys and decorations they can make.
10-8108 22 min. $16.95

SESAME STREET HOME VIDEO SERIES
The best segments of 17 years of the all time favorite children's TV shows, plus lots of brand new material, all combined in unique and exciting ways that will entertain, teach and delight youngsters. Each tape features a single learning goal or activity as presented by children's favorite Sesame Street characters. Plus each tape kit includes an activity book that educates and entertains after the TV is off, and is ideal for parent/child interaction. A great series! Closed captioned for the hearing impaired.

• **Bedtime Stories and Songs**
Getting ready for bed is a happy experience for children when their Sesame Street friends are there to help them along. Big Bird, Kermit the Frog, Cookie Monster and others tell wonderful stories and sing lullabies that children will ask for night after night. This unique program provides a "wind-down" for children getting ready for a nap, quiet time or bedtime. It touches on night-time fears and talks about imagination. Perfect for sharing those special quiet times while helping children get in the mood for bed. Closed captioned for the hearing impaired.
10-184 30 min. $14.95

• **Getting Ready to Read**
Getting ready to read is fun to do with this delightful program. Big Bird answers amusing questions about reading on his reading hotline while Cookie Monster, Ernie, Bert and other friends from Sesame Street present stories, songs and rhymes designed to show children how words look and sound alike and how letters can be blended together to form words. Young readers learn word blending, rhyming, phonics and seeing a word as a chunk of meaning. Closed captioned for the hearing impaired.
10-181 30 min. $14.95

• **I'm Glad I'm Me**
Children need to know that everything about them is special and unique-their bodies and how they look, what they think and what they feel. Presented in the form of a fairy tale, children learn to identify parts of their own bodies, learn their functions, and develop a sense of pride and self-esteem. They learn they are special! Closed captioned for the hearing impaired.
10-182 30 min. $14.95

• **Learning About Letters**
Big Bird and his friends present Alphabet Day on Sesame Street. Introducing all the letters from A to Z, children will sing along when Cookie Monster presents his letter C and his favorite word "cookie." Children learn how to recognize the form of the letter, hear the sound through repetition, and also how letters combine to become words and words become stories. Closed captioned for the Hearing impaired.
10-179 30 min. $14.95

• **Learning About Numbers**
Children will love to count along with the Count and Big Bird and their friends from Sesame Street. Through music, animation, and comedy children learn how to recognize numbers, distinguish one from another, recite the numbers, and count from 1-20. They also learn how to count objects and events. Closed captioned for the hearing impaired.
10-180 30 min. $14.95

• **Play-Along Games and Songs**
Play along with Big Bird and his friends as they present some of the most popular games and songs from Sesame Street. This is specially designed to help familiarize children with important reading, counting and reasoning skills; as well as

---

recognizing patterns and sorting. A fun tape for both children and parents. Closed captioned for the hearing impaired.

10-183 30 min. $14.95

• Visit The Hospital

The hospital can be frightening for young children, but with the Sesame Street gang along, it becomes an adventure. Kids join Big Bird and his friends as they learn all about what happens at the hospital in this reassuring program.

10-6761 30 min. $14.95

SHAMU AND YOU SERIES

Discover the wonder of wildlife as nature's most curious creatures are explored through fact-filled storytelling, catchy children's tunes, lively animation and up-close encounters in natural habitats.

• Exploring the World of Mammals
10-8016 30 min. $16.95

• Exploring the World of Fish
10-8017 30 min. $16.95

• Exploring the World of Reptiles
10-8018 30 min. $16.95

• Exploring the World of Birds
10-8019 30 min. $16.95

Sign-Me-A-Story

Linda Bove, a deaf actress children will know from Sesame Street, introduces children to a new way of communicating-American Sign Language. Starting with some simple signs, Linda and other performers act out Little Red Riding Hood and Goldilocks and the Three Bears.

10-3054 30 min. $14.95

Spinning Tops and Tickle Bops

The entire family will savor this richly entertaining video of three charming stories that tell children why we take care of property, why people have special jobs and why we need each other.

10-1917 30 min. $14.95

Student Life in Mexico

Visit Mexican children in their classrooms, at home, at work, and at play. See both city and country life in Mexico. Many questions are answered in this lively video which captures the spontaneity and interests of Mexican children. Some basics of the geography and history of Mexico are also included.

10-8179 18 min. $29.95

Telephone "Doctor"

Nationally-recognized authority on telephone

techniques, Nancy J. Friedman, The Telephone "Doctor", also shows her new friends Bink, Bobby and Abigail, how to make an emergency phone call if they're ever alone in the house and need help. This is one visit to the doctor kids of all ages will like.

10-5378 21 min. $24.95

Week in the Life of a Mexican Student

An overview of a week in the life of fourteen year-old high school student Xavier Sierra. Xavier work in a tortilla factory every morning before school to earn money for his schooling. This film shows Xavier in English, history, and chemistry classes; at work; and with his friends and family. Xavier goes with his class to Mexico City to visit the university; to the country with his family for a Mexican barbecue; and to a party where each girl is chaperoned by her mother.

10-8005 24 min. $69.95

Week in the Life of a Chinese Student

Young students of the fourth class of grade one of the Number Two Junior Middle School of Beijing are featured in this documentary look at life in the People's Republic of China. The school day includes an early reading session, math and English lessons, student-led physical exercises, and a snack break. At home, children help with chores and do homework in the evening--no TV for middle school students until the weekend. Saturday is the last day in the six-day Chinese school week.

10-8006 20 min. $69.95

When I Grow Up I Want to Be

This video features the insights and fantasies of young people about the world of work and how they relate to that world. Children will benefit from an increased awareness of these vocational alternatives and acquire useful knowledge about career development.

10-1929 45 min. $14.95

WHY WE CELEBRATE SERIES

This fascinating series explores the origins and significance of some of the holidays we celebrate. The intriguing presentations stimulate children's interest and help them gain a deeper appreciation of these special days. For grades 2-5.

• Columbus Day
10-2663 15 min. $39.95

• Halloween
10-2664 11 min. $39.95

• Independence Day
10-2662 12 min. $39.95

VIDEO TITLES LISTED IN THIS GUIDE ARE AVAILABLE FOR PURCHASE OR RENTAL. CONTACT YOUR LOCAL VIDEO STORE OR TELEPHONE (800) 383-8811

• **Memorial Day**
10-2661 10 min. $39.95

• **Thanksgiving**
10-2665 10 min. $39.95

**WILL ROGERS JR. PRESENTS:
STORIES OF AMERICAN INDIAN
CULTURE**
All are introduced and narrated by actor Will
Rogers Jr.

• **Hawk, I'm Your Brother**
This wonderful Byrd Baylor story is an enchanting,
warmhearted tale for the entire family.
10-9837 25 min. $16.95

• **Stories of American Indian Culture:
Other Ways To Listen**
This award winning Byrd Baylor story is about the
sound of night-blooming cactus, the sigh of a
mountain--and how just feeling good can be the
most natural felling in the world!
10-9838 20 min. $16.95

• **Stories of American Indian Culture:
The Way to Start a Day**
How do you "say hello to the sun" every morning?
You'll watch how people in many different
countries greet the new day. It's a fun and beautiful
voyage of discovery that will show you how you
too can take part in the magic of a new dawn!
10-9839 12 min. $16.95

Concerned About The Quality Of

Your Children's TV Viewing?

Take Them On Exciting Educational

Adventures With Tapes

From This Section.

VIDEO TITLES LISTED IN THIS GUIDE ARE AVAILABLE FOR PURCHASE
OR RENTAL. CONTACT YOUR LOCAL VIDEO STORE OR TELEPHONE (800) 383-8811

Classics

- ✓ *Classic Television*
- ✓ *Miscellaneous*

Classic Television

1950'S TV CLASSICS

• Jimmy Durante Show starring Jimmy Durante
36-6893 30 min. $14.95

• Jack Benny Show starring Jack Benny & Humphrey Bogart
36-6894 30 min. $14.95

• Jack Benny Show starring Jack Benny, George Burns, Bing Crosby & Bob Hope
36-6907 30 min. $14.95

• You Bet Your Life starring Groucho Marx & George Fenneman
36-6896 30 min. $14.95

• You Bet Your Life starring Groucho Marx
36-6903 30 min. $14.95

• This Is Your Life starring Stan Laurel & Oliver Hardy
36-6897 30 min. $14.95

• Adventures of Robin Hood starring Richard Greene
36-6898 30 min. $14.95

• Dragnet starring Jack Webb & Ben Alexander
36-6899 30 min. $14.95

• Cisco Kid starring Duncan Renaldo & Leo Carillo
36-6900 30 min. $14.95

• Flash Gordon starring Steve Holland
36-6901 30 min. $14.95

• Annie Oakley starring Gail Davis
36-6902 30 min. $14.95

• Hey, Mulligan! starring Mickey Rooney
36-6904 30 min. $14.95

• My Hero starring Bob Cummings
36-6905 30 min. $14.95

• Adventures of Ozzie & Harriet starring Ozzie, Harriet, David & Ricky
36-6906 30 min. $14.95

• Make Room For Daddy starring Danny Thomas
36-6909 30 min. $14.95

• Trouble With Father starring Stu Erwin
36-6910 30 min. $14.95

40 Years of Science Fiction Television
This is the story of those fantastic programs which captured our imaginations. You'll see clips from your favorites: "Outer Limits", "Lost in Space", and other sci-fi television favorites, including classic "Star Trek" bloopers.
36-8016 30 min. $16.95

40 Years of Television: Broadcast Journalism
Forty Years of Television Broadcast Journalism: Relive such classic moments as Bob Hope, an atomic bomb explosion, the spectacular Bel-Air fire, the Rose Parade, enjoy such unforgettable entertainment milestones as "Pantomime Quiz," "Beany and Cecil," "Lawrence Welk," and much, much more.
36-6361 120 min. $59.95

Amos 'n Andy: Anatomy of a Controversy
This is the complete story of the incredibly popular Amos 'n Andy, from its early days on radio to its boisterous days on America's first television screens. Hosted by comedian George Kirby, this special program is packed full of generous clips from both the radio and television show, including highlights of the now-classic episode "Kingfish Sells a Lot" and excerpts from the feature Check and Double Check.
36-5814 60 min. $29.95

Bang The Drum Slowly
Paul Newman, George Peppard and Albert Salmi star in this celebrated 1956 television production of Mark Harris' poignant story of a dying baseball player who wants to play one last season.
36-5623 60 min. $19.95

BURNS & ALLEN SHOW VIDEO LIBRARY

- "Meet the Mortons"
36-6887 30 min. $14.95

- "Car Accident"
36-6888 30 min. $14.95

- "Checking Account"
36-6889 30 min. $14.95

- "Income Tax"
36-6890 30 min. $14.95

- "Beverly Hills Uplift Society"
36-6891 30 min. $14.95

- "Nieces Visit"
36-6892 30 min. $14.95

- "Teen Visit"
36-6895 30 min. $14.95

- "Wedding Show"
36-6908 30 min. $14.95

Celebrity Commercials of the 60's
How did today's superstars get their start? In
television commercials! Let this hilarious video take
you back in time when today's most recognized
Hollywood stars were just beginning.
36-7047 30 min. $14.95

Courage Of Rin-Tin-Tin
Return to the days of yesteryear when the West was
young and Rusty, Rinny and Lt. Rip helped tame
the wild frontier.
36-6089 90 min. $24.95

Crazy Commercials of The 60's
Journey back to the 60's. Crazy, hilarious black &
white and color television commercials that depict
the trends, styles, and fashions of the 1960's.
36-6490 40 min. $16.95

FAN'S FAVORITES: LUCILLE BALL:
Two episodes per cassette.

- Lucy Does a TV Commercial - Lucy's
Italian Movie
36-6215 50 min. $19.95

- Job Switching - Fashion Show
36-6216 50 min. $19.95

- Lucy Meets Harpo Marx - L.A. at
Last! (With William Holden!)
36-6217 50 min. $19.95

- Lucy is Enceinte (Pregnant) - Lucy
goes to the Hospital
36-6218 50 min. $19.95

**Forty Years Of Science Fiction
Television Featuring: Star Trek**
This is the story of those fantastic programs which
captured our imagination. Beginning with Rocky
Jones, Space Ranger and Flash Gordon and
continuing through the 1990's we will glimpse the
best of occult and science fiction television. A rare
collection of "out-takes" from Star Trek's three
seasons on television is a major highlight of this
documentary.
36-6543 30 min. $14.95

It's a Wonderful Life
The original Frank Capra classic, starring
Jimmy Stewart.
36-9144 130 min. $16.95

Lassie: The Painted Hills
Splendid family entertainment starring America's
favorite collie.
10-9142 70 min. $16.95

**LONE RANGER WITH CLAYTON
MOORE & JAY SILVERHEELS**
Two episodes per cassette

- Fugitive - Message to Fort Apache
36-5865 55 min. $19.95

- Six Gun Sanctuary - Outlaw's Trail
36-5866 55 min. $19.95

- Texas Draw - Rendezvous At Whipsaw
36-5867 55 min. $19.95

- Code of The Pioneers - Heritage of
Treason
36-5868 55 min. $19.95

- Colorado Gold - Enfield Rifle
36-5869 55 min. $19.95

MILTON BERLE SERIES:

- Carnival of Comedy
This collection of comic highlights featuring Berle
and his guests Steve Allen, Basil Rathbone, Martha
Raye, Frank Sinatra, many others.
36-5627 62 min. $19.95

- Funny Fifties
Berle's hysterical comedy along with history-
making appearances by Elvis Presley (one of his
first TV performances!), Ronald Reagan, Bob

Hope, Martin & Lewis, Red Skelton, Jack Benny and many more.
36-5625 75 min. $19.95

• **Legends**
Uncle Miltie at his best with extraordinary comic guests-Jackie Gleason, Harpo Marx, Martha Raye, Peter Lorre - plus performances from true music immortals Cole Porte, Louis Armstrong, Frank Sinatra and Duke Ellington.
36-5626 61 min. $19.95

COOLEST PRIVATE EYE EVER: PETER GUNN

• **Death House Testament**
36-5860 $19.95

• **Rough Buck**
36-5861 $19.95

• **Lynn's Blues**
36-5862 $19.95

• **Comic**
36-5863 $19.95

• **Torch**
36-5864 $19.95

Rin-Tin-Tin Hero of The West
The best friend Justice ever knew, now in Color for the whole family!
36-6088 75 min. $24.95

ROY ROGERS SHOW
The original TV series! Not seen on network TV for 26 years. 2 fun-packed episodes per cassette.

• **Mountain Pirates - Empty Saddles**
36-5875 46 min. $19.95

• **Smoking Guns - Sheriff Missing**
36-5876 46 min. $19.95

• **Morse Mix Up - High Stakes**
36-5877 46 min. $19.95

• **Head For Cover - Paleface Justice**
36-5878 46 min. $19.95

• **Tossup - Brady's Bonanza**
36-5879 46 min. $19.95

• **Fishing for Fingerprints - Fighting Fire**
36-5880 46 min. $19.95

TV CLASSICS

• **Hollywood Half Hour & Public Defender**
36-5815 52 min. $19.95

• **Howdy Doody & Art Linkletter and the Kids**
36-5816 52 min. $19.95

• **Colonel March of Scotland Yard & Sherlock Holmes**
36-5817 52 min. $19.95

• **Arthur Godfrey's Talent Scouts & The Ed Wynn Show**
36-5818 52 min. $19.95

• **Burns and Allen Show & Heaven for Betsy**
36-5819 52 min. $19.95

• **Armchair Detective & Public Prosecutor**
36-5820 52 min. $19.95

• **Four Star Playhouse & the Stars and the Story**
36-5821 52 min. $19.95

• **Jack Benny Show**
36-5822 52 min. $19.95

• **Cisco Kid & The Roy Rogers Show**
36-5823 52 min. $19.95

• **Life of Riley**
36-5824 52 min. $19.95

TV'S MAGIC MEMORIES: SERIES
The best of classic television from the 50's featuring: action serials, science fiction, comedy and documentaries.

• **War Time Years Volume 3**
36-8001 60 min. $16.95

• **War Time Years Volume 4**
36-8002 60 min. $16.95

• **Christmas Memories**
36-8003 60 min. $16.95

• **Sky King Volume 2**
36-8004 55 min. $16.95

• **Atomic Memories**
36-8005 60 min. $16.95

• **One Step Beyond**
36-8006 55 min. $16.95

• **Today Show (11/20/57)**
36-8007 50 min. $16.95

• **Victor Borge Show (1951)**
36-8008 60 min. $16.95

• **Chicago & Northwestern Railroad Memories**
36-8009 60 min. $16.95

• **French & British Railroad Memories**
36-8010 52 min. $16.95

• **Those Fabulous Cars of Yesteryear**
36-8011 60 min. $16.95

• **Drag Racin' Yesteryear Style**
36-8012 60 min. $16.95

• **Dodge Rebellion Memories (1965-1968)**
36-8013 60 min. $16.95

• **Unaired Pilot Shows - Now is Tomorrow/Swingin' Together**
36-8014 60 min. $16.95

• **Rare Auto & Travel Thrills (1933)**
36-8015 60 min. $16.95

Miscellaneous

BACK TO THE 50'S

• **Volume 1**
A fascinating look at the fifties featuring original recordings by some of the top artists of that era--accompanied by incredible footage of all the fads, fashions and faces that have made the fifties memorable.
36-6461 33 min. $16.95

• **Volume 2**
Shows you a television advertisement featuring James Dean advising America to drive safely,

Humphrey Bogart selling Government Bonds, Elvis in the army and more.
36-6462 30 min. $16.95

Charlie Chaplin: Emerging Chaplin
Narrated by Douglas Fairbanks, Jr. An uproarious roller coaster ride of human comedy, this program features Charlie Chaplin during his early days as The Little Tramp. From early films to his stint at Mack Sennett's studios to the silent film classics that audiences have loved for decades, this profile gives you the emergence of a true genius. Includes clips from Kid Auto Races, The Bank, The Tramp, The Floorwalker, The Pawnshop, The Rink, and Easy Street.
36-5799 30 min. $19.95

CLASSIC CHAPLIN COLLECTIBLES

• **Charlie Chaplin At Keystone Studios (1914)**
36-6642 60 min. $19.95

• **Charlie Chaplin At Essanay Studios I (1915)**
36-6643 90 min. $19.95

• **Charlie Chaplin At Essanay Studios II (1915)**
36-6644 60 min. $19.95

• **Charlie Chaplin At Mutual Studios I (1916)**
36-6645 100 min. $19.95

• **Charlie Chaplin At Mutual Studios II (1916)**
36-6646 90 min. $19.95

• **Charlie Chaplin At Mutual Studios III (1917)**
35-6647 96 min. $19.95

Big Trees
A stunning western set in the High Sierras. Starring Kirk Douglas and Eve Miller.
36-9143 90 min. $16.95

Cruisin' Thru The 60's
An interesting and unusual look at the 60's, combining original newsreel footage and assorted clips with some of the hottest hits of that era. This video covers all the big moments and small wonders from space travel and peace rallies to the horror and tragedy of Vietnam.
36-6489 30 min. $16.95

VIDEO TITLES LISTED IN THIS GUIDE ARE AVAILABLE FOR PURCHASE OR RENTAL. CONTACT YOUR LOCAL VIDEO STORE OR TELEPHONE (800) 383-8811

GREAT EVENTS VIDEO LIBRARY:

- **Great Events 1950**
36-6696 30 min. $14.95

- **Great Events 1951**
36-6697 30 min. $14.95

- **Great Events 1952**
36-6698 30 min. $14.95

- **Great Events 1953**
36-6699 30 min. $14.95

- **Great Events 1954**
36-6700 30 min. $14.95

- **Great Events 1955**
36-6701 30 min. $14.95

- **Great Events 1956**
36-6702 30 min. $14.95

- **Great Events 1957**
36-6703 30 min. $14.95

- **Great Events 1958**
36-6704 30 min. $14.95

- **Great Events 1959**
36-6705 30 min. $14.95

- **Great Events 1960**
36-6706 30 min. $14.95

- **Great Events 1961**
36-6707 30 min. $14.95

- **Great Events 1962**
36-6708 30 min. $14.95

- **Great Events 1963**
36-6709 30 min. $14.95

- **Great Events 1964**
36-6710 30 min. $14.95

- **Great Events 1965**
36-6711 30 min. $14.95

- **Great Events 1966**
36-6712 30 min. $14.95

- **Great Events 1967**
36-6713 30 min. $14.95

- **Great Events 1968**
36-6714 30 min. $14.95

- **Great Events 1969**
36-6715 30 min. $14.95

Martin Luther
This film traces the life of Martin Luther in the
16th century, his beliefs, his battles with the
Roman Catholic hierarchy, and his vision. This
dramatic Academy Award nominated film portrays
the life of one of the most important men in history
and his contribution.
36-9118 115 min. $19.95

MOST AWESOME COLLECTION OF SUPERHEROES EVER:

- **Superman 1**
36-6195 50 min. $19.95

- **Superman 2**
36-6196 50 min. $19.95

- **Superman 3**
36-6197 50 min. $19.95

Rockin' The 50's
Dances, cars, TV, music - everything that made the
50's what it is today, namely a very marketable
commodity. With 50's nostalgia at an all-time peak,
radio stations converting everyday to a golden
oldies format, and even poodle skirts coming back
into style.
36-6488 30 min. $16.95

Quartet: Four Classic Tales by W. Somerset Maugham
An anthology of four of the best short stories by
W. Somerset Maugham. With a cast that includes
Dirk Bogarde, Honor Blackman, and George Cole.
36-8000 120 min. $69.99

TIME WARP SERIES:

- **Time Warp: 1954**
People: Ike and Mamie, The Honeymooners,
Liberace, Roy Chon, The Cisco Kid, the Reagans,
Howdy Doody, Marlon Brando, Betty Furness,
Rocky Jones, Space Ranger, Arthur Godfrey,
Groucho Marx, Roy Rogers, Speedy Alka Seltzer.
The Creature from the Black Lagoon. Events:
Battle of Dien Bien Phu, the Amy-McCarthy
Hearing, the Eniwetok Atoll H-Bomb Blast.
36-5769 79 min. $19.95

- **Time Warp: 1960**
People: The Kennedys, Castro, Khrushchev, Elvis,
Marilyn Monroe, the Flintstones, Princess

VIDEO TITLES LISTED IN THIS GUIDE ARE AVAILABLE FOR PURCHASE
OR RENTAL. CONTACT YOUR LOCAL VIDEO STORE OR TELEPHONE (800) 383-8811

Margaret, Barbie and Ken, Beaver Cleaver, Mickey Mantle, Richard Nixon, Alfred Hitchcock, Mr. Clean, Manners the Butler, Nick Adams (the Rebel), Jerry Lewis, Tennessee Ernie Ford. Events: The Nixon-Kennedy Debates, the Twist, the U-2 Incident, Crisis in Algeria, the Congo, South Africa.

36-5770 83 min. $19.95

• **Time Warp: 1964**

People: Lyndon and Lady Bird Johnson, Roy Orbison, Carol Doda, the Beatles, Jackie Kennedy, Fidel Castro, Malcolm X, Barry Goldwater, Cassius Clay, Dick Van Dyke, James Bond, Lester Maddox, Andy Griffith, the Beverly Hillbillies, GI Joe, General Mark Clark, Robert Kennedy, Martin Luther King. Events: Gulf of Tonkin Incident, The Long Hot Summer, California Surfing.

36-5771 85 min. $19.95

Turn the Past

into

Presents!

Nostalgia Videos

Make

Great Gifts.

VIDEO TITLES LISTED IN THIS GUIDE ARE AVAILABLE FOR PURCHASE OR RENTAL. CONTACT YOUR LOCAL VIDEO STORE OR TELEPHONE (800) 383-8811

Searching For

A Unique Gift That is

Informative and Appreciated?

The Video Titles

In This Guide

Make Wonderful Gifts.

Comedy

- ✓ *Comedy*
- ✓ *Sports Bloopers*
- ✓ *Miscellaneous*

Comedy

America's Funniest Dirty Jokes
This program is a collection of man-on-the-street jokes recorded all around the country. Some of the jokes are a little off-color and some are downright dirty, but they're all just plain funny.
33-8029 60 min. $16.95

Andy Kaufman - I'm From Hollywood
Known to millions as Latka from "Taxi", this is a comedic retrospective of the man who crowned himself the "Undisputed Inter-Gender Wrestling Champion."
33-9981 60 min. $19.95

BEST OF 50'S COMEDIES

• Volume I
Full of singing, dancing, stand-up comedy and clownish antics of some of the biggest names of the decade. Including Bob Hope, Red Skelton and more.
33-8008 28 min. $29.95

• Volume II
Featuring Bob Hope saluting servicemen, Burns & Allen, plus the hilarity of Red Skelton.
33-8009 29 min. $29.95

Best of Comic Relief, 1990
Dozens of America's most talented comedians present a live comedy event. Starring: Billy Crystal, Whoopi Goldberg, Robin Williams, Cid Caesar, John Candy, George Carlin, Jerry Lewis, Howie Mandel, Martin Short, "Weird Al" "Yankovic and others!
33-013 120 min. $29.95

Best of Saturday Night Live - Classics
The Not Ready for Prime Time Players in the most hilarious sketches from the immortal early years. (1975-1980)
33-8001 92 min. $39.95

Best of Saturday Night Live - Wayne's World
33-8003 90 min. $16.95

Billy Crystal: Don't Get Me Started
In this outrageously funny act, Billy Crystal plays "Fernando", "Sammy Davis Jr.", and his other wildly popular characters. A combination of Spinal Tap and Bring On The Night, Billy Crystal's video is absolutely "maahvelous!"
33-6658 60 min. $19.95

Bottoms Up "81"
Hilariously irreverent, raunchy, fast-moving, bawdy and packed with laughs, this video is a recreation for the screen of America's longest-running comedy revue. The unique mixture of humor and music has been a favorite of audiences worldwide since 1958.
25-254 72 min. $49.95

Bowery Boys Revisited
A look back at the lives and films of "The Bowery Boys" including never-before-seen interviews, out-takes and bloopers, rare stills and clips.
37-8000 30 min. $16.95

Business Woman's Guide to Dirty Jokes/ E. Wolynski
Billed as "Poland's only stand-up comic," Liz is described by the N.Y. Times as a "contemporary W.C. Fields".
33-8018 30 min. $19.95

Buster Keaton
Henry Morgan brings you the story of Buster Keaton, "The Great Stone Face, from his earliest childhood to his maturity as one of Hollywood's greatest comics. Includes seldom-seen footage from the classics "Fatty At Coney Island, "Cops," "Balloonatics," "Day Dreams" and "The General" from the Rohauer Collection.
06-034 60 min. $69.95

CAROL BURNETT'S MY PERSONAL BEST

• Went with the Wind
Everybody has his personal favorites from Carol Burnett's 1,000+ comedy routines telecast during 11 years of prime time television. These are Carol's favorites, personally chosen by her. Includes a new, live introduction and "wrap" by Carol.
33-1801 60 min. $29.95

• Little Miss Show Biz
More favorites from Carol Burnett's prime time comedy television show. This tape also includes a new introduction and "wrap," filmed where the show was originally shot.
33-1802 60 min. $29.95

Charlie Chaplin
Stan Laurel, Fatty Arbuckle, Mabel Normand and Ben Turpin join Charlie Chaplin, the "Funniest man in the world," in this video collection of the incomparable "Little Tramp" who captured the

Yes! *Please send me information about:*

_____ Renting special interest video tapes by mail

_____ The Complete Guide To Special Interest Videos on CD-ROM

_____ The Complete Guide To Special Interest Videos on floppy disk

- Please type, print or attach business card -

Name _____

Company/Institution _____

Address _____

_____

City _____ State _____ Zip _____

Yes! *Please send me information about:*

_____ Renting special interest video tapes by mail

_____ The Complete Guide To Special Interest Videos on CD-ROM

_____ The Complete Guide To Special Interest Videos on floppy disk

- Please type, print or attach business card -

Name _____

Company/Institution _____

Address _____

_____

City _____ State _____ Zip _____

PLACE
19¢ STAMP
HERE

Video Learning Library
15838 N 62ND ST STE 101
SCOTTSDALE AZ 85254-1988

PLACE
19¢ STAMP
HERE

Video Learning Library
15838 N 62ND ST STE 101
SCOTTSDALE AZ 85254-1988

hearts of the world with his comic portrayals of the little guy's contests with the "Machine" and an alien society.
06-006 105 min. $69.95

Comedy Classics: Bob Hope
Swing to the sound of Les Brown and his orchestra and crack up at the hilarious skits of Bob Hope, the King of Comedy.
33-8005 61 min. $19.95

Comedy Classics: TV Bloopers
Bloopers from the stars you grew up with like the Fonz, Dick Van Dyke, Laverne & Shirley, plus Alan Alda and the Mash crew.
33-8006 29 min. $16.95

Comedy Goes to Prison
Comedians Paul Rodriguez and Richard Belzer perform locked behind bars at the Arizona State Prison.
33-3061 80 min. $19.95

Comic's Line
Billy Crystal gets a chance to play all the parts in a zany and hysterical parody of rock videos and stand-up comics.
33-008 59 min. $19.95

Commercials from Around the World
Bask in an international glow of creativity as the brightest minds in advertising from around the world compete to fracture your funnybone. Award winning TV commercials from England, Australia, France, Japan, and other countries vie for the title of cleverest promotion.
33-8034 60 min. $19.95

Commercial Mania
Do you wonder where the yellow went? We'll put you in the driver's seat for an hour of the most incredible, insidious and entertaining commercials from the '50's and '60's. See President Reagan as a soap pusher and witness the debut of the "revolutionary" new Edsel.
13-464 60 min. $29.95

Commercials From the 50's
Take a break and journey back in time through the memorable commercials of the 50's with Mr. Clean, Lucky Strike, etc.
33-8014 36 min. $16.95

Deal
It's a wacky, behind-the-scenes look at the most famous comedy game show of all, "Let's Make A Deal." Incredible bloopers and highlights that made it one of the most popular shows ever.
13-155 84 min. $19.95

Delirious With Eddie Murphy
Eddie Murphy at his best, in concert.
33-002 69 min. $19.95

Evening With Lewis Grizzard
This exclusive video spotlights Lewis' classic stories as he casts his magic spell in a hilarious one-hour live comedy concert. Pull up a chair and get ready to laugh 'till you cry!
33-6213 60 min. $19.95

GALLAGHER COMEDIES

• Melon Crazy
America's most outrageous comedian has undergone melon craziness.
33-007 42 min. $19.95

• Over Your Head
A collection of craziness featuring a Gallagher's-eye view of politicians, ancient history, child rearing and anything else that opes into his bizarre brain.
33-011 42 min. $19.95

• Struck in the Sixties
Gallagher looks at the things that really matter in life-ugly bathrooms, bad drivers, hog futures and skeet golf.
33-004 58 min. $19.95

• Bookkeeper
33-001 58 min. $19.95

• Maddest
Gallagher lampoons everything from sex to school to hats without handles.
33-006 60 min. $19.95

Gary Shandling Show 25th Anniversary Special
One of America's hottest stand-up comedians headlines this salute to his nonexistent long-running cable show.
33-009 57 min. $39.95

George Burns and Gracie Allen Show
This tape takes you right on stage into the hilarious antics of the greatest husband wife team in comedy history.
33-8007 30 min. $16.95

George Burns: His Wit and Wisdom
Filled with hilarious, warmhearted insights on sex, exercise, Gracie and more!
33-9406 45 min. $9.98

VIDEO TITLES LISTED IN THIS GUIDE ARE AVAILABLE FOR PURCHASE OR RENTAL. CONTACT YOUR LOCAL VIDEO STORE OR TELEPHONE (800) 383-8811

George Bush: Favorite Bloopers

George shares his favorite bloopers by President Roosevelt, Kennedy, Carter, Reagan, Nixon, Ford, even Bush himself.

33-8017 30 min. $19.95

GEORGE CARLIN COMEDIES

• George Carlin: Playin' With Your Head

George Carlin makes the mundane funny, and reality hilarious in a night of ground-breaking comedy recorded live at Los Angeles' Beverly Theatre.

33-6649 60 min. $19.95

• Carlin At Carnegie

33-6650 60 min. $19.95

• Carlin On Campus

33-6651 60 min. $19.95

Golden Age of Comedy

Hilarious comedy clips from 1914-1929.

33-9411 78 min. $29.95

Howie Mandel - Howie Would

This hip, hilarious comedy concert takes audience participation to new heights and laughter into the stratosphere.

33-8033 60 min. $19.95

How to Become a Ventriloquist

This program teaches the art of ventriquest for all ages. Taught by America's Foremost ventriloquist, Paul Winchell. Includes vintage video clips of Winchell's TV shows to help demonstrate his instructions.

25-8022 60 min. $29.95

Hungry I Reunion

Comedy's best from the birthplace of stand-up comedy, including Mort Sahl and Lenny Bruce.

33-9409 90 min. $29.95

Jimmy Durante/Groucho Marx

Jimmy is featured with long time comedy partner, Eddie Clayton, then Groucho takes over the '57 classic "You Bet Your Life."

33-8012 60 min. $19.95

Joe Bob Briggs: Dead in Concert

Joe Bob is cleverly sarcastic, imaginatively offensive and genuinely All-American! You'll either love him or you'll hate him, but you won't be able to stop laughing at him. To say he's sexist is too limiting - he puts down everything! Not for sensitive viewers.

33-1657 42 min. $24.95

Joe Piscopo: New Jersey Special

You've seen him on Saturday Night Live. But not all of him...and not like this.

33-6653 60 min. $19.95

La Gran Scena Opera

There are times when things are not quite as they seem. Or are they? That's the question being asked when New York's incredible La Gran Scena Opera Company was videotaped in Munich for this hilarious release. The New York Daily News described it as "La Cage Aux Folles of serious music Lovers...A divine satire."

25-255 110 min. $39.95

Laughing Room Only

You've seen them on Johnny Carson, Late Night with David Letterman, Saturday Night Live...They include the star of NBC's "Night Court," co-star of "The Barbara Mandrell Show," and the star of "They Call Me Bruce." The best of everyone's favorites meet the hottest new young comics for a classic stand up comedy feast.

33-6091 52 min. $24.95

Laugh Along With (Lucy)

A video collector's dream--the first lady of comedy with Ed Sullivan and in comedy skits that include rare footage.

33-8010 30 min. $16.95

Laughter: America's Funniest Reel Moments

An unforgettable collection of American humor as it happened right in front of the motion picture cameras. These are the real life jokes, bloopers and blunders of some of our greatest citizens, from comedians like W. C. Fields and Bob Hope to Presidents Harry Truman and Richard Nixon.

13-248 60 min. $19.95

LAUREL & HARDY SERIES:

Rare home movie footage narrated by Stan's daughter Lois is just one of the many reasons why this collection of videos are such a hit. Each video is packaged in gold metallic and has a "collector's edition" look.

• Chump At Oxford

33-8019 35 min. $16.95

• Pack Up Your Troubles

33-8020 35 min. $16.95

• Saps At Sea

33-8021 35 min. $16.95

• At Work

33-8022 35 min. $16.95

• **On The Lam**
33-8023 35 min. $16.95

• **Sons of the Desert**
33-8024 35 min. $16.95

• **Swiss Miss**
33-8025 35 min. $16.95

• **Spooktacular**
33-8026 35 min. $16.95

• **Laurel & Hardy and the Family**
33-8027 35 min. $16.95

• **Stan "Helps" Ollie**
33-8028 35 min. $16.95

Live from Washington - It's Dennis Miller
Get ready for an hour of insightful and satiric comic brilliance recorded live in Washington D.C.
33-8032 60 min. $19.95

Louie Anderson: Mom! Louie's Looking At Me Again!
This guy is really a scream. In the tradition of Bill Cosby and Jack Benny, his impeccable timing, relaxed charm and outrageous body language never fail to have audiences rolling on the floor with laughter.
33-6291 60 min. $29.95

MICKEY ROONEY'S SILLY COMEDIES
Mickey hosts his early boyhood Mickey McGuire Silly Comedies films and after each film he tells stories of his experiences as a child star.

• **Volume 1**
33-6913 40 min. $14.95

• **Volume 2**
33-6914 40 min. $14.95

• **Volume 3**
33-6915 40 min. $14.95

Milton Berle/Jack Benny
A classic TV episode with Benny and famous friends, followed by Mr. Television, Uncle Miltie and his guest stars.
33-8013 60 min. $19.95

More Laughing Room Only
Starring Arsenio Hall, Richard Belzer, Milton Berle, Rip Taylor, Willie Tyler, and Lester. The

Hottest of the Hot! including Arsenio Hall performing live, hilarious stand-up comedy.
33-6090 60 min. $24.95

Nancy Reagan
Nancy and Ron's early years, the California years, the White House--all with Ronnie telling jokes.
33-8016 30 min. $19.95

Pardon My Blooper
The original Blooper Snooper Kermit Schafer, has compiled some of the greatest goofs in TV history in this uproariously funny feature film.
33-8004 75 min. $19.95

Redd Foxx: Video In A Plain Brown Wrapper
The infamous Redd Foxx-star of "Sanford and Son" and renowned standup comedian-live in his latest concert act, sharing his own outrageous brand of no-holds-barred ribald comedy.
33-6655 60 min. $19.95

Richard Pryor Live And Smokin'
Here is your chance to see the funniest comedian of our time in his very first complete, uncensored live concert performance.
33-6656 45 min. $19.95

Richard Pryor Live In Concert
33-6657 78 min. $19.95

Roast Tommy: With Tommy Lasorda
A 90 minute fast-paced tribute to Tommy Lasorda, the most colorful manager in baseball featuring America's top comics, entertainers and sports personalities. Taped in front of a live audience in Las Vegas' star-filled Bally's Hotel and Casino, this benefit for the Barbara Sinatra Children's Center is a comedy extravaganza in the true "roast" tradition. And we know it'll become a tradition in your home as well.
30-5460 90 min. $19.95

Robin Williams Live
Robin Williams Live at New York's Metropolitan Opera House! It's Robin Williams at his best and most outrageous.
33-6648 65 min. $19.95

Saturday Night Live - 15th Anniversary
Includes highlights of 92 unforgettable, totally hilarious sketches from 1975 to 1990.
33-8002 92 min. $39.95

Show Off
Join Malcolm-Jamal Warner, top-rated star of the Award-winning "The Cosby Show" and his zany

friends for an unbelievable hour of no-holds-barred hilarity-comedy for kids!
33-6660 60 min. $19.95

Steve Martin Live!
It's Grammy Award-winning comic Steve Martin, in a hilarious classic concert performance guaranteed to crack you up!
33-6659 60 min. $19.95

Steven Wright Live
It's an hour of laughs with Steven Wright-"the man with the monotone." Steven Wright Live features excerpts from his Grammy-nominated comedy album.
33-6652 53 min. $19.95

That's Black Entertainment
The all-star line up and many rare and unique film clips, make this a perfect tape for history and movie buffs alike. It is also ideal viewing during Black History month.
33-9426 60 min. $19.95

Unofficial Dan Quayle Video
A humorous collection of Quayle's speeches, press conferences and interviews.
33-8018 27 min. $16.95

Up The Creek
Starring Peter Sellers, the craziness abounds on a mothballed cruiser. Blackmarket navy supplies, rocket experiments and the admiral's surprise inspection-all in true Sellers style.
33-6093 83 min. $39.95

When Comedy was King
The clowns of the silent screen including: Buster Keaton and Charlie Chaplin.
33-9410 81 min. $29.95

Whoopi Goldberg Live on Broadway
Whoopi impersonates five characters: Fontaine, the junkie thief, goes to Amsterdam for a confrontation with the memory of Anne Frank. Her Valley Girl piece follows the same pattern-comedy with a chilling twist. The last three characters leave room for a glimmer of hope. A black girl who wears a shirt on her head to substitute for blond hair decides she's okay the way she is. A Jamaican woman who comes to America to keep house for a white man ends up rich. And a palsy victim gets married.
33-012 75 min. $19.95

World's Funniest TV Commercials
Here for the first time, are 41 hilarious creations from the "king of comic commercials", Joe Sedelmaier.
33-9344 25 min. $19.95

Wrong Arm Of The Law
Starring Peter Sellers in a rare show of cooperation, the bumbling police inspector and one of London's cleverest thieves strike an unusual deal.
33-6092 94 min. $39.95

Sports Bloopers

Amazing Sports Bloopers II
The video is the sequel to ESPN's top selling video. It includes action from our most popular sports as well as Biff! Bam! Boom! insanity from auto racing and rodeo. Hosted by Jay Johnstone.
30-8099 30 min. $16.95

Baseball Funnies
One of our top 10 titles! It's mixed up mayhem and some of the most spectacular plays ever filmed. Includes legends like Ty Cobb and Babe Ruth right up to today's star players such as George Brett and Dave Winfield.
30-6475 30 min. $16.95

Big Plays, Best Shots And Belly Laughs
The greatest moments and funniest plays of the 1989 season, including the conclusion of Seahawk Steve Largent's brilliant career and the coronation of the 49ers as the team of the decade.
30-6358 50 min. $19.95

Birdies And Bloopers
Hosted by Gary McCord, see some of the world's greatest celebrities, athletes and personalities in their pursuit of that wonderful little, dimpled ball. And with the help of the game's everyday hackers, you'll hear some of the game's funniest jokes and predicaments. All in all, we will show you the greatest and goofiest goings on in the game of golf.
30-6459 30 min. $16.95

ESPN's Amazing Biff Bam Boom Anything Goes Sports Bloopers
Also from the ESPN archives comes 45 minutes of side-splitting spoofs and goof! SportsLook host Ray Firestone and friends reveal the zany humor behind sports around the world, from football, baseball and hockey to skiing, tractor pulls and rodeo.
30-5481 45 min. $14.95

Football Follies on Parade
A historical look back at the most popular videotape series in NFL Films' history, from the tried and true to the one-shot wonders - all the best

---

follies are here. Brought to you by the creators of the first ever sports bloopers!
30-6352 50 min. $19.95

Pro Basketball: Hoops Bloops
You've never watched it like this before! Hoops Bloops shows you this fast-paced sport turned into complete mayhem on the court. It's fun...the silliest hoop action ever filmed.
30-6473 30 min. $16.95

Pro Football Funnies
Follow the action as Football's finest bungle, drop, fumble, stagger, stumble and trip through hysterically funny Pro Football low-lights. Eaves-drop on huddles and pep talks...then follow the hilarious action.
30-6472 30 min. $16.95

Pro Sports Bloopers
Are you ready for some great bloopers? Watch as Walter Payton, Bill Laimbeer, Isiah Thomas and dozens of other great pros stumble, fumble and bumble. The best collection of fast-paced foulups you will ever see. The NFL, NBA, PGA, and Major League Baseball Greats, plus great suprise bloopers.
30-6458 30 min. $16.95

Super Dooper Hockey
It's action on ice that wasn't planned. An exciting collection of the best bloopers, crunches, falls, slips and stumbles. Today's hockey greats at their funniest!
30-6474 30 min. $16.95

Miscellaneous

Car Funnies
Weird car tricks, impossible stunts, stunts go wrong-you name it. If it's a wacky car funny we have it in this wild video.
33-6477 30 min. $16.95

Clowns
Comic study of the circus clowns of yester-year. Directed by Fedrico Fellini, Produced by Elio Scardamaglia & Ugo Guerra, Script by Federico Fellini & Bernardino Zapponi, Photographed by Dario di Palma. In Italian with English Sub-titles.
33-6613 90 min. $59.95

Hollywood Bloopers
Forget the modern TV shows. Now see bloopers from the motion picture industry's true legends and their classic films.
33-8011 30 min. $16.95

Portrait of a Legend: Sammy Davis Jr.
Memorable performances that gained him the title of Mr. Entertainment, from dancing with his dad to his great songs.
33-8015 26 min. $16.95

Reagan Everyone Loves
Now, for the first time, Reagan's most humorous tales and most amusing anecdotes are combined on one delightfully entertaining collector's video.
33-6289 40 min. $19.95

If Laughter is Truly
The Best Medicine,
The Films In This Chapter
Should Cure All Ills!

VIDEO TITLES LISTED IN THIS GUIDE ARE AVAILABLE FOR PURCHASE OR RENTAL. CONTACT YOUR LOCAL VIDEO STORE OR TELEPHONE **(800) 383-8811**

New

Special Interest Video Titles

Become Available

Often.

Please Inquire

If A Title Or Subject

You Are Looking For

Is Not Listed.

Commercial Arts

✓ *Airbrushing*
✓ *Graphics & Design*

Airbrushing

AIRBRUSH TECHNIQUES WITH ROBERT PASCHAL

The intricate art of airbrushing began in 1881. Yet, no one has contributed more to this unique artform than Robert Paschal. A technical consultant for the Badger Airbrush Company, he teaches extensively at many of America's leading art schools. Mr. Paschal holds both a BFA and an MFA from the State University of New York and is a highly respected commercial artist.

• Introduction to Airbrushing: Volume 1
Includes explanations of equipment you will need, different types of airbrushes, accessories and air sources and basic exercises in line reading and masking techniques.
03-068 30 min. $69.95

• Value Exercise and Geometric Shapes: Volume 2
How to control the airbrush and the use of frisket film in airbrushing geometric shapes.
03-069 30 min. $69.95

• Frisket Cutting Procedures: Volume 3
How to develop spatial relationships by using a hard-edge line.
03-070 30 min. $69.95

• Rendering With Airbrush: Volume 4
How to use the airbrush to develop a finished painting.
03-071 30 min. $69.95

Graphics & Design

CALLIGRAPHY SERIES
Learn different styles of Calligraphy in this easy to follow program.

• Pointed Brush Writing
03-8005 56 min. $39.95

• Flat Brush Writing
03-8006 80 min. $39.95

• Pen Calligraphy
03-8007 60 min. $39.95

Computer Visions
A spectacular ride on the new wave computer animation. Multi-award-winning producer/director, Geoffrey DeValois, has created another gem of breathtaking and unforgettable computer animation.
03-8040 60 min. $19.95

GRAPHIC ARTS SERIES WITH NAT STARR
If you are looking for a principal authority in the graphics industry, look no more! Nat Starr, noted graphic arts consultant and educator, has more than 30 years experience in the field of Graphic Arts. In this video course, Nat covers all the main subjects, in a comprehensive manner.

• Basic Paste-up
Covers basic tools and equipment needed for paste-up work and step-by-step instructions on how to efficiently paste-up a mechanical.
03-072 30 min. $69.95

• Basic Layout and Clip Art
Shows how to design an attention-getting ad. Includes an explanation of how to use syndicated stock illustrations (clip art) as part of your layout.
03-073 30 min. $69.95

• Pressure Graphics
Explains how to use images available on self-adhesive acetate sheets (decorative borders, frames, illustrations, type, etc.), to finish an ad.
03-074 30 min. $69.95

Letraset-Design International
Letraset products are used around the world by highly creative designers. A type designer in Los Angeles, a car designer in Germany, an illustrator in Paris and a package designer in Japan show the "how" and "why" of their use of Letraset products. Good for rounding out the graphic designer's insight into Letraset products and for gleaning possible ideas on more creative uses of these products.
03-333 35 min. $24.95

LEARN AND EARN SERIES

• Desktop Design: 1, Basic Electronic Graphic Techniques
Thinking about getting into or expanding your desktop system? This stimulating introduction provides an objective presentation to help you make decisions for your individual situation, with a balanced overview of desktop design techniques and typesetting principles plus basic information on

VIDEO TITLES LISTED IN THIS GUIDE ARE AVAILABLE FOR PURCHASE OR RENTAL. CONTACT YOUR LOCAL VIDEO STORE OR TELEPHONE (800) 383-8811

software and hardware. The full color video takes a step-by-step approach to simple graphic projects to demonstrate the elements of good design and typography.
03-6960 30 min. $39.95

• **Desktop Design: 2, Creative Design with PostScript Drawing Software**
See how current draw software on the Mackintosh is being used to solve creative design needs. This video highlights five major applications, beginning with the finished project and retracing the designer's step to completion. Each project uses current draw programs such as Adobe Illustrator 88 and Aldus Freehand in conjunction with ancillary software and hardware. Projects covered include: charts/graphs, logo design, advertising illustration, font creation and a magazine cover.
03-6961 45 min. $39.95

• **Desktop Design: 3, Creative Design With Pagelayout Software**
See how current page-layout software on the Mackintosh is being used to creatively solve desktop publishing needs. This video highlights three major projects, beginning with the finished project and retracing the designer's steps to completion. Each project uses current programs such as Aldus Pagemaker, Ready, Set, Go! and Quark Xpress in conjunction with ancillary software and hardware. Projects covered include: a newsletter, a brochure, and a full-page ad layout.
03-6962 45 min. $39.95

• **Graphic Design: 1, Demonstrating The Values Of Good Design**
Learn the fundamentals of design (organization, proportion, unity, contrast, direction, etc.) as you watch actual studio and agency projects from conception to completion. A range of graphic designs is examined to show different approaches. This video emphasizes the importance of design in conveying information and provides a method for evaluating good design.
03-6963 45 min. $39.95

• **Graphic Design: 2, The Application Of Good Design**
Learn the application of the fundamentals shown in Graphic Design: 1 using typical tools, projects and media. You'll see how to create presentations that sell by watching professional designers working on rough layouts, comprehensive, and dummies. Computer aids for preparing effective designs are also demonstrated.
03-6964 45 min. $39.95

• **Paste-Up: 1, An Introduction To Production Art**
This basic level presentation provides an introduction to the tools and materials for keylining, including traditional methods of professional paste-up - assembling art and type on a base board to create a camera-ready mechanical. You'll learn about a variety of tools and materials needed for efficient production - and their application - as well as how to assemble a toolkit that is just right for you. Includes many professional, step-by-step tips to help new and less-experienced artists do fast, clean pasteups that will save time and money at the camera and plate-making stages.
03-6965 30 min. $39.95

• **Paste-Up: 2, Practical Examples Of Production Art**
Learn layout and production fundamentals common to a range of complex single and 2-color projects by following the techniques of skilled professionals. Media include: a trade publication ad, direct mail brochures and a die-cut invitation. Skills taught include: photo handling, type selection and specification, art sizing, ink selection and cost considerations.
03-6966 45 min. $39.95

• **Paste-Up: 3, Complex Examples Of Production Art**
Learn layout and production fundamentals common to a range of multi-color, advanced projects by following the production of a direct mail brochure, a package design and a corporate capabilities brochure. This video demonstrates the increasing complexity of preparing multiple-color mechanicals as compared to single-color projects. Particular attention is given to overlay cutting, tint specification and photo handling.
03-6967 45 min. $39.95

• **Studio Shortcuts: 1, Graphic And Production Tricks**
Learn contemporary production tips and tricks used by experienced and innovative graphics professionals. Time and money-saving procedures are demonstrated in a variety of projects show-casing processes, tools and techniques. An easy-to-follow, magazine approach to studio shortcuts for both new and experienced graphic artists.
03-6968 45 min. $39.95

• **Clip Art 1: Use & Fundamentals Using Pre-Prepared Art**
Learn the fundamentals of designing and producing effective finished artwork using limited-budget, camera-ready graphics. This video demonstrates and showcases exemplary choices and uses of clip art for a variety of applications, including newsletters, ads, brochures and T-shirts. Modifications of graphics, such as flopping, cropping, reversing, combining and extending

illustrations are shown via hands-on projects.
03-6969 45 min. $39.95

• Printing Basics for Non-Printers: 1, An Abridged Guide To Printing Fundamentals
This video de-mystifies the various steps leading to the printing of simple and complex projects. It is intended for designers, production artist, those in positions of purchasing printed materials and those dealing with print production people. This overview teaches you how to talk to printers in their own language and how to save money on printing by properly preparing materials for the job. Can do's and can't do's of the pre-press process are explained.
03-6970 45 min. $39.95

• Calligraphy: 1, Learning The Art Of Beautiful Writing
Learn the basics of beautiful writing with this fascinating introduction featuring a master scribe. You'll learn the tools and materials needed, the origins of the art, and the basic techniques of lettering. The video guides you through the complete upper and lower-case letters, numerals and punctuation in the Italic hand. You'll see the step-by-step procedures for pen manipulation, traditional methods of measuring letter height and width, spacing between letters and words, and an introduction to page layout. Winner of Certificate of Typographic Excellence from the Type Directors Club of New York.
03-6971 30 min. $39.95

• Calligraphy: 2, Learn & Earn with Calligraphy
A step-by-step guide on how to earn money for your work in Advanced Calligraphy. Learn the proper styles and techniques of lettering.
03-8003 30 min. $39.95

Printing with Light
03-8042 60 min. $39.95

State of the Art Computer Animation
A collection of computer animation shorts featuring one from George Lucas' Lucas Arts company.
03-8041 60 min. $39.95

Airbrushing!

Calligraphy!

Graphics Design!

You Can Do Them All With

the Help of our Videos.

VIDEO TITLES LISTED IN THIS GUIDE ARE AVAILABLE FOR PURCHASE OR RENTAL. CONTACT YOUR LOCAL VIDEO STORE OR TELEPHONE (800) 383-8811

Computers
&
Electronics

✓ *Computers*
✓ *Electronics*

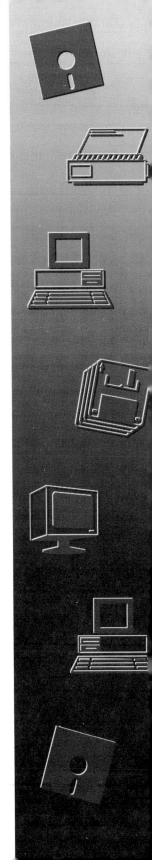

Computers

Advanced dBase II Plus Literacy
For experienced users, this comprehensive program will teach you how to learn database management.
09-8017 40 min. $39.95

Advanced dBase III Plus Literacy
Learn actual database commands and structure for reports and formats.
09-8018 40 min. $39.95

Advanced Wordperfect for Windows Version 5.1
This program covers nine topics for the more advanced user: Button bar, Outline, Styles, Headers and Footers, Footnotes, Endnotes, Table of Contents, Columns and Macros.
09-8029 54 min. $24.95

Age of Intelligent Machines
Stevie Wonder demonstrates two machines that widen his creative universe--a music synthesizer and a machine that reads books aloud.
09-8000 29 min. $89.95

BUSINESS GRAPHICS & CAD SERIES BY VIAGRAFIX

• **Learning Lotus 1-2-3: Introduction**
In this program you will learn the rudimentary skills of operating 1-2-3.
09-8051 47 min. $49.95

• **Learning Lotus 1-2-3: Macros**
Macros are the key to achieving the most with Lotus 1-2-3. This program will show you how to create and maintain self-running programs within 1-2-3.
09-8052 52 min. $59.95

• **Using Lotus 1-2-3: Advanced 2.3**
This video will show you many of the advanced features of Lotus 1-2-3, and how they are used in version 2.3. Learn how to create graphs and more.
09-8053 54 min. $49.95

• **Using Lotus: Advanced 3.1**
This will show you many of the advanced features of Lotus 1-2-3, and how to create graphs, reports, and more.
09-8055 65 min. $59.95

• **Using Lotus 1-2-3: Customizing**
You will learn advanced features to adapt 1-2-3 to meet your demands.
09-8055 65 min. $59.95

• **Freelance Plus: Introduction 4.0**
This tape will instruct you, in easy to follow steps, on how to generate professional presentations with Freelance.
09-8056 58 min. $49.95

• **Freelance Plus: Advanced 4.0**
Capture the best of Freelance Plus in your presentations. With the features and methods in this video, you will learn how to save time and increase the effectiveness of your work.
09-8057 60 min. $49.95

• **Harvard Graphics: Introduction 2.3**
You will learn quickly with this easy to follow video. You can rapidly master many of the fundamentals and become proficient in minutes.
09-8058 54 min. $49.95

• **Harvard Graphics: Advanced 2.3**
This video presentation will show you how to do the best in your presentations as you learn how to fine tune the many options.
09-8059 83 min. $49.95

• **Quickstart to DesignCAD 2-D/3-D** 5.0
These videos are for the beginning 2-D or the beginning 3-D user who wants to get up and running with the software quickly.
09-8060 58 min. $39.95

• **Customizing DesignCAD 2-D/3-D:** Any Version
This tape focuses on macros, icon menus, digitizer menus, and BasicCAD. This advanced tape is intended for the DesignCAD user who wants more.
09-8062 67 min. $59.95

• **Basics of BasicCAD (programming)**
Discover the fundamentals of BasicCAD programming in this video primer. BasicCAD can be a key to greater productivity with DesignCAD, but only if you know how to use it.
09-8065 63 min. $39.95

• **Learning DesignCAD 2-D (3-tape set)**
This three volume series covers the comprehensive command set of DesignCAD 2-D.
09-8063 111 min. $99.95

• **Learning DesignCAD 3-D (3-tape set)**
This three volume series covers the comprehensive

command set of DesignCAD 3-D.
09-8064 128 min. $99.95

• DesignCAD Seminar: The Complete Teacher (six tape set)
Learn from the seminar that American Small Business Computers uses to teach its employees. Conducted at a live seminar teaching DesignCAD 2-D and 3-D.
09-8066 552 min. $299.95

• Introduction to VinylCAD
This presentation is designed to give you a quick start in vinyl cutting with VinylCAD.
09-8067 53 min. $39.95

• Learning VinylCAD
This set of four tapes starts with the installation and setup of VinylCAD. You will see commands work and hear an explanation of the commands as they are being demonstrated.
09-8068 190 min. $199.95

• VinylCAD, the Complete Teacher
A complete set of six tapes. It includes the complete Learning VinylCAD set, a videotape on plotting and cutting, and also a tape on scanning images and using ScanPro.
09-8069 344 min. $299.95

Better Tools for a Better World
Demonstration on how to use a Sonic digitizer with Autocad.
09-8015 12 min. $19.95

COMPUTER LITERACY VIDEO SERIES
An easy to understand program on using MS-DOS, understanding macros, wordperfect and many of the other functions of the computer.

• Basic Computer Literacy
09-9463 20 min. $49.95

• MS-DOS Literacy
09-9464 20 min. $49.95

• Advanced MS-DOS
Version 1 through 3.3
09-9465 20 min. $49.95

• MS-DOS: Latest and Greatest
Version 4 through 5.0
09-9466 20 min. $49.95

• Wordperfect
Version 4 through 5.1
09-9467 20 min. $49.95

• Lotus Macros - All Versions
09-9468 20 min. $49.95

• Lotus 123 Literacy - Version 1 through 2.01
09-9469 20 min. $49.95

• Advanced Lotus 123 - Version 1 through 2.01
09-9470 20 min. $49.95

• Lotus: Latest and Greatest - Version 1 through 3.1
09-9471 20 min. $49.95

• Advanced Wordperfect - Version 4 through 5.1
09-9472 20 min. $49.95

dBase III Plus Level II
This video shows you how to copy and erase database files, sort and index records, create and modify reports, modify database files, create a query file and much more.
09-2891 62 min. $39.95

dBase III Plus Level III
Learn the most advanced dBase III Plus applications, such as importing and exporting files, programming concepts, and additional instruction on using the command line and memory variables.
09-2896 45 min. $39.95

dBase IV Level II
Planning and building a database structure, reopening a database file, adding data to an existing file, the sort command, deleting a database file, indexing a database file, building a report, adding a field to an existing database, making labels, setting up queries, and using forms.
09-6993 60 min. $39.95

dBase IV level III
Steps to build an application, designing the application, starting the application generator, designing the main menu bar, designing pop-up/pull-down menus, assigning action to objects, assigning actions to pull-down menus, organizing the screen, generating the documentation and program code, the dot prompt, running the application, and updating the application.
09-6994 60 min. $39.95

Business World's Guide To Computers
Hosted by Sander Vanocuer. Small and big businesses alike are confronted with a new wave of computer technology that is incredibly exciting and outrageously frustrating. This videocassette puts the choices into perspective and gives you a critical eye

toward the best in high technology. By tapping into the minds of the top decision-makers in the business world, this program gives you solid information regarding what may very well be the most important purchasing decision in business today.
09-5752 50 min. $19.95

Career Possibilities: Computer Programmer

Thinking of changing careers...or just starting out? This tape discusses the computer programmer-what employers want from a programmer, what fields are open to programmers, general responsibilities and the future of the job.
09-002 30 min. $29.95

Computability: Home Computers Made Easy for Everyone

Perfect for a brand new computer owner. Steve Allen and Jayne Meadows take you on a guided tour of computer language, financial programs, household systems, word processing and more. Designed for use with all makes and models, "Computability" gives you the knowledge and confidence to get the most out of your computer.
09-003 60 min. $39.95

Computer as an Art Tool

Taped in conjunction with the exhibition "The Computer as an Art Tool," Hurlbutt Gallery, Greenwich, CT explores the various techniques and programs used to create computer-generated art. The painting, assemblage, collage and video chosen for the exhibition feature pioneers in the use of computers to create art. Artists, educators and students included in the production: Manfred Mohr, Darcy Gerbarg, Mark Wilson, Isaac Victor Kerlow, Jeremy Gardiner, Margot Lovejoy, Haresh Lalvani, Robert Moran, Jerry McDaniel, Micha Riss, Eli Lapid, Roy Blomster and Olive Sabato. Synthesized music composed and performed by Toshi Hokari. An exhibition catalog is included with the videotape.
09-1734 12 min. $39.95

DESKTOP PUBLISHING

• Getting Started with Windows 3.1

Windows can make computing easier, and this video will make using Windows easier. Starting with installation, you'll learn the basics and become familiar with the Windows environment.
09-8042 79 min. $49.95

• Using Windows 3.1 Advanced

Learn how to customize and make your computing a breeze.
09-8043 71 min. $59.95

• Learning PageMaker for the PC 4.0

Desktop publishing is one of the growing areas in the computer arena. Learn to use Aldus Pagemaker the quick and easy way. Soon you will be able to produce ads, flyers, and brochures.
09-8044 82 min. $49.95

• Pagemaker: Advanced 4.0

This program is designed to give you training on the higher level features of the Pagemaker program.
09-8045 90 min. $59.95

• Pagemaker: Secrets and Timesavers

Learn the hard-to-find features of this program in this easy-to-follow presentation.
09-8046 64 min. $39.95

• Ventura: Introduction

You can start to learn to use Ventura in a matter of minutes with this video tutor.
09-8047 76 min. $49.95

• Ventura: Advanced

This program is designed to give you more instruction on the advanced capabilities of the program.
09-8048 65 min. $59.95

• dBase IV: Introduction

Learn many of the standard terms and procedures of this powerful software package.
09-8049 72 min. $49.95

• dBase IV: Advanced

This program will show you more of the complex capabilities of dBase IV, and still do it in a simple understandable manner.
09-8050 50 min. $49.95

Don't Be Afraid of Computers

This program identifies similarities between a typewriter and computer keyboard and explains that the computer cannot function without a human operator. Also-similarities shared by all computers and definitions of computer terminology.
09-011 30 min. $29.95

DOS AND OTHER PROGRAMS FROM VIAGRAFIX

• Learning DOS 5.0

In this video you will overcome your fear of DOS. This program covers files, directories and other DOS terms.
09-8070 81 min. $49.95

• Using DOS With a Hard Drive 5.0

This easy to follow video presentation presents

proper techniques for using your hard drive and your computer.
09-8071 60 min. $39.95

• **Learning About DOS Computers**
Computer literacy may be a better name for this tape.
09-8072 57 min. $39.95

• **Using Norton Utilities, Advanced**
09-8073 86 min. $39.95

• **Using PC Tools, Deluxe**
PC Tools can be a valuable addition to your computer, but only if you know how to use it.
09-8074 55 min. $39.95

• **Basics of BASIC**
You will learn how to actually write several short programs and get a feel for basic programming.
09-8075 63 min. $39.95

• **Programming in C**
Programming in C is intended to give the novice a programming foundation in this popular language.
09-8076 90 min. $39.95

• **Programming in PASCAL**
Learn the fundamentals of PASCAL, and also get information on programming in general.
09-8077 75 min. $39.95

• **Quicken, Quick and Easy**
Learn how to generate customized reports and keep on top of your bookkeeping needs.
09-8078 59 min. $39.95

• **Learning Peachtree, Complete Accounting 5.0**
You will learn to do payroll, create financial reports, and more.
09-8079 92 min. $49.95

• **Getting Started with DacEasy Accounting 4.2**
You will learn to install, setup accounts, generate reports, and more.
09-8080 79 min. $29.95

DOS Level III 2.0-3.3
Review previous terms. The CHKDSK (check disk) utility, using FC (file comparison), learn find utility, learn more utility, learn sort utility, learn to backup and restore and more on batch files.
09-6988 52 min. $39.95

Getting To Know Your Macintosh, MAC SE, Plus
Components, assembly, disk care, starting your

Macintosh, finder basics, finder menus, disk operations, document management, starting a Word Processor, emergency procedures and ten hints for successful computing.
09-7006 50 min. $39.95

Glenville School Computer Graphics
Produced by art teacher Oliver Sabato and her fifth and sixth grade students in Greenwich CT, this set shows animated designs created from original computer programming on an Apple II computer. A culmination of a unit designed to teach art, as well as the technical skills needed to be comfortable at the computer, the package includes a 36-page booklet, "An Easy Guide for Creating Computer Graphics in the Elementary Schools." The booklet contains a step-by-step lesson plan for a seven-week unit teaching computer-generated art, graphics and computer programming. It is suggested that the videotape and lesson plan be purchased together. The videotape is used for student motivation. It shows creative possibilities and contains no narration.
09-1735 80 min. $39.95

Hello PC
This exciting videotape will guide you through the starting steps of using your PC or PC compatible, and take you all the way to setting up subdirectories on your hard disk.
09-049 76 min. $29.95

Introducing Children To The World Of Computers
Spark your children's interest in computers with this entertaining, educational exploration of what computers are doing today. See how kids use computers to play games, practice math, invent toys, produce a school newspaper and learn about the latest technology. See how computers teach astronauts and pilots to fly, how TV weather maps are made and how the 911 phone system saves lives.
09-7003 24 min. $39.95

Introduction To 123 From Lotus
If you are a LOTUS owner or user, using your computer will be simplified after watching An Introduction to 123 From Lotus. The simple conversational approach is easy to understand, informative and convenient to use designed by a team of computer software specialists, Introduction to 123 From Lotus, shortens the learning cycle and reinforces the training.
09-5160 55 min. $29.95

Introduction to Appleworks Spreadsheet 2.0
Equipment needed and set up, defining a spreadsheet, starting the program, creating a file, learning the spreadsheet screen, creating a

VIDEO TITLES LISTED IN THIS GUIDE ARE AVAILABLE FOR PURCHASE OR RENTAL. CONTACT YOUR LOCAL VIDEO STORE OR TELEPHONE (800) 383-8811

spreadsheet, making formulas, the copy command, saving a spreadsheet, editing the spreadsheet, and printing the spreadsheet.
09-7004 59 min. $39.95

Introduction to dBase III Plus
Learn to use the assistant menus, plan and create a file structure, build a database, display records, browse the database, locate and edit records, how to use field list search conditions, and much more.
09-2890 68 min. $39.95

Introduction to dBase IV
Set up procedures, defining a database, starting dBase, creating a database file, entering data into the database, accessing a database, browsing a database, editing a database, and deleting a record.
09-6992 52 min. $39.95

Introduction To Excel 1.5
Set up procedures, starting Excel, learn about the Excel worksheet, entering data into the Excel worksheet, editing cell entries, entering numbers into Excel worksheet, changing cell appearance, adding dates and using series command, creating formulas, saving and printing a worksheet.
09-6999 56 min. $39.95

Introduction To Excel 2.01 (For The Macintosh)
Set up procedures and installation, starting Excel, learn about the Excel worksheet, entering data into the worksheet, editing cell entries, changing cell appearance, adding dates & using the series command, creating formulas, saving your worksheet, using the worksheet for analysis, and printing your worksheet.
09-7009 59 min. $39.95

Introduction to Lotus 1-2-3
Design and print a spreadsheet, learn the Lotus screen format, cells, rows and command line.
09-2877 45 min. $39.95

Introduction To Lotus 1-2-3 Version 2.2 & 3.0
Loading the program, moving around the spreadsheet, making cell entries, main menu options, erasing entries, types of ranges, creating a spreadsheet, entering formulas, the copy command, saving a spreadsheet, the sum function, printing your spreadsheet, and retrieving files saved to disk.
09-6990 47 min. $39.95

Introduction to Computers for Children
A simple and easy-to-understand video for kids with an interest in computers. The basics of computer jargon (bit, byte, RAM, ROM, etc.) as well as hardware, software and programming are explained by John Hynes, noted systems analyst, in a way kids will enjoy.
09-043 35 min. $29.95

Introduction to Microsoft Word
This tape will show you how to load and use this word processing program. You'll learn document creation, basic editing, basic formatting, spell-checking, saving, retrieving and printing a document and much more.
09-2893 53 min. $39.95

Introduction To Microsoft Word 1.04 (For The Macintosh)
Set up procedures, short menus command, saving a document, using the ruler (paragraph manipulation), editing your document, moving text, emphasizing text, fonts and point size, spell check, page review, page set up for the printer, and printing your document.
09-7008 43 min. $39.95

Introduction To Microsoft Word 5.0
Loading the program, creating a document, basic editing, block text operations, basic formatting, spell checker, saving and retrieving a document, and quitting the program.
09-6995 60 min. $39.95

Introduction To Multimate Advantage II
This tape covers set-up procedures, copying print files, loading Multimate, cursor movement, editing a document, the spell checker, moving text, the copy command, the place marker, centering, boldfacing, underlining, and printing your document.
09-6997 60 min. $39.95

Introduction To PFS: First Choice - The Word Processor
Installation & Startup, printer installation, entering text, saving text, cursor movement, editing a document, moving and copying text, find & replace, indents, tabs and margins, style options, spell check & thesaurus, and printing your document.
09-7000 54 min. $39.95

Introduction To PFS: First Publisher
Set up procedures, using the menus and tool box, using, editing and saving text, changing page format/using baselines, adding graphics and art, picture wrap, using graphic tools, printing a document, using the ruler, using the grid, creating boarders and title pages, and getting files from other programs.
09-7002 48 min. $39.95

VIDEO TITLES LISTED IN THIS GUIDE ARE AVAILABLE FOR PURCHASE OR RENTAL. CONTACT YOUR LOCAL VIDEO STORE OR TELEPHONE (800) 383-8811

Introduction To Ventura 1.1

Requirements and set up procedures, display overview and mouse control, loading a text file, typing text directly into Ventura, scrolling and viewing text, loading a different style, saving and retrieving a chapter, designing a page layout (framing), typesetting (paragraph tagging), and printing your document.
09-6998 68 min. $39.95

Introduction to Wordstar Professional

How to load Wordstar, make and save documents, use spell checker, move and delete text, use ruler, Introduction to Microsoft Word for Windows - Version 1.1. Proven teaching techniques make learning with the Video Professor fast and easy. For IBM and compatibles
09-8025 60 min. $19.95

Introduction To Wordperfect 5.0

Set up procedures and installation, installing and selecting printers, learn the screen and entering text, saving text, cursor movement, editing a document, using spell checker and thesaurus, learn to center, boldface, block, move, copy and underline text, printing your document, learn about reveal codes, and learn about file management.
09-5162 58 min. $39.95

Introduction to Wordperfect for Windows 5.1

This program covers the basic information that will help you master Wordperfect.
09-8027 54 min. $19.95

Introduction To Wordperfect For Apple, IIE, IIC

Set up & loading the program, cursor movement, editing your text, centering, boldfacing, underlining, the block command, spell check, saving & retrieving documents, printing, creating a macro for the printer and exiting the program.
09-7005 36 min. $39.95

Introduction to Wordperfect for Windows Version 5.1

This introduction covers 21 topics in a simple progressive manner.
09-8028 45 min. $24.95

IVS - INSTRUCTIONAL VIDEO SYSTEM

• Introduction To Personal Computers

Tape explains: the CPU, RAM, ROM, expansion slots, the floppy disk drive, hard disk drives, monitors, keyboard, printer, software, and more.
09-5340 30 min. $29.95

• Introduction To MSDOS

Tape reviews: booting up, dir, copy, delete, rename, erase, date, time, cd, md, rd, format, diskcopy, and more.
09-5341 30 min. $29.95

• Introduction To Wordperfect

Tape reviews: the Wordperfect keyboard and the editing screen, cursor movement, inserting and deleting text, undelete, canceling commands, help, bolding text, underlining, centering, reveal codes, moving text, printing, saving and retrieving files, spellchecking, formatting, list files, and more.
09-5342 30 min. $29.95

Investigating By Computer

More and more sophisticated data is being stored in on-line databases. Learn how to access with a computer and a modem. Perfect if you're a police officer, security type or private detective.
09-8014 50 min. $59.95

Just What Is a Computer, Anyway?

This overview of home computers gives you practical ideas of how your computer can solve home problems. Topics include computer codes, basic elements, the binary system, microchips, peripherals and more.
09-018 37 min. $29.95

Learning DOS

Shows how to connect the components of your computer, basic DOS commands, an overview of the keyboard, basic techniques and how to avoid common errors.
09-2853 42 min. $39.95

Learning DOS Level II

Learn all about sub-directories, batch and autoexec files, how function and hot keys work, as well as the fundamentals of hard drive operation and the most advanced DOS commands.
09-2872 41 min. $39.95

Learning Lotus Spreadsheets 1-2-3

Learn how make your own spreadsheets and presentations with this simple and easy-to-understand program.
09-9983 30 min. $39.95

Learning Microsoft Word for Windows

Learn how to use this data base in a simple easy-to-understand format.
09-9986 30 min. $39.95

Learning Windows 3.1

Learn how to master Windows like a pro!
09-8026 65 min. $19.95

VIDEO TITLES LISTED IN THIS GUIDE ARE AVAILABLE FOR PURCHASE OR RENTAL. CONTACT YOUR LOCAL VIDEO STORE OR TELEPHONE **(800) 383-8811**

Learning Wordperfect 5.1
Learn the reveal codes and how to create your own documents.
09-9982 30 min. $34.95

Lotus 1-2-3 Level II
Learn advanced commands, creating, saving, and transferring data, sorting and basic graphs.
09-2878 74 min. $39.95

Lotus 1-2-3 Level II Version 2.2 & 3.0
Creating a basic spreadsheet, writing and copying formulas, absolute and relative cell addressing, creating named ranges, the file combine command, using Lotus 1-2-3 for database operations, sorting records, criterion range headings, multiple criterion searches and printing reports.
09-6991 65 min. $39.95

Lotus 1-2-3 Level III
This video offers you a final graduate-level course in advanced Lotus spreadsheet applications.
09-2895 45 min. $39.95

Lotus 1-2-3 for Windows Level III
An introduction to planning a database, creating formulas within a database and planning and writing macros.
09-8086 30 min. $39.95

Lotus 2.2 & 3.0 Level III
File linking, Mixed relative and absolute address formulas, multiple ranges, calculating budget projections, worksheet windows, working with "undo" for budget projections, data tables, range search, database tables and database functions.
09-7010 60 min. $39.95

MICROCOMPUTER APPLICATIONS SERIES
This series of programs is designed for introducing people to the world of database management, using Wordperfect and the functions of the computer.

• **Computer Calc**
09-8003 28 min. $79.95

• **Wordprocessing**
09-8004 28 min. $79.95

• **Keeping Track: Database Management and Microcomputers**
09-8005 28 min. $79.95

• **Computer Talk**
09-8006 28 min. $79.95

• **Computer Careers**
09-8007 28 min. $79.95

• **Computer Peripherals**
09-8008 28 min. $79.95

• **Computer Crime**
09-8009 28 min. $79.95

• **Computer Images**
09-8010 28 min. $79.95

• **Computer Business**
09-8011 28 min. $79.95

• **Computer Sound**
09-8012 28 min. $79.95

Microsoft Word 5.5
An easy-to-follow program on how to use Microsoft Word to its best advantage.
09-8021 35 min. $24.95

Microsoft Word Level II
Learn search and replace, window operations, glossaries, thesaurus, text formatting, page formatting, tabs and tables, table of contents, and more.
09-2894 49 min. $39.95

Microsoft Works Word Processing Version 1.05
Set up procedures, creating a document, cursor control, choosing commands from a menu, basic editing, spellcheck, block text operations, search and replace, formatting text and tabs and tables.
09-6996 50 min. $19.95

Microsoft Works 2.0 The Word Processor
Setup procedures, creating a document, cursor control, choosing commands from the menu, editing a document, spell check, block text operations, search and replace, formatting text, tabs and tables.
09-7013 54 min. $39.95

Modems and Data Bases
Computer communications made simple-a look at modems and data bases: what they are, how they can be set up in your home computer, the functions of consumer data bases.
09-021 39 min. $29.95

National Geographic: Miniature Miracle, the Computer Chip
Witness the miracles of the technological revolution. Today, robots do jobs too dangerous for

humans, and computers help the disabled to walk again. At the heart of this new technological era is a miniature miracle-the computer chip. This power-packed chip, coupled with human ingenuity, is the key to the amazing inventions examined in this video.
09-1522 60 min. $29.95

OS/2 For DOS Users
The difference between DOS & OS/2, installation requirements and procedures, manipulate windows, running and adding programs, file manager, associating files, printing and command line operations, batch and command files, the command reference program, system editor, utilities and control panel.
09-7012 46 min. $39.95

Pagemaker 2.0a Level II
Introduction and set-up, creating a newsletter, setting up a tabloid newsletter and creating a headline, creating boxes for pictures and placing text, creating irregular columns, the drag place function, creating blow up quotes, flowing text around irregular shapes, printing out an oversized page using titles and creating graphics and special effects.
09-7007 58 min. $39.95

PERSONAL TUTOR SERIES
This series helps the computer novice gain understanding of the different programs they may have to use on a daily basis. Book and exercise diskette included.

• **WordPerfect 5.1**
09-8082 90 min. $69.95

• **Lotus 1-2-3 Release 2.2**
09-8083 90 min. $69.95

• **Lotus 1-2-3- Release 2.3**
09-8084 90 min. $69.95

• **Dos 5**
09-8085 90 min. $69.95

Personal Tutor for Dos 5
This program covers the use of DOS commands and how to use it to its full potential.
09-8016 90 min. $69.95

PC Tools Deluxe 6
Learn the basic and advanced use of PC Tools.
09-8019 30 min. $24.95

PFS: First Choice Level II: Database & Spreadsheet
Introduction to the database, planning and creating

a database form, building a database, exiting and retrieving a database, searching for files, using wild cards, printing a database, introduction to the spreadsheet, moving around in the spreadsheet, entering column and row headings, entering formulas, exporting files to the word processor and printing a spreadsheet.
09-7001 50 min. $39.95

PFS: Putting It All Together Level III
Creating and editing a database report, creating graphs, pulling graphs from a spreadsheet, creating slides on the word processor, using macros, setting bookmarks, creating and printing form letters, pulling mailing labels from the database and using a modem with PFS First Choice.
09-7011 40 min. $39.95

Robots: The Computer at Work
Robots are shown performing industrial work, assisting the handicapped, fighting fires and preventing crime.
09-8002 22 min. $69.95

Robotics: The Future is Now
Hosted and narrated by William Shatner. This introduces the concepts, capabilities and applications of industrial robots.
09-8001 20 min. $69.95

Step-By-Step PC Computer Assembly
Presented by Royal Maul who won a national award for the "1987 Course of the Year". This is the same course taught at many colleges and universities. With more than 20 years experience working with computers, Mr. Maul managed college computer centers, service bureaus, and computer installations for banks and manufacturing companies. A systems analyst and programmer, he designs systems for a wide range of businesses.
09-6307 30 min. $29.95

Understanding & Troubleshooting PC's
Learn how to troubleshoot and diagnose problems with your home computer.
09-8020 20 min. $24.95

VIAGRAPHIX WORD PROCESSING SERIES

• **Learning Wordperfect 5.1**
This video takes the computer novice by the hand and demonstrates keystroke-by-keystroke, how to begin with WordPerfect. You will install the program and learn rudimentary commands.
09-8030 69 min. $49.95

• **Journey Through WordPerfect 5.1, Volume 1**
In this video, the beginning WordPerfect user will

learn the entering and editing of text. Also presented are block commands, line and page formatting, printing and filling.
09-8031 58 min. $49.95

• **Journey Through WordPerfect 5.1, Volume 2**
After you learn the basics, this video presentation will give further instruction on advanced file management, basic mouse techniques, windowing options and more.
09-8032 82 min. $49.95

• **WordPerfect for Desktop Publishing**
Learn to create newsletters, brochures, and other useful articles. You will discover graphics, fonts and other design tools.
09-8033 89 min. $69.95

• **WordPerfect and Your Laser Printer 5.1**
Get the most from your laser printer. Learn to print different fonts, graphics and forms. Contains how-to information on Bitstream and HP font packages.
09-8034 56 min. $49.95

• **WordPerfect Secrets & Timesavers 5.1**
A concise assortment of simple but useful techniques, hidden features and over-looked devices for increasing your productivity with WordPerfect.
09-8035 50 min. $39.95

• **WordPerfect for the Office 5.1**
Manage mailing lists, speed up invoicing and automate other tasks in your office.
09-8036 84 min. $59.95

• **Customizing WordPerfect 5.1**
Macros, style libraries and many other "custom applications" are the heart of this video.
09-8037 81 min. $59.95

• **Microsoft Word: Introduction**
This program demonstrates the primary functions of Word. Learn editing, spelling and much more.
09-8038 50 min. $49.95

• **Microsoft Word: Desktop Publishing**
Desktop publishing with Word made easy. You will learn to create newsletters, brochures, letterheads and many other professional documents.
09-8039 78 min. $49.95

• **Writing with RightWriter 4.0**
RightWriter can help you produce high quality documents and this video will show you quickly, simply and easily how to use it.
09-8040 35 min. $29.95

• **Using Grammatik**
This can help you produce error-free documents, but only if you know how to use it. You are shown how to use Grammatik and also see the results in easy-to-understand terms.
09-8041 48 min. $29.95

Word Processor
Computer systems analyst John A. Haynes traces the merger of the typewriter, television and computer into one powerful communications device-the word processor. An overview is offered of the separate components, their functions and how they interrelate.
09-031 30 min. $29.95

Wordperfect 5.0 Level II
Learn the set up menu, color font attributes, fast save, initial settings & codes, auxiliary files, the shell feature, the format menu, line justification, margins, tabs, page numbering, page size and more, working on two documents at once, search and replace, learn macros and editing macros.
09-5163 60 min. $39.95

Wordperfect 5.0 Level III
Copying files in list files, creating merge files, setting your printer for labels, forms design, sorting documents, using fonts, inserting manual & automatic dates in documents, using automatic outlining & paragraph numbers, creating & using styles and using special tab techniques.
09-6989 60 min. $39.95

Wordperfect 5.0 Update
What's new with Wordperfect, set up procedures and requirements, loading printer and printer options, changing default settings in set up, file management and conversion, editing in reveal codes, macros: creation and editing, changes to control F8 (fonts), style sheet, view and graphics, and other changes in 5.0.
09-5164 54 min. $39.95

Wordperfect 5.1
Setup and installation, the mouse, menus, selecting printers, printing, entering, saving, and editing text, spell checker and thesaurus, page formatting and file management.
09-7014 57 min. $39.95

Wordperfect 5.1 Level I
An introduction to Wordperfect and its functions. Learn how to use commands, save documents and many other features.
09-8023 60 min. $19.95

Wordperfect 5.1 Level II
An advanced course on Wordperfect for those who

VIDEO TITLES LISTED IN THIS GUIDE ARE AVAILABLE FOR PURCHASE OR RENTAL. CONTACT YOUR LOCAL VIDEO STORE OR TELEPHONE (800) 383-8811

understand the basics of editing, saving page formatting and file management.
09-8024 60 min. $19.95

Wordstar 5.5
09-8022 30 min. $24.95

Your First Computer
An introduction for the first time computer owner. Learn basic operations and use of programs.
09-9984 20 min. $34.95

Electronics

DIGITAL ELECTRONIC SERIES

• **Introduction & Logic Gates**
09-6841 25 min. $69.95

• **Logic Conventions**
09-6842 15 min. $69.95

• **Logic Expressions & Diagrams**
09-6843 25 min. $69.95

Electronics Fundamentals and Terms
This module reviews the description, function and nature of electronic components, and covers semiconductors in depth. Characteristics of integrated circuits are dealt with and the learner is taught the identification of resistors and capacitors, and how to calculate metric and soft-metric values. The module concludes with a review and practice of methods used to voltage collage peak-to-peak and RMS values.
09-033 26 min. $99.95

Electronics Measurement Using the VOM
The VOM is the "bread and butter" test instrument of the electronics technician. This module demonstrates the purpose, function and use of the VOM and offers the learner practice in calculating current, voltage and resistance in parallel and series circuits. The function of the VOM is compared to the vacuum tube voltmeter (VTVM) and the digital voltmeter (DVM).
09-053 26 min. $99.95

Fault-Finding With Scope And VOM
A major task of the electronic technician/technologist is to locate, identify and correct system faults. Module 13 outlines a variety of systematic and proven methods of fault-finding. The substitution and the stage-by-stage methods, using the scope and the VOM are explained graphically, while specific troubleshooting techniques in active, capacitance and resistive components and in regulated power supplies, are dealt with step-by-step.
09-6844 30 min. $99.95

Solid State Motor Controls
This module focuses on motor controls, one of the more common applications of solid state electronic devices. Open and closed loop motor control systems are illustrated in detail, as are the characteristics and functions of stepper motor. This tape is of particular importance to those electronic technicians/technologists who are involved with solid state motor controls on a daily basis.
09-055 13 min. $99.95

Transistor Amplifiers
This module begins with common sense safety precautions to follow when working with transistor amplifiers. Include the function of transistors in RC coupling, transformer coupling and DC coupling amplifying chains. You will be shown how to discriminate between standard and non-standard Class A biased transistor amplifiers, and to describe the function of Class A, B and C transistor amplifiers. The learner is introduced to oscillators and practices as a way to identify, measure and correct the effects of negative oscillation.
09-056 25 min. $99.95

Transistor Switches
The module outlines the function of the transistor as a bistable switch with detailed explanations of the load line, maximum power line, cutoff state, full conduction state, saturation, region, bi-stable switching transistor and multivibrator circuits. The fabrication and function of logic gates and decoder circuits is also illustrated and explained in detail.
09-058 22 min. $99.95

Transistors
Transistor features and functions are covered in detail. The functions of common emitter PNP and NPN transistors are illustrated, while the user of is shown how to identify beta and gain with respect of common base, common emitter and common collector transistor circuits.
09-057 30 min. $99.95

VIDEO TITLES LISTED IN THIS GUIDE ARE AVAILABLE FOR PURCHASE OR RENTAL. CONTACT YOUR LOCAL VIDEO STORE OR TELEPHONE (800) 383-8811

Searching For

A Unique Gift That is

Informative and Appreciated?

The Video Titles

In This Guide

Make Wonderful Gifts.

Cooking, Food & Wine

Appetizers

Appetizers & Hors d'Oeuvres
Recipes for scallops in prosciutto, asparagus in pug pastry, sesame chicken strips, stuffed cucumber cups, barbecued shrimp, spicy ham phyllo triangles, and salmon dill crêpes.
11-154 30 min. $16.95

Great Chefs Appetizers
Chefs featured on this video are Chicago's John Draz and Jean Banchet; San Francisco's Adriana Giramonti, Max Schacher, Mark Miller and Werner Albrecht; New Orleans' Gerard Thabuis, Warren LeRuth, Daniel Bonnot, Gerard Grozier; and the Wong Brothers. Recipe booklet included.
11-224 60 min. $19.95

Breads

Basic Bread Baker
Recipes for sweet dough twist, sweet dough pretzel, whole wheat bread, dill bread, crusty rye bread, quick nut bread.
11-147 30 min. $14.95

Crusty Peasant Bread
Dr. Rosenbaum's easy instructions will turn you into a satisfied baker of healthy crusty peasant bread. You'll learn about the history of bread as you expand your fitness cooking skills.
11-8079 25 min. $29.95

Fitness Muffins
You'll love these fitness muffins. They're sweet, moist and delicious. With no fat, cholesterol, salt or refined sugar. A high fiber treat for the whole family.
11-8083 15 min. $29.95

French Bread, Brioche, Cheese Loaf
The French have a reputation for fine baking, as we all know. In this videotape, you will learn why, and how to recreate their results.
11-019 83 min. $39.95

Italian Bread, English Muffins, Crumpets
More international recipes mean more appreciation for your efforts with these tasty treats. It's easy to make wonderful breads, muffins and crumpets when you know how. Let Claudia Burns take you through these easy-to-follow instructions.
11-020 77 min. $59.95

PERFECT BREAD SERIES WITH BETSY OPPENNEER:

• Fun With Creative Shapes
Betsy demonstrates how to make dozens of shapes for breads, buns, and rolls. She presents dinner roll shapes including hard rolls, cloverleafs, knots, fantans, pretzels, and coils, plus hot dog and hamburger buns. This also features beautifully shaped breads including regular braids, double braids and multiple braids. Also includes instructions on making family favorites such as cinnamon rolls, Christmas trees and wreaths.
11-9576 45 min. $29.95

• How To Conquer Breadmaking
Master bread baking from the "Pied Piper" of breadbakers, Betsy Oppeneer, who travels the world over teaching and sharing her love of bread making. Learn techniques that are almost impossible to read and execute from books.
11-9575 45 min. $29.95

Chinese

ART OF CHINESE COOKING SERIES:

• Volume 1
Spring roll, wonton soup, deep fried wontons, moo goo gai pan, kung pao chicken, snow peas with shrimp, peeper steak, plum clouds.
11-167 58 min. $19.95

• Volume 2
Fried rice, quick chicken chow mein, Mandarin jade chicken, lobster Cantonese, crabmeat and asparagus, beef steak with scallops, prawns in lobster sauce, sweet and sour pork, Mongolian hot pot.
11-168 58 min. $19.95

Basic Chinese Cuisine
Recipes for spring rolls, wontons, egg fried rice, barbecued pork strips, sweet and sour sauce, hot and sour soup, vegetable stir-fry, fortune cookies.
11-153 30 min. $14.95

Chinese Cooking

With instructor Rosa Ross, you'll discover how to master Chinese utensils and the magnificent wok. Learn the secrets of perfect slicing, shredding, dicing and chipping; also the five cooking methods: stir-frying, deep-frying, steaming, red-stewing and poaching. Watch the step-by-step preparation of exotic foods from appetizers and soups to main courses and desserts. Hundreds of insider tips, plus a 192-page cookbook with over 220 recipes.
11-135 90 min. $39.95

Chinese Cooking Made Easy with Rocky Aoki

East meets West when Benihana's Rocky Aoki takes the mystery out of preparing great meals at home! His new quick and easy videos use no fancy ingredients or special cookware, and each meal takes only minutes to prepare.
11-2257 30 min. $14.95

Dim Sum

Miss Rhonda Yee, editor of Bon Appetit magazine, takes viewers through the complete preparation of exotic favorites of chinese cookery. She covers cooking methods that preserve vitamins and nutrients while offering the diner the savory flavor of the Far East.
11-228 60 min. $29.95

Flavors of China

Your getaway to the world's most fascinating culinary art! Master chef Titus Chan guides you through classic Chinese recipes you can prepare easily at home, using authentic Chinese ingredients and techniques.
11-198 119 min. $44.95

Guide to Chinese Cooking

Ken Hom, author of two books on Chinese cookery and an internationally acclaimed chef, shows you how to prepare a variety of delicious and easy-to-make Chinese dishes. You will learn the basic cooking techniques and ingredients that create authentic Chinese food.
11-001 87 min. $49.95

Wok on the Wild Side

Learn to "wok" a delicious seven-course Chinese meal. Stephen Yan, expert Chinese cook, starts out with mouth-watering prawns in a nest and proceeds to prepare a complete feast of gourmet dishes.
11-229 60 min. $19.95

Wok Before You Run

Expert Chinese Chef Yan brings his delightful cooking technique to this new video. He guides you step by step, from buying ingredients to seasoning your wok, making sauces, and actually cooking the complete meal.
11-120 60 min. $19.95

Creole/New Orleans

Basic New Orleans Cuisine

Recipes for sausage chicken gumbo, shrimp with remoulade sauce, black-eyed peas, trout pecan with meuniere sauce, muffuletta sandwich with olive salad, creme brule.
11-105 30 min. $14.95

CHEF PAUL PRUDHOMME'S LOUISIANA KITCHEN

In two companion volumes, Chef Paul takes us to Cajun country, to the Vieux Carre and into his kitchen. In a simple yet masterful demonstration, he shows how to prepare his legendary blackened redfish, jambalaya, chicken and andouille smoked sausage gumbo, bread pudding, mama's yeast rolls and Cajun popcorn.

• Volume 1
Complete Cajun meal featuring blackened redfish.
11-238 40 min. $19.95

• Volume 2
Cajun & Creole classics.
11-239 40 min. $19.95

GREAT CHEFS OF NEW ORLEANS SERIES:

Features the Chefs, their Restaurants and selection from their kitchens in this 13 volume series.

• Chris Kerageorgiou: La Provence
Fish paté, Noisettes D'Agneau, Salade D'Endives, Soufflé au Grand Marnier, Shrimp Saute St. Tropez, Quail "Roger Savaran" in Port Wine Sauce, Spring Salad, Gateau Saint-Honoré.
11-8096 60 min. $19.95

• Claude Aubert: Arnaud's Le Bec Fin
Saussarelle D'Escargots, Bourride a la Toulanaise, Salade de Laitue aux Noix, Tarte Aux Pommes a la Solognote, Oysters Bienville, Duck a L'Orange Soufflé Potatoes, Celery & Watercress Salad with Anchovy Dressing, Crêpes Soufflé.
11-8094 60 min. $19.95

• Daniel Bonnot: Louis XVI Eiffel Tower
Cream of Garlic Soup, Salade Tiede, Redfish en Croute Aux Deux Mousses, Paris Brest Crawfish

---

VIDEO TITLES LISTED IN THIS GUIDE ARE AVAILABLE FOR PURCHASE OR RENTAL. CONTACT YOUR LOCAL VIDEO STORE OR TELEPHONE (800) 383-8811

Beignets, Duck Confit, Potatoes Sarladaise, Pear Flan, Peppercorn Sauce, Strawberries Romanoff.
11-8090 60 min. $19.95

• **Gerard Crozier: Crozier's**
French Paté, French Onion Soup, Rabbit Chasseur, Ratatouille, Floating Island, Sea Scallop Appetizer, Asparagus with Homemade Mayonnaise, Chicken in Cream Sauce, Creme Caramel.
11-8100 60 min. $19.95

• **Gerhard Brill: Commander's Palace**
Artichoke & Oyster Soufflé, Shrimp Chippewa, Shrimp Fettuccine Tournedos Coliseum, Bread Pudding Soufflé, Sauté of Louisiana Crawfish, Oyster Marinière, Soft Shell Crab Choron, Pompano en Papillotte, Veal with Wild Mushrooms, Praline Soufflé Crêpes.
11-8091 60 min. $19.95

• **Goffredo Fraccaro: La Riviera**
Crabmeat Ravioli, Fried Calamari, Brociolone, Broccoli Italian Style, Custard Cups with Strega, Fettuccine Alla Goffredo, Scampi, Veal Piccata, Caponata Alla Sicilian, Rum Cake.
11-8093 60 min. $19.95

• **Gunter Preuss: Versailles**
Oysters Lafitte, Stuffed Cornish Game Hens, Potato Balls, Strawberry Crêpes, Bouillabaisse, Veal Steaks with Pink Peppercorns, Poached Pears.
11-8092 60 min. $19.95

• **Michel Marcais: Begue's**
Consommé des Ecrevisses Aux Truffles, Saumon en Paupiette au Beurre Blanc, Jambonnette et les Aiguillettes de Canard aux Myrilles, Patates Douces Dauphine, Salade Fromage, Pèche Royale dans son Panier Fleuri.
11-8089 60 min. $19.95

• **Michael Roussel: Brennan's**
Absinthe Suissesse, Oyster Soup, Eggs Hussarde, Eggs St. Charles, Eggs Sardou, Grillades and Grits, Bananas Foster.
11-8099 60 min. $19.95

• **Pierre LaCoste: Maison Pierre**
Paté Maison, Redfish Mousquetaire, Crown Rack of Veal, Strawberries & Cream. Gerard Thabuis: La Savoie Cold Cantaloupe Soup, Marinated Salmon Danish Style, Oysters La Savoie, Stuffed Flounder, Marquise au Chocolat.
11-8098 60 min. $19.95

• **Roland Hue: Christian's**
Mousseline of Redfish Nantua, Chicken Blackberry Vinegar, Profiteroles au Chocolat, Oysters Roland, Oyster Chowder, Smoked Redfish, French-Fried

Eggplant, Baked Alaska.
11-8097 60 min. $19.95

• **Warren LeRuth: Leruth's Restaurant**
Shrimp Remoulade Medallions of Pork Genoise with Amaretto & Chocolate, Oysters Belle Rive: Redfish a la Termereau Cassata Parfait Torte
11-8088 60 min. $19.95

• **Wong Brothers: Trey Yuen**
Hot and Sour Shrimp, Spring Rolls, Szechuan Spicy Beef, Kung Ming Shrimp, Whole Trout in Sweet and Sour Sauce, Beef with Watercress soup, Barbecued Ribs, Shrimp Kew, Lemon Chicken, Lobster in Black Bean Sauce.
11-8095 60 min. $19.95

New Orleans School of Cooking Workout Program
This is an exercise in Cajun and Creole cooking. The New Orleans School of cooking has been spreading the joys of Creole/Cajun food since 1980. Cooking instructor and New Orleans native Joe Cahn will teach you the basics "and then some" of his popular cuisine. His cooking exercises include gumbo, jambalaya, barbecued shrimp, blackened redfish, bananas foster and many more. This tape is highly instructional and hilariously entertaining.
11-194 75 min. $29.95

Desserts & Cake Decorating

Cake Decorating Easy as 1-2-3
Zella Junkin, director of the Wilton School, shows you the basics of cake decorating in simple terms. Learn baking and decorating techniques. This video shows you how to decorate five different cakes for fun entertaining.
11-2148 60 min. $24.95

Candy Making Easy as 1-2-3
Zella Junkin, director of the Wilton School, shows you how to make delicious candy with confectionery coating in this easy-to-follow video. Learn how to melt, mold, fill and roll candy and much more.
11-2147 80 min. $24.95

Cookies, Cakes, And Pies
In this program noted cookbook author and baking authority Rose Levy Beranbaum shows how to make a wide variety of delicious pastries as she

demonstrates the easy step-by-step preparation of such favorites as Downy Yellow Butter Cake, Orange Glow Chiffon Cake, Shortbread Cookies, Chocolate Butter Cake, Cherry Pie, Cordon Rose Cream Cheesecake, Apple Pie and more.
11-5148 90 min. $49.95

Guilt Free Brownies
Imagine enjoying chewy, moist and sweet brownies without the guilt of indulging in fatty calories! You'll learn all about the secrets of how to cook without fat or refined sugar as you add brownies to your menu of healthy foods. Dr. Rosenbaum also introduces the concept of fat and sugar triggers in our diets and how to overcome these threats to quality living. Recipe included.
11-8084 30 min. $29.95

Holiday Cookies and Treats
Recipes for pineapple bars, jewel bars, royal walnut crowns, yuletide cutouts, apricot fold-overs, coconut crisps, fudge nougats.
11-150 30 min. $14.95

Joy of Gingerbread Housemaking
Patti Hudson introduces you to a world in which houses are held together by icing and walkways are made of candy wafers and chocolate sprinkles. To the delight of everyone, the gingerbread family helps Patti demonstrate the art of building gingerbread houses, step by step.
11-253 70 min. $39.95

Judith Olney on Chocolate
For chocolate lovers everywhere-"the" complete guide to cooking and decorating with chocolate. You'll love the tantalizing recipes you'll see here, including how to make chocolate mousse, chocolate truffles and other imaginative and exotic chocolate creations.
11-072 60 min. $39.95

Magic of Gingerbread Houses
You too can build an elegant and truly beautiful gingerbread house. Included are demonstrated techniques that guarantee success for the first-time builder. Includes booklet.
11-8078 42 min. $16.99

Southern Desserts & Delights
Recipes for benne seed wafer cookies, chocolate mocha praline torte, pecan pralines, Williamsburg orange cake and lemon cheese pie.
11-179 30 min. $14.95

Sweet Satisfaction
Lynda Eggimann teaches you simple, easy tricks to create spectacular decorations. You'll learn how to ice your cake smoothly, master five basic borders and the tricks of cake writing neatly. Covers a

simple rainbow cake, rose buds and several scene cakes for children and adults. Themes include baby, bridal shower, birthday, sports and vacation. You also see a doll cake constructed and decorated and some simple piped figures being made. All instructions are given step-by-step for the beginner.
11-237 60 min. $29.95

Entertaining At Home

Art Of Dining
The Complete Guide on Dining Etiquette for Corporate Go Getters, Sales People, Professionals, Executive Housewives and anyone who entertains for business or social occasions. This guide will dramatically increase your social confidence when dining as a host or guest.
11-5396 60 min. $29.95

Candies, Champagne, & Romance
Recipes for tempura oysters, French mushroom soup, raspberry asparagus salad, rack of lamb with herb crust, broccoli with lemon curls and chocolate mousse tart.
11-174 30 min. $14.95

Cheers! Entertaining with Esquire
This is not just another cooking tape, but rather a fool-proof guide to entertaining at home with elegance. This program includes bar preparation, eye-catching table settings, four dinner party menus, dessert and after-dinner drink selections as well as party etiquette. A 24-page party planning booklet is included
11-246 40 min. $14.95

Chef Eric's Easy Guide to Holiday Cooking: Thanksgiving
Chef Eric will teach you the secrets behind preparing a delicious Thanksgiving dinner which will include:
Roast Turkey, Sage & Thyme Stuffing Mashed Potatoes, Spaghetti Squash, Cranberry-Orange Relish, Low-fat Pumpkin Pie.
11-8080 37 min. $24.95

Commonsense Hostess: New Party Secrets for the 90's.
A comprehensive guide to creative, hassle-free entertaining. Targeted for the economically-minded majority, it introduces viewers to the elegant alternatives to dining out at expensive restaurants. From deciding on a theme, through planning and organizing the entire party, this video covers every

---

VIDEO TITLES LISTED IN THIS GUIDE ARE AVAILABLE FOR PURCHASE OR RENTAL. CONTACT YOUR LOCAL VIDEO STORE OR TELEPHONE (800) 383-8811

thing. Plus the do's and don't's of being a success!
11-8122 30 min. $16.95

EVERYDAY GOURMET SERIES:

• Chocolate and Other Divine Desserts
You won't be able to resist this mouth-watering collection of luscious, easy-to-make dessert recipes.
11-2929 40 min. $14.95

• Easy and Elegant Holiday Dinner Party
Holiday entertaining has never been easier and more elegant thanks to Kathleen Perry, the everyday gourmet for all occasions. Mrs. Perry provides secrets to entertaining, including tips on table decorations, party "crowd control" and party preparations.
11-220 50 min. $19.95

• Family Gatherings and Celebrations
Now you can turn any family get-together into a gala celebration with easy-to-prepare foods and unique serving suggestions.
11-2033 60 min. $14.95

• Terrific Brunches for Two to Twenty
Whether you're planning an intimate meal for two or a brunch gathering for twenty, the sumptuous recipes on this video are prefect for the occasion.
11-2928 40 min. $14.95

• Winning Ways to Feed a Crowd
When you are having "the gang" over, you don"t want to miss all the fun by being stuck in the kitchen. By following the do ahead directions presented here, you don't have to.
11-2927 40 min. $14.95

Five Star Cooking
Discover Gourmet Cooking Secrets. Chef William Neal, America's hottest new chef, brings his outstanding cuisine into your home. This program is for the beginner as well as the expert and provides the ingredients for mastering the techniques of five star chefs around the world.Five Star Cooking Menu: miniature "BLTS", sweet golden pepper & garlic soup, pink grapefruit sorbet, wild mushroom and fontina cheese tartlet cheese puffs, and wine selections.
11-5316 50 min. $24.95

Guide To Dining Etiquette For Social & Business Occasions
We invite you to venture into the world of Etiquette training at the highest level. Includes: formal invitations, place settings, a complete seven course formal dinner, arranging and conducting a business luncheon, and hard to handle foods.
11-5655 60 min. $24.95

Guide to Entertaining
Host Beverly Sassoon, along with Beverly Hills Caterer, Randy Fuhrman show you that a great party doesn't have to cost a lot--it just requires imagination and preparation. This video offers a complete video manual for four great parties your guests will never forget!
11-8082 70 min. $24.95

Martha Stewart's Secrets for Entertaining: A Buffet Party
Follow Martha Stewart as she makes three tantalizing entrees, two tasty vegetable dishes and three desserts, then shows her lovely presentation for this festive feast.
11-2131 60 min. $24.95

Martha Stewart's Secrets for Entertaining: A Formal Dinner Party
Follow Martha Stewart into the kitchen to observe the preparation, and learn first hand about the tips and techniques for a successful formal dinner party-from salad to dessert.
11-2132 60 min. $24.95

Recipes for Brunch
Recipes for fruit shrub, marmalade walnut biscuits, Deer Creek french toast, glazed ham and pineapple rings, honey-oatmeal muffins, eggs a la king, buffet scrambled eggs, sausage balls with velvet gravy.
11-148 30 min. $14.95

Richard Sax: Secrets for Great Dinner Parties
Richard Sax shows you how to give great dinner parties with less anxiety and be able to spend more time with your guests by planning and cooking ahead. He gives you tips on what to prepare for both formal and informal dinner parties, as well as what recipes can be prepared ahead. He also shows you how to garnish. A must for anyone who would like to do more entertaining with less stress.
11-202 90 min. $29.95

Short-Order Gourmet
Esquire Magazine presents these cooking essentials for time-pressed professionals who still wish to enjoy the fun and rewards of cooking. Featuring Alice Waters (Chez Panisse) and Bradley Ogden (Campton Place), topics include techniques for sauteing, grilling, poaching, broiling and roasting; finding great kitchen equipment; getting all the elements of a meal to the table on time; and tips on how to give dinner parties, brunches and elegant picnics.
11-096 60 min. $29.95

Silver Palate Good Times Live
Good times, good food, good friends-it all comes together with ease and flair in this video. The

Silver Palate is more than food-it's a whole philosophy of entertaining. Recipes combine the finest ingredients with ease of preparation, so you can be out of the kitchen, mingling with the guests and enjoying the rave review.
11-1535 40 min. $19.95

Thanksgiving Dinner
Recipes for baked turkey, oyster dressing, apple pecan dressing, broccoli timbale, sweet potatoes with hot compote, scalloped potatoes, cranberry sauce, pastry shell, pumpkin tart, mincemeat pie.
11-110 30 min. $14.95

French & Continental

Craig Claiborne's New York Times Video Cook Book
Craig Claiborne demonstrates the preparation and presentation of over 20 recipes from his personal recipe collection, including: coquilles St. Jacques, soufflé, gravlax, chlodnik, guacamole, keema, mousse, pecan pie and cheesecake. Also includes a recipe booklet.
11-039 106 min. $29.95

JACQUES PEPIN'S GUIDE TO GOOD COOKING:

• **Chef's Secrets**
Jacques Pepin, formerly personal chef to three French presidents, is your host on this guide to the basics of cooking. Pepin, Gourmet magazine's resident columnist and author of best-sellers "La Methode" and "La Technique," offers a wide variety of time-and money-saving recipes, tips and techniques.
11-002 90 min. $49.95

• **Meat, Salads & Pastry**
In this third of the "Guide to Good Cooking" Series, this world renowned cooking teacher and author of cookbook classics, "La Methode" and "La Technique," shares a wealth of tips and techniques while preparing an abundance of mouth-watering recipes.
11-244 59 min. $39.95

• **Soup, Fish, Bread & Rice**
Renowned chef, author and teacher Jacques Pepin demonstrates a variety of delicious dishes while providing a wide range of insights into the art of preparing soups, fish, bread and rice.
11-204 72 min. $39.95

La Cuisine Pratique
Twenty delicious recipes that take about five minutes to prepare are demonstrated, including salads, Norwegian-style eggs, ham steak Viennese, Irish coffee and others.
11-073 60 min. $29.95

Master Cooking Course
Craig Claiborne and Pierre Franey leave the pages of the New York Times and come to life in this informative guide to gourmet cooking. See more than 100 actual techniques this famous culinary duo use to create tasteful and appealing foods of all kinds. You get to practice the recipes included with the guidance of real pros.
11-085 60 min. $24.95

Ingredients & Preservation Tips

Food Drying and Storage
Jack Jenkins, developer of the Equi-Flow Home Food Dehydrator, teaches you the techniques for drying foods by sun, oven and commercial home dryer.
11-062 52 min. $39.95

Game Processing
This video takes you through the most comprehensive instruction on processing game animals. It is hosted by professionals with over 30 years experience.
11-9587 90 min. $19.95

Garlic is as Good as Ten Mothers
An educational and entertaining video all about garlic and its history. Includes in-depth information on medicinal uses of the root and tips on cooking with garlic. With a jumping soundtrack of Cajun, French provincial, Flamenco, Swiss Italian, Moroccan and Mexican music.
11-063 55 min. $49.95

GREAT GARNISHES SERIES:
This three-part series is a "must" for the gourmet cook, food stylist or restaurateur serious about garnishing with fruits and vegetables.

• **Basics**
11-067 50 min. $39.95

• **Basics & Beyond**
11-068 50 min. $39.95

• **Advanced Course**
11-069 50 min. $39.95

Victory Garden Recipes: From the Garden to the Table
Marian Morash, who demonstrates vegetable cookery on the celebrated Victory Garden TV program, shares her favorite vegetable recipes. Starting with early spring vegetables, she takes you through the garden's seasons, showing you just how vegetable should look at their peak of ripeness, as well as sharing imaginative techniques for vegetable preparation.
16-053 90 min. $29.95

Italian & Pasta

All About Pasta
In this program, Giuliano Bugialli demonstrates a wide variety of classic Italian pasta preparation techniques while showing how to make many popular pasta dishes, including such favorites as Pasta alla Carbonara, Pasta alla Matriciana, Bigoli with Anchovy Sauce, Fazzoletti with Pesto Sauce, Cannelloni and much more.
11-8087 90 min. $49.95

Basic Italian Cuisine
Recipes for garlic bread, antipasto, stuffed mushrooms, minestrone, vegetable lasagna, beef lasagna, cheese-chocolate cannoli, almond cannoli.
11-106 30 min. $14.95

COMEDY COOKING SERIES:
Featuring Dom DeLuise. Based on Dom's best-selling cookbook.

• **Eat This - The Video: Volume I**
Dom takes you to Brooklyn, to "Mamma's house" where he and his loving mother prepare traditional Italian recipes. Anyone who loves to cook, eat or laugh will want this video for their very own.
11-6265 55 min. $19.95

• **Eat This - The Video: Volume II**
Featuring Dom DeLuise. Dom invites his Hollywood friends Carl Reiner, Dean Martin, Carol Burnett, and Burt Reynolds to ham it up in his kitchen. Dom's zany style of cooking will keep you laughing even while you're washing the pots.
11-6266 40 min. $19.95

• **Eat This - The Video: Volume III**
Featuring Dom DeLuise. Dom adds another dimension to his comedy cooking series when he

and his family prepare a seafood feast at their Malibu beach house. Mostly Italian recipes.
11-6267 35 min. $19.95

• **Eat This - The Video: Volume IV**
Featuring Dom DeLuise. Dom takes you to New York where Dom grew up to savor the tasty flavors of the Big Apple. Italian recipes and a cooking tour of this wonderful city.
11-6268 46 min. $19.95

Guide to Italian Cooking
Giuliano Bugialli, author, chef and 1984 Tastemakers Award winner, is your host on this video-guide to the basics of great Italian cooking. He takes you step-by-step through the preparation of a variety of delightful Italian dishes.
11-003 104 min. $49.95

Italian Cooking for a Healthy Heart
Join Nurse Joanne D'Agostino as she prepares low fat & cholesterol recipes for the Italian dish and dessert lover.
11-8077 58 min. $19.95

Pasta, Pasta, Pasta
Recipes for buttered ribbons, fettucini Alfredo, garden pasta, tortellini en broada, cannelloni with veal and spinach cannelloni with sausage and cheese, chicken with pasta.
11-104 30 min. $14.95

ROMAGNOLI ITALIAN COOKING SERIES:

• **Volumes 1 and 2**
Includes homemade pasta; ravioli filling; basic tomato sauce; fettucini with tomato and basil sauce; vermicelli with clam sauce; linguini with crabmeat; tomato, mussel and squid sauce; fettucini with peas and salmon; and crêpes with tomato and basil sauce.
11-254 60 min. $29.95

• **Volumes 3 and 4**
Includes basic meat sauce; Bologna meat sauce; lasagna alla Bolognese; white sauce; spaghetti alla carbonara; tomato, chicken giblet and mushroom sauce; basic tomato sauce; garlic, oil and hot pepper sauce; rich rigatoni with parsley; hot tomato sauce with penne; fettucini alla Romagnoli; tonnarelli with lemon and vodka sauce; fettucini with caviar; and fettucini with truffles and gorgonzola.
11-255 60 min. $29.95

Taste of Italy
In this video Giuliano Bugialli, renowned master of Italian cooking, takes the viewer on a gastronomic tour of his country as he demonstrates the step-by-

step preparation of such dishes as Duck with Capers, Stuffed Chicken Drumsticks, Chicken/Veal Galantine Sausage, Veal Scaloppine with Lemon Sauce, Fried Calamari and more. With his help you can delight your friends with gourmet Italian specialties.
11-8086 80 min. $44.95

Japanese

Japanese Sushi Made Easy with Rocky Aoki
11-2259 30 min. $16.95

Simply Sushi
Welcome to the sushi experience. This video reveals the many sushi styles and variations. You'll learn all about sushi history, traditions, preparation and presentation, cutting techniques and more. Join Rocky Aoki for this unique eating experience.
11-1928 60 min. $19.95

Sushi At Home
A very simple, basic instruction on how to prepare sushi, from preparation of the rice to the proper cutting of the fish.
11-191 40 min. $29.95

Mexican

Basic Mexican Cuisine
Recipes for guacamole, tortilla chips, chile con queso, flan, Mexican rice, chile rellenos and enchiladas.
11-172 30 min. $14.95

Guide to Tex-Mex Cooking
Learn the secrets to preparing authentic Tex-Mex chow from expert Jane Butel (author of "Chili Madness" and many other Tex-Mex cookbooks.) She will show you many mouth-watering recipes, including all the basic techniques that are needed to create outstanding Tex-Mex dishes.
11-004 85 min. $39.95

Microwave Cooking

Microwave Cooking
Award-winning book and cassette format. Comprehensive course on this modern cooking method for today's busy homemaker. Free cookbook with over 200 recipes. Starring best-selling author and TV personality Pat Hutt.
11-240 60 min. $34.95

Microwave Miracles
Recipes for bran muffins, scrambled brunch special, broccoli in cheese sauce, seashore dip, gingered meatballs, fiesta chicken, dill salmon, pineapple upside down cake.
11-176 30 min. $14.95

Microwaving Secrets
This is your introduction to the world of modern microwave cooking. We've taken the mystery out and replaced it with reliable information to help anyone who cooks. You'll learn how microwaves work, how to use covers and wraps for more even cooking, defrosting, browning, and how to use your conventional oven in combination with microwave. Successful use of temperature probes and varied power settings make complicated dishes easy to prepare with more confidence and in less time.
11-252 30 min. $39.95

One-Minute Cook: Microwave Made Easy
Your guide is best-selling author, B. Harris. High-tech cooking made fast, easy and delicious using your microwave.
11-086 42 min. $24.95

Yes! You Can Microwave
Donovan Jon Fandre hosts this common sense guide to the basics of microwave cooking. Learn the unique cooking techniques that will make your microwave the best investment you've ever made. Made-simple recipes are shown and reinforced by the cookbook that comes with the tape.
11-133 60 min. $29.95

Vietnamese Cuisine

VIDEO TITLES LISTED IN THIS GUIDE ARE AVAILABLE FOR PURCHASE OR RENTAL. CONTACT YOUR LOCAL VIDEO STORE OR TELEPHONE (800) 383-8811

GOURMET VIETNAMESE CUISINE SERIES:
Don't miss the opportunity to learn the secrets for preparing one of the world's greatest and most sophisticated cuisines. Learn as three star chef Rosalie Nguyen demonstrates step-by-step on each video, her own methods for preparing six delicious recipes.

• Part I
This video features Soup of the Chef, Vietnamese Famous Spring Rolls, Crispy Noodles, Butterfly Shrimps a La Vietnames Grilled Chicken with Curry Indochine Fried Rice.
11-8015 60 min. $29.95

• Part II
This video features Asparagus Soup with Crab, Salade De Fruits De Mer, Ravioli A La Vietnamese Chicken in Eight Delights, Grilled Beef Sate, Special Rice In Earthen Pot.
11-8016 60 min. $29.95

• Part III
Mixed Vegetable Soup with Shrimp, Soft Shell Crab with Sweet and Sour Sauce, Grilled Chicken with Fresh Lime, Rice Noodle Sautee with Vegetable, Shrimp and Pork Grilled Filet of Swordfish.
11-8017 60 min. $29.95

Wines & Spirits

Basics of Bartending
The California School of Bartending presents the basics of bartending for business or home entertaining. Chapters on party planning, champagne and wine, drink mixing, cappucino and much more. Bartending schools will charge $450 for this information.
11-021 60 min. $44.95

California Wines: The Red Varietals
In this program, you'll meet the mighty Cabernet Sauvignon; you'll explore the velvety smoothness of Merlot; you'll learn what gave Pinot Noir its softness. Then you'll delight in the festive simplicity of Gamay Beaujolais, the zestiness of Zinfandel, and the spicy depths of Petite Sirah. You'll learn all about them from the men who make them, and you'll know what to expect, and how to select...in any situation.
11-268 60 min. $14.95

California Wines: The White Varietals
From Chardonnay, to Sauvignon Blanc, to Chenin Blanc, you'll become intimately familiar with three of the most popular white varietal wines of California. Then you'll explore their more aggressive cousins: the intense Johannesburg Riesling, Gerwurztraminer, and French Colombard. And when you're through, you'll know how to "read" their colors, how to chill and serve them, and much more.
11-269 60 min. $14.95

Celebrity Guide To Wine
Hosted by international wine expert and Spago restaurant maitre d'Bernard Erpicum. Starring Whoopi Goldberg, Shelley Hack, Herbie Hancock, Kelly LeBrock, Robert Loggia, Dudley Moore, Steven Seagal, and Peter Weller. A fun, indispensable guide for everyone who owns a corkscrew.
11-6773 58 min. $19.95

Cooking With Wine
In this informative-and hilarious-collection of wine cookery recipes and anecdotes, John Pearse introduces us to dishes which he has collected over a concert career spanning thirty years and as many countries.
11-2889 60 min. $39.95

Enjoying Beer
Join Ray Mancini, Bill Saluga and Wolfgang Puck and learn everything you ever wanted to know about Beer, the history, the different types of Beer and what dishes go best with Beer. Also included are a bevy of "Boom Boom" Mancini's favorites, the Knockout Girls, who know how to hug and chug.
11-9357 35 min. $16.95

Homebrew Video Guide
This video is designed to take the novice beer maker through each step of beer making logically and comfortably. After watching this video you'll be able to brew a great tasting beer the very first time!
11-8183 41 min. $24.95

Homebrewing: An Introduction
Join Joe Sincuk as he shows you the equipment, the various ingredients and discusses the types of brew he prefers. Then he takes you through each step of the homebrewing process and lists phone numbers and addresses for businesses that sell home-brewing products.
11-8074 63 min. $19.95

Hugh Johnson's How to Enjoy Wine
From the world's foremost wine authority, Hugh Johnson, a fascinating video cassette that will help

turn any wine drinker into a true connoisseur.
11-071 60 min. $19.95

Joe the Bartender
Earn extra income Bartending, or be a great host at your next party. Learn the "ins" and "outs" of tending bar without spending the money for Bartending School. This easy, step-by-step video makes Bartending easy and fun.
11-8014 40 min. $19.95

Legends Of Napa Valley
California's serene and fertile Napa Valley produces wines of world-class stature. With host Adam Bronfman, you can now visit the distinguished men and women who produce these legendary vintages. Share the romance and secrets of America's finest winemakers.
11-5618 70 min. $14.95

Making Fine Fruit Wine at Home
In this program, James Barry, owner of the award winning Dover Winery located in upstate New York, demystifies the winemaking process while showing you how to create a wide variety of wines with fruit of your own choosing--all easily made in your own kitchen with readily available ingredients.
11-8085 45 min. $34.95

Video Guide To Homebrewing
Premium beer has been made in the home of centuries. Today, with the knowledge and materials available, homebrewing is easy as well as rewarding. You'll be able to treat yourself and your friends to a premium beverage as old as history itself.
11-267 47 min. $39.95

Video Wine Guide with Dick Cavett
Dick Cavett is your host for this informative program on the world of wine. Tour the wine-growing regions of the world-France, Italy, Germany and California-and see how wine is made; learn the how and why of wine tasting from renowned wine grower and author Alexis Lichine. Finally, you can join Cavett and critic Harvey Steiman in a series of wine tastings that includes explanations of the best food-wine marriages.
11-111 90 min. $39.95

Wine Advisor
Esquire Magazine has created this video for anyone who loves wine but has felt either intimidated of frustrated and confused by the incredible variety of wines available. Highlights include advice on serving, tasting and storing wines; deciphering European wine labels; how to get the best value for the price; and how to creatively combine wines with food.
11-118 60 min. $29.95

Wines of California
A stunning program, accompanied by William I. Kaufman's award-winning book, "The Pocket Encyclopedia of California Wine." Beautifully packaged as an heirloom book-and-video set.
11-119 240 min. $49.95

Wine Pure & Simple
This video demystifies the world of selecting, buying and enjoying wine. Join host Bob Bellus and Master Sommelier Fred Dame as they prove you don't need to be a connoisseur to enjoy wine.
11-5881 50 min. $24.95

Miscellaneous

American Barbecue & Grilling
American Barbecue and Grilling will help you excel, as you learn about meats, marinades and sauces; woods, chips and briquets; grills, grill positions and utensils.
11-5065 30 min. $29.95

Art of Napkin Folding
Learn how to fold napkins into 23 shapes that transform simple place settings into very special ones. Designs are divided into easy-to-make and a little harder.
11-9651 34 min. $24.95

Art of New York Deli Cooking with Abe Lebewohl
Acclaimed delicatessen cooking authority Abe Lebewohl, owner of the Second Avenue Deli on New York's Lower East Side, guides you in the step-by-step preparation of many authentic deli favorites.
11-2414 52 min. $29.95

Basic Middle Eastern Cuisine
Recipes for spinach salad with pomegranate, homos bi Tahiti, rice-orzo dressing, stuffed eggplant, stuffed kibbeh, grape leaf rolls and bablava rolls.
11-173 30 min. $14.95

Black Hat Chef/Chef Rene
Renowned Chef Rene shares secrets of the world's finest chefs while preparing two mouth-watering french meals, using veal and chicken.
11-8075 55 min. $19.95

BON APPETIT: TOO BUSY TO COOK?
Shortcuts, tips, cooking demonstrations,

suggestions for table settings, wine suggestions and knowledge, theme menus, bonus recipe cards with shopping lists, bonus wine and food pairing guide.

• **Easy Entertaining**
11-264 60 min. $19.95

• **Festive Desserts**
11-266 60 min. $19.95

• **Light and Fresh Cooking**
11-265 60 min. $19.95

• **Weeknight Inspirations**
11-263 60 min. $19.95

CELEBRITY CHEFS: COOKING WITH YOUR FAVORITE STARS

• **Volume 1**
Enjoy the humorous play between host Robert Morley and his star "chefs" while you learn the stars' secrets for preparing these luscious celebrity recipes for your own friends.
11-2517 60 min. $24.95

• **Volume 2**
Eight new stars join host Robert Morley in this second volume of the series.
11-1836 60 min. $24.95

CHEF TELL'S CARIBBEAN CUISINE SERIES:
Demonstrates how to prepare exotic Caribbean dishes quickly and easily in your own kitchen. Volumes 1 and 2 offer you a total of sixteen dishes -that are quick and easy to prepare in your own kitchen.

• **Volume 1**
11-2093 27 min. $24.95

• **Volume 2**
11-2092 27 min. $24.95

Convertible Cooking for a Healthy Heart
Learn how any recipe can become a healthy gourmet treat with almost no change in taste.
11-8076 60 min. $19.95

COOKING AT THE ACADEMY SERIES:
From poaching to pasta, chocolate to charcuterie, you'll see close-up demonstrations by chefs of the renowned San Francisco Culinary Academy in this acclaimed 13 part series.

• **Braising & Stewing**
11-8008 30 min. $19.95

• **Candy & Chocolate**
11-8009 30 min. $19.95

• **Charcuterie, Sausage, Paté**
11-8011 30 min. $19.95

• **Desserts**
11-8001 30 min. $19.95

• **Frying**
11-8010 30 min. $19.95

• **Grilling**
11-8002 30 min. $19.95

• **Ice Cream & Frozen Desserts**
11-8005 30 min. $19.95

• **Lighter Cuisine**
11-8012 30 min. $19.95

• **Pasta**
11-8003 30 min. $19.95

• **Poaching & Steaming**
11-8004 30 min. $19.95

• **Sauteing**
11-8000 30 min. $19.95

• **Soups**
11-8007 30 min. $19.95

• **Stocks & Sauces**
11-8006 30 min. $19.95

Cooking with Beefcake
Join Bernice and her bare-bottomed beefcake boys on a collision course with chaos in the kitchen. Together they cook up meals for six different special occasions, featuring selections from Carlos and Charlie's, Jimmy's Spago, the Beverly Wilshire Hotel, the White House and many more. Cooking was never like this!
11-250 60 min. $39.95

Cooking with Beefcake, Too!
Join Jaye P. Morgan and her saucy kitchen helpers as they prepare dishes from such world-class restaurants as Trumps, Bon Appetit and Le Dome.
11-2622 69 min. $39.95

Cooking with Country Music Stars
Down home dishes, created by your favorite personalities. Country cooking with country music

VIDEO TITLES LISTED IN THIS GUIDE ARE AVAILABLE FOR PURCHASE OR RENTAL. CONTACT YOUR LOCAL VIDEO STORE OR TELEPHONE (800) 383-8811

stars. Entertainment and information with each star sharing their favorite recipe.
11-1689 60 min. $19.95

Delicious Dishes To Go
Recipes for no-cook tabbouleh, fruited cheese packets, fruit and nut spread, vegetable medley, molasses muffins, Scotch eggs, deluxe peanut butter, chicken salad surprise, classic potato salad.
11-152 28 min. $14.95

Food Processor Video Cookbook
Jane Freiman, award-winning cookbook author and authority on food processor cooking techniques, reveals creative new ways to use a processor to quickly prepare a wide variety of delicious dishes.
11-1763 86 min. $39.95

Fold-Along Napkin Art
Learn to fold cloth or paper napkins into 47 dramatic sculptures, including eight charming animal characters.
11-9650 86 min. $39.95

Four Seasons Spa Cuisine Video Cookbook with Seppi Renggli
Chef Seppi Renggli of the famed Four Seasons restaurant in New York City demonstrates the preparation of various delicious dishes that are high in nutritional value yet low in fat, sodium and calories. This program is a result of over two years' collaboration between Chef Renggli and Dr. Myron Winick, professor of nutrition and director of the institute of Human Nutrition at Columbia University College of Physicians and Surgeons.
11-203 53 min. $39.95

Fun Meals for Kids
Recipes for blueberry muffins, chili con carne, macaroni and cheese, baked eggs and cheese, miniature pizzas, corn chow chili.
11-8026 30 min. $16.95

FRUGAL GOURMET COLLECTION:

Appetizers

- **First Courses and Wine**
11-8023 30 min. $16.95

- **Hors d'Oeuvres Buffet**
11-8021 30 min. $16.95

- **Tapas Buffet**
11-8022 30 min. $16.95

Soups & Salads

- **Chili**
11-8026 30 min. $16.95

- **Whole-Meal Salads**
11-8024 30 min. $16.95

- **Whole-Meal Soups**
11-8025 30 min. $16.95

Cheese & Eggs

- **Classic Omelet**
11-8029 30 min. $16.95

- **Quiche**
11-8028 30 min. $16.95

- **Yogurt and Cheese: Make Your Own**
11-8027 30 min. $16.95

Breads

- **Bread**
11-8032 30 min. $16.95

- **French & Italian Breads**
11-8030 30 min. $16.95

- **Sourdough**
11-8031 30 min. $16.95

Pasta & Rice

- **Addictive Pastas**
11-8034 30 min. $16.95

- **Pasta Buffet**
11-8035 30 min. $16.95

- **Rice**
11-8036 30 min. $16.95

Fruits & Vegetable

- **Apples**
11-8039 30 min. $16.95

- **Gracious Tomato**
11-8037 30 min. $16.95

- **Vegetables with Class**
11-8038 30 min. $16.95

VIDEO TITLES LISTED IN THIS GUIDE ARE AVAILABLE FOR PURCHASE OR RENTAL. CONTACT YOUR LOCAL VIDEO STORE OR TELEPHONE (800) 383-8811

Meats & Poultry

• Classic Beef Dishes
11-5040 30 min. $19.95

• Fancy Chicken Dishes
11-5041 30 min. $19.95

• Turkey
11-5042 30 min. $19.95

Fish & Seafood

• Clams
11-8044 30 min. $19.95

• Fish with a Flair
11-8043 30 min. $19.95

• Seafood and Wine
11-8045 30 min. $19.95

Sauces & Seasonings

• Garlic! Garlic! Garlic!
11-8046 30 min. $19.95

• Meat Marinades
11-8048 30 min. $16.95

• Sauces From Wine
11-8047 30 min. $16.95

Desserts

• Desserts
11-8051 30 min. $16.95

• Dine and Dessert
11-8050 30 min. $16.95

• Sherbets and Ice Creams
11-8049 30 min. $16.95

American Regional & Historical

• Barbecue, Southern Style
11-8052 30 min. $16.95

• New England
11-8053 30 min. $16.95

• Pacific Northwest
11-8054 30 min. $16.95

European Cuisines

• Edible Italian History
11-8057 30 min. $16.95

• French Kitchen
11-8056 30 min. $16.95

• Polish Kitchen
11-8055 30 min. $16.95

Middle Eastern & African

• Dishes of Africa
11-8059 30 min. $16.95

• Foods from Greece
11-8058 30 min. $16.95

• Lebanon
11-8060 30 min. $16.95

Far East Cuisines

• Dim Sum
11-8063 30 min. $16.95

• Hunan Treasures
11-8061 30 min. $16.95

• Japanese Kitchen
11-8062 30 min. $16.95

Entertaining at Home

• Molded Meal
11-8065 30 min. $16.95

• Sandwich Buffet
11-8064 30 min. $16.95

• Stand-Up Buffet
11-8066 30 min. $16.95

Cooking Methods

• Ancient Method of Steaming
11-8068 30 min. $16.95

• Cooking in Paper
11-8067 30 min. $16.95

• Grilling
11-8069 30 min. $16.95

VIDEO TITLES LISTED IN THIS GUIDE ARE AVAILABLE FOR PURCHASE
OR RENTAL. CONTACT YOUR LOCAL VIDEO STORE OR TELEPHONE (800) 383-8811

Potpourri

- **Coffee for Entertaining**
11-8071 30 min. $16.95

- **Firefighter Cooks**
11-8072 30 min. $16.95

- **Low Salt/Low-Fat Cooking**
11-8070 30 min. $16.95

GREAT CHEFS: A SHOW FOR ALL SEASONS SERIES:

- **Chocolate Edition**
Eight Great Chefs from Detroit, Chicago, New Orleans, Houston, Santa Fe, and San Francisco continue the love affair with chocolate.
11-8113 60 min. $19.95

- **Desserts**
Twelve of the finest chefs in America prepare their best desserts and show you how to make them yourself in your own kitchen.
11-8116 60 min. $19.95

- **Great Chefs: Great Bar-B-Q**
Narrated by Tennessee Ernie Ford. Barbecue hot spots, restaurants, cook-offs and contests, including Memphis in May. Many secret recipes for barbecue and much more.
11-8118 60 min. $19.95

- **Great Southern Barbecue: Grand Tour**
Country Western balladeer Tom T. Hall takes the viewer on a 4,000 mile trip through nine southern states, sampling the hottest restaurants and cooks in the barbecue belt. The musical track features Bela Fleck and His Bluegrass Band, Bill Monroe, Toots Thielemans and Charlie Byrd.
11-8117 60 min. $19.95

- **Great Southern Barbecue: Grand Tour**
Country Western balladeer Tom T. Hall takes the viewer on a 4,000 mile trip through nine southern states, sampling the hottest restaurants and cooks in the barbecue belt. The musical track features Bela Fleck and His Bluegrass Band, Bill Monroe, Toots Thielemans and Charlie Byrd.
11-8117 60 min. $19.95

- **International Holiday Table**
Share with ten international chefs a favorite holiday dish they remember as children in their homeland. France, England, Germany, Portugal and Cajun country are included.
11-8121 60 min. $19.95

- **New Orleans Jazz Brunch**
Narrated by famous jazz trumpeter Al Hirt. An entertaining look at the New Orleans tradition of brunches. Historical footage, rare interviews and over 20 on-camera recipes.
11-8114 60 min. $19.95

- **Seafood Sampler**
Great Seafood dishes from Great Chefs around the country including BBQ Shrimp and the first, exclusive, inside visit of the world famous 80-year-old Bozo's Seafood in New Orleans.
11-8115 60 min. $19.95

- **Southwest Thanksgiving Feast**
Featuring seven southwest chefs who prepare nine dishes for a complete menu that celebrates the traditional celebration, but in new ways, including: Sweet Potato Bisque with Avocado, Pear and Lime; Roast Wild Turkey; Maple-Pecan Sweet Potato Pie and Pumpkin-Chocolate Cheesecake.
11-8120 60 min. $19.95

- **Texas BBQ**
Features a tour of the Hill Country, including the Y.O. Ranch and Onion Creek Lodge, The Salt Lick in Driftwood, Kreuz's Market in Lockhart and Las Canarias in San Antonio.
11-8119 60 min. $19.95

GREAT CHEFS OF CHICAGO:

- **Carolyn Buster: The Cottage**
Features Smoked Duck, Sea Scallops in Spinach Leaves, Schnitzel, Raspberry Cake and Chocolate Rum Terrine. Michael Foley/Printers Row Features Wild Mushrooms flavored with Pine Needles, New York Duck Liver Terrine, Fluke and Daikon, Veal Done 6 ways, Macaroon Mocha Buttercream Cake.
11-8101 60 min. $19.95

- **Jean Banchet: Le Francais**
Features Squab Salad with Wild Mushrooms and Quail Eggs, Lobster with Noodles, Basil and Caviar, Roast Sweetbreads with Belgian Endives and Truffles, Noisette of Venison with Grand-Veneur Sauce, Raspberry Feuillete, Grand Marnier Soufflé. Roland Liccioni: Carlos' Flan de Foie Gras, Ravioli of Langoustine, Assiette of Squab with Wild Mushrooms, Night and Day Cake.
11-8104 60 min. $19.95

- **John Draz: Winnetka Grill**
Features Grilled Oysters with Smoked Ham and Fried Parsley, Butternut Squash, Ravioli with Cream and Asiago Cheese Mesquite Roast Loin of Pork with Apple and Corn-bread stuffing, Chocolate and Bourbon Peach Cake. Bernard Cretier: Le Vichyssois Seafood Pâte in Basil Sauce,

VIDEO TITLES LISTED IN THIS GUIDE ARE AVAILABLE FOR PURCHASE OR RENTAL. CONTACT YOUR LOCAL VIDEO STORE OR TELEPHONE (800) 383-8811

Salmon Baked in Puff Pastry, Tarte au Chocolat.
11-8103 60 min. $19.95

• **Pierre Pollin: Le Titi De Paris**
Features Sausage of Spinach Noodles, Saddle of
Lamb with Filet of Beef, Progres with Two
Chocolate Mousses, Pear Soufflé. Lamb Cake,
Warm Apple Tart.
11-8102 60 min. $19.95

• **Thierry Lefeuvre: Froggy's**
Features Seafood and Herb Sausage, Lobster in
Vanilla Sauce, Belgian Endive Salad with Sweet
Onion Confit, Breast of Duck with Green
Peppercorn Sauce, Lemon Mousse in pastry shell.
Lucien Verge: L'escargot Snail Torte Country
Style, Medallions of Venison with truffled Potatoes,
Dessert in all Simplicity, Pear Crêpes.
11-8105 60 min. $19.95

• **Yoshi Katsumura: Yoshi's**
Hot Duck Pâte in Puff Pastry, Dover Sole with
Scallop Mousse and Medallions of Lobster, Roast
Breast of Pheasant stuffed with Pheasant Mousse
and Foie Gras, Green Tea Ice Cream. Jackie
Etcheber: Jackie's Filo Nest with Exotic
Mushrooms, hot seafood salad, Striped Sea Bass
with Shrimp, Avocado and Peppers, Quail and
Duck with Radicchio, Mache and Green
Peppercorn Sauce, Chocolate bag filled with White
Chocolate Mousse.
11-8106 60 min. $19.95

GREAT CHEFS OF SAN FRANCISCO:

• **Bruce Le Fabour: Rose et Le Fabour**
Vegetable soup, Salmon with Asparagus Sauce,
Bombay Madness, Ann Kathleen Mckay's
Strawberry Cake a la Dacquoise. Also includes,
Rene Verdon: Le Trianon-Mousseline of Scallops
and Salmon, Chicken with Pink and Green
Peppercorn Gateau Nancy.
11-8107 60 min. $19.95

• **Christian Iser: Fournou's Oven**
Cassolette of Langoustine, Rack of Lamb with
Herb Sauce Salad, Cinnamon Peach Tart, Bread
Pudding. Barbara Tropp: China Moon-Steamed
Shao-Mai Dumplings with Young Ginger, Shrimp
and Crab Toast on French Baguettes with Fresh
Plum Sauce, Chicken with Hunan , Pan-Fried
Noodle Pillow with Stir-fried Chinese Greens and
Garlic, Mandarin Orange Tart.
11-8110 60 min. $19.95

• **Jeremiah Tower: Santa Fe Bar/Grill**
Santa Fe Black Bean Cake, Poached Fish with
Tomatoes and purple basil. Spit Roasted Sucking
Pig with Santa Fe Baby Garden Vegetables, etc.,
Masataka Kobayashi: Masa's-Green Pasta with
Tomato Sauce and Basil, Pasta with Cream Truffle

sauce & mushrooms, Medallions of Veal with
Sauce Nantua and Wine Butter Sauce, Baby Salmon
Stuffed with Caviar, White Chocolate Mousse in an
Almond Cookie Shell.
11-8108 60 min. $19.95

• **Mark Miller: 4th St. Grill**
Scallops Cerviche, Pepper Oysters, Swordfish,
Oysters with Lime-Chili Sauce, Yucatan Seafood
Stew, Mango Sorbet. Roberto Gerometta: Chez
Michel Mousseline of Frog Legs with Pasta,
Stuffed Leg of Duck with Red Wine Sauce, Progres
with Grand Marnier.
11-8112 60 min. $19.95

• **Max Schacher: Le Coquelicot**
Mousse of Duck Liver, Oysters Souvenir De
Tahaa, Saddle of Rabbit with Leeks
and Rosemary, Walnut Pie a la mode.
Jacky Robert: Ernie's-Shrimp Stuffed Ravioli with
Basil Sauce, Braised Squab in a Mold of
Vegetables, Gratin of Strawberries.
11-8109 60 min. $19.95

• **Udo Nechutnys: Miramonte**
Mousse of Poultry Liver, Salmon, Duck
Miraminte, Figs in Cabernet with Almond Ice
Cream, Egg Snowball. Werner Albrecht: French
Room Crayfish and Poached Quail, Eggs Salad
with truffle Vinaigrette, Cheese Pasta Roll with
Tomato Sauce, Rabbit with Apricots in Cabernet
Sauce, Hippennase.
11-8111 60 min. $19.95

GREAT CHEFS OF THE WEST HOME VIDEOS:

• **Volume 1**
Blue Corn Blini, Rabbit with Apple Cider, Ibarra
Chocolate Cake, Ranch Beans, Warm Lobster
Tacos, and many more.
11-6874 60 min. $19.95

• **Volume 2**
Peach Mousse, Chiles Rellenos, Goat Cheese
Rellenos, Egg White Rellenos, Refried Beans,
Barbecued Pork, and many more.
11-6875 60 min. $19.95

• **Volume 3**
Jalapeno Pasta & Sausage, Pork Tenderloin, Pashka
Mousse, Green Corn Tamales, Grilled Sea Bass,
Salzburg Nockerel, and many more.
11-6876 60 min. $19.95

• **Volume 4**
Spicy Gulf Shrimp, Fresh Berry Mousse, Lazy
Man's Peach Cobbler, Crab Balls, Chicken

Gonzalez, Chocolate Banana Cake, and more.
11-6877 60 min. $19.95

• **Volume 5**
Wild Rice Pancakes with Chicken, Lamb Loin, White Chocolate Ravioli, Fried Chicken, Salmon Pasta, and many more.
11-6879 60 min. $19.95

• **Volume 6**
Assorted hors d'oeuvres, Grilled California Chicken, Cuervo Biscochitos, Nuevo Biscochitos, Traditional Mexican, and many more.
11-6878 60 min. $19.95

• **Volume 7**
Guacamole, Grilled Squab, Mocha Framboise, Southern Fried Chicken, Avocado Shrimp Terrine, Duck Chili, Orange Zabaglione, and many more.
11-6880 60 min. $19.95

• **Volume 8**
Escargot Sombreros, Grilled Quail, Baked Peaches, Grilled Chicken Breasts, Corn Pasta Ravioli, Texas Rabbit, and many more.
11-6881 60 min. $19.95

• **Volume 9**
Sweet Potato Bisque, Pork Tenderloin, Chestnut Royal, Grand Prize Chili, Corn Fritters, Pheasant San Xavier, and many more.
11-6882 60 min. $19.95

• **Volume 10**
Cornmeal Pizza, Lamb Sausage, Chocolate Cream Pie, Home Style Biscuits, Texas Barbecue, Brisket & Ribs, and many more.
11-6883 60 min. $19.95

• **Volume 11**
Wild Mushroom Gratin, Border Grill, Catfish Mousse, Chicken Pueblo, Chocolate Roulade, Barbecue Sauce, and many more.
11-6884 60 min. $19.95

• **Volume 12**
Enchilada Filet Mignon, Rabbit Gumbo, Sweet Potato Pie, Tamales, Wild Game Terrine, Turkey Breast, and many more.
11-6885 60 min. $19.95

• **Volume 13**
Stuffed Prawns, Roasted Veal Rack, Rice Pudding, Quesadillas, Sweet Potato Tortellini, Sonoran Seafood Stew, and many more.
11-6886 60 min. $19.95

GOURMET MENUS:
No special talent is needed to prepare these sensational meals. Just follow the simple step-by-step instructions of Etta Sawyer, director of the Academy of Culinary Arts, and become an instant gourmet chef. Recipe card included.

• **Gazpacho/Paella/Chocolate Roulade**
11-259 30 min. $14.95

• **Salad Fruits/Chicken Florentine/Apple Charlotte**
11-260 30 min. $14.95

• **Zucchini Soup/Veal Ferdinand/Crêpes Margit**
11-261 30 min. $14.95

Healthier Cooking For Time-Pressed People
Chef Trainor demonstrates healthier cooking and will teach you how you can prepare delicious, healthier meals that take less than fifteen minutes to make.
11-5635 30 min. $16.95

Healthy Cooking By Melissa Ann Homann
New York Chef Melissa Homann makes an unusual yet healthy, low-cholesterol meal using ingredients found at the average green grocer and supermarket. Tasty soup, salad, grilled vegetables, and a delicious fish dish are prepared with a full ingredient list and instruction.
11-5397 30 min. $19.95

Hearty New England Dinners
Recipes for Boston brown bread, squash with pecans, boiled lobster, Camden fish chowder, New England boiled dinner and apple pandowdy.
11-175 30 min. $14.95

Holiday Gifts From Your Kitchen
Recipes for stollen, hot spiced tea, candied orange peel, fruitcake, chocolate pretzels, bourbon balls, spiced nuts.
11-149 30 min. $14.95

International Gourmet Delights with Chris & Goffredo
These two internationally recognized master chefs take a lighthearted, yet thorough, approach while demonstrating the preparation of classic international dishes, including such favorites as veal Sorrentina, red snapper with basil and tomato, minestrone Genovese, garlic roast duck, stuffed mushroom and crabmeat appetizers, homemade pasta, and more.
11-245 60 min. $29.95

VIDEO TITLES LISTED IN THIS GUIDE ARE AVAILABLE FOR PURCHASE OR RENTAL. CONTACT YOUR LOCAL VIDEO STORE OR TELEPHONE (800) 383-8811

Jewish Mothers Video Cookbook
Joanne Pepper and Jackie Frazin show you such traditional recipes as Gefilte fish, Matzo Balls, Kreplach, Kasha, and much more.
11-2844 90 min. $34.95

Kids in the Kitchen
Combine a creative cook with a couple of kids in the kitchen and you have a delightful program that will benefit everyone. Personable, vivacious Karen Underwood, assisted by Corey and Ashleigh, present some new recipe ideas as well as familiar favorites that children can easily prepare for themselves,   family and friends. Kit materials include a self-standing, smudge resistant recipe book, a wire whisk and a set of measuring spoons.
11-200 52 min. $19.95

Madeleine Kamman Cooks Chicken
In this tape Madeleine Kamman cooks the most successful chicken recipes from her acclaimed PBS series. She shows you how to cut up a whole chicken into various parts, how to bone, how to prepare both dark and white meat to best advantage-including cooking times and temperatures. She also teaches you what to do with necks, backs and wings, as well as techniques for roasting, broiling, frying and sauteing. The most comprehensive chicken preparation tape available.
11-201 90 min. $39.95

MADELEINE KAMMAN COOKS CHICKEN SERIES:

• Volume I
French chef, teacher and cookbook author Madeline Kamman introduces you to numerous techniques and recipes that will improve and enhance your cooking pleasure. This volume includes Caribbean shrimp salad and two ways to cut and prepare duckling.
11-077 60 min. $39.95

• Volume II
Learn the techniques for removing the sirloin and tenderloin cuts from veal and beef, and the uses of every segment of the cut from fat to bones. Also included are demonstrations of roasting, pasta making and creating a custard.
11-078 90 min. $49.95

Napkins...The Perfect Accent!
Explains step-by-step how to fold napkins as well as demonstrates the art of displaying the folds in various settings. This video also gives helpful tips on napkin selection and care instructions.
11-8081 30 min. $19.95

Noodle Making: Cheap & Easy
You'll find this easy to follow, step-by-step cooking class a great addition to your cooking skills. Jean Rosenbaum, M.D., Director of the American Aerobics Association, has devised a low fat noodle recipe during his research on nutrition for the AAA. You will learn to prepare healthy and delicious noodles for just pennies.
11-5127 19 min. $29.95

Meals for Two
Recipes for strawberry salad, pea salad, rice salad, London broil with mushroom sauce, teriyaki steak with marinade, pepper steak, ice cream crêpes with chocolate sauce.
11-107 30 min. $14.95

Mouth-watering Meatless Meals
Recipes for vegetable Wellington, sweet potato pancakes, vegetable curry, spaghetti squash, pasta presto primavera and veggie burgers.
11-177 30 min. $14.95

One Dish Meal
Recipes for lemon garlic salmon, German feast, veal au gratin, curried beef, scallop saute, oriental ham.
11-108 30 min. $14.95

San Francisco Firemen's Video Cookbook
Behind the station doors, San Francisco's fire-fighting chefs are cooking up some of the hottest gourmet meals in town. Features six of the fire department's most popular chefs, each with his own brand of wit and culinary wisdom. Includes 18 recipes from simple "door slammer" chicken dishes, soups salads, pastas, entrees, vegetables, to desserts such as a sublime gourmet French apple tart.
11-171 100 min. $19.95

Santa Fe Cuisine
The restaurants of Santa Fe turn out some of the most tongue tingling examples of southwestern cuisine to be found anywhere. Visit the kitchens of the Coyote Cage, The Shed, Pinon Grill and Rancho de Chimayo. Their chefs will demonstrate the preparation of five southwestern specialties. Recipes are included with the video.
11-1676 56 min. $29.95

Seafood Cookery
Don't let a fish intimidate you! With a little help from Sharon Kramis, award-winning author and food consultant, you can learn to prepare fish dishes perfectly every time. Included in this program are sections on selecting fish and shellfish, filleting, no-fail techniques for avoiding overcooking, plus demonstrations featuring saute meuniere, cioppino and other fish favorites. Don't miss the special section on salmon, cooked in tribal

fashion, complete with Indian music and dance.
11-095 57 min. $24.95

Secrets, Sauces & Savvy of American Barbecue and Grilling
An exciting menu of handy tips, demonstrations and recipes guaranteed to make your barbecue days joyful occasions.
11-235 30 min. $14.95

Sensational Soups
Recipes for beef stock, chicken stock, Mexican corn soup, artichoke mushroom chowder, French onion soup, black bean soup, cheddar cheese soup, gazpacho.
11-155 30 min. $14.95

Seven Simple Chicken Dishes
Recipes for stir-fry chicken and shrimp, lemon champagne chicken, sherry chicken, coq au vin.
11-109 30 min. $14.95

Single Serving
Easy recipes that will turn your simple dishes in "gourmet affairs". Ten different recipes: Garlic Shrimp Linguine, Italian Chicken, Chicken Breasts Dijon, Cheesy Stuffed Mushrooms, Meatloaf, etc.
11-9781 60 min. $24.95

Slim Gourmet
McLean Stevenson (of TV's MASH) narrates as Barbara Gibbons (who writes the "Slim Gourmet" column in Family Circle magazine) demonstrates gourmet recipes with calorie-counting substitutes. Gibbons reveals dozen of recipes for salads, meats, fish, pasta and desserts. Learn a professional's secrets on shipping, stocking a dieter's gourmet kitchen and how to avoid fat and cholesterol.
11-097 90 min. $39.95

Spago: Cooking with Wolfgang Puck
Chef Wolfgang reveals the exiting how-to of a wide array of tantalizing, easily-prepared Spago favorites. Puck has revolutionized the way America dines by popularizing "California Cuisine." This video features 15 Spago recipes, including Wolfgang Puck's famed pizzas and pastas.
11-1914 60 min. $29.95

Supermarket Savvy
An aisle to aisle tour of the supermarket giving tips on how to read product labels and understand what they mean as far as nutrition and calories.
11-2731 52 min. $24.95

Table Manners
A very funny videotape which seriously teaches adults and children about table manners for use in everyday situations. Can be used by parents and schools to teach table manners to young children and teenagers. Covers the basics of eating properly at the table for breakfast, lunch, and dinner in restaurants, fast food places, and at home.
11-5398 41 min. $19.95

VEGETABLE LOVER'S VIDEO COOKBOOK WITH BERT GREENE
A two-volume set by the noted food authority and author of the best-selling cookbook, "Greene on Greens". In these programs, Greene demonstrates the preparation of a wide variety of delicious vegetable dishes while providing the viewer with generous portions of vegetable lore and wisdom.

• **Volume 1**
11-242 82 min. $39.95

• **Volume 2**
11-243 86 min. $39.95

WAY TO COOK/JULIA CHILD SERIES:
This program looks at the way Julia Child is cooking today with new ideas, a light touch, and a versatile approach using the abundance of good, fresh ingredients that America has to offer. the series covers all of the basic areas of Julia's cooking repertoire.

• **First Courses & Desserts**
A master recipe for mousses and pâtes; for making crêpes and filling and gratineing them; for perfecting tarts, both savory and sweet; the versatile genoise and a chocolate-on-chocolate cake; plus a splendid trifle.
11-117 60 min. $29.95

• **Fish & Eggs**
From simple pan-fried and poached fish to sauteed shrimp and lobster dishes. All about the miraculous egg: poached, in omelettes, timbales, quiches, custards, in hollandaise and mayonnaise, and a spectacular soufflé.
11-116 60 min. $29.95

• **Meat**
Quick and easy steaks, chops and hamburgers; aromatic stews; majestic roast of beef and lamb. Includes tricks for trimming and carving meat and on flambeing for a dramatic finish.
11-113 60 min. $29.95

• **Poultry**
From the perfect chicken saute with its many variations, to tender ways with chicken breasts, to a classic coq au vin, to a festive holiday turkey and a very special roast duck.
11-112 60 min. $29.95

VIDEO TITLES LISTED IN THIS GUIDE ARE AVAILABLE FOR PURCHASE OR RENTAL. CONTACT YOUR LOCAL VIDEO STORE OR TELEPHONE (800) 383-8811

• **Soups, Salads & Bread**
Light and hearty soups from a variety of bases, including vichyssoise and French onion. Tossed and composed salads, with three American favorites: chicken salad, potato salad and coleslaw. Plus, how to make your own French bread.
11-115 60 min. $29.95

• **Vegetables**
From asparagus to zucchini, the best ways to maximize tenderness and flavor while preserving color. Plus Julia's favorite recipes for au gratins, tomatoes, Provencal, eggplant pizza and scalloped potatoes.
11-114 60 min. $29.95

WE'RE COOKING NOW SERIES:
Join Chef Franco Palumbo as he explores the wonderful world of cooking. The friendly host of a popular TV series and an instructor for the Culinary Institute of America, Chef Palumbo is also a noted restaurateur and cookbook author. He is responsible for the "Slim Cuisine" approach to food preparation and is the former executive chef of Weight Watchers International. Each tape includes a shopping list for ingredients and a recipe card.

• **Chicken Variations**
Recipes for chicken breasts with zucchini stuffing, chicken Cordon Bleu and seasoned butter, and breast of chicken (similar to chicken Kiev.)
11-164 30 min. $14.95

• **Crêpes**
Recipes for basic crêpe batter, desert crêpes, and chicken filled crêpes.
11-163 30 min. $14.95

• **Entertainment Night**
Recipes for bacon-wrapped dates, shrimp Budapest and chocolate truffles.
11-158 30 min. $14.95

• **Guests for Dinner**
Recipes for lamb chops with artichokes and endive, carrot orange soup, and coconut macaroons.
11-161 30 min. $14.95

• **Hors d'Oeuvres**
Recipes for clam rounds, brandied cheese balls, and smoked fish pâte.
11-162 30 min. $14.95

• **Omelets**
Recipes for basic omelet mixture, and three fillings: cottage omelet, spinach omelet and summer vegetable omelet.
11-159 30 min. $14.95

• **Pilafs**
Recipes for fruited pork pilaf, chicken pilaf and shrimp pilaf.
11-157 30 min. $14.95

• **Sunny Beef Salad**
Recipe and preparation instructions.
11-160 30 min. $14.95

Where's the Beef?
If you're like most North Americans, you are paying more for your meat. Now, you can provide your family with better quality meat and pay up to 50% less. You will be amazed at how a little knowledge of general butcher shop practices will revolutionize your shopping. This video points out the meat merchandizing tricks.
11-227 42 min. $24.95

A Loaf Bread, A Bottle of Wine, and a Video from This Chapter... The Key to Preparing the Finest Meals.

Crafts, Hobbies & Home Arts

- ✓ *Basket Making*
- ✓ *Carving*
- ✓ *Decorations & Gifts*
- ✓ *Flower Arranging*
- ✓ *Knitting, Crocheting, Needlepoint*
- ✓ *Sewing, Weaving, Quilting, Spinning*
- ✓ *Woodworking*
- ✓ *Miscellaneous*

Basket Making

Carving

Basket Weaving
Instructor: Grace Kable. Complete step-by-step demonstrations for the beginner. Begins by showing a variety of baskets and listing all the tools and supplies needed. The viewer is shown how cane first must be soaked and then is taken through the steps to complete a round basket all the way down to hiding spokes and weavers to weaving in the handle. Also how to decorate your basket by painting with hearts, ducks, etc., and how to stain the basket for added color.
12-208 95 min. $49.95

Make a Basket from a Tree
Estel Youngblood is a third generation Appalachian basket maker. Join him as he demonstrates his craft and shares his folksy anecdotes at a basketry workshop in California. Starting with white oak logs which were brought with him from Tennessee, you will watch the splitting of the log, whittling the ribs, splitting out the handle, tying the bow to attach the handle to the rim, splitting the weaver strands, and the weaving of the basket. There are long detailed close-ups so you can carefully watch and learn the process. A fascinating film and a tribute to an American craft.
12-183 60 min. $39.95

Splint Basketry Weaving I
The course begins with a bit of historical background on styles shapes and materials. You will learn which materials to use and how to prepare them as you weave an Appalachian egg basket. (The intricate "God's eye" that begins the basket is shown for both left and right handers.) You will learn several basket variations, and how to finish a basket. Technical tips solve many problems you might encounter and inspiration for other splint baskets concludes the course.
12-181 79 min. $49.95

Splint Basketry Weaving II
This course teaches you how to weave two distinctly different baskets, one round and the other square or rectangular. The two forms are presented together because they share the finishing steps for rims and handles.
12-292 96 min. $49.95

Art of Leather Carving and Figure Carving
Learn to use the most up-to-date leather crafting methods with your guide Joey Smith. Joey demonstrates and explains everything you need to know from casing to finishing. The second lesson of figure carving with leathercrafter Al Stolman, teaches you the basics of carving horses and other animals on leather.
12-152 50 min. $29.95

Basic Leathercraft/Stamping and Western Carving
This videocassette contains two complete lessons on one tape. Learn preparation of your leather for basic stamping, use of the six most common stamping tools, tracing and transferring design, proper use of your swivel knife, applying a protective finish, whip stitching and double loop lacing. The second lesson, on basic western carving, contains detail on the use of your swivel knife, plus how to use your six basic stamping tools to create a western floral design, how to color your design with antique stain, and how to carve a cartoon animal. Projects shown include a wristband, keycase and a wallet.
12-151 50 min. $29.95

Bird Carving: Art in Detail
The age-old art of bird carving comes to life before your eyes. Watch as today's generation of carvers transform blocks of wood into finely detailed sculptures while they share their secrets of a lifetime. They lead you from preparation, tool selection, design and individual techniques to final detailing.
19-245 30 min. $29.95

Carving Techniques and Projects with Sam Bush and Mack Headley Jr.
Discover the pleasures of carving with these two noted craftsmen with more than 40 years' experience between them.
12-269 90 min. $29.95

Decorations & Gifts

Art of Origami

You will learn how to make many different figures with only a piece of paper. Includes instruction for rabbits, ducks, swans, dogs, goldfish, and many others. This video can be used by adults or by children.

12-311 70 min. $29.95

Basic Christmas Designs: Nosegays and Centerpieces

Learn simple techniques to use in your holiday arranging including how to identify foliage and flowers, tie bows, and tips on caring for fresh greens. Covers the use of candles, lanterns and other decorative extras and props in your designs, and includes over a dozen ideas for dressing up your holiday tables.

12-038 60 min. $49.95

Calico/Memory Album

These lovely albums make beautiful gifts for family, friends new babies, graduates and travelers. They are easy-no sewing involved-and may be assembled quickly. Pattern pieces enclosed.

12-254 45 min. $39.95

CHRISTMAS DECORATION LIBRARY

Learn how to create wonderful seasonal decorations and ornaments. You will learn how to create wreaths, centerpieces, mantle arrangements and more!

• **Della Robbia Wreath/Kissing Ball**
Mistletoe
12-8028 30 min. $29.95

• **Table Centerpieces/Newel Post Decorations**
12-8029 30 min. $29.95

• **Two Mantle Arrangements, Vertical and Horizontal**
12-8023 30 min. $29.95

• **Window Wreath/Victorian Wreath/Pine Garland**
12-8031 30 min. $29.95

Christmas Tree Video

An electronic Christmas tree which can be used to enhance the holiday spirit & bring good cheer to the household with it's upbeat, positive music, and lovely visuals. This can be used in place of a traditional Christmas tree or to enhance the feeling wherever there is a VCR.

12-9899 40 min. $29.95

Course in Traditional Beading - Techniques and Applications

This can teach anyone, experienced or not, how to begin and complete a variety of stitches. In this one-on-one video training program, you will discover special pointers and tricks of the trade that Laura A. Lozano has learned from other traditional beaders. For two hours you will participate in the most comprehensive instruction on traditional beading techniques available anywhere. Laura guides you through the entire course by using real examples and illustrations.

12-8141 120 min. $34.95

Craft and Gift Ideas

Here's a sparkling collection of project ideas, so easy you can complete each one in just a few hours-or less. Easy-to-follow, all cutting dimensions are included. Perfect for the busy person who loves to create craft projects. No one will ever guess how long it took.

12-8035 30 min. $16.95

Creating a Merry Christmas

Make your own ornaments and learn how to "really" decorate a tree! Make Santa napkins, garland clusters, special gift wrappings and much more.

12-013 57 min. $24.95

Decorating on the Double

Nancy Zieman, hostess of TV's Sewing With Nancy brings her three part series to you. Also included is an illustrated booklet to help you in your decorating needs.

12-8026 30 min. $29.95

Decorating Your Home for Christmas

Learn how to make your own wreaths, swags and centerpieces for the holidays. Includes how to make bows, garlands, mantle decorations, wall trees and many tips to make your decorating easier.

12-017 59 min. $24.95

Eggery and Gold Leafing

This tape shows how to prepare, dye and cut eggs. Lee also creates things from eggs such as tree ornaments, birds, angels, pixies and jewelry boxes. Gold Leafing is also demonstrated.

12-021 58 min. $24.95

Flower Arranging, Holiday Wreath And Floral Design

Jim Manders presents simple wreath-making in easy-to-follow instruction, as well as floral design sure to enhance your holiday celebrations.

12-048 87 min. $ 59.95

VIDEO TITLES LISTED IN THIS GUIDE ARE AVAILABLE FOR PURCHASE OR RENTAL. CONTACT YOUR LOCAL VIDEO STORE OR TELEPHONE (800) 383-8811

FUN STAMPS SERIES:

• ABC's of Stamping
In this program you will learn how to stamp your own personalized card, inking your stamps, multi-colored impressions and more.
12-8166 26 min. $24.95

• Artistic Stamping
Learn how to create such things as spectacular garden scenes, use line or shape designs effectively, develop an eye for color and how to create a focal point.
12-8167 27 min. $24.95

• Special Effect Stamping
In this program you will learn a variety of ways to make your cards sparkle and shine, two new tricks for the back of stickers and highlighting effects with foils.
12-8168 49 min. $24.95

• Techniques of Stamping
Learn four tips for creating continuous patterns, soft color blending, paper punching techniques and simple methods to Pop-up any card in minutes.
12-8169 65 min. $24.95

Fun with Heritage Crafts
This extraordinary lesson will help mom, teachers, and scout leaders teach children basic American Heritage crafts such as pine cone crafting, lap weaving, handquilting, and embroidery. The extensive use of graphics makes everything simple and easy to do.
12-8017 30 min. $29.95

Gift and Bazaar Projects: Volume 1
Learn how to design and make greeting card baskets, tissue holders, fabric flowers and more.
12-044 58 min. $24.95

Gift and Bazaar Projects: Volume 2
Learn how to design kitchen witches, woven fabric baskets, decorate kitchen brooms and more.
12-045 60 min. $24.95

Holiday Angel Dolls
Learn how to design and make padded soft-sculpture angels, tree angels, stick angels, pixies and stuffed roly-poly angels.
12-047 60 min. $39.95

Instant Decorating
Add a new look to your home by changing the decor with fabric. Nancy and interior decorating sewing specialist, Gail Brown, explain unique and attractive decorating techniques for the bedroom, kitchen and living areas.
12-2475 60 min. $29.95

Introduction to Puppet Making
Follow along and learn the wonderful art of puppet making with award-winning puppeteer Jim Gamble. Using common household items, Gamble shows how to make an imaginative array of finger, book and rod puppets. This simple presentation is easy for children of all ages to understand.
12-8005 30 min. $16.95

Make Your Parties Fun
Children's parties are fun to plan and this tape gives you ideas for creating three memorable theme parties. Whether it's a clown party, a western party, or a teddy bear picnic, children will have fun making invitations, centerpieces, favors, placemats, etc. Suggestions are given for games and food to fit the occasion.
12-8018 30 min. $29.95

PAINTED LADY SERIES:
This series covers basic fabric painting techniques. Learn simple t-shirt designs, decorator wallpaper, Las Vegas costumes, prom dresses and furniture. Hosted by Peg Tuppeney.

• Introduction to Fabric Painting
12-8163 60 min. $29.95

• Home Decor
12-8165 60 min. $29.95

• More Fabric Painting
12-8164 60 min. $29.95

Peter Clark's Christmas Tree Tips
Everything you need to know to have a "professional" looking tree in your own living room! Easy-to-follow, step-by-step program includes tips on: selecting a tree, lighting, hanging garland, color schemes, coordinating a "theme" and much, much more!
12-1786 30 min. $19.95

Re-Do a Room In a Week with Donna Salyers
Donna Salyers gives easy instructions on how you turn old bedrooms into brand new ones--in just a single weekend.
12-8032 30 min. $16.95

Ribbon Magic
Anyone can learn to make a bow with this one hour easy-to-follow instructional tape which includes over ten different types of bows as well as how to make ribbon roses. Dozens of projects and ideas are given for using ribbons in decorating the home, wrapping gifts, making gift baskets and decorating for the holidays. All floral professionals and

beginners alike will be surprised and pleased with what they learn from this tape.
12-8019 60 min. $29.95

Styrofoam Wizardry
This exciting video lesson includes a comprehensive presentation of hints and techniques for working with Styrofoam brand plastic foam. Cutting, preparing, pattern making, painting and texturing are included. Dozens of projects and project ideas are presented including display work, seasonal items, party themes, floral and home decor.
12-8014 60 min. $29.95

Wall Hangings
Almost every room in your home can be enhanced by an attractive wall hanging. Learn how to use brooms, fans, frying pans, wicker baskets, mats and much more in your creative designs.
12-036 60 min. $49.95

Working with Colors
If you have ever been perplexed about how to match colors in your home decor, here's a quick and fun lesson in simple color coordination. Betty Ann explains the mystery of color and suggests how you can solve your color dilemmas. Also, you will learn three more popular styles including: the asymmetrical "L", crescent and vertical.
12-8009 60 min. $29.95

Flower Arranging

Advanced Centerpieces, One-Sided and Layered "Mass" Designs
Covers over two dozen different design ideas, including advanced design principles and material-selection tips.
12-035 60 min. $49.95

Art of Ikebana
This video thoroughly explains the art of Japanese flower arrangement. It covers various styles, containers, tools, and materials. Styles such as Nageire, Moribana, basic upright, slanting form, and free form are covered.
12-312 70 min. $29.95

Attendant's Flowers
This lesson includes hints and suggestions for selecting bouquet styles, flowers, and colors for all attendants. Step-by-step instruction is given for all

arrangement styles. Also included is a special section on how to carry bouquets.
12-8012 60 min. $29.95

Beginning: Bouquets and Headpieces for the Bride
Doing your own wedding flowers, helping a friend, or learning wedding work as a business can be a most rewarding and enjoyable experience. This program shows you where to begin and gives numerous selections for the bride's flowers and headpieces.
12-8011 60 min. $29.95

Blommor: Spring Blossoms
Covers garden flowers, foliage, outdoor arrangements, Easter baskets and more.
12-221 60 min. $39.95

Blommor: Autumn Arranging
Covers fresh flowers, dried and pods, indoor/outdoor arrangements, autumn wreaths and using an assortment of containers.
12-220 60 min. $39.95

Blommor: Florist Flowers
Covers working with florist flowers in creating a wedding basket, using glass containers, a silk planter and making Christmas decoration creations.
12-219 60 min. $39.95

Blommor: Holiday Arranging
Covers door swags, grapevine wreaths, a lantern of light and New Years novelties.
12-222 60 min. $39.95

Blommor: Variety
Covers vase arranging, potted flowers, silk flower selections and arranging, colors and natural colors, a basket of roses design and much more.
12-218 60 min. $49.95

Dried Flower Fantasy
Dried flowers are perfect for any decor. They are long lasting and easy to work with. Three styles of period arranging are taught (Williamsburg, Victorian, and Colonial) as well as contemporary design. A variety of methods are given for making wreaths, swags, and garlands as well as other decorative pieces such as topiary trees and baskets.
12-8015 60 min. $29.95

Driftwood and Other Naturals
Lee demonstrates how to clean driftwood; arrange with feathers, artificial flowers and nuts. Learn to make wreaths from dried flowers, pine cones and much more.
12-020 58 min. $39.95

Finishing Touch
This program gives you ideas and instructions for making those final and lovely touches to the wedding plans. You will learn how to make professional bows to enhance any part of your wedding.
12-8013 60 min. $29.95

Flower Arranging For Your Home
Jim Manders presents the principles of floral design in a series of mini-lessons using a variety of materials, designs and containers.
12-031 94 min. $39.95

Flower Arranging: A Step Further
Learn line arranging using different arrangement styles. Includes how to select materials for different kinds of arrangements.
12-033 56 min. $39.95

Flower Arranging: The Basics
Learn how to do elementary flower arranging using single-specimen flowers and basic arrangements in floral oasis. Includes all the mechanics involved with beginning an arrangement.
12-032 60 min. $39.95

FLORAL SERIES
An informative guide to creating floral arrangements for all occasions.

• Formal & Informal Flowers
12-8149 56 min. $29.95

• Wedding & Anniversary Arrangements
12-8150 56 min. $29.95

• Garden Party
12-8151 56 min. $29.95

• Williamsburg
12-8152 56 min. $29.95

Following the Seasons
The lesson explores the many and varied uses of this graceful floral design technique. You will not only make an elegant table top arrangement but learn to vary the style for a myriad of door and wall decorations.
12-8010 60 min. $29.95

Nosegays, One-Sided and Centerpiece Designs
Learn, step-by-step, how to make nosegays, one-sided and centerpiece designs. Pat Quigley discusses basic design theory and gives you an overview of all the materials you'll need for beautiful flower arrangements.
12-034 60 min. $49.95

Preserving Flowers and Foliage
Learn how to preserve garden flowers in silica gel using a new microwave oven technique. Includes tips on preserving foliage in glycerine solution and the art of pressing flowers.
12-096 61 min. $24.95

Secrets of Decorating with Flowers
Beautifully photographed, highly informative and extremely enjoyable, this program will open up a world of ideas for you. Join Renny Reynolds, renowned floral consultant to the White House, as he shares his tips and pointers on how to make decorating statements in your home.
12-9165 55 min. $24.95

Secrets of Entertaining with Flowers
Renny Reynolds demonstrates creative ideas for using flowers to create attractive and elegant settings for entertaining in your home.
12-9166 40 min. $24.95

Secrets Of Flower Arranging
This tape picks up where "Tips" leaves off as Zsuzsa creates a magnificent centerpiece and Japanese-style and Western-style arrangements right before your eyes.
12-5613 60 min. $19.95

Silk Flower-Making: Volume 1
Learn how to make silk carnations, rhododendrons, camellias, chrysanthemums and peonies.
12-139 60 min. $24.95

Silk Flower-Making: Volume 2
Learn how to make silk roses, gardenias, tulips, daffodils and delphiniums.
12-140 60 min. $24.95

Tips On Flower Arranging
Get the most out of your flowers with the secret skills used by the world's top flower designers. Beverly Hill's own Zsuzsa Cziraky demonstrates, in an easy, step-by-step way, how to achieve gorgeous results by developing an eye for color and balance.
12-5612 30 min. $19.95

Trinity Floral Design: The Basics
This program tells you all you need to know, about tools, supplies and the flowers you'll be using. Detailed step-by-step instructions lead you through the four floral design basics.
Closed captioned for the hearing impaired.
12-3099 60 min. $29.95

VIDEO TITLES LISTED IN THIS GUIDE ARE AVAILABLE FOR PURCHASE OR RENTAL. CONTACT YOUR LOCAL VIDEO STORE OR TELEPHONE (800) 383-8811

Working with Flowers

Begin your lessons on basic floral design with a comprehensive and fun lesson, giving all the helpful hints you need to know to make your flower arranging easy and quick. Learn simple and easy techniques for making all your arranging a creative joy whether it's silk or live flowers. You'll begin with three popular arrangements perfect for centerpieces.
12-8008 60 min. $29.95

Hobbies & Crafts

Barbie - Hall of Fame

This video captures all facets of the "Hall of Fame Barbie" museum and it's collection. High fashion and accessories, rare first Barbies, the original Lilli dolls, exclusive Barbies, International Barbies, Barbie's family and friends, and rare examples of Barbie collectibles. A must for any Barbie fan or collector.
12-8021 30 min. $24.95

Baseball Card Collector

An entertaining fact-filled look at America's favorite hobby from the days of the black and white Tobacco cards to the Golden Age of Baseball, from the modern era of the 70's and 80's to the Superstars of tomorrow.
12-8155 35 min. $19.95

Baseball Card Collecting for Big Bucks

Learn the secrets of profitable card collecting secrets that card dealers don't want you to know. This covers knowledge, planning purchases, market strategy, negotiation and card care.
12-8007 60 min. $39.95

Collecting Fashion Jewelry

You'll learn the answers about these wonderful pieces of art. Some of these old antique gems can be worth a great deal of money. Learn from the experts on collecting these little treasures.
12-8154 30 min. $19.95

Comic Book Collector

Hosted by Frank Gorshin, this fun-packed adventure into the history and highlights of comic books will take you through over 70 years worth of history. It's all here; hero's, villains and the golden age come together in this terrific program.
12-8156 40 min. $19.95

COMPLETE MINIATURE HOW TO WORKSHOP LIBRARY

A guide to miniatures hosted by Miniaturist, Vicki Metzger.

• **Fishbowl Filled, Fishbowl Spilled**
12-8036 42 min. $39.95

• **Vegetable Garden in a Tub**
12-8037 86 min. $59.95

• **Sparkling Goldfish Pond**
12-8038 63 min. $59.95

• **Secret Garden**
12-8039 72 min $97.50

• **Victorian Teddy Bear Box**
12-8040 86 min. $69.95

Coronation Story

A documentary video on the Coronation of Queen Elizabeth II and dolls produced by both European and American manufacturers, from 1929 -1992, on Princess Elizabeth, Queen Elizabeth, members of the royal family and Coronation memorabilia and souvenirs. Featured are the Coronation story, consisting of 36 dolls, custom produced by Madame Alexander, displayed from 1953 to the present at the Brooklyn Children's Museum; plus rare photos of Madame Beatrice Alexander and the Alexander Doll factory. An Alexander Masterpiece.
12-8004 72 min. $49.95

Dionne Quintuplet Dolls 1934 - 1939

This documentary video of the official Dionne Quintuplet Dolls, manufactured by the Alexander Doll Co., begins in 1934, with birth of the Five Famous Sisters, and ends with the last national ad for Quint Dolls. This history of Alexander Quintuplets includes 41 different styles of composition dolls, rag dolls and accessory sets; plus rare contemporary photographs of Madame Beatrice Alexander and the first Alexander catalog published in 1936. Added features: movie-news, rare clips, rare photos & memorabilia. An Alexander Exclusive.
12-8003 34 min. $49.95

Gemstones of America

Americans have a fascination with gemstones. Surprisingly, many don't realize that nearly every kind of precious gemstone is mined here in the United States. Hosted by Efrem Zimbalist Jr..
12-8162 60 min. $34.95

VIDEO TITLES LISTED IN THIS GUIDE ARE AVAILABLE FOR PURCHASE OR RENTAL. CONTACT YOUR LOCAL VIDEO STORE OR TELEPHONE (800) 383-8811

Gift of Heritage
Create your own family documentary! Learn how to retain your family-tree, history, stories and photographs on video in a very innovative and unique way with this extraordinary how-to video. This program takes the viewer through the process of gathering data, organizing material, interviewing, performing simple video techniques, and effectively telling your family story on video tape, providing a wonderful gift that can be handed down to future generations.
12-8025 60 min. $19.95

Making Doll Shoes
This video comes with a complete set of doll shoe patterns designed to make shoe making easy, fun, and profitable. Learn how to make custom shoes for your dolls with Greta Smith.
12-8161 81 min. $49.95

Practical Approach to Buying & Setting Up Your First Telescope
Charles Scovil has created this video in response to the many questions he has received about first telescopes. A perfect video for the beginning amateur astronomer.
12-9820 30 min. $29.95

Scarlett Dolls, An Alexander Tradition, 1937-1991
This documentary video traces the fascinating evolution of the Scarlett O'Hara dolls by Madame Alexander and the Alexander Doll Co.--from the early composition models in 1937, with footage of rare composition Scarletts, through the hard plastic and vinyl eras, and concludes with the porcelain Scarlett doll of 1991. More than 85 Scarlett dolls, plus "Gone With The Wind" memorabilia and rare photographs of Madame Beatrice Alexander are featured. This program also contains an original music score.
12-8002 72 min. $49.95

Video Guide to Stamp Collecting
Gary Burghoff hosts this introduction to stamp collecting. It covers all the basics of philately and it's a treat for the experienced collector, too. Featured are the types of stamps and where to get them, how to care for them and many other topics.
12-8153 50 min. $24.95

Knitting, Crocheting, Needlework

AMERICAN NEEDLEWORK COLLECTION

• Basic Cross Stitch on Linen with Marilyn Vredevelt
Delicate, rich designs evolve as cross stitching is worked into the even weave of linen and other novelty fabrics.
12-2042 55 min. $29.95

• Basic Custom Framing for Needlework with Kaye Evans
Demonstrates the necessary custom framing techniques that will give finished needlework the final creative touch.
12-2040 65 min. $29.95

• Learn to Crochet With Maggie Righetti
Demonstrates the basics of crocheting, an art form brought from Ireland to America in the 1800's.
12-2041 60 min. $29.95

• Learn to Cross Stitch with Marilyn Vredevelt
Instructs the viewer in the art of cross stitching, which dates back as far as the 1700's. Demonstrates how to create scenes of great beauty with just four stitches and a few simple tools.
12-2043 71 min. $29.95

Art Of Navajo Weaving
Explore the traditional art of Navajo weaving and its origins with visits to a contemporary Navajo weaving family. See how these beautiful artists create magnificent pieces of art that may take over a year to weave. In addition, you will see the Durango Collection, the most extensive private collection of Navajo weaving in the world.
12-6079 56 min. $29.95

Basic Crocheting
The easy basics of crocheting you need to create shawls, sweaters, afghans, granny squares and much more.
12-9343 30 min. $16.95

Basic Crochet
Basic Crochet is an introductory course leading the viewer through the selection of hook and thread, forming a slip loop and the proper way to hold the hook and thread for quick and easy crocheting. Also covered are chain stitch, single, double, half double and triple crochet stitch, slip stitch, shells, picot, popcorn and double treble stitch. The tape concludes with hints on counting stitches, hiding loose ends and finishing off. Instructed by Maggie Righetti.
12-207 52 min. $49.95

Basic Knitting
Learn CO, garter stitch, BO, stockinette stitch, ribbing, front cables, back cables, decrease/increase in knit, decrease/increase in purl, pattern stitch, reading pattern books.
12-275 120 min. $49.95

Basic Knitting
Linda Davis passes along the basics of knitting in easy-to-follow steps, learn at your own pace right at home.
12-8023 30 min. $16.95

Basic Knitting
Instructor: Maggie Righetti, School of Knitting. An introductory course for the novice, beginning with a brief history of knitting, then choosing yarn and needles, making a slip loop and casting on. Knit, purl, garter and stockinette stitch are demonstrated in the European and American methods for lefties and righties, followed by adding new yarn and concluding with binding off. Patterns included.
12-199 60 min. $49.95

Beginning Knitting
Kay Blanck takes you through the basics in a slow-paced introduction. Learn the basic beginning stitches, about your supplies and simple patterns.
12-007 93 min. $49.95

Chicken Scratch
Instructor: Stephanie Hedgepath of Pegasus Designs. Originating in Europe as the "lace stitch," Chicken Scratch is worked primarily on checkered gingham. In this tape, the viewer is instructed in the three basic stitches of this craft: double cross stitch, running stitch and the weaving stitch. Stitching on specialty fabrics is demonstrated as well as experimenting with ribbon. Instructions and pattern for a heart design are included.
12-198 28 min. $49.95

Circular Method Sweater
Instructor Kay Blanck shows you how to knit on circular needles with more complex stitches. Easy-to-follow instructions that take you into the more advanced knitting techniques.
12-010 118 min. $49.95

Contemporary Crochet Made Simple
Learn how to make three variations of granny squares with basic crochet stitches. Also, how to make pillow tops, tote bags, hot pads and afghans, slip stitching, and much more.
12-011 57 min. $24.95

Crochet
Watch the introduction to basic stitches, chain, single crochet, double crochet, triple crochet, changing colors, half double crochet, slip stitch, increasing and decreasing, granny square, finishing crochet and edgings and stitch gauge.
12-276 120 min. $49.95

Crochet Christmas Ornaments
Instructor: Helen Haywood. Basic crochet skills are assumed but the tape begins with a brief review of the stitches needed to create one-of-a-kind crochet snowflakes. These pieces can be used for a variety of purposes: pillows, framed on dark velvet, how to make angels, baskets, bells, etc. Supplies and materials are listed and precise instructions are given on stretching and stiffening your finished piece.
12-210 42 min. $49.95

Cross Stitch and Finishing Techniques
Instructor: Karen Dye. Demonstrates all phases of counted thread cross stitch, back stitch, quarter stitch, half stitch, three quarter stitch and French knot. Shows different techniques for stitching and many helpful hints. Proper care of floss and fabric is emphasized. Laundering instructions for finished design (a strawberry) are given. Charted design is included.
12-196 54 min. $49.95

Cross-Stitch with Erica Wilson
12-281 50 min. $29.95

Finishing Hand Knits
Instructor: Maggie Righetti. After the last stitch has been knitted the article must be put together and finished. How it is done can make the difference between a fine hand-made appearance and just a home-made look. This tape easily leads the knitter through all the steps of assembling and completing a garment. Invisible seam seaving, picking up stitches, crochet edges, concealing tag-ends, correcting loose stitches, duplicate stitch, button making and hand wash blocking.
12-309 90 min. $49.95

Fun With Ribbonstitch
Instructor: June B. Jones. Many ideas for creative ways to use 1/8" and 1/16" polyester ribbon including "Magic Ribbon-stitch." Demonstrates all types of needlepoint and embroidery stitches on canvas and evenweave fabric. Shows how to dress up lace edgings using ribbon.
12-195 17 min. $49.95

Intermediate Knitting
Instructor: Maggie Righetti. Basic knitting skills are required. Instruction includes increasing three different ways, decreasing in five different ways, multiple decreases, increases and decreases in pattern stitches and how to keep track of them and concludes with bind off in pattern. This tape

explains the things that a knitter will need to know to make a garment.
12-205 46 min. $49.95

Intermediate Knitting
Once you've mastered the basics of good knitting, Kay Blanck will show you how to do more complex stitches and patterning in this easy-to-follow program.
12-049 94 min. $59.95

Knit & Crochet Finishing
Learn how to knit seams: stockinette stitch, reverse stockinette, garter stitch, shoulder seams. Cut to shorten or lengthen. Add pockets, kitchner stitch. Cut buttonholes. Set in sleeve. Picking up edge and neck stitches. Crochet edge and buttonholes. Learn to crochet seams, slip stitch, weaving straight seams, shoulders, cross stitch.
12-274 120 min. $49.95

Knitting with Erica Wilson
12-278 50 min. $29.95

Knitting Pattern Stitches
Instructor: Maggie Righetti. Intermediate knitting skills are required. This tape is about learning to combine the knit and purl stitches to make a variety of textured patterns. Garter Stitch, Stockinette stitch, Quaker rib, one-by-one ribbing, seed stitch, Irish moss stitch, raised eyelet lace, feather and fan lace, snowdrop lace, front and back twist cable are all demonstrated and explained so that anyone can master these skills.
12-206 58 min. $49.95

Knitting, Crochet, Quilting: Advanced Methods
If you've mastered the basic needlecraft skills, you're ready to start on more challenging projects. You will get instructions for knitted garment construction and variations on basic crochet stitches that will change the pattern and texture. You'll also learn the easiest way to mark a quilt pattern and methods of two-dimensional quilting.
12-1502 57 min. $19.95

Knitting, Crochet, Quilting: The Basics
Don't let all those yarns, needles, fabrics and patterns intimidate you just because you're a beginner. This instructional video is a clear and concise introduction to needle arts. You'll learn: beginning knitting stitches, techniques for knitting colors, basic crochet stitches, how to put quilting blocks together and much more.
12-1501 57 min. $19.95

Needlepoint with Erica Wilson
12-279 50 min. $29.95

Needlepoint: Unique and Unusual Techniques
The student will learn how to transfer a design (enclosed) to needlepoint canvas, stitch the design using more than 20 different stitches and various fibers and objects including ribbon, perle cotton, beads, shiska mirrors, wool, velour, flosses and straw. Flowers will be stitched in a dimensional manner and the basket woven to look like a real basket. Ideas on mounting and framing are included. For beginners to very experienced.
12-294 102 min. $49.95

Rag Knit Sweaters
Instructor: Linda Bryant. The latest rage, sweaters made of "rags". Actual strips of fabric, ripped with the ends knotted together. Types of fabrics and needles are recommended. Demonstrates how to knit and assemble the sweater. Basic knitting skills are required. Materials are inexpensive and can be completed in a few evenings. Also shows ideas for making ensembles using the sweater fabric.
12-204 44 min. $49.95

Reading Knitting Instructions
Instructor: Maggie Righetti. Intermediate knitting skills required. This tape leads the viewer through learning to read, understand and interpret printed knitting abbreviations and directions. All of the steps and instructions necessary to make a long sleeved classic crew neck cardigan are explained both verbally and with captions on the screen.
12-209 65 min. $49.95

Tatting, Hairpin Lace & Broomstick Lace
Learn how to tat with heavy or fine cord and string, the right way to thread your shuttle, and how to make a shawl, blanket and belt.
12-144 52 min. $24.95

Sewing, Weaving, Quilting, Spinning

Alterations Hazel's Way
Hazel Howell brings 30 years experience into your home to show you the techniques you will need to do these common alterations and more.
12-8027 45 min. $34.95

Basic Log Cabin
Includes machine quilting, mitered bindings, machine tying and quilting, pin basting a quilt

---

together, and complete strip patchwork techniques from start to finish.
12-301 55 min. $29.95

Beginner's Patchwork Projects
Lee Maher demonstrates how to make a pillow, bookcover, potholder, muslin picture, tote bag and more.
12-006 60 min. $39.95

Beginning Four Harness Weaving
Whether weaving on a small table version or a large floor model, the weave structures and patterns possible with this type of a loom are almost limitless. First, the loom is described in detail, then you go through a thorough warping lesson (getting the loom ready for weaving) and work from one provided as you weave some of the many different pattern possibilities. Prerequisite: Introduction to Weaving.
12-180 86 min. $49.95

Card Weaving
This exciting weaving technique involves simple tools; cardboard cards and yarn. The weaving progresses very quickly. You will learn the basic techniques, several ways to measure the warp and thread the cards as you weave two projects: a belt and a tote bag made out of several woven bands. You are provided with a pattern design to follow as you weave many pattern variations. You will also learn how to design your own patterns.
12-177 97 min. $59.95

COUTURE TECHNIQUES
Roberta C. Carr demonstrates easy-to-follow methods designed to assure the fit of your hand-crafted clothing.

• **Couture Techniques for Fine Sewing**
12-9036 35 min. $34.95

• **Couture Techniques for Sewing Parties**
12-9037 40 min. $34.95

• **Couture Techniques for Special Occasions**
12-9038 35 min. $34.95

• **Couture Techniques for Designer Detail**
12-9039 36 min. $34.95

• **Couture Techniques for Tailoring**
12-9040 40 min $34.95

Cut Pile Rug Weaving
The step-by-step instructions on wrapping and weaving weft and pile yarns are so detailed that even a beginner will be proud of the first oriental, cut-pile rug. A design is provided for the project in this course, but you will learn how to prepare your own designs. Detailed instructions for building a small sturdy frame loom are also described.
12-178 101 min. $49.95

ELEANOR BURNS QUILTING SERIES:

• **Bear's Paw Quilt**
Learn this advanced quilt design. Eleanor Burns teaches her modern approach using a novel "multiple assembly" technique.
12-102 35 min. $44.95

• **Irish Chain Quilt**
12-8144 52 min. $44.95

• **Log Cabin Quilt, Quilt in a Day**
Eleanor Burns takes you from start to finish through the process of sewing a log cabin quilt in only one day! This video is organized into segments to allow you to stop conveniently and try each step according to Eleanor's precise instructions.
12-099 35 min. $44.95

• **Monkey Wrench Quilt**
Learn the unique monkey-wrench quilt design, also known as churn dash, lover's knot or hole-in-the-barn, combining only light and dark calicos. Eleanor Burns shows you how to be creative with color variations and gives you step-by-step, quick piecing methods.
12-100 35 min. $44.95

• **Ohio Star Quilt**
The Ohio star pattern made its way across the plains as the early settlers traveled West. Now this classic quilt pattern makes its way into your home. Eleanor Burns shows you how to piece the Ohio star together with quick and easy, non-traditional techniques.
12-101 35 min. $44.95

• **Block Party**
Join Eleanor in a quick and lively presentation as she shows you an easier approach to piecing a pineapple block than traditional methods.
12-9601 35 min. $44.95

• **Radiant Star Quilt**
12-8146 54 min. $44.95

• **Scrap Quilt**
12-8148 52 min. $44.95

VIDEO TITLES LISTED IN THIS GUIDE ARE AVAILABLE FOR PURCHASE OR RENTAL. CONTACT YOUR LOCAL VIDEO STORE OR TELEPHONE (800) 383-8811

• **Tulip Quilt**
12-8147 55 min. $44.95

• **Trio of Treasured Quilts**
12-225 55 min. $14.95

Fitting: The Sew/Fit Method
Making patterns fit, featuring Ruth Oblander. How to solve fitting problems on slacks, dresses, etc. by using the pivot and slide method with wax paper.
12-194 105 min. $34.95

Fun With Fabric with Lee Maher and Pat Quigley
Pat and Lee show you how to create clever gift and bazaar items from everyday budget fabrics, including hand puppets, felt cut-outs and yarn novelties.
12-042 61 min. $24.95

Fundamentals of Handspinning
This is a basic guide to handspinning, equipment, types of wool fibers and their preparation, and handspindle and spinning wheel techniques. Although designed for the novice, this course contains invaluable tips and techniques for the intermediate spinner and provides new insight for many expert spinners.
12-293 114 min. $49.95

Introduction to Weaving
Many people want to weave but do not know where or how to begin. What is weaving? This course answers those questions as it defines weaving terminology and explains looms, equipment tools and yarns, as well as projects that can be woven. It will help you choose a direction that is just right for you. It includes detailed exercises on how to figure yarn quantities needed for woven projects and many general topics that are common to most types of weaving. Therefore, this program is recommended as a prerequisite to other courses if you are new to weaving.
12-175 57 min. $39.95

Learn to Create Clothing
Learn how to redesign a sweatshirt or t-shirt into different fashions. Easy-to-follow steps and techniques are covered in this program.
12-9070 44 min. $24.95

Log Cabin Triangles
Step-by-step instructions for easy, accurate triangular designs for wall hangings and quilts.
12-302 55 min. $29.95

Making Soft Dolls
Follow along with this step-by-step instruction on body construction and contouring of five different dolls.
12-056 60 min. $24.95

Mastering Patchwork
This workshop by Jinny Beyers is the answer to any quilter's wish to make a quilt top as beautifully and effortlessly as Jinny does. It fills a need for something easy yet comprehensive enough for the beginner who wants to learn all about patchwork.
12-2499 120 min. $39.95

Palettes for Patchwork
This video gives you the chance to participate in a hands-on workshop which teaches a ground-breaking new method of selecting a color scheme for quiltmaking and other crafts. One of the unique features of this video is that it includes 85 solid color fabric swatches for your use.
12-1940 60 min. $29.95

Power Sewing: Designer Details Made Easy
Sewing mysteries, which frustrate the experienced sewer and intimidate the novice, are unraveled by detailed instructions shown with close-ups. Learn secrets of crisp detailing such as lapels, linings, fly fronts and more from Sandra Betzina, syndicated sewing columnist and TV personality.
12-2113 120 min. $34.95

Professional Techniques for the Million Dollar Look
Without proper techniques and quality workmanship, a million dollar look is almost impossible. The professional techniques taught on the tape include the easy insertion of a totally hidden zipper, a fast way to cut and mark, how to preshrink wool at home, application of a frustration-free waistband, a fast way to straighten fabric, and much more. Sewing should be enjoyable and exciting.
12-182 120 min. $44.95

Quilting
Learn to select fabric, cut, piece, assemble, applique and quilt. Suggestions as to how to use your quilted pieces to create a country warmth will also be demonstrated. Pattern pieces and quilting patterns are enclosed with tape.
12-256 55 min. $39.95

Quilting with Erica Wilson
12-280 50 min. $29.95

Reversible Quilts
Shows you how to assemble reversible quilts using a sewing machine.
12-303 55 min. $29.95

Rigid Heddle Weaving-Level 1

This unique loom offers many advantages to the weaver. It is small, inexpensive, light and very portable. And you will be amazed at what you can do. You will learn warping methods that are unique to these types of loom as you weave two projects; a beautiful wool scarf and a set of cotton placemats. Unusual weave structures are created with the use of a pick-up stick. Many problem-solving tips are included-as well as how to wash and finish your projects. Prerequisite: Introduction to Weaving.
12-179 87 min. $49.95

SEWING WITH NANCY SERIES:

• Begin to Sew

For anyone who really would like to sew but just doesn't know where or how to begin. Begin with Nancy from square one as she takes you slowly and patiently through the basics of how to choose a fabric, patterns, notions, pattern layout, cutting, marking and construction. Book included.
12-111 60 min. $29.95

• Busy Woman's Sewing Techniques I

In segments one and two of this tape, Nancy demonstrates how to sew a demi-lined blazer from a favorite lined or unlined blazer pattern. In the third segment, she shows updated techniques for sewing blouses. Book included.
12-227 60 min. $29.95

• Busy Woman's Sewing Techniques II

In the first segment of this tape, Nancy shows techniques for sewing casual tops. During the next segment she provides a fresh approach for sewing slacks. In the last segment Nancy outlines quick tips for skirt construction. Book included.
12-228 60 min. $29.95

• Contemporary Sewing

In this video Nancy starts with the basics of the four serger stitches-overlock, rolled edge, flatlock, chain stitch-and then shows how each stitch can be used for many different serging applications with just the changing of thread and/or tensions.
12-2473 60 min. $29.95

• Creative Accents
12-264 60 min. $29.95

• Creative Strip Quilting

Learn the various forms of strip quilting, including a speedy version of the log cabin method, a unique way to make a reversible quilt, Seminole quilting, and how to tastefully apply quilting to garments. Book included.
12-107 60 min. $29.95

• Fashion That Fits (No Matter What Size)

Because pattern companies often skip over the larger sizes, Nancy has developed this videotape to show you how to sew and fit for sizes 16 and above. She gives special attention to alteration techniques for patterns and ready-made, and to choosing the right pattern size, fabric and styles. Book included.
12-131 60 min. $29.95

• Fitting and Sewing Slacks

Learn how to fit and sew slacks, using pivot-and-slide instead of slashing and spreading your pattern, for easy alterations. Also learn how to convert a fitted waistband to an elasticized band and many other sewing hints for use with slacks. Book included.
12-135 60 min. $29.95

• Fitting the Bodice/Pivoting Techniques

Fitting the pattern, the first important step in sewing, raises the most questions. Nancy takes the guess work out of pattern alterations in this three-part tape by showing you how to use the pivot and slide techniques. Areas covered include fitting the bustline, shoulder, and back areas. Book included.
12-230 60 min. $29.95

• Fitting Slacks
12-263 60 min. $29.95

• Home Decorating-Window Treatments
12-265 60 min. $29.95

• Knit, Serge and Sew

Use a knitting machine, serger and conventional sewing machine to create one-of-a-kind fashions. Nancy takes a brand new approach in home sewing: knit panels of fabric with a knitting machine, outline the pattern shape on the knitted fabric, cut out the pattern shape by serging the edges and then sew/serge the pattern together!
12-2474 60 min. $29.95

• Machine Applique & Embroidery

Be an artist using your sewing machine to paint with thread! Joyce Drexler, author of the popular book "Thread Painting," joins Nancy to show you how to thread sketch, thread paint, shadow applique, monogram, satin stitch applique and much more. Book included.
12-137 60 min. $29.95

• Machine Monogramming

You'll get a great start and soon be able to monogram like a professional. Includes how to use a zigzag sewing machine to make both block and rounded alphabets, apply monograms to sweaters,

VIDEO TITLES LISTED IN THIS GUIDE ARE AVAILABLE FOR PURCHASE OR RENTAL. CONTACT YOUR LOCAL VIDEO STORE OR TELEPHONE (800) 383-8811

jackets, blouses and towels. Book included.
12-113 60 min. $29.95

• Machine Quilting
Learn how to machine quilt, including strip quilting, making three different designs using one modern quilting method. Also learn unique piecing techniques and how to put your quilt together using the machine. Book included.
12-123 60 min. $29.95

• Serging and Sewing Active Ware
12-262 60 min. $29.95

• Sewing for Children
Enjoy the fun of sewing for the children in your life. Learn how to design seven different styles of kids' clothes, including T-shirts, little girls' dresses, and little boys' pants and bib overalls. Book included.
12-115 60 min. $29.95

• Sewing Notions Know-How
Have a drawer filled with notions you don't know what to do with? Then this program is for you. Learn multiple uses for classic and newer notions like the pocket former template, bias tape marker, cone thread stand, as well as sewing tips for each notion. Book included.
12-121 60 min. $29.95

• Sewing Specialty Fabrics
Learn the how-to of sewing on specialty fabrics like silk, velvet and synthetic (e.g., "ultra" suedes), including cutting techniques, fusible interfacing methods, construction differences with specialty fabrics, and finishing steps. Book included.
12-125 60 min. $29.95

• Sewing Summer Activewear
Learn the "tricks of the trade" for sewing jogging suits, swimware, leotards, shorts and golf and tennis outfits for spring and summer wear. Includes a close look at elastic and closure construction methods and tips for working with specialty outerwear fabrics. Book included.
12-133 60 min. $29.95

• Slipping Patterns
You will learn how to make patterns from existing articles of clothing. A "must" for the home seamstress.
12-141 100 min. $29.95

• Successful Sewing Basics
Learn tips to successfully sew tailored and Peter Pan collars, zippers, facings and buttonholes-both machine and bound. In this video, Nancy gives hints for both the novice and experienced sewer.
12-2472 60 min. $29.95

• Tailoring Blazers
Learn how to tailor lined blazers using fusible interfacing and double fusibles; four-point closure, pressing and shaping; and how to sew a jacket together with two-unit and lining finishing techniques. Book included.
12-119 60 min. $29.95

• Tailoring Shirts for Women and Men
Step-by-step instructions on how to tailor a woman's or man's shirt, including how to sew on the front band, double yoke, two-piece collar with collar stays, sleeve placket and cuffs. Book included.
12-117 60 min. $29.95

Sew a Wardrobe in a Weekend
Imagine creating your own designer collection of six interchangeable separates: a jacket, skirt and pants to mix and match with a blouse, camisole and dress. Donna Salyers will show you how in easy to follow steps.
12-8033 30 min. $16.95

Sew Easy Sew Beautiful
Step-by-step instructions help make it easy for you to create your own stunning wardrobe. Includes a bonus Companion Guide Book that provides information for selecting patterns, fabrics and interfacing for successful shopping in fabric stores.
12-9278 30 min. $29.95

Smocking
Instructor: Karen Dye. This tape leads the novice through all the stitches necessary to complete a placket for a little girl's dress. Using the English method, all the basic stitches are demonstrated: outline, stem, cable, baby wave, two step and four step. Ideas are given in creative ways to use smocking-everything from pillows and hand bags to sportswear and Christmas ornaments. Kit sources included.
12-200 34 min. $49.95

Soft Sculpture Dolls
Instructor: Martha Holcombe of Miss Martha Originals. Comprehensive instructions on how to create a soft sculpture doll demonstrated on a Miss Martha doll. Tape begins with cutting the fabric, then goes on to show sewing, stuffing, dimpling and ends with applying the eyes and hair. Kit sources included.
12-202 81 min. $49.95

Super Time - Saving Sewing Tips
Get the fun and satisfaction of sewing like a professional, with these easy-to-follow tips from expert Donna Salyers. They'll help you save time and sew better.
12-8034 30 min. $16.95

Tapestry Weaving

Wall hangings and rugs can be woven in this pictorial weaving technique. You will learn how to weave many different shapes in different tapestry techniques as you complete three sample projects (pillows or wall hangings). Time-saving tips and problem-solving technical considerations help you weave a successful piece the first time. Instructions for making your own frame loom out of stretcher bars is included. Prerequisite: Introduction to Weaving.

12-176 110 min. $49.95

Video Guide to Quilting

Nine expert quilters undertake to make a quilt, a joint venture in which each shares tidbits of knowledge based on personal experience. Includes seven different lessons.

12-2716 120 min. $34.95

Weaving Without a Loom

Let Lee Maher change the way that you look at crafts as she shares secrets from the jungles of South America to the shelves of your kitchen. You'll be surprised at the possibilities!

12-9352 60 min. $29.95

Woodworking

Blizzard's Wonderful Wooden Toys

Parents, grandparents, and woodworkers will become expert toymakers when they watch Richard Blizzard's informative video. The charismatic craftsman demonstrates the skills needed to build seven safe, sturdy toys children will love. You'll learn to make a sandbox, a seesaw, a go-cart, a playhouse, a dollhouse, a scania truck, and even a Rolls-Royce. The 56-page booklet of assembly plans and cutting instructions that accompanies the tape is an integral part of the program.

12-5740 109 min. $24.95

Bowl Turning/With Del Stubbs

Del Stubbs, one of the leading woodturners in America, demonstrates how to lay out and mount a bowl blank; how to use different gouges and flat tools; and how to evaluate and sharpen cutting tools. See the striking effects of various tools and tool positions, grips and stances as you learn to turn thinwall, bark-edge and end-grain bowls. You'll enjoy Del's easy and enlightening approach as he leads you through the entire process.

12-025 120 min. $39.95

Build A Shaker Table with Kelly Mehler

Mehler shows the entire process of making a leg-and-apron table, from stock preparation to final scraping and sanding.

12-9512 60 min. $29.95

BUILD YOUR OWN SERIES:

• Computer Desk

Designed with space and style in mind, this drop leaf desk is perfectly suited for the compact computer set-up.

12-1931 30 min. $16.95

• Sketch and Storage Bench

Features large, built-in chalkboard, making it a perfect start at sparking your child's imagination.

12-1930 30 min. $16.95

• Welsh Cupboard

Can be used as storage space for china, crystal, or anything of value. This piece enhances any dining or living room.

12-1932 30 min. $16.95

Building Bookcases

Choosing the stock, tools and materials, designs and plans, cutting dadoes, rabbets, doweling, jointing the edges, building outer frame, shaping the molding, attaching molding and making the door. Booklet included.

18-232 30 min. $19.95

Building Cabinets

Choosing the stock, tools and materials, design and plans, preparing the stock, cutting shelves and rails, doweling, preparing sides, top and bottoms, cutting dadoes and rabbet, assembling face frames, cutting drawer fronts and glides, building doors, assembling the unit, building drawers and finishing touches. Booklet included

18-237 30 min. $19.95

Building Tables

Choosing the stack, tools and materials, design and plans, preparing the stock, preparing legs and rails, assembling the top, mounting the top, joinery, assembling the frame, attaching the top and finishing touches. Booklet included.

18-236 30 min. $19.95

Carve a Ball-and-Claw Foot with Phil Lowe

Woodworking instructor and specialist in period furniture reproduction, Phil Lowe, demonstrates how to make that hall-mark of 18th century furniture, the cabriole leg with a ball-and-claw foot, focusing on the colonial Philadelphia version. Learn to scale to your furniture plan; Bandsaw a

VIDEO TITLES LISTED IN THIS GUIDE ARE AVAILABLE FOR PURCHASE OR RENTAL. CONTACT YOUR LOCAL VIDEO STORE OR TELEPHONE (800) 383-8811

graceful cabriole ready for carving; lay out the ball-and-claw form; cut in the ball using a mallet and gouge; and shape the dragon's claw for a vigorous-looking grip.
12-028 115 min. $39.95

Carving Swedish Woodenware
Learn the grips, strokes and rhythms that make for successful Swedish wood carving. Learn from easy-to-follow instructions on technique, proper usage and handling of the carving tools.
12-9515 60 min. $29.95

Chip Carving with Wayne Barton
Using just a compass, a ruler and two knives, you can chip carve a dazzling array of incised borders, rosettes, letters and graceful free-form designs. An illustrated booklet includes plans for the designs covered, technical highlights and sources of supply.
12-2381 60 min. $29.95

Dovetail a Drawer with Frank Klausz
Watch as master cabinetmaker Frank Klausz shows you all the steps involved in sizing stock; running a groove for a drawer bottom; cutting quick, precise dovetails without the need for jigs or templates; and gluing up and fitting your completed drawer. Includes how to use the backsaw, chisel and smoothing plane; and how to rip, cross-cut and plow on power equipment.
12-024 60 min. $29.95

Easy to Build Woodworking Projects
Microwave cart, bandsaw box, cutting board and butcher block, videocassette holder, towel rack and name jigsaw puzzle. Booklet included
18-235 30 min. $19.95

Furniture Refinishing
Step-by-step instructions on how to disassemble hardware and mirrors; apply stripper; refinish sanding; apply stain; and seal and finish.
18-046 42 min. $19.95

Furniture Refinishing and Wood Care
Follow master furniture finished, Bill Richards, as he guides you step-by-step in how to bring back the natural beauty of your furniture. Bill will show you how to remove old varnish, shellac and lacquer from your furniture and demonstrates the proper method of applying and removing paint removers. Also learn how to apply tung oil and the best way to use stains.
18-178 53 min. $39.95

Furniture Refinishing
A step-by-step introduction to furniture refinishing demonstrating the three basic steps: 1) stripping and stain removal; 2) preparing the surface for refinishing, including removing gouges and sanding; and 3) refinishing with stains and/or varnish.
18-032 42 min. $29.95

Interior Wood Refinishing I: Stripping & Sanding
Learn how to plan, dismantle trim, strip with paste and liquid, and lots of time-saving tips.
18-061 45 min. $39.95

Interior Wood Refinishing II: Staining and Finishing
Learn how to reassemble, stain and finish trim.
18-062 42 min. $39.95

Jon Eakes Woodworking
Mr. Eakes, known as "Mr. Chips" in a popular woodworking show on Canadian television, has enjoyed an enthusiastic following. Part of the magic is the sense that a true master is revealing his secrets, combined with a warm, down-to-earth delivery.
18-218 60 min. $39.95

Making Mortise-and-Tenon Joints with Frank Klausz
Mortise-and-tenon joints are fundamental to good furniture making, and no one knows more about it than Frank Klausz. In this video he brings more than 20 years of cabinetmaking experience before the camera to show you how to make haunched, through/wedged and angled mortise-and -tenon joints. You'll learn how to determine which joint is best for which application, how to organize your procedures, and how to work with a variety of hand tools and common machines to increase your efficiency in the shop. Booklet included.
12-272 60 min. $29.95

Molding and Picture Frames
Molding. Choosing stock, tools and materials, design preparation and installation of baseboard, chair rail and crown molding, cutting profiles, bevel cuts, finishing touches. Picture Frames. Choosing stock, design cutting profiles, bevel cuts, assembly of frame and finishing touches.
18-234 30 min. $19.95

Outdoor Furniture
Hexagonal picnic table: Choosing stock, tools and materials design and plans, building center "wheels," cutting angles assembling top and seat, building and attaching legs, protecting wood. Planter: Choosing stock, cutting pieces, assembling legs and top. Booklet included.
18-233 30 min. $19.95

VIDEO TITLES LISTED IN THIS GUIDE ARE AVAILABLE FOR PURCHASE OR RENTAL. CONTACT YOUR LOCAL VIDEO STORE OR TELEPHONE (800) 383-8811

Radial Arm Saw Joinery with Curtis Erpelding

Craftsman Curtis Erpelding, the master who brought fine joinery to the radial-arm saw, shows you how to make impeccably precise cuts time after time. Learn how to set up and fine-tune your machine; lay out and cut a series of identical slip-joints; use these methods to cut increasingly complex joints; and how these artful jigging techniques liven up a host of new and exciting design possibilities.

12-027 110 min. $39.95

Refinishing Furniture: Volume 1 & 2

This video includes an introduction, stripping furniture, sanding furniture, staining, sealing, filling wood applying and rubbing out the finish and repairing the finish. Two tapes.

18-230 140 min. $39.95

Repairing Furniture with Bob Flexner

Expert furniture restorer Bob Flexner demonstrates each method and tells you how to decide which one is right for the job at hand. With Flexner's easy-to-follow instructions, and the information in the accompanying booklet, those wobbly chairs and banged-up bureaus are as good as fixed.

18-1534 70 min. $29.95

Repairing Furniture: Volume 1 & 2

This video includes an introduction, regluing, patching missing and broken pieces, tool sharpening, repairing veneer and using hide glue. Two tapes.

18-228 165 min. $39.95

Router Jigs and Techniques with Bernie Maas and Michael Fortune

The router is one of the most versatile tools in a woodworker's shop, but learning how to use one efficiently can be tough to figure out. That's why this video workshop is so helpful. With more than 30 years' experience between them, these two inventive woodworkers show you ways to use the router to increase your creativity and productivity in the shop.

12-271 60 min. $29.95

Sam Maloof: Woodworking Profile

Internationally recognized woodworker Sam Maloof displays his fluid style of woodworking. Viewers see how he builds his tables and chairs, including his distinguished rocker.

12-9510 60 min. $29.95

Small Shop Projects: Boxes

Great ideas for all those lovely bits of wood woodworkers can't bear to throw out. You'll learn how to make little things that you can use around your shop or your house.

12-9510 60 min. $29.95

Small Shop Tips and Techniques with Jim Cummins

In this video workshop, Jim shares some of the tips and tricks he has discovered, showing you how to use common machines such as the tablesaw, bandsaw and drill press to achieve uncommon results. Booklet included.

12-273 60 min. $29.95

Turning Wood with Richard Raffan

There's a new way to master the moves that are so important to skillful turning-a book and videotape combination by one of today's leading woodturners. In his book, Richard Raffan covers the basics and uses a series of exercises and projects to teach the skills involved in both centerwork and facework turning. The companion videotape features these projects and exercises, letting you see and hear the techniques you want to learn. Specific sections of the tape are keyed to pages in the book, so you can read along as Raffan teaches you his craft.

12-270 117 min. $39.95

Turning Projects

Twelve of the projects that are in the book. Turning Projects are clearly demonstrated in the video. By the end of the video and accompanying booklet you will have completed a satisfying course in woodturning.

12-9513 90 min. $39.95

Wood Finishing with Frank Klausz

Learn fine, durable finishes from 20-year cabinetmaking master Frank Klausz. Includes demonstrations on how to prepare an ideal surface for finishing: choose between oil, alcohol and water stains; apply tung oil or spar varnish for maximum wood penetration; spray lacquer; apply French polish; and even correct finishing goofs.

12-026 110 min. $39.95

Woodworking

An informative introduction to plywood and lumber; what you need to know to make cabinets, from cutting your materials to hardware installation; and power tools, such as table saws, routers, sanders, joiners and many more.

18-149 45 min. $29.95

WOODWORKING SERIES BY PUNKIN HOLLOW

Kenneth Bowers is one of the premier woodcrafters of our time. His reputation as a designer, builder and restorer of fine furniture is known throughout

England. Having built and restored pieces for clients from Hampton Court, he is now semi-retired and remains in great demand for lectures and seminars throughout Europe and America. This series is sure to increase your skills as well as your joy in woodworking.

• **Basic Tools**
In an eye-opening introduction Kenneth Bowers demonstrates the selection, use and care of basic tools for the woodcrafter. Do you know how to determine whether a tri-square is true? Or why you should always use a cutting gauge when planing end grain, but never when marking out a chamfer? How to adjust a plane correctly? A superb tape and a must for woodworking students, whether beginner or expert.
12-168 88 min. $39.95

• **Dovetails**
Ken has some stories about dovetails...he'll show you how to make them, and he'll show you some he's made. With practice, you'll be able to apply the knowledge to make through dovetails, lap dovetails, secret dovetails and others. Many woodcrafters say the dovetail is their favorite of all joints.
12-169 80 min. $39.95

• **Finishing and Polishing**
Many times a good woodworking job is ruined by a poor or inappropriate finish. This program is packed with more valuable knowledge and "secrets" than you ever imagined existed...and many of the techniques are surprisingly easy. Learn the correct techniques to show off your wookworking skills with a beautiful finish.
12-170 80 min. $39.95

• **Hinging, Clamping and Screwing**
Not knowing the proper techniques for putting things together can be costly. On this tape Ken shows you the preferred methods of assembling, gluing, and holding things together. Ken shows you what you how to make adjustments at this stage and also how to bring things into line so that the final product will reflect the work of a true craftsman.
12-171 74 min. $39.95

• **Mortice and Tenon/Dadoes**
Mortice and tenon is one joint, but two separate projects-and in the end they have to fit each other properly. There's no secret power tool which drills a square hole; it's all in knowing the proper techniques of marking out the pieces and where and how to cut, and with what tool. Also learn to make a through dada as well.
12-172 56 min. $39.95

• **Sharpening, Inlaying and Detailing**
The self-taught woodworker is prone to several

mistakes. One is selection of the wrong tools and materials. Another is lack of knowledge about how to properly sharpen tools. In less than an hour, the beginning craftsman will learn these techniques. The second part of the program is devoted to an introduction to inlaying and detailing.
12-174 86 min. $39.95

Miscellaneous

AMERICAN CRAFT COLLECTION

• **Basic Folk Art Painting with Peggy Caldwell**
Introduces the techniques of folk art painting for application on furniture, ornaments and other items.
18-2036 55 min. $29.95

• **Basic Stenciling Techniques with Jeannie Serpa**
Demonstrates stenciling techniques on fabric, wood and other hard surfaces. Covers how to cut stencils, the stenciling process, and the various stenciling surfaces.
12-2038 50 min. $29.95

• **Basic Tole and Decorative Painting with Peggy Caldwell**
Introduces the art of painting on tin, as well as decorative painting on wood, porcelain, and an assortment of fabrics.
12-2037 72 min. $29.95

• **Craft Medley and Gifts with Rose Ann Capiruscio**
This medley begins with an assortment of Victorian decorations, followed by projects created for special occasions. Includes crafts for children.
12-2039 62 min. $29.95

Bread Dough Folk Art
Lee Maher shows you how to mix dough recipes, from mushrooms and assemble to a plaque, paint bread dough and create different shapes and designs.
12-008 62 min. $24.95

Candlewicking
Instructor: Claire Bryant of the Berry Patch. Experience the old art of candlewicking. Master both the colonial figure eight candlewick knot and the fuzzy effect of tufting. A butterfly design is included with complete step-by-step instructions. Also, ideas on how to finish projects and how to

experiment with floss and colored yarns. Everything you need to know to create a colonial keepsake.

12-197 26 min. $49.95

Chair Caning

You can learn enough about caning to start your own business. If you are caning a heirloom or learning to cane chairs for extra income you will enjoy this interesting and rewarding video. Jane Nelson has over twenty-five years of experience in wicker repair. Both types of canning are demonstrated.

12-8020 105 min. $39.95

Coins: Genuine, Counterfeit, Altered

This program identifies the criteria for selecting a reputable dealer and demonstrates how to perform a preliminary examination at purchase. In addition, this informative program demonstrates what genuine coin characteristics can and do occur at the mint, including aberrations, weak strikes, hairline scratches, lint marks, die cracks, and clashed and altered dies. It also covers the characteristics of fake coins, including those coins that have been altered by additions, deletions and treated surfaces, as well as counterfeit coin characteristics including cast, electrotypes and counterfeits struck from copy dies.

07-162 50 min. $59.95

Collecting & Grading U.S. Coins

This video program grades a wide variety of coins to teach the basic principles. Copper coins are graded using the Lincoln cent and Indian Head cent; nickel coins are graded using the Buffalo nickel; silver coins are graded using the Washington quarter. Walking Liberty half dollar, Morgan dollar and the Peace dollar; gold coins are graded using the twenty dollar Liberty Head and Augustus Saint-Gaudins. Emphasis is placed on mint state or uncirculated coins. Two booklets included.

07-160 60 min. $79.95

Designer Sweatshirts

This video presents the process of sweatshirt decorating from the initial materials and tools needed to step-by-step procedures of altering.

12-3038 90 min. $24.95

Fun with Paints

Students will learn the art of stenciling and making their own stencils, water based paints are also used for easy clean-up. This lesson also includes potato stamping and personalizing with markers.

12-8016 30 min. $29.95

Gold Dredging Made Easy

Dave McCracken reveals his techniques for locating and dredging up paysteaks. Noted author of numerous books and articles on this timeless subject. Dave combines years of experience with advanced video effects and even underwater photography to bring you invaluable information on all aspects of gold dredging, from locating gold-bearing areas to reading rivers and useful tips on clean-up.

12-046 60 min. $49.95

Gunstock Checkering

A nationally-known custom gunstocker whose work has been illustrated in every major arms publication in the country, Joe Balickie discusses both past and current styles of intricate gunstock checkering patterns. He reviews the tools best suited for fine work and then proceeds to instruct the viewer in the intricacies of the layout, spacing, and pointing-up of the checkering pattern on a fine custom rifle stock.

12-212 120 min. $59.95

Gunstock Finishing

Joe Balickie demonstrates every facet of the application of the classic "in-the-wood" finish for gunstocks, one which duplicates the appearance of the hallowed and venerable London oilfinish used for centuries by the best English films. The materials discussed in this program represent the most modern and waterproof finishes available.

12-213 60 min. $49.95

How to Create Your Own Fantasy Horse

Dianne Headman will teach you how to create a beautiful fantasy carousel horse at the fraction of what it costs to buy one.

12-8142 45 min $29.95

How to Create Victorian Paper Scrap Art

Now there is a great new method for creating stunning decorator pieces from this lovely paper scrap. Whether you're a collector or just someone who loves Victoriana, you can bring the romance and style of a bygone era into your home.

12-8143 46 min. $29.95

How to Create Victorian Style Lampshades

Mary Maxwell has been specializing in making lampshades typifying turn-of-the-century styles. She feels that this is the best and most efficient way to share her talent with those who are interested in bringing back this art form.

12-8160 65 min. $49.95

How to Repair Plates, Pottery, Porcelain

This video was developed to satisfy the need for practical restoration and advice for household ceramic objects. So with a little patience and desire

VIDEO TITLES LISTED IN THIS GUIDE ARE AVAILABLE FOR PURCHASE OR RENTAL. CONTACT YOUR LOCAL VIDEO STORE OR TELEPHONE (800) 383-8811

you can do professional looking repairs effectively and inexpensively.
12-9699 60 min. $19.95

Introduction to Beekeeping
The film discusses package bee installation, catching a swarm, hive management, winterizing your colonies, honey removal, extracting and bottling.
12-253 58 min. $59.95

Lampshade Crafting
Instructor: Pam Bell of Make It Yourself demonstrates how to decorate paper lampshades using stencils, water colors, cross-stitch and cut and pierce. Everything from how to make scalloped edges to how to lace onto lampshade form. Includes pattern and materials sources.
12-203 43 min. $49.95

Making a Solid Body Electric Guitar
Build you own STRAT style guitar with instruction by Dan Erlewine, nationally know master repairman and columnist. Dan constructs a professional quality instrument "on camera" with complete instructions, close-ups and commentary for each step including: plans, layout, material, "squaring-up" the wood, constructing the neck and body, shaping and sanding, pre-fitting the hardware, final sanding and finishing, and final guitar assembly. A full-scale detailed blueprint, plus a parts and materials list is included with each tape.
12-223 120 min. $49.95

Making Stained Glass Windows
Tim Yockey is a master craftsman working in the Pacific Northwest. His original work in stained glass is well known and respected for its exquisite craftsmanship and skill. In this tape he shares the simplicity and the artistry of his method using clear and simple instruction, hints, close-ups and examples. Covers design and patterns, glass cutting, leading and soldering, puttying and finishing. A tape which will enable the novice to produce beautiful stained glass pieces.
12-161 100 min. $39.95

Maria! Indian Pottery of San Ildefonso
In this award-winning National Park Service program, noted Indian pottery maker Maria Martinez demonstrates the traditional Indian methods of pottery making. Beginning with the spreading of sacred corn, you will see gathering and mixing of clay, construction and decorating of pottery and building of the firing mound.
12-162 27 min. $29.95

PROFESSIONAL VIDEO LIBRARY
Learn how to create works of art or that little something to hang in the house.

• **Art of Cutting Glass**
12-9003 60 min. $29.95

• **Art Glass Construction**
12-9004 60 min. $29.95

• **Glass Fusion I**
12-9005 60 min. $29.95

• **Lamp Making with Joe Porcelli**
12-9006 60 min. $29.95

• **Professional Soldering Techniques**
12-9001 60 min. $29.95

PROJECT VIDEO SERIES
An informative series on glass etching, carving, staining, fusing and creating mirrors and decorations for around the home.

• **Brass and Bevel Cluster Construction**
12-9021 30 min. $19.95

• **Building a Victorian Lead Window**
12-9020 30 min. $19.95

• **Building a Window with Copper Foil**
12-9025 30 min. $19.95

• **Christmas in Stained Glass**
12-9019 30 min. $19.95

• **Decorative Soldering**
12-9011 30 min. $19.95

• **Glass Cabinet Doors**
12-9009 30 min. $19.95

• **Glass Candle Cubes**
12-9018 30 min. $19.95

• **Glass Etching Techniques**
12-9016 30 min. $19.95

• **Glass Jewelry Boxes**
12-9012 30 min. $19.95

• **How to Repair a Copper Foil Window**
12-9023 30 min. $19.95

• **Kaleidoscope**
12-9010 30 min. $19.95

• **Microwave Glass Fusing Art**
12-9014 30 min. $19.95

• **Panel Lamp Shades**
12-9007 30 min. $19.95

• **Pressed Flowers with Stained Glass**
12-9008 30 min. $19.95

• **Rapid Fusing Techniques**
12-9024 30 min. $19.95

• **Repair Techniques for Lead Windows**
12-9026 30 min. $19.95

• **Stained Glass Bird Houses**
12-9027 30 min. $19.95

• **Stained Glass Decorating Accessories**
12-9029 30 min. $19.95

• **Stained Glass Picture Frames**
12-9022 30 min. $19.95

• **Stained Glass Jewelry - Wearable Art**
12-9028 30 min. $19.95

• **Suncatchers and Nightlights**
12-9013 30 min. $19.95

• **Wall Lamp Sconces**
12-9002 30 min. $19.95

• **Wall Mirrors**
12-9015 30 min. $19.95

• **Working with Beveled Glass**
12-9017 30 min. $19.95

Shaker Chair: Weaving Patterns & Techniques
Turn an old chair into a family heirloom. Lenore Howe, an authority on Shaker chairs, teaches you how to weave five patterns used in cloth taped seats for Shaker-style chairs. Other subjects include calculating the amount of tape needed, tools, preparation of old chairs, splicing techniques, how to design custom patterns, and special tips for chair backs. Free supplier list for materials included.
12-8159 62 min. $24.95

Rainy Day Crafts: "Scissors, Paper & Glue"
This is a unique program created to introduce young children to arts & crafts techniques. This special inter-active video features 6 great fun projects with step-by-step instructions, that are easy to follow! This program will teach your child to create the following projects: super simple puppets,

hats & masks, my favorite things, paper animals, finger things and paper weaving placemat.
12-7048 30 min. $16.95

Rainy Day Crafts: "Stuff Around The House"
"Stuff Around The House" is a unique program created to teach and entertain young children for hours. This special inter-active video features 6 great fun projects with easy step-by-step instructions: printing with vegetables, noodles & yarn pencil holder, colorful greeting cards, old sock puppet, yarn people and pots and pans party.
12-7049 30 min. $16.95

Stamp Collecting Video
Hundreds of dazzling full-color stamps fill the screen as Gary Burghoff (M A S H's Radar O'Reilly) hosts the first home video on the world's most popular hobby. "The Video Guide to Stamp Collecting" is the perfect introduction for a beginner--it covers all the basics of philately--and it's a treat for experienced collectors too.
12-6270 50 min. $19.95

Stenciling
Learn to stencil on paper, fabric and wood. Many ideas will be shared for finishing projects to be used as gifts, greeting cards or for decorating with warmth.
12-255 35 min. $39.95

Stenciling
Instructor: Geanie Serpa. How to stencil on cloths, floors, walls, paper, canvas, fabric. Demonstrates how to cut your own stencil or use precut stencils. Proper shading and highlighting techniques are taught, along with a discussion of brush types, their use and care. How to line up register marks for perfect multi-part stencils. Also gives great ideas for decorating with stencils in unusual ways and how to combine stenciling with other crafts and needlework.
12-201 46 min. $49.95

Stenciling For Fabric and Walls
This course teaches the complete stenciling process from cutting the stencils to painting the design. You will learn many tips that would take years to discover as you learn how to stencil fabric, floor cloths and walls. The first project will give you a beautifully stenciled apron to wear while you stencil other projects. Several patterns are included as well as ideas for future projects.
12-291 98 min. $39.95

VICTORIAN VIDEO: TEXTILES, ARTS & CRAFTS SERIES
This series of programs features different ways of handling fabrics including: coloring, weaving,

handspinning and felt making.

• **American Tapestry Today**
An Exhibition - 1990
12-9405 28 min. $24.95

• **Bobbin Lace with Doris Southland**
12-9384 109 min. $39.95

• **Boundweave - Level I**
12-9400 140 min. $49.95

• **Color Interaction for Handweavers**
12-9398 40 min. $32.95

• **Doubleweave with Clotide Barrett**
12-9401 95 min. $44.95

• **Dressing the Loom with Constance LaLena**
12-9393 45 min. $19.95

• **Fabric Painting with Dyes on Silk and Cotton**
12-9388 118 min. $39.95

• **Feltmaking by Hand - The Basic Process**
12-9391 51 min. $39.95

• **Feltmaking - Garments and Surface Design Techniques**
12-9392 94 min. $39.95

• **Garments to Weave and How to Weave Them**
12-9395 37 min. $29.95

• **Handspinning - Advanced Techniques with Mabel Ross**
12-9390 112 min. $49.95

• **Handwoven Fabrics - Structure and Pattern**
12-9399 45 min. $39.95

• **Needlelace with Vima Micheli**
12-9385 109 min. $39.95

• **Quilted Painting with Ronni**
12-9389 68 min. $39.95

• **Supplementary Warp Patterning - Inkle Loom Techniques**
12-9402 87 min. $39.95

• **Tapestry Weaving - Level II**
12-9404 107 min. $49.95

• **Tatting I - The Basics with Mildred Clark**
12-9386 78 min. $29.95

• **Tatting II - Beyond the Basics**
12-9387 81 min. $39.95

• **Tips, Tricks & Problems with Sallie Guy**
12-9394 105 min. $39.95

• **Tubular Woven Finishes - Backstrap Loom Techniques**
12-9403 73 min. $39.95

• **Weave Drafting, The Easy Way Part I**
12-9396 69 min. $39.95

• **Weave Drafting, The Easy Way Part II**
12-9397 74 min. $39.95

Make a Quilt, Build a Cabinet

or Learn Ancient Folk Arts.

The Variety of Crafts in This Section is

Bound to please!

Documentary
&
History

- ✓ *Current Events*
- ✓ *Hollywood & Broadway*
- ✓ *Social & Political History*
- ✓ *War & Military History*
- ✓ *Miscellaneous*

HOLLYWOOD

Current Events

17 Days Of Terror: The Hijack of TWA 847

If you want a concise study of how a single incident of terror can render helpless a country and its resources, the textbook case would probably be this-the Hijacking of Flight TWA 847. Originally intended to fly 145 passengers (mostly Americans) from Athens to Rome, the airliner was hijacked in flight and rerouted to Beirut, where the terrorists began an odyssey of terror. On the spot news coverage with commentary from ABC news personalities such as Peter Jennings, Sam Donaldson, Pierre Salinger, and Peter Glass.
13-5761 60 min. $29.95

90's SERIES

This is a look at contemporary life in America. Culled from submissions by independent producers around the country, The 90's is a collection of reports, people, music, interviews and commentary organized around a weekly theme. People, places and ideas from around the world--fast paced, entertaining, funny and thought provoking reports from the creative edge of the video age.

* **America-Life, Liberty And...**
13-8314 60 min. $19.95

* **Anti-War Tapes**
13-8317 60 min. $!9.95

* **Bar Talk**
13-8312 60 min. $19.95

* **Food: You Are What You Eat**
13-8313 60 min. $19.95

* **It's Only TV**
13-8311 60 min. $19.95

* **Money, Money, Money**
13-8310 60 min. $19.95

* **Prisoners: Rights & Wrongs**
13-8319 60 min. $19.95

* **Race & Racism: Red, White & Black**
13-8315 60 min. $19.95

* **Street-Music And People**
13-8318 60 min. $19.95

* **Video Kids**
13-8316 60 min. $19.95

Animals Film

We skin them alive for furs, experiment on them and dissect them. This controversial program takes us inside the slaughterhouse, into the laboratory, and down the food processing line to create an experience that will change your life. Because of its graphic footage, this program has been banned from television.
13-1864 120 min. $79.95

Battered

At a rate of one every 15 seconds, acts of domestic violence strikes more women than automobile accidents, muggings and rapes combined. It's a leading cause of injury to women in the United States. This powerful video offers important information to families faced with domestic violence. This program won the John Muir Medical Film Festival Award.
13-8345 56 min. $99.95

Buster and Me

This Emmy Award-winning puppet show was created to address the feelings of helplessness, hopelessness, confusion and fear experienced by children as they become increasingly aware of the threat of nuclear war. Robin Goodrow stars as Robin, the hostess of the puppet program.
13-216 23 min. $49.95

Come Back, Africa

This film was made secretly in order to portray the true conditions of life in South Africa. This is the story of Zachariah...one of the hundreds of thousands of Africans forced each year off the land and into the gold mines by the regime.
13-2388 83 min. $59.95

Confessions of Bernhard Goetz

The "Subway Vigilante" who shot four teens while riding a New York subway, gave a lengthy videotaped confession to the police after turning himself in. For the first time ever, the public can now see the most complete account of this emotional, yet often vulgar, self-incrimination.
13-2315 80 min. $39.95

Convicts on the Street: One Year on Parole

Does the parole system offer promise for dealing with criminals? The Department of Justice predicts that the number of paroles will double in the next five years to 800,000. This documentary follows a parole officer and his 50 charges. He also makes surprise visits to the homes of those he suspects of violating their parole.
13-8348 60 min. $69.95

VIDEO TITLES LISTED IN THIS GUIDE ARE AVAILABLE FOR PURCHASE OR RENTAL. CONTACT YOUR LOCAL VIDEO STORE OR TELEPHONE (800) 383-8811

Day After Trinity
This video is a haunting journey through the dawn of the nuclear age, an incisive history of humanity's most dubious achievement and the man behind it J. Robert Oppenheimer, principal architect of the atomic bomb.
13-486 88 min. $79.95

Dear America
This landmark film captures the truth of Vietnam like no movie could. Actual letters from soldiers are read by such talents as Robert DeNiro, Kathleen Turner, Michael J. Fox, Sean Penn and William Dafoe, to a moving soundtrack of the music that rocked a generation.
13-8350 87 min. $69.95

Death Of The Nile: The Struggle For Peace And The Assassination Of Anwar Sadat
This program provides a public biography of Anwar Sadat's political life. Initiating a peace process that would forever change the dynamics of the Middle East, Sadat had to suffer the ultimate martyrdom for his efforts-death by an assassin's bullet. On-the-spot news coverage of key events, including the historic Camp David accords with President Jimmy Carter and Israeli Prime Minister Menachem Begin. Featuring ABC news personalities Frank Reynolds, Barbara Walters, Harry Reasoner, Howard K. Smith, and others.
13-5759 60 min. $29.95

Design For a Positive Future
Do you feel overwhelmed by media reports about polluted air and water? Are you searching for a new vision of a better life? On this tape, futurist Barbara Marx Hubbard and her "Design Team" propose an action agenda to solve society's dilemmas. They call for the creation of an "Office for the Future" to implement positive answers to pressing human needs.
13-9154 26 min. $16.95

Destination Nicaragua
A hard-hitting yet informative and entertaining program about this controversial issue and country. Experience the adventures of groups of American citizens as they embark on journeys to this hotbed of Central America. Hear mothers tell of the brutalities committed against their children, see the Contras as they embark on their covert mission, and make up your own mind who really represents the people of Nicaragua, the Sandinistas or Contras.
13-250 60 min. $49.95

Down and Out in America
This film, narrated by Lee Grant, takes us into the streets and brings the nightmare home. Truth is more fascinating than fiction.
13-1827 60 min. $29.95

Drugs: A Plague Upon The Land
Hosted by Peter Jennings. The gang-infested underworld of the drug trade is placed under the network microscope in this aggressive news investigation from ABC. With eye-popping footage from the underbelly of America, this program is testament to the fact that Cocaine, Crack, Heroin, PCP, and other illegal "recreational" drugs are truly destroying large segments of our society at every economic level.
13-5749 60 min. $19.95

Edge of History
Filmed in 1983 at a Physicians for Social Responsibility meeting, this program offers an updated description and analysis of the current nuclear threat. Twelve distinguished men and women discuss the need for a "new mode of thinking" about the nuclear weapons race. An important film on an important issue.
13-212 28 min. $49.95

Flip Side of Rodeo
Features the most outrageous highlights of the National Finals Rodeo from 1979 to 1987. Learn about cowboy superstitions, riding styles and much more.
13-8146 41 min. $16.95

Guns: A Day in the Death of America
America's death toll from handguns is rising. This program uncovers the human realities behind the statistics, in a chilling account of all gun-related deaths that occurred on a randomly selected day-- July 16, 1989. On that day 61 men, women and children were shot to death in murders, suicides, accidents, police actions and acts of self-defense. With 180 million guns in private hands (enough to put two firearms in every U.S. household) anyone is a potential victim.
13-8347 60 min. $99.95

Heil Hitler: Confessions of a Hitler Youth
A shocking true story based on the book by Alfons-Heck, recalling how he became a high-ranking member of the Hitler Youth during World War II. Heck pledged his life to Adolf Hitler as an impressionable 10-year-old. Could it happen again today?
13-8349 30 min. $69.95

In the Nuclear Shadow: What Can the Children Tell Us.
Children of various races and backgrounds openly discuss their responses to the threat of nuclear war.

VIDEO TITLES LISTED IN THIS GUIDE ARE AVAILABLE FOR PURCHASE OR RENTAL. CONTACT YOUR LOCAL VIDEO STORE OR TELEPHONE (800) 383-8811

In this deeply moving documentary they express their fear, anger and feelings of helplessness as well as their hope that the nuclear dilemma can and will be solved. A 1984 Oscar nominee.
13-215 25 min. $49.95

Inside The White House
Hosted by The President and Barbara Bush. With Sam Donaldson and Diane Sawyer. Unless you are Mikhail Gorbachev or Queen Elizabeth, you probably haven't been offered a true opportunity to tour the White House. The long wait is over. Also includes close-ups of the priceless treasures and artifacts contained that hang in the hallways. A collector's video treasure.
13-5748 50 min. $19.95

Last Epidemic
Conveys in plain language the effects of one or more nuclear weapons on a civilian population, while using visuals which actually show the effects of a nuclear explosion. It describes the drastic damage to the environment and the long-range devastation to the planet and features internationally recognized authorities from both the scientific and medical communities. This program has been described as "overwhelming," "harrowing" and "devastating."
13-211 28 min. $49.95

Line in the Sand: What Did America Win?
Peter Jennings examines the prospects for peace in the Middle East, the effects the war had on weapons build-ups and the political leadership of the region in the wake of Operation Desert Storm.
13-8295 50 min. $29.98

Oliver North: Memo to History
This video tells the whole story of Lt. Colonel Oliver North's role in the entire Iran/Contra scandal. Contains footage of North and the hearings and shows the considerable talents of the charismatic Colonel.
13-1587 90 min. $19.95

On Trial: The William Kennedy Smith Case
A chronicle of coverage by ABC News of one of the most celebrated court cases of our time. A charge of rape against a member of America's most prominent family and a plea of innocence by the accused, William Kennedy Smith. He and his alleged victim are face-to-face in a Palm Beach Florida courtroom, each telling their stories in fascinating detail.
13-8293 50 min. $29.98

Peter Jennings Reporting: Men, Sex & Rape
This examines the problem of rape and features interviews of both rapists and their victims in order to expose the motives and effects rape has.
13-8296 75 min. $29.98

Pushed to the Edge
This special edition of 20/20 focuses on the growing numbers of American women who are fighting back against abusive partners and rapists.
13-8292 50 min. $29.98

Rape: Cries from the Heartland
One in five women will be raped at some point in their lives, says the U.S. Senate report of March, 1991. This program reveals a disturbing portrait of rape as it really is; an act of violence, not sex. In addition to chronicling the efforts of police and sexual-abuse workers, this documentary explores the long term psychological effects of rape.
13-8346 45 min. $99.95

Rise and Fall of the Soviet Union
This epic film very clearly sets forth the dramatic events which occurred before, during, and after the Russian Revolution. This is the most complete and entertaining piece ever created on this subject. It will excite, inform, and above all, help the viewer understand what really happened to this once mighty nation.
13-8336 124 min. $89.95

Rodney King Case
Watch actual courtroom video of the Rodney G. King beating case.
13-8039 120 min. $59.95

Royal Wedding of H.R.H. Prince Andrew and Sara Ferguson
The sights and sounds of the royal wedding make a memorable keepsake and a rare family portrait to be shared and treasured. This is the official Buckingham Palace authorized video.
13-1593 100 min. $29.95

Sentenced for Life
Through candid discussions with young survivors of alcohol related accidents, this program provides a frank, first-hand look at the devastating effects of drunk driving. A film that gives teenagers an important edge-the facts about drinking and driving.
13-2293 40 min. $29.95

Situation
A frightening portrait of an American film crew who lived with a Salvadoran family for two tragic years in the hell of El Salvador's Civil War.

Features music by Bob Dylan; Peter, Paul and Mary; and Randy Master.
13-439 30 min. $34.95

Soviets, Meet Middle America!
Follow the adventures of Andrei, Boris, Lyubov and Petras as they travel from coast to coast, stay in people's homes and experience America in a thousand ways. Feel the excitement as people from both cultures, who have been denied access to each other for decades, meet face-to-face. See how these ordinary Soviet citizens become instant celebrities, representing their country to curious Americans.
13-5121 30 min. $39.95

Town Meeting: A Process Run Amok: Thomas/Hill Hearings
A discussion of the political and media issues surrounding the Clarence Thomas Anita Hill sexual harassment Senate hearings. Has the confirmation process in this country run amok? Ted Koppel is joined by Senators Alan Simpson, Bill Bradley and others with a an audience featuring Ralph Nader, Nina Totenberg and other Washington politicians and reporters to discuss these issues.
13-8294 90 min. $29.98

Wall: The Making And Breaking Of The Berlin Wall
At the Brandenburg Gate on New Year's Eve 1989 it was not just the new decade that the people were celebrating. History was in the making, 28 years of communist domination and unabridged rule had been demolished, and with it, the fall of the Iron Curtain. This fascinating and informative documentary traces the historical events of the past 28 years. From the horrifying erection of the Wall in 1961 through the celebration at the Brandenburg Gate on 12th December 1989, when the wall was finally smashed.
13-6450 50 min. $19.95

What About the Russians?
Are the Russians ahead in the nuclear arms race? Why the concern over the MX, Cruise, and Pershing missiles? Can we trust the Russians to honor a nuclear weapons treaty? How can we end the arms race and maintain our national security? These and other important questions are discussed by Robert McNamara, former defense secretary; George Kennan, former ambassador to the U.S.S.R; William Colby, former director of the CIA; and John Marshall Lee, Vice-Admiral U.S. Navy (Ret).
13-213 26 min. $49.95

Wise Use
A timberman's view of a properly managed southern forest. Accepted and shown on many PBS stations, this program depicts the lessons learned and the problems solved by today's lumberman.
13-8066 58 min. $99.95

Women: For America, For the World
This film celebrates women who have the vision, courage and determination to re-define the meaning of security for our nation and our world, and then confront the economic and political vested interests in the arms race. With common sense and compassion, they speak out for our health, educational and economic needs but, most importantly, for the future of our children. Features a roster of prominent American women.
13-214 28 min. $49.95

Hollywood & Broadway

25 Years of Entertainment
This program explores Hollywood in its heyday from 1942-1966. The stars, the premieres and much more make up this entertaining history.
13-3095 60 min. $14.95

Birth of a Legend
A marvelous documentary revealed in caring detail by producer Matty Kemp, from his personal knowledge of both Mary Pickford and Douglas Fairbanks. He has created a nostalgia packed film showing the on and off antics of this famous movie couple when they reigned as the king and queen of the movies. Here is an excellent perspective of their lives and times.
13-120 25 min. $29.95

Christmas at the Movies
A collection of clips highlighting favorite scenes from Hollywood's best movies.
13-8272 60 min. $19.95

Days of Thrills and Laughter
An expertly crafted look back at the action-packed, madcap days of slapstick comedy. Whether you're simply wondering what the era was all about or you want to review your old favorites, this compilation will leave you satisfied. Included are Mack Sennett, The Keystone Cops, Charlie Chaplin, Fatty Arbuckle and many more.
13-483 93 min. $29.95

Entertaining the Troops
This is a wonderful grab bag of nostalgic wartime vignettes assembled with obvious affection by Robert Mugge.
Featuring: Bob Hope, Dorothy Lamour and others.
13-9239 90 min. $16.95

VIDEO TITLES LISTED IN THIS GUIDE ARE AVAILABLE FOR PURCHASE OR RENTAL. CONTACT YOUR LOCAL VIDEO STORE OR TELEPHONE (800) 383-8811

GOLDEN MEMORIES FROM THE FIFTIES:

Milton Berl, Roy Rogers, Jackie Gleason, Art Linkletter, Jack Benny and over 50 other stars from the early days of television are showcased in this original, three-volume compilation series. Treat yourself to the vintage comedy, adventure, mystery and drama offered. These are rare, outrageous and nostalgic marvels from the archives of television's glorious past.

• **Volume 1**
25-233 60 min. $19.95

• **Volume 2**
25-234 60 min. $19.95

• **Volume 3**
25-235 60 min. $19.95

Great Romances of the Century

A nostalgic international journey with the headline heartthrobs, provocative pairings and wonderful weddings of the 20th century. From Rudolph Valentino to Prince Charles and Lady Diana--they are all here.
13-249 60 min. $19.95

Hollywood Home Movies

A documentary about the stars. See them behind the scenes! See them at their pools! See them as kids! See a hundred million dollar cast as they have never been seen before, in this never before revealed collection of home movies of the stars. With John Wayne, Marilyn Monroe, Robert Mitchum, Ann-Margaret, Gregory Peck and over 60 more celebrities. A must for collectors!
13-223 58 min. $19.95

Hollywood Stars Video Tour

This is an exciting tour through the movie capitol of the world. See where they live, shop, dine, and where their most popular movies where shot.
13-8118 45 min. $19.95

Ingrid: Portrait of a Star

Ingrid Bergman was more than a star, she was a legend. In this brilliant look at the woman, her career, and a woman not likely to be equaled in the kingdom of tinsel.
13-224 70 min. $24.95

Inside Hitchcock

Enter the mind of Alfred Hitchcock, one of the cinema's greatest directors. See clips from his best films and listen to the master himself discuss his techniques, his actors and his intentions.
06-016 55 min. $39.95

Inside the Labyrinth

A behind-the-scenes look at George Lucas' and Jim Henson's epic fantasy, "Labyrinth."
13-8269 57 min. $19.95

Ken Murray's Shooting Stars

Ken Murray has compiled an amazing assortment of rare "home movies" from 50 of our greatest Hollywood Celebrities, including Liz Taylor, Marilyn Monroe, Gregory Peck, Jayne Mansfield, Jack Lemmon and many more. Great fun!
13-132 62 min. $59.95

Lonesome Dove: The Making of an Epic

Includes a special behind-the-scenes look at the TV epic mini-series.
13-8147 50 min. $16.95

Love Goddesses

Documentary look at the goddesses of the cinema ranging from Little Egypt (1896) to Marilyn Monroe.
13-8263 83 min. $16.95

Maurice Chevalier

A portrait of the charmer in the straw hat, the most beloved of the song-and-dancemen, with archival footage tracing his career from Montmarte to Hollywood.
13-8060 58 min. $39.95

Oscar's Greatest Moments

Unforgettable highlights from the Academy Awards presentations, 1971-1991.
13-8662 110 min. $19.95

Power Profiles: The Folk Heroes

Charismatic western film actor Gary Cooper and world-renowned humorist/cowboy Will Rogers are featured.
06-071 50 min. $19.95

Power Profiles: The Legendary Ladies

Academy Award Winner Betty Davis and madcap comedienne Carole Lombard are featured.
06-072 50 min. $19.95

San Simeon

The Golden Age of movie stars; Hearst's opulent castle, their playground. Filmed by Ken Murray, his personal momento is a revelation of Hollywood's greatest including: Charlie Chaplin, Cary Grant, Carole Lombard, Hedda Hopper and others in a unique setting.
13-9000 20 min. $19.95

Woman's Place

A brilliant blend of rare photos and seldom seen motion pictures, this inspiring documentary is based on the LIFE Magazine special report

---

"Remarkable American Women." The material is paced in sequences such as women in the arts, in science, in business, in athletics...women who dared to be "first." Narrated by Julie Harris.
13-2452 25 min. $29.95

Women Who Made the Movies
Until now, little has been reported on the many contributions women have made to the motion picture industry. This unique documentary uses rare film clips and stills to trace the careers and films of Ann Baldwin, Ida Lupino, Lois Webb and others.
13-9427 56 min. $19.95

Yestereels of 1951
You will be thoroughly enchanted as you travel back in time to relive dramatic news stories that made lasting impressions forever.
13-8117 30 min. $16.95

Social & Political History

25 Years of News
This program highlights the historic events, tragic moments and the people who changed the world from 1941-1965. Includes many original film newsreels from this abundantly newsworthy time in history.
13-3096 60 min. $14.95

A. Einstein: How I See the World
To see the world through the eyes of Albert Einstein is to see some of the 20th century's most potent events from a unique perspective--and one much wilder than you may think.
13-8149 60 min. $19.95

Abraham Lincoln: Emancipation Proclamation
Step by agonizing step we are led along his path to his moment of decision. Here the program stops momentarily with the question for students: If you were President of the United States, what would you have done?
13-8285 25 min. $39.95

Age of Ballyhoo, Narrated by Gloria Swanson
The 20's roar in! A glittering time of speakeasies, flappers and the jazz age. Three Emmy Awards.
13-285 60 min. $24.95

Alcatraz
It's been called "The Island of No Return" and "The Devil's Island." But whatever name it goes by, this notorious parcel of land in San Francisco Bay is best known as the prison that housed the toughest criminals in the nation. Al Capone spent time there. So did Machine Gun Kelly and Frank Morris and Bob Stroud-"The Birdman of Alcatraz." the stories of these men and others who spent time in this infamous penitentiary are told in this fascinating and brutal documentary. Included in "Alcatraz" are scenes of "The Battle of Alcatraz" (1946), "Escape from Alcatraz" (1962), and the "Seizure of Alcatraz" by American Indians (late 1960's). Over 2,000,000 people have visited Alcatraz since it was turned over to the National Park Service in 1973.
13-226 54 min. $29.95

AMERICA AND THE WORLD SINCE WORLD WAR II
Hosted by veteran anchorman Ted Koppel and Peter Jennings, this unique four-volume set traces world history and culture from the end of World War II to the Geneva Summit. This is Fast-paced and offers a comprehensive look at the accomplishments and heartbreaking disappointments of one of history's most fascinating eras.

* **Volume 1: 1945-1952**
13-384 60 min. $29.95

* **Volume 2: 1953-1960**
13-385 60 min. $29.95

* **Volume 3: 1961-1975**
13-386 60 min. $29.95

* **Volume 4: 1976-1985**
13-387 60 min. $29.95

America Grows Up (1850-1900's)
America's growth from a nation of farms and villages to the leading industrial nation in the late 19th century is discussed.
13-008 50 min. $64.95

America's Public Enemies
The most famous and spectacular criminals of an era are now the subject of this penetrating program. Using rare and authentic footage, the lives of Al Capone, John Dillinger, Bonnie and Clyde, and a host of other gangsters will leave you spellbound. This is the real stuff,not Hollywood make believe.
13-425 60 min. $19.95

America, the Way We Were
Remember the home front and America's memory years 1940-45: Victory gardens, fireside chats, Your Hit Parade, Rosie the Riveter, Glenn Miller

VIDEO TITLES LISTED IN THIS GUIDE ARE AVAILABLE FOR PURCHASE OR RENTAL. CONTACT YOUR LOCAL VIDEO STORE OR TELEPHONE (800) 383-8811

and FDR teaching his grandchildren to swim at Hyde Park.
13-8077 180 min. $69.95

AMERICAN DOCUMENT SERIES

• America's Romance with Space
Col. William Anders USAF (Ret.) narrates this documentary about America's space program, as told by its first space pioneer, Dr. Robert Goddard.
13-2288 52 min. $24.95

• Black Shadows on a Silver Screen
The Black film industry co-existed with the Hollywood motion picture industry from 1915 to 1950, leaving little known from the era of segregated theaters and audiences. The story is a triumph of creativity and talent, a valuable source for our knowledge of Black culture in the 20th century.
13-2284 52 min. $24.95

• Building of the Capitol
Distinguished stage and screen actor Alexander Scourby provides a witty and informative commentary to this exclusive tour of one of our most cherished historical monuments.
13-2283 52 min. $24.95

• How We Got the Vote
Jean Stapleton effectively dramatizes the plight of early 20th century women stifled by an outmoded gender role and denied the right to vote.
13-2285 52 min. $24.95

• Inaugural Souvenir
Alexander Scourby narrates this collection of colorful stories surrounding our Presidential inaugurations.
13-2291 52 min. $24.95

• Legendary West
Ben Johnson narrates this documentary of how the film industry glamorizes the West while Westerners model themselves after fiction.
13-2287 52 min. $24.95

• Moment in Time
Gordon Parks narrates this history of photography and the social changes it effected in the United States.
13-2290 52 min. $24.95

• Patent Pending
William Shatner narrates this documentary where American ingenuity and the "better mousetrap" are whimsically and seriously treated.
13-2286 52 min. $24.95

• Working for the Lord
James Whitmore narrates this documentary about American religious communities of the 18th and 19th centuries, and the legacy they've left us.
13-2289 52 min. $24.95

American Gangster
A gripping look at the birth of organized crime in America.
13-8271 45 min. $16.95

Americans Courageous (1600-Today)
Two films featuring tales of courage: "The Gloucesterman," a filmed celebration of the townsfolk of a historic Massachusetts village who go down to the sea in ships, and "Not for Ourselves Alone", a 200-year history of America's armed forces.
13-002 50 min. $64.95

Anasazi
Why did a culture numbering into the hundreds of thousands suddenly disappear? Will the excavation of the Haynie Ruins reveal the secret of the Anasazi? Dozens of rooms have been excavated, unearthing many burial sites, arrowheads, stone and bone tools, pottery and jewelry.
13-487 37 min. $49.95

Anasazi: The Ancient Ones
The Navajo Indian meaning of "Anasazi" is "Ancient Ones." You will see the actual excavation of one of the largest mounds in the Southwest, a remnant of a culture numbering into the millions. Carbon dating in this mound goes back several thousand years. The Anasazi disappeared from the face of the earth 700 to 800 years ago, and no two authorities can agree on why, or on what became of them. Watch the actual unearthing of ancient burials, many stone tools, arrowheads, and pottery; and hear the story of what is known of the Anasazi.
13-142 24 min. $29.95

Ancient Indian Cultures of Northern Arizona
Explore the fascinating ruins of a mysterious prehistoric Indian people while visiting five national monuments: Montezuma Castle, Wupatki, Tuzigoot, Walnut Canyon and Sunset Crater. Learn how the ancient Indian civilizations of the Sinagua and Anasazi developed, survived and expired in this hostile environment.
13-141 30 min. $29.95

Animal Contact
A timely look at the relationship between all animals that walk the earth from the esteemed zoologist Desmond Morris. Three episodes look at the human animal's ascent to dominance, our

---

harvest of the animal world and the role of our former partners in building our civilization.
13-9455 180 min. $79.95

Arlington National Cemetery: Video Salute to America's Heroes
Take your own personal tour of America's most treasured national shrine. This official souvenir video, Pentagon approved, contains the entire Changing of the Guard Ceremony at the Tomb of the Unknown. Experience the story of the men and women of our great Nation who have paid the ultimate price to preserve our freedom.
13-8334 30 min. $19.95

Best Evidence: The Research Video
On November 22, 1963, shots rang out in Dallas, Texas, that were heard around the world: President John F. Kennedy was dead. The assassination remains a mystery to this day. But one man has uncovered shocking new evidence that must be seen to be believed.
13-6578 35 min. $19.95

Backstage at the White House
A rare, behind-the-scenes look at some great personal moments in the lives of our presidents and their families. Unforgettable moments that reveal the human side of the world's most powerful men.
13-146 60 min. $19.95

Belafonte Presents Fincho
Renowned singer Harry Belafonte hosts this colorful and exciting docudrama photographed by Sam Zebba on location in Nigeria. "Fincho" shows a single village's struggle to leap forward 1,000 years within a single decade.
13-023 120 min. $69.95

Buffalo Bill's Wild West Show
It was the circus, the Ice Capades, and the carnival all rolled into one. Fixing forever in the minds of Americans, and indeed millions of Europeans, the Wild West - as Buffalo Bill saw it. Contains rare footage taken between 1898 and 1912.
13-8015 45 min. $30.00

California Reich
Deals with a bizarre, complicated and frightening phenomenon: the rebirth of the Nazi movement in America. It took three months to get inside the front door of a Nazi household and another eight months before cameras were permitted to roll. The results are both poignant and chilling; the fear and hatred that motivates these individuals has roots in very real and recognizable frustrations the same frustrations that inspired an ex-paperhanger named Adolf Hitler to try to conquer the world. Be prepared, because the Nazis portrayed are not heel-clicking, Hollywood creations. More frighteningly,

they are the men, women and children who may live next door.
13-147 55 min. $49.95

Chicago Politics: A Theatre of Power
Enter the startling and dramatic world of Chicago politics-the naked prejudices, the rhetoric and the mechanisms of power.
13-1865 87 min. $29.95

Christopher Columbus Quincentennial
An artistic interpretation of historic reality based on documented accounts from European and American sources. This production is a pleasure and spectacle to be viewed by all ages...again and again.
13-8003 60 min. $19.95

Colonial History (1500-1600's)
A look at the period of history when France, Spain and England were fighting for the riches of the New World.
13-003 50 min. $64.95

COLONIAL WILLIAMSBURG SERIES:
Witness the life and times of the early American colonists in the original capital of Virginia. Filmed entirely on location, these programs provide a stunning portrait of what life in our country was like over 200 years ago.

• Basketmaking in Colonial Williamsburg
The crafting and many uses of one of man's oldest conveniences.
13-8085 28 min. $24.95

• Chelsea Porcelain from the Williamsburg Collection
An explanation of the history of Chelsea porcelain and how it came America.
13-8096 22 min. $24.95

• Christmas in Colonial Williamsburg
A sampling of the varied experiences enjoyed by Williamsburg's visitors during this special time of year.
13-8099 28 min. $24.95

• Colonial Clothing
The early Virginia colonists surrounded themselves with elegant, often extravagant fashions and furnishings.
13-8097 17 min. $24.95

• Colonial Naturalist
Based on the life and work of English naturalist Mark Catesby.
13-8086 55 min. $24.95

VIDEO TITLES LISTED IN THIS GUIDE ARE AVAILABLE FOR PURCHASE OR RENTAL. CONTACT YOUR LOCAL VIDEO STORE OR TELEPHONE (800) 383-8811

• **Cooper's Craft**
A demonstration of why the resident cooper was an indispensable craftsman.
13-8087 28 min. $24.95

• **Doorway to the Past**
Learn how archaeologists skillfully uncovered a host of artifacts to re-create the life of Colonial Williamsburg.
13-8101 28 min. $24.95

• **Flower Arrangements of Williamsburg**
See how the colonists brightened their lives with nature's bounty.
13-8100 30 min. $24.95

• **Forged in Wood: Building America's Blacksmith Shop**
The story of a blacksmith and entrepreneur who played an essential role in the American Revolution.
13-8102 32 min. $24.95

• **Glorious System of Things**
This dramatization shows how the American colonists learned through "circuit lecturers".
13-8098 58 min. $24.95

• **Gunsmith of Williamsburg**
A demonstration of the loving care that went into the making of each firearm.
13-8089 59 min. $24.95

• **Hammerman in Williamsburg**
The local blacksmith at a modest Williamsburg forge in the 1770 period.
13-8088 37 min. $24.95

• **Music of Williamsburg**
Virginia's eighteenth-century capital provides the background for the music of colonial America.
13-8095 40 min. $24.95

• **Musical Instrument Maker of Williamsburg**
You'll see and hear the results of one of our country's most specialized groups of artisan.
13-8103 53 min. $24.95

• **Search for a Century**
The excavation and interpretation of the early seventeenth century settlement of Martin's Hundred.
13-8094 45 min. $24.95

• **Silversmith of Williamsburg**
The art of silversmithing as it was practiced in eighteenth century Virginia.
13-8090 44 min. $24.95

• **Williamsburg File**
The role of archaeology in recreating the original capitol of Virginia. From forgotten maps to the diaries of Thomas Jefferson.
13-8093 45 min. $24.95

• **Williamsburg Sampler**
Architecture, gardens, textiles, furniture and other facets of our colonial heritage.
13-8091 28 min. $24.95

• **Williamsburg: The Story of a Patriot**
The colonist faces the issue of taxation without representation and the forces which led to their commitment to independence.
13-8092 36 min. $24.95

COMPLETE CHURCHILL SERIES:
An extraordinary four-part series chronicling the life of the twentieth century's greatest statesman. This four-part series is an integration of candid interviews, stark newsreel footage and fresh research unearthed exclusively for this series.

• **Maverick Politician**
Rarely seen footage of Churchill's incredible rise.
13-8062 50 min. $18.95

• **To Conquer or Die**
Behind the scenes during Britain's "darkest hour".
13-8063 50 min. $18.95

• **Beginning of the End**
From Yalta to a new world order.
13-8064 50 min. $18.95

• **Never Despair**
Victory over Germany, the Pulitzer Prize and knighthood.
13-8065 50 min. $18.95

Construction of the Hoover Dam
A fascinating return to a bygone era, this vintage 1936 documentary catalogues the dam's construction. Relive the almost insurmountable challenges faced by the engineers and builders of the mighty Hoover Dam.
13-028 35 min. $29.95

Contrasts
Performed by National Park Service employees, portrays the Plains Indians Warriors and the U.S. Cavalrymen that faced off against each other in the 1870's. Filmed at the actual site of the Reno retreat crossing at the Battle of the Little Big Horn.

Weapons, dress and gear, including cavalry horse gear, are displayed.
13-8011 48 min. $29.95

Courtesans of Bombay
Documentary about the young women of India who train in singing, dancing and the pleasing of men.
13-8270 74 min. $29.95

Custer's Last Fight
In 1912, Thomas Ince, one of the greatest American producers, turned his attention to Custer's Last Stand. It is the oldest film in existence. Filmed at a cost of $30,000 in 1912, Custer's Last Fight is a 45 minute treasure, filled with action and nostalgia.
13-8012 45 min. $29.95

Dark Days At The White House: The Watergate Scandal And The Resignation Of President Richard M. Nixon
Seldom in our history as a country has the nightly news been so important to us. During the Watergate scandal, we toned in ritualistically to see what new development had taken place. From the "Saturday Night Massacre" to the final resignation speech, this videocassette provides up-to-minute details on the doomed presidency of Richard M. Nixon.
13-5756 60 min. $24.95

DIVE WRECK VALLEY SERIES:
"Wreck Valley", a graveyard of ill-fated vessels lies off Long Island. Dive with award-winning cinematographer Daniel Berg as he searches for artifacts and explores such wrecks as a WWI navy cruiser, a rum runner and more.

• **USS San Diego and The USS Algol**
30-8278 48 min. $24.95

• **Lizzie D. & The R.C. Mohawk**
30-8279 48 min. $24.95

• **Kenosha & The Pinta**
30-8280 48 min. $24.95

• **Bronx Queen & The Propeller Salvage**
30-8281 48 min. $24.95

Declassified: The Plot to Kill President Kennedy
A fact-filled account of the nation's most tragic event.
13-9408 58 min. $19.95

Dwight D. Eisenhower Library and Museum
From documents, pictures, special displays and exhibits throughout the library; the video tells a story about President Eisenhower's personal life and how his presidency affected the United States. Also a tour of his boyhood home and Gettysburg farm.
13-8124 57 min. $24.95

Explore: Headhunters of Borneo
Join host James Coburn on an unforgettable expedition to the most dangerous jungle on earth. This exciting trek features killer ants, poisonous snakes, deadly crocodiles and blow- gun wielding natives.
13-1880 45 min. $29.95

EYES ON THE PRIZE SERIES:
A PBS special series on the evolution of black civil rights in America and the fight against racism.

• **Awakenings (1954-1956)**
13-8105 60 min. $19.95

• **Fighting Back (1957-1962)**
13-8108 60 min. $19.95

• **Ain't Scared of Your Jails (1960-1961)**
13-8107 60 min. $19.95

• **No Easy Walk (1961-1963)**
13-8108 60 min $19.95

• **Mississippi: Is This America? (1962-1964)**
13-8109 60 min. $19.95

• **Bridge to Freedom (1965)**
13-8110 60 min. $19.95

FABULOUS '60's
In a comprehensive year-by-year fashion, this series explores the fads and controversies, the global and political events, the fun and the tragedy, and the excitement that made the 1960's such a turbulent era.

• **1960**
13-408 60 min. $19.95

• **1961**
13-409 60 min. $19.95

• **1962**
13-410 60 min. $19.95

• **1963**
13-411 60 min. $19.95

VIDEO TITLES LISTED IN THIS GUIDE ARE AVAILABLE FOR PURCHASE OR RENTAL. CONTACT YOUR LOCAL VIDEO STORE OR TELEPHONE (800) 383-8811

- **1964**
13-412 60 min. $19.95

- **1965**
13-413 60 min. $19.95

- **1966**
13-414 60 min. $19.95

- **1967**
13-415 60 min. $19.95

- **1968**
13-416 60 min. $19.95

- **1969**
13-417 60 min. $19.95

Fall of the Roman Empire
Starring Sophia Loren, Stephen Boyd, Alec Guinness, Omar Shariff and others. The story traces the political and human reasons for the demise of the Pax Rimana and one of the greatest civilizations the world has ever known.
13-318 152 min. $29.95

Feathered Serpent
Quetzacoatl, "the feathered serpent," has been Mexico's symbol of spiritual practice since ancient times. About 1000 A.D. a Toltec priest and king revived this symbolic religion and led a cultural renaissance. 500 years later, Cortez used the prophecy of Quetzacoatl's return to overcome the Aztecs. His next foretold reappearance coincided with the recent worldwide Harmonic Convergence, when thousands reaffirmed his vision of universal enlightenment.
13-9163 40 min. $29.95

FEDERAL FOLLIES
Federal Follies is a collection of U.S. Government-produced films on a variety of topics. At the time they were made, each film approached its subject matter with the utmost seriousness. Today, they make for an extraordinary viewing experience, both for their unintentional humor and their historical content.

- **Volume 1**
"Blondes Prefer Gentlemen", "The Decision is Yours", "Duck and Cover".
13-482 50 min. $24.95

- **Volume 2**
"Cleanliness Brings Health", "Primordial Soup," "Our Job in Japan", "How to Succeed with Brunettes".
13-483 50 min. $24.95

- **Volume 3**
"Trip to Where", "Our Job in Germany".
13-484 50 min. $24.95

- **Volume 4**
"Tailgunner", "A Fool and his Money", "Civil Disturbances", "Time to Go".
13-2316 50 min. $24.95

- **Volume 5**
"Shadow of a Gunfight", "On Post Safety", "Code of Conduct", "Japanese Relocation".
13-2317 50 min. $24.95

- **Volume 6**
"Hookworm", "Curiosity Killed a Cat", "VD, One, Two", "The Big Lie", "World's Champion Hater".
13-2318 50 min. $24.95

Fire on the Rim
What kind of cultures develop in regions where the ground itself cannot be trusted? Where the earth explodes into molten destruction at a moment's notice? Volcanoes, earthquakes and tsunamis make their home in the area known as the "ring of fire". From Bali to New Zealand, from Japan to California. This series goes beneath the scientific surface to explore the ways the Pacific Rim cultures cope with the seismic and volcanic violence that frequents their world. This four part series interweaves the disciplines from social studies to science.
13-9453 240 min. $99.95

FRANK CAPRA COLLECTION: THE WAR YEARS
Army propaganda films directed by Frank Capra (It's A Wonderful Life).

- **Here is Germany**
13-8154 48 min. $19.95

- **Know Your Ally: Britain**
13-8155 48 min. $19.95

- **Know Your Enemy: Japan**
13-8156 62 min. $19.95

- **Negro Soldier**
13-8157 48 min. $19.95

- **Tunisian Victory I**
13-8158 48 min. $19.95

- **Tunisian Victory II**
13-8159 48 min. $19.95

- **Down and One to Go**
13-8160 51 min. $19.95

- **War Years: Attack! - The Battle for New Britain**
13-8264 48 min. $19.95

FRANK CAPRA COLLECTION: WHY WE FIGHT SERIES
Director Frank Capra's military documentaries.

- **Prelude to War and the Nazis Strike, Volume I**
13-8161 95 min. $24.95

- **Divide and Conquer, Volume II**
13-8162 57 min. $24.95

- **Battle of Britain, Volume III**
13-8202 54 min. $24.95

- **Battle of Russia, Volume IV**
13-8203 80 min. $24.95

- **Battle of China, Volume V**
13-8204 67 min. $24.95

- **War Comes to America, Volume VI**
13-8205 67 min. $24.95

Freedom: A Conflict of Interest
This takes you to the heart of Eastern Europe to see and hear first-hand interviews with Christian leaders. Dr. Reinhold J. Kerstan hosts this challenging documentary.
13-9110 60 min. $29.95

From the Czar to Stalin
Original footage, some never before seen, fills this fascinating view of Russia before, during and after the Revolution of 1917. See Czar Nicholas and his family; Rasputin; Lenin; President Woodrow Wilson; Stalin; and others who made history struggling for control or influence.
13-037 90 min. $29.95

Gathering Strength (1840-1914)
The differences between the old immigrants from northern Europe and the new wave of settlers from eastern and southern Europe are discussed.
13-006 50 min. $64.95

Gerald Ford: Oath of Office
Unelected as President of the United States, Gerald Ford takes that oath of office. Students are asked to analyze the interpretation.
13-8287 16 min. $39.95

Golden Door: Our Nation of Immigrants
This outstanding study of immigration in the United States gives the viewer a compassionate understanding of the immigrant experience as well as recounting the history of immigration laws.
13-2233 20 min. $74.95

Good Day to Die
Climb with Varum to the Crow's nest, charge down the valley with Reno and ride with Custer, Boyer and Curley into legend. Reno's river crossing, the fight on Last Stand Hill, scenes from the Indian village re-created and re-enacted by Sioux and Cheyenne Indians.
13-8010 60 min. $29.95

Grass: A Nation's Battle for Life
In 1924, neophyte film makers Cooper and Schoedsack, along with journalist and sometime spy Harrison, found excitement, danger and unparalleled drama in the migration of the Bakhtiari tribe of Persia (now Iran). This restored and full-length version, complete with an authentic new Iranian score, will astonish today's audiences with it's beautiful photography and heart-stopping adventure.
13-8025 70 min. $39.95

Great Decisions
Abraham Lincoln and the Emancipation Proclamation: We are led along his path to President Lincoln's moment of decision. Here the film stops momentarily with the question... "If you were the President of the United States, what would you have done?" William McKinley and American Imperialism: In 1908, President McKinley must make a fateful decision: whether or not to go to war with Spain and consequently, to embark on a policy of imperialism for the first time, acquiring colonies thousands of miles from America's shores. Woodrow Wilson: Fight for a League of Nations: Did Wilson help or harm his cause by trying to force the Senate to accept his views by making a direct appeal to the American public?
13-276 75 min. $39.95

Harry S. Truman Library and Museum
From documents, pictures, special displays and exhibits throughout the library; the video tells a story about President Trumans's personal life and how his presidency affected the United States. Also a tour of his birthplace home and the Truman farm.
13-8123 57 min. $24.95

HEADLINE STORIES OF THE CENTURY:
This series includes many of the headlines that captured America's attention.

• **America in the News**
13-8150 90 min. $29.95

• **America in Sports**
13-8153 90 min. $29.95

• **American Nostalgia**
13-8152 90 min. $29.95

• **World War II**
13-8151 90 min. $29.95

Immigrant Experience: The Long, Long Journey

An inspiring story told through the eyes of a young boy, Janek. His story is a moving portrayal of one turn-of-the-century immigrant family. Laden with traditions and dreams, they found a land full of opportunity and hardships. From his initial tagging and inspection, through the brutal realities of life among the poor, and finally to his initiation into the ways of his new country, a land where each can carve a small wedge of the American Dream.
13-367 30 min. $19.95

In the Land of the War Canoes: An Oram of Kwaktutl Life

Best known today as one of the premiere still photographers of the 20th century, Edward S. Cutris devoted his life to documenting the disappearing world and cultures of the American Indian.
13-8026 82 min. $39.95

Incas Remembered

Centuries ago, they performed miraculously technical brain surgery, built modern irrigation canals, and were master builders. They were the Incas, a wondrous people who once ruled half of South America before falling to the Spanish Conquistadors. Their miracles are presented in this fascinating exploration.
13-1871 60 min. $24.95

Independence

The dramatic events that led to the Declaration of Independence are powerfully recreated. Directed by one of Hollywood's great, John Huston, this video rings loudly the message of hope and freedom for an emerging nation.
13-419 30 min. $19.95

Independence: Birth of a Free Nation

Narrated by E.G. Marshall, this award-winning program recreates the dramatic events that led to the Declaration of Independence and the establishment of the United States Constitution.
13-2677 29 min. $29.95

Independence: Texas Gains Its Freedom-1836, Washington, Texas

In this dramatic re-enactment, Sam Houston and other legends of Texas history meet to declare Texas a free nation from Mexico. As the armies of General Santa Ana moved to crush the rebellious colonists, these brave men stayed behind to frame a constitution for the new republic. Official film of the Texas Sesquicentennial.
13-339 35 min. $29.95

INSIDE THE CIA: ON COMPANY BUSINESS

• **Assassination**
The CIA has played essential roles in the overthrow of foreign governments. U.S. officials and ex-CIA agents outline the strategies used in Iran and Central America.
13-445 60 min. $19.95

• **History**
This film takes us inside the most secret organization in our country, the CIA. The beginning of the CIA is outlined as WWII ends. Ex-agent Phillip Agee, reveals how the "Company" was initially conceived of as an intelligence-gathering agency, but actually became a force of assassination and subversion.
13-444 60 min. $19.95

• **Subversion**
The connections between large corporate America, the CIA, Nixon and coup attempts in South America are exposed in the segment of the CIA's history.
13-446 60 min. $19.95

Irish Homecoming

For the first time ever, an entertaining video has been released which enlightens Irish-Americans about the importance of tracing their roots, and how to go about the emotional journey.
13-9100 64 min. $29.95

It's Up to the Women

Featuring Joanne Woodward and Jane Alexander, this provides information on the number and cost of nuclear weapons as well as the ethical and political issues inherent in our nuclear policies. Taped in the U.S. House Representatives, this program combines interviews with experts and a cross-section of women with music and dramatic readings.
13-9809 27 min. $49.95

JFK: The Day the Nation Cried

James Earl Jones narrates this chronicle of Kennedy's life, times and untimely death. Remembrances of this great figure by those close to

VIDEO TITLES LISTED IN THIS GUIDE ARE AVAILABLE FOR PURCHASE OR RENTAL. CONTACT YOUR LOCAL VIDEO STORE OR TELEPHONE (800) 383-8811

him accompany historic, previously unseen footage, making this a remarkable piece of history.
13-8324 52 min. $24.95

JFK: Remembered
Award winning examination of JFK's 1000 days in office. Considered the best program ever done on Kennedy.
13-8298 54 min. $19.95

John F. Kennedy: Inauguration Speech
The complete speech of President Kennedy and the famous lines "Ask not what your country can do for you, but what you can do for your country" are included.
13-8290 13 min. $39.95

Just Around the Corner, Narrated by Alexander Scourby
Americans struggle through the bad times of the Great Depression. Winner of the New York International Film and TV Festival Silver Award.
13-288 60 min. $24.95

Kennedys
This is the definitive look at one of America's most powerful and controversial families. Beginning with the Kennedy's emigration during Ireland's potato famine in the 1860's, we learn what it means to be a Kennedy.
13-348 100 min. $24.95

KENNEDY'S
This film is about one of America's most influential political families. You'll see rare footage and learn the history behind one of America's first families.

- **Part I**
13-9978 120 min. $19.95

- **Part II**
13-9979 120 min. $19.95

Les Blank: Ziveli!: Medicine for the Heart
This video features the culture and music of the Serbian-American communities of Chicago and California. The video focuses on the vital cultural strengths of these immigrants from Yugoslavia, who helped form the backbone of industrial America. Featuring the Popovich Brothers, the Kupugi Brothers, and Dunav.
13-1623 50 min. $49.95

Liberty Weekend
Highlights of a once-in-a-lifetime event-the centennial celebration for the Statue of Liberty.
13-336 45 min. $19.95

Life and Death of Malcolm X
This fascinating documentary shows dozens of Malcolm X speeches, interviews and a special TV show. You'll also hear a secret recording of an FBI agent trying to bribe Malcolm and a never before seen confession from one of his assassins.
13-8299 90 min. $16.95

Life and Times of Buffalo Bill Cody
When Edison perfected the motion picture camera, Buffalo Bill Cody's Wild West was selected as the first subject. Cody starred in his own movies, as well as on stage and in the arena.
13-8013 20 min. $29.95

Lions of Capitalism: Great American Millionaires
Chronicles the achievements of great capitalists such as J.P. Morgan, Andrew Carnegie, Henry Ford and Ray Kroc. Men who forged the history and shape of American industry. Brings history to life with rare, archival footage, historical photos and riveting kinescope. With the compelling voices of Orson Welles, Robert MacNeil and broadcaster Lowell Thomas.
13-360 55 min. $19.95

MARCH OF TIME SERIES:

- **America's Youth 1940-1950**
Sheds new light on this subject in a series of case histories ranging from debutante children to the depression-ridden children of the poor.
13-2022 90 min. $19.95

- **American Family: The War Years 1941-1945**
Shows the contributions of peoples of diverse nations to the development of our cities, factories and industry, and much more.
13-2020 89 min. $19.95

- **American Family: The Postwar Years 1946-1948**
Presents facts about the family from a revealing study of child development to the steadily increasing life expectancy in adults during this time period.
13-2021 89 min. $19.95

- **Show Business: The Postwar Years 1946-1950**
Shows everything from pleasure-hungry Americans heading to the nightclub for entertainment by Jimmy Dorsey and Ed Wynn, to highlights of the early days of the musical cylinders that evolved into the popular LP record.
13-2019 92 min. $19.95

VIDEO TITLES LISTED IN THIS GUIDE ARE AVAILABLE FOR PURCHASE OR RENTAL. CONTACT YOUR LOCAL VIDEO STORE OR TELEPHONE (800) 383-8811

• **American Fashion and Leisure 1945-1950**
Takes a look at things such as the cost of being beautiful, from Fifth Avenue's most exclusive salons to mysterious beauty concoctions, and a funny look at the most vacationing people in the world- Americans.
13-2023 105 min. $19.95

March of Time
From a 40-year history of film making, including Charlie Chaplin and Al Jolson, to British film makers, challenge to Hollywood, including Stewart Granger and Ronald Coleman.
13-2018 73 min. $24.95

MARCH OF TIME: AMERICAN LIFESTYLES SERIES
A look back at the life and times of American families, fashion and leisure.

• **American Lifestyles 1939-1950/ America's Youth 1940-1950**
13-8216 90 min. $19.95

• **American Lifestyles 1939-1950/ American Fashion and Leisure 1945-1950**
13-8217 105 min. $19.95

• **Show Business: The War Years**
13-8212 73 min. $19.95

• **Show Business: The Postwar Years 1946-1950**
13-8213 92 min. $19.95

• **American Family: The War Years 1941-1945**
13-8214 89 min. $19.95

• **American Family: The Postwar Years 1946-1948**
13-8215 89 min. $19.95

MARCH OF TIME COLLECTION: THE COLD WAR SERIES:
A look at the start of the Cold War between the United States and the Soviet Union.

• **Cold War Part I**
13-8236 88 min. $19.95

• **Cold War Part II**
13-8237 90 min. $19.95

• **Cold War Part III**
13-8238 83 min. $19.95

• **Cold War Part IV**
13-8239 105 min. $19.95

MARCH OF TIME COLLECTION: THE GREAT DEPRESSION SERIES:
A look back at the great Stockmarket crash and it's aftermath in the mid-thirties.

• **Time Marches On 1935 Part I**
13-8230 88 min. $19.95

• **Economy Blues Part II**
13-8231 88 min. $19.95

• **Troubles Beyond our Shores Part III**
13-8232 82 min. $19.95

• **War and Labor Woes Part IV**
13-8233 111 min. $19.95

• **Prosperity Ahead Part V**
13-8234 106 min. $19.95

• **Reality and America's Dreams Part VI**
13-8235 97 min. $19.95

MARCH OF TIME: POSTWAR PROBLEMS & SOLUTIONS SERIES:
A look back at a soon to be changing America.

• **America's Post-War Problems Part I**
13-8240 119 min. $19.95

• **America's Post-War Problems Part II**
13-8241 119 min. $19.95

• **Post-War Problems Beyond Part I**
13-8242 107 min. $19.95

• **Post-War Problems Beyond Part II**
13-8243 125 min. $19.95

• **Modern Main Street U.S.A.**
13-8244 120 min. $19.95

Martin Luther King: I Have a Dream
One of the greatest speeches in American History was given on the steps on the Lincoln Memorial on August 28, 1963. That speech was so filled with eloquence and passion that it will live forever in our memories.
13-441 30 min. $16.95

Mein Kampf

This visually riveting documentary portrays the rise and fall of German fascism and the worldwide destruction that followed in its wake. Contains original footage from German archives and many other sources. B&W.
13-052 117 min. $39.95

Mesa Verde

Visit the world-famous cliff dwellings of Mesa Verde. Visitors from around the world come to study the ruins of an ancient Indian civilization that flourished for 1,000 years and then vanished forever. Mesa Verde's cultural sequence is interpreted for you in this excellent National Park Service film.
13-165 23 min. $29.95

Middle East: Cradle of Conflict

This documentary explores the 5,000 year-old culture, offering unique perspectives by religious and academic scholars and political leaders.
13-9146 30 min. $16.95

Millhouse: A White Comedy

This is one of the most controversial films ever made concerning one who has served in our nation's highest office. Utilizing film sequences from the career of Richard Millhouse Nixon, a comic yet terrifying portrait of the former President is drawn creating a political satire.
13-290 90 min. $39.95

MINI-DRAGON SERIES:

Known as the "mini-dragons", the Pacific Rim countries of Singapore, Taiwan, Hong Kong and South Korea are vigorous newcomers to the global marketplace. They continue to gain power and influence through trade, industrial growth and foreign investment, but at what cost? What are cultural and social forces that drive them? This four part series explores the personal stories of men and women within each distinctive country, piecing together a larger portrait of each nation and the region as a whole.

• **Taiwan**
13-8351 60 min. $99.95

• **Singapore**
13-8352 60 min. $99.95

• **Hong Kong**
13-8353 60 min. $99.95

• **South Korea**
13-8354 60 min. $99.95

Missiles of October

In October 1962, the world stood on the brink of destruction for 13 nerve-shattering days. Utilizing all available historical records, this video recreates the confrontation between the United States and the USSR over the placement of nuclear weapons in Cuba.
13-344 150 min. $59.95

Mr. Lincoln's Springfield

Return to President Lincoln's cherished home town and the only home he ever owned. Through historic photographs and the reminiscences of an 1860's photographer, this program conveys a vivid impression of Mr. Lincoln's relationship with his family and fellow townspeople. Lincoln National Historic Site now encompasses four city blocks in Springfield, Ill.
13-166 30 min. $29.95

MOYER'S GOD & POLITICS SERIES:

Join Bill Moyer's as he discusses the effects Politics and Religion have on one another in this three part series.

• **Kingdom Divided**
This program examines a clash between two distinct visions of Christianity that are not only helping to shape events in war-torn Central America, but are also having a significant impact on U.S. foreign policy.
13-8251 30 min. $19.95

• **Battle for the Bible**
A 10 year "holy war" among Southern Baptists, the largest denomination in the United States, sets the stage for a heated political battle that threatens to influence such volatile national issues as school prayer, abortion and foreign policy.
Fundamentalists seek to capture not only the control of their denomination, but our political structure as well.
13-8252 30 min. $19.95

• **On Earth As It Is in Heaven**
The holy hymn, "Onward Christian Soldiers" takes on new meaning for a radical new religious movement called Christian Reconstructionists, a group determined to base all of our government, laws and economic systems on a strict interpretation of the Bible.
13-8253 30 min. $19.95

NIXON INTERVIEWS WITH DAVID FROST

An in-depth interview with the former President of the United States.

• **Volume I**
13-8327 74 min. $19.95

• **Volume II**
13-8328 74 min. $19.95

• **Volume III**
13-8329 74 min. $19.95

• **Volume IV**
13-8330 74 min. $19.95

• **Volume V**
13-8331 74 min. $19.95

On the Bowery
Powerful documentary about a group of homeless alcoholics in New York's Bowery section.
13-2034 65 min. $29.95

Opening the West (1860-1900)
Lincoln's efforts to reunite the nation after the bloody Civil War and the beginning of epic westward expansion are discussed.
13-007 50 min. $64.95

Plot to Kill JFK: Rush to Judgment
The assassination of John F. Kennedy has been wrapped in conspiracy-oriented theories and undertones ever since the act was undertaken by Lee Harvey Oswald in 1963. This film explores the theories of lawyer Mark Lane and provides-better than any other document-a basis for further exploration.
13-342 60 min. $19.95

Plot To Kill Robert Kennedy
Containing newly released documents, film clips, and formerly suppressed testimony, this program will make you think twice about the single-assassination theory that centers on Sirhan Sirhan.
13-5767 95 min. $19.95

Pope, A Road to Glory
This colorfully memorable depiction of the life of Pope John Paul II is masterfully portrayed by Albert Finney. This story follows him through his teen-age years to his installation as the universal head of The Roman Catholic Church. Also starring Brian Cox and Patrick Stewart (Star Trek: The Next Generation).
13-8040 150 min. $59.95

Pope John Paul II Visits America
An informative look at Pope John Paul's visit to the United States with brilliant film footage, thrilling music, and stirring narration. Warmly greeted by more than six million Americans of every faith, age and race, the Pope expresses his concern for human rights, human dignity and peace throughout the world.
13-208 60 min. $29.95

Portrait of Great Britain
They dominated a fourth of the modern world... from a small island about the size of Oregon. This production penetrates the essence of the diverse people and cultures of Great Britain today. This four hour series is hosted by John Forsythe. Contains four video cassettes.
13-9454 240 min. $99.95

Proudly We Hail
This moving documentary of why Americans hold the flag so dear, offers a profound look at the major American wars. Beginning with the American Revolution, host Robert Stack takes us through the Civil War, both World Wars and the Korean and Vietnam conflicts.
13-9127 52 min. $19.95

Reagan Years in Pursuit of the American Dream
This traces the life from his childhood to his two terms in office as President of the United States.
13-8108 75 min. $29.95

Red Sunday
This is the story of the Custer's battle, told in art work, photos, modern re-enactment and aerial photography. Narrated by John McIntyre.
13-8014 30 min. $29.95

Remembering Life
A nostalgic look at the great years of Life Magazine. This documentary includes memorable photographs from the pages of Life, and interviews with the photographers who took them. Stories covered include World War II, the Korean War, the Civil Rights Movement, Hollywood, teenagers in the fifties, and the early years of the atomic bomb.
13-170 60 min. $24.95

Remembering Pearl Harbor: U.S.S. Arizona Memorial
America's "Day of Infamy" plunging her into World War II: the road to Pearl Harbor: the attack: war in the Pacific: atomic bomb: Japanese surrender: Punchbowl Cemetery: and Hawaii today. Underwater photography of the U.S.S. Arizona as archeological divers perform a fascinating survey.
14-8093 90 min. $29.95

Richard Nixon: Resignation Speech
Never before in the history of the United States has a president resigned. Never before have the governmental positions, that of President and Vice-President, been simultaneously assumed by unelected officials. This is the final minutes of Richard Nixon and his resignation from the highest

public elected office.
13-8286 16 min. $39.95

Road to the White House '92
The three way race to the White House by George Bush, Bill Clinton and Ross Perot. Narrated by Bernard Shaw and Catherine Crier.
13-8332 90 min. $19.98

Roots of Democracy (1700's)
This program portrays the relationship between foreign trade and domestic activities which led to the rebellion against English restraints and eventually to the american Revolution.
13-004 50 min. $64.95

Royal Wedding of His Royal Highness Prince Andrew and Sarah Ferguson
This is the official BBC-Buckingham Palace version taking us inside the Royal Family.
13-343 100 min. $29.95

Royal Wedding
For the first time in 300 years, the heir to the throne of Britain was to marry an Englishwoman. People all over the world looked forward to the wedding and the splendor and magnificence of a state ceremony that only Britain could stage. July 29, 1981-a day never to be forgotten, a glorious example of pageantry and color.
13-373 60 min. $29.95

Royal Wedding: His Royal Highness Prince Andrew and Sarah Ferguson
This official souvenir videocassette includes all the highlights of Thames Television's coverage of the wedding and honeymoon departure, with commentary by Sir Alastair Burnet and interview with the happy couple by Andrew Gardner and Sue Lawley. Relive Britain's most joyous event of 1986 and share the excitement of the day.
13-474 70 min. $19.95

Sacred Ground
Hosted by Cliff Robertson, this is a fascinating view of a society that believed that the land held the true meaning to life. The land is sacred to the American Indian--it is tied to their culture, their past and their future.
13-8131 60 min. $19.95

Salt of the Earth
One of the most gripping and controversial films ever made. This film tells of the true struggle of a small New Mexico mining community to achieve better working and living conditions.
13-1860 94 min. $29.95

Scotland Yard
The first inside look at that legendary institution of crimefighting. Hosted by David Niven, it's a rare, behind-the-scenes look at the history of British crime. Winner of the Christopher Award, Golden Mike Award, and nominated for an Emmy.
13-1870 60 min. $24.95

Second Gun
Robert Kennedy, about to make his charge at the Presidency, was gunned down in a kitchen of a Los Angeles hotel during the California Primary in 1968. Sirhan Sirhan is arrested and the eyewitness testimony is irrefutable. The bullets and gun match. It's an open and shut case! But is it? The autopsy raised questions yet uanswered. Was it conspiracy? Did two people, acting independently shoot RFK at the once? Who was the guard behind Kennedy? Why were key witnesses never interviewed?
13-326 110 min. $19.95

Sherrill Milnes: Homage to Verdi
This film takes you on a tour of Verdi's home region, the Po Valley, and creates the ambiance in which the Italian composer lived and worked.
25-278 60 min. $39.95

SPEECHES SERIES:
An historical look at the courageous and sometimes infamous speeches of the 20th century.

- **Adolf Hitler**
13-5802 50 min. $19.95

- **Douglas MacArthur**
13-5805 60 min. $19.95

- **Dwight D. Eisenhower**
13-5801 60 min. $19.95

- **Franklin D. Roosevelt**
13-5807 60 min. $19.95

- **Harry S. Truman**
13-5808 55 min. $19.95

- **John F. Kennedy**
13-5803 60 min. $19.95

- **Martin Luther King, Jr.**
13-5804 60 min. $19.95

- **Richard Nixon**
13-5806 60 min. $19.95

- **Robert F. Kennedy**
13-5809 60 min. $19.95

- **Winston Churchill**
13-5800 30 min. $19.95

VIDEO TITLES LISTED IN THIS GUIDE ARE AVAILABLE FOR PURCHASE OR RENTAL. CONTACT YOUR LOCAL VIDEO STORE OR TELEPHONE (800) 383-8811

Presidents
From George Washington to George Bush, no personality carries more weight than The President of the United States. This special videocassette is a tribute to all of the men who have served the people in this most prestigious of offices.
13-5746 60 min. $19.95

Spirit of the Salt River Valley
A documentary of the historic events leading to the dedication of Theodore Roosevelt Dam on March 18, 1911. Using original photographs and re-enactment of actual events, this program dramatizes the struggles of the Hohokam Indians and the early spirit of the pioneers.
13-369 17 min. $29.95

Streetwise
Children living on the streets, surviving on their wits as pimps, prostitutes, panhandlers and thieves. This is their true-to-life story. A haunting unforgettable look at "coming of age." It's about trying to find yourself, when all you really see is hell.
13-282 92 min. $24.95

Strengthening the United Nations
We can turn the United Nations into an effective instrument for planetary management. Suggested reforms include increasing the U.N.'s power to keep the peace, mediate regional conflicts, prevent environmental crises, prosecute international criminals and protect human rights.
13-9160 30 min. $16.95

Surviving Columbus: The Story of the Pueblo People
Another side of American history is now being told by the Pueblo people of the American Southwest. Explore the impact of the conquerors who followed Columbus and attempted to change America's native people--a 500 year
legacy that continues to this day.
13-8342 120 min. $19.95

Ten Days that Shook the Earth
This film is the definitive story of the 1917 Russian Revolution. No other film has captured those fateful days more completely than this historical classic narrated by Orson Welles.
13-1861 77 min. $39.95

Thank You, Mr. President
John F. Kennedy was a master of the press conference. Watch as this program highlights the best moments from his biweekly meetings with the White House Press Corps. Kennedy's wit, charm and intelligence shine through as always, as he discussed U.S.-Soviet relations, nuclear war,
women's rights and much more.
13-071 45 min. $19.95

Times of Harvey Milk
13-374 90 min. $19.95

Tosca's Kiss
This film by Daniel Schmid is a reverent and humorous look at the current residents of Casa Verdi, the musicians' retirement home founded by the great composer in 1902. "Inspired, insightful, life-affirming and entertaining."
25-125 87 min. $39.95

Touring Custer's Battlefield
Custer's Battlefield is the most famous site in all Indian Wars history. On this tour you will visit the museum and National Cemetery, the Indian Village site, the scene of Reno's fight in the valley of the Little Big Horn, the Reno Benteen defense site, Wier Point and Last Stand Hill.
13-8009 30 min. $24.95

TRIBAL LEGACIES COLLECTION:

• Incas
This takes us on the trail of one of the most impressive civilizations the world has ever known and reveals how they achieved their stunning success.
13-8339 60 min. $19.95

• Maya: Lords of the Jungle
This unlocks secrets of their splendid temples and magnificent moments the jungle swallowed centuries ago.
13-8340 60 min. $19.95

• Last Stand at Little Big Horn
It shines new light on this mythical and misunderstood battle. It completes this by including the views of the Lakota, Sioux, Cheyenne and Crow Indians. Through journals, archives, oral histories and drawings, it pieces together the truth behind the mythical tale.
13-8341 60 min. $19.95

Two Great Crusades (1930-1945)
The New Deal and World War II are the focus of this look at the U.S.'s two modern crises.
13-011 50 min. $64.95

U.N. Day: Nurturing World Peace
As a global citizen, each individual has a positive contribution to make towards world peace. Join the late Henry Fonda, Armand Hammer and others as they celebrate the U.N.'s achievements, such as eradicating smallpox and preventing many wars from escalating.
13-9158 24 min. $16.95

Underground
This controversial documentary brings the sixties and seventies vividly to life by interweaving the stories of The Weathermen, underground political activists, with the history of the times. "Underground" includes many significant events and personalities of the era: The Civil Rights Movement, Malcolm X, Martin Luther King, Bob Dylan and others.
13-346 88 min. $39.95

Video from Russia
Without asking for or obtaining permission, an American film crew traveled to the Soviet Union and talked freely with the Russian people. The results of those discussions are presented in this moving and startling videotape, in which Russians of all ages and orientations talk about war, work, friendship and rock n' roll.
13-440 45 min. $29.95

Vietnam: War at Home
Nominated for an Academy Award, this may be the only film made about the unrest at home during the Vietnam war years. College campuses were in chaos and many people thought we were headed for civil war. The sounds and images of that turbulent era make this video a time-tripping journey.
13-363 90 min. $29.95

War Between the States (1860's)
This program analyzes the institution of slavery and how it came to divide our country.
13-005 50 min. $64.95

Warring and Roaring (1914-1929)
This program examines U.S. involvement in World War I, the spirited 1920's, and the stock market crash of 1929.
13-010 50 min. $64.95

We All Came to America
The waves of immigration have helped build America as thousands of new Americans settle in. Freedom Foundation Award Winner. Narrated by Theodore Bikel.
13-287 60 min. $24.95

When Women Kill
Narrated and directed by Lee Grant. In this intensely powerful program, you will witness a horrifying close-up of seven psychologically trampled women who have been "forced" to kill. The stories are remarkably similar and their victims are most often domineering men-of-violence. This program includes an in-prison confession of Leslie Van Houton, who submitted to the violent will of Charles Manson. We are certain you will never forget this film.
13-5768 55 min. $29.95

Where America Began: Jamestown, Colonial Williamsburg and Yorktown
Join in a celebration of America's founding years as you explore the sites of some of the most dramatic chapters in American history.
13-2675 60 min. $29.95

William McKinley: American Imperialism
In 1898, President McKinley must make a fateful decision; whether or not to go to war with Spain and as a consequence embark on a policy of imperialism for the first time, acquiring colonies thousands of miles from America. As students face this decision, they begin to learn that our complex society holds no simple and easy solutions.
13-8289 25 min. $39.95

Wiping the Tears of Seven Generations
This program tells the story of the Lakota people and their attempts to deal with the memory of the "Wounded Knee" massacre. Inspired by dreams and visions, they attempt to bring themselves out of the mourning through a traditional Lakota ceremony which they call Washigila; "Wiping the Tears".
13-9976 57 min. $29.95

Wiping the Tears of Seven Generations
With Performance Rights
13-9977 57 min. $85.00

With Bard at the South Pole: The Story of Little America
Winner of the Academy Award for Best Cinematography and considered one of the Ten Best Films of the Year, "With Bard at the South Pole" is a celebration of the American hero at it's zenith.
13-8032 82 min. $39.95

Woodrow Wilson: A Fight for a League of Nations
This program presents a classic case in the problem of decision making. Did Wilson help or harm his cause by trying to force the Senate to accept his views with a direct appeal to the American Public? This program stimulates debate not only on the crucial issues of peace and World government, but the equally important issues of compromise and idealism.
13-8288 25 min. $39.95

World Survival Through Globalism
The United Nations is our best alternative to nuclear omnicide. Speakers Norman Cousins, Robert Muller and Burl Ives show how this world body offers a viable framework for peaceful conflict resolution.
13-9159 28 min. $16.95

VIDEO TITLES LISTED IN THIS GUIDE ARE AVAILABLE FOR PURCHASE OR RENTAL. CONTACT YOUR LOCAL VIDEO STORE OR TELEPHONE (800) 383-8811

World Without Walls: Beryl Markham's African Memoir

This PBS documentary (1987 Emmy Award Nominee) illuminates the life of the pioneering aviatrix, international adventuress, and best-selling author of "West with the Night." Archival footage offers a unique glimpse into the fast-living British East Africa society in the 1920's.
13-485 60 min. $29.95

Yesterday's Witness: A Tribute to the American Newsreel

A film by Christian Blackwood, narrated by Lowell Thomas. This film is a lively, provocative and amusing history of the American newsreel from 1911 until its disappearance in 1967, as told by narrators Ed Herlihy, Lowell Thomas and Harry Von Zell. This film is part journalism, part entertainment and part show business.
13-368 52 min. $19.95

War & Military History

1918 - 1941 BETWEEN THE WARS SERIES:

A look at America and it's place in the world during both World Wars.

• Versailles: Lost Peace/Return to Isolationism
13-9829 45 min. $19.99

• First Salt Talks/America in the Pacific
13-9830 45 min. $19.99

• Radio, Racism and Foreign Policy/Great Depression
13-9831 45 min. $19.99

• FDR and Hitler
13-9832 45 min. $19.99

• Recognition of Russia
13-9833 45 min. $19.99

• Italian-Ethiopian War/Spanish Civil War
13-9834 45 min. $19.99

• Phoney War
13-9835 45 min. $19.99

• Japan Invades China/War Comes to Pearl Harbor
13-9836 45 min. $19.99

Alaska At War

To an embattled United States the security of Alaska was crucial to the safety of America's North Pacific region. Through rare Japanese and American film footage, you'll see the rugged, inhospitable conditions under which this dramatic campaign was fought and the heroism of U.S. and Japanese soldiers in combat.
13-6590 60 min. $29.95

All the Unsung Heroes

Built to help heal a nation still torn by the Vietnam War, the hauntingly powerful Vietnam Veteran's Memorial pays tribute to all who served in that war.
13-8084 30 min. $19.95

Always Ready

The story of the U.S. Coast Guard, narrated by Ken Howard, and featuring exciting war footage at Guadalcanal and Iwo Jima. Always ready to rescue troubled ships at sea, the Coast Guard has been a strong naval presence for over two centuries.
13-001 45 min. $29.95

America at War

From Pearl Harbor to the Persian Gulf, this program covers 50 years of almost continuous action by America's military with fascinating footage of the American effort during World War II in the Pacific and European theaters, followed by Korea, the Bay of Pigs, Vietnam, Grenada, Panama and Operation Desert Storm.
13-8053 30 min $29.95

Anchors Aweigh

Witness the history of the U.S. Navy, from its birth to its struggles during Vietnam. Dramatic footage of both the Atlantic and Pacific campaigns in World War II, the Cuban missile crisis, and the Vietnam War. A collector's dream.
13-012 45 min. $29.95

Attack-Pacific!

The official Armed Forces footage of the savage and bloody Pacific battles and the most awesome air, sea and land conflicts in history. From Pearl Harbor to epic victories and the final confrontation in Japan. Experience this two-part visual masterpiece featuring the most nerve-jolting combat footage ever, from the front-line beachheads to a tribute to the fighting 1st Cavalry Division, "Hell for Leather", covering Los Negros, the Admiralties, Leyte and Manila, giving new meaning to jungle warfare.
13-014 65 min. $24.95

Attack and Reprisal
December 7, 1941: The Day of Infamy, when the Imperial Japanese fleet attacked the naval base at Pearl Harbor; this was the attack. On August 6, 1945, the U.S. Air Force dropped the first atomic bomb on the city of Hiroshima; this was the reprisal. This video is composed of two separate films combining to make one stunning military video.
13-422 52 min. $39.95

Battle for North Africa
This video includes spectacular footage of Rommel, the Desert Fox and his Afrika Korp Panzers up against Patton and Montgomery.
13-017 93 min. $24.95

Battle of Arnhem
This program details Field Marshal Montgomery's "Market Garden" Plan: the capture of all major river crossings in Holland in preparation for the final thrust toward Berlin.
13-8055 60 min. $29.95

Battle of the Bulge
As originally seen on NBC TV, the savage bloodbath in which America lost more men than in D-Day. Witness St. Vitch, Clervaux, Malmedy, the Screaming Eagles of the 101st Airborne, the "Hell on Wheels" 2nd Armored Division, and even Mac-Auliffe's famous "Nuts!" reply to the German surrender offer.
13-019 53 min. $24.95

Battle of Verdum
The battle that marked the turning point of World War I, Verdum was the epitome of trench warfare, so costly in human life that France may never have recovered.
13-8054 60 min. $29.95

Battle of Britain
Frank Capra's "Why We Fight" looks at England's heroic defense against the Nazi air onslaught during World War II. Original footage. B&W.
13-018 60 min. $19.95

Battle of China
Capra's lyrical and haunting narrative of the accomplishments of the Chinese people and their struggle against the Japanese military machine in World War II. B&W.
13-021 65 min. $19.95

Battle of Russia
Another in Frank Capra's award-winning "Why We Fight" series. This video shows the Nazis' invasion of Russia and their ultimate and first defeat at the hands of the determined Red Army. B&W.
13-020 83 min. $19.95

Battle Action
Over two hours of the most exciting combat footage in history, including air strikes, jungle beachheads, assault landings, the Battle of New Britain, the Battle for Leyte Gulf, the action at Angaur, and the Battle for Okinawa witships and their "cowboys" against the Viet Cong in the Iron Triangle, Operation Marauder, Crimp, Dexter, Yorktown, Aurora and more; 2) The Black Horse Regiment of the famed 11th Armored Cavalry, including Operation Thunderhorse, Elephant Ear and the Tet Offensive in steaming jungles; 3) The Air Mobile Division of the battling 1st Cavalry in helicopter battle; and 4) Know Your Enemy, a captured Viet Cong propaganda newsreel depicting the ambush and assault tactics of the 9th Viet Cong Main Force Division.
13-016 113 min. $24.95

Battle Hell Vietnam
This shows you choppers, air strikes and air troops and the tough, savage combinations that changed the face of modern warfare.
13-1609 113 min. $24.95

Blitzkrieg
A unique visual record of the most dramatic development of World War II-Blitzkrieg. From the German annihilation of Poland's defenses in 1939 to the final Russian onslaught against Berlin in 1945. All original archive material. This is World War II as it really happened.
13-1555 80 min. $24.95

BRUTE FORCE: HISTORY OF WAR TECHNOLOGY
A visual history of the military fighting machines and the use of them in the battlefield.

- **Helicopters**
  13-8303 48 min. $44.95

- **Fighters**
  13-8304 48 min. $44.95

- **Tanks**
  13-8305 48 min. $44.95

- **Artillery**
  13-8306 48 min. $44.95

- **Infantry**
  13-8307 48 min. $44.95

Cambodia: Year Zero, Year One
In one package: John Pilger's two award-winning documentaries depicting life in war-torn Cambodia. Historically relevant and emotionally harrowing, it's the story of millions killed, starving children, international politics and the world's attempts to

VIDEO TITLES LISTED IN THIS GUIDE ARE AVAILABLE FOR PURCHASE OR RENTAL. CONTACT YOUR LOCAL VIDEO STORE OR TELEPHONE (800) 383-8811

provide aid and relief.
13-148 120 min. $24.95

Citizen Soldiers
Ken Howard narrates this story of the U.S. Army, from the Revolutionary War to the Civil War, Indian Wars, 20th century conflicts in Cuba, World War I, World War II, the Korean War, the Vietnam War and more. Dramatic original footage.
13-025 45 min. $29.95

Civil War
Famous events from the Civil War are recounted and analyzed, including Lincoln's campaign for the Presidency; John Brown's Abolitionist Movement; the Battles of the Merrimac and the Monitor, Bull Run and Gettysburg.
13-152 30 min. $29.95

Civil War: The Fiery Trail
Recounts the enduring drama of America's bloodiest conflict. From Fort Sumter to Appomattox, this documentary tells the entire story of the war. On-site photography at more than a dozen battlefield parks puts the viewer on those fields of fire where the fate of the nation was decided. Archival photographs, Civil War art, handsome maps, and period music bring to life the war's major campaigns, battles and leaders.
13-5041 35 min. $19.95

Civil War Photographers
Step back into the past with Charlie Fifer, award-winning film director, to absorb the sound of muskets, cannons, beautifully scored period music and a compelling account of land and naval warfare produced especially for military enthusiasts.
13-5708 43 min. $16.95

Combat 'Nam
This is an all-Marine, six-part video with great combat coverage.
13-467 115 min. $24.95

Combat Fury
Witness: 1) The Bridge at Remagen: The race to the Rhine, the struggle to take and hold it; 2) The 3rd Army: The U.S. Army's own definitive study of the legendary 3rd and their immortal General George Patton in the 281-day race through France, Belgium and Germany: and 3) Only A Few Returned: Medal of Honor Series tribute to Gunnery Corporal Maynard Smith who stayed aboard his luftwaffe-hit B-17 to bring her home on a single engine. In all, unforgettable battle footage.
13-027 94 min. $24.95

Combat Vietnam: Air Power at Khe Sanh/Marines in Battle
Filmed under fire as it happened by combat cameramen of the Army, Navy, Air Force and Marine Corp. This is a not-to-be missed story of how air power helped win a decisive victory at Khe Sanh.
13-8343 30 min. $16.95

CRUSADE IN THE PACIFIC
This magnificent six-volume collection explores the land and sea battles that ravaged the Pacific during World War II. Spectacular wartime footage, and an exceptionally insightful narrative, combine to make history come alive again in this intriguing war record of the Pacific in transition.

• **Volume 1**
"The Pacific in Eruption'", "Awakening in the Pacific", "The Rise of the Japanese Empire", "America Goes to War in the Pacific".
13-402 115 min. $24.95

• **Volume 2**
"The U.S. and the Philippines", "The Navy Holds-1942", "Guadalcanal: America's First Offensive", "War in the North-The Aleutians", "The Rock Back-New Guinea".
13-403 130 min. $24.95

• **Volume 3**
"Up the Solomons Ladder: Bougainvillea", "Attack in the Central Pacific Makin and Tarawa", "The War at Sea", "Speeding Up the Attack-The Marshalls".
13-404 115 min. $24.95

• **Volume 4**
"Stepping Stones to the Philippines", "Battle for the Marianas", "The War in the China-Burma-India Theatre", "Paluau: The Fight for Bloody Nose Ridge", "MacArthur Returns to the Philippines".
13-405 130 min. $24.95

• **Volume 5**
"Bloody Iwo: The Capture of Iwo Jima", "At Japan's Doorstep: Okinawa", "The Air War on Japan", "The Surrender and Occupation of Japan".
13-406 115 min. $24.95

• **Volume 6**
"Shifting Tides in the Orient", "War in Korea (Part I)" ,"War in Korea (Part II)", "The Problem of Asia and the Pacific".
13-407 115 min. $24.95

D-Day Plus Forty Years
Share the emotion-filled memories of veterans who stormed the beaches at Normandy as Tom Brokaw salutes the 40th anniversary of D-Day.
13-2422 52 min. $24.95

D-Day: The Great Crusade
The storming of the Normandy beaches on D-Day, June 6, 1944, began the final chapter of World War II. This historic video is a unique and detailed record of the events of D-Day.
13-1828 112 min. $39.95

Day They Bombed Pearl Harbor
It was truly a surprise attack, and it forced America's hand-after the bombing, we were at war. This program tells the story of the attack, and is illustrated throughout with rare-archival footage from the historic Hawaiian island. George Bush may have thought it was a September event. but after viewing this film you'll never forget the date: December 7, 1941, "a day that will live in infamy."
13-5775 30 min. $19.95

December 7th, Midway, Bougainvillea
This award-winning film focuses on three crucial episodes in the Pacific Theater. First the infamous sneak attack on Pearl Harbor which threw the U.S. into the War against Japan. Then, the Battle of Midway, where the Japanese drive across the Pacific was halted. It ends with the invasion of Bougainvillea, an island in the Pacific which we took in 1943.
13-6082 60 min. $29.95

December 7: The Movie
Banned by U.S. Government censors since 1942, John Ford's lost movie has been restored to it's full-length version. This version has not been seen by the general public until now.
13-9035 82 min. $19.95

Desert Storm Gun Camera Footage
Navy and Marine Aircraft
13-8082 45 min. $16.95

Desert Victory
This clash on the sands of Egypt in 1942, injected a new spirit of confidence into the discouraged British force and sent the Germans on one of the longest retreats in military history. Acclaimed by many as the finest of war films, this combines captured German footage along with the superb filmwork of British Army cameramen.
13-8018 60 min. $29.95

Eagles Over the Gulf
Desert Storm pilots tell their stories with stunning scenes and footage, of the aircraft and their air crews.
13-8081 35 min. $16.95

Famous Generals
Generals Eisenhower and Patton led the fight to free Europe from Nazi despotism. This is a historical look at the lives of these two great American military leaders.
06-008 60 min. $39.95

Few Men Well-Conducted: The George Rogers Clark Story
This is the story of George Rogers Clark and his courageous army who fought on the Kentucky and Illinois frontier during the American Revolution. To help end British-inspired Indian attacks on Kentucky settlements, these brave men defied tremendous odds to capture Fort Sackville from the British in 1779.
13-320 25 min. $29.95

Fighting Generals
Four official U.S. Army programs on the great battlefield commanders: Omar Bradley, George S. Patton, Douglas MacArthur and Joseph W. Stilwell. The actual battle footage of the major campaigns and battles involving these four great men who made modern military history.
13-035 120 min. $24.95

Follow Me: The Story of the Six Day War
On June 7,1967, 14 Arab countries came thundering down on Israel. Yet in six dramatic days, the little country not only won a decisive victory, but also changed the map of the Middle East. Highlighted by previously censored footage, this film covers the three war fronts. A monumental work.
13-277 95 min. $49.95

Fort Phil Kearny
Take an exciting tour of historic Fort Phil Kearny, Fetterman Hill and the Wagon Box Fight, where the Sioux, under Red Cloud, clashed with the United States Army for control of northern Wyoming's Powder River Country and the Bozeman Trail.
13-8007 30 min. $29.95

Fortress Europe
This video includes action packed battles of northern Italy and southern France.
13-036 105 min. $24.95

From D-Day to Victory in Europe
A complete account of the most massive military maneuver in the history of warfare is now available. This film distinguishes itself by explaining and revealing both the brilliant and disastrous strokes of the war. Rare war footage and thrilling history for the student and military buff alike.
13-420 110 min. $39.95

Frontline Generals
This video illuminates the awesome spectacle, the

heroism and the sacrifice of World War II.
13-5714 30 min. $16.95

Gettysburg: The Final Fury July 1st-3rd 1863

The three-day battle is considered a major turning point in the Civil War, as it marked the unsuccessful culmination of Robert E. Lee's second and final attempt to invade the North. Fought on July 1-3, 1863, the historic battle was the bloodiest battle of the War, claiming 23,000 dead, wounded or missing Union Soldiers and 20,000 Confederate soldiers.
13-5709 30 min. $16.95

Gettysburg Battlefield Tour

Re-live one of the most significant battles in military history-- The Battle of Gettysburg-- with an inspiring tour of Gettysburg National Military Park in Pennsylvania. Through ingenious editing and photography the Park's statues and monuments become participants in this, the decisive and bloodiest battle of the American Civil War.
13-6086 35 min. $29.95

Great Battles Film Festival

This video shows battle film from some of the greatest directors such as John Ford and John Huston. Includes such films as World at War, Battle of Midway, Fury in the Pacific, and more.
13-040 120 min. $24.95

GREAT BATTLES OF THE WAR SERIES:

Some of the highlights of World War II's bloodiest battles.

• **Bulge**
13-9850 45 min. $19.99

• **German Invasion of Soviet Union**
13-9851 45 min. $19.99

• **Warsaw**
13-9852 55 min. $19.99

• **Cassino**
13-9853 55 min. $19.99

• **Burma**
13-9854 55 min. $19.99

• **Dien Bien Phu**
13-9855 45 min. $19.99

GREAT BATTLES OF WORLD WAR II SERIES:

• **Europe & North Africa**
This chronicles the most memorable battles in the African and Western Europe theaters of war.
13-8071 330 min. $79.95

• **Victory in the Pacific**
Relive the drama of Pearl Harbor, Battle of Midway, Iwo Jima and Okinawa.
13-8072 300 min. $79.95

Great Indian Wars 1840-1890

Exciting re-creations and authentic stills from Custer to Geronimo to Wounded Knee.
13-8148 96 min. $16.95

Guadalcanal & The Shores Of Iwo Jima

The Japanese depended heavily on two Pacific islands to mount their aggressive air and naval attacks: Guadalcanal and Iwo Jima. Armed forces from the United States were called upon to wrest these islands from Japanese rule, and both times the call was answered. This program examines the battles, which were unusually heavy in casualties and suffering. But the U.S. flag still flew-most famously at Iwo Jima, the inspiration for the Marine Memorial.
13-5778 60 min. $19.95

Guns of August: World War I

Based on the Pulitzer Prize winning book by Barbara Tuchman, "The Guns of August" combines extraordinary filmed footage, photographs and graphics to create one of the most absorbing, disturbing and candid accounts of World War I.
13-8337 100 min. $19.98

HEARST METRO-TONE VIDEO GAZETTE SERIES:

• **WWII Volume I**
From Hitler's early days to Pearl Harbor.
13-9432 51 min. $19.95

• **WWII Volume II**
USMC lands at Guadalcanal and the Battle of Stalingrad.
13-9433 51 min. $19.95

• **WWII Volume III**
Allies enter Naples, D-Day and more.
13-9434 51 min. $19.95

Hearts and Minds

An award-winning documentary exploring the events of the Vietnam War and the attitudes and values that lead America to both fight it and question its involvement later. An emotion charged journey for every American.
13-041 112 min. $24.95

Hell for Leathernecks
This includes classic hand-to-hand Marine combat footage where you stake your life out on a battle-ravaged beachhead.
13-468 60 min. $24.95

Hell on the Western Front
From the beaches at Normandy to the Siegfried Line and crossing the Rhine, this living document, taken from the Armed Forces Archival program, shows the greatest military campaign in United States history and has to be experienced to be believed.
13-042 80 min. $24.95

Heritage of Glory
The spirit of the U.S. Marines is captured in this visually exciting tale of marine development, featuring footage of Guantanamo Bay and Midway in World War II; Korean and Vietnam War action; and the Middle East.
13-045 45 min. $29.95

Hitler's Henchmen
Witness the graphic realities and horrors of Nazi death camps, powerfully depicted in this brilliant World War II German propaganda documentary.
13-046 60 min. $39.95

Holocaust
Writer and social critic Susan Sontag presents the realities and meaning of Hitler's genocide of the Jewish people. Includes "In Dark Places," "How Come Israel?" "The Good Omen," and Herschel Bernardi narrating "The Hangman," probing and elaborating on the same theme.
13-047 120 min. $69.95

How Hitler Lost the War
A unique video that details the critical mistakes that brought a regime from the brink of world domination to destruction and defeat.
13-8111 67 min. $59.95

In Country: Folk Songs of Americans in the Vietnam War
Hosted by Kris Kristofferson, this program is filled with lively and poignant songs, performed by veterans who turned their experiences into music.
13-8338 60 min. $24.95

Ironclads: The Monitor & The Merrimac
Ironclads tells the story of the two astonishing vessels that fought the most memorable naval battle of the Civil War and forever revolutionized maritime warfare.
13-6548 30 min. $19.95

Jimmy Doolittle: An American Hero
Narrated by Robert Stack, you'll see the triumphs and disasters of what is considered the greatest flyer America ever produced.
13-8115 60 min. $29.95

Korea: MacArthur's War
The Korean War was described by lifetime diplomat Averill Harriman as a "sour little war." Over 33,000 Americans and two million Chinese and Koreans died during the conflict and-most frustratingly-there was no resolution; the war ended in a stalemate that persists to this day. Perhaps the most indelible impression of the war was the fierce battle between General Douglas MacArthur and President Harry S. Truman.
13-5777 60 min. $24.95

KOREAN WAR:
This is a video documentary of the Korean conflict produced by Koreans. The Korean Television Network spent years compiling revealing information with never-before-seen film footage into chronological epic. This five-volume collection is a complete rendering of the conflict, beginning with the dividing of the Korean Peninsula after WWII and continuing right through to today, where an uneasy truce still exists.

• **Division & North & South**
13-8033 120 min. $19.95

• **Omens of War and Tempest**
13-8034 120 min. $19.95

• **To the North and A Different War**
13-8035 120 min. $19.95

• **Stalemate of Truce and War on the Homefront**
13-8036 120 min. $19.95

• **Truce & Epilogue: Reflections**
13-8037 120 min. $19.95

Last Full Measure
A video masterpiece about the Civil War battles at Gettysburg, taking you to the actual sites of the awesome confrontations. Stars Stacy Keach and includes maps of the battle zones, photos of America's leading Civil War historian; little Round Top; Cemetery Hill; Seminary Ridge; General Robert E. Lee and his army of Northern Virginia; Pickett's charge; as well as the short, "Gettysburg: The Final Fury."
13-050 30 min. $24.95

MacArthur In The Pacific
In the Pacific theater of war, MacArthur was a

VIDEO TITLES LISTED IN THIS GUIDE ARE AVAILABLE FOR PURCHASE OR RENTAL. CONTACT YOUR LOCAL VIDEO STORE OR TELEPHONE (800) 383-8811

general's general.
13-5716 30 min. $16.95

MARCH OF TIME COLLECTION: AMERICANS AT WAR SERIES:

• On the Homefront
13-8206 114 min. $19.95

• Friend or Foe Part I
13-8207 116 min. $19.95

• Friend and Foe Part II
13-8208 87 min. $19.95

• Friend and Foe Part III
13-8209 113 min. $19.95

• American Defense Part I
13-8210 122 min. $19.95

• American Defense Part II
13-8211 126 min. $19.95

MARCH OF TIME COLLECTION: TROUBLE ABROAD SERIES:

• War Abroad: Depression at Home 1937 Part I
13-8224 71 min. $19.95

• Tensions Increase 1937 Part II
13-8225 76 min. $19.95

• Germany and Other Problems 1938 Part III
13-8226 93 min. $19.95

• Spotlight on War 1938 Part IV
13-8227 91 min. $19.95

• Uncle Sam: The Observer 1938-1939 Part V
13-8228 75 min. $19.95

• War, Peace and America 1939 Part VI
13-8229 91 min. $19.95

MARCH OF TIME: WAR BREAKS OUT SERIES:

• Americans Prepare Part 1
13-8218 118 min. $19.95

• Americans Prepare Part 2
13-8219 113 min. $19.95

• Military Prepares
13-8220 124 min. $19.95

• Battle Beyond Part 1
13-8221 107 min. $19.95

• Battle Beyond Part 2
13-8222 117 min. $19.95

• Praying for Peace
13-8223 71 min. $19.95

Marines Have Landed
The Marines were unmatched in their fight against the Axis forces during World War II. This program tells the story of the Marines in their most celebrated battles.
13-5776 60 min. $19.95

Miracle of Survival: The Birth of Israel
The modern military miracle--the stunning display of Israel's courage, skill and perseverance in the face of the enemy.
13-8003 60 min. $19.95

Missing in Action: The Documentary
The search for American soldiers still missing.
13-8265 50 min. $14.95

Mondo World War II
For all the great programs that have come out of World War II, it remains the most "controlled" historical event, in terms of media coverage and exposure. This program changes that.
13-5774 60 min. $19.95

Mutiny on the Western Front: 1914-1918
Here for the first time on video is the untold story of World War I filmed on location in France, Germany and "Down Under." A starting portrait of the 200,000 Australian Anzac volunteers who suffered the largest percentage of casualties, in the war and mutinied against their incompetent and callous British and French commanders.
13-053 90 min. $69.95

Of Pure Blood
It was one of the most vicious and horrible schemes in history, the Nazi plan to breed and distill the children into a pure, Aryan race. In this program, this macabre notion is backed with real World War II footage and shocking interviews of Hitler's victims. This painfully graphic program is a filmed testimonial to one of the most bizarre and elitist aspects of Naziism.
13-292 100 min. $39.95

Our Fighting Navy
A rousing 90 minutes of naval aerial swash-

buckling- "Our Fighting Navy." Includes John Ford's classic Oscar winner record of Pearl Harbor; Ford's immortal documentary of the Battle of Midway; the Black Cats-Catalina PBY Night Bombers-taking on Japanese Zeros and Heavy Cruisers against overwhelming odds; and "Carrier Action-Korea" aboard the Valley Forge off Korea, with aerial action, Corsairs and AD Sky-raiders sharing scrap with F9F Panther Jets against enemy Migs, and rare footage of torpedo attacks on North Korean dams. Comes with Richard C. Knott's definitive book, "Black Cat Raiders of World War II' with 200 pages of photographs and maps of PBY raids.
13-060 90 min. $24.95

Payoff In The Pacific
From the attack on Pearl Harbor through much of the early Pacific campaign, this film focuses on the Army and Marine's assault on the Pacific Islands. Includes the Battle of Coral Sea, the invasions of Corregidor, Guadalcanal and Iwo Jima. It ends with the dropping of the atomic bomb and the Japanese surrender aboard the Battleship Missouri.
13-6081 59 min. $29.95

Quiet Hope
Seven Vietnam vets share their experiences and in so doing offer healing to those that fought and their families.
13-9126 60 min. $29.95

Rise & Fall of Adolf Hitler
This biography covers the tumultuous career of the failed Austrian artist who nearly conquered the world.
13-8056 60 min. $39.95

Road to War
Rare footage and the spirit of the 1930's highlight this foreboding chronicle (made in 1938) of the events leading up to WW II. You'll feel the tension of a planet in turmoil. You'll witness a defeated Germany regroup itself into an army of millions, the fiery Spanish Civil War, the Japanese invasion of China and Mussolini's attempt to create a second Roman Empire.
13-421 75 min. $39.95

Ship That Wouldn't Die
The powerful true story of the most decorated ship and crew in U.S. naval history, the aircraft carrier USS Franklin, or "Big Ben." Hosted by Gene Kelly and produced by NBC TV, this documentary takes you on board the historic vessel as she fought her way to Iwo Jima, the Philippines, Guam, Okinawa, Formosa, and finally the Japanese mainland itself, taking on Kamikaze onslaughts. Before the war was over, Big Ben's loyal crew had downed 160 ships and 338 aircraft, flown 3,971 sorties and

determined itself to be "the ship that wouldn't die.
13-065 60 min. $24.95

Situation
A chilling look at the Civil War in El Salvador. This program was also the basis of Oliver Stone's powerful film "Salvador."
13-9128 60 min. $19.95

SMITHSONIAN'S GREAT BATTLES OF THE CIVIL WAR SERIES:
This 6-part series from the National Museum of American History is a sweeping look at the military, political and social history of the Civil War.

• **Fort Sumter, First Manassas, Ironclads, Shiloh, etc.**
13-9685 60 min. $29.95

• **Battle for New Orleans and the Mississippi River, Antietam, Jackson in the Shenandoah Valley, etc.**
13-9686 60 min. $29.95

• **Battle of Corinth, The Battle of Perryville, Brandy Station, etc.**
13-9687 60 min. $29.95

• **Sieges of Vicksburg and Charleston, Chattanooga, etc.**
13-9688 60 min. $29.95

• **Battle of New Market and Atlanta, etc.**
13-9688 60 min. $29.95

• **Destruction of C.S.S. Alabama, Sailor's Creek, Siege of Petersberg, etc.**
13-9690 60 min. $29.95

Spanish Civil War
This is an unparalleled history of the bloody conflict of the 1930's that claimed three million lives. Hemingway fought there and the Abraham Lincoln Brigade died there. Double cassette.
13-1826 120 min. $79.95

Stillwell Road
This film tells the dramatic story of carving a land bridge from Burma to China, the effort by 200,000 laborers to keep China alive. You'll see dramatic air and ground action, jungle fighting and fierce combat in an effort to protect the laborers and complete the road. Narrated by Ronald Reagan.
13-257 60 min. $24.95

VIDEO TITLES LISTED IN THIS GUIDE ARE AVAILABLE FOR PURCHASE OR RENTAL. CONTACT YOUR LOCAL VIDEO STORE OR TELEPHONE (800) 383-8811

Task Force
This is a collection of the saga of sea power. Includes films such as Hook Down, Wheels Down and the Rise of the Soviet Navy.
13-069 120 min. $24.95

Television's Vietnam
Military experts, scholars, journalists and Vietnamese exiles contrast what actually happened in Vietnam.
13-8267 116 min. $14.95

Touring Civil War Battlefields
See the actual battlefields as they were and as they are today. Relive the story behind each conflict as thousands reenact the battles. A sensitive portrayal of the heroic soldiers who fought in this stirring, but tragic, chapter of our history.
13-2431 60 min. $29.95

Tried by Fire
This is the story of the 84th Infantry Division as they slug their way across Northern Europe. Soldiers from both sides, American and German, describe the awesome fighting that engulfed massive armies. A fascinating insight into their personal lives as they make history before the end of the war finally came.
13-247 60 min. $24.95

Triumph of the Will
This is a documentary record of the 1934 Nazi Party Congress in Nuremberg. It served as the rallying point for the Party in it's quest for world domination, and it's undoubtedly one of the most controversial films of all time.
13-9331 80 min. $19.95

Turbulent End To A Tragic War: America's Final Hours In Vietnam
On April 4, 1975, the last 2,000 Americans-both soldiers and civilians-were evacuated from Saigon, and thereafter the Vietnam war was finally over. This videocassette provides gripping on-the-site reporting from South Vietnam, as told by correspondents and anchorman like Ted Koppel, Frank Reynolds. Tom Jerrell, and Harry Reasoner. A Government in chaos. An evacuation plan. The end of a brutal chapter in American political history.
13-5755 60 min. $24.95

V FOR VICTORY
The original newsreel stories, V for Victory presents World War II's most momentous events and prominent personalities. The conflict's legendary leaders and soldiers, crucial campaigns and battles, and the important war at home come to life in this unique chronicle of global war.

• **Pearl Harbor to Midway**
13-5181 45 min. $19.95

• **Guadalcanal and the Pacific Counter Attack**
13-5182 45 min. $19.95

• **North Africa And The Global War**
13-7075 45 min. $19.95

• **Anzioa And The Italian Campaign**
13-7076 45 min. $19.95

• **D-Day And The Battle For France**
13-7077 45 min. $19.95

• **Tarawa And The Island War**
13-7078 45 min. $19.95

• **Women At War: From The Home Front To The Front Lines**
13-7079 45 min. $19.95

• **Battle Of The Bulge And The Drive To The Rhine**
13-7080 45 min. $19.95

• **Iwo Jima, Okinawa And The Push On Japan**
13-7081 45 min. $19.95

• **Eagle Triumphant**
13-7082 45 min. $19.95

VICTORY AT SEA SERIES:

• **Design for War**
The Battle of the Atlantic, 1939-1941.
13-8176 30 min. $14.95

• **Pacific Boils Over**
Pearl Harbor December 7, 1941.
13-8177 30 min. $14.95

• **Sealing the Breach**
Anti-Submarine Warfare, 1941-43.
13-8178 30 min. $14.95

• **Midway is East**
Japanese victories and the Battle of Midway.
13-8179 30 min. $14.95

• **Mediterranean Mosaic**
Gibralter, Allied and enemy fleets, Malta.
13-8180 30 min. $14.95

• **Guadalcanal**
13-8181 30 min. $14.95

• **Rings Around Rabuhl**
Struggle for the Solomon Islands.
13-8182 30 min. $14.95

• **Mare Nostrum**
Command for the Mediterranean, 1940-1942.
13-8183 30 min. $14.95

• **Sea and Sand**
Invasion of North Africa, 1942-43.
13-8184 30 min. $14.95

• **Beneath the Southern Cross**
War in the South Atlantic.
13-8185 30 min. $14.95

• **Magnetic North**
War from Mumansk to Alaska.
13-8186 30 min. $14.95

• **Conquest of Micronesia**
13-8187 30 min. $14.95

• **Melanesian Nightmare**
13-8188 30 min. $14.95

• **Roman Renaissance**
Sicily and the Italian campaign.
13-8189 30 min. $14.95

• **D-Day**
13-8190 30 min. $14.95

• **Killers And The Killed**
Victory - the Atlantic.
13-8191 30 min. $14.95

• **Turkey Shoot**
Conquest of the Marianas
13-8192 30 min. $14.95

• **Two If By Sea**
Peleliu and Angaur.
13-8193 30 min. $14.95

• **Battle For Leyte Gulf**
13-8194 30 min. $14.95

• **Return Of The Allies**
Liberation of the Philippines.
13-8195 30 min. $14.95

• **Full Fathom Five**
U.S. Submarines, 1941-45.
13-8196 30 min. $14.95

• **Fate Of Europe**
Black Sea surrender.
13-8197 30 min. $14.95

• **Target Suribachi**
Iwo Jima.
13-8198 30 min. $14.95

• **Road To Mandalay**
China, Burma, India and the Indian Ocean.
13-8199 30 min. $14.95

• **Suicide For Glory**
Okinawa.
13-8200 30 min. $14.95

• **Design For Peace**
Surrender of Japan and Aftermath of War.
13-8201 30 min. $14.95

Vietnam Experience
Country Joe McDonald weaves together the sights and sounds of that jungle conflict with his own original compositions to create a heartfelt journey that makes us come to grips with an era that changed us forever.
13-1847 30 min. $19.95

Vietnam: The News Story
You have never seen such a collection of indelible, vivid images which marked the 10,000 day war that nobody won. Only ITN could assemble such a powerful portrayal of a conflict that has, in some way, left it's mark on us all.
13-5174 60 min. $19.95

Vietnam Requiem
The story of five heroic soldiers who became victims of Vietnam, long after it was over. More absorbing and disturbing than any fictionalized account, this gripping documentary reports the horrors from those who survived that painful hell. Through interviews and authentic footage, this film pays homage to the valiant men and women who proudly served their country.
13-1551 48 min. $19.95

Vietnam: In the Year of the Pig
Emile de Antonio's powerful documentary which won the Grand Prize at the Cannes Film Festival and was nominated for an Academy Award. A harrowing look at the reality of the Vietnam War, the drama and bloodshed and our daily visual reminder

VIDEO TITLES LISTED IN THIS GUIDE ARE AVAILABLE FOR PURCHASE OR RENTAL. CONTACT YOUR LOCAL VIDEO STORE OR TELEPHONE (800) 383-8811

of it which made this war unlike any other. B&W.
13-089 103 min. $39.95

Vietnam: Remember!
Documentary footage tracing the pivotal battle of
Khe Sahn and American GIs surviving fierce jungle
fighting. Includes a patrol in search of Vietcong.
13-090 60 min. $39.95

Vietnam: The Air War
Through actual footage, you will see the story of
the men, the machines and the missions they flew
over the skies of Vietnam.
13-2485 30 min. $24.95

Vietnam: The Secret Agent
"I died in Nam and I didn't even know it." Thus
spoke a veteran dying from the effects of agent
orange. Max Gail (Sgt. "Wojo" on Barney Miller)
narrates this frank examination of the war and the
veterans who returned with problems.
13-362 60 min. $29.95

Vietnam: Time of the Locust
This film shows two distinctly different viewpoints
of the war. First, there is controversial, suppressed
footage as shot by a Japanese television crew. This
segment shows the brutality of the war and should
not be viewed by the delicate. The second part
deals with the official U.S. view of the war during
1965.
13-361 60 min. $29.95

War in the Pacific
A unique grouping of official World War II combat
films in a definitive visual portrayal of the Pacific
Campaign, Operation Cartwheel and the War in the
Pacific.
13-107 117 min. $24.95

WAR CHRONICLES SERIES:

• **Greatest Conflict**
Presents a breathtaking overview of World War II
from 1939 to 1945.
13-2644 35 min. $14.95

• **Desert War**
Depicts the battles between German forces, the
British First Army, and U.S. soldiers at Kasserine
Pass.
13-2708 35 min. $14.95

• **Beachhead at Anzio**
Masterfully retells the story of the key victory of
the Allied troops on Italian lines.
13-2646 35 min. $14.95

• **Normandy Invasion**
Puts you there on the beach for the day history will

never forget.
13-2647 35 min. $14.95

• **Pursuit of the Rhine**
Presents Patton's successful "Operation Cobra,"
sending Hitler's armies back in full retreat.
13-2648 35 min. $14.95

• **Bomber Offensive, Air War Europe**
Graphically depicts the most disastrous air
encounters of the War.
13-2649 35 min. $14.95

• **Battle of the Bulge**
Gives you a close-up look at the largest pitched
battle in the history of American arms.
13-2650 35 min. $14.95

• **Battle of Germany**
Shows the American forces breaking through at
Saint-Lo, and entering Nazi concentration camps.
13-2651 35 min. $14.95

War Comes to America
A sensitive and loving portrait of the American
people and the events that persuaded the United
States to enter World War II. B&W.
13-106 67 min. $19.95

Warlords
"The Warlords" is a series of biographies on the
European war leaders - Hitler, Mussolini,
DeGaulle, Stalin and Churchill - their personal
conflicts and liaisons. Each biography is separate in
its conception, giving 15 minutes per individual,
showing their triumphs and disasters.
13-1556 75 min. $19.95

WAR STORIES SERIES:
A tribute to the men and women who fought and
lived World War II. The history of that vast global
conflict, is presented through the eyes of those who
were there.

• **Remembering Pearl Harbor: Volume 1**
13-9094 50 min. $19.95

• **Airmen of World War II: Volume II**
13-9095 50 min. $19.95

• **Fighting Marines: Volume III**
13-9096 50 min. $19.95

• **Merchant Marines: Volume IV**
13-9097 50 min. $19.95

• **D-Day: Volume V**
13-9098 50 min. $19.95

VIDEO TITLES LISTED IN THIS GUIDE ARE AVAILABLE FOR PURCHASE
OR RENTAL. CONTACT YOUR LOCAL VIDEO STORE OR TELEPHONE (800) 383-8811

WAR YEARS: BRITAIN WORLD WAR II:

This series tells the stories of the familiar men and the famous battles of World War II as well as the lesser-known stories of those who stayed at home to endure the Blitz and to enlist in the Home Guard, with no weapons to fight off the feared invasion. The mood of fear and determination of Britain in it's darkest hours is underscored by some of that era's greatest music.

* **Phoney War**
13-8048 60 min. $29.95

* **Battle Of Britain**
13-8049 60 min. $29.95

* **Blitz**
13-8050 60 min. $29.95

* **Tide Turns**
13-8051 60 min. $29.95

* **Final Chapter**
13-8052 60 min. $29.95

We Can Keep You Forever

Now, for the first time, following a year-long investigation all over the world, a group of senior American and British journalists reveals what is already known to American intelligence about those brave servicemen and women of whom the Vietnamese once said, "We Can Keep You Forever."
13-5452 75 min. $19.95

WEAPONS OF WAR SERIES:

A visual chronicle of some of the most devastating weapons created for war.

* **YF 22A Fighter Plane**
13-9843 60 min. $19.99

* **Airshow**
13-9844 60 min. $19.99

* **Tank**
13-9845 60 min. $19.99

* **Hydrogen Bomb**
13-9846 60 min. $19.99

* **Atomic Bomb**
13-9847 60 min. $19.99

* **British Bomber**
13-9848 60 min. $19.99

* **First Jet Fighter**
13-9849 60 min. $19.99

Wings Over Water

A complete, dramatic documentation of American Naval Aviation in World War I and World War II.
13-8110 59 min. $59.95

WORLD AT WAR SERIES:

Narrated by Sir Laurence Olivier, this dramatic compilation of film from national and international sources is acclaimed as the definitive history of World War II and has won numerous awards. A superb collection with distinctive leather-like gold stamped spine labels. The series is presented in chronological order.

* **New Germany 1933-39**
Stricken by humiliating defeat and deep economic depression, Germany seeks new hope, pride and prosperity through national socialism. Adolf Hitler leads the Nazi movement with the fervent support of millions of German citizens. As Europe looks on apprehensively, Germany threatens to attack Poland.
13-181 60 min. $29.95

* **Alone Britain: May 1940-June 1941**
Nearly 350,000 Allied troops are dramatically rescued at Dunkirk. British morale plummets, but Churchill inspires his nation to fight on alone. The RAF heroically battles the Luftwaffe in the skies over London, and Britain gains a reprieve as Hitler's offensive turns to Russia.
13-184 60 min. $29.95

* **Banzai: Japan Strikes: December 1941**
Japan, seeking unrestricted access to raw materials she needs for expansion tires of negotiations and strikes at Pearl Harbor, inflicting a severe blow to American naval power. In a few months, Japan demonstrates how ill-prepared the Allies are, sweeping forward to capture Hong Kong, Burma, Malaya, Singapore, the Dutch East Indies (Indonesia) and the Philippines.
13-186 60 min. $29.95

* **Barbarossa: June-December 1941**
Germany, master now of all Europe, including Balkans, turns against Russia. The early stages are composed of devastating German victories as the Panzers sweep with appalling speed deep into Russia. But the German high command delays fatally, and the advance is held a few kilometers from Moscow when the mud and fierce cold take their grip.
13-185 60 min. $29.95

• **Bomb**
On August 6, 1945, an American B-29 bomber, the "Enola Gay," named after the mother of the pilot Paul Tibbetts, dropped the world's first uranium bomb on the Japanese city of Hiroshima. Four days later, a second bomb was dropped on Nagasaki.
13-204 60 min. $29.95

• **Desert: The War in North Africa**
The war in North Africa takes the better part of three years and is fought and refought over the same 600 miles of desert between Alexandria in Egypt and Benghazi in Cyrenaica (Libya) before Montgomery's "Desert Rats" defeat Rommel's Afrika Korps at El Alamein. The Germans are driven from North Africa and the way seems clear to the underbelly of Europe: Italy.
13-188 60 min. $29.95

• **Distant War 1939-1940**
Germany invades Poland and bombs Warsaw into submission. Prime Minister Chamberlain is forced to bring an unprepared Britain into the war. Following the failure of the British expeditionary force to Norway, the Chamberlain government falls and is replaced by Churchill's. The Nazi war machine rolls into the Low Countries and France.
13-182 60 min. $29.95

• **France Falls: May/June 1940**
The eyes of the world are on France, its huge army, its impregnable Maginot Line. Incredibly, the Wehrmacht skirts the line and forges south. As the humiliated French army collapse, Paris is occupied and France falls. The British retreat to the Channel coast as Hitler stands posed, ready to invade Britain.
13-183 60 min. $29.95

• **Genocide**
When the Nazis came to power in 1933, Heinrich Himmler was already Reichsfuhrer of the SS. The new eminence of the National Socialist Party allowed him to set about realizing his dream of awakening the Germanic race within the German people. He had already refined the philosophy of Nazism, its ideals on politics and on race. His aims lay in recreating an older Aryan Germany.
13-200 60 min. $29.95

• **Home Fires**
After the defeat in the Battle of Britain, the Luftwaffe changes the direction of their bombing raids from London to the provincial cities. Portsmouth, Sheffield, Glasgow and Bristol all suffer heavy casualties and damage, but Coventry and Plymouth are the worst hit. In Coventry, the heart is torn from the city and the situation is desperate.
13-195 60 min. $29.95

• **Inside the Reich: Germany 1940-1944**
In the summer of 1940, the German forces are the conquerors of Western Europe, and at home the feeling is that the war is over. German cities are untouched and there is thankfulness that scourge of the First World War has not been repeated.
13-196 60 min. $29.95

• **It's a Lovely Day Tomorrow**
Monsoon conditions for five months every year with attendant disease made serving in the Burma army "just a nightmare." Europeans found jungle conditions alien, and the Japanese's ability to endure and thrive in the those same circumstances helped build a "superman" myth among Allied soldiers.
13-194 60 min. $29.95

• **Japan 1941-1945**
Many Japanese were stunned and fearful when war was declared against the West in 1941. But after the victories of Hong Kong, Malaya, and Singapore, their earlier fears were lost in exultation. By 1944, the scales had tipped fully against Japan, but still they defended their homeland, unaware of the terrible weapon yet to be used against them, which would end the war.
13-202 60 min. $29.95

• **Morning**
In the early morning of June 5, 1944, the largest amphibian invasion force ever gathered reaches the beaches of Normandy. American, British and Canadian forces attack on five separate beaches, and although beachheads are made on all, the Americans meet strong opposition and have many casualties.
13-197 60 min. $29.95

• **Nemesis**
As the front lines shrink around Germany, the death toll mounts and many thousands die as the RAF and the USAF attack by night and by day. Allied prisoners of war are released by the advancing comrades, while German soldiers are captured by the thousands. In the bunker, Hitler and those around him face the end of the Reich. Goehring and Himmler betray their Fuhrer, and he decides on self-destruction, but not before marrying the faithful Eva Braun.
13-201 60 min. $29.95

• **Occupation**
The Netherlands, a neutral country, is attacked without warning in 1940. To stop more bloodshed, it capitulates quickly after Rotterdam is badly bombed. So subtly do German occupiers proceed with assurances of "no animosity," that most find it easy to carry on their normal lives.
13-198 60 min. $29.95

VIDEO TITLES LISTED IN THIS GUIDE ARE AVAILABLE FOR PURCHASE OR RENTAL. CONTACT YOUR LOCAL VIDEO STORE OR TELEPHONE (800) 383-8811

• On Our Way: America Enters the War

The conflicts in Europe and the Pacific are two separate wars. Many Americans are content to forget about Hitler and Europe and concentrate their war efforts on the Japanese. President Roosevelt is committed to the fight against Hitler, but Congress is not. Inexplicably, Hitler declares war on America, thus relieving Roosevelt of a difficult decision and, ultimately, altering the course of the war.

13-187 60 min. $29.95

• Pacific: The Island to Island War

The Allied Pacific offensive came under the command of two rivals: General MacArthur's mission was to sweep upwards from the Solomons and New Guinea to the Philippines, while Admiral Nimitz was to reclaim enemy-held islands, starting in November 1943 in the Gilberts at Tarawa. The Americans thought it would by easy; the casualties proved them wrong.

13-203 60 min. $29.95

• Pincers

With the liberation of Paris on August 25, 1944, the war seems to some to be as good as over. The Russians from the east and the Allies from the south and west are ready for the advance on the Fatherland. At this point, the disparity of views between Montgomery and Eisenhower reaches a critical point. The American plans advance on a broad front: Montgomery wants a narrow strike to burst through to the Ruhr and thus plans the Arnheim Raid.

13-199 60 min. $29.95

• Reckoning

Germany remains the key to European problems. Nobody wants Germany to be strong again, yet no one is ready to face the consequences of keeping her ruined forever. Thus, it was decided that four armies of occupation would supervise Germany's recovery so that she could make good what she damaged and destroyed. When the Japanese surrendered, the Americans decided that the occupation forces in Japan would be American troops. They wanted an industrialized Japan as quickly as possible in America's image and within the American political orbit. MacArthur begins the task.

13-205 60 min. $29.95

• Red Star

The story of Russia's massive, lonely war with its 20 million military and civilian casualties. In Leningrad 200,000 people were killed by German shells, and another 630,000 died of cold or starvation. Incredibly, the Russians not only survived but went on to rout the Germans.

13-191 60 min. $29.95

• Remember

In the second World War 20 million Russians died in action and captivity. Britain and the Commonwealth lost 480,000. Germany, lost nearly five million men and women. Two and a half million Japanese were killed. America lost nearly 300,000.

13-206 60 min. $29.95

• Stalingrad

The encirclement and defeat of the German army at Stalingrad holds more importance than the numbers of men lost - large though these were. For the first time, the Germans are beaten in the field. The legend of German mastery on land is dispelled as the people Hitler once called sub-human prove themselves more clever than he is.

13-189 60 min. $29.95

• Tough Old Gut

Winston Churchill describes Italy to Stalin as "the soft underbelly of the crocodile." His arguments persuade the Americans to join the Allies - reluctantly - on the road home. In November 1942, 11 months after Pearl Harbor, they meet the Wehrmacht for the first time. And in Tunisia they suffer their worst defeat of the war at the hands of the better equipped more experienced Afrika Korps.

13-193 60 min. $29.95

• Whirlwind

The blitz on Britain brings strident public demand for revenge bombing, but by the end of 1941 Britain's force of 700 aircraft is being eaten into by the demands of the North Africa and Atlantic battles.

13-192 60 min. $29.95

• Wolfpack

The German attempts to starve Britain by attacking ships bringing supplies from North America are very nearly successful. Many tons of shipping are sunk and many lives lost to the U-Boat attacks (Wolfpacks) of Gross Admiral Carl Doenitz. The allied merchant ships, despite convoy techniques, navy escorts and elementary underwater detection devices are extremely vulnerable.

13-190 60 min. $29.95

WORLD WAR II: A PERSONAL JOURNEY

An insightful look back at World War II and what it meant in the life of an individual soldier, as well as world.

• 1941-42: The First 1000 Days
13-8073 45 min. $24.95

• 1943 - At Home & Abroad
13-8074 48 min. $24.95

VIDEO TITLES LISTED IN THIS GUIDE ARE AVAILABLE FOR PURCHASE OR RENTAL. CONTACT YOUR LOCAL VIDEO STORE OR TELEPHONE (800) 383-8811

• **1944 Victory in Sight**
13-8075 47 min. $24.95

• **V for Victory**
13-8076 46 min. $24.95

Zero Pilot
The true story of Japan's number one fighter ace.
13-313 90 min. $69.95

Miscellaneous

---

25 Years of Sports
This program features newsreel footage of the greatest moments in sports, including the 1947 Yankee-Dodger World Series and the 1964 Olympic Games.
13-3097 60 min. $16.95

90 Degrees South: With Scott to the Antarctic
This chronicles Captain Robert Scott's heroic and untimely tragic race for the South Pole.
13-8027 72 min. $39.95

Above And Beyond The Call Of Duty
This is the definitive documentary on the Congressional Medal of Honor, this nation's supreme award for extraordinary heroism at the risk of life.
13-6187 60 min. $19.95

Agricultural Hall of Fame
Experience the rural world of your grandparents. Just a few of the historical relics and genuine artifacts you will see are the first farm truck 1903 Dart, 1781 Indian plow, 1912 Victor portable engine, steam engines, 1858 Chisholm trail saddle, 1850 prairie schooner, 1888 McCormick reaper and much more.
13-8125 32 min. $19.95

AMERICAN COWBOY COLLECTION:
This five-part series explores every facet of the New West: from the hard work that keeps a ranch in business, to the toe-tapping music that's the down-home spirit of the buckaroo. These programs vividly reveal the romance and the reality of cowboy life.

• **On the Cowboy Trail**
13-8246 60 min. $19.95

• **Do You Mean There Are Still Cowboys**
13-8247 60 min. $19.95

• **Cowgirls**
13-8248 30 min. $16.95

• **Salute to the Cowboy**
13-8249 60 min. $16.95

• **Buckaroo Bard**
13-8250 56 min. $16.95

Bart LaRue's Ark of Noah
A ship half the size of the Queen Mary lies frozen in a glacier at the 14,000 ft. level of Mt. Ararat. LaRue made this film under conditions ranging from impossible to illegal.
13-301 95 min. $39.95

Before Stonewall: Making Of A Gay & Lesbian Community
Narrated by Rita Mae Brown, this award-winning program documents the struggles of the gay and Lesbian community in the early days-before the 1969 riots outside a New York City gay bar called Stonewall Inn. Featuring interviews and rare footage from as far back as the 1920s.
13-5764 87 min. $29.95

Bermuda Triangle
Here is the spellbinding account of the actual documented incidents that have taken place within the latitudes and longitudes of the area in the Atlantic Ocean that comprises the Bermuda Triangle. It is taken from official reports, ships' logs and eyewitness accounts.
13-8325 94 min. $29.95

Bluffing It, A Nabisco Showcase Presentation
Nabisco's commitment to fighting illiteracy in America. This program stars Dennis Weaver and tells the story of an illiterate adult in America, that through the encouragement of his family, learns how to read.
13-8057 60 min. $29.95

Buckminster Fuller: Grandfather of the Future
Few men have had more impact on their times than Buckminster Fuller, designer of the geodesic dome. He discusses the revolutionary effect of new technologies.
13-9153 25 min. $24.95

Buried in Ice
In 1845, two ships, the Erebus and Terror, led by Sir John Franklin, set out to complete the charting

---

of the Northwest Passage. For 10 years, nothing was heard from the expedition. In 1855, a salvage operation (similar to that in "Aliens") uncovered the first evidence indicating the extent of the tragedy. Recently, Dr. Owen Beattie led an expedition to Beechey Island and exhumed the bodies to discover what caused this tragedy.
13-8122 60 min. $19.95

Chang: A Drama of the Wilderness
Available for the first time in 45 years, this was the obvious prototype for Cooper and Schedsack's later masterpiece, "King Kong". Shot entirely in Siam, this story tells of a farmer who settles a small patch of land on the edge of the jungle. Their existence is a constant struggle against many forms of wild animals.
13-8029 70 min. $39.95

Colt Firearms Legends
A history of the weapon that made all men equal-- the Colt handgun. Narrated by Mel Torme.
13-8268 66 min. $29.95

COUSTEAU I SERIES:

• **Alaska: Outrage at Valdez**
Jean-Michael Cousteau travels to investigate first-hand the devastating impact of the 1989 Exxon Valdez oil spill.
13-8278 57 min. $24.95

• **Amazon: Snowstorm in the Jungle and Ragging for the Amazon**
Journey into the Amazon Basin and confront the awesome power of the source of cocaine. Then see how the Cousteaus prepared for their most challenging expedition.
13-8274 90 min. $24.95

• **Lilliput in Antarctica**
Take an exciting trip to Antartica and find huge glaciers, Humpback whales, penguins and Elephant seals.
13-8276 48 min. $24.95

• **Papua New Guinea: Center of Fire**
Explore the remains of World War II battles including a 500 foot Japanese freighter and a B-17 Flying Fortress still remarkably intact.
13-8275 60 min. $24.95

• **Pioneer of the Sea**
A special 75th birthday salute to Captain Cousteau featuring rare photographs and more.
13-8273 60 min. $24.95

• **Tahiti: Fire Waters**
Travel to the beautiful islands surrounding Tahiti to examine the effects upon nature and the economics

of local cultures of continued nuclear weapons tests.
13-8277 60 min. $24.95

COUSTEAU II SERIES:

• **Bering Sea: Twilight of the Alaskan Hunter**
Jean-Michel Cousteau and his time travelers, sail to Alaska to witness the struggle for survival of bears, seals, walruses, Bowhead whales and the Eskimo people.
13-8279 48 min. $24.95

• **Borneo: Forests without Land**
In Borneo, the world's third largest island, live the sea's last Nomads. A people who eat, sleep and die on the water are poised between tradition and the challenges of the modern world.
13-8282 48 min. $24.95

• **Haiti: Waters of Sorrow**
Mysterious Haiti, once a tropical paradise, is now an impoverished land ravished by overpopulation and uncontrolled destruction of it's forests.
13-8280 48 min. $24.95

• **Riders of the Wind**
Cousteau unveils a new invention, a cylindrical high-tech turbosail system. Using this new system, he makes a daring voyage from Tangier to New York ushering a new era of windships.
13-8283 48 min. $24.95

• **Thailand: Convicts of the Sea**
In the gulf of Siam, Cousteau examines the effects of tin mining and overfishing of the sea floor and then explores the natural wonders of an unchartered coral reef.
13-8281 48 min. $24.95

• **Western Australia: Out West and Down Under**
Jean-Michel Cousteau and the windship Alcyone, venture into the waters off western Australia, where they encounter a healthy and protected marine life resulting from good management, ecological balance and planning for the future.
13-8284 48 min. $24.95

COUSTEAU ODYSSEY 10 SERIES

• **Blind Prophets of Easter Island**
Cousteau's fascinating quest to solve the many mind boggling riddles surrounding Polynesia's Easter Island. Who created the Pacific island's ancient, once revered, giant stone figures? Why do drawings in volcanic rock show trees and flowers, when virtually none exist today? Why is there evidence of cannibalism in a once peaceful and

VIDEO TITLES LISTED IN THIS GUIDE ARE AVAILABLE FOR PURCHASE OR RENTAL. CONTACT YOUR LOCAL VIDEO STORE OR TELEPHONE (800) 383-8811

flourishing society? This is Cousteau's mesmerizing human story lost in silence.
13-268 58 min. $24.95

• Calypso's Search for Atlantis
Two of the world's great unsolved mysteries center on the lost island of Atlantis: Where is it buried? Did it ever exist? Is it fact or legend that this advanced civilization flourished, then vanished from the face of the earth, destroyed by quakes and floods? Captain Cousteau sets out to find the answers, continuing the quest that has challenged explorers for centuries.
13-270 116 min. $24.95

• Calypso's Search for The Britannic
Captain Cousteau tells, for the first time, the full story of the sinking of Great Britain's majestic ship, The Britannic. The luxury-liner-turned-hospital-ship was on her sixth World War I journey of mercy when, suddenly, an explosion ripped her apart, and sent her to the bottom of the Aegean Sea. Was she torpedoed or mined? A gripping discovery of long held secrets.
13-271 58 min. $24.95

• Clipperton: The Island Time Forgot
Eerie and desolate Clipperton Island was once a stage for terror. Almost 70 years ago, a brutal rapist was murdered by an isolated group of women he had held captive there, along with their children. Captain Cousteau escorts one of the bloody scene's survivors, then one of the children, back to the Pacific island. They explore its harsh environment, amidst the lingering echoes of a violent tale.
13-265 58 min. $24.95

• Diving for Roman Plunder
Jacques Cousteau and the crew of the Calypso attempt to retrieve the art objects and golden plunder form a Roman galley sunk centuries ago.
13-029 59 min. $24.95

• Lost Relics of the Sea
Naval battles and natural disasters come vividly to life through the discovery of great ships in watery graves. Captain Cousteau and the Calypso pursue some of the most famous underwater shipwrecks, uncovering buried treasures from the time of an Athenian victory over Sparta to this century's volcanic eruption on exotic Martinique island.
13-266 58 min. $24.95

• Mediterranean: Cradle or Coffin?
Only 30 years after finding Mediterranean waters teeming with marine life, Captain Cousteau returns to discover much of the same sea floor to be a desert, the rich abundance gone. Pollution had taken its dreadful toll, like "an underwater dust storm." The world famous conservationist devotes the remainder of this voyage to visiting the Zulu

Nation, South Africa.
13-269 58 min. $24.95

• Nile
Explore the mysterious Nile in the style of adventurer and underwater scientist, Jacques Cousteau. Journey through the river's fabled past and equally amazing present in the spectacular Cousteau Society production.
13-030 116 min. $24.95

• Time Bomb at 50 Fathoms
Two ships collide off the southern coast of Italy. One ship, with a cargo of 900 drums of lead toxin, sinks to the bottom of the sea. Ultimately, the disintegration of the metal barrels could release a "time bomb" of toxin devastating fish, plant and human life in the area. Captain Cousteau's work inspires a dedicated and brave group of men to avert catastrophe.
13-267 57 min. $24.95

• Warm-Blooded Sea Mammals of the Deep
Dolphins, whales, seals-incredibly intelligent, mysterious and wondrous-they are the creatures of the sea most closely related to man. The Calypso team charts the marine mammals' amazing evolution, their spellbinding behavior, and their chances of surviving the recklessness of their distant human cousins.
13-272 58 min. $24.95

Custer's Last Trooper
Witness the fascinating archaeological dig where the haunting skull of Custer's last trooper is unearthed. Authentic artifacts, photos and diary excerpts punctuate the excitement.
13-8141 47 min. $24.95

Deadly Weapons
The most popular gun video ever made is used by CIA, FBI, U.S. Army, Navy, Marine Corps and over 600 law enforcement agencies. It features fascinating demonstrations of a wide variety of weapons in a no-nonsense, professional manner. Most interesting are the debunking of many common gun myths about such things as bullet penetration and "knockdown" power, use of silencers and the effectiveness of full auto fire. Excellent for both novice and the experienced.
13-430 105 min. $49.95

Dealers in Death
The most monstrous mobsters, madmen, murderers and maniacs of the 20th century are featured in this video. Notorious gangsters such as Al Capone, John Dillinger, and Bonnie and Clyde are revealed in rare live-action footage that was filmed during their short but boisterous careers. Includes some of the most powerful scenes of death and destruction

that have ever been filmed.
13-337 60 min. $19.95

Death Diploma
This documentary covers mass murderers and serial killers throughout history.
13-2009 50 min. $39.95

Disasters of the 20th Century
From the 1906 San Francisco earthquake; the incineration of the Hindenburg; the volcanic eruption of Mt. St. Helens; to the assassinations of the 60's: President Kennedy, Robert Kennedy, and the speech given by Dr. Martin Luther King, Jr. The night before he was shot. A chilling, warm, shocking and enlightening story of struggle and survival.
13-156 60 min. $19.95

Earthquake
Why take a risk? Prepare now, not just for an earthquake but for any emergency. Learn how you and your family can survive the first 72 hours following a major quake.
13-5157 30 min. $24.95

Earthquake: Disaster in L.A.
This authoritative video program lets you experience first-hand the devastation of a major earthquake, discusses, the likelihood and effects of a larger quake in Southern California, and tells what you can do to be prepared. A must for California residents!
13-2127 60 min. $29.95

Eruption of the Mt. St. Helens Volcano
Witness the incredible, explosive eruption of Mount St. Helens and the devastating aftermath as photographed by men who narrowly survived the mountain's wrath.
13-034 30 min. $29.95

Events That Shaped Our World
Specially priced videocassette featuring key news broadcasts from fourteen major events that helped shape world history, including: the last days of the Vietnam War; the assassination of Anwar Sadat; the glory days in space, and many more.
13-5754 30 min. $14.95

Eyes on Hawaiian Skies
The 1991 total solar eclipse in Hawaii was the most exciting astronomical occurrence of our lifetime! Journey through history and discover the myths and lore of this rare event.
13-8113 30 min. $29.95

First Ladies
What exactly does a First Lady do? This program has the answers, and some will surprise you. From

Martha Washington, our first Lady, to Barbara Bush, the program has much behind-the-scenes footage and information.
13-5747 60 min. $19.95

From Sheep to Sweater: Story of Wool
On a visit to a Colorado sheep ranch, visitors learn about how sheep are raised to produce high quality fleece which makes our warm and durable wool clothing.
13-8114 15 min. $29.95

Game of Monopoly (1870-1914)
This program examines the rise to wealth and power of industrial titans J.P. Morgan, Andrew Carnegie, John D. Rockefeller and Cornelius Vanderbilt.
13-009 50 min. $64.95

GANGSTER CHRONICLES SERIES:

• Part I
There was never anything like the blazing years between the bloody start of Prohibition and the death of John Dillinger. Behind the classic gangster myths from 1919-1935.
13-5710 46 min. $14.95

• Part II
This video delightfully mixes gripping original footage, uproarious sketches by the great illustrator Casey Jones and classic movie, newsreel and archival films.
13-5711 45 min. $14.95

Great Crimes of the Century
Five of the most bizarre, outrageous and shocking crimes of our century are explored in this amazing, and often brutal, videocassette. Using rare police and news footage shot during the investigations themselves, the stories behind Charles Manson, Leopold and Loeb, D.B. Cooper, Clifford Irving and the Boston Strangler are painstakingly recreated.
13-317 70 min. $39.95

GREAT WEST COLLECTION:
A look at the life of a cowboy takes a loving look at a truly American tradition. Through pictures and music, sit back and bring the tradition home.

• Last Cowboys
Journey to the ranges of southern Utah and northern Nevada and discover the legend and the reality of the cowboy.
13-8126 60 min. $19.95

• Ranch Album
Tracing the lives of a handful of Arizona ranchers and their families through the cycles of one year,

this finely crafted documentary presents a portrait of a way of life that is rooted in hard work, family, a love of nature and a hunger for independence.
13-8127 60 min. $19.95

• **My Heroes Have Always Been Cowboys with Waylon Jennings**
Join Waylon Jennings as he works the cattle by day and sings around the campfire at night. This program presents the rugged world of cowboys, against a background of Jenning's classic songs.
13-8128 60 min. $19.95

• **Great Ranches of the West**
Join Michael Martin Murphy for a visit to four of the largest and oldest family-owned ranches in America. This video documentary takes you to: Eaton's Dude Ranch, Parker Ranch in Hawaii, the Spanish Ranch in northern Nevada and CS Ranch in Cimmaron, NM, one of the largest family-owned ranches in America.
13-8129 60 min. $19.95

• **Working Cowboy: In Search of the Cowboy Song**
Country musician, cowboy poet and rancher, Ian Tyson, has always found inspiration in the cowboy's life. In this program, Ian's search for the cowboy song drives him to many of Canada's great ranches, underscoring the powerful link between true country living and Western music.
13-8130 60 min. $19.95

Guiness Book of World Records
Babe Ruth, Albert Einstein and a Himalayan ibex are just a few of the record-breakers featured in this collection of the most daring, fantastic and hilarious things people (and animals) do.
13-2324 30 min. $14.95

Guns of the Old West
Created entirely with footage shot for this production, this film tours the halls of the great gun museums and brings you as close as one can get to the firearms that shaped the most rugged era in American history.
13-8356 53 min. $19.95

Hearst Castle: The Enchanted Hill
Spectacular views of William Hearst's jewel of hilltop grandeur: incomparable antiques, arts, palatial gardens, bejeweled pools; stories of golden age movie stars, famous guests and historic construction scenes.
13-8096 75 min. $29.95

Hitler: The World of Tomorrow
Genius or madman - what was he? Watch this

video and you make the decision.
13-3065 30 min. $19.95

Hopi Pottery
The mysteriously rich heritage of an ancient civilization. Pottery making the old way is demonstrated in Hano village on First Mesa. Rare views over Hopi mesas, villages and Hopi ruins. This program covers the Anasazi, Spaniards, Nampeyo civilizations and pottery designs. Included is a segment on the evolution of Hopi pottery.
13-8095 65 min. $29.95

Hoover Dam: The Historic Construction
Reveals the perilous, arduous conditions the engineers faced during the 1931-1935 construction of the Hoover Dam, including the most powerful fear of all: the treacherous Colorado River. Lake Mead, created by the construction of the dam, is the host for many outdoor recreational activities such as, water-skiing, sailing, jet skiing and exploring the canyons.
13-8097 45 min. $29.95

How to Fix Up a Little Old American Town
A documentary about the historic, but dying downtown of New Bern, the colonial capital of North Carolina and the citizens who saved it.
13-9811 57 min. $59.95

John Muir: The Man, The Poet, The Legacy
The most comprehensive biography of John Muir, the man principally responsible for setting aside wild lands as National Parks and Forests. Ride speeding locomotives, stand atop Scottish castle walls, experience Yosemite's grandeur, relive his explorations and adventures.
13-8099 50 min. $29.95

Last Sailors
Narrated by Orson Welles, this stunning video documents the men who still harness the wind and the sea for their livelihood. Beautifully filmed in remote corners of the world with an original musical score, this is a thoughtful and fascinating presentation.
08-013 150 min. $39.95

LES BLANK DOCUMENTARY FILMS SERIES:
Les Blank began his film making career producing educational and advertising films. In 1967, he made his first independent film on Texas blues singer Lightin' Hopkins. This began a film series of intimate glimpses into the lives and music of people on the periphery of society: Rural French musicians, Chicanos, New Orleans blacks, garlic

fanatics and German film makers.

• A Well Spent Life
A deeply moving tribute to the Texas songster Mance Lipscomb, the survivor sharecropper who lived and worked in a system not much better than slavery. The film captures Mance's music, sets it off with scenes of his hometown of Navasota, and combines it all with the miracle of his love.
13-245 44 min. $49.95

• Always for Pleasure
An intensive insider's look at New Orleans, the myriad music traditions, Mardi Gras, and various celebrations and traditions of the black community.
13-230 58 min. $49.95

• Blues Accordin' to Lightnin' Hopkins
This film captures Lightnin's blues in their darkest power. It reaches past the impish bluesman into the blues itself, into the red-clay of Taxes, into hard times, into blackness, into the senses. A beautifully made film.
13-231 31 min. $49.95

• Burden of Dreams
A chilling but finely balanced account of what might ordinarily be considered artistic folly: German film maker Werner Herzog's obsession to complete the painfully plagued jungle shooting of "Fitzcalrado." Disaster after disaster befalls Herzog's tale of a penniless, opera-mad dreamer who risks everything to build a grand opera house in a jungle river port.
13-233 94 min. $59.95

• Chulas Fronteras
A magnificent chicano documentary featuring their music, home life, migrant farm life, rituals, food preparation and hardships.
13-235 59 min. $49.95

• Del Mero Corazon
A lyrical journey through the heart of the Chicano culture, as reflected in the love songs of the Tex-Mex Nortena music tradition. These love songs are the poetry of their daily life.
13-236 28 min. $49.95

• Dry Wood
Features the older, rural-style Cajun music of "Bois Sec" Ardoin, his sons, Canray Fontenot, and weaves together the lives of these two families.
13-237 37 min. $49.95

• Gap-Toothed Women
This film explores the self-image of women and the pressures they feel to conform to the ideals of mass media. It also reveals many unique and fascinating individuals who happen to be both women and gap-tooted. Featuring Lauren Hutton, Sandra Day O'Connor and many others.
13-1624 30 min. $49.95

• Hot Pepper
This film plunges the viewer deep into the music of Clifton Chenier and its source in the Louisiana surroundings. The great French accordionist mixes rock and blues with his unique version of Zydeco Music, a pulsating combination of Cajun French with African undertones.
13-239 54 min. $49.95

• In Heaven There is No Beer
A joyous romp through the dance, food, music friendship and even religion of the polka. The energy and bursting spirit of the polka subculture is rendered through this celebration of Polish-America.
13-240 51 min. $49.95

• Spend it All
A perceptive, lusty lyrical documentary of some true American originals, the bayou people in Cajun country. This film captures the intense bravado and old world spirit of these French speaking Acadian ancestors.
13-241 42 min. $49.95

• Sprout Wings and Fly
Featuring fabulous fiddler and ballad singer, Tommy Jarrell, this film also offers a fine old-time music, crazy jive, a fascinating cast of backwoods characters, and a look into the backwoods life.
13-242 30 min. $49.95

• Stoney Knows How
An extended interview with the late Leonard St. Clair, nick-named Stoney - a paraplegic dwarf, a carnival sword-swallower as a child and a tattoo artist since 1928. A fascinating film about an ebullient little man with the gift of gab and a fund of bizarre stories.
13-243 30 min. $49.95

• Werner Herzog Eats His Shoe
In 1979 German film maker Werner Herzog, honoring a vow he made to Errol Morris, came to the UC Theater at Berkeley and consumed one of his desert boots. Definitely one of the strangest of Blank's love letters to food.
13-246 20 min. $49.95

Les Blues de Balfa
This film features Louisiana's most renowned Cajun musician, Dewey Balfa, and his brothers, with other Cajun great: Rockin' Dopsie, Allie Young and Nathan Abshire.
13-232 28 min. $49.95

VIDEO TITLES LISTED IN THIS GUIDE ARE AVAILABLE FOR PURCHASE OR RENTAL. CONTACT YOUR LOCAL VIDEO STORE OR TELEPHONE (800) 383-8811

London Medley and City of the Golden Gate

A nostalgic tour back in time to London in 1938 and San Francisco in 1934. In London you'll see fishermen on the Thames, Hyde Park on a Sunday afternoon, an era of liveried footmen, and a time when everyone stops for tea. In San Francisco you'll see the ferryboats that carried commuters from "residential suburbs", the fishing boats at Fishermen's Wharf, Chinatown and the famous cable cars. Filmed in black and white.

13-067 19 min. $24.95

Made and Bottled in Kentucky

Whiskey has been made in Kentucky for more than 200 years. Today this ancient craft, little changed by modern technology, is threatened by contemporary tastes and attitudes. See the places and meet the people behind famous brands like Jim Beam, Maker's Mark, Wild Turkey and many others.

13-8106 59 min. $19.95

Memories of Mr. Jefferson's University

How many times have you tried to tell friends and family how special this university really is? Join fellow alumni Katie Couric, Brit Hume, and Senator Charles Robb as they reflect back on their years at the University of Virginia. Narrated by Charlie McDowell.

13-9783 47 min. $29.95

Mercenary Game

For the first time ever, film explores the private rites and rituals of a mercenary training camp. The best-known mercenary soldiers are interviewed on screen, and they frankly reveal who they are, how they train and how they're paid. Filmed at the "merc" camps in Georgia, this frightening and fascinating documentary features never-before-seen footage of an actual mercenary raid.

13-340 60 min. $39.95

Molokai Kalaupapa: The People, The Place, The Legacy

Breathtaking photography of the lavish tropical eden, where a community lived as exiles only to face death from their disease--leprosy. Heroic Father Damien lived and died for his commitment to bring dignity to their lives. Dramatic interviews with those living at that time and place.

13-8093 60 min. $29.95

Mysteries Of The Pyramids

Egyptian film star Omar Shariff takes you on a fascinating tour of the Pyramids and Sphinx at Giza. Go inside the 5000-year-old Great Pyramid and experience the mysteries of the ages.

13-5551 60 min. $19.95

National Geographic: Secrets of the Titanic

The fascinating story of the expedition and the amazing discovery of the doomed Titanic.

13-432 60 min. $19.95

Nature's Fury: A Decade Of Disasters

It was a decade in which the earth "rebelled." Natural disasters-truly acts of God-that rocked our ideas of stability and security. ABC News correspondents bring you to the sites of hurricanes, tornadoes, floods, earthquakes, and other disasters that demonstrate the planet's true capacity for destruction.

13-5762 60 min. $24.95

Navy Seals: The Real Story

Discover the incredible truth about how SEAL Teams really operated in Vietnam! Explosive action footage shows why Navy Seals were the most feared animals in the jungle.

13-6542 30 min. $14.95

Pot Shots: How They Grow Sensimilla

The most fact-filled documentary on sensimilla ever! Growers share their knowledge. Fun and informative.

13-8140 60 min. $39.95

Proudly We Hail

This is a moving documentary of why American's hold the flag so dear. This powerful film offers a profound historical look at the major American Wars.

13-6188 52 min. $19.95

Quest for the Monitor

Until 1973 the turbulent Atlantic waters hid the wreck of the USS Monitor, America's 1st ironclad warship that changed the course of the Civil War. In 1990 two diving teams captured a piece of history on film to share with the world.

13-8297 30 min. $19.95

Radio Days

This features remarkable stars from the golden era of radio. This program contains segments from 75 original broadcasts, over 200 archival photographs and classic film clips from radio's golden days.

13-9818 71 min. $29.95

Ranching: Living Legacy of the American West

It is a magical blend of original lyrics and music by rancher, singer, songwriter, Charlie Daniels in perfect union with the intimate and spectacular photography of Kathleen Jo Ryan, which features twelve Western States.

13-8145 31 min. $16.95

Red Baron

This looks at the most legendary ace of all--
Manfred Von Richthofen--"The Red Baron". He
was the nemesis of the Allied fliers of World War
I. Included are interviews, footage and the story
and controversy surrounding his death.
13-8019 60 min. $29.95

Ronnie Dearest

This is an amusing re-editing of Reagan's TV
commercials, out takes, war promos, features and
newsreels presenting a humorous history of the
famous Actor/President's diverse and controversial
career.
13-3094 45 min. $16.95

San Francisco Earthquake October 17, 1989

This program is a complete account of the fifteen
seconds when San francisco and the entire Bay
Area stood on the brink of annihilation. Thousands
of autos crowded the Nimitz Highway and Bay
Area Bridge on that day, some of them on their
way to Candlestick park and the third game of the
World Series. This tape features dramatic footage
of the victims and the heroes of the quake, and the
relief effort. Additionally, the video features safety
tips and precautions to take for those who may face
the shock of another deadly tremor.
13-5750 60 min. $16.95

Seven Wonders of the Ancient World

Philo of Byzantium compiled this remarkable list
approximately 2,000 years ago. Only one stands
today. While revealing the history and the original
purpose behind each monument, this video conveys
the story of the people responsible for each
wonder.
13-8020 60 min. $29.95

Shape of the World

The extraordinary story of how the world was
mapped is the essence of discovery in science,
math, religion and philosophy. This series shows
man's search over thousands of years to chart the
lands, the seas and the skies. In six one hour
videos, we travel with ancient Egyptian, Asian,
African and European explorers, up to the present
and the minute mapping of the DNA in our own
bodies.
13-9452 360 min. $149.95

SILK ROAD

This is the exclusive film about the Silk Road,
through which since pre-Christian times everything
from silk to stones to religious beliefs between East
and West has been transported. This film with its
splendid scenery, adventure, art, and a look into
the lifestyles of the people along the route, is truly
a fascinating rediscovery of the ancient and well

traveled path. This historical production was made
as a joint effort between NHK and CCTV. China
Central Television Network.

- **Glories of Ancient Changan**
13-6737 50 min. $29.95

- **Thousand Kilometers Beyond The Yellow River**
13-6738 50 min. $29.95

- **Art Gallery In The Desert**
13-6739 50 min. $29.95

- **Dark Castle**
13-6740 50 min. $29.95

- **In Search Of The Kingdom Of Lauian**
13-6741 50 min. $29.95

- **Across The Taklamakan Desert**
13-6742 50 min. $29.95

- **Kohotan - Oasis Of Silk And Jade**
13-6743 50 min. $29.95

- **Heat-Wave Called Turfan**
13-6744 50 min. $29.95

- **Through The Tian Shan Mountains By Rail**
13-6745 50 min. $29.95

- **Journey Into Music-South Through The Tian Shan Mountains**
13-6746 50 min. $29.95

- **Where Horses Fly Like The Wind**
13-6747 50 min. $29.95

- **Two Roads To The Pamirs**
13-6748 50 min. $29.95

Simba: The King of Beasts

Spectacular images and remarkable portraits of
Kenyan tribes and African wildlife highlight this
record of a lost world. Photography by Martin and
Osa Johnson.
13-8031 83 min. $39.95

Sky Above, Mud Below

In 1951, an international group of explorers set out
to cross the most dangerous, uncharted jungles of
Dutch New Guinea. In the 7 months it took them to
cover 1,000 miles, they came face-to-face with
bizarre native rituals and never-before-seen cannibal
tribes. Winner of the 1961 Academy Award for

VIDEO TITLES LISTED IN THIS GUIDE ARE AVAILABLE FOR PURCHASE
OR RENTAL. CONTACT YOUR LOCAL VIDEO STORE OR TELEPHONE (800) 383-8811

Best Documentary.
13-8061 92 min. $39.98

Son of a Gun
The legacy of Sam Colt, the man who made all men equal.
13-8261 50 min. $29.95

S.O.S. Titanic
The very mention of it's name is synonymous with monumental disaster. This production goes further and highlights the many famous personalities who were on board that fateful sailing and how they sacrificed their lives so that others could live.
13-8017 109 min. $29.95

Spectacular Disasters
Some of the world's greatest all-time tragedies are captured here in stunning, startling footage! Sci-fi star, George Takei, narrates this cavalcade of calamities. Included are: The Hindenburg Explosion, 1906 San Francisco earthquake and others.
13-8121 45 min. $19.95

Statue of Liberty
This unique program, which was nominated for a 1986 Academy Award, follows "The Lady" from her laborious construction in Paris to her controversial reception in the young United States. It includes stirring contributions by New York Governor Mario Cuomo, director Milos Foreman, poet James Baldwin, singer Ray Childs and many others.
13-315 30 min. $24.95

Stories of Change: Surviving Life's Challenges
Profiling the lives of four ethnically diverse young women, Stories of Change tells a timely and compelling story of survival: women who surmount alcoholism, drug abuse and cultural barriers, emerging with strength, confidence and a renewed sense of purpose.
13-8245 57 min. $99.95

Tabu: A Story of the South Seas
Two lovers are doomed by a tribal edict decreeing that the girl is "tabu" to all men. The lover's flight from judgment and the ultimate power of the tabu are reminiscent of Murnau's expressionist films. This unusual collaboration is by directors F.W. Murnau and Robert Flaherty.
13-8028 82 min. $39.95

Terrorism: The New World War
From sportscaster Jim McKay's memorable broadcasts from the Munich Olympics of 1972, this tape chronicles the accelerated rise of a new religious and political weapon: terror. Few areas of the globe are spared.
13-5758 60 min. $24.95

Terrorism: The Russian Connection
Watch as Soviet KGB head Yuri Andropov becomes Soviet Premier, and Polish Pope John Paul, is shot by a Turk with Bulgarian connections. Footage of the bombing of the U.S. embassies, the attempt on the full British cabinet, and on recruitment, training and techniques of the PLO and other terrorist organizations and their Soviet connections. The Canadian Broadcast Company's premier documentary on this timely and important subject.
13-070 60 min. $64.95

Treasures of the Titanic
The ultimate diving adventure takes you on the deep diving sub "Nautile" more than two miles down in the icy Atlantic to RMS Titanic's final resting place. Be there, as the sea finally surrenders the deepest secrets and priceless artifacts are recovered and brought to the surface.
13-8143 60 min. $16.95

Trolley
A nostalgic tribute to America's street cars and their significant contributions to the building of America's cities.
13-8038 60 min. $19.95

Turumba
Set in a tiny Philippine village, this film focuses on one family who traditionally made papier-mache animals to sell during the Turumba religious festivities, until a department store buyer shows up, buys all their stock, and then shows up again with an order for 500 more. The commercialization of a jungle village.
13-244 94 min. $59.95

U.F.O: The Unsolved Mystery
Do space aliens walk among us? Are the mysterious lights in the sky hallucinations or spaceships from other planets? Join M A S H star, Mike Farrell, in exploring the perplexing mysteries of the U.F.O. phenomenon.
13-5548 75 min. $19.95

USS Arizona: Life and Death of a Lady
Start with rare footage of the launch of the dreadnought in 1915, and follow the "life" of the ship through it's history. You will see rare footage of the ship where it lies today. And most historic, a former Arizona officer and the Japanese pilot who dropped the first bomb on the Arizona present a wreath in honor of the men still entombed aboard.
13-8142 47 min. $19.95

Volcano
A volcanic eruption in progress. Photographed at close range, the film illustrates the force, heat, lava flow, windstorm and destruction. Without narration but with music, this tape permits teacher commentary and a means of bridging the gap between scientific measurement and human emotion.
13-8058 29 min. $29.95

Wall In Jerusalem
A brilliant documentary on the history of 20th century Israel, vivid rare archive footage.
13-6614 91 min. $59.95

WEST OF THE IMAGINATION SERIES:
Here's the sweeping story of the American West as seen through the eyes of the artists, photographers, and film makers who helped create the myth which is our heritage...The West of the Imagination

• Romantic Horizon
Follow the path of Lewis and Clark, seeing the new lands through the eyes of artist-explorers George Catlin, Karl Bodmer and Alfred Jacob Miller.
13-8041 60 min. $29.95

• Golden Land
The saga of Manifest Destiny and the impact of the Texas Revolution, the Mexican War, the gold strikes and the pioneer spirit on a growing nation are examined in this program.
13-8042 60 min. $29.95

• Images of Glory
During the 1860's, artists paint a mythical Eden, while pioneer photographers whet America's appetite for Western adventure.
13-8043 60 min. $29.95

• Wild Riders
Here is the West of Fredric Remington and Charley Russell, who transformed the cowboy into an enduring hero in American folklore and created a gallery of heroes who live on, in our imaginations.
13-8044 60 min. $29.95

• Play the Legend
This program shows the west as the subject of popular culture and show business, from dime novels to Buffalo Bill's Wild West Show, from movie cowboy's to country singers.
13-8045 60 min. $29.95

• Enduring Dreams
The West has accommodated change while remaining a mythical land of freedom and possibility, thereby regenerating the Myth and redefining the American dream.
13-8046 60 min. $29.95

West That Never Was
The western is the most uniquely American form of film and it has been a vital part of the motion picture industry from the very start. From The Great Train Robbery in 1903 to the present there have been more than four thousand movies made about the American West. They have gone beyond mere entertainment--they have made the West a universal fascination and they have built that fascination into a form of mythology.
13-5037 58 min. $29.95

Winter's Quarters: Behind the Big Top
What really happens after "the smell of the grease paint and the roar of the crowd"? In "Winter's Quarters", we'll take you behind the scenes in a personal celebration and tribute to a very special breed of performer in the grand circus tradition. You'll learn first-hand from over 100 stars of the Circus past and present, the real meaning of, "The Show Must Go ON"!
13-8344 50 min. $19.95

Wonders of God's Creation
A contemporary look at what God has created on planet Earth. This three video collection, presents the beauty, wonder and miracle of God's creation. With each new discovery revealed, the viewer gains an even deeper appreciation for God's infinite power, wisdom and everlasting love.
13-8116 180 min. $59.95

Yellowstone Aflame
In this exciting, fast-paced film, you'll see Yellowstone before, during and after the Great Yellowstone fires and learn the complete fire story. Experience the raging Yellowstone fire-storms with incredible footage taken by people who risked their lives to film it. Discover the ecological role of fire as well as Yellowstone's beauty before and after the fires.
13-5042 30 min. $29.95

Yosemite's First 100 Years: 1890-1990
Centennial celebration of a national treasure. Wildlife, waterfalls, giant sequoias, the four seasons, rock climbing and skiing. 100 years of progress through historic photography: John Muir, paving Yosemite roads, Wawona tunnel construction and more.
13-8098 60 min. $29.95

Yosemite's Yesterdays
A fascinating look back at the "good old days" of Yosemite Valley. Leading expert and author Hank Johnston, presents rare photography in this historical account of the bygone days of rugged stage travel and the earlier daring attempts to reach the Valley by horseback.
13-9001 30 min. $19.95

VIDEO TITLES LISTED IN THIS GUIDE ARE AVAILABLE FOR PURCHASE OR RENTAL. CONTACT YOUR LOCAL VIDEO STORE OR TELEPHONE (800) 383-8811

New

Special Interest Video Titles

Become Available

Often.

Please Inquire

If A Title Or Subject

You Are Looking For

Is Not Listed.

VIDEO TITLES LISTED IN THIS GUIDE ARE AVAILABLE FOR PURCHASE
OR RENTAL. CONTACT YOUR LOCAL VIDEO STORE OR TELEPHONE (800) 383-8811

Drama
&
Literature

✓ *Drama & Literature*

Drama & Literature

Allen Ginsberg on Tour

On Feb. 16, 1983, Allen Ginsberg, together with fellow poet Peter Orlovsky and musician Steven Taylor, came to Wuppertal, West Germany for the final performance of their three-month tour through Northern Europe. This is a documentary of that extraordinary event. You'll see the poets on stage, in public interviews, in private situations and while walking around town. An 86-page book of the poems and songs from this event comes with each tape.

13-221 90 min. $79.95

AMERICAN SHORT STORY COLLECTION

Each of these videos is an adaptation of a classic American short story by such legendary writers as Mark Twain, Ernest Hemingway, F. Scott Fitzgerald, and many others. The list of performers is equally impressive: Tommy Lee Jones, Amy Irving, Ron Howard, Shelley Duvall, and more. So get ready to meet jazz babies, witness the supernatural, laugh on the Mississippi, or cry for a poor sharecropper's son. Your host is Henry Fonda.

• **Almos' a Man by Richard Wright**
Starring LeVar Burton and Madge Sinclair.
25-2614 51 min. $24.95

• **Barn Burning by William Faulkner**
Tommy Lee Jones and Diane Kegan star.
25-018 40 min. $24.95

• **Bernice Bobs Her Hair by F. Scott Fitzgerald**
Starring Shelley Duvall and Bud Cort.
25-091 49 min. $24.95

• **Blue Hotel by Stephen Crane**
Starring David Warner and James Keach.
25-2615 50 min. $24.95

• **D.P. by Kurt Vonnegut, Jr.**
Stars Stan Shaw.
25-1875 60 min. $24.95

• **Gift of Love**
Starring Timothy Bottoms
25-8011 96 min. $24.95

• **Golden Honeymoon by Ring Lardner**
Starring James Whitmore and Teresa Wright.
25-2616 50 min. $24.95

• **Greatest Man in the World By James Thurber**
Starring Brad Davis and Carol Kane.
25-2617 50 min. $24.95

• **I'm a Fool by Sherwood Anderson**
Starring Ron Howard and Amy Irving.
25-095 38 min. $24.95

• **Jilting of Granny Weatherall by Katherine Anne Porter**
Stars Geraldine Fitzgerald.
25-038 57 min. $24.95

• **Jolly Corner by Henry James**
Starring Salome Jens and Fritz Weaver.
25-2618 43 min. $24.95

• **Man Who Corrupted Hadleyburg by Mark Twain**
Starring Robert Preston.
25-047 40 min. $24.95

• **Man & the Snake/The Return**
Stars John Fraser & Peter Vaughan
25-8012 60 min. $24.95

• **Music School - John Updike & Parker Anderson, Philosopher - Ambrose Bierce**
Two stories on one tape: starring Ron Weyand in Music School and Harris Yulin in Parker Anderson, Philosopher.
25-2619 69 min. $24.95

• **Noon Wine by Katherine Anne Porter**
Stars Fred Ward.
25-1874 81 min. $24.95

• **Paul's Case by Willa Cather**
Starring Eric Roberts, Michael Higgins.
25-108 52 min. $24.95

• **Pigeon Feathers**
Stars Christopher Collet.
25-8013 45 min. $24.95

• **Rappaccini's Daughter by Nathaniel Hawthorne**
Kristoffer Tabori and Kathleen Beller star.
25-059 57 min. $25.95

• **Revolt of Mother**
Stars Amy Madigan
25-8014 60 min. $24.95

VIDEO TITLES LISTED IN THIS GUIDE ARE AVAILABLE FOR PURCHASE OR RENTAL. CONTACT YOUR LOCAL VIDEO STORE OR TELEPHONE (800) 383-8811

• **Sky is Gray by Ernest Gaines**
Starring Olivia Cole and Cleavon Little.
25-116 46 min. $24.95

• **Soldier's Home by Ernest Hemingway**
Starring Richard Backus and Nancy Marchand.
25-2620 41 min. $24.95

Becket
The church fights the power of the King in this
spectacular classic of 12th century England. Henry
II (Peter O'Toole) attempts to secure his power by
appointing his long-time wenching partner, Thomas
Becket (Richard Burton). Archbishop of
Canterbury. What ensues is an unexpected battle of
wills that leads to murder.
36-5793 150 min. $59.95

Call Of The Wild
Charlton Heston stars as John Thornton in this
rousing, authentic version of Jack London's classic
novel. It's a tough life for the dogs and men who
are looking for gold in the frozen tundra of the
Yukon. One very special German Shepherd, named
Buck, was plucked from his peaceful life in the
States and brought to Alaska to run the sleds. John
Thornton befriends this dog, and they team up for
adventure.
36-5794 105 min. $59.95

Christmas Carol
This movie version of Dickens' immortal tale has
long been considered the finest ever made. Some of
Britain's very best film makers united to produce
one of England's, and the world's, greatest classics
in this brilliant and moving film.
10-410 86 min. $29.95

Crime and Punishment
25-2262 40 min. $19.95

Cyrano de Bergerac
Cyrano de Bergerac-poet, philosopher, gallant
soldier extraordinaire-cannot win the love of the
beautiful Roxanne because of his large, deformed
nose. This acclaimed performance was translated
and adapted by Anthony Burgess with an award-
winning performance by Derek Jacobi.
25-267 176 min. $59.95

Four for Thrills
"Masque of the Red Death," by Poe; "The Hand,"
with Belafonte; "Casey at the Bat," and the story of
"The Hangman," as told by Herschel Bernardi.
25-027 120 min. $64.95

Fried Shoes, Cooked Diamonds
Features conversations and readings with poets
Allen Ginsberg, William Burroughs, Timothy

Leary, Meredith Monk, Miguel Pinero and Gregory
Corso.
25-2801 55 min. $29.95

GIELGUD'S CHEKHOV

• **Volume I**
Sir John Gielgud is your host narrator for these
dramatizations of three of the immortal
playwright's works. Contained within are "The
Fugitive," "Desire For Sleep" and "Rothschild's
Violin," stories dealing with the theme of escape.
25-029 60 min. $64.95

• **Volume II**
"Volodya" and "The Boarding House" are two of
the great Russian writer's best-loved works.
Dealing with illicit love, the twist endings are not
unlike O'Henry.
25-030 60 min. $64.95

• **Volume III**
"The Wallet" and "Revenge" deal with two classic
emotions as old as mankind and as contemporary as
today.
25-031 60 min. $64.95

Hamlet
The viewer will be led to reflect on death, evil and
decision-making in this short study of one of
William Shakespeare's most popular plays. Gain
insights into the person of Hamlet and the intricate
plot. What will Hamlet do to avenge the death of
his father? A good synopsis of a great classic.
25-087 40 min. $19.95

Iliad
25-282 40 min. $19.95

JAMES FENIMORE COOPER'S
LEATHERSTOCKING TALES
The true American myth, D.H. Lawrence. PBS's
authentic adaptation of "Deerslayer," "Pathfinder,"
"Last of the Mohicans," "Pioneers" and "Prairie,"
Natty Bumpo and Chingachgook bring alive the
early 1700's, when Americans, French and Hurons
were fighting for the vast uncharted wilderness.

• **Volume I**
25-035 60 min. $64.95

• **Volume II**
25-036 60 min. $64.95

Julius Caesar
William Shakespeare's classic play starring
Charlton Heston, Jason Robards, John Gielgud,

VIDEO TITLES LISTED IN THIS GUIDE ARE AVAILABLE FOR PURCHASE
OR RENTAL. CONTACT YOUR LOCAL VIDEO STORE OR TELEPHONE (800) 383-8811

Richard Johnson, Robert Vaughn, Diana Rigg and Richard Chamberlain.
25-150 116 min. $39.95

King Lear
Under Peter Brook's direction, Paul Scofield gives vibrant life to Shakespeare's tragedy of the conflict between parent and child, pride and wisdom, expectation and fulfillment.
25-2507 138 min. $29.95

Mark Twain's A Connecticut Yankee in King Arthur's Court
What does an innocent young citizen of Hartford, Connecticut do when he's plucked up from the 19th century and plunked down into King Arthur's medieval court? this tale of American ingenuity in Camelot stars Richard Basehart, Roscoe Lee Browne and Paul Rudd in a satirical spectacle.
25-048 60 min. $64.95

Medea
In her only non-operatic film, the incomparable Maria Callas gives a performance that left critics spellbound: "The greatest acting performance of her career...acting of a supreme dramatic achievement which will rank the film as a rare work of cinematographic art, "said The New Yorker."
25-122 100 min. $49.95

MEET THE CLASSIC AUTHORS
This unique series features fascinating portraits of outstanding authors whose works have weathered the test of time. Gives viewers insight into the lives and motivations of these great men and women and inspires them to read the works which are considered today's classics. For grades 5 and up.

• **Charles Dickens**
10-2070 20 min. $39.95

• **Edgar Allan Poe**
10-2075 18 min. $39.95

• **H.G. Wells**
10-2079 16 min. $39.95

• **Herman Melville**
10-2074 22 min $39.95

• **Jack London**
10-2073 16 min. $39.95

• **James Fenimore Cooper**
10-2069 20 min. $39.95

• **Jules Verne**
10-2078 15 min. $39.95

• **Louisa May Alcott**
10-2068 20 min. $39.95

• **Mark Twain**
10-2077 16 min. $39.95

• **Robert Louis Stevenson**
10-2076 17 min. $39.95

• **Rudyard Kipling**
10-2072 21 min. $39.95

• **Washington Irving**
10-2071 18 min. $39.95

Midsummer Night's Dream
Under the direction of Peter Hall, the Royal Shakespeare Company brings to life this brilliant production that captures both the play's comedy and its subtle undercurrent of melancholy.
25-2508 120 min. $19.95

Moliere
Based on events in the life of the renowned French playwright, the play shows Moliere as a man beset by church and state because of his sharp-penned satire of both in "Tartuffe."
25-268 112 min. $39.95

Moon Drum
An album of visual music by John Whitney, the pioneer of motion picture graphics and well-known creator of special effects used in 2001: A Space Odyssey and Star Wars.
25-8003 55 min. $29.95

Mr. Robinson Crusoe
Well-limbed adventurer Douglas Fairbanks makes a bet that he can live a year on a deserted South Seas island. Authentic locations and vintage Fairbanks acrobatics make this early sound film a rollicking, fun-filled yarn. Movie fantasy blends with exotic reality in plush odd detail. (Rumor has it that this film was made because the high-flying star wanted to sail his yacht to the South Seas on a vacation, anyway).
36-5795 80 min. $29.95

Raga
Legendary sitarist Ravi Shankar travels from the California sixties scene back to his spiritual roots in India. He performs with the likes of Alla Rakha and George Harrison.
25-8002 96 min. $29.95

Rime of the Ancient Mariner
Coleridge's epic poem, directed by Raul da Silva. This is an award-winning innovative work featuring a recitation by Sir Michael Redgrave, accompanied

VIDEO TITLES LISTED IN THIS GUIDE ARE AVAILABLE FOR PURCHASE OR RENTAL. CONTACT YOUR LOCAL VIDEO STORE OR TELEPHONE (800) 383-8811

by images both real and animated. Part 1: The Life of Samuel Colegridge; Part 2: The Rime of the Ancient Mariner.

25-061 60 min. $39.95

Sammie and Rosie Get Laid

Go slumming with some of the trashiest low-lifes around London. Sammie and Rosie want to inherit a rich old man's fortune, but they'll first have to come up with the grandchild he wants. Starring Claire Bloom and Roland Gift.

01-8033 97 min. $69.95

Scarlet Letter

25-2261 40 min. $19.95

SHAKESPEARE COLLECTION SERIES

These productions have recaptured the Elizabethan flavor of Shakespeare's own Globe productions by staging them just as they were seen in the 16th century.

The plays are complemented with meticulously constructed costumes and an artist's reproduction of the Globe Theater stage.

• Anthony & Cleopatra

Shakespeare's most popular tale of two of history's most famous personages. Starring Timothy Dalton, Lynn Redgrave and John Carradine.

25-8023 183 min. $89.95

• King Lear

Shakespeare's renowned story of familial deceit and murder. Starring Mike Kellen, Darryl Hickman and David Groh.

25-8027 182 min. $89.95

• King Richard III

Shakespeare's story of a self-centered weak king. Starring David Birney, Paul Shenar and William H. Bassett.

25-8024 172 min. $89.95

• Macbeth

Shakespeare's story of murder, greed and untimely death. Starring Jeremy Brett, Piper Laurie and Simon MacCorkindale.

25-8025 151 min. $89.95

• Merry Wives of Windsor

Shakespeare's timeless comedy about marital fidelity. Starring Leon Charles, Gloria Grahame and Joel Asher.

• Othello

Shakespeare's keen understanding of jealousy in love results in perhaps his greatest triumph as a stage play, and his prime example of the tragic

hero Othello. Starring Ron Moody and Jenny Agutter.

25-8029 195 min. $89.95

• Romeo & Juliet

Shakespeare's tragic story of young love thwarted by a family feud. Starring Alex Hyde-White, Blanche Baker and Esther Rolle.

25-8028 165 min. $89.95

• Taming of the Shrew

One of Shakespeare's most popular plays, "The Taming of the Shrew" examines the comedy of courtship. Starring Larry Drake, Karen Austin and Kathryn Johnson.

25-8031 115 min. $89.95

• Tempest

Shakespeare's classic tale of the fantasy world of spirits, sorcery, monsters, maidens and shipwrecked scheming noblemen is brought to life. Starring Efrem Zimbalist, Jr., William H. Bassett, Ted Sorel and Ron Palillo.

25-8026 127 min. $89.95

Steinbeck's The Pearl

Of the Nobel-prize-winning author's film, Time Magazine said: "As a fable of man's hope...it is close to perfect." Its breathtakingly beautiful photography has won a number of awards around the world. "The Pearl" tells the story of a poor Mexican fisherman whose dreams of wealth are both realized and shattered.

25-072 60 min. $69.95

Swan Lake

As seen on the Disney Channel, this beautiful story is reenacted on a cold wintery night as a grandfather tells his granddaughter the story of Swan Lake.

25-8010 28 min. $49.95

Strindberg's Miss Julie: Royal Shakespeare Company

August Strindberg is one of the prime innovators of out time. The impact of his dramatic method reflected in his "Miss Julie" is probably greater and less acknowledged than any other modern writer.

25-118 90 min. $74.95

Tale of Two Cities

Witness the love and anger of Dickens' characters as they live and die for loyalty to friends and justice. Gain knowledge of the complex characters of Charles Dickens and the French Revolution. What motivated the revolutionaries? What drove them to such extremes?

25-086 40 min. $19.95

VIDEO TITLES LISTED IN THIS GUIDE ARE AVAILABLE FOR PURCHASE OR RENTAL. CONTACT YOUR LOCAL VIDEO STORE OR TELEPHONE (800) 383-8811

Tartuffe

Posing as a holy man, the wily Tartuffe manages to gain favor with the believing and trusting well-to-do merchant Orgon, who bestows his worldly goods, social position and nubile daughter on the perfidious fraud. Tartuffe delights in accepting his all and also arranges a little depraved dalliance with Orgon's young wife, Elmire. A Royal Shakespeare Company production starring Antony Sher.

25-120 110 min. $29.95

Tempest

An ethereal production of this gentle comedy, Shakespeare's farewell. This is truly such stuff as dreams are made of. Designed by Rouben TerArutunian and starring Richard Burton, Maurice Evans, Tom Poston and Lee Remick.

25-8001 76 min. $39.95

Thornton Wilder's Our Town

Thornton Wilder's Pulitzer prize-and Emmy award-winning play is brought to the screen by Hal Holbrook, Barbara Bel Geddes, John Houseman, Robby Benson, Ronny Cox and Sada

Thompson. Love, life and death in a small American town.

25-052 120 min. $74.95

Turgenev's Month in the Country

"Burning hate is hidden within the most ardent love"--Ivan Turgenev. Here is one of the earliest and best Russian psychological dramas. Beautiful Natalia (Suzannah York) trifles with Rakitin's love for four years, then seeks to recapture the passions of her youth in an affair with young Beleyev (Ian McShane). This classic is both tragic and pathetically comic in the grand tradition of Chekhov.

25-077 87 min. $74.95

War and Peace

This epic production of Leo Tolstoy's great literary achievement has been hailed as the definitive transferal of literature to film. The six-hour and twenty minute feature is issued in a collector's case holding three videocassettes and program booklet.

25-3073 260 min. $99.95

Dramatic And Literary

Videos

Bring The Printed Page

To Life

Exercise
&
Fitness

- ✓ *Aerobics, Dance, Fitness*
- ✓ *Back & Stretching Exercises*
- ✓ *Jogging & Walking*
- ✓ *Yoga*
- ✓ *Miscellaneous*

Aerobics, Dance, Fitness

29 Minute Tummy Toner
Cynthia Targosz takes you through a three stage exercise routine designed to deliver a tighter, trimmer tummy in a minimum amount of time. Guaranteed to reduce your waistline with just 3 days of exercise a week.
15-9700 30 min. $16.95

5 Minute Workout With Sandy Duncan
Join Sandy Duncan, one of America's popular celebrities, for a head to toe workout that fits the lifestyles of men and women of all ages. Learn it in less than an hour, then do it anywhere, anytime.
15-8059 60 min. $16.95

Aerobic Dancing: Medicine, Health and Exercise
Before you move a muscle, the instructor discusses the physical aspects of aerobic dancing to make you aware of how your body is "strung together." Hints are also offered on how to avoid injury by maintaining proper alignment of the body.
15-005 30 min. $29.95

Aerobic Self-Defense
Ron Van Clief, World Martial Arts Champion, combines lively aerobics with basic self-defense movements.
15-006 60 min. $19.95

Aerobicise: The Beautiful Workout
Aerobic dancing to original music, produced by Ron Harris, fashion photographer. An erotic exercise program.
15-008 113 min. $19.95

Aerobicise: The Beginning Workout
A basic, simple exercise regimen for the uninitiated aerobiciser.
15-007 96 min. $19.95

Aerobicise: The Ultimate Workout
The last installment of the aerobicise trilogy is the most advanced, designed for those in excellent shape.
15-009 100 min. $19.95

Aerobics on the Easy Side
The only low-impact program recommended by Weight Watchers magazine. An hour of healthy, safe aerobics directed by the head of the American Aerobics Association.
15-145 60 min. $29.95

Aerobics: Medicine, Health & Exercise
Kim Blank explains the relationship between diet and exercise for effective weight control, then takes you through a series of simple aerobic exercises that can be done every day in your home.
15-004 30 min. $29.95

Aerobics: The Winner's Edge
Dr. Kenneth Cooper, an authority on aerobics-related conditioning, takes viewers through the development of a personal fitness program that is both practical and manageable.
15-003 30 min. $29.95

Anybody's Step Workout
This video offers two separate step workouts, the "interval step-plus aerobics workout", that alternates step training with aerobics and the "muscle step workout", a new muscle defining workout that uses hand weights and tubing.
15-8051 45 min. $24.95

Anybody's Workout With Len Kravitz
Len Kravitz was voted fitness instructor of the year by the 14,000 members from 38 countries of the International Dance Exercise Association. The "Anybody's Workout" has been named "excellent" in Shape Magazine's annual review of fitness videos and is highly acclaimed by Mademoiselle, Family Circle, USA Today, and the Complete Guide To Exercise Videos.
15-5704 90 min. $19.95

Armchair Aerobics
Armchair Aerobics is a fun exercise program designed to increase fitness. The program is unique because all of the exercises can be done while sitting. This easy-to-follow tape leads you through the exercises with lively music in the background. Kit includes an audio cassette and descriptive brochure.
15-2106 30 min. $34.95

Armchair Fitness
An aerobic workout in a chair for those who, because of preference, lifestyle, age or disability, need or want to avoid vigorous activity. Contains three 20-minute stretching and strengthening routines to Big Band music, that can be done by anyone who can sit up straight in a chair.
20-004 60 min. $39.95

Armed Forces Workout
Bill Dowers is your trainer and he'll work you as he did the stars of "An Officer and A Gentleman," using the same routines followed by the members of the American armed forces. This tape is for

women as well.
15-011 60 min. $19.95

Baby Boomer Light Impact Workout

Now you can have the best of two styles! Baby Boomer Light Impact workout features the superb aerobic conditioning of high intensity aerobics combined with all the low stress benefits of a low impact style. Plus you get the latest in multi-muscle conditioning along with the finest "anti-aging" workout ever to slow down you physical clock! You'll shape up, slim down and maintain all the qualities of a youthful, supple body.
15-5434 30 min. $14.95

Balanced Fitness Workout Program

A whole new concept in exercise that can be used at home with confidence. Two programs in one-a 30 minute "light-impact" aerobic workout and a 25-minute flexibility and muscle toning program-to alternate or combine. Emphasizes muscular strength and flexibility. Produced by Dr. Art Ulene.
15-144 58 min. $24.95

BALLETCISE

Prima Ballerina Marguerite Porter has developed a unique exercise program based on simple ballet steps for a perfect figure. The Balletcise routine conditions and trims the body by gently stretching and toning the muscles without the sweat and tears of other exercise routines.

• Beginners
15-8086 30 min. $19.95

• Advanced
15-8087 30 min. $19.95

Bellydance! Magical Motion

At last... a videocassette introducing the perfect dance exercise! Noted dance instructor, Atea, and five lovely dancers demonstrate the beautiful art of bellydance. Basic steps and more advanced techniques are clearly presented in an easy-to-learn format. Emphasis is on fun, creative expression, and safe, healthy exercise. Dazzling dance performances make this tape entertaining as well as educational. Come join us in our magic carpet ride!
15-132 60 min. $29.95

Bellydancing

This program is a complete course in the art of belly dance. A brief history of the dance origins and the making of a costume are included. Each body movement is explained fully and incorporated into the final dance sequence, designed for you to follow along, step-by-step.
15-9255 90 min. $19.95

Best Bust with Cynthia Targosz

No matter what size bustline you have, develop amazing shape, definition and beautiful curves. Cynthia takes you through a regimen that strengthens the underlying chest muscles. This will give the bust a youthful, uplifted, firmer appearance. A segment on "bust wellness" for early breast cancer detection, is also included.
15-9274 50 min. $19.95

Best Fat Burners

A high-energy workout, utilizing the latest research to trim fat and lose inches. No other workout is designed to attack stubborn fat zones and burn them up.
15-1912 30 min. $16.95

BETTY CROCKER EXERCISE AND LOOSE WEIGHT SERIES:

• Low Impact Aerobics

Join certified A.C.E. instructor Anne Barney as she leads you through a fun and upbeat low impact workout and helps you to design a healthier lifestyle and to achieve your weight loss goals.
15-9476 30 min. $16.99

• Stomach and Lower Body

Anne Barney leads you through an upbeat workout to flatten your stomach and firm your legs, thighs and buttocks; helps you design a healthier lifestyle and achieve weight loss goals.
15-9575 30 min. $16.99

Big On Fitness: Full Figure Aerobics

This is a carefully choreographed program to incorporate safe routines and exercises that tone muscles, burn fat, and increase cardiovascular fitness. This special approach was developed from a restricted program for large women conducted over the past 2 1/2 years. Every consideration is give to safety. For all fitness levels.
15-8010 53 min. $29.95

Body by Jake: Don't Quit!

Now you can work out with Jake Steinfeld, trainer to many Hollywood stars. Jake's workout combines speed and continuity to build endurance and tone muscles. Two levels, beginner and advanced, set to lively music.
15-014 60 min. $19.95

Body by Jake: Energize Yourself!

Hollywood's trainer to the stars Jake Steinfeld shows you how to get into shape with a new series of energizing, easy-to-follow aerobic exercise programs including the 30-minute body blitz and the 12-minute Jake quickie. Using ordinary household objects, Jake makes staying fit simple

VIDEO TITLES LISTED IN THIS GUIDE ARE AVAILABLE FOR PURCHASE OR RENTAL. CONTACT YOUR LOCAL VIDEO STORE OR TELEPHONE (800) 383-8811

and a lot of fun.
15-195 60 min. $19.95

Body In Progress with Jennie Garth

Jennie, of Beverly Hills 90210, has designed this program to show the young adult that being fit, feeling energized and looking terrific, comes from balancing "fun to do" exercises, with her "good for you" food program. In "Body In Progress" Jennie shows that "thin's out & healthy's in" as she demonstrates her fun and revolutionary new program.
15-8124 50 min. $19.95

Body Shaping

A dynamic and specially choreographed program designed to help shape and tone your body.
15-215 60 min. $19.95

Bodyband Workout

First home video exercise program to use elastic resistance. Produced by Dr. Art Ulene (The Today Show,) the program consists of a 35-minute muscle-toning workout and a 15-minute flexibility routine, designed by fitness expert Tamilee Webb. Packaged with a set of Bodybands and instruction booklet.
15-187 53 min. $19.95

Bruce Jenner's 29-Minute Workout

Bruce Jenner takes you through this solid, simple exercise program--no complicated routines, ideal for busy people.
15-2265 29 min. $14.95

Bunnetics: The Buttocks Workout

Finally, here's a video workout that really teaches you simply and directly the correct way to tone, trim and tighten what other workouts leave behind.
15-208 20 min. $16.95

California Calorie Burner

Madeleine Lewis helps you to slim down and shape up in this superbly choreographed, state-of-the art workout video.
15-8098 60 min. $19.95

Cathy Lee Crosby's 20 Minute Workout

Now, for the first time, the beautiful actress and former professional athlete Cathy Lee Crosby shares with you her amazing workout secrets. Let Cathy Lee show you how you can look and feel your very best in just 20 minutes a day!
15-5012 20 min. $14.95

Callanetics

The exercise book that's been storming the best-seller charts is now a video. Callan Pinckney demonstrates her revolutionary deep muscle exercise technique that can literally shed years off

your figure in hours without putting pressure on your back.
15-194 60 min. $24.95

Commuter's Workout

The unique fitness program you can do in your car! Too many of us waste valuable time sitting in traffic. Joy Bonner will help you use this time to stretch, relax and firm and tone your muscles and reduce stress. Get something useful out of your commute!
Includes audio tape.
15-8050 20 min. $19.95

CORY EVERSON SERIES:

• Body Shaping

The beautiful ESPN body shaping star takes you to the sexy, shapely body you have always wanted!
15-8033 50 min. $19.95

• Slender Thighs & Legs

Cory takes you step-by-step to trim and tone thighs and reduce hips while you flatten and tighten the stomach.
15-8034 50 min. $19.95

Couples Do It Debbie's Way

An exercise program that sets a new trend in fitness-sensible, evenly-paced exercises, set to Big Band music. Features Debbie Reynolds and husband Richard Hamlett plus Tom and Patricia Bosley, and Dick and Pat Van Patten.
15-2674 60 min. $29.95

Crystal Light Aerobic Workout

This video features Susan Anton and the Crystal Light national aerobic champions. A low-impact workout which includes toning for the arms, legs, stomach and buttocks.
15-1546 90 min. $29.95

Dance Yourself Fit

Dance your way to fitness with Melinda Field. This aerobic dancercise program combines easy-to-learn dance steps with aerobic exercise techniques, set to music with a strong beat. A great way to get fit and trim with a minimum of equipment and a maximum of fun.
15-141 60 min. $24.95

DENISE AUSTIN EXERCISE SERIES:

• High Energy Aerobics
15-1696 30 min. $16.95

• Hips, Thighs and Buttocks
15-1699 30 min. $19.95

• **Low Impact Aerobics**
15-1698 30 min. $16.95

• **Non-Aerobic Workout**
15-1700 30 min. $19.95

• **Super Stomachs**
15-1697 30 min. $19.95

• **30-Minute Fat Burning Workout**
15-5702 30 min. $19.95

• **Kicking with Country**
15-8118 60 min. $19.95

Disrobics
Physical fitness was never like this before! Eight gorgeous hunks bare their well-developed muscles. Each guy individually dances, sweats and pumps his way through a Disrobics workout. Our instructors will raise your pulse and give you a workout you'll never forget. Nudity.
15-199 60 min. $39.95

Disrobics: Advanced
Zip off your warm-up suits and get ready for the advanced workout. From top to bottom and head to toe, these sensuous hunks will raise your pulse and deliver a workout you will never forget. Nudity.
15-200 60 min. $39.95

Do It Debbie's Way
Debbie Reynolds has a new idea about exercise--it should be fun and not too strenuous. Debbie leads you in three separate exercise segments: for the beginner, the beginner-intermediate, and the beginner-advanced. She and her friends Teri Garr, Rose Marie, Florence Henderson, Shelley Winters and Dionne Warwick work out in a beautiful setting to the beat of Big Band music.
15-018 60 min. $29.95

Dolph Lundgren: Maximum Potential
He first exploded on the scene in "Rocky IV." Now, the body of the 80's comes to video and shares with you his secrets to ultimate fitness. With Dolph Lundgren's help, you can go all the way to achieve your maximum potential!
15-1636 60 min. $29.95

Ejercicios Con Clara
Clara Darnas ha creado un programa de ejercicios para buena salud, que le ayudara a quemar grasa, robustecer los musculos, y ponerse en forma optima. Este programa innovativo esta desenado cientificamente para quemar la grasa de su cuerpo en el menor tiempo posible.
15-9066 30 min. $29.95

ESQUIRE DANCE AWAY
Molly Fox, a former Jane Fonda Workout instructor, guides you through this four-part series. Features low-impact aerobics incorporating dance styles from different eras, such as the twist, to bop, the swim and the hustle.

• **Get Fit with the Hits-50's**
15-1968 30 min. $19.95

• **Get Fit with the Hits-60's**
15-1969 30 min. $19.95

• **Get Fit with the Hits-70's**
15-1970 30 min. $19.95

• **Get Fit with the Hits-80's**
15-1971 30 min. $19.95

• **Get Fit with the Hits-90's**
15-8100 30 min. $19.95

• **Get Fit with the Hits-Country Western**
15-8099 30 min. $19.95

• **Get Fit with the Hits-Oldies but Goodies**
15-9474 30 min. $19.95

ESQUIRE GREAT BODY SERIES
Produced in conjunction with Esquire magazine, this series is designed to be a total fitness program. The programs are hosted by Deborah Crocker, Director of Exercise Programming at Chicago's Charlie Fitness Club and Hotel.

• **Dynamite Legs**
15-124 30 min. $18.95

• **Low Impact Aerobics**
15-127 30 min. $18.95

• **Stretching for Energy**
15-129 30 min. $18.95

• **Super Stomach**
15-126 30 min. $18.95

• **Superbody: Aerobics Plus**
15-2001 40 min. $18.95

• **Superbody: Firm and Trim**
15-2003 40 min. $18.95

• **Superbody: Great Legs**
15-2002 40 min. $18.95

VIDEO TITLES LISTED IN THIS GUIDE ARE AVAILABLE FOR PURCHASE OR RENTAL. CONTACT YOUR LOCAL VIDEO STORE OR TELEPHONE (800) 383-8811

• **Total Body Tone Up**
15-128 30 min. $18.95

• **Upper Body Beautiful**
15-125 30 min. $18.95

• **Step Aerobics**
15-9477 30 min. $18.95

Esquire Ultimate Fitness
This program is ideal for toning up muscles, developing your strength and endurance, and conditioning your cardiovascular system. It's easy for both women and men to relate to: no complicated dance steps and easy-to-follow, sports training-like exercises.
15-020 60 min. $19.95

Esquire Ultimate Fitness: 30 Minute Workout
Deborah Crocker takes you through this new, brisk half-hour workout.
15-2263 30 min. $14.95

Exercise Now
This energizing exercise tape offers you the choice of two excellent workouts. The first is 10 minutes of warm-up and toning for those days when your schedule doesn't allow for the full program. The second is a complete 40-minute workout designed to release tension, firm muscles and increases aerobic capacity, with stretching and cool-down at the end.
15-024 60 min. $29.95

FIRM AEROBIC WORKOUT WITH WEIGHTS SERIES:

• **Volume 1**
Aerobic weight loss training, a revolutionary concept in exercise in which users typically report visible results within 10 workouts and one that creates a slender "swimmer's body." On the same tape: an exclusive information program, including a complete fitness encyclopedia with animated illustrations, anatomical models, charts and film clips. It explodes dozens of myths, and provides a scientific guide to fat loss and body shaping.
15-105 100 min. $49.95

• **Volume 2**
The second volume of this popular workout program features dancer/actress Janet Jones
15-3120 110 min. $49.95

• **Volume 3**
Introduces interval training. Actress/dancer Sandahl Bergman instructs. For men and women, the firm creates a slender swimmer's body.

Variable weights make it easy for beginners or maximum tough.
15-9358 105 min. $49.95

Fit and Physical
A short version of a Jazzercise workout for people on the run.
15-138 15 min. $16.95

Fit Forever
Fitness program for men and women, 55 or older. Level One shows how to exercise while seated in a chair. Level Two demonstrates how to exercise while alternating between sitting in a chair and standing while using the chair for support. Level Three exercises are freestanding and sometimes double-tempo.
15-217 46 min. $24.95

Fitness Experience: Strength Building Program for Mature Adults
Arnie Fonseca, MS, CSCS specializes in Senior Adult Fitness. This video will provide mature adults with a place to start. The program is divided into 8 sections. You may use all of the programs or only those sections for your specific needs.
15-8117 48 min. $24.95

Fitness Formula
Features America's leading fitness pioneer Judi Sheppard Missett, Jazzercise founder. Your individualized fitness formula contains: warm-up, aerobics, cool-down, and muscle toning.
15-5142 45 min. $14.95

Fitness Over Fifty
Put more life in your years is the message from this exercise video designed for older people and others who can benefit from an invigorating but non-strenuous exercise program. The objective is to improve the participants: strength, flexibility, energy level and muscle tone.
15-5470 100 min. $39.95

FLATTEN YOUR STOMACH SERIES:
Professional coaches guide viewers through three stages of exercise designed to trim down and firm up the stomach as never before.

• **Flatten Your Stomach - For Men**
15-025 30 min. $19.95

• **Flatten Your Stomach - For Women**
15-026 30 min. $19.95

Franco Columbo's Superset Shape-Up
A brisk and invigorating workout with or without weights...firms up muscles, flattens the stomach

---

and gets the body in shape with minimum effort.
15-1775 25 min. $19.95

Freedanse
This revolutionary dance fitness system is presented by Marine Jahan, the incredible dancer who caused an international sensation with her performance in "Flashdance." Work out with Marine as she exercise-dances in an exhilarating and fun series of movements.
15-027 60 min. $29.95

Freedanse II
Takes you through a dancer's series of stretches and exercises in uniquely developed series of dance movements that flow naturally from warm-up into combinations that become routines.
15-232 60 min. $29.95

Fun and Fitness Over 50
This tape show how mature adults can keep fit without a vigorous workout. Fitness instructor Phyllis Downey guides you through an easy paced workout to the music of international recording artist, Bob Kames playing the organ.
15-8083 42 min. $24.95

Funky Aerobics
This one-of-kind 30 minute workout is all you need to condition your total body, burn fat, improve your endurance and develop beautiful lean muscles.
15-5433 30 min. $14.95

Get Fit Rebounding
Sylvia Ortiz and Al Carter join forces to bring you this educational introduction video. Al presents the rebound exercise concept in a very simple and understandable way. Then Sylvia leads you step-by-step with an exhilarating ten-minute rebound exercise program.
15-8057 45 min. $24.95

Gymjazz: The Non-Impact Workout
A lively, MTV-style video featuring Gymjazz wrist/ankle weights. Features Sandahl Bergman and Josh Taylor. Weights not included.
15-2380 30 min. $19.95

Heidi Miller's Body Sculpting
This workout will not add bulk - it tones, firms and flattens. No necessity to purchase equipment, as Heidi illustrates the use of household objects. Start to shape up today, the body sculpting way.
15-1774 60 min. $19.95

Hooked on Exercise Classics
Now you can enjoy Louis Clark's brilliant arranging and conducting of the Royal Philharmonic Orchestra while exercising to a routine choreographed by one of America's most

popular fitness experts. It will firm your buttocks, shape your legs, flatten your stomach and provide excellent body tone, exciting results without the boredom!
15-8074 40 min. $16.95

High-Tech Workout
Rob Simonelli conducts this high charge workout featuring an innovative technique in fitness exercise.
15-2066 55 min. $19.95

Hot Bods Fat Burning Workout
This workout combines the latest scientific findings with high-sizzle excitement! Take it from AFAA - there's never been a more efficient way to burn fat. Hot Bods safely and easily lets you alternate a quick burst of high intensity with mellower, rhythmic segment - it's easy to master but it never gets boring.
15-5435 30 min. $14.95

How to Jump for Life
One of the best ways to get aerobic exercise without stress is to use a mini-trampoline. Jill Steinback has developed an energetic program, combining running, jumping and bouncing that will keep you fit.
15-042 30 min. $19.95

Idrea Presents the Larger Woman's Workout
Praised by fitness experts and health authorities as one of the most helpful and inspirational exercise videos ever made. The Larger Woman's Workout provides both a sensible low-impact aerobic program and high-spirited motivation.
15-5544 60 min. $19.95

If You Can Dance You Can Do It
The Bee Gees accompany you in this superb exercise tape. The musical background takes the boredom and repetitiveness out of the exercise routines and keeps you coming back for more.
15-180 60 min. $39.95

Jack LaLanne Way
America's favorite fitness expert now has a top-flight workout designed for men and women of any age. Jack's proven method: a two-part workout - 30 minutes of aerobics followed by 30 minutes of toning, firming and strengthening exercises.
15-069 60 min. $34.95

Jane Fonda's Prime Time Workout
This video is designed for everyone who wants to work at an average pace, at any age. You'll find calisthenics and aerobics to improve every part of your body without stress or overexertion. Whether you're slightly out-of-shape, in the prime of life, or

simply need to exercise more, this tape will get you going again. (Formerly titled Jane Fonda's Prime-Time Workout.)
15-035 60 min. $29.95

Jane Fonda's Low Impact Workout
Jane Fonda's newest workout focuses on stretching/toning and is exciting and fun. Jane has done it again!
15-177 50 min. $29.95

Jane Fonda's New Workout
Features expanded aerobics, state-of-the-art exercise techniques, all new music in stereo. Done in two segments - beginner and advanced.
15-108 90 min. $29.95

Jane Fonda's Pregnancy, Birth And Recovery Workout
Developed in conjunction with noted birth educator Femmy DeLyser to help women maintain a safe fitness regiment through the maternity process.
15-5691 89 min. $29.95

Jane Fonda's Workout: Lean Routine
Lean Routine features new low impact/high energy aerobics...20, 40, or 60 minute segments for every fitness level. And includes specially prepared segments on nutrition, fat-burning, and weight control.
15-5858 75 min. $29.95

Jane Fonda's Workout with Weights
15-2063 90 min. $39.95

Jane Fonda's Workout Challenge
A strenuous exercise program designed for experienced exercisers, dancers and athletes, featuring 20 minutes of advanced aerobics. You'll build strength, develop flexibility, and increase your endurance when you commit yourself to taking Jane Fonda's "Challenge."
15-036 90 min. $39.95

Jayne Kennedy's Love Your Body
Beautiful TV personality and actress Jayne Kennedy has her own unique system of conditioning and aerobics, designed to get you started and to keep you going to those great disco beats. She's full of an infectious vitality that won't let you down.
15-038 60 min. $59.95

Jazz and Exercise
A workout program that combines conditioning exercises with jazz dance movements, progressing from slow stretches to high-energy dance steps.
15-039 30 min. $29.95

Jazzercise: Funk Workout
This great combination of jazz dance and funk moves, features a blend of low impact and some higher impact aerobics.
15-8005 45 min. $16.95

Jazzercise: The Best Yet!
This Jazzercise video is easy to follow and fun to do, because it's an authentic Jazzercise class. Each routine is designed to keep your workout safe and effective and to monitor your exercise intensity and heart rate. Join the class for the fun, energy and enthusiasm, and enjoy the results!
15-137 60 min. $19.95

Joanie Greggains Firm Fannies
This workout is designed to strengthen, firm, and lift those gluteal muscles.
15-133 15 min. $19.95

Joanie Greggains High Energy Aerobics
This is an aerobic workout that is designed to increase your energy level, endurance, and zest for life. Aerobic exercises strengthen the most important muscle in your body - your heart. In addition, you'll be burning calories and replacing fat with muscle.
15-134 15 min. $19.95

Joanie Greggains Lean Legs
Designed for firmer and leaner legs, this workout will tone your calves, slim your inner and outer thighs and help eliminate that cottage cheese.
15-135 15 min. $19.95

Joanie Greggains Phenomenal Abdominals
A no-nonsense approach for men and women, that has been created specifically to strengthen and tone abdominal muscles.
15-8119 30 min. $19.95

Joanie Greggains Super Stomachs
This workout is designed to strengthen, tone and reduce you stomach. These exercises will help reduce fat, and tone those famous trouble spots, such as the overhang and love handles.
15-136 15 min. $19.95

Joanie Greggains Ultimate Buns
Created specifically for the buns and thighs. Strengthen and tone all of the muscles in your lower body.
16-8120 30 min. $19.95

Jody Watley - Dance to Fitness
Jody's hottest light aerobics are choreographed in her own street style and done to her music. A great dance and exercise combo.
15-8032 45 min. $19.95

Just Pump It
This is an all-in-one, interval aerobic training workout designed for men and women of all ages and fitness levels that will provide you with the key to achieving success in your personal fitness program.
15-8058 55 min. $24.95

KAREN VOIGHT'S WORKOUT SERIES:
Internationally acclaimed Voight's Fitness and Dance Center has led the fitness forefront in the last decade. Now Karen brings you her personal coaching and visual perspective on exercise that rivals even the best classroom experience.

• **Power Packed Workout**
15-8017 60 min. $24.95

• **Great Weighted Workout**
15-8018 85 min. $29.95

• **Lean Legs & Buns**
15-8019 45 min. $24.95

• **Pure & Simple Stretch**
15-8020 35 min. $24.95

• **Firm Arms & Abs**
15-8021 40 min. $24.95

Kathy Smith's Body Basics
Kathy Smith's exercise program really gets down to fitness basics. You'll appreciate the benefits of low impact aerobics that are easier on your body, while you get your pulse rate up and concentrate on problem areas such as fattening your stomach and firming your thighs.
15-103 60 min. $29.95

Kathy Smith's Starting Out
This video is a beginner's program that incorporates the innovative concept of "body awareness" into a dynamic new workout. This program develops that awareness and gets you into shape with an aerobics program designed to improve strength, flexibility and endurance.
15-1651 60 min. $19.95

Kathy Smith's Tone-Up
It's making your muscles work that really gives you the shape you're after. In this video, exercise instructor Kathy Smith makes use of industrial strength rubber bands (provided in the package) to give muscles the resistance they need to become lean and strong. Start with a warm-up and move through low-impact aerobics and spot-toning with the rubber bands to a final cool-down and stretch.
15-186 60 min. $19.95

Kathy Smith's Ultimate Video Workout
Kathy Smith's workout program combines variety and fun as essential components of a fitness routine that keep people motivated. A unique exercise program designed for individuals at all three levels - beginning, intermediate and advanced. Pays attention to the three essential components-cardio-respiratory, flexibility and strength.
15-044 60 min. $19.95

Kathy Smith's Winning Workout
This workout program uniquely combines the best features of both low and regular impact aerobics, plus the benefits of a progressive weight training program for maximum results in minimum time. A calendar is enclosed with each video to help you schedule regular workouts and chart you progress.
15-1605 105 min. $19.95

Kickstart
Unique workout combining the best of yoga, martial arts and non-strenuous aerobics. Follows natural body movements designed by Chaka Zulu, World Karate Champion.
15-2264 30 min. $19.95

LEE HANEY: MR. OLYMPIA BODY BUILDING SERIES:

• **Mr. Olympia Workout**
Share the secrets of "the biggest, the baddest and the best". Learn Haney's day- by-day routines.
15-8042 70 min. $16.95

• **Explosive Leg Workout**
Eight time Mr. Olympia reveals his leg blasting routines, grueling monster squats and pure power.
15-8043 50 min. $16.95

• **Massive Chest Workout**
Learn how you can pump those pecs, add massive muscular size and develop a truly titanic chest.
15-8044 50 min. $16.95

• **Power Arm Workout**
The master body builder shows arm routines that add power, size and strength while you sculpt and define.
15-8045 50 min. $16.95

LESLIE SANSOM SERIES

• **Firm Off Weight**
An excellent program designed to help you take off that extra weight and look better than ever. The first segment features exercises selected for their proven success as super firmers. It concentrates on the hips, thighs and buttocks. The second segment works on the upper body including a special set of abdonimals. The last segment is more leg work

VIDEO TITLES LISTED IN THIS GUIDE ARE AVAILABLE FOR PURCHASE OR RENTAL. CONTACT YOUR LOCAL VIDEO STORE OR TELEPHONE (800) 383-8811

with an intense set for the waistline. Can be used with or without weights.
15-8137 45 min. $24.95

• Weight Loss Walk
Divided into three segments, the first segment will have you walk one mile. The second will have walk one and half miles. The third will have you walk a challenging one and half miles. A great way to loose weight and never leave your living room.
15-8138 60 min. $24.95

Looking Good
If you're bored with the drab sameness of aerobics tapes on the market today, Looking Good might be the answer. Made in Europe with a different style of exercise, different pace and decidedly hipper music, Looking Good also features European film star Laura Gelmer (Emmanuelle) with extra fitness tips and encouragement.
15-188 60 min. $29.95

Look Good And Feel Terrific, With Dee Horn
Tone up and work out with New York fitness expert Dee Horn. A workout that works. You'll love every minute of this dynamic step-by-step program - warm up, aerobics, floor exercises and cool down - all enlivened by irresistibly energetic music. The program ends with Dee's proper diet and nutrition tips which will enrich your health and well-being.
15-5545 60 min. $19.95

Lorenzo Lamas' Self-Defense Workout
Hosted by Lorenzo Lamas, this program presents the perfect way to get and stay in shape, also outlines the right responses to situations requiring self-defense and agility.
15-3093 45 min. $14.95

Lou Ferrigno's Body Perfection
Want to learn how to attain body perfection? Then why not learn from the body perfect?
15-048 75 min. $14.95

Low-Impact No-Stress Workout
Especially for the overworked and overstressed! The most time efficient workout ever that cuts through the tedious repetitions and offers a fast-lane approach to a busy lifestyle. A low-impact, highly effective full exercise workout.
15-1910 30 min. $14.95

Margaret Richard's Body Electric
Based on her "Body Electric" program that is shown daily on PBS TV stations nationally. Margaret will motivate and inspire you to reach your fitness goals.
15-8122 60 min. $19.95

Margaret Richard's Forty & Fabulous
Safely and effectively exercise all major muscles groups for a shapely appearance. Margaret instructs clearly with good verbal and visual cues. Exercise I.O.U.'s (Intensity Options for You) are offered along the way to accommodate your current fitness level.
15-8116 60 min. $19.95

Margaret Richard's Home Improvement
Unlike other video workouts which require you to run and jump at home, this one offers you a safe, effective alternative with a series of dynamically sequenced exercises carefully designed to quickly tone and shape every major muscle in your body.
15-3098 60 min. $19.95

Margaret Richard's Knockout Workout
This video features low impact aerobic dancing that will work the arms, abdominals and gluteal muscles. If you're watching your diet and do this program, you'll be a total knockout.
15-8123 60 min. $19.95

Margaret Richard's Non Impact Fitness Formula
Quickly strengthen your stomach and buttocks with a no-nonsense program of controlled movements that will tone these common problem areas.
15-8121 60 min. $19.95

Marla Maples: Body Shaping Workout
Marla Maples now shares her secrets for keeping in shape. It's a complete workout, perfect for beginners through advanced stretching, muscle shaping and mental conditioning.
15-8065 45 min. $19.99

Maximum Workout
Rob Simonelli conducts an innovative technique in fitness exercise. Rob and the group will focus on cardiovascular development, muscle toning, and increasing flexibility.
15-8055 60 min. $24.95

Mid Eastern Dance: An Introduction to Belly Dance
Featuring Kathryn Ferguson, one of America's top oriental dance performer/instructors, this award-winning program teaches beginning and intermediate steps and movements with unique sections on oriental rhythms and abstract feelings of dance. A "one-on-one" teaching style combines with beautiful music, costumes and demonstrations to bring this ancient art to life. Professional dancers and choreographers will appreciate the beautifully-filmed program as a classic reference resource. Recommended by Dance magazine and Library Journal.
15-107 122 min. $39.95

More Alive

Improve your quality of life. 60 minute non-aerobic fitness program to exercise and tone every area of your body. It's safe, fun and effective while increasing flexibility, strength and endurance. The exercises are adaptable to all fitness levels. Each exercise is demonstrated in detail and you can gradually increase the repetition. You will look and feel better with each month and year.
15-5014 60 min. $39.95

Muscle Motion

Join eight handsome, virile Chippendale men as they lead you through an exercise program to progressively build up your strength, endurance and muscle tone. These guys combine aerobics and entertainment in a package that's guaranteed to get your heart beating faster - even if you just watch!
15-052 90 min. $39.95

NAUTILUS PLUS AEROBICS SERIES:

• **High Impact Aerobics**
15-8090 40 min. $16.95

• **Low Impact Aerobics**
15-8091 40 min. $16.95

• **Rubberband Workout**
15-8092 40 min. $16.95

• **Weight Loss Workout**
15-8093 40 min. $16.95

• **Body Shaping Workout**
15-8094 40 min. $16.95

• **Stretch to Perfection**
15-6471 40 min. $16.95

• **High/Low Impact Aerobics**
15-6470 40 min. $16.95

New Video Aerobics

A complete conditioning program starring Julie Lavin and Leslie Lilien, featuring new aerobic exercise routines done to a lively disco beat.
15-053 60 min. $59.95

No Jump Aerobics

Here it is! An aerobic workout with no jumping, but substantial cardiovascular challenge - at least one foot is always on the floor. This is a great benefit to pregnant women, folks with bad knees, beginners, injured jocks and anyone training in the alternating easy - hard format.
15-176 60 min. $19.95

No Flab Ab Workout

Designed to flatten the stomach while shaping and firming your mid-section, this workout is a must for most over 30 exercisers and some under 30.
15-8112 20 min. $16.95

Now You Can! Starring Rita Moreno

Rita Moreno leads women ranging in age from twentysomething to well into their sixties in an easy dance oriented workout that will get you fit and feeling fabulous about your body and yourself. Lively music and Rita's warm enthusiasm make this tape a sure bet to become a favorite.
15-5546 60 min. $19.95

One Step Beyond - Step Aerobics

Diane Springfield offers this complete step aerobics workout that is high intensity, low impact. Teaches you the basic steps plus interesting combinations and routines to keep your workout from become "hum drum." Safe, fun and easy to follow.
15-8113 50 min. $16.95

Original Non-Impact Aerobics

This new direction in aerobic exercise eliminates the stressful jarring and jumping of traditional aerobics. People of all ages and abilities can participate. Expert instruction by Debbie and Carlos Rosas.
15-211 42 min. $16.95

Plain Wrap Exercise for Men

The All-American video workout tape for men.
15-179 50 min. $19.95

Plain Wrap Exercise for Women

The All-American video workout tape for women.
15-055 50 min. $19.95

Playgirl Hunkercise

Exercise, and fantasize, with gorgeous "hunks" from Playgirl magazine's centerfolds, featuring Steve Rally, Man of the Year. Includes stretching, aerobics toning and cool-down.
15-057 55 min. $39.95

Playgirl Morning Workout

A unique exercise program conducted by fitness expert Jim Bolden, featuring the "hunks" of Playgirl magazine, including Man-of-the-Year, Steve Rally.
15-2413 50 min. $14.95

Power Funk

Join Thea White as she teaches you how to incorporate high energy funk movements into your low impact or funk class. Thea explains the components of each move during execution for easy understanding.
15-8000 60 min. $19.95

VIDEO TITLES LISTED IN THIS GUIDE ARE AVAILABLE FOR PURCHASE OR RENTAL. CONTACT YOUR LOCAL VIDEO STORE OR TELEPHONE (800) 383-8811

Power Stepping

A fun and effective way to workout. Power Stepping is a perfect form of cardiovascular exercise that helps you burn fat and tone muscle. Also includes an upper body toning section and abdominal work for the total body workout. With Lynne Brick, RN, BS.

15-8018 60 min. $24.95

Power Stepping II with Lynne Brick

This is a low impact/high intensity step training for intermediate to advanced steppers. Broken into 3 segments: warm-up, 30 minute workout and finally a cool down and sculpting section for your upper body. A complete, total body workout.

15-8052 60 min. $24.95

Prime Bodies

The prime bodies staff will introduce you to an overall total body cardiovascular workout which includes low impact aerobics and step training. The focus is on shaping the entire body. You will be shown proper warm-up/cool-down and stretching techniques, to achieve optimal conditioning.

15-8030 45 min. $16.95

Pump N' Step Workout

The total body conditioning program that utilizes the step and the APRI Xertube in a unique combination of aerobic conditioning and strength training.

15-8019 30 min. $24.95

Ray (Boom Boom) Mancini: My Knockout Workout

This film features the former world lightweight champion in a terrific workout for all fitness fans.

15-110 60 min. $19.95

Rebound And Beyond Aerobics

Now everyone can enjoy a program that's safe, effective and fun. Your rebound workout has been designed & choreographed to meet the latest industry guidelines, with particular attention to muscle balance and body alignment.

15-5188 28 min. $29.95

Richard Simmons: Reach For Fitness

This tape concentrates on special exercises for the physically handicapped. Richard Simmons once again demonstrates the versatility and warmth which has helped make his name synonymous with exercise and health care. Bodies are strengthened and hopes are renewed.

15-182 45 min. $14.95

Richard Simmons: Silver Foxes

A fitness plan for the more than 50 million Americans over the age of 50. Richard leads celebrity moms and dads through a warm-up

session, low-impact, non-impact, non-stress aerobics and a three-minute relaxation series that can be done morning or night. Approved by the Aerobics and Fitness Assn. of America and the American Longevity Assn.

15-196 45 min. $19.95

Richard Simmons: Sweatin' To The Oldies

Richard Simmons: Sweatin' To The Oldies. Join Simmons' "sock hop," featuring a live band playing 50's and 60's favorites, and dance your way to fitness through effective low-impact aerobics.

15-5694 45 min. $24.95

Rise Up With Rosie: Exercise and Dance Rhythms for Older Adults

Rose Metter, motivational specialist for older adults, has developed this special video to help men and women increase their physical stamina and enhance their quality of life. Her personalized approach is filled with joyfulness, rhythmic music, stimulating exercise sequences and Rose's unique brand of caring/sharing that motivates people.

15-8001 54 min. $24.95

Rock and Roll Step

Join Shemane Nugent, wife of legendary Rock Star, Ted Nugent, as she takes you through a high energy step workout that focuses on aerobics with a special segment on sculpting the upper body. All done to a rock and roll beat!

15-8054 60 min. $29.95

Sandahl Bergman's Body

Star of "Conan the Barbarian" and "All That Jazz," Sandahl Bergman has created a workout that combines the art of dance with a strengthening exercise routine.

15-067 60 min. $19.95

Senior Flex

This program provides a practical, safe and enjoyable way to stay in shape while allowing everyone to progress at their own pace.

15-2969 46 min. $29.95

Shape Up

Ballet coach David Howard hosts this exercise program including warm-up, beginner, intermediate, advanced and aerobic routines.

15-202 60 min. $24.95

SHAPE UP WITH MOLLY FOX SERIES:

Molly Fox has created workouts to meet your personal fitness goals. Her no-nonsense approach coupled with her encouraging and enthusiastic manner will help you tighten, tone and firm up for good!

VIDEO TITLES LISTED IN THIS GUIDE ARE AVAILABLE FOR PURCHASE OR RENTAL. CONTACT YOUR LOCAL VIDEO STORE OR TELEPHONE (800) 383-8811

• **Abs, Buns and Thighs**
15-8067 40 min. $19.95

• **Total Body Workout**
15-8068 40 min. $19.95

• **Fat Burning Workout**
15-8069 51 min. $19.95

Shirley Jones Lite Aerobic Workout
15-5431 40 min. $14.95

Shirley Jones/Lo-Cal Diet Exercise/Beauty Program
15-5432 90 min. $19.95

Solid Gold Five-Day Workout
The Solid Gold Dancers provide an easy-to-follow, five-day fitness program designed by a team of exercise specialists from the Alta Institute. Each workout is 20 minutes long.
15-073 106 min. $29.95

SPORTS ILLUSTRATED SUPER SHAPE UP PROGRAMS:
Collection of three physical fitness routines developed by experts of the Norwich Inn and Spa. These Sports Illustrated videos feature three world renowned models from the "Swimsuit Issue." Each program can be used individually, or in combination for a fully maximized cross training workout.

• **Aerobic Interval Training with Cheryl Tiegs**
15-8127 50 min. $24.95

• **Body Sculpting with Rachel Hunter**
15-8126 50 min. $24.95

• **Stretch and Strengthen with Elle Macpherson**
15-8125 50 min. $24.95

Stanford University Health and Fitness Program
A program that offers not only exercise, but an entire diet, nutrition and fitness regimen. Developed by the Stanford University Center for Research and Disease control. Includes a 40-minute workout, a 20-minute section featuring special exercises, and a 30-minute diet-and-lifestyle segment.
15-1962 90 min. $39.95

Stay Fit Rebounding Aerobic Workout
Many who couldn't and shouldn't exercise on hard surfaces because of back, leg or foot problems, can safely exercise on a mini-trampoline. This video offers an ideal aerobic exercise program for the safe alternative to jogging and floor aerobics.
15-2710 60 min. $34.95

Step Into Fitness with Karen Flores
Join Karen Flores, dance instructor, as she teaches you how to burn calories, and tone and sculpt your body utilizing step aerobics.
15-8079 45 min. $19.95

Step It Out with Dawn Brown
Join Dawn Brown in her new step workout designed for Intermediate to Advanced students.
15-9323 32 min. $19.95

SUPER BODY COMPLETE FITNESS SERIES:
Fitness expert Deborah Crocker, makes shaping up more fun and effective with her 4 program series.

• **Ultimate Low-Impact Aerobics**
15-1547 45 min. $16.95

• **Great Legs!**
15-8046 45 min. $16.95

• **Firm & Trim**
15-8047 45 min. $16.95

• **Aerobics Plus**
15-8049 45 min. $16.95

Super Callanetics
Callan Pinckney, your instructor on her previous video Callanetics, personally instructs viewers in unique new movements that challenge the body without stressing it.
15-2994 90 min. $24.95

Super Circuit: Pumping Rubber
David Essel, M.S. health and fitness expert can help you achieve the body you desire in just 10 minutes per day. With these incredible workouts you'll never get bored.
15-8024 60 min. $24.95

Susan Rasmussen: Total Body Workout
15-205 50 min. $19.95

Sweat Express with Kari Anderson
Kari's back with her high-energy all aerobic workout, combining her best multi-impact moves into an explosive program. She has created one of today's most challenging workouts for advanced, demanding aerobic enthusiast.
15-8080 60 min. $19.95

Sybervision: Lean Body Workout
This workout was designed by Cynthia Kereluk, an exercise physiologist and Miss Canada 1984. This scientifically developed low-impact exercise system was designed to enhance your body's ability to metabolize fat.
15-1557 45 min. $29.95

Texercise
The first country-western exercise program designed to condition, firm, and work your cardiovascular system. Stars Irlene Mandrell and includes special exercises "The Thighs of Texas," "The Big Bend," "The Saddle Bag Stomp" and "The Texas Hustle."
15-077 34 min. $24.95

Thin Thighs in 30 Days
Tired of not-so-perfect thighs, hips and buttocks? Wendy Stehling author of the best-selling book, "Thin Thighs in 30 Days," has designed this video exercise program to help you reduce and firm those problem areas.
15-078 60 min. $19.95

Tight and Toned
For firming the upper torso, hips, thighs, waist and abdominal muscles.
15-185 15 min. $16.95

Too Busy To Workout, Workout: Leslie Sansone's
A fast, effective workout to challenge the body to become fit and healthy in a short workout. Now you no longer need hours at the gym to get real health at home or in the office.
15-5706 30 min. $19.95

Toning the Total Body
Hips, thighs, buttocks and bellies...this video focuses on the hard-to-tone areas and shapes them up to beat the anti-gravity, sagging blues.
15-1911 30 min. $16.95

Video Aerobics Home Exercise Course
A stimulating total body conditioning routine, done to a lively disco beat. Features beginning and advanced programs.
15-080 60 min. $59.95

Walk Aerobics
Leslie Tommelleo takes you through this patented exercise program for everybody - all shapes, sizes and ages.
15-2632 30 min. $16.95

Warm Up with Traci Lords
Traci Lords, actress and physical fitness advocate, leads you through this fantastic, non-impact Jazzthetics workout designed safely and with no stress to any body joints. This program will exercise every body part and focuses on the Cardiovascular system with special emphasis on eliminating cellulite.
15-8115 49 min. $16.95

Your Guide To: Lean Legs
Work-out to tone your calves, slim your inner and outer thighs. Some of the exciting exercises in this work-out are the Down Hill Skier, the Lean Lift, and the Lamb Chop.
15-5120 15 min. $19.95

Back & Stretching Exercises

Back Health with Joanie Greggains
Revolutionary new way to eliminate back pain. Includes information from Joe Montana's back surgeon.
15-8064 40 min. $24.95

Back in Action
This program consists of informative information which addresses the problem of low back pain. Includes two 15-minute exercise segments and a segment on proper body mechanics to help you through daily activities. Safe and effective for eliminating both upper and lower back pain.
15-8114 40 min. $19.95

Back in Shape
The complete back pain prevention program brings the medical profession's most effective techniques to combat back problems in a convenient, no-nonsense video exercise format ideal for home use.
15-210 60 min. $19.95

Bob Mann's Isometric Stretch
Golfers, martial artists, bicyclists body builders and runners are among the athletes who will benefit by investing 15 minutes every other day in isometric stretch. Non-athletes find it the most efficient routine for improving muscle tone and posture.
15-212 25 min. $14.95

Denise Austin: Stretch & Flex
This 30-minute tension taming program will help you relax while listening to new age music. Stretching relaxes your mind and tones up your body. It reduces muscle tension, prevents injuries, increases your flexibility, and improves your circulation.
15-5703 30 min. $16.95

VIDEO TITLES LISTED IN THIS GUIDE ARE AVAILABLE FOR PURCHASE OR RENTAL. CONTACT YOUR LOCAL VIDEO STORE OR TELEPHONE (800) 383-8811

FITNESS FOR GOLF SERIES:

• **Stretching**
15-5436 30 min. $16.95

• **Manual Resistance Exercise**
15-5437 30 min. $16.95

• **Two-Weight System**
15-5438 30 min. $16.95

Healthy Back - Healthy Mind
A system of back exercises, which are a synthesis of classic yoga principles from the East. This program consists of fifteen-minute mini-routines, which fit the pace of today's fast-moving society. Many of the world's top film and TV stars, professional athletes, corporate executives, and other high-stress professionals offer testimonials to the program's effectiveness.
15-5126 60 min. $39.95

Keep Your Spine in Line
This video provides valuable information on the spine during stretching and strengthening exercises for the neck, mid-back, lower back, shoulders and knees. Also, special tips on everyday twisting, bending and lifting are included.
15-169 38 min. $39.95

No More Aching Back
In this comprehensive video, Dr. Leon Root and Chevy Chase, Dr. Roots friend and former patient, answer commonly asked questions about back pain and presents his clinically proven series of exercises to reduce or eliminate most back pain.
15-8066 60 min. $29.95

Revitalize Your Body
This video helps you to recover from illness or injury and to develop an active, vibrant body throughout life. Instructions are given for those who cannot stand or have other limitations. These exercises will raise energy level, dissolve physical and mental tension and create a positive, uplifting feeling.
15-8002 90 min. $29.95

Say Goodbye to Back Pain
This six-week series of easy exercises is a progressive program designed to eliminate or reduce back pain and prevent future problems. Learn the two causes of most back pain, six tests to find your real problem areas, seven tips on pain prevention, and ways to reduce stress and tension. Based on the work of Dr. Hans Kraus and the YMCA's exercise program, "The Y's Way to a Healthy Back".
15-068 96 min. $39.95

Stretching
A unique and different approach to the special needs of fitness for the older adult.
15-5165 28 min. $29.95

Stretching Video
The who, why, when and how of proper stretching. Includes instructions that lead you through easy-to-do stretches. Appropriate for people of all ages.
15-2496 60 min. $29.95

Jogging & Walking

Gary Yanker's Walking Workout
The first video cassette for America's number one exercise! Regardless of your age or lifestyle, injury-free exercise program which turns walking into an exhilarating aerobic workout.
15-115 56 min. $29.95

Marathon Challenge
Follow eight different people as they set out to meet the challenge of a marathon run. Learn proper training techniques, the proper shoes, diet advice, hill running, exercise timing and more. Also discussed are how to minimize injury and gain the most from running.
30-483 60 min. $29.95

Marty Liquori's Runners Workout
Liquori, the former class miler, covers it all: equipment, techniques, warm-ups, diets, race preparation and strategy.
30-241 60 min. $29.95

Running Great with Grete Waitz
Olympic Silver Medalist and eight-time New York City Marathon Champion, Grete Waitz has created the first running cassette designed for runners of all levels. This program is ideal for both men and women.
15-8070 60 min. $19.95

Running for Fun and Fitness
Marathon Champion Bill Rodgers sets the pace for safe and effective running standards. Whether you run for health and fitness or competition, Rodgers has some helpful tips for you
15-8071 47 min. $16.95

Stepping Out: A Complete Guide to Fitness Walking
Rita Moreno hosts. Video guide to fitness walking, America's fastest-growing exercise activity. Learn

---

VIDEO TITLES LISTED IN THIS GUIDE ARE AVAILABLE FOR PURCHASE OR RENTAL. CONTACT YOUR LOCAL VIDEO STORE OR TELEPHONE (800) 383-8811

about Rockport Fitness Walking Test, a scientifically proven method for determining a safe and effective walking program that's right for you.
15-2936 55 min. $19.95

Video Hiker - Grand Canyon

Join us on this motivational hike beginning at Phantom Ranch at the bottom of the Grand Canyon. From there it will take you all three workouts on this video, to reach the top. Works with all types of Stair Climbing Machines or Steppers.
15-8028 60 min. $24.95

Yoga

Aerobic Yoga

This flowing and dynamic Hatha Yoga practice is a complete balanced daily workout. It develops strength, flexibility, grace and beauty and contains all the major Yoga postures and elements needed for practice while combining movement, breathing and meditation. Featuring Ganga White and Tracey Rich of the White Lotus Foundation.
15-9093 64 min. $29.95

Introduction to Kundalini Yoga

Raise your life force (kundalini) energy. Very powerful and systematic. Includes some hatha which is incorporated into the kundalini system. Techniques are done to synchronized breathing exercises, giving increased benefit. Chakras (energy centers) are balanced while physical blocks are opened.
29-027 60 min. $39.95

Kundalini Yoga Workout

This video features an introduction to yoga and the basics of breathing techniques and relaxation. A series of stretching and flexing exercises will warm you up from head to toe, protecting against injury. The total body workout teaches bow pose, shoulder stand, locust pose, archer, cat and cow exercises. A meditation follows, balancing the energy and enhancing the effects.
29-151 72 min. $29.95

Lilias! Alive with Yoga

Now you can stretch, strengthen and relax at home with Lilias Folan, well-known health and fitness authority and star of the popular PBS-TV series, "Lilias, Yoga and You." Lilias combines strengthening exercises with yoga stretches and relaxation instruction to help you achieve and

maintain a healthy body and spirit.
15-229 60 min. $39.95

Mimmie Louis' Let's Do Yoga

This is a strong intermediate level class with detailed information for beginners. Persons in good health of any age may participate. This class teaches correct posture, and anatomical and kinesthetic awareness.
15-2204 90 min. $29.95

PRISCILLA PATRICK YOGA VIDEO SERIES:

• 15-Minute Tune-up

This unique workout is sure to help alleviate lower back pain and leave you feeling relaxed, through yoga.
15-2975 15 min. $15.95

• Priscilla's Upper Body Chair Exercises

Two 15 minute lessons designed for individuals with little or no mobility in their lower bodies. These sitting exercises will decrease muscular tension and increase range of motion.
15-8130 30 min. $24.95

• Ready, Set, Stretch!

These workouts are designed to encourage elementary school children to rid themselves of excessive energy through stretching and balancing exercises. Now the kids have their very own exercise video!
15-8131 30 min. $24.95

• Fit and Nifty Over 50

An exercise video for adults over 50 years of age. Divided into two segments, the first will ease you into stretches for flexibility, toning and strength. The second segment presents more challenging exercises for the participant.
15-8128 30 min. $24.95

• Stretch and De-Stress! The Executive's Office Workout

Divided into three segments to easily incorporate the busiest of schedules. Designed especially for those who have upper back and neck tension, or those that spend hours and a desk or computer terminal. It works wonders!
15-8129 30 min. $24.95

• Stretching for Athletes

Divided into two separate workouts to serve as warm-ups and cool-downs as well as to increase overall flexibility. These stretches are specifically targeted to include sports such as football, baseball, golf, tennis, running, bicycling and volleyball. Certainly a must for the weekend athlete.
15-8132 30 min. $24.95

VIDEO TITLES LISTED IN THIS GUIDE ARE AVAILABLE FOR PURCHASE OR RENTAL. CONTACT YOUR LOCAL VIDEO STORE OR TELEPHONE (800) 383-8811

• **Take a Break! Yoga Stretches with Priscilla Patrick**
In keeping with recent medical studies favoring low-intensity exercises over ballistic movements, these bends, twists, stretches and folds will safely increase flexibility, tone and strengthen the body and leave the practitioner feeling relaxed and energized.
15-6872 90 min. $39.95

PRISCILLA PATRICK TAKE A BREAK SERIES:
This full-length, award winning video, is also available as three separate videos to offer you the choice of individual lessons at a lower price.

• **Take a Break Lesson 1-Beginners**
15-8133 30 min. $24.95

• **Take a Break Lesson 2-Intermediate**
15-8134 30 min. $24.95

• **Take a Break Lesson 3-Advanced/Intermediate**
15-8135 30 min. $24.95

Richard Hittleman's Guide to Yoga Meditation
In this video Richard explains the meaning of meditation and how it is practically applied. Included, is a ten minute physical Yoga routine that may be used as a preparation for meditation and five separate meditation methods to help you discover the method that's right for you.
15-8012 60 min. $29.95

RICHARD HITTLEMAN'S YOGA SERIES:

• **Yoga I**
This video guides you gently through the elementary positions of the yoga exercises and breathing techniques. The benefits: firming and strengthening, promoting flexibility, reducing stress, increasing stamina, developing coordination, regulating weight, and quieting the mind and emotions. This program can help overcome various physical problems.
15-213 90 min. $39.95

• **Yoga II**
This video guides you through the more advanced positions and breathing techniques. This more advanced practice enables you to increase the overall benefits and to experience the profound effectiveness of yoga for stabilizing the mind and emotions.
15-214 90 min. $39.95

• **Yoga III**
Richard Hittleman guides you to the next level of your Yoga practice by incorporating breath-work and Yantra Visualization with the Yoga exercises. Yantras are geometric forms which, when visualized, stabilize the emotions and develop concentration making Yoga practice more effective. Contains two separate Yoga sessions.
15-8013 90 min. $39.95

Richard Hittleman's Yoga Workshop Lectures Video
In this 3-part lecture, Richard speaks about how the ego causes disturbance, the purpose of life and after death experiences. He also covers emotional balance, finding happiness from within, simplifying your life and the powerful benefits of Hatha Yoga.
15-8016 75 min. $19.95

Sivananda Yoga Video
A complete video guide to the physical postures, breathing exercises, relaxation and meditation techniques of yoga. Learn how to develop a fit and beautiful body, keep youthful through every stage of life, banish stress and tension.
15-9814 59 min. $29.95

Stretching With Priscilla: Yoga Stretches
With more than 20 different stretches, plus a shortened version of her well known limbering series. "Stretching With Priscilla" is a must for anyone who needs overall conditioning without pain, fatigue, or soreness. It's also a terrific way to get rid of tension and stress.
15-5095 60 min. $29.95

Stretching Your Whole Body with Jean Goulet
Loose relaxed muscles lead to inner calm and greater health. Jean helps you eliminate aches and pains and achieve a springy, youthful body. Especially useful for preventing injury during sports activities.
15-8003 60 min. $24.95

Yoga for Beginners
In this program, you will quickly master simple poses, breathing and relaxation techniques, as well as learn yoga's philosophy and how to create your own individualized routine. With booklet.
15-8082 75 min. $29.95

Yoga Maintenance With Priscilla Patrick
15-5096 60 min. $16.95

Yoga Moves
A step-by-step learning approach to yoga, starring yoga master Alan Finger--author and instructor of

---

VIDEO TITLES LISTED IN THIS GUIDE ARE AVAILABLE FOR PURCHASE
OR RENTAL. CONTACT YOUR LOCAL VIDEO STORE OR TELEPHONE (800) 383-8811

many Hollywood stars. You'll be guided through yoga exercises designed to tone and strengthen your muscles, provide you with suppleness and energy, and create a visually stimulating and joyous experience.
15-090 60 min. $19.95

YOGA: THE ART OF LIVING WITH RENEE TAYLOR

A two-videotape program of basic fitness for men, women and children.

• **Beginning Yoga: Volume I**
15-065 48 min. $29.95

• **Intermediate Yoga: Volume II**
15-066 48 min. $29.95

Yogaerobics
The best, fastest-paced exercises anywhere! Emphasize physical toning, stretching, rejuvenation techniques, breathing and deep relaxation techniques, and an introduction to yoga. Helps you not only look, but feel, great!
20-075 30 min. $39.95

YOGA FOR HEALTH T.V. SERIES WITH RICHARD HITTLEMAN

• **Programs 1-2-3: Introduction to Yoga**
The first three programs explain how Yoga works to reduce tension and stress and how to prepare for and benefit most from Yoga practice. He guides you through very gentle, basic Yoga exercises. A good introduction for the novice.
15-8014 60 min. $29.95

• **Programs 4-5-6: "Good Health Through Exercise"**
The focus of this video is to promote good health with Yoga exercise. You will learn exercises that provide the body with flexibility, circulation and stimulate health of the internal organs. Learn breathing exercises that energize, increase alertness, provide tranquility and deep relaxation.
15-8015 60 min. $29.95

Miscellaneous

BICYCLING AMERICA SERIES:
Make the time on your exercise bicycle fly as you and your video companions tour America's most scenic locations. Play this tape as you work out on your stationary cycle and you will no longer be alone at a tedious task. Set your spirits free with music composed and arranged especially for Bicycling America.

• **Volume 1**
Spectacular Yosemite National Park, picturesque country roads and the beautiful Oregon coast.
30-313 60 min. $29.95

• **Volume 2**
Colorful Bryce Canyon National Park, 14-mile fun bike race, majestic Grand Tetons.
30-315 60 min. $29.95

• **Volume 3**
Incredible Crater Lake National Park, Glacier National Park, sunny Maui, Hawaii.
30-314 60 min. $29.95

Bikercize
Review of proper bike use, step-by-step guide to finding your target heart rate. This video covers warm-up, upper body workout, leg work, free form and cool down. Features Kathy Yelverton, M.S.
15-5948 33 min. $29.95

Buns of Steel
A program created to help you improve the shape and tone of the arms, shoulders, hips, buttocks, thighs and lower legs.
15-2104 52 min. $16.95

Cross Training: 4 Power & Endurance
You'll learn about interval training, the new modern way to increase your endurance with shorter workouts. You'll then take a look at resistance training; how you can take a simple pair of dumbbells and do all the resistance work that you need to do right at home. Finally we will look at Isometric stretch. It's extremely productive and time efficient.
15-6544 40 min. $14.95

Cycling Experience
The tedium of stationary cycling quickly disappears as you experience the thrill of cycling through various landscapes, including Big Sur, Mt. Whitney, Death Valley, Mono Lake, the Sierra Nevada, King's Canyon, giant Redwoods, Joshua Tree National Monument and more. Includes training booklet.
15-2143 52 min. $29.95

Kung Fu Workout
Unlike aerobics and other exercise programs, Kung Fu and Tai Chi are the perfect answer to today's trend toward low-impact, all-around fitness. Hosted by David Carradine.
15-5338 50 min. $29.95

More Alive After 55
The exercises are adaptable to all fitness levels. Each exercise is demonstrated in detail and you can gradually increase the repetitions.
15-6177 30 min. $16.95

Stress Reduction Exercises
This video features relaxing movements derived from Chinese T'ai-Chi and Chi-Gung health exercises. You'll learn to combine flowing movements, concentration and proper breathing to create greater health and emotional stability.
15-8004 74 min. $24.95

Tai Chi Workout
David Carradine Host this program that features a thorough workout of the entire body. Unlike most of today's exercises, Tai Chi actually increases your mental and physical energy through systematic stress reduction. You'll learn graceful, flowing movements which tone muscles, firm the body and enhance flexibility.
15-5339 60 min. $29.95

Theracise
A home exercise video for everyone and not just the non-disabled. This program is designed with love to offer another option of exercise. This program is designed for individuals with a disability of the upper extremity.
15-6539 30 min. $34.95

Week with Raquel
This offers a complete 7-day interactive fitness program. Seven different and easy to do daily routines, no more than 15 minutes every morning. Designed to provide simple, easy instructions and great visual appeal, while allowing everyone to achieve and maintain higher levels of fitness and flexibility.
15-227 120 min. $29.95

Does Your

Current Exercise Video

Seem As Tired As You Do?

Put Some Bounce In Your Step

With A New Video

From This Section!

VIDEO TITLES LISTED IN THIS GUIDE ARE AVAILABLE FOR PURCHASE OR RENTAL. CONTACT YOUR LOCAL VIDEO STORE OR TELEPHONE (800) 383-8811

Searching For

A Unique Gift That is

Informative and Appreciated?

The Video Titles

In This Guide

Make Wonderful Gifts.

Fine Arts

- ✓ *Drawing & Painting*
- ✓ *Museum Guides*
- ✓ *Miscellaneous*

Drawing & Painting

American Impressionist-Richard Earl Thompson
This video captures on-screen the essence of Richard's lifetime of work; a visual feast, with classical musical accompaniment.
03-8034 30 min. $29.95

ART LESSONS FOR CHILDREN SERIES

• Easy Art Projects
Three step-by-step art lessons are demonstrated by using oil pastels, aluminum foil and printmaking.
03-8001 50 min. $29.95

• Easy Watercolor Techniques
An experienced elementary school art teacher demonstrates various watercolor techniques, using both transparent and opaque methods.
03-8000 50 min. $29.95

• Felt Pen Fun
A step-by-step guide on creating fun art using the felt pen and paper.
03-8065 58 min. $29.95

• More Fun with Watercolors
Demonstrations on how to create simple art in just four easy lessons.
03-8064 53 min. $29.95

Autumn Landscape
This video leads you step-by-step through the painting of this colorful and detailed autumn landscape. Special features are the magnificent clouds in the autumn sky, techniques for tree foliage, and a unique use of a long bristle brush for realistic foreground grasses and weeds. Color mixtures for each step are shown. Sketch and color print included.
03-6078 60 min. $29.95

BASIC ART SERIES

• Color
Demonstrates the poetic nature-color from the Renaissance through Impressionism to Modern periods, bypassing the raw beginners' color.
03-007 60 min. $74.95

• Drawing and Design
Demonstrates that, though intuitive, drawing and design skills must be consciously nurtured and developed under professional guidance.
03-006 60 min. $74.95

• Painting
Introduces drawing, design and color, the building blocks of painting, right in the instructor's own studio. Step-by-step, fine artist Charles Haddock teaches classic techniques in the tradition of the fine masters. Rewind and review at your own pace. All necessary tools demonstrated.
03-005 60 min. $74.95

Be a Cartoonist Video Learning Kit
It's easy and fun: Cartoonist Alan Silberberg demonstrates how to create cartoon figures utilizing familiar letters, numbers and figures. Drawing pad, pen, drawing pencils and eraser are included.
03-281 74 min. $19.95

Bob Ross Workshop - Wet on Wet Techniques
A three hour workshop answers in detail all of the questions about the "wet-on wet" technique with clear, understandable solutions.
03-8010 180 min. $29.95

CONNI GORDON PAINT-ALONG SERIES
Conni Gordon is listed in the Guinness Book of World Records as the World's most Prolific Art Teacher. Now her methods are presented in a thirteen volume series.

• Spring
Tips on oil painting for landscapes.
03-8043 29 min. $29.95

• Autumn
Tips on brush techniques and framing your painting.
03-8044 29 min. $29.95

• Winter
Learn how to mix and use color.
03-8045 29 min. $29.95

• Summer
Tips on how to make and use a color-star-chart.
03-8046 29 min. $29.95

• Floral
Tips on how to paint delicate oriental floral.
03-8047 29 min. $29.95

• Roses
Steps on creating your own painting.
03-8048 29 min. $29.95

• **Sunset**
Learning color secrets.
03-8049 29 min. $29.95

• **Seascape**
Learn how to create waves and moonlight scenes.
03-8050 29 min. $29.95

• **Tropics**
Tips on how to paint windblown palms along the seashore.
03-8051 29 min. $29.95

• **Horse**
Tips on how to paint animals in your own style.
03-8052 29 min. $29.95

• **Children**
Learn how to paint figures.
03-8053 29 min. $29.95

• **Clown**
Learn how to create a joyful clown.
03-8054 29 min. $29.95

• **Desert**
Learn how to develop your own desert scene with flowers.
03-8055 29 min. $29.95

Drawing with Harold Riley
Here is the artist at work with pencil, pen and charcoals. As he works, he offers insights into drawing.
03-299 60 min. $29.95

Everyone Can Learn To Draw Part 1
Capt. Bob uses a variety of animal drawings to illustrate his art techniques. The simple grace of a horse and the magnificence of a pheasant in flight are the main "Draw Along" subject for you to create in your own home.
03-5733 30 min. $19.95

Figure Drawing & Printing
James Kirk - artist, teacher and teacher of teachers has a main emphasis on artistic content rather than on depiction of reality. This video demonstrates and is developed for active participation.
03-8011 20 min. $29.95

GLENN VILPPU SERIES
Glenn Vilppu is known internationally as a master draftsman and an instructor of drawing in the tradition of the masters. His classes are filled with beginners, other teachers and professional artists. As an instructor of figure drawing at Walt Disney Productions, where he does layout in animation,

and at Brandes Art Institute, he brings a love and understanding of the craft of drawing which he developed from over 25 years of teaching, including 13 years at the Art Center College of Design.

• **Volume 1 and 2: Figure Drawing**
Analyzing the pose and starting the drawing.
03-243 60 min. $29.95

• **Volume 3 and 4: Figure Drawing**
The procedural approach to drawing.
03-244 60 min. $29.95

• **Volume 5 and 6: Figure Drawing**
The simplified figure and basic structure.
03-245 60 min. $29.95

• **Volume 7 and 8: Figure Drawing**
Sketching figures.
03-246 60 min. $29.95

• **Volume 9 and 10: Figure Drawing**
Analyzing form using direct and indirect light to model.
03-247 60 min. $29.95

• **Volume 11 and 12: Figure Drawing**
The classical approach to figure drawing.
03-248 60 min. $29.95

• **Volume 13 and 14: Figure Drawing**
Foreshortening.
03-249 60 min. $29.95

• **Volume 15 and 16: Figure Drawing**
Figure drawing for animation.
03-250 60 min. $29.95

• **Volume 17 and 18: Figure Drawing**
03-251 60 min. $29.95

• **Volume 19 and 20: Figure Drawing**
Direct drawing.
03-252 60 min. $29.95

• **Volume 21 and 22: Figure Drawing**
Drawing drapery-the clothed figure.
03-253 60 min. $29.95

• **Volume 23 and 24: Figure Drawing**
Head drawing.
03-254 60 min. $29.95

• **Volume 25 and 26: Figure Drawing**
Drawing children.
03-255 60 min. $29.95

VIDEO TITLES LISTED IN THIS GUIDE ARE AVAILABLE FOR PURCHASE OR RENTAL. CONTACT YOUR LOCAL VIDEO STORE OR TELEPHONE (800) 383-8811

• **Volume 27 and 28: Figure Drawing**
Drawing the figure with ink and wash.
03-256 60 min. $29.95

• **Volume 29 and 30: Figure Drawing**
Working on toned paper.
03-257 60 min. $29.95

• **Volume 31 and 32: Figure Drawing**
The air and space around the figure.
03-258 60 min. $29.95

• **Volume 33 and 34: Figure Drawing**
Rhythm.
03-259 60 min. $29.95

• **Volume 35 and 36: Landscape Drawing**
Thumb nails and blocking in.
03-260 60 min. $29.95

• **Volume 37 and 38: Landscape Drawing**
Drawing techniques: (A) Broad stroke.
03-261 60 min. $29.95

• **Volume 39 and 40: Landscape Drawing**
Drawing techniques: (B) Toned paper.
03-262 60 min. $29.95

• **Volume 41 and 42: Landscape Drawing**
Drawing techniques: Ink and wash.
03-263 60 min. $29.95

• **Volume 43 and 44: Landscape Drawing**
Drawing trees, bushes, grass.
03-264 60 min. $29.95

• **Volume 45 and 46: Landscape Drawing**
Buildings
03-265 60 min. $29.95

• **Volume 47 and 48: Landscape Drawing**
Sky, rocks and water.
03-235 60 min. $29.95

• **Volume 49 and 50: Landscape Drawing**
Transition to painting, materials and palette.
03-236 60 min. $29.95

• **Volume 51 and 52: Landscape Drawing**
Painting exercises for landscape, painting skills.
03-237 60 min. $29.95

• **Volume 53 and 54: Landscape Drawing**
Painting from sketches and color roughs, Part I.
03-238 60 min. $29.95

• **Volume 55 and 56: Landscape Drawing**
Painting from sketches and color roughs, Part II.
03-239 60 min. $29.95

• **Volume 57 and 58: Landscape Drawing**
Direct painting from nature, Part I
03-240 60 min. $29.95

• **Volume 59 and 60: Landscape Drawing**
Direct painting from nature, Part II
03-241 60 min. $29.95

• **Volume 61 and 62: Landscape Drawing**
Painting from photographs.
03-242 60 min. $29.95

HAL REED SERIES

• **Anatomy: Volume 1 and 2**
Skull and facial muscles.
03-197 60 min. $29.95

• **Anatomy: Volume 3 and 4**
Neck and shoulders.
03-198 60 min. $29.95

• **Anatomy: Volume 5 and 6**
Upper and lower arm.
03-199 60 min. $29.95

• **Anatomy: Volume 7 and 8**
Chest and pelvic front.
03-200 60 min. $29.95

• **Anatomy: Volume 9 and 10**
Upper and lower back.
03-201 60 min. $29.95

• **Anatomy: Volume 11 and 12**
Leg, front and back.
03-202 60 min. $29.95

VIDEO TITLES LISTED IN THIS GUIDE ARE AVAILABLE FOR PURCHASE
OR RENTAL. CONTACT YOUR LOCAL VIDEO STORE OR TELEPHONE (800) 383-8811

• **Anatomy: Volume 13 and 14**
Knee and calf.
03-203 60 min. $29.95

• **Anatomy: Volume 15 and 16**
Foot and toes.
03-204 60 min. $29.95

• **Anatomy: Volume 17 and 18**
Hands, back and palm.
03-205 60 min. $29.95

• **Anatomy: Volume 19 and 20**
Thumb and fingers.
03-206 60 min. $29.95

• **Anatomy: Volume 21 and 22**
Eyes and nose.
03-207 60 min. $29.95

• **Anatomy: Volume 23 and 24**
Mouth and ears.
03-208 60 min. $29.95

• **Anatomy: Volume 25 and 26**
Aging characteristics, masculine-feminine
characteristics.
03-209 60 min. $29.95

• **Anatomy: Volume 27 and 28**
Racial characteristics, facial expressions
03-210 60 min. $29.95

• **Color Comps: Volume 1 and 2**
One of the most valuable tools are color comps--
how to make and use them, including the basic
palette. All good paintings must first be good
abstract color designs.
03-171 60 min. $29.95

• **Color Comps: Volume 3 and 4**
Use of color wheel with comps, still-life color
comps.
03-172 60 min. $29.95

• **Color Comps: Volume 5 and 6**
Landscape color comps, seascape color comps.
03-173 60 min. $29.95

• **Color Comps: Volume 7 and 8**
Portrait color comps, genre color comps.
03-174 60 min. $29.95

• **Color Comps: Volume 9 and 10**
Enlarging comps to painting, enlarging
demonstration.
03-175 60 min. $29.95

• **Color: Volume 1 and 2**
How to bring forth from the discordant jazz of
nature, a symphony of color. Analogous color
theory and how to use a color wheel to improve
your painting.
03-169 60 min. $29.95

• **Color: Volume 3 and 4**
Mixing and matching color, not "stabbing and
guessing," but with knowledge. Analyzing the color
concept of all paintings.
03-170 60 min. $29.95

• **Composing Paintings: Volume 1 and 2**
The most important part of any painting or drawing
is the design or the composition. Includes such
items as scale, balance, negative and positive
shapes.
03-164 60 min. $29.95

• **Composing Paintings: Volume 3 and 4**
Symmetry versus asymmetry, eye path, line
continuation, rhythm.
03-165 60 min. $29.95

• **Composing Paintings: Volume 5 & 6**
Objectionable shapes, activation, unity,
center of interest, three tone.
03-166 60 min. $29.95

• **Elements of Art: Volume 15 and 16**
Plaster casting, waste molds.
03-218 60 min. $29.95

• **Elements of Art: Volume 17 and 18**
Latex and RTV molds.
03-219 60 min. $29.95

• **Elements of Art: Volume 19 and 20**
Bas relief coin medals.
03-220 60 min. $29.95

• **Elements of Art: Volume 21 and 22**
Bronze casting.
03-221 60 min. $29.95

• **Elements of Art: Volume 23 and 24**
Etching and engraving.
03-222 60 min. $29.95

• **Elements of Art: Volume 25 and 26**
Establishing yourself as an artist, selling.
03-223 60 min. $29.95

• **Elements of Art: Volume 27 and 28**
Art and teaching of Nicolai Fechin.
03-224 60 min. $29.95

VIDEO TITLES LISTED IN THIS GUIDE ARE AVAILABLE FOR PURCHASE
OR RENTAL. CONTACT YOUR LOCAL VIDEO STORE OR TELEPHONE (800) 383-8811

• **Perspective: Volume 1 and 2**
Perspective is not just for landscapes. To paint any subject you must know perspective; otherwise your painting will not look "right." Start from the beginning with a single point indoors and outdoors.
03-178 60 min. $29.95

• **Perspective: Volume 3 and 4**
Two point measuring methods.
03-179 60 min. $29.95

• **Perspective: Volume 5 and 6**
Three point measuring methods.
03-180 60 min. $29.95

• **Perspective: Volume 7 and 8**
Uphill and downhill. House from plans.
03-181 60 min. $29.95

• **Perspective: Volume 9 and 10**
Circles, arches, skies, lakes, streams.
03-182 60 min. $29.95

• **Perspective: Volume 11 and 12**
Perspective of shadows, light from side, front.
03-183 60 min. $29.95

• **Perspective: Volume 13 and 14**
Perspective of shadows, light from back, inside buildings.
03-184 60 min. $29.95

• **Perspective: Volume 15 and 16**
Perspective of shadows, steps, buildings, complex.
03-185 60 min. $29.95

• **Perspective: Volume 17 and 18**
Water and mirror reflections.
03-234 60 min. $29.95

• **Perspective: Volume 19 and 20**
Light and shade: If you want to achieve a three-dimensional effect on your two-dimensional surface, learn this magic starting from the basics: a vase, a tree, a head, are all spheres. Learn to give them form.
03-186 60 min. $29.95

• **Perspective: Volume 21 and 22**
Light and shade, blocks, donuts, curved surfaces.
03-187 60 min. $29.95

• **Perspective: Volume 23 and 24**
Light and shade, eyes.
03-188 60 min. $29.95

• **Perspective: Volume 25 and 26**
Light and shade, features of face, head.
03-189 60 min. $29.95

• **Perspective: Volume 27 and 28**
Folds of cloth. Learn the "law of folds." Don't just copy; know why they go the way they do.
03-190 60 min. $29.95

• **Perspective: Volume 29 and 30**
Folds of cloth, spiral, drop.
03-191 60 min. $29.95

• **Simple Series: Volume 1 and 2**
Planning and beginning paintings.
03-192 60 min. $29.95

• **Simple Series: Volume 3 and 4**
Color and its use.
03-193 60 min. $29.95

• **Simple Series: Volume 5 and 6**
Basic perspective.
03-194 60 min. $29.95

• **Simple Series: Volume 7 and 8**
Giving a painting depth.
03-195 60 min. $29.95

• **Simple Series: Volume 9 and 10**
Basic anatomy.
03-196 60 min. $29.95

Illustrated Figure with Jana Lynn-Holly
Art educator, Jana Lynn-Holly presents a condensed and clear overview over the process leading from figure drawing to finished illustration.
03-8014 30 min. $39.95

JAKE LEE SERIES

• **Volume 1 and 2: Fundamentals**
Fundamentals of watercolor, technique and application, demonstration of techniques on simple shapes and objects.
03-118 60 min. $29.95

• **Volume 3 and 4: Fundamentals**
Color and color mixing, color schemes, color harmony and color palette.
03-119 60 min. $29.95

• **Volume 5 and 6: Fundamentals**
Textures and how to achieve them, applying textures on sand, rock, wood and walls.
03-120 60 min. $29.95

• **Volume 7 and 8: Fundamentals**
Values, value scale, dimension, distances and form-space relationships.
03-121 60 min. $29.95

• **Volume 9 and 10: Fundamentals**
Using glass, wood, cloth, fur, metal, and demonstration of single items.
03-122 60 min. $29.95

• **Volume 11 and 12: Fundamentals**
Negative painting, cutting in, leaving white areas, signs, lettering and ornaments.
03-123 60 min. $29.95

• **Volume 13 and 14: Fundamentals**
Using sketchbook, calligraphy and techniques of brush drawing.
03-124 60 min. $29.95

• **Volume 15 and 16: Fundamentals**
Stretching paper, scaling for proportionate size, cutting mats.
03-125 60 min. $29.95

• **Volume 17 and 18: Intermediate**
Glass, metal, fences and roofs.
03-126 60 min. $29.95

• **Volume 19 and 20: Intermediate**
Waves, surf, waterfalls, rivers, lakes and ponds.
03-127 60 min. $29.95

• **Volume 21 and 22: Intermediate**
Windows, porches, verandas, doorways.
03-128 60 min. $29.95

• **Volume 23 and 24: Intermediate**
Ships and boats (fishing and sail), wharves and drydocks.
03-129 60 min. $29.95

• **Volume 25 and 26: Intermediate**
Barns, shacks, cabins, wagons, buggies, carts.
03-130 60 min. $29.95

• **Volume 27 and 28: Intermediate**
Bridges, towers, Victorian facades, missions and depots.
03-131 60 min. $29.95

• **Volume 29 and 30: Advanced**
Still life with fruit and flowers.
03-132 60 min. $29.95

• **Volume 31 and 32: Advanced**
Mist and mountains, storm at sea.
03-133 60 min. $29.95

• **Volume 33 and 34: Advanced**
Stormy skyscape, after the rain.
03-134 60 min. $29.95

• **Volume 35 and 36: Advanced**
A summer day, winter scene.
03-135 60 min. $29.95

• **Volume 37 and 38: Advanced**
Farm animals, scene with birds.
03-136 60 min. $29.95

• **Volume 39 and 40: Advanced**
Portrait of child, portrait of man.
03-137 60 min. $29.95

• **Volume 41 and 42: Advanced**
Experimental techniques.
03-138 60 min. $29.95

Jon Gnagy - Learn To Draw: Volume 1
Subjects include snow scene, Canadian geese, grist mill, fishing dock and ocean liner.
03-024 60 min. $29.95

Jon Gnagy - Learn To Draw: Volume 2
Subjects include winter scene, harbor scene, bucking bronco, old oak tree and mountain lake.
03-025 60 min. $29.95

JOURNEY INTO ART WITH BEN STAHL
Ben Stahl (1910 - 1987) received more than 50 national awards in his lifetime; his work was in the Saturday Evening Post, Cosmopolitan, Esquire and many others. This series demonstrates his technique, art and philosophies.

• **Introduction and painting tips.**
03-8037 30 min. $39.95

• **Painting and review**
03-8038 30 min. $39.95

JOYCE PIKE SERIES

• **Volume 1 and 2**
Pink roses and silver.
03-139 60 min. $29.95

• **Volume 3 and 4**
Mums with black background and cooper.
03-140 60 min. $29.95

• **Volume 5 and 6**
Iris with handpainted china.
03-141 60 min. $29.95

VIDEO TITLES LISTED IN THIS GUIDE ARE AVAILABLE FOR PURCHASE OR RENTAL. CONTACT YOUR LOCAL VIDEO STORE OR TELEPHONE (800) 383-8811

• **Volume 7 and 8**
Watermelon and cantaloupe with green glass jug.
03-142 60 min. $29.95

• **Volume 9 and 10**
Shasta and marguerite daisies with lemons.
03-143 60 min. $29.95

• **Volume 11 and 12**
White and pale yellow roses.
03-144 60 min. $29.95

• **Volume 13 and 14**
Raggedy Ann and Andy dolls.
03-145 60 min. $29.95

• **Volume 15 and 16**
Pink gladiolus in crystal vase.
03-146 60 min. $29.95

• **Volume 17 and 18**
Geraniums with pottery jug.
03-147 60 min. $29.95

• **Volume 19 and 20**
Clear-colored glass objects with fruit.
03-148 60 min. $29.95

• **Volume 21 and 22**
White mums shown with silver.
03-149 60 min. $29.95

• **Volume 23 and 24**
Poinsettias with copper.
03-150 60 min. $29.95

• **Volume 25 and 26**
Zinnias with antique coffee grinder.
03-151 60 min. $29.95

• **Volume 27 and 28**
Apples with eggs, iron pot and wine bottle.
03-152 60 min. $29.95

• **Volume 29 and 30**
Blue hydrangeas in antique pitcher.
03-153 60 min. $29.95

• **Volume 31 and 32**
Red roses with large hat.
03-154 60 min. $29.95

• **Volume 33 and 34**
Brass samovar with large and small yellow mums.
03-155 60 min. $29.95

• **Volume 35 and 36**
Chinese magnolias in basket with roses.
03-156 60 min. $29.95

• **Volume 37 and 38**
Antique china doll in wicker chair.
03-157 60 min. $29.95

• **Volume 39 and 40**
Brown-eyed susans with tin water can.
03-158 60 min. $29.95

• **Volume 41 and 42**
Large white magnolias with violin.
03-159 60 min. $29.95

• **Volume 43 and 44**
Indian corn, Indian basket, matillaja poppies.
03-160 60 min. $29.95

• **Volume 45 and 46**
Antique clock with bronze mums.
03-161 60 min. $29.95

• **Volume 47 and 48**
Iceland poppies in clear glass.
03-162 60 min. $29.95

• **Volume 49 and 50**
Calla lilies and lace tablecloth.
03-163 60 min. $29.95

Landscape Painting with Harold Riley
This tape is a working conversation with the renowned artist in which he offers first-hand information about what he does as he works on his latest landscape.
03-302 60 min. $29.95

LEARNING TO PAINT WITH CAROLYN BERRY

• **Field Flowers**
You will learn what supplies are needed and how you can go from a blank canvas to your own finished field flower creation. Easy to follow style of teaching is ideal for beginners or more accomplished artists eager to learn a new technique.
03-6631 25 min. $29.95

• **Portrait Drawing**
Learn the techniques needed to master the art of Portrait Drawing. This easy to follow video starts by showing you what materials you will need to get started. There are also valuable tips on how to better see your subject.
03-6632 25 min. $29.95

• **Portrait Painting**
An accomplished artist herself, she shows you what supplies and strategies you will need to paint a portrait. Watch Carolyn as she paints the portrait of a model, all the while explaining what colors are needed and how you can learn to create a successful portrait painting.
03-6633 25 min. $29.95

Let's Draw with Captain Bob
Capt. Bob uses a variety of his animal drawings to illustrate this art technique. The simple grace of a horse and the magnificence of a pheasant in flight are the main subjects.
03-307 51 min. $19.95

Magic Gallary: Mona Lisa to Dada
Children are sure to open their minds to the unusual movement known as the dada period. This would later open the doors to what we now refer to as "pop art".
03-8039 60 min. $89.00

Mastering Calligraphy
This video has been prepared by art teachers who designed and are teaching this course. The course has been successful for many years for students who are not skillful in the arts, as well as those who are. This video has been carefully prepared to present only those salient aspects of calligraphy that are necessary for a competent beginning.
03-6292 45 min. $39.95

Mountains - A William Palluth Workshop In Oils
Develop your artistic abilities as you learn how to paint this dramatic scene of the Mount of the Holy Cross in Colorado. Follow noted landscape artist William Palluth as he mixes and applies each color with brush and knife. Also learn how to achieve the illusion of depth, one of the most sought after effects in landscape painting. Sketch enclosed.
03-6796 60 min. $29.95

Norman Rockwell & the Saturday Evening Post
This inside story of the best twenty years of Norman Rockwell's memorable Saturday Evening Post covers offers a unique new view of America's most popular artist and his finest work.
03-8033 30 min. $29.95

Mystery of Picasso
Here, Picasso is shown creating 15 original paintings especially for this film, but after they were completed they were burned by the artist.
03-2806 85 min. $39.95

Oil Painting Techniques
Paint your own masterpiece in the time it takes to watch the video. Learn William Alexander's proven secrets to creating beautiful landscapes in your own home.
03-090 60 min. $19.95

Oil Painting: Teton Country
Art Kerner's "touch painting" is demonstrated using palette knives.
03-8009 30 min. $29.95

PAINTING LANDSCAPES IN OIL WITH WILLIAM PALLUTH
William Palluth is a painter and artist, as well as the author of three Walter Foster Art instructions books. His paintings are sold in 12 countries. The artist takes you through step-by-step instructions for transferring sketches to the canvas, brush choices and how to use them, color mixtures and how to mix them, The thickness of the paint, and much more. A sketch to transfer to canvas comes with each tape.

• **Autumn Landscape**
03-094 60 min. $29.95

• **Winter Landscape**
03-095 60 min. $29.95

Portrait Painting with Harold Riley
This internationally respected artist offers a unique insight into portrait painting in a candid commentary as he works. His suggestions are invaluable.
03-301 60 min. $29.95

Portraits in Watercolor: Volume 1, The Elements of Design
03-2920 60 min. $39.95

Portraits in Watercolor: Volume 2, The Magic of Light and Dark
03-2921 60 min. $39.95

Starting To Paint
For the beginning artist! Needing only a bare minimum of supplies, This video will introduce you to the basic brushes, brushstrokes and paints to show you exactly how to apply oil paints to canvas while keeping your colors clean and rich. Using a small, simple painting that can be completed in a short time, learn how to mix colors and use the enclosed 8 x 10 transfer sketch.
03-6076 60 min. $29.95

Sunset - A William Palluth Workshop In Oils
See your canvas come to life as you paint this

serene summer sunset, complete with warm evening light reflecting off a quiet stream. In this video workshop, artist William Palluth shows how mixing large pools of color can make painting so much easier and also promote color harmony in you paintings.
03-6795 60 min. $29.95

TOLE PAINTING SERIES WITH PRISCILLA HAUSER

• **Tole Painting - Apples**
Priscilla Hauser turns a simple wooden towel rack into a lovely decorative home accessory. Step-by-step instructions include the preparation of the wood surface for oil painting, a review of basic brush strokes and tips on how to paint dimensional apples. Includes patterns.
03-065 60 min. $69.95

• **Tole Painting - Daisies**
A simple daisy design enhances a lap desk. Instructions include how to transfer the enclosed pattern onto the painting surface, a review of basic brush strokes and step-by-step instructions on how to paint daisies and leaves.
03-067 60 min. $69.95

• **Tole Painting - Poppies**
Priscilla Hauser shows how her techniques in decorative oil painting make it easy to paint a colorful bouquet of poppies on an oval canvas. Includes patterns.
03-066 60 min. $69.95

UNI MARTCHENKO SERIES
Uni Martchenko, noted painter and teacher, is admired for her outstanding portrait and figure paintings. She is represented in many collections: Metropolitan Opera Gallery, La Mirada City Hall and Occidental College. She has exhibited widely and received numerous awards from Frye Museum, Seattle; Riverside Museum of Art; Redlands Museum; San Bernardino County Museum; and Los Angeles Municipal Galleries. Uni shares her methods and various approaches in painting the head and figure.

• **Volume 1 and 2**
Structure of head and correct placement of features, essential elements in beginning your portrait.
03-225 60 min. $29.95

• **Volume 3 and 4**
Development of portrait, blocking in composition, mood, color and tonal relationships, explored.
03-226 60 min. $29.95

• **Volume 5 and 6**
Painting the male portrait, problems of

backgrounds, search for characteristics.
03-227 60 min. $29.95

• **Volume 7 and 8**
Lighting the subject, selecting pose, gesture of hands, dull or intense color.
03-228 60 min. $29.95

• **Volume 9 and 10**
Angle of head, clothing and accessories, spatial elements considered, color contrasts, warm and cool.
03-229 60 min. $29.95

• **Volume 11 and 12**
Commissioned portrait, formal or informal, size of portrait, personality of the client and ways to achieve a likeness.
03-230 60 min. $29.95

• **Volume 13 and 14**
Painting from photographs, high or low-key profiles, improvisation.
03-231 60 min. $29.95

• **Volume 15 and 16**
Spontaneous figure gesture, exploring shapes as design elements.
03-232 60 min. $29.95

• **Volume 17 and 18**
Interplay between tradition and innovation. Patterns and rhythm.
03-233 60 min. $29.95

UNIQUE VIDEO WORKSHOP
Each tape in this art instruction video series is hosted by an award winning artist. They'll teach you the proper techniques required to fully develop your artistic potential.

• **Explosion Of Color**
Abstraction of still-life using knife and brush technique by Bob Tapia.
03-6220 60 min. $39.95

• **Harmonies In Red**
Impressionistic still-life in Oil by Anita Wolff.
03-6222 60 min. $39.95

• **Man From El Dorado**
Paster portraiture by Anita Wolff.
03-6219 60 min. $39.95

• **Sand Dollar Seascape**
Coastal Landscape in Oil by K. Susan Swenson.
03-6223 90 min. $39.95

• **Sentinels In Time**
California Coastal Redwoods in oil by Griselda
Tello.
03-6221 60 min. $39.95

Watercolor Fast and Loose
Ron Ranson follows up his first watercolor art
instruction video with this new video, designed to
show artists that watercolor painting can be fast,
loose and fun!
03-1679 60 min. $29.95

**Watercolor Painting with Judy Howard:
Part I: Wet and Spontaneous**
You don't need to be able to draw when you follow
this watercolor technique. This program
demonstrates just enough color theory and exercises
to help you understand he behavior of watercolor
paint. As you work along, you will be creating
attractive paintings of your own, using this wet and
free technique.
03-314 60 min. $39.95

**Watercolor Painting with Judy Howard:
Part II: Taming the Wet Medium**
This program teaches more exacting control of the
wet painting process taught in Part I. The subjects
are more defined, but achieving harmonious colors
and looseness remain the main goals. You will
understand the step-by-step development of a
painting, as well as some special watercolor
techniques.
03-315 60 min. $39.95

Watercolor Painting: Letting it Happen
03-2922 55 min. $39.95

**Watercolor Pure and Simple with Ron
Ranson**
Ron Ranson, author of one of England's top-selling
watercolor painting books, has led hundreds of
artists around the world through his watercolor
workshops. His basic palette of seven colors and
his mastery of the hake brush have made him a
popular instructor. This new video is packed with
ideas and techniques such as: wet-into-wet
techniques, color mixing figures in landscapes, fast
action demonstrations of clouds and skies, faults in
composition and how to correct them.
03-282 60 min. $29.95

Winter Landscape
You'll love doing this nostalgic snow scene
featuring a magnificent bare tree with snow-covered
limbs in the warm light of early evening. Each
color is mixed as you watch, making it an
especially valuable lesson. Shows how to give form
to trunk and limbs to make them look realistic, and
how to use complimentary colors to get interest and

sparkle into your paintings.
03-6077 60 min. $29.95

**Workshop In Oils With William Palluth
Oil Painting Technique**
In this fascinating video, noted landscape artist
William Palluth reveals techniques that would
otherwise take years to develop, packing literally
dozens of lessons into one invaluable program.
From painting wood textures, shadows and
reflections, to soft edges, wet-on-wet, and painting
in glazes, Bill shows you how to obtain a higher
form of realism in your painting.
03-6794 60 min. $29.95

Your First Steps to Watercolors
This in-depth program presents basic watercolor
techniques. Artist/teacher Gene Pollock begins with
preliminary essentials such as selection of paper,
brushes and pigments and proceeds with close-up
demonstrations of specific strokes and techniques.
All the instruction needed to get started on creating
your own watercolor paintings.
03-280 110 min. $49.95

Museum Guides

AMERICAN ART SERIES
This documentary series views the Whitney
Museum's exhibition with a lively commentary by
artists, critics and the curators who assembled it.
Artists interviewed are Dara Birnbaum, Robert
Breer, Eric Fischl, Donald Judd, Elizabeth Murray,
Susan Rothenberg, David Salle, Kenny Scharf and
Ned Smyth. Critics are Arthur Danto and Carter
Ratcliff.

• **1985**
03-304 28 min. $29.95

• **1987**
03-8070 30 min. $29.95

• **1989**
03-8071 30 min. $29.95

Louvre
The Louvre museum was founded and opened to
the public in 1793. Masterpieces from the Palace of
Versailles, collected over several centuries by the
Kings of France, form the core of this magnificent
museum. Additional works were appropriated
during the Revolution, and still others were
commissioned by Napoleon.
03-029 105 min. $29.95

Prado
The Prado proudly displays more than six thousand painting in its extensive and beautiful collection. To pay them due tribute, they are presented to you in two sections: European painting and Spanish painting.
03-049 60 min. $29.95

Vatican Museum
The works of Michelangelo, Raphael, Martini, da Forli and other classic artists are contained in the galleries of the Vatican Museum. Come on a fascinating tour of the Vatican galleries and see the papal apartments and the Sistine Chapel, as well.
03-055 53 min. $29.95

Miscellaneous

20th Century American Art
This award-winning documentary presents the dramatic story of American art in our century based on the Whitney Museum's third floor exhibition. Beginning with the neglect of American artists at the turn of the century, the film traces American art history from the opening of the museum in 1931, to abstract expressionism, and the subsequent impact of pop art and minimalism.
03-303 26 min. $44.95

Andrew Wyeth: The Helga Pictures
Charlton Heston hosts this beautiful program filmed in Chadds Ford on the Kuerner Farm, where many of the Helga pictures were painted, and at the Wyeth home nearby. Explores the meaning and the mystery of Wyeth's work.
03-2509 36 min. $39.95

Art of Making Pictures: A Guide to Creating Art
Hosted by award-winning artist and author Lee Hanson, this program familiarizes the viewer with various art media available covering pen and pencil, tempera, crayons, collage, watercolor, markers and a brief introduction to anatomy.
03-004 51 min. $29.95

Batik as Fine Art with Helen Carkin
Helen Carkin takes a Textile Art into the realm of Fine Art with a minimum of expense.
03-8015 60 min. $39.95

Day in the Country: Impressionism & the French Landscape
One of the best programs ever! Features 40 of the most important paintings from the largest exhibition of impressionist landscape paintings ever assembled. Monet, Van Gogh, Pissarro, Sisley, Cezanne and other masters are represented in an inspiring overview of the late 19th century movement. Musical accompaniment by Debussy.
03-092 27 min. $29.95

Day On The Grand Canal With The Emperor Of China
World-famous artist David Hockney takes you down a magical journey through a legendary 17th-century Chinese scroll. Hockney spins a dazzling discourse on eastern and western perspectives and his own artistic vision.
03-9063 60 min. $39.95

Degas, Erte and Chagall
Three of this century's most influential artists are studied in this video trio. "Degas in New Orleans" portrays the artist's little-known visit there. Diana Vreeland tells the story of Erte, his life and works, from Paris to Hollywood. In the third segment, Marc Chagall gives a personal view of some of his greatest works.
03-012 100 min. $69.95

FILMS OF CHARLES & RAY EAMES
Charles and Ray Eames were among the most influential American designers of our time. Each volume includes an introduction by Gregory Peck.

• Volume 1: Powers of Ten
The film that revolutionized the way we view our world.
03-8035 21 min. $59.95

• Volume 2
The second in the series consists of seven short films.
03-8036 21 min. $59.95

Filigree EmbossArt
Filigree EmbossArt is a new and refreshing way to decorate with acrylic paint. A unique applicator is used to delicately apply a raised bead of paint to almost any surface, creating beautiful decorative designs.
03-015 30 min. $29.95

Learn the Art of Pinstriping
Learn the applications of Paint, Brushes and Design Strokes. The lesson includes an actual Field Application of Pinstriping on the body of a white Mercedes-Benz.
03-6929 45 min. $39.95

MAGIC GALLERY SERIES

• Marc Chagall
This exciting introduction to the world of art

utilizes the magic of video to explore the world of Marc Chagall. The children in the show are transported to Chagall's village in Russia and learn about his life and his colorful imaginative style of painting.
03-6240 90 min. $69.95

• Picasso's Cubism
The Magic Gallery provides an opportunity to explore this unique style by several examples of cubism. Presented in an interesting and informal manner, the children have an opportunity to examine the artist' use of line' color,and symbolism, as well as to create their own example of cubist art.
03-6241 90 min. $69.95

• Pop Art
Rows of Coke bottles? Combat cartoons? The American flag? Clothespins? Presenter, Jackie Copeland, explains why these common objects became the subjects for art in the 1960s. Ms. Copeland, with the help of The Magic Gallery really "gets into" these works of art to show the children some of the unusual techniques used to create these works of art.
03-6243 90 min. $69.95

Mind's Eye
A spectacular odyssey of breathtaking computer animation imagery. Set to an original music soundtrack.
03-9307 40 min. $19.95

MUSEUM WITHOUT WALLS

• Crete and Mycenae
Filmed on the island of Crete and at Mycenae on the Greek mainland, this film offers an incredible view of the lands and legacies of two magnificent ancient cultures. It explores the connections between the Minoan civilization and Mycenae, probes the ruins at Knossos, and adds yet another piece to one of the most fascinating archaeological puzzles of our time.
03-323 54 min. $19.95

• Cubist Epoch
This documentary studies the works of the brave generation of Cubists: Picasso, Braque, Gris, Leger, Gleizes, Villon, Delaunay and their followers. It presents a comprehensive survey of almost all of the significant art and artists of this important movement, shedding new light on the short but turbulent Cubist Epoch.
03-328 53 min. $19.95

• Germany-Dada
The Dada movement, grandfather of pop art and surrealism, is delightfully displayed by original

Dadaists, including Hans Richter and Richard Huelsenbeck, in this unique film collage of art, music and poetry. According to The Wall Street Journal, "Germany-Dada' faithfully creates not just Dada art but the times that spawned it."
03-324 55 min. $19.95

• Giotto and the Pre-Renaissance
All of the remarkable innovations and major frescoes that made Giotto di Bondoni the undisputed master of the Florentine painters are filmed here in vibrant detail. This program records each of the major cycles of Giotto's frescoes in superb detail, conveying the powerful emotion and shimmering three-dimensional quality of the great master's work.
03-327 47 min. $19.95

• Goya
This documentary led Films in Review to proclaim, "The cinematography is of an exceptionally high order-the lighting is so faithfully reproduced it's breathtaking." "Goya" probes the brilliant Spanish master's most prominent works, including his etchings, tapestries, portraits, frescoes, and even the famous "black paintings" from his own home.
03-329 54 min. $19.95

• Greek Temple
This unique film takes you on an exploration of the remains of the colossal sacred cities at Paestum, Delphi, Agriegento, Sounion and the Acropolis. It traces the evolution of the temples through the Doric, Ionic and Corinthian styles, including models and animations of many of the ancient shrines that span the golden age of the Greek Empire.
03-326 54 min. $19.95

• Le Corbusier
From the hills of France to the Himalayas of India, you'll witness a stunning portrait of the life and works of Le Corbusier. "Le Corbusier" conducts an interesting tour of his most important buildings, explores his revolutionary ideas on architecture and urban renewal, and studies both the man and the vision that changed the face of 20th century architecture.
03-330 46 min. $19.95

• Picasso: War, Peace, Love
Beginning with the famed Guernica mural, this critically lauded film artfully documents the master's later accomplishments, including many previously undiscovered pieces. It travels through 22 museums, seven galleries and 11 private collections to create a moving tribute to the most influential artist of the 20th century.
03-325 51 min. $19.95

VIDEO TITLES LISTED IN THIS GUIDE ARE AVAILABLE FOR PURCHASE OR RENTAL. CONTACT YOUR LOCAL VIDEO STORE OR TELEPHONE (800) 383-8811

Philip Pearlstein Draws the Artist's Model
Focuses on the painting and teaching ideas of one of the most important and influential artists of the 20th century.
03-308 42 min. $69.95

PICASSO: THE MAN AND HIS WORK SERIES:
Produced and directed by Edward Quinn. Quinn has created a screenplay showing Picasso as if he were going through the scrapbook of his life, with many flash-back sequences showing the evolution of his work and the episodes of his life drawn in parallel.
03-290 90 min. $79.95

• **Volume 1**
03-045 45 min. $39.95

• **Volume 2**
03-046 45 min. $39.95

• **Collector's Dual Pack**
03-290 90 min. $79.95

Raku Ceramics with Jim Romberg
This program teaches you all you need to know for making Raku pieces. Jim Romberg has written extensively on the technical and philosophical aspects of Raku.
03-8016 75 min. $39.95

Remington and AVA: American Art
Frederic Remington immortalized the Wild West in his paintings and sculpture, capturing for all time the intimate drama of the unbridled American Spirit. The spirit of Remington himself lives on in the contemporary frontiers of American art, paired on video with AVA, the prestigious Awards in the American Arts, and narrated by Arthur Godfrey.
03-050 100 min. $64.95

Return to Glory: Michelangelo Revealed
This is the story of the restoration of the Sistine Chapel. Edwin Newman narrates this documentary describing the twelve-year project. Up on the scaffolding, the cameras offer close-ups of the painstaking cleaning of the fresco surface, revealing a wealth of information about Michelangelo and his techniques. You can see the original color of the paintings as the controversial restoration wipes away centuries of dirt.
03-1607 60 min. $39.95

Sculpting with Fred Rowe: Sheriff Figure
Fred Rowe has been dedicated to the art world for over twenty years. His three-hour instruction of his "free-form" sculpture style is detailed as he transforms clay into anatomy.
03-8008 60 min. $29.95

The Videos In This Section

Will Help You

Savor The Work Of Masters

Or

Create Your Own

VIDEO TITLES LISTED IN THIS GUIDE ARE AVAILABLE FOR PURCHASE OR RENTAL. CONTACT YOUR LOCAL VIDEO STORE OR TELEPHONE (800) 383-8811

Fishing

- ✓ *Equipment*
- ✓ *Fishing Trips*
- ✓ *Tips & Tactics*
- ✓ *Miscellaneous*

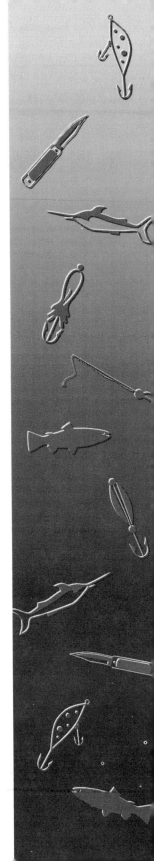

Equipment

Bass Tackle: How to Buy and Save
An indispensable guide to buying tackle. A must for every fisherman who wants to buy the best and save money.
19-2267 90 min. $29.95

Building Your Own Rod
Build a better rod than you can buy...exactly suited to your own fishing needs. Discover just how fun and rewarding rod building can be. Dale Clemens, master rodcrafter and author of the bible on rodcrafting, gives you step-by-step instructions to build any type of rod you want...fly, spinning, trolling or casting.
19-010 100 min. $39.95

Creative Rod Crafting
Few hobbies offer as much creative satisfaction as crafting your own custom rod. Dale Clemens, master rodcrafter, takes you beyond rod building to beauty-enhancing techniques for creating your own unique work of art.
19-013 110 min. $39.95

Dry Fly
Stoneflies, caddis, scuds and leeches are favorites of trout big trout. Discover how to tie and fish them to increase your sub-surface fishing success.
19-043 90 min. $39.95

Fishing Knots
This video teaches you easily and effectively, the best ways to perfect knot tying techniques.
19-8032 30 min. $19.95

POUL JORGENSEN ON FLY TYING
Poul Jorgensen is one of America's best known fly tiers. This is his first appearance on home video.

• **My Favorite Fishing Flies, Vol. 1**
Learn how to tie lures and basic ties.
19-8000 100 min. $29.95

• **My Favorite Fishing Flies, Vol. 2**
Learn how to tie advanced flies and lures.
19-8001 100 min. $29.95

Tying Trout Flies
Gary Borger shows you step-by-step techniques needed to tie 90% of all dry flies, nymphs and streamers. Go underwater with the camera to observe how the imitation matches the natural.

Gary's instruction will speed your fly-tying development and enhance your understanding of this sport.
19-081 60 min. $39.95

Ultimate Lure
Join Charlie White and his special guest Arte Johnson as the give you an insightful view of what happens when a fish strikes a lure.
19-8008 88 min. $19.95

Fishing Trips

Alaska: Once in a Lifetime?
Share the experience of two men who said, "Just once in my life I'd like to see and fish Alaska," and did it! Fish from one of Alaska's premier "fly-out" fishing lodges. Catch silver salmon, rainbow trout and arctic char as fast as the fly hits the water. See grizzly bears and other wildlife. This is an adventure of your dreams.
19-119 72 min. $29.95

Alaska: Rivers Full Of Silver
Follow a group of fishermen as they travel to a remote Eskimo village on Alaska's beautiful and rugged northwest coast to fish for all five species of Pacific salmon and trophy size trout.
19-6595 45 min. $29.95

Alaskan Angler
Join Bob Stearns as he heads upriver to Alaska's Togiak Wildlife Refuge for a remarkable fishing adventure.
19-2754 85 min. $39.95

America's Hottest Bass Lakes
The perfect travel program for today's fishermen who want to fish the greatest lakes in all 50 states. Information on travel arrangements, who to contact, what supplies to bring and much more.
19-2268 60 min. $19.95

Away From It All
Malcolm Florence and Vic McCristal, Australia's foremost fishing author, wander in an unwished tropical paradise. With a variety of light tackle they explore this uninhabited area of the Great Barrier Reef and catch a great variety of tropical sportfish.
19-052 53 min. $49.95

Barramundi Fever
Barramundi is one of "down under's" most sought after sportfish. Join a host of Aussie sportfishing legends as they tell you all about this elusive and

intense trophy.
19-8071 35 min. $29.95

Bermuda's Yellowfin Tuna
The viewer sees a day's outing on a top charter boat for yellowfin tuna on Bermuda's Challenger Bank. All the techniques used to catch this great game fish are discussed. The viewer gets a first-hand underwater look at how tuna feed in the chum. The finish of the film shows a world-record catch taken on 16-pound test. Good information and plenty of action.
19-053 30 min. $34.95

Beyond the Edge-Professionals at Play
A rare Coral Sea exploration to a remote reef 150 miles off the Great Barrier Reef. A group of Australia's best known sports fishermen fish for yellowfin tuna, red bass, giant dogtooth tuna and sharks. This is a place where fish do not know man. Lots of action.
19-054 54 min. $49.95

Black Marlin-The Ultimate
Spectacular tag and release battles with giant black marlin off Australia's fabulous Ribbon Reefs. Also, night diving and fun fishing the Barrier Reef. Great action shots.
19-055 54 min. $49.95

Bow Hunting for Shark
This video documents a bow hunt for shark in the Florida Keys with bow hunter Nelson Poyer
19-8003 30 min. $29.95

British Columbia's Babine Steelhead
Fall at a remote fishing lodge in British Columbia, Canada is the setting for this film. The story is of two men who go after the big steelhead trout of the Babine River. Their goal is to catch one weighing over 20 pounds and to do it on a fly rod... something only one out of five hundred steelhead fishermen ever succeeds in doing.
19-120 50 min. $29.95

Bronzebacks of the North: Smallmouth Spectacular
Join Babe Winkelman on a tour of scenic unspoiled waters as he explores the mystery of the smallmouth bass.
19-1996 50 min. $19.95

Canoe Country Fishing: Angling in the Quetico-Boundry Waters
A trip to a wilderness area requires preparation; this tape shows how to plan the trip, set up camp, portage a canoe and catch smallmouth bass and

walleye.
19-1950 60 min $39.95

Cowboys and Cutthroats: A Rocky Mountain Fishing Adventure
The viewer will join two fly fisherman as they take a 100-mile horse pack trip through the famous Bridger Teton Wilderness area south of Yellowstone Park. Enjoy the journey across the Continental Divide and experience the parting of the waters--where a stream actually splits.
19-196 50 min. $29.95

Cozumel Sailfish
Fishing for this symbol of all fish in the blue waters of the Yucatan Peninsula area at world-famous Cozumel, Mexico.
19-115 30 min. $49.95

Deep Sea Fishing-The Baja Coast
Prepare for excitement and the grueling action of a long-range fishing trip. You will see yellowfin tuna and wahoo off the Baja California, coast and experience luxury hotel-like accommodations.
32-114 23 min. $29.95

Fishing Alaska
If you're a sportfishing enthusiast, Fishing Alaska is a special way to enjoy one of the largest and most varied fishing resources in the world.
19-6596 70 min. $29.95

Fishing Canada
Get the inside scoop from Roland Martin on the best places and times to game fish in Canada.
19-8146 60 min. $19.95

Fishing in Alaska
Rainbow trout fishing at its very best! Filmed on the magnificent Kvichak River, this is the heart of world famous rainbow fishing. The river is also brimming with silver, king and chum salmon and arctic greylings.
19-107 60 min. $39.95

Fishing the Canadian Shield: The Ultimate Experience
Join Babe Winkleman as he experiences the "lakes of life" in the rugged waters of Ontario.
19-1997 50 min. $19.95

Fishing the Gulf of Mexico
Cobia, wahoo, grouper, amberjack, marlin, barracuda, mackerel, snapper, trout, tarpon, sailfish and others. The most saltwater action ever compiled in one video. Instructions, times, places and methods.
19-109 60 min. $39.95

VIDEO TITLES LISTED IN THIS GUIDE ARE AVAILABLE FOR PURCHASE OR RENTAL. CONTACT YOUR LOCAL VIDEO STORE OR TELEPHONE (800) 383-8811

Fishing with Roland Martin: Volume 5
Roland Martin tangles with bass and catfish in South Carolina.
19-2787 60 min. $29.95

Fishing with Roland Martin: Volume 6
Roland Martin and fellow fishermen seek out New York salmon.
19-2788 60 min. $29.95

Fishing Montana's Famous Salmon Fly Hatch
One of the great world fishing experiences is the famous salmon-fly hatch on several of Montana's renowned blue-ribbon trout streams.
19-2161 60 min. $59.95

Fishing Ontario: It's Incredible!
Babe Winkelman treks to one of his favorite places on earth to fish for walleye, smallmouth bass, northern pike and brook trout.
19-1951 60 min. $39.95

Fishing Pacific Panama
A potpourri of light tackle fishing around the island of Coiba off Panama's West Coast. This is an entertaining and informative film that shows how to take tropical species with light-weight tackle.
19-132 28 min. $29.95

Fishing Yellowstone Country
Discover and explore Yellowstone National Park and surrounding areas. Follow fishermen on a day on the water. See the catches, hear the conversations and learn proper fishing techniques.
19-190 60 min. $24.95

Fly Fishing New Zealand
Three world class fly fishermen travel by plane, car, boat and helicopter to some of the most pristine fly fishing waters in New Zealand.
19-2067 30 min. $19.95

GIANT BLACKS AND GREAT WHITES SERIES

• Volume 1
Part 1: Black Marlin-Dream Fish: Fishing for giant black marlin along Australia's Great Barrier Reef. Part 2: Golden Fins of Montagu: Light tackle and yellowfin tuna off the Coast of New South Wales. Good action.
19-056 52 min. $49.95

• Volume 2
Part 3: Pedder-Lake Super Trout: Fishing in Tasmania off Australia's south coast for monster brown trout. Part 4: Great White Sharks: Coming face-to-face with one of nature's most perfect

killers off the Australian coast. Lots of action.
19-057 52 min. $49.95

Great Plains Reservoir
Winkelman unravels the secrets to catching walleye and bass in a world where river fish have become lake fish.
19-1998 50 min. $19.95

GREAT EXPLORATION SERIES

• Part 1
You'll be treated to some of the most action packed tropical sportfishing ever seen. This video takes you from Lizard Island to the Great Barrier Reef.
19-8072 48 min. $29.95

• Part 2
In part two of this exploration, you'll see the Barrier reefs untouched by man for centuries.
19-8073 48 min. $29.95

Great Whites Off Dangerous Reef
An extended version of Part 4 of Giant Blacks & Great Whites. Malcolm Florence dives with great white sharks off the Dangerous Reef on South Australia's Coast. Then he battles one of these giant sharks for a tag and release. Action packed.
19-058 53 min. $49.95

Island Holiday
A young family's adventure on a tropical island in the Great Barrier Reef chain. Surrounded by beautiful coral reefs, Palm Island offers breath-taking diving, spectacular light tackle sportfishing and great hiking. A special vacation in the sun. Variety of action.
19-059 53 min. $49.95

Jimmy Houston Goes Salt Water Fishing
Relive some great moments of Jimmy Houston in this series of saltwater fishing experiences. See barracuda fishing off the Florida Keys, redfish and speckled trout at Cocadrie, Louisiana, plus a show on blue runners.
19-6563 60 min. $29.95

Of Tigers, Sails and Crocodiles
From the Northern tropics to the Southern Ocean this is an explorer's dream come true. Tremendous battles with awesome prizes make this Malcolm Florence show a must for any angler's collection.
19-8069 52 min. $29.95

Ribbons
A dream trip to fish the pristine edge of the Ribbon Reef off Australia's Coast. Jigging and trolling with light tackle where 50-pounders get eaten whole on the way up and 600-pound marlin get hooked on

jigging tackle. Great action.
19-060 53 min. $49.95

Roland Martin's Bass Tales
Follow Roland to all his favorite fishing holes,
from Florida's Lake Okeechobee and Clearwater
Pond to Washington D.C.'s famous Potomac River.
19-2515 47 min. $19.95

Sailfish-A Young Man's Challenge
The very special adventure of a 14-year-old boy in
search of his first light-tackle sailfish. Plenty of
action with tuna, mackerel, dolphin and marlin.
19-061 53 min. $49.95

Sailfishing with Roland Martin
This video puts the viewer in the sailfishing action
off Florida's gold coast.
19-2790 30 min. $29.95

Saltwater Smorgasbord
Fishing action in the Gulf of Mexico and the
Cayman Islands. You'll get expert advice on ways
to catch a variety of grand blue water species.
19-116 30 min. $39.95

**Spring Fishing: The Cure for Cabin
Fever**
A celebration of spring in the north country after a
long winter indoors.
19-1999 50 min. $19.95

Stoneflies and the Big Hole
The stonefly hatch on Montana's Big Hole River is
world famous among fly fishermen. Spend four
days in June with two men as they fish the beautiful
Big Hole, casting dry flies for rainbow and brown
trout. The river, the float trip, the wildlife, and
much more, all set in the exquisite Montana
country.
19-121 53 min. $29.95

Trout Fishing: Northern California
More than 30 prime trout fishing spots thorough
Northern California are highlighted. From "urban"
fisheries where marshmallows and salmon eggs are
the featured bait to pristine wild trout rivers for the
expert fly rodder, this video has something for
every type of trout fisherman and someplace to go
where you'll usually get good results.
19-1722 60 min. $29.95

Wild Times in Paradise
Join Mal and his mates for an angler's adventure to
the outer limits of the Great Barrier Reef and see
the boys pull in seven high flying sailfish in one
day!
19-8070 50 min. $29.95

World of Fishing
Spend a few days at Yellowstone fishing with
expert fisherman Jerry Cobb. Learn the rules and
regulations of the park, how to acquire a license
and how to fish the area.
19-174 60 min. $29.95

**Yellowstone and The Madison: One
After Another**
Yellowstone Park gives rise to two magnificent
rivers, the Yellowstone and the Madison. Come
along with fly fisherman Alton Coulter as he floats
and fishes the mighty Yellowstone with John Bailey
of Livington, Montana and then crosses the Divide
to fish the beautiful Madison, often referred to as
the "100-mile riffle".
19-122 50 min. $29.95

Tips & Tactics

Advanced Trolling for Saltwater Fish
Learn highly advanced methods including outrigger
release mechanisms, slow trolling methods and
more.
19-8151 60 min. $29.95

America's Favorite Sportfish
In this tape, Uncle Homer teaches you all the
details you need to know to hook the top six
freshwater game fish. The best baits, locations,
times of the day, and much more are covered.
19-8123 38 min. $19.95

Basic Fly Fishing
Greg Lilly and Dave Corcoran combine 25 years of
guiding experience to teach you everything from fly
selection to casting techniques and locating fish.
19-5509 58 min. $19.95

Basic Nymph Fishing With Jim Teeny
Fish feed below the surface 90% of the time, so to
catch more fish, improve your wet fly techniques
with Jim Teeny, 9-time world fly rod record
holder. Teeny explains wet fly, or "nymph" fishing
strategy in-depth, including fish location, natural
presentation of the fly, reading the water, line
control and more.
19-5510 50 min. $19.95

Basics of Bass Fishing
Hank Parker, host of the syndicated television
series "Hank Parker's Outdoor Magazine" is ranked
as one of the top professional fishermen in the
nation. Winner of the 1983 B.A.S.S. Angler of the
Year title. Hank is now ranked third on the all time

money list. Hank's video series offers useful and practical tips that every viewer from novice to expert can use and apply in their quest for the outdoors. Volume One covers four basic points: (1) consider the fish, (2) consider your boat position (3) consider your tackle and (4) consider your technique. Hank Parker is a devoted sportsman of proven talents who shares his secrets for success in this entertaining, yet informative video.
30-565 60 min. $29.95

Bass in Heavy Cover
Trees, stumps and weeds hold bass, but they are difficult to fish. See how the pros actually use these obstacles to catch more fish.
19-005 30 min. $29.95

Bass Fishing on The East Coast
The best techniques, the best time, the best place to bass fish. With Rowland Martin.
19-8144 60 min. $19.95

Bass Fishing the Fly Rod with Wendell Hise
Wendell Hise, a fly-fishing guide and instructor for 20 years, maintains a busy schedule of seminars, lectures and appearances at major tackle shows. His techniques are simple to learn and effective. He covers casting correctly, left-hand action, single and double haul, bringing in the catch and where to fly fish for bass.
19-246 60 min. $29.95

Bass Fishing Technique
A detailed and comprehensive presentation on how Bass behavior is affected by weather frontal systems and barometric pressure. Professional advice on locations and conditions that will improve Bass angler's success.
19-8150 60 min. $19.95

Bass Fishing: Top to Bottom
Features three-time Bass Masters Classic winner Ricky Clunn, who shows you how to recognize bass feeding patterns, how to fish at all depths, seasonal movements, structure, casting, special techniques like "flippin" and more.
19-004 60 min. $49.95

Bass Magic
Babe Winkelman teaches the techniques of spinner-bait fishing for big bass.
19-8143 50 min. $19.95

Bass Tactics that Work
Larry Nixon has the distinguished honor of being named Bass Angler of the Year and is a Bass Master Classic Champion. Larry covers every aspect of the sport from live bait, topwater plugs, crankbaits, spinners, jigs, soft-plastic lures and

much more. He'll also give you some tips on casting techniques, how to read the water and habitat used by these very elusive fish.
19-066 30 min. $29.95

Bass Strategies
Dave Embry shows you the best kept secret of catching big bass. You will learn all about rod & reel selection, casting & retrieving techniques, crank baits, spinners, plastic lures & jigs and where to find bass.
19-6483 30 min. $14.95

Bigmouth Bass
Go below the surface to the private world of the largemouth bass. Gain a better understanding of their behavior and temperament. A fascinating study of the bass life cycle.
19-007 60 min. $49.95

Bluefish on Light Tackle
Learn proven methods for locating and catching bluefish on spinning, plug casting, and fly-fishing gear. No matter what conditions or season, you can improve your fishing success. Packed with dramatic action.
19-009 60 min. $19.95

Bluewater Fishing Tips
This tape teaches advanced anglers the many things they need to know about catching Big Game fish. This is serious, hard core stuff.
19-8088 60 min. $29.95

Catch the Big Ones
Welcome to the world of fly fishing. Come on a tackle store tour. Learn how to properly select rods, reels, lines, leaders, clothes and flies. Then you're off to the stream (conveniently located in your living room of course) for a slow motion lesson in casting technique. John Tibbs demonstrates his world famous techniques for tying flies. He talks about proper choice and selection of flies too.
19-011 49 min. $24.95

Catching Big Bass
Shows the tactics and proven strategies that have helped Doug Hannon catch and release more than 400 bass over ten pounds.
19-2395 60 min. $49.95

Catching More Bass
Get ready to "Catch More Bass" with Renaud Pelletier! The Northwest's all-time leading tournament money winner shares the secrets of his "seasonal approach" to fishing, adjusting to changes in water temperature and bass habits.
19-5508 58 min. $19.95

Catching Pan Fish

Have you ever tasted fresh fish? Uncle Homer explains the tried and true methods to land yourself the best tasting Bluegill and Crappie.
19-8122 55 min. $19.95

Cliff Craft's Spinnerbait Tactics

Cliff Craft has won more than 75 fishing tournaments, placing him on the list of leading money winners. Cliff will show you how to master this big bass bait to improve your catch of largemouth bass. Unique underwater footage is used to illustrate the techniques taught in this video.
19-1544 47 min. $29.95

Crappie Magic

Go after monster Crappies! Babe Winkleman will teach you how to find and catch them.
19-8145 50 min. $19.95

Deep Sea Fishing

Beginner or expert, you will enjoy the great saltwater fishing action and tips on bait, rod handling, filleting, etc. So join us for some fun in the sun as we go fishing!
19-6479 30 min. $16.95

Down Rigging Techniques for All Fishermen

Down rigging is the fastest growing fishing system in the U.S., and millions of fishermen will want to watch John Fox demonstrate the right equipment and the proper techniques.
19-2269 45 min. $19.95

Drift Fishing in the Pacific

Full of facts, fishing tips and tricks, this video will give you many pleasant hours of armchair fishing enjoyment and result in more productive fishing trips. An absolute must for any serious fisherman who wishes to improve.
19-239 60 min. $39.95

Essence of Fly Casting

Important facets of casting, interspersed with some exciting sequences of largemouth trout, bonefish and silver salmon. Course has been patterned after a curriculum that has taught thousands of students and covers the mechanics of the fly cast, good form in casting, roll cast, the pick-up and lay-down cast, recognizing and understanding the casting loop, false cast, the "feel" of fly casting, shooting line, the double haul, the Belgian cast and various presentations.
19-019 60 min. $39.95

Feeding Habits of the Bass

Discover when and why bass strike and feed and how to use this information to catch more-and bigger-bass.
19-020 30 min. $49.95

Fishing for Albacore Tuna

Everything from tackle to test line is covered in a thorough guide to seeking the spirit of big game fishing.
19-2789 30 min. $29.95

Fishing The Wet Fly and Nymph

Hal Janssen will show you ways to increase the skills needed to enjoy more fly fishing success.
19-2391 90 min. $49.95

Fishing for Florida Bass

Great fishing spots that promise exciting fishing adventures. With Roland Martin.
19-8141 60 min. $19.98

Flippin' School for Big Bass

Jason Turley has gained the reputation of being the Flippin' Machine. The Flippin' rod has become a permanent tool for every top tournament angler. All the Basics are covered plus a new method of setting the hook that assures success.
19-279 60 min. $16.95

Fly-Fishing

Step-by-step instruction on fly casting, tying flies and selection of equipment.
19-8142 90 min. $19.98

Fly-Fishing for Trout

An on-the-stream course in successful trout-fishing strategies with Gary Borger as you private tutor. Learn how to read a river, where to find trout, casting techniques, matching the hatch and more.
19-027 60 min. $49.95

Fly-Fishing: The English Way

Learn from some of England's finest fly-fishermen as they share their proven methods for casting trout on beautiful English lakes and streams.
19-026 60 min. $49.95

Flyfishing Strategies

Dave Embry teams up with Jerry Johnson of The Federation of Flyfishing. They discuss all aspects of how to become a great fly fisherman.
19-6484 30 min. $16.95

Gamefish

This how-to video has some of the most exciting fresh water game sequences ever captured on video. Fishing, field care, cleaning and cooking are demonstrated by top Wisconsin fishing guides.
19-8022 55 min. $39.95

VIDEO TITLES LISTED IN THIS GUIDE ARE AVAILABLE FOR PURCHASE OR RENTAL. CONTACT YOUR LOCAL VIDEO STORE OR TELEPHONE (800) 383-8811

Hooked on Fly Fishing
In this video, John Tibbs clues you in on most aspects of fly-fishing, from buying the proper equipment to tying your own flys, and much more.
19-2965 30 min. $16.95

How to Catch Bass
It is true that 10% of the bass fishermen catch 90% of the bass because they have taken the time to learn how to use fish-catching secrets for consistent success. Professional bass fisherman Roger Moore takes you through one hour of the most extensive bass fishing schools ever filmed. He will cover how to use live bait, soft-plastic lures and jigs, crankbaits, and spinners...plus dozens of Roger's own private bass catching secrets.
19-067 60 min. $16.95

How to Catch Walleye
Babe Winkelman will cover every aspect of catching walleyes using soft-plastic lures and jigs, crankbaits, spinners and live bait. Fantastic underwater shots of walleyes in their natural habitat as never before seen on film. Plus live action shots of all the lures in action. Without fail, this show will take the novice as well as the seasoned pro angler and turn them into consistently successful walleye fishermen.
19-069 60 min. $14.95

How to Fish a Lake You've Never Seen Before with Ken Cook
Ken Cook tells you how he approaches a lake he has never fished before and what to look for-structure, cover and areas where bass would most likely be. He explains pre--fishing preparations and how to obtain maps and helpful information. Ken describes how to eliminate areas that may not be productive, and explains how to detect a fish feeding pattern. He covers what baits and lures are best in certain areas of the lake.
19-197 60 min. $29.95

How to Fish for Trout
Rex Gerlach has had numerous books and magazine articles published on the subject since 1954. He will show you over three decades of successful trout fishing techniques, including the art of fly-fishing, fly selection, how to read trout water, how to select the right equipment and his special techniques for using spinners and other forms of hardware for trout. Most other forms of fishing are referred to as sport, but with Rex trout angling is an art, and he will show you how to become a true angling artist.
19-068 30 min. $16.95

How to Troll for Fish
Through consistent success on Lake Michigan, Peter Ruboyianes has become known as the "Trolling King." Peter has spent nearly two decades defining the art of trolling for all species of fish and has won many fishing tournaments. Whether you enjoy trolling big water in a boat with a dozen or so lines out, or the peace of cruising your favorite waters in a one-man boat, this film was produced with your success in mind. His methods are universal and can be used anywhere on any species of fish.
19-072 42 min. $29.95

How, When, & Where to Catch Bass with John Fox
Learn to become a master bass fisherman from the Pro's Pro, John Fox. Helpful hints on the right locations, high tech electronics and much more. "How, When & Where to Catch Bass" is a fisherman's "must-have" video.
19-8009 117 min. $19.95

Ice Fishing
Wisconsin guide and fishing educator Tom Newbauer runs you through an A to Z hard water primer. Segments include making lures, picking a spot, jigging, tip-ups, and even an on-the-ice hot lunch.
19-8023 72 min. $39.95

In Pursuit of Salmon: The Hakai Experience
This film shows the huge chinook salmon of British Columbia's wilderness Hakai Pass. It also details how to catch these exciting 50-pound (and heavier) world-class trophy fish with cut-plug herring on the lightest of sport fishing tackle.
19-240 60 min. $29.95

Insider's Guide to Bass Fishing
Marlin Gibbs and Keith Clow show where quality bass are found and other bass fishing tips.
19-2935 40 min. $19.95

Insider's Guide to Salmon Fishing
Learn how to combine natural bait with artificial lures, how to cure roe to keep it fresh, and many other tricks and techniques, hosted by Marlin Gibbs.
19-2933 40 min. $19.95

Insider's Guide to Trout Fishing
Marlin Gibbs teaches you how to rig a weight that you make yourself, how to fish with roe, and the most ingenious method ever invented for threading an nightcrawler.
19-2934 40 min. $19.95

Introduction to Structure Fishing for Bass
Begins with what structure is and then tells you how to find it and fish it.
19-2394 60 min. $49.95

John Fox's How, When and Where to Catch Bass

A complete guide to bass fishing: bass locating secrets, catching techniques, equipment selection, and much more, plus highlights of great bass fishing moments. Perfect program for beginner and expert.
19-2266 60 min. $29.95

Look, Mom, I'm Fishing

Get the whole family out fishing right away! Tim Manion shows how to keep fishing inexpensive, uncomplicated and fun. Packed with instruction and information, this video is aimed at the non-expert, but even experienced anglers will pick up new tips.
19-1831 40 min. $19.95

Mayfly

A complete guide to the most advanced techniques available to the modern fly-fisherman. Hal Janssen reveals his techniques for tying and fishing all the stages of the mayfly, the most popular insect used in fly-fishing today. Also an in-depth biology of the mayfly life cycle and explosive fishing action.
19-124 60 min. $39.95

Muskie Fishing Magic

Learn the techniques the nation's best muskie fishing guides use - on North America's finest muskie waters.
19-050 55 min. $49.95

Northern Pike Fishing in the West

Learn about the lures and tackle you need to land these monster freshwater barracuda.
19-2750 45 min. $19.95

Nymphing with Gary Borger

A streamside lesson in the best techniques to catch trout subsurface, where they do 90% of their feeding.
19-051 30 min. $59.95

Quest for the Record

Secrets to trophy fishing in the famous Flaming Gorge Lake in Utah. Learn where to go, what to use, when to go, and what methods are the most successful.
19-2686 60 min. $39.95

Sailfish Technique

Learn methods of rigging natural and artificial baits along with essential information on techniques. A must have for sailfishers.
19-8152 60 min. $29.95

Secrets for Catching Walleye

Babe Winkelman takes you further into his secret world of consistently catching this exciting sportfish of the north. He will show you how to work his special rigs that have made him the tournament champion he is. He covers new ways to rig live bait, work spinners, crankbaits and soft-plastic lures.
19-074 30 min. $29.95

Secrets of Spinner Bait Success with Ken Cook

Drawing on his experience as the first $100,000 Super B.A.S.S. tournament winner and over 13 years as a fisheries biologist, Ken Cook covers all aspects of fishing spinner baits. Finding bass in heavily covered areas. Common mistakes in spinner bait selection. How to cast and retrieve spinner baits for best results.
19-223 30 min. $14.95

Secrets of Steelheading

Experienced fishing guide Marlin Gibbs shares his expertise and knowledge of the four basic elements of trout fishing: preparation, locating the fish rigging, presentation of the bait, and hooking and landing the fish--all in a simple and concise manner. Both the beginning and the experienced fisherman will benefit from the basic procedures and insider tips that give the extra edge!
19-125 40 min. $19.95

Shark Fishing Made Easy

Catching one of these babies is easier than you think! In this video, you'll learn all about the special tackle, baits and equipment needed for shark fishing.
19-8064 40 min. $29.95

Smallmouth Bass

Increase your fishing success by using the methods experts use in lakes and rivers to consistently take smallmouth.
19-063 30 min. $39.95

Steelheading 1: A Primer

To freshwater sports fishermen, steelheading is the ultimate challenge. It may take up to two years to learn all the skills necessary to catch these fighting fish, and many steelheaders prefer to hoard their hard-won knowledge. Here, at last, is on master fisherman who tells it all.
19-238 60 min. $29.95

Striper Fishing with Charlie Mayes

Charlie Mayes has packed this 30-minute video with a wealth of information on striper fishing. Charlie covers all the bases for the beginner and has some important tips for the pros, such as using live bait and artificial lures. What is the best and most durable tackle for striper fishing? How important are electronics in striper fishing? How to locate big schools of stripers.
19-224 30 min. $14.95

VIDEO TITLES LISTED IN THIS GUIDE ARE AVAILABLE FOR PURCHASE OR RENTAL. CONTACT YOUR LOCAL VIDEO STORE OR TELEPHONE (800) 383-8811

Surface Lures & Buzz Baits
Learn exciting top water techniques for taking bass. Watch surface busting action and see how you can improve your top water fishing.
19-077 30 min. $49.95

To Catch a Thrill
This unique, first-of-its-kind provides insight into different fishing techniques and seldom-seen fish. First-ever underwater film in 35mm color. See for yourself the many kinds of fishing surprises and the best fishing in North and South America, both fresh and saltwater. The program took five years to produce and includes almost every type of fish known to man, from sunfish to shark, sturgeon, chad, piranha and many more. See the pros taking catfish by hand or out of hollow logs and the southern caller who actually summons fish to his boat and bait! Over 40 types of fishing covered. You won't believe it until you've seen it.
19-091 100 min. $39.95

Top 100 Fishing Tips
If you're hungry for information, this is the tape for you. Learn all the quick tips to bringing them in! No matter what waters you fish, this information will help you do one thing--catch more fish!
19-8121 55 min. $29.95

Trolling for Saltwater Fish
The most informative trolling excursion you will ever experience. In short, everything you'll need to insure trolling success.
19-8102 60 min. $29.95

Tuna, Tuna, Tuna
Yellowfin tuna can be the hardest fish to find and land. This video covers all the information you need to catch this highly sought after fish.
19-8087 40 min. $29.95

Ultimate Blue Marlin
The Blue Marlin is one of the hardest fish to catch in the sportsfishing world. This video will teach you everything you need to know to catch the ultimate prize.
19-8051 40 min. $29.95

Uncle Homer's Best Secrets for Catching More Fish
Uncle Homer shows you backlash to de-hooking your hand, rescuing a lost lure to desperation tactics and other helpful hints.
19-8124 55 min. $19.95

Understanding Bass
In this comprehensive videotape, "bass professor" Doug Hannon shows you how big bass stick to the rules more so than lesser fish. Learn the physical and sensory characteristics, learning capabilities, metabolism and feeding habits of big bass and how they absolutely determine how they track and out-maneuver prey, and how you can use this knowledge to catch the Big One. Doug has caught over 400 bass exceeding 10 pounds each.
19-089 60 min. $49.95

Walleye Strategies
Dave Embry teams up with Earl Mockellky of Black Bear Island Lake Lodge. He will show you all his secrets for catching big walleye.
19-6485 30 min. $14.95

Walleye Fishing Basics
Gain a better understanding of the walleye. Learn proven methods for fishing lakes, rivers and structure, and how to change your techniques to match water and weather conditions.
19-082 60 min. $49.95

Way of a Trout
A fly-fishing classic! Gives you insight into the habits of the trout.
19-083 30 min. $49.95

Wet Fly and Nymph
Hal Janssen discloses his theories and methods for some of the most rewarding fly-fishing you'll ever experience.
19-044 90 min. $39.95

Why Fish Strike! Why They Don't!
Charlie White takes anglers underwater clearly showing, in slow motion, what happens at the exact moment a fish strikes.
19-8007 83 min. $19.95

Worm Fishing Techniques
There really are no secrets to successfully fishing plastic worms-just good equipment, proper techniques and a little experience. In this video you'll see first hand how to choose proper equipment and learn new techniques for worm fishing.
19-198 30 min. $14.95

Miscellaneous

Beginnings
The story of how and where the world's greatest sportsfishing began. The north part of Tropical Australia is teeming with fish, including marlin, and you'll see amazing footage from the 50's that

will prove it.
19-8074 60 min. $29.95

Encyclopedia of Saltwater Sport Fish
This excellent production will answer your
questions regarding fish identification, locations,
patterns, and most importantly how to catch forty-
eight of the most popular sport fish around
the country.
19-8104 60 min. $29.95

National Fishing Tackle Museum
The seasoned fisherman will find this filled with
artifacts of the past, bringing back memories from
long ago. For the novice, it will be useful resource
for future fishing.
19-1784 50 min. $29.95

**SPORTSMAN'S VIDEO
COLLECTION, TROUT SERIES:**
A book is included with each tape in this series
about trout fishing

• **Fishing the dry fly**
19-259 42 min. $49.95

• **Basic fly-casting**
19-260 42 min. $49.95

• **Advanced fly-casting**
19-261 42 min. $49.95

• **Strategies for selective trout**
19-262 42 min. $49.95

• **Advanced strategies for selective trout**
19-263 42 min. $49.95

• **Anatomy of a trout stream**
19-264 42 min. $49.95

• **Fly-fishing for Pacific steelhead**
19-265 42 min. $49.95

• **Advanced fly-fishing for Pacific
steelhead**
19-266 42 min. $49.95

• **Fly-fishing for trophy steelhead**
19-276 42 min. $49.95

Don't Let The Big Ones

Get Away!

These Videos Will Show You

Where The Fish Are Biting And

How They Can Be Caught.

VIDEO TITLES LISTED IN THIS GUIDE ARE AVAILABLE FOR PURCHASE
OR RENTAL. CONTACT YOUR LOCAL VIDEO STORE OR TELEPHONE **(800) 383-8811**

New

Special Interest Video Titles

Become Available

Often.

Please Inquire

If A Title Or Subject

You Are Looking For

Is Not Listed.

VIDEO TITLES LISTED IN THIS GUIDE ARE AVAILABLE FOR PURCHASE
OR RENTAL. CONTACT YOUR LOCAL VIDEO STORE OR TELEPHONE (800) 383-8811

Games
&
Magic

- ✓ *Board Games*
- ✓ *Card Games*
- ✓ *Gambling & Betting*
- ✓ *Juggling & Clowning*
- ✓ *Magic*
- ✓ *Miscellaneous*

Board Games

Doorways to Horror

The thrills and spine-tingling chills of the classic Hollywood horror movies with stars such as Bela Lugosi, Boris Karloff and Lon Chaney have been captured in this exciting game. Trapped in a hunted estate, the players vie to capture vampires, monsters, werewolves and other creatures of the night, while trying to amass the most gold.
17-074 42 min. $39.95

Isaac Asimov's Robots VCR Mystery Game

The master of science fiction turned all his creativity toward creating this intriguing, exhilarating video game. It starts with a mystery and brings to life an epic conflict among earthlings, aliens and robots. With over thirty different solutions, it's a game that will fascinate for years!
17-5619 40 min. $19.95

PLAY CHESS SERIES

This series presents a clear explanation of the game of chess: the pieces, the board, the basic moves and key terms.
Featuring International Chess Master, Vince Cambridge.

• Volume I
17-9480 50 min. $19.99

• Volume II
17-9481 65 min. $19.99

Pro Chess: Novice to Intermediate
17-2721 120 min. $29.95

Pro Chess: Intermediate to Advanced
17-2722 120 min. $29.95

Card Games

Bridge Lessons From Shelley De Satnick

Learn the fundamentals of standard American bridge from the top New York bridge instructor. You play as the "fourth," learning bidding, scoring and basic strategy.
17-007 60 min. $29.95

Casino Gaming

Don't go near a casino without viewing this tape! This is the best approach to casino gaming in trying to buck the odds. It teaches self control, self respect, win/lose profits, techniques of winning and gaming plans.
17-009 50 min. $29.95

How to Read Playing Cards: Beginning Level

This program includes step-by-step instructions for interpreting the cards, examples of actual readings, techniques for laying out and reading the cards, plus much more.
17-2121 60 min. $39.95

Kids N' Cards

This is a fun, entertaining and educational means by which to teach children to play several popular children's card games: Crazy Eights, Go Fish!, War and Train Solitaire. This video was designed in a manner that children see as a simple and fun way to learn games.
17-8039 45 min. $16.95

LEARNING BRIDGE THE RIGHT WAY

It's time to learn that sensational game over 40 million Americans play. Lee Henry will show you how easy it is in this personal tutorial. Take private lessons from Lee as he guides you through the rudiments of the game in the first volume. In the advanced volume, Lee show you how to put more power into your game with his winning strategies and new techniques.

• Bridge the Social Gap with Cards
17-094 60 min. $19.95

• Winning Strategies for Advanced Players
17-095 60 min. $19.95

Play Bridge with Omar Sharif

Play bridge with Omar Sharif and Grand Master Dorothy Hayden Truscott in this exciting video experience that takes you through step-by-step bidding and play off of 15 challenging games. Each hand was selected to demonstrate a wide variety of techniques and strategies. You'll learn how to establish an early game plan and take control, how and when to use the classic bidding conventions, the advantages of a short suit, the secret of finding a fit with your partner's hand, how to master the rough and the finesse, plus much more.
17-042 55 min. $29.95

Win at Bridge

Player on the U.S. World Championship team and author of 14 books on bridge, Eddie Kantar tells all

---

the tricks experienced players use to locate key honor cards and finesse them right out of their opponents' hands.

17-092 60 min. $29.95

Gambling & Betting

Business of Blackjack
Powerfully effective training techniques are used in this presentation to teach you how to play a winning game of blackjack. The basic strategy of play and count strategy are taught with high-tech electronically generated Video Flash cards, the most efficient memory training tool available. Although valuable information for the beginner is included and highly recommended, this video is geared for the intermediate and advanced players.

17-8002 40 min. $29.95

Casino Gaming: Business Persons Guide to Gaming
Learn the real odds and how to put them to work for you. Taken seriously, this tape will help change your approach to more profitable casino gaming.

17-8014 50 min. $39.95

Casino Survival Kit
A beginner's guide to blackjack, roulette and craps. Covers the rules, procedures and betting options for each game, as well as simplified playing strategies for the entry-level player. Each package contains a unique set of "survival cards" for in-casino use.

17-8020 45 min. $24.95

Charting the Tables
An important treatment of one of the most underrated and neglected aspects of casino gambling-and one of John Patrick's most important disciplines. Examines the techniques expert players use to isolate favorable betting situations by illustrating actual playing sequences in blackjack, roulette and craps.

17-8019 60 min. $39.95

College Football Handicapping
Start the season right with John Patrick's in-depth video on college football (contains more than a dozen proven handicapping strategies) plus an advance scouting report for early season use. An unbeatable combination.

17-8026 90 min. $39.95

Day at the Greyhound Races
This video features racing footage and offers in-depth interviews and tips from track officials, greyhound owners and trainers and a professional handicapper. This is designed to teach consumers how to get the most out of their visits to any of the 63 tracks around the country.

17-8001 41 min. $29.95

Harness Racing
An indispensable guide to sensible harness race handicapping for the novice to intermediate player. John Patrick and track analyst Alan Mitchell discuss the theories expert players use to isolate winners. Contains a special segment with famous money winning driver, Herve Filion.

17-8025 60 min. $39.95

Horse Racing I
This tape is about handicapping the races. It shows you how to use the Daily Racing Form to analyze the races the way the professionals do.

17-8006 30 min. $39.95

How To of Horse Race Wagers
Bine Master, an expert in the horse racing industry, will instruct you on how to place bets, and how to understand the different types of bets.

17-2723 19 min. $29.95

Learn to Play to Win: The Basics
This tape is designed to help increase your odds of winning by playing the game of black jack properly. It will also help eliminate first time player's embarrassment and confidence in approaching any table. Hosted by Jimmy "The Scot" Jordan.

17-8003 58 min. $19.95

LEARN HOW TO WIN SERIES:

• Advanced Blackjack (Card Counting)
Counting cards is easier than you think! In just a few hours of study and a little practice with John Patrick's simplified, easy-to-follow methods, you can learn the counting techniques and money management methods expert players use to beat the house.

17-8022 60 min. $39.95

• Advanced Craps II (Super Craps)
Expansion and elaboration on sophisticated playing and hedging concepts introduced in Advanced Craps I. (See 17-8016)

17-2991 85 min. $39.95

• Baccarat
John Patrick shows how to win by demonstrating proven money management systems through actual playing situations.

17-2990 60 min. $39.95

• Blackjack
John Patrick, professional gambler, cautions that blackjack is one game you shouldn't play unless you know what you're doing. This tape gives you the knowledge, discipline and money management skills necessary to perfect your basic strategy and become a more consistent winner.
17-083 60 min. $39.95

• Craps
John Patrick teaches you how to win at craps. In this tape, you'll learn the basic theory of right betting, how and when to play the odds, and how to maximize your returns on place bets. You will gain the knowledge and skills you need to minimize the house edge and come out a winner.
17-082 60 min. $39.95

• Craps: Intermediate
For the player who is ready to learn more advanced betting and money management techniques.
17-8028 60 min. $39.95

• Craps: Advanced
For the experienced player, John Patrick reveals the sophisticated hedge bets and money management methods he uses to reduce the house edge.
17-8016 60 min. $39.95

• Draw Poker
Actual playing situations are used to illustrate the "Big 6" of poker: Tactics, Knowledge, Deception, Money, Management, Psychology, and Guts.
17-8029 60 min. $39.95

• Seven Card Stud Poker
Actual game simulations are used to demonstrate tactics and playing strategy.
17-8030 75 min. $39.95

• Video Poker
Analyzes the various kinds of machines in Atlantic City and Nevada and how the differences in their pay-tables affects the house edge.
17-8031 60 min. $39.95

• Roulette
Professional gambler John Patrick says there are no guarantees, but if you follow his step-by-step advice, starting with the "Big 4"-bankroll, knowledge of the game money management and discipline and then move on the "Little 3"-logic, theory and trends you'll have a simple formula for success
17-081 60 min. $39.95

• Roulette: Advanced
Introduces a variety of playing strategies favored by expert roulette players, including off-shoots of the

Action Number system, the Z system, the Labouchere and the 31 .
17-8021 60 min. $39.95

• Slots
John Patrick, a professional gambler, hosts this tape about slots. It's been created with one goal in mind-to teach you to win.
17-2423 60 min. $39.95

• Lottery Video
Learn the techniques experienced lottery players use to improve their chances of winning a major lottery.
17-8023 45 min. $24.95

• Pai Gow Poker
John Patrick teams up with expert Bill Zender to bring you a rare insight into this popular card game. All aspects are covered.
17-8018 60 min. $39.95

• Pai Gow Poker: Charting the Tables
17-8019 60 min. $39.95

Poker with the Joker
What do celebrity couples Jo Anne Worley & Roger Perry and Fred & Mary Willard do when they get together and want to have fun? They play poker. But not just ordinary poker, they play all the wild and unusual games demonstrated in this fun video.
17-8015 40 min. $19.95

Pro Blackjack
Blackjack is the first and only game in the history of organized casino gaming that can be systematically won, and this home video course teaches you how.
17-019 120 min. $24.95

Pro Football
A comprehensive guide to successful pro football handicapping from basic fundamentals to advanced statistical theory. Covers John Patrick's personal handicapping approach, his teaser method, and money management system.
17-8027 90 min. $39.95

Secrets of Winning Sweepstakes
This program analyzes why and how sweepstakes are run as well as how you can increase your chances of winning prizes. Created in conjunction with the editorial staff of the Contest News-Letter, whose readers have won millions of dollars of prizes annually.
17-8011 49 min. $16.95

VIDEO TITLES LISTED IN THIS GUIDE ARE AVAILABLE FOR PURCHASE OR RENTAL. CONTACT YOUR LOCAL VIDEO STORE OR TELEPHONE (800) 383-8811

Secret to Blackjack
Learn how to enhance the odds of coming home a winner with this easy, new technique from one of America's most successful blackjack players.
17-2249 40 min. $29.95

Secret to Poker
Maximize your skill and become a consistent winner at the major forms of poker. Learn your opponent's telltale signs and how to gain control of the game.
17-2250 50 min. $29.95

Secrets To Slots
17-6139 60 min. $29.95

Texas Hold'em Poker
Learn to play and bet with confidence as you master the fundamental strategies used by expert players. Watch as hands are played and analyzed.
17-8009 52 min. $29.95

Thoroughbred Horse Racing
John Patrick teams up with Rick Lang, track analyst for the New York Post, to show you how to interpret the past performance charts to pick winners.
17-8024 110 min. $39.95

Winning at Blackjack
It's now possible to learn the professional game of blackjack in less than an hour simply by watching your television. Let Glenn Porter show you how.
17-8017 30 min. $19.95

Juggling & Clowning

Jugglercise
Join Professor Confidence and a dozen of his out of shape friends as they take you step-by-step through twelve exciting music videos.
17-8010 30 min. $16.95

Juggletime
Children learn to juggle with a scarf by following the lead of Professor Confidence. Ages 6-11.
17-9280 26 min. $19.95

Juggler's Jam
Learn to juggle and manipulate rings, clubs, cigar boxes, diabolo, devil stick, ball spinning and five balls with Professor Confidence and his friends.
17-9282 30 min. $19.95

Juggling Star
Learn to juggle three and four balls or beanbags with Professor Confidence and his young friends as they take you step- by-step through twelve music videos.
17-9281 30 min. $19.95

Juggling Step-By-Step
This instructional and entertaining tape covers every aspect of juggling. Includes instruction in scarves, bean bags, balls, rings, clubs, cigar boxes, top hats, spinning balls and torches. It also covers passing and advanced skills with four to eight objects.
17-056 120 min. $29.95

Let's Juggle
Virtually anyone can learn the basics of juggling with this entertaining and clearly demonstrated tape. Improves eye-hand coordination, rhythm, timing and reflexes while developing confidence through the learning of new skills. Includes set of 3 custom mako juggling balls.
17-6627 60 min. $34.95

T-Bone's World of Clowning
Explore the world of clowning with T-Bone and his friends as they laugh and share the basic principles of clowning. Juggling, balloon animals and characterization are just some of the topics covered in this educational and highly entertaining program. Through T-Bone's special blend of magic, he informs and mystifies as he brings out the clown in all of us. Great for children ages 5-9 or adults who resist "growing up!"
17-061 35 min. $29.95

Magic

AMAZING THINGS SERIES
He's a magician. He's a prankster. He's the life of every child's party and he's bringing his Amazing Things to home video. Dr. Misterio hosts this pair of creative interactive, make-it-yourself videotapes in which children are taught how to transform simple, household items into spellbinding objects of fantasy. Whether he's demonstrating how a bleach bottle can become a powerboat or simply dangling a spoon off his nose, Dr. Misterio encourages the child to participate in the creative process. This tape was made for every child who has ever wondered "How did he do that?" Perfect for birthday parties, Sundays and rainy afternoons.

• **Volume 1**
17-051 60 min. $19.95

• **Volume 2**
17-052 60 min. $19.95

Be a Magician Video Learning Kit
Master magician Martin Preston demonstrates on stage in full costume his feats of illusion. Then he takes you backstage to explain the "trick of the trick." The one-hour program is segmented to present each trick as a separate step. Magic equipment includes a magic wand, cards, sponge balls, metal rings, rope and laces.
17-063 54 min. $19.95

Blockbuster Magic
Wonderama's Bob McAllister stars on this new videotape that will give you hours of fun. Learn how to amaze the kids with these sleight of hand tricks. Seventeen tricks in all, showing side, and front views in slow motion, and with detailed instructions. Remember! Never reveal how they're done!
17-005 30 min. $14.95

Balloonacy
This colorful video features 18 balloon animals, each made step-by-step before your eyes. The illustrated book compliments the video and shows you how to make an additional 12 balloon animals. That's a total of 30 balloon animals!
17-5385 40 min. $24.95

Card Magic
In this video Mr. Hassini will teach you, step-by-step, a fascinating selection of card tricks. Also he will show how to make your own magical props. Within minutes of viewing this video, you will be performing amazing card tricks with an ordinary deck of cards.
17-5631 30 min. $16.95

Kids Video Magic
A child's introduction to the fine art of magic. The child will be able to put on their own magic show. The video comes with a magic wand and an official handbook. Kid's love it! Recommended for kids ages 6-12.
17-8005 30 min. $16.95

Learn How To Do Magic With Ordinary Objects You Have At Home
Mr. Hassini will teach you how to do tricks with cards, coins, paper, ropes, and other small objects that you have around the house. And the Famous Cut and Restored Newspaper Trick. You will learn a complete magic act (requires no skill) you can do right after viewing.
17-5638 40 min. $16.95

Learn The Secrets Of Magic From The World's Six Best Magicians
You will learn from Paul Harris, Frank Garcia, David Roth, Derek Dingle, Bernard Bills, Tony Hassini. Each will fascinate you with an amazing trick. Then, each will teach you step-by-step, how to perform these amazing tricks.
17-5640 40 min. $16.95

Magic Secrets with Steve Dacri
All ages, 8 to 80, will love this fascinating videotape starring magician and actor, Steve Dacri, who has been on "That's Incredible", the Merv Griffin Show and has appeared with Bob Hope and Steve Martin. Watch as Steve performs spellbinding magic feats and baffling illusions for magicians, aspiring magicians and audiences everywhere. Then go behind the scenes as Steve reveals the masters' secrets with expert, step-by-step instruction. Includes magic trick props and gimmicks, including those for the "Magic Bunny," "Rabbit in the Hat," "Rope Mystery," "Triple Coincidence" and many more.
17-015 60 min. $24.95

Magic That's Fun! An Introduction Into the World of Magic
An introduction into the world of magic is an interactive and educational way for kids to learn basic magic effects using everyday household items. The program is broken into easy-to-learn segments. Each segment shows a magic trick in performance and then teaches how the trick was done.
17-8000 30 min. $19.95

Magic: The Sleeveless Way
Learn simple magic tricks in detail, to amaze and astound the kids and your friends. Follow the three "P's" and you'll be a magician in no time at all!
17-016 47 min. $29.95

Mr. Wizard's World: Puzzles, Problems and Impossibilities
In this video, Don Herbert (TV's Mr. Wizard) uses a few common household objects--a drinking straw, scissors and string-to create optical illusions and puzzles. Tape may be stopped for step-by-step guidance in duplicating stunts such as pulling a tablecloth off a table without disturbing anything or jumping through an 8 1/2" by 11" piece of paper. Close-captioned for the hearing impaired.
10-420 46 min. $19.95

Party Magic For Fun Or Profit!
In this video, Mr. Hassini will teach you a fascinating selection of party tricks that you will be able to perform at parties. These tricks will light up any party, and put a smile on everyone's face.
17-5639 40 min. $16.95

Sleight of Hand with Derek Dingle

Sleight of hand card tricks are simple when you learn them from Derek Dingle-the man Time magazine called "the greatest card manipulator in the world." Derek will teach you all about equipment, card control, misdirection of attention, forcing, top change and lots of card tricks themselves.
17-024 60 min. $39.95

Miscellaneous

Basic Handwriting Analysis

Learn how your handwriting reveals the secrets of your personality through slant, base line and pressure. The tape includes full instructions on identifying emotional responsiveness and moods from the handwriting. Learn to recognize an analytical, intuitive, or methodical thinker by merely glancing at a writing sample.
17-106 60 min. $39.95

Cruel Tricks for Dear Friends

America's foremost rip-off artistes show you how to use your VCR to pull seven mean-spirited practical jokes.
17-2256 60 min. $19.95

Frisbee Disc Video

It floats! It flies! It produces pure fun out of thin air! It's Frisbee, America's favorite outdoor toy, and now there's a video to help you master it. "Crazy John" Brooks, World Frisbee Champion, guides you step-by-step from basic catching and throwing to games like Disc Golf, Guts, and Ultimate Frisbee. Packaged with a free official Wham-o Frisbee.
17-5622 35 min. $19.95

How to Play Pool with Minnesota Fats

Learn how to play pool from the king. Instructional as well as highly entertaining with a special guest appearance by Waylon Jennings.
17-053 60 min. $19.95

HOW TO SCORE MORE POINTS ON NINTENDO GAMES

Nintendo is the home entertainment phenomenon of the decade whose popularity is still soaring. Every player will want to share the inside tips and tricks provided by these videos for increasing point-scoring skills. Take advantage of the secret clues obtained directly from the game companies.

• Volume 1

Top Gun, Wizards & Warriors, Platoon, Mega Man 2, Metal Gear.
17-5620 34 min. $14.95

• Volume 2

Blaster Master, Double Dragon, Simon's Quest, WrestleMania, Town & Country, Surf Designs.
17-5621 23 min. $14.95

MASTER POOL TECHNIQUES

• Power Pool
17-6132 58 min. $39.95

• Pool School
17-6133 61 min. $39.95

• Trick Shots
17-6134 49 min. $39.95

Rich Little's Great Hollywood Trivia Game

Play Trivia by video?! Sure! With this entertaining videogame hosted by comic Rich Little and his famous Hollywood "friends"- his impressions of Bogart, Grant, Wayne and many others. Over 200 questions, ranging from movie musicals to TV sitcoms, for your enjoyment and edification.
17-021 60 min. $59.95

SECRET VIDEOGAME TRICKS

• Codes & Strategies I

Tricks for twenty-two games, including Simon's Quest, Contra, Blaster Master, Adventure Island, Rambo, Metal Gear, Adventures of Lolo, Star Soldier, Double Dragon, Life Force, and Iron Tank.
17-5810 60 min. $19.95

• Codes & Strategies II

P.O.W., Milon's Secret Castle, Ironsword, Twin Cobra, Rambo, Guerrilla War, Silkworm, Three Stooges, Airwolf, and Thundercade.
17-5811 40 min. $14.95

• Codes & Strategies III

Wrestlemania, Bad Dudes, Ikari Warrior II, Operation Wolf, The Guardian Legend, Demon Sword, Bubble Bobble, Baseball Simulator, and Sky Shark.
17-5812 40 min. $14.95

Video Bingo

America's favorite game is now on video! "Video Bingo" contains everything you will need to play for hours and hours, and with over 500 game variations! Comes with bingo markers and game

---

cards, packaged in a resealable case for easy storage.
17-027 120 min. $29.95

Video Guide to Creative Revenge
This program shows you over 50 hilarious, all purpose, non-violent revenge tactics. In this professionally produced, 1 hour feature you'll see how to turn the tables on anyone who's hurt or betrayed you.
17-8040 60 min. $24.95

Yo-Yo Man Instructional Video
In the talented hands of Tommy Smothers, one of the world's oldest toys becomes a brand new sensation. As the hilarious "Yo-Yo Man", Tommy shows you how to yo-yo like a pro-from basic techniques to amazing tricks.
17-5611 33 min. $19.95

Frustrated By Being
The Dummy At Bridge?

Some Of These Videos
Can Help You
Bid For Success!

VIDEO TITLES LISTED IN THIS GUIDE ARE AVAILABLE FOR PURCHASE OR RENTAL. CONTACT YOUR LOCAL VIDEO STORE OR TELEPHONE (800) 383-8811

Gardening

- ✓ *Indoor*
- ✓ *Outdoor*
- ✓ *Miscellaneous*

Indoor

Design with Plants

Television's most popular gardener and plant enthusiast, Ed Hume, shows you how to create a delightful environment using a variety of houseplants. Learn to select healthy plants, provide them enough moisture and humidity, nip nasty insects and diseases in the bud, propagate your plants properly, and feed them the nutrients they need to thrive. Ed demonstrates the pinch-and-save method to groom your plants and gives you tips on how to obtain cuttings to start new ones.

16-026 57 min. $19.95

Hydroponics: Set Up, Care & Maintenance

This is a step-by-step instructional video on home hydroponics. This comprehensive video teaches you everything you need to know to get started and growing hydroponically, pesticide and herbicide free, using a minimum of space and water.

16-8022 24 min. $29.95

Mr. Green Thumb's Guide to Successful House Plants

Stan DeFreitas (Mr. Green Thumb) presents his informative and fun approach to plant growth, covering a number of indoor plants and more.

16-8008 60 min. $29.95

Outdoor

Alternative Pest Control

If you'd rather not use chemicals in your garden, this tape is for you. John Bryan discusses the dangers and disadvantages of chemical sprays while suggesting natural alternatives for controlling pests. Learn how to order and release insect predictors like the ladybug and preying mantis and how to use natural products and even plants to fight insects.

16-2342 28 min. $19.95

Art of Landscaping: Design

Howard Garrett, widely read author and landscape architect, applies his creative flair in this dynamic informational video. His maverick philosophy that "rules are made to be broken" helps the homeowner address his own needs and desires--

regardless of geographic location.

16-1588 52 min. $29.95

Art of Landscaping: Shopping

This video takes the homeowner on a guided shopping trip through a nursery explaining in detail the specific differences between good and bad plants, container sizes, soil amendments, and working with nursery personnel. This video can save the landscape do-it-yourselfer valuable time and money in addition to helping avoid the frustration of ineffective shopping.

16-1589 30 min. $19.95

Blue Ribbon Veggies

Ed Fume shows you the simple steps to successful vegetable gardening. See and hear about using the wide row method; tilling and cultivating; slug and insect control; effective watering methods; and how to grow corn, peas, berries, beans, tomatoes, potatoes, asparagus and many other nutritious crops abundantly.

16-012 60 min. $16.95

Children's Garden Project

Children, educators and parents will enjoy this video visit to a children's garden, a summer recreation program which teaches the magic and mystery of gardening. How to set up, coordinate and make gardening fun for kids are detailed during the video and in the accompanying booklet.

16-8007 20 min. $29.95

Custom Landscaping

In this program you will learn the basic of lawn care and how to landscape your yard. Ed Hume discusses indoor and outdoor plants, and how to plant and take care of them properly. Learn about hanging baskets, the right way to start seeds in your flower and vegetable gardens, and the right way to water and weed for the best results.

16-003 53 min. $19.95

Exclusive Lawns

This program teaches you how to seed your own lawn and how to maintain it. Topics covered include liming and moss control, raking, thatching, mowing, trimming and more.

16-020 48 min. $19.95

First Time Garden

How well does your garden grow? Develop a green thumb with the help of this information-packed video, which traces the transformation of a bare and muddy building site to a flourishing garden.

16-5741 91 min. $29.95

Fun With Herbs

This program covers planning and planting an herb garden, drying, preserving and cooking with herbs,

wreath-making, pot pierre, herbal cosmetics and much more. Short interludes between segments offer additional useful tips, for example, on soil testing and using "good" insects to control harmful insects without the use of pesticides. Hosted by well known lecturer and teacher, Beverly Fennell.
16-8023 60 min. $24.95

Garden Pruning
Ed Hume shows you how, when, where and why to prune your trees. You will learn what tools to use and professional methods for pruning a wide variety of trees and bushes.
16-024 56 min. $14.95

Garden: Annuals/Hanging Baskets
Annuals are plants that grow, flower, go to seed and die in one year, and are often the plants that add the most beauty to your garden. Ed Hume shows you the black-eyed Susan, lobelia, sweet peas, coleus and many other blooming annuals, and demonstrates the proper way to pinch them to encourage growth and control direction. Many other helpful hints.
16-001 38 min. $19.95

Gardening And Insects
Linda Naeve, horticulture associate, and Ken Holscher, entomologist, discuss insect infestation of garden plants and harvesting garden vegetables.
16-6853 28 min. $39.95

Ground Covers
Ground cover plants serve many uses in your flower garden. Learn how to grow and direct juniper, English ivy, boxwoods and many more. Ed Hume is your host.
16-011 60 min. $19.95

Landscape Gardening
Extension ornamental horticulturist Jim Midcap answers questions on selecting ornamental trees, shrubs, annual and perennial flowers planting techniques, and maintenance practices such as pruning and fertilization.
16-6851 28 min. $39.95

LANDSCAPING VIDEO GUIDE SERIES
Tom Lied is a landscape architect nationally known for his design ability and for his commitment to construction excellence. Tom's excellent step-by-step instruction will give you the knowledge and confidence you need to successfully complete your landscaping projects.

- **Design, Soil Preparation & Planting**
  16-8009 60 min. $39.95

- **Lawn Installation and Maintenance**
  16-8010 60 min. $39.95

- **Pruning and Plant Care**
  16-8011 60 min. $39.95

- **Roses & Bulbs**
  16-8012 60 min. $39.95

- **Garden Steps/Landscaping Steep Slopes**
  16-8013 60 min. $39.95

- **Patios and Decks**
  16-8014 60 min. $39.95

- **Fences and Hedges**
  16-8015 60 min. $39.95

- **Stone and Wooden Walls**
  16-8016 60 min. $39.95

- **Low Maintenance Landscapes**
  16-8017 60 min. $39.95

- **Garden Pools/Berm Gardens**
  16-8018 60 min. $39.95

- **Selecting Fruit Trees and Shade Trees**
  16-8019 60 min. $39.95

- **Managing Wooded Lots**
  16-8020 60 min. $39.95

Lawn Care with The Garden Doctor
This video covers such subjects as soil conditioning, proper nutrition, pest disease control, getting rid of weeds, properly watering and mowing lawns for a healthy and green lawn.
16-9672 30 min. $19.95

MASTER GARDENER SERIES:

- **Maintaining Landscape Shrubs And Evergreens**
  16-6845 22 min. $39.95

- **Maintaining Landscape Trees**
  16-6846 17 min. $39.95

- **Plant Pathology**
  16-6847 29 min. $39.95

- **Selecting And Planting Landscape Plants**
  16-6848 19 min. $39.95

VIDEO TITLES LISTED IN THIS GUIDE ARE AVAILABLE FOR PURCHASE OR RENTAL. CONTACT YOUR LOCAL VIDEO STORE OR TELEPHONE (800) 383-8811

• Tree Growth And Identification
16-6849 20 min. $39.95

Organic Gardener
This method produces healthier plants with high yields in small areas through manageable techniques which can be mastered by anyone interested in gardening. Master gardener Loren Burkhart takes you through the steps of preparing raised beds, demonstrates planting methods, and covers important elements of successful gardening such as composting, fertilization of beds, double digging, bed layout, companion planting and transplanting. This method of gardening results in a larger growing season, and produces more vegetables in less space with less work and less water.
16-034 30 min. $24.95

Perennial Gardening
A novice or veteran perennial flower gardener will enjoy the information and fun of designing an island, building a small rock wall, soil preparation and planting, plus easy methods of plant and bulb propagation. Planting guidebook included.
16-051 60 min. $19.95

Pest and Diseases
John Bryan discusses the effect of various plant diseases, then takes you shopping for some of the common remedies for home pest and disease problems. You'll learn which insecticides are correct for particular problems and how to use them properly.
16-2341 28 min. $19.95

Professional Planting
An in-depth look at plant propagation, from seed to tissue culture, with instructions on the planting and transplanting methods used by plant specialists at the renowned Brooklyn Botanical Gardens. An especially valuable guide for your backyard garden or front lawn landscaping.
16-022 120 min. $64.95

Professor Greenthumb's Guide to Good Gardening
16-049 60 min. $16.95

Queen's Garden
A rare and enchanting look at the Queen's Garden at Buckingham Palace.
13-466 52 min. $29.95

Spectacular Roses
The rose is one of the most popular flowers in the world. Join Ed Hume as he explains the difference between hybrid tea roses, grandifloras, pillars and the miniature roses. You will also learn how to grow climbing and tree roses; how to select and use

fertilizers; and the how to's of insect control especially for rose gardening.
16-025 47 min. $19.95

Success with Roses by the Garden Doctor
This comprehensive video teaches you visually how to choose roses, where & when to plant, condition soil, feeding, watering and pruning.
16-9673 30 min. $19.95

Vegetable Gardening Basics
Gardening is an enjoyable activity for many people. This program covers several basic aspects of gardening that can help ensure a good crop. Topics include soil management, how to plant covers, irrigation, and mulch. Linda Naeve, ISU Extension horticulture associate, narrates this program.
16-6850 19 min. $39.95

Victory Garden
Hosts Bob Thompson and Jim Wilson take you month by month through an entire year of planning, maintaining and reaping the benefits from your vegetable and flower gardens. Contains all new instructions from the original producers of the television series, "The Victory Garden."
16-028 60 min. $19.95

War of Weeds
Find out how to win the eternal battle facing every gardener...weeds! John Bryan explains when and how to beat pesky weeds. You'll learn to use cultivators and hoes to remove weeds. You will also learn two methods of composting and how to use compost material to fight weeds.
16-2340 28 min. $19.95

Waterwise Gardening
Beautiful gardens with less water. Gardening tips include: Using mulches, drip irrigation systems, soil conditions and more.
16-8006 32 min. $16.95

Miscellaneous

DISCOVERING GARDENS SERIES
This series of entertaining and informative visits to many of England's most beautiful gardens will delight you. Hosted by Gyles Brandrell and Michele Brown.

• Trelissick, Cornwall/East Lambrook, Somerset
16-8000 60 min. $29.95

VIDEO TITLES LISTED IN THIS GUIDE ARE AVAILABLE FOR PURCHASE OR RENTAL. CONTACT YOUR LOCAL VIDEO STORE OR TELEPHONE (800) 383-8811

• **Cotehele, Cornwall/Docton Mill, Devon**
16-8001 60 min. $29.95

• **Bicton Park, Devon/Mapperton, Dorset**
16-8002 60 min. $29.95

• **Stourhead, Wiltshire/Glendurgan, Cornwall**
16-8003 60 min. $29.95

• **Tresco, Isles of Sicily/Mount Edgcumbe, Cornwall**
16-8004 60 min. $29.95

• **St. Michael's Mount, Cornwall/Trewithen, Cornwall**
16-8005 60 min. $29.95

GARDENING FROM THE GROUND UP

• **Annuals, Biennials and Perennial**
Discusses many of your favorite flowers, including sweet william, delphinium, snapdragons, marigolds and petunias.
16-2357 28 min. $19.95

• **Bulbs and Rhododendrons**
Takes you shopping to demonstrate the selection of flowering bulbs and gives you tips on their cultivation and placement in the garden.
16-2356 28 min. $19.95

• **Cacti and Succulents**
Explains everything from the differences between cacti and succulents to their propagation and cultivation.
16-2361 28 min. $19.95

• **Citrus**
Takes you to a nursery specializing in citrus plants to discuss cultivation of dwarf citrus trees. Covers everything from proper growing climates and soil preparation to tips on growing and planting.
16-2355 28 min. $19.95

• **Containers**
Demonstrates how to select the correct containers for various plants and discusses the relative merits of containers made from plastic, wood, terracotta, and ceramic.
16-2346 28 min. $19.95

• **Cover-Ups**
Demonstrates how pretty cover-ups can also be practical exterior insulation against heat or cold, and how trees can be pruned to provide lovely shaded areas.
16-2365 28 min. $19.95

• **Especially from Holland**
Covers how to select tulip bulbs as well as how, where and when to plant these easily-grown flowers.
16-2360 28 min. $19.95

• **Ground Covers**
Various types of ground covers are discussed and you'll learn which ones are suitable for different purposes, and how to care for them.
16-2363 28 min. $19.95

• **Growing Roses**
Takes you from planting to pruning, and discusses the special problems for gardeners in various climates.
16-2358 28 min. $19.95

• **Herbs**
Instructs you on selection, soil requirements and uses of various herbs. Also, discover the many ornamental possibilities for herbs in your garden.
16-2353 28 min. $19.95

• **Indoor Operations**
Shows you everything from repotting and mixing soils, to watering and maintaining your house plants so they stay looking beautiful.
16-2351 28 min. $19.95

• **Landscaping**
Discusses planning and design, teaches you how to achieve an aesthetic balance by combining trees and other plants by color, texture and form.
16-2362 28 min. $19.95

• **Lawns**
Instructs you on everything from dethatching and feeding, to reseeding and returfing. Learn proper watering and fertilizing and how to repair lawn burns and depressions.
16-2364 28 min. $19.95

• **Lilies**
Teaches home gardeners how to plant and nurture lily bulbs and tells about the interesting history and significance of these splendid flowers.
16-2359 28 min. $19.95

• **Love Your Plants**
Shows you how to select the best house plants for your home and then demonstrates how to care for them properly.
16-2350 28 min. $19.95

VIDEO TITLES LISTED IN THIS GUIDE ARE AVAILABLE FOR PURCHASE OR RENTAL. CONTACT YOUR LOCAL VIDEO STORE OR TELEPHONE (800) 383-8811

• **Propagation**
Shows you various ways of propagating plants, including cuttings, layering and division.
16-2345 28 min. $19.95

• **Pruning**
Takes you shopping for the proper tools for the job, and then explores the broad aims and methods of this necessary skill.
16-2347 28 min. $19.95

• **Salad Days**
Learn how to maximize the number of vegetables per plot, tips on watering, protecting your seeds from birds, and how to use compost to grow vine vegetables.
16-2352 28 min. $19.95

• **Seeds of Spring**
Shows you how to raise flowers from seeds, care for seedlings and how to plant these seedlings in your garden.
16-2344 28 min. $19.95

• **Soils**
John Bryan discusses the advantages and disadvantages of clay and sand and various qualities of soils you are likely to find in your garden.
16-2343 28 min. $19.95

• **Unnatural Habitats**
Demonstrates the use of a hydroponic kit and shows how it enables you to grow larger plants in less time.
16-2349 28 min. $19.95

• **Vegetables**
Explains how to plan and plant various vegetable crops. Learn how to properly mix and prepare soil, and how to increase your vegetable yield.
16-2354 28 min. $19.95

• **Warmer Climates**
Looks at the amazing variety of plants that can be grown in temperate climates.
16-2348 28 min. $19.95

Old Farmer's Almanac Video
This collector's edition is jam-packed with lively humor and amazingly useful information that you and your family will love. Hosted by Willard Scott and Special Guest Star Johnathan Winters.
16-8021 52 min. $19.95

Plant Diseases And Horticulture Tips
Richard Jauron, extension horticulture associate, and Mark Gleason, extension plant pathologist, field questions on diseased house and garden plants

as well as offer handy horticulture tips.
16-6852 28 min. $39.95

Professional Techniques: Pruning, Bonsai and Dye Making
Learn the sophisticated pruning techniques used by the Brooklyn Botanical Garden; the art of growing potted dwarf trees, or bonsai; and the secrets of obtaining natural dyes from plants and trees.
16-023 120 min. $64.95

YARDENING

• **How to Care for Your Lawn**
Jeff Ball teaches proven techniques for choosing the right lawn, preparing soil, seeding a new lawn, laying sod, mowing and dethatching, controlling weeds, and giving old grass new life.
16-1514 53 min. $17.95

• **How to Design & Build a Vegetable Garden**
A step-by-step guide for building a vegetable garden that can produce 400 pounds of vegetables in just 200 square feet! Includes building a time-saving raised bed system, preparing soil, extending season, plus tips on new developments.
16-1505 53 min. $17.95

• **How to Design a Flower Garden**
Here's a lush, low-maintenance flower garden that you'll be proud of. Includes selecting the right flowers and garden site, creating an attractive layout, preparing soils, watering, mulching, and techniques to keep your garden productive.
16-1512 48 min. $17.95

• **How to Grow & Cook Fresh Herbs**
Jeff Ball teaches you how to make common dishes extraordinary by seasoning with fresh-grown herbs. You'll learn how to grow herb plants in your garden and how to make culinary magic with herbs.
16-1511 60 min. $17.95

• **How to Grow Cool-Weather Vegetables**
Now you can extend your growing season by a full three months! You'll learn how to use simple season-extending "tunnels" for an early start and a late harvest, and master nurturing methods designed especially for cool-season crops.
16-1503 57 min. $17.95

• **How to Grow Flowers**
Now you can learn the easy, time-saving way to grow beautiful flowers! Jeff Ball shows you how to plant perennial, annuals and bulbs, apply mulch, water like an expert, and create a lush, long-lasting

cut-flower display.
16-1504 50 min. $17.95

• **How to Grow Healthy Houseplants**
Here's all you need to learn on how to grow and
maintain healthy houseplants. It includes choosing
containers, customizing potting soil, maintaining
the right water and humidity levels, cleaning,
pruning and much more.
16-1506 60 min. $17.95

• **How to Grow Plants in a Greenhouse**
Now you can grow vegetables, flowers and
houseplants all your 'round. You'll get expert tips
on where to put your greenhouse, design options,
managing micro-climates, growing a variety of
produce, watering, feeding, and greenhouse
maintenance.
16-1508 47 min. $17.95

• **How to Grow Plants in Sunspaces**
This program will show you how to create a
successful sunspace in your home, how to choose
the right plants and where to put them, feeding,
pest control and more. It's the perfect way to
beautify your home!
16-1513 54 min. $17.95

• **How to Grow Roses**
This program proves it doesn't take a green thumb
to grow roses. Includes testing and preparing soil,
transplanting container and bare-root roses, "dual
mulching," pest control, and lots more.
16-1507 48 min. $17.95

• **How to Grow Warm-Weather
Vegetables**
Learn the special warm-weather techniques that will
make your garden flourish! You'll see how to grow
warm-weather seedlings, set up trellises, control
pests and harvest a bumper crop of summer
vegetables.
16-1510 55 min. $17.95

• **How to Grow & Nurture Seedlings**
This program will give you the same head start the
experts get by growing their own seedlings! It
includes proven ways to water and feed seedlings,
choose the right container and soil, use grow lights,
control pest and set seedlings.
16-1509 49 min. $17.95

Is Your Garden

In The Weeds?

These Videos Can Help Put

the Bloom

Back On Your Rose.

VIDEO TITLES LISTED IN THIS GUIDE ARE AVAILABLE FOR PURCHASE
OR RENTAL. CONTACT YOUR LOCAL VIDEO STORE OR TELEPHONE (800) 383-8811

Searching For

A Unique Gift That is

Informative and Appreciated?

The Video Titles

In This Guide

Make Wonderful Gifts.

Health
&
Medicine

- ✓ *Disease*
- ✓ *Drug & Alcohol Abuse*
- ✓ *First Aid*
- ✓ *Massage & Acupressure*
- ✓ *Nutrition & Weight Loss*
- ✓ *Stop Smoking*
- ✓ *Stress Reduction*
- ✓ *Miscellaneous*

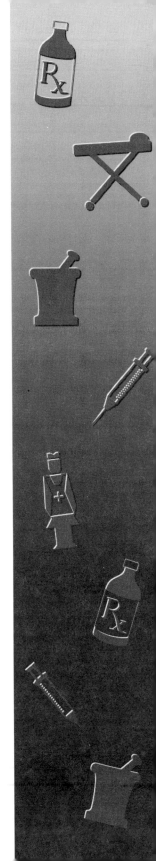

Disease

An Affair of the Heart
A complete video guide to the care of the recovering heart patient, complete with nutritious, doctor-approved recipes.
20-2460 60 min. $19.95

AIDS
This program addresses the myths and realities of the disease. It covers the history of AIDS and its probable origin, how it is proliferated, efforts devoted to screening and finding a cure, symptoms and progressing of the disease, the most frequently expressed fears, preventive measures, risks in receiving blood and how to support a patient both physically and emotionally.
20-111 30 min. $79.95

AIDS: Answers For Everyone
An in depth review of the world's most devastating, incurable disease-the AIDS virus. Featuring noted medical experts including Dr. C. Everett Koop, nurses of AIDS patients, mothers of AIDS victims and moving interviews with several persons with AIDS. An informative, compelling and human look at the killer virus and its impact on our lives at work, at school and at home.
20-6204 60 min. $79.95

AIDS: Everything You and Your Family Need to Know...But Were Afraid to Ask
Former Surgeon General, C. Everett Koop provides level-headed specifics in this current program from HBO. He gives information that people want and need to know. Complete with discussion guide.
20-8058 38 min. $99.95

AIDS: Profile of an Epidemic
Narrated by Ed Asner, this program provides information everyone should know about the most controversial, misunderstood and dreaded disease of out time.
20-109 60 min. $29.95

AIDS: What You Need to Know
This program will shatter the myths surrounding AIDS, and will shed needed light on a problem labeled by many as "the plague of the 20th century".
20-2519 44 min. $19.95

Allergies: Coping With Allergies
This is your guide to quick relief from sneezing, coughing and congestion. Find out what causes allergies and which common testing procedures are available. Learn about traditional and non-traditional treatments and how to allergy proof your home.
20-6557 34 min. $24.95

Almost Like You and Me
A documentary about people with severe behavior disorders and how they are working in the community, paying taxes and getting better and better. A story of a parent who found a new, humane way to help people with autism and other challenging behavior problems.
11-9808 27 min. $59.99

ARTHRITIS: BEST USE OF THE HANDS
These videos are designed to teach arthritis patients to lessen damage done to their hands by improper usage. Each tape is divided into three parts. The first deals with anatomy of the hand, in laymen terms, on how the bones, muscles, ligaments and joints work. Next, the person is taught how to protect their hands. The final part shows common aides and useful tools to reduce stress on the hands.

• Rheumatoid Arthritis
20-9572 22 min. $39.95

• Osteoarthritis
20-9573 22 min. $39.95

Behavior Technology for Living & Working in the Community
Psychologist, Marcy Smith of Community Services for Autistic Adults, discusses the behavioral approach to treatment of people with mental developmental disorders. She explains the usefulness of this therapy and compares it to more traditional practices.
20-9812 60 min. $69.95

Breast Cancer....A Curable Disease
Remarkable medical advances in recent years have made it possible to cure or control 90% of all cases of breast cancer when they are detected early. This film tells the story of a few ordinary women who, with the help of dedicated professionals and family support, face their fears and conquered a potentially deadly disease.
20-8032 45 min. $29.95

Cancer
It may be news to you that cancer is not an automatic death sentence. Dr. David Hawkins has taken a lifetime of psychiatric experience, combined it with a "new age" consciousness and demonstrates

most effectively... the only way to beat this or any man made disease. In his practice and in his own personal life, Dr. Hawkins recounts his own elimination of 20 life threatening illnesses...how they came... and how he eliminated them.
20-6786 60 min. $39.95

Cancer: Just A Word
The very personal, revealing and uplifting story of Joy Hopkins-Hausman, actively involved in healing from her breast cancer. A holistic approach which includes: Chemotherapy, Guided Visualization, Massage Therapy, Cancer Support Groups, Yoga and Meditation, Hands-on Reiki Therapy, Nutrition, Exercise, Humor, Mammography & Breast Reconstruction Surgery.
20-6787 45 min. $29.95

CARDIAC REHABILITATION: "CARDIAC COMEBACK"
"Cardiac Comeback" is a three-part exercise program created to guide low-risk cardiac patients through a progressive home conditioning and education program.

• Level 1:
Initiates recovery with light daily exercises and motivational testimony.
20-6617 39 min. $24.95

• Level 2:
Builds on progress made in Level 1 and moves to a more intense level of cardiac recovery.
20-6618 50 min. $24.95

• Level 3:
Level 3 builds on Level 2, advancing to a dynamic workout using wrist weights and vigorous exercise routines.
20-6619 50 min. $24.95

Cathy Rigby: On Eating Disorders
This video is a must for anyone involved with treating this problem. Medical, health and fitness, education and athletic professionals will find this program to be an important resource in their library of tools. "Cathy Rigby on Eating Disorders" can help you help others begin a dialogue of trust, and help patients better understand their illness.
20-7062 30 min. $29.95

Dangerous Affair: A Teenage Story of AIDS
Aids in teenage women increased 70 percent last year. This program, based on a true story, demonstrates that AIDS can happen to anyone. Complete with discussion guide.
20-8057 30 min. $69.96

Diabetes
This program discusses the history of the disease, symptoms, foot care, home care tips, diet, medication guidelines, exercise and emotional coping. It also answers the common questions patients ask, and encourages viewers to assume greater responsibility for their health.
20-112 40 min. $49.95

Diabetes: A Positive Approach
Tom Parks, Comedian and Diabetic, takes us on a funny and informative jaunt around his home town introducing us to other successful diabetics in film, television and professional sports.
20-8062 43 min. $29.95

Diabetes: "Living With Diabetes"
Diabetes does not need to be debilitating. Follow along with this positive approach to healthy living. Learn the best techniques for self-monitoring and how to avoid common complications. Experts from the Joslin Clinic of Boston discuss alternatives to insulin therapy and how to achieve healthy weight loss. Learn exciting recipes that fit your lifestyle.
20-6561 35 min. $24.95

Feeling Good With Arthritis
Finally, reliable information and advice is available for the more than 37 million Americans who suffer from arthritis. Join baseball legend Mickey Mantle and leading national arthritis experts who share practical information on diet, medical treatment, positive attitude and exercise. Follow along with a daily program of stretching and strengthening exercises designed to improve mobility.
20-6553 60 min. $24.95

Fight for Your Life
A complete program that teaches those with cancer how to become involved in their own healing process. Designed to be used on a daily basis as a vital part of your ongoing medical treatment.
20-2228 150 min. $64.95

Food Allergies and How To Overcome The Problem
Dr. Joseph Cannillo, a leading research scientist and food allergist, shows you how to detect hidden food allergies often mistaken for other discomforts. Food allergies often cause arthritis, asthma, skin problems, sinus discomfort, hyperactivity and learning disabilities in children, plus many more problems. Learn how to detect and treat food allergies, and live a healthier and happier life.
20-5643 30 min. $16.95

Growing up in the Age of AIDS
Hosted by Peter Jennings this video focuses on AIDS, the HIV virus and what children, teenagers

and parents should know about this disease.
20-8047 75 min. $19.99

Healthy Heart: "Say Goodbye To High Blood Pressure"

Left undetected and untreated, high blood pressure greatly increases your risk of stroke, heart disease, kidney disease, diabetes, eye disease and even sudden death. Join Leslie Charleson of the hit series "General Hospital" and Dr. William Castelli, Director of the Framingham Heart Group, for an informative look into the causes, effects and best treatments of high blood pressure.
20-6558 45 min. $24.95

Living With Arthritis

All-Pro NFL quarterback Boomer Esiason, who had arthritis as a teenager, hosts this program filled with valuable tips to help you live better with the disease.
20-8019 60 min. $34.95

Living With Arthritis: Self-Help

Morning Workout with Darlene Cohen. A 50-minute period of exercises you can use every morning to get your stiff or painful body moving with ease; Movements for loosening every joint in Lying, Sitting and Standing positions; Five people with different arthritis difficulties demonstrate the movements; A section on What to do when it hurts.
20-5067 50 min. $39.95

Living with Diabetes: A Winning Formula

Whether you or someone you love is challenged with diabetes, understanding the disease and being motivated to lead a healthy lifestyle is your key to good health and satisfaction.
20-8024 60 min. $24.95

Living With High Blood Pressure

Hosted by tennis legend and heart attack victim, Arthur Ashe, this highly acclaimed video presents vital information you need to know to help your doctor control high blood pressure.
20-6234 59 min. $34.95

Managing Your Arthritis (In Control)

An arthritis self-management program designed by the Arthritis Foundation to develop an effective way to "manage" your arthritis. Hosted by James F. Fried, M.D., Director of the Arthritic Clinic at Stanford University.
20-2668 68 min. $74.95

Natural Therapies for Healing Cancer

This program reports findings from specialists such as Nobel Laureate Linus Pauling on natural therapies. Raw food diets, megavitamins, and pancreatic enzymes are proven alternatives to

standard cancer treatments. This information could save the life of someone you know.
20-9147 52 min. $24.95

Straight From the Heart with Mike Ditka

Six leading experts help Mike show you how to live better and longer with some simple changes in your lifestyle. They give you valuable private counsel on vital topics such as: What is a heart attack? Minutes that can save a life. How to defy time. Good news about nutrition and weight control. Secrets of mealtime magic and getting fit and staying fit.
20-8033 77 min. $39.95

Drug & Alcohol Abuse

Cocaine: The Source & Consequences

This film chillingly portrays narco terrorism; how cocaine is grown by mountainous native tribes in Colombia, sold through huge drug cartels that control entire governments and ultimately finances Third World unrest and revolutionary movements.
20-6202 45 min. $49.95

Crack U.S.A.

Narrated by Joe Mantegna, the program shows a cross section of abusers, primarily teenagers, who have fallen under the spell of the most addictive and affordable drug in America. Interviews with addicts and their families reveal that crack knows no socio-economic boundaries. Also explored is the overwhelming frustration felt by police and the community in the face of the problem. Discussion guide included.
20-8056 42 min. $99.95

Downfall: Sports and Drugs

A documentary that shows the consequences of drug use today. Features stories of students, amateur and professional athletes, their families and coaches. It illustrates how alcohol, cocaine, marijuana and steroids destroy health, opportunities, career, self respect and finally the happiness of those who are involved with them. It concludes, with a look at the lives of athletes that made the choice to live "drug free".
20-8060 51 min. $39.95

Drug Education for Young People

A series of three popular drug films. The first films deals with young people and places them in situations where they must often make a decision that could change the rest of their life. The second film deals with abuse of amphetamines, or "uppers," drugs that can be more dangerous than heroin or LSD. The third in the series deals with barbiturates, or "downers". See the facts about dependency, addiction, overdose and possible death.

26-079 48 min. $49.95

Drug Free Kids: A Parents' Guide

An up-to-the-minute educational and entertaining program designed to help parents identify and deal with the urgent problem of childhood drug abuse. Through role-playing to depict intimate family situations and professional advice given by America's leading experts in the field of drug and alcohol abuse, you will gain valuable knowledge and learn constructive ways to handle this issue within your own family.

20-108 70 min. $29.95

Drug Free Zones: Taking Action

A fast paced, inspirational video that offers hope and motivates communities to take action against drug dealing and alcohol-related problems in schools, neighborhoods, parks, and housing developments.

20-9676 27 min. $39.95

MOST OUTSTANDING DRUG PREVENTION PROGRAMS AVAILABLE:

• High On Life

How teenagers can live a happy and Drug-Free lifestyle as taught at the F.B.I. National Academy!

20-6199 35 min. $29.95

• 3 Ways To Keep Your Kids Off Drugs

Don't wait until it's too late! Use the drug prevention program taught at the F.B.I. National Academy!

20-6200 46 min. $29.95

Say No to Drugs

This is a practical, easy-to-follow approach for parents and families who want to keep their children off drugs. This program combines interviews and dramatic vignettes with solid advice and techniques you can use to teach your children the truth about drugs and alcohol.

26-115 45 min. $14.95

Shattered if Your Kid's on Drugs

Hosted by Burt Reynolds and Judd Nelson, this engrossing presentation profiles two everyday teens seemingly free of the temptations to use drugs. Yet, due to peer pressure and ready availability, we see how experimental use of so-called harmless drugs can quickly escalate to full-scale dependency, shattering promising futures and tearing apart

loving families.Included is an on-screen list of drug and alcohol help and rehabilitation referral centers. This program offers a message of understanding and hope for every parent and child.

10-463 59 min. $24.95

Teenage Drug and Alcohol Abuse

In this dramatization of individual case histories, a psychologist, a teenager and his mother give their perspectives and feelings regarding these problems. Information is offered as to how to contact agencies and organizations who can assist families troubled by teen alcohol and drug abuse.

20-071 30 min. $29.95

Twelve Steps

Based on the Alcoholics Anonymous program, this sensitive, dramatic interpretation is for individuals and their families touched by alcoholism, drug addiction, overeating, gambling and other life-stress problems. Through the artistic blending of original music and stirring cinematography, you see individuals from all walks of life practicing the steps. This uplifting presentation is designed to offer general understanding of the program and its principles, as well as to encourage individuals and their families to participate.

20-101 35 min. $49.95

Victory Over

Alcohol
Jean and Veryl Rosenbaum well-known therapists and recovered alcoholics, interview real people who have successfully battled alcoholism. They offer encouragement, advice and hope for a healthy productive future.

20-5004 30 min. $39.95

Waking Up from Dope

This unique presentation on drugs and alcohol abuse speaks to young people in their own language. Drama and humor are used to drive home the hard facts of substance abuse and chemical dependency.

20-123 39 min. $69.95

First Aid

Baby Alive

Phylicia Rashad and medical experts present a step-by-step guide for prevention and treatment of life-threatening situations facing children from birth to 5 years old, including: choking, drowning, poisoning, head injuries, cuts,burns, first aid, and

injury prevention.
20-5409 60 min. $19.95

CPR-You Could Save A Life: A CPR Quiz and Trainer

Combines two programs that carefully and clearly illustrate cardio-pulmonary resuscitation, step-by-step on simulated victims. The newest method for clearing obstructions in the windpipe is also featured. Offers questions and answers, realistic emergency situations in a variety of locations, and gives an ideal first exposure to life-saving procedures.
20-158 35 min. $49.95

CPR for Bystanders

Basic life-support training classes for the public and school age students. Training modules include assessment, the ABC's of CPR, one rescuer CPR, infant and child CPR, choking, risk factors and more. Terrific training aids for CPR classes at work or off the job. Produced according to guidelines published by the Journal of the American Medical Association.
20-8044 30 min. $19.95

CPR For Everyone

In accordance with the most current standards of the American Heart Association and the American Red Cross, Anne Demmon, RN, MN, demonstrates in detail the steps of CPR and Emergency Choking Procedures (Heimlich Method) for the Infant, Child and Adult. Would you be prepared in a family emergency?
20-8054 45 min. $29.99

Dr. Heimlich's Home First-Aid Video

Here, Dr. Henry Heimlich offers an incisive, no-nonsense guide to treating, and when possible, preventing the most common home emergencies in this vital addition to every home library.
20-2993 36 min. $19.95

First Aid for the Home

Saving a Life: Every year more than 176,000 people are killed in accidents in the United States. Half of them die needlessly because bystanders are helpless. The answer: everyone should have basic first-aid instruction. This program concentrates on the ABC's of emergency rescue-airway, breathing and circulation. The emphasis is on speed, simplicity and efficiency. Shock and fractures are discussed. Questions with multiple choice answers are visually and dramatically posed. Scenes are cinematically displayed so viewers can analyze and respond. Treating Injuries: Some 36 million Americans are injured in the home each year; 6,000 die of poisoning. Many of these injuries are not life-threatening, but improper care can result in fatal complications. This program concentrates on specific treatment for burns, choking, poisoning

and heat stroke. Questions with multiple choices are posed within accident vignettes. Cinematic delays enable viewers to identify and respond as through it were an actual emergency.
20-157 45 min. $39.95

Home Emergency Video

This tape dramatizes the need for and explains the method of dealing with the following emergencies: heart attack (CPR), choking (the Heimlich maneuver), drowning, shock and poisoning.
20-193 30 min. $29.95

How to Save Your Child's Life

This video instructs adults and children how to perform CPR, mouth-to-mouth breathing, the Heimlich Maneuver and other lifesaving techniques on infants and children.
20-209 45 min. $29.95

Learn How To Save A Life With First Aid

A skilled emergency physician and advanced emergency medical technicians will show you step-by-step what to do when faced with a life threatening emergency. You will learn the proper techniques for C.P.R. for infants, children, and adults.
20-5637 30 min. $16.95

MOUTH TO MOUTH BREATHING TECHNIQUES:

• Version 1: First Responder
This version is for EMS, police and general work force personnel.
20-8048 30 min. $295.00

• Version 2: Medical
This version is designed for medical employees.
20-8049 30 min. $295.00

Seconds Count

This video reviews the Heimlich maneuver and basic CPR for infants and children. Narrated by a paramedic, the video dramatizes a child losing consciousness in a bathtub, choking on food and then shows you how to react quickly and appropriately. Available in English & Spanish.
20-2541 18 min. $19.95

Until Help Arrives: A Video First-Aid Guide

Minutes, even seconds, can make the critical difference! Would you know what to do? Who to call? How? This program gives you the answers in easy-to-understand words and pictures.
29-146 60 min. $19.95

Massage & Acupressure

Acupressure
Dr. Michael Smith teaches simple acupressure techniques to relieve common ailments such as headaches, asthma, arthritis and others.
20-001 30 min. $39.95

Acupressure Facelift
A total, interactive video experience, this ancient massage system from the Orient will stimulate and tone your skin, actually making it more supple and young looking. Add it to your daily ritual and it can help prevent the need for a facelift, now or in your future. You'll discover a dynamic difference in the way you look and feel within just a few sessions. And as a simple, natural way to relieve stress and tension at the end of your busy day, the effect will be immediate.
05-067 45 min. $19.95

Aromatherapy and Massage
Aromatherapy essential oils work not only on the physical level, but on the emotional and spiritual levels too. Gain valuable insight into this natural therapy, and learn which oils will uplift, revive and stimulate and which oils help soothe and relax.
20-8051 80 min. $16.95

Art of Massage
Now you can enjoy massage techniques used for centuries to relax over-stressed bodies. This program combines techniques from Swedish, Neo-Reichian and Shiatsu traditions.
20-006 59 min. $39.95

Art of Shiatsu Massage
Shiatsu massage is one of the oldest and most natural methods of healing. Its techniques and uses are based on the philosophy that a complete system of energy is in circulation throughout the body.
20-007 120 min. $49.95

Bum Back
Author of The Bum Back Book, Michael Reed Gach, demonstrates how to prevent and relieve backaches.
20-117 60 min. $39.95

Don Wright's Basic Massage
In this instructional tape Don Wright, internationally known masseur, shows you the highly effective techniques of good massage.
29-147 60 min. $19.95

Fundamentals of Acupressure
An introduction to the major acupressure techniques including jin shin, shiatsu and do-in (self-acupressure.) Oriental breathing exercises, self-acupressure techniques and reflexology are demonstrated.
20-118 90 min. $39.95

Healing Massage for Lovers & Friends
Join French Physical Therapist, Ghisaine Borg as she skillfully explains and demonstrates the "language of one's hand and body". She explains three types of massage: relaxation, pain relief and rejuvenation.
20-8009 90 min. $29.95

HEALTHY MASSAGE:
The benefits of massage are well known relieving tension, stress and muscle strain. In this series Rebecca Klinger reveals the step-by-step secrets of giving a professional, relaxing and enjoyable massage.

• **Back**
20-3082 30 min. $16.95

• **Legs and Feet**
20-3083 30 min. $16.95

• **Scalp, Face, Neck and Chest**
20-3081 30 min. $16.95

Infant Massage
This video teaches you how to massage your baby tenderly and naturally. It teaches a full body massage, with 32 specific strokes. Massage improves the emotional communication between parent and child and helps parents feel competent in their baby's daily care.
20-208 28 min. $39.95

Introduction to Acupuncture
After tracing the history of acupuncture, this film shows never-seen-before sequences of acupuncture actually being used--a hernia operation, acupuncture anesthesia used for a thyroidectomy and treatment of nerve deafness. An excellent foundation for a subject which remains complex and often misunderstood.
20-127 22 min. $49.95

Learn How To Massage Your Loved Ones
Dr. R. Michelli will teach you how to find the therapeutic points of the human body, while Mary-Rose Ventrilli, a licensed Massage Therapist, demonstrates step-by-step the correct use of Massage Techniques to help reduce stress, ease tension, promote relaxation, and create an "overall feeling" of "well-being". Dr. Michelli also shows

VIDEO TITLES LISTED IN THIS GUIDE ARE AVAILABLE FOR PURCHASE OR RENTAL. CONTACT YOUR LOCAL VIDEO STORE OR TELEPHONE (800) 383-8811

you how massages can be used to ease the pain and tension caused by back & neck problems.
20-5644   30 min. $16.95

Light Touch
This is a step-by-step guide in which the viewer will learn how to utilize the power of human touch to help or heal others.
20-3024   90 min. $54.95

Massage: Simple
This is a pleasing and practical program, a restful and relaxing late-night treat. It features one woman and one man, both young and athletic, both sensual and natural. This fully-narrated video is accompanied by New Age piano solos, there are many close-ups and the instruction is easy to follow.
20-1674   50 min. $19.95

Massage for Everybody
Over the last few years, medical science has taken a renewed interest in the benefits of hands-on therapy. It has been shown that massage improves circulation, relieves fatigued muscles, increases joint range of motion, speeds healing after injury, improves respiration, and hastens elimination of metabolic wastes. Massage is psychologically relaxing and it is a natural antidote for stress. Massage enhances your most precious possession-- your health. Taught by Sharon Weinstein, M.D.
20-154   60 min. $29.95

Massage for Health
Join Shari Belafonte-Harper as she puts herself into the practiced hands of two acclaimed massage professionals. Discover the healing power of touch as you learn Swedish/Western style massage techniques.
20-2142   65 min. $29.95

MASSAGE INSTRUCTION:
This massage video series presents therapeutic massage techniques for anyone who wants to understand and master the art of massage. The instructor, Dietrich Miesler, Ph.D., brings over 30 years experience to this information-packed program, providing valuable insights into anatomy, physiology, theory and technique. The series is designed to become part of a program that will lead to certification as a massage technician, but is also excellent for the casual beginner.

• Back Massage
The back massage is the key element of any body massage. Dietrich covers this complex area thoroughly, demonstrating various techniques such as shiatsu, traeger, Swedish, and deep tissue massage, and evaluating each of these as a choice. This tape is a must for any serious student or practitioner of massage.
20-095   42 min. $49.95

• Choreography of the Full Body Massage
The term "choreography" was suggested by a ballet dancer, and this is a seamless performance of a variety of massage techniques. Dietrich deals with the awe-inspiring system of muscles, tendons, ligaments and other connective tissues which move and shape the body, and hold it together.
20-096   42 min. $69.95

• Massage During Pregnancy
In an unusually enthusiastic, sensitive and thorough demonstration, this tape covers all aspects of pregnancy massage in a very concise manner. It covers not only techniques of manipulation but addresses philosophical, psychological and medical questions.
20-2492   45 min. $54.95

• Massaging the Extremities
Depending on inherited body structure and type of activity, muscle groups in arms and legs vary from person to person. This tape shows how to deal with various conditions and special attention is paid to the complex anatomy of the joints.
20-2491   48 min. $49.95

• Massaging Your Friends
This program is designed for people who simply want to learn how to give nice massages to their close friends and who are not seeking all the knowledge required for a professional career in massage. It teaches simple but effective methods for giving a massage.
20-092   42 min. $49.95

• Nine Basic Massage Strokes
The following five basic massage strokes are discussed in this tape: stroking, petrissage (kneading), tapotement (tapping), friction and vibration (augmented by shaking, stretching, acupressure and skin rolling).
20-094   42 min. $49.95

• Pain-in-the-Neck Workshop
This tape is devoted to couples in stressful jobs because it deals with the elimination of tension headaches and neck and shoulder pain.
20-093   42 min. $49.95

Massage Made Simple
This program will teach you basic, easy-to-learn massage techniques to relieve the aches and pains of today's lifestyle. Learn how to relieve stress, ease tension and soothe those sore muscles. Enjoy total relaxation in the privacy of your own home through massage.
20-1673   60 min. $29.95

Massage: Instruction for the Beginner

This program is an overview of Swedish massage. Following a brief history and explanation of its benefits, the video instructs you in a full-body Swedish massage. It is a demonstration of strokes, an easy-to-follow lesson in "How to Touch," presented in a manner that is as safe as it is wholesome. It is a high quality, state-of-the-art product that entertains as it educates.
20-184 90 min. $39.95

Personal Massage

Presents tips on self-massage.
20-2010 40 min. $29.95

Releasing Shoulder and Neck Tension

This tape teaches you to release tension in the shoulder and neck areas using finger pressure on key acupressure points in the shoulder and neck areas, both for yourself and others.
20-119 40 min. $39.95

Reversing Disabilities

This summation of the actual filmed case histories of physically traumatized patients, offers new hope of rehabilitation. Therapist Eleanor Gibbs shows how she has successfully used a process of muscle manipulation and exercise to help improve disabled clients' vital functional activities.
20-8015 53 min. $16.95

Shiatsu Massage

Complete instructions for a full body, Japanese massage with detailed explanations and close-ups. Releases deep seated tension and dissolves aches and pains. Basic techniques are shown for beginners.
20-8000 90 min. $39.95

Shiatsu Massage: Advanced

How to find and work acupressure points and meridians. Explanation of Oriental medical theory and diagnosis. Very detailed demonstrations of treatment. Many angles and close-ups are used for ease in learning.
20-8001 115 min. $39.95

Shiatsu Massage with Pat Morita

Pat Morita of Karate Kid fame shares his knowledge of Shiatsu, a time honored method of hands on Oriental massage for the entire family. Demonstrating a 5-step process, Morita emphasizes the relationship between himself and his subject as being one of giver and receiver and suggests breathing in sync to establish rhythm.
20-8017 32 min. $24.95

Swedish Massage

Experience an overwhelming sense of vitality and rejuvenation with Swedish Massage. With a gentle touch of symmetrical movements, alleviate stress and gain tranquility and relaxation.
20-8036 60 min. $29.95

Tai-Chi-Ch'uan: Movements of Power and Health

Detailed classroom instruction for the "yang short form" of these ancient health exercises, based on the natural movements of animals. Includes training in basic coordination, the flow of internal energy concentration exercises and the use of Tai-chi-Ch'uan for stress reduction.
20-8004 120 min. $29.95

Tai-Chi-Ch'uan-Chinese Moving Meditation

Demonstration of the slow, flowing movements practiced since ancient times in parts of China, "yang short form" is shown from two angles in natural surroundings with simple instructions.
20-8005 48 min. $24.95

Tai-Chi Massage

Now you can learn to give a very gentle pleasurable and relaxing massage, based on the natural, meditative movements of Tai-Chi-Chuan. You will learn to release deep-seated tension and invigorate the body as each muscle and nerve is refreshed.
20-8003 60 min. $19.95

Touch For Health

John Thie, D.C., President of the Touch for Health Foundation, demonstrates techniques for removing toxins from the body, relieving energy blockages, reducing tension and enhancing the body's natural tendency towards health. The techniques involve muscle testing, massage of acupressure points, and activation of meridian energy.
20-132 47 min. $39.95

Zen Shiatsu

Based on the Acupressure Institute's course, the tape demonstrates how to release tension in the neck, shoulder, back, legs and face.
20-120 60 min. $39.95

Nutrition & Weight Loss

Home Video Weight-Loss Program (In Control)

A 30-day program with weight loss authority Dr. Albert Marston and gymnast Cathy Rigby. Features techniques for changing your eating habits, handling difficult food pressure situations at restaurants, parties and holiday gatherings, how to

VIDEO TITLES LISTED IN THIS GUIDE ARE AVAILABLE FOR PURCHASE OR RENTAL. CONTACT YOUR LOCAL VIDEO STORE OR TELEPHONE (800) 383-8811

control binge eating and much more. Includes a Viewer's Guide and two personal record diaries. Following the procedures on this tape, the average person should lose one to two pounds each week, and what's even better, keep it off! This set includes two videotapes.
20-040 240 min. $98.95

Alive and Well Diet
A preventive health diet intended to keep you healthy and lose weight by showing you how to make great meals! If you enjoy what you're eating, you are more likely to stick with it! With Diane Jouganatos and Mike Jerrick.
20-203 42 min. $19.95

Cellulite! Cellulite! Cellulite!: Removal in Five Easy Steps
See how these five easy steps--self-massage, proper exercise, nutrition, herbal cleansing and other proven European techniques--can lead to a slender silhouette.
20-2118 46 min. $24.95

Count Out Cholesterol By Dr. Art Ulene
Using this program most people can expect to see a medically significant reduction in blood cholesterol levels within a 30-day period. Count out cholesterol is unique because it shows you how to address the cause of high blood cholesterol. It's a safe approach that will help you lower your cholesterol level without boring menus, rigid diets, or forbidden foods.
20-6068 75 min. $24.95

Dieting
What makes people diet? How do they determine the best way to lose weight? In this dramatization of typical dieters and their special problems, find out about "miracle" diets and their successes and failures; fad diets; the special problems and diseases associated with being overweight; and how to help your body adjust to weight loss without risking your short-term or long-term health.
20-017 37 min. $29.95

Eat Smart
Learn the truth about nutrition for the 90's. This investigative report is filled with tips to help Americans make better choices in their diets to enhance their lives and health. See a remarkable 20% reduction in heart disease and 50% reduction in cancer, according to the Food and Nutrition Board.
20-8045 60 min. $16.95

Eat to Win
Lionel Richie and Martina Navratilova agree that "Eat to Win" is the best system of nutrition and fitness available today. Work with Dr. Robert Haas to develop a winning diet and exercise regimen just

for you. You'll improve your fitness and sports performance by following Dr. Haas' 14-day diet plan and by using the daily aerobic workout on the tape. With Ivan Lendl and Audrey Landers.
20-018 72 min. $39.95

Eating Healthy: The High Fiber, Low Cholesterol Way
Five leading nutritionists provide expert advice on healthier eating. They demonstrate healthy breakfasts, lunches, and dinners. They compare good choices with bad choices - and explain the calorie, fat, and cholesterol counts. You'll learn the importance of high fiber and the best sources to get it from. You'll learn how to reduce cholesterol in your diet.
20-5636 45 min. $16.95

Fit for Life
At last! Discover the permanent weight loss plan that proves it's not what you eat, but when and how. Learn the simple secrets of America's all-time number on health and diet plan in this innovative, self-help videocassette based upon nutrition experts Harvey and Marilyn Diamond's multimillion-copy best-seller. The Diamonds share their revolutionary new eating plan in an informative, entertaining program that: offers a personal coaching program centered around the easy-to-apply principles of permanent weight loss and lifelong health; and provides a handy 14-day meal plan for weight loss and permanent maintenance-including menus, recipes and a personal diary to chart progress.
15-216 75 min. $24.95

Fit or Fat for the 90's
Covert Bailey, a nutritional biochemist and best selling author, presents new information on the physiology of fat cells; caffeine and smoking; alcohol and biochemistry and the medical benefits of exercise.
20-8046 60 min. $16.95

Lose Weight with Alf Fowles
Deep relaxation techniques and self-hypnosis are taught to help viewers lose weight in a safe, easy way.
20-090 60 min. $39.95

No Effort Weight Loss: Subliminal Video by Dick Sutphen
This tape is structured to assist you in losing weight by watching the TV screen. It is a beautifully produced movie-quality production of exciting visual fantasies and relaxing music. Although you can't see the visual subliminal and you hear only the music, you are actually being subjected to intense programming communicated to your subconscious mind without resistance.
20-190 20 min. $19.95

No-Nonsense Cholesterol Guide
Learn to prevent heart attacks for you and for your children.
20-8028 60 min. $24.95

Nutrition
Renowned health authority Paavo Airola summarizes his findings about nutrition, drawn from studies of the world's longest-lived peoples. The tape also includes a graphic demonstration of the weakening effect sugar has on the body, plus a short play. A fun way to learn about good and bad eating habits.
20-9148 30 min. $24.95

Psychology of Weight Loss: Resolving Emotional Eating for a Lighter and Healthier You
This program explains at a feeling level, the Why, What and How, to correct emotional eating behavior, the major missing link in "diet" programs and the reason they fail at a 90 percent rate. Included in this informative and inspirational format are personal experiences about emotional eating and a simple nutritional formula to achieve weight loss goals and more.
20-9628 47 min. $29.95

Rotation Diet, Martin Katahn, Ph.D.
The Rotation Diet was developed by Martin Katahn, Ph.D., director of the nationally acclaimed Vanderbilt University Weight Management Program. This diet is a product of Dr. Katahn's personal victory: losing over 75 lbs. of excess weight. The dieting formula that worked for Dr. Katahn and thousands of other has been researched and tested with amazing results...now it's available to you! Includes a complete pocket version of the 21-day meal plan and maintenance guidelines; personal advice on how to "live" with The Rotation Diet, including how to live it up and keep it off; fitting fitness into your lifestyle; mixing food and feelings; resisting temptation; specially developed low-fat, not-fat recipes for cooking the rotation way; and "The Rotation Rap" music video.
20-163 59 min. $19.95

Sports Nutrition: Facts and Fallacies
A guide for athletes. Improve your performance by knowing more about nutrition, the timing of meals relative to workouts, carbohydrate versus fat consumption, and much more.
20-067 30 min. $29.95

Sybervision: Weight Control & the Will to Change
This video is an overview of the sound principles on which the neuropsychology of weight control is based, including: set-point theory, sound eating habits, gentle exercise, and improved self-image.

Includes eight audiocassettes and study guide.
20-1500 60 min. $89.95

Vanna White's Get Slim, Stay Slim
It's Vanna White's Get Slim, Stay Slim, her new, safe, medically sound diet and lifestyle video program. Created with the cooperation of top nutritionists and doctors at UCLA, this video reveals her personal weight loss and maintenance secrets to her legion of fans.
20-211 60 min. $19.95

Vegetarian Protein
This is designed for high school students in home economics class. Through the creative use of animation and live action students will learn about the four food groups, balanced diets, fats and cholesterol and alternatives in food choices. The program comes complete with recipes, classroom activities and a quiz for evaluation.
20-9662 30 min. $79.95

Vitamins & Nutrition For A Healthier Life
Four leading doctors and nutritionists collaborate in this important video. They teach you good nutrition and explain about the vitamins that are needed daily. You learn what each vitamin is good for. You learn how vitamins work against cancer and heart disease.
20-5641 30 min. $16.95

Weight Watchers: Guide to Dining and Cooking
Join Host Lynn Redgrave as she and Weight Watchers magazine resident experts explore some no-nonsense techniques for dining out and cooking in-deliciously.
20-102 55 min. $29.95

Stop Smoking

Home Video Freedom from Smoking Program (In Control)
The American Lung Association presents this unique smoking control program. Comprised of 13 segments, including why people keep smoking; handling withdrawal systems, including the use of nicotine gum; weight management; and coping tools. With the support of Dr. Nina Schneider, Dr. Albert Marston and Steve Garvey, you'll stop smoking within 10 days. Package includes a two-hour videotape, 124-page Viewer's Guide, and audiocassette.
20-039 120 min. $79.95

VIDEO TITLES LISTED IN THIS GUIDE ARE AVAILABLE FOR PURCHASE OR RENTAL. CONTACT YOUR LOCAL VIDEO STORE OR TELEPHONE (800) 383-8811

Death in the West

One of the most powerful anti-smoking films ever made. Originally produced for British T.V. and vigorously suppressed by tobacco interests, it juxtaposes the healthy independent image of the Marlboro Man, defended in interviews with cigarette company executives, with the stark reality of 6 smoking cowboys, all dying of smoking induced illnesses.
20-8043 32 min. $29.95

Dirty Business

This is about a media genius named Tony Schwartz, who decided to battle to cigarette industry after he found out his best friend was dying of lung cancer. An effective and moving anti-smoking message designed for junior and senior high levels.
20-2698 30 min. $99.95

Fresh Start: 21 Days to Stop Smoking

The American Cancer Society's own one-day-at-a-time program that uses proven, how to stop smoking techniques. The 21 day-by-day segments will guide, cancel and encourage you from Day 1, "Quit Day," to "Off the Hook"--the day you did it!
20-025 75 min. $29.95

Smoke That Cigarette

This program is a nostalgic, archival, thoughtful film about America's very strange and very powerful attraction to the cigarette. It probes our reasons for smoking, investigates truth in advertising and explores smoking in the bedroom and hospital room. It is filled with movie stars and lung operations; with hit songs and funeral dirges; with medical endorsements and medical atrocities. In short, it's a lot of fun. And it hurts.
20-5763 51 min. $59.95

Stop Smoking Programming/Hypnosis

Designed to help you stop smoking one day at a time. Combines a variety of persuasion techniques with the soothing voice of the narrator.
20-036 22 min. $29.95

Stop Smoking With Alf Fowles

Alf Fowles has combined deep relaxation techniques with visual messages aimed below the level of conscious perception to produce a therapy to stop smoking.
20-2986 60 min. $29.95

Stress Reduction

Can't Sleep? Count Our Sheep

Throughout history, counting sheep has been one of the most productive methods of falling asleep. In this video you simply count our sheep as they jump a fence in a beautiful sylvan setting, to lovely symphonic strains of the classic Brahms Lullaby. You'll be carried off to a peaceful rest long before you realize it.
20-8040 58 min. $19.95

Coping with Stress

Effective methods for dealing with stress, including a self-hypnosis technique.
29-095 60 min. $39.95

Dr. Art Ulene's Stress Reduction Program

If stress is interfering with your enjoyment of life, this program will help you find relief. It will show you how to reduce the amount of stress in your life. You'll also learn how to cancel the effects of any stress you can't avoid.
20-6067 60 min. $24.95

Friendly Flames Stress Reduction Program

In this program you are invited to join Dr. Kabat-Zinn, a leading authority on stress reduction, as he builds you in the practice of easily performed meditative exercises designed to reduce feelings of stress and anxiety and help you become more resistant to the negative effects of stress. You will find that these exercises, practiced to the softly flickering light of the "friendly flames," will quickly enable you to attain a state of deep relaxation, in which your physical and mental tensions melt away as you are filled with a sense of alert and relaxed well-being.
20-1766 60 min. $29.95

Hypertension: The Mind/Body Connection

Biofeedback has been a successful method for treating migraine headaches and some vascular diseases. Now techniques have been developed for the control of hypertension, and they are clearly demonstrated in this film. The success rate of this treatment has been outstanding. Of those treated, as many as nine out of ten are returned to good health and are permanently free of the many side effects of drugs used in other forms of treatment.
20-128 28 min. $89.95

Joy of Stress

Dr. Peter Hanson shows you how to make the stresses in your life work for you with a rare combination of medical insight and humor.
20-2082 30 min. $19.95

Learn Tai-Chi with Master Erle Montaigue

The ancient art of Tai Chi remains one of the most effective forms of exercise for increasing mental and physical energy through systematic stress reduction. Join Master Erle Montaigue as he teaches you the 90's way to workout and reduce stress!

20-8055 90 min. $19.99

Light in the Darkness

Dr. Gary Koppel leads meditations through the minds' eyes of his students, and their images are recreated through magnificent sights, sounds and music. Includes audio cassette.

20-2846 43 min. $49.95

Morgan Fairchild's Stress Management Program

Learn to manage stress with our celebrity host! Endorsed by leading medical authority! Comprehensive system covering active and passive stress reducing techniques!

20-5412 45 min. $29.95

Relax With Dennis Weaver

Dennis Weaver's powerful and captivating video will leave you feeling relaxed & refreshed. See an extraordinary flow of images, hear soothing music and be guided through a series of relaxation techniques that really work!

20-5408 60 min. $29.95

Stress: A Guide to Better Living

This tape offers positive suggestions on avoiding stress in our daily lives. The information in this program will enable many people to recognize stress and change their habits to avoid negative stress. Stress: Relaxation Techniques: Presents special methods of meditation, biofeedback and relaxation therapy that are highly effective means of reducing stress.

20-159 44 min. $39.95

Vermont on Video: Winter Edition

This relaxation video is edited to soothing New Age music. The visual presentation depicts the ethereal beauty and splendor of the Vermont landscape in winter.

20-3040 20 min. $19.95

Video Fireplace

The one you've heard about! No logs to haul! No ashes to clean! A real fire burning in real-time, from roaring flames down to glowing embers. Now you can have the cozy fireplace you've always wanted without the fuss. A treat for the holidays, family times or just the two of you.

14-047 60 min. $19.95

Miscellaneous

Aura Reading and Healing

Reverend Rosalyn Bruyere shows her accuracy in direct intuitive knowing through an aura reading demonstration. She identifies the status of a woman's health from the color of her energy field and even teaches how to sense these subtle hues yourself.

20-9152 23 min. $24.95

Ayurveda: The Science of Self-Healing

Foremost exponent of Ayurvedic medicine in the United States, Dr. Vasant Lad presents an overview of this 5,000-year-old science of self-healing first recorded in the ancient Hindu Vedas.

20-2463 91 min. $29.95

BACK-CARE-CISE: THERAPEUTIC EXERCISE PROGRAM:

Top Specialist Dr. Linda J. Nelson shows how to eliminate back and neck pain, strengthen back muscles, increase flexibility, shorten recovery time and reduce stress.

• Back-Care-Cise A

Moves slowly and gently to help quickly relieve pain. For people with less exercise experience, in pain or recovering.

20-6150 45 min. $24.95

• Back-Care-Cise B

Increased stretching and strengthening for those with less or no pain.

20-6151 45 min. $24.95

• Back-Care-Cise C

A complete body stretch and tone for those with more exercise experience or have mastered A & B.

20-6152 45 min. $24.95

Back Pain Relief

A remarkable routine for reconditioning your back and relieving pain. Developed in cooperation with the American Academy of Orthopaedic Surgeons (AAOS)--America's expert on the treatment of back pain.

20-6071 60 min. $29.95

Coming of Age

As life expectancy increases, staying healthy and enjoying life longer becomes more and more important. Coming Of Age is a practical lifestyle guide to help maintain and improve your health after 40. Includes helpful information on cancer

prevention, healthy heart, skin care, strong bones, mental fitness.
20-5092 64 min. $24.95

Biofeedback: The Yoga of the West
"If we can make ourselves sick, then perhaps we can learn to make ourselves well". Based on that assumption, Dr. Elmer Green, his wife Alyce, and colleagues at the Menninger Foundation research the ability of the mind to control the body.They test Indian yogis who can stop their hearts at will or remain in a airtight box for hours. They study pain, bleeding and infection. And through the use of biofeedback training, they help patients overcome disease and develop a sense of self-mastery and deeper insight into the subconscious.
20-133 40 min. $49.95

Breaking Silence: Healing Incest and Child Sexual Abuse
A definitive film on incest and child sexual abuse. Personal stories told by survivors and their families, woven with telling drawings by abused children, give viewers understanding of this difficult issue. Never sensational or exploitative, Breaking Silence celebrates those who are finding the courage to "break silence" and regain their lives.
20-8034 30 min. $99.95

Breast Center Video
This video dispels the many myths about breast cancer and contains up-to-date information on: low-dose mammography, breast self-exam, cancer treatment options, breast reconstruction, and much more. Hosted by TV's Marcia Wallace.
20-2989 37 min. $24.95

Coming of Age
Discover the latest medical research on how to positively affect the aging process of your body and mind.
20-8030 60 min. $24.95

Computers in Diagnostic Medicine
An overview of the use of computers in the medical field today. Includes demonstrations of CAT scans, EKGs, angiography and nuclear medicine techniques. For general information, and especially for anyone who will be experiencing one or more of these tests for the first time and would like to overcome anxiety about the procedures.
20-015 30 min. $29.95

Crystal Healing: Activating Energy Centers
Oh Shinnah Fastwolf, a healer and entertainer of Mahawk and Apache ancestry, shares with you Native American traditions on how to use healing crystals such as amethyst, garnet, and quartz to

reduce stress and recharge the aura. Her songs, stories, and practice with gemstones show how to induce harmony and heal sickness.
20-9161 25 min. $16.95

DR. BERNARD JENSEN HEALTH SERIES:
Tissue cleansing-rid your body of the accumulated toxic wastes through Dr. Jensen's tissue cleansing program. Do the revitalizing "total cleanse" in your home with the doctor's information at your fingertips. Then start with a "clean slate" on a sensible nutrition program.

• Nutrition
20-126 60 min. $39.95

• Tissue Cleansing
20-125 60 min. $39.95

• World Search for Health
This is the documentation by renowned author and nutritionist Bernard Jensen of the various health and eating habits of the different cultures of the world and how they affect longevity. Narrated by Dennis Weaver.
20-110 75 min. $39.95

Emotions of Life
Three critical crises are examined: aggression, depression and addiction. "Aggression" deals with the fears and frustrations of commonplace situations and how to overcome them. "Depression" is a study of abnormal behavior and how to deal with it. "Addiction" deals with alcoholism as a model of drug dependence, how to manage and overcome dependence, and its impact on the family and a society.
20-020 60 min. $64.95

Essence of Crystals: Science of Metaphysics
This documentary describes the origin and formation of crystals, their current popularity, and the belief that quartz crystal will be the computer of the future. Well-known professionals will explain their view of crystals as tools for enhancing communications, healing, and spiritual development.
20-8020 60 min. $29.95

Everywoman's Guide to Breast Self-Examination
Provides a complete demonstration of proper BSE technique and the most up-to-date information about how you can make an important first step in the early detection of breast cancer.
20-2724 18 min. $19.95

Everywoman's Guide to Osteoporosis
Provides the most up-to-date information available about the prevention, detection and treatment of this crippling disease.
20-2725 28 min. $19.95

EYE CON SYSTEM SERIES:
Now, with the aid of video technology, you can improve and enhance your health with Eye Con Home Hypnosis videocassettes. The tapes in this series are designed for use in the comfort and privacy of home.

- **Losing Weight**
29-129 45 min. $39.95

- **Reduce Stress**
29-130 45 min. $39.95

- **Stop Smoking**
29-131 45 min. $39.95

Freedom From Back Pain
The most comprehensive and effective program for total back health: why your back hurts, how to fix it yourself, and how to keep it pain-free.
20-6322 55 min. $39.95

From the Edgar Cayce Readings:
Natural Remedies and Cures
The success of Edgar Cayce's diagnosis of disease and the remedies received from his clairvoyant medical "reading" has astounded scientific experts through the world. In this lively interview, Drs. Williams and Gladys McGarey, foremost medical practitioners of the Cayce cures, and Jess Steam, award-winning journalist and authority on the life of Cayce, discuss and demonstrate how you can easily apply many of these practical remedies at home.
20-2464 57 min. $29.95

Get Up And Go: After Breast Surgery
Developed for use after breast surgery, this program includes five different sequence levels that can be used immediately following breast surgery or utilized even if the surgery was some time ago. The women performing the exercises have all undergone breast surgery and exercise has been very beneficial to their recovery. The tape was developed in conjunction with the American Cancer Society, Michigan Division, Inc. and the University of Michigan Medical Center.
20-5469 60 min. $39.95

Get Up And Go: With Parkinson's
This exercise video was designed specifically for all levels of Parkinsonians because of its free flowing easy movement exercises. The exercises are performed by actual patients and focus on improving the patient's ability to sit, rise, reach and walk, and can be done standing, sitting or lying down. The tape was developed by a team of physicians and professionals in rehabilitative medicine, neurology and physical therapy.
20-5468 60 min. $42.95

Guide to Family Care Giving
This program is designed to provide basic training and support for the Home Care Giver. Developed by specialists in health care training and presented by a registered nurse, the video offers solutions to the every day problems encountered when caring for a loved one at home. Easy to understand step-by-step procedures are demonstrated. Topics include: How to move your patient safely, walking, toileting, bedmaking and bathing.
20-9794 58 min. $39.95

Harmonic Convergence
For many, August 16-17, 1987 marked a new epoch in human development predicted by several ancient civilizations. Ceremonies around the globe heralded a world spiritual renaissance. Share in the joyful celebration at Mt. Shasta, California and become a part of this ongoing process of planetary healing.
20-8012 45 min. $16.95

Healing Way Song: Tuning Body Energy
Chanting can affect your aura, which is a biomagnetic halo encircling the human body. Medicine woman Oh Shinnah Fastwolf teaches you to sensitize your hands to the field of energy that flows between them. You'll learn an ancient therapeutic song, while witnessing a rite of healing never before allowed to be recorded.
20-9164 25 min. $16.95

Healing with Crystals
Dr. Frank Alper, a pioneer in healing with magnetic energies, demonstrates a series of geometric configurations for using quartz crystals to produce energies where they are most needed. In an interview with Dr. Alper, he explains the nature of crystals' healing powers, as well as some caveats.
20-114 54 min. $39.95

Healing Power of Herbs: The European Tradition for Natural Health
Discover many herbal cures that grow right under your feet. Dr. Theiss, graduate of the renowned Max Planck Institute, is a practicing pharmacist, well qualified to show you how to combine European herbal traditions with modern pharmacology.
20-2465 58 min. $29.95

Health and Beauty with Lillian Grant
The human body is a marvelous, intricate machine

VIDEO TITLES LISTED IN THIS GUIDE ARE AVAILABLE FOR PURCHASE OR RENTAL. CONTACT YOUR LOCAL VIDEO STORE OR TELEPHONE (800) 383-8811

that is not replaceable. You have only one. Lillian Grant will give you the guidelines to guard it well. You will learn how to minimize stress, slow down the aging process and maintain your beauty, health and vitality.
20-8041 30 min. $29.95

Health Through God's Pharmacy: A Plant for Every Illness
Study herbal medicine with Europe's most renowned herbalist. Maria Treben, author of the European best-seller "Health Through God's Pharmacy," gives you in-depth instruction in how to heal yourself and your loved ones with herbs.
20-2462 57 min. $29.95

Helping Hands: The Right Way to Choose a Nursing Home
There comes a time when someone you love is better off in a nursing facility because he or she will receive better care. Family members can't deliver the same level of care at home without great difficulty and sometimes overwhelming expenses. This program offers a practical approach to finding the care you need.
20-8008 45 min. $39.95

Holistic Health: The New Medicine
Twelve physicians specializing in holistic medicine demonstrate their methods for controlling pain, healing cancer and promoting optimum health, emphasizing, each in their own way, the key relationship between body, mind and spirit and the link between western and traditional philosophies, attitudes and methods. Recipient of the Cine Gold Eagle Certificate and first place in the National Press Women's Contest, 1978.
20-030 35 min. $49.95

Homeopathy: The Non-Toxic Approach to Illness
Learn From Dr. Bill Gray, Stanford-trained physician and one of the nation's most preeminent homeopaths, how this medical science stimulates the body-s natural healing forces. In this video, Dr. Gary unfolds the history of homeopathy, its uses in healing acute and chronic diseases, and the preparation of homeopathic remedies.
20-2461 58 min. $29.95

Lumbar Laminectomy & Spine Fusion
Dr. Dodge, a world renowned neurosurgeon, has performed numerous lumbar surgical procedures. This program demonstrates the procedure of the lumbar laminectomy and spine fusion. The anatomy of the lumbar spine, history taking, physical examination, X-rays, and the various tests for the herniated lumbar disc are presented. An educational tape for anyone with disc-related problems, as well

as for nursing and medical students.
20-091 22 min. $99.95

Native American Prophecy and Ceremony
Gain insight into the Native American sacraments of the peace pipe, sweat lodge and ritual dancing. Honored medicine men present challenging prophecies regarding how our civilization must return to a way of life in harmony with nature and the Great Spirit or else face destruction.
20-9162 25 min. $24.95

Natural Therapies for Colds, Flu and Allergies
Four leading experts on natural health discuss and demonstrate a variety of easy ways to help everyone overcome three of the most common health problems--colds, flu and allergies--the natural way.
20-3028 60 min. $24.95

Pathways To Parenthood
Fifteen percent of all American couples have trouble conceiving a child. Find out all there is to know about what's considered "normal" and what's not. Learn when to see a specialist and what to try at home. Learn about drug therapies that work and surgery as an alternative. Options such as in-vitro fertilization and donor programs are explored.
20-6559 35 min. $24.95

POLARITY THERAPY SERIES:
Alan Siegel, N.D., director of the Polarity Therapy Center of San Francisco and the author of Life Energy: The Power that Heals (the science of polarity therapy), demonstrates hands-on healing techniques for balancing life energy. The easy-to-follow, step-by-step instructions can be used effectively by lay persons or professionals for self-learning and/or teaching others. Health practitioners, therapists, bodyworkers and chiropractors have added to their skill and effectiveness by incorporating the principles of polarity therapy.

• Basic Course
Includes theory and principles, history, how to give a polarity session, a general energy balancing session, a specific manipulations for digestion, the lymphatic system, diaphragm, chakra balancing, stress reduction and more.
20-121 70 min. $59.95

• Advanced Course
Includes theory specific manipulations for neck, back, shoulder and hip pain, colon, kidney, foot reflexology, gas release, headaches, emotional stress and more.
20-122 65 min. $59.95

Prepare for Care
This video addresses the problems associated with long-term health care and offers an objective, no-nonsense approach to solutions that work! This could be the most important time you've ever invested in you own or a loved one's long term security.
20-8027 25 min. $29.95

Radon Free
Radon is the nation's second leading cause of lung cancer. The EPA estimates that up to 20,000 Americans die each year from lung cancer caused by radon. The good news is that radon can be easily detected and eliminated from your home. This tape describes: what Radon is, how Radon affects your family, how to test for Radon, and how to eliminate Radon.
20-5093 32 min. $24.95

Right To Kill
Is mercy killing a blessing which society needs as an answer to terminal illness and intractable pain, or is it an open door to a new holocaust? This thought provoking question is explored in depth in this compelling documentary featuring noted author and editor, William F. Buckley, Jr.
20-6203 60 min. $59.95

Sound of Healing with Alana Woods
A documentary taking you on a journey into a "music medicine". You will learn the basic historic and scientific foundations of this dramatic healing tool and how sound moves matter.
20-9679 50 min. $29.95

Sportsmedicine
This problem investigates the different kinds of medical care at one of the country's best sportsmedicine clinics.
20-162 30 min. $24.95

SUBLIMINAL PERSUASION AUDIO/VISUAL SERIES:
This is a truly unique system to help you awaken your unlimited potential. It incorporates all the aspects of learning: sight, sound and repetition. Each system package includes both a video and an audio tape, designed to change and improve your life.

- **Relaxation**
20-147 30 min. $39.95

- **Relieve Stress & Anxiety**
20-152 30 min. $39.95

- **Stop Smoking**
20-143 30 min. $39.95

- **Weight Loss**
20-141 30 min. $39.95

Sugar Trap
In this video, you'll learn the truth about sugar-- where it comes from, what it does to you, and why it has you hooked. You'll also see how and where sugar is hidden in processed foods, how sugar affects your emotions and health, what sugar does to your teeth, and why some people are "sugar-holics". Features Dr. Linus Pauling and Dr. Lendon Smith.
20-207 58 min. $39.95

Tai-Chi for Health
An innovative workout for the mind and body. Tai Chi is an exercise form that tones muscles, improves flexibility and reduces stress. It provide all the benefits of a rigorous workout, without the harmful side effects. With easy to follow demonstrations and health tips, you will notice what a dramatic difference it can make for a healthier, happier you.
20-8007 60 min. $16.95

Taking Control of Depression: Mending the Mind
For millions of American's who suffer from clinical depression, take heart; it's a controllable disease and not a frame of mind. Take control of your life!
20-8029 34 min. $24.95

Tibetan Medicine: A Buddhist Approach to Healing
This was filmed at the Tibetan Medical Center established in exile by the Dalai Lama in the Indian Himalayas--the only remaining center for Tibetan medicine. Ama Lobsang Dolam, Tibet's first woman doctor, shows how medicines are made from animal, vegetable and mineral substances and how acupuncture and moxibustion was used during her daily rounds as a practicing physician. The video explores the relationship of physical health to magnetic and other forces in the environment, showing how Tibetan medicine heals both the physical and the psychic being by treating the patient rather than the disease.
20-160 29 min. $39.95

TOUCH FOR HEALTH I & II
Learn Touch for Health techniques from the system's founder, John Thie, D.C., as he demonstrates methods for reducing tension and enhancing the body's natural healing abilities. In Part II Dr. Thie shows you how to do a complete Touch for Health balancing treatment on a person.

- **Part I**
20-9149 25 min. $24.95

VIDEO TITLES LISTED IN THIS GUIDE ARE AVAILABLE FOR PURCHASE OR RENTAL. CONTACT YOUR LOCAL VIDEO STORE OR TELEPHONE (800) 383-8811

• Part II
20-8011 50 min. $39.95

Understanding Hyperactivity
In this video a group of skilled professionals explain the symptoms and the consequences of this disorder. Effective treatment approaches are outlined, along with the experiences of one particular child and family as they learn to deal with hyperactivity.
20-8016 35 min. $39.95

U.S. News Fitness Guide Best Ways to Stay Healthy
A survey of the latest findings and innovations in nutrition, medicine and fitness.
20-8052 45 min. $24.95

You Can Heal Your Life
An "at home" workshop designed especially for in-depth study. The program includes a book to read, a tape to watch and exercises to do. It is suggested that you be open to the ideas and possibilities suggested as you work on yourself.
20-130 120 min. $49.95

Worried About

Your Weight?

Questions About AIDS?

Trying To Quit Smoking?

Looking For A Healthier Life?

These Videos Can Help!

VIDEO TITLES LISTED IN THIS GUIDE ARE AVAILABLE FOR PURCHASE
OR RENTAL. CONTACT YOUR LOCAL VIDEO STORE OR TELEPHONE (800) 383-8811

Home Improvement

✓ *Building, Maintenance & Repairs*
✓ *Home Security*
✓ *Insulation & Energy Conservation*
✓ *Interior Design*
✓ *Miscellaneous*

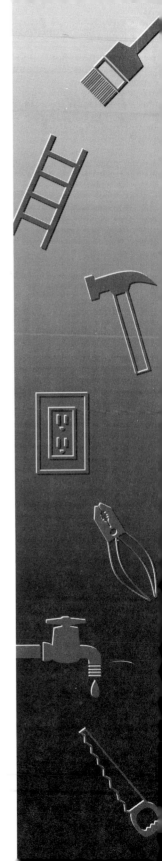

Building, Maintenance & Repairs

APPLIANCE DOCTOR VIDEO SERIES
Dr. Bob presents an instructional program which will teach everyone how to maintain their appliances, regardless of their technical background. He solves the simplest to the most complex problems, along with disassembling and testing of parts. Each tape includes a list of symptoms and solutions to help you. He also provides suggestions for preventive maintenance to help your appliance run better and last longer.

Washing Machines

• **Washing Machines**
Kenmore & Whirlpool
18-9629 74 min. $39.95

• **Same as above in Spanish**
18-9630 74 min. $39.95

• **Covers General Electric, Hot Point & Penncrest**
18-9631 106 min. $39.95

• **Same as above in Spanish**
18-9632 106 min. $39.95

Dryers

• **Gas Dryers**
Covers Kenmore & Whirlpool
18-9633 56 min. $39.95

• **Covers General Electric, Hot Point & Penncrest**
18-9634 53 min. $39.95

• **Covers Frigidaire, Norge, Signature & Westinghouse**
18-9635 59 min. $39.95

• **Electric Dryers**
Covers Kenmore & Whirlpool
18-9636 55 min. $39.95

• **Covers General Electric, Hot Point & Penncrest**
18-9637 52 min. $39.95

• **Covers Maytag**
18-9638 60 min. $39.95

• **Covers Speed Queen**
18-9639 55 min. $39.95

Dishwashers

• **Dishwashers**
Covers Kenmore & Whirlpool
18-9640 74 min. $39.95

• **Covers General Electric, Hot Point & Penncrest**
18-9641 41 min. $39.95

• **Covers KitchenAid & Hobart**
18-9642 57 min. $39.95

• **Covers Admiral, Chambers, Coloric, D&M, Frigidaire (early), Norge, Philco, Preway, Modern Maid, Magic Chef, G&S, Gibson (early), Kelvinator, Kenmore (early), Roper, Welbilt, Wedgewood, Westinghouse & Whirlpool (early)**
18-9643 60 min. $39.95

Ranges

• **Generic**
Covers Ovens/Ranges (electric self-clean)
18-9644 40 min. $39.95

Refrigerators/Freezers

• **Covers Refrigerators/Freezers (with ice-makers)**
18-9645 85 min. $39.95

• **Covers Freezers (upright model shown in video)**
18-9646 77 min. $39.95

Air Conditioning

• **Air Conditioners (window units)**
18-9647 56 min. $39.95

• **Refrigerator/Freezer**
18-8020 85 min. $49.95

Attic Conversion
Step-by-step instructions on how to fur out rafters; insulate your attic; install a vapor barrier; apply and finish drywall; work on curved surfaces;

VIDEO TITLES LISTED IN THIS GUIDE ARE AVAILABLE FOR PURCHASE OR RENTAL. CONTACT YOUR LOCAL VIDEO STORE OR TELEPHONE (800) 383-8811

prepare floors; apply a vinyl tile floor; and install skylights.
18-043 30 min. $19.95

Basic Carpentry
Step-by-step instructions on how to choose and use tools, including a tape measure, combination square, level, power saw, drill , sander and metal fastener; frame a wall; apply paneling at irregular corners; install a wall shelving system; and use an air compressor and accessories.
18-044 30 min. $19.95

Basic Home Repair
Many basic home repair projects are clearly explained. Subjects include replacing a faucet and toilet, sweating copper pipe, unclogging drains, caulking a tub, replacing light fixtures and switches, repairing lamps, repairing broken tile, running toilets and leaky faucets and replacing a shower head.
18-2098 30 min. $19.95

Be Your Own Plumber
There is no need to call a plumber for minor home plumbing jobs when you have this program. Jerry Jones will show you how to make basic plumbing repairs and what tools to use for each job. You'll be able to fix a leaky faucet; unclog a clogged drain; tackle common toilet problems; and install a new shower head. A sure time and money saver.
18-180 60 min. $24.95

BUILD YOUR OWN SERIES:

• Re-Side Your House
With siding panels and a few simple tools, your home's appearance and resale value can be improved dramatically.
18-1934 30 min. $16.95

• Store-it-All Barn
Styled after the "little red barn," this rustic and functional structure is well-suited for your garden area.
18-1933 30 min. $16.95

Ceilings: Ceiling Tile Installation
Learn how to install ceiling tiles, including planning, tools and materials, safety tips and hints.
18-074 45 min. $19.95

Ceilings: Suspended Panel Installation
Learn how to install suspended ceilings, including planning, repair, hanging the grid, tools, materials, and the most common mistakes and how to correct them.
18-073 45 min. $39.95

Ceramic Tile: Floors and Countertops
Surface preparation, establishing working lines, spreading the adhesive, laying tile, grouting, installing trim and marble threshold, caulking and sealing, removing and installing toilets, and designing and choosing the proper tile.
18-2095 27 min. $19.95

Ceramic Tile: Walls
Wall surface preparation, establishing working lines, spreading adhesive, laying tile, grouting, installing trim tile and accessories such as soap dishes and towel rack, caulking and sealing, designing and choosing the proper tile.
18-2094 27 min. $19.95

Constructing Stud Walls
Learn the components of stud walls and how to correctly cut, measure and nail these pieces together into a solid wall. Includes how to space studs; build a corner, make a door opening, use hand and power tools, and much more.
18-021 30 min. $29.95

Domestic Dishwasher Repair
With this video learn how to properly diagnose and repair nearly any domestic dishwasher. Instruction for today's servicing procedures. Illustrates basic component functions, specific brand theory and operations plus tips for the customer to make their appliance last longer. Covers solutions to common problems ranging from no-run conditions to poor washability.
18-8009 60 min. $39.95

Drywall
Applying to walls, ceilings and curves, including measuring, cutting and attaching. Taping and mudding seams, corners and curves. Sanding and finishing techniques.
18-053 42 min. $19.95

Electrical
Running new wiring in open stud walls. Wiring receptacles, switches and lights. Installation of exterior lights, overhead lights and new outlets in existing circuits. Also safety, codes, tools and materials.
18-063 42 min. $19.95

Electrical-Made Easy
18-184 30 min. $14.95

Exterior Projects
Step-by-step instructions on how to install a shingle roof; install a garage door opener; install a lockset and deadbolt lock; build a deck install a door threshold; and use an air compressor and accessories.
18-038 39 min. $19.95

Fixed Bench/Storage/Barbecue Cart

Pete Priain designs and builds an interesting, two-level redwood lumber bench and a basic redwood shelving unit with decorative lapping corner joints. A roll-around patio serving cart features interior storage, built-in barbecue grill, and maple chopping block. Pete shows you how easily this versatile unit goes together.
18-177 60 min. $39.95

Floor and Ceilings

Step-by-step instructions on how to install sheet vinyl flooring; install vinyl tile; install hardwood parquet tile; install a suspended ceiling; and install a tile ceiling.
18-039 30 min. $19.95

Garage Door Openers

Learn how to install an electric garage door opener, including trolley and chain hook up, connecting the electricity and adjusting the tension.
18-080 45 min. $19.95

GE Self Cleaning Ranges

This video places strong emphasis on diagnosing a complicated appliance with the use of the schematic. Learn the theory of how self cleaning ranges work. The method used will show you how to diagnose any self cleaning range. See how to check electrical components with your VOM. Covers bake, broil and self cleaning problems.
18-8006 77 min. $39.95

Home Repair

This video manual provides step-by-step instructions on how to deal with the repair problems that are most likely to arise in your home. Repair leaking faucets, rewire defective light switches, replace broken windows and more. 48-page booklet is included with video index for quick reference
18-243 110 min. $29.95

HOME REPAIR AND REMODELING LIBRARY

• Basic Landscaping

This video discusses how to plan and design your landscape. Learn the correct way to prepare the site, transplant an existing tree, and layout planting beds. Also shows how to plant trees, shrubs and other plants and put in edging, landscape fabric and mulch.
18-6798 40 min. $19.95

• Bathrooms

This video demonstrates how to rough-in plumbing for bathroom fixtures, install a vanity cabinet, and fabricate and laminate a countertop. Also shows how to plan for and install ceramic tile on walls

and floor and accomplish final hookup of plumbing fixtures.
18-6797 40 min. $19.95

• Fence And Gates

This video explains how to layout a fence squarely using the 3-4-5 method and construct a fence on a hill using a "step-down" method. Shows how to locate, dig holes (using a digger and auger), align and set supporting posts. Explains the use of dado cuts for fitting rails and depicts building and installing a gate. Demonstrates the use of traditional hand tools as well as power and pneumatic equipment.
18-6805 40 min. $19.95

• Framing

This video demonstrates how to plan and design a new addition. Explains how to frame out a two story addition including rough openings for windows & doors. Shows how to install joists, subfloor, rafter ties and joist hangers. Also includes installing roof trusses and sheathing that tie into existing roof and framing interior walls. Demonstrates the use of traditional power tools and pneumatic equipment.
18-6806 40 min. $19.95

• Hand And Power Tools

This video covers how to work with measuring and layout tools. Demonstrates how to use hand saws, circular saws, power miter saws, table and radial arm saws. Shows how to choose the correct hammer for your project and how to add accessories to your drill for a variety of tasks. Also deals with how to use chisels for mortising a door, using a plane and working with a router.
18-6799 40 min. $19.95

• Hardwood Floors

This program covers topics including repairing, sanding and refinishing existing hardwood floors, as well as floor preparation and installing prefinished parquet and plank floors.
18-6800 40 min. $39.95

• Home Security

Teaches the necessary prevention measures to be safe and secure in your own home. Topics covered include installing a locking door knob, a dead bolt and anti-jimmy devices in a door. Also discusses how to install locking devices on windows, a home security survey and installing an electronic alarm system.
18-6802 40 min. $39.95

• Roofing

This video deals with how to tear off old shingles and prepare for new by installing underlayment and different types of flashing. Shows how to install shingles for professional looking results, including

hip and ridge shingles. Also explains how to safely deal with heights.
18-6803 40 min. $19.95

• Siding

This video shows how to tear off old siding and/or replace existing sheathing and correctly estimate material requirements. Demonstrates applying house wrap for weatherization. Also includes installing necessary flashing and siding and caulking the finished job. Also explains how to safely deal with heights.
18-6804 40 min. $19.95

• Underground Sprinklers

This video demonstrates how to design an effective underground sprinkler system and select the proper equipment for various landscape situations. Shows how to utilize a pipe puller to efficiently install underground sprinkler pipe. Explains how to tap into existing water systems, install proper backflow controls, and install and adjust a varied selection of sprinkler heads. Also shows how to take the necessary precautions to protect the sprinkler lines during winter in cold climates.
18-6801 40 min. $19.95

• Windows And Doors

This video explains how to install interior prehung hollowcore doors, exterior door jamb, threshold, lockset, strike plate and weather stripping. Demonstrates the process to rough-out an opening in an existing wall and install a casement window and a patio door. Also shows how to remove and replace a double-hung window with a box bay window.
18-6807 40 min. $19.95

How To Diagnose Whirlpool Direct Drive Washers

A must for servicemen to properly diagnose direct drive washers. See step-by-step how the main components in the Whirlpool Direct Drive washer are taken apart. Covers mechanical and electrical aspects. Learn how to solve the following problems: dead washer, agitation, no drain, no spin, shaking, vibrations, water and oil leaks. Demonstrates removal of pump, motor, gearcase, clutch and basket drive.
18-8007 77 min. $39.95

HOW TO HANG DOORS SERIES

• Fundamentals

This video will give you invaluable information on door hanging procedures and many door hanging tips.
18-9556 42 min. $19.95

• Interior Doors I

This will show you the proper procedure for replacing an interior door slab, hanging a double acting hinge door, and cafe doors.
18-9557 47 min. $19.95

• Interior Doors II

This video will show you how to install a pocket door and a dutch door.
19-9558 37 min. $19.95

• Interior Doors III

This video has detailed installation procedures for bifold doors, double doors and bypass doors.
18-9559 35 min. $19.95

• Exterior Doors I

This video has all of the detailed procedures for installing a jamb and then later installing the finishing door.
18-9560 48 min. $19.95

Installing A Lockset

An easy-to-follow video showing you how to install almost and king of lockset. Includes locating, marking, and chiseling the door and frame, then drilling and installing the lockset or deadbolt lock.
18-023 30 min. $29.95

Installing A Pre-Hung Door

You'll learn all the professional tips and tricks for installing a door, insuring the proper fit and level hang.
18-024 30 min. $29.95

Installing A Suspended Ceiling

Learn the main components of a suspended ceiling and the proper way to install a perfect ceiling.
18-025 30 min. $29.95

Interior Design with Brick & Stone

Ideas and designs for home buyers, builders, remodelers and designers. More than 100 ideas and designs for fireplaces, lobbies and entries, floors and stairways, stoves and inserts, kitchens with bricked in appliances, curved and arched walls, sculptured brick scenes, and even brick ceilings.
18-8001 36 min. $29.95

Interior Projects

Step-by-step instructions on how to install wall shelving; install kitchen counter tops; install a kitchen sink; install a washing machine/dryer; ventilate your attic; use an air compressor and accessories; repair holes and cracks in walls and ceilings; remove wallpaper; and add a new electrical outlet.
18-037 30 min. $19.95

Video Titles Listed In This Guide Are Available For Purchase Or Rental. Contact Your Local Video Store Or Telephone (800) 383-8811

Kitchen Cabinets
Step-by-step instructions on how to remove your existing cabinets; remove existing appliances and sinks; install new uppers; install new lowers; install countertops; and install a new kitchen sink.
18-045 30 min. $19.95

Kitchen Remodeling
This tape has two major benefits. One, it provides the home handyman with a step-by-step procedure from planning through construction of kitchen remodeling. Second, it provides the information needed to make the best possible decisions concerning contracting and the total scope of kitchen remodeling.
18-217 60 min. $19.95

Learning the Art of Laying Brick
A step-by-step procedure from mixing mortar and proper tools needed, through building your own walls and other small projects. A three-tape series.
18-8000 45 min $79.95

Microwave Oven Repair
If you can use a volt-ohm meter (VOM) you can correctly diagnose 98% of microwave problems. Learn how a microwave oven works. Understand schematics, solid state touch boards, components and functions in relationship to the schematic, safety precautions and trouble shooting. This program also lists part suppliers for microwave parts.
18-8003 85 min. $39.95

NEW HOME BUILDING SERIES

• **Framing Floors with Larry Haum**
18-9500 60 min. $34.95

• **Framing Walls**
18-9501 60 min. $34.95

• **Framing Roofs**
18-9502 60 min. $34.95

• **Basic Stairbuilding**
18-9503 60 min. $29.95

• **Making Kitchen Cabinets**
18-9504 60 min. $29.95

• **Laying Floors (Hardwood)**
18-9505 60 min. $29.95

• **Sanding & Finishing Hardwood Floors**
18-9506 60 min. $29.95

• **Installing Kitchen Cabinets & Countertops**
18-9507 60 min. $29.95

• **Trim Carpentry Techniques: Installing Trim**
18-9508 60 min. $29.95

• **Trim Carpentry Techniques: Installing Doors & Windows**
18-9509 60 min. $29.95

Paint and Wallpaper - Made Easy
18-186 30 min. $14.95

Paint Like a Professional
The steps are thorough: from preparing surfaces and buying the proper supplies to painting evenly and attaining maximum coverage in minimum time. After you're through, "Paint Like a Professional" demonstrates how to clean, store and maintain your painting materials.
18-1677 30 min. $14.95

Paneling and Shelving
Installing 4' x 8' panels over new or existing walls, and trim techniques. How to install various types of shelving. Installing individual plank boards to walls, with trim techniques.
18-069 42 min. $19.95

Plumbing
Bathroom/laundry installation of rough plumbing for water and waste lines. Installation of toilet, vanity faucet and sink, tub and shower, and a washer and dryer. Also safety, codes, tools and materials.
18-065 42 min. $19.95

Plumbing - Made Easy
18-185 30 min. $14.95

Plumbing and Electrical
Part I: Plumbing. Overview of plumbing systems; and step-by-step instructions on how to work with cooper pipe; plumb for a shower and tub; install a bathroom sink; install a toilet; and install a washing machine/dryer. Part II: Electrical. Step-by-step instructions on how to connect outlets and switches; connect outdoor fixtures; connect overhead lights; and install a new outlet in an existing wall.
18-040 30 min. $19.95

Principles of Paneling
Paneling, from start to finish, is the topic of this videotape. Learn to cut, glue nail, and finish off a paneled room, and how to get professional results.
18-026 30 min. $29.95

Railing/Roofing

Sturdy railings add both safety and practicality to any deck project. Peter Priain demonstrates typical post and rail construction plus several ideas for decorative and functional railing treatments.
18-176 60 min. $39.95

Remodeling - Made Easy
18-183 30 min. $14.95

Secrets of Basic Electrical Troubleshooting

This video, and accompanying reference book, covers the basics of troubleshooting almost any electrical appliance. Straight forward and easy to understand. Explains how to use various meters, how to test for hot, ground and neutral. Also covered are electrical basics, trouble shooting motors, relays and transformers
18-8008 60 min. $39.95

Secrets of Troubleshooting Refrigerators

This is the video you need if you want to successfully begin diagnosing and repairing refrigerators. Revealed are many secrets of troubleshooting and repair. You will learn theory and operation of both manual and automatic defrost models. Also included are schematics to help visualize how the defrost system operates. Many complaints and solutions are covered.
18-8002 72 min. $39.95

Skylights

How to plan, locate, layout, cut opening, make structural changes and frame opening. How to install skylights and roof windows. Also installing flashing, shingles, insulation, drywall and finishing the opening.
18-085 42 min. $19.95

Substructure/Decking

Pete Priain simplifies a major deck project by showing you a step-by-step approach.
18-175 60 min. $39.95

SUNSET VIDEOS - THE EXPERTS SHOW YOU HOW

Sunset brings you home improvement know-how on video. Expert hosts, working in actual home or workshop settings, demonstrate step-by-step procedures for each project area: planning and design considerations, selecting and using tools, choosing and working with materials, and completing the project or installation. Each Sunset Video program is accompanied by an illustrated 16 to 48 page booklet packed with additional information and helpful tips.

- **Bookshelves**
18-6505 30 min. $19.95

- **Cabinets**
18-6506 30 min. $19.95

- **Carpentry**
18-6507 30 min. $19.95

- **Ceramic Tile**
18-6508 30 min. $19.95

- **Decks**
18-6509 30 min. $19.95

- **Drywall & Paneling**
18-6510 30 min. $19.95

- **Flooring**
18-6511 30 min. $19.95

- **Furniture Refinishing**
18-6512 30 min. $19.95

- **Home Inspection**
18-6513 30 min. $19.95

- **Home Repair**
18-6514 30 min. $19.95

- **Insulation & Weatherstripping**
18-6515 30 min. $19.95

- **Kitchen Remodeling**
18-6516 30 min. $19.95

- **Painting & Wallpapering**
18-6517 30 min. $19.95

- **Plumbing**
18-6518 30 min. $19.95

- **Skylights**
18-6519 30 min. $19.95

- **Wiring**
18-6520 30 min. $19.95

This Old House

Material from the Emmy Award-winning, how-to television series on home repair and restoration. Now updated and revised to bring you even more easy-to-duplicate basic and advanced projects.
18-110 60 min. $24.95

Tiling Countertops with Michael Byrne

Watch professional tilesetter Michael Byrne demonstrate his craft. Byrne shows you how to use traditional techniques and modern materials to tile attractive easy-to-clean countertops. You'll learn

how to work with both backer-board and mortarbed substrates, lay tile around a sink and detail your countertop.
18-2382 60 min. $29.95

Tiling Floors with Michael Byrne
The focus is on a watertight bathroom floor and a sloping shower pan, but the techniques can be applied anywhere in your home. You'll learn how a border can simplify a diagonal layout, how to mix and float mortar for a substrate that's flat, level and sturdy, how expansion joints can keep your floor from cracking and more.
18-2384 60 min. $29.95

Tiling Walls with Michael Byrne
Byrne covers all of the techniques you need, from layout to grout. Working on a bathroom job site, he shows you how to handle out-of-plumb walls, how to maneuver around bathtubs, plumbing and windows, how to cut tile using biters, snapcutters and a wetsaw and much more.
18-2383 75 min. $29.95

Tools
Use and care of hand tools, including measuring, leveling, attaching, dismantling, finishing, and safety and time saving tips. Use and care of power tools including cutting, drilling, assembling and finishing, and safety tips.
18-049 42 min. $19.95

Tools for the Beginning Carpenter
Pete Priain explains the basic tools you will need for the beginning carpenter's tool box. Areas include striking tools, measuring tools, cutting tools, fastening tools, and miscellaneous specialty tools.
18-181 60 min. $39.95

Truth About Sealed System Repair
Using animated graphics and live demonstrations simplifies the information to make cap tube systems easy to understand. Tools, theory and operation and sealed system diagnosis are covered as well as compressor installation, contaminated systems, soldering techniques and much more. Learn about evaporator punctures and five steps to repairing them.
18-8005 77 min. $39.95

Vinyl Floors
Installing sheet vinyl, including making a paper template and cutting and installing the vinyl for both perimeter bond and full spread adhesive floorings. Installing self-adhesive vinyl floor tiles including planning, layout, cutting border tiles and curves, tips, tools and materials.
18-071 42 min. $39.95

Walls
Step-by-step instruction on how to install and finish drywall; prepare your wall for paint and wallpaper; paint large surfaces and trim; remove wallpaper; apply wallpaper; install paneling and apply trim.
18-042 30 min. $19.95

Walls/Framing and Removal
Learn how to frame a wall with window and door openings and how to remove a wall to open up a room.
18-081 45 min. $19.95

WOODWORKING CARPENTRY: DO-IT-YOURSELF SERIES
The video programs contain practical, step-by-step instruction on how to undertake all kinds of fun and economical projects that may be used in educational settings and in do-it-yourself/home improvement activity. Each video includes a free set of plans or instruction guides.

• **Woodworking Techniques**
18-6860 25 min. $39.95

• **Workbench Storage Cabinet**
18-6861 25 min. $39.95

• **Store-It-All Barn**
18-6862 25 min. $39.95

• **Computer Desk**
18-6863 25 min. $39.95

• **Welch Cupboard**
18-6864 25 min. $39.95

• **Sketch & Storage Bench**
18-6865 25 min. $39.95

• **Re-side Your Home**
18-6866 25 min. $39.95

• **Downhill Racer**
18-6867 25 min. $39.95

• **Remodeling Decision**
18-6868 25 min. $39.95

• **Add-A-Room**
18-6869 25 min. $39.95

• **Gabled Garden Shed**
18-6870 25 min. $39.95

Home Security

Consumer Report: Home Safe Home
An essential guide to keeping your home safe and secure. A guided room-by-room tour of your home, showing how to child-proof your home, fire protection and safety tips, security devices and how to get the best homeowner's insurance.
28-042 50 min. $19.95

Consumer Reports: Burglarproofing Your Home & Car
Every 10 seconds a home is broken into and a car is stolen...don't let it happen to you.
28-082 60 min. $19.95

Crime Prevention in the Home
Videoguide to crime prevention, covering many aspects of home protection, including crime deterrents like alarms, solid wooden doors and deadbolt locks; means of entry and common tools used by thieves; what to do in the event of a break in; and safety tips within the home.
18-029 30 min. $29.95

Principles of Home Defense
For the single resident or a family, this program is designed for those who are serious about safety and security at home. Gives realistic alternatives to being a victim of crime. Deputy J.D. Harris of the L.A. County Sheriff's Department shows you how to develop a home defense plan that makes it too costly for a criminal to violate your castle.
28-020 60 min. $29.95

Wally's Workshop: Alarms & Safes
Wally shows how to select the best security plan. He demonstrates how to mount the unit so that it's inconspicuous and how to attach the wires to detection devices. You'll learn how to create secret compartments in drawers, bookcases and books. And he'll give you pointers for choosing a safe that provides protection from fire as well as robbery.
18-5108 30 min. $19.95

Insulation & Energy Conservation

Energy Conservation
Step-by-step instructions on how to install a new threshold; weatherstrip a door; apply caulk; weatherstrip a window; install a programmable thermostat; insulate a hot water heater; install both insulation; install vapor barriers; and insulate the attic floor.
18-041 30 min. $19.95

Installing Insulation and Sheetrock
Find out all about vapor barriers, "R" value, and how to measure, cut and install insulation. Then explore how to install sheetrock: measurement, cutting, handling and installation, including doors and electrical box openings. Just like a pro!
18-022 30 min. $29.95

Insulation
Installing fiberglass batts in walls, roofs and attics. Ventilation, vapor barriers, and time-saving tips. Installing blown-in insulation and rigid foam panels. Also, attic ventilation, wind turbines, tools and materials and safety.
18-067 42 min. $19.95

Interior House Painting
Jerry Jones shows you which brushes, rollers and pads are the right ones for your job; how to save time and money; and the right way to spray paint.
18-179 58 min. $39.95

Weatherization
Weatherstripping and caulking doors, replacing door threshold and home weatherization audit. Weatherizing windows, caulking foundations and cracks, insulating hot water heaters and energy conservation projects.
18-051 30 min. $39.95

Interior Design

Art Of Interior Design
Whether you are redecorating one room or an entire home. The Art Of Interior Design can provide the information and skills you need to create a functional and beautiful interior.
18-5365 60 min. $29.95

Be a Stripper
This program was developed to help solve the sticky problem of wallpaper removal. It shows detailed step-by-step instructions by a professional for preparing for repapering or painting.
18-3003 10 min. $19.95

VIDEO TITLES LISTED IN THIS GUIDE ARE AVAILABLE FOR PURCHASE OR RENTAL. CONTACT YOUR LOCAL VIDEO STORE OR TELEPHONE (800) 383-8811

Decorating: Selecting the Right Carpet

Cathy Crane, author of "Personal Places" and "What Do You Say to a Naked Room," co-hosts this video. In each room she discusses the basic decorating and design concepts to consider to make your house feel like your home. A special section explains how to make the right choice in carpets for each room.

18-2096 25 min. $19.95

DECORATIVE PAINTING VIDEO SERIES: THE FINISHING SCHOOL

These tapes demonstrate the glazing, marbling and graining decorative painting techniques included in the book entitled "Professional Painted Finishes".

* **Glazing**
18-8015 85 min. $49.95

* **Graining I**
18-8014 120 min. $49.95

* **Graining II**
18-8010 83 min. $49.95

* **Marbling I**
18-8011 73 min. $49.95

* **Marbling II**
18-8012 73 min. $49.95

* **Marbling & Stone**
18-8013 70 min. $49.95

Faux Fun

Anyone can paint decorative wall finishes by using Faux Fun's easy to follow step-by-step instructions. Comes complete with demonstrations on sponge painting, dragging and from rag painting to marbleizing.

18-8024 50 min. $34.95

Finishing Touch Interior Design Tour

An interior designer, Sherry Lynn, who has been helping people with their interiors for over 20 years, takes you on a lighthearted yet educational tour of her home. She explains, by example, how beautiful real life interiors can be achieved. You will be shown how to begin and develop a plan. She shares ideas on lighting, layout and the use of color. Sherry Lynn's inspiration and encouragement will guide you to create unique interiors of your own.

18-8019 46 min. $24.95

Interior Paint and Wallpaper

Wall repair and preparation; how to paint walls, ceilings and trim; removing old wallpaper; time-saving tips; common mistakes; wallpaper planning and hanging; outside and inside corners; and papering around openings.

18-240 30 min. $19.95

New American Home: A House of Ideas

See the latest in home design and innovative building products. You will get a wealth of ideas and information as well as inspiration about home building and decorating. The New American Home has a house full of ideas for you!

18-9598 35 min. $19.95

Professional Tips for Easy Wallpapering

Nancy Mitchell, with almost 10 years experience as a professional paperhanger, walks you through all aspects of papering your room.

18-103 56 min. $29.95

Step-By-Step Guide To Basic Wallpapering

Professional paper hanger Mark Florian demonstrates the fundamentals of his craft in this step-by-step approach. The tape and accompanying leaflet cover all essentials - how to calculate the amount of wallpaper needed, preparing the walls, how to choose a starting point, pattern matching, ceiling lines, adhesives, inside corners, working around windows and papering electrical outlet covers.

18-3501 25 min. $19.95

U-DO-IT AND TILE-IT-YOURSELF SERIES

* **Counters**
Demonstration of tools and materials needed to install countertops. Two complete jobs. First, the installation of a full mortar system. Shows how to layout all types of counters, prepare the surface, mix mortar and leveling the mortar bed. How to mix and apply the proper adhesive and grout. Learn how to tile different types of kitchens and on almost any surface from old tile to wood.

18-9552 35 min. $19.95

* **Glass Block**
Teaches all the basic techniques of installing glass block. Laying out the job. Using tools, spacers, panel anchors, expansion materials, reinforcing and mortar are shown in detail. How to install glass block inside and out.

18-9550 35 min. $19.95

* **Wallpaper**
Shows the proper use of tools and hanging different types of wallpaper. Stripping, prepare and fix holes, cutting, booking, matching are shown.

Papering around doors, windows, soffitts, cabinets and archways, covering switchplates are demonstrated in detail.
18-9548 50 min. $19.95

● **Saltillo Mexican Tile**
How to seal, grout care and maintenance tips.
18-9549 35 min. $19.95

● **Walls**
Complete demonstration of installing wall tile on a three walled tub/shower enclosure. The techniques will work on any wall surface. Bruce shows the tile layout to achieve symmetry and have the fewest cuts necessary. Keeping level working lines and how to make cuts of tile around fixtures are also demonstrated.
18-9551 50 min. $19.95

Warm & Inviting: Home Interior Design
This video presents the basic principles of home design by identifying and illustrating the integration of: color, furnishings, arrangement, and accessories. Your house can be a "Warm and Inviting" home, when you apply these basic principles.
18-5100 40 min. $29.95

Window Principles - Custom Balloon Shades
This video takes the mystery out of planning and constructing these charming Balloon Shade window treatments. These detailed instructions will help you achieve a professional look with the satisfaction of knowing you did it yourself.
18-6237 103 min. $29.95

Window Principles - Custom Draperies
The first in the Window Principles series of custom window treatment instructional videos covers traditional pinch-pleat styles, a more contemporary french pleat and the ever-popular rod-run. These detailed instructions help you achieve a professional look and the satisfaction of knowing you did it yourself.
18-6236 112 min. $39.95

Miscellaneous

BETTER HOMES AND GARDENS VIDEO SERIES
Six titles help you capitalize on the opportunities from Better Homes and Gardens books/video.

● **Room Arranging Do's And Don't's**
18-6161 25 min. $19.95

● **Building A Deck**
18-6162 20 min. $19.95

● **Preparing Your Home To Sell**
18-6167 45 min. $19.95

● **Refinishing Furniture**
18-6168 57 min. $19.95

● **Making Your Kitchen Store More**
18-6164 23 min. $19.95

● **Wallpaper Like A Pro!**
18-6169 55 min. $19.95

Safe and Warm: Made Easy
This is an instructional program on a variety of projects. Building fireplaces, installing locks, storm windows and many other projects are included in this video.
18-187 30 min. $14.95

Earth Ponds: Introduction to Pond Design & Construction
You've dreamed of building a pond--for a place to swim and skate, a pool to catch fresh fish. These are a few of the rewards for the backyard pond owner. Let Tim Matson show you how these ponds are designed and built, as well as the exciting ways that they can be enjoyed.
18-9693 48 min. $29.95

Full Access: The Contractor's Guide to Selling and Building for Disabled and Elderly Communities
Codes, regulations and more are covered in this hour long feature. This video targets a specific industry and shows how to find a lucrative niche.
18-9565 60 min. $39.95

How to Prepare Your Home for Sale
Make selling your home a lot easier and more profitable. Just let Barb Schwartz show you what to do to prepare your home for sale...so it sells!
18-8023 30 min. $39.95

Tips From the Pros: Pool Care
This easy-to-follow video is consumer oriented, showing you everything from how to shop for pool products to troubleshooting and much more.
18-3037 50 min. $39.95

VIDEO TITLES LISTED IN THIS GUIDE ARE AVAILABLE FOR PURCHASE OR RENTAL. CONTACT YOUR LOCAL VIDEO STORE OR TELEPHONE (800) 383-8811

New

Special Interest Video Titles

Become Available

Often.

Please Inquire

If A Title Or Subject

You Are Looking For

Is Not Listed.

Horses

English Horsemanship & Training

ABC's of Basic Dressage
Olympic bronze and Pan American gold medal winner, Hilda Gurney, explains and teaches you by demonstration the philosophy of dressage, reveals proper tack and equipment, shows how to use the aids properly. Graphics and animated illustrations make it easy to understand the sometimes mystifying components of one of America's fastest growing sports, the art of dressage riding. The program is a pleasure to watch and of instructional value to riders of all disciplines.
21-001 60 min. $49.95

Basic Dressage for North America
Christolot Hanson Boylen. No matter how proficient a rider you may be, if you are new to dressage you must begin at Step One. Christolot Boylen stresses the fundamentals that are essential to good performance at every level. The instruction includes demonstrations of lunging technique, rhythm and suppleness, rider's aids and beginning competitive skills. This tape is a visual training manual that will provide a sound foundation in the art and science of dressage.
21-259 46 min. $49.95

Basic Dressage with David Hunt
English Olympic Team Member gives three basic lessons: 1) type of horse and tack; the three basic paces; 2) lateral work: shoulder in, traverse, half pass, walk pirouette; and 3) the flying change in four, three, two and one time sequence; the pirouette, the half pirouette, the piaf, the passage, the into and out of the piaf, and the into and out of passage.
21-002 70 min. $49.95

Basic English Horsemanship
Jill Clark and Jerry Hull show you the basic skills of English riding. Equipment and how to use it, as well as how to get your horse ready to show. Hunt seat.
21-5990 45 min. $49.95

Basic Hunt Seat
Lee Troup Johnson, trainer of national and world champions, shows you how to select the right horse, how to approach the sport...stresses the rider's attitude.
21-5991 45 min. $39.95

Basic Jumping Clinic
The sound basics of starting your horse over the jumps, from trainer of world champions, Lee Troup Johnson. You'll watch a young filly on her first day of jumping.
21-5992 45 min. $39.95

Basic Flatwork 1
Captain Phillips assumes in this cassette that the young horse has no education beyond handling and backing. It also assumes the rider's knowledge is reasonably basic. By the end of the tape horse and rider are acting as a team with the horse quiet, attentive, confident and starting to supple up. Specific areas covered include: 1) How to establish a system of communication with your horse. 2) Why horses will not perform to your wishes. 3) How to establish basic control; overcoming various forms of resistance. 4) How to obtain complete relaxation and receptiveness. 5) How to settle an excitable horse. 6) How to determine your educational goals and objectives. 7) Basic two track exercises. 8) Improvement of activity, rhythm and balance.
21-013 30 min. $49.95

Basic Flatwork 2
In this tape Captain Phillips takes you from where your horse can walk, trot, canter in an open frame without resistance to the stage where he moves freely on the bit, is supple, active and attentive to the aids. Your horse reaches the point where he is ready for specialized education. Specific areas covered include: 1) The mystery of being "on the bit" and how it is achieved. 2) Two track exercises and overcoming specific resistance. 3) Correcting the horse's "line". 4) How to execute a correct turn, the myth of the inside rein, how to keep your horse moving forward through turns. 5) Half halts, their benefits and implementation. 6) Development of flexibility of stride. 7) Refinement of upward and downward transitions.
21-014 30 min. $49.95

Basic Jumping 1
To achieve maximum benefit from this tape you will need: a reasonably basic knowledge of horsemanship; a secure position; a confident approach; your horse trained to the level of Basic Flatwork 2 in this video series. Specific areas covered include: 1) Free jumping on the lunges. 2) Introductory exercises over poles and suitable distances. 3) Trot exercises over fences. 4) Introduction to cantering over fences. 5) Introduction to related lines of fences. 6) Establishing correct distances. 7) Introduction to combination.
21-015 30 min. $ 49.95

Basic Jumping 2
In Basic Jumping 1 the young horse was introduced to jumping and his skills developed to the point where he was quietly and confidently cantering

---

VIDEO TITLES LISTED IN THIS GUIDE ARE AVAILABLE FOR PURCHASE OR RENTAL. CONTACT YOUR LOCAL VIDEO STORE OR TELEPHONE (800) 383-8811

around a straightforward course. In this tape through a series of further exercises Captain Phillips shows how to improve the horse's technique, balance and confidence and how to overcome any of the more subtle problems that may develop. The flat preparation is designed to improve balance and flexibility of the canter and teach and refine the flying change and counter-canter. The detailed jumping exercises will sharpen his reactions, improve his technique by encouraging him to use neck, shoulders, back and hocks correctly.
21-016 30 min. $59.95

Basic Techniques of Riding and Jumping
Famous Olympic Gold Medalist, Chairman of the USET Board and national TV equestrian sports commentator William Steinkraus covers basic techniques for both horse and rider for world-class show jumping. Good for the beginner, too!
21-030 58 min. $49.95

Bruce Davidson: Horse Management
Covers in great detail those aspects of Eventing which are of vital importance to any rider's daily schedule. Here Bruce deals with different kinds of tack, bandaging, and boots, explaining his preferences for the various kinds of equipment and demonstrating how they should be used. An invaluable film for anyone concerned with the day-to-day care and management of horses in all disciplines.
21-5995 50 min. $39.95

Bruce Davidson: Water Schooling
This film will appeal to a wide audience, from pony club members to advanced riders, dealing as it does with the water schooling of a novice horse right from the beginning of its career onwards. Under the expert hands of Bruce Davidson twice World Champion Three-Day Eventer, a young horse is taken with patience and care through all the stages of approaching and jumping in and out of water.
21-5996 30 min. $39.95

Concepts of Dressage
This is a moving talk given at Cal Poly University by Charles De Kunffy, world authority with European training and background in the field of dressage. Mr. De Kunffy addresses the motivation of riders, their relationships to their horses, and generally what it actually means to call oneself a horseman. Clips of the Western U.S. Olympic Dressage Trails at the Los Angeles Equestrian Center superimposed with Mr. De Kunffy's talk help make this tape a real treasure of information and enjoyment not readily available in most dressage clinics.
21-022 40 min. $49.95

Cross Country: Part 1
Interval training; roads and tracks; steeplechase. For the rider starting out or wishing to advance his skills, this video is a valuable addition to any riders' store of knowledge and a must for any rider seriously considering competing in Three-Day Eventing.
21-004 90 min. $49.95

Cross Country: Part 2
Actual cross-country phase. Bruce Davidson walks and rides you through all kinds of cross-country jumps, including water jumps, gates, coffins, Normandy banks, bullfinches, etc. He also deals with horse care during this demanding part of the endurance phase.
21-005 80 min. $49.95

Day-to-Day Care of Your Horse
Captain Phillips makes the young and fairly inexperienced horse person aware of the basic everyday care required to keep your horse in top condition. He talks about 1) Good stabling, the best size, construction and types of bedding. 2) The requirements of field and fencing. 3) the daily routine including mucking out, rigging, stable bandaging, grooming kits, dressing feet, cleaning tack. 4) Exercise: how to correctly bandage your horse's legs, exercise boots, saddling up, food to work ratio, washing the horse down. 5) General veterinary notes: diagnosis of problems and treatment, symptoms of colic and its causes.
21-012 30 min. $49.95

Dressage
Bruce Davidson rides both Might Tango and JJ Babu and demonstrates all aspects of dressage from an Eventing point of view, including initial training, position of rider and importance of correct use of aids, correct equipment and medical advice applicable to dressage.
21-003 90 min. $49.95

Dressage: Official U.S.D.F. Introduction
Featuring Kathy Connelly and narrated by Bill Woods, this talented team explains and demonstrates what the judge looks for in a dressage test, from basic training level through Grand Prix. They also demonstrate how to achieve constant non-verbal communication through use of seat, leg and rein aids producing accurate ring fingers, symmetrical circling, suppleness and smooth obedient transitions. An invaluable training seminar for beginners and experienced riders alike!
21-248 50 min. $69.95

English Pleasure Horse: Beginning to Champion
Cal Poly University's 17th Annual Horsemanship Seminar features noted Arabian trainers Tom and Sandy Sapp. They demonstrate their techniques

---

VIDEO TITLES LISTED IN THIS GUIDE ARE AVAILABLE FOR PURCHASE OR RENTAL. CONTACT YOUR LOCAL VIDEO STORE OR TELEPHONE (800) 383-8811

with the early training of a horse, with the final stages being devoted to the development of a quality English pleasure horse.
21-023 50 min. $49.95

Equestrians: 1984 Summer Olympic Highlights
A limited edition! Produced by ABC Sports, this 90-minute production includes footage not broadcast to the general public. Includes winning dressage tests, the USET's three-day squad in its gold medal winning performance, as well as both the gold and silver winning performances of the show jumping team.
21-057 90 min. $49.95

General Horse Management
Covers in great detail those aspects of eventing which are of vital importance in any rider's daily schedule. Bruce Davidson deals with different kinds of tack, bandaging and boots among other things, explaining his preferences for the various kinds of equipment and demonstrating how they should be used.
21-009 50 min. $49.95

George Morris: The Science of Riding
Olympic medalist George Morris brings his teaching techniques to riders who may never otherwise have the opportunity to train with him. Three half-hour segments cover the basics used as the foundation of his training program. Techniques are demonstrated with the help of the 1984 Malcay and the American Horse Show finals.
21-223 90 min. $69.95

Gridwork
Careful ground work and a gradual building up of a horse's confidence are essential to prepare him for the fences he is going to encounter during a Three-Day Event. This video should be essential viewing for anyone wishing to learn or improve their own or their horses ability to jump.
21-007 55 min. $59.95

Horse Trials 1
This tape assumes that the horse is educated at least to the levels described at the end of Basic Flatwork 2 and Basic Jumping 2. Captain Phillips explains the particular problems faced by the Horse Trails competitor and advises on the selection of a suitable horse. The development of the cross-country seat is explained in detail as are exercises designed to accustom the horse to traveling easily over uneven country. The horse's introduction to cross-country obstacles is examined at length with particular attention being paid to: water, bank and steps, drop fences, ditches and slides. General consideration regarding fitness and preparation for a One-Day Event are discussed as is the actual event itself including warm-up and dressage, walking the cross-

country and showjumping.
21-018 30 min. $49.95

Hunt Seat Horsemanship
Lee Troup Johnson shows you the vital basics as well as the fine points of training to win. Useful instruction for people showing at the various breed and open shows.
21-6000 45 min. $39.95

Introduction to Horseback Riding & Horse Care
Internationally recognized sports woman and motion-picture/television star Stephanie Powers and famed horse trainer Art Gaytan present a comprehensive, authoritative guide for beginning riders in both English and Western styles. Topics include: mounting, trail etiquette, safety tips and much more.
21-8003 52 min. $29.95

Jeffery Method of Horse Handling
Featuring Maurice Wright and sons as instructors, this very enlightening program demonstrates in detail the complete process of this amazing method. The subject horse is gathered with its herd from the rugged, picturesque range country of New England, Australia. Over a period of two days the horse learns to accept its handler and rider completely, with obedience, trust and affection. The technique is presented in a step-by-step, professional way. Excellent.
21-227 75 min. $49.95

Jimmy Williams: "A Bit About Bits"
Jimmy Williams, one of the most respected and knowledgeable horsemen, discusses the characteristics and proper usage of bits. He tells how to select the right bit, how to avoid problems, how to use snaffles, pelhams, kimberwick, and gags. Learn why a bit is only as good as the person using it.
21-225 90 min. $59.95

Preparing the Horse with Jimmy Williams
This tape concentrates on technique and proper equipment for training hunters and jumpers for the show ring.
21-026 60 min. $49.95

Preparing the Rider with Jimmy Williams
Jimmy Williams has 50 years of experience with stock, hunter and jumper horses. This "Horseman of the Year" for the American Horse Show Association has had six of his students become members of the USET. This tape centers on how to develop proper and effective skills as a rider interested in competition in hunter and jumper

classes.
21-025 60 min. $49.95

Rider Over Jumps

No matter how capable or well educated your horse may be, both his happiness and any long-term success are dependent on his being correctly ridden. In this tape Captain Phillips explains the forward jumping seat and how to maintain perfect harmony and control over the horse when jumping. The rider's position and application of the aids are dealt with in great detail stage by stage, including the line, the turn, the approach, the take-off, through the air, the landing and getaway. Also included are a number of exercises designed to enable the rider to develop an "eye for stride" thus ensuring his horse meets every jump at the correct point of take-off.
21-020 30 min. $69.95

Selection of Your Horse

In this cassette Captain Phillips helps you, the prospective purchaser, to determine your requirements in a saddle horse and shows you how to look for a suitable animal. He explains in clear terms the individual attributes of a horse that are important for you to consider and he pays particular attention to the following areas: 1) Confirmation, 2) Soundness, 3) Temperament, 4) Performance, 5) Dangers and pitfalls and how to avoid them, 6) Veterinary report and how to evaluate it.
21-011 30 min. $69.95

Show Jumping

The different kinds of jumps in the show ring are considered by Bruce Davidson as he walks and jumps you through each of them. He also covers in detail all the rules relating to a show jumping round which can often be overlooked.
21-006 55 min. $49.95

Show Jumping World Cup

A complete film record of the 1980 horse show jumping competition for the Federation of Equestrians International World Cup, a must-see for any horseman interested in improving his riding skills or for anyone who truly enjoys the highest level competition among the world's top horses and riders.
21-031 120 min. $69.95

Spanish Riding School: The First 400 Years

Produced in Austria, this is the first time the public has had behind-the-scenes film access to the famous Spanish Riding School of Vienna. An incredible documentary on the breeding, history, tradition and actual performance of the Lippizaners. This video is a limited edition.
21-074 60 min. $39.95

Stallions of Distinction

Some of the most beautiful Arabian stallions in the world. The 8th Annual Arabian Riders and Breeders Society of San Diego presents their All-Arabian Show at the Griffith Park Equestrian Center in Los Angeles and gives you an opportunity to see the elegance and beauty of the purebred Arabian Stallion.
21-075 30 min. $49.95

Starting The Show Jumper

In this unique video tape, Bill Robertson explains his system, a combination of the teachings and philosophies of Europe's leading masters such as Bertalan De Nemethy and Richard Watjen and a touch of West Texas "real cowboy" psychology. We'll see him start a young prospect in the round pen, test his ability in the jumping chute, move him through basic lunging and gymnastics, and finally observe him as he walks and rides a horse-show course.
21-6001 45 min. $59.95

Strategy of Dressage

1984 Olympian, Sandy Pflueger Clarke, offers the opportunity for American dressage riders to share in the lessons she has learned while studying and competing in international dressage. Emphasis is placed on the entry, use of the corners, transitions, preparations for movements, attitude of the rider, accuracy, and above all, homework. Gain experience and knowledge in what the judge would like to see in your test.
21-224 60 min. $49.95

Water Schooling

A young horse is taken with patience and care through all the stages of approaching and jumping in and out of water. As the horse's ability and confidence grows, more is gradually asked and expected of him.
21-008 30 min. $39.95

Three-Day Gold

The U.S. Three-Day Team's preparation and the 1976 Olympic Three-Day Equestrian Event in Quebec, Canada. Highlights of the triumphs of dressage, the grueling cross-country endurance test and stadium jumping.
21-032 70 min. $49.95

Your First Pony

Your First Pony is Captain Phillips' guide to both parents and children of the pleasures, responsibilities and possible pitfalls of owning a pony. He talks about the selection of pony gear and tack, housing the pony and its daily care and he pays particular attention to the safety of both pony and child. Topics covered include: 1) Qualities to look for in the ideal pony. 2) Trying out the pony. 3) Necessary requirements at home-stabling, field

VIDEO TITLES LISTED IN THIS GUIDE ARE AVAILABLE FOR PURCHASE OR RENTAL. CONTACT YOUR LOCAL VIDEO STORE OR TELEPHONE (800) 383-8811

and fencing. 4) Rider requirements, equipment and veterinary care. 5) Daily routine for general care and feeding. 6) Grooming, hosing down, exercise and saddling up.
21-010 30 min. $69.95

Health, Maintenance, Grooming

Art Of Braiding
Lyra Parks, an expert in the area of grooming and braiding, presents this step by step tape in a very thorough manner. She shows the tools needed and demonstrates many styles of braids on manes and tails, discusses care techniques, pulling manes and in general the time tested methods she has used.
21-6012 60 min. $29.95

Basic Horsemanship with Odette Larson
Horse trainer Odette Larson has developed a program for teaching primary concepts to those needing a fundamental education in horse handling, grooming, feeding and horse psychology. She also covers such topics as administering shots, feed requirements, appropriate tack, grooming tips and much more. Must viewing for any new horse enthusiast as well as some old hands!
21-254 80 min. $79.95

Blue Ribbon Grooming
Grooming for health and comfort is covered, as well as proper feeding and hygiene, You will also watch as a champion Arabian stallion is prepared for show.
21-280 45 min. $24.95

Body Clipping Your Horse
This video demonstrates how to body clip your horse in three general styles: the Trace, the Hunt, and the Full; plus their variations total 7 clip styles. The various body clip styles are outlined on the horse showing their boundaries, and an explanation is given as to the importance of each style.
21-6054 60 min. $49.95

Breeding By Artificial Insemination
Cal Poly University vet Dr. Gerald Hackett, Jr. demonstrates the essentials of a successful artificial insemination program. Presented are the actual collection of semen from a stallion, methods of semen evaluation, requirements of semen handling and the insemination of mares that resulted in pregnancies. Also includes discussion of the

advantages of artificial insemination programs.
21-6014 28 min. $39.95

Common Sense Approach To Handling The Young Horse
Cal Poly University's 17th Annual Horsemanship Seminar highlights with noted Arabian trainers Dan and Rhita McNair. They demonstrate their approach to handling and gentling the young horse in preparation for further training as a saddle or driving horse. Basic principles of training a horse to show at halter are a portion of the tape.
21-6015 37 min. $29.95

Emergency First Aid For Your Horse
Dr. Gerald Hackett, Jr. of the W.K. Kellogg Arabian Horse Unit of Cal Poly University covers many aspects of first aid, including founder (laminitis), how to take pulse and temperature, colic, and various life threatening and non-life threatening emergencies. Also, basic for a first aid kit.
21-104 42 min. $59.95

Equine Nutrition
Whether you have one horse or a hundred - ride for pleasure or compete for gold and glory - here is a down to earth, no-nonsense video which will help you attain optimum performance from your horse.
21-2732 65 min. $49.95

Farrier's Forge Work
The Oklahoma Farrier's College staff shows you the art of forge work. How to build the shoe (or anything else you want!) Step-by-step, easy-to-understand instruction.
21-114 45 min. $39.95

Feeding Your Horse: Ron Palelek
A no-nonsense approach to the proper use of roughage and concentrates. Important differences between feeding the young horse and the older horse. Our horses are what they eat!
21-6016 28 min. $29.95

First Horse: A Beginner's Guide
Good for teen! Covers basic guidelines on horse care and handling, as well as equipment needs, catching your horse, leading, safety, boarding, feeding, grooming, etc.
21-058 28 min. $59.95

Fitting The Show Horse For Halter
Topics included in the very instructional tape designed for fitting the western show horse for halter include: grooming, clipping the bridle path, legs, ears and face, hoof care, application of commercial products for highlighting or de-emphasizing both good and bad features and proper

fitting of your equipment.
21-6051 48 min. $29.95

Foaling Process
The complete process of foaling. Included is everything from the mare lying down and entering labor to the foal standing and nursing. Information is also given on what to look for when the mare is approaching parturition as well as what to do for the mare and foal before, during and after the birthing process.
21-6052 17 min. $29.95

Foaling Your Mare
This is a beautiful video complete from conception to weaning. Actually experience the birth of several foals, including hard deliveries. You'll learn what to look for in case of trouble and how to help your mare deliver a healthy foal.
21-6053 50 min. $49.95

From the Ground Up: Care and Handling
Featuring Don Burt and Heather Bender. Safe and correct horsemanship from the ground up! Together with an equine vet, Dr. David Ramey, Don and Heather cover basic health considerations, and what to do until the vet gets there. Topics include safety for horse and handler, correct bathing and grooming, exercise for the horse at liberty and on the lunge line, and the proper care of the legs.
21-116 60 min. $59.95

Grooming Your Horse: Ron Palelek
Grooming equipment needed, brushing techniques, bot egg removal, bathing, hoof care, clipping. Bandaging for transport and injury as well as for working sessions.
21-6017 61 min. $29.95

Heartbar Shoe
The lecture and step-by-step procedure for treatment of acute and chronic laminitis (founder) as developed and demonstrated by Burney Chapman. This is a remarkable and tested procedure developed during years of research and practical application that can save even the most severely crippled horse. A must for all farriers, equine practitioners and university libraries.
21-119 90 min. $89.95

Hoof Care And Basic Shoeing
Oklahoma Farriers College with the nationally respected Bud Beaston and his staff. They show you what you can do for yourself and when to call a corrective farrier. The solid basics of shoeing.
21-6018 45 min. $59.95

Horseshoeing
An "oldie but goodie" in which a draft horse with long, clipped cracked hooves is trimmed and shod by a farrier. Great for trail riders who want to learn the correct way to pull a loose shoe and to "do it yourselfers" who wish to learn the basics of shoeing. A "no glitter" production made in 1946, but the information is still sound. US Office of Education.
21-6019 18 min. $19.95

Horses Talk: Where It Begins
To own a horse - at some time, everybody's dream. Live the event through this video. Foaling, the young horse learning at mother's side. The Yearling Sale. Formal training, care, and nutrition, equipment. The grace and beauty of the Thoroughbred in motion. Experience your dream with every viewing. Enjoy!
21-9816 46 min. $39.95

Influencing the Horse's Mind: Horse Psychology
How can the behavior of an ill-mannered horse who is headshy, does not allow his feet to be easily handled and continuously fights his handler be modified in just a few minutes? Dr. Robert Miller, vet correspondent for Western Horseman magazine, provides the answers to this question plus much more helpful information. The techniques developed by Dr. Miller over 26 years of medical practice are humane, easy to learn and can be of great benefit to you. They are all demonstrated for you on this video.
21-125 40 min. $49.95

Lameness: Fore & Hindlimb
Wobbler syndrome, compressed spinal cord, cut flexor tendons, fractures of the first and second phalanges. Related arthritis, toe cracks and 1/4 cracks. Several wound types including wire cuts and lacerations, some fundamentals of wound therapy, cast. The bandaging of hoofs and sarcoid.
21-6020 53 min. $59.95

Linda Tellington-Jones: Starting a Young Horse
Linda has developed a training method called T.E.A.M., an approach to horse training that reduces behavioral problems, and enhances the horse's performance potential. This unique program is divided into three stages: Body Work, which relieves tension and pain; Ground Exercises, to enhance coordination, balance, obedience, self-control, focus, and willingness to learn; and Riding Awareness, how balance, breathing and visualization affect your horse's attitude, stride, confidence and performance. Perfect for any horse owner, whether you are starting a young horse or want to improve communication or solve problems with an older horse.
21-238 90 min. $69.95

VIDEO TITLES LISTED IN THIS GUIDE ARE AVAILABLE FOR PURCHASE OR RENTAL. CONTACT YOUR LOCAL VIDEO STORE OR TELEPHONE (800) 383-8811

Loading and Hauling Horses
Some methods to use for the safety of you and your horses. How to handle difficult loaders and how to protect your valuable horses in transport. Walt Searle and Pat Patterson.
21-228 45 min. $39.95

Linda Tellington-Jones: Teaching the Touch
A demonstration of the methods that have proven so successful in the relatively new frontier of physical therapy and communication with horses.
21-127 120 min. $49.95

Maintenance and Show Grooming
Step by step instructions covering complete grooming techniques including body clipping, mane and tail care, hoof preparation for show and discussion of the modern products used in these procedures highlight the video clinic.
21-6021 72 min. $29.95

Performance Feeding for Your Horse
Proper nutrition from colt to maturity is covered. You'll see the results of champion Arabians fed a proper diet over the years and how you can also attain these results.
21-290 60 min. $24.95

Performance Hoofs
Your horse's performance is based on its hoofs. No matter how beautiful the conformation, if there's a problem with the hoofs, you have a problem. Stuart Greenberg takes you through the fascinating history of the farrier's art, demonstrates the proper way to care for hoofs for optimum performance.
21-5423 45 min. $29.95

Resistance Free Training: The Older Horse
Retrain your horse by knowing his abilities and then establishing a program that works. Study drills and collection exercises that will shorten or lengthen your horse's stride, speed up or slow down your horse's gaits...learn how to establish a ground work program to teach confidence and obedience. Master lead changes, spins and stops with your horse being your "willing partner".
21-8001 30 min. $34.95

Safe Handling of Foals & Yearlings
Hosted by Prof. Norman K. Dunn, Director of the W.K. Kellogg Arabian Horse Unit at Cal Poly, Pomona University, this tape covers a mini-clinic in detail on methods of working with new foals to introduce them to handling, halter breaking, loading and unloading out of a trailer and basic ground handling.
21-133 51 min. $59.95

Vet First Aid
Dr. R.R. Domer and Walter Searle tell you what to do for your injured or sick horse after you have called your vet and before he can get there.
21-136 45 min. $39.95

When Should I Call The Vet? - Part I
Is it an emergency or just a minor upset? Do you try to handle it yourself, or, if you need to call the vet, what do you do till he arrives? You'll learn how to establish the "normals" for your horse and how to use the stethoscope. You'll be able to check pulse, respiration, hydration, intestinal sounds, capillary refill and condition of mucous membranes.
21-5424 53 min. $29.95

When Should I Call The Vet? - Part II
You'll see examples of wounds, founder, and the dreaded colic. You'll learn how to cleanse a wound, how to control bleeding and how to bandage properly. With this video, you'll be prepared to administer first aid and give your horse a better chance of avoiding serious problems.
21-5425 50 min. $29.95

Racing

Body Language Of The Race Horse
1987 Kentucky Derby winner Chris McCarron and best-selling author Bonnie Ledbetter are featured in this exciting video. You'll learn to spot the Sharp Horse, the Dull Horse, the Nervous Horse, the Frightened Horse, the Unfit and the Fit and Ready Horse.
21-5430 40 min. $49.95

Breeder's Cup-1984
Pick the winners at horse racing's most prestigious and exciting day at the races! All seven races of this unique $10,000,000 race series are profiled in depth.
21-137 120 min. $29.95

Breeders Cup-1985
From Legendary Aqueduct Racetrack in New York comes the second edition of the "Super Bowl" of thoroughbred horse racing.
21-229 120 min. $29.95

Harness Racing: The Horse In Sport
From the wild and furious chariot races of the Ancient Greeks to the floodlit track of the Meadowlands in New York comes a thrilling sport that seems to have been made for filming. Though

the races have changed, they have never been tamed: top horses leave the starting gates at 35 mph - almost as fast as a thoroughbred can gallop, and they can earn thousands of dollars with one winning circuit of the track.
21-6025 60 min. $39.95

Horses Talk: The Paddock and Post Parade

For all who love horses, this video is a must! You'll view it again and again. Let author-producer Trillis Parker introduce you to the Thoroughbred race horse, the supreme professional athlete-- and the many positive and negative body signs related to physical fitness, health, and mental attitude--and the special signs of a Champion.
21-9817 47 min. $39.95

Thoroughbred Heroes

A quarter of a century of dynamic, exciting thoroughbred history. See the great ones in action, including citation, Swaps, Round Table, Duckpasser, Northern Dancer, Majestic Prince, Bold Ruler, Silky Sullivan, Secretariat and others. Great racing and training scenes.
21-145 55 min. $89.95

Western Horsemanship & Training

Barrel Racing Clinic

World champion Marlene Eddleman shows you **how to train, practice and win. She won $67,000** and the world title without knocking over a single barrel!
21-161 45 min. $39.95

Barrel Racing with Martha Josey

WPRA and AQHA Champion Barrel Racer Martha Josey teaches the approach, posture and mindset that shaves seconds from your time around the barrels. Learn from one of America's best.
21-147 45 min. $49.95

Basic Stockhorse Training

S.W. Searle, Jill Clark and Edsel Brashear show you how to start your horse on cattle for basic ranch use...cutting, roping and general ranch work.
21-6037 45 min. $69.95

Bill Freeman: Approaches to Cutting

Bill Freeman is well known in the cutting industry for his winning ways. He has won the Triple Crown of Cutting on Smart Little Lena. In his video, Bill discusses the correct techniques he uses for preparing his horse to enter the herd and cutting out a calf. He discusses his methods of preparing his horses for showing. He emphasizes the importance of a positive attitude while showing your horse.
21-247 42 min. $49.95

Calf Roping Clinic

World All-Around Champion Dee Pickett shows you the basics and the really fine points. The best Video on roping available--without exception.
21-165 45 min. $39.95

Calf Roping with Roy Cooper

Learn calf roping from the best...Roy Cooper, winner of five PRCA World Roping Championships and four Calf Roping Championships. Learn how to practice to win!
21-148 40 min. $39.95

Care of the Western Saddle

This tape takes you through a careful step-by-step disassembly and reassembling of the saddle. It shows how to make minor repairs, check for safety measures and failure prevention, cleaning and conditioning. Gail Denman, horsewoman and saddle maker is the featured instructor.
21-232 45 min. $39.95

Championship Barrel Racing With Martha Josey

This video tape is for anyone, from beginner to amateur to professional. If you have wanted to attend a Josey clinic, but haven't been able to, here is your chance. Now you can learn everything you need to become a champion yourself.
21-5985 45 min. $29.95

Colt Training Clinic

Veteran trainer and author Walt Searle shows you a quiet, effective method of starting two-year-olds that's easy on everyone!
21-149 45 min. $39.95

COMPLETE HORSEMANSHIP SERIES

The Complete Horsemanship series is an instructional video series for the pleasure horseman featuring B.F. Yates, Dean of the Horse Extension School of the Texas A & M University. This series takes you all the way from buying your horse to the show ring.

• Basic Maneuvers

Walking, trotting and loping. Leads. Perfect circles. Correct stopping with no rearing.
21-172 30 min. $39.95

VIDEO TITLES LISTED IN THIS GUIDE ARE AVAILABLE FOR PURCHASE OR RENTAL. CONTACT YOUR LOCAL VIDEO STORE OR TELEPHONE (800) 383-8811

• **Bits and Biting**
Different types of bits and their use. Teach response to bit pressure. Use of principles of reinforcement.
21-174 30 min. $39.95

• **Collection and Flying Lead Changes**
Simple and flying lead changes. Lateral movement, plus 360 degree spins on haunches or forehand. Roll backs and pivots.
21-176 30 min. $39.95

• **More Basic Maneuvers**
More about leg pressure. Side passing. The two-track maneuver.
21-175 30 min. $39.95

• **Owning Your First Horse**
Buy enjoyment, not headache with the right horse! Facilities and equipment you will need. Approach, catch and handle your horse. Leading, tying and saddling. Your first ride. Care, feeding and exercise.
21-170 30 min. $39.95

• **Psychology of Training**
The importance of contingency obedience and the principle of reinforcement. How to ask, receive and reinforce the response. Communicate with auditory, tactile and visual stimuli.
21-171 30 min. $39.95

• **Rider Skills**
In "Rider Skills" you will learn to use your hands, feet, legs and body position to more effectively communicate with your horse.
21-173 30 min. $39.95

Cow Cutting Clinic
Filmed at Clark's Doc Bar Syndicate Ranch, this video shows how trainer Don Taylor starts two-year-olds, and works horses at all stages to the finished open horse.
21-160 45 min. $39.95

Cowboy Up
Experience the spirit of courage and grit that settled the American West and lives today in the thrilling sport of rodeo. It's danger, pageantry and competition--all in the same arena. Hosted by Cliff Robertson.
21-239 30 mi. $29.95

Cutting Horse Training with Joe Helm
Cutting clinic for amateurs and professionals by the winner of 1984's Cutting Triple Crown and the '81 and '83 NCHA Futurities. Winning cutting techniques from A to Z.
21-177 40 min. $69.95

Don Shugart--Professional Horse Photography--Photographing the Halter Horse
Don Shugart is the nation's leading quarterhorse photographer today. In this video, Don shares with you how to position the horse for that perfect rear-end shot, profile shot and head shot. He demonstrates his equipment and discusses the best lighting and weather conditions needed for the perfect shot.
21-245 45 min. $39.95

Draft Horses Come in Handy
Narrated by "All American Cowboy" Bob Tallman, this video is packed with valuable ideas and specific instruction for incorporating draft horses into farm and ranch operations. You'll get a first hand look at the equipment, handling and training techniques that make working with horses increasingly popular today.
21-8000 45 min. $39.95

Good Horse Keeping
Covers the basics of proper grooming and bathing of horses. It introduces and explains the various tools and supplies that are required and demonstrates how to use them correctly. It also tells the viewer when to groom, when to bathe a horse or when merely to spot-wash the animal. Also included are little-known grooming tips and tricks from the experts.
21-9571 35 min. $19.95

Girl's Rodeo Clinic
Breakaway Roping and Goat Tying skills, by Marlene Eddleman. She is assisted by PRCA roper and veteran horse trainer Dan Eddleman. A fine instructional video.
21-6033 60 min. $49.95

Halter Showmanship, Fitting
Trainer of world champions Chip Knost demonstrates his entire program for getting a champion ready to show. Feeding, the lighting program, exercise, grooming.
21-6040 30 min. $39.95

Horse Conformation
How to really evaluate a horse, point by point. Dr. R.R. Dolmer pays special attention to conformation flaws that can lead to injury. Basically western "stock horse" but of value to all beginners and novices.
21-060 30 min. $39.95

Horsemanship: Richard Shrake
Step by step see the drills and exercises for both horse and rider to help establish that "oneness with your horse." Helpful ideas for both split rein and the romal rider. Comments about coordinating

outfits and how to achieve the look of the "finished rider."

21-6042 40 min. $39.95

Horse Sense

Valuable tips for trail riders from the U.S. Forest Service. An oldie but goodie and great for beginners as well as experienced riders. Covers horse handling while out in the "back country"! (1953).

21-062 23 min. $39.95

LARRY ROSE TRAINING SCHOOL SERIES:

Larry Rose, National Riding Champion, trainer, instructor and NRHA judge has developed this modern and scientific way to ride and train your horse. Techniques are taught step-by-step and each point is demonstrated along the way.

• Volume 1

Starting a green colt, educating the mouth and educating the sides, proper headset and basics.

21-179 42 min. $69.95

• Volume 2

Developing the real mouth, spins, rollbacks, circles and lead changes are skills covered.

21-180 42 min. $69.95

• Volume 3

Sliding stops, backups, show preparation and style.

21-181 42 min. $69.95

Lynn Salvatori Palm--Hunt Seat Equitation

The 1985 Winner of the Skoal/Copenhagen Super Horse Award at the AQHA World Championship Show and the 1985 Congress "Superhorse" Award Winner demonstrates why a good hunt seat equitation foundation is essential for competition in hunt seat events. Lynn demonstrates exercises for a balance seat, common equitation patterns, and shows correct posture, equipment and tack use.

21-242 72 min. $29.95

Reining Futurity Horse

Bob Loomis is the leading reining horse champion with five NRHA Futurity wins and seven AQHA World Championships to his credit. In this video, Bob explains the importance of suppleness and gentle handling in training the young horse. He demonstrates exercises to achieve correct circles and lead changes, spins and stops.

21-241 53 min. $39.95

Reining with Craig Johnson

Craig Johnson starting winning championships when he was only 18. In 1981 he was Junior Reining Champ at the AQHA World Show. In this video, Craig covers the critical selection of a reining horse, working with the young horse, special reining maneuvers and the pros and cons of reining bits, bridles and more.

21-203 60 min. $49.95

Resistance Free Training I

Watch a young horse be saddled, bridled and ridden for his first time. In less than two hours, he is taken through an easy to follow, step-by-step program that eliminates the need to use the old-fashioned, forceful methods of training a horse. This video allows you to master the fundamentals to gain the confidence of your horse by having the confidence in yourself as a trainer.

21-6146 60 min. $39.95

Resistance Free Training II

Richard Shrake gives you the building blocks to teach that "young horse under saddle". Learn the step-by-step process that will create a willing partner of your horse. From walking, circling, lateral bending and hip movement, you will go on to learn to cue for relaxed and controlled transitions.

21-6147 60 min. $39.95

Resistance Free Training: The Wild Mustang

No other horse is like the wild mustang and he should not be started out like other horses. Richard Shrake has created a training program especially for the wild mustang in a simple, easy to follow program that teaches herd behavior, pecking order, bonding, patterning, halting, corral and pen work, teaching to lead, schooling for backing, picking up feet and safety. This video is a must for every wild mustang owner!

21-8002 30 min. $39.95

Resistance Free Training - The Problem Horse

The Resistance Free method is the most powerful achievement tool that exists today. Learn to retrain the spoiled, problem horse to become a long-term, quiet, obedient horse. Correct your horse's "bad habits" such as lack of concentration, unresponsiveness and stiffness and unpredictable behavior. Through the basics of ground work, bitting and relaxation exercises, see immediate results in your horse's behavior.

21-6149 30 min. $39.95

Resistance Free Riding

The Resistance Free method is the most powerful achievement tool that exists today. It gives immediate results by developing a "bond" between horse and rider for total communication and "feel." Whatever level the rider, from beginner to advanced, will learn through exercise drills and mental preparation the secrets of balance, timing

VIDEO TITLES LISTED IN THIS GUIDE ARE AVAILABLE FOR PURCHASE OR RENTAL. CONTACT YOUR LOCAL VIDEO STORE OR TELEPHONE (800) 383-8811

and rhythm in an intelligent, easy-to-follow, common sense approach.
21-6148 30 min $39.95

Roping Basics I: In The Practice Pen With Roy Cooper

Whether you have never roped before in your life, or you need to sharpen and refine your roping skills, this video will help you. Watch the methods that made Roy Cooper a World Champion from your favorite armchair. Then put his methods to the test on your own horse. You'll want to watch this tape several times to pick up every tip.
21-5983 36 min. $29.95

Ross Carnahan: Championship Pole Bending

Ross Carnahan has been the world champion pole bender seven times at the Quarter Horse World Championship Show. Each World Championship was won on his own horse. Ross is more than qualified to teach his championship style. He walks through the course and describes step by step where the position of the horse and rider should be. His video shows how he teaches a young horse to run the poles. Finally, Ross describes how he maintains his finished horse in top running condition.
21-246 42 min. $39.95

SUPER PRO SERIES:

• Dale Youree: Barrel Racing the Youree Way

A legend in barrel racing shares his technique for training champion barrel horses. He covers the vital areas, hot spot and burn areas. He shows the different approaches to run the barrel.
21-243 62 min. $49.95

• Jody Galyean: Snaffle Bit Futurity Horse

The renowned two-time winner of the prestigious "Triple Crown" series of two year old Snaffle Bit Pleasure Futurities. Jody Galyean shares his ideas on selecting the correct horse for snaffle bit competition, ground and round pen work, supplying exercises and equipment.
21-240 52 min. $49.95

• Mary Burger: Futurity Barrel Racing

Champion barrel racer, Mary Burger along with her husband Kerry, discuss the importance of choosing the right barrel prospect, equipment and correct shoeing. She has won at all the major barrel futurities.
21-244 40 min. $49.95

Tack Tape

This is the most comprehensive guide ever assembled for the horse owner. It's a richly detailed yet simple introduction to Western saddles, bridles, bits halters and more--how they work and how to choose the right combination for you and your horse. Includes tips from professional horse people and a fascinating historical look at the evolution of tack.
21-9570 35 min. $19.95

Team Roping Clinic

World Champions David and Dennis Motes, with a combined 20 trips to the National Finals Rodeo, show you how to practice to win. Equipment, ropes and horse training.
21-163 30 min. $39.95

Tommy Manion: Trail Horse Clinic

The winner of 27 World Championship Quarter Horse titles introduces the training and show techniques to win trail horse classes.
21-209 45 min. $49.95

Tommy Manion: Western Riding Clinic

World Champion horseman Tommy Manion demonstrates how to choose the right western riding horse and gives tips on training and polishing both you and your horse to become a winning team. Tommy covers different gaits, lead changes, horse's response to rider, correct hand position, stopping, backing and other important techniques that judges look for in western riding competition.
21-255 60 min. $49.95

WESTERN EQUITATION & THE WESTERN SHOW HORSE:

Don Burt reveals what the judge is looking for in western pleasure, stock horse and western equitation classes. This judge of national and world championships in every major breed of horse is also a published author.

• Western Equitation
21-210 40 min. $49.95

• Western Show Horse
21-211 40 min. $49.95

WESTERN HORSE TRAINING SERIES:

• Colt Training Skills

Starting the two-year-old with a trainer of champions, you'll see how to get one going quickly and with control.
21-150 45 min. $39.95

• Hackamore Magic

From tying the mecate and fitting the hackamore properly, to the art of using this ancient method, Tom Chown shows you what he learned growing

up in the world of California reinsmen.
21-153 30 min. $39.95

• Snaffle Bit Horsemanship
Trainer of champions, Tom Chown, shows you the art of training with the snaffle bit. Headset and body position of the horse, leads and training routines.
21-152 30 min. $39.95

Western Pleasure
What to look for in the ideal western pleasure horse with tips on conformation, attitude and training for both horse and rider. Drills and exercises that can change your horse's stride plus improve cadence. Finer points on the turnout and way of going for the super winning ride.
21-282 40 min. $39.95

Western Pleasure with Tommy Manion
Champion of Quarter Horse Showing shares his western pleasure training and showing techniques. Covers movement, headset, attitude and tack.
21-212 60 min. $49.95

Western Pleasure Advanced
Tom Chown shows you his program of finishing a training program for the competitive pleasure horse. This is a good video for those looking for the winning edge and the finer points of showing.
21-155 30 min. $39.95

Western Pleasure Basics
Tom Chown shows the secret of making your pleasure horse go smoothly and relax under your control, without intimidation or gimmicks.
21-154 30 min. $39.95

Western Riding Clinic
Easy to follow basics and fine points for this event. Counter leads are illustrated. The pattern is discussed and how to handle it to your advantage. Training routines.
21-156 45 min. $39.95

Miscellaneous

AMERICAN HORSE AND HORSEMAN TELEVISION SERIES:

Hosted by television personality Dale Robertson, this classic television series, from the 1970's, was acclaimed for its then unique presentation of its format as an electronic magazine. Its popularity was well documented by the fact that it received more fan mail from devotees than the then number one television show, "All In The Family" during one particular weekly time period.

• Volume 1
Santa Anita: a behind-the-scenes look at one of America's loveliest race tracks. The Acrylic Foot: affecting the foot of the horse, founder is a condition that can severely damage a horse's usefulness. The Proud Breed: The story of the Arabian horse. Halter Breaking a Foal: How top Arabian trainer Tom McNair uses his halter-breaking method with a young Arabian foal.
21-312 60 min. $49.95

• Volume 2
The Gentle Giants: The story of the Budweiser Clydesdales; J. Trump, the only American bred, owned, trained and ridden horse to win the Grand National; Quarter Horse Conformation with B. F. Yates; Horse Specialist at Texas A&M University; and the War Admiral/Sea Biscuit match race from the 1930's.
21-033 50 min. $49.95

• Volume 3
The Pony Express; the immortal trotter, Greyhound; and the 30-mile Levi-and-Tie Race.

• Volume 4
The Road to Duquoin...and the Hambletonian; Senator Thurston Morton and the American Horse Council; Floating Teeth and its importance to a horse's health.
21-035 50 min. $49.95

• Volume 5
A biography of Ted Keefer, Texas thoroughbred horse trainer, "Nobody Winked", the story of Shelbyville, Tennessee and home of the Shelbyville Walking Horse Celebration; the story of the American Saddlebred.
21-036 50 min. $49.95

• Volume 6
The American Quarter Horse Congress in Columbus, Ohio; the ins and outs of trailering--a comical view of the do's and don't's; the story of Dr. Linfoot, an American Indian and a qualified equine vet, who uses the techniques of his ancestors to break a wild mustang to ride in just 20 minutes, right in front of your eyes!
21-037 50 min. $49.95

• Volume 7
Rex Cauble and Cutter Bill, one of the world's most famous cutting horses; how to barrel race; a look at the Oklahoma Farrier's School; and "Racing Luck".
21-038 50 min. $49.95

VIDEO TITLES LISTED IN THIS GUIDE ARE AVAILABLE FOR PURCHASE OR RENTAL. CONTACT YOUR LOCAL VIDEO STORE OR TELEPHONE (800) 383-8811

• Volume 8
The Cowboy Hall of Fame in Oklahoma City; the story of the Pony of the Americas; and a broad overview of unsoundness.
21-039 50 min. $49.95

• Volume 9
California match race between Typecast and Convenience, two remarkable thoroughbred mares in a winner-take-all race, Appaloosa confrontation with B. F. Yates, horse specialist from Texas A&M; and the story of the Welsh pony today.
21-270 50 min. $49.95

Arabian, Palomino and Saddlebred
Breed biographies on the Arabian with Wayne Newton; the Palomino-the color of gold; and the horse America made, the Saddlebred. All in one volume.
21-041 80 min. $49.95

Ballad of the Irish Horse
This is a breathtaking film. It is a poetic blend of music and scenery with spectacular horses and horsemanship. Highlights include the Irish Sweepstakes, racing at Leopardstown, the National Hunt, Connemaras and show jumping at Ballsbridge. A horseman's holiday!
21-052 48 min. $59.95

Horse America Made
The American quarter horse in all it's glory from beginning to the present.
21-5097 40 min. $29.95

How to Buy a Horse
A checklist of ways to wisely choose a horse that fits your purposes. Walt Searle and Dr. R.R. Domer explain conformation, action, and how to spot weaknesses.
21-226 45 min. $39.95

Imprint Training the Foal
From the moment of birth, foals have the capacity to learn, and due to the "imprinting phenomena" can absorb more information than at any other time. You learn how to condition your foal at a very early age through this process. Dr. Robert Miller demonstrates with thoroughbreds and other breeds of horses. Foals are gentled and prepared for the schooling they will receive later in life.
21-124 60 min. $59.95

Intuitive Communication
This unusual tape features well-known and respected California psychic Cynthia Lester, who shows us methods to more effectively relate to our horses by utilizing color imagery and picture visualization. Cynthia has worked extensively at UCLA and has consulted with horse owners for

many years.
21-064 40 min. $39.95

John Lyons Symposiums - Leading And Loading Safely
21-5150 60 min. $59.95

John Lyons Training Clinic - Round Pen Reasoning
21-5149 60 min. $59.95

Lead Your Horse
In this program, learn the steps of leading your horse properly at your side. The tape covers the training from foal to maturity.
21-281 60 min. $24.95

Long Distance Riding
Matthew Mackay-Smith, DVM, Dane Frazier, DVM and Darolyn Butler, 1984 American Endurance Riding Conference National Champion, on competitive endurance trail riding. Covers training, tack and much more.
21-066 60 min. $69.95

Mount Up: Riding Skills with Don Burt
Mount-up with Don Burt and learn the riding skills that lead to complete riding proficiency. Be it English or western, this video clinic will show you how to correctly walk, trot or jog, canter or lope, make simple lead changes and pick-up the proper diagonal. Learn how to communicate with your horse and how to interpret the ways he communicates with you. Become familiar with different types of bits and saddles as you learn how they can help you. Understand what is meant by "Be firm, but think soft" and "Impulsion plus collection equals balance."
21-067 60 min. $49.95

National Geographic: Ballad of the Irish Horse
Over the centuries, horses have captured the hearts and minds of the Irish people. Nurtured by the mild Irish climate and rich grasses, the horses of Ireland have always flourished. From the magnificent wild stallions to the sturdy work ponies and the elegant racing thoroughbreds-Ireland's horses are an enduring part of the country's history.
21-1649 60 min. $29.95

Prepare Your Halter Horse for Show
Learn feeding, conditioning and schooling necessary for getting your horse ready to compete at halter. Teach your horse the ideal head and neck positions and how to demonstrate.
21-289 60 min. $24.95

Resistance Free Riding
The rider learns to develop a "feel," where there

---

are no resistant moves against the horse.
21-2924 60 min. $39.95

Resistance Free: Training the Problem Horse
This video teaches you how to turn the problem, spoiled horse into a quiet, obedient horse.
21-2925 60 min. $39.95

Rider's Workout: Conditioning
A program of exercises and aerobics designed specifically for the horse enthusiast. Cheryl Schuhmann, a registered physical therapist and active horsewoman, designed this workout for all riders, no matter what their field of interest. It we

expect our horses to be well-conditioned athletes, shouldn't they expect the same from us?
21-072 60 min. $59.95

Year of the Quorn
A full year in the life of the Quorn Hunt in High Leicestershire, England, recorded as it happened. Follow the Hunt throughout the year-- you'll see the hunting fields; hounds in full cry; the spirit and excitement of the chase; scenes from the point-to-point, the cross-country team event at Muxlow Hill and the hunt's social activities. A film crew actually followed the hunt for three seasons. Michael Clayton, the editor of "Horse and Hound," is the narrator.
21-258 44 min. $59.95

Got A Burr Under Your Saddle?

These Videos Will Soon Have You Riding Tall!

Searching For

A Unique Gift That is

Informative and Appreciated?

The Video Titles

In This Guide

Make Wonderful Gifts.

Hunting

- ✓ *Guns & Shooting*
- ✓ *Hunting Trips*
- ✓ *Tips & Tactics*
- ✓ *Training Hunting Dogs*
- ✓ *Miscellaneous*

Guns & Shooting

Basic Guide to Handguns

Jeff Cooper, handgun expert, is right on target in this program for shooters of all abilities. Lesson one is the safe handling of the weapon, a must for anyone who owns a gun or shoots. Cooper covers safety, grip and stance, target shooting, rapid fire and gun care. Jeff has served as the director of the American Pistol Institute and president of the Gunsite Raven Corp.
19-002 59 min. $24.95

Basic Guide to Shotguns

This program starts with fundamentals: how to choose and fit a gun, correct gun mount, sight picture, trigger pull, dealing with recoil, target acquisitions and methods of lead. John Satterwhite is your teacher, the only man in U.S. Skeetshooting history to have won the U.S. Olympic Committee as Athletic Advisor for Shooting. The highlight of this video is his trick shooting exhibition. It's an exciting glimpse of what is possible by a master of this sport.
19-003 45 min. $24.95

Basics To Bullseyes

NRA pistol champion, John Pride demonstrates his proven techniques for winning in competition and survival in the streets.
19-8006 30 min. $29.95

Mastering Shot Placement

This video solves the age-old problem of where to aim on big game. With detailed analysis and instruction from experts, the guesswork of placing that perfect shot is made easy.
10-8019 30 min. $44.95

Masters International Shooting Championship

Competitive shooting at it's best. Three-hundred shooters from around the world compete in this three-day, three-gun, pro-am match that test skills for speed and accuracy.
19-9694 60 min. $19.95

Rifle Shooting Tips and Techniques

A must for every hunter or target shooter regardless of experience level. Former national champion marksman Glen Pearce and Olympic team gunsmith Jim Carter will show you invaluable techniques for fitting your rifle, dry firing, sighting in, wind doping, range, bullet drop estimation and trigger squeeze. From different angles you will see the recommended positioning for shooting while prone, sitting, kneeling and standing.
19-151 48 min. $49.95

Shotgun School with Ken Robertson

Ken Robertson is a California state champion and a winner of the Grand Prix of Europe. But more importantly, he is an excellent instructor. The course of instruction includes proper stance, weight distribution, swing and pointing with both eyes open. Shooting includes simulations of driven grouse, ducks over blinds and flushing quail and pheasants.
19-134 60 min. $49.95

Skeetshooting with Ken Robertson

Top instructor Ken Robertson demonstrates proper skeetshooting technique and strategy to students with a variety of abilities. Ken will teach you proper stances, gunholds, eyeholds where to break the target and how much to lead.
19-137 51 min. $49.95

SUCCESS LIBRARY

• **Understanding Arrow Making**
Step-by-step instruction for consistent arrow fletching and building.
19-8014 30 min. $44.95

• **Selecting, Tuning & Shooting Guide for Modern Compound Bows**
What every beginner should know about selecting, Setting up and shooting his first compound bow.
19-8015 30 min. $44.95

• **Understanding Arrow Flight**
A how-to guide for proper arrow selection and bow tuning for proper arrow flight.
19-8016 30 min. $44.95

• **Understanding Release Aids**
Pro shooter Terry Ragsdale shows you how to select, set up and shoot today's release aids.
19-8017 30 min. $44.95

• **Understanding Shooting Form**
Pete Shepley and TV host Wayne Pearson outline ten basic steps of shooting form for consistent and accurate shooting for bow hunting or competition.
19-8018 30 min. $44.95

Hunting Trips

Adventures of Hunting Trophy Caribou
This takes you to the far north in pursuit of Quebec-Labrador Caribou with expert bowhunters Bill Krenz and Jay Scholes.
19-2688 70 min. $49.95

African Adventure Safari
Relive this colorful safari with Guns & Ammo magazine's Black Powder Editor Phil Spangenberger as he hunts with famed Professional Hunter, Kelly Davis. Stalk the "wait a bit" thorn bush country with them as Phil takes three world class plains animals with the Kodiak MK IV .45-70, a sidehammer double rifle, reminiscent of 1880's Africa--the Dark Continent's Golden Age of Hunting. See Africa as Phil lived it, while sighting down the barrel of his rifle. Share with them the excitement of a Zulu village, as half naked maidens dance alongside their men in ritual tribal dances. Feel as they did, the tension in the air, as they intruded upon the feeding grounds of a mother rhino and her young, and have a near-miss with the deadly black mamba snake.
19-6465 30 min. $16.95

Alaska Mixed Bag With Lynn Castle
Hunt for: moose, sheep, and caribou. High quality shot on 16mm. A George Kucky hunting video.
19-6325 60 min. $49.95

Bowhunting for Black Bear
Bob Eaton, professional bow hunter, takes you on an actual hunt for black bear in Canada. This complete how-to video is for all bow hunters. Whether you're a novice or a pro, this video will be an enlightening experience.
19-1682 60 min. $39.95

Bowhunting for Russian Boar
Bob Eaton, professional bow hunter, hosts this complete how-to video on hunting Russian boar. Filmed at Telico Junction in the foothills of the Great Smokey Mountains. Witness actual footage of the killing of a 350 lb. Russian boar.
19-1683 60 min. $39.95

Catching "Crocs"
Malcolm Douglas is the only man in Northern Australia licensed to hunt these dangerous maneaters, alive. This is a real life action adventure.
19-2693 36 min. $16.95

Columbia Basin Waterfowl
This program is packed with dynamic hunting scenes and lots of no-nonsense hunting instruction. Expert guides take you to the Columbia Basin of Washington State to hunt mallards, pintails and Canadian geese.
19-2683 68 min. $59.95

Elk Hunting in the Rocky Mountain West
This program features some of the most stunning elk photography you'll ever see...close-ups such as a bull elk completely dismantling a lodgepole pine while scraping his antlers, bugling scenes, elk in the process of raising their young, activity during the rutting season, a bowhunting sequence, rifle hunting and some of the most awe-inspiring habitat scenery in the Rocky Mountains.
19-191 54 min. $49.95

Grizzly
Join Pete Shepley as he travels to Alaska and the Yukon to hunt black bear and the grizzly. Share in the hunting adventure and enjoy the magnificent scenery of the Northern Wilderness, an area accessible only by bush plane, horseback and wild rivers. Bowhunting thrills await you as Pete encounters the unpredictable grizzly bear.
19-129 74 min. $34.95

Harvesting Fall Turkeys
Shows the unique challenges of hunting wild turkeys in the fall by focusing on changes in wild turkey behavior and demonstrating special strategies for fall scouting, positioning, setting up and calling.
19-2406 60 min. $49.95

Hunting the North American Wild Turkey
Join expert turkey hunters/callers as they show how to successfully call turkey under varying conditions from Missouri and Arkansas to Montana.
19-2689 60 min. $49.95

Hunting Desert Bighorn in Northern Baja
Filmed in Baja Norte, Mexico in 1983 and 1984. Three successful hunts (by Ken Wilson, Bud Hartman, and Dave Harshbarger) with the highlight being the harvesting of a Boone and Crockett record book trophy by Harshbarger on El Diablo Mountain. The Wilson and Hartman hunts are home movies which Harsbarger views before departing on his hunt, which was capably filmed by Bill Hodkin. You will see incredible sequences of the kill and of numerous magnificent rams.
19-153 36 min. $19.95

Hunting Rocky Mountain Mule Deer
Not only does this video emphasize the hows and wheres of hunting trophy mule deer bucks in the Rocky Mountain West, it also dramatically shows several hunters taking bucks with the bow in Nevada's Humboldt Range, and the rifle in Idaho.
19-2160 70 min. $59.95

Hunting Trophy Whitetails
This program explores the mystique, but it also

goes beyond to present practical insights into the whitetail species and the best methods of hunting them.
19-2158 60 min. $59.95

In The Blood
Based on President Theodore Roosevelt's African Game Trails, the classic memoir of the hunter's role in wildlife conservation, In the Blood skillfully weaves the retelling of two safaris, separated by 80 years, into a breathtaking action film. Rare historical footage from the Smithsonian Institute shows President Roosevelt in 1909 hunting African game with his son Kermit.
19-7092 90 min. $39.95

Javelina: Made for Bowhunting
Travel to San Carlos Indian Reservation in scenic Arizona to hunt one of bowhunting's most popular game animals, the Javelina.
19-2968 55 min. $44.95

Moose Hunt - Talkeetna River
This video documents a bow hunt for Moose along the Talkeetna River in Alaska. Witness the hunt of a Bull Moose and the beautiful mountains from the fall colors to the snow.
19-8002 30 min. $29.95

North American Big Game
The most fabulously photographed program featuring the ten most sought-after big game animals of North America ever filmed. Narrated by Curt Gowdy, this exciting film takes you into the heartlands of Alaska after moose, dall sheep, caribou, and grizzly bear - to the majestic Rocky Mountains where you will seek out the haunts of elk and mule deer - you'll go into the wilds of whitetail deer country and enter the southwestern territories after javolina and mountain lion. This is truly a spectacular film that also tells you what caliber rifle is best for each species of big game and geophysically shows you where to place your shots.
19-073 30 min. $16.95

Planning Your Rocky Mountain Hunt
This video will provide both entertainment and solid information on how to plan that hunt in the Rocky Mountains west, so it will be an unqualified success. Video includes actual hunting sequences and stunning wildlife. You'll find this video helpful in putting you on the right track to make your dream hunt.
19-251 54 min. $59.95

River Bottom Mallards
This takes you into the flooded timberlands of Arkansas to hunt a variety of duck species with expert caller Mike Morton.
19-2687 58 min. $49.95

Rocky Mountain Goat: Quest for a Trophy
Experience the beauty and ruggedness of a mountain goat hunt in the majestic splendor of British Columbia. This video takes you on a trip into the Rocky Mountain Outfitters area, a 320,000 acres, true wilderness area that shows fishing and wildlife and culminates in the taking of a record-class Billy.
19-273 48 min. $29.95

Scoring North America's Big Game Species
Shows footage of most of the North American big game trophies in the wild - from elk to grizzly bear, moose, caribou, mule deer, bighorn sheep, Dall sheep and many others.
19-2159 85 min. $59.95

Spring Trophy Hunting
Explains the special problems and challenges expert trophy turkey hunters face, shares secrets of hunting "hushed up" and "hung up" gobblers, shows how to track a large gobbler on the move and demonstrates techniques for calling in gobblers late in the day.
19-2405 60 min. $59.95

Successful Spring Turkey Hunting
Outlines proven spring turkey hunting strategies and techniques, illustrating the fine points of roosting a gobbler and choosing alternate hunting sights.
19-2404 60 min. $59.95

Wapiti Creek: Story of American Elk
If you're an outdoorsman, you have a favorite place. For outdoor photographer Bill Grunkemeyer it's Wapiti Creek. This is the story of the elk of Wapiti Creek. Grunkemeyer's camera captures these majestic animals as they follow the snowline to their summer range. You'll see a two-day-old calf take its first swim in the swirling water, and hear the bugling bulls during the September mating season.
19-123 74 min. $29.95

Waterfowl Hunting: Pacific Flyway
This video is absolutely packed with dynamic hunting scenes and lots of no-nonsense hunting instruction. Expert guides take you to the Columbia Basin of Washington State to hunt mallards, pintails, and Canadian geese.
19-2163 68 min. $59.95

VIDEO TITLES LISTED IN THIS GUIDE ARE AVAILABLE FOR PURCHASE OR RENTAL. CONTACT YOUR LOCAL VIDEO STORE OR TELEPHONE (800) 383-8811

Tips & Tactics

Archery Hunting Tactics for Deer
Chuck Adams is unquestionably America's most widely published bowhunting writer. He has taken over 100 deer of various kinds with a bow, including record-sized animals of every North American species. In this beautifully filmed production, you can join Chuck right in the heart of whitetail and mule deer country where he will show you how to use his secrets for success.
19-064 30 min. $16.95

Art Of Deer Calling & Other Hunting Tips
Learn to call in and bag Whitetail, Blacktail and deer predators using the little-known doe-call and other hunting techniques. You'll learn to make your own deer call in minutes and for just pennies. While other hunters rattle horns, walk, wait, or drive, you can successfully call in and kill deer in less time than you ever imagined, using the doe call techniques.
19-6247 70 min. $29.95

Basic Bird Hunting
Be a better birder! Kay Ohye, championship shooter and top shotgun shooting instructor, gives you an in-depth look at bird hunting. Kay addresses proper gun fit, accurate aiming, load selection, walking a field, working with dogs, field safety and much more.
19-5512 50 min. $19.95

Big Game Hunting Skills
Professional outfitters/guides Al Novotny, Don Shult and Walt Searle discuss and illustrate the basic skills, and the fine points, for stalking and taking trophy deer and elk.
19-006 30 min. $39.95

Bowhunter with Curt Gowdy
See superb whitetail deer hunting by bow, actual kill sequences are gracefully presented. Enjoy an historic journey through time of bowhunting with Native American Indians hunting in the great North Woods.
19-2047 52 min. $49.95

Bowhunting for Gator Gar
Non-stop bowfishing action on the murky backwaters of the Mobile Delta. The experts show the tactics and equipment necessary to shoot and land these 100-plus pound beasts.
19-8010 40 min. $44.95

Bowhunting for Whitetail Deer
Jim Dougherty dispels the myth that bow hunting is essentially the same as hunting with a gun. Learn the special attitudes and skills of the expert whitetail bowhunter.
19-2401 60 min. $49.95

Bucks on the Fringe
Bowhunting Rocky Mountain mule deer in Utah and Nevada with Pete and Laura Shepley. The use of treestand and ground blind techniques to take advantage of mule deer feeding and watering movements.
19-8020 30 min. $44.95

Critter Callin'
The sport of predator calling can offer the bowhunter and sportsman year round shooting opportunities. Dr. Ed Sceery exhibits the techniques to "bring 'em in"!
19-8012 30 min. $44.95

Decoys and Duck Calls: Two Secrets for Success
Bob Brister, shooting editor for Field & Stream magazine, is an internationally recognized authority on waterfowling who has proved his expertise in the field of duck calling competition. He holds the all-time record in the North American Duck Shooting Championship with 37 ducks downed with 40 shots. In addition to learning the secrets for using decoys and duck calls, Bob will tell you dozens of additional secrets for success - everything from gun selection to what kind of shell or shot size is best for specific situations. Now you will have the exclusive opportunity to hear his secrets for duck hunting success.
19-065 30 min. $16.95

Deer Calling Techniques
Bob McGuire teaches you the complex vocalization vocabulary of the whitetail, how to make the sounds, when to use them, rattling with calling, how to call does, tending bucks, dominant bucks, and more! Actual successful deer hunt with Ben Rodgers Lee.
19-144 48 min. $49.95

Doves & Sporting Clays
A pre-season warm-up designed to develop your wingshooting skills.
19-8147 30 min. $19.95

Duck and Goose Hunting
With expert guide and dog trainer Mike Mathiot, this is a comprehensive lesson in duck hunting concepts and techniques.
19-2400 60 min. $49.95

VIDEO TITLES LISTED IN THIS GUIDE ARE AVAILABLE FOR PURCHASE OR RENTAL. CONTACT YOUR LOCAL VIDEO STORE OR TELEPHONE (800) 383-8811

Duck Calling with Bill Harper

Bill Harper demonstrates and explains the art of calling all types of ducks on this informative video.
19-015 33 min. $49.95

Duck Hunting Secrets

Expert hunter, Jim Fernandez teaches us the secrets that make him so successful. You'll venture out into the marsh and learn what kind of guns, decoys and the most durable clothes to use when you hit the reeds.
19-8021 30 min. $16.95

Duck Identification

A foggy morning. A whistle of wings. And in the flutter of an eye, a duck is down. Identifying that duck before you shoot can be the difference between bagging more ducks and bagging your day. The information in this tape will sharpen your eye by showing you what to look for.
19-016 60 min. $49.95

Ducks Unlimited Video Guide to American Waterfowl and Game Birds.

The most complete identification guide for the field. The result of over two years of effort by Ducks Unlimited, the pioneering wetlands conservation and sportsmen's organization, this first-of-its-kind videotape documents all 43 species of waterfowl and 20 wetland upland game birds. Identifications include complete descriptions, sounds and calls, still photos, film footage, and computer-generated video techniques to provide actual wing beats both above and below water in low-light conditions found in the field. Narrated by acclaimed naturalist/photographer Michael Godfrey.
19-021 72 min. $39.95

Early Season Elk Hunting

You'll watch bull elk being called in and taken with the bow and arrow, plus some dramatic big game hunting sequences with two of the top elk callers in the country: Larry D. Jones of Oregon and Rob Hazlewood of Montana. You'll also see and hear these two experts outline techniques for bugling elk in the early season - techniques applicable to the rifle or bow that can help you become a better elk hunter. Filmed on actual hunts in Montana by noted wildlife photographers Gary Holmes and Ed Wolff.
19-193 60 min. $59.95

Elk Calling with Bill Harper

See a monster bull elk called in, and learn the basic techniques of calling and hunting elks from Bill Harper. Shot on location in Idaho.
19-017 33 min. $49.95

Elk Fever

Catch elk fever along with these hunters as they bring rut crazed bulls to their call. Learn how to excite bulls by raking, bugling, and using cow talk. Discover how to read sign, work bulls, and how to team up to bag your trophy. Experience the excitement of elf fever while watching close up footage of three bulls being taken with bow and arrow.
19-5662 60 min. $49.95

Elk Memories

Watch as Dwight Schuh calls a six point bull to five yards of Steve Jones. Then Larry D. Jones using Steve's six point will step by step show you how to handle and butcher your elk once he's down. Larry has bagged 25 elk and even the seasoned hunter can learn from this informative video. You will learn to preserve your elk memory by caping, boning, quartering and transporting it.
19-5669 60 min. $39.95

FIELD TO FEAST SERIES

Each tape tells the complete story of handling wild foods with clear instructions and easy-to-follow recipes.

• Small Game

This tape features some great hunting sequences and tips on improving your skills. Learn easy skinning and cleaning methods and dynamite recipes.
19-8026 52 min. $39.95

• Wild Turkey

This tape features spectacular footage of a large Tom taken with a bow. Plus a step-by-step preparation of the big game bird.
19-8027 55 min. $39.95

• Pheasant

Tips on shooting and retrieving as well as three superb recipes for pheasant are included.
19-8028 56 min. $39.95

• Waterfowl

Guide and dog trainer Glen Kania teaches us how-to set decoys and duck calling basics.
19-8029 51 min. $39.95

• Ruffed Grouse

Segments include how to choose the most productive hunting habitat, a terrific hunt, color phases, sexing and field care. Also, two recipes that respect the delicate flavor of the bird are included.
19-8030 43 min. $39.95

• Wild Edibles

You can learn how to make delicious meals out of spring and fall mushrooms, cattails, Queen Anne's Lace, milkweed, and other wild plants. It's your guide to identification, harvesting and food

preparation for a wide variety of wild edibles, featuring Nancy Frank.
19-8031 52 min. $39.95

Fox and Coyote Trapping East to West: Volume 1
All aspects of trapping these predators are covered, including trap selection, laying out the line, longlining, sets, lure use, location for sets, ethics and more.
19-276 110 min. $49.95

Fox and Coyote Trapping East to West: Volume 2
This video shows the little secrets which turn good trappers into top notch predator men. Topics include aerial locations, set variations, digger animals, snow methods, hiding catches, snares, draw stations and much more.
19-277 70 min. $34.95

Foxhunting
A video on modern day foxhunting in England and Whales as well as it's varying forms and immense cross-section of society are also featured.
19-8004 60 min. $39.95

Gobbler
Join accomplished bowhunter Pete Shepley and a pair of national turkey-calling champions, Billy Macoy and Dick Kirby, as they exhibit their skills while hunting the wild turkey. Through the concerted efforts of game departments and sportsmen across the country, the once-threatened American wild turkey now flourishes and is quickly becoming the most popular game bird in the U.S.
19-131 75 min. $44.95

Goose Calling with Bill Harper
Bill Harper conducts a seminar on calling and hunting geese, including several styles of calling, and tips to improve your hunt.
19-041 90 min. $49.95

Gun Dogs & Ringnecks
Uplandbird expert Ted Dewey shares pro tips on hunting pheasant.
19-8148 30 min. $19.95

High Plains Mulies: Method for Stalking and Driving
Guides Buff Terril and John Anderson explain two completely different mule deer hunting methods.
19-8149 30 min $19.95

Hog Hunting: Bowhunting Backwoods Rooters
Enjoy the fun and excitement of wild hog hunting

in the beautiful southeast.
With Pete Shepley and his PSE crew.
19-8013 30 min. $44.95

How to Find and Call the Wild Turkey
Shows how to plan a successful turkey hunt, demonstrating techniques of scouting hunting locations, identifying signs that indicate turkeys are nearby, identifying gobbling and responding with convincing calls.
19-2403 60 min. $49.95

How To Hunt Javelina
Enjoy a hunt with Reed Peterson, John West, Neil Rodgers, and Larry D. Jones. Besides watching footage of Javelina, Coues and mule deer, fox, bear, elk, quail, hawk, and rabbit, you will see stalks that end in close up arrow striking kills, Learn how to find Javelina where they feed, bed, and how to hunt them.
19-5663 60 min. $49.95

How to Hunt Whitetail Deer
John Wootters is the best authority on whitetail deer hunting in the world. Here are John's secrets for stalking whitetails in all types of habitat and how to perfect the art of horn rattling. Learn his secrets for locating buck rubs and scrapes and how to hunt these productive areas. John's information covers a span of decades devoted to the sport of hunting whitetail deer.
19-070 30 min. $16.95

How to Hunt Wild Turkeys
J. Wayne Fears has worked with hunting operations throughout North America. His career as a wildlife biologist led to a second career in outdoor writing, with over 1,500 feature articles appearing in major outdoor publications. He will show you which calls are best and how to use them; how to hunt various kinds of turkey habitat in all parts of the country. The wild turkey is the most sought-after trophy in secrets you need to know in order to bag your trophy tom.
19-071 30 min. $14.95

Hunting and Games Calling Tips
Learn from expert hunter and game caller Larry D. Jones in this comprehensive tape with instructions and demonstrations concerning the use of elks calls, predator calls and other hunting tips.
19-192 35 min. $39.95

Hunting Big Muleys
Features successful on-camera hunts for mule deer bucks. Outfitter Lad Shunneson guides successful early and late season hunts and shows trophy judgment, shot placement and game management.
19-163 40 min. $49.95

VIDEO TITLES LISTED IN THIS GUIDE ARE AVAILABLE FOR PURCHASE OR RENTAL. CONTACT YOUR LOCAL VIDEO STORE OR TELEPHONE (800) 383-8811

Hunting For Pheasant

Dave Embry takes you in search of the premier upland game bird, the pheasant. You'll see lots of hunting action as Dave shows you the techniques that produce the very best in pheasant hunting. You will learn: where to find pheasant, best shotguns and loads to use, how to hunt with or without dogs, how to hit flying pheasants, field dressing your birds, plus lots of exciting fast action footage.

19-6481 30 min. $14.95

Hunting Trophy Hogs

Hunt along with Cliff, Larry & Mike and learn the techniques of hog hunting. Watch dramatic stalks as Cliff and Larry move in for close shots. Enjoy the fun of being there, missing and bagging hogs with these outstanding hunters!

19-5664 60 min. $49.95

Hunting Whitetail Deer with Bob Mc Guire

Follow Bob McGuire and Alan Altizer as they film over-the-shoulder action in various mid-western habitats.

19-8005 30 min. $29.95

Insider's Guide to Duck Hunting

Mel Freitas, the nation's top professional waterfowl guide and duck calling champion, show you the tricks and techniques he has developed to bring the wariest of ducks right over the blind.

19-2932 45 min. $19.95

Introduction to Duck Calling

Learn to speak "duck" from the real experts, the ducks themselves. Waterfowl guide Flip Pallet and championship caller Harold Knight show you the concept and purpose of interpreting duck calls, and how to translate those calls, and how to translate those calls into proven techniques. You can talk more ducks into your line of thinking and your line of fire.

19-046 45 min. $24.95

Production Line Water Trapping

This video concentrates on pro methods of trapping mink, raccoon, beaver and muskrat. Topics include pro equipment location, sets for all species, land raccoon trapping, drowning techniques, actual catch footage and more.

19-278 100 min. $49.95

Pronghorn Hunting

Elk bucks and does taken on camera, plus lots of "how to" including trophy judgment and hunting techniques.

19-161 43 min. $49.95

Quest For Moose

You can learn how to hunt and call moose as you watch veteran guide John Blackwell and expert hunters Neil Summers and Larry D. Jones hunt Canadian moose. Watch and listen as these hunters point out moose sign, the sounds to use when calling moose and other important keys for successful hunting. You'll see Larry complete his quest for moose as he successfully stalks and bags Pope & Young bull.

19-5667 60 min. $49.95

Secrets for Hunting Black Bear

Featuring Dick Ray and Roger Moore and hosted by Jay S. Warburton, this video shares secrets and tips for hunting black bear.

19-2905 30 min. $16.95

Successful Duck Hunting

No freezing at 5:00 a.m. for you! Learn the art of duck hunting comfortably at home. "Cowboy Jim" Fernandez, manufacturer of Yentzen Duck Calls, and Cam Sigler, take you step-by-step through the basics. You learn how to call the duck, set decoys and select a blind. See and hear what works best in various ponds and marshes. Every step is described in detail, so when you hit the reeds, you'll know how it feels to be "The Complete Duck Hunter."

19-075 44 min. $19.95

Successful Elk Hunting Techniques

Join Pete Shepley and Jerry Morrison as they hunt elk in the Rocky Mountains. You will learn the successful techniques they have acquired during 27 years of elk hunting experience. Learn to locate elk habitat and how to bugle in trophy bulls during the rut. Share the secrets of experts that can make you a successful elk hunter.

19-130 80 min. $44.95

Successful Mule Deer Hunting

Jim Zimbo will put you closer to your trophy, make you a more knowledgeable mule deer hunter, and take you on a learning adventure in the Wyoming high country.

19-2227 60 min. $49.95

Successful Whitetail Deer Hunting

Successful whitetail hunting depends on a full understanding of the deer. Based on 30 years of research and hunting experience, Jerry Chiappetta shares his knowledge of the whitetail's finely-tuned defense mechanism, feeding habitats and preferred locations during the season. You'll learn how to select hunting regions, scouting and hunting methods, choosing the right firearm and ammunition, plans for driving deer and how to avoid the mistakes most hunters make.

19-175 55 min. $49.95

Tree-Stand Techniques for Hunting Big Game

The growing popularity of the tree-stand as a method of hunting big games has brought with it a need for the expert information provided in this video.

19-2162 46 min. $49.95

Turkey Calling and Hunting Techniques

A complete course in turkey calling, including techniques, safety tips and hunting techniques. Bill Harper is your host.

19-080 93 min. $49.95

Turkey Hunting

A thru Z of turkey, as five time world champion turkey caller Ben Rodgers Lee instructs you on types of calls, hunting equipment, calling techniques, scouting, and turkey sign. Actual bowhunt for Alabama gobblers. Bob misses the first bird, but Ben calls in another for a successful hunt! Explicit kill footage shown.

19-142 30 min. $49.95

Ultimate Bear Hunt

Expert Jim Ponciano gives you the details on baiting bears. You'll know how to pick the area, the bait site, stand height and location, type of bait to use, the best time to hunt, and where to shoot your bear. This video is packed with close up footage of bear, deer, small game, and three kill shots.

19-5666 60 min. $49.95

Understanding Elk Sounds

Larry demonstrates and discusses bugles, grunts, barks, and cow talk. He supports his statements with actual hunting footage so you will know which sounds to use on your hunts. If you hunt with bow or rifle you can find out which sounds to use in early or late season for effective hunting.

19-5670 30 min. $29.95

Understanding Wild Turkey

Covers how to quickly locate and identify gobblers and hens under difficult hunting conditions, and explains the sophisticated senses and defenses used by the elusive wild turkey.

19-2402 60 min. $59.95

Way of the Whitetail

The basis of the system presented in this fascinating study is best stated by your guide trophy deer hunter Jerry Chiappetta, "Only when you understand the whitetail will you be able to enter the world and find deer on purpose - not just by accident." Every hour you spend observing the "Way of the Whitetail" represents hundreds of hours of field study by white tail expert Jerry

Chippetta and his crew.

19-084 55 min. $49.95

Whitetail Video Magazine

An information-packed video certain to increase your knowledge of the whitetail deer and improve your hunting odds.

19-8024 53 min. $39.95

Training Hunting Dogs

Competition Coon Hunting

This video contains instructional tips on how to prepare both hound and handler for a competition hunt, how to call your hound during the hunt and the strategy used against other dogs and handlers. Dale Chain's Special guest is Jimmy Houston. Their lively personalities combine to make this video both instructional and humorous. Join the excitement of an actual coon hunt and see, firsthand, how a champion coonhound should work during a hunt.

30-567 58 min. $29.95

Hunting Dog Magazine

A dynamite tape that offers loads of great information: tips from trainers on how to start your pup on the right foot; demonstrations of various breeds to show what each does best, including the German wire hair, English spaniel, golden retriever and a breed from Germany that's new to the U.S.-- fabulous Meunsterlander.

19-8025 50 min. $39.95

Hunting Retriever Training Complete

A complete guide to training your retriever pup, from basic commands to retrieving.

24-023 120 min. $49.95

Miscellaneous

Archery Strategies: How To Get Started

Join Dave Embry and special guest Jim Dougherty as they discuss what to look for when selecting a new bow, arrows and other archery equipment, along with deer sightings, techniques and strategies.

19-6480 30 min. $16.95

Basic Archery Guide

An instructional video that teaches proper tuning

and shooting techniques for compound bows.
19-241 42 min. $44.95

Caping and Field Dressing Big Game

You'll witness the actual field caping and field dressing of a bull elk. The purpose of the video is to assist you in the proper caping of trophies you want to mount and also in the techniques of field dressing big game to achieve maximum flavor and texture of wild meat. With Rob Hazlewood and Steve Musick.
19-195 30 min. $39.95

Deer Hunter's Guide to Processing and Cooking Venison

How to prepare for a hunt, field dress, skin, quarter and butcher. Includes gourmet recipes.
19-2053 97 min. $29.95

Elusive Whitetail Deer

Step into the world of the elusive whitetail deer and see deer as few have ever seen them: undisturbed, in their natural habitat. This video journey through the secretive world of the majestic North American whitetail features valuable information for hunters and outdoor enthusiasts.
19-2107 37 min. $49.95

Field to Feast Venison

This video contains complete information on field dressing, skinning, and processing the venison. Also, you'll learn kitchen-tested recipes for some of the best venison dishes, including BBQ ribs, stroganoff, and pepper steak.
19-275 $39.95

JOHN FOX'S HUNTING SERIES

• Art of Bow Hunting

This is professional advice on equipment, camoguise, survival gear and much more.
19-2271 48 min. $19.95

• Art of Turkey Calling

This video features Leroy Braungardt, the greatest turkey caller of all time.
19-2272 42 min. $19.95

• Deer Hunting Made Easy

Starring Darrell LaMonica, former Oakland Raiders quarterback, this is exciting big buck footage.
19-2270 60 min. $19.95

• Spring Hunting Wild Turkey

Starring Walter Payton, NFL champion, this is winning advice on locating and stalking the magnificent "big birds."
19-2273 51 min. $19.95

OUTDOOR FUNDAMENTAL SERIES

• Basic Bird Hunting

This is the video encyclopedia of bird hunting. Kay Ohye gives you an in-depth look.
19-8091 50 min. $24.95

• Championship Skeet Shooting

It's like having your own personal shooting instructor! Join former Olympian and Trap Shooting Hall of Famer Frank Little as he helps you visualize proper bird-to-bead aiming relationships.
19-8090 53 min. $24.95

Has Your Aim Gone

To The Birds?

Steady Your Sights With A

Hunting Video!

VIDEO TITLES LISTED IN THIS GUIDE ARE AVAILABLE FOR PURCHASE
OR RENTAL. CONTACT YOUR LOCAL VIDEO STORE OR TELEPHONE (800) 383-8811

Investment
&
Personal
Finance

- ✓ *Financial Planning*
- ✓ *Real Estate*
- ✓ *Stocks, Bonds, Commodities*
- ✓ *Tax Preparation*
- ✓ *Miscellaneous*

Financial Planning

Bankruptcy

At last--a plain english explanation of the most helpful Government program that is available, to help debt-ridden consumers. In addition to answering the most common asked questions about the filing of a Bankruptcy petition, lists of attorneys and telephone numbers of every Bankruptcy Court in the United States are also covered. Hosted by attorney Eugene Grossman.

07-8073 100 min. $29.95

Credit Clear: A Guide to Clearing Your Credit

This video presents clear and concise techniques to help you prevent and/or repair credit problems. Learn how to solve credit problems yourself!

07-8080 33 min. $39.95

Financial Workout with Meg Green

Meg Green will show you how to get your finances in shape through a series of simple exercises and no nonsense tips. Discover the secrets of: taxes, investments, insurance, retirement and estate planning. This set iIncludes a financial planning workbook.

07-8134 59 min. $49.95

How To Repair & Re-establish Your Credit

This video will show you how to repair, re-establish your credit in the comfort of your home. You will learn how to: obtain immediate Visa/Mastercard, repair your credit, re-establish your credit, establish credit for first time, obtain copies of your credit files and negotiate with creditors.

07-5013 30 min. $19.95

Learn to Use Money Wisely--for Children

Problems faced by young people regarding money management are addressed, with particular attention paid to budgeting, avoiding impulse buying, comparison shopping and the dangers encountered with charge accounts and credit cards.

07-016 30 min. $29.95

Making Your Money Count

This video offers ten tips for financial security from the editors of Money Magazine--expert guidance on managing personal finances for everyone 18 to 80.

07-3076 60 min. $19.95

Mastery Of Money

In this entertaining video seminar, lecturer - author Stuart Wilde talks about money as energy. It is a vital part of your spiritual quest, for you need money to buy life's experiences. Once you can see money as energy there is really no limit to how much money you can acquire. Stuart's highly successful metaphysical approach shows you how to get into the flow of "easy money". He discusses practical techniques on how to raise your energy quickly. Once you do, people will be naturally attracted to what you are. When they show up, bill'em.

07-5838 71 min. $34.95

Meyer's Guide to Consumer Bankruptcy

Jerome Meyers has specialized in bankruptcy for the past 20 years. In this video you'll learn how to take advantage of this unique and forgiving law. All questions are answered in simple, layman's terms.

07-9782 45 min. $39.95

NIGHTLY BUSINESS REPORT SERIES:

Take the mystery out of money with these programs designed to help you make the most of your money.

• Guide to Retirement Planning

Most of today's retirees count on their financial support from Social Security and company pension plans; but financial experts agree that "baby boomers" may not be able to count on these safety nets in the future. Starting to save for retirement now has become crucial, but the question is how? Tips included in this video are: how to "watchdog" your company pension plans, how to evaluate an early retirement offer, explanation and listing of tax deferred savings plans and special retirement considerations for women.

07-8081 47 min. $19.95

• Guide to Buying Insurance

Gain a better understanding of what you are buying when you purchase insurance. Experts give buying tips for life, health, homeowner's and auto insurance including terms and how to choose a financially secure company.

Plan your family's future and security without being "over-insured".

07-8082 50 min. $19.95

• How Wall Street Works: Guide to Investing in the Financial Markets

An in-depth, behind the scenes look at the way the financial marketplace works for the novice investor interested in concise explanations of commonly used terms and inside information including basic do's and don'ts. Learn how to read a stock listing,

the difference between trading "at the market" and placing a "limited order" and much more.
07-8083 38 min. $19.95

Planning for Your Retirement and Financial Freedom
This will take you through a step-by-step approach to defining your retirement goals, determining your retirement budget and calculating your financial resources.
07-2051 40 min. $29.95

Planning Your Financial Future
Helps explain the financial planning process in easy-to-understand terms. It can help you make realistic decisions based on individual needs and current financial limitations. Includes a copy of the "Consumer Guide to Financial Independence" booklet.
07-2448 60 min. $39.95

Practical Guide to Getting More Life Out of Your Money
Help make your retirement more comfortable and rewarding with less worry about money. Workbook and public performance rights are included.
07-8022 40 min. $29.95

Socially Responsible Investing
Would you like to learn to invest in a way that fits your values while fulfilling your fiscal goals? Find out how to make money supporting companies meeting ethical criteria. This video contains enough information for you to instruct your broker to base your portfolio on firms that earn profits without exploitation.
07-9156 35 min. $24.95

Sylvia Porter's Personal Finance Video
Using clear examples and state-of-the-art graphics, this video gives viewers 21 money-making tactics which put them in control of their investments. These strategies were developed by Sylvia Porter, America's most trusted financial advisor.
07-1650 30 min. $29.95

U.S. NEWS FINANCIAL SERIES:

• Investment Guide: Best Investments
An offering of smart investment options for the future, as well as a retrospective analysis of last year's major investment performances.
07-8124 45 min. $24.95

• Personal Finance Guide: Building Your Future
Information on financial planning and investment and tax strategies to help you plan and prepare for your future.
07-8126 45 min. $24.95

Understanding Living Trusts
Your financial affairs are, and should remain, private. No one wants the government meddling in their family's inheritance proceedings. A living trust is the answer: By setting up a living trust you can avoid probate and government interference. Taped live at an "Investors Club of the Air" meeting, this in depth seminar program focuses on explaining the advantages and disadvantages of the living trust.
07-5981 45 min. $19.95

Real Estate

Are Your Buying a Home?
Follow home buying experts, Don Booth and Mitch Kuffa, as they walk you through real homes, discover typical problems and explain how to deal with them. Learn how to protect yourself by avoiding costly surprises and gaining a better understanding of the home structure.
07-8062 63 min. $24.95

Basic Real Estate Investing With Chuck Baker
This video will provide you with some of the "secrets" of basic real estate investing...what to look for, how to get financing, and where to locate sale property that is priced fairly.
07-6598 47 min. $29.95

Buy a Home
Robert Allen, best-selling author of Nothing Down, gives a seminar just for you...in your home and at your convenience. Learn the 10-step approach to buying a home that has helped Allen make millions of dollars in real estate. Allen shares his valuable tips on negotiating, financing (even with no money down), property appraisal and pitfalls, plus a formula to determine your price range. Learn how to save $1000's and avoid costly mistakes.
07-004 60 min. $24.95

Buying Your First Home
Buying your first home can be a confusing experience. This video explains everything about home buying: the difference between houses, condos and co-ops, how to decide what you can afford, how to find a home without a broker, the steps between contract and closing, the type of mortgage that's right for you and much more.
07-208 40 min. $29.95

VIDEO TITLES LISTED IN THIS GUIDE ARE AVAILABLE FOR PURCHASE OR RENTAL. CONTACT YOUR LOCAL VIDEO STORE OR TELEPHONE (800) 383-8811

Buying Your First Home

This 1992 production presents an overview of all the necessary information a first-time buyer needs before purchasing a home. From defining needs and price range to financing and closing, this program prepares the buyer for the purchasing procedure.
07-8017 30 min. $19.95

Homeseller's Primer

There is more to selling a home than putting it on the market, if you want to maximize your dollars and expedite the sale of your home. This video will show you how.
07-2720 22 min. $16.95

How to Buy a House, Condo or Co-op

The most important decision of your life shouldn't be uninformed. Many people who are interested in buying a home become victims of unscrupulous real estate agents, uncooperative sellers and inflexible loan officers. Here, the editors of Consumer Reports give information on choosing, financing and buying houses (and condos) so you can help make yourself an expert.
07-168 60 min. $19.95

Preparing Your Home for Sale

This program explains how to prepare and package your home for the most expedient and profitable sale. We compare two homes, one professionally prepared for sale and one not. Aside from a room-to-room tour such issues as odors, noises, conducting the tour, and more, are covered.
07-1857 25 min. $19.95

U.S. News Home Owner's Guide: How Much is Your Home Worth?

Practical advice on buying and selling homes, financing, renovations and repairs, renting and home technology are included in this video.
07-8125 45 min. $24.95

Stocks, Bonds, Commodities

Bonds

Looking for a long-term investment? Bonds may be the answer. This videotape gives you an understanding of bonds and acquaints you with short-term money market investments. Covers the types of bonds available, the terminology and the basic market principles that affect their value. Whether you want to save or trade bonds, Roma

Sinn shows you how to become a knowledgeable creditor of American industry or government.
07-039 59 min. $29.95

Introduction To Investing In Mutual Funds

In this video, Paul Scheibner introduces the viewer to the world of Mutual Funds, their types, fund organization and history, fund growth and development, diversification and risk.
07-5016 30 min. $39.95

Marketplaces

Learn about opportunities to invest. Covers arenas for investing, from the most conservative to the riskiest: New York Stock Exchange. American Stock Exchange, Over-The-Counter market, Penny Market and Commodities Market. You'll learn financial vocabulary, the broker/dealer's role, some of the rules and projections of each market, and receive the knowledge you will need to make financial decisions that are right for you.
07-037 55 min. $24.95

Mutual Funds

Investing in mutual funds is often a good way for small investors to get involved in the market. In this program, an expert who trains mutual funds representatives teaches you how a mutual fund works, the types and features available, the vocabulary of funds, and the projections the industry provides to the investor.
07-040 51 min. $24.95

Stock Market

An introduction to corporate investment. Explains market order, bids, price-earning ratios, index and market prices, and how to read and understand stock market information listed in newspapers.
07-028 30 min. $29.95

Stock Selection Guide

Endorsed by National Association of Investors' Corporation, this stock guide is designed to assist the investor in selecting a common stock that will achieve the financial goal of 100% increase from price appreciation and dividends over a five-year period. It is simple enough to help new, inexperienced investors, and yet contains enough detail for the most sophisticated investors.
07-166 46 min. $39.95

Ultimate Wall Street Trader: Paul Tudor Jones

If you're interested in the stock market and want to know what it's really like on Wall Street, this one-hour documentary, Trader, offers a fascinating education. Filmed before the 1987 crash, this show follows famed financial wunderkind Paul Tudor Jones, one of Wall Street's most successful security

VIDEO TITLES LISTED IN THIS GUIDE ARE AVAILABLE FOR PURCHASE OR RENTAL. CONTACT YOUR LOCAL VIDEO STORE OR TELEPHONE (800) 383-8811

traders. This award-winning film gives viewers an inside look at Jones' lifestyle and examines his prediction that America is nearing the end of a 200-year bull market.
07-5979 60 min. $39.95

Understanding Wall Street
Explains what all investors should know about the stock market. Viewers learn how to read the financial pages and what to look for in evaluating a company for potential investment.
07-2055 110 min. $39.95

Tax Preparation

How to Benefit from Tax Reform
Taxes have always been a complex issue. With the sweeping changes in the federal tax bill of 1986, they are more complicated than ever. This video includes an introduction to and history of tax laws, an outline of the new tax bill, the new law's overall impact on the economy, in-depth discussion of the new tax bill, and what the consumer can do to benefit from tax reform.
07-269 60 min. $29.95

Tax-Ease!
Larry Robinson and Joanne Luciani of the I.R.S. host this friendly, simple guide to completing your tax form. By just following along with your form and a pencil, you'll see what information is needed on each line! "Tax-Ease!" is broken up into four segments: the introduction, the 1040 EZ form, The 1040 A form, and the 1040 with schedules A & B.
07-6927 75 min. $24.95

Tax Tips on Tape
This video was produced by the Internal Revenue Service to help clergy and church leaders calculate their federal income and social security taxes. Included, are instructions for: figuring estimated tax, calculating annual income, filing self-employment tax, keeping business and travel expense records and many more issues.
07-9137 15 min. $16.95

Miscellaneous

Common Sense Law
Volume 1: Wills, contracts, moving/movers, employment rights, homesteads, bankruptcy, divorce, child support, bad checks and small claims court. Volume 2: Traffic tickets, drunk driving, credit awareness, credit ratings, loans/foreclosures, parent responsibilities, personal injury, lemon law, power of attorney, civil harassment and tele-law.
07-271 108 min. $49.95

How to Finance a College Education
Video includes how to increase your chances of receiving financial aid, why everyone should apply for aid regardless of income, how to avoid costly errors in filling out financial aid forms, how to use non-traditional financial sources, and how tax reform will affect financing a college education.
07-266 60 min. $39.95

Smart Investing From Consumer Reports
There are a million millionaires in the U.S. today. You could be one, too! Also covers new tax laws.
07-268 60 min. $19.95

Buy Low And Sell High!
These Videos Will Give You
An Edge On The Market.

VIDEO TITLES LISTED IN THIS GUIDE ARE AVAILABLE FOR PURCHASE OR RENTAL. CONTACT YOUR LOCAL VIDEO STORE OR TELEPHONE (800) 383-8811

New

Special Interest Video Titles

Become Available

Often.

Please Inquire

If A Title Or Subject

You Are Looking For

Is Not Listed.

VIDEO TITLES LISTED IN THIS GUIDE ARE AVAILABLE FOR PURCHASE
OR RENTAL. CONTACT YOUR LOCAL VIDEO STORE OR TELEPHONE (800) 383-8811

Jobs
&
Careers

✓ *Descriptions*
✓ *Training, Planning, Preparation*
✓ *Miscellaneous*

Descriptions

Accounting
Accountants working either as consultants or employees are presented in various private and public sectors. Areas of involvement include costing, budgeting, taxes and property. The accountant as an auditor, concerned with control of records and statements, is examined. Education and professional associations are discussed.
07-217 15 min. $24.95

Acting Careers
Ever thought of being an actor? In this program all the mystery is taken out of the successful pursuit of an acting career in film and television. If you have ever dreamed of being an actor, then this is for you!
07-8040 30 min. $39.95

ACTOR'S VIDEO LIBRARY SERIES

• Building a Character
25-8005 86 min. $39.95

• Combat for the Stage
25-8008 96 min. $39.95

• Creative Drama & Improvisation
25-8004 110 min. $39.95

• Directing Process
25-8009 110 min. $39.95

• Make-up Workshop
25-8007 104 min. $39.95

• Mime over Matter
25-8006 101 min. $39.95

Advertising: Tricks Of The Trade
A highly successful merchant and an advertising executive talk about what they do to get you to buy products and services.
07-078 30 min. $89.95

Air Transport/Flight Services
This program presents the flight crews of commercial airlines, pilots of smaller commercial aircraft and helicopters and flight attendants. Those involved detail their duties when preparing for a flight during and after a flight. Educational requirements, training procedures and background experience is noted.
07-218 15 min. $24.95

Air Transport/Ground Services
Ground service personnel such air traffic controller, radio operator, crew scheduler and ramp attendant portray their roles in the operation of an airport. Training and lifestyle are mentioned.
07-219 15 min. $24.95

Architecture
The many activities of an architect are examined to emphasize the scope and complexity of this profession, as assignments can vary from the design of a residential landscape to the supervision of a world's fair site. Young grads are contrasted with accomplished masters. This program is interspersed with outstanding examples of architectural design work.
07-220 15 min. $24.95

Assembling A New Bicycle
This video is an entry level training tool for the purpose of identifying Bicycle Components. Bicycle Shop Tools, and assembling a New Bicycle (using an ATB as the main model). This video is designed to save bicycle shops & retailers valuable time and expense.
07-5054 37 min. $39.95

AUDITION POWER SERIES
"A real asset", says Gene Kelly. This resourceful program covers all the strait talk, strategy, and inside information from Hollywood's top dancers and choreographers. It's important knowing what it takes to be chosen.

• Volume I
07-8020 51 min. $39.95

• Volume II
07-8021 45 min. $39.95

Auto Assembly Line General Repairman
Learn what it's like to be on the auto assembly line from a 15-year veteran of a Westland, Michigan auto manufacturing company. See how the cars are put together and learn the importance of Tom Molesky's "last man on the line" job.
07-061 30 min. $89.95

Bartending
Jeff Madden started Madden Educational Videos when he decided to use his expertise in the field of bartending to produce a "How To" video that could be used to replace the expensive bartending schools that are springing up throughout the country. The video guide, along with a handy drink recipe sheet that is included, covers everything the prospective bartender needs to know and do to obtain his first

bartending job and adapt into anyone's system quickly and easily.
07-6695 29 min. $29.95

Being A Car Dealer
The business person Americans love to hate tell his side of the story.
07-069 30 min. $89.95

Big Time Talent Management
Stan Kamen, talent manager for such stars as Barbara Streisand, Warren Beatty, Goldie Hawn and Diane Keaton, talks about what is involved in becoming a talent agent, helping his clients reach stardom and keeping them there.
07-106 30 min. $89.95

Business and Data Processing Machine Operators
Men and women who operate the machines developed to improve the efficiency of business and data processing are featured. The machines used today vary from adding machine and simple calculator to the mainframe computer. Operators discuss the variety of skills required and the applications served. Required special training will be discussed.
07-221 15 min. $24.95

Careers In Sales
A sales trainer, and employment agency owner, and an employer of sales people explore the varied and often lucrative careers available in sales.
07-080 30 min. $89.95

Carpentry
This program includes occupations concerned with constructing, renovating and maintaining wooden structures using power saws, planes, hammers and other carpentry tools. Levels of advancement are noted from apprenticeship to journeyman, foreman and contractor. The role of the union in hiring practices is also explained.
07-222 15 min. $24.95

Chips: Highway Patrolman
Join Rick Porterfield, 34, on a typical day as one of the elite California Motorcycle Patrol: and find out what it took to get there. Rick started riding motorcycles when he was 15 and waited nine years for his dream assignment with the patrol to become a reality. Rick feels television portrayals of this profession are false and tells you why.
07-055 30 min. $89.95

Civil Engineering
Civil engineers work in a variety of responsibilities in government, industry and private consulting practice. They are shown at their jobs in design, quality control, project supervision and top-level

administration in such areas as transportation, building construction, utilities and environment-related projects. Educational background and professional associations are noted.
07-223 15 min. $24.95

Clerk: Bank, Insurance And Commerce
Clerks responsible for the maintenance of financial records, the exchange of funds and statistics are the subject of this program. They discuss their duties at insurance, banking and customer service facilities. Brief mention will be made of advancement opportunities and amenities.
07-224 15 min. $24.95

Coal Miner
At age 32, Eddie Gilmore has spent one-third of his life in the coal mines of Big Stone Gap, Virginia. Come with Eddie, section foreman, at 8:00 in the morning as he and his crew put on their "bankers' suit" - what they call their work clothes-and travel two and one-half miles underground to their destination deep within the black caverns of the mines.
07-045 30 min. $89.95

Coast Guard Pilot
Take a look at how Chris Dewhurst flies dangerous search and rescue missions for the U.S. Coast Guard as a helicopter pilot. Go along with Chris as he patrols to save lives over the nation's coastlines and waterways.
07-058 30 min. $89.95

COLD READINGS MADE EASY SERIES
A three part series created by Noelle Nelson to help you get that important part or series regular. Each program covers preparation for reading and reading with confidence, call backs and understanding the character that you're reading. Remembering the do's and don'ts is an important first step in obtaining the part that you want.

• Basic Cold Readings
07-9269 47 min. $29.95

• Personalizing Your Cold Reading (Intermediate)
07-9270 43 min. $29.95

• Getting the Job (Advanced)
07-9271 51 min. $29.95

Community Planning
This video program presents an in-depth look at the role and importance of a community planner in today's society. Planners come from different educational backgrounds and are engaged in solving problems such as densely populated areas, traffic,

VIDEO TITLES LISTED IN THIS GUIDE ARE AVAILABLE FOR PURCHASE OR RENTAL. CONTACT YOUR LOCAL VIDEO STORE OR TELEPHONE (800) 383-8811

the need for parks and green belts, easy accessibility to schools and churches and the protection of the environment.
07-226 15 min. $24.95

Computer Programming And Systems Analysis

Enter the world of computers as systems analysts and programmers. Plan, implement and control electronic data processing services and computer systems. Featured areas of specialization include the use of electronic resources and computer graphics. Educational programs at the university level are discussed.
07-227 15 min. $24.95

Cosmetic And Personal Services

Occupations concerned with grooming and personal care for men and women are the topic of this informative video. Cosmetologist, barbers, hairdressers and manicurists are spotlighted at their jobs, discussing their backgrounds and interests. Various training procedures and opportunities are also included.
07-228 15 min. $24.95

Dental Hygienics

Private practice, public clinics and the military provide the background for an occupation concerned with supportive work in the field of dentistry. Hygienists demonstrate their duties in the care and treatment of patients. Educational programs are reviewed, with career opportunities noted.
07-229 15 min. $24.95

Dentistry

Dentists are shown at different stages of their careers examining, diagnosing, preventing and treating ailments of the gums, teeth and jaw structures. A comprehensive picture is presented as family dentists and specialists discuss the rewards, demands and stresses of the field. Degree programs and professional associations are reviewed.
07-230 15 min. $24.95

Doctor

Dr. Warren Strudick, surgical intern at Stanford University Medical Center, shows you what it's really like to be a first-year medical school intern. He talks about the rewards and drawbacks of working long hours taking care of patients while also learning the science of medicine.
07-057 30 min. $89.95

Drafting

Those who prepare detailed drawings to specified dimensions are spotlighted. Typical areas of specialization include architectural, engineering, commercial and topographical drafting. Management views of skills, amenities and training

programs are discussed.
07-231 15 min. $24.95

Electrical And Electronic Engineering

Here is a comprehensive survey of engineers in occupations related to electrical energy. Areas of specialization covered are fiber optics, satellite, telephone, recording, audio and electrical power. Educational requirements via university or technical school programs are discussed.
07-232 15 min. $24.95

Elementary And Secondary Education

While the motivations to teach are unique to individual educators, certain elements are common to all. This program attempts to point out these shared characteristics and to emphasize that teaching cannot be reduced to a mechanical process.
07-233 15 min. $24.95

Financial Business Services

Occupations featured in this program are concerned specifically with the management of money within the business world. Included are investment counselors, securities brokers, trust officers and mortgage underwriters. Bank, insurance companies, stock brokerage firms and other large corporations provide the setting. Educational backgrounds often include degrees in commerce and accounting.
07-234 15 min. $24.95

Finding And Landing The Right Job

The personnel director of Oscar Mayer Corporation, and employment agency owner and a university career counselor talk about some little known and effective techniques for finding job openings and how to proceed to increase your chances of getting the job you want.
07-077 30 min. $89.95

Fire Prevention And Firefighting

Featured are occupations concerned with the general prevention and fighting of fires in both government service and private industry. Several locations are used to demonstrate the wide range of equipment employed, the skills required and the types of emergencies that may arise. Related roles such as emergency rescue and disaster relief are introduced. Senior personnel discuss the training programs for new recruits and their respective organizations.
07-235 15 min. $24.95

Fireman

This is the story of George Kreuscher, 40, who has been a veteran of the New York City fire department for the previous 18 years. George put his degree in respiratory training to good use as a member of the highly trained Rescue Company

Number 1 in Mid-town Manhattan.
07-042 30 min. $89.95

Fisherman
Come with fisherman Lennon Nance, 49, at 4:00 a.m. as he takes off from Calabash, North Carolina in his shrimp boat, "The Hank." Then join Lennon and his wife and brothers as they prepare the day's catch in the family's coastal seafood restaurant.
07-054 30 min. $89.95

Forestry Sciences
Occupations concerned with studying, developing and controlling forest lands are examined. Scientists and technicians involved in these areas are shown at their jobs from research to its practical application. Conservation categories are included from tree nursery superintendents to forest fire fighters. Educational background is included.
07-236 15 min. $24.95

Graphic Arts
Occupations in this program include commercial design, artists, layout, scenery, display, sign painters, art supervisors and medical illustrators. Shown at work in advertising agencies, design firms, manufacturing companies and others, the people doing these jobs outline the skills and training required and explain how they become involved in their particular occupations.
07-237 15 min. $24.95

Home Economics
This exciting video presents a variety of career opportunities for both males and females in the field of Home Economics. A series of interviews with persons working in each field explores careers in dietetics, foods and nutrition, child development, interior design, and fashion. Working with cooperative extension, in education, and with business and industry, are among the career profiles presented. Educational, personal and professional requirements are given for each field. The video concludes with suggestions for becoming an entrepreneur in their chosen occupation. Don't pass on this opportunity to expose students to the exciting career possibilities in Home Economics.
07-6936 30 min. $79.95

Horse Trainer
Join Florida cutting horse trainer, Ralph Adkinson, as he trains horses for competition. Watch as Ralph teaches his horse how to run fast and make precise pivot turns.
07-059 30 min. $89.95

Household Economics
The science of household economics in both private industry and government service is examined. Shown are the design of consumer appliances, research, and implementing public programs. The various occupations in this category are highlighted with respect to required educational background, nature of work and employer organization.
07-238 15 min. $24.95

HOW TO BE AN OUTSTANDING RECEPTIONIST
This program can assist you in building your receptionist skills. Both volumes cover techniques to help make you a more effective and satisfied receptionist.

• **Volume I**
Ten qualities that enhance the value of a receptionist and those that detract.
07-8043 90 min. $99.95

• **Volume II**
Learn how to screen calls, handle stress, manage your time, and getting along with all types of people.
07-8044 90 min. $99.95

Information Hollywood
Twelve steps to becoming a successful actor and what to watch out for.
25-9122 55 min. $24.95

Insulating And Roofing Occupations
Construction workers who specialize in reducing the passage of heat, cold or sound are shown in on-the-job situations. Varied occupations demonstrate the skills required in working with asbestos, fiberglass and styrofoam for insulation; asphalt, tar, cedar and concrete for roofing. Union representatives explain their role in this fascinating career.
07-239 15 min. $24.95

Library And Archival Science
Cataloguer, film librarian, archival documenter, music librarian and archival conservator are examples of the specialized areas presented. In addition to independent activities, those involved are shown serving the public in a variety of ways. Basic educational requirements as well as grad studies are noted.
07-240 15 min. $24.95

Management - Private Enterprise
The role of management in the corporate world is examined. While the actual positions vary widely, basic skills and duties are consistent throughout sales, personnel, production, advertising, purchasing, transportation and communications, to name a few. Management is presented from a range of firms up to the multinational corporation. Educational and personal backgrounds are offered for a better understanding of these positions.
07-241 15 min. $24.95

VIDEO TITLES LISTED IN THIS GUIDE ARE AVAILABLE FOR PURCHASE OR RENTAL. CONTACT YOUR LOCAL VIDEO STORE OR TELEPHONE (800) 383-8811

Mechanics

Automotive aircraft, motorcycle, diesel, refrigeration and heavy equipment mechanics are shown working at various repair facilities. The major area of concern is the maintenance and repair of equipment powered by electrical and internal combustion engines. Progression through the trade from apprenticeship to journeyman certification is examined.
07-243 15 min. $24.95

Medical Laboratory Technology

This program studies those who are involved in the laboratory procedures that provide the medical profession with support in the prevention and treatment of disease. Specialization areas included are blood bank, biochemistry, hematology, histology and microbiology.
07-244 15 min. $24.95

Medicine

The practice of medicine is presented so that one can understand medical career areas of specialization such as psychiatry, neurology, radiology and the family practitioner. Educational requirements and medical associations are also discussed.
07-245 15 min. $24.95

Mickey Rooney - On Acting

Join Mickey as he motivates his students to think creatively and build confidence in themselves. Learn techniques like, improvisation, auditioning, memorizing, and body movement. Everything you need to know from the ultimate performer.
07-9478 48 min. $29.95

Modeling, Commercials & Acting

Exciting interviews of your favorite TV stars and models who give their formulas for success. Leading Hollywood Agents tell how it all works. All the do's and don'ts of the business.
07-8057 45 min. $16.95

Modeling Made Easy

Jill Donnellan is a working model and actress. She teaches us all of the indepth instruction and step demonstrations of runway techniques for men and women.
07-8058 70 min. $19.95

Music

Musical occupations can range from full symphony orchestras to night club entertainment. The career development of selected musicians is presented to show typical examples of background and training.
07-246 15 min. $24.95

Nursing And Paramedical

The well-known aspects of nursing and specialties such as outpost nursing and public health nursing are featured as well as paramedical services. Filmed on location, individuals involved discuss their training and motivations for selecting this field.
07-247 15 min. $24.95

Optometry

Optometrists are presented examining eyes, prescribing and fitting eye glasses and contact lenses. Areas of responsibility with respect to referring patients to medical practitioners are noted. Special skills required in the use of optometric aids are demonstrated by those involved, and licensing procedures are mentioned.
07-248 15 min. $24.95

Paramedic

Join paramedic Bill Olsen, whose job is to save lives by bringing the "emergency room on the road" to the patient. Learn what is really takes to be in this "no second chance" profession preparation, a strong stomach, faith,--patience and complete confidence in one's teammates.
07-060 30 min. $89.95

Parole Agent

G.A. Patrick has been a parole agent for the California Department of Corrections for 26 years. Learn what it's really like to work in the law enforcement from a man who began his career as a correctional officer at San Quentin Prison.
07-046 30 min. $89.95

Performing Arts Technologies

Production assistants, make-up artists, special effects technicians, wardrobe supervisors, recording and audio engineers are examined at various facilities where they work, along with the equipment they operate. These technical occupations are specialized areas within the operation of television studios, theaters, motion picture studios and concert halls. Mention is made of the appropriate union involved with each profession.
07-249 15 min. $24.95

Pharmacy

In this program the pharmacist's job is examined in the retail outlet and in the hospital. Industrial pharmacists are studied as they are involved in the development of new drugs, the improvement of existing ones and the development of equipment for production of new products. The pharmacologist is shown in the research of the relationship between drugs and other substances which eventually lead to the development of new drugs.
07-250 15 min. $24.95

Photographic Processing

Photographic and motion picture processing

laboratories are the subject of this video program. Occupations such as color timers, printer operators, film mounters, copy camera persons and developing machine operators are examined. Also included is a discussion of optical sound transfer in the context of the overall working environment. Internal training programs and the unique working conditions are introduced.
07-251 15 min. $24.95

Picture Perfect: How To Become a Model
Ever wanted to know what it takes to become a model in today's world of fashion? Super-model Denise, is your guide to this in-depth tour of the basics of modeling. Let Denise show you how.
07-8064 30 min. $24.95

Photography
The diverse field of photography is examined, from medical photographer to the cinematographer, including news, portrait and television. Various individuals are shown to contrast the artistic and technical aspects of practicing photography. The mobility of the freelancer is introduced.
07-252 15 min. $24.95

Pipefitting And Plumbing
Tradespersons concerned with installing and repairing pipelines and plumbing for distributing water, gas, steam and other materials discuss the nature of their job and working conditions. A brief outline of the apprentice and journeyman certification program is included.
07-253 15 min. $24.95

Police
Police service on a local and county basis is examined. The training, day-to-day duties, shift work, motivation and risk factors involved with police work are brought to light. Areas of duty, such as traffic, fraud, theft and morality are mentioned along with promotion possibilities. Both urban and rural situations are shown.
07-254 15 min. $24.95

Printing
The people of the printing industry are featured in various printing and binding operations. The different duties and processes are discussed by those who are responsible for the operation of the equipment. A union rep comments on the overall industry and opportunities in general.
07-255 15 min. $24.95

Professional Sports
Athletes are examined in terms of skills, demands and requirements, uncertainties that are common to most major sports, as well as the rewards. While the participation of these athletes in actual competition is featured, they are also shown in

business and community responsibilities. Mention is made of the increasing role of agents and associations.
07-256 15 min. $24.95

Promoting Concerts From Rock To Pop
Art D'Lugoff, a New York impresario, and Ron Paskin, a midwest attorney turned promoter, talk about the nuts and bolts of promoting headline concert events.
07-100 30 min. $89.95

Psychology
The application of experimental, therapeutic, research and applied psychology within business, universities, government and private practice is examined. Besides defining the distinctions between various disciplines, the education and experience required to fill this type of occupation is described. Information pertaining to certification procedures is noted.
07-257 15 min. $24.95

Radio And Television Production
Sound recorders, video equipment operators, switchers and transmitter operators discuss their jobs and the prerequisite training found within a technical school program. Specializations such as record production are included. Filmed within radio stations, television stations and recording studios.
07-258 15 min. $24.95

Retailing And Merchandising
This program presents a cross-section of employees in retail sales from small outlets to department store chains. Featured are occupations which provide a service, a convenience or a resource to customers. Furniture, clothing, shoe and ski stores are typical of the background locations used.
07-259 15 min. $24.95

Sales - Commodities
The general role and lifestyle of commodity salespersons is depicted with special mention of irregular hours, commission income and other considerations unique to sales positions. Commodity sales represented include automobiles, furniture, appliances, business machines, electronic products and publications.
07-225 15 min. $24.95

Secretarial Services
From the executive and administrative secretary with top-level responsibilities, to the clerk typist who has just left high school, the essential role this occupation plays in any organization is examined. The scope and variety of opportunities with secretarial sciences in explored. Specific skills, advancement procedures, advantages and amenities are also mentioned.
07-260 15 min. $24.95

VIDEO TITLES LISTED IN THIS GUIDE ARE AVAILABLE FOR PURCHASE OR RENTAL. CONTACT YOUR LOCAL VIDEO STORE OR TELEPHONE (800) 383-8811

Selling Houses For A Living

Most realtors do not make a living at what they do and, sooner or later, they quit. Given this background, three successful realtors share with you the whys and hows of making it in their field.
07-068 30 min. $89.95

Social Work

Occupations featured are those involved in the diagnosis, treatment and counseling of social problems affecting individuals and communities. Examples are home visitor, guidance counselor, case worker and group home counselor. Educational requirements and association affiliations are mentioned.
07-261 15 min. $24.95

Sports - Attendants And Support

Services
The many support occupations necessary to the function of professional sporting operations are investigated. The duties and qualifications required for such occupations as equipment manager, caddie, ice maker, jockey, valet and scoreboard operator are explained. While working, these people discuss their jobs and their relationship with players, coaches, officials and management.
07-262 15 min. $24.95

Stuntman

Conrad Palmisano, 34, is one of the 200 active, working stuntman in the United States today. In the profession for 14 years, Conrad is a California native, husband and father of two, and loves the challenge of his work.
07-043 30 min. $89.95

Three Cops

Three police officers, two men and a woman, compare the portrayal of their profession on television with the real day-to-day life of a cop.
07-110 30 min. $89.95

Three Surgeons Open Up

Three surgeons share their experiences in coping with the pressures of life and death. Two videotapes, 30 minutes each, available as a set.
07-109 60 min. $179.95

Two Successful Trial Attorneys

Two successful trial attorneys, Jack McManus and Don Eisenberg, talk about the joys and personal costs of being a courtroom gladiator, and reveal the unique make-up of verbal battlers.
07-107 30 min. $89.95

Utilities Equipment Operation

The operators of a variety of stationary equipment such as air compressors, boilers, heating and ventilation systems, pumps and refrigerators are depicted. Included are utilities operators involved with powerhouses, substations and pumping stations. Internal procedures and certification regulations are explained.
07-263 15 min. $24.95

Veterinarian

Spend time with Dr. Nora Matthews, Cornell Graduate and Veterinarian, as she treats domestic pets and also helps farmers with their cattle in upstate New York.
07-056 30 min. $89.95

VIDEO CAREER LIBRARY SERIES

Individual occupations correspond to standard occupational classification titles found in many other sources of career information. Each tape contains descriptions of occupations within a broad segment of the work world.

• **Careers In The Literary And Performing Arts**
07-191 40 min. $79.95

• **Careers In The Physical And Life Sciences**
07-192 25 min. $79.95

• **Careers In The Repair Field**
07-184 25 min. $79.95

• **Careers In The Social Sciences**
07-193 25 min. $79.95

• **Careers In Administration & Management**
07-177 30 min. $79.95

• **Careers In Allied Health Fields**
07-190 40 min. $79.95

• **Careers In Clerical And Administrative And Support Occupations**
07-181 25 min. $79.95

• **Careers In Construction**
07-185 35 min. $79.95

• **Careers In Education**
07-194 25 min. $79.95

• **Careers In Engineering And Related Occupations**
07-178 45 min. $79.95

- **Careers In Marketing And Sales**
07-180 20 min. $79.95

- **Careers In Mechanical Occupations**
07-183 25 min. $79.95

- **Careers In Medicine & Related Fields**
07-189 30 min. $79.95

- **Careers In Production I**
07-186 30 min. $79.95

- **Careers In Production II**
07-187 30 min. $79.95

- **Careers In Public And Personal Services**
07-182 35 min. $79.95

- **Careers In Technical Occupations**
07-179 35 min. $79.95

- **Careers In Transportation & Material Moving**
07-188 20 min. $79.95

Visual Arts
A realistic view of those who have chosen careers in the world of art. Included are realist and abstract painters, sculptors in steel, bronze, stone and wood, print makers and ceramicists. Each artist is shown creating his or her special form of art. The formal development of artistic talent is introduced.
07-264 15 min. $24.95

VOCATIONAL VISIONS CAREER SERIES
The Vocational Visions Career Series is designed to increase career awareness by providing high school and vocational students with information that will help them make appropriate career decisions. It includes interviews with people in various occupations to provide useful information in a lively and personal format that makes viewing fun as well as educational!

- **Auto Mechanic**
07-6946 15 min. $39.95

- **Band Director**
07-6945 15 min. $39.95

- **Chef**
07-6941 15 min. $39.95

- **Florist**
07-6944 15 min. $39.95

- **Insurance Agent**
07-6940 15 min. $39.95

- **Letter Carrier**
07-6938 15 min. $39.95

- **National Park Ranger**
07-6943 15 min. $39.95

- **Paralegal**
07-6937 15 min. $39.95

- **Physical Therapist**
07-6939 15 min. $39.95

- **Potter**
07-6942 15 min. $39.95

Writing And Journalism
Within broadcasting, newspapers and advertising, literature and industry, there are a large number of writing and journalism occupations. A spectrum of possibilities ranging from novelists to technical writers is surveyed. Various employment situations from freelance to salaried are highlighted. Editors give their input on what they expect from writers and journalists.
07-265 15 min. $24.95

Writing & Selling Your First Screenplay
A master class from a leading Screenwriter and lecturer at UCLA Extension and the American Film Institute. This video gives instruction on structure, dialogue, scene construction and seven other crucial subjects. Also includes interviews with a leading Hollywood literary agent and a top production executive.
07-9252 90 min. $39.95

Training, Planning, Preparation

Art of Competitive Interviewing
In this one-hour condensation of a live four-hour seminar, you will meet Peter D. Leffkowitz nationally acclaimed consultant to the professional search and employment industry. He will offer insight and energy to this often emotionally-charged proposition.
07-8061 60 min. $39.95

VIDEO TITLES LISTED IN THIS GUIDE ARE AVAILABLE FOR PURCHASE OR RENTAL. CONTACT YOUR LOCAL VIDEO STORE OR TELEPHONE (800) 383-8811

Auditions And Insights With Terrence Mann
A video workshop for serious actors taught by one of Broadway's leading talents. Contains valuable information about the business of acting, including audition preparation and presentation, hiring an agent, equity and open calls, plus many of Terry's personal experiences and insights. An invaluable teaching tool and reference guide for actors and teachers.
07-6638 30 min. $39.95

CAREER HUNTERS SERIES
Today's competitive job market is no place to enter unprepared; all too often mistakes are unknowingly made that automatically screen you out. You'll see top professionals reveal the secrets of successful career hunting. They'll also show you the "do's" and "don'ts" that are critical to this process.

• You And The Market
Part A. Getting Ready, This program deals with the importance of knowing your interests, aptitudes, hobbies, accomplishments and personal characteristics - all necessary in deciding what you want to do in life. Part B. The Market, A look at where job openings exist in a variety of areas, covering apprenticeship, clerical, on-the-job training and summer employment.
07-214 30 min. $19.95

• Selling Yourself
Part A. Your Calling Card selling yourself on paper is often an important step in obtaining a job. Tips on writing resumes, cover letters and filling out application form are included. Part B. First Impressions, A program that looks at how to sell yourself the first time around, in person, on paper and on the telephone.
07-215 30 min. $19.95

• Getting Hired
Part A. The Interview, Blowing smoke in an employer's face can cost you a job: the "do's" and "don'ts" of handling an interview in a professional manner. Part B. Climbing the Ladder A wrap up program that examines the qualities an employer looks for in an new employee and why it's important to be aware of these.
07-216 30 min. $19.95

Career Strategies Part I
In this videotape by Esquire, top corporate leaders reveal the secrets of their success and tell aspiring young executives how to zoom into the fast lane. Features "In Search of Excellence" co-author Robert J. Waterman, Jr. and top executives at companies from Citicorp to Burger King.
07-006 60 min. $29.95

Career Strategies Part II
In this Esquire videotape, headhunters, executives, and other experts share inside knowledge of changing jobs and leveraging careers. Features hiring consultant Kurt Einstein, headhunter Putney Westerfield, and many others.
07-007 60 min. $29.95

Change Your Mind: Inner Training for Women in Business
An effective program designed to help you be the very best you can be and reach your full potential. With Dr. Kay Porter and Judy Foster's five step inner training program, you will learn to deal with the issues of time, power, balance and confidence. Targeted for Corporate Training and Development.
07-8018 30 min. $199.95

EARN BIG BUCKS SERIES
Learn how to start a video production company. These series of tapes covers the basics of getting started, finding business, equipment, marketing and other important steps into building a profitable and successful video production company.

• Business End of Video
07-8073 30 min. $29.95

• Editing Theory & Practice
07-8071 30 min. $29.95

• High End Weddings
07-8067 40 min. $29.95

• Industrial Video Production
07-8066 40 min. $29.95

• Producing & Marketing Videos
07-8072 30 min. $29.95

• Professional Equipment & Techniques
07-8068 45 min. $29.95

• Toaster Basics
07-8070 45 min. $29.95

• Video Depositions
07-8069 30 min. $29.95

Employment Agency Business
Ruth Clark, President of Clark Unlimited Personnel of New York City, and Roger McDowell, owner of a Snelling & Snelling personnel franchise business in Wisconsin, talk about the employment agency business. Learn about the hows and whys of the trend toward part-time employment and toward the "department store" approach, which they believe these businesses will have to take in the future in order to be successful. Lots of tips for job seekers

VIDEO TITLES LISTED IN THIS GUIDE ARE AVAILABLE FOR PURCHASE OR RENTAL. CONTACT YOUR LOCAL VIDEO STORE OR TELEPHONE (800) 383-8811

as well as for potential employment agency owners.
07-090 30 min. $79.95

FIND THE JOB YOU WANT AND GET IT

Pat Sladey offers you tips to gain an advantage over other job applicants. These four tapes help you find the hidden job market, gain the necessary self-confidence, prepare a winning resume, anticipate problems, sell yourself in the interview and more.

• **Being Prepared for the Interview**
07-2087 45 min. $59.95

• **Job Search**
07-2086 45 min. $59.95

• **Marketing Yourself**
07-2088 45 min. $59.95

• **Selling Yourself in the Interview**
07-2089 45 min. $59.95

Getting Your Kids Into Commercials

This video tape presents interviews with top industry insiders: Agents, Producers and Directors. They offer you and your children the knowledge and experience they have acquired through years in the business. In less than one hour you will gain knowledge that otherwise might take you years of frustration and cost your child dozens of lost chances.
07-6264 60 min. $19.95

Good Job After College - How To Get

One - The Visual Advisor Volumes I & II Recommended for recent college graduates or current students preparing for the future. Contains vital information from senior recruiters and vice presidents from some of the country's leading companies, such as Kraft Foods, GTE, Ernst & Whinney and others. These specialists provide what companies expect from you, how to prepare yourself and more. Experts also tell you how to take advantage of special opportunities and internships while still in college.
07-6639 80 min. $49.95

How To Interview For A Job

Joy Booth, Assistant Director of education for the University of Washington; Nancy Chellevold, employment consultant; and May Fraydas, career counselor, give you tips and advice on how to interview successfully for a job. Some of their ideas are probably new even to seasoned job seekers.
07-092 30 min. $89.95

How To Read A Financial Statement

It's not surprising that many business persons do not know how to read a financial statement. Here is a video that takes the viewer step by step through a sample financial statement.
07-8047 30 min. $59.95

How To Write A Resume

In the modern marketplace, you need a modern resume to compete effectively for the job you want. This program shows how to prepare a resume that sells you, from choosing the most effective style and content to selecting the right type face and paper, and teaches how to avoid the pitfalls of an old-fashioned "employment history" by presenting examples of modern functional and chronological resumes. Step-by-step instructions show how to compose and organize content to put your best foot forward. Pointers are given for those who feel their work history is too short, or too long. Examples of effective resumes of various types and styles are shown, including typewritten, word processor, and professionally printed. The video concludes with a list of "do's" and "don'ts" for resume preparation and comments on making yours stand out from the pack.
07-126 22 min. $59.95

If You Really Want To Get Ahead

Discover why some people climb the ladder to corporate success while others don't. Let the editors of "Communications Briefings", newsletter, give you a step-by-step plan to reach the top.
07-8054 48 min. $79.00

Inside Secrets Of Interviewing

This program offers the key to landing the job of your future. It provides the secrets of saying the right thing at the right time to make the best impression.
07-2054 30 min. $29.95

Interviewing: Employment, Evaluation, Termination

Personnel interviewing techniques can make or break a management career, or even a company. This video training program covers the three main types of personnel interviews: candidate selection, performance reviews and exit interviews. Roleplay shows how good interviewing is done, including how to prepare and ask the right questions and avoid the wrong ones. The program also illustrates how techniques used in the hiring interview also apply to performance evaluation, disciplinary conferences and terminations. Major emphasis is placed on getting and giving the right information in the right way to accomplish objectives of selecting the right candidate, improving employee performance, and minimizing hard feelings and lawsuits when the employee must be terminated.
07-127 25 min. $59.95

VIDEO TITLES LISTED IN THIS GUIDE ARE AVAILABLE FOR PURCHASE OR RENTAL. CONTACT YOUR LOCAL VIDEO STORE OR TELEPHONE (800) 383-8811

Interviewing with Confidence
College prepares our young people for success, but it fails to prepare them for a successful job interview. Peter D. Leffkowitz will take the viewer through a step by step process of being interviewed and leave you with the tools to do it right.
07-2841 105 min. $69.95

It's Your Life - It's Your Career
Susan Levine formed one of California's most successful career placement agencies. The secrets of marketing yourself effectively are revealed.
07-8059 30 min. $29.95

On Camera: Breaking Into Television Commercials
Iris Acker, star of over 200 commercials, presents her secrets with segments on preparation, resumes wardrobe, auditioning, script reading and agents.
07-2182 45 min. $29.95

Platinum Rainbow Video
Get an inside look at the recording industry and learn how to think realistically in a business based on fantasy. Learn how to promote yourself, find a manager, producer or agent, get free recording time, how to make a deal, recognize and record a hit song and what record companies look for.
07-8024 122 min. $29.95

Power Interviewing
An effective guide to being hired. Patrick J. Atkinson shares his professional expertise as an executive recruiter as he takes the viewer through what it takes to succeed in a job interview.
07-9291 30 min. $19.95

Successful Interviewing: How To Interview Others
A look at interviewing from the other side, how the interviewer can best get what she or he wants from the interview. Equally useful to those on both sides of the interviewer's desk.
07-093 30 min. $89.95

SYBERVISION PERSONAL ACHIEVEMENT SERIES
The nation's best management consultants identify the three most essential managing skills. These three highly effective courses were designed to teach these.

• Decision Making
07-8087 35 min. $69.95

• Effective Presentations
07-8088 37 min. $69.95

• Time Management
07-8086 34 min. $69.95

Techniques to Improve Your Writing
Gives the viewer the short course on how to write logical, organized reports, memos and letters; writing clearly and how to get answers to tough punctuation and grammar questions. Includes the "Techniques to Improve Your Writing" handbook.
07-8015 38 min. $79.95

Three Great Sales People
Three successful sales people share their secrets in this look at what motivates the motivators.
07-114 30 min. $89.95

What Everyone Should Know About The Real Estate Business
Inside secrets to acquire real estate at below market prices. Excellent ideas to generate leads, find buyers and sellers to make profits in real estate.
07-8001 30 min. $59.95

Winning at Job Hunting in the 90's
Presents a solid, aggressive and effective total job hunting system. By following this system you can find satisfying employment, learn networking strategies techniques and more.
07-9821 60 min. $59.95

Winning Job Interview
John C. Crystal, expert career development counselor, guides you through all aspects of career change, whether you're a student, an executive or retiree. Ten proven steps to create the right image for your aspirations are explored; the result - improvement in interviewing skills.
29-053 60 min. $39.95

Miscellaneous

Barter For Fun And Profit
Owners of a for-profit barter agency dealing with business people and a founder of a nonprofit barter exchange for consumers tell you the benefits of barter for everyone.
07-079 30 min. $89.95

FYI VIDEO SERIES
This video series covers different work related subjects. You can learn how to become a leader and be recognized, how to re-define your skills, how to network and how to become successful at what you do best.

VIDEO TITLES LISTED IN THIS GUIDE ARE AVAILABLE FOR PURCHASE OR RENTAL. CONTACT YOUR LOCAL VIDEO STORE OR TELEPHONE (800) 383-8811

• **Bringing Out the Leader in You**
07-8002 23 min. $79.95

• **Coaching For Top Performance**
07-8010 25 min. $79.95

• **Juggling Your Work & Family**
07-8003 30 min. $79.95

• **Making Your Point Without Saying a Word**
07-8004 27 min. $79.95

• **Networking Your Way to Success**
07-8008 30 min. $79.95

• **Re-Energize Yourself**
07-8006 25 min. $79.95

• **Setting & Achieving Your Goals**
07-8011 25 min. $79.95

• **Smart Risk Taking**
07-8005 28 min. $79.95

• **Successful Negotiating**
07-8009 25 min. $79.95

• **Tapping Into Your Creativity**
07-8007 30 min. $79.95

Hazards Of Being A Therapist
Dr. Goldberg, a part-time psychotherapist, trades stories with three other therapists about the joys, risks and bruises of their business.
07-113 30 min. $89.95

How To Get Along With Your Boss
Presented in a humorous documentary style using monster movie scenarios. Not only will you learn about monsters, mummies and assorted aliens, You'll learn how to get along with your supervisor. Look at the different types of bosses: Authoritarian, Democratic, Laissez-Faire and Combination.
07-8053 17 min. $98.00

I'm Tired of a Messy Desk
Learn tips on increasing personal work space efficiency. Each step is taught in an easy-to understand system. Accomplish urgent tasks with minimal repetition and wasted motion.
07-8052 25 min. $98.00

Interviewing With Confidence: The Complete Guide for Successful Interviewing
This is a condensed version of a live seminar conducted by Peter Lefkowitz. Featured is

information directed toward the job-seeking applicant with some work experience. Includes manual.
07-2841 105 min. $69.95

Midlife Career Change
Three people who have faced the challenge of changing an established career at midlife talk about the impact that it had on their lives.
07-112 30 min. $89.95

Smart Solutions for Managing Your Time
Learn how to manage your time better and find the time to do it! Learn to communicate, use quality control mechanisms, handle interruptions and more.
07-8037 40 min. $49.95

US News Career Guide: Jobs For the Future
A survey of job trends and salaries, training in the workplace, benefits and growth industries.
07-8123 45 min. $19.95

WINNING CASE: SUCCESSFUL LITIGATORS GUIDE TO SUCCESS IN THE COURTROOM
Acclaimed author and respected consultant Noelle Nelson, Ph.D, has helped attorneys at the nation's top law firms win cases and maximize jury awards. Learn what it takes to prepare for that important litigation and to present yourself and your witness in a credible manner.

• **Credibility in the Courtroom**
07-9346 40 min. $39.95

• **How to Prepare Your Witness Successfully for Deposition**
07-9349 45 min. $39.95

• **How to Prepare Your Witness for Trial**
07-9350 45 min. $39.95

• **Persuasion**
07-9347 40 min. $39.95

• **Strategy**
07-9348 45 min. $39.95

Searching For

A Unique Gift That is

Informative and Appreciated?

The Video Titles

In This Guide

Make Wonderful Gifts.

Languages

- ✓ *English As A Foreign Language*
- ✓ *Foreign Languages*
- ✓ *Sign Language*

Grazi
(Italian)

Thank You
(English)

Merci
(French)

Todah
(Hebrew)

Gracias
(Spanish)

Arigato
(Japanese)

English As A Foreign Language

Basic English for Hispanics: (ESL) By Video
Hispanics can learn English as a second language (ESL) for school, business and daily living. Read, write and speak a 1,000 work-and-phrase vocabulary. Offers dimensions of learning that audiotapes alone cannot provide. Rewind and review at any point so you can learn at your own pace.
01-037 60 min. $74.95

English as a Second Language (ESL)
Non-English-speaking people can learn reading, writing and speaking in this introduction to English as a second language. Two volumes.
01-2870 240 min. $79.95

ESL: English as a Second
Language I
Get started learning English with confidence. Learn the easy way, in your home and at your own pace. Learn faster and be better prepared. For beginners.
01-158 60 min. $39.95

ESL: English as a Second
Language II (Finding A Job)
Just learning to speak English? An experienced teacher guides you through the easy way to learn English pronunciation and conversation patterns.
01-159 60 min. $39.95

Foreign Languages

Basic Hebrew 1 and 2
This is an introductory course to the Hebrew language. This program is designed to teach Hebrew as a second language, it is suitable for use by individuals, community organizations, universities and schools - no previous knowledge of Hebrew is required.
01-123 141 min. $99.95

BASIC LANGUAGE SERIES BY MASTERVISION
Learn a second language for travel, business or pleasure by seeing as well as hearing. Read, write and speak a 1,000 word and phrase vocabulary using 43 of the most often encountered life situations. Instant video replay lets you review and learn at your own pace.

- **Basic Arabic by Video**
01-2109 60 min. $74.95

- **Basic Chinese by Video**
01-1947 90 min. $74.95

- **Basic French by Video**
01-039 60 min. $74.95

- **Basic German by Video**
01-040 60 min. $74.95

- **Basic Hebrew by Video**
01-2506 60 min. $74.95

- **Basic Italian by Video**
01-041 60 min. $74.95

- **Basic Japanese by Video**
01-042 60 min. $74.95

- **Basic Portuguese by Video**
01-9626 40 min. $74.95

- **Basic Russian by Video**
01-2110 60 min. $74.95

- **Basic Spanish by Video**
01-043 60 min. $74.95

BERLITZ LANGUAGE SERIES
Berlitz videos for travelers combine computer graphics with live action and freeze frames to produce a new and exciting interactive language learning video series. Now you can make your trip more meaningful, interesting and fun. Taught by Professor Berlitz, who leads you through each step in language proficiency. A booklet is included with each tape.

- **French**
01-044 85 min. $29.95

- **German**
01-046 85 min. $29.95

- **Italian**
01-047 85 min. $29.95

- **Spanish (Latin American)**
01-045 85 min. $29.95

VIDEO TITLES LISTED IN THIS GUIDE ARE AVAILABLE FOR PURCHASE OR RENTAL. CONTACT YOUR LOCAL VIDEO STORE OR TELEPHONE (800) 383-8811

GET BY LANGUAGE SERIES
The BBC quick-learning system for travelers uses sight, sound and exercises to help you learn and remember each language. The package includes a videotape with familiar sights that guides you step by step through the course. Includes audio tape and instruction book.

- **Italian**
01-8096 30 min. $69.95

- **French**
01-8097 30 min. $69.95

- **Spanish**
01-8098 30 min. $69.95

- **German**
01-8099 30 min. $69.95

JAPANESE: THE SPOKEN LANGUAGE SERIES

- **Part 1**
The basics; introductions, telephoning, asking directions, etc.
01-8053 45 min. $29.95

- **Part 2**
More basics: ordering food, clothing, transportation, etc.
01-8054 40 min. $29.95

- **Part 3**
More advanced situations: how to complain, offer opinions, criticize, etc.
01-8055 20 min. $29.95

JOY OF TALKING SERIES
Each tape includes an audio cassette and phrase book.

- **French**
01-136 60 min. $39.95

- **German**
01-137 60 min. $39.95

- **Hebrew**
01-139 60 min. $39.95

- **Italian**
01-138 60 min. $39.95

- **Spanish**
01-135 60 min. $39.95

LIVING LANGUAGE SERIES
Learn basic languages in just six weeks--simply look, listen and repeat the phrases. You will be able to carry on everyday conversations with fluency and the correct accent - at airports, hotels, stores and on the street. English subtitles help you learn from native-born actors.

- **French**
01-051 60 min. $24.95

- **German**
01-052 60 min. $24.95

- **Spanish**
01-053 60 min. $24.95

Mexican Pizza: Lively Conversation in Spanish
An interesting way to train the ear and to motivate intermediate and advanced students of Spanish. Recommended for classroom use and for tourists traveling to Spanish-speaking countries.
01-9799 20 min. $40.00

Spy Who Spoke Spanish
In this program the viewer listens and learns as a man and a woman meet in Mexico and fall in love. The student begins to learn immediately because every word is subtitled in Spanish with the English equivalent directly below on the screen. Colorization of key words allows the student to make connections quickly and easily. Learning Spanish has never been more fun...or easy!
02-8070 39 min. $29.95

Sign Language

AMERICAN SIGN LANGUAGE SERIES

- **Christmas Stories**
Brings your favorite stories to life through sign language as well as a full voice over so everyone can enjoy the Christmas spirit.
01-8067 80 min. $29.95

- **Fairy Tales I**
Brings to life your favorite Fairy Tales through sign language and full voice narration. Stories include: Rapunzel, The Frog Prince, and more.
01-8068 110 min. $29.95

VIDEO TITLES LISTED IN THIS GUIDE ARE AVAILABLE FOR PURCHASE OR RENTAL. CONTACT YOUR LOCAL VIDEO STORE OR TELEPHONE (800) 383-8811

• **Fairy Tales II**
Brings to life your favorite Fairy Tales through sign language and full voice narration. Stories include: Sleeping Beauty, Little Red Riding Hood, and more.
01-8061   100 min. $29.95

Basic Sign Language
Genuine professional sign language instruction in a full-length video course. Based upon proven classroom methods.
01-8063   120 min. $49.95

Granny Good's Signs of Christmas
You'll all enjoy the beauty of sign language as Granny and Hans demonstrate Christmas signs and the alphabet song. Recommended for preschool through first grade.
01-8001   27 min. $29.95

Say it by Signing
This videotape can help people of all ages communicate with the hearing-impaired, or with others who want to use hand-signing just for the fun of it. The basics of sign language are taught, with an emphasis on everyday, useful words and phrases. Signing becomes simple, while communication with a deaf friend or family member is dramatically increased.
01-054   60 min. $29.95

STORIES FROM THE ATTIC
These stories are told by master children's storyteller, Billy Seago. Billy is a deaf adult with extensive experience in capturing young audiences with his acting and storytelling abilities.

• **Village Stew**
01-8119   15 min. $29.95

• **Father, Son & The Donkey**
01-8120   15 min. $29.95

• **House That Jack Built**
01-8121   15 min. $29.95

• **Magic Pot**
01-8122   15 min. $29.95

Talking Hands with Suzanne
Learn basic sign language: signing a song, tips for communication, manual alphabet, exact English sentences, counting 1-1000, weekdays, communication for emergency situations, word signs, American sign language dialogues and signing at restaurants.
01-130   60 min. $29.95

These Videos Speak Your

Language…

And Just About Any Language

You Want To Speak!

Marriage, Family & Relationships

- ✓ *Adolescence*
- ✓ *Being Single*
- ✓ *Communication & Intimacy*
- ✓ *Marriage & Divorce*
- ✓ *Parenting*
- ✓ *Weddings*
- ✓ *Miscellaneous*

Adolescence

Belonging Game
Wendy moves to a new city and school and longs
to be as popular as she was back home. When the
"in" crowd of girls test her allegiance through
actions she knows are wrong, Wendy has a tough
choice to make between being popular and doing
what's right as a Christian.
27-193 30 min. $49.95

Better Way: Addressing the Issue of Teen Suicide
This program has been created to help motivate
teens away from suicide. This teaches you to
become involved and for the teen, parents and
peers to develop a healthy environment in which to
discuss suicide.
23-9582 27 min. $59.95

Dating Movie
Drama, comedy and interviews present dating with
its pitfalls and glories from first dates to breaking
up and everything in between. Christian humorist
Pat Hurley helps teens laugh at themselves and take
other people's feelings seriously. An honest look at
an awkward subject.
26-095 45 min. $49.95

Dating: Turning Your Love Life Over to Jesus
Going steady, the kiss, sexual temptations-- Dr.
Campolo deals with these and other issues with
humor, good taste and biblical standards. He also
dares Christian youth to be sensitive to the less
"datable" among them.
23-004 49 min. $69.95

Drug Education for Young People
This looks at drug and alcohol abuse and it will
enable the viewer to weigh the facts. It will fully
explain what drugs and alcohol do to us physically
as well as mentally. If you have waited for that one
film that will push the point across without being
over dramatic then we urge you to get this film.
23-8068 48 min. $49.95

Drug Free Kid: A Parents Guide
Hosted by Ken Howard and starring Elliot Gould,
Paul Winfield, Bonnie Franklin and Ned Beatty,
this is an excellent guide for parents on how to
identify, confront and deal with the serious problem
of childhood drug use.
23-8057 70 min. $29.95

Friend of the Lonely Heart: Helping Students overcome Feelings of Loneliness & Boredom
Josh McDowell and Dick Day have developed this
program to help young people deal with loneliness.
They teach you to appreciate your uniqueness,
building friendships and finding a purpose in life.
Along with this video are a leader's guide for
group use and a book on loneliness.
23-8054 60 min. $79.95

Grounded For Life: Teenage Pregnancy: Afraid To Say NO!
Confronting the problem of teen pregnancy using
student discussions and information, Grounded for
Life examines the rising national trend of
unplanned pregnancies in the teen population.
Utilizing actual case studies and interviews with
teenage mothers, this presentation graphically
illustrates the risk factors, motivations and thought
processes associated with the rapidly growing
teenage pregnancy problem. This program not only
covers pregnancy-related problems, but also
provides an in-depth discussion of methods of
prevention. One of the most informative, intriguing
classroom videos available today.
23-6935 60 min. $79.95

How to Get Along with Your Parents
Part 1: Seeing God Through Your Parent's Eyes. A
good relationship with parents affects many areas of
teens' lives, especially their relationship with God.
Part 2: Being a Peacemaker in Your Home. Young
people can assure successful communication with
their parents by taking on the role of family
peacemaker. Part 3: Learning to Obey Your
Parents. Parental discipline is a form of love and
by accepting it teens are following God's guidance
and counsel. Part 4: Seeing Life From Your
Parents' Point of View.
23-050 115 min. $159.95

How Can I Tell If I'm Really In Love?
Justine Bateman ('Family Ties') hosts this guide to
dating made especially for teenagers. Jason
Bateman ("Valerie") and Ten Danson ("Cheers")
are featured.
23-052 51 min. $29.95

It Can Happen to You: What You Need to Know About Date Rape
This illustrates the true-to-life date rape scenario
with cutaways to real victims and their testimonies
and to the comments by professionals in law,
psychology and social services. This video/booklet
offer is essential information for dating teens and
their parents as well as for pastors and other
counselors who attempt to heal the aftereffects of

this violent crime.
23-8053 60 min. $49.95

POWER OF CHOICE SERIES:
How to be a V.I.P. by using vision, initiative and perspective as tools for making the best choices. This series, hosted by Michael Pritchard, helps teens have a clear vision of goals and put things into proper perspective, For ages 13 to adult.

- **Acting on Your Values**
23-3007 30 min. $79.95

- **Communicating with Parents**
23-3016 30 min. $64.95

- **Coping with Pressures**
23-3009 30 min. $64.95

- **Depression and Suicide**
23-3015 30 min. $64.95

- **Drinking and Driving**
23-3012 30 min. $64.95

- **Drugs and Alcohol, Part 1**
23-3010 30 min. $64.95

- **Drugs and Alcohol, Part 2**
23-3011 30 min. $64.95

- **Friendship and Dating**
23-3014 30 min. $64.95

- **Power of Choice**
23-3006 60 min. $79.95

- **Raising Your Parents**
23-3017 30 min. $64.95

- **Self-Esteem**
23-3008 30 min. $64.95

- **Sex**
23-3013 30 min. $64.95

PREPARING FOR ADOLESCENCE SERIES:

- **Part 1**
The process of preparing for adolescence begins as early as ages two or three and continues throughout childhood. Dr. James Dobson offers suggestions to parents on how they can make adolescence less painful for themselves and their children.
23-014 50 min. $69.95

- **Part 2**
Taking a close look at puberty, Dr. James Dobson recommends open discussions between parents and pre-adolescents about inferiority, conformity, love, sexual development and masturbation.
23-015 48 min. $69.95

Saving Yourself: 12 Signs of Suicide
Become familiar with the warning signs for yourself or someone you know, that may be indicative that there are some serious problems, possibly suicidal tendencies. You can make a difference.
23-9583 60 min. $69.95

Sexual Puzzle
Through true-to-life dramatic vignettes, Josh shows how sexual intimacy gets its best star in caring values, responsible actions and healthy self-esteem.
23-6263 30 min. $29.95

STOP, LOOK AND LAUGH WITH PAT HURLEY
Christian humorist Pat Hurley offers insight, understanding and lots of laughs while helping teens deal with typical problems.

- **Life in the Herd**
Can you be popular and still be a Christian? Pat Hurley challenges teens to follow Christ's example and to use peer pressure wisely, to share the gospel and to create meaningful relationships.
27-180 25 min. $39.95

- **Moms, Dads and Other Endangered Species**
Parents and kids want the same things from one another - respect honesty, communication, gratitude and most importantly, love. Hurley points out that it's not so hard to have a great relationship with parents - it just takes a little effort and understanding.
27-179 30 min. $39.95

- **There's More to Life Than the Weekend**
Hurley urges teens to get out of their ruts, to quit griping about being bored and do something about it. He shares with them that a Christ-filled life can be exciting. This lively, lesson-filled program is a favorite among Christian youth.
27-181 30 min. $39.95

Straight Up
Starring Academy Award winner, Lois Gossett Jr., Straight Up is an entertaining way to educate about the realities of drugs and alcohol, the negative influence of peer pressure and the satisfaction a drug and alcohol free life can be.
23-8055 90 min. $29.95

VIDEO TITLES LISTED IN THIS GUIDE ARE AVAILABLE FOR PURCHASE OR RENTAL. CONTACT YOUR LOCAL VIDEO STORE OR TELEPHONE (800) 383-8811

Strangers

Hank, Nancy, son Scott and daughter Meg appear to be a normal, church-going family. In reality, they are devoid of understanding, love and communication. When Scott runs away, the family is ready to change. Their pastor and friends use God's work and a frank exchange of feelings to encourage the gradual growth of a loving relationship among family members.
27-182 30 min. $24.95

Suicide: Call for Help

A group meeting at a teen center provides a basis for discussion on why young people try suicide and what can be done to prevent it. The film encourages viewers to offer help to friends they suspect of being seriously depressed, stressing that talking about suicide does not cause it--it's more apt to prevent it.
23-8010 23 min. $69.95

Teenage Confidential

Collection of previews from teen flicks, as well as an overview of juvenile delinquency as taken from 1940s and 1950s newsreels and government scare films.
23-2027 60 min. $16.95

Teens Clean & Sober

Teenagers share their experiences with alcohol and drug addiction in this straight forward program.
23-8047 20 min. $29.95

TEENAGE DATING SERIES:

• Volume 1

Have the sexual revolution and feminism of the 1970s and 1980s affected the high school dating scene? Learn the facts in this enlightening videotape on teenage dating today.
23-037 30 min. $89.95

• Volume 2

Four teenagers talk about what it means to "go steady".
23-038 30 min. $89.95

THAT TEEN SHOW

These videocassettes deal with social issues such as drugs, teen suicide, diet fads, peer pressure, prejudice, religion, mind control and many other topics. That Teen Show is filmed on location across the country in high schools, colleges, half-way houses and hospitals for discussions with young people about there problems.

• Acne, Dating and Self-Confidence
10-518 30 min. $34.95

• Career Opportunities of the Future
10-507 30 min. $34.95

• Coexistence
10-525 30 min. $34.95

• Diet Fads
10-505 30 min. $34.95

• Drug and Alcohol Abuse Among Parents
10-512 30 min. $34.95

• Martial Arts
10-509 30 min. $34.95

• Mind Control
10-513 30 min. $34.95

• Peer Pressure
10-503 30 min. $34.95

• Prejudice
10-510 30 min. $34.95

• Religion: Life After Death
10-515 30 min. $34.95

• Rock Concert Violence
10-502 30 min. $34.95

• Sense of Humor
10-511 30 min. $34.95

• Sports Scholarships: Volume 1
10-523 30 min. $34.95

• Sports Scholarships: Volume 2
10-524 30 min. $34.95

• Teen Rights
10-519 30 min. $34.95

• Teen Runaways: Volume 1
10-521 30 min. $34.95

• Teen Runaways: Volume 2
10-522 30 min. $34.95

• Teenage Crime
10-517 30 min. $34.95

• Teenage Entrepreneurs: Volume 1
10-526 30 min. $34.95

VIDEO TITLES LISTED IN THIS GUIDE ARE AVAILABLE FOR PURCHASE OR RENTAL. CONTACT YOUR LOCAL VIDEO STORE OR TELEPHONE (800) 383-8811

• **Teenage Entrepreneurs: Volume 2**
10-527 30 min. $34.95

• **Teenage Immigrants**
10-516 30 min. $34.95

• **Teenage Marriage**
10-506 30 min. $34.95

• **Teenage Pregnancy**
10-514 30 min. $34.95

• **Teenage Suicide**
10-504 30 min. $34.95

• **Testing, Tension and Competition**
10-520 30 min. $34.95

• **What My Parents Didn't Tell Me**
10-508 30 min. $34.95

YOU CAN CHOOSE SERIES:
A series designed for teenagers to help them to deal with the everyday problems that occur in their lives and practical solutions.

• **Appreciating Yourself**
23-8033 30 min. $59.95

• **Asking for Help**
23-8034 30 min. $59.95

• **Being Friends**
23-8035 30 min. $59.95

• **Being Responsible**
23-8028 30 min. $59.95

• **Cooperation**
23-8027 30 min. $59.95

• **Dealing with Disappointment**
23-8032 30 min. $59.95

• **Dealing With Feelings**
23-8029 30 min. $59.95

• **Doing the Right Thing**
23-8031 30 min. $59.95

• **Resolving Conflicts**
23-8036 30 min. $59.95

• **Saying No**
23-8030 30 min. $59.95

Tough Questions About Sex
Straight talk on love, sex and dating by Dawson McAllister. "Most dating relationships can not withstand the stress of being too physical. They self-destruct," says McAllister. Explore the tough issues that confront teenagers today.
23-055 36 min. $49.95

Being Single

Art & Science Of Flirting
Join nationally known flirting expert, Kathryn Brown, as she presents a step-by-step approach to meeting eligible men and women. She will teach you to flirt, using a practical formula designed to shatter social barriers. Her lively video seminar covers all the bases - including strategies for overcoming shyness and initiating that all-important first conversation.
23-5118 30 min. $16.95

Art of Meeting Men
This is a practical, step-by-step guide that will teach you the fine art of meeting men. This entertaining video, designed by a team of psychotherapists and authors, will show you: how to use verbal and non-verbal flirting techniques to draw the man to you.
23-8000 45 min. $29.95

Being Single
Dr. Goldberg and his guests discuss their mixed feelings of freedom, loneliness and being single.
23-030 30 min. $89.95

How to Meet Women Easily
This is a practical, step-by-step guide that will dramatically increase your ability to meet the kind of woman that you really want. You will learn by actually seeing the most effective techniques demonstrated for you. You'll see beautiful women tell you what they really want.
23-8001 50 min. $29.95

Single After 60
Four senior citizens talk about dating, working, traveling and how they deal with the loneliness of being single after age 60.
23-036 30 min. $89.95

Video Guide to Successful Seduction
An entertaining "hands-on" guide for keeping relationships fresh and exciting. Learn how to keep passions alive and change "not now" into "how

VIDEO TITLES LISTED IN THIS GUIDE ARE AVAILABLE FOR PURCHASE OR RENTAL. CONTACT YOUR LOCAL VIDEO STORE OR TELEPHONE (800) 383-8811

about it?"
23-2613 60 min. $24.95

Communication & Intimacy

Friendship
Three people, including Madison attorney Donald Eisenberg, look at the impact of friendships on their lives.
23-031 30 min. $89.95

Givers, Takers, & Other Kinds Of Lovers
Josh McDowell presents three dramatic stories of young love and weaves them into a total statement contrasting the world's current standards of love between young people. Included are the demanding lover who loves only if the lover meets his or her demands, the desperate lover who will sacrifice anything to keep the object of his or her love and a couple who are working out a Christian standard for their loving relationship. A timely subject for your youth group or young adult Sunday School Class.
23-6260 50 min. $29.95

Love is a Decision
Learn what you can do to make your marriage and family stronger and more fulfilling. This video course will teach the five keys to loving and lasting relationships, the tremendous value of a man, the incredible worth of a woman, how to energize your mate in 60 seconds the secret of a close-knit family and finding more fulfillment in your life. This video course consists of two video cassettes. divided into six, 50 minute sessions, leader's guide with discussion guide and a hardcover book.
23-8052 300 min. $129.95

Loving Relationships
Popular human relations expert, Dr. Leo Buscaglia, explores a myriad of personal relationships from lovers and family to friends and coworkers.
23-6912 55 min. $19.95

Politics of Love With Leo Buscaglia
Leo Buscaglia is a best-selling author on the subjects of love and relationships. He is also a professor, lecturer and humanist. Recorded live in Chicago, he shares his experiences and gives you tips on creating dynamic relationships.
23-053 60 min. $69.95

What Men Want From Women
Four men and women talk candidly about what men want from woman and what women think men want from women in an intimate relationship.
23-042 30 min. $89.95

What Women Really Want
In this video, you'll find out what women wish you knew about them but will rarely tell you. In candid interviews, beautiful women share with you the secrets for winning their hearts. Join your host, Steven Newmark, as he guides you through the female psyche so that you can be successful with the opposite sex.
23-8073 60 min. $29.95

What Women Want From Men
Four women and men talk candidly about what women want from men and what men think women want from men in an intimate relationship.
23-044 30 min. $89.95

Why Are Women So "Weird" and Men So "Strange"?
Tim Timmons of the highly acclaimed series "Maximum Marriage", explains that men and women are different. According to Timmons, a successful relationship depends on getting them "together" like a lock and key, fitting and functioning properly. " He takes a fresh look at critical issues, giving gut level, practical answers combined with humor.
23-057 53 min. $69.95

Marriage & Divorce

BUILDING A CHRISTIAN MARRIAGE
This comprehensive, two-part series helps pastors and lay people counsel couples before the wedding as well as after the honeymoon's over. Each is designed as a four-week course and comes with an extensive leader's guide, exercise sheets and homework for the couple.

• Marriage Enrichment
The same two couples as in the first program are featured. This time with topics relevant to married couples. They include finances, how to disagree constructively, sexual relations and children. Encourages sharing, mutual love and understanding to enrich Christian marriages.
23-002 30 min. $59.95

• Premarriage Counseling

Bill and Laura, Rick and Jane are in love and ready to be married. In several short vignettes, they deal with topics such as honest communication, family, friends and jealousy, annoying habits and realistic expectations.

23-001 30 min. $59.95

Divorce Can Happen to the Nicest People

Designed to answer kids' tough questions about why Mommy and Daddy are getting divorced, this animated program is based on the book by Peter Mayle and Arthur Robins.

23-1859 30 min. $19.95

Divorce Counseling

Ann Milne returns to talk about which divorcing couples are good candidates for divorce counseling. She talks about how it's different from marriage counseling, when it's appropriate to seek it and explains why issues around kids, money, relationships and the law are often best resolved with the aid of divorce counseling. Finally, Ms. Milne discusses mechanics such as how many sessions it takes and how to find a competent divorce counselor.

23-6859 22 min. $89.95

Divorce Process

Ann Milne, a divorce counselor and divorce mediator, explains the predictable emotional stages a person will experience during and after a divorce. Addressed are why some stages are tougher than others for different individuals, the appropriateness of divorce counseling, the risks to kids during a divorce and whether a divorce is a tragedy or a transition. Ms. Milne discusses both the pain and the opportunity for personal growth.

23-6858 22 min. $89.95

ENRICHING YOUR MARRIAGE WITH DR. DAVID MACE SERIES:

• Clergy: Marriages in Crisis

Clergy marriages face the added stress of being constantly on display. Dr. Mace's timely insight helps husbands wives and congregations understand and cope with marriages that are lived "on a pedestal."

23-009 34 min. $49.95

• Is Disagreement Natural?

Can conflict ever be positive? Is disagreement even natural? Why are we the only ones with problems? Dr. Mace urges couples to welcome conflict as an opportunity for growth.

23-006 40 min. $49.95

• Love, Anger and Intimacy

Few people ever attain the goal of an intimate marriage relationship. By applying Dr. Mace's suggestions, you and your spouse can be among the few. Learn the proper use of anger spouse can be among the few. Learn proper use of anger and how intimacy can be promoted rather than destroyed.

23-007 40 min. $49.95

• Marriage From the First Critical Year

Only 10% of all married couples achieve happy and satisfying relationships. In an eye-opening examination of the pivotal first year of marriage, a respected marriage counselor reveals problems - and solutions - that can enrich the marriage of couples of all ages and situations.

23-008 48 min. $49.95

• Three Essentials for Marriage

In a world where mediocrity in marriage is the norm rather than the exception, Dr. Mace presents the secrets to an effective "coping system" that his 40-year counseling experience has proved essential for a fully successful marriage.

23-005 50 min. $49.95

FIGHTING FOR YOUR MARRIAGE SERIES:

• Ground Rules for Fighting & Loving
23-9580 30 min. $29.95

• How to Manage Conflict
23-9581 30 min. $29.95

How To Establish & Maintain A Rich Marriage

Patricia Clason and Bob Grieves return to demonstrate how to establish and maintain a rich marriage once you've defined one. The experts discuss how often couples need to tune-up their marriage, how they go about communicating to do it successfully and whether some extremely well-matched couples can avoid the work others must do to maintain their marriage.

23-6856 22 min. $89.95

How To Marry Right

Patricia Clason, Director of the Center for Creative Learning in Milwaukee, explores who is likely to choose a partner who will enhance their lives and who is likely to pick a conflict-riddled marriage. She looks at the process of falling in love, making choices and trying to relive our pasts with the mates we choose. In addition, Ms. Clason explains how people might prepare themselves to make successful choices or minimize damage from destructive choices already made.

23-6854 22 min. $89.95

VIDEO TITLES LISTED IN THIS GUIDE ARE AVAILABLE FOR PURCHASE OR RENTAL. CONTACT YOUR LOCAL VIDEO STORE OR TELEPHONE (800) 383-8811

John Bradshaw on Surviving Divorce

John Bradshaw lays the groundwork for helping people to move on with their lives. Bradshaw, divorced himself, walks his viewers through the emotional trauma and self-denials of divorce. With the aid of a live audience, John offers tools for survival and warns of pitfalls to avoid on the road to recovery.

23-8002 60 min. $29.95

Let Him Who Steals, Steal No Longer

A subtle form of abuse permeates Christian marriages today. Dr. Dennis Guernsey discusses how we steal from one another by using one another rather than by serving one another. This film is a must for partners who want to make their union the best it can be.

23-028 60 min. $49.95

Surviving a Dual Career Marriage

John and Susan Van Vleet tackle one of the most pressing problems in our culture.

23-2242 105 min. $39.95

Two Ex-Couples and What They Know Now

Two couples who have experienced the pain of divorce share the lessons they learned from breaking up.

23-040 30 min. $89.95

Two Good Marriages and Why

An encouraging report on the survival of marriage, from the personal stories of two couples who found that marital bliss can exist.

23-041 30 min. $89.95

What Is A Good Marriage

Patricia Clason is joined by clinical psychologist and marriage counselor Bob Grieves. These guests zero in on the importance of defining a good marriage before you marry. Coming from very different clinical backgrounds, they wind up agreeing on the four most important ingredients in a successful marriage and on the methods the engaged or dating couple could use to examine whether these elements exist or can be achieved in a marriage. In the process, some elements typically thought of as a key to a good marriage are down played while other elements are identified as essential.

23-6855 22 min. $89.95

What Wives Wish Their Husbands Knew About Them

Dr. James Dobson discusses the principles of a secure, healthy marriage as well as some common difficulties. He deals especially with women's struggles with depression and low self-esteem and couples' problems with money and romance.

23-010 49 min. $69.95

When Should A Couple Divorce

Marriage counselor and divorce mediator Ann Milne and psychologist Jim McGloin discuss when divorce is the best solution for both parties. They address cases where the divorce is good for one and bad for the other, or couples have grown far apart, or one has fallen in love with another person and how all these tie into the appropriateness of dissolving a marriage. Also examined is whether it's wise to stay together for the kids. Finally, they look at whether a wound can be so deep, that it cannot be healed.

23-6857 22 min. $89.95

Parenting

ART OF PARENTING SERIES:

Evelyn Petersen has created a three part series on the problems and solutions to today's parenting problems.

• **Young Child**
23-8064 52 min. $69.95

• **School Age Children**
23-8065 52 min. $69.95

• **Teenagers**
23-8066 52 min. $69.95

Baby-Safe Home

Emmy Award winning television consumer expert David Horowitz and his wife, Suzanne McCambridge, take you on a guided tour through a typical home, pointing out hazard areas and potential killers and offering simple life-saving suggestions.

23-6791 60 min. $19.95

Breastfeeding: The Art Of Mothering

It is recommended for mothers who are breastfeedling, intend to breastfeed or are just thinking about it. For a mother considering breastfeeding, it is a frank presentation which will help her decide what is best for her. The mother who has already made the decision will benefit from the recommendations for preparing to breastfeed, while the mother who is already nursing will appreciate the detailed instruction in the techniques of successful breastfeeding. Approved by the American Academy of Pediatrics.

23-5410 40 min. $29.95

Child Development: The First Two Years

This video will provide you with helpful guidelines for enhancing your child's development. From 0 to 24 months.

23-9283 30 min. $19.95

Child Molestation: A Crime Against Children

This program teaches children to be careful without teaching them to be paranoid. Questions are answered by children who have been sexually molested and who have been helped by counseling. But most of all they learn they are not to blame.

23-8012 11 min. $69.95

Child Molestation: When to Say NO

Without sensationalism or scare tactics, this program shows that child molesters exist and teaches young viewers the things they can do to protect themselves. They learn the right way to say "no", politely, yet firmly.

23-8013 13 min. $69.95

Christian Fathering

Dr. James Dobson points out what he believes to be the most important need among families today - responsible Christian fathering. He urges dads to make their families top priority and to become leaders in their homes.

23-012 60 min. $69.95

Creative Parenting: The First 12 Months

New parents express their feelings and relate their experiences. Hosted by actor Beau Bridges, this videocassette walks the viewer through the first year of life and deals with such issues as nutrition, psychological and physiological changes, the father's involvement and quality day care. Most worthwhile is a demonstration of the different plateaus of development, from newborn through one year.

26-110 60 min. $19.95

Infant Development: A First Year Guide To Growth And Learning

A Johnson & Johnson Parenting Video by author and child care expert Dr. T. Berry Brazelton. The first video to explore the physical, cognitive and emotional development of the newborn. Topics include: Developmental norms and sequences, what babies know at birth, development of motor skills, taste/touch/sight/sound, bonding, language and smiles.

23-6789 45 min. $24.95

Infant Health Care: A First Year Support Guide

A Johnson & Johnson Parenting Video by author and child care expert Dr. T. Berry Brazelton.

Shows parents sensitive and caring ways to respond to: crying, colic, breast and bottle feeding, mother's nutrition, bath time, care of the umbilical cord, fever and getting baby to sleep.

20-6793 45 min. $24.95

Infantasia

Presents basic shapes, primary colors, enchanting animals and easily recognizable objects in charming and imaginative animation set to familiar nursery songs.

23-2767 25 min. $19.95

I Know Better: On Missing Children

No parent wants their child to be one of the many children each year that turns up missing. Phil Foster, M.S. Ed., narrates this educational tape which shows situations, such as playgrounds and parking lots and how to respond properly to potentially dangerous situations without being alarming to you children.

23-8049 60 min. $39.95

Newborn Care: Step-by-Step

Two registered nurses use their medical expertise to help new parents through the sometimes confusing early stages of their new baby's infancy.

23-2970 30 min. $19.95

Prejudice: Answering Children's Questions

Hosting an audience of young children as culturally diverse as our nation, Peter Jennings leads an exploration of prejudice or what he terms as "the child of ignorance". This program provides people of all ages, answers to the question of whether we have to be the same to be equal.

23-8069 75 min. $29.95

Questions Parents Ask

Can parents enjoy their children during the "terrible twos"? Does discipline always mean "the belt"? Is there hope for harried parents? Dr. Dobson deals with these questions and others on temper tantrums, learning difficulties and even inferiority in a witty style as he shares proven methods for coping with children through successful and enjoyable parenting.

23-019 60 min. $49.95

RAISING GOOD KIDS IN BAD TIMES SERIES:

Millions of kids today are in trouble and they need our help. This nationally acclaimed series conveys the problems we face and the solutions at hand.

• American Dream Contest
Hosted by Michael Landon.

23-8061 30 min. $29.95

VIDEO TITLES LISTED IN THIS GUIDE ARE AVAILABLE FOR PURCHASE OR RENTAL. CONTACT YOUR LOCAL VIDEO STORE OR TELEPHONE (800) 383-8811

• **New & Improved Kids**
Hosted by Loni Anderson.
23-8062 30 min. $29.95

• **See Dick & Jane Lie, Cheat & Steal**
Hosted by Tom Selleck.
23-8059 30 min. $29.95

• **Take Me to Your Leaders**
Hosted by James Garner.
23-8063 30 min. $29.95

• **Truth About Teachers**
Hosted by Whoopi Goldberg.
23-8060 30 min. $29.95

Roughhousing: A Guide to Safe, Fun, Physical Play
This educational video for parents, teachers and children shows the importance of rough and tumble play for children. Rules for safe and fun physical play are described for home, chid care centers, preschools and elementary schools.
23-8003 28 min. $29.95

Selecting Daycare for Your Child
The placement of a child in a day care environment is one of the most important issues facing parents in today's society. This has been developed to help parents formulate and answer the numerous questions that should be considered before placing a child in day care.
23-9258 30 min. $29.95

Self-Esteem: Building A Strong Foundation For Your Child
This video program addresses the problems associated with child development. Specifically the effect that self-esteem has on the interpersonal relationships of the child and his/her ability to succeed. Dr. Brooks and Mr. Dalby suggest techniques for developing and improving the child's self-esteem. They also recommend methods for reversing the downward slide of low self-esteem as evidenced by self-doubt, bad attitude, poor behavior and school problems.
23-5105 41 min. $29.95

Sibling Rivalry
Narrated by Jean Rosenbaum, MD, this program is for mothers and fathers having more than one child. Discussions with parents and children explore what to expect when siblings are jealous and how to make the situation smoother and more positive. A charming section features children drawing with Dr. Rosenbaum explaining how the drawings reveal the kids' feelings about their parents and siblings.
23-5003 28 min. $39.95

Single Parenting
Explores the joys and difficulties of single parenting. Both single mothers and fathers, interviewed by Psychoanalyst Veryl Rosenbaum, give advice from their own experiences on what works and what to avoid. An excellent guide through the complexities of single parenting.
23-5002 30 min. $39.95

Somebody New Lives At Our House
Originally written from a foster home point of view, feelings expressed in these resources branch out into adoption & multiple marriage homes.
 Brings out hidden feelings to build better relationships in the home.
23-5051 27 min. $39.95

Step Parenting
The authors of the book, "Stepparenting", Jean Rosenbaum, MD and Veryl Rosenbaum, PSA, discuss the inevitable problems of this delicate form of parenting. Couples share their experiences, frustrations and solutions in a helpful and informative manner.
23-8046 28 min. $29.95

STRAIGHT ANSWERS TO QUESTIONS PARENTS FACE SERIES:

• **Ages 1-5**
This is about questions regarding discipline, divorce and others.
23-8042 30 min. $24.95

• **Pre-Teens Ages 6-12**
This provides several answers to the many questions and problems that face children and parents.
23-8043 30 min. $24.95

• **Teens Ages 13-18**
This is about questions like Sex, drugs, alcohol and many others.
23-8044 30 min. $24.95

Strong Willed Child
Dr. James Dobson discusses the difference between "willful defiance" and "childish irresponsibility" and explains how parents can find the important balance between love and authority.
23-011 63 min. $69.95

What Do You Really Want for Your Children
Few of us are naturally great parents, but we all cherish the opportunity to nurture a young life. With this thoughtful program, clarify your objectives and help your children make the most of

their talents and abilities.
23-1842 60 min. $69.95

WHAT EVERY BABY KNOWS SERIES:

• Volume I
Dr. T. Berry Brazelton, with a studio audience, discusses the newborn, the infant and the toddler.
26-066 100 min. $14.95

• Volume II
Dr. Brazelton discusses the real issues of today: separation from the child, the working parent and the best type of day care.
26-067 100 min. $14.95

• Volume III
Dr. Brazelton discusses pregnancy and childbirth, and answers questions for mothers nearing delivery, as well as thoroughly explaining the birth process.
26-068 60 min. $14.95

• Volume IV
Dr. T. Berry Brazelton discusses the expanded role played by contemporary fathers in raising children.
10-484 70 min. $14.95

What My Parents Mean to Me at 40
A trio of 40-year olds examine how they relate to parents at middle-age and to what degree their parents still affect their lives.
23-043 30 min. $89.95

What Kids Want to Know About Sex & Growing Up
The most complicated and often embarrassing conversations parents ever have with their kids have just gotten easier. This is an extensive program that discusses puberty, sexuality and reproduction in language easily understood by pre-teens.
23-8024 60 min. $19.95

Weddings

Do Your Own Wedding, Elegantly & Affordably
This elegantly produced video makes wedding plans fun while saving thousands of dollars. Experts give detailed information in areas including photography, flowers, invitations and wedding attire.
23-9249 40 min. $29.95

How to Plan a Perfect Wedding
Today's "average" wedding costs thousands of dollars. It has created a multi-billion dollar industry which affects everything from tuxedo rentals to travel agents. Marion Ross leads the prospective bride through every facet of planning, from the engagement right through the honeymoon.
05-044 60 min. $19.95

It's Your Wedding Reception: Consumers Guide to Planning a Wedding Reception.
Covers location, food/beverage, entertainment, flowers, photo/video. Concise and entertaining with informative interviews of industry professionals.
23-9032 37 min. $19.95

Miss Manners on Weddings: For Better Not Worse
This video is not a step-by-step guide, rather, it is designed to identify acceptable and unacceptable behavior in every facet of wedding planning. With wit and charm, Miss Manners guides viewers through those touchy situations that may detract from the bride and groom's perfect day, dispelling many common misconceptions on wedding etiquette.
12-277 50 min. $19.95

PLANNING YOUR WEDDING SERIES:

This series covers everything you need to know for planning your wedding and reception.

• Selecting Your Formal Wear
23-8014 37 min. $19.95

• Selecting Your Wedding Cake
23-8016 16 min. $19.95

• Selecting Your Photographer
23-8017 41 min. $19.95

• Visit to Your Caterer
23-8015 24 min. $19.95

• Visiting Your Travel Agent
23-8018 32 min. $19.95

Shopping For Your Wedding
Shopping For Your Wedding can save the bride-to-be from making costly and embarrassing planning mistakes. This video will take you right to the experts with valuable tips and indispensable advice

---

on everything from catering and photography to dressmaking, tuxedos, music, florists, limousine, jewelry and even travel.
23-5653 30 min. $19.95

Steps Down the Aisle
This video and companion workbook will help you plan the wedding of your dreams. Join Debby Boone as she visits with bridal consultants, floral arrangers, a diamond expert and entertainers to learn the easiest and most enjoyable ways to plan a wedding.
23-3004 60 min. $29.95

Miscellaneous

1-2-3 Magic
1-2-3 Magic utilizes non-violent discipline to stop undesirable behavior and positive reinforcement to start desirable behavior. The video also addresses how to control sibling rivalry, how to handle misbehavior at home and in public and how to respond to children's attempts to test and manipulate their parents.
23-6982 120 min. $39.95

Gathering of Men with Bill Moyers and Robert Blye
An introspective look at the spiritual journey a man must take in order to finally achieve happiness. The sharing of prospectives between men, to help overcome the fears, confusion and myths that they have about life.
23-8008 90 min. $29.95

In Defense of the Housewife
Four homemakers who have found sincere fulfillment in their role share insights about their choice, as well as common stereotypes.
23-032 30 min. $89.95

Is Portnoy Still Complaining
Dr. Goldberg and guests examine author Phillip Roth's Jewish male stereo type to see if it ever had validity.
23-033 30 min. $89.95

Joey & Me
In animation, a twelve-year-old boy reminisces about his friendship with Joey, a star high school basketball player whose strength of character makes him memorable.
23-8011 10 min. $69.95

Lifestyle "The Working Mom's Survival Guide"
An ideal video for women who don't have time to read how-to books. "The Working Mom" is the perfect video companion to "managing it all!" Tips on time management, stretching the family budget and raising happy children are discussed by leading experts. The program features a special follow along section on preparing quick and nutritious meals to fit into your busy schedule.
23-6560 45 min. $24.95

Mother
Ann Sweeney probably receives more Mother's Day cards than anyone else in her Greenwich, Connecticut community. Ann is "Mom" to 18 children! Herself an only child, she has raised seven of her own and with husband John, adopted 11 more multinational and multiracial kids. Find out why Ann loves her life and job and how cooking and caring for the whole family, she still finds time to teach piano and cello to 50 kids, six days a week.
07-044 30 min. $89.95

Secrets About Men Every Woman Should Know
How much do you really know about men and sex? Take the quizzes and find out. There are exercises, checklists, do's, don't's and proven-effective tools and techniques that can turn you into a more powerful woman and absolutely transform your relationships with men.
23-8058 80 min. $24.95

Structured Intervention: How to Deal With the Addict in Your Life
Hosted by Ken Howard and enthusiastically endorsed by the NCADD/California, this provides a structured intervention program, the first step for recovery from chemical and/or alcohol dependence.
23-8071 50 min. $39.95

To Be a Woman
Homemaker versus career woman - the struggle continues. Opinions on the roles and attitudes of-toward women are constantly changing. Dr. James Dobson discusses solutions to the concerns of depression as a result of low self-esteem, fatigue and loneliness and women's physical make-up. A humorous and disarming presentation that offers stability in a fluctuating world.
23-018 60 min. $49.95

When Bad Things Happen to Good People
This is a source of comfort and insight for anyone confronted by tragedy and suffering. Dr. Harold S. Kushnerspeaks from his own painful experience, the loss of his young son, Aaron, to a rare illness.

Kushner's answer is as practical as it is theological. It provides a reaffirmation of a belief in God and offers a compassionate direction for those in pain.
23-8004 60 min. $16.95

Where Do Babies Come From
Animated program that offers a sensitive way to help you explain God's gift of sexuality to your children. Perfect for six to eight year olds.
23-9326 45 min. $29.95

Working Mom's Survival Guide
Working moms are caught in a trap of trying to do it all. Being a good parent, partner and professional means being good to yourself first. "The Working Mom's Survival Guide" will help you sort through what's important and what's not, when time is your worst enemy.
23-8041 50 min. $19.95

Planning a Wedding?

Hoping To Strengthen Your Marriage?

Looking For Ways To Get Along Better With Your Children?

These Videos Have Many Answers.

New

Special Interest Video Titles

Become Available

Often.

Please Inquire

If A Title Or Subject

You Are Looking For

Is Not Listed.

VIDEO TITLES LISTED IN THIS GUIDE ARE AVAILABLE FOR PURCHASE
OR RENTAL. CONTACT YOUR LOCAL VIDEO STORE OR TELEPHONE (800) 383-8811

Metaphysical
&
Supernatural

- ✓ *Astrology & Tarot*
- ✓ *Occult*
- ✓ *Miscellaneous*

Astrology & Tarot

21st Century Astrology
This program combines scientific facts gathered by NASA and astronomers from around the world, Astrological knowledge gained over the centuries, to give us a greater understanding of the life paths we travel. Sheds light on your daily horoscope.
17-9425 45 min. $19.95

Advanced Tarot
Includes the role of counseling in to card reading, how to explore psychological and spiritual levels through instruction, and examples of three original spreads. These advanced spreads will give the student answers to questions relating to the key issues in the past and present, life's purpose and lessons to be learned, areas of their personality which need development and how to choose between conflicting life paths.
17-040 58 min. $29.95

Astrology of Romance
A complete analysis of love and compatibility as seen through the twelve astrological signs. Each sign is examined carefully. Learn the answers to such questions as: What causes you to fall in love? How should you begin and end relationships? What do you need to learn to be a better partner? Learn the secrets of romance through the stars.
17-002 118 min. $39.95

Astrology Lesson
In an interview format, noted astrologers Jeff Jawer, Angel Thompson, Jim Lewis, Karma Welch and others introduce you to the signs of the zodiac along with dozens of living examples of each sign. The elements (fire,earth, air and water) as well as the modalities (cardianl, fixed and mutable) are also thoroughly described. This tape has been highly acclaimed by astrology circles.
17-048 120 min. $39.95

Basic Palmistry
Learn to interpret the destiny in your hands through an understanding, of the life, head and heart lines. This tape explains the significance of the shape of the palm and fingertips with special emphasis on specific areas of the palm and hand.
17-110 60 min. $39.95

Intermediate Tarot
Professional tarot card reader Laura Clarson includes full instructions and examples for reading four original spreads to help students answer questions about relationships, career, love and home life.
17-039 58 min. $29.95

Minor Arcana
Includes in-depth meanings of each of the minor arcane cards, both upright and reversed, with Ms. Clarson's professional insights. Included are specific combinations of cards which allow the reader to choose the best interpretation of the spread.
17-109 120 min. $49.95

Read your Tarot
All the tarot tips you need plus a free deck of cards. Learn how to give readings to family and friends with easy to understand interpretations.
17-8004 60 min. $24.95

Secrets of the Tarot Revealed
A precise course of instruction in the tarot, the ancient divinatory system using card readings. The beginning tarot student will learn how to read the past and present and predict the future. Learn the secrets of your destiny and hidden potential. Includes a 19-page instructional guide.
17-022 42 min. $39.95

Occult

America's Best Kept Secret
Were there really people in America in the 1980's who actually worshiped the devil in a formal, ritualistic manner? This documentary examines the frightening increase of devil worship in today's America and the devastating effects it is having on society in general.
13-9135 57 min. $29.95

First Family of Satanism
Noted religious journalist Bob Larson interviews Zeena LaVey, daughter of Church of Satan founder Anton LaVey, and Nikolas Schreck, head of the Werewolf Coven, in a no holds barred discussion about Satanism and it's horror. Find out what Satanism has in store for the 90's--and beyond.
13-9132 90 min. $39.95

Occult Experience
This is a documentary on the world of witchcraft, magic, satanism and exorcism.
17-2826 87 min. $59.95

Witchcraft Throughout the Ages

Explore the history, facts and theories of witchcraft through the ages.

17-029 90 min. $29.98

Miscellaneous

Amazing World of Psychic Phenomena

Raymond Burr, along with respected psychics like Jeanne Dixon and Uri Geller, host an exciting new look at the supernatural world of ghosts, seances, reincarnation and much more.

17-001 60 min. $19.95

Basic Numerology

Explore the hidden potential in your numbers. Points covered include: exploration of the personality traits of each number from 1 to 9 and the master numbers 11 and 22: how vowels in your name act as a motivating force in your life; and much more.

17-2120 60 min. $39.95

Bermuda Triangle

Take an exciting look at the facts and theories about the "Bermuda Triangle," that triangular area in the Atlantic Ocean near Bermuda where ships and planes have been mysteriously lost.

17-003 30 min. $29.95

Beyond Belief

Can we communicate with the spirit world? This film offers sights not often seen. You will learn about telepathy, reincarnation, automatic writing, unidentified flying objects. If you think these things don't exist, think again!

17-9435 94 min. $19.95

Contact UFO: Alien Abductions

The first video to examine the frightening phenomena of alien abduction. Through probing interviews with abductees and a full presentation of the evidence, including unexplainable scars, implants and tape recordings of hypnosis sessions, you'll learn what it means to be taken by a force you don't understand. Featuring: John Mack, Bud Hopkins, author of Intruders and Betty Hill, an abductee.

13-8291 90 min. $79.98

Mysteries From Beyond Earth

Witchcraft, psychokinesis , ESP, UFOs and many other things are explored in this startling film. Lawrence Dobkins hosts.

17-9430 95 min. $19.95

Nostradamus

His name has resounded through the centuries - shadowed in legend and mystery. He has predicted actual events more than 400 years before they actually happened. What does he have in store for our time? It could be the most unnerving of all!

17-8035 100 min. $24.95

Outer Space Connection

Was life on earth carried here by a highly advanced civilization of intergalactic travelers thousands of years ago? Narrated by Rod Serling, this video explores the theory of "Earth Base One" in the Peruvian Andes, where ancient Mayans were performing brain surgery while the world still lived in the darkness of the Stone Age. "The Outer Space Connection" takes a bold step in the search for man's beginning.

17-1927 94 min. $59.95

Overlords of the U.F.O.

Incredible UFO appearance and kidnappings that have baffled scientists of the world are investigated. Proof that not all Extra-terrestrials are friendly.

17-9429 92 min. $19.95

UFO's: A Need to Know

Features never before seen interviews with people involved in UFO sightings, abductions and cover-ups, including drawings of the Alien bodies recovered in Roswell, New Mexico and accounts of the Fyffe, Alabama sightings. Also speculates the purpose of "Area 51", located in the Nevada desert.

13-8107 90 min. $29.95

Take a Look at What Can't Be Seen.

Metaphysical Tapes Provide a

Look at the Unknown.

VIDEO TITLES LISTED IN THIS GUIDE ARE AVAILABLE FOR PURCHASE
OR RENTAL. CONTACT YOUR LOCAL VIDEO STORE OR TELEPHONE (800) 383-8811

Searching For

A Unique Gift That is

Informative and Appreciated?

The Video Titles

In This Guide

Make Wonderful Gifts.

Music
&
Dance
Instruction

- ✓ *Dance*
- ✓ *Guitar*
- ✓ *Other Instruments*
- ✓ *Piano & Organ*
- ✓ *Voice*
- ✓ *Miscellaneous*

Dance

All American Girls Funk Dance Workout
Workout designed to teach you the funky new dance steps.
22-8120 30 min. $19.95

Argentine Tango
This easy to follow video features the Argentine Tango for beginners and intermediate students. The emphasis is on basic technique, lead/follow, line of movement, and how to improvise. It includes 15 patterns and 4 dance demonstrations.
22-8127 45 min. $29.95

Bailar Lambada
Scorching lambada lessons including hot dance tracks of Dance Lambada. Learn how to do one of the hottest latin dances!
22-9321 45 min. $19.95

Ballet for Beginners
Basic ballet movement techniques taught by David Howard, Baryshnikov's coach. Perfect for that young dancer!
22-003 40 min. $39.95

Ballet Class for Intermediate/Advanced
Now, amateur dancers can perfect ballet movement, kinetic awareness and dance vocabulary at home and without paying a fortune. This video, taught by coach David Howard features Cynthia Harvey and Peter Fonseca of the American Ballet Theatre.
22-729 60 min. $39.95

Beginning Appalachian Clogging with Sandy Silva
Included on this tape are basic steps (including: Chug. Tennessee Walking Step, The Indian, Buck & Wing, and Wagon), stretching, choreography and a creative approach that allows you to combine the various steps in your own arrangements.
22-289 60 min. $39.95

Breakin' In The USA
Sony presents break dancing, taught by the dance pros from New York dancers. Practice with this tape and soon you'll be breaking, spinning, doing body rock, and 17 other outrageous moves! Includes slow-and super-slow-motion view of all the steps.
22-025 60 min. $29.95

Breaking New York Style
Now, at great price, you too can learn to break like the best New York dancers. Practice with this tape and soon you'll be breaking, spinning, doing body rock, and 17 other outrageous moves! Includes slow-and super-slow-motion views of all the steps.
22-026 60 min. $19.95

Bujones in Class
Fernando Bujones demonstrates the personal ballet technique that has made him one of the most sought-after guest artists in the world. This instructional program is an excellent learning and teaching tool. It is especially designed by ballet master Bujones to teach the technique of classical ballet with emphasis on posture, placement, and the classical ballet movements.
22-1628 31 min. $39.95

Cajun Dancing-Allons Danser! (Let's Dance!)
It's easy and fun to learn to Cajun dance! You'll learn the traditional Cajun Waltz, Jitterbug, Two-step. Features Rand Speyrer, one of the countries foremost Cajun Dance instructors. The step-by-step approach makes it fun and easy.
22-9658 30 min. $29.95

CAL DEL POZO'S LEARN TO DANCE

• Basic Lesson
22-5734 30 min. $19.95

• Latin Dances
22-5736 30 min. $19.95

• Swing Era
22-5735 30 min. $19.95

Cha Cha/Polka
Learn two complete combinations in each dance. Cha Cha patterns like the Side Basic, Arch Turn and Cross Body Lead. Polka steps such as the Turning Basic and Flip Flop.
22-2999 50 min. $39.95

Cheerleading and Dance
Learn more about cheerleading and dance than you can learn at camp.
22-9317 30 min. $19.95

Country Dancing for Kids
Kids can have fun moving while learning some of the most popular country dance steps. Dances include: Cowboy Countdown, Slap Leather Twist, Cowboy Polka, Peter Push and Electric Slide. Designed for kids 4 through 12 years of age.
22-8195 35 min. $19.95

Country Dance Styles

Valerie and Scott will teach you the popular country and western dances as well as the Texas special dances like the Cotton-eyed Joe, Texas Polka, Texas Two-Step, Texas style waltzes and other favorites. A lot of fun for all ages!
22-8075 30 min. $29.95

Country Line Dancing

Learn how to do the Electric Slide, Honky Tonk Stomp, Slap Leather, Tush Push, Achy Breaky and the Cotton Eyed Joe. Unlike other dance videos that "break away" for you to practice alone, this program allows you to practice each basic step until it becomes automatic.
22-8192 35 min. $19.95

Country Partner Dancing

You will learn all of the basics of Country Partner Dancing--traditional dance position, footwork, simple turns, promenade position and cuddle. Dances include: Three Step, Two Step and a bonus line dance, the Cowboy Motion.
22-8194 35 min. $19.95

Dance Master: Ballet

Lucia Hatcher and Janet Beyers, of the Frethon Dance Company in an exercise and technique session for grace and beauty.
22-030 60 min. $49.95

Dance Master: Ballroom

Blanche and Emilio, of the Royal Academy of Dance, show you how to do today's popular ballroom favorites.
22-029 60 min. $49.95

Dance Masters: Frisco Disco

Dance Fever contest winners show you how to move like the pros. Stay in shape and have fun.
22-431 60 min. $49.95

Dance Masters: Modern Jazz

Instructor Henry Parish puts you through the paces and exercises that lead to improved grace and style.
22-027 60 min. $49.95

Down & Dirty

Contemporary versions of the great all-time dances.
22-9325 30 min. $19.95

East Coast Swing

Learn three fun combinations of Swing patterns and two Waltz patterns.
22-2998 57 min. $39.95

Easy to Learn Texas Dance Styles

Learn country and western dancing! Easy to follow instruction featuring: Texas Two Step, Cotton

Eyed Joe, Texas Style Polkas, Texas Waltzes, Schottische and others.
22-9342 30 min. $24.95

Folk Dance Aerobics

Learn Miserlou, Alundel, Hora, Savilla Se Bela Loza and Harmonica. Then dance along for fitness and fun.
22-3001 64 min. $39.95

FRED ASTAIRE DANCE STUDIO SERIES:

The internationally acclaimed Fred Astaire Dance Studios, founded by Fred Astaire in 1947, have now created a series of how to dance videos. You'll learn with proven techniques, each new step and routine with the demonstration of the man's position, woman's position and the complete dance as a couple. Instructed by Peggy and Lee Santos.

• **Ballroom Dancing**
22-9823 30 min. $19.95

• **Country Western Dancing**
22-9824 30 min. $19.95

• **Dancing to the Top 40's**
22-9825 30 min. $19.95

• **Latin Dancing**
22-9822 30 min. $19.95

• **Swing Dancing**
22-9826 30 min. $19.95

Fun and Fancy Texas Two-Step- Advanced

Learn the fancy steps, spins and turns for these dances featuring: Texas Twister, Rib Tickle, Tula Tangle, Eighter from Decatur, Laredo Wrap and Texas Tumbleweed.
22-8008 30 min. $24.95

Fun & Funky Freestyle Dancing

This tape will give you everything you need to look and feel confident on the dance floor. It has separate sections for kids, teens and adults. No matter what the age or ability level, this video has something for everyone.
22-8099 60 min. $24.95

FUN OF TOUCH DANCING

This series provides you with the instruction you will need to learn these dance patterns, so you to can discover the "fun of touch dancing."

• **Cha Cha**
22-2835 30 min. $39.95

VIDEO TITLES LISTED IN THIS GUIDE ARE AVAILABLE FOR PURCHASE OR RENTAL. CONTACT YOUR LOCAL VIDEO STORE OR TELEPHONE (800) 383-8811

• Fox Trot
22-2832 30 min. $39.95

• Hustle
22-2837 30 min. $39.95

• Mambo
22-2839 30 min. $39.95

• Merengue
22-2838 30 min. $39.95

• Rumba
22-2836 30 min. $39.95

• Samba
22-2840 30 min. $39.95

• Swing
22-2831 30 min. $39.95

• Tango
22-2834 30 min. $39.95

• Waltz
22-2833 30 min. $39.95

Fun with Foxtrot
22-1646 58 min. $39.95

Hip Hop Dancing
Have fun learning the latest steps like Robo-cop,
Mike Tyson and more.
22-8122 30 min. $19.95

Hot Country Dancin'
This high-quality videocassette is hosted by Melanie
Greenwood, star of "Dancin USA" with special
guest Lee Greenwood. Learn country music's
hottest dance steps to songs by MCA artists.
22-037 60 min. $29.95

Hot Dancin'
Four hot contemporary original dance routines on
one tape! High energy and style make it the
perfect instructional video for dance teams,
cheerleaders, aerobic enthusiasts, gymnasts and
dance studio performers. Jazz routine, Funky Mix
routine, High Energy routine and Character
routine.
22-8104 60 min. $19.95

Hula: Lessons 1 and 2
Learn the hula with two of Hawaii's most popular
songs, "Lovely Hula Hands" and "Little Brown
Gal".
32-243 30 min. $39.95

Hula Dancing for Fitness & Fun
A complete course that features Beginner,
Intermediate, and Advanced instruction in: Hula,
Tahitian, Poi Balls and Fire/Knife. This offers a
total body workout and is suitable for women and
men of all ages.
22-9109 48 min. $29.95

**Introduction to Belly Dance with
Kathryn Ferguson**
An excellent way to learn Belly Dance and it's a lot
more fun than aerobics. This tape has been
recommended by top professional dancers. Suitable
for men & women alike.
22-8142 120 min. $39.95

Jazz Dance Class with Gus Giordano
Jazz dance legend Gus Giordano leads you through
a complete jazz dance class. Designed for the
beginning to intermediate dancer, this program
covers warm-up, basic technique, jazz walks,
center barre and a special section on the
professional dancer.
22-2119 60 min. $59.95

**JAZZ DANCE SERIES WITH
CHRISTY LANE:**
This sensational video series consists of 4 videos
that will teach you all the techniques from basic to
advanced for Jazz dancing.

• **Beginning**
22-8100 50 min. $24.95

• **Low Intermediate**
22-8101 50 min. $24.95

• **High Intermediate**
22-8102 50 min. $24.95

• **Advanced**
22-8103 50 min. $24.95

Let's Learn How to Dance Tango
You'll see how the tango was danced in its early
days, and you'll see the updated version. You'll be
able to dance a complete tango plus you'll learn the
most important fancy steps. Comes with
audiocassette featuring 14 of the most famous
Argentinean tangos.
22-804 21 min. $29.95

**LET'S LEARN HOW TO DANCE
SERIES FROM KATHY BLAKE
DANCE STUDIOS**
This series will teach you all the dances you've
always wanted to know. Learn at your own pace,
convenience and in the privacy of your own home.

- **Ballet for Kids**
22-773 60 min. $39.95

- **Ballet for Preschoolers**
22-770 60 min. $39.95

- **Beginner's Tap**
22-9918 60 min. $39.95

- **Bolero**
22-9917 60 min. $39.95

- **Bossa Nova**
22-9916 60 min. $39.95

- **Cha Cha**
22-322 60 min. $39.95

- **Charleston**
22-9919 60 min. $39.95

- **Creative Dance For Preschoolers**
22-768 60 min. $39.95

- **Dirty Dancing**
22-9320 60 min. $39.95

- **Fox Trot**
22-323 60 min. $39.95

- **Fox Trot II**
22-763 60 min. $39.95

- **Fox Trot III**
22-6100 60 min. $39.95

- **Jazz Dance**
22-9920 60 min. $39.95

- **Jazz Dance II**
22-9921 60 min. $39.95

- **Jazz Dance for Kids**
22-771 60 min. $39.95

- **Jitterbug**
22-324 60 min. $39.95

- **Jitterbug II**
22-764 60 min. $39.95

- **Jitterbug III**
22-6102 60 min. $39.95

- **Lambada**
22-9931 60 min. $39.95

- **Line Dance**
22-9930 60 min. $39.95

- **Mambo I**
22-6106 60 min. $39.95

- **Mambo II**
22-6107 60 min. $39.95

- **Nightclub**
22-325 60 min. $39.95

- **Nightclub II**
22-9932 60 min. $39.95

- **Paso Doble**
22-9915 60 min. $39.95

- **Peabody**
22-9922 60 min. $39.95

- **Polka**
22-326 60 min. $39.95

- **Rumba**
22-327 60 min. $39.95

- **Rumba II**
22-766 60 min. $39.95

- **Rumba III**
22-6105 60 min. $39.95

- **Salsa**
22-9914 60 min. $39.95

- **Samba**
22-328 60 min. $39.95

- **Samba II/Cha Cha II**
22-767 60 min. $39.95

- **Shag**
22-9924 60 min. $39.95

- **Tango (Argentine)**
22-329 60 min. $39.95

- **Tango II**
22-765 60 min. $39.95

- **Tango III**
22-6104 60 min. $39.95

- **Tap Dance For Adults**
22-774 60 min. $39.95

• Tap Dance For Kids
22-772 60 min. $39.95

• Tap Dance For Preschoolers
22-769 60 min. $39.95

• Waltz
22-330 60 min. $39.95

• Waltz II
22-762 60 min. $39.95

• Waltz III
22-6101 60 min. $39.95

• West Coast Swing
22-9923 60 min. $39.95

KATHY BLAKE COUNTRY DANCE SERIES:

• Country Two-Step
22-9896 60 min. $39.95

• Country Two-Step II
22-9897 60 min. $39.95

• Country Two-Step III
22-9898 60 min. $39.95

• Country Waltz
22-9899 60 min. $39.95

• Country Waltz II
22-9900 60 min. $39.95

• Country Waltz III
22-9901 60 min. $39.95

• Shuffle
22-9902 60 min. $39.95

• Shuffle II
22-9903 60 min. $39.95

• Shuffle III
22-9904 60 min. $39.95

• Schottische
22-9905 60 min. $39.95

• Schottische II
22-9906 60 min. $39.95

• Schottische III
22-9907 60 min. $39.95

• Pony Swing
22-9908 60 min. $39.95

• Pony Swing II
22-9909 60 min. $39.95

• Pony Swing III
22-9902 60 min. $39.95

• Country Line Dancing
22-9911 60 min. $39.95

• Country Line Dancing II
22-9912 60 min. $39.95

• Country Line Dancing III
22-9913 60 min. $39.95

KATHY BLAKE TECHNIQUE SERIES:

It's all a matter of styling and technique. Kathy Blake, award winning dancer has created this series of videos and shares with you her secrets of winning dance competitions and looking fantastic on the dance floor. If you are interested in polishing up your skills, Kathy will explain to you, in understandable detail, how you can learn everything you need to know to look your very best on the dance floor.

• Technique 1: Posture & Balance (Smooth Ballroom)
22-9925 60 min. $39.95

• Technique 2: Posture & Cuban Motion (Latin)
22-9926 60 min. $39.95

• Technique 3: Rhythm & Styling (Smooth Ballroom)
22-9927 60 min. $39.95

• Technique 4: Rhythm & Styling (Latin)
22-9928 60 min. $39.95

• Technique 5: Competition & Exhibition Dancing
22-9929 60 min. $39.95

Learn How to Square Dance
Step-by-Step introduction to the world of American Square Dancing.
22-8121 30 min. $19.95

Let's Dance America! Modern Freesytle & Hip Hop Dance Styles of the 90's

People across the world want to learn party/club dancing but are hesitant to join dancing schools. Private lessons are expensive. Let's Dance offers you a step-by-step dance instructional video that will teach you the most popular dances of the 90's. The same steps you see on MTV, VH1, etc. Nineteen different dance steps in all.

22-8162 45 min. $19.95

LETS DANCE SERIES! WITH THE WORLD FAMOUS STAR DJ'S

Features the dances and hits of different era's. It's a Party on Tape and you're invited! Whether you're practicing for a party or you want to invite your friends over to dance on your coffee table, get ready for the ultimate entertainment experience.

• 60's Party Hits

Learn to dance to the most popular party hits: the Twist, Soul Man, Shout, Dance to the Music, Locomotion, and Greased Lightnin'.

22-8005 40 min. $24.95

• 70's Party Hits

Learn to dance the most popular hits of the 70's: The Hustle, Disco Inferno, Turn the Beat Around, Play That Funky Music, Le Freak and many more.

22-8006 40 min. $24.95

• All Time Popular Party Hits

Learn to dance to the most popular party hits: Electric Slide, Time Warp, the Bird, Hands Up and two new Star DJ original hits, Get Funky and I'm a Jammer.

22-8007 40 min. $24.95

Let's Get Busy

How to Dance video that teaches all the latest dance steps. Learn how to dance Funk, Hip-Hop, House and Hammer Style in the comfort of your home.

22-8086 47 min. $29.95

LINE DANCING SERIES:

• Volume 1

Dances included: Kansas City Stomp, Walkin Wazi, Cowboy Cha Cha, Pasadena, California Coast, Whiskey River, Rockabilly Boggie, Horse Feathers.

22-9337 55 min. $29.95

• Volume 2

Dances included: Freeze, Cowboy Boogie, Traveling 4 Corners, Flying 8, Shotgun, Austin, Roundup, Tush Push.

22-9338 55 min. $29.95

Line Dancing For Seniors

Perfect for Senior Citizens, this video teaches the techniques of Line Dancing, while providing exercise and fun. Join Dr. Grant Longley, an expert line dance instructor, as he guides a class step by step through five dances. This video's popular dance music creates the perfect setting for learning and having fun with a group of friends.

22-8187 30 min. $19.95

Line Dancing With Christy Lane

Line dancing with professional dancer & instructor, Christy Lane is unique because it is Country & Funky! Featuring five of the hottest, most popular line dances sweeping the country today.

22-8098 95 min. $19.95

More Country Line Dancing

Now that you can do the basic country steps you are ready to learn more country line dancing and increase your repertoire. Dances include: T.C. Electric Slide, Country Strut, Southside Shuffle, Cowboy Cha Cha and Achy Breaky.

22-8193 35 min. $19.95

More Texas Honky Tonk Dancin'

Taped live at the National Dance Championship of Texas - more Texas Honky Tonk Dancin'.

22-042 55 min. $39.95

Polka

Clear step-by-step instruction available anytime. Slow motion and close-ups of important points. Instruction by nationally recognized professionals. Lot's of fun patterns. All for about the price of a private lesson.

22-6496 23 min. $24.95

Polka Dancin' Texas Style

Nowhere in the world do they country/western dance like in Texas. Begin learning from this easy-to-understand lesson, allowing you to learn at your own speed with or without a partner.

22-2695 50 min. $29.95

Social Dance Aerobics

Whether you want to learn a fun way to get and keep fit or would just like to learn to dance socially, you'll find this instructional video invaluable. You will learn to dance some of today's favorite dances - Swing, Polka, Cha Cha, Viennese Waltz, and Samba - and combinations that will add variety to your dancing. This is really two tapes in one - instruction plus aerobic workout.

22-647 100 min. $39.95

Steppin' Out: Ballroom Dancing

Two professional ballroom dance teachers introduce you to the fox trot, tango, waltz, rumba, cha cha

VIDEO TITLES LISTED IN THIS GUIDE ARE AVAILABLE FOR PURCHASE OR RENTAL. CONTACT YOUR LOCAL VIDEO STORE OR TELEPHONE (800) 383-8811

and swing, as well as the elements of dance, positions and music.
22-2973 56 min. $19.95

Swayze Dancing
The Swayze family share their talents in "Swayze Dancing", starring renowned choreographer Patsy Swayze. Guest stars include Patsy's star son Patrick Swayze, his wife Lisa and his sister Bambi. Have fun, work out and learn to dance by watching four couples develop from beginners to dance competitors.
22-6183 60 min. $19.95

Tap Dancing for Beginners
Learn tap step-by-step from Henry Le Tang, choreographer of "Sophisticated Ladies". This video features a special appearance by the legendary Honi Cole.
22-065 60 min. $39.95

Tap Dancing Advanced Routine with Charles Goddertz
For those with a background in dance or tap and for those who have always dreamed of dancing on a Broadway stage, this unique tap routine will put a spring in your step! Charles Goddertz has created this tap routine using his progressive, step-by-step, sound by sound system for teaching tap. He draws on the best of his background as dance educator, performer and choreographer.
22-8002 40 min. $39.95

Texas Honky Tonk Dancin'
Taped live at the National Dance Championship of Texas with music by Pure Texas. With guest Eddie Lopez and the best Honky Tonk Dancin' in Texas.
22-041 55 min. $39.95

Two-Step Dancin' Texas Style
Learn the most popular of all country western dances at home. This videocassette allows you to learn at your own speed, with or without a partner. Lessons include basic step. beat recognition, dance hold, balance step, forward turn, underarm turn, the promenade, the whip, belt loops, double cross turn and sweetheart wrap.
22-788 50 min. $29.95

Viennese Waltz
Learn the Box Step, Arch Turn, Point and Balance and more. Two complete combinations of patterns.
22-6495 24 min. $29.95

Waltz Dancin' Texas Style
Begin learning country/western dance Texas style from this easy-to-understand lesson, allowing you to learn at your own speed with or without a partner.
22-2696 50 min. $29.95

Wedding Day Dancing
If you are getting married. This tape will help you look great. It will teach you an easy Waltz routine, Fox Trot routine, Jitterbug and Triple Swing, as well as provide you with helpful dance hints. Our list of 100 romantic love songs and 50 big band tunes can help your band or D.J. provide you with the music that you want to dance to.
22-5380 60 min. $39.95

West Coast Swing
This is the dance that's perpetually 'IN;. Learn turns, whips, loops and much more, four complete combinations. This video includes a dance-along section for practice and fitness.
22-3000 76 min. $39.95

Guitar

Adrian Belew Electronic Guitar
This video provides an instructive look at Belew's incredible arsenal of electronic effects, along with clear explanations and demonstrations. He thoroughly explores such areas as creative soloing, alternate turnings, two-handed fingerboard techniques and fretless guitar.
22-795 60 min. $49.95

Advanced Rock and Roll Bass
Kevin Kelley teaches this course for Al Di Meola. Al shows his scale choices for soloing over various chords including a special section on "the dominant 7th-diminished connection". Many of his melodic lines, licks, rhythm patterns and solos have been transcribed in the accompanying booklet.
22-8226 60 min. $49.95

Arlen Roth: Advanced Rock and Lead Guitar
Arlen Roth made this video lesson for the more advanced player. It shows with pinpoint accuracy and detail how to play chromatic style rock leads, volume control effects, advanced single and double-note bends. Arlen's unique harmonic hammer-ons, advanced scales, tricks and countless licks. Truly a master class.
22-243 60 min. $49.95

Arlen Roth: Chicago Blues Guitar
Arlen Roth recorded this tape for the intermediate through advanced blues player. You'll learn, up close, blues string being vibrato, improvisational skills, rhythm work, ninth chord licks, and countless blues licks and scales, as well as the

styles of some of the most famous blues guitarists. You'll learn how to get the most emotion out of every note!
22-245 60 min. $49.95

Arlen Roth: Hot Country Lead Guitar
Arlen Roth, author of the acclaimed Oak bestseller, Nashville Guitar, and the popular Hot Licks audio series of the same title, has packed this video with some of the hottest country picking you'll ever learn! You'll work on country string bending, unique "pedal steel" licks, pick and finger technique, chicken pickin', false harmonics, double - note bends, rapid-fire picking and many other techniques that make this the greatest country lead guitar lesson you'll ever take.
22-242 60 min. $49.95

Arlen Roth: Learning Rock and Heavy Metal Guitar
Arlen Roth has recorded this video lesson with the beginning through intermediate player in mind. You'll learn, first hand, proper string bending, vibrato, whammy bar style, right-hand metal hammer-ons, hammers and pulls, "flash" tricks, various harmonic techniques and all the scales and licks to get you on the way to becoming a rock and metal player.
22-244 60 min. $49.95

Arlen Roth: Slide Guitar
Arlen roth, one of the world's great slide guitarists, and guitar consultant and coach for the film "Crossroads," overseeing all of the scenes involving slide guitar. You'll learn proper slide technique, "box" patterns, blues, country, and rock styles in open E and G tunings, as well as standard tuning slide crucial right and left-hand damping, slide tilting, hammer-ons, pulloffs, harmonics and vibrato. This is a definitive study on slide guitar.
22-241 60 min. $49.95

BACKSTAGE PASS INSTRUCTIONAL VIDEOS: GUITAR

• **Andy West: "Creative Musical Approaches For Progressive Electric Bass"**
22-6418 51 min. $49.95

• **Bruce Bouillet: "Improvisation For Progressive Hard Rock Guitar"**
22-6422 50 min. $49.95

• **Jeff Richman: "Creative Composition And Improvisational Techniques For Guitar"**
22-6413 82 min. $49.95

• **Steve Bailey: "Advanced Bassix" Contemporary Practice And Performance Techniques**
22-6421 84 min. $49.95

Basic Chords and Accompaniment Styles with John Hartin
Designed for the individual with no playing experience or a beginning guitarist with some basic skills, this course provides a comprehensive introduction to chord forms and rhythm styles. Over fifteen songs including country, blues, folk, gospel and blue grass are presented in several keys. Simple step-by-step and easy-to-follow examples teach you how to accompany the songs, using a variety of strumming and finer picking styles.
22-635 100 min. $29.95

Basic Guitar Chords
In this video John Hartin teaches you how to connect all chords with fun to play "bass runs." He also teaches advanced strums, fingerstyle accompaniments, Merle Travis style picking, and country folk melody picking. John also teaches many new chords, Major 7ths, minors, and how to use diminished and augmented chords. A good follow-up video to Basic Chords and Accompaniment Styles.
22-8251 60 min. $29.95

Bass Guitar Master Class with John Entwistle
One of rock's most influential bassists, John Entwistle helped rewrite rock'n roll history as a member of "The Who" for nearly 20 years. John shares with you his unique experiences and techniques as you learn fingering, licks, octave style, chords, hammer-ons, pull-offs, picking techniques, harmonics, soloing concepts, walking bass lines, string bending, and phrasing. This is your chance to learn at your own pace with one of rock's all-time greats!
22-225 60 min. $49.95

Bassist Survival Manual
A practical look at what you need to know about becoming a working professional bassist. Clear explanations and advice designed to increase your chance for survival. Sections deal with: Basic and necessary music theory, rhythmic reading, reading chord changes, basic chord substitutions, patterns for scales and chords, tips for soloing, hot tricks to help you stand out from the crowd and sage advice on when to keep your head low. Dean Peer is one of the most innovative bassists on the scene today.
22-8052 60 min. $29.95

B.B. KING: BLUES MASTER SERIES:
An intimate documentation for the style and technique of the most influential blues guitarist in

VIDEO TITLES LISTED IN THIS GUIDE ARE AVAILABLE FOR PURCHASE OR RENTAL. CONTACT YOUR LOCAL VIDEO STORE OR TELEPHONE (800) 383-8811

history. B.B. discusses many of the essential elements of his brilliant approach including vibrato, bending, picking, influences, phrasing and more.

- **Blues Master 1**
  22-8227 60 min. $49.95

- **Blues Master 2**
  22-8228 60 min. $49.95

- **Blues Master 3**
  22-8229 60 min. $49.95

BeBop & Swing Guitar with Emily Remler
This is an opportunity to learn with one of jazz guitar's most unforgettable artists, the late Emily Remler. All of the essentials of true jazz Bebop and Swing are taught here including working with the metronome on two and four, identifying changes, jazz-style blues, turnarounds and tips.
22-8107 60 min. $49.95

Beginning Bass Guitar
This video Bass Guitar lesson features colorful graphics, vivid closeups, split screen closeups, detailed illustrations, highlighting and instruction book. You will learn all about tuning, chords, tablature, right & left hand positioning, bass parts, triads, octaves. Major/minor scale construction, arpeggios, walking base lines and more.
22-8170 57 min. $29.95

Beginning Folk Guitar
In this Beginning Folk Guitar video, Evo Bluestein teaches how to hold and tune your guitar, chords for the keys of D,A,G and C, basic strum, flatpicking for accompaniment in 4/4 and 3/4 (waltz) times, bass runs, and beginning melody flatpicking. You will learn a series of songs while learning these techniques.
22-2455 50 min. $39.95

Beginning Guitar
You will learn Tuning, Chords, Tablature, Rhythm, Accompaniment, Fingering, Melody arrangements, Scale runs, Endings and a variety of songs all using detailed, vivid closeups and colorful graphics.
22-8170 60 min. $29.95

Beginning Guitar with Will Schmid
Will Schmid is one of the world's leading guitar teachers and authors. Through the use of on-screen music and guitar diagrams, and close-up hand positions and demonstrations, he gives you a beginning guitar lesson. You will learn how to play chords, read music, play solos and duets, how to improvise rock and how to accompany singing in a wide variety of musical styles.
22-630 60 min. $29.95

Beyond Acoustic Guitar: Adrian Legg
Adrian Legg, one of England's musical treasures, shows you advanced single, double and even triple-note country stringbending, fingerpicking, open tunings, banjo-peg tricks, special effects and so much more. He uses electric guitar light gauge strings on his acoustic, so all techniques covered can also apply to electric guitar.
22-8250 60 min. $49.95

Bluegrass Bass with Ed Marsh
This is the easy way to get started on the upright or "doghouse" bass. Ed teaches the fundamentals for playing basic as well as advanced bass lines for a wide variety of bluegrass styles. Ed teaches the important right and left hand techniques and essential chord theory for learning new material.
22-8046 60 min. $29.95

Bluegrass Guitar Video Lesson
This beginning/intermediate program includes all the details of right hand and left hand technique, hammer-ons, pull-offs, finger and rhythm exercises, strumming techniques, bass runs, proper method of changing strings, cassette recorder, turning and more.
22-671 90 min. $39.95

Chord-Solo Jazz Guitar
In this highly systemized approach, you'll learn one of the most satisfying and impressive methods of playing guitar. Steve Wohlrab teaches you to improvise full-sounding guitar solo pieces by harmonizing the melody notes of standard, jazz and pop tunes, with techniques for adding fills and bass lines to your chord solo arrangements.
22-8040 60 min. $29.95

Classical Rock Guitar: Michael Fath
This is video for today's lead guitarists who wants progressive and classically flavored chops. Michael shows you techniques such as: sweeping arpeggios, triad stacking, Paganini-style classical licks and exercises, double-stops, tapping, mirror octaves, cross string tapping, just to name a few.
22-8114 60 min. $49.95

Country Jazz Guitar: Joe Dalton
This video has been prepared to bridge the gap between country and jazz styles for you! Joe Dalton will teach you, double-bends, pedal steel jazz licks, chord melody and substitutions, licks using a pentatonic scale as a chromatic guide, combining blues, country and more.
22-8113 60 min. $49.95

Composing and Arranging for the Guitar with Jorge Morel
Enlist in Jorge's master class and learn the many facets of composition and arranging as well as

VIDEO TITLES LISTED IN THIS GUIDE ARE AVAILABLE FOR PURCHASE OR RENTAL. CONTACT YOUR LOCAL VIDEO STORE OR TELEPHONE (800) 383-8811

technique as you work with tremolo, tambora, vibrato, special E tuning, dropped-D tuning and so much more. A rare and unique opportunity to work with a master.
22-8111 60 min. $49.95

Dave Crigger: Slap & Tap
Dave reveals his amazing techniques from right hand tapping with double stops and chords to combinations of taps, hammers, slides, slaps, plucks and pull-offs. He performs a mind-boggling solo piece and discusses the various concepts and techniques. Then he gets downright funky and demonstrates slapping and popping.
22-8221 60 min. $49.95

Easy Gospel Guitar with Alan Munde
If you can play a few chords and strum a little, you will be playing Alan's arrangement of "Where The Soul Never Dies", "I'll Fly Away", "Blessed Assurance", "The Old Rugged Cross" and many others. Alan includes a section on improving rhythm, fingering techniques and arranging tunes.
22-8028 60 min. $29.95

Electric Bass with Ed Marsh
In this course you will learn to play bass parts for over 15 songs. Even if you have never held an electric bass, you will soon have the basic skills to play in the country, bluegrass, gospel and rockabilly styles. This course includes many examples of chord theory and chord progressions, and also prepares you for developing bass lines for your favorite types of music.
22-636 100 min. $29.95

Electric Guitar: Rock & Blues
Jesse Taylor is a technical expert and an emotionally "live" guitarist. Jesse teaches you his searing electric blues, rock-a-billy, rapid fire hot licks and chicken picking, in this complete study.
22-8037 60 min. $39.95

Eric Johnson: Total Electric Guitar
This video deals with every subject important to guitarists such as: Advanced picking techniques for speed and accuracy, left/right muting, blues bends, country "pedal steel" bends, different positions for different sounds, unique chord voicings, harmonics, dynamics, vibrato, equipment, etc.
22-8105 90 min. $49.95

FINGERPICKING COUNTRY BLUES SERIES:

• Fingerpicking Country Blues I
Great for the beginning fingerpicking blues guitarist. John Reid takes you step-by-step through 8 traditional country blues tunes while learning the

basic techniques you'll need to handle more difficult tunes as you progress.
22-8029 60 min. $29.95

• Fingerpicking Country Blues II
The next step for beginning/intermediate fingerpicking country blues guitarists. Step by step instruction will guide you through more of your favorite country blues tunes while you increase your skill and learn more advanced techniques including rolls, bends, alternate tunings, and advanced chording.
22-8030 60 min. $29.95

Flatpicking with Joe Carr
Joe Carr is one of the world's foremost flat picking experts. Joe was featured for several years with the famous Country Gazette band. This course is designed for the intermediate to advanced player, and includes a number of Joe's recorded solos, and detailed comparisons of right and left hand techniques. Joe reveals the secrets to his great sound, and shows you how to master flatpicking guitar.
22-644 100 min. $49.95

Flatpicking Guitar
This is an excellent beginner's course for learning the basic skills for guitar flatpicking. Clear, step-by-step examples show you how to develop your flatpicking techniques. You will learn 15 fun-to-play flatpicking experts. Each song is exciting and fun to learn.
22-637 100 min. $29.95

FRANK GAMBALE SERIES:
Frank is the unique guitar player with Chick Corea's Elektric Band and has gained international recognition with his solo recordings.

• Monster Licks & Speed Picking
This video details Frank's innovative speed/sweep picking technique and presents a method for developing monster licks. He demonstrates picking techniques, playing slowly so you can play along then at lightning speed to give you something to strive for.
22-8231 68 min. $39.95

• Modes: No More Mystery
The second video features Frank in a clear and easy to understand guide to using modes in soloing, a subject that guitarists often find confusing and explains it in simple terms. He covers all 7 major modes and demonstrates the use of each in the context of some extraordinary solo work. Level: Intermediate to Advanced.
22-8230 65 min. $49.95

VIDEO TITLES LISTED IN THIS GUIDE ARE AVAILABLE FOR PURCHASE OR RENTAL. CONTACT YOUR LOCAL VIDEO STORE OR TELEPHONE (800) 383-8811

George Lynch On Guitar
George demonstrates shapes, tapping, string skipping, vibrato techniques and whammy bar effects plus several favorite licks. He also teaches excerpts from some of his famous recorded solos. The video follow George right into the recording studio where he's creating solo overdubs for the Lynch Mob album "Wicked Sensation."
22-8232 50 min. $49.95

Gerald Veasley: Solo Bass Techniques
Gerald covers right hand techniques including the free stroke, hammer stroke and slap style. Then focuses on the left hand, discussing minimal motion and includes permutation exercises to build dexterity and finger independence. The video includes scale and arpeggio sequences and the modal playing demonstration.
22-8223 70 min. $49.95

Get Started on Guitar with Chet Atkins
This audio-visual lesson shows Chet Atkins teaching and playing with two young students. Through split-screen closeups and on-screen chord symbols, you will learn key fingering techniques and how to play along with the tape. Plus, you'll enjoy Atkins' easy manner and excellent choice of material. An audio cassette of the soundtrack, and a 112-page guidebook are included with this tape.
22-423 60 min. $69.95

Great Rock and Roll Solos with Jerry Tubb
If you have covered the essentials of rock and roll guitar and are ready to start learning some of the great solos that have been recorded over the years, this video will provide a lot of fun and a new challenge for you. Jerry teaches you lead guitar parts for many hits of the 50's, 60's, and 70's.
22-8036 60 min. $29.95

Guitar Basics with Mike Christiansen
Learn to play guitar at home. Video covers fundamentals, accompaniment styles, and more. For beginners through advanced.
22-9530 100 min. $19.95

Heavy Metal Primer with Jay Jay French of Twisted Sister
Jay Jay will show you special left hand exercises, power warm-ups, heavy metal power chords, heavy metal lead scales, licks, string bending and many metal flash techniques that only he knows.
22-8115 60 min. $49.95

Instant Jazz Bass with Ed Marsh
Jazz is one of the most challenging and fun styles of music for the electric bass player. Ed Marsh teaches the student the great bass lines of the professional artists. Ten standards are taught step-by-step and the student will quickly learn the concepts of playing good jazz lines for major, minor, augmented, diminished and several types of seventh chords. Ed shows how chord substitution can be used to embellish even a three-chord tune.
22-8047 60 min. $29.95

Instant Jazz Guitar with Slim Richey
Slim shows you the correct chord types to use for jazz guitar and he starts you out playing great jazz licks like you've heard on his "Jazzgrass" album. You'll learn to play Jazz like the pros.
22-8039 60 min. $29.95

Jesse Taylor Electric Guitar: Rock and Blues
Jesse Taylor is a technical expert and an emotionally "alive" guitar player. He has the ability to mesh blues, rock and country into a powerful fury. While the lead guitarist for the Joe Ely Band, Jesse received international acclaim for his brilliant "stringing" guitar style. In this video instruction tape, Jesse teaches you his searing electric blues, rockabilly, rapid fire hot licks, chicken picking and a complete study of Jesse's outstanding talent.
22-645 100 min. $39.95

Joe Beck: Jazz Chord Workouts
Joe Beck offers his unique approach to chords and theory. You'll learn about chord configuration, structure, common tones, common melodies, chord soloing, envisioning intervals, sub-situations, "hearing" the chord before you play it, bassline theory, relationships of bassnotes to chords, etc.
22-8110 60 min. $49.95

Larry Coryell: Advanced Jazz Guitar
Larry's focus in this lesson, is to teach you how to play over changes, substitute jazz chords and licks, turnarounds, complex single-note lines, Blues/Jazz styles, "swing" with modern "walking" bass lines, "waterfall" harmonics and more.
22-8109 60 min. $49.95

LEARNING CLASSICAL GUITAR SERIES:
These programs provide a comprehensive, step-by-step method for students to learn classical guitar at their own pace. Booklet included.

• Volume 1
Introduction, proper playing position, tuning, right hand technique and basic arpeggio technique.
22-045 90 min. $69.95

• Volume 2
Left hand technique, single line melody playing, and musical rudiments including eighth notes, rests, key signatures and dynamics.
22-046 90 min. $69.95

VIDEO TITLES LISTED IN THIS GUIDE ARE AVAILABLE FOR PURCHASE OR RENTAL. CONTACT YOUR LOCAL VIDEO STORE OR TELEPHONE (800) 383-8811

• Volume 3

Left hand technique expanding on first position, solo music in two parts, and musical rudiments including chromatic, new key and time signatures.

22-047 90 min. $69.95

• Volume 4

Completion of first position, musical rudiments, solo pieces and their related techniques, care and use of fingernails and rest ringing the guitar.

22-048 90 min. $69.95

Let's Do A Session: Lead And Rhythm Guitar

Have you ever watched a music video and wished you could join in? Here's your chance! For the first time this program will let you play lead and rhythm guitar to entire selections of rock, blues, ballads and funk tracks. The ultimate in interactive video.

22-5789 55 min. $19.95

MICHAEL LAUCKE CLASSICAL GUITAR SERIES

Michael Laucke is one of Canada's finest guitarists. He has given highly successful concerts in some of the world's most prestigious venues: Carnegie Hall, Wigmore Hall, the National Gallery of Budapest and others. His numerous recordings, publications and films are distributed worldwide. In this unique series, even the person without musical training can progress beyond simple strumming to mastery of the guitar as solo instrument. In the tradition of his teachers, Segovia, Bream, Diaz and Blain, Michael explains every phase of solo classical guitar playing, from fundamentals to concert level.

• Lesson 1

Intro: Technique, Tuning, Beginning to Play (Strokes, Alternation, Naming the Fingers, Left Hand, Right Hand,) Chords, Arpeggios. Michael Laucke in Concert-Danza Negra by Antonio Lauro. Enclosed in tape box: Complete Notes of the Fingerboard.

22-233 45 min. $49.95

• Lesson 2

Intro: Lagrima by Francisco Tarrega Reading Music: The Staff and its Notes. Duration of Notes, Bars and Time Signatures. Reading on Guitar: 1st String; Music-Jingle Bells, English Carol, French Round, 3rd String, 4th String; The Half Note: Music-House of the Rising Sun, Frere Jacques, Skip to My Lou. Technique Review: 5th String Music - The Frog Galliard (excerpt) by John Dowland, 6th String. Note Review: Music Leyenda by Isaac Albeniz: Malaquena; Michael Laucke in Concert with Sonia Del Rio, Flamenco Dancer: Playing Panaderos Flamencos by Paco De Lucia and Soleares. Leyenda by Albeniz and Malaguena.

22-234 45 min. $49.95

• Lesson 3

Intro: Adelita by Tarrega Completion of the First Position: Sharps and Flats, Natural Signs, Key Signatures, Chromatic Scale; Music-Au Clair de la Lune, Aire by Mauro Giuliani. Arpeggio Review: Music-Prelude by Matteo Carcassi, Study by Ferdinard Carulli Legado (Slur). Techniques: Ascending, Descending, Two Slur Patterns for Daily Practice. Michael Laucke in Concert-Las Abejas (The Bees) by Agustin Barrios. Enclosed: Complete Notes of the First Position.

22-235 45 min. $49.95

• Lesson 4

Intro: Romance (Anon) Dotted Notes: Counting, The Dotted Quarter Note. Music-Greensleeves; Saraband by Robert DeVisee. Chromatic Exercise, Slur Exercise, Arpeggio Exercise. Five Major Scales, Second Position: Music-Folk Theme. Michael Laucke in Concert-Bourree and Double by J.S, Bach. Sheet music enclosed: Greensleeves; Bourree and Double by Bach.

22-236 45 min. $49.95

• Lesson 5

Intro: Leyenda by Albeniz, with Castanet accompaniment. Third Position: New Notes, The Mobile Major Scale. Fifth Position: Music-Catalan Folk Song. Position Shifts, Dynamics, Nuances and Tempo Indications: Music-Andante by Carulli. New Time Signatures: 3/8 and 6/; Music-Andante by Sor, Minuetto by DeVisee. Michael Laucke in Concert: The Emperor's Song by Narvaez. Sheet music enclosed: (A) Cancion del Emperador by Luis de Narvaez; (B 7th Position Chart.

22-237 45 min. $49.95

• Lesson 6

Intro: 3rd Gymnopedie by Satie. Tone Production: Vibrato, Slide, Tone Contrast, Nails. Melody and Arpeggio: Music study by Sor. Seventh Position: Music-Prelude by DeVisee; Study by Carcassi. Michael Laucke in Concert-Vals by Barrios. Sheet music enclosed: (A) 3rd Gymnopedie by Satie; (B) 7th Position Chart.

22-238 45 min. $49.95

• Lesson 7

Intro: Passameze by Adrien Le Roy. Scales, Contrapuntal Music: Music-Fantasia XIII by Narvaez; Study by Sor. Harmonics: Natural, Artificial, Chord with Harmonics. Advanced Techniques and Effects: Tremolo, Pizzicato, Tambor. Michael Laucke in Concert-Fantasis XIV and Baxa de Contra punto by Narvaez. Sheet music enclosed: (A) Passameze by LeRoy, (B) Narvaez, Fantasia XIII, Fantasia XIV, Baxa de Contrapunto.

22-239 45 min. $49.95

• Lesson 8

Intro: (VL & GT) Giga by Arcangelo Corelli.

VIDEO TITLES LISTED IN THIS GUIDE ARE AVAILABLE FOR PURCHASE OR RENTAL. CONTACT YOUR LOCAL VIDEO STORE OR TELEPHONE (800) 383-8811

Ninth Position: Mastery Hints for Completion of the Fingerboard. Four Popular Works: Adelita By Tarrega, Lagrima by Tarrega, El Testamente de N'Amelia by Miquel Llobet, Romance (Magazine Advice). Flamenco: Rasqueado, Alzapua. Michael Laucke in Concert-Prelude No. 1 by Heitor Villa-Lobos. Sheet music enclosed: (A) Adelita by Tarrega: (B) Lagrima by Tarrega; (C) El Testamente de N'Amelia by Llobet; (D) Romance.
22-240 45 min. $49.95

Mick Taylor: Rock, Blues & Slide Guitar
Former Rolling Stone, Mick Taylor, takes you through some of his most challenging styles and techniques including blues bends, vibrato, standard tuning slide, slide in open E tuning, soloing concepts, country string bending and more.
22-8106 60 min. $49.95

Nashville Guitar 2000 A.D.
Joe Carr picks up where his "Nashville Style Electric Guitar" video left off. This video won't cover the fundamentals, however it will teach you a lot of the hottest licks and blazing country picking that you've heard today. You will use these ideas immediately! If you want to play hot and flashy guitar, this video teaches you how.
22-8032 60 min. $29.95

Nashville Style Electric Guitar
Fast picking, "Hot Rod Licks," and unique string bending licks which are heard on so many of today's records are presented in this exciting guitar course. Over 15 songs are included to thoroughly develop the techniques for playing "Nashville Style" electric guitar. This course also includes numerous examples of unique fingering and picking techniques and practical applications of scales and chords. With John Hartin, Joe Carr and Tim McCasland.
22-642 100 min. $29.95

Nathan East: Contemporary Electric Bass
Take private lessons with the bass wizard who tours with stars like Anita Baker, Eric Clapton, Michael Jackson, Phil Collins, and Lionel Richie. ps, turnings, grooves, and more. You can learn at your own pace and take a lesson as often as you want. If you're an advanced player, hone your skills with advice from this master musician.
22-6140 60 min. $49.95

PAUL GILBERT: INTENSE ROCK SERIES:

• Intense Rock I
Intense Rock takes you step-by-step through the techniques that will enable you to play terrifying licks. In this video, Paul Gilbert teaches you his personal exercises and sequences for incredibly fast and clean alternate picking and string skipping.
22-8235 60 min. $49.95

• Intense Rock II
Volume II goes where no guitar instructional video has gone before. Paul Gilbert explains how to approach "unteachable" skills such as phrasing, dynamics, improvisation and "feel". Also comes complete with a healthy dose of techno-terror licks.
22-8236 60 min. $49.95

PEDAL STEEL GUITAR SERIES WITH TIM McCASLAND:

• Volume I
This course is designed for the beginner or player with limited experience. It provides an excellent introduction to the "Nashville Style" pedal steel guitar. Includes a comprehensive introduction to the mechanics of the pedal steel and professional tuning information. Also included is an introduction to chord and scale theory and numerous examples for technical development, as well as twelve complete songs to learn the principles of introductions, fills, back up, solos and endings.
22-641 100 min. $29.95

• Volume II
Tim McCasland knows what should be played on the steel guitar and he has included his great solos for "Blue Eyes Crying in the Rain, Pride, Steel Guitar Rag, Mama Tried, Mojo Hand, and Amazing Grace". Tim's relaxed, method will teach you how to get the most from your pedal steel.
22-8082 90 min. $29.95

Rhythm and Blues Electric Guitar
Tim McCasland one of the best known artists, and studio players in the Southwest, has prepared this video for the guitarist who wants to play rhythm and solo guitar in the rhythm and blues styles of the master artist. He includes 5 of his greatest solos and note-for-note instruction of some of the hottest rhythm and blues guitar ever!
22-8038 75 min. $29.95

Rick Derringer: Guitar Secrets
The examples in this video are not only useful as exercises, they also form the basis for building great rock guitar solos. Some exercises may appear difficult at first, but if you watch the video and practice carefully, they become easier.
22-797 40 min. $39.95

Rock and Roll Bass
Kevin Kelley teaches the essential skills for playing today's rock and roll bass. He covers the important scales and fingerings and teaches the

professional right/left hand techniques. Kevin teaches numerous popular bass lines to help the student sound professional. Practice techniques are included to help the student develop "super chops."
22-8048 58 min. $29.95

Rock and Roll Bass: Advanced
This new advanced rock and roll bass is designed for the player with basic skills who is ready to move ahead. Kevin's method is an outstanding way to learn metal, pop, and soul bass styles and techniques. Kevin also teaches many examples of tunes that use the slap styles and tap techniques of today's famous bass artists. If you want to learn bass lines that drive, this is a great way to learn!
22-8049 60 min. $29.95

Rock and Roll Guitar with Jerry Tubb
This video provides the fundamentals for becoming a good Rock guitar player. Jerry teaches creative soloing, power chords, and the important right/left hand techniques used by today's superstars. He teaches fundamentals of rock, blues, and metal styles and teaches the harmonic and melodic devices to help you become great!
22-8035 60 min. $29.95

ROOTS OF ROCK 'N ROLL: GUITAR COURSE BY JOHNNY KAY SERIES
Johnny Kay was the lead guitarist with Bill Haley and the Comets from 1959 to 1967. He has appeared on stage with the Beatles, The Rolling Stones, The Who, Chuck Berry and The Manfred Mann Band. Johnny has taught guitar since 1967, and his former students are now becoming the leading rock guitarists of today. The more you use the course, the more effective it becomes. No music reading is required. Video graphics, broadcast quality and split screens enhance and reinforce each concept.

• Volume 1
This tape takes the student from the basic open chords of G-D-A-E on through bar chords I and V completely over the entire finger board. Video graphics enhance and reinforce each concept.
22-050 60 min. $19.95

• Volume 2
The 8th Note Rock Rhythm, the 12/8 Ballad Rhythm is demonstrated. The "Moving 5th" style of strumming is fully explained by live close-ups and video graphics.
22-051 60 min. $19.95

• Volume 3
The open, moveable and major scales are taught. Also, the student will learn how to bend, slide, and perform various professional playing techniques.
22-052 60 min. $19.95

• Volume 4
This video offers the student the opportunity to learn how to improvise solos using various rock-blues scales in all positions. Blues-rock forms 1-2-3-4 are also presented.
22-053 60 min. $19.95

• Volume 5
This video examines just how to finger the most frequently used major, minor and seventh chords in all keys.
22-054 60 min. $19.95

Southern Gospel Bass Playing
In this video, we will examine the techniques and essential elements necessary to successful bass playing in the Southern Gospel style. We will start at the beginning level and move through material for all level players. Southern Gospel employs elements from as many different styles of music from blues to country, and including funk, so hang on, this will be fun!
22-8045 60 min. $29.95

STAR LICKS MASTERS SERIES:

• Al McKay of Earth, Wind and Fire
On this special edition of the Star Licks Master Series, Grammy award-winner Al McKay of Earth, Wind and Fire serves up a man-sized portion of his specialty rhythm guitar. Al carefully takes you step by step through an exciting array of tasty fills and funky rhythms to such Earth, Wind and Fire hits as: "In the Stone," "I'll Write a Song for You," "Power," "Shining Star," "Get Away," and more.
22-057 42 min. $44.95

• Albert Lee Country Super Picker
Watch out as super picker Albert Lee, winner of Guitar Player magazine's Best Country Guitarist award for the last four years in a row, and session man for such stars as Eric Clapton, Emmylou Harris, Willie Nelson and Jerry Lee Lewis takes you step-by-step through a fantastic assortment of his hottest licks and leads. You'll Learn "Slick Chicken Pickin'", "Flowing Double Stops", "Speedy Scale Runs" and more
22-059 42 min. $44.95

• Brian May of Queen
Hold on as one of rock's finest guitarists, Brian May of Queen, takes you step-by-step through a fantastic selection of his classic licks and solos featuring material from 11 different Queen albums. You'll learn the licks and leads from such songs as: "Brighton Rock," "Bohemian Rhapsody," "Tie Your Mother Down", "Dragon Attack", "Crazy Little Thing Called Love" and more. Plus a section devoted to harmony soloing.
22-063 42 min. $44.95

VIDEO TITLES LISTED IN THIS GUIDE ARE AVAILABLE FOR PURCHASE OR RENTAL. CONTACT YOUR LOCAL VIDEO STORE OR TELEPHONE (800) 383-8811

• Carlos Cavazo of Quiet Riot

You'd better buckle up tight for this one, as one of heavy metal's hottest new ax-blasters, Carlos Cavazo of Quiet Riot, takes you step-by-step through an explosive collection of his greatest licks and solos. You'll learn the licks and leads from such Quiet Riot hits as: "Metal Health", "Cum on Feel the Noise", "Battle axe", "Run for Your Life" and "Red alert"plus an exciting look at Carlos' tap on technique.

22-064 42 min. $44.95

• Earl Greco: Advanced Bass

Learn bass guitar in this easy-to-follow session. Master two-hand chord extensions, sliding harmonics, rapid fire motor snaps, sequencer grooves and other bass techniques.

22-034 25 min. $44.95

• Jimi Hendrix Heavy Guitar Hero

You're going to start playing heavy rock guitar like you never dreamed possible as Mike Wolf, takes you step-by-step through the most unbelievable collection of Jimi's greatest licks and leads from such songs as "Voodoo Chile," "Come On," "Hey Joe," "Foxy Lady" and many more. Plus rare Hendrix footage on each video.

22-060 42 min. $44.95

• Louis Johnson: The Brothers Johnson

Get ready to start thumpin' and snappin' with the best in the business as Grammy award-winner Louis Johnson, bass guitarist for such super stars as Michael Jackson, Paul McCartney, Stevie Wonder, John Cougar, Stanley Clarke and Stevie Nicks takes you step-by-step through unbelievable assortments of thundering licks, grooves and solos featuring material from Brothers Johnson hits as "Tokyo", "Street Wave", "Stomp" and more.

22-062 42 min. $44.95

• Steve Lukather of Toto

All we can say is, you ain't heard nothin' yet, as Steve Lukather, super guitarist for Toto and one of today's premier rock 'n roll session players, takes you step-by-step through an exciting assortment of his greatest licks and solos from such hits as "Rosanna," "Carmen", "Hold the Line" and more. Plus tips on equipment, effects and soloing.

22-061 42 min. $44.95

• Tony Iommi of Black Sabbath

Prepare yourself, as one of heavy metal's greatest guitarists, Tony Iommi of Black Sabbath, takes you step-by-step through a blistering selection of his hottest licks and leads, featuring material from Black Sabbath favorites, plus a fully notated solo section featuring improvisation of some of the most incredible lead guitar around.

22-058 42 min. $44.95

• Wolf Marshall: Beginning Lead Guitar Power Builder

Wolf Marshall, featured guitarist on the original Star Licks and Star Guitar series, now makes his popular and proven method for beginning lead guitar available to you. This unique program is designed not only to teach you the kind of hot rock guitar you really want to learn but to get you immediately involved and playing lead guitar the very first day! Plus, exciting rock riffs, licks, technique, practice rhythm section and more.

22-056 42 min. $44.95

STRING ALONG: LEARN GUITAR WITH JOHN PEARSE

This series is a carefully developed teaching program that shows how easy it is to play the guitar. John Pearse, guitarist, writer and instrument maker, has put together this fascinating series of lessons based on his PBS-TV series.

• Volume 1
22-2884 90 min. $49.95

• Volume 2
22-2885 90 min. $49.95

• Volume 3
22-2886 90 min. $49.95

• Volume 4
22-2887 90 min. $49.95

Teach Yourself Lead Guitar

This video is about lead guitar. Specially filmed for the beginner or guitarist with some experience. Steve Tarshis brings you professional know-how, creating exciting leads coupled with clear explanations and demonstrations on how you can learn to play professional sounding lead guitar. Steve teaches you, in easy steps, techniques, fingerings, riffs, blues, scales, soloing and more.

22-5138 50 min. $39.95

Traditional Irish Fiddle Tunes for the Fingerpicking Guitarist

With step by step instructions, you'll learn how to change a string, use a capo and more. Then you'll play in a concert with a professional band. The guitar part has been dropped out so you can join in, using everything you've learned.

22-802 120 min. $69.95

WESTERN SWING GUITAR STYLES WITH JOE CARR

• Volume 1
Joe Carr teaches you all the chords and the harmonic theory to sound like a professional and he

includes many famous songs for you to perfect your western swing playing. Your guitar playing friends will want to take lessons from you!
22-8033 60 min. $29.95

• **Volume 2**
More great guitar chords and bass lines in the Western Swing style are included. Using common Western Swing chord progression, Joe explains the principals of chord substitution in an easy to understand method. You will learn how to spice up even the simplest two chord song with sixth, ninth, minor seventh, augmented and diminished chords!
22-8034 60 min. $29.95

Other Instruments

Advanced Country and Blues Harmonica
With this tape, the advancing "harp" player will learn the techniques and tricks used by the highly sought-after pros session players. Bending notes, playing rhythm chops, fills and solos will be demonstrated in the video. Useful scales and rushes will be introduced. Learn to play songs in minor keys. A great selection of country and blues songs is included. This program is a must for serious players.
22-8067 60 min. $29.95

Alan Munde Banjo Workshop
Alan Munde, long time banjo player for "Country Gazette" and innovative solo artist, is a frequent instructional contributor to Banjo newsletter and Frets magazine. His impressive discography includes sessions with Jimmy Martin, Clarence White, Sam Bush, Linda Ronstadt, The Flying Burrito Brothers, The Eagles and many more. This course offers the intermediate to advanced banjo player an opportunity to learn the secrets of Alan's techniques of solo development, applications of chordal and melodic theory and unique approaches to arranging music for the banjo.
22-646 100 min. $49.95

All Time Fiddle Favorites
Ed Marsh teaches you note by note, how to play many fiddle favorites such as:
"Orange Blossom Special", " Listen to the Mockingbird", "Faded Love" and many favorite waltzes and breakdowns. This video will put you at a much higher level of fiddle playing.
22-8054 60 min. $29.95

Arranging for Folk Harp with Kim Robertson
Folk harpist Kim Robertson has created a unique style of playing. On this tape you can learn many of her techniques and arranging ideas. Explained are left hand chord patterns, bass lines, dampening, tremolo, ethnic tunings and improvisation. Many sample tunes are included.
22-282 60 min. $39.95

BACKSTAGE PASS INSTRUCTIONAL VIDEOS: DRUM

• **Carmine Appice: Rock Drum Clinic**
22-6425 60 min. $49.95

• **Scott Travis: Progressive Hard Rock and Double Bass Drum Techniques**
22-6420 60 min. $49.95

• **Vinny Appice: Hard Rock Drum Techniques**
22-6426 60 min. $49.95

Basic Irish Fiddle with Dale Russ
Dale shows you the elements of the Irish Fiddle style. Included are exercises to develop coordination in both hands, basic bowing techniques, slides, grace notes, or bowed triplets. He demonstrates combining these techniques within various dance rhythms to make the traditional Irish fiddle style available to the student.
22-288 60 min. $39.95

Basic Jazz Improvisation for Saxophone
Let Lynda Reid teach you the basic skills to create your own sax lines over jazz chord changes. Learn to read chord symbols and apply the correct scales and modes to common jazz chord progressions. Recommended for the intermediate level player.
22-8070 60 min. $29.95

Basic Jazz Saxophone Techniques
Lynda Reid explores the basic techniques used by the pros, including articulations, vibrato, subtones, ghosting, falls, turns, bending, alternate fingerings and more. If you're an intermediate level player and are ready to take a giant step forward with your playing, this is the video for you.
22-8069 60 min. $29.95

Beginning the Appalachian Autoharp with Evo Bluestein
In this beginning autoharp tape, Evo demonstrates three main steps that make up his style of playing: pinch strum for rhythm accompaniment, pinch strum for melody picking and full rhythm strum for melody picking. Start at the beginning of the tape,

repeat each segment along with Evo, until you can duplicate what Evo is doing.
22-287 60 min. $39.95

Beginning Appalachian Dulcimer with Mark Nelson
This tape gives you everything you need to start playing music on the Appalachian dulcimer, including tuning, strums, finger positions and movement, ornaments and more. It Starts with the basics and teaches you how to develop your own style for maximum enjoyment.
22-283 60 min. $39.95

Beginning Banjo
If you are a beginner, this instruction is for you. Special emphasis is placed on helping the beginner. The first song opens the door to accomplishment. The beginner can take advantage of split-screen views and special effect not possible with book or even private music lessons. Graphic illustrations of every detail are fully explained. Songs are broken down into small sections and demonstrated slowly.
22-778 50 min. $29.95

Beginning Drum Set Techniques
No matter what type of music you want to play, this tape will get you off to the right start. Al Gardner explains basic set-up and address of the instrument, stroke/hand technique with simple rudiments and developing simple coordination and reading rhythms. You'll also learn the concept of time, style, sound and groove.
22-8079 60 min. $29.95

Beginning Folk Harp with Kim Robertson
A step-by-step approach to learning the nylon-strung folk harp. Starting with beginning exercises to develop tone and strength, continuing on to chords, beginning pieces, chord patterns and special effects. The beginner is taught a personal approach to accompaniment and improvisation.
22-281 60 min. $39.95

Beginning Old Time Banjo
Evo Bluestein is a well-known teacher and performer of many folk instruments and has recorded a number of albums with the Bluestein Family and as a solo artist. Evo teaches you the basic frailing (clawhammer), double thumbing, drop thumbing, hammer-ons, pull-offs and slides. Tunings included are open G, double C, G modal, using a capo for other keys.
22-2457 50 min. $39.95

Bluegrass Banjo with Tim McCasland
This course starts with very easy chord forms for song accompaniment and progresses to a variety of five string banjo techniques. Even the absolute

beginner will soon be playing his favorite bluegrass songs and having a great time with this video course. Over 15 all time favorite bluegrass banjo songs are presented in this exciting banjo course.
22-638 100 min. $29.95

Bluegrass Banjo Video Lesson
This easy, step-by-step course is for the beginner or intermediate player. Learn to read tablature, develop all right and left hand techniques, efficient practice habits, several great tunes and more.
22-670 120 min. $39.95

Bluegrass Bass Video Lesson
This lesson for beginners contains everything you need to get started as the stand-up bass player in a bluegrass band. You will learn where the notes are, scales, chord progressions, basic music theory for bass, how to watch the guitar chords, bass runs, technique for both hands, tuning, several and more.
22-667 120 min. $39.95

Bluegrass Dobro Video Lesson
This program includes detailed study of bar technique, pick technique, chimes, trills, bending strings, hammer-ons, pull-offs, slants, rhythm chops, the cassette recorder, slow songs, fast songs and more.
22-668 90 min. $39.95

Bluegrass Fiddle Video Lesson
Although fun, the fiddle is more difficult to learn in the beginning than other instruments. This lesson is designed to start you off right, with hints to make your progress fast and painless. Includes: holding the fiddle and bow, detailed technique for both hands, proper form, tuning, hints, double stops, beginning shuffle, scales, exercises and much more.
22-666 90 min. $39.95

Bluegrass Mandolin with Joe Carr
In this step-by-step method you will quickly learn the skills to become a good bluegrass mandolin player. The course includes 20 fun-to-play bluegrass mandolin songs and incorporates professional technique. Numerous examples include hammer-ons, pull-offs, scales and solo development, as well as chopping and rhythm playing.
22-643 100 min. $29.95

Bluegrass Mandolin Video Lessons
This program includes all the details of right hand technique, left hand technique, hammer-ons, pull-offs, finger exercises, rhythm strumming techniques, chopping, proper method of changing strings, the cassette recorder, tuning and more.
22-669 90 min. $39.95

Blues Style Harmonica Made Easy

Lonnie Joe Howell is a well known song writer, and session musician. He was formerly with the Nashville Songwriters Association and is now working as a writer, publisher, studio player and entertainer. Lonnie Joe teaches the modern "blues" style of harmonica that is heard on today's records. Included is a unique graphic display that makes it as easy as possible to learn quickly. You can sound like a "Pro" with this great method. Lonnie Joe teaches several songs and includes numerous special harmonica techniques like train sounds, fiddle sounds and many others.

22-6521 60 min. $29.95

Country Fiddle with Ed Marsh

This course is designed for beginning players and provides an outstanding introduction to country style fiddle set-up and tuning. It also includes examples of country intros, back up styles and practical exercises for technical development.

22-640 100 min. $29.95

Dobro with Tim McCasland

A very easy and enjoyable course which provides the basic techniques for playing the fascinating Dobro. This course includes many songs and the beginning Dobro player will be able to play accompaniment, backup and solos for these well known songs. Easy, step-by-step presentation of chord progressions and essential music theory will help the new student work out material by ear.

22-8056 60 min. $29.95

Dynamic Dulcimer with Mark Nelson

The ideal self instruction for dulcimer players wishing to expand their repertoire and learn new techniques. Mark demonstrates flatpicking and modified fingerpicking, tuning, cross-tuning and left hand positions. Includes 12 tunes from around the world played on French epimette, Swedish hummel and Hungarian citera, which you can play on your Appalachian dulcimer.

22-284 60 min. $39.95

Easy Solos for 5-String Banjo

With just a few elementary right hand roll picking patterns and some easy left hand fretting positions, you can learn to play ten all-time great country, gospel and bluegrass standards and participate in informal jam sessions with your picking friends.

22-8042 60 min. $29.95

Ed Thigpen: On Jazz Drumming

Join Ed Thigpen as he covers the basics of jazz drumming. Also included are several outstanding drum solos, which illustrate Ed's mastery of the drums and his wide range of ability. A must for every serious jazz drummer.

22-2634 60 min. $49.95

Harp and Voice

This is an excellent guide introducing simple techniques that will enable you to develop your own accompaniment arrangements, freeing you from written music and enhancing your creative ability. Easy-to-understand explanations of techniques for all levels.

22-2453 50 min. $39.95

How To Play Drums From Day One

Relax, get comfortable, pick up your sticks and get ready to play the drums! This video lesson is designed to get you playing actual drum set rhythms as fast as possible. Veteran drum instructor Jim Payne will have you playing a drumbeat in the very first lesson. You'll learn everything from holding the sticks to proper motion to hand-foot coordination. Play along with nine songs, including rock, blues, funk and shuffle - and have some fun. 38-page booklet included.

22-6141 54 min. $39.95

How to Play the Flute in the Traditional Irish Style with Mickie Zekley

Instruction on how to hold the flute, embouchure and breathing technique (the secret of Irish flute tone.) Mickie demystifies ornamentation including taps, cuts, rolls, multiple rolls, slides, triplets, finger vibrato and diaphragm pulsing. Also includes examples of tunes in different rhythms including the jig, slip jig, reel, hornpipe, polka and air.

22-285 60 min. $39.95

HOW TO PLAY HARMONICA INSTANTLY:

A must for anyone who wants to learn to play harmonica! It will teach you what you need to know, to be playing right away!

• Volume 1

22-805 30 min. $24.95

• Volume 2

For anybody who wants to learn to play blues harmonica. Teaches you how to bend the missing blues notes and cross harp style. Book included.

22-2449 30 min. $24.95

Hammered Dulcimer

In this lesson, Robin Petrie shows how to understand and play the hammered dulcimer by ear. Robin fully explains how to tune and find your way around the instrument, how to hammer and pick out scales, chords and arpeggios.

22-716 55 min. $39.95

Jaco Pastorius: Modern Electric Bass

Jaco Pastorius has been recognized as the world's number one electric bassist. He has consistently topped readers' and critics' polls in music

---

VIDEO TITLES LISTED IN THIS GUIDE ARE AVAILABLE FOR PURCHASE OR RENTAL. CONTACT YOUR LOCAL VIDEO STORE OR TELEPHONE (800) 383-8811

magazines worldwide and has won many awards, including Japan's Jazz Musician of The Year. He was a key member of Weather Report and has three solo albums to his credit. Includes 24-page book.
22-801 90 min. $59.95

Kenny Aronoff: Laying it Down
John Cougar Mellencamp's drummer gives pointers on rock drumming, hand-foot exercises, setting up the groove, independence and more. Perfect for beginners or intermediate players. Book included
22-2328 52 min. $39.95

Learn the Hammered Dulcimer
Famous Arkansas dulcimer artist, Dennis Lee has produced this beginning video. He teaches tuning, ear training, chord progressions and tablature reading for this unique instrument. He also teaches several beautiful songs for the hammered dulcimer.
22-8071 60 min. $29.95

Learn the Mountain Dulcimer
Dennis Lee, famous Arkansas dulcimer artist, has developed this new course for playing the mountain dulcimer. He teaches ionian tuning and several strumming patterns. He also teaches how to use the noter, read tablature and develop chords. He also teaches several fun to play songs.
22-8072 60 min. $29.95

Learn to Play the Fiddle Appalachian Style with Evo Bluestein
Evo Demonstrates the proper old time fiddle techniques of bowing, finger position, slides, rhythmic emphasis and a selection of tunes including: the Appalachian fiddle style stems from the unique combination of Celtic dance music and Afro/American tradition. This tape is ideal for the beginner or the folk music enthusiast wanting an authentic approach to the Appalachian folk style.
22-286 60 min. $39.95

Making the Most of MIDI
This video gives you the practical information you need for success with the new music technology. Along with a brief history and the basics of Musical Instrument Digital Interface, you'll learn about the devices, language and uses of MIDI.
22-3036 120 min. $49.95

Mandolin Lesson with Jody Stecher
This lesson is for the mandolin player who has reached a plateau and wants more techniques and inspiration.
22-648 60 min. $39.95

Melodic Autoharp
If you would like to play the melodies of favorite songs on the autoharp, this video is for you! Using traditional country songs, autoharp master, Carol

Stober takes you step-by-step from basic accompaniment patterns to advanced melodic solos. Includes ear training tips for the play by ear student as well as tablature and notes for sight readers.
22-8073 60 min. $29.95

Play the Accordion with Rusty Hudelson
Even if you have never tried the accordian before, Rusty will soon have you playing this popular instrument. Rusty teaches the standard "piano accordian" in a fun to learn style. You will soon be playing many of your favorite waltzes, polkas and popular music.
22-8068 60 min. $29.95

Playing the Drum Set
This covers the basics of commercial drumming and also provides useful information on the basic equipment. Richard Barnett performs several songs with the combo to teach the basic rock, country, blues and swing styles. He teaches all of the essential skills that the professional drummer must have.
22-8078 60 min. $29.95

Rhythm Section Workshop
John Reid, drummer Al Gardner and keyboard artist Rusty Hudelson teach the essential elements of a wide variety of grooves from country to rock, jazz, R & B, fusion and funk. Learn the essentials of putting together a tight rhythm section. Learn how to listen to each other, work off of each other and compliment each others lines.
22-8077 60 min. $29.95

Seaman's Concertina
You will learn a basic approach to the 3-row anglo concertina that requires no previous knowledge of music or music training. Techniques include basic, melody, harmony, left and right hand accompaniment, arpeggios, inverted positions, ornamentation and more.
22-2456 50 min. $39.95

Secrets of Analog and Digital Synthesis
A simple, no-nonsense guide to making any sound on any synthesizer with valuable insights into stage and studio performance techniques, includes 130 page manual.
22-2333 120 min. $69.95

Snare Drum Rudiments
This tape is comprised of a clear demonstration of all the key rudiments including many of the more advanced P.A.S. rudiments. The rudiments are divided into four main categories: rolls, flams, diddles and drags. Each one is played at several tempos and written clearly on the screen. Workbook included.
22-1773 30 min. $29.95

Steve Smith
This tape offers a revealing look at a great drummer and an understanding of the methods, techniques, and approach that have helped him develop into a highly skilled musician. His band, Vital Information, is featured throughout the video. Workbook included.
22-1771 60 min. $39.95

Video Drum Method
Covers matched grip, basic rudiments, simple note reading and drum set studies. Your teacher is Richard Petrie, a professional freelance drummer and educator.
22-2209 60 min. $39.95

Video Maestro Beginning Fiddle
Learn tuning, finger positions, timing, key scales, a variety of fiddle tunes and much more.
22-2881 55 min. $29.95

Zildjian Day in New York
See this historic day of percussion available for the first time. Each of these great drummers gives an excellent clinic with plenty of solos, playing examples, and a question-and-answer period. Vinnie Colaiuta's clinic features bassist Tim Landers and Alex Acuna performs with a brilliant percussion ensemble.
22-1772 50 min. $39.95

Piano & Organ

BACKSTAGE PASS INSTRUCTIONAL VIDEOS: KEYBOARD

• **Claude Schnell: Multi-Keyboard Techniques for Hard Rock**
22-6427 60 min. $49.95

• **T. Lavitz: "Around The Modes In 80 Minutes"**
22-6423 80 min. $49.95

Beginning Keyboard
In this video the various switches & controls common to Yamaha and Casio keyboards are identified and explained. You'll learn how to select/coordinate basic keyboard operations and combine the various rhythm and voice options to perform your favorite songs. You'll be instructed in basic music reading for playing melodies with your right hand then you'll learn to combine right hand melodies with the automatic rhythm abilities of your keyboard.
22-8173 55 min. $29.95

BEGINNING PIANO SERIES: AN ADULT APPROACH WITH DR. ALAN GILES

• **Lessons 01 and 02**
22-004 60 min. $39.95

• **Lessons 03 and 04**
22-005 60 min. $39.95

• **Lessons 05 and 06**
22-006 60 min. $39.95

• **Lessons 07 and 08**
22-007 60 min. $39.95

• **Lessons 09 and 10**
22-008 60 min. $39.95

• **Lessons 11 and 12**
22-009 60 min. $39.95

• **Lessons 13 and 14**
22-010 60 min. $39.95

• **Lessons 15 and 16**
22-011 60 min. $39.95

• **Lessons 17 and 18**
22-012 60 min. $39.95

• **Lessons 19 and 20**
22-013 60 min. $39.95

• **Lessons 21 and 22**
22-014 60 min. $39.95

• **Lessons 23 and 24**
22-015 60 min. $39.95

• **Lessons 25 and 26**
22-016 60 min. $39.95

• **Lessons 27 and 28**
22-017 60 min. $39.95

• **Lessons 29 and 30**
22-018 60 min. $39.95

Blues Piano with Rusty Hudelson
Rusty teaches you many world famous blues licks he learned in the French Quarter in New Orleans. He teaches you to how to incorporate these great

musical licks into many songs and to create new and great solos.
22-8060 60 min. $29.95

Chick Corea: Keyboard Workshop
Invaluable insights into developing technique, practicing and composing. Features John Patiticcu (bass) and Tom Brechtlein (drums). Extensive booklet included
22-2329 60 min. $39.95

Contemporary Keyboardist Basics by John Novello
Designed for the serious beginner or intermediate level musician, this video provides a step-by-step approach to the fundamentals of keyboard playing with just enough theory to understand the material covered.
22-8241 74 min. $39.95

ELECTRONIC KEYBOARD VIDEO SERIES
Johnny Mann, well-known entertainer, musician, composer, arranger, conductor and recording star, as well as star of the weekly syndicated television series "Stand Up and Cheer", takes you through a step-by-step approach to learning to play your electronic keyboard, through the use of contemporary, standard and 50's classic songs, the Casio Electronic Keyboard Video introduces you to such concepts as music notation, automatic rhythm and chord performance.

• Casio Electronic Keyboard Video
This tape covers: how to create exciting sounds and effects, how to play a melody, left hand accompaniment using the Casio chord system, 3-step learning approach to quickly learn new songs, various automatic-drum patterns on the keyboard and their use, explains fill-in and variation settings for accompaniment, explains and uses the tempo lamp.
22-628 60 min. $29.95

• Yamaha Electronic Keyboard Video
This covers: how to create great sounds and effects, play a melody, left hand accompaniment using the auto bass chord system, 3-step approach to quickly learn songs, various automatic-drum patterns on the keyboard and their use, full-in and variation settings for accompaniment and uses the tempo lamp.
22-629 60 min. $29.95

George Duke: Keyboard Improvisation
A video seminar during which George Duke discusses left hand comping, phrasing techniques, soloing, chord constructions, voicing and other tricks of the trade. Booklet included.
22-2330 60 min. $29.95

George Duke: Keyboard Vocal Accompaniment
Here, George Duke concentrates on introductions to songs, chord substitutions, voice leading, and phrasing. Booklet included.
22-2331 60 min. $39.95

GOSPEL SERIES WITH RUSTY HUDELSON

• Beginning Gospel Piano
Everybody loves good gospel music. Now you can learn to play great, old time gospel music on the piano even if you've never played a note in your life. You'll be playing these fun, gospel arrangements in no time! With the beginner in mind, Rusty Hudelson has prepared an easy method that will amaze yourself and friends.
22-8063 64 min. $29.95

• Intermediate Gospel Piano
Now you can learn to play beautiful gospel piano by ear with Rusty Hudelson's easy step-by-step method. Designed for the student with some piano experience, Rusty unlocks the secrets of bass, chord, and melody laying that will give your piano playing that something extra!
22-8064 52 min. $29.95

• Advanced Gospel Piano
Pianists of all levels enjoy this gospel video. Advanced players will quickly learn the right and left hand techniques that will give your gospel songs that finishing touch. A special section will teach you to take just the melody and chords found in many songbooks and develop your own full arrangement on the piano--by ear!
22-8065 60 min. $29.95

Hot Country Piano
Rusty Hudelson is one of the few artists who has the ability to play and teach great country piano in a way that's fun to learn. If you really want to play amazing country piano solos, Rusty will show you how!
22-8061 60 min. $29.95

Hot Licks and Solos for Country Piano
Paul Goad has developed a great new method for learning Nashville piano styles. He teaches several complete songs and numerous special techniques to make your piano playing what you want it to be. This video will have you playing today's hits whether you're in a band or just playing for fun.
22-8059 60 min. $39.95

How to Play Blues Piano with Richard Bradley
An effective video for players ranging from beginner with just basic keyboard knowledge

---

(reading, rhythm, some chords and scales) to more experienced players who want to learn blues playing and improvisation. Companion booklet.
22-8203 60 min. $39.95

How to Play Jazz Piano with Richard Bradley

This course is for beginning to more experienced players. You will be playing and sounding good almost immediately. It can be used independently, however it works best when combined with Richard's "How to Play Blues" video.
22-8204 60 min. $39.95

HOW TO PLAY PIANO SERIES:

This three part series is designed for the beginner/hobbyist. Featured is Bradley's highly successful method for piano and portable keyboard. Each course comes with a booklet. It provides a simple way to learn piano at your own pace.

* **Lessons 1, 2 and 3**
22-1767 45 min. $39.95

* **Lessons 4, 5 and 6**
22-1768 45 min. $39.95

* **Lessons 7, 8 and 9**
22-1769 45 min. $39.95

How to Play Rockabilly Piano

If you want to play Rockabilly Piano, Rusty Hudelson has a great method! He teaches the chords, the hot licks, the famous "killer" licks and the hot bass lines of many famous songs. If you love Rockabilly Piano, you'll have a great time!
22-8062 60 min. $29.95

How to Play the Piano

If you are undecided about taking piano lessons, try this video. You'll see if you like piano after you're able to play a few songs. All you need is a TV, VCR and keyboard. Instruction manual included.
22-676 60 min. $34.95

LEARN THE ESSENTIALS OF PIANO WITH TALC TOLCHIN:

* **Volume 1**
This video for beginners contains the equivalent of six to ten weeks of lessons, beginning with the names of notes, scales, chords, rhythms and improvisation.
22-2502 120 min. $49.95

* **Volume 2**
Using the Beatles' tune, "With a Little Help from

My Friends", Talc will show you how to learn a tune from a recording.
22-2503 60 min. $49.95

* **Volume 3**
This tape is an introduction to the blues - its simplicity, variety and intricacy. Includes blues licks, progressions, rhythms and improvisation.
22-2504 60 min. $49.95

* **Volume 4: Intermediate Series**
The first half of this tape is an exercise tape, which will develop speed, strength and independent hand movement. Talc will demonstrate how some of these exercises will aid you in writing your own music and develop your own improvisational lines. More advanced scale work, arpeggios and patterns are shown. The second half of the tape goes more in depth with chords, covering 9ths, 11ths, 13ths and chords based on 4th intervals. The tape closes with chord resolutions.
22-5335 52 min. $39.95

* **Volume 5: Intermediate Series**
With all the information presented in the prior volumes, you are now ready to write your own music. This tape covers the most popular song forms and how to approach beginning and completing a song. Specific suggestions are illustrated using 10ths, progressions, pedal tones, bass lines and repetitive rhythmic lines, aided by the use of drum patterns and a sequencer.
22-5336 44 min. $39.95

* **Volume 6: Intermediate Series**
This tape is a demonstration showing how to demo a tune. You will be taken from conceptually the beginning of a tune through the completed version. You will be introduced to the benefits of a sequencer and how it is an integral part of song writing and production today. Also multi-track recording is utilized to further layer and fill out the composition.
22-5337 40 min. $39.95

Let's Play The Piano

Lets Play the Piano and All Those Keyboards" is a teaching technique which has been developed as a self-programmed approach to play the piano. This method will have the student reading music and playing a popular tune with chord accompaniment after only two half-hour lessons.
22-6308 140 min. $39.95

Master Lessons on Your Favorite Piano Pieces with Margaret Ott

Learn the piece you always wanted to play quickly, accurately and beautifully with this unique method. You will acquire insight and access into the structure of compositions and the intentions of

composers. Includes booklet.
22-2244 60 min. $49.95

Piano Magic with Patty Carlson

In less than 45 minutes, you will be playing advanced and sophisticated music. Patty's revolutionary new technique of teaching Piano will prove to you that playing piano is actually very simple. You'll be playing so well after one lesson that your friends will think you've been studying for years.
22-8151 37 min. $49.95

PLAY COUNTRY PIANO BY EAR WITH RUSTY HUDELSON

• Volume 1

Rusty Hudelson teaches you how to play the chords and rhythm parts that you always hear in blues, country and gospel music. You will learn to play by ear, even if you have never tried to play the piano or any other instrument. Since you don't have to learn to read music, you'll be playing your favorite songs right away!
22-8057 60 min. $29.95

• Volume 2

In this follow-up to Volume 1, Rusty teaches you many more of the world's most famous country piano styles. Rusty's "hot" chords and solos will make you sound like a professional player and his teaching method is relaxed and stress free. You'll have a great time!
22-8058 60 min. $29.95

Play Blues Piano By Ear

Rusty Hudelson will teach you many of the world famous blues licks that he learned in the French Quarter of New Orleans. Those licks are heard in many kinds of music, R&B, Country, Rock and Gospel. Rusty teaches you how to incorporate these in songs and solos.
22-8145 54 min. $19.95

PLAY PIANO THE FUN WAY

A beginning, interactive video course designed for children and adults.

• Volume 1: Comes with 26 page Interactive Workbook
22-9516 60 min. $24.95

• Volume 2: Comes with 34 page Interactive Workbook
22-9517 60 min. $24.95

Richard Tee: Contemporary Piano

Features a performance with Steve Gadd.
22-2332 60 min. $49.95

Video Course for Casio Keyboards

In this video you will welcome Kate Joseph into your home as she teaches you to master any keyboard from 32 keys to 88 keys. Her pleasant demeanor and proven teaching technique will embark you on a lifetime of music enjoyment.
22-2205 85 min. $29.95

Videoano: Beginning Keyboard for Real People

Innovative exercises are coordinated with animated video graphics, making music fun for all ages. Complete with cross referenced book.
22-2117 36 min. $39.95

Voice

Beatles Sing-A-Long

Bring Karaoke into your living room and sing-a-long to some of the greatest Beatle's hits of all time while classic Max Fleischer cartoons tell the story. Songs are presented in two ways: with and without the lead vocal track so you can step in and become one of the Fab Four. Songs included: "Yesterday", "Good Day Sunshine"," Let It Be"," Michelle" and "Hey Jude".
22-9318 30 min. $19.95

Body, Mind, Spirit, Voice: Developing the Young Singer

Mrs. Helen Kemp, well-known for her work with children's choirs, works one-on-one with young singers. In each session she shares methods that music directors can employ when working with a variety of voices. How do you encourage the shy singer? What can you do to help with intonation problems? What about the singer whose voice is changing? Mrs. Kemp demonstrates simple non-threatening techniques that can be used to help these children and others sing better.
22-031 45 min. $49.95

Born To Sing

Born To Sing equals hundreds of hours of voice lessons and brings the voice teacher to you.
22-5360 60 min. $29.95

Enter the Vocal Zone

This tape shows you exercises and techniques on how to sing developed by singer/songwriter/vocal instructor Buddy Mix. Includes exercises for both male and female voices.
22-2501 105 min. $24.95

Learn to Sing Like the Stars

Join Vocal Coach Roger Love as he teaches you the most famous vocal technique ever taught. Uncover the secrets that make the superstars shine and turn your own dreams of singing into reality. Learn male/female exercises, breathing techniques, definition of terms, plus original songs to learn and perform. For beginners to advanced.

22-9316 78 min. $24.95

Sing-A-long Christmas

Follow the lyrics on the screen and join in the singing as we take you through the Christmas season in sight and sound. For every holiday party!

22-8143 30 min. $16.95

Sing it Right: From Bach to Rock

Muriel Brown Older brings a wealth of knowledge to each of her voice students. In over 20 years of teaching, she's trained thousands of successful singers. Muriel covers the four basic elements required for developing your abilities as a singer.

22-777 35 min. $34.95

Singercize Vocal Workout

This entertaining, video shows you exercises for the muscles used in singing. Designed to maintain and develop upper, lower and middle vocal registers for trained vocalists and beginners.

22-2992 30 min. $29.95

Vocal Ease: Care and Exercise for the Singing Voice

A masterful vocal lesson by artist, Pamela Polland. She's worked with Joe Cocker, Leon Russell, Ry Cooder, Jackson Browne, Van Morrison, Kenny Loggins and others and has become one of the most respected and sought after vocal coaches.

22-8248 78 min. $49.95

Vocal Workout Video With Chris & Carole Beatty

This video workshop will teach you the importance of proper posture, breathing and vocal warm-up technique for your singing and speaking voice. Ideal for choirs, pastors, teachers and speakers.

22-9459 78 min. $19.95

Miscellaneous

EARLY MUSICAL INSTRUMENTS SERIES:

The entire range of instruments which are ancestors to our modern instruments is the subject of this series. The Early Music Consort of London demonstrates how the instruments look and sound and how they are played.

• Reed Instruments

The development of reeds from those played by the Saracens to the 17th century forerunners of today's instruments.

22-8088 60 min. $29.95

• Flutes and Whistles

Primitive peoples developed the first musical instruments when they used tubes of bamboo, bone or wood to produce whistling sounds. This program shows what happened as the same principle was applied to a wide range of instruments.

22-8089 60 min. $29.95

• Plucked Instruments

The roots and foreign branches of the guitar-family tree. This program looks at the more important relatives.

22-8090 60 min. $29.95

• Bowed Instruments

In order to make their instruments sound like the human voice, musicians began drawing a piece of wood or bone across the strings to sustain the tone. This program traces the development of bowed instruments.

22-8091 60 min. $29.95

• Keyboard or Percussion

A close look at such rarities as the dulcimer and the hurdy-gurdy, as well as better-known instruments like the organ, harpsichord and kettledrums.

22-8092 60 min. $29.95

• Brass Instruments

The trumpet fanfares and brass bands developed relatively recent in the history of music. David Munrow explains how pitch variations are achieved with these brasses.

22-8093 60 min. $29.95

How to Read Music with Frederick Noad

The most important aspects of reading music and demonstrated by leading music educator Frederick Noad in this self-contained, full-color course, ideal for the beginner or the musician looking for a refresher course. Covers pitch, duration, rests and ties, familiar tunes, new time signatures, sharps and flats, chords and counterpoint.

22-038 42 min. $39.95

VIDEO TITLES LISTED IN THIS GUIDE ARE AVAILABLE FOR PURCHASE OR RENTAL. CONTACT YOUR LOCAL VIDEO STORE OR TELEPHONE (800) 383-8811

John Scofield: On Improvisation

Techniques of improvisation that apply to any instrument. Use of models and scales, chromatic, passing tones and picking techniques.
22-2334 60 min. $49.95

Killer Demos

If you're a musician, songwriter or hobbyist who wants to get the most out of your home studio, you need this tape. Bill Gibson, producer, composer and recording engineer, will take you step-by-step through the recording process. You'll learn everything from equipment selection to recording, effects, equalization and mixdown.
22-8132 60 min. $39.95

Learning About Music

Preschoolers through age 8 will enjoy this clever duo, Mif and Morf, two cute space aliens enroute to Earth to learn about Earth Music, as they learn about lines and spaces, rhythm, high and low notes and the musical alphabet.
22-8150 51 min. $19.95

Major Lingo: Live at the Mansion

A definitive exposition of a rare American instrument, the Lap Steel Electric Guitar. Styles range from Celtic to Reggae to 60's Psychedilia.
22-8252 60 min. $16.95

Read Music Today with Paul Wayne Beach

Learn how to read music today whether your are a beginner or just need a refresher course!
22-9532 120 min. $24.95

READING MUSIC NATURALLY SERIES:

Learn how to read music for the first time or adapt what you've learned to a specific instrument with these comprehensive, instructional videos.

• Reading Music Naturally for the Guitar Player with John Reid
22-8041 60 min. $29.95

• Reading Music Naturally for Piano
22-8666 60 min. $29.95

• Reading Music Naturally for Fiddle
22-8055 60 min. $29.95

• Reading Music Naturally for Bass Players
22-8053 60 min. $29.95

ROCKSCHOOL SERIES:

• Elementary Equipment and Basic Technique: Volume 1

Learn the basic techniques of rock...proper tuning...and how to select the equipment that's right for you.
22-1896 80 min. $19.95

• Blues to Heavy Metal: Volume 2

The simplicity of blues and the flash of heavy metal...every good musician should master these staples.
22-1897 55 min. $19.95

• Funk, Reggae and New Music: Volume 3

In this program you'll feel right at home in what might otherwise by alien landscapes.
22-1898 80 min. $19.95

• Digital Age Hardware: Volume 4

Experts help you find your place in the brave, new world of synthesizers and MIDI.
22-1899 80 min. $19.95

• Melody and Soloing: The Lifeblood of Rock: Volume 5

This program can help any musician or vocalist become a better performer.
22-1900 55 min. $19.95

• Arrangements, Putting it all Together: Volume 6

The elements come together in this final program with advanced insights into rhythm, sampling and harmony, and rock arrangement.
22-1901 80 min. $19.95

Songwriter's Video

Prepare to arm yourself with the proper tools to attack songwriting from a professional approach! Lonnie Joe Howell is well known for this work with the Nashville Songwriters Association and his outstanding harmonica playing. Lonnie teaches the craft of songwriting and the fundamentals of the music industry. He also teaches song analysis, and a simple and fun method for understanding music theory, the Nashville Number System, and tips to improve and market your original songs. Includes a reference manual and will be a great asset to developing your songwriting skills.
22-6522 45 min. $29.95

STAR LICKS STAR STYLE SERIES:

This series helps to teach you licks in the style of today's most popular musicians. Top recording and session players are featured, demonstrating 20 of the most blistering licks you would ever want to learn, in the style of your favorite group or instrumentalist.

• **Beginning Rock Drum**
22-8253 45 min. $19.95

• **Beginning Rock Guitar**
22-8254 45 min. $19.95

• **Eric Clapton Style**
22-8255 40 min. $19.95

• **Guns 'N' Roses Style**
22-8256 52 min. $19.95

• **Jake E. Lee Style**
22-8257 35 min. $19.95

• **George Lynch Style**
22-8258 45 min. $19.95

• **Yngwie Malmsteen Style**
22-8259 40 min. $19.95

• **Randy Rhoads Style**
22-8260 40 min. $19.95

• **Steve Vai Style**
22-8261 35 min. $19.95

**STUDIO-ON-A-BUDGET'S GUIDE TO
HOME RECORDING SERIES:**

• **Getting Started: Volume 1**
A clear, user friendly lesson for singers, players, and song-writers with a 4-track recorder (or two cassette decks) who want to record music at home for demos, practice or fun. You'll learn multi-track recording techniques, Jargon, Computer Sequencing, Reducing Tape Hiss, Correcting Mistakes, etc. On-screen charts and graphics make learning fun and easy.
22-8244 60 min. $29.95

• **Top Secret Home Recording Techniques: Volume 2**
Here are the specific techniques the pros use to achieve that "professional" sound you've been striving for. Techniques for recording vocals, using compressors, microphones, MIDI sequencing in the home studio, Recording Guitars and Bass Guitars, using SMPTE Time Code and more.
22-8245 60 min. $29.95

• **More Top Secrets: Volume 3: Techniques**
More professional techniques you'll use to record music at home. Hear the difference in the mix as we add Reverb, Delay and EQ. Watch as we go through the intricate mixing-down process of a song. Learn the best way to "monitor" your mix, how to use Parametric EQ and when to use a "Noise Gate". These secrets and more will sharpen your skills and creativity.
22-8246 60 min. $29.95

Writing and Selling Your Song
Join Redd Stewart and learn the secrets to effective song writing and how to sell your song. Video contains Publishers who are willing to listen to your song!
22-8144 60 min. $29.95

Writing Songs for Fun and Profit with Tom T. Hall
Tom T. Hall, master storyteller and songwriter, guides you through an informal look at the mechanics of songwriting. Tom talks about the rules and tools of songwriting: where to get your ideas; publishing and copyrights; getting paid; recording; and what to do with your song after you've written it.
22-1941 93 min. $39.95

Jazz Up Your Life!

Play the Piano...

Dance the Schottische..

Or Sing Along With Englebert.

VIDEO TITLES LISTED IN THIS GUIDE ARE AVAILABLE FOR PURCHASE OR RENTAL. CONTACT YOUR LOCAL VIDEO STORE OR TELEPHONE (800) 383-8811

New

Special Interest Video Titles

Become Available

Often.

Please Inquire

If A Title Or Subject

You Are Looking For

Is Not Listed.

Music
&
Dance
Performance

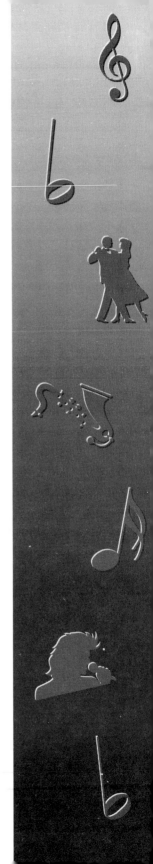

- ✓ *Ballet & Dance*
- ✓ *Big Band & Swing*
- ✓ *Blues*
- ✓ *Classical Music*
- ✓ *Country & Western*
- ✓ *Gospel*
- ✓ *Jazz & Dixieland*
- ✓ *Opera*
- ✓ *Rock & Other Contemporary*
- ✓ *Miscellaneous*

Ballet & Dance

Ailey Dances
This video is a wonderful dance program featuring four of the group's most famous dances: "Cry","The Lark Ascending", "Revelations", and "Night Creatures". The performances were recorded live at New York City's Center Theatre, and introduced with firsthand knowledge by former Ailey star, Judith Jameson. Presentations are choreographed by Alvin Ailey.
25-1608 85 min. $39.95

All the Best from Russia!
For the best in ballet, folk dancing and all-around entertainment from inside Russia, don't miss this tape. You'll see the Bolshoi Ballet, the Don Crossack Dancers. the Armenian Folk Ensemble, the Moscow circus as well as treasures from the fabulous Hermitage Museum. "All the Best from Russia!" presents a dramatic variety of colorful, exciting entertainment.
25-004 60 min. $64.95

Anyuta
A ballet based on characters from Chekhov. Yekaterina Maksimova and Vladimir Vasiliev perform to the music of Gavrilin along with dancers from Leningrad, the Kirov and Maly theaters.
25-089 68 min. $39.95

Backstage at the Kirov
The epitome of ballet companies, the Kirov, is seen from the personal viewpoint of the Russian dancers and teachers - their fears, joys and lifestyles.
25-259 80 min. $59.95

Ballerina: Karen Kain
Rudolph Nureyev has said of this dancer that "in her, the star quality is unmistakable." The first American ballerina to perform with the Bolshoi Ballet. "Carmen", "Coppelia" and "Romeo and Juliet".
25-014 100 min. $64.95

Ballerina: Lynn Seymour
Nureyev is but one of many male stars performing here in Kenneth MacMillian's "Romeo and Juliet", Sir Fredrick Ashton's "Two Pigeons" and "Intimate Letters" with Galina Samsova. Also, the world premier of "Mac and Polly".
25-015 100 min. $64.95

Ballerinas
Features Carla Fracci in a lavish re-creation of the Golden Days of ballet in Paris. Includes excerpts from such classics as Giselle, Coppelia, and Sleeping Beauty.
25-1760 108 min. $39.95

Baryshnikov by Tharp
This dance special features Baryshnikov and dancers of the American Ballet Theatre in three ballets by the great choreographer, Twyla Tharp.
25-1761 59 min. $39.95

Baryshnikov: The Dancer and the Dance
Shirley MacLaine narrates this intimate profile of Baryshnikov's life and work - the first he has ever allowed. The film captures him working with the ABT and follows him as he exercises, coaches and rehearses a new ballet called "Configurations," choreographed by Choo San Goh.
22-760 82 min. $39.95

Black Tights
Four sparkling ballets by Roland Petit featuring Petit and three legendary partners: Zizi Jeanmaire as Carmel in The Diamond Cruncher; Moira Sherer as Roxanne in Cyrano de Bergerac; and Cyd Charisse in a Merry Mourning. Maurice Chevalier is your host.
25-147 126 min. $ 29.95

Bolshoi Ballet
Excerpts from eight ballets, with music performed by the Bolshoi Symphony, permitting viewers to see the Corps de Ballet prepare. Spectacular color and motion are displayed in: "Paganini," music by Rachmaninoff; Ravel's "Bolero" and "Waltz;" and Prokofiev's "Stone Flower."
25-1632 90 min. $39.95

Bolshoi Ballet: Les Sylphides
Music by Chopin, whose most famous melodies accompany this production featuring Natalie Bessmertnova, Alexandre Beofatyriov, Galina Kozlova and Irina Kholina. Chopiniana: a complete one act ballet.
25-017 34 min. $39.95

Bujones: In His Image
Fernando Bujones, considered one of the leading male ballet dancers in the world, debuts his newest film. The program is a compilation of his greatest performances with excerpts from "Le Corsaire," "Raymonda," "Don Quixote," "Swan Lake," "Giselle," and "La Bayadere."
25-1633 57 min. $39.95

Carmen Ballet
Maya Plisetskaya, the supreme Russian ballerina of the 1950's and 1960's is featured in four of her

greatest roles; The Dying Swan, Bach prelude, Raymonda Variations and Carmen. A tape to watch over and over again.
25-131 73 min. $59.95

Catherine Wheel
Twyla Tharp's inspiration for this dance came from a fascination with Saint Catherine, the 4th century martyr who was condemned to die on a spiked wheel. This video presentation, completely refashioned by Twyla Tharp herself, is set to an original score by David Byrne, the lead singer/composer of the Talking Heads; has been described as "a major event in theatre" with "dancing of astonishing beauty and power." Superbly alive.
25-092 87 min. $39.95

Children of Theatre Street
The late Princess Grace Kelly takes us on a memorable trip to Leningrad in this Academy award nominee. Unprecedented filming in the Soviet Union shows in detail the training at the Kirov ballet school, where Baryshnikov, Makarova and Nureyev all studied.
25-021 92 min. $39.95

Cinderella/Lyon Opera Ballet
Choreography by Maguy Marin Maguy. Marin's magical version of Prokofiev's Cinderella was an unparalleled success! Marin envisions her characters as live dolls, whose story unfolds in a fabulous dollhouse world. In this imaginative setting, the fairy godmother uses a high-tech wand; Cinderella travels in a toy pink convertible, and the prince searches for his love on a rocking horse.
25-5738 87 min. $39.95

Cinderella Ballet
Berlin Komischen Opera. Grimm's wonderful fairy tale as enchanting as ever. Superbly danced by Hannelore Bey and Roland Gawlick.
25-012 75 min. $39.95

Dance Theater Of Harlem
Choreography by Agnes de Mille, Robert North, Lester Horton, Arthur Mitchell. The New York Times called the Dance Theater of Harlem "an all-black ballet company of stature and integrity." Here, the influential company displays its energy, creativity, and classical perfection in four signature pieces: Fall River Legend, Troy Game, The Beloved, and John Henry.
25-5739 117 min. $39.95

Der Rosenkavalier
Elisabeth Schwarzkopf, Sena Jurinac, Anneliese Rothenberger and Otto Edelmann recreate their roles in Richard Strauss' most popular opera filmed at the world-famous Salzburg Festival by Paul Czinner and conducted by Herbert von Karajan.
25-133 190 min. $69.95

Fernando Bujones in Sleeping Beauty
Fernando Bujones performs "The Sleeping Beauty" as guest artist of the Ballet del Teatro Municipal in Santiago, Chile, in this 1982 performance.
25-026 90 min. $39.95

Fernando Bujones In Coppelia
25-025 90 min. $39.95

Fonteyn and Nureyev: The Perfect Partnership
A video retrospective of the fabulous partnership of Margot Fonteyn and Rudolf Nureyev. This program contains much archival footage. Included are excerpts from their memorable performances in "Le Corsaire," "Les Sylphides," "Romeo and Juliet" "Swan Lake" and more. This program both illustrates and explains "The Perfect Partnership."
25-1629 90 min. $39.95

Godunov: The World to Dance In
An in-depth portrait of Alexander Godunov, ballet's most exciting and sensual dancer performing today. From his Russian background and 1979 defection to the West, this is the story of Godunov's dominance of his profession. Dazzling.
25-032 60 min. $39.95

Golden Age: The Bolshoi Ballet
Erek Moukhamedov, Natalia Bessmertnova; choreography by Yuri Grigorovich.
25-5737 113 min. $39.95

I Am a Dancer: Nureyev
The legendary performer practices and discusses his art, offering intimate glimpses of his offstage life.
25-127 60 min. $49.95

Israel Folk Dance Festival
This rare and exciting collection of the best Hebrew folkloric dance groups performing in Israel today was filmed at picturesque Zemach, on the shore of the Sea of Galilee.
25-280 60 min. $59.95

Kirov: Classic Ballet Night
This live performance by the world-renowned Kirov Ballet Company brings to life some of the famous "Pas de Deux" of the Classic Repertory. Included are "Diana and Actheon," "Esmeralda," Flower Festival in Genzano," "The Canteen-Keeper," "The Venice Carnival" and "Pas de Quatre."
25-042 99 min. $39.95

VIDEO TITLES LISTED IN THIS GUIDE ARE AVAILABLE FOR PURCHASE OR RENTAL. CONTACT YOUR LOCAL VIDEO STORE OR TELEPHONE (800) 383-8811

La Bayadere
La Bayadere (The Temple Dancer) is a three act ballet staged by Marina Petipa with music by Ludvig Minkus. A stunning performance is given by Gabriella Komleva and Tatyana Terekhova. Filmed on the stage of the Kirov theatre in Leningrad.
25-096 125 min. $39.95

La Fille Mal Gardee
One of the great masterpieces of the Royal Ballet's repertory, Frederick Ashton's lyrical comedy, "La Fille Mal Gardee" tells the story of Lisa and how she manages to win the hand of the man she loves, the young farmer, Colas, despite her mother's determination to marry her off to the dim-witted son of a wealthy vineyard owner. Danced by world famous prima ballerina, Lesley Collier, and performed at Covent Garden in London.
25-097 98 min. $39.95

La Sylphide
This 1982 VIRA Award winner, a reconstitution of the original Talioni ballet performed in Paris in 1832, was completed in 1971 by Pierre Lacotte. This features the original costume and set designs and stars Michael Denard, Ghislaine Thesmar and the Paris Opera Ballet Company.
25-043 81 min. $39.95

Lovers of Teruel
The Lovers of Teruel was heralded by Paris Critics as revolutionary. Ludmila Tcherina's inspired performance unqualifiedly established her as the tragedienne of dance. Chosen as France's official entry at the Cannes Film Festival.
25-104 90 min. $39.95

Martha Graham Company
This video offers two vintage Graham works from the late 1940's "Errand into the Maze" and "Cave of the Heart." Also included is the more recent "Acts of Light," which preserves what Miss Graham refers to as "the regality of order."
25-257 85 min. $39.95

Martha Graham: An American Profile
Shown here are rare performances of a passionate artist who exemplifies the American Spirit in its purest form. This video contains three historic performances by Miss Graham.
25-3074 93 min. $39.95

Medea
This Soviet ballet is based on the tragedy by Euripides: the ancient tale of Jason, his lover Creusa, and his revengeful wife Medea. Features the artistry of Goderdziashvili set to the music of Soviet composer, Revaz Gabichvadze.
25-107 70 min. $39.95

Moiseyev Dance Company
The non-stop excitement and acrobatic dancing of this world famous dance ensemble introduces the viewer to the many faces of folk dancing in the Soviet Union. This live spectacle was presented as part of the 1980 Olympic cultural program at the Congress Hall of the Kremlin in Moscow.
25-049 42 min. $39.95

Natasha
Natalia Makarova, who is universally acknowledged as one of the greatest ballerinas of our age, stars in this award-winning film. Includes excerpts from "Romeo and Juliet," "Manon," "A Month in the Country," "Carmen," "Dying Swan," and "Les Sylphides."
25-1558 70 min. $39.95

Nicolai Ghiavrov
25-045 60 min. $29.95

Nureyev's Don Quixote
Rudolf Nureyev stars and co-directs this film version of the famous ballet. The dancers of the Australian Ballet are featured in this elaborate production.
25-2700 110 min. $39.95

Nutcracker - A Fantasy on Ice
Dorothy Hamill skates to the music of Tchaikovsky in an ice ballet like you've never seen before!
30-569 85 min. $79.95

Nutcracker
This version of everyone's favorite Christmas story was performed at the Bolshoi Theatre in Moscow and stars Yekatrina Maximova and Vladimir Vasiliev.
25-1684 120 min. $29.95

Opera Ballet: Six Ballets
A series of pas de deux, ensembles and variations danced by the Ballet Company of the Paris Opera.
25-016 95 min. $39.95

Pas de Deux
This is a collection of pas de deux by 16 outstanding international ballet stars. Highlighted are Patricia McBride, New York City Ballet; Wayne Eagling, Royal Ballet; Ghislaine Thesmar and Michael Denard, Paris Opera Ballet; and Yoko Morishita, Matsuyama Ballet, Tokyo. The ballets include Sleeping Beauty, le Corsaire, Don Quixote and La Sylphide. Dancer/choreographer John Clifford hosts the program.
25-256 80 min. $29.95

Pavlova
New performances of Pavlova's dances have been staged and choreographed with leading dancers

from the world's most prestigious dance companies including Ronald Reagan and Amanda McKerrow. Film clips and photographs have been included in this spectacular video narrated by Leslie Caron.
25-2335 90 min. $69.95

Peter Martins: A Dancer
Peter Martins, one of the male principals of the New York City Ballet, explains his feelings about himself, his work and the City Ballet. The film shows rehearsals, three full pas de deux, and scenes with the late George Balanchine.
25-109 54 min. $39.95

Plisetskaya Dances
The immortal Plesetskaya is shown in all phases of her remarkable career along with thrilling film footage of some of her most outstanding roles, in such ballets as Romeo and Juliet, Swan Lake, Sleeping Beauty and Don Quixote. Exhilarating dancing.
25-146 70 min. $59.95

Portrait of Giselle
This program features Sir Anton Dolin in conversation with eight of the greatest Giselles of this century, illustrating their comments on the role with rare film of their performances dating from as early as 1932. With Alicia Alonso, Carla Facci, Natalia Makarova, Galina Ulanova and more.
25-1631 98 min. $39.95

Queen of Spades
A production from the Bolshoi Theater in Moscow, Tchaikovsky's tale of horror, with a plot involving obsessive love and gambling, hallucinations and descent into madness.
25-2623 174 min. $69.95

Raymonda
A glorious ballet that boasts a magical score by Alexander Glauzunov, filled with melody, color, dazzling costumes, grand scenery and effects, performed at the Bolshoi Theater in Moscow.
25-2624 146 min. $39.95

Romantic Era
This video offers four of the world's prima ballerinas in performances and conversations illustrating the romantic style as evident in the ballet. The legendary ballerinas are: Alicia Alonso of the Ballet National de Cuba; Carla Fracci of La Scala; Ghislaine Thesmar of the Paris Opera Ballet; and Eva Evdokimova of the Berlin Opera.
25-1559 89 min. $39.95

Romeo & Juliet
Ballerina Galina Ulanova created the role of Juliet when Prokofiev originally wrote his most famous ballet, and here is her historic interpretation

preserved for posterity-the 1985 VIRA Award Winner. Miss Ulanova is extraordinary.
25-129 95 min. $59.95

Romeo & Juliet with Nureyev
25-238 129 min. $39.95

Romeo and Juliet
The Bolshoi Ballet Company brings to life the world's most tragic love story. Features Natalia Bessmertnova and Mikhail Lavrosky.
25-2699 108 min. $39.95

Romeo and Juliet, the Royal Ballet
Danced by The Royal Ballet at the Royal Opera House, Covent Garden, one of the most famous stories of all time is spectacularly brought to life in this exciting performance. Superbly danced and unrivaled in presentation.
25-115 128 min. $39.95

Royal Ballet
Features three segments filmed on-stage at London's Covent Garden Theatre, starring Dame Margot Fonteyn, Michael Somes and the Royal Ballet Company.
25-1942 132 min. $29.95

Russian Folk Song and Dance
Tony Randall narrates the performances of these four great Russian troupes. The exciting and colorful film features dance and song from the Ukraine, Siberia, Samarkand and northern Russia.
25-063 70 min. $59.95

Spartacus
A story based on Thracian Spartacus' fight to free himself and his followers from the slavery to which they had been subjected by Crassus, leader of the Roman legions. Danced by Erek Moukhamdeov and Mikhail Gabovich.
25-117 128 min. $39.95

Stars of the Russian Ballet
Highlights from three ballets are seen in this document which brings together for the only time on film Maya Plisetskaya and the legendary Galina Ulanova in The Fountain of Bakhchisarai. Ulanova is also seen in highlights from Swan Lake, and the videotape ends with the Flames of Paris, a stirring tribute to the French Revolution.
25-132 80 min. $59.95

Swan Lake
The world-renowned Bolshoi Theatre is the site of this "live" filming of Tchaikosky's most famous ballet masterpiece with the great Maya Plisetskaya in the dual roles of Odette/Odile.
25-130 130 min. $59.95

VIDEO TITLES LISTED IN THIS GUIDE ARE AVAILABLE FOR PURCHASE OR RENTAL. CONTACT YOUR LOCAL VIDEO STORE OR TELEPHONE (800) 383-8811

Swan Lake, Kirov Ballet
Tchaikovsky's complete ballet is given an exciting interpretation by the Kirov Ballet and the Leningrad Philharmonic, as performed in 1981.
25-074 90 min. $39.95

Swan Lake: Vienna State Opera Ballet
Filmed during an actual stage performance of this full-length work starring Margot Fonteyn and Rudolf Nureyev, Choreographed by Nureyev.
25-1922 113 min. $39.95

Tango
The Ballet Company of the Grand Theatre Company of Geneva dance a series of pieces to the vibrant and throbbing rhythms of the tango. Choreographed by Oscar Ariaz with a great originality and performed with flair and precision by some of the finest dancers in Europe.
25-075 100 min. $39.95

Ultimate Swan Lake
The Bolshoi Ballet Company and the Moscow Symphonic Orchestra combine for this magnificent rendering of ballet's classic Swan Lake. Natalia Bessmertnova, Boris Akinov and Alexander Bogatyrev star in this opulent production. Gene Kelly is your host and narrator.
25-078 126 min. $39.95

Big Band & Swing

All-Star Swing Festival
For the first and only time, the legendary greats of the swing jazz era appear together in a gala concert hosted by Doc Severinsen and recorded live at Lincoln Center. Features Ella Fitzgerald, Count Basie, Benny Goodman, Duke Ellington and Dave Brubeck. The joint is jumpin'!
22-649 52 min. $29.95

BIG BANDS SERIES:

• Volume 101
Count Basie, Lionel Hampton and Duke Ellington strut their stuff in this outstanding video featuring the music that made them famous.
22-081 46 min. $19.95

• Volume 102
Harry James, Ray McKinley, Si Zentner, and Ralph Marterie - swinging sounds that make this a best buy for big band buffs.
22-082 52 min. $19.95

• Volume 103
Tex Beneke, Ralph Flannigan, Les & Larry Elgart and Vaughan Monroe had a lot to do with the post-war baby boom with hits like "At Last," "Hot Toddy," and the classic "Racing with the Moon."
22-083 53 min. $19.95

• Volume 104
Tex Beneke directs the Glen Miller Orchestra, Krupa does his thing, Jerry Wald swings and Stan Kenton introduces a promising young singer named June Christy. Outstanding video album.
22-084 53 min. $19.95

• Volume 105
Larry Clinton, Jimmy Dorsey, Red Nichols, Bunny Berigan, Ina Ray Hutton - five of the great swing bands of the 30's and 40's play some of the tunes of the day.
22-085 50 min. $19.95

• Volume 106
Lawrence Welk, Russ Morgan, Hal Kemp, Jan Garber - the sweet domesticated sounds of the country's leading "society" bands of the 30's will be music to the ears of the grown-up children of the Depression.
22-086 53 min. $19.95

• Volume 107
Guy Lombardo with His Royal Canadians - the ultimate "sweet" band of all times performs 20 of its all-time favorites, including "Sioux City Sue," "Toot Toot Tootsie" and "On a Slow Boat to China."
22-087 54 min. $19.95

• Volume 108
Duke Ellington, Count Basie and Lionel Hampton play hits that make this an absolute must for jazz lovers: "Supercalifragillisticexpialidocious," Shake Rattle and Roll" and "Flying Home".
22-088 47 min. $19.95

• Volume 109
Hal Kemp, Johnny Long, Frankie Carle, Jan Garber and Art Mooney provide a real walk down memory lane. This one is worth it just to see and hear the great Frankie Carle.
22-089 51 min. $19.95

• Volume 110
This is what the Big Band sound is all about with Ray McKinley, Dick Stabile, Sam Donahue and Stan Kenton setting your toe tapping and blowing your ears off.
22-090 44 min. $19.95

• Volume 111
Count Basie, plus some outstanding solo work by

Johnny Hodges, Harry Carney, Cootie Williams with Corky Corcoran, and Buddy Rich with the Harry James band as well. Great stuff!
22-091 50 min. $19.95

Cobham Meets Bellson
Can a couple of drums have a conversation? Yes! Especially when they're played by two all-star drummers like Louie Bellson and Billy Cobham. Listen and watch as the two performers face each other, alternating in virtuosity and using all kinds of tones from the "whispering" to the "fortissimo." A continuous flow of rhythm punctuated by the Louie Bellson Big Band that provokes contagious movement.
22-194 35 min. $24.95

Louie Bellson and His Big Band
This inventor of the two bass drum kit is famous for his memorable participation in the big bands of Ellington, Basie, Dorsey and Benny Goodman. Bellson keeps up the big-band tradition with this video of his own orchestra with a superb live concert performance.
22-166 55 min. $29.95

Mel Lewis and His Big Band
Here is a top-flight 19-piece jazz band in a live outdoor concert in Jerusalem. This swinging big-band jazz at its best.
22-170 38 min. $24.95

Blues

Ladies Sing The Blues
The "Ladies" who created an art form and sang their way into legend...a bygone era is recaptured in this filmed salute to the women who started it all...whose turn of a phrase made musical history. Priceless footage of the great American divas (complete songs, not just tantalyzing excerpts) Billie Holiday, Bessie Smith in her only film appearance...Dinah Washington from the stage of The Apollo Theatre...Peggy Lee, Sarah Vaughan, Lena Horne, and others, singing their classics.
25-5099 60 min. $29.95

Mississippi Blues
Award winning director Bertrand Tavernier (Around Midnight) gives us a fascinating close-up look at the true folk music of the South: the delta blues. In a musical journey to Oxford, Mississippi, we meet up with great blues legends who still produce this inspirational form of music.
25-5791 92 min. $24.95

Classical Music

All That Bach
A galaxy of international performers got together in Canada to celebrate Bach's 300th birthday, and the result was this remarkable film. Performers include Keith Jarrett, Maureen Forrester, the Canadian Brass and many others.
25-2538 50 min. $49.95

Arturo Toscanini Conducts the Music of Giuseppe Verdi
Toscanini's exceptional performance of Verdi's Hymn of Nations.
25-080 30 min. $19.95

At the Haunted End of the Day: A Profile of Sir William Walton
Profile of the British composer, produced by London Weekend Television. Includes over 20 pieces of his work, including "Crown Imperial," which was written for the coronation of King George Vi, never before shown in the United States.
25-1902 100 min. $59.95

Beethoven, Schumann, Brahms
Selections include "Sonata for Violin and Piano No. 7 in C Minor," "Arabeske in C Major," lieder and more.
25-090 90 min. $39.95

Classical Images
A musical and visual delight featuring several popular classical selections interpreted through scenic and natural images from the four seasons. Features Debussy's "Afternoon of a Faun," Grieg's "Piano Concerto," Mozart's " A Little Night Music," Pachelbel's "Canon in D Major," Beethoven's "Fur Elise" and much more.
25-1915 45 min. $29.95

Claudio Arrau: The Emperor
Opens with a documentary tracing the remarkable life of this unique artist. Then the scene shifts to the Metropolitan Cathedral in Santiago, Chile for his performance of Beethoven's "Emperor Concerto."
25-2319 60 min. $49.95

Concert Aid
The BBC Symphony Orchestra performs Beethoven's "Symphony No. 5" with Sir George Solti conducting. Profits from the tape are directed

VIDEO TITLES LISTED IN THIS GUIDE ARE AVAILABLE FOR PURCHASE OR RENTAL. CONTACT YOUR LOCAL VIDEO STORE OR TELEPHONE (800) 383-8811

to the famine relief fund for Ethiopia and the Sudan.
25-258 40 min. $19.95

David Oistrakh: Remembering a Musician
In rare footage from the musical archives of the Soviet Union, Oistrakh plays scintillating and emotional performances of the "Intermezzo" movement from Lalo's Symphonie Espagnole, excerpts from Shostakovich's F Minor Sonata and much more.
25-271 60 min. $39.95

Erick Friedman Plays Fritz Kreisler
Friedman plays the works of the beloved Kreisler. The recital includes 10 pieces, including "Liebesfreud" and "The Old Refrain."
25-022 90 min. $39.95

From Mao to Mozart
Isaac Stern's fascinating Academy award-winning journey to China is now on video, featuring the glorious music of Mozart. Stern's 1979 visit created a spirit of friendship and cultural exchange rarely experienced with the Chinese people.
25-028 90 min. $59.95

Going on Fifty
The Israeli Philharmonic began fifty years ago in Tel-Aviv. Its musicians were Jewish refugees from Europe. Zubin Mehta has been musical director for the last 25 years and he hosts this historical program. Musical highlights include Puccini's "Madam Butterfly," Tchaikovsky's "1812 Overture," and much more.
25-1916 50 min. $39.95

Handel's Messiah: Complete Performance
Maestro Robert Shaw conducts the Atlanta Symphony Orchestra and the Atlanta Symphony Chamber Chorus in this monumental performance.
25-2527 141 min. $49.95

Hansel and Gretel by Engelbert Humperdinck
This presentation in English was taped during a 1982 performance at the Metropolitan Opera. The charm of this production is well known in New York, where its popular Christmas season performances are greeted by audiences and critics alike.
25-286 104 min. $29.95

Heifetz
The greatest violinist of the 20th century performs Bruch's Scottish Fantasy and Bach's Chaconne,

plus works by Mozart, Debussy, Rachmaninoff, Korngold, Prokofiev and Gershwin.
25-121 63 min. $49.95

Horowitz in London
Vladimir Horowitz is featured on this music video playing Scarlatti, Chopin, Schumann and Rachmaninoff. He reminisces about his career and personal life during the intermission.
25-034 116 min. $39.95

Joan Sutherland in Concert
This program is rich in classical numbers from the dramatic to the lighthearted and displays the wide range of "La Stupenda," whose voice has thrilled music lovers throughout the world for a quarter of a century.
25-273 49 min. $39.95

John Kim Bell
Traces the interest and musical development of this young North American Indian pursuing his career as a symphony conductor by starting as a promising pianist. Filmed in New York, Toronto and Montreal.
25-2629 41 min. $29.95

Jose Serebrier
The master of orchestral balance conducts three selection from Prokofiev, Tchaikovsky and Beethoven. Performed are "Alexander Nevsky," "Symphony No. 1" by Tchaikovsky and "Symphony No. 3" (Eroica) by Beethoven.
25-040 134 min. $39.95

Kyoto Vivaldi
Antonio Vivaldi's Baroque masterpiece, "The Four Seasons," is one of the most popular classical pieces of all time. This program is a lyrical yet passionate portrait of the year's shifting moods. Performed by the Japanese Koto-Ensemble, Vivaldi's musical seasons provide the background for this visual discovery of the ancient city Kyoto.
25-2338 45 min. $29.95

Leonid Kogan
With piano accompaniment by his daughter Nina, we experience Kogan's performances of Tchaikovsky's "Melodie and Valse Scherzo," Glazunov's "Entr'acte," Brahms's "Scherzo," Kreisler's "Liebesfreud," Bizet's "Carmen" and a set of Paganini variations.
25-275 60 min. $39.95

Looking at Music with Adrian Marthaler
Directed by Adrian Marthaler, performed by the Basel Radio-Symphony Orchestra, conducted by Matthias Bamert. Swiss TV director Marthaler helms four classical music video performances:

Gershwin's Rhapsody in Blue, Bach's Brandenburg Concerto No. 2, Honegger's Concertino and Saint-Saens' Danse Macabre.

25-1946   50 min. $29.95

Mozart
Concerto for Flute in D Major; K314/Andante for Flute in C Major; K318/Concerto for Piano in E Flat Major; and K271.

25-177   55 min. $39.95

Neville Marriner
The historic, stately home of Longleat House provides the ideal setting for the music of Bach, Handel, Mozart, Grieg, Pachelbel, Borodin, Gluck and Rossini, as performed by the Academy of St. Martin in the Fields.

25-270   55 min. $29.95

Newborn King
This joyful, traditional holiday celebration features bariton Benjamin Luxon from VAI Glyndebourne Opera performances, boy Soprano Aled Jones, the Westminster Cathedral Choir and actor Emlyn William reading brief selections from Charles Dickens and Thomas Hardy.

25-249   60 min. $29.95

Polish Chamber Orchestra, Conducted by Jerry Maksymiuk
This brilliant performance of Mozart's "Eine Kleine Nachtmusik Divertimento," K.136 (First Movement) and Haydn's Symphony No. 45" (Farewell) is a rare treat.

25-274   60 min. $29.95

Rostropovich: Dvorak Cello Concerto, Saint Saens Cello Concerto No. 1
Filmed in London and conducted by Carlo Maria Cuilini, this incorporates two concert performances by the magnificent cellist Rostropovich.

25-2628   65 min. $29.95

Scarlatti, Debussy, Ravel
Let Nelson Freire, Martha Argerich and Maisky thrill you with their interpretations of Ravel's "La Valse" and "Gaspard de la Nuit," Debussy's "Sonata for Cello and Piano in D Minor" and Scarlatti's "Sonata in D Minor" on this video.

25-064   47 min. $39.95

Tchaikovsky Competition: Violin & Piano
All the musicality of the event laced with all the tension of a thriller... "London Times." Absolutely spellbinding... technique, virtuosity and style...it is Mullova's presence and performance that are the core of the tape... some of the finest sound engineering for home video... "Rob Baker, N.Y.

Daily News. P. Kogen conducts the Moscow Symphony.

25-076   120 min. $74.95

Tropical Sweets
Award winning violinist, Bill Patterson, has sensitively interpreted some of the best known classical pieces, carefully matching each video sequence to the nuances of the music score. The result is an exhilarating, yet relaxing way to actually visualize these great classical works while listening to some of the world's most celebrated orchestras.

22-8027   37 min. $29.95

Verdi Requiem
Filmed live at the Edinburgh International Festival in Usher Hall, this performance is conducted by Claudio Abbado, and features are rare gathering of four distinguished soloists: Jessye Norman, Margaret Price, Joe Carreras and Ruggero Raimondi.

25-149   86 min. $39.95

Viktoria Mullova and Maxim Shostakovich in Performance.
Two of the most important Soviet music defectors took part in this historical all-Russian concert, with the London Symphony Orchestra. Presented by the BBC.

25-2000   95 min. $29.95

Yehudi Menuhin: Brahms Violin Concerto in D
Recorded at the Gewandhaus in Leipzig, East Germany, this performance sparkles with outstanding brilliance.

25-272   60 min. $29.95

Yehudi Menuhin: Concert for the Pope
Yehudi Menuhin and the Polish Chamber Orchestra play for the Pope in a private performance in beautiful Castelgandolfo. Vivaldi "Concerto in D, op. 89, No. 11." Vivaldi "La Caccia" concerto in B flat, op. 8, No. 10. Bach "Erbarme Dich, mein Gott" aria (Mira Zakai). Mozart Adagio K261 and Rondon K373.

25-001   52 min. $29.95

Yehudi Menuhin: Tribute to J.S. Bach (1865-1750)
The English Chamber Orchestra. "Concerto for Violin in A Minor," "Cantata des Paysans" BW212, Partita in E Major for solo violin, "Cafe Cantata," BWV211.

25-013   86 min. $29.95

Video Titles Listed In This Guide Are Available For Purchase Or Rental. Contact Your Local Video Store Or Telephone (800) 383-8811

Country & Western

Alabama in Concert: Collector's Edition
Relive the excitement of Alabama's early years of
stardom in this historic release that anyone who
has ever heard the hit sounds of Alabama will be
proud to own..
25-8262   60 min. $16.95

Banjos, Fiddles & Riverboats
A magical mix of images from other times, other
places and of some extraordinary people whose
lives have been shaped by the love of riverboating.
Taped aboard Opryland USA's famous General
Jackson Showboat, John Hartford is the host and
central character of this "Living Diary" in which he
shares his own memories, along with some of his
special friends.
22-8197   45 min. $16.95

Behind the Scenes of Full Access
Be part of superstar Hank Williams Jr.'s platinum
award-winning Full Access video as it was filmed;
in concert, at his ranch and behind the scenes.
22-8168   30 min. $16.95

Christmas Past: Grand Ole Opry
This is a rare experience in entertainment: an
original, uncut Grand Ole Opry Christmas show
from the stage of the famous Ryman Auditorium in
Nashville, Tennessee. Filmed in 1967, the featured
artists included: Porter Wagoner, Dolly Parton,
Dottie West and many others.
22-8196   30 min. $16.95

Conway Twitty: # 1 Hits
Featured are such hits as: Make Believe, Hello
Darlin,' Slow Hand and others.
22-8155   45 min. $16.95

Conway Twitty: King of Hits
Featured are such hits as: To See My Angel Cry,
Linda on My Mind and others.
22-8156   45 min. $16.95

Full Access: Hank Williams Jr.
See, hear and feel Hank's hits as only he can
perform them in his electrifying concerts. Full
Access features all-new footage produced
exclusively for this video.
22-8165   80 min. $19.95

George Jones - Same Ole' Me
Legend George Jones, is featured in clips
throughout his thirty year career.

In addition, anecdotes and comments are featured
form such greats as Johnny Cash, Randy Travis,
Buck Owens, Ricky Van Shelton, and others.
22-9437   30 min. $19.95

**GREATS OF THE GRAND OLE
OPRY:**
Join Willie Nelson, Reba McEntire and Roy Clark
as they host these video programs featuring some of
the "greats" of country music.

• Train Songs
Hosted by Boxcar Willie.
22-8198   40 min. $29.95

• Leading Ladies
Hosted by Reba McEntire.
22-8199   40 min. $29.95

• Movin' Home
Hosted by Roy Clark.
22-8200   50 min. $29.95

• Song Masters
22-8201   55 min. $29.95

**Hank Williams, "The Show He Never
Gave"**
Country singer "Sneezy" Waters portrays Hank
Williams, giving an imaginary impromptu concert
to everyday folks--a small, intimate concert in a
roadside bar. Waters' performance is a touching
tribute to the young country star.
22-8087   86 min. $24.95

**Hank Williams, Jr.: A Star Spangled
Country Party**
22-726   60 min. $29.95

Johnny Cash: Ridin' the Rails
Johnny Cash sings more than a dozen great railroad
songs including: "Casey Jones," "Wreck of the Old
97," "The City of New Orleans," "Brother Can
You Spare a Dime" and many more.
22-268   52 min. $29.95

Loretta Lynn: Honky Tonk Girl
This is the lively and personal portrait of an
entertainer who has truly lived the American
dream.
22-9439   60 min. $19.95

Nashville Goes International
Join host Charlie Daniels and some of Nashville's
and country music's greatest stars for a look at
country music in concert at different places around
the world. Featuring: Emmylou Harris, Barbara

Mandrell, Oak Ridge Boys, etc. 22-8164 59 min.
$16.95

Real Patsy Cline
The complete, true story of Patsy Cline's brilliant rise to stardom and her tragic death at the pinnacle of her career. This classic biography features rare performances of Patsy's hit songs, such as "Crazy", "I Fall To Pieces" and more.
22-8163 48 min. $16.95

Some Enchanted Evening with Willie Nelson
It's been called a "gala tribute". Over 400 entertainment industry leaders, dignitaries and friends gathered to pay tribute to Willie and his record-setting "Stardust" album.
22-8166 60 min. $16.95

Telluride 17th Annual Bluegrass Festival
A remarkable collection of musicians creating the unique blend of music found only at Telluride entertained sell-out crowds for four days under Colorado's skies. Featured are: James Taylor, Mary-Chapin Carpenter, and Mark O'Connor.
22-8001 90 min. $19.95

Waylon Jennings: The Lost Outlaw Performance
Now for the first time you can enjoy an exciting country concert that has long been forgotten. Experience the evening of August 12, 1978, when Waylon Jennings and the Waylors performed on the concert stage of The Grand Ole Opry in Nashville, Tennessee.
22-9444 60 min. $19.95

Waylon Jennings: Renegade, Outlaw, Legend
This production features classic performances (some never before released), including home video (some Buddy Holly footage never before released), photos and his music. Interviews and anecdotes from such greats as: Herb Albert, Hank Williams Jr. and Robert Duvall.
22-9438 61 min. $19.95

Willie Nelson: On the Road Again
This features such hits as: "Blue Eyes Crying In The Rain", "Crazy" and others.
22-8153 45 min. $16.95

Willie Nelson: Great Outlaw Valentine Concert
Features Willie Nelson singing: "You Are Always On My Mind", "On The Road Again" and other great songs
22-8154 45 min. $16.95

Willie Nelson Special
Willie, and guest star Ray Charles, sing five songs together including a duet version of "Georgia" But what makes this show even more special is a rare behind-the-scenes glimpse of two musical superstars in rehearsal.
22-263 60 min. $19.95

Will the Circle be Unbroken II
This goes beyond documenting how the album was made. It's lots of great music performed by great musicians. And it's an insight on how they got together to make it happen.
22-8167 87 min. $19.95

Gospel

Gospel
A concert extravaganza featuring five of the top acts in Black gospel music. Filmed at the paramount Theater in Oakland, California, this film captures the spirit of this unique American art form.
22-2621 92 min. $39.95

Gospel According to Al Green
Famous as a seductive purveyor of soul in the early 1970's Green become a Pentecostal preacher in 1977 and has been inspiring audiences with his funk-laced, fever-pitched gospel songs ever since.
22-2377 94 min. $29.95

Gospel Road
The story of Jesus sung and told by Johnny Cash with June Carter Cash and Kris Kristofferson. Filmed entirely in Israel, the movie faithfully follows in the footsteps of those who walked these ancient roads 2,000 years ago. Glorious music!
22-253 62 min. $39.95

GOSPEL SOUND MUSIC SERIES:

• **Volume 1**
Tennessee Ernie Ford, Della Reese, the Fisk Jubilee Singers, Miss Micki Ferman, the Happy Goodman Family.
27-234 45 min. $29.95

• **Volume 2**
Tennessee Ernie Ford, Della Reese, the Fisk Jubilee Singers, the Jordanaires
27-235 45 min. $29.95
• **Volume 3**
Tennessee Ernie Ford, Andre Crouch, Della Reese,

VIDEO TITLES LISTED IN THIS GUIDE ARE AVAILABLE FOR PURCHASE OR RENTAL. CONTACT YOUR LOCAL VIDEO STORE OR TELEPHONE (800) 383-8811

Grandpa Jones and Ramona, The Nashville Sounds and the Happy Goodman Family.
22-2375　45 min.　$29.95

• **Volume 4**
22-2376　45 min.　$29.95

Irish Music

Dubliners With Paddy Reilly & Jim McCann
Great Irish music, recorded live in Dublin, with songs like "Molly Malone" and others.
22-8123　75 min.　$19.95

Frank Patterson: Ireland's Golden Voice
Filmed at several great Irish locations featuring 16 great Irish songs like "Danny Boy", "The Last Rose of Summer" and others.
22-8125　60 min.　$19.95

Paddy Noonan's Let's Have An Irish Party
The world's first Irish video is a fun filled hour of music, humor, bagpipes, dancing and great Irish sing-a-longs.
22-8126　60 min.　$19.95

Paddy Reilly Live
Ireland's favorite singer in a live performance of well-loved songs.
22-8124　51 min.　$19.95

Jazz & Dixieland

America's Music: Jazz Then Dixieland 2
Starring Teddy Buckner, Bob Crosby, The Hessions, Al Hirt, Scatman Crothers, Judy Carmichael and Irma Thomas.
22-2305　60 min.　$19.95

Celebrating Bird: The Triumph of Charlie Parker
The first and only authorized documentary on Charlie Parker, includes on-camera interviews with Rebecca Davis Parker, Dizzy Gillespie, Louis Armstrong, Thelonious Monk, and others. This very special program moves beyond the focus of Parker and traces the evolution of jazz from the Armstrong era of the 1920s to bebop--the new music of the 40s and 50s, a music Parker brought to its highest level. This is a must for any jazz lover!
22-1758　58 min.　$29.95

Chet Baker: Candy
Includes an extremely imaginative treatment of Cole Porter's "Love for Sale". Hailed by Europajazz as one of its most ambitious jazz video projects to date.
22-2390　30 min.　$19.95

Different Drummer: Elvin Jones
This is an excellent visual and aural study of the great drum innovator, with some smoking with from his quartet with saxist Pat La Barbara, guitarist Ryo Kawasaki and bassist David Williams.
22-2636　30 min.　$39.95

Dizzy Gillispie: A Night in Tunisa
A musical portrait of the jazz legend.
22-8157　30 min.　$24.95

Dukes of Dixieland and Friends
Celebrating their 40th anniversary, the Dukes with their "Friends (the New Orleans Pops Orchestra) feature standard straw hat fare like "Fidgety Feet", "Rampart Street Parade,""Basin Street Blues" and "Sensation Rag". The orchestra backs them on "Midnight in Moscow, "Star Wars" and Bourbon Street Parade".
22-8189　60 min.　$29.95

Ellyn Rucker in New Orleans
Following three successive years at the Northsea Jazz Festival in Amsterdam, this fresh, sultry vocalist and brilliant pianist will soon be one of the top female jazz singers around. She is backed up by Carmen McRae's bassist, Mark Simon and Jill Fredrickson on drums.
22-8191　60 min.　$29.95

George Shearing: Lullaby of Birdland
Features one of the most popular pianists of all time. His lasting legacy is still played by musicians today!
22-8211　57 min.　$19.95

Good Morning Blues
This program is an entertaining, informative color documentary on the country blues--from turn of the century roots in the Mississippi Delta through work songs and field shouts to Memphis and up Highway 61 to Chicago. Narrated by B.B. King.
25-8019　60 min.　$24.95

VIDEO TITLES LISTED IN THIS GUIDE ARE AVAILABLE FOR PURCHASE OR RENTAL. CONTACT YOUR LOCAL VIDEO STORE OR TELEPHONE (800) 383-8811

Herbie Hancock Trio with Billy Cobham & Ron Carter

The master pianist goes back to his jazz roots to capture the full spectrum of the art, a display of sensual touch and sizzling pyrotechnics.
22-8158 60 min. $19.95

JAZZ GREATS: THE PERFECT GIFT FOR JAZZ FANS:

Treat yourself or a jazz lover you know to rare performance footage. Now, some of the best footage has been made into superb a video series. The Piano Legends, hosted by Chick Corea. The Trumpet Kings, hosted by Wynton Marsalis. John Coltrane helps unravel the web of mystery which surrounds the legendary saxophonist.

- **Piano Legends**
  22-2547 63 min. $39.95

- **Trumpet Kings**
  22-2436 72 min. $39.95

- **John Coltrane**
  22-2435 61 min. $39.95

Jazzball

This Nostalgic look at America's jazz greats features rare screen performances of stars like Duke Ellington, Artie Shaw, Louis Armstrong, Cab Calloway, Gene Krupa, Buddy Rich and more.
22-158 60 min. $29.95

Louis Bellson: The Musical Drummer

Demonstrates brush and double-bass technique, covers swing, samba, shuffle, bossanova, and jazz/rock beats. Highlights include two classic solos in the Bellson tradition.
22-2635 60 min. $49.95

Mable Mercer: Cabaret Artist

This video was recorded live from Cleo's in New York, Mabel Mercer will touch you Forever and Always with this 20-song selection of Great American Popular Song.
25-5171 58 min. $29.95

Monterey Jazz Festival

Captures three of the greatest jazz musicians ever during the 10th annual Monterey Jazz Festival. Features Mel Torme, Woody Herman and Joe Williams.
22-2785 60 min. $29.95

Moscow Sax Quintet: Jazznost Tour

Whether it is classic Fats Waller or The Beatles or Charlie Parker solos in blazing 5-part harmony, you can hear the mastery of the music. Russia's

foremost jazz group totally capture the jazz feeling with their magical sounds.
22-8161 60 min. $29.95

ONE NIGHT WITH BLUE NOTE:

Thirty major jazz artists salute Blue Note Records in an historic evening of performances.

- **Blue Note: Volume I**
  22-173 60 min. $29.95

- **Blue Note: Volume II**
  22-174 60 min. $29.95

OUT OF THE BLACK, INTO THE BLUES:

This is a two part series that focuses on the story of the blues using live interviews and performances.

- **Along the Old Man River: Part I**
  Featuring: Bukka White, Sonny Terry, Brownie McGhee and more.
  25-8020 60 min. $24.95

- **A Way to Escape the Ghetto: Part II**
  Featuring: B.B. King, Willie Dixon, Sonny Terry and more.
  25-8021 60 min. $24.95

Ron Carter & Art Farmer: Live at Sweet Basil

The heartland soul of jazz are captured by this all-star quartet, from deep in the heart of New York's jazz nightlife.
22-8160 60 min. $29.95

Salute to Jelly Roll Morton

Taped live at Lulu White's Mahogany Hall in New Orleans' French Quarter. Banjo/guitarist Danny Barker (who performed with Jelly Roll in the 1930's) and the Dukes of Dixieland collaborate on fifty-eight minutes of the composer's tunes.
22-8189 60 min. $29.95

Sarah Vaughan: Live from Monterey

Recorded live in September 1983 during the Monterey Jazz Festival, the program features this premiere jazz singer at her best.
22-2786 60 min. $29.95

Saxophone Colossus

The career of jazz great Sonny Rollins is examined through the use of interviews and filmed performances.
22-1853 101 min. $29.95

SHANACHIE JAZZ SERIES:

VIDEO TITLES LISTED IN THIS GUIDE ARE AVAILABLE FOR PURCHASE OR RENTAL. CONTACT YOUR LOCAL VIDEO STORE OR TELEPHONE (800) 383-8811

• **Gypsy Guitar: Legacy of Django Reinhardt**
His name is synonymous with gypsy guitar. This program explores the influence of this great jazz guitarist and how his music has spread worldwide.
25-8017 60 min. $24.95

• **Ben Webster: Brute & the Beautiful**
Considered one of the great saxophonists in jazz. In his era, only Coleman Hawkes and Lester Young were his equal. Filmed in Britain, America, Holland and Denmark, The Brute and the Beautiful traces the evolution of Webster's style from his origins in Kansas City in the 1920's, to his last professional engagement in Holland in September 1973.
25-8018 60 min. $24.95

Woody Remembered
When Woody Herman died, American music lost the last of the big band giants. Like the other greats, Woody was an original. His artistry and energy spanned a half century, and through it all he retained humor and integrity while leading some of the greatest big bands in jazz history.
22-8190 60 min. $29.95

Opera

Abduction from the Seraglio
25-142 130 min. $49.95

Abduction of Figaro
Prof. Peter Schickele has unearthed P.D.Q. Bach's first full length operatic misadventure: "The Abduction of Figaro," as given in its world premiere by the stellar Minnesota Opera featuring a stellar cast chorus and "corpse" de ballet.
25-127 144 min. $49.95

Abduction From The Seraglio
Wolfgang Amadeus Mozart's masterpiece, performed by The Dresden State Opera and conducted by Harry Jupfer. This merry song-play illustrates how profound human ideas, love and faith can overcome power and egotism.
25-003 130 min. $39.95

Amahl and the Night Visitors
This production stars Metropolitan Opera diva Teresa Stratas, who has appeared in the hit Broadway show "Rags," as well as Giorgio Tozzi, Wilard White and Nico Castel.
25-251 50 min. $29.95

Arabella
Soloists: Ashley Putman, Glanna Rolandi, Regina Sarfaty. This opera, with its romantic Viennese plot and its lush waltz-time melodies, was often labelled a second "Rosenkavalier." This amorous comedy about the complications surrounding the heroine's betrothal to a rich landowner benefits from careful staging, scrupulous preparation and intimacy.
25-202 154 min. $39.95

AUSTRALIAN OPERA SERIES:
Four classic operas, performed by Dame Joan Sutherland with Richard Bonynge conducting the Elizabethan Sydney Opera. Each in stereo, and purchase includes a libretto and a playbill.

• **Adriana Lecouvreur**
25-008 135 min. $79.95

• **Dialogues of the Carmelites**
25-009 155 min. $79.95

• **Die Fledermaus**
25-010 142 min. $79.95

• **Il Trovatore**
25-011 138 min. $79.95

Boris Godunov
Universally acknowledged as the greatest of all Russian operas, this dazzling Bolshoi production was taped in 1978. The program is in Russian and distinctively subtitled in English. This rare performance of "Boris Godunov" is the finest full-length version on videocassette.
25-252 181 min. $69.95

Centennial Gala
An operathon celebrating the Met's 100th year. One hundred singers! Seven conductors! Two cassettes.
25-100 231 min. $39.95

Christmas With Flicka
Opera star Frederica Von Stade celebrates the holiday season with the music of Christmas in a picture-postcard Alpine village, with friends Melba Moore, Rex Smith and Julius Rudel.
25-3087 60 min. $29.95

Composer's Notes: Philip Glass and the Making of Akhnaten
Directed by Michael Blackwood, narrated by Philip Glass. A documentary about how avant-grade composer Glass created his third opera, Akhnaten, which premiered in 1985 simultaneously in Stuttgart and Houston.
25-1945 87 min. $49.95

Cosi Fan Tutte
Once again, John Pritchard is on the podium for a sparkling performance of Mozart's delightful farce on romantic foibles. Thomas Allen, Franz Petrie and Helena Dose head the cast.
25-143 150 min. $49.95

Don Carlo
One of Verdi's labyrinths of sex and violence with Placido Domingo in the title role. Two cassettes.
25-101 214 min. $39.95

Don Giovanni
Mozart's most famous opera stage work features Benjamin Luxon as the Don in Peter Hall's vibrantly dramatic production.
25-141 173 min. $59.95

Ernani
In the tittle role, Pavarotti's voice rings out like a clarion trumpet. As Elvira, Michell's singing is glorious, while Milnes spins out Don Carlo's music with tonal beauty and suave refinement. Ruggero Raimondi also gives a solid performance, musically and dramatically.
25-245 142 min. $29.95

Eugene Onegin
An operatic production in three acts of the Kirov Leningrad Opera and Ballet Theatre. Music by Tchaikovsky, an adaptation of the novel by Alexander Pushkin. Stars Evguenia Gorokhovskaya, Tatiana Novikova and Larissa Dyadkova. Russian language, subtitled in English. Two cassettes.
25-1627 155 min. $69.95

Falstaff
The late Donald Gramm stars as the Fat Knight in this glistening performance conducted by John Pritchard. Well acted, charming and moving.
25-136 123 min. $49.95

Fidelio
International star Elisabeth Soderstrom is the courageous Leonore in Beethoven's only opera. Bernard Haitink conducts the Peter Hall Production. A compelling documentary.
25-135 130 min. $49.95

Francesca Da Rimini: Riccardo Zandonai
This Metropolitan Opera production may be one of the most beautiful in the company's recent history. Subtitled in English, recorded in 1984.
25-288 148 min. $29.95

I Live for Art
Fifteen opera divas gather to discuss their "Tosca" roles, and are featured in live performances. Includes Maria Callas, Renata Tebaldi, Kiri Te Kanawa, Montserrat Caballe, Birgit Nillson and Eva Turner, among others.
25-2017 98 min. $39.95

I Lombardi
Verdi was commissioned to write "I Lombardi" as a direct result of his successful opera, "Nabucco, "the year before. It was first produced at La Scala in 1843 at a time when Verdi was becoming increasingly popular not only in Italy, but abroad as well. This production from La Scala is the first there for more than 50 years, headed by a cast of international opera stars.
25-094 126 min. $39.95

Idomeneo
Mozart's dramatic opera series stars Richard Lewis as Idomeneo with Josephine Barstow as Electra and Leo Goeke as Idomeneo's son Idamante. John Pritchard conducts.
25-138 127 min. $49.95

Joan Sutherland: The Making of Lakme
Joan Sutherland, diva colortura soprano, and Richard Bonynge musical director, feature in the making of Delibes' "Lakme," from elaborate costume and scenic sketches to elaborate execution. From rehearsals to opening night. Students and buffs alike will be enchanted and delighted with production and performance.
25-039 120 min. $64.95

Julius Caesar
The Berlin State Opera. A superior performance by the great Theo Adam is the highlight of this production of the story of Julius Caesar, Cleopatra and her brother Ptolemy, King of Egypt. Conducted by Hans Krenitz.
25-041 122 min. $39.95

Khovanshchina - Bolshoi Opera
Mussorgsky's "Khovanshchina" is one of Russian opera's masterpieces. It's a sprawling tale of the struggle for power in Russia at the beginning of the reign of Peter the Great. Stars Yevgeni Nesterenko as Dosifei. "Khovanshchina" is a riveting operatic experience, here vividly brought to life. Two cassettes.
25-1626 172 min. $69.95

Kiri Te Kanawa at Christmas
Accompanied by over 100 musicians and singers from the Philharmonic Orchestra and the Tallis Choir, this international Diva offers us an extraordinary gift of a gala concert of her favorite seasonal music.
25-3086 60 min. $29.95

VIDEO TITLES LISTED IN THIS GUIDE ARE AVAILABLE FOR PURCHASE OR RENTAL. CONTACT YOUR LOCAL VIDEO STORE OR TELEPHONE (800) 383-8811

L'Incoronazione di Poppea
This is Monteverdi's last opera, often considered his best. It tells the story of the Roman emperor Nero's love affair with the scheming and seductive Poppea, with evil triumphing over good. Performed by the Glyndeborne Festival Opera with the London Philharmonic Orchestra.
25-099 148 min. $39.95

La Boheme
A stunning production of this Puccini crowd-Pleaser with Teresa Stratas as Mimi, Jose Carreras as Rodolfo, and Renata Scotto as Musetta followed by an interview with director Franco Zeffirelli.
25-102 125 min. $29.95

La Cenerentola
Soloists: Kathleen Kuhlmann, Marta Taddel, Laura Zannini. This opera is Gioachino Rossini's version of the story of Cinderella - a sparkling favorite in his repertoire. This new Glyndelbourne production captures perfectly the fairy tale spirit of the piece. Directed by John Cox.
25-203 152 min. $39.95

La Cenerentola (Cinderella)
By Gioacchino Rossini. A classic for all time, starring Fedora Barbieri.
25-019 94 min. $39.95

Legend of the Tsar Saltan
By Nikolai Rimsky-Korsakov with the Dresden State Opera. A highly imaginative and innovative production, with special effects animation offers an original and entertaining spectacle, including such well-known works as "Flight of the Bumblebee."
25-023 95 min. $39.95

Les Troyens
This was the first uncut performance of Berlioz's masterpiece at the Met. These sold-out performances revealed the magic of Les Troyens to audiences and critics alike - work of outstanding artistry, one of the monuments of the operatic repertoire.
25-246 253 min. $39.95

Live From the Met Highlights
25-220 70 min. $29.95

Lucia Di Lammermoor
It was as the frail Lucia that Met Opera star Anna Moffo achieved many of her early triumphs. In this version, the beautiful Miss Moffo is seen amidst the real highland castles in which the story is set.
25-123 100 min. $49.95

Macbeth
Verdi's setting of Shakespeare's dark tragedy stars Kostas Paskalis and Josephine Barstow as the scheming Macbeth with Met star James Morris as Banquo. John Pritchard conducts a performance that bristles with excitement.
25-137 148 min. $59.95

Magic Flute
Mozart tells the story of a handsome young prince's quest to save a beautiful princess from the forces of evil. It's a marvelous tale of mysticism, good versus bad, and the power of love.
25-247 134 min. $29.95

Manon Lescaut: Giacomo Puccini
This opera is Puccini's ultimate story of youth and love. Director Gian Carlo Menotti gave us fluid movement, eye-catching invention, sex appeal, and above all, a sense of humor. This presentation, subtitled in English, was taped at the March 29, 1980 performance at the Metropolitan Opera.
25-287 135 min. $29.95

Maria Callas: Life and Art
Celebrates her singing and dramatic skills, and explores the woman behind the public person. Features extracts from Tosca, La Traviata, and Norma.
25-1762 78 min. $29.95

Marriage of Figaro
Kiri te Kanawa, Lleana Cotrubas and Frederica von Stade highlight this performance of Mozart's comic masterpiece in the Peter Hall Production. (Two Cassettes.)
25-139 168 min. $59.95

Mary Stuart
In this performance from the English National Opera is London, Dame Janet Baker portrays Mary Stuart as she experiences a memorable range of human emotions in the scenes leading to her execution in the climactic scene of the fictitious encounter with her persecutor. Elizabeth I.
25-106 138 min. $39.95

Magic Flute
The stunning David Hockney production conducted by Bernard Haitink and featuring Benjamin Luxon and Felicity Lott. A quality production of musical honesty, careful preparation, attractive sets and world-class singing.
25-134 164 min. $49.95

Operafest
A gala of stars never seen in North America. Enjoy Mirella Freni, Jose Carreras, Lucia Popp, Gwyneth Jones, Alfredo Kraus, Nicolai Ghiaurov and many others in arias, duets and ensembles.
25-2546 90 min. $59.95

VIDEO TITLES LISTED IN THIS GUIDE ARE AVAILABLE FOR PURCHASE OR RENTAL. CONTACT YOUR LOCAL VIDEO STORE OR TELEPHONE (800) 383-8811

Phillip Glass and the Making of Akhnaten
Part of Phillip Glass' popularity derives from the hugh success of his trilogy of operas, the third of which is Akhnaten. Award winning director Michael Blackwood worked with Glass as he prepared for two simultaneous premieres in Stuttgart and Houston to create this cinema verite portrait of an artist at work.
25-2550 87 min. $49.95

Rakes's Progress
Stravinsky's sardonically witty opera stars Leo Goeke as Tom Rakewell and bass star Samuel Ramey as Nick Shadow. Felicity Lott and Rosalind Elias co-star in the David Hockney Production conducted by Bernard Haitink. Two cassettes.
25-144 146 min. $59.95

Renata Scotto: Prima Donna in Recital
Metropolitan Opera star Renata Scotto is seen in one of the frequent recitals, this one taped in Tokyo in 1984. Miss Scotto sings music of Verdi, Rossini, Puccini, Liszt, Scarlatti, Mascagni, Handel and Respighi. The Washington Post describes her as "the greatest singing actress in the world."
25-124 152 min. $39.95

Return of Ulysses to His Homeland
Dame Janet Baker and Benjamin Luxon join to bring Monteverdi's music drama to vivid life. Early music expert Raymond Leppard conducts one of the best opera productions one is ever likely to see. Two cassettes.
25-140 152 min. $59.95

Rigoletto
By Giuseppe Verdi. Directed by Carmine Galone. The Unforgettable Gobbi in a film from 1946.
25-060 80 min. $39.95

Sherrill Milnes: An All Star Gala
Baritone Sherrill Milnes has invited some of his friends and colleagues to join him: tenor Placido Domingo, sopranos Julia Migenes-Johnson and Mirella Freni, tenor Peter Schreier and host Burt Lancaster. Together, they perform works by Verdi, Mozart, Leoncavallo, Romberg and Brahms.
25-250 55 min. $39.95

Tannhauser
Few productions in the Metropolitan Opera's repertory have been so unanimously admired as Richard Wagner's "Tannhauser." Richard Cassily gives a masterful performance in the title role. A splendid viewing as well as listing experience.
25-119 176 min. $39.95

Thespis
"Thespis - or, The Gods Grown Old." The "Lost Opera" by Gilbert and Sullivan. Staged by the Connecticut Gilbert and Sullivan Society in 1989, this is the only Performing Edition of "Thespis" ever seen in this century!
25-6985 110 min. $79.95

Tosca
Critics showered praise on this production, describing Behrens in the title role as "regal and proud, and one responded strongly to her power of conception and intelligent realization of her difficult role".
25-248 127 min. $29.95

Un Ballo in Maschera
In this Verdi opera, a governor of colonial Boston is fatally stabbed. But before he dies, he sings one final aria in which he pardons his assassins and promotes his secretary.
25-103 150 min. $29.95

Verdi's Otello
The Berlin "Komischen Opera" conducted by Kurt Mesur. The legendary story of Otello the Moor, Desdemona and the jealous Iago. A spectacular performance with a cast of hundreds in a one-of-a-kind production.
25-051 123 min. $39.95

Verdi's Rigoletto At Verona
The grand opera of grand master Giusseppi Verdi performed at the ancient Roman amphitheatre at Verona, Italy. Acoustic sound in a dramatic setting, staged regally for the tragic tale of Rigoletto, court jester and his daughter, Gidla. The performance digitally mastered for the discriminating opera-loving audience.
25-079 120 min. $74.95

Rock & Other Contemporary

America's Music: Folk 1
Theodore Bikel hosts this folk music jamboree featuring Buffy Ste. Marie, the New Christy Minstrels, Odetta, Hoyt Axton and Glenn Yarbrough.
22-072 58 min. $19.95

America's Music: Folk 2
Starring: Doc Watson, Limeliters, Josh White Jr., Jean Richie, Dave Van Ronk, Mary McCaslin and Jim Ringers, and John McEuen.
22-2303 60 min. $19.95

VIDEO TITLES LISTED IN THIS GUIDE ARE AVAILABLE FOR PURCHASE OR RENTAL. CONTACT YOUR LOCAL VIDEO STORE OR TELEPHONE (800) 383-8811

America's Music: Soul 1

Get down and funky with these soul superstars - James Brown, Ben E. King, Mary Bond Davis, Tyrone Davis and Maxine Nightingale.
22-076 60 min. $19.95

America's Music: Soul 2

Starring: Gladys Knight and the Pips, Rufus Thomas, Carla Thomas, Jerry Butler, Freda Payne and Percy Sledge.
22-2307 59 min. $19.95

Beach Boys

A candid look at America's favorite clean-cut, candy-striped and harmonic family: Brian, Dennis and Carl Wilson, cousin Mike Love, and Al Jardine. The surf, the fun, the magic and the sorrow of the legendary Beach Boys all come to life in this expansive film biography.
22-261 105 min. $24.95

Beatles: Live

Rare live footage of John, Paul, George and Ringo in concert. Songs include "Twist and Shout," "I Wanna Hold Your Hand" and more.
22-258 156 min. $16.95

Beatles: Magical Mystery Tour

The Fab Four created this freaky TV special in 1967, a video fantasy for collectors of all ages. John, Paul, George and Ringo Perform "I Am the Walrus," "Fool on the Hill," "Magical Mystery Tour" and more.
22-080 60 min. $19.95

BEE GEES ONE FOR ALL TOUR:

• Volume One

After ten years of studio sessions, the Bee Gees returned to the live stage during the triumphant "One For All" tour. This stunning, digitally recorded concert, lit by award-winning designer Allen Brantion, and shot with over 16 cameras, is a joyful celebration of 27 Multi-Platinum Bee Gees' hits spanning 20 years. Volume One includes: Ordinary Lives, Givin' Up the Ghost, To Love Somebody, I've Gotta Get a Message to You, One, Tokyo Nights, Words, Juliet, and an incredible medley of top hits.
25-5786 57 min. $16.95

• Volume Two

More hits from the celebrated "One For All" live concert. Volume Two includes: How Deep Is Your Love, Neighborhood, How Can You Mend a Broken Heart, House of Shame, I Started a Joke, Massachusetts, Stayin' Alive, Nights on Broadway, Jive Talkin', You Win Again and You Should Be Dancing.
25-5787 55 min. $16.95

BEST OF NEW WAVE THEATER:

Highlights from the highly acclaimed nationally broadcast cable program that literally revolutionized rock 'n roll television during its three year run. Hosted by the late Peter Ivers and featuring new wave luminaries 45 Grave, The Blasters, The Dead Kennedys, Black Flag and more.

• Volume 1

22-314 60 min. $29.95

• Volume 2

22-315 60 min. $29.95

Crosby Stills & Nash: Acoustic

When they first electrified the music world at Woodstock, they did it with their acoustic music. Now they capture another memorable acoustic show: performing their greatest hits live in concert at San Francisco's Warfield Theatre in November, 1991.
22-8186 80 min. $16.95

Crosby, Stills & Nash: Long Time Comin'

A band like Crosby, Stills & Nash comes along but once in a generation. This program celebrates the 21 years of their union by exploring the inspiration for their music: the history of our times. The program is intensely rich with historic materials from numerous film and video archives: feature film, televisions shows, documentaries, out-takes, lifted sequences, concert films, newsreels, home movies, plus rare and never-before-seen Crosby, Stills & Nash performances. From their early days with The Byrds, The Hollies, and Buffalo Springfield to their 1990 world wide tour, this is the ultimate tribute to a landmark rock group.
25-5792 60 min. $19.95

David Bowie: Glass Spider Tour

With the spectacular Glass Spider Tour, David Bowie has achieved what the New York Times calls "rock-driving, imagistic music theatre." Since his early days in England where he was influenced by American rhythm and blues. Bowie's harmonies and vocals have always been outrageous and controversial. He has cultivated a well-crafted and innovative sound that, says critic Robert Hilburn, may "not have been equalled since Presley." Including such songs as "Never Let Me Down," "Jean Genie," "Let's Dance," "Fame," and "Fashion," Bowie's digitally recorded concert, attended by over 6 million people worldwide, marks the culmination of his superlative musical insights and explorations.
25-5788 110 min. $19.95

DICK CLARK'S BEST OF BANDSTAND SERIES:
Features guests from American Bandstand hosted by Dick Clark.

• Volume 1: Dick Clark
Dick Clark has reached into the Bandstand vault and selected some of the best performances to create this video of wall-to-wall rock 'n roll classics. Features: Bill Haley and the Comets, Buddy Holly, Jerry Lee Lewis, the Big Bopper, the Everly Brothers, Chubby Checker and more.
22-257 60 min. $29.95

• Volume 2: The Superstars
It's got a great beat, and you can dance to it - Dick Clark has searched the Bandstand archives again! This video features The Supremes, The Jackson 5, The Beach Boys, Roy Orbison, The Four Seasons and much more.
22-1892 47 min. $29.95

Elvis: Aloha From Hawaii
Relive the King's legendary performance - an entertainment event watched by the world.
22-306 75 min. $29.95

Hard Day's Night
The Beatles' first movie is a whimsical look at the moptops on tour, Through the imaginative eye of director Richard Lester. Where is Paul's grandfather now?
22-070 85 min. $39.95

HELP!
The Beatles' wildest, wackiest adventure ever. Ringo discovers a ruby ring and adds it to his personal collection. Unbeknownst to him, however, the ring has secret powers and is coveted by a strange Indian cult. Many of the Beatles' greatest tunes were written for this film, including "Ticket to Ride," "You've Got to Hide Your Love Away." "I Need You" and of course, "HELP!"
22-776 90 min. $69.95

John Lennon: Imagine
John Lennon reaches out to us in a hauntingly beautiful film that sings, laughs and loves. The action in punctuated with thirteen inspired songs from the #1 album.
22-2337 55 min. $29.95

John Lennon: Live in New York City
August 30, 1972. John Lennon and Yoko Ono, backed by the plastic Ono Elephant's Memory Band, played at a benefit concert to raise money for mentally handicapped children. It was their last concert together.
22-2339 55 min. $29.95

Linda Ronstadt
With hits ranging from country to rock'n roll to operetta, Linda Ronstadt is one of today's best loved and most versatile performers. When she turned her extraordinary talents to classic ballads - by such songwriting legends as Irving Berlin and George and Ira Gershwin - the result was the phenomenally successful album" What's New." This enchanting performance includes Linda Ronstadt's stirring renditions of "What's New," "Lover Man," "I've Got A Crush On You" and other hits from the chart-topping "What's New" album.
22-5119 60 min. $29.95

Marvin Gaye
An intimate look at the legendary performer. Featuring 28 songs.
22-5049 60 min. $19.95

MOTOWN TIME CAPSULE SERIES:

• 1960's
Various Motown artists, including the Temptations and the Supreme, perform their greatest hits of the '60s.
22-704 50 min. $29.95

• 1970's
Various Motown recording artists from the '70s, including Edwin Starr and Marvin Gaye, perform.
22-705 119 min. $29.95

Nancy Wilson: At Carnegie Hall
Nancy Wilson, the great vocal communicator, in a memorable concert with full string orchestra, direct from Carnegie Hall, New York.
25-5091 52 min. $29.95

Nat "King" Cole: Unforgettable
Nat King Cole was indisputably one of the greatest musician singers of the century. This video presents filmed recollections of Quincy Jones, Frank Sinatra, Harry Belafonte, Mel Torme, Ella Fitzgerald, Eartha Kitt, Oscar Peterson, and others who knew him well. Songs include: Unforgettable, These Foolish Things, Hush Hush, Mona Lisa, Nature Boy, The Christmas Song, Route 66, Sweet Lorraine, Dance, Ballerina Dance, Yes, We Have No Bananas, Bewitched, Bothered and Bewildered, Stardust, and more.
25-5790 90 min. $24.95

Police: Around the World
In 1980 and 1981 the Police toured through more than a dozen countries. This film features highlights of that tour which included stops in Japan, Hong Kong, India, Egypt, Australia and Latin America. Features 16 songs.
22-316 77 min. $29.95

VIDEO TITLES LISTED IN THIS GUIDE ARE AVAILABLE FOR PURCHASE OR RENTAL. CONTACT YOUR LOCAL VIDEO STORE OR TELEPHONE (800) 383-8811

Rainbow Bridge
This film has Hendrix acting, rapping, philosophizing and most importantly, performing. Hendrix is shown in his last photographed performance, the historic Maui concert of 1970. Hendrix is unquestionably one of the greatest rock guitarists of all time.
13-304 74 min. $19.95

Rainbow Goblins Story
Masayoshi Takanaka, Japan's virtuoso rock/jazz fusion guitarist, pushes your imagination to the max with this live concept concert at Japan's famed Budokan Theatre.
22-718 53 min. $19.95

Real Buddy Holly Story
Paul McCartney's film of the life and music of Buddy Holly, paints an historic portrait charting his school life to the formation of the Crickets, the Pilgrimage to Nashville with the first "demo," to the sold-out tours in America, Canada and Europe. Here is history being made: the first recorded footage of Elvis Presley; clips that capture Buddy and Jerry Lee Lewis in those early concerts; Paul McCartney playing and paying tribute to one of his great influences; and those few precious television appearances Buddy made.
22-1757 90 min. $29.95

Russian Rock & Roll
Participate in the excitement as Soviets and Americans join together at the Moscow Winter Festival. Rock songs and costumed dances express their desire for a world at peace. Enjoy the clowning and camaraderie of people building bridges of love.
22-8210 30 min. $16.95

Steve Gadd in Session
This video features Steve Gadd in the studio with two all-star rhythm sections including Jorge Dalto, Eddie Gomez, Richard Tee and Will Lee. Players arrange and perform tunes that illustrate a variety of styles, including funk, be-bop, reggae and ballads.
22-798 90 min. $59.95

Takanaka World
Masayoshi Takanaka, Japan's virtuoso rock/jazz fusion guitarist, presents a feast for your eyes an ears. This video is a collection of eight exciting songs, written and performed by Takanaka.
22-719 42 min. $19.95

Windham Hill: In Concert
Virtuoso performances by guitarists Michael Hedges and Will Ackerman, Pianist Scott Cossu, and Shadowfax. Experience the magic of a live Windham Hill concert.
22-1985 68 min. $29.95

Woodstock Rock Festival
This is a two-part chronicle of the original and greatest rock festival of them all, Woodstock. Experience, or re-experience, the August 1969 performances of The Who, Santana, Jimi Hendrix, Joan Baez, Jefferson Airplane, Crosby, Still, Nash and Young and countless others.
22-472 95 min. $29.95

Miscellaneous

AMERICAN COMPOSERS SERIES:

• John Cage
Avant-garde legend John Cage, one of the world's most revolutionary and influential modern American composers explores his fascination with environmental sounds.
22-8128 60 min. $19.95

• Philip Glass
He is one of the most successful living American composers today.
22-8129 60 min. $19.95

• Meredith Monk
Her work has influenced many English and American singers, including Kate Bush and Lene Lovich.
22-8130 60 min. $19.95

• Robert Ashley
Ashley performs excerpts from Perfect Lives, a work created exclusively for video. It is the start of a new musical genre.
22-8131 60 min. $19.95

Celebration of Music and Dance
This was filmed at the 1985 session of the Lark In The Morning Traditional Music and Dance summer camp. It captures the spirit of this exciting event attended by over 300 people. Enjoy the teaching, dancing, storytelling, cooking and eating, music, and more. A good time.
22-222 48 min. $34.95

Andrew Lloyd Webber's "Requiem"
From the creator of "Jesus Christ Superstar," "Evita," and "Cats," this is a special film with Placido Domingo and Sarah Brightman, the Choirs of Winchester Cathedral and St. Thomas' Church,

---

together with the orchestra of St. Luke's conducted by Lorin Maazel.
22-1625 19 min. $19.95

Anna Russell: The (First) Farewell Concert

"The world's funniest woman" - says The London Times. This recital features Miss Russell's now-infamous analysis of Wagner's Ring Cycle plus many of her hysterical sketches. No wonder the Washington Post has described her as "a lady who has been reducing audiences to helpless laughter for nearly half a century."
25-128 85 min. $49.95

BEST OF REGGAE SERIES:

• Sunsplash 1

1982 Jamaican concert with performances by Chalice; Steel Pulse; Eek-A-Mouse; Lloyd Parkes & We the People; Aswad; Burning Spear; Mutabaruka; Big Youth; Marcia Griffiths; Home T. Four, Mighty Diamonds, Blue Riddim.
22-199 60 min. $19.95

• Sunsplash 2

Jamaican concert with performances by Byron Lee and the Dragonairs; Big Youth; Toots & the Maytals; Home T. Four; Taj Mahal; Mutabaruka; Yellowman; Lloyd Parkes; Deniece Williams; Twinkle Bright and many more.
22-200 60 min. $19.95

BEATS OF THE HEART MUSIC SERIES:

• Shotguns and Accordions: Music of the Marijuana Growing Regions of Columbia

Vallenata music is a hot, jumpy dance music that mixes accordions, electric bass, percussion and lusty, open-throated singing.
22-8177 30 min. $24.95

• Konkombe: Nigerian Pop Music Scene

This is the perfect introduction to the endlessly fascinating world of African pop's dizzying array of sounds, rhythms and melodies.
22-8178 30 min. $24.95

• Rhythm of Resistance: Black South African Music Under Apartheid

This takes you across forbidden boundaries of apartheid to experience the authentic joy and sorrow of black South African music.
22-8179 30 min. $24.95

• Spirit of Samba: Black Music of Brazil

This offers a glimpse of such major stars as Gilberto Gil and Milson Nascimento and enters areas tourists are warned to avoid.
22-8180 30 min. $24.95

• Roots, Rock, Reggae: Inside the Jamaican Music Scene

Take a rare look into the roots of reggae, featuring performances and interviews with Jimmy Cliff, Bob Marley, Toots and the Maytals and more.
22-8181 30 min. $24.95

• Chase the Devil: Religious Music of the Appalachian Mountains

In the remote backwaters of the Appalachians, two powerful forces, music and religion, animate people's lives. "Chase the Devil" delves into the region's intense preaching and singing.
22-8182 30 min. $24.95

• There'll Always Be Stars in the Sky: Indian Film Music Phenomenon

This video takes you behind the scenes of India's booming "Hollywood" where you'll meet the stars, singers and directors in the studios, on the sets and in the streets.
22-8183 30 min. $24.95

• Tex-Mex: Music of the Texas-Mexican Borderlands

Tex-Mex music, an exuberant style with a Mexican soul and a rock 'n' roll heart, is a joyful, energetic party music with lyrics commenting on social issues.
22-8184 60 min. $24.95

• Salsa: Latin Pop Music Scene

This captures the influence and essence of this joyful music.
22-8185 60 min. $24.95

Beyond the Mind's Eye

Beyond is a surreal voyage bridging the gap between reality and imagination. Travel through the inner depths of the human psyche. Music by Jan Hammer
22-8208 45 min. $19.95

BUDDY RICH MEMORIAL SCHOLARSHIP CONCERT:

Six of the world's finest drummers came together with the Buddy Rich Big Band to honor Buddy Rich. The historic event was taped live at the Wiltern Theater in Los Angeles.

• Volume I

Offers brilliant playing and solos by Louie Bellson, Gregg Bissonette, and Dennis Chambers with the big band.
22-8214 64 min. $49.95

• **Volume II**
Features classic performances and solos by Vinnie Colaiuta, Steve Gadd, and Dave Weckl along with the band.
22-8215 64 min. $49.95

• **Volume III**
Features Neil Pert, Smitty Smith, and Steve Smith plus a duet by Smitty and Steve.
22-8216 73 min. $49.95

• **Volume IV**
Features Omar Hakim, Wil Calhoun, and Neil Pert.
22-8217 60 min. $49.95

Black and Tan: Duke Ellington and St. Louis Blues: Bessie Smith
Two great music videotapes in one: Duke Ellington's first screen appearance in only the second year of sound. And Bessie Smith singing the blues in a smoked filled speakeasy in the late 20's, her only film.
22-195 36 min. $19.95

Bob Marley and the Wailers
When Bob Marley, the king of reggae, died in 1981, popular music lost one of its most creative forces. His influence on rock music was immense. This cassette brings back one of the last live concerts given by Bob Marley.
22-793 60 min. $19.95

Bobby Short at the Cafe Carlyle
Join Bobby at the Cafe Carlyle for this thrilling 25-song set, delivered with his usual verve and charm. He also invites us into his home for an exclusive and intimate look at the man behind the music.
22-781 75 min. $29.95

Canyon Consort
Join the Paul Winter Consort in the Grand Canyon as they improvise, rehearse and record music that responds to the magic and mystery of the canyon. The film begins with the Consort recording in one of the largest gothic cathedrals in the world, St. John The Divine, in New York City. It concludes with the Consort riding the powerful white rapids while we hear music inspired by the experience - transcendental music that, in Paul's words, "is of the canyon rather than about it."
22-291 42 min. $19.95

Christmas Across America
This is a musical portrait depicting some of the ways this most holy and joyous of holidays is celebrated in the United States. With all of your favorite carols and hymns, this is the perfect inspirational experience for the Christmas holidays.
22-9112 40 min. $29.95

Christmas Carol Video
The joys of Christmas come alive in this enchanting musical videocassette. Snowy country landscapes, stained glass, yule logs, snowmen, a sleigh ride and the bright happy faces of children. Features the choristers and cathedral singers of the Cathedral Church of Saint John the Divine.
22-1835 30 min. $19.95

Classical Christmas
An opulent presentation that places the most treasured classical Christmas music to the sights of the holiday season.
22-1685 30 min. $19.95

Dances From the Casbah
A collage of four works, explores new dimensions in mid-eastern dance. This features Kathyrn Ferguson and the Xanadu Dancers.
22-8000 48 min. $29.95

Danny Kaleikini:A Very Special Aloha
Hawaii's "Ambassador of Aloha" presents Hawaii in his own special way. Danny narrates this one-hour special filled with the music of the islands. The beauty of Hawaii comes alive in Danny's musical tribute to his island home.
32-241 60 min. $49.95

Don Ho: In Love with Hawaii
Don Ho presents a love letter to Hawaii, Combining his favorite Hawaiian songs with breathtaking footage.
32-005 30 min. $49.95

Edith Piaf: La Vie en Rose
Here is Piaf's life story told through archival footage and the recollections of her friends, from her beginnings as a street singer to stardom in the boites of Paris.
22-8096 58 min. $39.95

Fela in Concert
Recorded live in Paris in June 1981, during an all-night concert, this extraordinary program features the music of the famous Nigerian musician and composer Fela Anikulapo Kuti and The Africa 70. Fela is the most celebrated black musician today and a revolutionary, cultural and political symbol, often misunderstood by the Western mind. A charismatic performer, Fela projects the imperial trappings of power. He has assembled over 20 musicians and six singers in a performance that is punctuated by the exotic and highly suggestive tribal dances and rituals performed on stage by his 15 wives. Fela has recorded more than 50 albums.
22-417 57 min. $29.95

Further on Down the Road
Here is genuine house-rocking' music. Digitally

recorded live at Carnegie Hall and on locations around the country. Guitar playing legends perform together for the first time and tell about the long road to this historic night. Features Albert Collins, Lonnie Mack and Roy Buchanan.
22-2218 90 min. $29.95

Flamenco
A magnificent panorama of Flamenco and it's performers, for whom the rhythms and lyrics are inherited folklore and part of daily life--but the techniques are studied.
22-8095 55 min. $39.95

Gil Evans and His Orchestra
In this 1983 live concert from Switzerland, Gil Evans conducts a 20-piece orchestra interpreting his arrangements of Gershwin, Charlie Mingus, Theolonius Monk and Jimi Hendrix, as well as his own compositions. Soloists include Michael and Randy Brecker, Lew Soloff, Howard Johnons, John Clark, Mike Manieri and Billy Cobham.
22-708 57 min. $29.95

Greenpeace: Non-Toxic Video Hits
Greenpeace, an organization dedicated to preserving the environment and improving global ecological conditions, is the inspiration for this program. Features 14 of today's top recording artists including Tears For Fears, Peter Gabriel and George Harrison.
22-255 59 min. $29.95

Grokgazer
A video concert of moving forms and colors that will help you feel more relaxed and harmonious. Scored with original sound by Tod Rundgren.
22-8149 40 min. $29.95

Hawaii's Magic: Prince Lot Hula Festival
This made-for-TV special captures some of the magical moments of 11 Halu Hula (dance schools) from Hawaii at the 1985 Prince Lot Festival.
32-242 80 min. $39.95

Heartland Reggae
The immortal Bob Marley is joined by Peter Tosh and a dozen other reggae stars in his only concert film. It delves into the philosophy behind the music and provides a rich musical documentary of a classic concert.
22-124 90 min. $29.95

Hugh Shannon: Saloon Singer
When Billy Holiday heard Hugh Shannon for the first time, she said to him "Man, you don't sound like nobody. You gotta sing. "However, it was John S. Wilson of the New York Times who dubbed him "saloon singer." from New York to

Paris to Capri, Spain and the French Riviera, he has performed around the world. Counts and movie stars, millionaires and musicians have all cried for more as he entertained them into the wee small hours of the morning. He weaves magic in this live performance from David K's in New York.
22-420 42 min. $29.95

In Our Hands
James Taylor, Carly Simon, Peter, Paul and Mary; and other notable performers, join with Meryl Steep, Dr. Helen Caldicott and others, in this 1982 concert for peace and nuclear disarmament, staged in New York's Central Park.
22-129 90 min. $29.95

Jacques Brel
The life and music of the inimitable French composer-singer, the tough Parisian with the guitar, who looked life in the eye unflinchingly.
22-8094 58 min. $39.95

JUDY GARLAND IN CONCERT:

• Volume 1
A 1964 television special, singing favorites, such as "That's Entertainment," "Liza" and others.
22-161 60 min. $29.95

• Volume 2
The second of Judy's celebrated television concerts features many of her classics.
22-162 60 min. $29.95

Julie Andrews Sings her Favorite Songs
Join Julie in a live concert evening of the songs she made famous on the stage and in motion pictures as well as those songs which she loves. Featuring such classics as: "Camelot","The Sound of Music" and "On A Clear Day".
22-9996 60 min. $29.95

Lena Horne: The Lady and Her Music
Here's Lena's classic renditions as performed in her broadway show.
22-165 134 min. $39.95

Mabel Mercer: A Singer's Singer
"Miss Mercer is the grande dam of popular song," said John S. Wilson of the New York Times. "The audience sat transfixed, sensing her wit and supernatural class, felling her discipline and craftsmanship, being touched by her sorcery," said Rex Reed. This 17-song set, shot at Cleo's in New York, captures her vocal artistry. Her matchless phrasing gives new dimension to some of the greatest songs ever written, and she is the quintessence of New York night life.
22-419 42 min. $29.95

MUSICAL CLASSICS FOR CHILDREN:

• Adventures of Peer Gynt
Follow Peer Gynt into an enchanting world of witches, trolls and animals as award-winning puppeteer Jim Gamble creates a delightful marionette story. Based on the classic story by Henrick Ibsen.
22-8021 30 min. $14.95

• Nutcracker
Based on the classical musical tale by Peter Tchaikovsky and performed by The Berlin Symphony Orchestra, this wonderful puppet performance will charm children of all ages.
22-8022 30 min. $14.95

• Carnival of the Animals
Based on the classical musical story by Carmille Saint-Saens and accompanied by a full orchestra, this wonderful puppet performance will enchant children of all ages.
22-8023 30 min. $14.95

• Peter & the Wolf
Based on Sergei Prokofiev's famous musical work, Peter & the Wolf features a wide variety of puppet characters portraying people, animals, and animated instruments accompanied by the Hamburg Symphony Orchestra.
22-8024 30 min. $14.95

Photonos
Emmy Award winning "Emerald Web" in an hour of swirling laser graphics and stunning music.
22-8159 60 min. $19.95

ROMANY TRAIL GYPSY SERIES:
Join in the search for the lost Gypsy tribes and their music, from different parts of the Europe and Africa.

• Gypsy Music Into Africa
This searches for the lost gypsy tribe of Egypt. Along the way, you meet gypsy dancing girls, magicians, acrobats, fortune tellers and even mystics conducting an exorcism.
22-8175 60 min. $24.95

• Gypsy Music Into Europe
This video takes you to India to find the original gypsy families and the music from that area.
22-8176 60 min. $24.95

Sentimental Journey
The late Pearl Bailey hosts "Sentimental Journey", a trio of specials dedicated to some of the greatest moments in musical television. Featured are classic performances by many of the giants of the music industry in the 1960's.
22-8152 147 min. $29.95

True North: Discover the Spirit of the North
A timeless journey into the expanse of the northern wilds. This video will transport you over mammoth glaciers, along rugged coastlines, into primeval forests and through time. Featuring music by: Tangerine Dream, James Reynolds, John Serrie and Paul Speer.
22-8209 45 min. $19.95

We Shall Overcome
This traces the fascinating story of how an old slave spiritual was transformed into a labor organizing song before becoming the well known anthem of the civil rights movement. Early versions reveal the role played by both Black and White musicians in transforming the song that helped bring an end to segregation.
22-9223 58 min. $19.95

Great Performances

Right In Your Own

Living Room!

VIDEO TITLES LISTED IN THIS GUIDE ARE AVAILABLE FOR PURCHASE OR RENTAL. CONTACT YOUR LOCAL VIDEO STORE OR TELEPHONE (800) 383-8811

ORDER FORM

Name _____ Phone ( ) _____

Company Name _____

Address _____

City _____ State _____ Zip _____

NOTE: All addresses must include street name for UPS delivery.

Please send me the following items:

ITEM	QTY	TITLE	PRICE
PC COMPATIBLE COMPUTER DISK		The Complete Guide To Special Interest Videos $69.95 + $4.00 Shipping. *Specify 3 1/2 or 5 1/4*	
CD-ROM		The Complete Guide To Special Interest Videos $69.95 + $4.00 Shipping.	
GUIDE		The Complete Guide To Special Interest Videos $19.95 + $2.50 Shipping.	

SHIPPING CHARGES
Purchases: $4.00 for first tape, plus $1.50 for each additional tape. Alaska and Hawaii residents, add $1.00 for each tape.

Please make your check or money order payable to: **Video Learning Library.**

SUBTOTAL	
(Sales Tax 6.7% AZ)	
SHIPPING	
TOTAL	

☐ Please send me the 110-page book entitled **Selling Special Interest Videos As A Profitable Home-Based Business** @ $39.95 + $4.00 shipping.

✔ **Telephone Orders:** Call 800-383-8811 toll-free. Visa, MasterCard, Discover, American Express

✔ **FAX:** (602) 596-9973

✔ **Mail Orders:** Video Learning Library, 15838 N. 62nd Street, Scottsdale, AZ 85254

✔ **Payment:** ☐ Check   ☐ Visa   ☐ MasterCard   ☐ Discover   ☐ AMEX

Credit Card #: _____ **Expires** _____

Signature: _____

Please allow 4-6 weeks for delivery

Nature
&
Environment

✓ *Oceans & Coastline*
✓ *Wilderness & Preserves*
✓ *Wildlife & Zoos*
✓ *Miscellaneous*

Oceans & Coastline

Ocean Waves
Landlocked? Or don't you get down to the ocean as often as you'd like? Well, now you can! White caps, breakers, crashing water! A real-time view of Pacific Ocean waves for ocean lovers everywhere!
14-009 60 min. $19.95

Solitudes: Wave Watching
14-1671 30 min. $24.95

Surf
Let the surf's gentle rippling against the Pacific coastline transcend your mood while you watch seagulls quietly sitting atop one of the hugh rocks in this peaceful setting. Music combined with sounds of ocean waves add to this relaxing program.
14-016 60 min. $19.95

Wilderness & Preserves

Alaska Stories
Alaska Stories is docu-drama about the human experience. It is about quest and discovery. It is about the unexpected. Watch as the past and present merge together in this moving and compact production.
14-8061 47 min. $39.95

AMERICAN VISIONS
These stunning videos are portraits of America's most visited National Parks.

• **Acadia**
14-6145 30 min. $19.95

• **Great Smokey Mountains**
14-6143 30 min. $19.9

• **Olympic**
14-6144 30 min. $19.95

Acadia National Park and Cape Cod National Seashore
Two programs in one! In this nature-oriented National Park Service program, you will explore glacier-carved Acadia National Park, where forest-draped mountains descend to the sea. Next, travel to charming Cape Cod, where a special blend of natural beauty and historical heritage make it one of the East Coast's most special places.
32-151 30 min. $29.95

Arches
Experience the rich geological gifts and photographic challenges of southern Utah's Arches National Monument. Learn how wind, sand and water collaborated to create the park's panorama of freestanding stone arches, rock formations and gullies.
32-311 30 min. $19.95

Bent's Old Fort & Great Sand Dunes National Monument
Bent's Fort a Castle on the Plain - a story of Indians, of Mountain men and of Texas and Mexico during war and peace. Also features the Great Sand Dunes in Colorado- -geology in motion, nature's mystifying processes creating dunes up to 700 feet high.
32-154 46 min. $29.95

Big Bend National Park, Texas
Explore the remote beauty of Big Bend's rugged Chisos Mountains, vast Chihuahuan Desert wilderness and river-carved canyons along the Rio Grande. Discover the tremendous variety of wildlife and plants, the park's spectacular hiking trails and its incredible geology.
32-295 30 min. $29.95

Bryce/Zion National Park
Enjoy the beauty and splendor of Utah's finest. See Nature's handiwork in Bryce's pinnacle formation and its natural bridges. Enjoy Zion's mighty canyons and cliffs accented by the colorful beauty of Fall. Experience the fury of passing lightning storms and the gentle side of nature, beautiful rainbows, spectacular sunrises and sunsets.
14-2215 60 min. $29.95

Bryce, Zion & Grand Canyon's North Rim
This program lets you visit the most popular features of these three treasured national parks, with the emphasis on Bryce and Zion in Utah. From the fairy-land pinnacles of Bryce to the towering monoliths of Zion, you will enjoy the very best of each park. Includes spectacular vistas overlooking the North Rim of the Grand Canyon.
14-025 25 min. $29.95

California Big Sur
This is considered by many to be the most scenic stretch of coastline in America. Many artists and poets have made Big Sur their home, and for good reason. The natural setting provides beauty, peace and inspiration, key ingredients for artistic

expression. Feel the excitement of passing storms and pounding waves crashing on the cliffs. Enjoy magnificent sunsets as you explore Big Sur from San Simeon to Monterey.
14-001 60 min. $29.95

Carlsbad Caverns
Carlsbad Caverns is one of the most inspiring sights in the entire world. It is a place of rare beauty and a place of discovery. Journey into the caverns' depths with this unique video expedition. Filmed in cooperation with the National Park Service. A fascinating and educational video tour.
14-028 20 min. $29.95

Chrono's
This epic visual music journey captures more than 50 of the world's greatest wonders including the Sphinx, the Great Pyramids and the Vatican. Transcend history form the cradle of civilization to modern day Paris.
14-9680 40 min. $19.95

Death Valley
Come with us on enjoyable and educational visit to Death Valley. Learn of its geological treasures and of man's struggle to survive here. Indians, the early settlers, the Borax Boom, Scotty's Castle, Dante's View, Devil's Golf Course, Artist's Pallet and more. Includes complete tour of Scotty's Castle. National Park Service-approved.
32-334 26 min. $29.95

Denali Wilderness, Alaska
Set amidst the pristine wilderness of Denali National Park, this award-winning program lets you join moose, wolves, grizzly bears and caribou in a four-season struggle for survival. Outstanding photography of an incredible landscape. Dramatic life-or-death sequences as predators and prey struggle for survival.
24-038 30 min. $29.95

Desert Vision
The renewal of life after a desert rain... sparkling stalactites dripping in the deep recesses of a cave. "Desert Vision" takes you on a phenomenal visual/musical journey over and through ten magnificent national parks and monuments in the desert southwest. From an eagle's point of view you will soar over mesas, along cliffs and through arches, guided by the original music of David Lanz and Paul Speer.
14-1777 50 min. $29.95

Empire of the Red Bear
Explore the breathtaking landscape of Russia as few have ever seen it in this two tape set. See unspoiled landscapes, active volcanoes and the largest forest on earth.
14-8074 180 min. $39.95

ESPN EXPEDITION SERIES:
This exciting series features nature and wildlife at their "wildest". Interesting and educational programs for the whole family.

- **Africa's Cat's: Fight for Life**
  14-8051 48 min. $16.95

- **Bio Bio: Lost River of Mapuchi**
  14-8052 48 min. $16.95

- **Cocos Island: Treasure Island**
  14-8060 48 min. $16.95

- **Earth Winds: The Test Flight**
  14-8058 48 min. $16.95

- **Grand Canyon: River of Dreams**
  14-8057 48 min. $16.95

- **Himalayas: Kingdom of Sherpa**
  14-8053 48 min. $16.95

- **Nameless Tower**
  14-8049 48 min. $16.95

- **Sharks: Predators in Peril**
  14-8054 48 min. $16.95

- **Soviet Union: Rafting to Freedom**
  14-8055 48 min. $16.95

- **Timbuktu: Off the Wall**
  14-8056 48 min. $16.95

Giant Sequoias
Largest of all living things! Learn about these amazing trees and their relationships with other forest inhabitants. In this excellent nature-oriented program, you will experience the splendor of the Giant Sequoia groves found in Sequoia and Yosemite National Parks. Produced by the National Park Service.
14-032 30 min. $29.95

Glacier National Park
In this breath-taking program, you will discover a land where sunshine plays on snow-shrouded peaks, where waterfalls dance downward and crisp mountain air sends shimmers across countless emerald lakes. Glacier National Park is carved by glaciers, and dominated by massive peaks and endless forests. Spectacular wildlife, wildflowers, geology and scenery are here for you to learn about and enjoy!
32-298 30 min. $29.95

VIDEO TITLES LISTED IN THIS GUIDE ARE AVAILABLE FOR PURCHASE OR RENTAL. CONTACT YOUR LOCAL VIDEO STORE OR TELEPHONE (800) 383-8811

Grand Canyon & Petrified Forest

Capture the Grand Canyon experience. Spectacular vistas, summer thunderstorms, raft and mule expeditions and the ever-changing moods of the canyon walls. Plus, visit the petrified Forest National Park - Arizona's prehistoric wonder. Learn of a once-lush topical jungle where dinosaurs roamed. Includes the Painted Desert.
14-033 45 min. $29.95

Grand Canyon National Park

This video travel experience takes you on a tour of the popular South Rim of the Grand Canyon with breathtaking aerial shots from season to season, as well as fascinating on-land views. You'll see sunrises and sunsets and out-of-the-way waterfalls, all accompanied by classical music arranged for maximum enjoyment and relaxation. No Narration is used.
32-223 45 min. $29.95

Grand Canyon

Go on the most incredible and breathtaking helicopter journey of your life as you sweep through the Grand Canyon itself! You'll enter the deepest chasms and narrowest gorges; zoom over rapids inches above the water; and sweep majestically into panoramic heights as you listen to Tchaikovsky, Wagner, Metheny and Jarre. Truly a magnificent way to witness one of the world's greatest natural wonders--and safe, too!
14-005 60 min. $29.95

Grand Tetons

Western Wyoming's picturesque mountain range and Snake River provide breathtaking scenery and inspiring messages. Experience the incredible beauty and contrasts of the Snake River, from a rollicking float trip to serene moments on the valley floor near Jackson Hole. Feel for the next hand or foothold as you climb the Grand Tetons under your own power. The park offers an infinite array of possibilities for human enjoyment.
32-312 30 min. $24.95

Glacier National Park

The majestic grandeur of the many glaciers, emerald lakes and streams creates a magical feeling, as if all of nature's gems were gathered and placed in this magnificent park.
14-2667 57 min. $29.95

INFINITE VOYAGE SERIES:

• Search for Ancient Americans

The secrets of our own past are unlocked during this search for ancient civilizations in the America's. Relive the excitement of five astounding discoveries
that became archeological landmarks.
14-8090 58 min. $19.95

• Keepers of Eden

This environmentally conscious video takes you on a tour of innovative zoos and parks that are struggling to stop the onslaught of our rapidly disintegrating species of wildlife.
14-8091 58 min. $19.95

• Living with Disaster

This timely video takes a fascinating look at the ongoing effort scientists are employing to be able to predict when and where disasters, such as earthquakes, volcanoes and hurricanes will occur.
14-8092 58 min. $19.95

Kilauea Volcano

Experience close-up the awesome majesty of Hawaii's Kilauea volcano in full eruption, accompanied by stirring background music. Impossible to believe until you've seen it.
14-006 30 min. $39.95

LIVING PLANET SERIES:

This is the ultimate guided tour of planet earth. A video expedition that educates as it entertains, led by one of the world's foremost natural scientists, David Attenbourough. This award-winning BBC/Time-Life Video production lets you steal into a hibernating bear's den, wade with piranhas and crawl across glaciers. Attenbourough's enormous enthusiasm and offbeat personality makes the complicated concepts seem simple.

• Baking Deserts
14-8082 60 min. $99.95

• Building of the Earth
14-8077 60 min. $99.95

• Community of the Skies
14-8083 60 min. $99.95

• Frozen Forests
14-8078 60 min. $99.95

• Jungle
14-8080 60 min. $99.95

• Margins of the Land
14-8085 60 min. $99.95

• New Worlds
14-8088 60 min. $99.95

• Northern World
14-8079 60 min. $99.95

• Oceans
14-8087 60 min. $99.95

• **Sea of Grass**
14-8081 60 min. $99.95

• **Sweet Fresh Water**
14-8084 60 min. $99.95

• **Worlds Apart**
14-8086 60 min. $99.95

Loon Country By Canoe: Solitudes
For ears and eyes abused by the 20th Century, this tape provides a wilderness refuge. Enjoy the steady stroke of the paddle, pushing and slicing cool waters. Rest tired eyes with wilderness green, and embers glowing in the late night campfire. Hear water sounds, songs of birds, the wail of a timber wolf, wind through the trees, thunderous skies and the echoing cry of the loon. No narration.
14-048 30 min. $29.95

LORNE GREENE'S WILDERNESS
Lorne Greene hosts this series of nature programs covering animals from a wide variety of environments worldwide, from Japan to Colorado to Yugoslavia and many other beautiful and exotic locations.

• **Close Encounters of the Deep Kind**
14-2008 30 min. $16.95

• **Enchanted Forest**
14-2024 30 min. $16.95

• **Huntress**
14-2025 30 min. $16.95

• **Inky, Dinky Spider**
14-2013 30 min. $16.95

• **Love Story: Canada Goose**
14-2014 30 min. $16.95

• **Master Hunter**
10-102 60 min. $16.95

• **Tales of the Snow Monkey**
14-2026 30 min. $16.95

Meadows
The world's most beautiful meadows in springtime fill this program, taken in the High Sierras of Northern California. Relax as tall grass and trees blow in the wind to soothing music.
14-007 60 min. $29.95

Mount Rainier
Discover the scenic and geological wonders plus early pioneer history of this mountain paradise.

Washington State's Mt. Rainer National Park is the crown jewel of the Cascade Range. Lush forests of cedar, hemlock and fir flourish on its volcano born slopes. Learn the mysterious forces of nature which created this exquisite mountain.
32-026 28 min. $29.95

Mt. Rushmore and the Black Hills of South Dakota
Come explore Mt. Rushmore and the surrounding Black Hills with all its unique natural wonders and Old West heritage. This was the stomping grounds of Wild Bill Hickok, Calamity Jane and others. See the Badlands, Custer State Park, Wind Cave and more. Plus, learn the inspiring Rushmore story. Russ Finley photography.
32-168 30 min. $29.95

Mt. Rushmore: Four Faces on a Mountain
In this inspiring National Park Service film, you will see the faces of Presidents Washington, Jefferson, Lincoln and Roosevelt being carved from Mt. Rushmore in rare black and white film. Plus, see the struggles and challenges that each of these four great presidents overcame to help make our great nation what it is today.
32-027 30 min. $29.95

National Monuments of Southern Arizona
Explore the splendid scenery and fascinating natural and cultural history of several national Park Service locations in southern Arizona. Visit Saguaro, Organ Pipe Cactus, Tonto, Tumacacori, Chiracahua, Casa Grande, Coronado and Fort Bowie.
32-282 30 min. $29.95

Natural States
A beautiful visual tribute to the rivers, lakes, snowy peaks, valleys and ocean shores of the Northwest. This is a restful land and air excursion enhanced by trick photography, mirrored images, the gliding Steadicam Camera, slow and fast motion.
14-036 45 min. $29.95

Nature's Serenade
Savor the seasons. Revel in the changes they bring to the spectacular natural world of our national parks. Enjoy it through magical film footage set to the lilting musical seasonings of Venetian composer Antonio Vivaldi's, "The Four Seasons".
14-8000 60 min. $29.95

Nature's Symphony
Nature's Symphony is a program which explores water's natural paths, from wintry alpine lakes and

roaring waterfalls in Yosemite National Park to geysers and bubbling pots in Yellowstone. Viewers relax in lush spring meadows, blanketed with colorful flowers. The journey continues downstream through precipitous granite river canyons that open onto spectacular desert sunsets in the Grand Canyon. And along the way, elk, moose chipmunks, birds and other native creatures add to the visual exhilaration of this program.
14-5888 60 min. $29.95

Olympic Range
Experience the variable moods and majestic rain forest of Olympic National Park on the rocky, northwest coast of Washington State. Lose yourself in lush overgrown streams, broad alpine meadows, snow-covered mountains, unspoiled stretches of ocean beach, and majestic cedars and firs shrouded with fog.
32-314 30 min. $24.95

Rivers
Winding rivers flow gently by you in this soothing nature video. The only sound comes from the rivers themselves.
14-011 60 min. $19.95

Rivers of Fire
This is the official National Park Service documentation of the 1984 eruption of Mauna Loa Volcano in Hawaii's Volcanoes National Park. Spectacular shots of volcanic eruption.
32-236 30 min. $39.95

Shenandoah: The Gift
Shenandoah National Park is a symbol of renewal, or reclaiming an exploited land. Here is a hidden jewel, tucked away in the sleepy hollows of Virginia's mountains. Through amazing black and white footage, see Shenandoah as it was developed in the 1920's and 30's. Visit CCC camps and see President Franklin Roosevelt deliver a memorable dedication speech.
32-170 20 min. $29.95

Story of America's Canyon Country
This video features untamed landscape encompassing four states: Utah, Arizona, Colorado and New Mexico. Visit Monument Valley, Cedar Breaks, Canyonlands, Arches, Capitol Reef and Lake Powell and hear the story of America's truly wild West.
14-8011 60 min. $29.95

Streams
Watch and listen as beautiful mountain streams and creeks wind their way thought crevices of the High Sierras. Natural wildlife sounds complement this viewing experience.
14-015 60 min. $19.95

Teton Country: Grand Teton National Park
Set in Wyoming's Grand Teton National Park, this nature-oriented video program lets you explore the park's incredible wildlife and breathtaking landscapes from a wholly natural perspective. No roads, no cars - just the fantastic wilderness and wildlife for which the park is noted. See moose, elk, buffalo, bear, marmot and more.
32-171 30 min. $29.95

Touring America's National Parks
Celebrate America's national parks with a video journey through the scenic beauty of the nation's greatest natural treasures. You'll visit: Acadia, Mt. Rainer, the Olympics, Mesa Verde, the Everglades, Crater Lake, Carlsbad Caverns, and others, as well as the most popular parks: Yellowstone, the Grand Canyon and Yosemite.
32-264 60 min. $29.95

Vanishing Wilderness
German photographer Heinz Sielman uses his camera to capture the magnificence of the North American wilderness and its many species of wildlife.
14-2822 90 min. $19.95

Walk in the Forest
Journey into the heart of America's rain forests: the old-growth of the Pacific Northwest. Feel the warmth of summer, the terror of fire and the blessing of rain. This video portrait details the delicate balance of plants and animals that make this region a living whole.
14-8047 30 min. $24.95

Wilderness Rhapsody
Let your mind relax and your spirits soar as nature's magic unfolds accompanied by the inspiring selections of Mozart, Beethoven, Handel, Tchaikovsky, Grieg and Strauss. A gratifying orchestration of light and music flora and fauna.
14-8001 31 min. $29.95

Yellowstone Fire
It was the worst fire since 1910. The Yellowstone National Park Fire destroyed over 1 million acres, and caused untold millions of dollars in damages. This amazing video, filmed with the help of the US Forest Service, shows dramatic close-up footage of the largest fire in US history. View aerial shots of such intense force they put you right on the fire line!
14-7050 30 min. $19.95

Yellowstone in Winter
Yellowstone is the largest and oldest national park,

VIDEO TITLES LISTED IN THIS GUIDE ARE AVAILABLE FOR PURCHASE OR RENTAL. CONTACT YOUR LOCAL VIDEO STORE OR TELEPHONE (800) 383-8811

and famous for its magnificent geysers. Two million people visit Yellowstone every summer. But, beyond the crowds and cars, there's a Yellowstone that few of us ever see. It's a spectacular place that belongs to the wildlife, a challenging place where animals struggle desperately to survive and it's a place that up until now only the animals have known.
14-1566 60 min. $19.98

Wild Australia
This is a wildlife adventure through the wonders down under, tracing the history of animals rarely seen even by Australians. You will also learn revealing little-known facts about well-known animals.
14-2669 60 min. $29.95

Yellowstone
A photographic study of the world's first national park. Explore Yellowstone's rock formations, geyser activity, plant life and wildlife. Begin to understand the fragility of the park's ecosystem in this vast thermal basin, as seen through a naturalist's eyes.
32-316 30 min. $24.95

Yellowstone & Grand Teton
Discover the wonders and wildlife in two of America's most inspiring parks. Yellowstone, a geological showcase, features the most spectacular geyser field in the world. See Old Faithful, emerald hot pools and more. Grand Teton simply features the most dramatic mountain landscape found anywhere. This video features great wildlife photography.
14-041 42 min. $29.95

Yellowstone National Park
As one of America's most popular parks, Yellowstone abounds in wildlife, incredible sights including Old Faithful. Included also is the majestic Grand Tetons mountain range with its rugged peaks, and beautiful lakes and streams. You'll experience the park from season to season, so sit back and relax to the sights and sounds of Yellowstone National Park.
14-022 60 min. $29.95

Yosemite National Park
Here you'll find soothing relaxing images of cascading waterfalls, flowing rivers and spellbinding videography of the changing seasons. See Yosemite as never seen before, viewed from the air, from a raft, and at the top of its famous waterfalls. Take a deep breath and relax as these powerful images and beautiful music invigorate your own passion for life.
14-023 60 min. $29.95

Wildlife & Zoos

AFRICA ARMCHAIR SAFARI SERIES:
Learn a new way of "seeing" wildlife. "Look" at the animals like a safari guide. "Hear" like a wildlife researcher.

• Masai Mara Lions/Virunga Gorillas
Masai Mara Reserve in Kenya is the best place in the world to see lions. Visit them in the middle of their summer feasting. Trek to the Virunga Mountains of Rwanda into the domain of the endangered mountain gorilla. See the dominant silverback males and the warm family community they so zealously protect.
14-8043 45 min. $29.95

• Serengeti Migration/Amboseli Elephants
See thousands of zebra, wildebeest and Thomson's gazelle follow ancient rarils in their annual quest for fresh pasture. Visit the elephants of Amboseli National Park in Kenya. Learn the behavioral links that bind elephant society.
14-8044 45 min. $29.95

ALL ABOUT ANIMALS ACADEMIC SERIES FOR CHILDREN:
Youngsters are introduced to the amazing world of animal behavior and adaptation. Concepts are introduced in songs that children can learn to sing, and key works are captioned on screen to expand children's vocabulary.

• Amphibians
01-8014 10 min. $49.95

• Birds
01-8015 10 min. $49.95

• Dolphins: Our Friends From the Sea
01-8017 10 min. $49.95

• Fish
01-8016 10 min. $49.95

• Mammals
01-8013 10 min. $49.95

• Miracle of Reproduction
01-8018 15 min. $49.95

• **Microbes: Bacteria and Fungi**
01-8019 17 min. $49.95

• **Reptiles**
01-8012 10 min. $49.95

• **Seasons: A Year of Change**
01-8020 15 min. $49.95

ANIMALS OF AFRICA SERIES:
As you travel to the pulsating African Continent, you will witness exquisite photography of animal life in its natural habitat filmed over a 10 year period.

• **Africa in Flight**
24-9414 70 min. $16.95

• **Between Two Worlds**
24-9420 70 min. $16.95

• **Big Cats of the Kalahari**
24-9412 70 min. $16.95

• **From the Sky to the Sea**
24-9417 70 min. $16.95

• **Hippos, Baboons & African Elephants**
24-9413 70 min. $16.95

• **Impalas, Wildebeests & the Gemsbok**
24-9416 70 min. $16.95

• **Land of the Elephants**
24-9418 70 min. $16.95

• **Paths of Survival**
24-9419 70 min. $16.95

• **Reserve**
24-9416 70 min. $16.95

• **Wondrous Works of Nature**
24-9420 70 min. $16.95

Attracting Birds to Your Backyard with Roger T. Peterson
In lyrical motion footage, this cassette visits over 80 species of North American birds who accept relationships with us.
14-2058 60 min. $29.95

AUDUBON SOCIETY'S VIDEO GUIDE TO THE BIRDS OF NORTH AMERICA SERIES
Written, produced and narrated by acclaimed naturalist Michael Godfrey, this video series covers all the birds of North America. Includes still photos and moving film footage by the world's greatest bird photographers, including Porter, Eisenstaedt, Pettinggill, Greenwalt, Goldman and the Cruickshanks. Introduction by Roger Tory Peterson, author of the celebrated Field Guide to the Birds of North America. You will not only see and hear each bird in flight, but through special multi-vision animation techniques, see them dive, feed and play above and below the waterline. Complete descriptions and animated range maps showing each bird's migration patterns completes this first-of-its-kind video guide.

• **Volume 1**
Features 116 species of loons, grebes, pelicans and their allies, swans, geese and ducks, hawks, vultures and falcons and chicken-like birds (pheasants, grouse, quails, ptarmigans).
24-010 94 min. $74.95

• **Volume 2**
Features 105 species of water birds including herons and egrets, cranes, shorebirds, gulls, terns and alcids.
24-2637 76 min. $74.95

• **Volume 3**
Features 77 species of pigeons and doves, cuckoos, owls, nighthawks, hummingbirds and swifts, trogons, kingfishers and woodpeckers.
24-2638 61 min. $74.95

• **Volume 4: Songbirds I**
Features 98 species of flycatchers, larks, swallows, crows and jays, titmice and chickadees, nuthatches, creepers, wrens, thrushes, waxwings, shrikes, thrashers and vireos.
24-2639 75 min. $74.95

• **Volume 5: Songbirds II**
Features 109 species of warblers, orioles and blackbirds, tanagers, grosbeaks, finches, buntings and sparrows.
24-2640 80 min. $74.95

Awesome Bucks
Filmed entirely on location in Nevada, Colorado and Utah, concentrating on antler spreads from 26 inches to 38 inches. Large Muleys are shown in velvet antler stage with many abnormal points and cheaters.
14-5667 45 min. $39.95

Bighorn Sheep: Their Life Story
Follow the life cycle of the majestic bighorn sheep with stunning footage of the animals throughout the different phases of their life cycle. Filmed throughout the Rocky Mountain region.
24-2685 60 min. $29.95

BIRDS SERIES:

The grandeur of great birds of prey; the spectacle of thousands of wading birds turning in unison above the water; the miracle of naked, newly hatched chicks--just a few of the sequences that will have you spellbound in these award winning programs.

• Concerning Swans

All the beauty and serene majesty of swans is captured in this award-winning program.
24-8013 60 min. $29.95

• Feathered Athletes

This program examines the swiftest and most agile members of the bird world, relating their abilities to the skills of our Olympic athletes.
24-8012 60 min. $29.95

• Getting to Know Birds

Are you a beginning bird watcher? Let this video start you off on an exciting pastime that will last throughout your life.
24-8016 60 min. $29.95

• Little Owl's Story

This enchanting program documents the life of a little owl called Athene. From her birth to her courtship, we see how Athene learns how to contend with life's hazards.
24-8015 60 min. $29.95

• Migration of Birds: Flight for Survival

Migration is one of the mysteries and marvels of the bird world. This feature maps out the journeys made by migrating birds which are indeed "flights for survival".
24-8009 60 min. $29.95

• Talons, Beaks and Nests

This show examines a variety of birds and how their talons, beaks, and nest have adapted to fit their particular environment.
24-8008 60 min. $29.95

• Year of the Stork

The striking beauty of the white stork, the legendary "bringer of babies", has inspired man since the earliest of times. This program follows the daily lives of a family of storks in northern Germany, We soar effortlessly alongside them as they migrate southward to feed alongside the game animals of the African plains.
24-8014 60 min. $29.95

EAGLES INTERNATIONAL

These award-winning programs, filmed on five continents, reveal the variety, beauty and secrets of the world's supreme birds of prey. Soaring in the upper air currents, with their hugh wings outstretched, eagles typify freedom, power and grandeur.

• Eagles: The Majestic Hunters
24-8005 60 min. $29.95

• Where Eagles Fly
24-8006 60 min. $29.95

Dolphin Touch

A very special relationship exists between humans and dolphins. This captivating documentary presents a number of cases where people have had first hand experiences with wild dolphins and the effects such an encounter had on them. The Dolphin Touch explores the future of the human-dolphin connection and the exciting possibility that we may one day learn to communicate directly with our friends in the sea.
14-5745 49 min. $24.95

Ducks Unlimited's Video Guide to Waterfowl and Game Birds

For the hunter and naturalist, accurate bird identification is a must in order to protect endangered species. This 75-minute video is a comprehensive system of sight and sound identification for the 43 species of waterfowl and 21 upland game birds. Wing beats are accurately animated to each bird's actual cycle and silhouetted flock formations aid identification in low light conditions.
24-9691 75 min. $39.95

Falcons of Arabia

Learn the centuries old trapping and training techniques of the world's best falconers. Witness the deadly air-to-air combat as the falconers and their elusive prey fight in a life and death struggle in the unforgiving desert.
24-8029 60 min. $49.95

Forgotten Wilderness with Stan Brock

Preservation of endangered species has been the life work of Stan Brock, seen here in a true story with beautiful, natural wildlife.
14-8002 67 min. $19.95

Friendly Gray Whales

Take a journey to the turquoise tranquility of Mexico's lagoons. Encounter these friendly whales and witness their peculiar habits. Their awesome size will fill you with wonder as sounds of their blows echo in your mind. Additionally, discover the pristine beauty of the islands off the west coast of Baja, Mexico and their unique wildlife including elephant seals, seabirds, and sea lions.
14-6597 30 min. $29.95

Friends From the Sea
For years the killer Whale has been a mystery of
the sea. Witness the whales in their natural settings
as well as in the sanctuary of an oceanarium. Join
the experts as they discuss and demonstrate the
behavior of the Killer Whale. This is a close-up
and fascinating glimpse of 4 tons of coordinated
flesh and muscle.
24-8034 30 min. $19.95

Humpbacks of Maui
A documentary about Pacific Humpback whales,
co-produced with the Pacific Whale Foundation.
24-2800 30 min. $39.95

In The Kingdom of Dolphins
In this definitive documentary, marine scientists
explore and research the dancer of the depths. This
program sets out to examine this most intelligent
and ancient creature of the sea.
24-8038 50 min. $39.95

Land of the Leopard
Travel with John Varty and Elmon Mhlongo as
they develop a unique relationship with a family of
wild leopards. Includes numerous segments
capturing much of Africa's unique wildlife.
24-2670 60 min. $29.95

LORNE GREENE'S NEW WILDERNESS

• Ascent of the Chimps
Take a trip to the Arnhem Zoo in the Netherlands,
where in 1971, they opened a chimpanzee
enclosure that accurately mimics the conditions of
the wild. Since then a whole generation of scientists
have watched the community develop. Remarkably,
this community has displayed all the dramatic
elements of any human community - love, power
struggles, reconciliation, and even murder!
24-1564 22 min. $16.95

• Frozen Eden
Journey to the vast Ungava Peninsula where the
world's last great caribou herds thunder over a
frozen Eden on their annual thousand mile
migration. You'll first meet the herd in winter
while they move along in small segregated groups
of male and female. For half the year, the females
are alone, fighting off the elements, until the males
catch up. Then the 500,000 head caribou herd
grazes on - only to separate again when winter
comes.
24-1563 22 min. $16.95

• Hunters of Chubut
Visit the rugged Atlantic coast of Argentina where
sea lions and penguins battle and breed in a packed
and frenzied colony. It's a beautiful, violent world,
where even these large hunters tall prey to the
biggest, most powerful predators on earth - the
killer whale!
24-1560 22 min. $16.95

• Master Hunter of the Night
Come explore the true nature of the fabled night
predator - the great horned owl. Meet Kay
McKeever, a pioneer in the rehabilitation of owls,
and see what happens when a male owl is injured,
and the effects the injury has on its family. You'll
be surprised at how much human and owl families
have in common!
24-1561 22 min. $16.95

• Old Dogs, New Tricks
Travel to the mountains of Montana and Wyoming
to meet the smart, adaptable new king of the wild -
the coyote. You'll learn how man's effect on nature
has changed the coyote from a clever, cunning
hunter to a lethal part of a powerful pack. Nothing
seems to stop them - not guns, traps or poison. The
coyote is an old dog who's learning a whole new
bag of tricks!
24-1562 22 min. $14.95

• Pretty Poison
Fly along the path of the monarch butterfly.
Physically fragile and helpless, this black and gold
creature migrates more than 2,000 miles each year.
However, it travels the round-trip journey well-
armed - with its body glutted with enough poison to
kill five humans. Discover how such a seemingly
strange contradiction occurs!
24-1565 22 min. $14.95

Meet Your Animal Friends
Lynn Redgrave hosts this video designed to
introduce young children to the varied world of
animals. Over 20 short segments emphasize
mothers and their young.
24-019 52 min. $29.95

NATIONAL GEOGRAPHIC SERIES:

• African Wildlife
Witness the realities of birth, death and survival in
this vivid and exciting encounter with the animal
world. This program was filmed over the course of
two years, capturing extraordinary close-ups of
various animal behaviors.
13-450 60 min. $19.98

• Among the Wild Chimpanzees
In 1960 Jane Goodall set out for Tanzania's remote
Gombe Stream Game Reserve to study the behavior
of the chimpanzee. This is the story of two decades
of dedication and perseverance working with and
studying man's closest living relative.
13-1893 59 min. $19.98

VIDEO TITLES LISTED IN THIS GUIDE ARE AVAILABLE FOR PURCHASE
OR RENTAL. CONTACT YOUR LOCAL VIDEO STORE OR TELEPHONE (800) 383-8811

- **Atockha**
13-449 60 min. $29.95

- **Creatures of the Namib Desert**
For hundreds of thousands of years, the sun's rays have baked the Namib Desert in southwestern Africa, where ground temperatures reach 170 degrees. Narrated by Burgess Meredith, this acclaimed program takes a fascinating look at the desert's vast wilderness and sand, sea and open spaces where nature has learned to adapt and flourish.
14-1521 60 min. $19.98

- **Gorilla**
Presents an informative and engaging look at the mysterious mountain gorilla of central Africa. Featured are segments with renowned scientists Diane Fossey, zoo director John Aspinall, and an entertaining look at the famed gorilla Koko, who communicates in American Sign Language.
13-452 60 min. $19.98

- **Great Whales**
Once feared and hunted almost to extinction, the whale now commands worldwide attention. Join scientists and conservationists as they study and document the anatomy, communication and migratory patterns of killer, pilot and humpback whales.
13-461 60 min. $19.98

- **Grizzlies**
Monster of the imagination and monarch of the wild, the great grizzly bear has long played a part in myth and legend. Despite man's combined fear of and fascination with the grizzly, the bear survives today only by consent of his one real contender - man.
13-1647 60 min. $19.98

- **Himalayan**
River Run
A team of adventurers risk their lives as they navigate the raging, unpredictable white water of Nepal's Dudh Kosi River. Using ultralight aircraft as airborne troubleshooters, their goal is to kayak the distance of the bitter cold river that has its source in the glaciers of the world's tallest peak, Mt. Everest.
14-1648 60 min. $19.98

- **Iceland River Challenge**
From National Geographic's daring "Explorer" series, follow 12 modern-day pioneers as they run a wild Icelandic river through glacial caverns, violent gales and crashing rapids.
14-034 60 min. $19.98

- **Land Of The Tiger**
Majestic, powerful, sleek, and mysterious - National Geographic comes closer than ever to the enormous jungle cats for a rare and fascinating adventure in the tiger's world.
13-455 60 min. $19.98

- **Polar Bear Alert**
Narrated by Jason Robards, this video takes viewers on a journey to Churchill, Manitoba, where the residents have learned to live with a unique wildlife problem. Each fall the largest, most deadly carnivore in the Arctic Migrates through this isolated Canadian village on an annual northward trek. For scientists, the migration presents a unique chance to observe the bears. For residents, it is a season of apprehension.
13-1520 60 min. $19.98

- **Rain Forest**
The tropical rain forests of the world are home to nearly half the animal species. More than 100 inches of rain fall each year sustain this lush environment, where some of the most fascinating examples of natural adaptation can be found. Fascinating and thought-provoking, Rain Forest is an eloquent warning of the natural wonders we stand to lose if human encroachment of the world's rain forests continues.
13-462 60 min. $19.98

- **Realm of the Alligator**
Enter the mysterious wilderness of Okefenokee, 700 square miles of swampland on the Georgia-Florida border. Okefenokee is dominated by a descendant of the dinosaur: the fearsome alligator. Join scientists as they study the behavior of these powerful reptiles.
13-1895 59 min. $19.98

- **Save The Panda**
In the bamboo forested mountain ranges of Central China lives the elusive and endangered giant panda, join scientists as they track these rare creatures.
13-451 60 min. $19.98

- **Sharks**
One of the most famous programs in National Geographic's archives, following sharks around the world and challenging the myths surrounding these creatures of the deep. Watch experiments with a stainless steel suit which enables a person to survive a shark attack. Unbelievable!
13-454 60 min. $19.98

NOVA ANIMAL SERIES:
An educational and exciting series of programs designed to entertain and educate children and adults.

VIDEO TITLES LISTED IN THIS GUIDE ARE AVAILABLE FOR PURCHASE OR RENTAL. CONTACT YOUR LOCAL VIDEO STORE OR TELEPHONE (800) 383-8811

• All American Bear
The remarkable hibernation of the shy and intelligent North American black bear.
14-8065 30 min. $19.95

• Animal Olympians
Marvel at the amazing athletes of the animal world.
14-8063 30 min. $19.95

• Cities of Coral
The spectacular life of the Caribbean coral reef.
14-8069 30 min. $19.95

• In The Land Of The Polar Bears
Take a wondrous look at an unspoiled Arctic habitat.
14-8068 30 min. $19.95

• Signs Of The Apes, Songs of the Whales
A fascinating "conversation" with the animal kingdom.
14-8067 30 min. $19.95

• Visions Of The Deep
Explore the awesome underwater world of animal life.
24-8066 30 min. $19.95

• Whale Watch
Get an up-close look at the world's greatest mammal.
14-8064 30 min. $19.95

Of Sharks And Men
Narrated by Bruno Vailati, this video takes you on an exciting voyage from the Red Sea to the Yucatan, from Tahiti to Australia, following different breeds of the world's most deadly species, the shark. Eerie underwater encounters with these deadly creatures show how man has learned to live with, but never control, this brutal, fascinating creature.
24-045 93 min. $19.95

Rattlesnake Country?
This video is designed with outdoors people in mind. Included are many interesting and helpful facts about rattlesnakes such as what to do in case of snakebite, how to avoid being bitten, and different areas where rattlesnakes can be found.
24-9569 60 min. $29.95

Return of the Great Whales
Not Long ago, the humpback and blue whales faced almost certain extinction at the hands of ravenous fishing and whaling industries. This program documents the triumphant return of the whales to Northern California coastlines and the people who

are fighting to see that history doesn't repeat itself.
24-8037 50 min. $39.95

Rocky Mountain Big Horn Sheep: Their Life Story
Witness the rewards of the cameramen's effort as you watch tiny newborn lambs frolic and huge dominant rams fight the long, vicious winters of the Northern Rockies. This is the story of the Rocky Mountain Bighorn Sheep and the magnificent land in which it lives.
24-8027 60 min. $29.95

Rocky Mountain Elk: Their Life Story
Share in the elk's life story from birth to death as it is captured in all phases of its life. Filmed throughout the Rocky Mountain region.
24-2684 54 min. $29.95

Savage and Beautiful
A documentary look at nature's wildlife, narrated by Donald Sutherland. Music by Vangelis.
14-8050 60 min. $19.95

Search for Survival
Every living creature requires water to live. This program show the different ways animals search for this precious link to survival.
24-2805 94 min. $19.95

Shark Hunter
Demonstrates how Vic Hislop tracks and catches whalers, hammerheads, tiger sharks, and the great whites. Spectacular underwater shots support Vic's theory that sharks are not friends of man.
24-2671 60 min. $29.95

Sharks
A close look at one of the Sea's most ancient creatures, one that actually predates the dinosaurs! This program traces the development of this predator while dispelling many of the myths that have grown up around the creature. An excellent, scientific presentation - not an adventure story.
24-025 28 min. $29.95

Sharks! Pirates Of The Deep
This film has some of the most terrifying footage of sharks ever shot. During the filming you will witness the dissection of a shark containing human remains, of one shark cannibalizing another and many close brushes with death.
24-8036 87 min. $29.95

Sharks: The True Story
Experience the danger that lurks beneath the ocean's surface as you explore the mystery surrounding the deadliest predator in the sea - the Great White Shark. Join Peter Benchley and marine biologists as they reveal the truth behind the

---

terrifying man-eating legend.
14-2486 60 min. $29.95

Shooting Africa
This is a photo safari of over 30 animals in their natural environments. It includes animal behavior rarely seen, with magnificent sequences of predators stalking, ambushing and running down prey in their struggle to survive.
24-8007 30 min. $19.95

Snake's: Natures Armored Warriors
Poisonous snakes are among the most deadly feared, yet fascinating creatures on earth. They strike their prey with pin-point precision, injecting lethal doses of poison. Now, for the first time on video, you can take an inside look at the exciting world of these intriguing reptiles. Witness lightening quick strikes and live capture scenes of America's most deadly snakes, the Rattler, Water Moccasin and the Coral Snakes. Join host and expert snake handler Bob Popplewell as he separates myth from reality!
14-7052 40 min. $16.95

Spirit Of The Eagle
Join a young boy and his friends as they discover the Masters of the Sky. Experience bald eagles as they hunt prey, raise their young and soar across the skies of the Pacific Northwest and Alaska.
24-9305 30 min. $19.95

Tropical Birds
This tape shows a collection of six South American birds which are studied by the camera. The camera is stationary so the viewer can enjoy the movement and natural sounds that the birds provide. There is no narration or music - just natural sound.
14-051 60 min. $19.95

UNDERSEA WORLD OF JACQUES COUSTEAU

• Sound of Dolphins
Captain Cousteau and his crew sail the Straits of Gibraltar and Mauritania, Africa, to unravel the mysteries surrounding one of the world's most intelligent creatures, the dolphin.
24-081 60 min. $24.95

• Desert Whales
The Calypso crew set sail to track, study and film the enigmatic California grey whale during its annual 5,000-mile migration from the Bering Sea to the warm inland lagoons of Baja, California.
24-084 60 min. $24.95

• Dragons of Galapagos
On this expedition Cousteau studies the little-known marine iguana, an exotic remnant of a reptilian order which became extinct more than 100 million years ago.
24-083 60 min. $24.95

• Flight of Penguins
On a space-age Antarctic expedition, Captain Cousteau and the Calypso crew film in exciting detail the life of the penguin, above and below the surface.
24-085 60 min. $24.95

• Forgotten Mermaids
Captain Cousteau explores the cypress glades of east Florida to film the huge manatee, about which Columbus noted: "Sighted three mermaids. They were not as beautiful as had been painted."
24-086 60 min. $24.95

• Octopus-Octopus
The crews of the Calypso and her sister ship, Espadon, sail the Mediterranean and the Pacific to film one of the most serious creatures on the planet, the octopus.
24-082 60 min. $24.95

• Singing Whale
In the West Indies, the Cousteau crew searches out mysterious voices and records a concert sung by hundreds of humpback whales converging on a large expanse of water.
24-078 60 min. $24.95

• Smile of the Walrus
The Calypso journeys to the Arctic to conduct a detailed film study of the massive walrus, both above the surface and below.
24-080 60 min. $24.95

• Unsinkable Sea Otter
The Calypso sails the sea lanes used by early fur traders from frigid Alaskan waters to picturesque Monterey, California, for some never-before-filmed glimpses of the "Old Man of the Sea."
24-079 60 min. $24.95

• Whales
The Calypso sails the Indian Ocean off the coast of Madagascar, then the Pacific Ocean off the Baja coast, in search of the most intelligent inhabitants of the sea - the finback, sperm and killer whales.
24-087 60 min. $24.95

Video Aquarium
At last, fish that don't die. Over 25 colorful marine fish turn your TV into their water-filled tank. No fish to feed! No tank to clean! Includes a picture card identifying the fish. Great for parties!
14-018 60 min. $19.95

VIDEO TITLES LISTED IN THIS GUIDE ARE AVAILABLE FOR PURCHASE OR RENTAL. CONTACT YOUR LOCAL VIDEO STORE OR TELEPHONE (800) 383-8811

Watching Birds with Roger Tory Peterson

In this program you'll see 52 common birds in detail; and learn to identify them using the principles of the trusted Peterson Identification System with world-renowned naturalist Roger Troy Peterson as your guide. You'll see vivid closeup scenes and live action photography giving you the colors, calls and characteristics of everything from the Great Horned Owl to the Ruby-throated Hummingbird from the White-breasted Nuthatch to the Indigo Bunting. A great study guide.
24-060 60 min. $49.95

Whale-Song

Enter the world of the cetaceans - creatures that breathe air like us, feel like us, and possess intelligence that rivals all other species in the animal kingdom. Lloyd Bridges is our escort and guide to "the people that live in the sea" singing, dancing, ancient mammals - that have graced our planet for 50 million years - are still endangered by senseless slaughter and ocean pollution.
14-5122 60 min. $39.95

What In The World Is A Manatee

Sparked by a chance encounter with a manatee, three young explorers learn about this endangered species through reading, fossil collecting, viewing a manatee skeleton in a museum and visiting with an expert about their finds. Engages young viewers to actively participate in wildlife conservation.
24-8028 25 min. $24.95

Wild Body Language

This video demonstrates how wild life communicates with body language. It teaches what to look for and what it means. Your enjoyment of watching wildlife will be greatly enhanced by learning a few simple techniques for interpreting wild body language.
24-8026 60 min. $39.95

WILDLIFE IN ACTION

Each of the "Wildlife in Action" videos, feature two separate documentaries to entertain and educate you and your family.

• Grizzlies of the Great Divide:

Three years were spent filming grizzlies in the high country of the Rocky Mountains Great Divide. Braving many trails and dangers, the filmmaker captured breathtaking scenes of the grizzly's behavior, never before filmed.
Wild Dogs of Jasper: This is a story of the wolves and coyotes which inhabit the Canadian Rockies. Follow a large pack as it kills a moose and see how a new wolf pack is formed.
24-098 50 min. $54.95

• Giants of The Forest:

In the rugged mountains of northwest America during autumn, bull moose and bull elk joust like medieval knights to win female favor. Bighorns of Beauty Creek: Bighorn sheep form a strange society in which repeated fighting helps preserve the species. This film tells the story of one band of sheep, and their natural leader, the Old Ram, who confronts the supreme challenge to his leadership.
24-099 50 min. $54.95

• Hunters of The Sky:

Anywhere in North America, you're within earshot of an owl or within sight of a hawk...owl with their remarkable hearing and soft silent plumage; and hawks, with their great vision and flying abilities. Filming The Fish Hawk: It took four years of great risk to film the life cycle of the great osprey, sometimes known as the fish hawk. Our filmmaker constructed his own "osprey nest" to live in and has captured both comic and tragic moments.
24-100 50 min. $54.95

• High Arctic Close-up:

North America's high arctic is a forbidding region of dry polar deserts and thick permanent icecaps. We accompany a veteran nature filmmaker to explore the wildlife on this harsh and challenging land. Destroyers of Mountains: The giant glaciers relentlessly grind down seemingly indestructible mountains. From that destruction spring up many forms of life including the sure-footed bighorn sheep, the cougar, and the remarkable bird, the dipper.
24-101 50 min. $54.95

• Survivors Of The Short Grass:

The short grass prairie of America's western mountains are forever altered by man, but still the pronghorns, bullsnakes, badgers, long-billed curlews, sage grouse and more survive. Call Of The Loon: No sound is more symbolic of the North or more thrilling than the call of the loon. This film pulls aside the curtain of mystery surrounding the life story of this bird so symbolic of the great Northern Woods.
24-102 50 min. $54.95

• Lure Of The Rockies:

North America's longest mountain range, the Rockies are magnificent from their snowcapped peaks to their green-carpeted valleys. But the real lure is the wildlife: black bear, pine martin, elk, ptarmigan, high country caribou and grizzly bear. Animals in Action: A series of six vignettes emphasizing animal behavior through picture and sound as it relates to establishing and defending territories and courtship during the breeding season. Many birds and animals on display.
24-103 50 min. $54.95

Wildlife Of A Prairie River

The Prairie Rivers water is the catalyst of life. The land that surrounds the river appears desolate, but a closer look reveals the beauty of some of America's most precious wildlife resources. This video is a procession of wildlife.
24-8030 50 min. $39.95

Wildlife Of Alaska

Wildlife of Alaska brings the icy grip of an Alaskan winter to your living room, along with small animals like the willow ptarmigan and the snowshoe rabbit who fight the blistering elements to survive. You'll see nomadic caribou ceaselessly wander the tundra in route to their traditional calving ground and brown bear as they congregate in spring at shallow river rapids to gorge on spawning salmon.
14-6591 60 min. $29.95

World Alive

A World Alive profiles the myriad creatures of the planet, their activities and interactions. Its dramatic musical score and powerful narration are blended with some of the most spectacular wildlife footage ever assembled. Learn through its entertainment.
14-6409 25 min. $24.95

Miscellaneous

Accident Hazards Of Nuclear Power Plants

Nuclear Physicist, Dr. Richard Webb, gives a clear informal explanation of the potential for serious accidents in nuclear plants today. Especially poignant in the light of 3 Mile Island and Chernobyl.
14-8040 30 min. $49.95

AFTER THE WARMING SERIES:

In the tradition of the hit series "Connections" James Burke takes us into the future to see what could have been done in the 1990's to slow the Greenhouse Effect. Using a device called the "virtual reality chamber", Burke guides us through scenarios of global warming in the year 2050, simulating the future based on today's actions.

• Volume I
14-8075 55 min. $99.95

• Volume II
14-8076 55 min. $99.95

Amazing World Below

This beautifully filmed program explores the ecological world of Blanchard Springs Caverns in Arkansas. Discover a living cave, where nature continues with its work of creation, constantly carbing and transforming the cavern walls, includes great animation on how caverns are formed and close-ups of bats, cave crickets and other dwellers of the dark.
14-2678 20 min. $29.95

AMERICA BY AIR

From inches above the Earth to a mile high in the sky, you'll experience the wonders of America's heartland as you fly above canyons, badland, glacial peaks, remote islands, dunes, mountains and great rivers. It's like no other aerial film ever produced.

• From the Mississippi to the Rockies
14-8012 48 min. $24.95

• Treasures of the West
14-5130 47 min. $29.95

• Wonders of the East
14-8013 47 min. $24.95

AUSTRALIAN ARK SERIES

• Amazing Marsupials
The koala is Australia's best known cuddly creature, but are you familiar with other marsupial natives of the land "down under?" Truly unbelievable animals that will intrigue and fascinate you.
14-1787 60 min. $19.95

• Changing Face of Australia
Once part of a huge land mass that split into pieces more than 200 million years ago, this continent is forever changing - in response to environmental forces. Vivid, engrossing, and absorbing, this program is strikingly spectacular.
14-1788 60 min. $19.95

• Coming of Man
Discover the riddles posed by man's 50,000 year presence on earth. Travel deep inside an Ice Age quarry and visit an Aboriginal encampment. Tribesmen practicing Stone-Age rites might suggest what was any viewer's ancestral past!
14-1789 60 min. $19.95

• Farthest West
Boisterous technicolor parrots and cockateels gather by the hundreds as miniature dragon-like lizards scurry underfoot. Journey to a very unfamiliar

VIDEO TITLES LISTED IN THIS GUIDE ARE AVAILABLE FOR PURCHASE OR RENTAL. CONTACT YOUR LOCAL VIDEO STORE OR TELEPHONE (800) 383-8811

west, rich with flora and fauna.
14-1790 60 min. $19.95

• **Green World**
Enter a world rich and dense with forests, surpassing a surrealist's dream filled with abundant life. Nature's delicate, experimental workshops are a delight of many colors.
14-1791 60 min. $19.95

• **Land of the Birds**
Unique and beautifully feathered, the cassowary, lyrebird and bowerbird take flight in one's imagination as well as in the wide blue sky. Soar with nature's first aeronautical pilots!
14-1792 60 min. $19.95

• **Last Wilderness**
Frazier Island, a magical fairy-tale landscape, is made entirely of sand, woven together by the protective roots of the trees that populate its soil. Explore this fragile island off Australia's coast!
14-1793 60 min. $19.95

• **Life and Death in the Great Barrier Reef**
The manta ray merely seems dangerous. The great white shark is a killer. Learn who will perish and who will survive the Great Barrier Reef, the mightiest of Earth's edifices, covered with tiny coral polyps!
14-1794 60 min. $19.95

• **Life in the Desert**
Nothing moves under the infernal mid-day sun. At dusk however, the desert blossoms with mammals, birds and reptiles. A desperate struggle for survival amongst the heartiest of creatures is about to begin.
14-1795 60 min. $19.95

• **Life in the Southern Seas**
Come face to face with a curious pack of sea lions or find out that a hole in the ground is really a snug little home to a muton bird and a tiger snake...not your ordinary trip to the seaside.
14-1796 60 min. $19.95

• **North of Capricorn**
Home to two of the world's highest waterfalls, incredibly long snakes, fat toads and giant butterflies, this is not just a latitudinal line on a map...it is a land that is larger than life!
14-1797 60 min. $19.95

• **Return to the Dreaming**
From twigs and ground pigment to fantastic beasts and the mystical world of spiritual beings, an Aborigine guides one through the primeval

"dreaming time" of his people.
14-1798 60 min. $19.95

• **Small World**
Insects seems alien to man at first glance, yet on closer inspection they share many human traits. Examine this habitat of the miniature, filled with industrious, sociable and sexually active creatures. It is truly remarkable.
14-1799 60 min. $19.95

• **Survivors**
The platypus' duck bill, a mole's fur, a beaver's tail and a lizard's gait might be one of nature's more humorous "mistakes," or they might be living fossils the forces of evolution have simply bypassed - relics that live today.
14-1800 60 min. $19.95

Canyon Dreams
Breathtaking aerials, skirting the canyon rim, expose the Grand Canyon's overwhelming majesty. Discover rarely seen side canyons, raft through churning white waters and dive underwater for a unique new perspective.
14-1778 40 min. $29.95

Clouds
A collection of magnificent time-lapse cloud formations composed with music - a magical vision of atmospheric moods.
14-2780 60 min. $29.95

Concert in Flowers
Refresh your spirit, relax and rejuvenate your mind with the beautiful de-stressor of Rocky Mountain flowers and accompanying soothing music in stereo. This video brings a sense of harmony to viewers-relieving anxieties, promoting serenity and a sense of inner harmony, while soothing away stresses.
29-163 60 min. $39.95

Conversations With A Survivor
A conversation with a survivor of Hiroshima, Ms. Shigeko Nimoto. She shares her personal experience living with the consequences of the first atomic bomb used in war. She was one of the groups of women called the Hiroshima Maidens, who were treated for their wounds in the United States.
14-8041 15 min. $16.95

Country Barns
You can almost feel the gentle breezes that blow in the wheat fields near the country barns, while flocks of blackbirds fly by. The only movement in this video is that of nature herself.
14-002 60 min. $19.95

Country Roads
Experience the serenity of country roads and lanes as light and wind play in the leaves.
14-003 60 min. $19.95

Drought
What are the causes and consequences of drought? This evocative documentary looks at the devastating impact of drought on Australia's flora and fauna, and upon the people who have tried to carve a livelihood out of the most unforgiving continent of all. It explores the Australian aboriginal attitude toward drought and examines the latest theories on it's causes: sunspots, volcanic eruptions, or eccentricities in the earth's orbit.
14-5743 59 min. $24.95

Down In The Dumps
A video classic, foreshadowing today's recycling efforts with wit and ingenuity. Tells the story of a young couple buying country property sight unseen and moving from the city to discover they have bought the town dump. They decide to stay and build a home from the available resources. Join them for funny look at a serious problem.
14-8037 15 min. $16.95

EARTH AID--OUR WORLD: A USER'S GUIDE
Ed Begley Jr., provides information on water conservation and recycling in your home each day. Many suggestions will be given so that you and your family can easily apply these without changing your lifestyle.

• **Water Conservation**
14-9284 25 min. $19.95

• **Recycling**
14-9285 22 min. $19.95

End Of Nuclear Power
This program covers topics from the conference sponsored by The Citizen's Energy Council, on dangers from continued use of nuclear power plants. Included are research papers on health effects of low-level radiation, and the rise of excess deaths attributed to Three Mile Island, Chernobyl and operating nuclear power stations.
14-8038 55 min. $29.95

Fireside Moments
Enjoy a raging fire without the need for a fireplace. Turn your television on, pop in this video and feel the warmth it will add to any room.
14-8010 60 min. $19.95

Greenpeace: Greatest Hits
These are the real adventures of the Greenpeace members--and they'll thrill you more than any action movie could. This video puts you right in the middle of the excitement as you see these valiant activists risk arrest, assault and even their lives to protect our world.
14-8049 60 min. $29.95

Help Save Planet Earth
Reviewed and approved by some of the most respected environmental organizations representing millions of concerned citizens this video urges everyone to start making a difference today.
14-5859 30 min. $19.95

Just Cows
Cows staring at you, while you stare at them brings the viewer to bovine heaven. "Just Cows", provides a tranquil depiction of these beautiful creatures in their own environment.
24-8025 17 min. $16.95

Nature: The Volcano Watchers
Two daring scientists, Maurice and Katia Krafft, take a look at some of the world's most spectacular volcanos - up close and personal! Incredible footage of actual eruptions and lava flows.
14-6911 60 min. $19.95

Portable Aquarium
This is a clean, safe and easy way to turn any TV into an aquarium for an hour. The soothing and relaxing benefits can be enjoyed anywhere. Great for tropical fish lovers or as a relaxation tool.
14-9554 60 min. $9.95

Quiet Garden: Impressions Volume 2
Three visits to a quiet garden: for guided relaxation, active visualization, and for tranquil sights and sounds.
14-2782 60 min. $29.95

Reflections in a Forest: Impressions Volume 1
For your relaxation, three moments in the forest: the first guides you in relaxation, the second offers access to your inner resources, the third provides a soothing ambience without dialogue.
14-2781 60 min. $29.95

SEEDS OF CHANGE SERIES:
The Seeds of Change conference was held in Aspen, Colorado in August 1988. It's purpose was to bring attention to the ways in which environmental ecology affects food production. Listed below are three of the best presentations.

• **Recent Trends in Global Warming**
Dr. Noel J. Brown is a citizen of Jamaica and is directly involved in the United Nations Environment Program for North America. She has an understanding of the facts, trends and inter-

VIDEO TITLES LISTED IN THIS GUIDE ARE AVAILABLE FOR PURCHASE OR RENTAL. CONTACT YOUR LOCAL VIDEO STORE OR TELEPHONE (800) 383-8811

relatedness of global ecology and presents this with warmth, humor and simplicity.
14-8014 60 min. $24.95

• **Secrets of the Soil with Peter Tompkins**
The true story of a largely unseen war being perpetrated on the Earth for the life on the planet.
14-8016 60 min. $24.95

• **Where is The Future?**
Mr. Trombly, the featured speaker, is the director of Project Earth which is pursuing revolutionary research contributing to changing our world view of our vulnerable and endangered planet and how we can change our relationship to it.
14-8015 90 min. $29.95

Solo
Follow a lone mountain climber as he journeys from a misty predawn canyon floor to a windswept mountain top. This wordless and hypnotic masterpiece, is accompanied by a behind-the-scenes look at the risks and challenges of filming such an adventure.
14-8048 30 min. $29.95

Survival of Spaceship Earth
Ecological Film by Dirk Summers that humbles mankind into realizing that without our planet we cannot survive. Narrated by Raymond Burr, Hosted by Hugh Downs.
14-8009 63 min. $16.95

Water Journey
An aquatic voyage through marshes, ponds, lakes and rivers. Winner of "Film as Environment" award. Natural sounds of water, birds and insects.
14-2779 60 min. $29.95

Waterfalls
Majestic waterfalls in Yosemite and along the California coast show their inherent beauty in this unique video program.
14-019 60 min. $29.95

Wild California
Wild California is a collection of journeys, each journey is different...in mood, in tempo, in habitat, and in sound. Each takes your imagination to a special part of the wilderness of California.
14-5373 40 min. $29.95

Will Our Children Thank Us?
Dr. Benjamin Spock narrates a documentary about people working for social change.
14-8042 60 min. $49.95

WINDHAM HILL SERIES:

• **Autumn Portrait**
Sample a wonderful video portrait of the beautiful colors of Fall containing beautiful "New Age" music.
14-069 42 min. $29.95

• **China**
This video features "New Age" music set to rich imagery. Imagery provided by Chinese locations only recently opened to Western visitors.
14-1905 55 min. $29.95

• **Seasons**
Sample another selection of beautiful moments from the Windham Hill collection. It's a musical and scenic masterpiece.
14-1986 46 min. $29.95

• **Water's Path**
Since 1976, the music of Windham Hill has captivated music lovers around the world. Listen as "The Hill" brings this beautiful music to life with these breathtaking visual interpretations of their music.
14-020 42 min. $29.95

• **Western Light**
Let the enchanting music of Windham Hill come to life with images "The Hill" has named "Western Light."
14-021 42 min. $29.95

• **Winter**
Witness the spectacular beauty of winter in this wonderfully serene portrait set to music.
14-052 42 min. $29.95

WINDSTAR CHOICES FOR A HEALTHY ENVIRONMENT SERIES:

• **Learning From the Earth with Shakti Gawain**
Shakti Gawain is a leader in the consciousness expansion field. It is her special gift to bring matters of spiritual nature into practical application in people's lives.
14-8017 104 min. $49.95

• **1990's: The Decade of the Environment**
Jay D. Hiar Ph.D. is President of the National Wildlife Federation in Washington D.C., the nations's largest conservation organization. He has received awards for outstanding performance in the management of environmental enterprises.
14-8021 74 min. $29.95

VIDEO TITLES LISTED IN THIS GUIDE ARE AVAILABLE FOR PURCHASE OR RENTAL. CONTACT YOUR LOCAL VIDEO STORE OR TELEPHONE (800) 383-8811

• **Business, Technology and Our Future: Stanley Marcus**

Mr. Marcus, Chairman Emeritus of Neiman-Marcus since 1976, is the legendary force behind the phenomenal growth of the original Neiman-Marcus in Dallas, which is known throughout the world as the epitome' of quality. He brings the wisdom and perspective of an elder statesman and successful businessman to the environmental issues facing this generation.

14-8036 50 min. $24.95

• **Ceremonies, Ritual and Our Connection With Earth**

Brooke Medicine Eagle was raised on a reservation in Montana. She's a ceremonial leader, singer, healer, licensed counselor, practitioner of Neuro-Linguistic Programming and a certified Feldenkrais practioner. She leads and encourages people to heal themselves through spiritual action on the land.

14-8022 43 min. $24.95

• **Challenge of the Future-Noel J. Brown, Ph.D.**

Dr. Brown has many publications about global warming and world ecology to his credit. He has a comprehensive understanding of the facts, trends and inter-relatedness of ecology and global warming.

14-8024 65 min. $29.95

• **Choice For a Loving Environment: Marianne Willamson**

Ms. Williamson is an entertaining and dynamic transformational speaker whose teaching focuses on A Course In Miracles. In this lively and humorous presentation she illustrates the relationship between the physical environment and the metaphysical aspects of the attitudes and consciousness in the human beings who make it up.

14-8031 127 min. $49.95

• **Current State of the Planet: Schneider, Ph.D.**

Dr. Schneider is frequently called as an expert contributor to print and broadcast media on climate and environmental issues. He has authored over 160 papers and books and his most recent book is entitled "Global Warming".

14-8028 75 min. $39.95

• **Dance of the Tiger: Chungliang Al Huang**

Al Huang is President of the Living Tao Foundation in Illinois and Director of the Lan Ting Institute in China. He is a Tai Chi Master, dancer, calligrapher, musician, author and lecturer whose playful and provocative spirit inspire all who come

in contact with him.

14-8023 57 min. $24.95

• **Global Climate, Change and You: Earth Pulse Panel I & II**

Earth Pulse Panel is a forum on global climate change and what individuals can do about it. It is comprised of experts and scientists from diverse fields of environmental study.

• **Panel I**
14-8032 110 min. $49.95

• **Panel II**
14-8033 105 min. $49.95

• **Global Environmental Security: The Greenhouse Crisis-Jeremy Rifkin**

Jeremy Rifkin dynamically involves every audience member in an eclectic exploration of history, politics, economics, personal belief systems and world views and their relationship to the current global environmental crisis.

14-8035 75 min. $29.95

• **Heroes and Heroines: The Journey of Choice**

Jean Houston, Ph.D. is nationally recognized as a leading pioneer in the development, exploration on application of human potentials, consciousness and the mythic structures of the psyche.

• **Part One**
14-8026 110 min $49.95

• **Part Two**
14-8027 123 min. $49.95

• **On Commitment: Dennis Weaver**

Dennis has fashioned a successful career complimented by a strong commitment to world peace, the ending of hunger and homelessness in America, drug abuse prevention and the exploration of personal and spiritual growth.

14-8020 23 min. $16.95

• **Our Diet and the Future of Life: John Robbins**

John Robbins, son of the founder of Baskin-Robbins ice cream empire, renounced the family business and fortune to chart his own course to the truth about life and oneness with the Earth. He is the president of EarthSave, a non-profit foundation, and tells the story of how people's choice to eat animal products has resulted in horrible suffering of many species of creatures, death and disease in humans and environmental devastation.

14-8029 62 min. $29.95

VIDEO TITLES LISTED IN THIS GUIDE ARE AVAILABLE FOR PURCHASE OR RENTAL. CONTACT YOUR LOCAL VIDEO STORE OR TELEPHONE (800) 383-8811

• **Personal Responsibility and the Need For Individual Action: Graham Nash**
From his beautiful opening rendition of "I Am A Simple Man", through a captivating and humorous series of reminiscences from his musical career and personal journey, to the intimate and heartfelt finale performance of "Wind On The Water" and "Teach Your Children Well", Mr. Nash delivers an inspiring musical message of personal responsibility and human commitment.
14-8034 48 min. $24.95

• **Planetary Smile: Barbara Marx-Hubbard**
Barbara is the founding director of Global Family, a non-profit organization committed to networking people and organizations throughout the world working for the peaceful transformation of our planet.
14-8019 20 min. $16.95

• **Politics of a Healthy Environment**
Rep. Claudine Schneider of Rhode Island has championed a wide range of legislation to protect the environment, preserve endangered species and to promote a balanced use of natural resources. Her widely acclaimed Global Warming Prevention Act will be introduced in the 101st Congress.
14-8025 65 min. $29.95

• **Recycling: Progressive Waste Management for the 90's with Peter Grogan**
Peter is an associate and Director of Materials Recovery for R.W. Beck & Associates in Seattle where he coordinates the largest staff dedicated to waste reduction, recycling and composting. He has developed programs for governments throughout the country and educational programs for schools. He is joined by Lorie Parker who directs one of the most successful recycling programs in the world .
14-8030 100 min. $39.95

• **Windstar Award-Tom Crum & Wangari Maathai**
Windstar Award is presented to a global citizen who is contributing to the creation of a healthy, peaceful future. Dr. Maathai has been recognized for her work in establishing a reforestation program and reversing the serious decertification of her native Kenya. Tom Crum, Aikido Master and author of "The Magic of Conflict", which demonstrates how to turn the energy of conflict into the magic or resolution.
14-8018 62 min. $29.95

Worldlink: Spaceship Earth
This is a thought-provoking video magazine designed to inform, inspire and motivate. Hosted entirely by young people, this contemporary program travel around the world to explore three primary environmental issues: deforestation, global warming and ozone depletion.
14-8046 25 min. $29.95

Swim With The Whales...

Fly With The Eagles...

And Learn How You Can

Help Protect Their World.

Personal Development

- ✓ *Attitude & The Inner Self*
- ✓ *Beauty & Grooming*
- ✓ *Community Service & Personal Safety*
- ✓ *Public Speaking*
- ✓ *Miscellaneous*

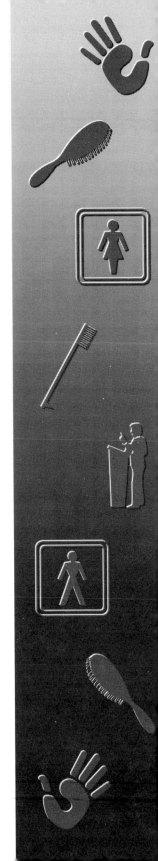

Attitude & The Inner Self

5 Components Of Self-Esteem
This video is a must for every teacher to help improve student performance, create a positive climate and to achieve success with "at risk" and "gifted" students. Gail Dusa, acclaimed self-esteem consultant, offers practical ideas that really work that are as enjoyable for the teacher as they are successful for the student.
01-8003 30 min. $79.95

Alchemy Of Love
This tape brings to life Joseph Campbell's insights into the universal application of myth. Two playlets, one revolving around a contemporary talk show and the other presented as a stylized mythic dance, dramatize the elemental archetypes at work within us. Both are based on the classic love story, which show us the path to personal fulfillment. The hero is separated from his beloved by an evil force, which he must defeat through the use of magical power in order achieve reunion. In the same way, we can overcome inner resistance to growth by contacting our instinctive drives, giving us intuition and strength to help us realize our dreams.
29-8002 45 min. $16.95

Angela Lansbury's Positive Moves
In this program Ms. Lansbury shares her secrets and simple techniques for building strength, stamina and a great mental outlook.
29-3084 50 min. $29.95

Basics To Improve Your Memory
Never again face the embarrassing situation of forgetting the name or telephone number of that important client. Let noted expert Madelyn Burley-Allen teach you the practical skills you need to improve your memory and never forget. This program comes complete with workbook and audiocassette.
29-8012 42 min. $95.00

Being Different
A touching documentary about and tribute to the women and men who have overcome their physical disabilities or disfigurement to live full and productive lives. These victorious individuals were once forced into the fringes of society but now live in the mainstream.
13-022 102 min. $59.95

Components of Self Esteem
Gail Dusa is a motivational speaker who with humor and charm emphasizes practical, easy ways to implement strategies for building self-esteem. She is nationally recognized as an expert in creating self-esteem building strategies that are adaptable on the personal level and in a school or business setting.
28-8001 30 min. $79.95

Dr. Wayne Dyer: How To Be A No-Limit Person
Showcased with an enthusiastic studio audience and in a personal interview, Wayne reflects on his own life experiences and, in so doing, shows the stuff that goes into the making of a strong, secure "no-limit" person.
29-150 60 min. $79.95

Everybody Rides the Carousel
Enter an animated world that illustrates Erik Kriksen's theory of personality development. It shows and explains his eight stages of life, with each stage represented as a ride on the carousel of life.
01-015 72 min. $39.95

Expert Body Language
Combines psychological studies of several scientists into a step-by-step guide that gives you the advantage in any social, business or law enforcement type interview situation. By reading, and controlling a persons proxemic zones, facial expressions, verbal clues, and autonomic body reactions, you will be able to judge a person's stress levels, sensory type, verbal modality and tell if they are being truthful or deceptive.
29-8014 48 min. $59.95

Fabulous 50+
In this upbeat documentary you will meet people of various backgrounds who in some way or another are doing wonderful things with their lives. From Las Vegas showgirl grandmothers, to vintage race car drivers, to the Senior Olympics, you will hear first-hand their secrets for living a healthy and happy life over 50. Featuring a jazzy original theme song and narration by 40's film star Marcy McGuire, this inspiring, entertaining and educational program is sure to motivate anyone to chase their dream, simple or elaborate as they may be.
29-6374 50 min. $39.95

How To Attain Prosperity
Prosperity is a feast for the senses, brimming with rich images and proven techniques for self-empowerment. It's never been done like this before! Dr. Brenda Wade introduces a unique, multi-faceted system for achievement. Learn the keys to success, and how to apply them in your life

today. Your mastery will grow with each successive viewing. Experience the elegance of abundance. The answers are here, NOW!

29-5393 60 min. $39.95

How to Get Results with People

You'll learn how to gain credibility and the respect of others, get people to support you and your ideas, handle conflict with confidence and ease, motivate others and much more. By knowing how to get more cooperation from others, you'll not only improve your relationships, but greatly increase your success.

29-2246 105 min. $69.95

How To Use Dianetics

This video reveals, in simple terms anyone can understand, the single source of stress, tension, depression, psychosomatic illness, compulsion, addiction and insanity and gives you something you can do about it. Based on the #1 self-help bestseller, learn how to open the door to your full potential and achieve what you want in life!

29-8011 60 min. $24.95

Image and Self-Projection for Today's Professional Woman

This program reveals the secret of how to project authority and credibility - and make an impact! You'll learn how to be seen as a winner, establish respect, rid yourself of power-robbing mannerisms in speech and body language and much more. Two tapes.

29-2247 173 min. $199.95

L. Ron Hubbard: An Introduction to Scientology

In this unique video, today's #1 self-help author deals directly with the problems that most often trouble people and provides actual solutions to better your relationships with others, to help you to really understand the mind, body and spirit. Discover how to improve the quality of your life and reach your goals.

29-8071 58 min. $24.95

Meditation

A complete introduction to the concept of meditation and concentration, it's benefits, philosophy and practical application. Also contains a special section for daily practice to quiet and energize body and mind.

29-9813 60 min. $29.95

MASTER OF LIFE TRAINING SEMINAR:

Each tape contains 2 Video Hypnosis sessions. You'll learn who you are beneath your programming and how to end suffering, attain peace of mind and make your life work.

• Dharmic Destiny & Soul Goals
29-8021 120 min. $29.95

• Liberation
29-8022 120 min. $29.95

• Self-Creation
29-8020 120 min. $29.95

• Success on Every Level
29-8023 120 min. $29.95

Norman Vincent Peale: The Power of Positive Thinking

Listen to conversations on how to achieve daily positive living. Topics include motivating yourself, overcoming tension and stress, defeating defeat, finding happiness, believing in yourself, a winning attitude, faith and more.

29-171 60 min. $29.95

Optimal Thinking

This is the realistic mental technology which empowers peak performance. We cannot function at our peak when we think in sub-optimal terms. This video is interactive and offers the most practical techniques to maximize productivity, profitability and daily life.

29-8072 36 min. $59.95

Overcome Your Fear Of Flying

Hundreds of people now fly without white knuckles thanks to anxiety specialist Dr. Ralph Tassinari and veteran commercial pilot Roger Martin. Using the latest research on stress management, this program gives you the knowledge about airplanes and the effective in-flight relaxation techniques that will finally put you in control of your fear.

29-8018 48 min. $39.95

Overcoming Procrastination

Almost everyone procrastinates from time to time. Why? To escape unpleasant or seemingly overwhelming tasks--to get someone else to do them or fear of failure. This video program gives you proven, powerful techniques to start any project with energy and enthusiasm.

29-8073 62 min. $99.95

Peacemakers

You could alter your family life for the better if you knew how to skillfully facilitate peacemaking. Learn the art of conflict resolution from international authorities. Ceremonial songs and dances will help you find the dwelling place of peace within you.

29-8002 30 min. $16.95

VIDEO TITLES LISTED IN THIS GUIDE ARE AVAILABLE FOR PURCHASE OR RENTAL. CONTACT YOUR LOCAL VIDEO STORE OR TELEPHONE (800) 383-8811

Peak Performance
Your guide is a mathematician, psychologist, computer analyst and world-class weight lifter, to boot. Dr. Charles Garfield teaches you how to become a top performer by developing the key skills common to most successful people.
07-020 60 min. $19.95

Psychology of Winning in Action with Denis E. Waitley, Ph.D.
Denis Waitley teaches principles of thought and behavior you can use immediately--in your organization, your career and your personal life. You will learn how to eliminate self limiting thoughts and behavior, action steps to enhance self-esteem, accepting responsibility for your actions, the importance of setting attainable goals and much more.
29-145 60 min. $99.95

Ransack, Wrestle & Roll
Learn how to recapture the spirit of discovery...how to take risks...how to solve problems. Let Miggs B. show you his secret. The 3 R's of creativity: Ransack...the closet of your mind and discover a new world of ideas. Wrestle...with each idea until you come up with a winner. Roll...into action by putting your skills and determination to work.
29-8013 20 min. $29.95

Secrets of Style
This video shows you how to identify your face, body type and color palette to choose flattering silhouettes, accessories and make-up. A study guide helps you plan a personalized, flexible basic wardrobe for all seasons and circumstances, building on the pieces you already have.
29-8019 60 min. $69.95

Secrets of the Stars: Shirley Jones and Sheila Cluff
This program is designed for the total woman, without regimented exercise routines or fad diets that take the joy out of living. Live in the "natural high" of having your life reflect the woman you can and want to be. You can also tailor the lessons to your individual needs and tastes.
15-148 90 min. $29.95

SELF CHANGE PROGRAMMING SERIES:

Each set contains 1 video, 4 audio tapes.

• Accelerated Learning
Power-boost your brain. We only use 10 percent of our brain's power. In the 90 percent of unused potential is the power to accelerate learning to an incredible degree if you have the self-discipline to incorporate the latest medical/nutritional research into your lifestyle and regularly use the latest programming technology.
29-8030 30 min. $59.95

• Attract Love & Create a Successful Relationship
Do you want a warm, loving relationship in which you share experiences and mutual personal growth? Techniques that tap the power of your subconscious mind program your subconscious with new beliefs about love and relationships.
29-8031 30 min. $59.95

• Incredible Self-Confidence
Self confidence is critical to your success in all areas of your life, including business, relationships, emotional well-being and even your health. If your self confidence is low, it is the result of negative subconscious programming. Use this self-programming video set to change these negative beliefs.
29-8027 30 min. $59.95

• Lose Weight Now
Dick Sutphen approaches weight loss from the position of cause and effect.. the only way to solve the weight problem and keep the weight off. He combines up to date medical research with the latest brain/mind technology that when incorporated into your life, your goal soon becomes your reality.
29-8026 30 min. $59.95

• Self Healing
Well documented research shows that your mind has the ability to assist in the healing process. The use of altered-state sleep and subliminal programming and mind imprinting maximizes positive healing suggestions to your subconscious minds. Beliefs generate thoughts and emotions, which create emotions. Change those beliefs and change your life.
29-8032 30 min. $59.95

• Seven Keys to Greater Success
Invest in your future by applying the powerful principles of self-image psychology to your life. Learn and understand how to redesign your self-image so you can realize your full, untapped potential.
29-1841 48 min. $79.95

• Stop Smoking Forever
Research has proven that nicotine is as addictive as heroin. Almost every smoker wants to quit, but it's a much tougher battle than most people realize. For this reason, we have gathered together the very latest knowledge and the world's most powerful reprogramming techniques to help you "stop

VIDEO TITLES LISTED IN THIS GUIDE ARE AVAILABLE FOR PURCHASE OR RENTAL. CONTACT YOUR LOCAL VIDEO STORE OR TELEPHONE (800) 383-8811

smoking forever".
29-8028   30 min. $59.95

• Succeed By Listening
Effective listening is truly the foundation of business success, yet today it's becoming a "lost art". In this exciting multi-media program, Madelyn Burley-Allen reveals the keys to effective, active listening. Contains video/audio/book
29-8006   35 min. $94.95

• Ultra-Monetary Success
No matter how hard you work, if you violate any of the basic laws of success, you will never attain your goals. If you are willing to devote a small portion of your day to brain/mind programming, you are halfway there. 90 percent of success results from 4 factors: energy, enthusiasm, self-image, and discipline.
29-8029   30 min. $59.95

• Un-Stress
To reduce stress, you need to understand it. One of the latest findings is that the daily hassles of life may have a more stressful effect than larger misfortunes. This is the ultimate approach to resolving stress in your life.
29-8033   30 min. $59.95

Self Discipline Seminar With Dick Sutphen
In this video seminar, Dick Sutphen talks, conducts demonstrations and in-depth processing sessions, and interacts with participants. This video set helps you manifest increased self-discipline whether it revolves around weight loss, smoking, procrastination, self confidence, it works with all areas to help do what you need to do and stop doing what doesn't work.
29-8025   420 min. (4-tape set) $79.95

Shirley Maclaine's Inner Workout
There is no escaping stress in the world, no matter who you are. That's why Shirley Maclaines's inner workout is such a breakthrough. It's the definitive stress-reduction program - a highly repeatable workout for mind, body and soul that can reduce stress in everyone!
29-5835   70 min. $29.95

Strangest Secret
Earl Nightingale, can help you achieve improved performance in every area of your personal life and career with a "checklist for living," based on his Gold Record award-winning message. Create good attitudes and improve your ability to set and achieve goals on schedule.
29-149   21 min. $69.95

Ten Keys to a More Powerful Personality
A highly regarded consultant in personal and professional development, Brian Tracy reveals the ten traits shared by all winners. Called the "Ten Cs of Success," they comprise a strategic plan you can easily put to work in your life.
20-1839   64 min. $69.95

Three Happy People
Three happy people reveal the personal formulas, insights and circumstances that keep them that way.
23-039   30 min. $89.95

VIDEO HYPNOSIS SERIES:
Dick Sutphen combines 2 kinds of hypnosis with 2 kinds of subliminals, suggestions that you can see and hear, then the same suggestions repeated as visual and audio subliminals that only your subconscious can perceive.

• Accelerated Learning
29-8043   30 min. $19.95

• Accomplish Your Goals
29-8049   30 min. $19.95

• Attracting Love
29-8042   30 min. $19.95

• Boost Your Brain Power
29-8067   30 min. $19.95

• Chakra Balance
29-8041   30 min. $19.95

• Channel for the Light
29-8053   30 min. $19.95

• Charisma-Drawing People to You
29-8054   30 min. $19.95

• Develop Psychic Ability Now
29-8045   30 min. $19.95

• Golf
29-8062   30 min. $19.95

• Good Health-Strong Immune System
29-8051   30 min. $19.95

• Good Life-Health, Wealth, Happiness
29-8064   30 min. $19.95

• Healing Acceleration
29-8043   30 min. $19.95

VIDEO TITLES LISTED IN THIS GUIDE ARE AVAILABLE FOR PURCHASE OR RENTAL. CONTACT YOUR LOCAL VIDEO STORE OR TELEPHONE (800) 383-8811

• **Increase Self-Discipline**
29-8070 30 min. $19.95

• **Incredible Concentration**
29-8047 30 min. $19.95

• **Incredible Self-Confidence**
29-8038 30 min. $19.95

• **Intensifying Creative Ability**
29-8046 30 min. $19.95

• **Lose Weight Now**
29-8035 30 min. $19.95

• **Love & Believe In Yourself**
29-8048 30 min. $19.95

• **Master of Life-Personality Transformation**
29-8037 30 min. $19.95

• **Mind Over Muscles**
29-8061 30 min. $19.95

• **Overcoming Addictions**
29-8063 30 min. $19.95

• **Past Life Regression**
29-8060 30 min. $19.95

• **Perfect Weight, Perfect Body**
29-8068 30 min. $19.95

• **Physical & Mental Fitness**
29-8065 30 min. $19.95

• **Positive Thinking**
29-8050 30 min. $19.95

• **Quick Thinking**
29-8058 30 min. $19.95

• **Sensational Sex**
29-8069 30 min. $19.95

• **Sports Improvement**
29-8057 30 min. $19.95

• **Stop Punishing Yourself**
29-8055 30 min. $19.95

• **Stop Smoking Forever**
29-8036 30 min. $19.95

• **Successful Independent Lifestyle**
29-8056 30 min. $19.95

• **Tennis Programming**
29-8065 30 min. $19.95

• **Ultimate Relaxation**
29-8066 30 min. $19.95

• **Ultra-Monetary Success**
29-8040 30 min. $19.95

• **Un-Stress**
29-8039 30 min. $19.95

• **What Do I Really Want**
29-8052 30 min. $19.95

Voices Of Peace
Peace will come when the masses demand it of our politicians. Relive June 12, 1982, when nearly one million people marched through Manhattan calling for disarmament and attended a concert featuring Bruce Springsteen, Jackson Browne and Joan Baez.
29-8003 25 min. $16.95

Win Through Relationships
Jim Cathcart and Tony Alessandra show how to analyze a person's behavior and interact with that person to get the result you want. Enjoy satisfying, conflict free achievements. One video and two audio tapes included.
29-8005 43 min. $95.00

Winning in Life: Walter Payton
The Chicago Bears Super Bowl XX champion shares his exciting game plan for winning. He emphasizes the importance of a winning attitude, enthusiasm and a relentless pursuit of excellence. An inspiring look at how to be a winner in life.
29-152 60 min. $59.95

You Determine Your Success With John Wooden
The "Wizard of Westwood", UCLA's legendary coach, John Wooden, presents his winning philosophy and discusses how to apply it towards gaining success in all areas of life.
29-8000 20 min. $19.95

Your Thoughts Create Your Life
Louise L. Hay D.D. is a metaphysical counselor and teacher whose work is based on loving the self. During the past 16 years, she has helped individuals and groups realize their self worth and self esteem. Through her techniques and philosophy, many have learned to create more of what they want, including wellness in body, mind and spirit.
29-5836 60 min. $29.95

VIDEO TITLES LISTED IN THIS GUIDE ARE AVAILABLE FOR PURCHASE OR RENTAL. CONTACT YOUR LOCAL VIDEO STORE OR TELEPHONE (800) 383-8811

Beauty & Grooming

5 EASY PIECES SERIES

• Wardrobe Strategy-Part I

Watch image consultant Judith Rasband show you
how to build a wardrobe to suit your needs and
style. She will show you how to begin a cluster
with clothes you already own reducing clothing cost
and shopping time. Coordinate your clothing and
makeup colors, make a positive impression and
look and feel beautiful! Whatever your age or
lifestyle you'll enjoy this creative strategy for
building a wonderful wardrobe.
05-9562 70 min. $39.95

• Strategy In Action-Part II

See wardrobe clusters in different price ranges,
worn by different women, each with different
personal styles. You'll see a variety of colors,
fabrics, fashions and accessories, guaranteed to fire
your imagination and add individuality to your
wardrobe.
05-9563 70 min. $39.95

Beautiful! The Total Look

Starring health and beauty expert Beverly Sassoon.
Features tips from guest stars Cathy Lee Crosby,
Eva Gabor and Maria Gibbs. An informative,
entertaining guide to total beauty for today's active
woman. Step-by-step instruction.
05-002 120 min. $29.95

BEAUTY DEFINED SERIES

This series is designed to help you with choosing
the right look and make-up that best suits you.
Hosted by Elaine Maike.

• Volume I
05-8020 30 min. $24.95

• Volume II
05-8021 30 min. $24.95

BEAUTY KNOWLEDGE SERIES:

Learn the inside secrets for applying make-up that
will bring out your best features, how to have
beautiful nails that look like you had them
professionally done and the secrets to help you
maintain youthful, healthier looking skin and hair.

• Hair Care Knowledge
05-8019 30 min. $16.95

• How to Make-Up Knowledge
05-8016 30 min. $16.95

• Nail Care Knowledge
05-8017 30 min. $16.95

• Skin Care Knowledge
05-8018 30 min. $16.95

Beauty On The Go

Invite Jackie Zeman, General Hospital star and her
friends into your home and take advantage of her
secrets for a great life, loving romance and beauty
tips which will make you look and feel wonderful.
She will be your personal trainer and show you her
40 workout exercises, demonstrate sexy, fun
flirting, show you how to look like a million with
out spending it. Jackie's common sense ideas are
perfect for today's active woman.
05-8007 107 min. $19.95

Color Me Beautiful

Author Carole Jackson and image consultant Cindy
Howard show you how to discover your natural
beauty through the colors that make you look
great... and feel fabulous. Includes book.
05-004 60 min. $14.95

Color Me Beautiful Makeup Video

Carole Jackson, author of Color Me Beautiful, now
shows you how to choose and use makeup colors
that will help you look your best.
05-3051 60 min. $19.95

Cover Girl Video Guide to Basic Make-Up with Christie Brinkley

Modeling's most famous face, Christie Brinkley,
hosts a behind-the-scenes look at make-up and the
fast-paced world of fashion and modeling.
05-1620 60 min. $19.95

DAVID NICHOLAS MAKE-UP ARTIST SERIES:

• 40 & Over Make-Up Techniques:

For women 40+, 60+, 80+. The older face
benefits from David's make-up technique by
accentuating the positives of aging and looking
more beautiful.
05-9934 60 min. $39.95

• Ethnic Make-Up Techniques

This demonstrates how to maximize the beauty of
various racial characteristics of Black, Hispanic,
and Oriental woman.
05-9936 60 min. $39.95

• Rubenesque Make-Up Techniques:

This video is specifically designed to assist

heavyset women in developing their full beauty potential.
05-9935 60 min. $39.95

• Basic Make-Up Techniques
Detailed demos show you how to condition and care for your skin and correctly apply day or evening make-up.
05-9933 60 min. $39.95

• Reconstructive & Corrective Make-Up
This program demonstrates how to hide birthmarks and scars, whether from acne, burns or other accidents. This kind of make-up application is more complex than applying regular make-up. Even the best plastic surgery often leaves tell-tale scarring that can be carefully camouflaged with corrective make-up.
05-9937 30 min. $39.95

• Men's Skin Care & Make-Up
Teaches men how to use cosmetics to camouflage those early signs of male pattern baldness. David shows how to use make-up so that scars and tattoos vanish for more than 24 hours and are waterproof. He demonstrates how you can select the most flattering individual beard style and how to trim a beard or mustache correctly. Many other grooming secrets are shared in this tape so that men can look their best.
05-9938 60 min. $39.95

• Professional Photographic Make-Up
Be prepared for any type of still photo work, B & W or Color, with the lessons taught in this video. Male and Female models.
05-9939 60 min. $39.95

• Video/TV Make-Up Techniques
Improve your look when you are a guest or perform before the television camera. Male and female models.
05-9940 60 min. $39.95

THEATRICAL AND FANTASY MAKE-UP SERIES:
Three special videos show you how to apply make-up for the right look for opera, ballet, runway or theatre. You'll learn techniques to adapt to other characterizations from these examples.

• Animation (Cat), Street Punk, Nautical (Facial Hair), Stylized Geisha
05-8013 60 min. $39.95

• Clown, Geisha, Ballet/Stage/Opera
05-9941 60 min. $39.95

• Female Impersonator, Aging (man), Dracula
05-8014 60 min. $39.95

Eight Minute Makeovers
Author Clare Miller stars in this 60-minute video program based on her best-selling book, "Eight Minute Makeovers". Clare shows how any woman can look glamorous, earthy, romantic or classic with simple make-up techniques. Includes book.
05-034 60 min. $19.95

Eyes Have It - With Donna Mills
Donna Mills is one of the few actresses who actually applies her own make-up both on a off the set. Now you, too, can share in all her beauty secrets in this easy-to-follow guide that takes you through each of the steps necessary to become a more beautiful you.
05-060 55 min. $19.95

Faces For Teens
Faces for teens is an up-beat, totally "now" look at the basics of good skin care and makeup. It provides easy, step-by-step demonstrations for your individual needs. Join eight lively models showing you how to care for and compliment your features so you can look you best, starting today!
05-8010 45 min. $24.95

Face Workout with Deborah Shelton
The former Miss America and star of T.V.'s "Dallas" shows viewers how to build facial tone and keep their skin looking young with the help of exercises developed by cosmetic and plastic surgeons.
05-1903 36 min. $16.95

French Braiding Fast and Easy
Learn to french braid your own or someone else's hair using one simple step-by-step fingering technique.
05-2709 15 min. $24.95

Great Face
Makeup expert Zia Wesley-Hosford provides no-nonsense skin care tips, including masque, astringent and deep-cleansing techniques.
05-1980 30 min. $16.95

Hair: Know it...Grow it
Marc Rosenbaum, Researcher for the American Fitness Association, explains his uni-sex, non-magical program to stimulate hair growth and strengthen existing hair. Viewers of all ages will benefit from this 3 step program: Cleanliness, brushing and massage.
05-8008 45 min. $29.95

VIDEO TITLES LISTED IN THIS GUIDE ARE AVAILABLE FOR PURCHASE OR RENTAL. CONTACT YOUR LOCAL VIDEO STORE OR TELEPHONE (800) 383-8811

Hair Loss Connection

This video clears up the confusion and frustration often encountered by people losing their hair. It's a no-nonsense video, five years in the making, that will answer questions about what you can do about hair loss.

05-9286   100 min. $29.95

Haircutting at Home

Haircutting is actually one of the easiest "do-it-yourself" tasks to accomplish, but also one of the most intimidating. Patty, a professional hair stylist for 12 years, will guide you through a step-by-step process for layering, trimming bangs and long hair, plus proper use of combs and scissors. You can beat the increasing costs of professional hair styling and save time too.

05-009 50 min. $29.95

Hairstyling At Home

Create the look and style you've always wanted. You'll learn how to cut and style the latest hair designs, how to roll and process permanents properly to get the style you want. This instructional tape shows you everything you need to know to look great.

29-9669 57 min. $29.95

Health & Beauty

Nutritionist, Lillian Grant will teach you how to minimize stress, slow down the aging process and maintain your beauty, health and vitality.

05-8000 30 min. $29.95

How to Cut Your Child's Hair

Michael Herber, a professional haircutter, shows you hot to cut a child's hair, giving the child a good haircut without spending money and expensive cuts.

05-3029 32 min. $24.95

Improve Your Smile

"Improve Your Smile" is a non-clinical video program for Dentists that motivates patients to seek cosmetic dentistry procedures. It presents the success stories of three real people whose confidence and self-esteem were boosted by esthetic improvements to their smiles. The video, which depicts technique verbally and visually, can be shown in the reception area, in the operatory prior to examination and consultation, or in the patient's home.

29-6636 10 min. $29.95

Joy Of Color

Learn how to contour with color makeup and coordinate this with your skin tone and clothing colors to create a dynamic image that makes you look terrific. Joy of Color shows you how to connect with the positive energy of color around

you to enrich your daily life.

05-5001 60 min. $29.95

Lookchangers

Image consultant, Judith Rasband, will show you how to experiment with what's in your closet and how to change the look of a basic outfit for a variety of personal styles, moods and occasions.

05-9561 40 min. $39.95

Looking Great, Feeling Great With Florence Henderson

Florence shares the simple, quick and inexpensive tricks she's learned in her 30 years of show business. Her secrets include: 20 minute make-up magic, do-anywhere exercises, stress reduction and fashion tips.

05-8009 60 min. $19.95

Looking Your Best

Learn the makeup secrets of the Hollywood stars. During Michael Westmore's 25-year career as one of Hollywood's top make-up professionals, he has worked his magic on such superstars as Natalie Wood, Elizabeth Taylor, Cher, Farrah Fawcett, Liza Minelli, Bette Davis, Shirley MacLaine, and Sally Field. Now for the first time these secrets from Hollywood's royal family of beauty are revealed in this exciting new video, expertly designed for women of all ages who want to look their best with a minimum of effort and expense.

05-6182 60 min. $16.95

Looks

Three attractive people are asked to reflect candidly on the pluses and pitfalls of going through life good-looking.

23-034 30 min. $89.95

Make-Up: Dramatic By Night

This program is for a more "glamorous" or night-time look. It guides the viewer through the application of the kind of make-up that can be used for evening or to achieve a dramatic effect.

05-2115 30 min. $16.95

Make-Up: Subtle by Day

This program presents a very natural approach to make-up. It is for the person who wears little make-up, but wants to look better than if they had none at all.

05-2114 30 min. $16.95

NEW FACES SERIES:

Coreen Cordova is one of Northern California's leading experts in make-up fashion. Her tips have been published in Harper's Bazaar, she has lectured for Mademoiselle magazine, and has had her own column in the San Francisco Chronicle. She is a licensed cosmetician whose skills are utilized by

VIDEO TITLES LISTED IN THIS GUIDE ARE AVAILABLE FOR PURCHASE OR RENTAL. CONTACT YOUR LOCAL VIDEO STORE OR TELEPHONE (800) 383-8811

plastic surgeons for post-operative patients, and has been instrumental in developing make-up techniques for burn patients in her work with the Northern California Burn Council. She is also a consultant to a major cosmetics firm.

• Beauty After 50
Adding years - Not make-up. "More is less as the years go by". These are key concepts in this program.
05-024 30 min. $39.95

• Color in Make-up and Clothes
Coreen Cordova tells about color, clothing, and make-up. She shows how fabric, fashion and make-up are all coordinated and enhanced through color.
05-013 30 min. $39.95

• Fabulous 40's
You're looking good, maybe even your best ever. Coreen talks about the use of color and make-up in these fabulous years.
05-023 30 min. $39.95

• Face on the Go
Coreen shows you how to get your drawers of cosmetics and treatments into one small bag for traveling. No excess!
05-016 30 min. $39.95

• Glasses Get Passes
The tint of glasses, the material and color of the frames, the shape to fit the face. Coren looks at these points plus make-up to enhance the eyes and glasses to get the best looks.
05-025 30 min. $39.95

• Grooming for Men
Coreen discusses skin care, shaving tips, tinting lashes, bronzing gels and the use of fragrance.
05-007 30 min. $39.95

• Hair and Make-up
Just as there is good and bad make-up, there are good and bad hair styles. Which one is most flattering to you? A guest hair stylist will appear with Coreen to show different styles.
05-017 30 min. $39.95

• Make-Up Artist Exposed
A "before and after" of the professional make-up artist. Coreen starts the program with no make-up on her face, and then demonstrates step-by-step how a professional applies make-up.
05-020 30 min. $39.95

• Million Dollar Face
Not everyone can afford the most expensive make-up, but she still wants to look fashionable and up to date. Coreen lets the viewer in on creating the "in"

look without a lot of investment.
05-014 30 min. $39.95

• Plastic Surgery: Part I
When is the right time for surgery, if at all? Descriptions and slides of face lifts, rhinoplasty (noses), eyes, chin implants. The present and future of plastic surgery. Dr. Roger Greenberg will help Coreen Cordova discuss this subject.
05-026 30 min. $39.95

• Plastic Surgery: Part II
When is the right time for surgery, if at all? This program continues the advice and concepts of "Plastic Surgery Part I".
05-027 30 min. $39.95

• Questions and Answers
Ten good questions about make-up, and ten good answers from Coreen.
05-022 30 min. $39.95

• Skin Care
How to maintain good skin: facials, everyday cleaning, special problems and how to correct them. Bella Schneider, skin care expert, will help Coreen in the demonstration.
05-015 30 min. $39.95

• Three Faces of Beauty
Coreen takes one face and gives it three entirely different looks: casual, work and night.
05-018 30 min. $39.95

• Tools of the Trade
Brushes, sponges, applicators, etc. Coreen runs through all of these "tools of the trade" for viewers.
05-019 30 min. $39.95

Outside Tells Us About the Inside
Coreen talks with a dermatologist on the care of the most common skin problems and how they can be corrected. Dr. Marshall Goldberg will assist.
05-021 30 min. $39.95

Patricia's Accessory Allure
Patricia answers the big accessory question - How, What and When to wear scarves and other accessories? See the impact of pulling outfits together with a simple scarf or a colored necklace. Watch Patricia as she creates one outfit after another with her original pairs of accessories formula. Create dozens of coordinated outfits with only 3 scarves, 3 necklaces, and 3 belts.
05-4039 30 min. $16.95

Patricia's Scarf Sensations
30 fun-filled minutes of follow along scarf tying with Patricia - 30 easy and wonderful, ways with

scarves - step-by-step action with the bias, oblong and square shapes - Patricia's ties have names to jog your memory - peak your self confidence with a sensational scarf tie on your neck, around your head, your waist - as a blouse under your jacket.
05-4038 30 min. $16.95

Professional Style - Esquire
Esquire has designed this videotape with the well-dressed man in mind. Competing in a business environment is tough enough, but this tape will help. It is full of advice on how to develop professional style and to create a powerful look. Expert clothing designer Alexander Julian is featured, along with Sassoon salon grooming specialists and several executives who discuss how appearance has helped them rise to the top. You'll learn how to choose the right wardrobe for your body type and profession; how to get perfect alterations for the perfect fit; how to put together the right ties, shoes, belts and accessories; how to use formal wear as a business asset; and much more.
05-028 60 min. $29.95

RAQUEL: TOTAL BEAUTY & FITNESS
Stunning actress Raquel Welch brings her special regimen of beauty and fitness to this video, combining the following areas for that total look and feel.

• **Hair Care**
05-8005 30 min. $19.95

• **Make-up**
05-8003 30 min. $19.95

• **Nails & Nail Care**
05-8004 30 min. $19.95

Swimwear Illustrated
Swimwear Illustrated takes you on location with photographers to a golden sunlit beach, a steamy steam bath, a seductive spa and even a boxing ring, for an inside look at the year's hottest swimsuits and models.
05-066 32 min. $19.95

Ultimate Face
Take charge of your appearance with the ultimate facial exercises designed to prevent wrinkles, remove sags, tighten muscles and reverse aging. These easy to perform facial exercises and relaxation techniques were designed by Jean Rosenbaum, M.D., to keep you looking youthful and vigorous.
05-8001 30 min. $29.95

Why Do I Call You Sexy
In this program, Jose Eber gives you the opportunity to look like the stars of Hollywood. This new make over program demonstrates all of his Hollywood secrets in action on 12 unique women.
05-033 90 min. $39.95

Community Service & Personal Safety

Be Your Own Traffic Policeman
"Be your own traffic policeman," is another way for saying, "be responsible for your own actions". This film stimulates youngsters to set up their own "let's pretend" traffic situations around the school and around the neighborhood and to discuss how individuals should respond in each situation. Primary grades.
28-8010 10 min. $49.95

Bicycle Drivers Don't Have To Have Accidents
Research shows that ten-to-fourteen-year-old boys have most of the serious bicycle accidents. They need to see this film. Accident-causing behaviors are depicted with the objective of increasing awareness of cause and effect relationships between such behavior and serious injuries. Intermediate-junior high school.
28-8012 14 min. $49.95

Chen Style T'ai Chi-Ch'uan
Tseng, Yun Xiang is one of S.E. China's top champions. In this video he demonstrates the original style. The form is shown from several angles and step-by-step instructions are given with self-defense applications for each movement demonstrated.
28-8020 90 min. $29.95

Common Sense Defense
Lisa Sliwa is a high-fashion model by day, a Guardian Angel by night. Here are her no-nonsense tips on how to recognize and respond to the dangers all women face. A practical, instructional and informative tape that can help women regain control of their lives by boosting self-confidence with knowledge that can save lives.
28-050 60 min. $29.95

Curiosity Without Tears: Childproofing Your Home
In this information-packed program you will learn

VIDEO TITLES LISTED IN THIS GUIDE ARE AVAILABLE FOR PURCHASE OR RENTAL. CONTACT YOUR LOCAL VIDEO STORE OR TELEPHONE (800) 383-8811

about hazards to children from birth to school age. You will also learn easy, childproofing techniques to help ensure safe environment for these precious family members. Parents, grandparents and babysitters will want to view this video so they can encourage baby's natural curiosity, without tears.
20-8006 20 min. $24.95

Eagle Claw Kung-Fu
Eagle Claw Kung-Fu is a very powerful style practiced in the Shaolin Temples of China. It uses strong ripping strikes as well as fast multiple punches, high kicks, ground work and finger strikes to accupressure points. Join Master Tseng, Yun Xiang as he gives you step-by-step instructions with the fighting applications of each movement included.
28-8021 90 min. $29.95

Firearms Safety & Your Family
This video covers loading and unloading procedures for the most common types of rifles, shotguns, and handguns including break, lever, bolt and pump actions as well as semiautomatics, revolvers and black powder guns. It also deals with child prevention training and covers both improvised and commercial locking devices and storage containers. Other topics include eye and ear protection and proper procedures and equipment for carrying or transporting firearms.
28-8015 30 min. $29.95

Getting Smart
This is an appealing and useful program that advises young people on how to deal with the violence that occurs in schools. For junior and senior high school levels.
28-2697 32 min. $99.95

GOOD KIDS-KARATE KIDS SERIES:
This is a unique & fun program designed to give children of all ages greater self-esteem, confidence and fitness through the study of Karate. Each "Good Kids" video contains a different series of lessons.

• **Confidence Makes Me Special**
28-8003 58 min. $19.95

• **No More Bullies**
28-8024 58 min. $19.95

• **Nobody Picks on Me**
28-8002 58 min. $19.95

Great Southwest Desert Survival Test
A humorous but critical look at Emergency Preparedness and Self-Reliance when living in (or just driving through) southwestern U.S.A. desert regions; presented as an easy-to-take, self scoring

quiz which immediately evaluates viewer readiness to combat various desert/wilderness emergency situations.
28-8027 23 min. $29.95

Handgun Safety
A certified NRA representative teaches how to use handguns safely.
28-8029 30 min. $16.95

Instant Self-Defense Guide For Women
This is a step-by-step guide that offers a straight forward approach to protection from "date rape" and "assault defense". Let experts in Karate and Aikido turn your normal, everyday reflex motions into devastating escape maneuvers for you.
29-9540 30 min. $19.95

Introduction To Rope Rescue
This video overviews the history and philosophy of rope rescue as well as step-by-step instruction in mountaineering, as it relates to rope rescue, non-technical/technical evacuations, terrain evacuation scenarios, consequences of error in the vertical realm. The teaching approach is clear and concise.
28-8008 45 min. $99.95

Karate For Kids: Easy Instruction and Exercise
Karate instructor Ted Nordblum takes kids through a workout teaching basic karate stretches and techniques. The focus is on self-improvement rather than competition and is great for promoting self esteem, health, fitness and positive values. Hip, upbeat music adds to fun!
28-8007 35 min. $16.95

Kids Have Rights Too!
An entertaining, informative and educational presentation to help children stay safe by making them aware of their rights. Designed as a loving and supportive parent/child communication tool that will give your child a message of strength and confidence.
28-8017 40 min. $19.95

Martial Art of Self-Defense
Starring Kazja. A Martial Arts expert with over 25 years experience demonstrates easy self-defense techniques for men and women.
28-1960 60 min. $16.95

MARTIAL ARTS SERIES WITH T'AI-CHI-CH'UAN MASTER BOB KLEIN

• **Chinese Kickboxing (2 tape set)**
Complete instructions for full contact T'ai-chi'Ch'uan style Chinese kickboxing. Includes punching, kicking, grappling, groundfighting and use of animal style, snake, tiger, mantis, monkey,

crane and drunken. Classroom training with corrections of students and detailed explanations of training methods.
28-8002 225 min. $69.95

• Kung-Fu Exercise Workouts
Two vigorous workouts using Kung-fu movements, including warm-ups. Develops flexibility, fluidity, speed and stamina. Self defense applications demonstrated.
28-8003 120 min. $39.95

• Practical Self Defense
Now the average person can learn to defend themselves even if they are not muscular. Master Klein shows you how to use the opponent's force against him. He reveals how to control the attacker's attention and balance and neutralize his force. Excellent for women/children. Step-by-step classroom instruction.
28-8006 90 min. $29.95

• Praying Mantis Kung-Fu
The Northern mantis form is shown from two angles in natural surroundings. Step-by-step instructions are given along with self-defense applications for each movement and the "mantis stances". This is a vigorous exercise which revitalizes the body.
28-8005 94 min. $39.95

• Push Hands-Kung-Fu's Greatest Training Secret
A unique, Chinese two person exercise which develops fluidity, internal energy, concentration and the ability to neutralize aggression. You will learn to sense the other person's intentions before they materialize physically. Complete instructions with applications to self defense, health and meditation. Very important for all martial arts students.
28-8004 120 min. $39.95

• T'ai-chi-Ch'uan Kung-Fu
Step-by-step instructions for the ancient Chinese movements which serve as the basis for "kung fu", considered the most devastating form of self defense. Applications for each movement, weight distribution, breathing and beginning "push hands".
28-8000 120 min. $39.95

• T'ai-chi Sword Forms
Graceful sword movements with step-by-step instructions, fighting applications for each movement, sword exercises and demonstration of free style swordfighting practice.
28-8001 120 min. $39.95

People Tracking: You Can Find Anyone
Find anyone with this step by step video that will teach you how to access public records, government agencies, newspaper morgues, online computer databases, credit reporting agencies, motor vehicle departments and a whole slew of special sources to help you track or build a dossier on anyone. "People Tracking: You Can Find Anyone" lists exact search paths, methodologies and addresses so you can find anyone in the most efficient method possible.
28-8014 75 min. $69.95

Protect Yourself! A Woman's Guide To Self Defense
Robin Cooper, a 3rd-degree black belt, presents an easy to follow exercise program that combines straight forward common sense with a series of defense techniques to help women of all ages deal effectively with an assault.
28-8019 60 min. $16.95

Protect Yourself with Simon Rhee
L.A. Raiders stars Marcus Allen and Obis McKinney help Tae Quon Do master Simon Rhee show the finer points of mauling any attacker.
28-072 45 min. $16.95

Safely-Walk To School
This video follows the route of two children walking to school and illustrates to children the importance of safety while teaching about crossing the street, accepting rides, obeying traffic signals, and walking on sidewalks. Also available in Spanish. Primary grades.
28-8011 12 min. $49.95

Safety Rules For School
The Safety Gremlin guides students through safety rules they should observe on the way to school, inside school, and on the playground. This puppet character intervenes in a variety of near-accidents, and helps youngsters understand what can happen if safety rules are ignored.
28-8013 11 min. $49.95

Self Defense: An Instructional Video For Everyone
Practice the techniques on this video and stop living in a state of fear. Learn how not to be a victim. Learn how to escape. Crime does not discriminate among men and women or the young and old. Be a survivor instead of a statistic. Practice "Self-Defense". It's easy and effective.
28-5375 60 min. $19.95

Self Defense For All Men & Women
Master Instructor Personious, along with three martial arts students, demonstrates and explains dozens of self-defense techniques in this helpful video. These techniques are easy to learn and remember and applicable to both men and women.
28-9586 45 min. $26.95

VIDEO TITLES LISTED IN THIS GUIDE ARE AVAILABLE FOR PURCHASE OR RENTAL. CONTACT YOUR LOCAL VIDEO STORE OR TELEPHONE (800) 383-8811

Self Defense for Women

Discover an attacker's weak points and your own strong points in a practical illustration of self defense especially designed for women. Steve Powell offers advice, exercises and instruction on basic methods of defense against purse snatching and sexual assault. An important tape for every woman to view.

28-026 60 min. $29.95

Self Defense With Steve Powell

Chief instructor at England's Chosen-Kai School, Steve Powell shows how to discover opponent's weak points and use your own strong points.

28-045 60 min. $29.95

Self-Defense Workout With Lorenzo Lamas

Strengthen and tone your body while learning self-defense techniques that increase your agility and flexibility. In this video, Lorenzo Lamas presents the perfect way for men and women to work out while practicing exciting self-defense exercises.

28-8018 45 min. $16.95

Split Second Self-Defense

Specifically for women, this tape condenses 23 years of Martial Arts experience into a few essentials. Learn basic escape moves and common holds criminals use against women.

28-8026 32 min. $24.95

Steve DeMasco's Aerobic Defense Workout

Through a simple step-by-step process, learn to apply this workout to attack situations. By mastering the application of the workout, you will develop the confidence to perform in high stress situations.

28-8028 60 min. $16.95

Teenage Ninja Karate Lessons

Hey Dudes...like, let two awesome Karate Champs show you how to be really, really good at defending yourself or your friends. This rad video makes it easy to do perfect wheel kicks, cobra strikes, front jump kicks, plus 18 other radical moves.

28-6463 30 min. $16.95

Woman's "How-To" of Self Defense

What to do. What not to do. A simple-to-learn, practical, illustrated guide of different ways to defend yourself against bullies, drunks, rapists, flashers and degenerates. This tape features case histories of rape victims. It gives you 25 strike points to attack. Woman's "How-To" of Self Defense is a videotape that could save your life.

28-049 60 min. $29.95

Public Speaking

Be Prepared to Speak

A step-by-step guide to public speaking, presented by Toastmasters International and designed to provide you with the skill and confidence to stand up and speak effectively in any situation. Its three-part structure takes you through speech presentation, control of stage fright and also covers preparation.

07-002 27 min. $89.95

Expressively Speaking

Expressively Speaking presents an hour of speech improvement exercises to give your speaking voice power, clarity and flexibility. Each lesson builds on the preceding lesson and lessons are numbered for easy reference. The daily speech aerobics segment is an abbreviated compilation of exercises positioned at the head of the tape to be used as a daily warm-up. The confidence and expression segment of the tape is 30 minutes long and presents actors' techniques to insure that you will be confident, expressive, and in-control in any context of presentation. With the advantage of these techniques you can be more dynamic, and you can be sure that your message will be heard.

29-5132 60 min. $59.95

How to Speak with Confidence

It isn't what you say that counts; it's how you look, act and speak that sells your message. Sound familiar? Expert communications trainer Bert Decker demonstrates a step-by-step program to help you master facial expressions, features and humor.

07-1840 46 min. $69.95

Persuasive Speaking

Distinguished speakers and speaking coaches from the worlds of business, politics, and theater explain the keys to the essential skill of speeches and presentations. Features clips of speeches by master speakers President Ronald Reagan and New York Governor Mario Cuomo.

07-021 60 min. $29.95

Miscellaneous

Smart Cookies Don't Crumble

Based on the best selling book, "Smart Cookies" delivers life-changing insights to today's American

women. Dr. Sonya Friedman shows you how to take control of your life, how to create your own second chances, and how to minimize self-defeating behavior.
29-176 30 min. $24.95

SUBLIMINAL PERSUASION AUDIO/VIDEO SERIES

This is a truly unique system to help you awaken to your unlimited potential. It incorporates all the aspects of learning: sight, sound and repetition. Each system package includes a video and audio tape designed to help you change and improve your life.

• **Concentration**
29-103 30 min. $29.95

• **Creative Thinking**
29-111 30 min. $29.95

• **Develop Enthusiasm**
29-109 30 min. $29.95

• **Good Study Habits**
29-107 30 min. $29.95

• **Memory Improvement**
29-105 30 min. $29.95

• **Money - Prosperity**
29-112 30 min. $29.95

• **Self-Confidence**
29-110 30 min. $29.95

• **Subconscious Sales Power**
29-106 30 min. $29.95

TEEN TOPICS SERIES:

• **Time Management For Teens "Getting Your Act Together" Vol I**
This classroom-tested program will improve your skills in handling these and other important problems. The lessons learned will be of great benefit throughout your lifetime. This program was developed and tested by experts to increase your confidence and self-esteem, preparing you for success in whatever endeavor you choose. It is a great reference tool which you can review as often as you like. Teen Topics is your partner for a prepared future.
29-5355 52 min. $29.95

• **"Study Skills For People Who Hate To Study" Vol II**
Here's a very special classroom-tested program designed for people who hate to study. It covers fundamentals of study skills necessary for success. Review as often as you wish...your Teen Topics is your partner for a lifetime.
29-5356 83 min. $29.95

You Can Win! Negotiating For Power, Love and Money
Follow the techniques of Dr. Tacet Albert Warschaw (as revealed in entertaining scenarios) and learn to get what you want from your boss, your kids, even your lover! Master the art of reading body language, controlling emotional reactions and handling intimidation. You'll soon find that you can easily negotiate to your advantage.
29-057 55 min. $29.95

Zig Ziglar: Goals
With this video, you'll get a step-by-step approach that you can tailor to your immediate needs for setting goals and achieving them and how to enjoy their benefits. Zig Ziglar is a master at helping people reach their maximum potential.
29-1642 70 min. $79.95

These Videos Will Help You

Develop Qualities, Attitudes and

Talents that Will Improve Your Life.

Searching For

A Unique Gift That is

Informative and Appreciated?

The Video Titles

In This Guide

Make Wonderful Gifts.

VIDEO TITLES LISTED IN THIS GUIDE ARE AVAILABLE FOR PURCHASE
OR RENTAL. CONTACT YOUR LOCAL VIDEO STORE OR TELEPHONE (800) 383-8811

Pets

- ✓ *Dogs*
- ✓ *Cats*
- ✓ *Miscellaneous*

Dogs

ALL STAR DOG TRAINING PROGRAM:

• Advanced Behaviors
Joel Silverman instructs you how to teach your dog such things as: Head down, Head up and other Advanced Behaviors.
24-8001 30 min. $39.95

• Basic Behaviors
Presented by Birds & Animals Unlimited, leading animal training company in Hollywood for 25 years. Trainer Joel Silverman will teach you positive training methods for your dogs.
24-8000 30 min. $39.95

• Health, Nutrition and Safety
This tape gives advice on the proper care of your dog including: health tips, nutrition and your dog's safety.
24-8002 25 min. $39.95

ARF!
Starring: Merlin Pekinese, Lob Baker, Miss Julia Chow. At last! A video program just for dogs. ARF! is the canine video that everybody is barking about with shows like Mild Kingdom, with Merlin Pekinese; Recipes To Lick Your Chops Over, with Julia Chow; the popular game show Boners, with Lob Barker... and many more! It's the perfect gift for Fido (and a great one for your dog-loving friends).
24-058 30 min. $14.95

Barbara Woodhouse Goes to Beverly Hills
Barbara Woodhouse, the world famous dog trainer, goes to Beverly Hills and visits a host of stars and their dogs in this look at extraordinary world of canine culture among the very rich.
24-011 52 min. $16.95

Caring for Your Dog
24-077 45 min. $19.95

Complete Canine Training Video
This video training program was created by Paul Moran. The techniques are so successful that the "Moran" method is known by many as "The World's Most Advanced Basic Training Program". All that you need is contained on this four tape set.
24-8050 200 min. $69.95

Dog Care Guide
Here's a videocassette your customers will be eager to get their paws on. "The Westminster Kennel Club Dog Care Guide" for dog owners. This videocassette offers the knowledge and experience of the prestigious Westminster Kennel Club for the selection, training, and overall care to raise a healthy and happy dog.
24-6380 45 min. $19.95

Dog Training With The Grossmans
Tips for training puppies and older dogs from world-class dog trainers.
24-015 30 min. $39.95

Good Puppy
An easy step-by-step training program on housebreaking, nipping and prevention, learning to be alone, calming techniques and more!
24-8028 56 min. $19.95

Guide to Complete Dog Care
Roger Caras gives in-depth information on dog care, including exercise, nutrition, grooming, health and behavior training.
24-012 60 min. $29.95

How to Train Your Dog at Home
Have you been envious of dog owners whose animals are responsive and obedient? Now you can gain similar control of your dog by using the method presented in this tape.
24-076 55 min. $39.95

Leading the Pack: The Ultimate Dog Training Video
This is an easy-to-follow program that educates owners in state-of-the-art dog training. Through advanced computer graphics and special slow-motion training sequences, you will learn commands and develop a great relationship with your dog. Reviewed "excellent" by Humane Societies nationwide.
24-8052 60 min. $24.95

Menu For Manners
Robert Milner guides you through a simple and workable instruction of dog obedience that will housebreak, train and maintain a family dog.
24-039 60 min. $39.95

Man's Best Friend
We feed them, breed them, muzzle them, nuzzle them, walk them, talk with them and give them free run of our homes. Over 30% of Americans live with a dog. Why of all the many different animals do we choose to share our lives with dogs? Nature explores the special relationship between man and dog that has lasted over 1000 years.
24-1568 60 min. $19.95

VIDEO TITLES LISTED IN THIS GUIDE ARE AVAILABLE FOR PURCHASE OR RENTAL. CONTACT YOUR LOCAL VIDEO STORE OR TELEPHONE (800) 383-8811

NOW YOUR TALKING DOG! VIDEO SERIES:

Dr. Dennis Fetko is recognized as one of the nation's foremost authorities on canine behavioral therapy. Dennis' training began as a youth. His formal practice has been in operation for over fifteen years. He specializes in the elimination and reversal of negative behaviors in dogs.

• **Eliminate Excessive Barking Behavior In Your Dog**
24-5305 30 min. $19.95

• **Prevent Your Dog From Leash Pulling And Door Dashing**
24-5303 30 min. $19.95

• **Reverse Destructive Digging And Chewing Habits**
24-5304 30 min. $19.95

• **Stop Unwanted Jumping In 3 Easy Steps**
24-5302 30 min. $19.95

• **Successfully Housebreak Your Dog**
24-5301 30 min. $19.95

Obedience And Behavior: You Can Train Your Dog

Anyone can train a puppy or adult dog in obedience and solve some annoying behavioral problems. The training methods are gentle, fast and very effective. You will learn how to teach your dog to sit, stay, heel and lie down; also, how to correct behavioral problems such as jumping on the furniture and excessive barking. Tape also includes tips on housebreaking, nutrition and grooming.
24-033 30 min. $39.95

Puppy's First Year

This video is designed to help you understand and train your puppy to become an enjoyable companion and family member. Topics include picking a puppy, housebreaking, diet, socialization, puppy problems, puppy training, grooming and more.
24-105 90 min. $19.95

Tellington Touch for Healthier, Happier Dogs

This informative program introduces you to the Tellington Touch, a magical method for healing and communicating with your favorite dog.
24-9798 60 min. $29.95

TLC Way Of Training Your Dog

Hosted by "Dallas" star and life-long dog owner, Howard Keel. This is a complete guide for training dogs and works with all breeds and ages, especially for first time dog owners or newly acquired dogs. The TLC package includes two booklets, one to chart your dogs daily progress and a special tips booklet by canine therapist, Martha LaBaugh covering problems like housetraining, barking, digging, chewing and more.
24-6212 72 min. $24.95

Train Your Dog Before Your Dog Trains You

Learn The Secrets Of Professional Dog Training. This video program demonstrates the most effective, successful and easy to follow methods of obedience and behavior training ever presented.
24-6142 90 min. $19.95

Training Your Best Friend: With Elke Sommer

This entertains and educates the dog owner on how to train his best friend. Elke Sommer is the program host. Features the Kamer Praise technique for training untrained dogs, as well as partially trained dogs that are a nuisance. Michael Kamer, dog trainer to the stars, brings you his techniques.
24-5038 71 min. $19.95

Cats

Cat Care Video Guide

This video features healthcare, nutrition, grooming and playtime tips. The program highlights home health exams, neuter/spay and vaccination information, flea control, pet exercise and basic diet requirements.
24-097 20 min. $29.95

Cat Show

Breeders and exhibitors discuss showing their particular breed and what judges are looking for. Very educational!
24-8033 30 min. $29.95

Just Call Me Kitty

This is a purr-fectly charming video all about cats. It takes the viewer to a major cat show, a cat specialty store, a cat groomer, and the ever-popular "Pet Limo Service" plus much more.
24-2116 60 min. $14.95

Kittens to Cats

Designed to help you understand your cat through all stages of its life, from picking a kitten to coping

VIDEO TITLES LISTED IN THIS GUIDE ARE AVAILABLE FOR PURCHASE OR RENTAL. CONTACT YOUR LOCAL VIDEO STORE OR TELEPHONE (800) 383-8811

with grief. Practical, effective and easy-to-follow information.
24-2059 60 min. $19.95

Longhaired Cat Breeds
Loads of Persians and others are included on this informative video. Coat care is discussed as well.
24-8032 30 min. $29.95

Shorthaired Cat Breeds
A down to earth look at the many individual shorthaired breeds that make up this group of cats.
24-8031 60 min. $29.95

Tellington Touch for Happier, Healthier, Cats
Learn how to communicate and heal your cat. Gain a deeper connection with your favorite feline from birth to death.
24-2976 60 min. $29.95

Miscellaneous

Barnyard Babies
These barnyard babies will charm and fascinate the entire family! Ranchers and their children show us their spring crop of animals and talk about the joys of rearing new life.
24-5005 30 min. $29.95

Basic TTeam with Llamas
Marty McGee studied intensively with Linda Tellington-Jones, who created TTeam as an innovative way of working with horses. Marty applied the TTeam approach to hundreds of llamas, adapting the techniques as the llamas showed her what worked best with them. The results are remarkable.
24-8051 120 min. $64.95

Bird Basics
Fun and easy guide for new and experienced bird owners. Featuring avian expert, Dr. M. Lintner.
24-8003 30 min. $19.95

Boas & Pythons
This will teach you everything you need to know about taking care of Boas and Pythons. Topics include: health problems, caging and feeding.
24-8004 30 min. $19.95

Five Star Llama Packing
This entertaining program is loaded with information and demonstrations. The five stars are experienced commercial packers who share insights

gained from years of experience.
24-9081 120 min. $39.95

Kuddly Kittens
Every child dreams of having a kitten of their very own. Now, "Kuddly Kittens" lets you make your child's dream come true! "Kuddly Kittens" features all the real live bouncing, running, wrestling, sniffing, tail-wagging baby kittens any child could possibly want! Set to an original musical sound track, this program will delight children while stimulating them to discuss their feelings and emotions.
24-7053 30 min. $14.95

Llama Reproduction: Neonatal Clinic
This informative video covers reproductive anatomy, breeding, fetal development, birthing and newborn care. It also contains several live llama births. Includes book.
24-9802 210 min. $94.95

Llama Training with Bobra Goldsmith:
What Every Llama Should Know
A popular tape for people who are thinking of acquiring llamas as well as very useful for llama owners. Bobra Goldsmith demonstrates specific methods for both young and adult llamas.
24-9803 120 min. $64.95

Pets And Their Care
Children learn that fresh food, clean water, love and affection, a clean home, exercise, baths, grooming and regular medical care are as important to their pet's well-being as they are to their own.
24-8017 15 min. $49.95

Puppy Pals
Every child dreams of having a puppy of their very own. Now, "Puppy Pals" lets you make your child's dream come true! "Puppy Pals" features all the real live bouncing, running, wrestling, sniffing, tail-wagging baby puppies any child could possibly want! Set to an original musical sound track, this program will delight children while stimulating them to discuss their feelings and emotions.
24-7054 30 min. $14.95

Telepathic Communication with Animals
Have you ever wondered what an animal was thinking? Penelope Smith talks with animals all the time. An inspiring program that even skeptics will enjoy, including many tips on how you can communicate with animals.
24-9797 40 min. $29.95

Training Llamas to Dance with Bobra Goldsmith
Topics include preparing the llama for driving, fitting the harness, the first driving lesson, the

touch of the reins, ground driving, introducing the llama to the cart, riding in the cart and safety.
24-9804 120 min. $64.95

Tropical Fish On Video
An introduction to tropical fish as a hobby. With an instruction manual for the aquarium and trouble shooting guide for occasional problems.
24-6934 40 min. $24.95

Why Llamas
If you've ever wondered, "Why llamas?" you will wonder no more after seeing this delightful

videotape. You'll hear the humming, shrieking and ogling of llama language. Taking care of llamas and their history are also covered. Features a soundtrack by the Andean music of Sukay.
24-9805 52 min. $29.95

Your Pet, Your Pal
This program presents kids with a selection of different pets, ranging from dogs and cats to boa constrictors and cockatiels. Children are encouraged to handle the animals, ask questions and familiarize themselves with the responsibilities of pet care.
24-034 45 min. $29.95

Training Your Dog?

Picking Out A New Pet?

Thinking About Llamas?

Or Fish?

Or Boas?

The Videos In This Chapter

Can Help.

VIDEO TITLES LISTED IN THIS GUIDE ARE AVAILABLE FOR PURCHASE OR RENTAL. CONTACT YOUR LOCAL VIDEO STORE OR TELEPHONE (800) 383-8811

New

Special Interest Video Titles

Become Available

Often.

Please Inquire

If A Title Or Subject

You Are Looking For

Is Not Listed.

Photography,
Film
&
Video

✓ *Commercial Photography*
✓ *Instruction & Technique*
✓ *Video Art*
✓ *Miscellaneous*

Commercial Photography

Glamour Through Your Lens: How to Shoot Your Own Centerfold

Will give photographers, novices and serious amateurs alike, the tips they'll need to know to take their best shots. Learn the fundamentals of a shoot, from styling and make-up to lighting and posing.

03-8059　60 min.　$19.95

Perfect Picture System

With this program you can be certain that you are seeing and hearing the absolute best that your home video system can create.

03-8067　30 min.　$19.95

Instruction & Technique

Action Photography

Join action photographer John Vaeth for an in-depth look at the lenses, films and techniques that make sports photography an exhilarating pursuit. See how to take dynamic pictures of bicycle moto-cross, water-skiing, snow-skiing, basketball, diving, swimming, gymnastics and wrestling. Learn to adapt to any situation in which your subject can't or won't sit still.

03-108　30 min.　$19.95

Art of Photo Composition

Prize-winning photos illustrate the value of strong composition in the creation of better-than-average 35mm pictures. Learn to bring out your own natural sense of design by following six simple guidelines for better photo composition. See how prize winners break, as well as abide by the compositional rules. Add impact to every picture.

03-099　30 min.　$19.95

Art of Videography

Presented with a refreshing style and simplicity, the techniques used may be easily applied to any situation. You'll see the principles at work in story plots and direct examples, with a wealth of information on virtually every aspect of videography. Repeated viewings will be required as you begin to master the greatest story teller

ever...the video camera.

35-9083　60 min.　$29.95

Basic Photography

Photo journalist and Seattle University photography instructor Bruce McKim quickly takes you through all the basics of how to operate the Polaroid, 220 and 35mm cameras. Learn about various lenses, how to load your camera, the meaning of labels on various types of film packages, and the basics of good composition.

03-064　49 min.　$39.95

Basic Picture-Taking

Build better pictures from your 35mm camera of just about anyone or anything, step-by-step. Learn how to express what you see photographically. Get expert advice on how to take exciting, humorous and memorable photos of your favorite subjects. Improve your chances of snapping that "lucky" shot.

03-098　30 min.　$19.95

Camcorder Class

Whether you've invested in a VHS, Beta or the new 8mm camcorder system, invest a little more and learn to use the system properly. This program is packed with information that will make your video projects look professional.

03-2171　35 min.　$29.95

Camcorders: Shoot Like the Pros

Top professionals show you how to use a camcorder and how to shoot quality home videos. Includes shot planning, transitions, pans and zooms, lighting tips and editing between a camcorder and VCR. Easy to follow demonstrations.

03-9995　60 min.　$29.95

Creating The Image

In three diverse locations - a studio in Kansas City, Martha's Vineyard, and Elko, Nevada - master photographers show how they achieve their award-winning and powerful black and white images. Scott Griswold, Nick Vedros, and David Burnett share their expertise and show you how to create fascinating and unusual images.

03-5570　50 min.　$19.95

Creating The Print

Taking the shot is only the beginning of a photographer's creativity. The darkroom is his second stage and in this informative video three master black & white printers demonstrate various useful techniques and show you how they apply to every aspect of photography from fine art to photojournalism. Whether or not you make your own prints, you will learn how to direct this highly

VIDEO TITLES LISTED IN THIS GUIDE ARE AVAILABLE FOR PURCHASE OR RENTAL. CONTACT YOUR LOCAL VIDEO STORE OR TELEPHONE (800) 383-8811

creative step.
03-5571 50 min. $19.95

Effective Use of Lenses
Deepen your knowledge of interchangeable lenses. Discover what lens focal length can tell you about angle of view and magnification. Learn to use the relationship between focal length and minimum shutter speed for maximum picture sharpness. Examine normal, wide-angle and telephoto lenses in terms of use, perspective and distortion. Start manipulating depth of field to your picture-taking advantage.
03-100 30 min. $19.95

Existing Light Photography
Enjoy taking unobtrusive (without flash) pictures by natural light. Choose the proper film, filters and processing for different types and intensities of light. Discover how to judge, and work with, lighting situations encountered in everyday life. Improve your pictures of sporting events and those taken after sunset.
03-101 30 min. $19.95

Existing Light Photography: Advanced
Join master photographer Gary Whelpey as he shows you what beautiful pictures you can take using only "the light that happens to be on the scene." Tour Walt Disney World's EPCOT Center from twilight through starlight. Slip indoors for the action-packed Empire State Games in Syracuse, New York. Even step inside a typical home for soft, natural portraits of children as you learn to capture all the moods and colors you see.
03-110 30 min. $19.95

Glamour Photography
Peter Gowland's photographs of the female face and form have been appearing in magazines, books, calendars and ads for more than 35 years. In this cassette, Peter and his wife, Alice, take you along with them on several shooting sessions where they demonstrate ways to capture the beauty in their subjects for stunning results.
03-114 30 min. $19.95

Guide to Home Video Camera Use
A complete guide to home video camera use, including camera movement, framing and composition, lighting and sound, and how to plan your production.
03-010 60 min. $29.95

How to Light for Videography
Lighting equipment, the concept of lighting, the control of light, creative lighting and basic safety are covered in this how-to program for the beginning videographer.
03-020 30 min. $16.95

How to Record Sound for Video
This program shows and tells how to listen like a microphone, how to eliminate ambient noise, how to add sound afterwards. It also covers innovative uses of sound and audio legalities you need to know.
03-019 30 min. $16.95

How to Shoot Home Video: The Basics
A "must" program for the beginning home videographer covering the basic techniques of sound, lighting, composition and directing.
03-018 30 min. $16.95

How to Shoot Sports Action
How-to tips for shooting eight different sports, including equipment, camera placement, sound techniques, and dramatization of the story.
03-022 30 min. $16.95

IMAGES: 150 YEARS OF PHOTOGRAPHY SERIES:
Culled from over 20 different collections of photographs in museums, archives and private collections in the U.S., Canada, Britain and France.

• Best or Nothing
Only in the last 20 years have photographs become objects to be traded through auction rooms; as their value increases, so does their status as art. This program explores the passions of the private collector.
35-8002 60 min. $29.95

• Domestic Memories
The amateur documentary tradition is seen through the eyes of two photographers from northern Britain.
35-8001 60 min. $29.95

• Eyes of the Empire
Photography in the 19th century was often a tool of imperial science and exploration. Numerous anthropological photographic collections are examined in this program.
35-8003 60 min. $29.95

• Magic Mirror
Selecting their own favorite photos from contemporary works back to 1839, the producers of this program trace the lineage of photography as art and present a glorious parade of great photographs drawn from the great museum collections of the world.
35-8005 60 min. $29.95

• Pencil of Nature
This program follows the technical and aesthetic strides made by the early practitioners of

VIDEO TITLES LISTED IN THIS GUIDE ARE AVAILABLE FOR PURCHASE OR RENTAL. CONTACT YOUR LOCAL VIDEO STORE OR TELEPHONE (800) 383-8811

photography.
35-8000 60 min. $29.95

• **Real Thing**
Focusing on the Farm Security Administration, which set out to document America in the 1930's, this program looks at the results achieved when photographers are commissioned to reflect the world or aspects of it.
35-8004 60 min. $29.95

Images with Imagination
Enter the special tabletop/still-life/derivation world of Joe Timmer, winner of over 500 photo-competition awards in more than 25 countries. Joe explains how competition photography is a game that you can play and win with your camera. He shows you how you can manipulate your subjects and use trick photography to create slides with immediate impact.
03-113 30 min. $19.95

Imaginative Use of Filters
Explore these interesting add-ons that feed your creative impulses. Discover the versatility of a polarizing screen and the practical and psychological joys of color conversion filters. Find out how to let one filter do the work of several, how to fine-tune your color slides, how to add softness, blur, star bursts, rainbows, even mind-boggling, multi-image effects to your pictures.
03-102 30 min. $19.95

Introduction to Photography
Basic photographic instruction for learning how to get the most from your 35mm camera and how to start taking pictures you can be proud of. Learn how to get sharp, correctly exposed pictures instead of fuzzy, faint near-misses. Start capitalizing on such camera features as adjustable shutter speeds, lens openings, built-in exposure meters and interchangeable lenses. Increase your percentage of good results.
03-097 30 min. $19.95

Kodak's How To Take Better Pictures
If the pictures you just picked up disappointed you, this video program is just what the doctor ordered. Filled with simple, easy-to-understand information, it can help anyone take better pictures. Travel around the country, from vacation spots like Sea World to a child's birthday party, and gain valuable tips on making your photos the best they can be.
03-5568 30 min. $19.95

KODAK'S LEARNING PHOTOGRAPHY SERIES:

• **Art Of Composing Pictures**
Understand lighting and learn how to use it to

improve your photographs by varying mood and emphasis. Also, includes a strong introduction to composition and framing.
03-5576 45 min. $19.95

• **Basics Of Taking Better Pictures**
Learn the basics of shutter speed, lens openings, exposure meters, flashes, setting up shots and much, much more!
03-5575 45 min. $19.95

• **Choosing The Right Film, Lenses, And Advanced Flash Techniques**
Various film types and various lenses can create a wide range of results that you can use to enhance your pictures. Learn how to choose the right type, size and speed of film and explore the uses of the wide-angle, normal, and telephoto lenses.
03-5578 45 min. $19.95

• **Using Filters, Creative Techniques And Photographing People**
Discover how lens filters can create new and exciting pictures. Learn the pro's secrets for photographing people, in candid and portrait style.
03-5577 45 min. $19.95

Kodak Presents How To Make Better Home Videos
Designed for every skill level of video-camera user, this easy-to-understand instructional guide covers every essential area, from basic operation and maintenance to making good sound recordings and using light to improve picture quality. Learn how easy it is to tell stories and relive memorable events by using a video camera.
03-5569 45 min. $19.95

Language of Light
Begin to understand the nature and qualities of light. Learn to recognize and control light direction. Work with contrast to bring out the best in your subjects. Use the color of light to express your moods or feelings. Turn even bad weather lighting conditions into opportunities for atmospheric pictures.
03-103 30 min. $19.95

Lights-Camera-Action
Fifty basic shooting and production techniques. Covers: Children, Weddings, Sports, Lighting and lots of professional tips. This tape has been rated highly by critics and is recommended as an introduction to using home video equipment.
03-6637 30 min. $19.95

Magic Moments: Capture Them in Pictures
A program for people who aren't "photographers," but rather "aim and shoot" picture-takers who want

to improve their skills. Comes with a pocket-size photo tips card.
03-1966 30 min. $19.95

Magic Of Photography
This video is geared toward the novice photographer who wants to learn the techniques of lens selection, lighting, model placement, camera angles, exposure ratios, composition, and much more.
12-8006 45 min. $29.95

Nature Photography
Join wildlife photographer Tom Mangelsen in Grand Teton National Park for an insider's perspective on the joys of photographing animals in their natural environments. Get up and out early to photograph ducks, geese, osprey, swans, even elk and moose. Learn what lenses, films, shutter speeds and techniques to use. Camouflage yourself and your camera to take pictures of birds attracted by decoys and callers.
03-111 30 min. $29.95

ON ASSIGNMENT:

• Basic 35 mm Photography
A video for the serious photographer. Divided into three 30-minute segments, it deals mostly with various aspects of lighting. The first portion outlines the "nature of light" as it applies to professional photography. From understanding light, the program moves into the control factors and various exposures. Then the viewer is shown how to use available light for both portraits and product illustrations.
03-115 90 min. $29.95

• Basic Videography
This is the starting point for anyone wishing to learn the exciting, colorful world of video.
03-2064 90 min. $29.95

• Business Of Photography
Topics include preparing your portfolio, selling yourself and your services, and career opportunities.
03-320 90 min. $29.95

• Darkroom
This video outlines in detail the basic skills and knowledge needed to build, equip and work in a darkroom environment.
03-6323 90 min. $29.95

• Photographic Design
Topics include camera vision, composition, and designing with light and color.
03-318 90 min. $29.95

• Photographic Light
Uses an entertaining and highly visual style to build an essential foundation for understanding the concepts of light.
03-2065 90 min. $29.95

• Studio
Topics include large format cameras, studio and product lighting, and people photography.
03-319 90 min. $29.95

Photographers and Their Films
Look at color and black-and-white films with an improved eye. Learn to choose the right type, size and speed of film to meet your particular picture-taking needs. Get an insider's understanding of why photographers sometimes choose a black-and-white film or a slow color film. Find out how to turn the "wrong" film into a good, sometimes even great, spontaneous picture!
03-104 30 min. $19.95

Photographing the Nude with James Baes
James Baes presents a step-by-step instruction in directing a model, lighting techniques, backgrounds and props, creative composition, filters and special effects. Appeals to both the professional and amateur photographer.
03-044 42 min. $39.95

Photographing People
Focus on photography's most popular subject - people! Discover how to make a subject's face "light up" rather than "freeze up." Learn to make choices that will flatter your subject with indoor as well as outdoor settings. Perfect posing and camera-handling techniques that will transform you into a popular photographer.
03-105 30 min. $19.95

Prize-Winning Pictures
Eavesdrop on two photo experts as they talk about what turns a picture into a prize winner. Find out how you can improve your chances of clicking a "lucky" shot. Practice seeing the world with an imaginative eye. Learn when, where and how to look for the contest picture. Discover how to plan a posed shot so that it looks spontaneous and how to capture a spur-of-the-moment shot with prize-winning ease.
03-106 30 min. $19.95

PRO PHOTO TECHNIQUES SERIES:

• How to Paint Portrait Backdrops
Modern and traditional designs for high and low key photography, studio and location work. Easy instruction ensures professional results even if

VIDEO TITLES LISTED IN THIS GUIDE ARE AVAILABLE FOR PURCHASE OR RENTAL. CONTACT YOUR LOCAL VIDEO STORE OR TELEPHONE (800) 383-8811

you've never painted before. This video shows the procedure for painting five backdrops.
35-8063 60 min. $59.95

• Problem Portraits
How to use clothing, posing and lighting to produce beautiful portraits of clients with less than perfect faces or figures. You will be able to achieve the best possible photos of your clients, using the minimum of equipment.
35-8062 60 min. $59.95

• Wedding Photography Part 1 & Part 2
A complete "study video" on wedding photography. The emphasis is on simplicity and working quickly to produce a series of exceptional wedding portraits that will not fail to sell. Master photographer Ian Hawthorne guides the viewer through each stage demonstrating 100's of poses.
35-8061 210 min. $99.95

• Windowlight Photography
International portrait photographer, Joy Henry, explains how all photographers can take award winning photos by windowlight using only a camera and a reflector. Full lighting and posing techniques for bride and groom, teenagers, children and babies are clearly explained.
35-8060 90 min. $59.95

Secrets of Successful Film-To-Video Transfers
Expert videographers teach you the professional secrets of how to transfer 8mm, Super 8mm and 16mm home movie film to videotape. Whether you want to transfer your own home movies to video or make money providing this professional service, you'll learn all you need to know about equipment options, pricing, adding music, titles and much more! This program is endorsed by the APV (Association of Professional Videographers), and hosted by award-winning producer Steve Yankee.
03-8068 29 min. $39.95

Scenic Photography
Join scenic photographer Abi Garaman for a breathtakingly beautiful look at the Grand Tetons. Practice composing scenic photos, framing them to lead a feeling of depth, manipulating their horizon lines and varying them by choosing different camera angles. See the effect of different focal-length lenses on a frequently photographed cluster of pines. View a barn in just the right position amidst picturesque mountain peaks.
03-112 30 min. $19.95

Underwater Photo Clinic
At last, a real down to earth instructional video teaching the Cathy Church technique of underwater photography. Learn how to select the right camera, lens, strobe and other equipment.
30-8113 48 min. $29.95

Using Flash
Brighten your picture outlook with automatic or manual flash equipment. Learn how you can improve on natural lighting with a "dash" of flash. Discover the advantages of bounce flash, multiple flash, even painting with flash. Come to know your flash equipment so that you'll think of it as a helpful, photographic companion.
03-107 30 min. $19.95

Way I See It
Four experienced professional photographers talk about how and why they selected their specialties and what tricks of the trade they have discovered over the years. Learn from a people photographer who likes to portray active subjects in natural settings, a nature photographer, an action photographer who tries to be in the right place at the right time, or a scenic photographer who insists that you leave your imprint on every picture you take.
03-109 30 min. $19.95

Video Art

American Image: 150 Years Of Photography
This dazzling array of unforgettable images composes an unforgettable chronicle of America. From the landscapes of Ansel Adams through the social realism of Jacob Riis to the art of Steiglitz and Steichen, this is a history through the eye of the camera, a permanent visual record of who we are, where we've been and what's been important to us.
03-5573 60 min. $29.95

Andromeda: Crystal Light
A sensory experience beyond comparison, a new art form, and more: a window into another time and space, an ever-evolving dimension of light and energy, rarely witnessed and never before dynamically recorded.
04-153 30 min. $39.95

Aurasound
This is the beautiful music of William Aura and the dreamlike imagery of Kinetic Collage softly woven together to elevate the consciousness of the viewer. An audiovisual experience that transcends.

VIDEO TITLES LISTED IN THIS GUIDE ARE AVAILABLE FOR PURCHASE OR RENTAL. CONTACT YOUR LOCAL VIDEO STORE OR TELEPHONE (800) 383-8811

Excellent for pre-meditative relaxation.
22-631 60 min. $29.95

Brink
A poetry jazz film by Ruth Weiss. A "synthesis of poetry and images highly structured but containing a residue of very real immediate, almost haiku, feeling..."Stan Brakage, 1963. B&W.
22-220 40 min. $74.95

California Images: Hi-Fi for the Eyes
This absolutely unique collection of visual-musical shots presents the viewer with a stream-of-consciousness-imagery contemporary fantasy world through incredible animated environments. laser light shows, and computer graphics creations, all played to symphonic, new-wave and pop-rock musical backgrounds.
03-009 54 min. $19.95

Dog Star Man
One of the major works of the experimental cinema, this is an epic visionary challenge. Stan Brakhage sees with a universal eye the cycles of time and space, the theme of the struggle of man to ascend.
03-2387 75 min. $74.95

ENCHANTED LANDSCAPES SERIES:
Mary Walsh's and Ken Jenkins' visionary montage of nature images for relaxation and visual meditation. Photographed in Hawaii and Northern California. Music by Emerald Web, Schawkie Roth, and Danna and Clement.

• Volume 1
14-027 40 min. $39.95

• Volume 2
22-210 40 min. $39.95

Galen Rowell: Mountain Light
Both nature lovers and photographers will thrill to this exploration of the vision of Galen Rowell. America's foremost wilderness photographer. Travel to some of the most awesome landscapes on the continent as Rowell demonstrates his astonishing gift for capturing nature in all its resplendent glory. It's inspirational.
03-5572 60 min. $29.95

Harmony
A "New Age" musical/visual experience designed to heighten awareness, develop creative thinking, reduce stress, accelerate learning and concentration, and energize the mind/body complex. Kaleidoscopic rainbow colors are artistically integrated and synchronized with beautiful music.
22-211 26 min. $29.95

Hypnotic Places, Exotic Spaces
Four dream vignettes designed around four dynamic musical sound tracks ranging in feeling from a light and airy tropical piece to a haunting track composed by Vangelis. This video takes the viewer through an ethereal dream sequence.
03-1783 30 min. $19.95

Illuminated Music
Experience Stephen Beck's video art - shapes and forms designed on the computer and on the video synthesizer. Featuring music of Yusef Lateef, Jimi Hendrix, and Joynt Effort, this is video art at its finest. Pieces from the collection are on display at the Whitney Museum, the San Francisco Museum of Modern Art, and at the Video Plaza in Tokyo.
03-023 36 min. $39.95

It's In Every One of Us
Enchanting to both adults and children, this unforgettable video blends heartwarming images of our global family with music and lyrics in a celebration of the human spirit.
03-2778 50 min. $19.95

Light Sculpture
Fascinating! A work of art! Enjoy the moving, changing choreography of patterns and rhythms in light and color floating on a background of velvet black. Beautiful imagery to the lilt of tranquil music. A sculpture in light as exhibited in art museums.
14-046 60 min. $19.95

Moodtapes: Tranquility
"Tranquility" is designed to create a soothing and harmonious atmosphere in any environment. By blending exquisite visuals with serene New Age music, this video features glowing sunrises, whispering clouds and peaceful ocean waves that are synchronized in perfect harmony with a calming and rhythmic concerto. It can be played over and over again to fully caress your senses into a tranquil mood. Perfect for relaxing or entertaining.
03-332 47 min. $29.95

Natural Light: Windance
David Fortney's camera dances of light, motion and substance, are as sensual and alive as the natural world he photographs.
03-2777 30 min. $24.95

Nudes in Limbo
The beauty of the human form in motion is explored through a series of scenes of the nude body in abstract settings. A visual feast for the lover and artist of the body beautiful.
03-032 53 min. $29.95

VIDEO TITLES LISTED IN THIS GUIDE ARE AVAILABLE FOR PURCHASE OR RENTAL. CONTACT YOUR LOCAL VIDEO STORE OR TELEPHONE (800) 383-8811

Peace/Allelujah
An inspirational visual music experience of the Allelujah Spirit and the Spirit of Peace. C.H. Deuter's "Whirling" and Raphael's "Alleluia."
22-214 30 min. $29.95

Private Music
Peter Baumann produces and directs superb imagery to the music of Private Music artists: Jerry Goodman, Patrick O'Hearn, Eddie Jobson, Sanford Ponder and Lucia Hwong.
22-224 25 min. $29.95

Radiance/Celebration
Dorothy Fadiman's journey from the light in nature to the luminous spirit in humanity; and a celebration of inner wholeness. Narrative accompanied with music by Klaus Schulze, Will Ackerman, Alex de Grasse, et al.
22-215 30 min. $39.95

Structures from Silence
A dream flight through soft liquid universes on waves of transparent music, motion paintings offer celestial navigation for our imagination.
03-2784 30 min. $24.95

Thursday Afternoon
Brian Eno's ambient music and images. Seven sensuous video music paintings.
22-206 82 min. $19.95

Visual Dynamics
Vince Collins' five surrealistic animation. Award-winning explorations of visual music fantasies. "A tour de force of optical stimulation and metamorphic imagery," said Norman McLaren.
22-208 21 min. $29.95

Watercolors
Synopsis video artist Denise Gallant paints 14 impressionistic vignettes. The mood moves from soft and ethereal to the scintillating and futuristic. Music by S. Roach, R. Burmer, L. Monahan, K. Braheny and M. Christopher.
22-223 50 min. $39.95

Miscellaneous

Cleaning/Repairing VCR's and Camcorders
Contains an audio cassette and two video tapes. Cassette covers running a business, how and where to market your service and many other tips. Close-ups of every aspect of head-cleaning, common repairs, disassembling and cleaning video heads.
18-8004 120 min. $59.95

Home Video System Maintenance
Learn the best ways to clean and maintain your VCR. Topics include cleaning the audio and video heads, degaussing and trouble-shooting problems.
03-017 30 min. $29.95

How to Shoot a Wedding
Whether for fun or for profit, shooting a wedding is a complex challenge. This program covers pre-production, scouting of locations, choosing camera angles and shooting the reception.
03-021 30 min. $14.95

LAYMAN'S GUIDE TO MINOR VCR REPAIR SERIES:

• Volume 1
Covers lubrication, replacing belts, idler assembly and tape sensor lamp.
03-8057 45 min. $39.95

• Volume 2
Explains replacement of RF modulator, tape end sensors, reel table sensors and cassette loading motors, all with tools you probably already have.
03-8058 45 min. $39.95

• Volume 3: Professional VCR Cleaning
Learn how to keep $50.00 in your pocket instead of sending your VCR to a repair shop to be cleaned.
03-8056 30 min. $29.95

Movie Magic
This brings you the very best special effects from Hollywood's biggest movies. In addition, this program takes a fascinating inside look at the special effects created for the blockbuster hits. You'll see techniques such as computer graphics, blue-screen and stop motion animation, motion control, blue-screen and rear-screen projection.
03-8066 30 min. $19.95

Video Tape Repair VHS
What is repairable on 1/2 inch tape. Contents: discussion of most common problems, glossary of terms, step-by-step disassembly and re-assembly of a VHS tape, basic splicing technique, dealing with labels, and removing tamper-proof screws.
03-5151 30 min. $39.95

VIDEO TITLES LISTED IN THIS GUIDE ARE AVAILABLE FOR PURCHASE OR RENTAL. CONTACT YOUR LOCAL VIDEO STORE OR TELEPHONE (800) 383-8811

Pregnancy & Childbirth

✓ *Pregnancy & Childbirth*

Pregnancy & Childbirth

ACOG: Postnatal Exercise Program
A complete home exercise program for women after childbirth.
26-042 55 min. $19.95

ACOG: Pregnancy Exercise Program
A home exercise program for women in all stages of pregnancy. The program emphasizes safety while exercising all parts of the body. Maintain muscle tone, strength and endurance during your pregnancy.
26-002 42 min. $19.95

Birth Class: Focus on Labor & Delivery
Covers major concerns from fetal development to maternal nutrition and exercise, with a segment on stages of labor highlighted by visual aids, including clips of women during actual labor and birth. This is a "home birth class" designed for women with their spouse or support person. A highly accurate and enthusiastically presented instructional program.
26-9585 120 min. $29.95

Birth Of The Lamaze Method
You've probably heard of the Lamaze birthing method - the special breathing and relaxation techniques that are intended to ease pain in the delivery room (and decrease the dependence on drugs). Lamaze, a French physician, developed his method after observing the breathing techniques practiced by Soviet women preparing for delivery. This amazing film goes to the original source - the history of psychosomatic treatment, hypnotic suggestion, and "shock and counter shock", portrayed in this film with all the sensationalism of faith-healing.
26-5813 50 min. $19.95

Basic Baby Massage - Birth To Six Months
Learn why pediatricians recommend this light fingertip massage to enhance parent/child bonding and communication skills. Baby massage has been proven to promote brain development, reduce crying, and help baby sleep better.
26-116 60 min. $39.95

Caring for Your New Born with Dr. Benjamin Spock
World-renowned infant and child care adviser Dr. Benjamin Spock, M.D. gives advice and guidance when you need it most. A comprehensive video manual on baby care for parents.
20-012 60 min. $16.95

CHILDBIRTH-FROM INSIDE OUT SERIES:

• Part I: Pregnancy & The Pre-Natal Period
26-5089 78 min. $29.95

• Part II: Delivery & The Post-Natal Period
26-5090 72 min. $29.95

Childbirth Preparation Program
Created by the American College of Obstetricians and Gynecologists for home use, this program is specially designed to help pregnant women practice techniques that promote relaxation and relieve discomfort during labor and childbirth. Narrated by Dr. Art Ulene.
26-001 56 min. $19.95

Complete Birth/El Nacimiento Completo
This comprehensive childbirth video features childbirth educator, Royal Phillips. This program includes a helpful written manual and convenient video locator and is available in both English and Spanish versions.
26-8005 96 min. $34.95

Giving Birth
Pioneering video documentary of a home birth. Shot in the Yucatan, Mexico, where the child is delivered by a Mayan midwife in a hammock, Mayan style. The result is graphic as planned, and hilarious as not planned.   Black & White.
26-8007 25 min. $34.95

Having Your Baby
This is a complete Lamaze-prepared childbirth program. It is designed to take you from the classroom to the delivery room. Includes breathing exercises, relaxation techniques, and complete Cesarean preparation.
26-120 125 min. $39.95

Infertility Tape: A Couple's Guide
A video guide for couples dealing with infertility & recurrent pregnancy loss. First hand stories and current information on the infertility evaluation process combined to give couples clear, incisive information. Also included is an overview of assisted reproductive technologies. Facts, advice and encouragement are presented by Dr. John Stangel and Dr. William Butler.
26-9795 40 min. $29.95
Classroom Version $69.95

Jane Fonda's Pregnancy, Birth & Recovery Workout

Designed for pregnant women who want to keep in shape while baby grows, and need a less strenuous workout than Jane's original. This excellent workout includes segments on skills for birth and on baby massage and infant care.

15-037 90 min. $39.95

Joy of Natural Childbirth

Lorenzo Lamas and wife host this look at natural childbirth, featuring discussion and demonstration of the Lamaze Method. Other celebrity parents featured include Kenny Rogers, Jane Seymour, John Ritter and "Famous" Amos.

26-027 59 min. $39.95

Lamaze Method: Techniques for Childbirth Preparation

A guide to the popular, prepared childbirth method, Lamaze, developed by the American Society for Psychoprophylaxis (ASPO) and supervised by the Lamaze organization. Hosted by actress Patty Duke Astin.

26-028 45 min. $19.95

Modern Moves for Pregnancy Fitness

A pre-natal yoga and contemporary non-impact exercise video for conditioning and stress reduction for pre and post-natal fitness. Elize St. Charles instructs this video in her 8th month of pregnancy in a soothing yet precise style. Acclaimed by the American Journal of Nursing.

26-9289 60 min. $19.95

Motherwell: Maternity Health & Fitness

A comprehensive, adjustable pace home exercise program taken from the nationally acclaimed "Motherwell Classes", that conforms with the guidelines of the American College of Obstetricians and Gynecologists.

26-8000 90 min. $29.95

Newborn Care

This is a delightful and reassuring program that guides parents through the basic skills they need to care for their infants. This specially priced cassette includes a 20-page booklet that explains many subjects new parents will encounter during the first months of their child's life. From bottle-feeding to bathing, Newborn Care is a must for anyone with a new baby.

26-8007 43 min. $24.95

Now is the Future: Pre-natal Care

Being a young mother (13 years old is not uncommon) is no picnic. It's lonely and debilitating. If you do get pregnant, here's what you need to do for your health and the health of your baby.

26-9671 20 min. $19.95

Pathways to Parenthood

In this video, discover the latest information on conception from the nation's leading experts. You will learn what is normal, why couples have trouble conceiving and what options are best for you.

26-8003 45 min. $24.95

Pre & Postnatal Yoga

A powerful and safe exercise system. Fifteen minutes of specialized exercises help you prepare for birth and fifteen minutes help you to shape up gently but firmly afterward.

26-8008 35 min. $24.95

Rock-A-Bye Baby

Prenatal exercise video that follows the guidelines of the American College of Obstetricians & Gynecologists. Instructor Shemane Nugent interviews an Obstetrician and tours a labor and delivery room. Music and cameo appearance by her husband, musician Ted Nugent.

26-8002 45 min. $16.95

Water Baby: Experiences of Water Birth

A unique 57 minute video documentary that provides comprehensive information on the use of water for labor, birth and early childhood development. Shot in the USA, France and the USSR, with the world's leading experts in the field.

26-6615 57 min. $99.95

When Baby Comes Home

This is an innovative "how to" for caring for your newborn child. Over 40 topics are detailed, including bath, breast feeding, teething and much more. It is sure to alleviate the apprehensions of first-time parents.

26-108 60 min. $29.95

Your Baby with Penelope Leach

Penelope Leach noted child development expert and mother of two, demonstrates techniques of everyday care and teaches you exactly what your baby needs from you in a variety of situations that you'll encounter.

26-9041 75 min. $29.95

Your First Baby

A well-balanced program to prepare parents and home for the new arrival. Learn what to expect from newborns, how to deal with problems that might arise and how to get an early start stimulating your baby's mind and senses.

26-057 40 min. $29.95

VIDEO TITLES LISTED IN THIS GUIDE ARE AVAILABLE FOR PURCHASE OR RENTAL. CONTACT YOUR LOCAL VIDEO STORE OR TELEPHONE (800) 383-8811

Your Newborn Baby

Joan Lunden, of Good Morning America, and mother of two will answer your questions, calm your fears and reinforce your self-confidence in this informative tape on caring for your newborn. You will also get invaluable information from Jeffrey Brown, M.D., F.A.A.P. Topics covered include choosing your doctor, preparing the nursery, your baby's body, feeding, bathing, crying, sleep and when to call the doctor. Excellent for prospective and new parents.

26-069 60 min. $16.95

Considering Lamaze?

Thinking About Natural

Childbirth?

Preparing To Bring Your New

Baby Home?

Videos In This Chapter Can

Help You Prepare For This

Glorious Time!

VIDEO TITLES LISTED IN THIS GUIDE ARE AVAILABLE FOR PURCHASE OR RENTAL. CONTACT YOUR LOCAL VIDEO STORE OR TELEPHONE (800) 383-8811

Religion
&
Philosophy

- ✓ *Bible*
- ✓ *Christianity*
- ✓ *Philosophy*
- ✓ *Miscellaneous*

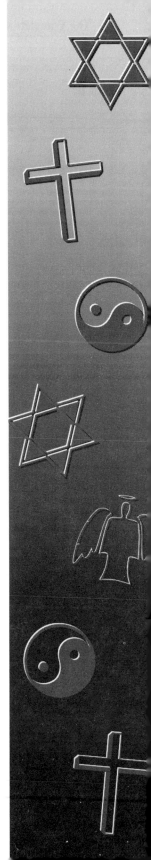

Bible

Abraham's Sacrifice
Gene Barry portrays Abraham, one of the Bible's most stalwart heroes. In this memorable Biblical tale, his rock-solid faith is put on its fiercest test when King Harabal announces to his people that Isaac, Abraham's beloved only son, is to be executed. When Abraham hears of this evil plan, he fights for justice and, with God's help, makes an incredible sacrifice that has endured throughout the ages as a sacred act.
27-229 50 min. $19.95

A.D.
The book of Acts comes alive in this live action, three tape epic covering the years 30-69 A.D. This program comes with a Study Guide outlining a 12-week course of study. Performances from an all-star cast.
27-8040 360 min. $149.95

Adam's Garden
Set in the ancient land of the Bible where Adam once dwelled in harmony with nature in a paradise on earth, Adam's Garden examines the contrast of nature and the human condition in a Biblical and philosophical context. Light background music and quotations from the Bible are interspersed throughout.
27-147 27 min. $24.95

ADVENTURES IN CHARACTER BUILDING
This program teaches kids modern day values through examples from stories from the past.

• Story of Joseph
10-9131 30 min. $19.95

• Good Samaritan
10-9132 30 min. $19.95

ANCIENT TALES FROM THE PROMISED LAND SERIES:
This animated series features some of the most well known bible stories presented in a progressive, up-to-date manner that children and young adults can relate to. Each video contains two separate stories.

• Joshua Smashes Jericho:
The Israelites, led by Joshua, come out of the desert after forty years to take over the land of Canaan.

Joshua In Trouble Valley:
Joshua continues his strikes against Canaanite towns, but runs into momentary trouble with a dishonest soldier and a doublecrossing mayor.
27-8055 30 min. $19.95

• Deborah and the Headbanger:
Sisera leads a Canaanite offensive and the Israelites turn to their prophet Deborah for help. The streetfighter Barak is asked to go up against Sisera.
Gideon Gets His Woolly Wet:
Gideon strikes a blow for the Israelites' by smashing up the Canaanites' Corn Goddess.
27-8056 30 min. $19.95

• Gideon's Exploding Pickle Pots:
Led by the cunning Gideon, the vastly outnumbered Israelite army gets the better of the Canaanites. But just up the coast, the Philistines are landing.
Samson Gets Knotted:
The strong and not to bright Samson, marries a Philistine girl, which leads to big trouble.
27-8057 30 min. $19.95

• Samson Gets a Haircut:
Samson falls for another Philistine girl, Delilah, who betrays him by revealing the secret of his strength.
Samuel and the Spooky Godbox:
Samuel emerges as a leader of the Israelites and their Ark of the Covenant is stolen by the Philistines.
27-8058 30 min. $19.95

• Saul Rips Up His Camel:
The prophet Samuel elects Saul to help establish a proper kingdom for the Israelites. But Saul is disowned by Samuel after getting too big for his boots.
David Gets a Good Gig:
Big things lie ahead for the young harp playing shepherd, David after he makes a striking impression on Saul.
27-8059 30 min. $19.95

• David and the Hairy Man Mountain:
David becomes a hero after dispatching the Philistine giant, Goliath, but Saul becomes jealous of David's increasing influence.
Saul Goes Bonkers:
Saul is still King, but is humiliated by David and vows to get rid of him once and for all.
27-8060 30 min. $19.95

• Saul Bumps Into a Witch:
Saul seeks spiritual guidance from the Witch of Endor, but only learns of his own impending death.
David Gets to Number One:
David is proclaimed King of the Israelites and settles into Jerusalem, only to have his comfort

disrupted by ominous visions painted by Nathan.
27-8061 30 min. $19.95

ANIMATED STORIES FROM THE NEW TESTAMENT SERIES:

This animated series will teach children all about the bible and Christian values, while entertaining them.

• **King is Born**
27- 8016 25 min. $16.95

• **John the Baptist**
27-8017 25 min. $16.95

• **Prodigal Son**
27-8018 25 min. $16.95

• **Good Samaritan**
27-8019 25 min. $16.95

• **Miracle of Jesus**
27-8020 25 min. $16.95

• **Saul of Tarsus**
27-8021 25 min. $16.95

• **He is Risen**
27-8022 25 min. $16.95

• **Righteous Judge**
27-8023 25 min. $16.95

• **Forgive Us Our Debts**
27-8024 25 min. $16.95

• **Kingdom of Heaven**
27-8025 25 min. $16.95

• **Who is Rich?**
27-8026 25 min. $16.95

• **Ministry of Paul**
27- 8027 25 min. $16.95

AMAZING BOOK

A wonderfully animated look at the Bible. Features animation by a former Disney team with catchy songs about the Old & New Testament. Let Doc, Reever Mouse and Dewey Decimole take you on a fun filled "good look at the Good Book".

• **Amazing Book**
27-6193 30 min. $19.95

• **Amazing Children**
27-9133 30 min. $19.95

• **Amazing Miracles**
27-9134 30 min. $19.95

BIBLE LIFE AND TIMES SERIES

• **Abraham**
Look at the Abraham's civilization and his travels in Canaan and Egypt. See how the Covenant was forged against a background of pagan gods. This tape also discusses hospitality, visitation by angels and sacred altars.
27-238 60 min. $49.95

• **First Christmas**
This cassette covers Annunciations and the Nativity, the temple and its priesthood, Jewish birth rituals, angels and archangels, sacrifice and dedication, Simeon and Anna, the Messianic expectation, baptism, and the Dead Sea sect, among its many notes.
27-241 72 min. $49.95

• **In The Beginning**
Illuminates the background of the Creation, Adam and Eve, Cain and Abel, and Noah and the Flood. It looks at similar accounts from other cultures, the importance and meaning of names, and other fascinating details.
27-237 60 min. $49.95

• **Isaac, Esau and Jacob**
This program reveals the treachery in the universal story of desperate twins, the sorrows of barrenness and its cultural disgrace, bloodshed and tribal vengeance, household gods and cleanliness in this saga of the patriarchal family's second, third and fourth generations.
27-239 60 min. $49.95

• **Joseph**
We are taken from Canaan to mighty Egypt with its cultural sophistication where the covenant family is reunited and prepares for a journey that would last 400 years.
27-240 60 min. $49.95

Bible Music Video
Beautiful songs especially composed and orchestrated for the video, offer inspiration and praise to the Lord. The entire family can sing-a-long as the words are highlighted on the screen.
27-9067 30 min. $19.95

Daniel and the Lion's Den
Daniel's faith is put to the ultimate test when he is thrown into a den of hungry lions. Stars Gavin Macleod.
27-132 30 min. $14.95

VIDEO TITLES LISTED IN THIS GUIDE ARE AVAILABLE FOR PURCHASE OR RENTAL. CONTACT YOUR LOCAL VIDEO STORE OR TELEPHONE (800) 383-8811

Daniel and Nebuchadnezzar
Starring: Donny Most, Hans Conreid. The Hebrews, dead-set on living their own lives and following the tenets of Judaism, are enduring yet another vicious wave of religious persecution from the Babylonians. But one Jew will not compromise: Daniel, a young firebrand of faith.
27-090 51 min. $19.95

Daniel in the Lion's Den
Alone in a den full of lions, his faith was his only weapon. Starring Robert Vaughan and Dean Stockwell.
27-2379 39 min. $19.95

David and Goliath
Armed only with a sling and his faith, David defends the Kingdom of Israel against the mighty Philistine warrior, Goliath. Stars Robby Benson and Herschel Bernardi.
27-128 30 min. $14.95

David and Moses
This animated film tells the life stories of two great Biblical characters in a delightful way. Ideal for children.
27-045 46 min. $39.95

David And Goliath
Starring: Ted Cassidy, Jeff Corey. Teenage Israelite David tries to live his life as best he can, obeying the laws of God, and helping out his brethren at every turn. But he grows annoyed at Philistine giant Goliath, who taunts the Israelites daily and dares them to pit their fiercest warrior against him in a one-to-one battle.
27-091 37 min. $19.95

Early Ministry
Jesus heals the sick, confronts the pharisees, selects his disciples and teaches the Great Sermon on the Plain. He calms a storm on the lake, exorcises an outcast and instructs His disciples in the Lord's Prayer.
27-2254 75 min. $49.95

Easter Story
Portrays the last days of Jesus on Earth and the wondrous events of his resurrection and ascension to Heaven.
27-2612 40 min. $19.95

First Easter
The events surrounding the Crucifixion, Resurrection and Ascension are recreated as told in the Gospel according to Luke with a beautiful and moving narrative of the scriptures.
27-113 70 min. $49.95

HOLYVISION SERIES:
This live-action series takes you on a journey from the birth of Jesus, his life and the miracles he displayed and finally the death, resurrection and ascension.

• Birth of Jesus
Shows us the early years of Jesus' life from when he was born to Mary and Joseph in the Bethlehem stable, to when the Wise men follow the star to Bethlehem and offer gifts. Later, at the age of 12, Jesus' parents take him to Jerusalem for the Passover. The last part tells us about the first disciples Jesus meets.
27-8042 55 min. $19.95

• Jesus the Healer
As Jesus and his Disciples travel through Samaria on their way to Galilee, he stops to talk with the woman at the well about living water. Later, when Jesus encounters the nobleman from Capernaum he brings life to his dying son. Finally, Jesus heals ten lepers, but only one of them, a samaritan, returns to thank him.
27-8043 45 min. $16.95

• Betrayal of Jesus
Judas bargains with the chief priests to betray Jesus and turn him over to them for 30 pieces of silver. Meanwhile, Jesus and his disciples assemble in the upper room for their meal together. As Jesus prays in the garden of Gethsemene, Judas betrays his master with a kiss. Jesus is arrested and taken away. In remorse, Judas goes out to hang himself.
27-8044 50 min. $16.95

• Jesus Has Risen
Jesus is brought to Pilate for trial, but Pilate can find no fault in him and sends him back to Herod. Herod returns him to Pilate who turns Jesus over to the mob to be crucified. After the crucifixion, when the three women come to anoint Jesus' body, they find the stone rolled away and the tomb empty. In the last part Jesus appears to the disciples behind closed doors and later meets them at the sea of Galilee. He makes a final appearance on the mount of Olives and ascends to his father.
27-8045 50 min. $19.95

How the Bible Came to Be
A carefully documented presentation of the origins of Scripture beautifully photographed in the Holy Land.
27-8036 60 min. $29.95

In Search of Noah's Ark
It's one of the oldest stories known to man, but is it merely folklore or is it fact? This question and more are answered as you witness the fascinating story of Noah's Ark.
27-2326 95 min. $39.95

VIDEO TITLES LISTED IN THIS GUIDE ARE AVAILABLE FOR PURCHASE OR RENTAL. CONTACT YOUR LOCAL VIDEO STORE OR TELEPHONE (800) 383-8811

Jacob: The Man Who Fought with God

Jacob's struggle to receive his father's blessing and inheritance is depicted as well as his marriage to Rachel and the return of his brother Esau.

27-036 118 min. $49.95

Jacob's Challenge

Isaac fathers twin sons, Jacob and Esau. But although born at the same moment, the two boys are quite different from each other. Esau is a hard worker but somewhat irresponsible, while his brother Jacob is intelligent and sensitive. This creates a feeling of jealousy in Esau, which is brought to a frantic head when their father Isaac bestows a blessing upon Jacob that was originally intended for Esau. Esau's fury explodes and he vows to kill his brother, leaving Jacob with the choice of exile or death. Jacob does not want to bring sadness to his father's family, so he leaves his homeland and receives a promise from God that he will one day be able to return.

27-092 50 min. $19.95

Jesus and His Times

This live action, three volume set, comes in a handsome, protective case and comes with a full-color viewer's guide. The videos in this set are: The Story Begins, which covers the story of Christ's birth: Among the People, which covers the miracle Christ performed, and The Final Days. which covers the Crucifixion, Resurrection and Ascension of Christ.

27-8031 180 min. $59.95

Joseph and His Brethren

This program stars Gregory Home and Robert Morley. A dramatization of the Biblical story of Joseph, whose jealous brothers sell him into slavery.

27-037 103 min. $19.95

Joseph in Egypt

Joseph arouses deep resentment among his older brothers when he is chosen by their father to be his deputy and wear the multi-colored coat, symbolic of his new station, a post normally reserved for one of the elder sons. The resentment is so deep, in fact, that his brothers sell Joseph as a slave and then tell their father that he was attacked and killed by animals. Time and events soon change the course of Joseph's life and, despite some setbacks, he is eventually appointed as a first deputy by the Pharaoh, a position which leads him to a dramatic reunion with his family.

27-093 52 min. $19.95

Joshua and the Battle of Jericho

Joshua leads his army in a march around the walled city of Jericho, culminating in a spectacular entrance to the Promised Land. Stars Edward Asner and Mariette Hartley.

27-129 30 min. $16.95

Joshua At Jericho

After years of wandering in the wilderness, the Israelites are led into Canaan by Joshua only to be faced with the virtually impenetrable walls of the fortress city of Jericho. Having neither the weapons nor the manpower to breach this mighty fortress, the Israelites have only their faith in God, which proves to be the greatest weapon of all.

27-094 59 min. $19.95

Judgment of Solomon

King David is becoming old and his throne must go to one of his sons, Solomon or Adonijah. The rivalry for the throne becomes heated and bitter, spilling out into the kingdom and causing tribal rebellions. The unrest in the kingdom is becoming critical and a new king must be chosen soon before chaos takes over and order can no longer be restored. Finally, the tide of opinion is turned in Solomon's favor when he impresses leaders of opposing tribes with his wisdom, courage and sense of justice in a dispute over a baby by two women who both claim to be its mother.

27-098 54 min. $19.95

King David

Richard Gere, Edward Woodward Denis Quilley, Niall Buggy, Alice Krige. Director Bruce Beresford's ("Tender Mercies") story of the shepherd boy who grew to be King of Israel. Entertaining Biblical drama.

27-038 114 min. $79.95

Moses

Starring: John Marley and Robert Alda. Through the miracle of the burning bush, God instructs Moses to deliver his people from their Egyptian oppressors. After negotiating in vain with the stubborn Pharaoh, Moses brings a terrifying series of plagues upon the Egyptians, forcing them to their knees. Reluctantly, the Pharaoh agrees to free the Hebrews, and Moses leads them towards the Promised Land.

27-095 58 min. $19.95

Mysteries from the Bible

Documentary explores many amazing Biblical stories and the events that surrounded them.

27-139 100 min. $19.95

Moses

Moses confronts the evil Pharaoh and, after a series of destructive plagues, leads the Israelites out of slavery. Stars James Whitmore and James Earl Jones.

27-127 30 min. $16.95

VIDEO TITLES LISTED IN THIS GUIDE ARE AVAILABLE FOR PURCHASE OR RENTAL. CONTACT YOUR LOCAL VIDEO STORE OR TELEPHONE (800) 383-8811

Nanny and Isaiah Easter Today, Easter Forever
Nanny Feather's first experience dealing with death helps her understand the reason for Jesus' death and resurrection.
27-2643 60 min. $29.95

Nativity
Travel back in time to the tiny village of Bethlehem and witness the world's most miraculous event - the birth of the Christ Child. Experience the faith of Mary and Joseph (voices of Helen Hunt and Gregory Harrison) and the evil of King Herod (voice of Vincent Price).
27-1776 30 min. $16.95

Noah: The Deluge
God has created a bountiful world, and yet man has poisoned it with lust, greed, and sin. Now God will destroy it all. Only obedient Noah and his family will survive the mightiest flood in history.
27-096 49 min. $19.95

Noah's Ark
The heavens unleash a torrent of rain, but Noah, his family and animals of every kind are ready. Stars Lorne Greene and Charlotte Ray.
27-130 30 min. $16.95

Old Testament I
Outstanding characters and events of the Old Testament are dramatized: Abraham, Man of Faith; Jacob, Bearer of the Promise; Joseph, The Young Man; Moses, Called by God; Joshua, The Conqueror; Gideon, The Liberator.
27-046 120 min. $19.95

Old Testament II
Outstanding characters and events of the Old Testament are dramatized: Ruth, A Faithful Woman; Samuel, A Dedicated Man; David, A Young Hero; David, King of Israel; Solomon, Man of Wisdom, Elijah, Fearless Prophet.
27-047 120 min. $19.95

ONE-MINUTE BIBLE STORIES SERIES:
This series features Shari Lewis and Florence Henderson as they tell stories from the Old and New Testament with some of their favorite puppet friends.

• **Old Testament**
27-226 30 min. $19.95

• **New Testament**
27-225 30 min. $19.95

Parables
Jesus continues His teachings using parables, including the mustard seed, the prodigal son and the sick man and his steward. While Jesus is in Jericho, on His way to Jerusalem for the Passover, He cures a blind man who has recognized Him.
27-2255 57 min. $19.95

QUIGLEY'S VILLAGE
Quigley's Village is a series designed to teach children biblical values through the adventures of lovable puppet friends.

• **Danny Lion: Always Tell the Truth**
Here, Danny Lion is given money to buy decorations for the Fun Day Picnic, but ends up buying a pet "Blobit" instead.
27-2551 40 min. $19.95

• **Lemon Lion: That's Not Fair**
Here, Danny Lion, Bubba the Orangutan and Spike the Porcupine each want to pick the watermelon they grew together.
27-2552 30 min. $19.95

• **Spike: Be Kind to One Another**
In this episode Danny Lion and Spike the Porcupine compete for the title in the World Championship Hide-and-Seek Contest.
27-2553 35 min. $19.95

Samson and Delilah
The Philistines resort to treachery, bribing Delilah to obtain the secret of Samson's strength. Years later Samson's strength returns and he seeks revenge against the Philistines. Stars Perry King and Linda Purl.
27-131 30 min. $16.95

Saul and David
A beautifully filmed story of David's life with King Saul, David's battle with Goliath, and the tragic end of Saul.
27-052 120 min. $19.95

Sodom and Gomorrah
Starring: Ed Ames, Dorothy Malone, Gene Barry. Lot leads his people through the wilderness, desperately hoping to find a peaceful place to settle down for good. But after a series of brutal setbacks, these luckless but determined wanderers stumble upon Sodom and Gomorrah, where the wicked citizens fall further and further into an abyss of debauchery.
27-097 50 min. $19.95

Ten Commandments
Out of the misery and oppression of Egypt, emerge Moses and his people, scaling the spectacular heights of Mount Sinai. Moses then leaves them in

order to receive the most important gift ever from the heavens: the Ten Commandments. However, without the charismatic and unifying presence of their leader, the Israelites fall into a state of utter chaos and sin. Moses returns, carrying the tablets of righteousness, saves his people and a new era is born.
27-227 58 min. $19.95

TESTAMENT: BIBLE & HISTORY SERIES
This series covers the story of the Bible told from an historical point of view. Using archaeological and scientific evidence as well as the ancient texts themselves, this series explores the cultures and historical events that molded the Bible.

• As It Was in the Beginning
The development of ideas about gods and holiness from the East to the God of Moses and the Exodus; a story of nomadic people living at the edge of the great civilizations and developing a concept of one God.
27-8000 60 min. $29.95

• Chronicles and Kings
The rise and fall of ancient Israel and the role of Jehovah in the development of the Jewish nation. The period between the establishment of the kingdom in the Promised Land and the exile of the Jews in Babylon.
27-8001 60 min. $29.95

• Mightier than the Sword
The historical context into which Jesus was born, the background against which the New Testament was written and the period in which the Old Testament achieved it's final shape.
27-8002 60 min. $29.95

• Gospel Truth
The historical remains of the time, place and perhaps the life of Jesus and how the Christian Bible came into being.
27-8003 60 min. $29.95

• Thine is the Kingdom
The story of Christianity from the transformation of the Roman Empire into a Christian one, the conversion of Constantine, the correspondence between Sts. Jerome and Augustine and how the Bible stories came to be used.
27-8004 60 min. $29.95

• Power and the Glory
The sole source of learning during the Dark Ages, the Bible was used to justify the social order. The artistry lavished on it made these stories and characters central to medieval culture.
27-8005 60 min. $29.95

• Paradise Lost
The evolution of the Bible from unquestioned sacred book to object for study and the historical and cultural influences that generated this changing point of view.
27-8006 60 min. $29.95

Tower of Babel
The Mighty King Amathar wishes to walk with God, and in order to achieve this goal he commands the building of a huge tower to be his stairway to heaven. The people of his kingdom are not happy with this gigantic task, but Amathar's vanity blinds him to the protests of his subjects. Soon the king begins to think of himself as a god and orders his likeness to be placed on the tower. God's wrath is unleashed as he destroys the tower and gives the people different languages so that Amathar can no longer effectively command them.
27-099 50 min. $19.95

WHERE JESUS WALKED
Depicts the life of Jesus, commencing at the Qumran Caves in the Judean Desert, where the scroll of Isaiah announcing the coming of Jesus was found, passing through places related to his life.

• Prophecy: Volume 1
27-2599 26 min. $19.95

• Birth of Jesus Christ: Volume 2
27-2600 26 min. $19.95

• Childhood and Baptism of Jesus: Volume 3
27-2601 26 min. $19.95

• Transfiguration: Volume 4
27-2602 26 min. $19.95

• Jesus in Galilee: Volume 5
27-2603 26 min. $19.95

• Jesus and the Samaritan: Volume 6
27-2604 26 min. $19.95

• Parables: Volume 7
27-2605 26 min. $19.95

• Jesus in Jericho: The Ascent to Jerusalem: Volume 8
27-2606 26 min. $19.95

• Last Supper: Volume 9
27-2607 26 min. $19.95

• Agony in Gethsamene: Volume 10
27-2608 26 min. $19.95

VIDEO TITLES LISTED IN THIS GUIDE ARE AVAILABLE FOR PURCHASE OR RENTAL. CONTACT YOUR LOCAL VIDEO STORE OR TELEPHONE (800) 383-8811

• **Crucifixion: Volume 11**
27-2609 26 min. $19.95

• **Resurrection and Ascension of Jesus: Volume 12**
27-2610 26 min. $19.95

• **Message of Jesus Christ: Volume 13**
27-2611 26 min. $19.95

Where Jesus Walked
Walk in the footsteps of Jesus through Bethlehem, Nazareth, Jericho Capernaum and Jerusalem. Captures the beauty of the Holy Land, yesterday and today.
27-2673 55 min. $29.95

Christianity

Born Again
Dean Jones and Anne Francis star in this compelling true story of the political downfall and spiritual rebirth of Charles Colson, former Nixon White House special counsel. Inspirational.
27-001 110 min. $59.95

Champions
Features champion Christian athletes speaking out and interviewing others on issues vital to youth, and sharing their faith, feelings and experiences. Includes discussion guides.
27-2578 120 min. $159.95

CHILDREN'S STORY OF JESUS
In wonderful animated color, the life and times of Jesus Christ is recounted with a young audience in mind. Each feature (Part 1 and Part 2) is dramatized to provide both uplifting instruction and a solid example to live by.

• **Part 1**
27-064 60 min. $19.95

• **Part 2**
27-065 60 min. $19.95

China Passage
What started as a run for the record books became an education and a test of spiritual strength for Stan Cottrell, a share-cropper's son who ran through sections of China previously closed to outsiders.
27-2572 24 min. $39.95

Christians And Christianity In Jerusalem
The site of Jesus' trial and Crucifixion has drawn both pilgrims and protection of its holy places from all corners of the Christian world. Traces Christianity's link with Jerusalem from the New Testament to the crusades.
27-6493 47 min. $29.95

City That Forgot About Christmas
This program features Benji and Waldo who learn about a city that neglected Christmas until it was almost too late.
27-168 55 min. $19.95

COLOR ME A RAINBOW SERIES:
Four charming videos that feature Jana Wacker and her lively puppets, communicating Jesus' love by teaching who he is through music, crafts, Bible verses and interaction with children. Each video describes an aspect of who Jesus is.

• **Friend**
27-2569 25 min. $19.95

• **God's Son**
27-2570 25 min. $19.95

• **King**
27-2568 25 min. $19.95

• **Savior**
27-2571 25 min. $19.95

Christmas Gift
A high quality live action adventure series portraying real life situations. This video shows Christian solutions to problems children face through a natural, realistic format which does not rely on sensationalism or violence.
10-8069 25 min. $29.95

Cross and The Switchblade
Starring Pat Boone and Erik Estrada and based on the book of the same title, this film presents a now legendary story. David Wilkerson's mission sent him from the tranquil countryside of rural Pennsylvania into the midst of gang violence in New York's urban ghettos.
27-215 105 min. $29.95

Cry For Freedom
This award winning documentary addresses the drug problem from a Christian perspective. Winner of the prestigious CINE Golden Eagle Award as well as the U.S. Film and Video Festival's Silver Screen Award, this honest, sometimes startling look

at the drug problem explores the ultimate solution to drug abuse.
27-8032 39 min. $24.95

CRY FOR YOUNG AMERICA SERIES
This series represents an honest and bold attempt to grapple with the challenging issues faced by Christian families in our complicated society. Each program uses the power of music and song to uplift, inspire and reinforce its message of Christian solutions to contemporary problems.

• Cry of Young America
The talents of Greg Volz and The Ministers highlight this program with the lively sounds of Christian rock.
27-8046 60 min. $29.95

• Cry of Young Black America
Daniel Winans, Lynette Hawkins Stephens, Ben Tankard and Yolanda Adams inspire black youth to solve the complicated problems facing them today.
27-8047 60 min. $29.95

• Guilt and Adjustment
Featuring Carla Riehl, this volume explores feelings of guilt and adjustment, rules in the home, friends and divorce.
27-8048 60 min. $29.95

Devil at the Wheel
Ken Pestana reenacts his conversion to Christ in this powerful video drama. Formerly a member of a gang of rebellious, trouble-making teenagers. Pestana finds himself in jail-where he also finds the word of God. A true-life story with an important lesson for all teenagers.
27-184 40 min. $24.95

Easter Collection
A collection of two films: "Nail", a contemporary parable of the Biblical "Upper Room" and "Dawn of Victory", a drama visualizing events of the crucifixion and Easter Sunday.
27-015 50 min. $19.95

Evidence for Faith
Josh McDowell marshals evidence that enables the Christian facing skepticism to back up his belief. Two audiocassettes supply additional resources.
27-2581 240 min. $179.95

Fiesta
The parable of the prodigal son as illustrated by a Mexican-American family. A fine celebration of forgiveness, love and God's presence in life, set against the majestic background of the Arizona countryside.
27-224 30 min. $24.95

Fill All the World with Songs of Praise
Not only does the glory of nature await us at some of the world's most lovely spots, but God Himself is also waiting for us. All of nature unites in a symphony of which man plays a vital part in praise to God.
27-211 30 min. $24.95

First Fruits
Over 250 years ago, two young Moravians left their comfortable community of Herrnhut convinced that they had been called by God to preach to slaves in the West Indies. They went, willing to become slaves themselves, in order to minister to these oppressed people. In this film, you will share the suffering which these young men endured for their missionary zeal.
27-230 70 min. $59.95

FITNESS FOR THE SPIRIT SERIES WITH REV. BILLY GRAHAM

• How to Get Into the Kingdom of Heaven
People are always ready with excuses for not attending God's great feast. Dr. Graham offers answers and examples of meeting Jesus Christ personally.
27-245 50 min. $29.95

• New Birth
This program focuses on the hope we have that God will accept us "just as we are."
27-244 50 min. $29.95

• Road to Armageddon
We do not know when the last great battle will take place, but we do know that we are hurtling down the road toward that unimaginable day.
27-246 50 min. $29.95

• Secret of Happiness
What we pursue lies in Jesus Christ's eight beatitudes. This formula for happiness includes the undeniable truths that control our daily lives.
27-243 50 min. $29.95

Follow Me
A Christian family resolves to heed Christ's command. "Take up your cross and follow Me." Each family member encounters setbacks, challenges and humorous moments as they practice Christian discipleship in their daily lives.
27-205 30 min. $24.95

Freedom Is
Follow the adventures of Benji, Waldo and Jason as they race to deliver a letter to the founders of the Declaration of Independence. Watch as they turn a

temporary defeat into an eternal victory in Christ.
10-8055 25 min. $16.95

God Lives and Works Today
The story of revival among a group of young German girls which led to the founding of the Evangelical Sisterhood of Mary. Share in their experience of miracle upon miracle in answer to prayer and repentance as they follow the dark pathways of faith.
27-212 30 min. $24.95

Golden Life: Lines of Sinai
Many have reached a dead end since God's commandments were pushed aside. This film, made on location, comes like the outstretched arm of God's love as we find renewed meaning in the laws given at Sinai.
27-210 30 min. $24.95

Hazel's People
Geraldine Page, Pat Hingle, Graham Beckel. Bitter and hostile, a college student attends his friend's funeral in Mennonite country. He discovers not only a way of life he never knew existed, but a personal faith in a living Christ.
27-032 105 min. $29.95

Holy Land and Holy City
The Holy Land at Christmas offers a heartwarming look at the Holy Land during the season when many Christian sects gather to share a common legacy, while The World of the Vatican II offers an artist's chronicle of the activities in the Holy City of Rome during the reign of Pope John XXIII.
27-034 120 min. $64.95

How to Strengthen Today's Family
Covers seven topics such as pornography, child development, adolescent well-being, adolescent pregnancy plus three more subjects affecting today's Christian family. Includes a detailed leader's guide.
27-2555 105 min. $159.95

If I Had it to Live Over Again
This video follows up on a survey of elderly people who were asked what they would do differently if they had their life to live over. Lively illustration and the author's energetic presentation drive home this Christian message.
27-2574 50 min. $39.95

Impact of Cultural Trends on Today's Family
Covers six topics, including commitment, problem-solving in a crisis, religious involvement and three more subjects that present practical answers to the challenges of building a strong Christian family in

today's world. Includes a detailed leader's guide.
27-2556 90 min. $159.95

Jesus: His Life and His Land
An expertly filmed, present day experience of the places and events of the New Testament. It guides you through the historically rich Holy Land with a lively narration that gives specific references to the Scripture as it follows the footsteps of Jesus Christ, exploring scene by scene His life and His ministry. You'll be inspired and the Gospel will come alive when you visit places like Bethlehem, the Mount of Olives, Gethsemane and others.
27-102 60 min. $29.95

Jesus of Nazareth
The highly acclaimed portrayal of the life of Christ in s stimulating three-tape, 12-week study format, complete with Leader's Guide. This three tape production, noted for its complete research, provides a moving spiritual experience. Use this inspiring teaching tool to begin Bible study.
27-8041 371 min. $129.95

John Hus
Intrigue and false promises weave a powerful story of one man's commitment to faith in Jesus Christ. In the end, Hus was accused, imprisoned, charred with heresy, condemned and burned at the stake as a heretic. John Hus died singing on July 6, 1415.
27-216 55 min. $49.95

Joy Of Passover: How To Create One Passover Seder You'll Never Forget
Step-by-step explanation of the ceremony, rituals and food preparation for the Passover Seder. Suitable for all ages and faiths.
27-6229 30 min. $19.95

Learning to Teach Sunday School
An intensive, six-session course that helps teachers create exciting and effective Sunday school classes. Features examples of teachers in actual Sunday school settings. Topics include teaching law and gospel, using questions, communication, discipline, active learning activities, and student involvement techniques. The detailed Leaders Manual that comes with the tape makes it easy to use. Also included are 10 guides to help teachers apply these concepts effectively.
27-040 120 min. $149.95

LIFE OF CHRIST SERIES:
This live-action series re-enacts the story of Christ: from his birth through the resurrection and ascension.

• Volume I
Biblical events from the birth of Christ to the Lord's Ascension, as told in the four gospels: Birth

VIDEO TITLES LISTED IN THIS GUIDE ARE AVAILABLE FOR PURCHASE OR RENTAL. CONTACT YOUR LOCAL VIDEO STORE OR TELEPHONE (800) 383-8811

of the Savior; Childhood of Jesus; First Disciples; Jesus, Lord of the Sabbath; Jesus teaches Forgiveness; The transfiguration.
27-041 120 min. $39.95

• Volume II
Biblical events in life of Christ are depicted: Last Journey to Jerusalem; Thirty Pieces of Silver; The Upper Room; Betrayal in Gethsemane; Jesus Before the High Priest.
27-042 100 min. $39.95

• Volume III
Biblical events from the life of Christ; Trial Before Pilate; The crucifixion; Nicodeemus; The Lord is Risen; The Lord's Ascension.
27-043 100 min. $39.95

Lion is Out of His Cage
Here, Pa Hurley dispels many of the fears Christian young people have about acknowledging their commitment and sharing their faith.
27-2580 30 min. $29.95

Little Visits With God
Family devotions are very important to spiritual growth but are often difficult to get started or keep meaningful. You and your children will enjoy meeting the delightful, life-like puppets which with animation, live actors and a grandfatherly storyteller, present adapted and updated devotional stories.
27-197 70 min. $19.95

Martin Luther: Heretic
This dramatic film follows Luther's 10-year quest for the surety of salvation and climaxes with his excommunication, condemnation, kidnapping and eventual return to Wittenberg, home base for the Reformation. This edition is edited for four study sessions. A superb youth and adult study program.
27-198 70 min. $49.95

Magic Boy's Easter
Josh has a serious problem--too serious, some might say, for a 12-year old to bear alone. What he discovers, through a vivid dream experience is that he need never be alone again. Christ's merciful love will see him through the life of faith that is just beginning for him. Starring Bernie Kopell of "The Love Boat".
27-8038 25 min. $16.95

Maximum Marriage
Four lively sessions presented for Christian marriages both new and established. Whether couples are newlyweds, or struggling in a problem marriage-the principles here will help. Includes study guides.
27-2575 210 min. $159.95

NANNY AND ISAIAH SERIES:
A five-part program designed to help children put faith into action.

• Nanny & Isaiah Learn to Follow Jesus
Nanny and Isaiah struggle to form a church softball team while demonstrating love and concern for others.
27-171 50 min. $39.95

• Nanny & Isaiah Learn to Share Jesus
Are you looking for an enjoyable way to teach evangelism? This is an excellent program that's ideal for Sunday School.
27-170 40 min. $39.95

• Secret of the Second Basement
Viewers of all ages will be moved by the story of "street people" who live in the sub-basement of a church. Join their quest for Christmas joy and their discovery of Jesus' love. Includes a copy of Carol Greene's modern classic, "Christmas on the Street."
27-169 30 min. $19.95

• Welcome the Stranger
Nanny and Isaiah imagine what it would be like to witness the first Christmas. They meet the shepherds, Mary, Joseph and the baby Jesus. Includes a copy of the book, "What Child Is This"?
27-172 20 min. $19.95

No Escape from Christmas
An angry young woman and her husband, Alan, whose only son had died, attempt to escape from Christmas by taking a back-packing trip. But Alan's Christian faith, witnessing and cheerfulness help change Margo's bitterness.
27-204 30 min. $39.95

Others
Jerry doesn't have a job and Becky, his wife, takes in laundry. Their daughter, Amy, tapes a poster made in school to the dashboard of Jerry's truck. The poster uses the first letters Jesus, others, and you spell out "JOY". Jerry picks up a hitch-hiker, Roger, who is also looking for work. They talk about Amy's poster and the real world. yet, in the end, each man is led to work for the benefit of others.
27-186 30 min. $24.95

Our Daily Bread
Film genius King Vidor produced and directed this award-winning story of a young couple struggling through the Depression. Stars Karen Morley and Tom Keene.
27-050 74 min. $59.95

Pope John Paul II: Seven Days Of Eternity

Narrated by Joseph Campanella. This is a lavish keepsake of the celebration of Holy Week in Rome --one of the most inspiring events of recorded time. Rich in emotion and faith, this program captures all the pomp and pageantry of an unforgettable week of worship - from the majesty of Palm Sunday, through the somber rites of Good Friday, to the glorious observance of Easter Sunday. Archival clips from great moments in the life of John Paul II are also included, as is a reading of the Pope's poetry by Orson Welles.
27-5766 48 min. $19.95

Power of the Resurrection

The passion of Christ, as seen through the eyes of Simon and Peter.
27-051 60 min. $19.95

Prayers

An inspirational collection of Christendom's most popular spiritual meditations brought to dramatic life. It's a true sharing experience.
27-247 25 min. $14.95

Psychic Confession

This is the compelling story of how Danny Korem, a world-class magician and expert on deception, unmasked a man heralded as the world's leading psychic: James Hydrick. A leading Christian spokesman in psychic deception, Danny comments on how Christians can avoid deception by those who fraudulently claim to have psychic or supernatural powers.
27-232 44 min. $49.95

Relationships

A unique video set for teens that opens up vital communication, stimulates group discussions and offers solid, Biblical answers to the relationship issues teens face today. Includes a detailed leader's guide.
27-2557 90 min. $159.95

SCRIPTURE SERIES:

A life-action series that re-enacts many of the most well known stories in scripture.

• Betrayal Of Jesus

Judas! Thirty pieces of silver! A kiss! These are the essential elements of the most infamous betrayal in history. See Judas Iscariot as he bargains with the high priests to betray his master for "30 pieces of silver", unbeknown to Jesus and the other eleven disciples, who were assembled in an upper room for their last supper together.
27-5718 50 min. $14.95

• Birth Of Jesus

Journey with the three wise men as they are guided by the star to that stable in the little town of Bethlehem. Born to Mary and Joseph, and ultimately to the world, little Jesus is welcomed with worldly gifts and love. Later, at age 12, as is the custom, Jesus is taken to Jerusalem for the traditional passover.
27-5720 55 min. $14.95

• Jesus Has Risen

Jesus, of Nazareth is brought forth before Pontius Pilate for trial. Pilate, finding no fault in Jesus, returns him to King Herod for disposition. Herod, after a time again sends Jesus back to Pontius Pilate, who in apparent frustration gives Jesus over to the clamorous mob. The mob crucifies Jesus.
27-5717 50 min. $14.95

• Jesus The Healer

Jesus and his disciples, enroute to Galilee, stop at a well in the region of Samaria, and talk with a woman at the well about "living water"...Further along in the journey, encountering a nobleman who hails from the city of Capernaum, Jesus brings life to the dying son of the nobleman.
27-5719 50 min. $14.95

Peace and Joy, Songs of Faith and Inspiration

Join Frank Patterson and his special guests, the Little Gaelic Singers of New York for a program of inspiring songs.
27-8015 60 min. $16.95

Rosary

New creative ways for you and your family to pray with the use of visual imagery and a musical background.
27-8014 60 min. $16.95

Silent Witness

This video is an investigation into the authenticity of the Shroud of Turin. Italy's Turin Cathedral is the home of an ancient burial cloth bearing an image many believe to be that of Jesus Christ. Medical examiners, theologians, physicists, and historians use modern science to trace the probable history of the cloth.
27-248 55 min. $39.95

Stained Images

Negative images from church politics and media reports influence impressions of Christianity. Do these stained images create unfair stereotypes? In this video, people talk honestly about Christianity and Christians. Colorful animation sequences combine with interviews that explore these misconceptions: Why are so many Christians hypocrites? Who defines morality? If you're good,

---

you go to heaven. Right?
27-8034 25 min. $29.95

Strengthening Your Grip
This presentation challenges the viewer to resist the steady pressures that always threaten to wear down their resolve and loosen their grip on the Christian values they cherish most. Includes study guides.
27-2577 234 min. $179.95

Sunday School Stories
This videotape features "The Creation," "What is Christmas?" "What Is Easter?" "Right and Wrong," and "I'm Somebody Special." Ages 3-8 years.
10-037 51 min. $16.95

Truce in the Forest
Set on Christmas Eve 1944 during the Battle of the Bulge, this is a powerful drama about Christian brotherhood and visualizes the reality of the Bible message, "Peace on earth, good will to men."
27-195 30 min. $39.95

Using Video in Ministry: A Guide for the Local Congregation
The program provides a section directed to members of your congregation to interest them in using video in church as a motivational and reference tool. Then, it shows those more directly involved in video using-the youth group, committees and staff members.
27-223 60 min. $24.95

Waiting for the Wind
Starring Robert Mitchum, Rhonda Fleming and Jameson Parker. This is Christian video at its most compelling: contemporary, relevant, filled with the drama of real life. "Waiting for the Wind", is the story of a land locked farmer with a dream as big as an ocean. Walter's rugged faith in the face of terminal illness is conveyed to his adoring grandson in a final scene viewers will never forget.
27-8037 30 min. $19.95

When God's Heart Breaks With Love
This presentation of God's holiness puts a perspective on the strife-torn world in which we live and seeks to answer the agonizing question: "If God is live, why doesn't he intervene?" With rebellion, war and disaster all around, here is a reminder of hope for the future.
27-209 30 min. $49.95

Who Are My Own
As a priest from a wealthy and aristocratic family, La Salle was given a prestigious position at the Cathedral of Rheims. But he could not ignore the hunger, ignorance and despair in the city. Here is a story of love and dedication. LaSalle's story is

disconcerting, unbelievable, paradoxical and true.
27-217 90 min. $49.95

Within Thy Gates, O Jerusalem: The City And The Temple
Unfolds sites and events during the birth of Christianity, based on Josephus Flavius, rich archaeological findings and a mini-model of Jerusalem at the Holy Land Hotel.
27-6494 32 min. $24.95

Wrestling with God
This is one of those rare Christian films that opens doors to new spiritual journeys. Its compelling message is delivered by asking questions rather than imposing answers. Based on the early life of Alexander Campbell, an Irish intellectual who immigrated to America. Campbell's personal conflicts are the same battles Christians wrestle with today; the day-to-day tests, the hard fought triumphs and the faith shaking tragedies of real life.
27-9111 72 min. $29.95

You Can Make a Difference
Tony Campolo cuts through pretense and good intentions to compel young people to come to grips with the issues of commitment, vocation, dating and discipleship. A survival kit for maintaining Christian values in today's culture.
27-2582 220 min. $159.95

Your Personality Tree
Florence Littauer's practical sessions urge self-acceptance and honestly. She helps you evaluate the affect your personality has on your family and others, and achieve inner peace through God and personal effectiveness. Includes study guides.
27-2576 105 min. $159.95

Philosophy

Climb A Tall Mountain
A spiritually uplifting film photographed entirely on location in the majestic Swiss Alps, its message of love and forgiveness comes alive in a heart-warming way through the lives of Heidi, Peter, Hans and the Swiss woodcarver. The message is meaningful for all ages--from youngsters to grandparents. "Climb A Tall Mountain" will be an inspiration to your church members and will provide an excellent opportunity for an invitation to others.
27-6259 45 min. $29.95

VIDEO TITLES LISTED IN THIS GUIDE ARE AVAILABLE FOR PURCHASE OR RENTAL. CONTACT YOUR LOCAL VIDEO STORE OR TELEPHONE (800) 383-8811

Course in Miracles

In this leisurely dialogue with longtime student Charles Johnson, Tara Singh offers a comprehensive overview of his inspirational teachings. Exploring the requirements for meditation, the role of miracles in self-correction, and the need for passion in the search for truth, Mr. Singh also reflects on the nature of "problems", and on the necessity for a self-reliant, ordered life.
27-8028 60 min. $29.95

God of Stones and Spiders

We live in a post-Christian society. Morality is scorned. Ethical absolutes are ridiculed. Evil is called good and good evil. In this provocative video series (based on the best-selling book by the same title), Charles Colson speaks the prophetic voice against this new dark age. With rare insight, Colson looks at what happens to a culture that has lost common standards of beauty, truth and goodness.
27-8039 60 min. $49.95

Heavensent

A typical Junior High student, Chris is bored with most of the formal settings in his life, including his Sunday School class as it studies what Heaven will be like. Chris comments, "What's so special about Heaven? It sounds boring!" His comment results in a special dream where he learns that in Christ, he is truly special and that Heaven is so much more than he ever imagined. A delightful original music score by David Maddux, winner of the best musical score award for a 1982 film release, compliments the funny but meaningful story.
27-6258 30 min. $29.95

In Search of Historic Jesus

Relive the life and times of the most revered figure in human history in this stunning quest. Based on the best-selling book.
27-8066 91 min. $19.95

Life After Life

Since the beginning of time, people have pondered what happens to them when they die. This program offers what some believe is strong evidence that death is just a transition to another state. Share the experiences of those who have been there and returned to their normal lives--forever changed. In this video, Dr. Raymond Moody interviews people who have "survived death" and who are alive to give us first hand reports of what they witnessed.
27-8009 60 min. $19.95

LONG SEARCH SERIES:

This series takes an in-depth, philosophical look at the many religions that are practiced throughout the world today.

• **Alternative Lifestyles in California: West Meets East**
27-8078 52 min. $99.95

• **African Religion: Zulu Zion**
27-8076 52 min. $99.95

• **Buddhism: Footprint of the Buddha: India**
27-8069 52 min. $99.95

• **Buddhism: Land of the Disappearing Buddha: Japan**
27-8075 52 min. $99.95

• **Catholicism: Rome, Leeds and the Desert**
27-8070 52 min. $99.95

• **Hinduism: 330 Million Gods**
27-8068 52 min. $99.95

• **Islam: There Is No God But God**
27-8071 52 min. $99.95

• **Judaism: The Chosen People**
27-8073 52 min. $99.95

• **Orthodox Christianity: The Rumanian Solution**
27-8072 52 min. $99.95

• **Protestant Spirit USA**
27-8067 52 min. $99.95

• **Reflections On the Long Search**
27-8079 52 min. $99.95

• **Religion in Indonesia: The Way of the Ancestors**
27-8074 52 min. $99.95

• **Taoism: A Question of Balance**
27-8077 52 min. $99.95

Power of Attention

In this compelling hour, Tara Singh shows what attention is, what it can do and challenges the viewer to find the power inherent in the state beyond the intellect.
27-8030 60 min. $29.95

POWER OF MYTH VIDEO SERIES:

VIDEO TITLES LISTED IN THIS GUIDE ARE AVAILABLE FOR PURCHASE OR RENTAL. CONTACT YOUR LOCAL VIDEO STORE OR TELEPHONE (800) 383-8811

• **First Storytellers**
29-6364 58 min. $29.95

• **Hero's Adventure**
29-6362 58 min. $29.95

• **Love and the Goddess**
29-6366 58 min. $29.95

• **Masks of Eternity**
29-6367 58 min. $29.95

• **Message of the Myth**
29-6363 58 min. $29.95

• **Sacrifice and Bliss**
29-6365 58 min. $29.95

SOUL SERIES:
In three visually stunning programs produced for the BBC, Soul explores the spiritual implications of this new scientific thinking with noted thinkers such as Stephen Hawkins, Paul Davies and Danah Zohar.

• **Soul of the Universe**
This fascinating program takes a fresh look at the universe.
27-8062 45 min. $19.95

• **Evolving Soul**
This program examines the changing world of life sciences.
27-8063 45 min. $19.95

• **Silicon Soul**
This program explores the human mind.
27-8064 45 min. $19.95

Still, Small Voice
Former CBS News corespondent, Bill Kurtis, hosts an examination of modern mystical experiences.
27-8008 60 min. $19.95

There Must Be Another Way
The story of how A Course In Miracles was given in response to humanity's cry for help. Filmed at a workshop with Tara Singh, this video explores the significance of the encounter which precipitated the writing of the course. Mr. Singh explains that the course was given to meet the depths of human sorrow and despair and release us.
27-8029 60 min. $29.95

WISDOM OF ALAN WATTS SERIES:
Perhaps the foremost interpreter of Eastern philosophy for the contemporary West, Alan Watts provided timeless insights on life and death, God and time, work and play, reproduction and our planet's future. Just before his death in 1973, Alan Watts foresaw the coming video revolution, and with the help of his son Mark, summed up a lifetime of thought via the powerful medium of video. Throughout Watts' presentations, his wit and clarity underline a timeless message.

• **Clothing**
Cultural garb and the fabric of life.
29-083 30 min. $39.95

• **Coming to Our Senses**
Do you smell? Our most repressed sense springs to life.
29-086 30 min. $39.95

• **Cosmic Drama**
In which God is the actor who plays all parts.
29-087 30 min. $39.95

• **Death**
The universe as an on/offing process.
29-080 30 min. $39.95

• **Ego**
Myself, a case of mistaken identity.
29-079 30 min. $39.95

• **God**
The ultimate being or the ultimate idol.
29-078 30 min. $39.95

• **Man and Nature**
We didn't come into this world...we came out of it.
29-077 30 min. $39.95

• **Meditation**
We begin by listening without naming.
29-085 30 min. $39.95

• **More it Changes**
Three philosophical fantasies.
29-084 30 min. $39.95

• **Nothingness**
You can't have something without nothing.
29-081 30 min. $39.95

• **Time**
Does the past really determine the present?
29-082 30 min. $39.95

• **Work as Play**
The art of working is to be paid for play.
29-076 30 min. $39.95

VIDEO TITLES LISTED IN THIS GUIDE ARE AVAILABLE FOR PURCHASE
OR RENTAL. CONTACT YOUR LOCAL VIDEO STORE OR TELEPHONE (800) 383-8811

Miscellaneous

Beyond the Next Mountain
This is the true story of a missionary at the turn of the century who brought the gospel to the Indian tribe of a young man, Ro, and in the process, converted his father.
27-2579 97 min. $59.95

God Views
A multi-talented actor and writer, Curt Cloniger, explores some of the ways we view the God who loves us and cares for us. "God Views" will keep you laughing as it starts you thinking about your own perspective and the way you view God.
27-9461 42 min. $24.95

Holy Koran
The Holy Koran is a penetrating study of the holy book of Islam which explains for the Western mind why this religion is such a force in the modern world today. Islamic Science shows in detail how the people of the Moslem world have contributed to today's civilization and culture. The Religious Experience compares Islam with the world's other great religions.
27-033 120 min. $64.95

Human Value
This collection of 3 films spans the spectrum of human liberty: Keith - a mime dramatizes an internal battle for freedom, Mimi - gifted woman's struggle with limited physical abilities, and Holy War - a graphic denunciation of war.
27-140 31 min. $29.95

Inner Circle of Life: Part I
These powerful films enhance awareness about inner struggles people face in life, providing insights into moral strength and responsibility. This video includes To Be Aware of Death, To Be Alone, To Be Afraid and To Be Continued.
27-137 59 min. $29.95

Inner Circle of Life: Part 2
This part includes, To Be True to Yourself, To Be Creative, To Be the Most You Can Be and To Be Assertive.
27-138 63 min. $29.95

Jimmy and the White Lie
When nine-year-old Jimmy accidently breaks cranky Mr. Crankshaw's window he learns the hard way that a lie can be quite difficult to live with! Jimmy's lie grows and grows until Jimmy confronts it and asks God for guidance. A delightful, imaginative program for children-with an important lesson, too!
27-178 20 min. $19.95

Morals By Monsters
These delightful, animated films for children communicate a potent dose of self-acceptance to enhance self worth, aimed at solving the problems of small children in building a positive self-image.
10-048 25 min. $29.95

Nepal, Land of the Gods
Examines the ancient civilizations still thriving in this Himalayan kingdom, focusing on Nepal's unique mixture of Buddhism and Hinduism. It shows the ritual invocation of deities, meditation and training for young Tibetan monks, and depicts belief in local spirits, mountain gods and folk figures (such as Yehti) into daily Sherpa life in the Everest region. It culminates in a dramatic evocation of a shaman's journey through the landscape of the psyche. The narrative explains how lamas have taken over the shaman's role as psychic healer and guide of souls, and how Tantra is an integral part of daily life, harmonizing the relationship between man, woman, nature and a higher spiritual reality.
27-150 62 min. $69.95

ONLY FOR CHILDREN SERIES
These delightful cartoons capture young imaginations entertainingly while teaching children moral integrity in solving problems and confronting life situations.

• Lion and the Turtle
27-2567 12 min. $12.95

• Volume 1
27-2564 30 min. $19.95

• Volume 2
27-2565 30 min. $19.95

• Volume 3
27-2566 30 min. $19.95

Ripped Down the Middle
The word "family" evokes feelings of warmth and security for some, but hurt for others. An emotionally wounded generation affects the church, the workplace and society as a whole. In this video men and women talk about growing up in homes marked by abuse, alcoholism and other trauma. And you'll hear how to move beyond hurt into hope.
27-8035 27 min. $29.95

SUNSHINE FACTORY SERIES:
A very special fix-it factory shop where neighborhood children learn biblical values from P.J. the repairman and an enthusiastic group of delightful characters. Each episode deals with a particular value.

• **Honesty**
27-2560 23 min. $19.95

• **Obedience**
27-2562 23 min. $19.95

• **Responsibility**
27-2563 23 min. $19.95

• **Sharing**
27-2561 23 min. $19.95

Tantra of Gyuoto (Sacred Rituals of Tibet)
An account of the secret Tibetan Buddhist ceremonies by monks of Gyuoto Tantric College. Through ritual and mantric power, the Guyoto monks use sound to effect a change in the individual and his environment. By their sheer inherent potency and disciplined execution, these concentrated essential energies bring about direct spiritual phenomenon. It is only in this exceptional time, an age of massive world changes, that the lamas have reversed their traditional practice of secrecy and have allowed certain chants to be heard. These rituals were filmed by authorization of his Holiness the Dalai Lama, who introduces the ceremonies.
27-151 52 min. $59.95

This Section Brings You Tapes That...

Dramatize the Old Testament

Present the Life & Time of Jesus

and

Explore the World's Religions

VIDEO TITLES LISTED IN THIS GUIDE ARE AVAILABLE FOR PURCHASE OR RENTAL. CONTACT YOUR LOCAL VIDEO STORE OR TELEPHONE (800) 383-8811

Searching For

A Unique Gift That is

Informative and Appreciated?

The Video Titles

In This Guide

Make Wonderful Gifts.

VIDEO TITLES LISTED IN THIS GUIDE ARE AVAILABLE FOR PURCHASE
OR RENTAL. CONTACT YOUR LOCAL VIDEO STORE OR TELEPHONE (800) 383-8811

Sex
Education

Sex Education

BEST OF PLAYBOY SERIES:
This series was designed to help couples enhance their sexual relationships.

• Secrets of Euro Massage
Set your senses tingling with the intimate art of Swedish, French and German massage.
31-8033 60 min. $29.95

• Intimate Workout for Lovers
Try these wet and wild exercises to enhance your health and sexual gratification.
31-8034 60 min. $29.95

• Erotic Fantasies I
Enjoy these sensual seduction scenarios. Allow them to enhance your relationship.
31-8035 60 min. $29.95

• Erotic Fantasies II
Share the intimate desires of provocative playmates.
31-8036 60 min. $29.95

• Secrets of Making Love to the Same Person Forever
Learn the secrets of turning routine sex into a life-long erotic adventure.
31-8037 60 min. $29.95

BETTER SEX VIDEO SERIES:

• Better Sex Basics
This introductory course focuses on the sexual experiences of several couples. Each couple explains (and illustrates) experiences from their past and shows how a better understanding of their sexuality, together with improved communication skills, helped them to enjoy greater sexual pleasure.
31-5465 90 min. $39.95

• Advanced Sexual Techniques
In Video One you saw what is important to know about the basics of your sex life. In video two, Advanced Sexual Techniques, we will discuss exactly how to perform more advanced sexual practices, taking the time to dwell on detailed methods of giving and enjoying pleasure.
31-5466 90 min. $39.95

• Sex Games And Toys
Video Three covers the all-important issue of including sex toys to change the nature of the interaction and bring newness and freshness into an established and loving intimate relationship.
31-5467 90 min. $39.95

Chinese Lovemaking Secrets
Ancient Chinese lovemaking secrets revealed for the first time on video without nudity or explicit sex. Western sex researchers have only recently discovered what the Chinese have known for over 4,000 years - how to derive the maximum male/female sexual pleasure using the G-spot, acupressure, breathing control and sexual positions.
31-048 40 min. $39.95

CHRISTIAN APPROACH TO SEX EDUCATION SERIES:
This series fills the missing gap in teaching your children Christian sexual values. Don't let the media and the schools be the final word on what is right or wrong.

• Volume 1
Introduction to this series is designed to help parents realize the focus of this program. This video will motivate parents to become a more active participant in their children's sexual education.
31-8007 65 min. $29.95

• Volume 2
This program will help you set up an environment that encourages Christian sexual values. Become responsible for your child's sexual education at all ages. Don't let schools be the only form of Sex Education your child receives.
31-8008 50 min. $29.95

• Volume 3
It's never too early or too late begin educating your children in Christian sexual values. Learn how to communicate God's word in a comprehensive manner your children will understand.
31-8009 55 min. $29.95

• Volume 4
Is sex education helping our teens or contributing to the problems teen pregnancy and sexually transmitted disease. This video explores these questions and more.
31-8010 55 min. $29.95

Common Sexual Problems
Sex counselors Jane James and Lloyd Sinclair help define a happy, healthy sex life and how it contributes to the overall success of a marriage. They also discuss some of the common sexual problems in American marriages. Among the

issues discussed are: whether these problems are different according to age or to sex and how a couple's sex life changes as they move from dating to the honeymoon, to a long-term marriage.
31-8011 22 min. $89.95

CONCORDIA SEX EDUCATION SERIES:

• **Each One Specially**
Explains the differences and similarities between boys and girls. For children ages 3-5.
26-096 6 min. $19.95

• **How You Got to be You**
Helps children understand body changes. For Children ages 8-11.
26-098 15 min. $19.95

• **I Wonder Why**
Visualization and discussion of specific body parts, body functions and the birth process. For children ages 6-8.
26-097 10 min. $19.95

• **New You**
Explains that the feelings of masculinity and femininity are healthy and normal. For children ages 11-14.
26-099 15 min. $19.95

• **Sexuality: God's Precious Gift to Parents and Children**
An overview of the other four tapes. Deals with adult sexuality and designed to build the self-confidence of sex educators. For parents and teachers.
26-101 20 min. $19.95

Everything You Always Wanted To Know About Safe Sex...But Were Afraid To Ask
You'll learn more about safe sex in 60 minutes than you've ever learned before. This program offers a practical, authoritative, straight-forward and entertaining approach to a subject that to date, has been treated clinically, often without consideration of the realities of sexual conduct.
31-8004 60 min. $29.95

FACTS, FEELINGS AND WONDER OF LIFE SERIES:
This series provides the straight-forward answers to questions posed by young people. It provides a safe, comfortable atmosphere for young people to express their feelings and find out what they need to know about their changing bodies.

• **Physical Changes**
31-8013 23 min. $69.95

• **Sexual Changes: Boys**
31-8014 19 min. $69.95

• **Sexual Changes: Girls**
31-8015 19 min. $69.95

GREAT SEX SERIES WITH FRANK G. SOMMERS, M.D.

• **Taking Time to Feel: Volume I**
A real couple, married 14 years explicitly demonstrate how they make love without intercourse. With pressure to perform put aside, they explore each other in a gentle, erotic way, utilizing a variety of positions.
31-8001 30 min. $24.95

• **Mutuality: Volume II**
This video is a loving celebration of unrepressed, playful human sexuality featuring a real couple. Fellatio, cunnilingus and self-pleasuring, in the context of a couple relationship, are lovingly, explicitly illustrated.
31-8002 46 min. $29.95

• **Sexual Pleasures: Volume III**
A real couple in their 20's show how they make their sex life exciting and keep it alive. Their creative lovemaking includes oral fantasy and positional variations. Exercises for premature ejaculation and a method of quiet, relaxed intercourse are all clearly illustrated.
31-8003 75 min. $39.95

How To Be A Good Lover
Jeff faced the problem of finding the perfect lover. He was thrilled with his computerized list of ideal qualities until a friend pointed out that his approach doesn't work. Then Josh McDowell lectured in their human sexuality class about what does work. To find a good lover, you must be one first and Josh shows how. An ideal program for young people's meetings or retreats.
31-6261 45 min. $29.95

L'Amour
An erotic, humorous program which shows you what you should and shouldn't do to maximize your pleasure and that of your partner.
31-006 56 min. $29.95

Lovers Guide to Sexual Ecstasy
The ultimate handbook for anyone in search of more satisfying romance and greater pleasure in their relationships. Four beautiful couples tastefully and sensually demonstrate easy-to-learn techniques on seduction, foreplay, oral sexuality,

VIDEO TITLES LISTED IN THIS GUIDE ARE AVAILABLE FOR PURCHASE OR RENTAL. CONTACT YOUR LOCAL VIDEO STORE OR TELEPHONE (800) 383-8811

fantasy role playing and a variety of sexual positions. Features the Grafenberg orgasm.
31-8000 75 min. $39.95

Love Skills
Five beautiful couples reveal ways to enhance your sexual pleasures in this tastefully (yet erotic and explicit) presented guide. Chapters include: foreplay, positions, fantasies and obstacles.
31-007 56 min. $29.95

Massage for Couples
This program is designed for those who wish to share the joy and intimacy of soothing, helpful and energizing massage. You will learn the basic massage techniques designed to reduce stress and promote relaxation and result in an overall feeling of well-being. Presented by Elaine Hyams, M.Th., formerly head instructor of massage at the Swedish Massage Institute in New York.
31-010 45 min. $29.95

Massage Your Mate
Rebecca Klinger, a N.Y. State licensed massage therapist and a leading authority on massage, guides you through five segments of massage techniques and demonstrations. She covers both Swedish massage and Shiatsu acupressure techniques. You will learn the correct hand strokes, how to deal with ticklish or sensitive areas and tips on preparation. An excellent tape on massage for both home use and for beginning professionals.
31-024 90 min. $29.95

Massage: The Touch of Love
Sensual massage is demonstrated by couples, revealing how to stroke and relax each area of the body.
31-009 30 min. $39.95

Out In the Open: Plain Talk About Sex
This video provides a unique opportunity for young adults to hear peers talk frankly about sexual struggles. They explain common problems in depth and speak of God's principles, forgiveness and healing.
31-8022 28 min. $29.95

Playboy's Art of Sensual Massage
This visual feature on the science of sensation is a hands-on, how-to guide for couples. Viewers will enjoy attractive male and female nude models demonstrating sensuous, yet serious massage techniques. Couples will learn how to unlock their bodies' pleasure centers in ways never before imagined.
31-053 45 min. $19.95

Playgirl Magazine's Sexual Secrets
This guide to sexual awareness was created to help couples express their sexuality in an open and honest manner. Two sex therapists, provide enlightened instruction to couples whose explicit demonstrations reveal the joys of making love.
31-001 60 min. $29.95

Reproduction of Life
This video tastefully and scientifically presents the entire process of human reproduction from conception through pre/natal development to birth itself. With "Kittens Are Born", younger viewers learn firsthand about birth and are helped to develop an enlightened and positive attitude toward this natural phenomenon.
01-026 120 min. $64.95

Safe Sex? Don't Buy The Lie!
Buster Soaries has become one of the most sought-after speakers for youth. In a world filled with double talk and hidden messages, Buster communicates. Youth and their parents find his style compelling: his content life-changing. Here he takes on one of today's most important issues. Today's kids are being cheated by people who are asking them to believe a lie! The world's idea of "Safe Sex" is leading our kids to a poor self-image and many unwanted pregnancies. This tape is ideal for youth group programming, for peer group parties and young adult discussion.
31-6262 45 min. $29.95

Safe Sex for Men and Women: How to Avoid Catching AIDS
Morgan Fairchild hosts this program that deals with the AIDS issue in a realistic way and educates people about the facts. Features interviews with Dr. Laura Schlessinger and Dr. Michael Gottlieb. Appropriate for all audiences.
31-1972 60 min. $29.95

Self-Loving: Video Portrait of a Women's Sexuality Seminar
Join Betty Dodson and a dozen women of various ages and sizes, discovering their own power and sexuality as they masturbate in a workshop environment. Also includes a "show and tell" segment where each woman explores her sexual organ with wonder and praise.
31-8024 60 min. $39.95

Sensual Pleasuring
This video cassette is designed to increase the viewers sexual focus by exploring the act of sensuous non-verbal communication. Learn through a series of techniques how to prolong sexual activity, and gain control over your body. The viewer learns how to introduce his or her partners to a variety of physical pleasures. Used world wide

by leading professional sex therapists with thousands of couples.
31-7094 60 min. $49.95

Sex After 50: What Every Adult Should Know About Sexuality and Aging

This video deals with all of the sexual topics that affect maturing adults: the inability to communicate with each other about their sexuality, the lack of desire, menopause & hormone replacement therapy, the effects of illnesses and medications on sexuality, erection difficulties, the loss of a partner and much more is presented by one of the greatest teams of psychologists and sex educators assembled.
31-8023 90 min. $39.95

TEENAGE YEARS SERIES:

These four programs were designed for young people in junior and senior high to help address the physical and psychological concerns of adolescence and prepare teenagers for sexual maturity. Features actor Scott Baio.

- **Sexual Development**
  31-8017 29 min. $69.95

- **Physical Development**
  31-8018 26 min. $69.95

- **Understanding Feelings**
  31-8019 26 min. $69.95

- **STD's and Sexual Responsibility**
  31-8020 35 min. $69.95

Treatment for Sexual Problems

Jane James and Lloyd Sinclair talk about treatment for common sexual problems. They discuss when professional help is needed and reveal self-help techniques that may solve sexual problems. The guests discuss how to pick competent sex counselors, what to expect in treatment and the likelihood of a positive outcome.
31-8012 22 min. $89.95

Ultimate Kiss

This how-to video passionately explores the joys of oral lovemaking. Intimate narration and original music accompany the soft-focus cinematography that demonstrates both male and female participation.
31-2747 30 min. $29.95

What's Happening To Me?

Everybody goes through it but nobody feels comfortable talking about it. This program solves the puzzle of puberty and offers quick relief for

the growing pains we've all experienced. Learning about puberty can be fun with this humorous fully animated video.
31-055 30 min. $19.95

Where Did I Come From?

Sex education can be fun. This animated videocassette tells the story of conception through birth in a way that lets children (and sometimes their parents) learn while they laugh. In half an hour of full color animation, it answers all those awkward and unavoidable questions that have embarrassed mothers and fathers ever since kids and curiosity were invented. From the sperm race to the fertilization tango, from the comforts of womb service to the joys of the birth day, the facts of life are presented with the same love and humor that have made "Where Did I Come From"? a best-selling book all over the world.
10-264 27 min. $24.95

Who Do You Listen To? Sex In the Age of Aids

In an age where promiscuity is rampant and can be fatal, this video encourages our young people to be responsible in making the best decisions. It creates lively discussion to help our youth see God's plan for relationships. This is an important film featuring noted author and communicator, Josh McDowell.
31-9460 37 min. $49.95

Why You're Feeling Different

Psychologists say that young people beginning puberty often experience a lot of stress. This program takes a look at the feelings, emotions and coping mechanisms of youngsters during this time. A group of preteens share feelings about sex, childbirth and growing up. They also discuss their fears about AIDS. Bob Emerson, from the Centers for Disease Control, explains how AIDS is transmitted and discusses the symptoms and treatment of other sexually transmitted diseases such as herpes and chlamydia.
31-8016 26 min. $69.95

Miscellaneous

Chippendales: Tahitian Adventures

This video documents the exciting sights and sounds of a sizzling photo shoot. It presents an intimate, candid and uncensored look at the behind the scenes moments that made this a video hot!

VIDEO TITLES LISTED IN THIS GUIDE ARE AVAILABLE FOR PURCHASE OR RENTAL. CONTACT YOUR LOCAL VIDEO STORE OR TELEPHONE (800) 383-8811

Now you can be stranded on a tropical island with over a dozen sexy men.
31-8005 65 min. $19.95

How to Strip for Your Lover
An entertaining light-hearted, yet scintillating and seductive look at the art of taking it all off. Explores in rib-tickling detail, the enticements and ecstasies of stripping.
31-023 60 min. $29.95

Mermaid Fantasy
Come along as four beautiful girls dive "au natural". Swim with some of the ocean's most beautiful creatures off an almost deserted tropical island.
31-8025 60 min. $19.95

Party Games: For Adults Only
John Byner hosts the fun in this videoguide to adult party fun. Treat your guests to such risque games as Ride 'Em Cowboy; Tipsy; Marshmallow Kiss; Body Painting; and many others. The games adapt to large and small groups and are designed to make your party the one no one will ever forget.
17-018 53 min. $29.95

Procreation In The Wild
An unbelievable, incredible video based upon three years of filming, from Antarctica to Africa and Asia. Hi-tech camera work has captured Nature's most intimate moments - lovemaking in the Animal Kingdom! For the first time ever, you can view sex between turned on turtles, happy-hippos, mingling minks, gentle giraffes, ecstatic elephants, pulsating penguins, romantic monkeys, torrid tigers and many more.
31-6599 90 min. $39.95

Sexyexercises
A workout program designed for couples, featuring such exercises as the kiss 'n kurl and the clutch 'n crunch. The exercises encourage flexibility and sexiness. Includes two sets of rubber workout bands.
31-8026 43 min. $29.95

Starlet Screen Test
What's it like to audition for a part in a major motion picture? Now, consider that your role involves total nudity! What's it like for the producer who is in charge of the casting session?
31-5039 60 min. $16.95

Note: Massage videos for couples are listed in the "Health & Medicine" section of this Guide.

Get A Little Closer To Someone You Love; Find Some Help and Advice on Topics That Are Often Difficult to Discuss.

Sports

- ✓ *Baseball*
- ✓ *Basketball*
- ✓ *Bicycling*
- ✓ *Boxing & Wrestling*
- ✓ *Football*
- ✓ *Golf*
- ✓ *Gymnastics*
- ✓ *Martial Arts*
- ✓ *Soccer*
- ✓ *Tennis & Racquet Sports*
- ✓ *Track & Field*
- ✓ *Water Sports*
- ✓ *Weight Lifting & Body Building*
- ✓ *Wilderness Sports*
- ✓ *Winter Sports*
- ✓ *Miscellaneous*

Baseball

1992 Atlanta Braves-Lightning Strikes Twice
Enjoy these great Braves moments and more in this official story of the Braves 1992 championship season.
30-8277 40 min. $19.98

500 Home Run Club
Only 14 players in history have 500 career homers. See this elite group in action in this award winning video, hosted by Mickey Mantle and Bob Costas.
30-8157 55 min. $16.95

Ball Talk: Baseball Voices of Summer
Larry King, America's top television and radio host, guides you through this nostalgic odyssey. And while the announcers give you behind-the-plate scoop, he tells you the fan's side of the story with incredible insight and the special memories that come from living in the very shadow of Ebbets Field.
30-8202 50 min. $19.95

BASEBALL IN THE NEWS:
Watch many of baseball's greatest heroes make sports history. Witness some of baseball's greatest moments! All-Star games and the World Series. Plus much much more!

- **Volume I: 1951-1955**
30-5184 60 min. $29.95

- **Volume II: 1956-1960**
30-5140 60 min. $29.95

- **Volume III: 1961-1967**
30-7083 60 min. $29.95

Baseball with Rod Carew - Sybervision
Rod Carew, seven-time American League batting champion, shares with the beginner a wealth of hitting experience. Watch Carew's perfect stance, grip, and follow-through as he hits to all fields.
30-005 60 min. $69.95

BASEBALL BUNCH SERIES:
Baseball great Johnny Bench, the Baseball Bunch helpers and a bull pen of major league superstars join together to help kids become better ball players. Each engaging "Baseball Bunch" title features easy-to-follow drills designed specifically for video. And there's lots of fun with footage of major league bloopers and great plays, too. Kids are sure to turn to these tapes time and time again to brush up on the basics.

- **Fielding**
With Ozzie Smith, Craig Nettles and Gary Carter.
30-267 59 min. $16.95

- **Hitting**
With Lou Piniella, Jim Rice and Ted Williams.
30-266 59 min. $16.95

- **Pitching**
With Dan Quisenberry, Tom Seaver and Tug McGraw.
30-268 59 min. $16.95

Baseball Our Way
Personal baseball instruction from six major league stars: Tommy Lasorda, Steve Yeager, Don Sutton, Bill Russell, Eric Davis, and Wally Joyner.
30-2962 90 min. $29.95

BASEBALL THE RIGHT WAY
Let New York Mets coaches Bill Robinson, Mel Stottlemyre and Bud Harrelson, show you how to hit, pitch and field like a world champion.

- **Fielding for Kids**
30-2471 30 min. $16.95

- **Hitting for Kids**
30-2469 30 min. $16.95

- **Pitching for Kids**
30-2470 30 min. $16.95

Baseball - The Pete Rose Way
Baseball superstar Pete Rose makes learning baseball fun and easy on this informative video for young players and adults alike. Get the inside story on how America's baseball legend battled his way to the top and set more individual baseball records than any other player in history.
30-269 60 min. $19.95

Baseball - The Yankee Way
The 1960's era New York Yankees. Filmed in their prime just after their 1964 pennant-winning season, you'll see Mickey Mantle and Roger Maris share the secrets of their slugging success, learn pitching proverbs from Hall-of-Famer Whitey Ford, and fielding finesse from Yankee legends like Bobby Richardson. The ultimate in nostalgia entertainment.
30-393 45 min. $16.95

VIDEO TITLES LISTED IN THIS GUIDE ARE AVAILABLE FOR PURCHASE OR RENTAL. CONTACT YOUR LOCAL VIDEO STORE OR TELEPHONE (800) 383-8811

Baseball: Fun and Games
Here's a brand new collection of baseball's most hilarious bloopers, with Joe Garagiola hosting the hit-and-run fun. A must for every sports fan.
30-2320 53 min. $16.95

Baseball: Funny Side Up
Hosted by Tug McGraw, former major league All-Star and renowned baseball humorist, and narrated by Mel Allen, this program takes a laughing, loving look at the lighter side of our national pastime.
30-1661 45 min. $19.95

Baseball: Legends of the Game
Babe Ruth, Lou Gehrig, Willie Mays, Ty Cobb, Jackie Robinson. These are some of the all-time all-stars who made baseball America's pastime. This is a look back at the great games and moments that became the legends of baseball.
30-387 60 min. $16.95

Baseball Time Capsule
A remarkable journey through the world's largest private collection of Baseball Memorbillia. The Barry Halper collection with special guests: Mickey Mantle, Don Mattingly, Nolan Ryan and the late Billy Martin.
30-8159 49 min. $16.95

Baseball's Hall of Fame
Donald Sutherland is your host for a spellbinding tour of the Hall of Fame in Cooperstown, New York. Exciting rare footage, too.
30-006 50 min. $29.95

Baserunning Basics with Maury Wills
Maury Wills says a baseball player doesn't need blazing speed to be a good baserunner: "Good baserunning is simply getting the most out of what you have on the base paths." Since Maury is the man who broke Ty Cobb's base-stealing record, he ought to know. Watch Wills demonstrate good techniques. You'll pick up tips on stealing, sliding, leading off, the hit and run play and more.
30-001 45 min. $24.95

Battlin' Bucs: The First 100 Years of the Pittsburgh Pirates
This is the story of the Battlin' Bucs, a vivid account of dramatic moments and revealing interviews that recapture all the memorable names and games of 100 Pirate seasons.
30-1668 60 min. $19.95

Billy Martin: The Man, The Myth, The Legend
Just prior to his untimely death, Billy Martin recorded what was to be his last interview. It's the most powerful, emotional, and revealing one he ever gave. One of Baseball's most controversial figures talks in depth on baseball and managing-no-holds-barred.
30-8162 60 min. $16.95

Boys of Summer
The Brooklyn Dodgers, they were the "bums" America loved. From Roger Kahn's best seller, this is their heartwarming story - then and now.
30-2321 90 min. $19.95

Centennial: Over 100 Years of Philadelphia Phillies Baseball
This video is a complete visual history of the Phillies, from the 1800's to the present, charting the course of the club's past success and failure. It follows the Phillies from the era of Grover Cleveland Alexander, through the Whiz Kids of the 50's with Dick Sisler and Richie Ashbury, to more recent times with Mike Schmidt and Steve Carlton.
30-1667 60 min. $19.95

Charley Lau - The Art of Hitting 300
Professional baseball coach Charley Lau explains and demonstrates his "Ten Absolutes of Hitting," with help from baseball players Carlton Fisk and Greg Luzinski. You'll improve your stance, shift your weight, adjust your swing - and raise your batting average to hit like the pros!
30-009 50 min. $29.95

Chicago and the Cubs - A Lifelong Love Affair
The Chicago Cubs begin playing baseball in the 1870's, and since then no other team has held such a spell over its fans. This program captures all the emotion between one of America's greatest cities and one of sport's greatest franchises.
30-1663 60 min. $19.95

Chicago White Sox: A Visual History
Writer and humorist Jean Shepherd is your guide on this visual journey through the entire history of the White Sox, from the Hitless Wonders of 1906, through the GO-GO era of the 50's, to the present.
30-1664 60 min. $19.95

COACHING BASEBALL: SKILLS AND DRILLS SERIES
The complete video coaching series for kids' baseball. This series of tapes is endorsed by the Little League, Babe Ruth Baseball, the National High School Athletic Coach's Association, Dixie Youth Baseball and Pony/Colt. It's the best. Your coach instructor is Dr. Bragg Stockton, head baseball coach at Texas Christian University, whose teams have won over 80% of their games. Dr. Creighton Hale, President of Little League Baseball says: "Little League certainly recommends

that all managers and coaches in our program take advantage of this excellent presentation."

• Coaching Psychology
How to handle parents. Getting the best performance from any player. Helping the player define and meet his goals. How to maximize the youth baseball experience and handle parents.
30-011 57 min. $39.95

• Defensive Skills by Position
The six basic drills applied. Infield positions. Pitcher. Turning double plays. Outfield. Cut-offs. Catcher.
30-014 45 min. $39.95

• Fundamentals of Baserunning
The key to maximizing offensive output. Getting a good lead. Sliding. Situational strategies.
30-015 45 min. $39.95

• Fundamentals of Fielding
The key to solid defense. Five basic defensive drills. Critical body positions. Visual aids designed to develop a "kinesthetic image" of the proper throwing motion.
30-013 40 min. $39.95

• Fundamentals of Hitting
A revolutionary system of coaching hitting. Understanding the elements of sound swing. Visual aids to help develop a "kinesthetic image" of a proper swing. Physical, visual and mental drills for players.
30-010 55 min. $39.95

• Fundamentals of Pitching
Correct body mechanics - the best preventive medicine for arm jury. Five phases of the pitching motion. Body mechanics. A safe and effective curve and change-up.
30-012 57 min. $39.95

Dodger Stadium: The First 25 Years
A look back at the first quarter of century of Dodger Stadium, from Koufax to Valenzuela, through special interviews and rare film footage of the memorable men and moments of the great Dodger teams that played there.
30-1665 60 min. $19.95

Forever Fenway: 75 Years of Red Sox Baseball
From Babe Ruth to Jim Rice and all that's in between, this is the official story of the team and the players that have called Fenway Park home since 1912.
30-1662 60 min. $19.95

George Brett's Secrets of Baseball
Learn the secrets of hitting from All-Star Kansas City Royal, George Brett. This is an entertaining lesson in all aspects of baseball hitting.
30-2938 60 min. $16.95

Giants History: The Tale of Two Cities
From their beginnings at Coogan's Bluff in New York City to their triumphs in the City by the Bay, this video captures the memories of one of baseball's oldest franchises, the San Francisco Giants.
30-1669 60 min. $19.95

Glory of Their Times
Documentary on turn-of-the-century baseball. Includes footage of Ty Cobb, Christy Matthewson, Honus Wagner, and many other greats of the time.
30-2012 55 min. $29.95

GOLDEN DECADE OF BASEBALL
The greatest players and events of Major League Baseball form the years 1947-1957.

• Part 1 (1947-1952)
30-8193 60 min. $16.95

• Part 2 (1953-1957)
30-8194 60 min. $16.95

Greatest Comeback Ever
Bucky Dent and Phil Rizzuto give you an insider's locker-room-view of the Yankees' incredible 1978 season, starting with the injuries and clubhouse strife, and ending in tumultuous victory.
30-550 58 min. $16.95

History of Baseball
It's all here: from the earliest origins of a child's game in the playing fields of America to the twenty-six Major League franchises of today, this video is the definitive account of the growth and development of our national pastime.
30-1660 120 min. $29.95

Little League's Official How-to-Play-Baseball by Video (8-12-year-olds)
For half the cost of a good baseball mitt, give your child or coach the first-time-ever Little League instructional video designed especially for beginning players. Teaches all the skills needed to play the game: gripping, throwing, hitting, pitching, sliding, and playing all the defensive positions, using kids to demonstrate.
30-017 90 min. $19.95

Lou Piniella's Winning Ways
The skipper of the Cincinnati Reds teaches the

fundamentals of batting.
30-8192 60 min. $19.95

Mantle vs. Mays
Mickey Mantle is hosted by Paul Hornung. Willie Mays is hosted by Reggie Jackson.
30-497 45 min. $24.95

Major League Hitting Secrets
Former player and current major league batting coach Vada Pinson is your private instructor in this fast-paced lesson.
30-2966 30 min. $16.95

MARK CRESSE SCHOOL OF BASEBALL SERIES:
Los Angeles Dodger's Coach Mark Cresse offers helpful hints, strategies, and different techniques to the aspiring big-leaguer. If you can't attend his successful baseball camp, this video is the next best chance to gain from his expertise.

• Volume I - Offensive
Lessons on bunting, hitting, pitching and baserunning.
30-8214 60 min. $16.95

• Volume II - Defensive
Lessons on catching infield and outfield play.
30-8215 60 min. $16.95

Meet Babe Ruth
A thrilling journey of the life and times of "The Babe", including rare footage of his early days as the pitcher in Boston, to career heights during his New York years.
30-8158 30 min. $16.95

Mickey Mantle: American Dream Comes To Life
The hall of famer Mickey Mantle reminisces about his career. Never-before released footage of game highlights.
30-8260 60 min. $24.95

Pete Rose - Winning Baseball
Superstar Pete Rose, 1985 Athlete of the Year and breaker of Ty Cobb's Major League record for most hits, gives you his personal tips and secrets on hitting and bunting from the batter's box. Also learn how to get the most out of each pitch with pitcher Claude Osteen, as well as defensive catching techniques from Sonny Ruberto. Also includes historical footage of Pete's record-breaking hit - a collector's item.
30-290 55 min. $19.95

Red Sox '86
The complete season championship series and World Series highlights! Red Sox '86 - the official video yearbook - captures all the excitement of the spectacular season.
30-677 60 min. $29.95

Science of Pitching - Wes Stock
Have a real pro coach your Little League team, or show you some major league pitching tips in your living room. Former Major League pitcher and pitching coach Wes Stock runs through basics, such as grip, four fundamental pitches, position, wind-up, follow-through and more. He demonstrates helpful practice drills and points out causes for throwing high or low, inside or out. High school and college teams will benefit from this video, as well as weekend jocks of all skill levels.
30-019 60 min. $19.95

Slow Pitch Softball
600-plus hitter Ray DeMarini's reflex hitting system will help you become a better, more consistent hitter regardless of your size and power.
30-8098 55 min. $16.95

Sports Clinic Baseball
Dick Williams, Seattle Mariners manager, is your pitching, batting, fielding and baserunning coach in this information-packed video.
30-018 80 min. $19.95

Sports Pages: Baseball Bloopers
Get ready for some of the silliest, strangest and goofiest goofs, blunders and mishaps you have ever seen in Baseball Bloopers. Featuring: Pedro Guererro, Kirby Puckett and George Brett.
30-8134 30 min. $16.95

Steve Garvey's Hitting System
This unique program demonstrates what it takes for a hitter to raise his bating average, hit with consistency and eliminate flaws in his swing. Segments include: the mental side of hitting; lost art of bunting; before you hit; what the hitter sees or doesn't see; getting the bat head to the ball; a firm base to a firm base; problem solving; exercises for improving and maintaining good habits; and a word to hitting instructors.
30-689 45 min. $29.95

Story of America's Classic Ballparks
A baseball fan's dream! Join baseball fan Jeff Daniels on a nostalgic journey to some of the greatest ball parks in America and the history behind them.
30-8167 60 min. $29.95

Strategy of Slow Pitch Softball
This video will show you, the Slow Pitcher, how to locate and exploit a batter's weaknesses.
30-8286 45 min. $29.95

VIDEO TITLES LISTED IN THIS GUIDE ARE AVAILABLE FOR PURCHASE OR RENTAL. CONTACT YOUR LOCAL VIDEO STORE OR TELEPHONE (800) 383-8811

Teaching Kids Baseball With Jerry Kindall

Coach Jerry Kindall's dedication to fundamentals, effort and teamwork has made champions of his University of Arizona Wildcats. In this video he shares his winning coaching techniques to build solid skills in youngsters just starting out in the game with instruction on running, throwing, hitting, fielding and team play.
30-5494 75 min. $29.95

Ten Greatest Moments in Yankee History

Mel Allen narrates this potpourri of highlights of the team with perhaps the richest, most colorful history of any in baseball.
30-1965 30 min. $19.95

TOTAL BASEBALL SERIES

In this two part series, Tony shows you the batting, fielding, base stealing and training techniques that have made him a winner. With Tony Gwynn.

• King of Swing
30-8033 35 min. $19.95

• Play to Win
30-8034 35 min. $19.95

Williams vs. Rose

Ted Williams and Pete Rose are showcased here, hosted by Tom Seaver.
30-500 45 min. $24.95

Winner's Edge: Baseball

Former Chicago White Sox manager Don Kessinger gives young players tips on pitching, batting, fielding and baserunning.
30-002 25 min. $16.95

Winning Softball

Howard's Western Steer softball team has earned the title "World's Best Softball Team," having won four national championships since 1973. Join the team and see how the best hone their skills for slow pitch softball.
30-2981 45 min. $19.95

You Be the Judge: An Introduction to Basic Umpiring Skills for Baseball & Softball

An ideal instruction tape for umpire training at all levels of youth, recreational, intramural or military baseball and softball leagues, as well as umpiring associations.
30-9990 31 min. $39.95

Basketball

BASKETBALL SKILLS AND DRILLS

It all starts with team attitude. After that, practice makes permanent. This is a comprehensive 14 part program developed by Don Meyer and Jerry Krause. This gives coaches of all levels a guide to the important skills and drills of basketball.

• Field Goal Shooting (set/jump shots)
30-8068 15 min. $19.95

• Field Goal Shooting (layup/3 points)
30-8069 30 min. $19.95

• Footwork
30-8071 15 min. $19.95

• Free Throw Shooting
30-8070 30 min. $19.95

• Get Open to Score
30-8073 15 min. $19.95

• Individual Defense
30-8077 15 min. $19.95

• Pass & Catch
30-8072 15 min. $19.95

• Perimeter
30-8074 30 min. $19.95

• Post Play
30-8075 30 min. $19.95

• Rebounding
30-8078 30 min. $19.95

• Setting & Using Screens
30-8076 30 min. $19.95

• Teaching Tips
30-8080 15 min. $19.95

• Team Attitude
30-8079 30 min. $19.95

Basketball With Gail Goodrich

The Celtics star demonstrates and explains the basic fundamentals of basketball - dribbling, shooting,

defense, jumping techniques.
30-022 30 min. $19.95

BUILDING A CHAMPIONSHIP PROGRAM SERIES:
Find out what high school coaches from all 50 states and over 100 universities have learned which has helped them improve their basketball program. With Don Meyer.

• **Becoming a Great Shooter**
30-8056 30 min. $29.95

• **Building a Championship Program Through Team Attitude**
30-8051 30 min. $29.95

• **Championship Preparation for Games**
30-8060 30 min. $29.95

• **Championship Approach to Strength Training and Conditioning**
30-8063 30 min. $29.95

• **Developing Your Post Players**
30-8057 30 min. $29.95

• **Developing Your Perimeter Players**
30-8058 30 min. $29.95

• **Drills for Teaching Individual Fundamentals and Team Offense**
30-8065 30 min. $29.95

• **Drills for Teaching Individual and Team Defense**
30-8064 30 min. $29.95

• **Practice Planning, Organization & On-the-Floor Demonstration**
30-8066 30 min. $29.95

• **Pressure Man-to-Man Defense System**
30-8052 30 min. $29.95

• **Match-Up Zone**
30-8055 30 min. $29.95

• **Motion Offense**
30-8053 30 min. $29.95

• **Traditional Game**
30-8062 30 min. $29.95

• **Utilizing and Defending the Three Point Shot**
30-8059 30 min. $29.95

• **Winning Special Situations**
30-8061 30 min. $29.95

• **Zone Attack**
30-8054 30 min. $29.95

Chamberlain vs. Abdul-Jabbar
Wilt Chamberlain is hosted by Tom Seaver. Kareem Abdul-Jabbar is hosted by Jayne Kennedy.
30-499 45 min. **$24.95**

Coach to Coach: The Ultimate Clinic
The top coaches in the NBA lead in-depth clinics on their respective areas of expertise. Some of the topics include: Teaching techniques, game strategies, motivation and other crucial coaching skills designed to enhance performance on and off the court.
30-8010 70 min. $39.95

Converse Basketball Tips with "Dr. J", Julius Erving, Kevin McHale and Dale Brown
A unique collection of inspirational tips, personal insights and motivational strategies, as well as offensive moves, free throw instruction, practice tips, mental training and personal inspiration.
30-8067 20 min. $19.95

Fundamentals of Women's Basketball - Offensive Play
Cathy Benedetto, head coach at Seattle University and New Mexico State University (her current team), includes everything from shooting mechanics to offensive strategy in this complete program on basketball offense. Members of the New Mexico State University women's varsity team demonstrate a variety of offensive drills for improvement in shooting, dribbling, passing and rebounding. Benedetto gives perhaps the most detailed section on "shooting" that has ever been presented in video form. This will be a valuable addition to every coach's team library.
30-025 61 min. $29.95

JIM HARRICK APPROACH TO WINNING BASKETBALL
Jim Harrick has vaulted to the top of college basketball's coaching elite. Now Coach Harrick opens his playbook and team practices for this great video series! Perfect for the serious coach who is looking for a greater understanding of what it takes to build a basketball dynasty.

VIDEO TITLES LISTED IN THIS GUIDE ARE AVAILABLE FOR PURCHASE OR RENTAL. CONTACT YOUR LOCAL VIDEO STORE OR TELEPHONE (800) 383-8811

- **Balance Court High Post Offense**
30-8084 30 min. $29.95

- **Beating the Zone & Matchup**
30-8083 30 min. $29.95

- **Fast Break**
30-8081 30 min. $29.95

- **Playing Basic Defense**
30-8082 30 min. $29.95

- **Preparing for Special Situations**
30-8085 30 min. $29.95

- **Winning Difference**
30-8086 30 min. $29.95

Men's Basketball: Defensive Play

Marv Harshman believes a basketball team must play good, sound defense if it is to be a winning team. Says Harshman, "Your offense will have its good nights and its off nights, but tough defensive play will keep you in the game even on the off shooting nights." Harshman demonstrates the drills he uses to school his teams on sound defensive principles. Marv begins with individual reaction drills and progresses to team defense in this excellent hour on defensive play. The program deals with both man-for-man and zone defensive strategy.
30-100 56 min. $29.95

Men's Basketball: Offensive Play

In four decades of organized basketball, Marv Harshman, University of Washington coach, has devised and revised a number of drills to help build an offense. In this program Marv demonstrates the drills he believes are important in learning the proper mechanics of offensive basketball. The drills cover shooting, passing, dribbling, screening, rebounding and movement without the ball. These drills are applicable to high school and college basketball.
30-101 59 min. $29.95

NBA COMMEMORATIVE COLLECTION

- **Milestones: Record Breakers of the NBA**
A remarkable compilation of the most amazing performances in NBA history!
30-9681 30 min. $19.95

- **Champions: The NBA's Greatest Teams**
See the most memorable teams and players in basketball history are all here.
30-9682 40 min. $19.95

- **Classic Confrontations**
The greatest one-on-one challenges in NBA History, from the legendary confrontations of Wilt Chamberlain and Bill Russell to the more recent duels between Larry Bird and Magic Johnson.
30-9683 45 min. $29.95

North Carolina System

Dean Smith, along with former assistants Eddie Fogler and Roy Williams, cover defensive stance, balance and movement; individual skills such as denying the ball, playing off the ball, handing screens, and shooting techniques
30-8011 36 min. $19.95

Philadelphia Big Five

Hosted by Al Meltzer. A salute to the conference that spawned many exciting basketball memories. Features La Salle, Temple, St. Joseph's, Villanova and the University of Pennsylvania, as well as the coaches who led their teams to victory and the arena where the action took place.
30-1943 60 min. $29.95

Pyramid of Success with John Wooden

A motivational and educational program by the most successful coach in basketball history. Ideally suited for coaches, educators and administrators as a means of appealing to and promoting The achievement desires of boys and girls, young adults--and their parents.
30-8028 27 min. $29.95

Red Auerbach - Red on Roundball

Red Auerbach, the most successful basketball coach, conducts an up-close look at the sport with the greatest pros in NBA history. You'll see Julius Erving, Bob Cousy, Bill Russell, Dave Cowens, Wes Unseld, Bill Walton, John Havlicek, Kareem Abdul-Jabbar and others. Watch the pros demonstrate the fundamentals of dribbling, shooting, rebounding, shot blocking, passing, playmaking and much more.
30-028 109 min. $29.95

Shaq Attack: In Your Face & Off the Court

Highlights of one of the NBA's hottest stars. See footage of his now famous backboard shattering slam dunks.
30-8303 45 min. $19.95

Sports Clinic: Basketball

Bill Walton, Walt Hazzard and Greg Lee teach you the basics of solid basketball.
30-026 75 min. $19.95

Sports Pages: Basketball Funnies

This is the strange collection of the silly goof-ups and the goofy pratfalls just not found in the other blooper shows. Backboards crumble, players tumble, coaches mumble! It is all in Basketball Funnies--and basketball fans will love it!
30-8169 60 min. $16.95

Spud Webb: Reach for the Skies

The NBA superstar shares his philosophies and techniques. You'll see Spud in action on the court as he demonstrates his tricks of the trade.
30-8169 60 min. $14.95

Swish: Shooting By Herb Magee

Now you too can learn from the master. Follow the coach through step-by-step instructions, from "shooting hand" to practice techniques. Everything needed to improve your performance. No matter what age, whether a beginner or professional, Coach Magee will teach you how to put the ball through the hoop.
30-6540 58 min. $39.95

Teaching Basketball Offensive Tips with Morgan Wootten

A concise video clinic composed of several short sessions which concentrate on specific aspects of the offensive game. Each session features direct and to the point teaching techniques, drills and explanations.
30-8027 60 min. $29.95

Teaching Kids Basketball With John Wooden

Coach John Wooden brought UCLA ten national championships by helping each player achieve his own personal best. In this video the Wizard of Westwood shows you how to teach your kids the right techniques and attitude to make basketball more rewarding and fun.
30-5505 75 min. $29.95

Three Point Shot

Coach Mike Fratello, formerly of the NBA's Atlanta Hawks, demonstrates creative plays for implementing the three-point shot in transition and half-court situations and shows how you can put these innovative ideas and strategies to work in your game.
30-8005 42 min. $29.95

Winner's Edge: Basketball

NBA pro Paul Westphal (Coach of the Phoenix Suns) concentrates on shooting, rebounding, dribbling, passing and defense.
30-029 25 min. $14.95

Winning Basketball Featuring Larry Bird and Red Auerbach

Red Auerbach has led the Boston Celtics to 16 world championships, and conveys his winning strategies and secrets. Larry Bird's unparalleled talents and methods in every important aspect of the game are clearly and completely illustrated with Red's guiding presence.
30-1538 60 min. $19.95

Your Best Shot

Basketball All-Stars Bill Russell, Michael Cooper and Chris Thompson team up with "Voice of the Lakers" Chick Hearn to show you what it takes to become a shooting sensation.
30-2429 32 min. $29.95

Bicycling

Anybody's Bike Video

This is a clear and simple introduction to bicycle repair. It shows how to diagnose and fix common bicycle problems, from flats to front wheel wobbles, and maintain any bike so it will run safely and smoothly. It also explains when to go to a bicycle shop for expert help.
30-660 50 min. $19.95

Battle of Durango: The First Ever World Mountain Bike Championship

See the fiery action of the 1990 World Championships at Durango in this spectacular hour-long race documentary. Captures all the action and aerial acrobatics of some of the best racers in the world.
30-8200 45 min. $29.95

Bike Experience

A unique visual experience which gives you a chance to experience the thrills of high speed dicing from the sharp end of motorcycle road racing and marvel at the expertise and courage of the experts.
30-8092 60 min. $29.95

Bike Tripping

This film introduces bicyclists to the basics of riding safely, as well as covering the many kinds of bikes available and the specific ways they can be used. Subjects include learning to ride a bike; learning to ride safely in traffic, choosing and using a good helmet; and avoiding the difficulties that can take the joy out of joy-riding. There are hints on planning, packing and preparing both the bike and

VIDEO TITLES LISTED IN THIS GUIDE ARE AVAILABLE FOR PURCHASE OR RENTAL. CONTACT YOUR LOCAL VIDEO STORE OR TELEPHONE (800) 383-8811

rider for any bike trip.
30-661 50 min. $19.95

Build Your Own Bike Wheel
This easy-to-follow, step-by-step demonstration shows you how to build your own wheel using spokes, hub, and rim without special equipment. Also included is an instruction booklet outlining the procedures.
30-212 60 min. $29.95

BMX X-Treme
Takes a look at all the wild and bizarre new aspects of the sport of bicycling. You'll see GPVs (gravity-powered vehicles) downhilling at dangerous speeds. There is an in-depth look at all aspects of BMX, ranging from head to head racing, to outrageous aerial maneuvers, to the wildly complicated flatland freestyling.
30-1810 60 min. $29.95

Complete Cyclist
Whether you're new to cycling or ready to race, this video will get you moving and keep you rolling. Olympic Gold and Bronze cycling medalists Connie Carpenter Phinney and Davis Phinney steer you safely through every facet of the cycling experience, including: bicycle selection, cycling techniques, training and exercise routines, nutrition and more.
30-684 80 min. $29.95

Cycling Warm-Up
Warming up before any sport protects muscles, joints and tendons. This short program will help you to achieve peak performance and your personal best.
30-1610 20 min. $16.95

Freestyle Biking Aerials
A video documentary of the NFA 1985 Grand National Freestyle Championships. Watch the pros as they compete in daring feats and stunts. Highly entertaining. Watch the tape over and over to learn how they do it!
30-317 30 min. $14.95

Freestyle's Raddest Tricks
More incredible freestyle antics with new tricks and new riders, with step-by-step instruction on over 30 of the most happening maneuvers.
30-2167 30 min. $29.95

Freestyling Fanatics
This video captures the most exciting, up-to-the-minute action taking place in the world of freestyle/BMX bicycling. See the top pros performing outrageous aerial maneuvers, and the newest, most bazaar forms of flatland freestyle

bicycling.
30-1807 30 min. $14.95

L. L. Bean Guide to Bicycle Touring
L. L. Bean, the Maine outdoors specialty company, and Dennis Coello, a well-known author who literally "lives on two wheels," bring you the joys of bicycle touring. Join Dennis and learn how to select the right touring bike, how to ride safely, perform basic roadside repairs, and how to have fun touring. Filmed on location in and around Acadia National Park, Bar Harbor, Maine.
30-319 80 min. $29.95

No Competition Freestyle Biking
Fred Blood, Chris Day, and a host of other top freestyle bikers do their stuff at The Spot in Redondo Beach, California.
30-1983 30 min. $19.95

Rad TV: The Sequel
Here, by popular demand, yet another BMX Plus! Rad video with even more tricks and top riders to help you do tricks that fit your own skill level.
30-2166 30 min. $29.95

Showin' Off Freestyle
The first of it's kind ever Super Sho' on how to do some of freestylin's hottest tricks. But that's not all! This also brings you up to date on the newest in bike features, accessories and the all important safety gear. Join the nationally acclaimed Evans Brothers Freestyle Team as they help you go through the steps of learning the Squeaker Peg Picker, the Bar Hop Switch Stance, the 360 Cherry Picker and many other rad flatland tricks.
30-8129 35 min. $19.95

Boxing & Wrestling

Boxing Bloopers and K.O.'s
Join us in this hilarious slug-fest, which also features interviews with legendary boxer's Smokin' Joe Frazier and Evander Hollyfield. Hosted by Al Bernstein, ESPN's Boxing analyst.
30-8216 30 min. $16.95

Boxing Greatest Knockouts
At last, here's a fight fan's dream come true! In this unique "fight-documentary" you will be ringside for all the top main events. See Muhammad Ali, the charismatic, motor-mouthed heavyweight champion in his spectacular, bone-crushing fights against other greats like Leon Spinks and Joe Frazier. Also included in this

powerful video you'll see other greats like Joe "The Brown Bomber" Louis, Rocky Graziano, Sugar Ray Leonard and many many more.
30-6457 30 min. $16.95

Grudge Fights
This is boxing at its passionate best. The furious and ferocious rematches that give the ring its glamour, its lore and its gore. Thirty-four of the most devastating knock-outs in ring history.
30-2322 60 min. $19.95

Hagler vs. Hearns
It's 1985's sporting event of the year - the spectacular middle-weight championship fight held at Caesar's Palace in Las Vegas. It is a ringside seat with instant replay at your fingertips.
30-292 60 min. $29.95

Legendary Champions
A unique Oscar-nominated feature film spanning 47 years of boxing (1882-1929). Featuring rare footage of John L. Sullivan, James J. Corbett, Gene Tunney and many more.
30-2323 90 min. $19.95

Masters Of Mayhem
Outrageous, out-of-control, headslamming action! Title matches! Tag Teams! Caged no-holds-barred fights to the finish! You'll see some of the greatest wrestlers ever to hit the mat.
30-5441 90 min. $19.95

Mike Tyson's Greatest Hits
Non-stop ring action of boxing's most exciting star since Ali. This is the only history of Tyson available anywhere.
30-2942 60 min. $19.95

Power Profiles: The Champs
There's boxing excitement and human drama with "The Brown Bomber", Joe Louis and "The Manassa Mauler", Jack Dempsey.
06-070 50 min. $19.95

Sports Pages: Boxing Bloopers
Welcome to the Boxing Hall of Shame, where the very worst in boxing will be featured in this non-stop exercise in hilarity.
30-8143 30 min. $16.95

Sports Pages: Killer Boxing
Boxing's baddest! See Ali, Shavers, Foreman and more in this high octane, body crunching video.
30-8145 30 min. $16.95

Sports Pages: Wrestling Funnies
If you think the world of Pro Rasslin' is crazy, wait until you see this! Get ready to shake your head in amazement as these crazy guys show just how wild

and funny pro wrestling can be.
30-8138 30 min. $16.95

Triple Hitting Boxing
Bouts taped live June 23, 1986 at Caesar's Palace, Las Vegas: Thomas Hearns vs. Mark Medal, Roberto Duran vs. Robbie Sims, Barry McGuigan vs. Fernando Ssoza.
30-579 145 min. $29.95

Tyson vs. Spinks: Once and for All
This was the most eagerly anticipated heavyweight championship fight in years between two undefeated fighters, fought on June 27, 1988.
30-2943 60 min. $19.95

Coaching

Coaching Clinic with Tom Tutko
This program discusses many of the most common personality and competitive situations that you, as a coach, will face both on the field and off, in dealing with your athletes.
30-8296 45 min. $49.00

Introduction to Coaching Kids
Highlights include: diverse roles the coach must play, defining clear goals for the program, teaching young athletes how to compete and sports psychology for youth coaches.
30-8106 25 min. $29.95

Sports Psychology for Youth Coaches
This film is designed to examine the role of the coach as both a communicator and a motivator. If a coach cannot communicate and does not understand athletic motivation as it relates to youth, he or she will have great difficulty in teaching and in motivating their athletes.
30-8292 20 min. $59.95

TEACHING KIDS SERIES:

• Teaching Kids Baseball
Coach Jerry Kindall's dedication to fundamentals, effort and teamwork has made champions of his University of Arizona Wildcats. In this program he shares his winning techniques on how to play the game.
30-8225 75 min. $19.95

• Teaching Kids Bowling
Championship bowler Gordon Vadakin shows you how to teach your kids the right techniques and proper attitudes that will help them the bowl better

VIDEO TITLES LISTED IN THIS GUIDE ARE AVAILABLE FOR PURCHASE OR RENTAL. CONTACT YOUR LOCAL VIDEO STORE OR TELEPHONE (800) 383-8811

and have more fun.
30-8226 40 min. $19.95

• **Teaching Kids Football**
Bo Schembechler is one of the game's greatest coaches. Learn the safety and the fundamentals of offense and defense of the game.
30-8227 75 min. $19.95

• **Teaching Kids Golf with Ben Sutton**
30-8228 50 min. $19.95

• **Teaching Kids Skiing with Hank Kashiwa**
30-8229 50 min. $19.95

• **Teaching Kids Soccer with Bob Gansler**
30-8230 75 min. $19.95

• **Teaching Kids Swimming with John Naber**
30-8231 40 min. $19.95

• **Play Ball with Reggie Jackson**
30-8232 35 min. $19.95

Teaching Sports Skills to Young Athletes
This film gives coaches the basic guidelines for the planning and conducting of efficient practices and how to effectively teach sport skills to the young athletes.
30-8291 20 min. $59.95

Youth Sports: Is Winning Everything?
A philosophy film edited from the TV Emmy award winning documentary which examines the effect that the professional sports ethic of "winning is everything", has on today's youth sport programs. Are our youth coaches caught up in the "win at all cost" syndrome, sacrificing the child's emotional and physical development for that league title.
30-8105 29 min. $69.95

Football

COACHES VIDEO NETWORK
The Coaches Video Network now gives you the winning techniques of America's top ranked university coaches. Each action packed video demonstrates basic skills, "special" drills, position strategies and expert demonstrations as well as each coach's inspiring motivational, philosophy. Don't

miss this opportunity to be trained by the best college football coaches in America.

• **Defensive Ends**
30-7033 50 min. $39.95

• **Receivers**
30-7035 54 min. $39.95

• **Quarterbacks**
30-7036 56 min. $39.95

• **Defensive Line**
30-8288 55 min. $39.95

• **Offensive Line**
30-7037 53 min. $39.95

• **Linebackers**
30-7038 60 min. $39.95

• **Defensive Secondary**
30-7039 57 min. $39.95

• **Offensive Backs**
30-7040 60 min. $39.95

Disposable Heroes
A stunning, critically acclaimed HBO "American Undercover" presentation about the staggering price of professional football fame and fortune.
30-2292 60 min. $29.95

Football Legends
Beyond a doubt, football has earned it's place as one of America's favorite sports. Relive the history of football and see the players who have become football's greatest heroes and legends. The most remarkable and memorable plays, victories, and defeats. The real people, real football, that have made football the great game it is today.
30-6456 40 min. $16.95

FOOTBALL WITH TOM LANDRY SERIES:
Coach of the Dallas Cowboys for 25 years and All-Pro tackle Norm Evans teach you everything you ever wanted to know about football.

• **Defensive Line**
Outwitting the offense and holding the line are the jobs of the defensive lineman. Veteran lineman Mike McCoy has played every spot on the defensive line and he shows you what it takes. Big Mike starts off with the nose guard position, outlines tackle play, then ends with defensive end play. Defensive linemen and their coaches will appreciate this step-by-step guide to tough defense.
30-052 60 min. $29.95

VIDEO TITLES LISTED IN THIS GUIDE ARE AVAILABLE FOR PURCHASE OR RENTAL. CONTACT YOUR LOCAL VIDEO STORE OR TELEPHONE (800) 383-8811

• Offensive Line

This program is a textbook on offensive line play. Center Pete Brock of the New England Patriots, host Norm Evans and Tom Landry give you the benefit of their years of experience in detailing the basics of interior line play and its importance in football play at any level, from Pop Warner to the NFL.

30-048 60 min. $29.95

• Playing to Win for Backs & Receivers

Great running back Archie Griffin is featured on this program. You'll see why Archie won the coveted Heisman Trophy twice as he outlines the duties of the tailbacks and fullbacks, demonstrating the proper techniques for running, pass receiving and blocking. Steve Largent, wide receiver for the Seattle Seahawks, joins the "seminar" and demonstrates getting open and catching the ball.

30-069 60 min. $29.95

• Quarterbacking to Win

Jim Zorn, veteran quarterback of the Seattle Seahawks, joins Tom Landry to show and tell what it takes to be the leader on the field. Learn how to find receivers, read the defense, use the cadence count as a weapon and pass the football right on the money. Zorn and Landry also cover developing arm strength, quick release and "going deep."

30-073 60 min. $29.95

• Winning Linebacker

Dallas Cowboy star Bob Breunig knows about great linebacker play. He shows you how to read on play quickly and react properly. Perennial All-Pro cornerback Mike of the L.A. Raiders, Super Bowl Champs of '84, demonstrates methods and techniques for playing the defensive backfield positions.

30-096 60 min. $29.95

Football: Legends of the Game

This is a collector's edition of the mighty men and towering teams of the gridiron. Football's rise from a "minor league" sport to a national obsession is chronicled "live" by the cameras, spanning the college greats and the pro dynamos.

30-388 60 min. $16.95

Giants Forever - History of the NY Giants

Few teams have had more impact on the growth and development of the NFL than the New York Giants. Relive the different eras in Giant history.

30-8128 45 min. $19.95

How To Play Winning Football, Featuring Jim McMahon

This tape is "basic training" for gridiron champions from the top men on the field, including the Superbowl quarterback for the Chicago Bears, Jim McMahon, longtime Dallas coach Tom Landry, Sonny Jurgenson and Jay Hilgenberg. Get the real scoop on game preparation. Mental preparation. Conditioning. Strength building skills, drills, and much more!

30-5592 60 min. $19.95

How to Watch Pro Football

A step-by-step guide designed to enhance every fan's enjoyment of the game. Top coaches Tom Landry, Don Shula and Dick Vermeil take you through everything an armchair quarter-back needs to know. Produced by the National Football League.

30-531 53 min. $39.95

Jim McMahon: No Guts No Glory

He's the punky quarterback who captured the public's imagination and in the process breathed new life into the stuffy image of the professional athlete. Hear firsthand how to have the confidence to be your own man. Find out just how much hard work it takes to make it look so easy. He's wild and unpredictable! Experience the wit and wisdom of Jim McMahon.

30-496 40 min. $29.95

JOHNSON & JOHNSON: PRO FOOTBALL TRAINING ROOM WITH PROFESSIONAL TRAINERS SOCIETY

Johnson and Johnson and the Professional Trainers Society present a four part educational series that demonstrates the evaluation treatment and rehabilitation of football injuries.

• Shoulder & Knee Injuries

30-8029 40 min. $19.95

• Hand, Wrist & Elbow Injuries

30-8030 50 min. $19.95

• Soft Tissue Injuries

30-8031 55 min. $19.95

• Neck, Head & Facial Injuries

30-8032 40 min. $19.95

Ken O'Brien's Quarterback Clinic

New York Jets quarterback Ken O'Brien hosts this instructional video designed to improve quarterbacking techniques.

30-2817 30 min. $16.95

Man Named Lombardi

Vince Lombardi was one of America's greatest

football coaches; this is history. Narrated by George C. Scott and featuring clips from Lombardi's most memorable games with the Packers, this is a touching look at a true spiritual leader. Candid interviews with Hornung, Starr, Thurston, Jurgenson and others give us an insider's view of the man and his methods.
30-046 55 min. $29.95

Most Memorable Moments In Super Bowl History
The most memorable moments in the history of the Super Bowl. From the good and bad to the funny and sad, like Broadway Joe's prediction of victory in Super Bowl III and Joe Montana's record-shattering performance in Super Bowl XXIV.
30-6354 50 min. $19.95

Official Pop Warner Football Video Handbook
Pop Warner remains the standard by which fundamental football is coached and played. This video handbook brings the philosophy and techniques of this tradition to life. This is an entertaining and educational program.
30-2201 50 min. $19.95

Pro Football Funnies
This hilarious video will let you eavesdrop on huddles and pep talks, then follow the action as football's finest stumble and bungle their way through pro football low-lights.
30-2690 30 min. $16.95

Silver/Black Attack
The winningest team in sports rap/sing and smash their way onto the music scene. See your favorite Los Angeles Raiders as you've never seen them before.
30-534 30 min. $19.95

Sports Clinic: Football
Coach George Allen and a crew of all-star pros teach the power basics of lineplay, receiving, and quarterbacking. Each segment is carefully designed to increase your skills.
30-070 75 min. $19.95

Sports Pages: Football Bloopers
Football's zaniest moments can happen at any level--small college and even pro football has seen it's share of the unbelievable.
30-8136 30 min. $16.95

Starr vs. Unitas
Features Bart Starr, hosted by Paul Hornung and Johnny Unitas, hosted by Jayne Kennedy.
30-498 45 min. $24.95

Super Bowl Shuffle
It took a great team, a popular tune and a lot of nerve, but the 1985 World champion Chicago Bears produced some real musical mayhem here. Included with this musical classic are the blunders and mishaps of the mighty Bears struttin' their stuff.
30-621 30 min. $19.95

Super Sunday: A History of the Super Bowl
From Super Bowl I to Super Bowl XXI, see the unprecedented footage of some of football's greatest players, coaches and dynasties.
30-1782 55 min. $19.95

Tackling Football: A Woman's Guide to Watching the Game
The definitive explanation of how history's most exciting game is played.
30-532 35 min. $24.95

Teaching Kids Football With Bo Schembechler
Former coach of the University of Michigan, Bo Schembechler is one of the game's greatest coaches. Bo stresses that safety and proper mental attitude are as important to the young player as technique. He points out that winning is not the most important part of playing football, and stresses the importance of kids having fun. Bo then teaches the fundamentals of offense and defense, including blocking, receiving, passing, tackling, running and the kicking game.
30-5507 75 min. $29.95

Tyler Rose: The Legend of Earl Campbell
Contains spectacular footage of Earl's greatest accomplishments on the grid-iron. Includes special appearances and interviews with celebrities from the world of sports and entertainment. This program presents a positive attitude and inspirational message of personal accomplishment attained through hard work, discipline and dedication.
30-8304 60 min. $19.95

Winner's Edge: Football
Quarterback Jeff Kemp and receiver Mike Barber focus on the quarterback-receiver relationship and how to execute the passing game.
30-094 25 min. $16.95

Golf

60 Yards with Ray Floyd
Ray Floyd, winner of more than twenty tour events, hosts this instructional program on the "short game". There is no other area of the golf game where improvement will help a player better his score than getting it "up or down".
30-8124 45 min. $29.95

Advanced Chipping
Chipping may be one of the most important strokes in golf and certainly one of the most misunderstood strokes. Bob Kesler discusses chipping from the advanced player's perspective by covering types of chipping irons, how many kinds of chips there are, how to stand for each type, how to swing, hold the club and impact the ball. Theory of chipping, sighting the pin, and reading the green; creating bite, head speed and control. Loft, skip and run are also covered.
30-123 30 min. $39.95

Advanced Golf Swing
Proper timing of all of the body components are covered in detail from left foot action to the top of the swing. Creating snap at impact, releasing the right side and maximizing distance make this program a must for advanced golfers. Power loss, hitting the low drive, and advanced techniques are discussed as well.
30-124 30 min. $39.95

After the Driving Range... Then What?
Bob Kesler shows how to get a starting time, how to keep score. He talks about renting or buying the clubs, what a golf cart is, and how to obey the rules of the game. Whom to play with or without, and the importance of good golf etiquette. What's a birdie, bogey and eagle? Who ever heard of a bingo, bango or bongo - they're also discussed.
30-132 60 min. $39.95

An Inside Look at the Game for a Lifetime
Bob Toski, Jim Flick, Peter Kostis and John Elliott.
30-543 56 min. $49.95

Arnold Palmer - Play Great Golf: Fundamentals
30-691 69 min. $39.95

Arnold Palmer - Play Great Golf: Course Strategy
Includes developing a clear plan of attack, finding your individual strengths, playing boldly not wildly, sound course strategy, bunker shots, bad lies, water hazards, course obstacles and wind.
30-692 69 min. $39.95

Arnold Palmer: Play Great Golf
This is a set that includes volumes 1 and 2.
30-1612 120 min. $79.95

Azinger Way
Every player could learn a valuable lesson from Paul Azinger's amazing career. Ranked as one of the top in his class, all the things he has learned is in this tape.
30-8150 55 min. $16.95

Beginning Chipping
Bob Kesler covers all of the fundamentals in this show. Stance, how to hold the club, types of chips, sighting the pin, reading the green, and many other aspects are examined from the beginner's point of view. The basics of club and ball impact are also covered.
30-127 30 min. $39.95

Beginning Golf for Women
Designed specifically for those women who have never played or are just beginning, Donna White, 14-year LPGA tour veteran, will show you how simple learning golf can be.
30-8300 45 min. $16.95

Beginning Golf Swing
Golf pro Bob Kesler introduces the beginner to the golf club and, through careful instruction, demonstrates what a good golf swing should look like, why the golf swing seems to defy the body's natural motion, and how the beginner can develop personal checks and balances to maintain a proper golf swing.
30-122 30 min. $39.95

Beginning Putting
In this video Bob Kesler discusses in detail how a golf ball is made, and how its construction causes the ball to roll on a putting surface. Sighting the pin, and "reading the green" are also covered in this program, as well as stroke; what causes the ball to track left or right of the hole: and types of greens and green construction.
30-126 30 min. $39.95

Bob Toski Teaches You Golf
30-545 70 min. $74.95

VIDEO TITLES LISTED IN THIS GUIDE ARE AVAILABLE FOR PURCHASE OR RENTAL. CONTACT YOUR LOCAL VIDEO STORE OR TELEPHONE (800) 383-8811

Chipping and Putting Video

Golf pro Charlie Schnaubel is ready to show you how to quickly improve your score. The chipping lesson stresses wrist action, backswing and the role of the golfer's head, while the putting lesson emphasizes stance, arm action and takeback. Charlie also shows when to use for specific shots.
30-1659 30 min. $16.95

COMPLETE HISTORY OF GOLF SERIES:

This remarkable program spans the entire history of golf. Set amidst the breath-taking landscapes of the world's most combative courses, this monumental series uses exclusive interviews and rare archival footage to reveal the full dimension of a rich and wondrous sport. Hosted by Pat Summerall.

• **Let the Game Begin (1100-1916)**
30-9001 30 min. $24.95

• **Boom Between the Wars (1917-1944)**
30-9002 30 min. $24.95

• **Into the Television Age (1945-1962)**
30-9003 30 min. $24.95

• **The Past Meets the Future (1963-1991)**
30-9004 30 min. $24.95

Crash Course

To enjoy the game of golf you have to understand the fundamentals. Keith Lyford sets the stage with information that every golfer must know. It's like going to golf school without leaving your own living room.
30-8097 35 min. $16.95

Curtis Strange

The champion golf pro demonstrates ways to improve one's game.
30-8191 71 min. $19.95

Daley's The Long Shot: 1991 PGA Championship

The memorable "Cinderella" story of John Daly that launched him into the national spotlight and one of the most dramatic matches in golf history.
30-8099 52 min. $24.95

Exercise Fitness for Golf

Improve your golf at home or office with daily 10 to 30 minute workout sessions. You'll lower your score and increase muscle strength and endurance.
30-1585 60 min. $29.95

Fit for Golf

Eight easy-to-do exercises that add distance to your shots, improve ball control and increase endurance.

Includes a bonus section with five easy pre-game stretches to improve flexibility and reduce muscle strain.
30-2102 30 min. $19.95

Games Golfers, Hustlers and Cheaters Play

Bob Kesler spends time describing some of the cute and funny, and not-so-cute and funny things golfers do. How to spot them, recognize them, take advantage of them. Further, Bob goes on to finer points of etiquette and manners - good and bad - on the course.
30-133 30 min. $39.95

Golden Tee

Legendary golf professionals reveal the secrets of their specialties. From long ball hitting, to delicate wedge shots and putting wizardry, you'll see the techniques and savvy that have earned these gifted players over 6 million dollars in PGA and LPGA tournament play!
30-285 72 min. $16.95

Golf for Kids of All Ages

A fun, instruction-packed golf video from PGA Tour veteran Wally Armstrong, son Scott, and host Gabby Gator that makes the fundamentals of golf exciting and easy to remember.
30-1936 50 min. $29.95

Golf the Miller Way

Golf pro Johnny Miller hosts this golf instructional golf video.
30-576 30 min. $19.95

Golf Course Equipment

What every golfer should know about taking care of a golf course is shown in detail by a careful look at equipment used in mowing, cutting, sanding, edging, grooming and fertilizing the course. Examined are how and when the ground crews prepare surfaces, and the equipment needed to keep the grounds in good condition.
30-128 30 min. $39.95

GOLF DIGEST SERIES

Learn the techniques and basic fundamentals for playing golf or just improving your game.

• **Driving for Distance**
Bob Toski and John Elliot.
30-468 25 min. $29.95

• **Find Your Own Fundamentals**
Bob Toski and Jim Flick.
30-467 25 min. $29.95

- **Sharpen Your Short Irons**
Bob Toski and Jim Flick.
30-469 25 min. $29.95

- **Swing for a Lifetime**
Bob Toski and Jim Flick.
30-466 25 min. $29.95

Golf for Women
This is a complete introduction to golf specifically for women. More than an explanation of technique, this shows what is needed to take up the game, how to warm-up, practice and exercise.
30-8087 60 min. $19.95

Golf Gadgets & Gimmicks
Wally Armstrong is one of golf's great innovators. In his 20 years of teaching the game of golf, and in his experience on the PGA tour, he's found that training aids and swing enhancement tools can be invaluable in teaching the game of golf.
30-8149 30 min. $16.95

Golf Lessons From Sam Snead
Golf's grand master demonstrates and explains all aspects of golf, from drives to putts. Recommended by Golf Magazine.
30-105 60 min. $49.95

Golf Like a Pro with Billy Casper
Have a private lesson with Billy Casper, winner of the prestigious Masters Tournament and twice champion of the U.S. Open. Casper shows you the fundamentals of good golf from the grip to the swing. Slow motion and stop action photography show you how to hit the ball with every club. Casper includes a section on putting that's a must. Watch and learn about accuracy with short irons, pitch shots, how to get close to the pin out of sand traps, and more.
30-106 51 min. $19.95

Golf My Way with Jack Nicklaus
An easy-to-follow guide for the beginning and intermediate golfer, starring Jack Nicklaus, offering tips on all aspects of the game.
30-107 128 min. $84.95

Golf - The Perfect Passion
Golf's most colorful players, pros and amateurs, share their personal thoughts and memories about America's fastest growing sport. Hosted by John Brodie, this tape provides insight into the history, spirit, challenge and fun of the game!
30-8154 30 min. $16.95

Great Golf Courses of Ireland
This is a unique opportunity to tour Ireland's finest golf courses. Many of them are set amongst the most breathtaking scenery in the world and have played host at one time, or another, to all the great names in golf.
30-8107 60 min. $29.95

GREAT GOLF COURSES OF THE WORLD SERIES:
Breathtaking and beautiful landscapes highlight this fascinating history from the world's greatest golf links. Perfect for the golf trip planner, or a terrific experience for the devoted spectator.

- **Pebble Beach**
Hosted by Jack Whitaker.
30-8151 54 min. $19.95

- **Scotland**
Narrated by Sean Connery.
30-8152 72 min. $19.95

- **Ireland**
Hosted by Pierce Brosnan.
30-8153 58 min. $19.95

Greater Golfer In You: A Total Approach
Dr. Gary Wiren, Director of Learning and Research, PGA, hosts this stimulating seminar on two video cassettes, reinforced with three audio cassettes. It will help you enjoy golf to the fullest, improve your technique, overcome problem situations and lower your handicap. Twelve vital sessions on developing a repeating swing, chipping and pitching, putting, handling unusual lies and trouble shots, and much more. Printed practice guide included.
30-110 42 min. $69.95

History & Traditions Of Golf In Scotland
This dramatic video takes you on a pilgrimage to the heart and home of golf, Scotland. A rare look inside the R&A Clubhouse in St. Andrews with historian Bobby Burnet reveals treasures of the past never seen by the public. From feathery balls and longnose clubs to the steel shafted blades of today, experts give new insight into the evolution of golf.
30-6448 45 min. $29.95

Hit It Farther With Betsy Cullen
In this video you will see Betsy Cullen's easy-to-learn system that teaches women the body movements and positions that maximize power for a better game of golf.
30-2169 60 min. $69.95

How Clubs Are Made
Very few golfers, including many pros, have been inside a golf manufacturing plant. Bob Kesler discovers with the viewer all about grips, shafts, and heads. The differences between laminated and

---

VIDEO TITLES LISTED IN THIS GUIDE ARE AVAILABLE FOR PURCHASE OR RENTAL. CONTACT YOUR LOCAL VIDEO STORE OR TELEPHONE (800) 383-8811

persimmon heads for woods. How clubs are built and bent based upon the height and arm length of the golfer. Bending, drying, sleeving, pinning and other club-building techniques are shown in detail.
30-130 30 min. $39.95

Intermediate Putting
How putters are made and how their construction affects the rolling action of the ball are covered in detail. Stance, sighting and stroke analysis are also discussed. Care of the grip, selection of the shaft and type of head are examined carefully in this program.
30-125 30 min. $39.95

Jan Stephenson's How To Golf
A comprehensive program for golf enthusiasts of all ages and abilities, starring one of the most recognized sports personalities world-wide, Jan Stephenson. Jan addresses each and every aspect of the game from driving off the tee to effective hazard play.
30-432 50 min. $29.95

Jimmy Ballard Golf Collection
Jimmy Ballard is the pro's pro, whose instruction as improved the games of PGA golfers like Sutton, Miller and Player. Now the top pro at the Doral Country Club, Ballard's system involves hitting with "connection," and practical tips on driving, pitching, putting, fades and draws. Recommended for the more advanced golfer, but useful for beginners as well.
30-111 90 min. $49.95

JoAnne Carner's Keys to Great Golf
Demonstrates in clear detail almost every situation one faces during the playing of a game, perfectly shown in regular speed and slow motion. Run through this tape before each game you play.
30-2633 90 min. $49.95

Junior Golf "The Easy Way"
Instruction covers all aspects of golf: the grip, stance and posture; the swing, woods, irons, chipping, putting and sand play. Each section shows the techniques involved and lists important key reminders to simplify learning.
30-667 43 min. $59.95

MASTER SYSTEM TO BETTER GOLF SERIES:
Learn the fundamentals and techniques to help improve your golf game. This 3 volume series features many of the game's greatest players.

• Volume I
Master the fundamentals with help from the masters of golf. Including Davis Love III and Craig Stradler.
30-8263 60 min. $24.95

• Volume II
Play like a pro with PGA's top performers Paul Azinger, Fred Couples and Bobby Wadkins.
30-8264 60 min. $24.95

• Volume III
Improve your game and lower your score. Master the basics with Miller Barber, Orville Moody and Dale Douglas.
30-8265 115 min. $24.95

Mastering The Basics: A Guide For The Woman Golfer
Whether you're a beginner or an experienced player, this informative video will help you shave strokes off your score and enjoy the game that you love even more. Take "private lessons" from pros Michelle Bell and Annette Thompson and improve every aspect of your play. Introduction by Patty Berg, member of the LPGA Hall of Fame.
30-5590 40 min. $19.95

Nancy Lopez: Golf Made Easy
Learn the techniques that made this superstar golfer a Hall-of-Famer.
30-8261 48 min. $19.95

One Move to Better Golf
The professional that teaches the professionals - Carl Lohren will show you many of the tips he shares with fellow PGA members, including his miracle move that could slash your handicap up to 50%.
30-287 30 min. $19.95

Orville Moody
Proven PGA performer, and one of the Senior Tour's top putters, demonstrates his innovative shot.
30-8255 25 min. $19.95

Outrageously Funny Golf
Hosted by Paul Hahn Jr., a trick shot artist, stand up comic and golf pro, combines comedic antics with solid, useful golf tips to improve your game.
30-2919 30 min. $19.95

PGA TOUR GOLF SERIES:
Each of the three tapes in this series presents five PGA Tour Pros, Hal Sutton, Craig Stadler, Lanny Wadkins, Payne Stewart and Tom Kite, giving you tips on a better golf game with in depth instruction.

• Course Strategy
30-2656 60 min. $59.95

• **Full Swing**
30-2654 60 min. $59.95

• **Short Game**
30-2655 60 min. $59.95

Pictures Worth 1000 words
Wally Armstrong builds two large pictures that every golfer should to have in his mind.
30-8148 30 min. $16.95

Play Better Golf: Pat Simmons
This video contains complete information and demonstrations on the proper way to hit the golf ball.
30-8126 20 min. $24.95

REACHING YOUR GOLF POTENTIAL SERIES:

• **Developing Maximum Consistency**
This video features Tom Kite & Friends: Claude Akins, Ron Masak, Julius Erving, and Cindy Rarick. Sit back and relax as I teach golf's fundamentals to my friends in a way designed to improve your game regardless of its current level.
30-6184 50 min. $24,95

• **Strategies & Techniques**
This video features Tom Kite & Friends: Claude Akins, Ron Masak, Julius Erving, and Cindy Rarick. Strategies & Techniques are emphasized during a fun-filled round. Study, Practice and watch your game improve.
30-6185 50 min. $24.95

Rules & Etiquette of Golf
Hosted by Tommy Horton, Rules Of Golf: The Heart Of The Game
1982 U.S. Open Champion Tom Watson, three-time U.S. Woman's Amateur Champion Juli Inkster and ABC Sports and BBC commentator Peter Alliss take an entertaining you informative look at the rules.
30-5634 24 min. $29.95

Senior Swinger with Don January
Is the "swat"leaving your swing? Is the aging process whittling away your distance off the tee? Here are a few tips on how to keep a competitive edge to your game. If you're over 40, this video will help you cut strokes from your score and make golf the "fun game" it really is.
30-668 60 min. $69.95

Sports Pages: Golf Bloopers
This is the most unusual golf bloopers tape you have ever seen! And, it's the top players doing the goofing up!
30-8137 30 min. $16.95

Stretching For Better Golf
Bob Anderson author of the best seller Stretching which has sold 1,000,000 copies. Bob has been a stretching consultant to College, Professional, and Olympic Teams.
30-5407 40 min. $29.95

Sudden Death & the Play-Offs
The history of major golf tournament play-offs, 1962-1990. Narrated by Harry Carpenter.
30-8168 59 min. $19.95

Sybervision: Bobby Jones - How I Play Golf (Limited Collector's Edition)
This special collector's edition set includes eighteen recently discovered instructional films featuring the "greatest golfer of all time". The set includes two 90-minute videocassettes, a Bobby Jones book and a certificate of authenticity.
30-3068 180 min. $249.95

Sybervision: Difficult Shots with Hale Irwin
World famous golf pro Hale Irwin demonstrates difficult shots and teaches you how to master them by using the Sybervision neuromuscular training techniques. Difficult shots include: uphill and downhill lies, tall grass and sand traps.
30-436 60 min. $59.95

Sybervision: Golf with Al Geiberger
This original Sybervision title features pro tour golfer Al Geiberger, whose score of 59 for 18 holes is the lowest ever recorded on the tour. Every element of golf is presented and reproduced dozens of times to enable you to imprint this perfection into your mind. Experience the perfect form of the drive, fairway wood, 1-iron, 5-iron, 9-iron, pitch, chip and putt.
30-108 60 min. $69.95

Sybervision: Golf with Patti Sheehan
Improve your golf game with LPGA star Patti Sheehan. This Sybervision tape includes repetitive views of many golf shots, including the drive, chip and putt. Patti's perfect form is imprinted in your neuromuscular memory resulting in better performance on the course.
30-109 60 min. $69.95

Sybervision: Power Driving with Mike Dunaway
This tape is guaranteed to improve your driving distance and accuracy. Featuring legendary hitter Mike Dunaway, you will learn flawless driving techniques through Sybervision's innovative method

VIDEO TITLES LISTED IN THIS GUIDE ARE AVAILABLE FOR PURCHASE OR RENTAL. CONTACT YOUR LOCAL VIDEO STORE OR TELEPHONE (800) 383-8811

of neuromuscular training.
30-434 30 min. $49.95

Sybervision: Precision Putting with Dave Stockton

PGA Champion Dave Stockton teaches you precision putting through the Sybervision neuromuscular training technique. This tape will teach you the correct grip, alignment and set-up, how to read the green, and putting from 5-35 feet.
30-435 30 min. $49.95

Teaching Kids Golf With Ben Sutton Golf School

Instructors from the famous Ben Sutton School was bright computer graphics, props and fun drills to demonstrate all the basics from tee to green, including etiquette, in a way that's easy for kids to understand and remember.
30-5497 75 min. $29.95

Three Men and a Bogey

A comedy hole-in-one. A side-splitting spoof on bending the rules to improve your game.
30-8262 30 min. $19.95

TIGER SHARK PLAY BETTER GOLF SERIES

This four part series presents expert instruction from golf pro and club designer Pat Simmons. Pat demonstrates and discusses all aspects of the game.

• Irons-Hitting with Power and Accuracy
30-8024 30 min. $19.95

• Putting - The Science and the Stroke
30-8026 30 min. $19.95

• TroubleShots - Recovery Strokes Made Easy
30-8025 30 min. $19.95

• Woods-Hitting for Distance
30-8023 30 min. $19.95

Total Golf-Saving Strokes with Bruce Crampton

A 15-tournament winner on the PGA Tour, Bruce Crampton is a two-time winner of the Vardon Trophy, which is awarded to the player with the lowest scoring average each year. When he decided to end his nine-year layoff to join the Senior PGA tour, his comeback was a resounding success and he is one of the tour's top moneymakers. In this video, the "Ironman" of the Senior Tour shares his fitness program, golf techniques, mental keys, and selection of proper

equipment.
30-1586 92 min. $49.95

Trick Shots

In this show Bob Kesler shows how the beginning golfer can develop a repertoire of trick shots to augment his golf game when he gets into trouble with hazards. Also covered in this program, are typical problems beginning golfers have with their golf swing.
30-129 30 min. $39.95

Ultimate Drive

Learn how you can increase your drive distance and club speed with Golf Digest's National Long Drive Champion Art Sellinger! Learn proper positioning for both your club and body, as well as club selection. What have you got to lose? Except a stroke or two!
30-1687 30 min. $16.95

Video School of Golf

Featuring one of America's top teaching professional golfers, Jim Chenoweth, and his revolutionary "Toe Up/Toe Up" teaching method with his "Triangle Swing" concept.
30-536 60 min. $39.95

War by the Shore: 1991 Ryder Cup

Recall the joy, pressure and suspense of the 1991 Ryder Cup matches as the United States regains control of the cup.
30-9000 40 min. $24.95

Water, Trees and Tall Grass... Or Where Did My Ball Go?

Every golfer has been in water, trees and tall grass; unfortunately most don't know how to get out of trouble...effectively. This program covers in detail the many rules that apply to hazard shots. Bob Kesler also demonstrates which special strokes to use; the club, the stance and the attitude required to reduce your score. What to do if your ball is lodged in a tree branch, water tactics and rules, and how to get out of a culvert are situations Bob Kesler covers with practical strokes and humor.
30-134 30 min. $39.95

What's a Hazard?

Bob Kesler shows in this program the many types of hazards found on a golf course. Rough, trees, traps, water and other hazards are discussed in detail. The rules for getting out. The shot and club to use. When and how to gamble against the odds. What trick shots work best in which hazard.
30-131 30 min. $39.95

Winner's Edge: Golf

With PGA pro Kermit Zarley.
30-332 25 min. $16.95

Women's Golf Guide

A video for novice women golfers who know how to swing their club and are now ready to play the game, learn the rules and behave as a golfer. Helene Landers hosts this informative program.
30-8271 60 min. $19.95

Gymnastics

Champion Women Acrobats of China

Unbelievable performances filled with grace, beauty, skill and daring... a lasting legacy of an ancient art.
30-8155 60 min. $19.95

GYMNASTICS SERIES:

• Gymnastic Exercises for Men

The Class III and IV Compulsory Exercises were developed by the National Gymnastics Federation to start athletes in the sport of gymnastics. This program is designed to help gymnasts master individual skills and coordinate these beginning level routines. One of the gymnast's primary requirements is proper flex. Coach Paul Ziert begins this program with a comprehensive examination of stretching exercises designed to prepare the athlete for an intense workout while providing an ongoing program of improved flexibility. Each of the Class III and IV events are then performed and examined step-by-step through their component skills. National champion Bart Conner provides his personal insights as you see him perform from the best camera angle and in slow motion.
30-237 50 min. $39.95

• Gymnastic Exercises for Women

This program is designed to help gymnasts master individual skills and coordinate beginning routines. Coach Paul Ziert begins this program with a comprehensive examination of stretching exercises designed to prepare the athlete for an intense workout while providing an ongoing program of improved flexibility. Each of the Class III and IV events are then performed and examined step-by-step through their component skills. Coach Ziert features Becky Dunning in this program. Becky has been coaching gymnastics for over 14 years.
30-236 60 min. $39.95

GYMNASTIC EXCELLENCE SERIES:

A four part series that presents safe, progressive instruction to enhance gymnastic development. This series is highly recommended for young gymnasts, their parents, teachers and their coaches.

• Advanced Tumbling
30-8009 30 min. $29.95

• Beginning Tumbling
30-8007 30 min. $29.95

• Intermediate Tumbling
30-8008 30 min. $29.95

• Pad Drills
30-8006 30 min. $29.95

NBC Sports Presents: America's Best: The U.S. Gymnastics Championships

Watch as the top male and female gymnasts in the United States compete for the honor of being crowned national champion. From the grace and beauty of the Women's floor exercises, to the power and strength of the Men's rings, you will witness the courage, skill and determination that makes these gymnasts the very best.
30-8094 50 min. $19.95

U.S. Men's Gymnastics Championships

A filmed record of the top male gymnasts in the U.S. competition for the 1981 title. Of all the team competition enjoyed by Americans today, gymnastics is considered the fastest growing.
30-248 120 min. $64.95

U.S. Women's Gymnastics Championships

A filmed record of the top female gymnasts in the United States competition for the 1981 title. A must for gymnasts interested in championship techniques.
30-249 120 min. $64.95

Martial Arts

BILL WALLACE MARTIAL ARTS AND TRAINING SERIES:

World Karate Champion, Bill "Superfoot" Wallace, is recognized by martial artists everywhere as being the world's foremost authority on flexibility training. He has written two best-selling books on the topic, and has presented over 2,000 seminars. The following series is designed to improve the physical condition and performance of all athletes.

• Super Kicking Techniques

Bill Wallace kicks at clocked speeds close to 70

VIDEO TITLES LISTED IN THIS GUIDE ARE AVAILABLE FOR PURCHASE OR RENTAL. CONTACT YOUR LOCAL VIDEO STORE OR TELEPHONE (800) 383-8811

miles per hour. He teaches you how to use your legs like hands to reach under, over and around your opponent's blocks with amazing precision. These dazzling kicks are broken down into slow motion so you can understand how to perform each movement.
15-100 90 min. $59.95

• **Super Sparring Techniques and Fight Strategy**
Bill Wallace teaches you over 100 offensive and defensive techniques that are sure to score points on your opponent. Covers proper stances, footwork, speed, power, timing, distance, combinations, and how to set up your opponent. Designed to build endurance and confidence.
15-101 90 min. $59.95

• **Super Stretching and Conditioning**
A must for not only marital artists but all athletes wishing to improve their flexibility and endurance. At a pace you can easily follow, he starts with basic stretches, gradually working into advanced splitting routines. You should be able to do a split within 3-6 months. Good for beginners and recommended as a prerequisite to the next tapes.
15-099 60 min. $59.95

Black Belt Karate: Volume I
This is the first of a series of three instructional films dealing with the ancient and increasingly popular art of self-defense. Your instructor is Jay T. Will, 7th Degree Master, and member of the United States Karate instructors Hall of Fame. The first of the three editions introduces the novice to the basic stances and moves.
28-006 120 min. $64.95

Black Belt Karate: Volume II
Here is the second in a series of three instructional films dealing with the ancient and increasingly popular art of self-defense. Your instructor is Will, 7th Degree Master, and member of the United States Karate Instructors Hall of Fame. This second of three editions takes the serious student to the second level of expertise.
28-007 120 min. $64.95

Black Belt Karate: Volume III
This is the third in a series of integrated films dealing with the ancient and increasingly popular art of self-defense. Your instructor is Jay T. Will, 7th Degree Master and member of the United States Karate Instructors Hall of Fame. In this edition, the serious student is taught to function on the level of championship belt holders.
28-008 120 min. $64.95

Black Belt: T'ai Chi Ch'uan
The program presents step-by-step, detailed instruction in a daily repeatable format: the Nine

Temple Exercises, traditionally used by Chinese monks to exercise their muscles after long hours of meditation; the Short Form, a series of pre-arranged movements to be executed slowly and effortlessly - it consists of 27 techniques performed consecutively; Push Hands involves pushing and yielding in a continuous exchange of force; Self-Defense Applications - the movements explored in the Short Form are applied to self-defense situations. This program includes an instructional booklet.
28-078 90 min. $29.95

Budo
The techniques of the oriental - "art of killing" 'kendo, karate, aikido, and judo - are explored in this astonishing look at Japan's martial arts, featuring the master practitioners of hand-to-hand fighting.
28-003 90 min. $39.95

Karate & Self-Defense
The classic defensive art of karate is easy to learn with this complete training program. Black belt Ivan Rogers welcomes you to his private dojo (training school) for your series of personal lessons with a karate master.
28-017 90 min. $19.95

Karate Exercise
Designed to teach you self-defense techniques through combining karate moves and aerobic exercise.
15-109 50 min. $29.95

Karate Master: Learn Karate
International champions Pat Worley and Gordon Franks teach you the flexibility, strength and mental conditioning that is involved in karate. The basic movements for self-defense as well as various kicks and strikes are demonstrated in this instructional video.
28-064 40 min. $16.95

Karatecise Workout
Dominick Giacobbe, black belt karate master, takes you through lessons and exercises using the techniques of the ancient art of Tang Soo Do karate. An excellent fundamental tape featuring an exciting "mind over matter" sequence with Master Giacobbe.
15-043 60 min. $24.95

Lesson #1 Buddy Hudson's: Kicks For Kids
Follow along at home instruction for kids. High action black belt demonstration, designed especially for kids, a great workout for moms & dads, and home and playground safety tips.
30-5652 60 min. $29.95

Pro-Karate Championships
Here are the highlights of the best Full Contact Championship Matches held under the auspices of the United States Professional Karate Association from 1976 to 1981. Any practitioner of the ancient art will profit from repeated viewing of these matches which demonstrate the skills and techniques the best American karate masters have to offer.
28-021 60 min. $64.95

Self-Defense for Kids
Fundamental and practical techniques to enable children to defend themselves in crisis and abuse situations. This tape gives a clear step-by-step description of the disciplines and strategies to enable a smaller person to control tough and dangerous situations.
28-077 40 min. $39.95

Sybervision: Defend Yourself! (Women's)
Being physically attacked seems impossible, until it happens to you. Then you wish you had been prepared. Cynthia Rothrock, a five-time Women's Martial Arts Champion, teaches you 10 easy-to-execute moves that can save you from being hurt, even save your life.
28-040 60 min. $69.95

T'ai Chi Ch'uan with Nancy Kwan
The health enhancing "meditation in motion" of t'ai chi, a centuries-old Chinese spiritual exercise, is adapted from the classic maneuvers of the martial arts. Learn this fatigue-free yet energizing exercise to develop breathing, and a balanced, relaxed posture.
15-076 75 min. $39.95

T'AI CHI CH'UAN SERIES:
Professionally-produced state-of-the-art instructional videos in Chinese holistic health practices. These programs are a must for all t'ai chi and yoga enthusiasts-beginning and advanced. Experience and understand t'ai chi's open secrets and become proficient in daily practice of this treasured art.

• T'ai Chi Ch'uan
The Chinese method of calisthenics for health and self defense. Graceful in movement, slow in tempo, relaxed and aware in continuous postures. T'ai Chi Ch'uan is meditation in movement, practiced the world over for its great health benefits. Good for all ages, Tai Ch'uan is a timeless and proven method of self-empowerment that addresses the totality of the human process.
20-185 30 min. $39.95

• T'ai Chi Ruler
A very rare system of Taoist yoga, or chi-kung ("energy cultivation") consisting of eight exercises utilizing a specially designed wooden dowel or ruler. Each exercise coordinates movement, breath, mental and visual focus along a T'chi physical and energy pathway. The t'ai chi ruler is a powerful and dynamic system of yoga that promotes robust health and longevity.
20-186 50 min. $49.95

• T'ai Chi Sword
Practiced as a spiritual discipline, it becomes an extension of the T'ai chi player's energy and consciousness as both move as one. The classics say that after 10,000 rounds of practice of the sword exercise, the T'ai chi sword will move like a "dragon swimming in the clouds." In this program, Master York Loo demonstrates superb fencing techniques at just such a level.
20-188 50 min. $49.95

World of Martial Arts
Today's foremost martial arts experts offer basic self-instruction in Budojujitsu, a combination of seven distinct forms of martial arts are recognized as one of the most effective forms of martial arts in the world.
28-071 60 min. $39.95

Soccer

GRADUATED SOCCER METHOD:
This outstanding three-volume program is designed especially for young players and their coaches who have dreams of The World Cup dancing in their heads. Featuring Gary McKinley a renowned soccer teacher and Division I head coach, the series starts with the basics, and moves on to developing fast feet, skill in changing directions, and outwitting opponents, all the while stressing the fun that youngsters can have with the world's most popular sport. For Boys And Girls Age 7 To 14.

• Volume I
Building a relationship with your soccer ball, developing ball handling skills, the confidence to be competitive, and the vision to apply techniques as you master them.
30-5607 30 min. $39.95

• Volume II
Developing fast feet and the speed and coordination necessary for good ball control.
30-5608 30 min. $39.95

VIDEO TITLES LISTED IN THIS GUIDE ARE AVAILABLE FOR PURCHASE OR RENTAL. CONTACT YOUR LOCAL VIDEO STORE OR TELEPHONE (800) 383-8811

• Volume III
Learning to take on your opponent with various techniques used to outwit the competition.
30-5609　30 min.　$39.95

Head to Toe: Soccer for Little Leaguers
This is a comprehensive how-to-program for junior players starring Wayne Jenkes, the only pro soccer star to play in all four major leagues, NASL, ASL, MISL and AISL.
30-2386　30 min.　$19.95

SOCCER IS FUN SERIES
An instructional series designed to help kids learn the "ins" and "outs" of the game, offensively and defensively.

• Part 1
With Bobby Charlton.
30-079　60 min.　$29.95

• Part 2
With Bobby Charlton.
30-080　60 min.　$29.95

SOCCER SERIES:
Morris video brings you this soccer series that will teach the beginning player the fundamentals of the game and is also instructional for the more advanced player as well.

• Attack
30-081　60 min.　$29.95

• Creating Space
30-087　60 min.　$29.95

• Defending
30-086　60 min.　$29.95

• Goal Keeping
30-082　60 min.　$29.95

• Passing and Support
30-083　60 min.　$29.95

• Set Plays
30-084　60 min.　$29.95

• Shooting
30-085　60 min.　$29.95

Soccer Skills from Head to Toe
The U.S. Soccer Federation presents this exceptional program featuring Rick Davis, former U.S. World Cup and Olympic team captain. He begins with a basic introduction to the rules of the game and proceeds with instruction on fundamental skills. Also included are drills and exercises for individuals and teams.
30-8110　40 min.　$29.95

Sports Clinic Soccer
Hubert Vogelsinger and his international staff of experts efficiently teach you everything you'll need to know about the fast-paced, fast growing sport of soccer.
30-071　75 min.　$19.95

Sports Pages: Soccer Funnies
Goofy goals, crazy coaches, wacky plays and pitiful pratfalls are what this unique show is all about.
30-8140　30 min.　$16.95

Teaching Kids Soccer With Bob Gansler
Help kids find their soccer balance early with this teaching video featuring Bob Gansler, coach of the U.S. World Cup Team. Coach Gansler teaches the magic of ball control, passing, heading, dribbling, shooting and shielding. The video also includes simple drills to help sharpen kids' skills.
30-5506　75 min.　$19.95

VIDEOCOACH SOCCER SERIES:
A comprehensive series of instructional programs from the world renowned player, coach and author Hubert Vogelsinger.

• Soccerobics
30-8012　30 min.　$29.95

• Kicking
30-8013　30 min.　$29.95

• Ball Control
30-8014　30 min.　$29.95

• Dribbling & Feinting
30-8015　30 min.　$29.95

• Super Skills & Heading
30-8016　30 min.　$29.95

• Soccer Tips
30-8017　30 min.　$29.95

Winner's Edge: Soccer
Seven-year pro veteran Steve Long takes the intermediate player beyond the basics, helping with dribbling, passing and scoring.
30-095　25 min.　$16.95

Tennis & Racquet Sports

30-Minute Tennis Lesson

This complete thirty minute lesson shows you everything you need to know to have a winning game.

30-2967 30 min. $16.95

Attack

Personal insights, tips & strategies from Andre Agassi & Nick Bollettieri

30-8190 52 min. $19.95

Best of U.S. Open Tennis: 1980-1990

Some of the most exciting tennis in the history of the sport is included on this tape. Featuring: Jimmy Connors, Ivan Lendl, Boris Becker and many other greats.

30-8121 45 min. $19.95

Body Prep: Tennis

This action packed tape contains the most effective tennis related exercises ever assembled in a video. Tim Mayotte, and other outstanding players show you how to get into shape. You'll will learn how dozens of exercises and sports directly benefit your tennis skills.

30-8089 105 min. $16.95

Championship Tennis

Learn the game of tennis from an insider's view and increase the level of your game with World Cup Champion Tony Roche. Learn the moves that will give you the "winning edge!" Superstars featured include: John McEnroe, Martina Navratilova, Bjorn Borg, Ivan Lendl, Stan Smith, Jimmy Connors, Arthur Ashe and others!

30-1688 60 min. $19.95

CHRIS EVERT WINNING TENNIS COLLECTION:

Chris Evert and Sybervision team up to bring you the first and only instructional tapes with Chris Evert. Excellent for players of all levels of ability.

• Evert on Winning Fundamentals
30-8204 70 min. $49.95

• Evert on Advanced Shots
30-8205 70 min. $49.95

• Evert on the Competitive Advantage
30-8206 70 min. $49.95

DENNIS VAN DER MEER'S TENNIS TALK SERIES:

Sports author and founder and president of Van der Meer Tennis University, Dennis Van der Meer has designed this unique and systematic method of teaching tennis using teaching aids and the educational psychology of the game. This method applies to all players, with the average student gaining a 42 percent increase in his match play ability. Dennis has successfully coached hundreds of tennis pros, including Billie Jean King, Margaret Court, Julie Heldman, Jeff Borowiak and many others.

• Backhand Drive

Understanding the fundamentals of a backhand drive is critical to developing a complete tennis game. Dennis Van der Meer demonstrates correct and incorrect strokes, techniques, and shot development. High bouncing balls, the slice and topspin are also covered. How to approach the net, and the two-handed backhand are also demonstrated.

30-158 30 min. $39.95

• Blackboard Tennis

Dennis Van der Meer demonstrates proper techniques in using various tennis teaching tools. The blackboard, ball machines and rally techniques are covered in detail. All are designed to improve the player's skill level.

30-165 30 min. $39.95

• Corrective Tennis

Dennis Van der Meer demonstrates improper stroke techniques in the lob, drop shot and overhead smash; the serve, backhand and forehand. More important, corrective stroke techniques are shown. This program is must viewing for the experienced player who has problems with any of these strokes.

30-164 30 min. $39.95

• Doubles Tactics Tennis

"Don the Dictator" or "Harry the Hog" may someday be your doubles partners. Dennis Van der Meer shows that knowing how they play and how they relate to your game may be important. "Doubles Tactics" is required viewing for any tennis player who needs to know where to stand, what to hit, winning tactics, and how to exploit the opposing team's weaknesses.

30-162 30 min. $39.95

• Forehand Drive

Teaching the forehand drive is fundamental to a good tennis game. Wrong strokes and corrective action grounded in an excellent teaching method make this program valuable to any tennis player. Dennis Van der Meer teaches the fundamentals of a good forehand drive, high bouncing balls, slice, approach shots and topspin shots. All are tied to

an understanding of where the players should position themselves on the court, and how to practice the forehand drive.
30-155 30 min. $39.95

• Instant Tennis
All beginners love this show...it describes the basics and shortcuts to immediate performance on the tennis court. All strokes... serve, volley, lob, backhand are taught by the Van der Meer shortcut to results. If you have never hit a tennis ball, this program is designed for you.
30-159 30 min. $39.95

• Mixed Doubles
Mixed doubles is not a body contact sport. Dennis Van der Meer covers court courtesy, how to play the weak player, where the most vulnerable spot on the court is, using the lob, how to hit to the net person, and other mixed doubles fundamentals.
30-156 30 min. $39.95

• Serve in Tennis
Dennis Van der Meer demonstrates the role of the serve in winning the point. Proper and improper serves are covered in detail, as well as how to return different types of serves. Dennis teaches the viewer how to develop his serve; topspin, flat, and other serving techniques are demonstrated.
30-161 30 min. $39.95

• Singles Tactics
Dennis Van der Meer starts by discussing and demonstrating proper singles tactics and ends this program talking about how to play against the strengths and weaknesses of opponents. Scouting the opponent, serve placement, covering the net, return placement, safety, approach shot placement, geometry of the game and judgment are also covered. Playing against the power server, hard hitter, rusher, heavy topspin, undercut, net rusher and two-handed players are also demonstrated. Wind, court surfaces and other conditions are discussed.
30-160 30 min. $39.95

• Specialty Strokes
In the repertoire of all tennis players are a number of important shots which are winners. Dennis Van der Meer demonstrates the lob, topspin lob, overhead smash, drop shot, half volley and "television" or show-off shots to the viewer.
30-157 30 min. $39.95

• Tennis
This program serves to enhance your game whether you are a novice or a seasoned player.
30-2523 30 min. $39.95

• Tennis Equipment
Dennis Van der Meer will cover everything from where to stand to what to say. Racquet, balls, shoes, clothes, courts and lines will be demonstrated.
30-166 30 min. $39.95

• Volley
A blinding exchange at the net and Dennis Van der Meer demonstrates the volley...both good and bad. The importance of standing, running and footwork is integral to a good volley. Dennis also covers in great detail the importance of exercise to improve the volley and strengthen the grip. Practice in the low volley, split step and grip change provides a well-rounded approach to improving the viewer's understanding of the volley. Court position with respect to approach, hot seat and closing the hole complete this program.
30-163 30 min. $39.95

How Tennis Pros Win
Beginners and advanced players learn from this step-by-step video on tennis fundamentals. Trish Bostrom was the third-ranked women's doubles player in the U.S. in 1979. She'll show proper grip, stance and weight transfer. learn about forehand, backhand, volley, overhead, serve and service returns. Learn strategy for singles and doubles. Slow-motion and stop-frame photography help Trish provide analysis of touring pros Tracy Austin, Rosie Casals, Andrea Jaeger and Virginia Wade.
30-141 51 min. $19.95

Platform Tennis
Whether you're a beginner or a top competitor, this video is guaranteed to improve your game! Rich Maier, 7 time APTA National Champion guides you step by step as you: improve your serve, volleys, overheads, and screen shots, refine your strokes, discover winning strategies, and learn the secrets of ball control and consistency.
30-8120 52 min. $29.95

Power Racquetball: Marty Hogan
Regardless of your level of skill right now, this program will give you more control, more confidence and a deeper understanding of the game. Six lessons from the champ. Six weeks to power performance.
30-442 30 min. $16.95

Racquetball with Dave Peck
Dave Peck, top professional racquetball player, performs all the fundamentals of racquetball. Experience, through the Sybervision neuro-muscular technique, the perfect serve, fore-hand and backhand serve return, pinches, "Z" ball,

ceiling ball, straight-in, cross-court skills and more.
30-146 60 min. $49.95

Rod Laver Introduces Tenniscise
Featuring two-time Grand Slam Champion Rod
Laver, Tenniscise is a revolutionary new method of
exercise designed to develop and increase tennis
skills such as balance, footwork, and racket
preparation, while simultaneously providing an
invigorating aerobic workout.
30-1584 60 min. $19.95

Stretching for Winning Tennis
Stretching could be the key to reaching your
playing potential. Learn to warm-up for success.
Play injury free. Build fluid strokes. Compete
choke-free. And reach like the Pros.
30-9064 30 min. $19.95

Teaching Kids Tennis With Nick Bollettieri
Nick Bollettieri, teaches his method that makes
tennis fun, natural and rewarding for the child just
starting out in the game. His program teaches
parents and youth coaches how to give a child
relaxed confidence and solid skills - the foundations
of lifetime tennis pleasure.
30-5498 60 min. $19.95

Tennis For Life: Understanding the Game
In addition to actual on-court demonstrations by
tennis coach Peter Burwash, strokes and other key
elements in a tennis game are shown here through
computer animation.
30-3032 60 min. $39.95

Tennis For Life: Winning Strategy
In addition to actual on-court demonstrations by
tennis coach Peter Burwash, key points for tennis
strategy are shown here through computer
animation.
30-3031 60 min. $39.95

Tennis Our Way
Whether you're an advanced tennis player or a
beginner, this film is a wonderful instructional tool
which will help improve your game. Three of
tennis' all-time greats give valuable pointers on all
aspects of the game. Vic Braden has been called
the "Number One Tennis Coach in America," and
Arthur Ashe and Stan Smith are pros who have
literally won every championship title. Learn how
tennis their way can become tennis your way!
30-690 151 min. $39.95

TENNIS SERIES: FEATURING DENNIS VAN DER MEER
Dennis Van Der Meer has taught millions of people
to play tennis. He teaches a standard method of

tennis which has become recognized worldwide.
No matter what your age or level of experience, his
method of teaching and progressive steps will
greatly improve and fine tune your game.

• Attacking Game
Be aggressive. Learn the simple twists and turns
that transform basic shots into crushing points.
30-614 60 min. $29.95

• Essential Strokes: The Basic Game
Master these breakthrough strokes, based on
biomechanical principles, to develop the sound
tennis skills required to build a devastating game.
30-613 60 min. $29.95

• Strategy, Tactics and Mental Side
The essential psychology of tennis that teaches you
how to out-think your opponents is made vividly
clear through overhead video shots or pros
executing tactical maneuvers.
30-615 60 min. $29.95

Tennis Warm-Up
Warming up before any sport protects muscles,
joints and tendons, these short warm-ups will help
you to peak performance and personal best.
30-298 20 min. $16.95

Tennis with Stan Smith
Smith's pure, flawless tennis form comes to life on
this interesting tape. Used successfully by the
Stanford University Men's Tennis Team (1980 and
1981 NCAA Champions) and many tennis pros,
this video imprints tennis strokes into your body's
"muscle memory": the serve, forehand and
backhand groundstroke and service return, volley,
backhand approach and overhead smash.
30-167 60 min. $69.95

Tennis: Workout to Win with Virginia Wade
This program combines instruction on all the basic
strokes with aerobics, stretching and weight lifting.
It features a comprehensive, overall fitness routine
designed to condition the specific muscles used in
tennis, as well as all racquet sports. It will help
tennis players develop balance, coordination and
stamina while honing the skills and reflexes the
game demands.
30-557 75 min. $29.95

VIC BRADEN SERIES:

• Faults & Cures
30-542 26 min. $29.95

• Science and Myth of Tennis
30-8036 60 min. $29.95

VIDEO TITLES LISTED IN THIS GUIDE ARE AVAILABLE FOR PURCHASE
OR RENTAL. CONTACT YOUR LOCAL VIDEO STORE OR TELEPHONE (800) 383-8811

• Strokes & Strategy
30-541 26 min. $29.95

• Vic Braden Teaches You Winning
Tennis Strokes
30-539 56 min. $49.95

• Vic Braden's Quick Cures for
Common Tennis Problems
30-540 56 min. $49.95

• Women's Doubles
30-8305 60 min. $29.95

VIC BRADEN'S TENNIS FOR THE FUTURE SERIES:
This series covers a broad range of tennis shots and techniques.

• Volume 1
This volume covers four tennis fundamentals;
forehand, backhand, serve and volley. From
Braden's successful PBS program, "Tennis for the
Future."
30-168 120 min. $29.95

• Volume 2
This segment covers the approach shot (spin and
service return,) the overhead shot, lob and drop
shots, and conditioning.
30-169 120 min. $29.95

• Volume 3
This program is rich in useful, hands-on
information and demonstrations of techniques.
30-170 125 min. $29.95

Virginia Wade's Visual Tennis
Visual Tennis gives every player a revolutionary
method for playing improved, inspired tennis on a
regular basis, presenting the first comprehensive
approach to learning and improving tennis based on
visualization and mental imagery.
30-5186 50 min. $29.95

Winner's Edge: Racquetball
Long-time pro Al Chassard shares his expertise in
the basics of a strong all-around game, including
proper stroke execution and game strategy.
30-171 25 min. $19.95

Winner's Edge: Tennis
Long-time captain of the U.S. Davis Cup team,
teaching pro Dennis Ralston offers guidance with
forehand, backhand, volley and serve, along with
helpful strategy tips.
30-172 25 min. $19.95

Track & Field

CHAMPIONSHIP TRACK & FIELD WITH BILL DELLINGER
Bill Dellinger, Head Track Coach at the University
of Oregon, presents a phenomenal 17 part series
on techniques and conditioning. Dellinger himself
was an NCAA and Olympic medalist and he has
coached athletes in 118 All-American
performances, plus 2 Olympic gold medalists!

• Long/Triple Jump Techniques
30-8034 30 min. $29.95

• Pole Vault Techniques
30-8035 30 min. $29.95

• Discus Techniques
30-8036 30 min. $29.95

• Javelin Technique
30-8037 30 min. $29.95

• Hammer Technique
30-8038 30 min. $29.95

• Distance Technique
30-8039 30 min. $29.95

• Hurdle Technique
30-8040 30 min. $29.95

• Shot Put Technique
30-8041 30 min. $29.95

• Sprint Technique
30-8042 30 min. $29.95

• Relay Technique
30-8043 30 min. $29.95

• High Jump Technique
30-8043 30 min. $29.95

• 400/Intermediate Hurdle
30-8044 30 min. $29.95

• Distance Conditioning
30-8045 30 min. $29.95

• Pole Vault Conditioning
30-8046 30 min. $29.95

VIDEO TITLES LISTED IN THIS GUIDE ARE AVAILABLE FOR PURCHASE
OR RENTAL. CONTACT YOUR LOCAL VIDEO STORE OR TELEPHONE (800) 383-8811

• **Weight Events Conditioning**
30-8048 30 min. $29.95

• **Sprint Conditioning**
30-8049 30 min. $29.95

• **Jump Conditioning**
30-8050 30 min. $29.95

Fifty-Plus Celebration
During the weekend of the 8th Annual Fifty Plus 8K at Stanford, Emil Zatopek vividly recalls his legendary 1952 Olympic victories, recounting in hilarious fashion his experiences as a neophyte marathoner. This is one of the most exciting running events of the year.
30-8203 55 min. $24.95

Ligamentous Injuries of the Ankle
One of the most common injuries encountered in athletics is acute sprain of the ankle. UCLA's athletic trainer, Ducky Drake, demonstrates his method of taping the ankle to prevent injury and to protect the sprained ankle. This tape also describes the anatomy of the ankle joint, so that the viewer better understands what happens when it is injured.
20-196 23 min. $69.95

Musculotendinous Injuries in Track Athletes
UCLA's athletic trainer, Ducky Drake, demonstrates early and late management methods of track injuries. The tape also illustrates the biochemical analysis of the running stride using footage of top sprinters' running gate. Educational viewing for any athlete.
20-097 20 min. $69.95

Olympia I
Leni Riefenstahl's documentary of the 1936 Olympics, as hosted by Nazi Germany.
30-8195 119 min. $19.95

Olympia II
More of the 1936 Olympics, as hosted by Nazi Germany.
30-8196 96 min. $19.95

TRACK AND FIELD SERIES WITH RON PICKERING:
The series consists of five volumes. Presented by Ron Pickering, athletics advisor and former Olympic gold medalist. Through exhilarating action and slow motion sequences, world class athletes demonstrate the techniques and beauty of top track and field events. Designed for young people who either wish to participate in sports, or just learn more about particular events. These programs may be used as a teaching tool, or as pure family entertainment.

• **How to Attain Basic Physical Fitness, Strength and Endurance**
Fitness for Sport: More than 50 exercises are demonstrated, which show how to attain the basic physical fitness for success. Strength Training for Sport: Once basic fitness and endurance have been attained, the athlete moves to the next step...strength training. This begins with exercises using the body's own weight. Coaching Young Athletes: Training young people is quite different from coaching mature athletes. Beginning principles as well as the where and when it is best to start training are emphasized in this video.
30-617 62 min. $59.95

• **Track Events and Running**
Here we fully cover the sprint, relay, hurdles and middle distance running. Aerobic and anaerobic training are shown by top athletes. Full speed sprinting, smooth and efficient baton handover, principles of basic hurdling and finally, how winning performances can be achieved through dedicated training.
30-618 48 min. $59.95

• **Track Events - Javelin and Jumps**
This program demonstrates the long jump, triple jump, high jump and javelin. Animation, stop-frame and slow-motion photography illustrate the fluid action of the long jumper. Weight training and jumping activities are demonstrated along with sprinting techniques in the triple jump. In the high jump, two dominant styles are analyzed, the Fosbury flop and the straddle. The whole action of the throw is broken into its component parts. The intricate and smooth timing of the movements are displayed in the javelin.
30-437 49 min. $59.95

• **Track Events - Shotput, Pole Vault, Discus and Hammer**
Athletes see exactly how muscular force should be applied through the body to the shot. The pole vault is broken down into teaching phases and there is a spectacular slow-motion section which should motivate both athletes and youngsters. Discus and hammer throwing are technically demanding sports requiring training and discipline from the outset. Illustrating basic movements for both events, the viewer sees the training involved for this demanding sport.
30-438 49 min. $59.95

WOMEN'S TRACK AND FIELD SERIES:
This is a video series on a wide range of women's track and field activities.

• **Conditioning**
Perhaps the most important overall program offered by Coach Foreman is this program on conditioning

of the female athlete. It's a comprehensive approach to developing both strength and flexibility.
30-257 33 min. $39.95

• **Discus/Shot Put**
Coach Foreman shows how to develop a beginner in the discus or the shotput. Of particular interest in this program is overhead photography in the discus event.
30-254 48 min. $39.95

• **High Jump**
Through liberal use of slow motion and stop frame photography, Ken Foreman teaches the mechanics of the back flop high jumping technique. A number of drills away from the high jump pit are included.
30-253 23 min. $39.95

• **Javelin**
One of the world's finest javelin throwers, Karin Smith, is Dr. Ken Foreman's demonstrator. Proper technique is emphasized by the coach and the athlete and slow motion photography helps show that technique.
30-251 53 min. $39.95

• **Long Jump**
Olympic Games veteran Martha Watson is the demonstrator for Coach Foreman in this demanding event in women's track and field. Foreman shows the step-by-step procedure he uses to bring along a beginning long jumper.
30-252 46 min. $39.95

• **Middle Distance Running**
Dr. Foreman's holistic preparation of middle distance runners is featured in this program. He spends a great deal of time in off-track training programs to keep the runner's interest. "Middle Distance Running" is an excellent training tool.
30-619 42 min. $39.95

• **Sprints, Hurdles & Relays**
Each of these events requires the use of sprinting techniques, so Dr. Foreman has combined the three into one teaching tool. You'll gain a number of drills to develop sprinters, hurdlers and relay runners.
30-255 48 min. $39.95

• **Talent Search**
In this program, Dr. Ken Foreman provides coaches and athletes with a variety of tests which will help determine each potential athlete's best event.
30-250 60 min. $39.95

Water Sports

4th Annual Maui Grand Prix
This is a detailed look at the sport of windsurfing. Enjoy incredible footage of the most prestigious event in windsurfing.
30-546 60 min. $49.95

Air Born
Sailboard jumping from chophops to back loops, this is a revolution in learning. Teach your body and your head will follow & you will fly like Ian Boyd.
30-8118 27 min. $24.95

Aloha Classic
Setting new standards for surf-sailing competition, this event exploded the Hookipa scene with radical action, peak performances and new equipment.
30-2544 60 min. $49.95

Bali High
Surfing at its best: 90 minutes of exciting surf footage from exotic locales. Ride the waves in Java, Bali, Hawaii, and even the mysterious "Isle of Kong," then revel in the bikini-clad girls from around the world.
30-173 90 min. $59.95

BEST OF DAREDEVIL SPORTS - SERIES

• **Ultimate Super thrills**
Watch as these sports crazies water ski barefoot behind a helicopter, kayak over waterfalls, ride Motocross and sailboard on the edge. It's a sports video and an adrenaline rush all in one.
30-8249 35 min. $16.95

• **Ultimate Ski Thrills**
Watch daredevil skiers freestyle on the edge. It's the ultimate ski video that will make your wildest ski fantasies come true.
30-8250 35 min. $16.95

• **Ultimate Motorcross Thrills**
The excitement of the Super Bowl of Motocross plus motocross music videos make this a tape a must for any motorcycle enthusiast.
30-8251 35 min. $16.95

• **Ultimate Surf Thrills**
Travel around the world for the most exciting

surfing imaginable. Totally tubular!
30-8252 35 min. $16.95

Blue Highway
Expert Herbie Fletcher takes you wave jumping on the North Shore of Oahu. He launches his jet powered craft off the top of some of the biggest waves you'll see.
30-8273 25 min. $19.95

Blue Water Hunters
An extraordinary film, narrated by Peter Fonda. Travel with the divers who dive to depths of up to one hundred feet with only the air in their lungs to breathe. Featuring champion spear fisherman Terry Mass.
30-8248 58 min. $29.95

BOARDSAILING

• Learning The Basics
If you want to learn sailboarding, the long board is the place to begin. This comprehensive look at sailboarding basics features champion board sailor Nevin Sayre who demystifies the challenge of this increasingly popular sport.
30-5499 60 min. $19.95

• Short Board
Once you've mastered the basics of boardsailing, go for the excitement of a short board. They're light, fast and designed for sailing in winds over 15 knots. Take your boardsailing to the edge as Nevin Sayre shows you how to control your shortboard and get the best ride when the waves and wind leave others on the beach.
30-5500 40 min. $19.95

DIFFERENT STROKES SERIES:

• Olympic Style Back Stroke, Breaststroke and Turns
A coach or swimming teacher can use this program as a tool to help break down the two strokes into progressive steps for coaching or teaching. Coach Dick Hannula has world-class swimmers demonstrate proper arm and leg action, breathing and turns. He then shows a variety of drills swimmers can use to develop these techniques. Because of extensive slow motion and stop frames, the viewer is able to see exactly how each stroke should be performed and how to go about developing the strokes through practice drills. An ideal teaching and coaching aid, this program is "must" viewing for high school, college and club swimmers, teachers and coaches.
30-182 39 min. $39.95

• Olympic Style Crawl & Butterfly
Coach Dick Hannula breaks down both of these competitive strokes into progressive steps to be used in teaching the strokes. Hannula has elite-class swimmers demonstrate the proper techniques for the arm actions, leg kicks, breathing, etc. He also shows numerous drills to be used in developing these techniques. Extensive use of underwater photography in regular speed, slow motion and stop frame, allows the viewer to see exactly how each stroke should be performed through practice drills. This program is an ideal teaching and coaching aid for every level of swimming. "Must" viewing for club, high school and college swimmers, coaches and teachers.
30-183 41 min. $39.95

Dive Scapa Flow
On June 21st, 1919, the entire German High Seas Fleet, some 74 ships dramatically scuttled itself at Scapa Flow in the Orkney Islands off Northern Scotland. Today, seven of those ships lie still and silent, a veritable magnet attracting thousands of divers each year. Come and discover the unknown.
30-8113 30 min. $29.95

Extreme Surfing
The beauty, excitement and danger of surfing the North Seas.
30-8175 46 min. $19.95

Force 10: Sail the Gorge
A sailor's guide to windsurfing in the Gorge. Tour one of the world's top high wind sailing spots.
30-8119 65 min. $29.95

Go with the Windsurfer
The hottest windsurfing action ever filmed.
30-8177 52 min. $19.95

Hot Boards
Amazing feats of body boarding, windsurfing, sand skiing, snow boarding and trick water skiing. A thrill a minute.
30-304 30 min. $16.95

How to Use Dive Tables
A complete instructional program covering the use of dive tables by sport divers, and recommended safety precautions. A training guide is enclosed including guidelines for use, definitions, dive tables, sample problems and a repetitive dive planning guide.
30-480 36 min. $49.95

Impact Zone
Experience the fastest growing sport of our time. Featuring an award winning soundtrack from Grammy award winner, Clarence "Gatemouth" Brown. Watch as the windsurfers take on towering waves and brave razor sharp rocks in the most

VIDEO TITLES LISTED IN THIS GUIDE ARE AVAILABLE FOR PURCHASE OR RENTAL. CONTACT YOUR LOCAL VIDEO STORE OR TELEPHONE (800) 383-8811

exciting sport today!
30-8272 35 min. $29.95

Jet Ski: World Tour Warm Up
For personal watercraft fans this is a great compendium of racing, wavejumping, pretty girls, technique tips and action that'll leave you sitting on the edge of your TV.
30-8274 30 min. $19.95

Learn Snorkeling
Snorkeling is safe and requires very little training. The equipment is inexpensive and with this video, anyone can learn snorkeling.
30-1863 32 min. $29.95

LIFEGUARD SYSTEMS SERIES:

• Black Water Contingency
This video demonstrates how to do a proper gear check. Reviews underwater signals , covers all the minimum clothing and equipment needed by tenders and demonstrates use and techniques of alternate air sources (pony bottles) for emergency conditions, and depicts the "Hendrick Hand Signals".
30-8254 28 min. $29.95

• Dress and Care of a Drysuit
This video demonstrates how a professional team (Police, Fire, Underwater Rescue) dresses for the job at hand, it then continues methodically to demonstrate exactly how to dress and care for the dry suit system.
30-8256 27 min. $29.95

• Flooding of Drysuit
This video discusses the problem of a dry suit flooding and over weighting. We completely open and flood a dry suit at a depth of 100 feet and then proceed to demonstrate. If weighting is done properly, there will be no effect on a diver's ability to surface.
30-8255 22 min. $29.95

• Sport Diving Rescue
This video is structured in two parts. The first part covers 120 seconds to save a life. The second part is a video of a 4-minute slide show demonstrating two separate rescues, one done correctly and one done incorrectly and 17 minutes of what a rescue diver course should entail for sport divers.
30-8253 30 min. $29.95

Northwest Diver
Filmed entirely in the Pacific Northwest, this diver's guide brings all of the pristine beauty of these waters. Giant Octopi, wolf eels, swimming scallops, dancing nudibranch, poisonous jellyfish

and much more!
30-8243 30 min. $29.95

Offshore Pipeline Masters
Come to Oahu's Bonzai Pipeline and enjoy the 14th Annual Masters Surfing Classic. World-renowned surfers compete for the coveted championship on the most challenging and savage waves known.
30-180 60 min. $39.95

Open Water Experience
This video program introduces you to the exciting world of SCUBA diving. One of the fastest growing sports in the world today. The emphasis of the program is placed on skills you will learn on your way to becoming a certified open water diver. Sections on beach diving and boat diving will show you just how easy it is to explore the mysteries of the underwater world.
30-5145 50 min. $39.95

OPEN WATER VIDEO COURSE

• Advanced Open Water Video Course
The advanced audio-visual course is completely coordinated with the Advanced Sports Diver Manual and Workbook. Under-water film sequences were filmed off Santa Catalina Island in California. The advanced audio-visual course covers diving equipment, boat diving, underwater navigation, limited visibility, diver's stress and rescue, deep diving.
30-179 111 min. $35.95

• Open Water Video Course
The audio-visual course is completely coordinated with the Open Water Manual and Workbook. Underwater film sequences were filmed on San Salvador Island in the Bahamas. The audio-visual course covers the following subjects: skin diving equipment, scuba diving equipment, the diver underwater, the diver at depth, underwater environment, underwater life.
30-0178 126 min. $29.95

PSAA SURFING

• Volume I
Joey Buran's PSAA Summer shows you what it takes to become a pro surfer. What the judges are looking for and what to expect from the competition. Joey Buran is your coach, and California is the training ground. Oceanside, Huntington, Malibu, and Ventura provide the arenas for the most hardcore surfing to hit the American coast. And don't miss the outrageous bikini action.
30-7069 80 min. $29.95

VIDEO TITLES LISTED IN THIS GUIDE ARE AVAILABLE FOR PURCHASE OR RENTAL. CONTACT YOUR LOCAL VIDEO STORE OR TELEPHONE (800) 383-8811

• Volume II

This is the most incredible slicing, dicing, aerial experience ever recorded. Highlights of the Pro Surfing Association of America's 1986 season show California's best surfers performing the most up to date surfing techniques (such as floaters, aerials, vertical re-entries, and 360's), at such famous beaches as Malibu, and in giant waves in San Francisco. Ex-world champion Peter Townend with Superbowl champ Mike Cruickshank and hot rookie sensation Richie Collins offer expert coaching advise. And blast off on a bonus treasure hunt to the world's longest ride - surfing the rapids of the Snake River in Wyoming.
30-7070 85 min. $29.95

Scuba Diving Across the USA

Includes ice diving and warm water snorkel racing from Texas to Minnesota.
30-8244 30 min. $19.95

Scuba Diving in America

Now see the America most American's have never seen! Marvel at the treasures to be found in the depths of such foreign lands as Lake Michigan, California and Florida.
30-8242 51 min. $24.95

Scuba Gear Maintenance

Learning proper upkeep and routine repair of your dive equipment will insure years of exciting, adventurous and safe expeditions.
30-8258 18 min. $16.95

Scuba: The First Time

This is the official PADI diving instructional video with Australia's Paul Mugglestone. It is a great aid to those who are learning to dive in cold water areas.
30-8257 50 min. $29.95

Scuba Video Refresher Course

NAUI and PADI instructors conduct a complete review of basic techniques and safe practices providing detailed underwater demonstrations that can be easily followed and independently practiced. Content includes segments on health and physical fitness, basic pool training, diving hazards, advance pool training and open water diving.
30-479 37 min. $34.95

SHORT BOARD SAILING TECHNIQUES SERIES:

• Volume I

Fundamentals, waterstarts, stance, jibes and more.
30-8236 40 min. $29.95

• Volume II

Jibes/Duck jibes in swells & high wind.
30-8237 40 min. $29.95

Ski Boarding Made Easy

One of the hottest new watersport today is also known as wakeboarding or skufing. This sport derives most of it's maneuvers from snowboarding and skateboarding rather than waterskiing.
30-8275 45 min. $24.95

SOLO SPORTS SURFING SERIES:

• Ocean Action Video Magazine

Ocean Action brings you the very latest in surfing, windsurfing, boogie boarding and underwater action from Hawaii the year-round water sports capital of the world!
30-371 45 min. $16.95

• Storm Riders

The greatest rides you've ever seen, on the most perfect tubes you've ever imagined, set to today's hottest rock sounds. The fastest moving, most thrilling surfing video ever made with Shaun Tomson, Ho Richards and many more attacking the sets in Australia, South Africa, Hawaii, and never-before-seen secret spots in Bali and Thailand.
30-372 92 min. $39.95

Surf City

This video is everything you have ever wanted to see about surfing...and more. You'll see the top surfers up and down the California coast. You'll have an insider's look at Surfer Magazine's 25th anniversary party and a guided tour of legendary Surf City. All of this action and fun are set to a soundtrack of the west coast's hottest new bands.
30-1809 60 min. $29.95

Surf's Up

Electrifying footage of the Men's Pro Cup and World Cup filmed at Sunset Beach, Hawaii!
30-306 30 min. $16.95

SURFING'S SUPER

Travel around the globe with the world's top professional surfers on the international championship tour in their quest to be crowned Number One. Surfing the exotic shores of southern France, Japan, South Africa, Australia, Israel and Hawaii. Hosted by Shaun Tomson.

• Hawaii, Australia
30-370 60 min. $39.95

• Israel, France, Hawaii
30-369 60 min. $39.95

• Japan, South Africa

VIDEO TITLES LISTED IN THIS GUIDE ARE AVAILABLE FOR PURCHASE OR RENTAL. CONTACT YOUR LOCAL VIDEO STORE OR TELEPHONE (800) 383-8811

• **Japan, South Africa**
30-368 60 min. $39.95

Swimming Warm-Up
Warming up before any sport protects muscles, joints and tendons. This short program will help you to peak performances and personal bests.
30-307 20 min. $16.95

Treasure Hunting
Take a vagabond excursion around the Caribbean and Indian Ocean. Visit ships of the past and present. Learn the secrets and legends of lost treasure of the deep. Interviews with the greatest treasure hunter of them all, Mel Fisher.
30-8246 30 min. $19.95

Tricks of the Trade
A sailboard instructional tape that uses a unique visual teaching format that relies on a solid visual image rather than lengthy verbal explanations. You will establish an accurate mental picture and convert them to actual experiences.
30-8117 22 min. $19.95

Underwater Navigation Made Easy
You'll expertly navigate the most challenging underwater terrain following the methods of underwater self-orientation taught on this tape. This program teaches you the most effective methods such as compass use, landmarks, safety procedures and tide and drift control.
30-8282 40 min. $29.95

Water Workout
Join Candy Costie, 1984 gold medalist in synchronized swimming, for an exhilarating water workout that builds aerobic fitness while helping every major muscle group in the body develop more strength and improved stamina.
30-186 60 min. $39.95

Water-Rowing, Sculling
The most demanding of all sports - sculling. The full power of the oarsman's body must be applied to the oar and combined with the current movement and coordination for maximum efficiency. Single scull-blade work is the basis of sound sculling techniques. The film illustrates common faults and shows how to amend these at various points. Land training with weights is an essential part of the rower's technique which is often neglected by both coach and oarsman.
30-439 52 min. $59.95

Waterskiing Fun-Damentals
Learn the basics of waterskiing with this informative video that teaches proper form and technique for one ski or two. Expert waterskiers demonstrate different starts and landings, crossings and jumping the wake, safety rules, hand signals, even hints on how to drive the boat. You'll get good tips on selecting and using the right equipment.
30-185 30 min. $19.95

Watersports World Tour
Watersport thrills and beautiful girls. Excitement from Oahu's North Shore surfing to thrilling Jet-crafts in Mexico. All this plus great hot music and the most sensational sexy ladies and beach fashions ever.
30-8276 38 min. $19.95

WET AND WILD WORLD OF WATERSKIING:

• **Beginning Water Skiing**
Learn to master the basics of this sport. Also, a special section is included on how to teach kids to ski.
30-8208 30 min. $19.95

• **How to Drive a Ski Boat**
Learn the correct techniques for water starts, throttling up, skier down maneuvers and others.
30-8209 60 min. $29.95

• **Show Ski Competition**
If you are inspired by the elegance and grace of synchronized team skiing, exhilarated by electrifying barefoot action or amused by the burlesque antics of ace trick skiers, then this is for you.
30-8210 60 min. $29.95

• **Improve Your Waterskiing Skills**
Learn how to do the big spray and jumping wakes. A great video for intermediate waterskiers.
30-8211 30 min. $19.95

What Dreams Are Made Of
The treasures of the 1715 Plate fleet. Everyone has a secret fantasy of discovering sunken treasure. Join Mel Fisher and Dan Wagner as they dive of Florida's east coast to uncover a king's ransom of days long ago.
30-8247 30 min. $19.95

Whitewater Bloopers
River runners from all over the world come to Northern California's Salmon River, looking for a good time. Watch as they get more fun than they bargained for! You'll see it all in this hilarious video.
30-8127 40 min. $19.95

Wild Winds: Windsurfing Hawaii
Experience the incredible sport of windsurfing in the beautiful, picturesque waters of Hawaii to the

beat of a super soundtrack.
30-373 20 min. $39.95

Windsurfing with Murray Willet
Learn to windsurf with Australia's own wild man,
Murray Willet. This world-class windsurfer will
show you all the ropes you need to know to get
started in this action-packed sport.
30-1583 30 min. $19.95

Weight Lifting & Body Building

Arnold Schwarzenegger: The Comeback
Arnold Schwarzenegger is Mr. Olympia in this
exciting filmed record of the 7th Annual
Bodybuilding Contest for the world title as the
controversial Schwarzenegger comes out of
retirement to recapture the crown. Among the
contestants here are former Mr. Universe title
holders: Roy Callender, Boyer Coe, Frank Zane
and others.
30-031 120 min. $64.95

BUILDING THE BODY BEAUTIFUL
A step-by-step regimen, presented in three
volumes. Designed to build, tone and define the
body. With instructors Jim Yount, Jeff DeYoung
and Diane Marin.

• **Body & Arms**
30-1988 24 min. $16.95

• **Body & Chest**
30-1989 24 min. $16.95

• **Body & Stomach**
30-1990 24 min. $16.95

Iron Bodies
A behind-the-scenes look at the workout sessions of
both male and female bodybuilders.
15-031 60 min. $19.95

Leslie Chazin's Light Weight Training
The benefits of light weight training are
tremendous, toning and shaping your body to the
best it can be. National Aerobics Champion Leslie
Chazin has designed an effective program to get
you started safely.
30-2692 30 min. $16.95

Pumping Iron II: The Women
The film that is reshaping the world's view of the
female physique. Struggle with the competitors,
from the sweat of the gym to the glory of the stage,
as they attempt to stretch the limitations of both
mind and body.
15-168 107 min. $79.95

Weightlifting: Training and Conditioning
Designed to condition and strengthen the body, this
program starts with a brief history of weightlifting
and moves on to segments focusing on warm-up,
stretching exercises, and eight separate exercises
using various types of body building equipment.
Even includes pointers on stress moderation for use
in conjunction with bodybuilding.
15-086 30 min. $29.95

Wilderness Sports

Backpacking America with Kent and Donna Dannen
These two professionals cover the full gamut of
backpacking needs. They have spent most of their
lives in the Rocky Mountains and feel a deep
concern for the environment and the need to
preserve it for future generations.
30-607 70 min. $29.95

FAMILY CAMPING SERIES:

• **Camping Activities**
Entertaining family travel games, orienteering,
stargazing, adventures in hiking and valuable
watercrafting advice.
30-686 40 min. $19.95

• **Essential Planner**
How to plan, what to pack, what to buy and wear,
setting up camp, and campfire cooking secrets!
30-685 40 min. $19.95

• **Family Camper on Wheels**
Adventures in pop-up camp trailers or motorized
RVs with tips on packing, driving, parking,
emergency procedures, and campsite hookup
information.
30-688 40 min. $19.95

• **Safety: A Guide to Being Prepared**
Basic first aid and safety precautions every family
member should know before hitting the trail.
30-687 40 min. $19.95

VIDEO TITLES LISTED IN THIS GUIDE ARE AVAILABLE FOR PURCHASE
OR RENTAL. CONTACT YOUR LOCAL VIDEO STORE OR TELEPHONE (800) 383-8811

Hiking the West Coast Trail

Take on the rugged wilderness and explore the intriguing surroundings of Vancouver Island. The incredible story behind the West Coast Trail, and the tragic shipwrecks leading to its inception, are also revealed.
30-2982 60 min. $29.95

Solo

Follow a lone climber from a canyon floor into a breathtaking panorama of snow, sky, and forbidding peaks. You'll find out why climbers take such extraordinary risks. You'll gain insight into climbing philosophy and techniques, as well.
30-682 30 min. $29.95

West Coast Trail

This film serves as a magnificent setting for exploring the relationship between the wilderness and man. You'll learn the most up-to-date minimum impact camping techniques, as well as fundamental skills applicable to any wilderness environment.
30-643 60 min. $29.95

Winter Sports

Avalanche Awareness

Snow avalanches are the single greatest hazard to the unwary backcountry traveller. Combining spectacular live footage with practical safety tips and the fundamentals of avalanche safety.
30-8166 30 min. $29.95

Best of Killington: America's 6 Mountain Ski Resort

With six beautiful mountains interconnected by a system of 107 trails, Killington is the most popular ski resort in the eastern United States. This is your guide to the unparalleled diversity of this famous resort.
30-8116 45 min. $19.95

Beyond the Edge

Knowing your limits is good sense. Pushing your limits, challenging them, is taking your capabilities Beyond the Edge! You're right there in the action with cliff jumpers, snow boarders, freestylers and speed burners - with the usual complement of misfits and celebrities on both sides of the edge.
30-1701 90 min. $19.95

Bill Johnson's Pre-Ski Workout

This workout is divided into four sections: warm-up, moderate impact aerobics, muscle conditioning, and cool down, designed to improve skiing performance and minimize fatigue.
30-2820 60 min. $29.95

Billy Kidd: Ski Racing

No matter what your ability - beginner, intermediate, expert - if you can turn your skis, you can learn to race. Billy Kidd shows you the fast way to improve your skiing.
30-2327 30 min. $19.95

Body Prep: Skiing

This contains the most effective ski-related exercises ever assembled in a video. Pro racers teach you how each exercise and sport directly benefits your skiing skills.
30-8090 101 min. $16.95

Breakthrough Basics Of Downhill Skiing

Let premier ski instructor Hank Kashiwa push you off your beginner or intermediate plateau. His back-to-basics emphasis in conditioning, turn perfection, and timing makes this one of the most effective ski improvement courses available.
30-5517 45 min. $29.95

Brian O'Shea's Extaski

Join a group of World Class skiers as they escape for the ultimate three-day ski adventure. Desert dry powder, aerial insanity and hair-raising moguls face each skier on the scenic slopes of Snowbird, Utah.
30-2220 30 min. $19.95

Canadians - "A Saga"

This is the extraordinary adventure of the Montreal Canadians hockey team, a team that has had so many records, success stories and renowned players that a whole library could be devoted to it. You will have the opportunity to look back on this amazing story through unpublished documents, stunning interviews and outstanding events. Every true hockey fan will greatly enjoy this story of the team that is the pride of Canada.
30-324 52 min. $19.95

Cross-Country Skiing with Jeff Nowak - Sybervision

Sybervision's system of repeated athletic form is the basis of this tape. Jeff Nowak, one of the world's top cross-country skiers, demonstrates every important fundamental of Nordic cross-country skiing, including the perfect diagonal stride; double pole technique; telemark position, etc. Beautifully filmed in Colorado.
30-189 60 min. $69.95

Distinctive Skiing

The twelve basic rules of distinctive skiing - fully

VIDEO TITLES LISTED IN THIS GUIDE ARE AVAILABLE FOR PURCHASE OR RENTAL. CONTACT YOUR LOCAL VIDEO STORE OR TELEPHONE (800) 383-8811

demonstrated in a simplified format (skiers learn at home - then practice on the mountain.) Skiers learn how to look good and have more fun skiing. This program also features a special skier's workout and a segment of ski care.
30-2181 82 min. $39.95

Don't Pat the Dog
A snowboard video that relies on solid video imaging rather than lengthy verbal explanations to help the beginner snowboarder get started. You will establish an accurate mental picture which you will replace with actual experience.
30-8115 15 min. $19.95

How to Ice Skate
Aa tape for beginners through experts that includes tips from professional skaters, Tai Babylonia and Randy Gardner, and top skating coach, John W. Nicks
30-1952 60 min. $16.95

Introduction to Cross-Country Skiing
This program is the perfect tool to remove anxiety from the beginning cross-country skier. To take the guesswork out of selecting your equipment, you'll tour the shop, gaining a practical knowledge of what is best for your budget and for your style of skiing. Then you take to the back country to learn the simple progression from walking to cross-country skiing. You'll see how to take advantage of downhills and save energy when climbing. This program can show the novice how to take the fear out of unexpected steep terrain. You'll learn the elegant telemark turn and how to cross-country parallel.
30-192 45 min. $39.95

Learn to Ski Better
Unparalleled ski instruction for all levels, endorsed by the Professional Ski Instructors of America. Tips on all aspects of performance, conditioning and equipment. Plus, a section on mind/body awareness to improve overall ability.
30-600 90 min. $24.95

Maltese Flamingo
The real life and times of the strangest band of ski bums ever assembled. Les Arcs, Tignes, Val d'Isere, Geneva, London, Steamboat Springs, Squaw Valley and Aspen are just a few of the locations visited.
30-2559 75 min. $39.95

Nordicross
Cross country skiing has gone through exciting changes recently. The first half of this tape teaches you traditional Nordic techniques which still form the basis for cross country; the second half introduces you to the new world of freestyle skiing.
30-8207 88 min. $39.95

Peter Bogner's Skiing Techniques
This all-inclusive video covers: warm-up and freestyle skiing exercises, tips from world champion skiers, skiing through gates, start and finish pointers, tactics and mental preparation, pre-season conditioning, injury prevention, ski tuning, and what to look for in ski equipment.
30-2641 45 min. $19.95

Private Lessons: Skiing with Bob Muran
Bob Muron has over 25 years of ski instructing experience. His students have included personalities such as Ivan Lendl and Ed McMahon and Edward Kennedy. Bob is a full time ski instructor trainer and examiner for the Professional Ski Instructors of America.
30-8096 60 min. $16.95

Rossignol - A Cross Country Celebration
A collection of programs from the Rossignol Ski Company featuring selections on equipment, the evolution of cross country skiing and action scenes.
30-8003 35 min. $19.95

Ski Better Now
Whether you're a beginning skier or an aspiring expert, this program will push you to new levels of ability and open the door to new ski experiences. This is designed to help you learn exactly what you need to know to ski better.
30-8091 25 min. $16.95

Ski Champions: The Winners
Suzy Chaffee and David Soul host this spotlight on men's and women's professional skiing and speed skiing, featuring the creme-de-la-creme on snow!
30-330 30 min. $19.95

Ski Country: The Ultimate Downhill Adventure
Produced and narrated by Warren Miller, a renowned sports filmmaker, this breathtaking adventure takes you to 25 locations around the world, including the Alps, New Zealand, the Rockies, Vermont and Canada. Includes acrobatic feats, Olympic champions Bill Johnson and Phil and Steve Mahre, as well as 78-year-old ski pioneer, Otto Lang. A must for ski enthusiasts
30-331 93 min. $29.95

Ski Magazine's: Learn to Ski
Filmed on location in Deer Valley, Utah, and featuring the world's leading skiers, this step-by-step instructional tape is geared to the beginning and re-entry level skier. Includes guidelines on equipment usage, exercises, basic ski techniques, how to ski bumps and downhill race; how to walk and climb on skis, traverse, ride the lift, parallel turn and ski moguls. Supported by the U.S. Ski Team, National Ski Patrol and Professional Ski

---

VIDEO TITLES LISTED IN THIS GUIDE ARE AVAILABLE FOR PURCHASE OR RENTAL. CONTACT YOUR LOCAL VIDEO STORE OR TELEPHONE (800) 383-8811

Instructors of America.
30-334 60 min. $24.95

SKI: THE BEST OF THE WEST:

• Volume 1
Includes Aspen, Colorado; the Victorian Silver
Queen with four great ski areas; the Grand Teton
powder paradise of Jackson Hole, Wyoming; Park
City, Utah; Steamboat Springs, Colorado; and the
sunny slopes of "Baldy" in Sun Valley, Idaho.
30-2424 60 min. $39.95

• Volume 2
Includes Taos, New Mexico; quaint and colorful
Victorian Telluride, Colorado; glitzy Vail,
Colorado; the Canadian Rockies' Sunshine Village
and Lake Louise, Alberta; and the giant Canadian
Coast Mountains, Whistler, British Columbia.
30-2425 60 min. $39.95

Skier's Dream
Action footage of top skiers Nelson Carmichael ,
Jean Marc Rozan and Lloyd Langlois.
30-8197 75 min. $16.95

Skiing with Gordy Skoog: Downhill Skiing Basics
Before you "hit" the slopes, take advantage of some
helpful tips from an expert. Gordy Skoog starts
you out with advice on picking the best equipment
for your ability and budget. Gordy offers two
approaches to skiing: that of the aggressive skier
with average ability, or of the beginner who needs
more time to develop confidence. Learn various
techniques, from the snow-plow to parallel skiing,
at your own pace.
30-197 45 min. $24.95

Skiing Lessons with Gene Heinz Landsmann
Skiing expert Gene Heinz Landsmann guides the
beginning skier from the simple straight fun and
basic wedge turns through basic christie turns and
the early stages of parallel skiing.
30-195 60 min. $29.95

Snow Motion
Willie Bogner directs this collection of incredible
ski stunts.
30-8198 40 min. $16.95

Snowthrills
A must for the serious ski enthusiast. Snow Thrills
show-cases the top ranked ski and snowboard Hot
Doggers ever to slash and thrash their way down
the slopes! Thrill to the practitioners of the
winterland's wildest, new, high-flying sport -
Snowboarding, combining the skills of surfing,
skiing and skateboarding into one exciting package.
30-5446 60 min. $16.95

Snowonder
Top skiing spots from around the world. Includes
footage of the Swiss Alps, volcano skiing in
Mexico, helicopter skiing in Canada, snowcat
skiing in Oregon, and lots more.
30-260 98 min. $19.95

Steep and Deep
Breath-taking, action-packed ski adventure in the
high country of Canada, Asia, Europe, New
Zealand and U.S. featuring daredevil stunts by cliff
jumpers, helicopter skiers, ski bunnies and even
breakdancers on skis.
30-538 92 min. $19.95

Suzy Chaffee's Ski Workout
Helps you hit the slopes in peak condition! A
home-conditioning program that promotes strength,
balance and agility. Contemporary music and
inspiring ski footage included. The official
workout of the U.S. Recreational Ski Association.
30-639 60 min. $29.95

Sybervision: Black Diamond Skiing
Follow Jens Husted and Chris Ryman as they show
you a ski training system that can help you master
difficult skiing, from steep, smooth terrain to steep
mogul runs. Includes a training guide.
30-3070 60 min. $49.95

Sybervision: Skiing with Jean-Claude Killy
Three-time Olympic gold medalist Jean-Claude
Killy demonstrates all the fundamentals of downhill
skiing. Improve your skiing technique by
neuromuscular visual programming. Jens Husted
and Chris Ryman are also featured on this tape,
which is endorsed by the Professional Ski
Instructors of America.
30-198 60 min. $69.95

Sybervision: The Fundamentals of Downhill Skiing
Here, you'll learn the building blocks of ski
mastery from former U.S. Demonstration Team
instructors Jens Husted and Chris Ryman. Includes
a training guide.
30-3069 60 min. $49.95

Teach Your Child To Ski At Home
Eliminate all the negatives of teaching little children
how to ski with this wonderful new video. Watch
Emily demonstrate the basic ski maneuvers on the
slopes of Sugar Bowl and Alpine Meadows. See
Davey start out from the beginning lesson, learning
about his new equipment and follow him step by

step as the fundamentals of skiing are taught to him (and you). Then watch him go from the living room to the ski slopes for his first day of skiing. Davey is 3 1/2 years old.
30-5143 32 min. $29.95

Telemarking
Come experience the new adventure in skiing. Learn the turn that's revolutionizing the slopes! Telemarking is for the skier who's looking for a new challenge. Using the lighter gear for the downhill thrill of alpine skiing, skiers will discover an exciting new way to enjoy the slopes. Cross-country skiers will thrill to find new back country to explore. Instructor Steve Terry presents the telemark turn in easy-to-follow instructions with repeated demonstrations, so the viewer can visualize and practice the correct movements.
30-337 50 min. $39.95

Torvill & Dean
A fascinating documentary chronicling their rise to the top of the skating world.
13-473 52 min. $19.95

WARREN MILLER COLLECTION:

• Best of Warren Miller Comedy
Unfortunate skiers meet with skiing related disasters.
30-8185 55 min. $19.95

• Born to Ski
The excitement and danger of skiing, from Chile to Squaw Valley.
30-8171 92 min. $19.95

• Escape to Ski
Features helicopter skiing in Canada, France and the Atlas Mountains of Morroco.
30-8172 92 min. $19.95

• Extreme Skiing
A ski adventure through deep powder, cliff jumps, bumps and outrages stunts.
30-8173 46 min. $19.95

• Extreme Skiing III - The Scot Schmidt Story
The life story of the man who defied the term extreme skiing.
30-8174 60 min. $19.95

• Extreme Winter
An all skiing high-country tour across 6 countries and 4 continents.
30-8176 92 min. $19.95

• How the Super Skiers Ski
Focuses on the hottest skiers of all time, including Stein Erikson and Scott Schmidt.
30-8178 52 min. $19.95

• Skiing Bloopers
The King of Skiing comedy presents crashes, clutzes and calamities covering the gamut from beginners to Zudnick the dog.
30-8182 46 min. $19.95

• Ski Film Festival
Contains: Ballet of Competition, Skiing Movement & Motion, Seven Days in Paradise.
30-8180 70 min. $19.95

• Ski Time
Radical skiers demonstrate 100 foot drops, treacherous downhill speeds and glacier skiing in 1600 feet of snow.
30-8181 107 min. $19.95

• Snow Boarding - Tweaked and Twisted
Collection of snowboarding action featuring half-pipe competition, heli-boarding, slalom & super G racing and extreme boarding.
30-8183 46 min. $19.95

• Snowonder
Witness unbelievable volcano skiing in Mexico, snowcat skiing in Oregon, helicopter skiing in Canada, and more.
30-8184 98 min. $19.95

• To the Extreme
Take a journey to the most exotic and fascinating places on Earth.
30-8186 52 min. $19.95

• Truth About Skiing
Teaches the physical and mental skills needed to reach the level of expert skiing.
30-8187 60 min. $19.95

• Warren Miller's Ski Time
Come on an exciting ski adventure to the world's greatest mountains and experience incredible downhill racing and terrifying cliff jumping. Then ascend to the peaks by helicopter, bush planes, and sno-cat to witness the beauty of nature in winter.
30-201 60 min. $19.95

• White Magic
Features paragliding over the Austrian Alps, heli-skiing in the Caribous and more.
30-8188 91 min. $19.95

VIDEO TITLES LISTED IN THIS GUIDE ARE AVAILABLE FOR PURCHASE OR RENTAL. CONTACT YOUR LOCAL VIDEO STORE OR TELEPHONE (800) 383-8811

Miscellaneous

Amazing Sports Bloopers II
This tape is the sequel to ESPN's top selling video. It includes action from our most popular sports as well as Biff! Bam! Boom! insanity from auto racing and rodeo. Hosted by Jay Johnstone.
30-8099 30 min. $16.95

ATHLETIC CLINIC
The highly skilled professional athletic trainers of the National Basketball Trainers Association bring their knowledge and experience to this series of four videos that will help improve the health and performance of all athletes. Sponsored by Johnson & Johnson.

• Ankle Injuries
30-8018 20 min. $19.95

• Shoulder Injuries
30-8019 25 min. $19.95

• Foot Injuries
30-8020 20 min. $19.95

• Knee Injuries
30-8021 25 min. $19.95

Athletic Taping
Taping procedures for injury prevention and for providing support to injured muscles. Techniques can and should be used in any sport at any level of competition. This program is sponsored by Johnson & Johnson.
30-8033 40 min. $19.95

Bizarre Sports and Incredible Feats
30-1939 36 min. $16.95

Bob Uecker's Wacky World of Sports Tips
All you ever need to know about playing every sport to perfection. Only Bob Uecker, that crazy guy with the shy personality, can show you the way not to play every sport like the pros!
30-9857 30 min. $19.95

Bowl to Win
Called the greatest bowler in pro tour history, Earl Anthony takes you through the basics of good bowling. Learn to select, and use your own equipment. Anthony demonstrates how a beginner can throw a controlled hook, using a smooth delivery. Learn to recognize common errors and how to avoid them. Earl, a left-hander, bowls right-handed through the miracle of electronics on this video.
30-209 61 min. $24.95

Bowling with Marshall Holman and Johnny Petraglia - Sybervision
Perfect bowling form - for left-or right-handers - from pro bowlers Holman and Petraglia; instruction through perfect body positioning and balance, back swing, delivery, release and follow-through.
30-210 60 min. $69.95

Bowling: Going for 300
This video is a guide to raising your bowling score. Expert Earl Anthony shows how to handle difficult lane conditions. He analyzes wrist, arm, body and foot positions. Earl demonstrates the winning techniques that he developed to maintain a high average year after year.
30-235 60 min. $24.95

Bull's-Eye Archery
You can learn archery from the man who coached the '80 U.S. Olympic archery team, Dwight Nyquist. He shows and tells about various bows and arrows used in this fascinating sport. Learn the proper stance and how to load the bow. Nyquist explains arm action, string arm action, anchoring, aiming, release and follow-through. This program will be helpful to potential archers of all ages.
30-233 50 min. $24.95

BYRNE'S STANDARD VIDEO OF POOL AND BILLIARDS SERIES:

• Volume I
This video is a complete course in the game of pool, taught by acclaimed instructor Robert Byrne. The program covers all areas from the basics to game-winning techniques, and extensive computer-generated graphics make everything clear.
30-678 60 min. $29.95

• Volume II
For the more advanced and intermediate player. This course covers trick shots and other hard to do tricks.
30-8308 60 min. $29.95

SPORTS SEMINAR SERIES:

• College Dream: For Male Athletes
Will your male student athletes be ready when the college coach calls to begin the recruitment process? All too often, high school athletes think that their sports skills will guarantee them a college education. This program presents leading coaches,

---

VIDEO TITLES LISTED IN THIS GUIDE ARE AVAILABLE FOR PURCHASE OR RENTAL. CONTACT YOUR LOCAL VIDEO STORE OR TELEPHONE (800) 383-8811

admissions personnel, and former recruited student athletes who will guide you through this complex experience.
30-8269 25 min. $59.95

• Challenge: For Female Athletes
Female student athletes at the high school level are being recruited to play college athletics in record numbers. This program will feature leading women who are coaching women at the college level. In addition, admissions directors and former recruited student athletes will share information about financial aid, scholarships, campus visits and home visits along with recruiting guidelines.
30-8270 25 min. $59.95

Champions of Death Defying Sports
This explosive video catches the world's most outrageous thrillseekers on film in the wildest collection of death-defying heroics that you're ever going to see anywhere. An absolutely heart-stopping collection of sports--and the champions who dare to perform them!
30-8163 30 min. $16.95

Cheerleading Routines
Carol and Lance will guide you through the fundamental exercises and movements of cheerleading. Each technique will be demonstrated by the award-winning cheerleaders from Richardson High School in Dallas, Texas. Carol and Lance are both on the staff of the National Cheerleaders Association.
30-230 49 min. $19.95

Cheerleading Tryout Secrets
Here's your chance to learn from the National Cheerleaders Association. You will learn conditioning and flexibility exercises; beginning and advanced tryout routines; personal grooming tips; plus top-notch squads demonstrating cheerleading technique, style and enthusiasm.
30-1658 30 min. $19.95

CHEERLEADING SERIES:

• Partner Stunts
This video shows you step-by-step action of stunts and all levels of partner stunts including beginning, intermediate and advanced.
30-2829 70 min. $29.95

• Pyramids
This tape outlines the construction of a variety of pyramids for squads sized from 3 to 14. Shows pyramids being built from the front, side and back views.
30-2830 76 min. $29.95

• Basics
This informative tape teaches all the basic principles of cheerleading for girls and guys, including how to try out.
30-2828 46 min. $29.95

Conditioning the Young Athlete
This film introduces the coach to the "principles of training" and how to develop a training program that will effectively take the athlete from pre-season through the competitive season.
30-8293 20 min. $59.00

DO IT BETTER SERIES:

• Baseball
California Angles pitching coach Marcel Lacheman and Cleveland Indians field scout Vincent Cappelli join up to offer expert instruction on throwing mechanics and hitting techniques to help you play better baseball.
30-8221 35 min. $16.95

• Basketball
NBA Bigman's Camp Coach Peter Newell demonstrates the methods he uses to improve his NBA players' skills. He covers footwork, handling and shooting, along with the psychological aspects of the game.
30-8217 35 min. $16.95

• Beach Volleyball
Kathy Gregory shares her expertise to help you cross-over from indoor to two person beach play. Includes clips from professional tournaments and demonstrations from world class players.
30-8218 35 min. $16.95

• Running
Distance world record holders Ingrid Kristiansen and Steve Scott team up to share their training secrets to help you run better and further. This video includes advice on exercise selection for strength, mental training for marathoning and winter training.
30-8224 35 min. $16.95

• Soccer
Learn how to master the two soccer extremes--controlled touch and explosive power, and apply these principles to dribbling, passing, collecting and shooting. Hosted by John Boyle, and players Gregg Murphy, John Benbow and Peter Ferrel.
30-8223 35 min. $16.95

• Slow Pitch Softball
Three softball legends, Rob Whittleton, Rick Wheeler and Mike Cullura, demonstrate how you can improve your softball team by demonstrating

pitching, team positioning and practice techniques.
30-8219 35 min. $16.95

• **Women's Basketball**
Joan Bonvicini presents a comprehensive look at
the philosophies, strategies and skills that have
made L.B.S.U. a perennial powerhouse in NCAA
Women's Basketball.
30-8222 35 min. $16.95

• **Wrestling**
Freestyle wrestling is one of the greatest challenges
in the world of sports, requiring strength, balance
and stamina. In this video, Bob Douglas shares his
unique formula for wrestling success. Includes
actual match footage.
30-8220 35 min. $16.95

Drill Team Techniques
A chirographical approach to cheerleading,
including methods to building a program, steps and
exercises, and tips to take you through a good half-
time show.
30-482 60 min. $24.95

Duel at Diablo
Part One of exciting footage of the NSA Pro-Am
Skateboard Contest held at the Tempe Diablo
Stadium in Tempe, Arizona.
30-2530 60 min. $34.95

Freewheelin'
Coming at you with some of the hottest, most
incredible Bicycle MX Freestyle and skateboard
stunt action ever filmed. "Freewheelin" brings the
excitement and fascination of these two dynamic
street sports together as never before seen! Here's
your chance to get in on the newest gravity defying
skateboard and BMX freestyle moves on the
pavement!
30-5444 60 min. $14.95

Going for It!
Go with superstar athletes on some of the most
exciting sports adventures possible: surfing giant
waves, hot dog skiing, hang gliding in Yosemite,
rock climbing in the Grand Tetons. Push it to the
limit with these amazing adventurers.
30-234 90 min. $16.95

**GREATEST SPORTS LEGENDS
COLLECTOR SERIES:**
Relive the action of the sports world's all-time
greats in this award-winning series. Featuring live
interviews and original film highlights, these tapes
are sure to please the sports enthusiast.

• **Arnold Palmer-Golf**
30-355 30 min. $16.95

• **Bart Starr-Football**
30-339 30 min. $16.95

• **Bjorn Borg-Tennis**
30-346 30 min. $16.95

• **Bobby Hull-Hockey**
30-358 30 min. $16.95

• **Bobby Orr-Hockey**
30-338 30 min. $16.95

• **Bruno Sammartino-Wrestling**
30-360 30 min. $16.95

• **Gordie Howe-Hockey**
30-351 30 min. $16.95

• **Jesse Owens-Track & Field**
30-352 30 min. $16.95

• **Jimmy Connors-Tennis**
30-343 30 min. $16.95

• **Johnny Unitas-Football**
30-340 30 min. $16.95

• **Larry Holmes-Boxing**
30-342 30 min. $16.95

• **Mickey Mantle-Baseball**
30-357 30 min. $16.95

• **Pete Rose-Baseball**
30-353 30 min. $16.95

• **Phil Esposito-Hockey**
30-349 30 min. $16.95

• **Sam Snead-Golf**
30-361 30 min. $16.95

How to be a Great League Secretary
The secretary of a bowling league has a thankless,
tireless job that has to be done--and done right. A
secretary's job begins weeks before the first ball is
bowled and doesn't end until all the paper work is
completed. This is a step-by-step training guide on
all the ins and outs of being the league secretary
including helpful hints and tips from professionals.
30-8201 75 min. $29.95

Jane Fonda's SportsAid
"SportsAid" explains how to recognize sports
injuries, treat them at home and prevent them from
happening again. From the devoted runner to the
weekend tennis player, from the aerobic dancer to
the occasional walker, from parents to children,

VIDEO TITLES LISTED IN THIS GUIDE ARE AVAILABLE FOR PURCHASE
OR RENTAL. CONTACT YOUR LOCAL VIDEO STORE OR TELEPHONE (800) 383-8811

"SportsAid" is for anyone who leads an active life.
30-1702 90 min. $39.95

KAY CROWFORD PEP ARTS TRAINING - SERIES

• **Cheerleading**
30-6661 60 min. $59.95

• **Songleading**
30-6662 60 min. $59.95

• **Majorette And Baton Twirling**
30-6663 60 min. $59.95

• **Tall Flags**
30-6664 60 min. $59.95

• **Field Shows**
30-6665 60 min. $59.95

Let's Bowl with Dick Weber
Learn to bowl with a master of the sport who holds 28 PBA titles. Begins with the basics and goes on to demonstrate technique and explain the benefits of bowling.
30-2035 40 min. $16.95

Mental Athlete - Mental Training for Peak Athletic Performance
Mental conditioning is being used by athletes worldwide with stunning results. Judy Foster and leading sports psychologist Dr. Kay Porter discuss goal setting, positive self-affirmation, progressive relaxation, creative visualization and keeping a mental log as part of a step-by-step program. Designed in a concise and easily understood language to be applied to established training regiments.
30-8022 31 min. $39.95

Miracle Moments in Sports
A collector's edition of the great events and the great athletes of sports history. These are the immortal moments that have taken on a life of their own, enduring in the memories of millions of fans everywhere.
30-389 60 min. $19.95

Mud Fight Wrestling
This video contains an assortment of beautiful models wrestling in mud, boxing and also wrestling in an arena. The mud match will delight your senses as this tape features our Golden Girls in real competition. All these girls really slip and slide to sexy victory.
30-5449 72 min. $29.95

Not So Great Moments in Sports
Hosted by Tim McCarver, this is a collection of film footage and photos documenting athletic bloopers, bleeps and blunders.
30-1948 54 min. $16.95

NBC Sports Presents: AVP Pro Beach Volleyball
Pro Beach Volleyball, America's fastest growing sport, guarantees non-stop action on the hottest sand courts in the country. Watch as AVP beach volleyball stars including Sinjin Smith, Randy Stoklos, Kent Steffes and Tim Holland compete for the right to be crowned "King of the Beach".
30-8093 55 min. $19.95

NCAA SPORTS: INSTRUCTIONAL VOLLEYBALL

• **NCAA - Serving, Blocking and Individual Defense**
30-9333 30 min. $34.95

• **NCAA - Passing, Setting and Spiking**
30-9334 30 min. $34.95

Oil Wrestling
This video contains an assortment of beautiful ladies wrestling and boxing in oil! Wrestling in hot oil has been a craze in recent years in the U.S.A. The oil makes the swim suits cling like cellophane to the bodies of our magnificent maulers. All these girls really slip and slide to sexy victories.
30-5448 72 min. $29.95

On the Edge
Athletes from around the world participate in the most dangerous sporting events on Earth.
30-8179 47 min. $19.95

Prevention and Treatment of sport Injuries
This film examines the roles of the coach in the prevention of injuries, basic first aid for common athletic injuries and guidelines for proper rehabilitation of injuries.
30-8294 23 min. $59.00

PRO'S GUIDE TO BETTER BOWLING
Don Johnson was one of the greatest bowlers in the history of the game. This fantastic bowler is now a world-famous bowling instructor who has put many of his secrets to being a better bowler in this program.

• **Volume I**
30-8131 57 min. $19.95

VIDEO TITLES LISTED IN THIS GUIDE ARE AVAILABLE FOR PURCHASE OR RENTAL. CONTACT YOUR LOCAL VIDEO STORE OR TELEPHONE (800) 383-8811

• Volume II
30-8132 57 min. $19.95

Roller Derby Mania
Catch Roller Derby Mania - the all-star action and thrills of hard-hitting sports entertainment. The best of today's wall-to-wall skating excitement as the gals battle it out and the guys stomp each other from Los Angeles to Madison Square Garden. Excerpts from the good old days included.
30-367 58 min. $24.95

Rowing Machine Companion
Hosted by former Olympic rower Stephen Kiesling, this program allows the viewer to sit in the front seat of a four-man racing shell and row down Boston's Charles River.
30-1855 34 min. $14.95

Skateboarding
Joe Lopes, John Lucero and Monty Nolder star in a day of training and competition with the Schmidt Stix skate team, along with a demonstration by top pro Hans Lindgrien.
30-1984 30 min. $19.95

Slippery When Wet
The slickest Hot Bods in Ladies Professional Oil Wrestling compete in this exciting, exotic, single elimination tournament. It's not just another swimsuit show!
30-8283 95 min. $29.95

Slow Pitch Softball Reflex Hitting Techniques
600-plus hitter Ray DiMarini's reflex hitting system will help you become a better, more consistent hitter regardless of your size and power. Ray explains stance, swing, batspeed, timing, pitch selection, and attitude. This tape is a "must" for even casual softball players!
30-5493 60 min. $19.95

Sports Colossus - Heros of the 20's, 30's and 40's
This exceptionally entertaining two hours of sports nostalgia from the famed Grantland Rice collection highlights the epic-making performances of yesteryear. Through these clips of a matchless galaxy of world champions, The Golden Age can be enjoyed and preserved forever. Narrated by Bob Mathias.
30-8125 109 min. $24.95

SPORTS ILLUSTRATED: GET THE FEELING
This series from Sports illustrated puts you in the action, giving you the feeling of speed, of untamed power and the ecstasy of triumph and the agony of defeat.

• Power
30-3078 50 min. $16.95

• Speed
30-3079 69 min. $16.95

• Winning
30-3077 60 min. $16.95

SPORTS PAGES SERIES:

• Killer Hockey
Hockey is fast paced and its action non-stop. And now, all of the violent sides of the game are gathered into one unforgettable video--meant to be watched again and again!
30-8146 30 min. $16.95

• Killer Rodeo
Rodeo action has never been like this. The bucking broncos! The raging bulls! The elusive calves! The stubborn steers! Killer Rodeo is cowboys crashing to earth from a hostile horse. It's bulls tossing their riders like ragdolls--and then stomping them. It's just plain pain on the range!
30-8144 30 min. $16.95

• Kooky Smashes & Crashes
You won't believe just how many kooky smashes and crashes you'll see. This is fun for the entire family--a tape you'll watch again and again!
30-8142 30 min. $16.95

• Rodeo Funnies
Every rodeo fan will want to add Rodeo Funnies to their collection of home videos--it's a must see even for tenderfoots.
30-8139 30 min. $16.95

• Sports Funnies
It is simple…bloopers happen! And in this program you will see the weirdest collection of the goofy, the crazy and the unusual. Basketball players bumble, football players fumble, skiers land face first, gymnasts miss the beam, cowboys on bulls get creamed! It's all about great athletes having a bad day.
30-8141 30 min. $16.95

Streetstyle in Tempe
Part two of the exciting highlights of the NSA Pro-Am Skateboard Contest held at Tempe Diablo Stadium in Tempe, Arizona.
30-2531 60 min. $29.95

Strikes, Spares, And Strategy With Lou Scalia
This video is a series of outstanding bowling tips and guides that Lou Scalia compiled from his

Television series "The 10th Frame." Lou's insight and understanding of the necessary tips and techniques is conveyed in this easy to follow instruction video. Topics range from strikes, spares, strategies on gaining more lift, releases for changing surfaces, urethane balls and much more.
30-6555 30 min. $19.95

Super Bowling with Earl Anthony
Prepare at home and get your game coached before taking it to the alley, and build up your strike force with bowling champion Earl Anthony.
30-2516 30 min. $16.95

Sybervision Bowling with Marshall Holman and Johnny Petraglia
Viewing this video will do as much for your average as several hours of perfect practice. This set includes one video cassette, four audiocassettes and a training guide.
30-3071 60 min. $69.95

Teaching Kids Bowling With Gordon Vadakin
Champion bowler and youth coach Gordon Vadakin shows you how to teach your kids the right techniques and proper attitudes that will help them bowl better and have more fun. Features Olympic bowler Mark Lewis.
30-5513 75 min. $29.95

Teaching Kids Speed
Regardless of size or ability, all kids can get faster, and you can help. Improving speed is a function oftechnique and movement efficiency. Now you can apply the very same methods used by world class sprinter Carl Lewis.
30-8123 51 min. $19.95

Triathalon: Training and Competing
A program for total physical and mental fitness featuring top triathalon athletes including: Scott Molina and Julie Leach covering swimming, Scott Tinley and Kathleen McCartney covering cycling, and Dale Basescu and Julie Moss covering running. In addition, there is a 20-minute segment called "Ironman", which is an award-winning documentary of the February 1982 mariathlon. It is hosted and narrated by Bruce Dern.
30-374 60 min. $39.95

Winning Trap: Sports And Our Kids
Featuring Peggy Fleming, Olympic and World Champion Figure Skater, Bob Chandler, NFL App-Pro/Super Bowl Champion Oakland Raiders. In a thoughtful, sensitive program, Peggy and Bob examine the roles of parents and coach and the damaging consequences of the "win at all costs" attitude can have on our children.
30-8108 37 min. $59.95

Wrecks of the Caribbean
Dive some of Caribbean's better known dive wrecks, including some recent wrecks. See the Lockheed Constellation that landed intact in 40 feet of water.
30-8245 30 min. $19.95

Develop Your Drive...

Build Your Backstroke...

Or Just Relish the Opportunity

To Watch Others

Sail, Swim & Ski

VIDEO TITLES LISTED IN THIS GUIDE ARE AVAILABLE FOR PURCHASE OR RENTAL. CONTACT YOUR LOCAL VIDEO STORE OR TELEPHONE (800) 383-8811

New

Special Interest Video Titles

Become Available

Often.

Please Inquire

If A Title Or Subject

You Are Looking For

Is Not Listed.

VIDEO TITLES LISTED IN THIS GUIDE ARE AVAILABLE FOR PURCHASE
OR RENTAL. CONTACT YOUR LOCAL VIDEO STORE OR TELEPHONE (800) 383-8811

Trains

- ✓ *Steam*
- ✓ *Model Railroading*
- ✓ *Miscellaneous*

Rail

Along the Hudson Division
Possibly the most beautiful commuter ride in the U.S. is Amtrak's Hudson Division running north from New York City's Penn Station to Albany along the course of the Hudson River. The scenery is beautiful, with charming vistas, vintage railway stations and plenty of lineside action.
02-8065 60 min. $39.95

Berkshire: Best of a Breed
Takes a look at the Fort Wayne Railroad, Historical Society's 2-8-4- on runs east out of Fort Wayne, Indiana to Cleveland, Ohio.
02-2281 45 min. $24.95

Berkshire's Montage Series: Volume 1
This starts with coverage of the Kentucky Railway Museum's Ex-L & N, Light Pacific and ends with a final story about a new home for an old friend-Steamtown, USA, now in Scraton, PA.
02-2279 58 min. $49.95

Berkshire's Montage Series: Volume 2
Starts with coverage of the Blue Mountain and Reading Railroad's first annual railfan weekend, then ends with a story about 765's remarkable comeback in 1986.
02-2280 58 min. $49.95

Colorado's Narrow Gauge Railroads
Relive the 1800s with trips aboard four famous narrow gauge lines still in operation, and learn about railroading's colorful past.
02-2514 55 min. $29.95

Forty Feet Below: The Video
Here is the fascinating tour of the Chicago underground freight tunnels back when tiny electric locomotives pulled trains of short, heavy cars through a maze of sharp curves and endless tunnels to service the needs of the busy metropolis above. Then fast forward to 1992 when the tunnels flooded the basements of Chicago's Loop. You'll see repair crews at work and listen to experts talk about the history and problems of this forgotten labyrinth.
02-8064 25 min. $16.95

Flying Scotman
This tape features one of the worlds greatest steam locomotives during its never to be repeated visit to Australia. It shows the locomotive in the U.S.A. and England as well as footage of it being loaded and unloaded for its visit to Australia. This tape is certain to become a collectors item.
02-6452 55 min. $16.95

Little Engines that Could
This fascinating program is about the oldest narrow gauge rail-road in the U.S., the East Broad Top Railroad. You'll learn the history of the line, and relive those days through still photographs and rare vintage 16mm Film. You'll see the "truck swap" from standard to narrow gauge trucks, double-headers in the snow, and a triple-header on a special run.
02-085 52 min. $39.95

Majestic Mikado
Built by the Baldwin Locomotive Works in 1911, the "Majestic Mikado" joined the mighty Southern fleet and ran the rails for 37 years. You'll see a "fun run" of this old locomotive, on an excursion called the "Dixie Limited". Leaving Richmond, Virginia, you'll hear her sprinting for Keysville where you'll disembark and join the "Dixie Days Festival" which features jazz bands, home cooking, and handmade arts and crafts. Then it's back to Richmond. A fine tribute to a great locomotive.
02-087 40 min. $39.95

Mighty J
This video provides an in-depth look at Norfolk & Western's big 4-8-4, Class J. Number 661 runs east out of Bellevue, Ohio to Buffalo, New York, and south out of Bellevue to Columbus, Ohio. We'll take you trackside over 30 different times.
13-443 30 min. $19.95

Pacific Princess
Finally, after 13 years of hard work and dedication by the Kentucky Railway Museum, ex-L&N 4-6-2, No. 152 is back in service. Built in 1905 by ALCO's Rogers Works in Paterson, New Jersey, No. 152 is the oldest active 4-6-2 operating in the U.S. today. After a brief recap of its history, you'll see some of the other Kentucky Railway Museum equipment.
13-442 45 min. $39.95

San Diego Model Museum
The largest indoor model railroad museum in the U.S. is located in Balboa Park, in San Diego, California. Four permanent displays include O-scale, N-Scale, and two HO-Scale layouts. Pentrex captures the realistic detail of these painstakingly-crafted and smooth-running model railroads, complete with music, narration, and dubbed-in appropriate railroad sound effects.
02-8068 30 min. $19.95

Santa Fe 3751: Return to Steam
The long-awaited return to steam power to Santa Fe rails took place in December, 1991, after 10 years

of restoration effort. The 4-8-4 Northern type steam locomotive performed flawlessly on its maiden run from Los Angles, over Cajun Pass to Barstow, then around Tehachapi Loop to Bakersfield and return. This program shows the restoration story and covers this historic trip in its entirety.
02-8066 60 min. $29.95

Steam Alive
Steam locomotives puffing their way into country towns were the life blood of the countryside, bringing in supplies and visitors and taking away produce and goods. Today the steam locomotives have been replaced. Many were left to rust and decay, but a number of them have been restored by dedicated groups of volunteers, determined to preserve this exciting part of our heritage. Steam trains are alive again in this magnificent video. This tape is a tribute to those groups who have kept the locomotives on the tracks to give pleasure to those who love steam travel. You can enjoy the thrill of the journey, the heat of the firebox, the shrill of the whistle as you watch "Steam Alive."
02-6451 55 min. $16.95

Steam Still Stands
Located in the quiet Amish farmlands of Lancaster County in Pennsylvania are two fine examples of our American railroad heritage-the Railroad Museum of Pennsylvania and the Strasburg Railroad. In this tape you will visit both, learning some of the background of steam locomotion. Then you'll see locomotives under steam pulling train loads of passengers through the scenic Lancaster countryside.
02-086 52 min. $39.95

Trolley - The Cars That Built Our Cities
Meticulously researched over four years, this lyrical documentary, seen on the Arts & Entertainment network, presents a comprehensive collection of trolleys, seen in motion picture footage dating from the 1890's to the 1990's.
02-8064 60 min. $19.95

Trolley Treasure
This is a program about Trolleyville-U.S.A. in Olmsted Falls, Ohio. Trolleyville is an active, operating museum depicting the era of the streetcar and inter-urban. This show will tell you how Trolleyville was founded, and how a handful of dedicated people have kept this part of our heritage alive. You'll see many rare old photographs from the Trolleyville collection as well as observe the operations of the line today.
02-088 41 min. $29.95

Union Pacific's Clinchfield Challenge
In November, 1992, Union Pacific Challenger steam locomotive #3985 made its first-ever trip into the Appalachian Mountains to head the 50th running of the Clinchfield Santa Claus Special. This special train, operated by former Clinchfield Railroad and successor CSX, pulls Santa Claus and his helpers as they toss candy and gifts to the children of the coal-mining towns that line the route. The 3985 underwent a name and number change for the event to become "Clinchfield 676".
02-8069 120 min. $29.95

A Video Adventure By Train…

The Perfect Gift for a

Railroad Buff

VIDEO TITLES LISTED IN THIS GUIDE ARE AVAILABLE FOR PURCHASE OR RENTAL. CONTACT YOUR LOCAL VIDEO STORE OR TELEPHONE (800) 383-8811

Searching For

A Unique Gift That is

Informative and Appreciated?

The Video Titles

In This Guide

Make Wonderful Gifts.

VIDEO TITLES LISTED IN THIS GUIDE ARE AVAILABLE FOR PURCHASE
OR RENTAL. CONTACT YOUR LOCAL VIDEO STORE OR TELEPHONE (800) 383-8811

Travel
&
Adventure

✓ *Africa & Middle East*
✓ *Alaska*
✓ *Asia & South Pacific*
✓ *California*
✓ *Caribbean*
✓ *Cruises*
✓ *Europe & British Isles*
✓ *Hawaii*
✓ *Mexico, Central & South America*
✓ *Other United States & Canada*
✓ *Wilderness Vacations*
✓ *Miscellaneous*

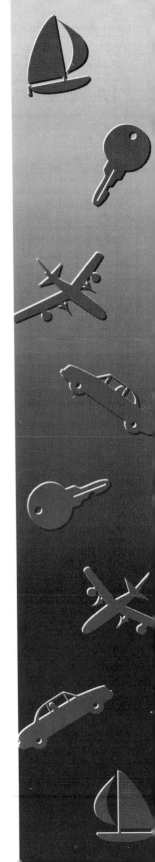

Africa & Middle East

Cairo/Luxor
Walk in the Land of Pharaohs through the ruins of a 5,000-year old civilization. Travel by camel caravan to the Great Sphinx and Pyramids of Giza. We also take you on an overnight train to Luxor to see the Temple of Karnak. Sail like Antony and Cleopatra along the historic Nile and visit the Valley of Kings. Also included is a reference guide to resorts and hotels plus travel tips by Berlitz travel guides.
32-041 60 min. $29.95

Christmas in Bethlehem
Beautiful one-hour program capturing the beauty and majesty of the annual Christmas Mass in the Church of the Nativity of Bethlehem.
27-146 58 min. $19.95

Egyptian Adventure: Tour of Ancient & Modern Egypt
Sample the ancient mysteries, exotic beauty, music, art and people of modern and ancient Egypt. A horseback ride among the pyramids of Giza. Visit Cairo, Alexandria, the Sinai Peninsula and Mt. Sinai. Bargain in bazaars, cruise the River Nile through upper Egypt and explore ancient temples. All music recorded in Egypt.
32-8001 20 min. $24.95

GIANT NILE SERIES:
Traveling through five countries in three engrossing one hour documentaries, The Giant Nile winds from the most isolated regions of Africa to the splendors of the pharaohs, in the journey of a lifetime.

• Volume I: Wild River
32-8234 60 min. $19.95

• Volume II: White Nile, Blue Nile
32-8235 60 min. $19.95

• Volume III: Egyptian Journey
32-8236 60 min. $19.95

His Land
A musical journey into the soul of a nation. This award-winning film is a compelling and colorful musical tour of Israel, filled with the sights, sounds and history of this vibrant land.
22-254 67 min. $29.95

Holy Land: 5,000 Years, an Incredible Journey
A magnificent tour of the Holy Land which presents every major Holy Land site, from the biblical era to present-day Israel. Filmed by an award-winning production team, viewers are offered a unique historical perspective of biblical geography. Including over 42 sites, this outstanding production captures the signs and sounds of the lands of the Bible.
32-088 60 min. $29.95

India
Tour India, visit the holy city of Varanasi, where pilgrims bathe in the healing waters of the River Ganges. Travel to Agra and visit, the famed Taj Mahal and much more!
32-5031 55 min. $24.95

Israel - The Holy Land
Relive the history of the Holy Land in this colorful Video Visits production depicting the beauty and contrasts of God's promised land.
32-1743 60 min. $24.95

Israel - This Land Is Yours!
Explore Israel as it is today, as well as its fascinating people and historic sites, dating back thousands of years. This is a land holy to Muslim, Christian and Jew. Visit Masadea, Nazareth, Galilee, Jerusalem and more.
32-164 28 min. $29.95

Jerusalem: Of Heaven and Earth
An eight-part series that draws you into Jerusalem's past and present, peeling away the many layers of a city that still represents the conflicts of humanity. Learn the forces that separate, yet strangely bind the people of Jerusalem.
27-101 200 min. $59.95

Jerusalem - Within These Walls
Jerusalem's Old City is a tiny, historic enclave. It is the fountainhead of three major religions and home to thousands of people of profoundly different cultures living side by side in a fragile peace. Here is a view of a city within a city.
32-1894 59 min. $24.95

Kenya Safari - Essence of Africa
Join Video Visits as they traverse the jungles of Kenya in search of the essence of Africa, encountering its indigenous people and wildlife in this remarkable journey.
32-1736 45 min. $24.95

Laura McKenzie's Travel Tips: Egypt and the Nile River
Enjoy the fascination and the mystery of ancient Egypt. Laura McKenzie takes you to Cairo,

Sakkara, Alexandria, and Luxor, the modern cities of this historic land. Cruise on the Nile River, experience the Great Pyramids and Sphinx in Giza. Tour the Valley of the Kings and the tomb of King Tut, and visit the Aswan Dam. She also gives you tips on what clothes to wear, where the best outdoor cafes are located, and what sights to see in the cities you visit.

32-177 56 min. $24.95

Laura McKenzie's Travel Tips: Morocco

Enjoy the fabulous and exotic mix of cultures that make this area so rich in historical landmarks, architecture, and people. Learn how to get around in a city like Casablanca, and what sights to see. Visit Rabat, Fes, Tangiers and bargain at the Marrekesh markets. Discover the interesting sights in the countryside, and take day trips to Taroudannt and Agadir.

32-182 56 min. $24.95

Passport Travel Guide - Egypt And Morocco

Morocco's magical kingdom is bordered by the warm Atlantic and the crystal clear Mediterranean, with wonderful cuisine, fine handicrafts at bargain prices and belly dancing. This is the home of exotic cities - Marrakesh, Casablanca, Tangier. However, the true beauty of Morocco lies in the many faces of it's people and their wonderful hospitality. Take advantage of this chance to travel to Egypt, 1,000 miles up the Nile and back 5,000 years in history to visit the ancient temples at Luxor and Abu Simbel and the fascinating excavations along the river banks.

32-6430 35 min. $16.95

This is Israel

Explore this land of contrasts, mystery and beauty. Relive your visit to the home of three world religions or use the film for an educational adventure through the land of the Bible. Experience the historical majesty of Israel as you travel to such sites as Bethlehem, David's Tomb, the Wailing Wall and Solomon's Pools.

27-145 53 min. $29.95

Zambian Safari

See the enchanting beauty of Zambia and the warm smiles of its people. Filmed mostly in South Luangwa and Kafue National parks, you will participate in wildlife safaris by open vehicle, foot, canoe, and boat and will visit several lodges and bush camps. This is your chance to visit Lusaka, Livingstone and Victoria Falls. See cultural dancing, crafts, and a "sundowner cruise" on the Zambezi River.

32-8002 40 min. $24.95

Alaska

Alaska

Discover the rugged, untouched beauty of Alaska's magnificent natural wonders with Laura McKenzie as your guide. Be prepared to "rough it" when you step ashore to pan for gold or explore the face of a glacier. Every breath of crisp, pure air will remind you that you're at the edge of civilization!

32-1515 60 min. $24.95

Alaska - A Portrait Of The Last Frontier

This program introduces you to every corner of this enormous state, region by region. On each stop along the way, you'll experience many of the unique characteristics of the land, the wildlife, the cities and the history of the Last Frontier.

32-6592 60 min. $29.95

Alaska Outdoors

Experience the great outdoors of beautiful, rugged Alaska, America's last wilderness. Discover the lore and legends that make this romantic state "The Great Land".

32-221 50 min. $19.95

Alaska Experience with Video Visits

Journey across this great land and marvel at the diversity of its people, its wildlife and its unmatched scenic beauty.

32-1748 50 min. $24.95

Cruising Alaska's Inside Passage

Follow Alaska's marine highway along the course of a tour that highlights history, geography, geology and wildlife. Slip between islands to see Indians carve totem poles, cruise through Misty Fiords, drive to Mendenhall Glacier fly over Juneau Icefield and more.

32-8093 60 min. $29.95

Denali National Park, Alaska

Join Video Visits in a powerful display of nature's never ending life cycle on the slopes of majestic Mt. McKinley.

32-1752 45 min. $24.95

Explore America's Last Frontier: Alaska

This video highlights the rich history of the people of Alaska. From the ancient Siberians, to the Russian colonists in 1763 and finally the tragic journey of American gold-seekers to the Klondike.

32-8281 60 min. $29.95

VIDEO TITLES LISTED IN THIS GUIDE ARE AVAILABLE FOR PURCHASE OR RENTAL. CONTACT YOUR LOCAL VIDEO STORE OR TELEPHONE (800) 383-8811

National Geographic: Yukon Passage
Narrator Jimmy Stewart takes viewers on a wild Yukon adventure through the frozen reaches of Canada and Alaska. Journey back in time with four courageous young men who brave the roaring rapids of the Yukon River and biting cold of the Arctic Circle in their quest for adventure.
32-251 60 min. $24.95

Passport Travel Guide - Alaska
Our 50th state is more than ice, snow, igloos and eskimos. Let's go North to Alaska.
32-6443 30 min. $16.95

Round About Anchorage
Join Video Visits and Capture the awe-inspiring beauty of this city and its natural surroundings while you enjoy numerous outdoor activities.
32-1750 30 min. $24.95

See Alaska
See Alaska is a treat for your senses; an experience that will open eyes and fill your ears with the wonders of Alaska. Eskimo cultures, massive mountain ranges, jagged glaciers, adventuring in the bold outdoors, and wildlife are just a few of the sights that will come alive in your living room.
32-6593 30 min. $29.95

Touring Alaska
Filmed over the course of three years, this film captures the uniqueness of the country from the wilderness of the great parks to the life of the people in the cities and countryside. You'll cruise up the Inland Passage, explore Glacier Bay's fjords and glaciers, ride the Alaska railroad and discover many more of the wonders of Alaska.
32-262 30 min. $29.95

Video Trip Guide to Alaska
Discover America's last frontier in all its unspoiled splendor with host Lorne Greene.
32-2275 60 min. $19.95

Voices from the Ice, Alaska
A breathtaking journey into the rugged Chugach National Forest and Portage Glacier area in South central Alaska allows you to explore the ice-carved landscape and its plant and animal communities. This is a land still dominated by active glaciers where you will hear the roar of crashing ice and see the exquisite beauty of a timeless, yet constantly changing land.
32-288 20 min. $29.95

Wild Alaska
Dale Johnson, whose credits include films for National Geographic, BBC and Nova takes you to the Alaska wilderness to view its wildlife. A heartwarming look at their life and death struggle

for survival.
32-2430 60 min. $29.95

Asia & South Pacific

Bali: A Window on Paradise
Journey to the exotic island of Bali, a mystical melding of religion, art and music. Visit the temple at Lake Bratan, Tour Ubud, the country's cultural center where painting, poetry and dance flourish. Stroll through Mas, explore the port town of Singaraja. Enjoy the beaches of Sanur, where world class resorts abound.
32-8029 53 min. $24.95

Bali: Life in the Balance, a Personal Journey with Rick Ray
Go deep into the heart of Indonesia with Rick Ray and his family as they explore the island of Bali. Ray and his family live in a native village where they discover a world where life is expressive with festivals, ceremonies, artists and craftsmen. Bali's Hindu-influenced way of life is explored in depth.
32-9697 79 min. $29.95

Bangkok by Fodor's
Begin your visit to Bangkok with William Warren, author of Thai Style to view the ornate architecture of the Grand Palace which houses the most revered object in the Thai kingdom, the Emerald Buddha, and much more.
32-6062 45 min. $29.95

Beyond the Great Wall
Journey into Old China with newsman Bob Jones, into a world of snake-eaters and dragon dancers, a world far away from modern times.
32-002 60 min. $49.95

China
From the grasslands of Inner Mongolia to the center of government at Beijing and the cosmopolitan savvy of Canton, this immense country emerges from centuries of mystery. Meet China's people - the energetic young, the revered old and the minority inhabitants who lend their own enchantment. Discover China's Great Wall and Yangtze River. Learn how today's China lives, eats, travels, works and plays.
32-309 30 min. $24.95

China and the Forbidden City
A very special look at the mystery, opulence, and grandeur of one of mankind's greatest treasure; a city, Peking, and a civilization that has survived

and endured. Winner of the Peabody and Christopher Awards.

32-1873 60 min. $24.95

China: World of Difference (Video Visits)

This is a fascinating view of The Peoples Republic of China with an in-depth look at the people and places of this country so unknown to most tourists. Visit the circus and take part in a dance recital to gain even more insight into this vast country. Take a journey to the Great Wall and visit small villages to see people in their everyday activities. An excellent introduction to China for most viewers.

32-215 50 min. $24.95

Fiji

Included in this tour of the quiet south Pacific paradise are water sports, rivers and the friendly people of the Fiji islands. Also included is a tour of the best hotels.

32-375 30 min. $14.95

Great Barrier Reef

"Here is footage of extraordinary beauty that makes great viewing for science lovers and offers a timely message for anyone concerned with ecology - the Great Barrier Reef, most magnificent of the world's barrier reefs..." is fittingly presented by Prince Phillip, the Duke of Edinburgh, assembled with affection and painstakingly edited.

32-010 120 min. $69.95

HONG KONG

Embark on the fabulous Oriental adventure of your dreams with Laura McKenzie as your guide. Visit the thrilling international duty-free port of Hong Kong, where East meets West, renowned as a shopper's paradise and gourmet's delight. This tour includes Kowloon, Wanchai, Causeway Bay, Aberdeen, Repulse Bay and Victoria Peak.

32-1517 60 min. $24.95

Impressions of Hong Kong

Join Video Visits and experience the essence of Hong Kong, an intricate mosaic of ancient Oriental culture and the most modern Western influences.

32-1737 24 min. $24.95

JAPAN WITH JANE SEYMOUR

Join Jane Seymour as she examines how Japan's ancient traditions have blended with new technology and modern trends to shape the society and its people today in this four-volume beautiful documentary series.

• Electronic Tribe

Focuses on the contrasts between the present day life of factory workers and the inherited religious and rural customs still found in the ordinary home.

• Legacy of Shogun

Looks at the continuing effect of the 17th century Shogun philosophy of hard work, discipline and hierarchy. It also explores the law-abiding nature of contemporary Japan where Tokyo has one of the lowest crime rates in the world.

• Proper Place in the World

Looks at Japan's intervention on the world's stage during the 20th century and its likely future as a world economic superpower.

• Sword and the Chrysanthemum

Takes a close look at what the West sees as a paradox in Japanese society as represented by Samurai warrior, who combined an appreciation of beauty and high culture with fighting aggression.

• Four Volume Boxed Set

32-8134 240 min. $79.95

Japan - Island Empire

Join Video Visits in Japan where bullet trains streak into the past. Enter a Zen temple, then witness an ancient ritual in a Shinto shrine. Travel south to the resort of Ibusuki, you'll marvel at the guests buried to the neck in steaming volcanic sand. Admire the Great Buddha of Kamakure, the architecture of 400 year old Himeji Castle and more.

32-8231 50 min. $24.95

Mystical Malaysia-Land of Harmony

Your "Video Visit" to exotic Malaysia begins in the capital Kuala Lumpur. Peer inside the Batuk Caves, where Hindu shrines are tucked away in the limestone recesses. Travel to the trading port of Malacca with it's Dutch Architecture. Journey to Sarawak and ride a native longboat deep into the Borneo jungle to encounter some former headhunters. Continue on to Sabah and Mt. Kinabalu.

32-8168 45 min. $24.95

Singapore

Travel to exotic Singapore, the ancient trading port poised on the top of the Malay peninsula that has become a 21st century commercial center. Stroll across the Padang to admire Parliament House and the Singapore Cricket Club.

32-5033 30 min. $24.95

Singapore by Fodor's

Explore the bustling island of Singapore, a sightseeing, shopping and dining hub of cultural diversity. Host Mike Gorrie describes Singapore's evolution from an ancient island culture to the international port it is today.

32-6064 45 min. $29.95

VIDEO TITLES LISTED IN THIS GUIDE ARE AVAILABLE FOR PURCHASE OR RENTAL. CONTACT YOUR LOCAL VIDEO STORE OR TELEPHONE (800) 383-8811

South China Seas: Singapore and Borneo with Rick Ray

With a blend of humor and insight, Rick Ray unveils the multicultural city-state of Singapore and the vast, uncharted island of Borneo. Modern Singapore, Lee Kuan Yew's legacy, is seen as a rigidly disciplined world of high rise apartments and clean, safe parks and streets, yet mystical rituals still take place in the shadow of skyscrapers.
32-9695 85 min. $29.95

Taiwan - Exotic Blossom

Land of jade temples and cities of marble. Join Video Visits and roam the beaches and listen to the stories of its charming people. Experience one of the oldest and most refined cultures on this modern and beautiful island.
32-1751 50 min. $24.95

Thailand-The Golden Kingdom

Marvel at the architectural splendor of the Grand Palace and tour Bangkok's labyrinth of narrow streets and winding canals. Visit Wat Po where the colossal reclining Buddha resides. Witness the art of silk weaving, visit an orchid farm and watch artisans paint colorful parasols. Bask on the sun-drenched beaches of Koh Samui, Phuket and Koh Phi Phi. A Video Visits presentation.
32-8030 56 min. $24.95

California

Cabrillo National Monument

First Europeans discover California: Cabrillo's historic voyage and landing at Point Loma, 1542; human, natural history; the settlement of San Diego, from mission to urban city.
32-8266 75 min. $29.95

Discover California

Discover this state of unsurpassed beauty, of dynamic cities and cultural wealth. From the fabulous coastline to the towering Sierra; from the sun-drenched cities and deserts, to the inspiring scenery of Yosemite, Sequoia, Kings Canyon and the Redwoods - you will discover California as never before. Includes almost every major tourist and scenic attraction.
32-159 60 min. $29.95

Golden Gate Bridge

This unique video presents an historical overview using rarely seen photographs and film of the Bridge's original construction which took place from 1933 to 1937. You will see how the Bridge,

which is a major highway, has to be greased like a car. Also featured is the 1987 50th Anniversary celebration.
32-8179 28 min. $19.95

Knott's Berry Farm, California

Knott's Berry Farm and Ghost Town in Buena Park are where the Old West meets the 20th century, head on! Ride a steam locomotive, stage coach or a thrill ride like the Corkscrew. Enjoy the romping fun of Camp Snoopy or watch a western stunt show. Great family fun.
32-286 40 min. $29.95

Lake Tahoe's Video Postcard

This program contains facts, history and breathtaking aerials of Lake Tahoe. Features Gatekeeper's Museum, the Truckee River, Meeks Bay, Horsetail Falls, Emerald Bay, Vikingsholm, Teahouse on the island and more. You'll see information on beaches, hiking, bicycling and skiing.
32-2172 27 min. $24.95

Los Angeles/Laura Mckenzie

The Los Angeles area is so large that having some good advice before you go really helps make the most of your time there. Laura McKenzie answers questions like how long will it take to tour Disneyland, how to get around Los Angeles, what interesting places should be seen and visited. You'll see Hollywood, Beverly Hills, Malibu, Santa Monica, San Diego and Palm Springs. She'll take you to the beaches, amusement parks, star/celebrity homes, shopping areas, night clubs, cultural centers and much more
32-181 56 min. $24.95

Los Angeles

Welcome to one of the most talked about places in the world! Discover L.A. earliest beginnings at Mission San Gabriel and the busy marketplace on Olvera Street. Experience the renaissance of downtown L.A.'s at the Music Center and Museum of Contemporary Art. See the Rose Bowl and Pasadena's Huntington Gardens. Have fun at famous amusement parks and Griffith Park, then hello to Hollywood and all its glitter! Tour Universal and NBC Studios. Stroll down the Walk of Fame and stop by the trendy boutiques on Melrose Avenue. Revel in the opulence of Beverly Hills' mansions and Rodeo Drive shops before heading west to Howard Hughes' Spruce Goose, the Queen Mary and the sunswept beaches of Malibu and Venice.
32-5144 55 min. $24.95

Monterey Peninsula and Carmel-by-the-Sea

See the Monterey Bay Aquarium with its one-of-a-kind showing of bay sealife and multi-storied display tanks. Visit historic Monterey, Mission Carmel, the Customs House, Cannery Row and old Fisherman's Wharf. Marvel at the awe-inspiring beauty of the Pacific Coast, Big Sur and Pebble Beach's 17-mile Drive.

32-111 40 min. $24.95

Pebble Beach Then and Now

Capture the sparkling beauty of Pebble Beach and the Del Monte Forest - dedicated to recreation and gracious living on California's Monterey Peninsula. This video features world-famous golf courses, the 17-Mile Drive and much more.

32-379 40 min. $39.95

San Diego: America's Historic Cornerstone

The rich heritage of the modern city where California history began; San Diego Zoo, one of the world's largest; missions; Balboa Park; Del Coronado; Cabrillio National Monument that preserves the discovery of California and the human, natural history of Point Loma.

32-8272 75 min. $29.95

San Diego Zoo

From earliest dawn to lights out, this intimate look at the San Diego Zoo brings to life the spirit and wonder of this world-renowned Zoo. Spectacular footage of the Zoo's most popular animals including the koalas, pygmy chimpanzees, and baby animals in the nursery...Rare behind-the-scenes visits with the keepers and the animals they care for.

32-5146 30 min. $19.95

San Francisco

This majestic city captured in spectacular photography. Old San Francisco highlights include: historic scenes of 1906 earthquake, rare footage of Alcatraz: Al Capone's incarceration, prisoner's escape attempts, as well as other famous sites.

32-8271 90 min. $29.95

San Francisco With Laura Mckenzie

Probably everyone's favorite American city, San Francisco is also one of the most energetic and diverse. Laura McKenzie will take you on the cable cars, suggest good restaurants, and what shoes to wear. You'll see the Golden Gate Bridge, the Embarcadero, Chinatown, Union Square, Coit Tower, Alcatraz Island and much more.

32-185 56 min. $24.95

San Francisco Bay Cruise

Cruise past San Francisco Bay's most famous landmarks - Alcatraz, Fort Point, Angel Island, Telegraph Hill, the Golden Gate and Bay Bridges - and experience the bustle and colorful sights of both the San Francisco and Sausalito waterfronts.

32-033 24 min. $24.95

San Francisco Golden Gateway

Come on a whirlwind tour of San Francisco and savor the excitement and beauty that makes it such a unique city. See the cable cars, Coit Tower; Fisherman's Wharf, Chinatown, Nob Hill and more!

32-034 24 min. $19.95

San Luis Obispo County

Discover California's "Middle Kingdom". Between Los Angeles and San Francisco, San Luis Obispo is one of the most beautiful coastal counties in the country. See world famous Hearst Castle, visit a traditional farmers market and one of our many wineries. See beautiful beaches and majestic mountains. Relax, sit back and enjoy.

32-8167 40 min. $24.95

Southern California

Finally, a video that captures the excitement, glamour and scenic beauty of Southern California. From San Diego to Santa Barbara, including L.A. and Hollywood, this stimulating film whisks you to the most exciting scenic, cultural, and tourist attractions in the Southland. Plus fascinating early history of the area.

32-036 30 min. $29.95

Singles' Guide To Los Angeles

Beaches, hot tubs, nightlife, Hollywood! It's all Los Angeles, and this revealing video lets you in on "the inside story" of how to make the most of your visit to one of the most exciting cities on earth. From restaurants and shopping, through health clubs and museums, to movie studios and discos; it's all here for you!

32-5628 60 min. $16.95

Caribbean

10 Hottest Caribbean Resorts

Preview your ultimate vacation and explore the wonderful resorts in the Caribbean. Even travel on a Windjammer Cruise through some of the most exotic islands in the Caribbean. See for yourself!

32-8164 60 min. $29.95

Aruba

Explore the fascinating landscape of Aruba's north coast-exotic cactus mix with the island's trademark "Watapana" or Divi Divi Trees. From old pirates lairs to abandoned gold mines, the romance of this

VIDEO TITLES LISTED IN THIS GUIDE ARE AVAILABLE FOR PURCHASE OR RENTAL. CONTACT YOUR LOCAL VIDEO STORE OR TELEPHONE (800) 383-8811

Dutch island will capture your imagination! Catch the shows complete with "Copa dancers" and exciting international entertainers - or try your luck at the many casinos. Get away from it all to Aruba...your escape to Paradise!
32-5221 50 min. $29.95

Bahamas - Holiday in the Bahamas

Start your visit to this nation of 700 islands in Nassau, where pirates, slave traders, and rum runners used to rub elbows. Take a carriage ride to Prince George Wharf then continue on to Parliament Square, with its pink colonial buildings. Stroll through the shopper's paradise of Bay Street and the Straw Market, where bargains are everywhere. Walk past marching pink flamingoes, dive among coral reefs, and go para-sailing at one of the fabulous beaches of the Bahamas. A Video Visits program.
32-5032 40 min. $24.95

Bermuda

A detailed, guided tour to beautiful Bermuda. A delightful vacation spot for young and old, a charming and active island retreat.
32-2426 40 min. $29.95

BEST OF THE CARIBBEAN SERIES:

• Volume 1

A detailed guide to 10 favorite spots: Anguilla, Barbados, Cancun, Cozumel, Jamaica, Key West, Martinique, St. Barth, St. John and St. Martin. Each segment begins with a colorful overview of the spot's unique flavor, followed by a detailed tour of all there is to see and do. There is a preview of 75 recommended hotels and hideaways - the grounds, beaches, pools and rooms. Includes booklet.
32-358 90 min. $39.95

• Volume 2

Takes you to Antigua; Dominic, the jungle island; and Grand Cayman, the underwater mecca for diving enthusiasts.
32-2427 60 min. $29.95

• Volume 3

Tours French Guadeloupe; the quiet emerald isle of Montserrat; and the beautiful beaches of the British Virgin Islands Tortolla and Virgin Gorda.
32-2428 60 min. $29.95

• Volume 4

Tour the French Guadeloupe, with its beautiful topless beaches and steaming volcanos, with a side trip to the charming offshore islands of Les Saintes, plus much more!
32-5661 60 min. $29.95

British Virgin Islands - Yacht Chartering

Charter a yacht and stop at uninhabited islands, with turquoise water and secluded white beaches.
32-351 35 min. $29.95

Cayman Islands

Where the sun, sand and surf of these Caribbean West Indies islands beckon the water-sports enthusiast or the harried vacationer who just wants to unwind. You'll also find good shopping in Georgetown's Freeport shops, and a variety of dining options.
32-126 30 min. $19.95

Cayman Islands

This video takes you on a tour of Grand Cayman, little Cayman & Cayman Brae. You will get a look at the beaches, dinning, restaurants, hotels and clubs that make the Cayman Islands one of the hottest vacation destinations in the world.
32-5008 25 min. $24.95

Freeport, Bahamas

World-class hotels and matchless beaches are the focal point of the adventure to this tropical paradise of floral-lined streets.
32-046 60 min. $44.95

Grand Cayman

Included in this tour of Grand Cayman are duty-free shops, windsurfing, Hobie cat sailing, jet-skiing, hidden beaches and the Cayman Turtle Farm.
32-376 30 min. $16.95

Islands of the Caribbean

Join Video Visits and discover the Dominican Republic, where you'll see cane harvested. Experience Puerto Rico's high-rise towers, dazzling casinos, hidden retreats and protected rain forest parks. Enter St. Thomas, a shoppers's paradise or go sailing on turquoise waters. Sway to the rhythms of calypso and reggae in Trinidad.
32-8033 53 min. $24.95

Jamaica

Join us on Jamaica's magnificent north coast from Ocho Rios to Montego Bay and Negril. Sunny, white beaches, green forest mountains and silken waters streaming down the mountain sides. View breath taking sights from Richmond Hill in historic Montego Bay, the palatial great house Rose Hall and much more. Also included is a reference guide to resorts and hotels plus travel tips by Berlitz travel guides.
32-048 60 min. $29.95

Jamaica: Land Of Wood And Water

Join Video Visits and discover the lush tropical

---

paradise of Jamaica, 3rd largest island in the Caribbean. Begin in Spanish Townand continue on to Kingston, the nation's business and cultural center. Take in a cricket match, visit a coffee plantation, then learn about the Hollywood stars who made Port Antonio a playground of the 40's. Then off to Montego Bay, where open-air markets, glorious beaches, and exciting nightlife beckon.
32-5191 50 min. $24.95

Nassau, Bahamas
Nassau, the cosmopolitan playground of the Bahamas. Spin the wheel in lavish casinos. Experience the local cuisine and bargain-hunt duty-free for watches, jewelry, cameras, and perfume. Enjoy parasailing, windsurfing, tennis, golf and scuba diving. Climb to Fort Fincastle on the queen's steps dating back to 1770. Also included is a Reference Guide to resort and hotels plus travel tips by Berlitz travel guides.
32-051 60 min. $29.95

Passport Travel Guide - Bahamas
Bahamas...meet the fascinating people of the Bahamas. Visit the exotic surroundings of Nassau, Freeport and the many out islands with their perfect weather and charming customs.
32-6439 35 min. $16.95

St. Croix
Live the Caribbean legend, where visitors are spoiled by natives, cuisine is exotic and accommodations are pampering. Such a place is St. Croix in the U.S. Virgin Islands.
32-054 60 min. $29.95

St. Kitts - The Video Guide
This video is perfect for those who want to learn more about St. Kitts, those interested in visiting St. Kitts, and a must for anyone eager to share their Caribbean experience with others. This program highlights the fascinating history, the natural beauty, pristine beaches and many activities available around the island.
32-8233 43 min. $29.95

St. Martin
Delightfully Dutch and fantastically French, this dual nation Caribbean island is a little bit of Europe under the sun.
32-147 60 min. $29.95

St. Thomas/St. John
These cities of the U.S. Virgin Islands are explored for their beautiful beaches, wonderful water sports and duty-free shopping.
32-055 60 min. $29.95

WEST WIND RESORT GUIDE SERIES :

• Antiqua
Gaze out over Antiqua's breathtaking beaches, wander through a charming restored dockyard and the bustling capital of St. John's. You will also take a tour through 19 resorts from deluxe properties to holiday hideaways. to hotels best for those on a budget.
32-6629 30 min. $24.95

• St. Maarten
With it's Dutch influence, St. Maarten gives you a taste of Europe in the Caribbean.
32-8171 30 min. $24.95

• St. Thomas And St. John
A comprehensive video tour of 26 resorts on St. Thomas and St. John. This resort guide takes the guesswork out of choosing a place to stay. It also gives viewers an overview of St. Thomas from it's beautiful beaches to it's lively shopping district. There is also a section on what travelers should know and a list of resort telephone numbers.
32-6628 30 min. $24.95

Cruises

10 Hottest Cruises
Preview your ultimate vacation and explore 10 wonderful cruises through some of the most exotic islands of the Caribbean.
32-8176 45 min. $24.95

CARIBBEAN CRUISING SERIES:

• Cruising the U.S. Virgin Islands
This is a cruising and navigation guide to the U.S. Virgin Islands. Beautiful beaches, superb anchorages and all the best shoreside facilities are shown. Includes navigation charts, route planning, dive spots and more. For Power and Sail alike. The Virgin Islands offer an almost perfect combination of history and beauty set in an area of almost no nautical hazards.
32-8193 55 min. $29.95

• Cruising the British Virgin Islands
This is a cruising and navigation guide to the British Virgin Islands. Beautiful beaches, superb anchorages and all the best shoreside facilities. Includes navigation charts, route planning, dive spots and more. For Power and Sail alike. The British Virgin Islands offer an almost perfect combination of history and beauty set in an area of almost no nautical hazards.
32-8194 46 min. $29.95

VIDEO TITLES LISTED IN THIS GUIDE ARE AVAILABLE FOR PURCHASE OR RENTAL. CONTACT YOUR LOCAL VIDEO STORE OR TELEPHONE (800) 383-8811

Cruise with Royal Viking Line

Provides the flavor and practical travel tips for the vacationer who has never been on a cruise as well as the experienced cruise traveler seeking new adventures. You'll really get the feel for what is's like to take a "legendary voyage" with Royal Viking Line.
32-129 30 min. $19.95

Fantome Windjammer, Bahamas

The ancient art of seamanship unfolds in this look at the vacation adventure aboard the flagship of the Windjammer fleet.
32-044 60 min. $29.95

Flying Cloud Windjammer, British Virgin Islands

Quiet coves, hidden bays and pristine uninhabited islands are only part of the beauty captured in this video show aboard one of sailing's "tall ships".
32-045 60 min. $29.95

San Francisco Bay Cruise-Video Visits

Sail beneath two of the world's great bridges the Bay Bridge and the commanding Golden Gate. Cruise past Telegraph Hill, Angel Island, and more. Your adventure will also take you beyond the ship's deck, as you walk the streets for a closer look and experience breathtaking views from aloft.
32-8124 24 min. $24.95

World By Sea

Cruise to discovery with this gorgeous documentary that lets you sample life at sea and a variety of countries around the world, from the Caribbean and the South Pacific to Alaska and Australia. A special photography section helps you improve your travel photos with Kodak know-how.
32-5630 65 min. $19.95

World of Cruise Ships

Join Video Visits and the late Pulitzer Prize winning travel writer, Stan Delaplane, for a fast-paced introduction to the cruise liners of the world. Learn how to select a cruise. Travel to the Caribbean, Mediterranean, Mexico and Alaska. Dock at Rio de Janeiro for Carnival. Get a preview of future, exotic cruise ship designs. Get insider tips to make your voyage a success!
32-8125 45 min. $24.95

Europe & British Isles

Algarve, Portugal

The Portugal coast is a dramatic stretch of secluded coves and rocky cliffs, amid the Old World charm of the European countryside.
32-136 60 min. $29.95

Alps

Explore the Alpine areas of Austria, Italy, Switzerland, Yugoslavia and West Germany. Thrill to such sports as mountaineering, world-class skiing, skijoring and horse racing on the frozen lake at St. Moritz. Fall in love with the gentle sounds that echo through the spectacular peaks. Meet Alpine cookie bakers, lace makers, brewmasters, glass painters, wrought-iron workers and violin makers. Go behind the scenes of the Salzburg Marionette Theater, Spanish Riding School and Vienna Boys Choir.
32-306 30 min. $24.95

Amsterdam

The land of windmills, tulips, and Hans Brinker is brought to life as you glide along the canals in the "Venice of the North".
32-039 60 min. $29.95

Athens and the Greek Spirit

Join Video Visits and capture the life and color of the Mediterranean by land and sea in this tour of Greece and her islands.
32-104 60 min. $24.95

Balloon Adventures in Spain

This is a tour across the Spanish country-side: Andalusia, Cordoba, Granada and the Costa del Sol. The fleet of colorful balloons attracts the smiles and hospitality of the Spanish people - over the vineyards, hills, villages,. beaches of Spain.
32-224 25 min. $39.95

Bath: England's Roman Spa/Video Visits

Enjoy a delightful visit to England's elegant Georgian city of Bath. Visit the hot springs where Romans built a temple in 65 A.D. and where, later English royalty came to "take of the waters".
32-001 30 min. $24.95

Classic Tour of Germany

Steeped in legend and magical beauty, the Rhine and Moselle Rivers make for a spectacular tour of medieval castles, Roman monuments, colorful wine towns and historic cities.
32-8227 60 min. $29.95

COUNTRYSIDES: CASTLES & CITIES OF THE BRITISH ISLES SERIES:

• Touring England

All the things you'd want to see in England are included in this lively video jaunt around this island country. It covers the countryside, cities, castles

---

and cathedrals that have become legendary. The royal palaces, events, and historic landmarks and a journey to Wales with native son, Richard Burton. From royals to rogues, you'll see the heritage of what was once the world's greatest empire.
32-8082 60 min. $29.95

• Touring Scotland
This video spans a panorama of this country and adds the unexpected--from palm trees to semi-tropic gardens-inter-woven with the history, culture and natural character of the land. Travel from misty mountains to ancient cities, on to the city of Glasgow and to Loch Lomond. Search Loch Ness for "Nessie". Visit the courses of Gleneagles, Turnberry and that shrine of golf, St. Andrews. As a finale, a lone piper stands on the battlements of Edinburgh Castle; piping a plaintive skirl.
32-8083 65 min. $29.95

• Touring Ireland
From Shannon to Kilarney, County Clare to County Cork--home of the Blarney Stone, then to Galway, the Arran Island, Connemara, the hills of Sligo, on to Donegal, Waterford, Wexford, Dublin and more. It's home to poets, potato farmers and plentiful pubs. This video explores Ireland's Gaelic soul through centuries of turbulent history. It reflects the irrepressible spirit of Ireland.
32-8084 60 min. $29.95

Czechoslovakia: Triumph & Tradition
Join Video Visits as East meets West to weave a fascinating cultural tapestry. Tour the capital city, Prague, with it's historic Old Town Square, the Prague castle, and the St. Vitus cathedral. Experience this proud nation and celebrate the awakening of its triumph and tradition.
32-8018 55 min. $24.95

Denmark: The Jewel of Europe
Join Video Visits and explore the tiny kingdom of Denmark, with its pristine islands and winding coastline. In the bustling seaport of Copenhagen, take an inside peek at the Carlsberg Brewery. Discover the diversity of Danish design reflected in Denmark's cozy thatched-roof cottages and sleek modern-day furniture. Indulge in the toy fantasies of Legoland Park and the real life charm of Skagen a quaint fishing port.
32-8010 52 min. $24.95

Discovering England
Begin with London and the changing of the Guards at Buckingham Palace. Visit Cornwall, land of fishing villages and pirate coves; the whitewashed cottages and green countryside of Devon; the Regency city of Bath; the monoliths of Stonehenge. Stroll through Oxford and Cambridge and the woods of Sherwood forest and Stratford

upon Avon, Shakespeare's birthplace.
32-8025 85 min. $29.95

Discovering Ireland
Tour the Ring of Kerry, the ancient Aran Islands and the Giant's Causeway. Then visit Blarney and Bunratty castles. Watch horse races at Curragh. See the creations of Waterford's crystal factory. Discover the cities of Belfast and Dublin. Stop at their pubs before enjoying the Galway Oyster Festival.
32-8011 85 min. $29.95

Discovering Wales
Discover a land of ancient legends, eccentric charm and fierce pride. Find adventure shooting the rapids of wild rivers in North Wales. Climb the slopes of majestic Snowdonia by steam train. Then see modern Wales and attend the joyous Eisteddfod celebration.
32-8013 55 min. $29.95

Dragonquest, Sacred Sites of Britain
Begins and ends with the Earth itself, the ruins of ancient temples, stones that have survived the ages, standing quiet and still, speaking a silent language that crosses the great expanse of time, compelling us to explore their mysteries. Join the quest on a journey that fills mind with wonder and the eyes with new vision.
32-8172 42 min. $24.95

East of England Heritage Route
Explore the lesser-known delights of the Eastern side of England with its ancient heritage and national parks. The six cathedral cities are gems just waiting to be discovered, each set in an unspoiled landscape that ranges from peaceful farmland to rugged coast and heather-clad hills. Visit the following cathedral cities: Durham, York, Lincoln, Peterborough, Ely and Norwich.
32-210 28 min. $19.95

Eternal France
From the Roman ruins in Provence to Napoleon's Arc de Triomphe in Paris, the rich history and culture of France await you. Wander inside the majestic cathedrals of Reims and Chartres. Watch the artistry of glass-makers in Baccarat, the lace-makers in the Auvergne and silk painters in Lyon. Then marvel at the beauty and mystery of Brittany's stunning abbey of Mont-Saint-Michel.
32-8021 60 min. $24.95

Eternal Greece
Experience Delphi - to early Greeks the center of the universe, the site of the Delphic oracle, and the location of a great temple of Apollo. Explore the fertile Ionian island of Corfu in a colorful horse-drawn taxi. Savor the blended fragrance of fruit and flowers on the "perfumed island" of Zakinthos,

known for its centuries-old olive trees and as producer of half the world's raisin.
32-5063 60 min. $29.95

Europe Through the Back Door
Get off the tour bus and experience Europe as a temporary European. Travel with Rick Ray to Europe's most memorable destinations: the ancient hill town of Civita near Umbria, the Cinque Terre on the Italian Riviera, Brugge, the late-medieval Belgian city and Gimmelwald in Switzerland. Learn the basics of do-it-yourself travel!
32-9329 45 min. $39.95

Finland-Fresh and Original
Begin your Video Visits journey in the capital city of Helsinki. Visit the neoclassical Senate Square and striking monument to composer Jean Sibelius. Join the Finns in a sauna, then travel to the unspoiled wilderness of Lapland, where reindeer herding is an ongoing tradition for the friendly Lapps.
32-8020 50 min. $24.95

Florence: Cradle of the Renaissance
In this video experience the essence of the century that was to become known as the cradle of rebirth in art, architecture, letters and philosophy.
Come and celebrate this fateful century. Come with us to Florence, Museum city of the World.
32-8076 30 min. $19.95

Florence
This video is a beautiful introduction to Florence, as well as a valuable and interesting guide for those already familiar with the city. The English-speaking narrator puts each masterpiece in its historical context.
32-360 50 min. $24.95

France-Fodor's Travel Video
In Paris, visit the Avenue Montaigne to see the world's most fashionable names and meet the people who create haute
couture. Then move on to wineries in Bordeaux and Champagne and see the majestic castles of the Loire. Meet fashion designer Pierre Cardin and the Queen of the Jasmine Festival in Grasse. Then visit Europe's highest mountain, Mont Blanc and the Cote d'Azur.
32-8128 90 min. $29.95

Germany-Fodor's Travel Video
Journey to the hidden corners where East meets West. You'll meet the people who make Germany so fascinating--a piano maker at Hamburg's Steinway factory, a beer maker and a fashion designer in Munich. Your tour begins in Berlin the takes you to Heidelberg University before turning towards the beautiful Black Forest and the
Hohenzollern castle nearby.
32-8129 90 min. $29.95

Glacier Express: Swiss Adventure in 4 Moods
This is a journey through some of the most spectacular vistas in the world: elegant Zurich and sophisticated St. Moritz, the famous Rhone Glacier, the majestic Matterhorn towering over Zermatt, and Geneva, the city on the lake - all stops on the breathtaking route of the legendary all-electric train known as the Glacier Express.
32-277 20 min. $39.95

Great Britain: Fodor's Video Guide
One of the best known names in travel brings you a video full of tips for travelling in Great Britain.
32-1641 75 min. $29.95

Great Cities of Europe
Join Video Visits tour of Europe's most renowned cities: London, Dublin, Amsterdam, Munich, Vienna, Salzburg, Paris, Madrid, Athens, Rome. Join the famed Oktoberfest, climb the Acropolis, throw a coin in the Trevi Fountain. See romantic castles, picturesque canals, lively piazzas, and parks and meet the Europeans at work and play.
32-8019 60 min. $24.95

Greece
Visit classic, cosmopolitan Athens, one of the world's great cities. Share in the traditional music and dance, work alongside a modern Greek sculptor, a rural wood-rug maker and an expert in Greece's fur-coat craft. Cruise the islands of Corfu, Crete, Mykonos, Patmos, Rhodes and Santorini. Discover a donkey taxi service, Plato's Lost City of Atlantis, an artists' and writers' colony, a model fishing-boat carver, and the nearly 30-year-old Petros, the Pelican. Soak up the clear, bright sun and immerse yourself in the rich Greek Orthodox pageantry.
32-308 30 min. $24.95

Greece: Playground of the Gods
Explore with Video Visits, the famed Aegean architecture and enjoy the volcanic beaches of Santorini. Marvel at the Acropolis where the spirits of Greek Mythology still preside. View the wind-mills of Mykonos the monoliths of Meteora. Mingle with the locals and venture to Crete to uncover the arid ruins of Knossos, palace of King Minos.
32-8029 58 min. $24.95

HERITAGE TRAVEL SERIES:
Have you already made, or are you planning a trip to trace your family's Irish, Scottish, or Welsh roots and heritage? Here's the perfect preview or reminder of that exciting journey. Discover the language, legends and traditions of your native

land. See the role your ancestors played in the history and culture of their birthplace as the country's story unfolds. Tracing your ancestors booklet included.

- **Wales & Your Welsh Ancestry**
32-8121 60 min. $29.95

- **Ireland & Your Irish Ancestry**
32-8122 60 min. $29.95

- **Scotland & Your Scottish Ancestry**
32-8123 60 min. $29.95

Hungary
Welcome to Hungary, land of baroque palaces and cobblestone streets echoing with gypsy rhapsodies. Journey to Budapest, the magnificent city along the Danube River where old world charm mixes gracefully with modern vitality. Tour the Royal Palace, rejuvenate in the thermal waters of a world-class spa, bask in the sun at the Hungarian Riviera. Discover the medieval city of Pecs and tour the renowned Zsolnay procelain factory. Ride horseback with the csikos on the prairies of the Great Plain.
32-7090 55 min. $24.95

Hungary: Fodor's Video Guide
World-famous travel writer, Eugene Fodor hosts your journey to his enchanting native homeland of Hungary to explore the colorful traditions, alluring history and pastoral countryside. Check in at the Forum Hotel in Budapest, one of the city's finest. Visit Heroes' Square, build to celebrate the one thousandth anniversary of the nation. Enter Jak Abbey, the finest example of Romanesque architecture in the country. Delight in the historic music, operas and concerts of Budapest. Travel southwest of Budapest to Lake Heviz Europe's largest spring-fed warm water lake. And much more!
32-6063 60 min. $29.95

Iceland: Europe's Outback, A Personal Journey With Rick Ray
Join us in this in depth often humorous look at pure old Norse Vikings who inhabit a land of fire and ice. Get a comprehensive look at the history, culture, religion and pastimes of these geothermally heated Scandinavians..
32-9696 82 min. $29.95

In Love with Paris
Join Video Visits and see this special city up close in this excellent production. Go shopping, eat at the best restaurants and sample the night life in this unique video tour. See Montmartre, Notre Dame, the Eiffel Tower, the Arc de Triomphe, Versailles, the Louvre, Tomb of the Unknown Soldier and much more. Stroll the Champs Elysees and enjoy the view from your sidewalk cafe. Learn the history of this world-famous city and enjoy your trip to Paris.
32-218 55 min. $24.95

Ireland
Ireland is a land shaped by the proud people who live there; visit Dublin, Galway and Cork. Discover Tipperary, Kilkenny, Limerick and Kerry. This is an island of sweeping hillsides laced with stone fences, ancient castles perched upon cliffs overlooking the sea. Also included is a reference guide to resorts and hotels plus travel tips by Berlitz travel guides.
32-139 60 min. $29.95

Ireland: Emerald Treasures
Go with Video Visits on a journey through a country filled with natural scenic beauty, rich culture and some of the friendliest people in the world.
32-1741 50 min. $24.95

Italy: Fodor's Travel Video
Roam through a delightful country that truly bridges the centuries. Stroll the streets of Pompeii. Visit violin shops of Crimona. See the Uffizi Museum in Florence through the eyes of a painter and wander through the ages in Milan, where national treasures like La Scala and the venerable cathedral inspire today's fashion houses and designers.
32-8130 90 min. $29.95

King Arthur & His Country - Southern England
Return to centuries past and to the true-to-life legend of King Arthur. Learn the story of King Arthur and explore his kingdom - Southern England - as it is today, visiting the very places where he lived and ruled. Includes outstanding views of Tintagel, Cadbury, Slaughter Bridge, Glastonbury Abbey and more.
32-165 25 min. $29.95

LAURA McKENZIE'S TRAVEL TIPS FOR EUROPE SERIES:

- **Athens and the Greek Isles**
Laura McKenzie takes you on a fascinating tour of the Olympic Stadium, Parliament house, the Acropolis, and the Roman Forum. She'll tell you how to get around in the city, good places for Greek food, and what shoes to wear. Day trips include Cape Sounion and Temple of Poseidon, Delphi, and Naplion, as well as a cruise of the Greek isles.
32-176 56 min. $24.95

VIDEO TITLES LISTED IN THIS GUIDE ARE AVAILABLE FOR PURCHASE OR RENTAL. CONTACT YOUR LOCAL VIDEO STORE OR TELEPHONE (800) 383-8811

• **Austria**
From Vienna's Lippizan Stallions to Salzburg - "The City of Mozart," to Innsbruck's Olympic Village, ski resorts and famous castles. You'll see them all!
32-1868 60 min. $24.95

• **Ireland**
How long will it take to kiss the Blarney Stone? Ireland is a country of magic and beauty. You'll learn the best places to eat real Irish cooking, where to shop, how to get a VAT refund, and what the weather will be like as you tour Dublin, Kildare, Cork, Kenmare, Killarney, Limerick, Shannon and Tralee. You'll see castles, famous landmarks, lush countryside and fascinating sights.
32-179 56 min. $24.95

• **London and Surrounding Day Trips**
Laura McKenzie answers questions, such as how to get around in the city, what type of coat to pack, when is the best time to see the changing of the guard and much more. You'll see the Tower Bridge, Westminster Abbey, Hyde Park, and Covent Garden. You'll also take exciting day trips to Windsor Castle, Blenheim Palace, Stratford-Upon-Avon, Ragley Hall and Warwick Castle.
32-180 56 min. $24.95

• **French Riviera**
Laura McKenzie, noted travel expert, shares her knowledge with you in this entertaining and informative videocassette. You'll travel through the world of the international jet set, stopping along the way at Nice, Cannes, St. Tropez, Antibes as well as the principality of Monaco and the casinos of Monte Carlo. Take side trips to the towns of Portofino, Eze and visit the famous castle at Cagnes.
32-5135 60 min. $24.95

• **Munich and Bavaria**
An introduction to King Ludwig's Castle, the salt mines of Berchtesgaden, Bavarian beer halls, medieval towns and more!
32-1866 60 min. $24.95

• **Paris and Surrounding Day Trips**
Everyone loves Paris, but you'll enjoy it even more when you know how to get around, what clothes to wear, where to eat, and what sights to see. Laura McKenzie will answer these questions and more. You'll visit the Pantheon, Bourbon Palace, Arc de Triomphe, Champs Elysees, Royal Palace, Louvre Museum, Notre Dame cathedral, and more day trips include Fountainbleau, Versailles and Chartres.
32-183 56 min. $24.95

• **Rome and Surrounding Day Trips**
Covers tips on how to get around Rome, what clothes to take, how long to allow to tour the Colosseum, where to go for real Italian foods and many other tips. You'll visit the Roman Forum, Vatican City, St. Peter's Square, Piazza Venezia, Arch of Drusus, Presidential Palace and much more. You'll take exciting day trips to Tivoli, Pompeii and the Amalfi Coast.
32-184 56 min. $24.95

• **Spain and the Costa Del Sol**
Visit the Spanish cities of Madrid, Segovia, Toledo, El Escorial, Granada, Tangiers and Morocco. See the exquisite cathedrals and historical landmarks. Learn about the bullfights, festive places to eat, how to bargain at the flea markets in Morocco. See the sights in the Spanish countryside, and tour the beautiful Costa del Sol.
32-186 56 min. $24.95

• **Switzerland**
A land of fairy tale beauty, colorful and challenging places to ski, sophisticated cities, and lovely lakes. You'll see famous churches, bridges, forts, towers, and castles in Zurich, Brunnon, Lucerne, Loukerbad, and Geneva. You'll also visit Lake Vierwaldstattersee, the Matterhorn and other beautiful wonders of nature.
32-187 56 min. $24.95

• **Venice**
Visit and learn all about St. Mark's Square, The Doges Palace, the famed canals and gondolas, Venetian glassworks, plus other popular attractions.
32-1869 60 min. $24.95

Lincoln: England's City on a Hill
This production features the beautiful city of Lincoln, with its fine architecture and historical past. Learn about the origins of the city, its evolution and its present-day activities in this unique production. Little-known stories about the people and places in the city to make this tape a must for students of English history.
32-216 25 min. $24.95

Lisbon
Lisbon, capital of Portugal, home of Magellan and Ponce de Leon. Discover Lisbon with its old world charm. A city built on seven hills, filled with museums, and monuments erected when Portuguese explorers set sail to discover new worlds in the 15th Century. Also included is a reference guide to resorts and hotels plus travel tips by Berlitz travel guides.
32-049 60 min. $29.95

Loire Valley
The Loire Valley brings to life the 16th century among its chateaux, palatial gardens and abundant vineyards. Experience the opulent decor and culture of royal medieval times, in the countryside

VIDEO TITLES LISTED IN THIS GUIDE ARE AVAILABLE FOR PURCHASE OR RENTAL. CONTACT YOUR LOCAL VIDEO STORE OR TELEPHONE (800) 383-8811

of central France.
32-141 60 min. $29.95

London
The River Tahmes, Buckingham Palace, the Tower of London, Big Ben, the House of Parliament, Hyde Park, Piccadilly Circus, Trafalgar Square; names that ring with pageantry, tradition, courage, and history. Visit theaters, ride on double-decker buses and stroll in parks. An exciting tour through London's past and present. Also included is a reference guide to resorts and hotels plus travel tips by Berlitz travel guides.
32-352 40 min. $29.95

London
A splendid tour of the capital, with exciting views of this bustling city with all its colorful extravaganza, signs and sounds. See all those well-known and best-loved places: Buckingham Palace, The Houses of Parliament, Westminster Abbey, Trafalgar Square, Downing Street, Tower Bridge, along with dramatic views of the Thames. A tour that captures the flavor of London Town and its unique atmosphere.
32-149 60 min. $39.95

London: Heart of a Nation
From high above the River Thames to the gates of Windsor Castle. Witness the Royal wedding of Prince Charles and Lady Diana. Visit Trafalgar Square and stop by Simpsons to savor the country's best roast beef and Yorkshire pudding. From Buckingham Palace to the Notting Hill Carnival, join Video Visits and meet the people, the heart of London.
32-8026 58 min. $24.95

Moscow And Leningrad
Journey to Moscow, the soul of Mother Russia. Enter the Kremlin, a walled city within a city and seat of government. Enjoy the pageantry of Red Square, then pause before the tomb of Vladimir Lenin. Witness the true spirit of Russia at the Bolshoi Ballet and Moscow Circus. Visit the Winter Palace, home of the Hermitage Museum, and the extravagant Palace of Petrodvorets with miles of waterfalls and fountains.
32-7091 50 min. $24.95

Norfolk Broads of England
Sail on the waters of the Broadlands of Norfolk in this peaceful view of the waterways which are found in Northeastern England. Whether by barge or sailboat, you will enjoy the scenic beauty and interesting historical information featured in this delightful production.
32-213 25 min. $19.95

Norway: Nature's Triumph
From the peaceful, sun-glistening fjords to wildly, rugged peaks, you'll see a true wonderland of creation in Norway. Join Video Visits and explore Oslo's medieval Akershus Fortress, travel to Bergen's colorful waterfront, to Trondheim's Nidaros Cathedral and see the awesome, beauty of Geiranger Fjord.
32-8012 53 min. $24.95

Norwegian Saga
Join us in this fast moving, colorful and informative story of Norway and the modern Vikings. Journey to Oslo and Bergen, in this travel documentary of Norway and her people.
32-9668 60 min. $29.95

Oktoberfest from Munich
Join the biggest folklore celebration in the world. Bavarian "Gemutlichkeit," the atmosphere of the beer tents, sensational sideshows and swift rides, including roller-coasters and a ferris wheel! The Oktoberfest is depicted in a colored, magnificent array of video pictures!
13-465 30 min. $29.95

Orient Express
A five day romance over an 1800 mile journey from Paris to Istanbul aboard the elegant blue train that was once the transportation of aristocracy and where every meal is a gourmet's feast. As well as savoring the old world elegance of Reims, Salzburg and Vienna, we can glory in the steam locomotives of days gone by, the excitement of train chasing through the mountains and an excursion with masked Hungarian horsemen into the sinister Puszta forest. This trip of sophistication and historical intrigue will be one you want to take over and over again.
32-1714 62 min. $29.95

Paris
Paris, magical capital of France. Enjoy a city tour that shows you the Arc de Triomphe, the Obelisk, Napoleon's Tomb, and the Bastille. Stroll through exquisite gardens and charming parks along the Champs-Elysees, Eiffel Tower, and Notre Dame along with the many other sites and activities featured on this Travelview International travel tape. Also included is a Reference Guide to resorts and hotels plus travel tips by Berlitz travel guides.
32-145 60 min. $29.95

PASSPORT TRAVEL GUIDE SERIES
Gunther Less, winner of 13 major travel journalism awards and the host of the longest running travel program on T.V., has received the prestigious Gold Award of the International Film and T.V. Festival of New york for this exciting travel guide series. If you are planning a trip, this video is a must. Or, if you have already completed your trip this video is a wonderful way to share your experience with friends and family.

VIDEO TITLES LISTED IN THIS GUIDE ARE AVAILABLE FOR PURCHASE OR RENTAL. CONTACT YOUR LOCAL VIDEO STORE OR TELEPHONE (800) 383-8811

• **France - A Heritage Of Beauty**
32-6432 35 min. $16.95

• **Germany**
32-6433 35 min. $16.95

• **Ireland - A State Of Mind**
32-6434 35 min. $16.95

• **Italy**
32-6444 35 min. $16.95

• **Sweden And Denmark**
32-6442 35 min. $16.95

Poland

The hospitable people of Poland welcome you to their friendly country. Journey to Warsaw, the capital, filled with newly restored historical buildings. In Castle Square, gaze at the Royal Castle and Sigmund's column, the symbol of the city. Tour Cracow's Wawel Hill, the ancient seat of Polish kings, and enjoy Polish folklore in the Tatras mountains. And much more!
32-5189 55 min. $24.95

Portrait of the Isle of Man

This is a tour of the Isle of Man, located in the Irish Sea - a historic, beautiful island. From the oldest continuous parliament established by the Vikings, to the horse tram service along Douglas Promenade, to tales of romantic legends about Celtic Sea gods of magical powers, the film also covers the steam railway, Silverdale Glen, the water wheel in Laxey, as well as many other interesting areas, and includes coverage of the international motorcycle races that attract thousands of enthusiasts.
32-200 16 min. $29.95

Portugal: Land of Discoveries

From the beautiful shores of the Algarve to the lush forests of Bucaco, Portugal is full of treasures. Journey through one of the oldest countries in Europe and uncover the history of kings, religion, and exploration. Cheer for the cavaleiro as he battles the mighty bull. Savor the rich wines of the Douro. Join Video Visits and enjoy the charm, warmth and spirit of Portugal's people.
32-8022 57 min. $24.95

Reflections: The Soviet Union with Hart

Have you ever wondered what it's really like in the Soviet Union? Cheerful young people eating ice cream. High school students playing American jazz. Russian Orthodox church services. A grandmother speaking of her desire for a happy future for her children. New Year's celebrations and folk dancing. When Kelly Hart visited the Soviet Union with a group of fellow Americans

they were free to go anywhere in the cities they visited, mingle with people, go into their homes, and make friends. Poignant, heartwarming and just plain fun.
32-175 60 min. $34.95

Romantic Road

Come join us on the Romantic Road, enchanting, charming, filled with dreams. We'll take you to the magnificent towns of Wurzburg and Rothenburg, lovely Dinkelsbuhl and Nordlingen, 2000 year old Augsburg, and on the Alps for Fussen, with it's splendid mountain lakes.
32-8169 60 min. $29.95

Rome: Portrait of a City

A tour of Rome and the Alban Hills featuring art and architecture as well as fascinating insights into the ancient Roman World. See how Napoleon copied monuments in the Roman Forum for the City of Paris. Highlights include the Campidoglio, Piazza Narona, the Appian Way, the Vatican and treasures of the Sistine Chapel.
32-1845 50 min. $24.95

Scandinavia: Land of the Midnight Sun

Come with Video Visits and meet the friendly people of Scandinavia. Begin in Denmark with a tour of romantic Copenhagen. See the famous Tivoli Gardens, Kronbrog Castle--home of Hamlet. See Stockholm and Norway's rugged coast and crystalline fjords. Explore Oslo and visit Trondheim, the ancient seat of the Viking Kings.
32-8023 57 min. $24.95

Scotland

Scotland, a land of castles and bagpipes. Edinburgh, Scotland's capital. Walk the Royal Mile from Edinburgh Castle to the Palace of Holyroodhouse, once home to Mary Queen of Scots. At nearby St. Andrews play 18 holes on one of the world's oldest golf courses. Visit: Burrell Gallery, George Square, Aberdeen, Balmoral Castle and much more!
32-5228 50 min. $29.95

Scotland: Land of Legends

Sporting fans will appreciate the lush greens of St. Andrews, while shoppers delight in the century-old shopping district of Barras. Encounter the mystery of Loch Ness and the somber castles of Aberdeen, the battlefield of Culloden, the famous Glenfiddich distillery and Abbotsford, home of Sir Walter Scott.
32-8027 52 min. $24.95

Song Of Ireland

Share in the sights and sounds of Dublin, a city bustling with the experiences that fill a traveler's heart with pleasure and his mind with memories. Meander through the markets on Henry and Moore

---

streets, stop by colorful pubs, tour the famous Phoenix House Zoo, and refresh your spirit at St. Patrick's Cathedral or St. Steven's Green.
32-5131 60 min. $29.95

Spain
Enjoy this wonderful overview of Spain with its beautiful and dramatic landscapes, architecture and cities. Visit Madrid, Segovia, Avila, Cordoba, Seville, Granada, Costa del Sol and Barcelona. Learn the age-old craft of sword-making in Toledo and sample the outstanding cuisine of this fascinating land.
32-217 55 min. $19.95

Spain: Fodor's Travel Video
Discover the multifaceted character of the Spanish people and Spain's most revered cities...Segovia, Salamanca, Toledo, Granada, Madrid and of course, Barcelona. See Seville's Feria festival, the Royal Palace and the memorable exhibits at the Salvador Dali Museum.
32-8130 90 min. $29.95

Sweden: Nordic Treasures
Experience Sweden's glacial beauty with it's landscape dotted with islands, farms and snow-capped mountains. Stroll through Skansen to see Sweden "then" and "now". Come with Video Visits and witness the serenity of Fjord country & the culture of Stockholm.
32-8024 53 min. $24.95

Swiss Story
Come with us on this fast, colorful journey through Switzerland and meet the amazing people that live here while they work and play. See Zurich, Bern, Geneva and Luzern. Join us in this informative documentary of the Swiss people and their home.
32-8000 60 min. $29.95

Switzerland: Alpine Winter
Experience the breathtaking beauty of the Swiss Alps during an Alpine winter.
32-302 45 min. $29.95

Switzerland: Glacier Express
This highly-acclaimed film form Video Visits features the "Glacier Express" train of the Swiss National Railway as it journeys from St. Moritz to Zermatt. The production features dramatic aerials of the alps, intimate coverage of the villages along the route and gives the viewer a true sense of this spectacular rail journey.
32-208 52 min. $24.95

Thailand
Thailand, a kingdom shrouded in the Oriental mystique and imagery of ancient Siam, is Southeast "Asia's" Land of Smiles". Here, Bangkok reveals the magnificent Grand Palace, ornate Buddhist temples, food hawkers, antique bazaars, and Thai classical performances. Imagine cruising the Chao Phraya River aboard a long-tail boat; shopping from a tiny sampan at the floating market; exploring Bangkok's celebrated nightlife in Patpong. This videocassette contains a feature on Thailand; a Reference Guide to accommodations, shopping and services; and Travel Tips by Berlitz Travel Guides.
32-5136 50 min. $29.95

Touring London, Paris and Rome
Come join us as we tour the well known cities of London, Paris and Rome--the best of Europe's Great Cities. See all the famous landmarks that make these cities world renowned--from London's Big Ben and Paris' Eiffel Tower to Rome's Spanish Steps.
32-8073 60 min. $29.95

TRAVELOGUER COLLECTION:
Journey with professional travel filmmakers as they capture the beauty, spirit, history and culture of European destinations. Each video takes you on a personal, educational tour. Your guide knows the area intimately and has lived and traveled in this country. Visit famous landmarks and explore places most tourists never see.

• **Austrian Odyssey**
32-8105 60 min. $29.95

• **Bonjour France**
32-8107 60 min. $29.95

• **Bonny Scotland**
32-8110 60 min. $29.95

• **Charm of Holland**
32-8102 60 min. $29.95

• **Discovering Denmark**
32-8109 60 min. $29.95

• **Eternal Greece**
32-8223 60 min. $29.95

• **Glory of England**
32-8100 60 min. $29.95

• **Romantic Germany**
32-8111 60 min. $29.95

• **Romance of Vienna**
32-8106 60 min. $29.95

• **Russian Journey**
32-8108 60 min. $29.95

VIDEO TITLES LISTED IN THIS GUIDE ARE AVAILABLE FOR PURCHASE OR RENTAL. CONTACT YOUR LOCAL VIDEO STORE OR TELEPHONE (800) 383-8811

• **Si Spain!**
32-8112 60 min. $29.95

• **Spirit of Sweden**
32-8098 60 min. $29.95

• **Song of Ireland**
32-8101 60 min. $29.95

• **This is Switzerland**
32-8222 60 min. $29.95

• **Treasures of Italy**
32-8221 60 min. $29.95

• **Wonder of Norway**
32-8099 60 min. $29.95

Venice
Gore Vidal traces his roots back to Venice, Italy, taking you along as he peers into Venice's mysterious history. In this beautifully filmed tour of Venice past and present, Vidal tells about the Venetian people and their Empire. Visit Crete and Naxos, Venetian strongholds of the past. This is a two tape set.
32-1843 55 min. $59.95

Venice: Queen of the Adriatic
Come join us on a tour of the city seen through the eyes of artists, architects and poets. Come and linger in the sublime beauty that is Venice, Museum City of the World. This tour includes the well-known cathedrals, canals and museums of Venice.
32-8075 30 min. $19.95

Yorkshire Dales of England
Enjoy this delightful and peaceful journey through one of England's most scenic and unspoiled landscapes.
32-220 45 min. $24.95

Hawaii

10 Hottest Hawaiian Resorts
Come and see for yourself why the enchantment still lives in Hawaii. You will experience a guide to fun and information to help you plan your next vacation.
32-8226 45 min. $19.95

Adventures of Kauai
Explores Hawaii's magnificent "garden isle" of Kauai, commonly regarded as the most beautiful of the Polynesian string. Aerial and ground views present such points of interest as the mountain area boasting the world's greatest rainfalls, the cliff coast, the awesome craters and mammoth humpback whales photographed both above and below the ocean's surface.
32-195 30 min. $39.95

Explore Hawaii
Explore Hawaii is a fact-filled, no nonsense video guide to Hawaii. Covering all six of the major Hawaiian Islands, it is a must for anyone planning a trip to Hawaii. In just 30 minutes, "The Hawaii Traveler" covers every conceivable visitor destination in the 50th state. It gives travel tips, seasonal information and interesting facts - everything you need to plan a perfect Hawaiian vacation. It's Hawaii without the hope.
32-240 30 min. $19.95

Feel Hawaii: Oahu
A visually exciting look at Oahu, Hawaii's most popular island. Visit Pearl Harbor and the Arizona Monument, then continue on with the sights and sounds of this beautiful paradise to Sunset Beach, a surfer's dream. Feel the South Seas culture and hospitality of this vacation paradise.
32-007 30 min. $29.95

Fodor's Hawaii Video Guide
Experience all the sights and sounds of this island paradise.
32-1640 75 min. $29.95

Forever Hawaii
An artistic blend of stunning visuals and the finest Hawaiian music, this program is a video portrait of all six of the major Hawaiian Islands. The one-hour feature includes breath-taking aerials, spectacular volcanic eruptions, and incredible underwater footage. From sun-drenched beaches to snow-capped peaks, from busy Waikiki to the untouched wilderness of Kauai's Napali Coast, "Forever Hawaii" is a comprehensive video program about Hawaii.
32-245 60 min. $39.95

Forever Maui
An in-depth visit to the Valley Isle of Maui from the producers of the award winning "Forever Hawaii". Includes breathtaking video, a Hi-Fi stereo soundtrack, and interesting stories about this lovely and popular island.
32-5844 30 min. $29.95

Hawaii
From Hawaii's black sand beaches to the beaches to the craters of active volcanoes, the Big Island's scenic beauty is a fitting backdrop to the friendly

Polynesian people.
32-137 60 min. $29.95

Hawaii
Travel to the Hawaiian Islands. Explore the beauty of their many beaches, abundant flowers, varied wildlife, miles of volcanic mountains and modern cities. Shoot the pipeline with some of the world's greatest surfers. Experience the serenity of this tropical paradise during sunset.
32-310 30 min. $24.95

Hawaii: Islands of Relaxation
Enjoy the sights and sounds of the most beautiful islands in the world - the Hawaiians. Visit all the islands and revel in the natural beauty and awesome spectacle that make Hawaii unforgettable experience.
32-012 60 min. $29.95

Hawaii: Sights and Sounds of the Islands
An in-depth look at the beauty and history of the Islands from Video Visits.
32-110 60 min. $24.95

Hawaii: A Pacific Paradise
Hawaii, the Big Island: Travel from Hilo Bay to the Kona Coast. Visit Rainbow Falls, Lava Tree park, the Black Sand Beach at Kaimu and the historic Parker Ranch. Kauai, the Garden Island: Ride the Waimea River to the beautiful Fern Grotto, travel through the tunnel of trees to Poipu Beach and Spouting Horn, then soar over Waimea Canyon and the rugged Napali Coast as you enjoy the lush beauty of this tropical paradise. Maui, the Valley Island: travel the Hana Highway to the Seven Pools, marvel at the awe-inspiring spectacle of the crater on Haleakala, then on to West Maui. Oahu, the Gathering Place: go aboard the USS Arizona Monument in Pearl Harbor and visit the national cemetery at Punch Bowl. See the Pali Lookout, Waikiki Beach and famous Diamond Head.
32-305 45 min. $29.95

Hawaii's Underwater Paradise: Adventure Beneath the Sea
Features undersea footage of tropical marine life and reef and wreck locations.
32-2798 30 min. $39.95

Hawaiian Islands
Enjoy Kauai, Maui, Oahu, Molokai, Hawaii. It's an island adventure of the many faces of the Hawaiian Islands, a South Pacific celebration.
32-138 60 min. $29.95

Hawaiian Paradise: Reader's Digest
Feast your eyes and relish the opulent scenic splendors of the island paradise of Hawaii. Feel the breezes on the cliffs of Na Pali. Hear the legend of Pele, ancient Goddess of Fire. Tremble as the Kilauea volcano erupts. Stroll the grounds of Iolani Palace and bask in the sun on a black sand beach.
32-8131 90 min. $29.95

Insiders Guide to Oahu
Long-time Hawaii resident Jim Nabors hosts this entertaining, humorous and information-packed visit to the island of Oahu. Journey through Hawaii's history and culture with Palani Vaughan. See all the sights with Karen Keawahawaii. Sample Hawaii's unique and exotic foods with Wally "Famous Amos".
32-247 60 min. $39.95

Kauai
Kauai's deserted beaches, remote canyons and mountain wilderness have earned it the name, "Garden Isle".
32-140 60 min. $29.95

Kauai - Flight Of The Canyonbird
Kauai, "the Garden Isle", has been called the most beautiful island on earth. But much of Kauai is inaccessible wilderness. Here are secret and sacred places - ancient valleys, ribbon-thin waterfalls spilling thousands of feet down sheer cliffs, and verdant rainforest surrounding Waialeale, the wettest spot on earth - sights witnessed only by our helicopter and the island's graceful birds. Experience the magic and the true spirit of Kauai, as no other program has ever revealed it, in "Flight of the Canyonbird".
32-5848 30 min. $19.95

Hawaii With Laura Mckenzie
Laura McKenzie takes you to all the islands: Oahu, Maui, Kauai, and Hawaii (the Big Island), and she explains how to get from island to island. You'll experience beautiful beaches, magnificent waterfalls, powerful volcanoes, and some of the most inspiring natural landscapes in the world. She also gives you tips on where to attend a good luau.
32-178 56 min. $24.95

Maui
This video features magnificent location footage and background information about the island of Maui.
32-2799 30 min. $29.95

Maui
From sparkling beaches to the heights of volcanic Haleakala, Maui is a Pacific paradise. Besides its contrasting natural beauty, Maui also offers luxurious resorts, recreational sports and unlimited shopping.
32-142 60 min. $29.95

VIDEO TITLES LISTED IN THIS GUIDE ARE AVAILABLE FOR PURCHASE OR RENTAL. CONTACT YOUR LOCAL VIDEO STORE OR TELEPHONE (800) 383-8811

Oahu

Venture to the awesome beauty of Diamond Head, catch a wave on Waikiki or traverse the bustling city of Honolulu. Enjoy true island beauty and excitement.
32-144 60 min. $29.95

Passport Travel Guide - Hawaii

Rich in 20th century history. The islands have beauty from the warm beaches to the volcanic mountains inland. See the real Hawaii.
32-6445 30 min. $16.95

Polynesian Cultural Center

Share the fabulous polynesian experience with your family and friends back home. Enjoy it again and again. Relive your visit to Hawaii in your own home for years to come. This high-quality video cassette provides you, your family and friends with a stunningly beautiful 38-minute replay of Hawaii's number one visitor attraction.
32-5660 38 min. $24.95

Touring Hawaii

Hawaii abounds in surprises: vibrant people, exotic cultures, exciting history, beautiful seas and scenic wonders. This film captures the uniqueness of a vacation wonderland going beyond the usual to sites seldom seen. A sporting paradise, you'll dive the coral reefs, sail the majestic seas and surf the ocean's waves. A video vacation you can take anytime you wish.
32-263 30 min. $29.95

Mexico, Central & South America

10 Hottest Mexican Resorts

Travel to some of the hottest spots in Mexico. You'll visit Los Cabos, Old Mexico and other great vacation spots.
32-8238 59 min. $14.95

600 Days to Cocos Island

Join Gene and Josie Evans as they leave the rest of the world behind and take their small sailboat on an incredible 600-day adventure. See Mexico, Central America, Galapagos and the Cocos Islands.
32-8186 93 min. $39.95

Acapulco

Watch the cliff divers and discover the night life this jet-set resort city has to offer.
32-038 60 min. $29.95

Argentina

Your visit to Argentina begins in Patagonia with its diverse terrain, from spectacular mountain scenery and endless wind-swept desert to its rocky coast line. Hear the legacy of the gaucho, the Argentinean cowboy. Explore Glacier National Park and Perito Moreno Glacier, the only growing glacier in the world. Enter the storybook resort towns of San Martin and Bariloche. Survey the Arrayanes Forest's dramatic cinnamon-colored trees, inspiration for the forest in Disney's "Bambi". Venture into Argentina's "Misiones Provence", a tropical rain forest and amazonian jungle full of exotic sounds.
32-7089 60 min. $24.95

Brazil

Brazil, tropical land of the future, home of macumba and emeralds, welcomes you with open arms. Meet the warm people of Bahia and dance with them in an umbanda ceremony. Feel the rhythm of Rio de Janeiro, where sun-worshipping Cariocas play on Copacabana Beach, showgirls prepare for Carnival, and everyone sambas to the sultry music. Complete your journey in Brasilia.
32-5029 55 min. $24.95

Cancun

Jetset for Caribbean adventure. Scuba, snorkel, ski and sun in Mexico's newest and most exciting resort. Return in time to the coastal Mayan ruins of Tulum. Explore a natural aquarium in Xelha's seven freshwater lagoons. Catamoranto the Lagoon of Love and the ruins of El Rey - harem of Mayan kings. Also included is a reference guide to resorts and hotels plus travel tips by Berlitz travel guides.
32-042 60 min. $29.95

Costa Rica - Land of Pure Life

Join Video Visits and discover magical Costa Rica, where mist-shrouded peaks loom over fertile valleys and lush, tropical forests. Tiptoe around Irazu' volcano and visit the village of Sarchi where traditional wooden oxcarts are colorful works of art. Breathe in the fragrance of wild orchids at Lankester Gardens and join the struggle this pacifist nation faces in preserving its fragile natural wonders.
32-8014 56 min. $24.95

Cozumel

Off the Yucatan coast Cozumel is a diverse vacation destination. From scuba diving to windsurfing and parasailing, a wide variety of possibilities awaits you. Indulge in Yucatanian delights of conch, Mayan seafood and succulent shrimp. Explore sunken ships off Isla Mujeres or return in time to the ruins of Chichen-Itza. Also included is a reference guide to resorts and hotels plus travel tips by Berlitz travel guides.
32-043 60 min. $29.95

VIDEO TITLES LISTED IN THIS GUIDE ARE AVAILABLE FOR PURCHASE
OR RENTAL. CONTACT YOUR LOCAL VIDEO STORE OR TELEPHONE (800) 383-8811

DESTINATION MEXICO SERIES:

This series presents in-depth information about the hotel systems of Mexico's resort areas. It takes you into the lobbies of 10-30 hotels in each area, as well as visiting rooms and suites. There is also a "What to See" selection on each tape, and includes restaurants, shopping areas, sporting activities, nightlife and natural wonders. Must viewing for vacation planning by individuals and travel agents.

• **Video Hotel Directory and Travel Guide to Acapulco**
32-254 55 min. $24.95

• **Video Hotel Directory and Travel Guide to Baja California**
32-255 55 min. $24.95

• **Video Hotel Directory and Travel Guide to Cancun**
32-256 55 min. $24.95

• **Video Hotel Directory and Travel Guide to Cozumel**
32-257 31 min. $24.95

• **Video Hotel Directory and Travel Guide to Ixtapa**
32-258 30 min. $24.95

• **Video Hotel Directory and Travel Guide to Mazatlan**
32-259 30 min. $24.95

• **Video Hotel Directory and Travel Guide to Puerto Vallarta**
32-260 30 min. $24.95

Don't Blame Us If You Love Rio

This video adventure features the beaches of Copacabana and Ipanema and the beautiful people that relax there. Candid and exciting this is people watching at its best.
32-8237 30 min. $19.95

Ghosts of New Mexico

Documentary filmmaker J.C. Cale takes you on a journey of discovery through New Mexico's original pioneer settlements. See the remains of towns that settled the west and hear the stories of their birth...the hardships and trials of their growth...and the reasons behind their passing. Hosted by Hi Busse.
32-8232 70 min. $29.95

Guatemala

A country of contrasts is featured here, as Travelvision International leads viewers from sophisticated hotels to Mayan ruins to the fabled sinking city of Flores. This destination is a pleasant surprise.
32-047 60 min. $29.95

INSIDE MEXICO SERIES:

• **Folkloric Dances Of Mexico**
This program celebrates the 30th Anniversary of the Ballet Folclorico Nacional de Mexico, founded in 1960 by Silvia Lozano.
32-6285 108 min. $29.95

• **Mexican Prehispanic Cultures**
With this program, you will obtain a panorama of the various Pre-Columbian Civilizations that existed in the Mexican territory.
32-6286 26 min. $29.95

• **Mexico On Video**
Visit the National Museum of Anthropology and Teotihuacan. Explore the mysterious past and richness of the Pre-Columbian Civilizations.
32-6287 37 min. $29.95

• **Sounds Of Mexico**
Get to know the most representative music of Mexico, complemented with typical handicrafts and folk dresses.
32-6288 45 min. $29.95

Ixtapa-Zihuatanejo

The twin destinations of Ixtapa/Zihuatanejo offer the dual attraction of a contemporary resort city with a traditional Mexican village of Zihuatanejo, situated on a stretch of beautiful bay and Ixtapa, its more contemporary counterpart. Also included is a reference guide to resorts and hotels plus travel tips by Berlitz travel guides.
32-303 40 min. $29.95

Merida

Once celebrated as the "Paris of the West," Merida, located on the tip of the Yucatan peninsula, is a modern day combination of Spanish and French colonial influences, blended with a Mayan heritage. Parisian styled sidewalk cafes and 16th century Spanish courtyards remind you of yesteryear. Visit the Centenario Zoo, the Archeological Museum or the three story mercado. Also included is a Reference Guide to resorts and hotels, plus travel tips by Berlitz travel guides.
32-143 60 min. $29.95

Mexican Beach Resorts and West Coast Cruise With Laura Mckenzie

Acapulco, Cancun, Manzanillo, Las Hadas, plus a cruise to Puerto Vallarta, Mazatlan and Cabo San Lucas.
32-357 56 min. $24.95

VIDEO TITLES LISTED IN THIS GUIDE ARE AVAILABLE FOR PURCHASE OR RENTAL. CONTACT YOUR LOCAL VIDEO STORE OR TELEPHONE (800) 383-8811

Mexico City

Mexico City, a vibrant, thriving metropolis. Stroll the Chapultepec Park, shop international boutiques in the avenue of the Zona Rosa. Colonial churches and Aztec ruins overwhelm the senses, along with mariachi bands that mingle with contemporary night life. See for yourself this intriguing and exhilarating destination. Also included is a Reference Guide to resorts and hotels plus travel tips by Berlitz travel guides.
32-301 40 min. $29.95

Mexico Coast On Your Budget

This tape gives you actual interviews with people in Mexico, sharing invaluable facts covering each of these areas: health, activities, banking, climate, transportation and safety, shopping, accommodations, cost of living and recommendations, and RV living.
32-5631 30 min. $19.95

Mexico Inland On Your Budget

This tape gives you actual interviews with people in Mexico, sharing invaluable facts covering each of these areas: health, activities, banking, climate, transportation and safety, shopping, accommodations, cost of living and recommendations, and RV living.
32-5633 30 min. $19.95

Mexico: Journey to the Sun

Come with Video Visits and discover Mexico, from its ancient ruins to its intriguing and sunny beaches. View the Pyramid Tenochitlan. Visit Cuerna-vaca and its perfect climate, Visit Taxco, a colonial town decorated with flowers of every kind and Oaxaca, Acapulco, along Mexico's Riviera.
32-8031 60 min. $24.95

On the Road in Baja !

Take a trip down the 1000 mile Baja California peninsula in this colorful, informative video designed for the Baja traveler. Visit cities and villages from the Pacific Coast to the Sea of Cortez. You'll meet natives and also two noted baja authorities, Walt and Tom. Experience the natural beauty of this "forgotten land". The rich panpipe music of "Alturas" is a delightful plus!
32-9000 40 min. $24.95

Mexico Video Guide/Fodor's

One of the best known names in travel brings you a video full of tips for traveling in Mexico.
32-1639 75 min. $29.95

Passport Travel Guide - Mexico

Ole! A land rich in notable treasures. Vanished civilizations have left behind for us dance, precious stones and architecture. Beauty abounds.
32-6447 30 min. $16.95

Peru - A Golden Treasure

Begin in Lima, exploring with Video Visits the legacy of the Incas, and continue to Cuzco, the "City of Kings". Then, discover the beautiful oceanside resort of Las Dunas and view the Nazca lines, giant linear patterns that have puzzled scientists ever since their discovery.
32-8032 53 min. $24.95

Puerto Vallarta

Enjoy a wonderful blend of new and old in this seaside village. From burros transporting goods, to outstanding seaside restaurants, breathtaking views of cliffs, mountains and sunsets, it is a combination of fun and relaxation. Activities featured are sailing, parasailing, fishing, tennis, etc. Also included is a Reference Guide to resorts and hotels plus travel tips by Berlitz travel guides.
32-052 60 min. $29.95

Ronnie's Rio

A captivating look at a place, a people - and a man. Here is one of the world's most fabulous cities as seen by someone who knows it on both sides of the tracks: its famous beaches and its crowded back streets, its sophisticated night clubs and its bacchanalian "Carnivale". The man is Ronald Biggs, who engineered England's "Great Train Robbery" of 1963. He surfaced in Rio with new papers, a new face and new life.
32-226 48 min. $39.95

Singles' Guide To Rio De Janeiro

An absolute must for anyone planning to visit Brazil, even if it's only in their dreams. Learn about food, climate, special events, accommodations, and Rio's most incredible natural resource, its beautiful women. This video provides everything that the intrepid traveler needs in order to enjoy the warmth and sensuality of this great city,
32-5629 60 min. $19.95

This...Is Costa Rica

Ride the jungle train and the white-water rapids, experience a mystic rain forest and pull in the biggest deep-sea game fish ever. Stand on the edge of an active volcano and marvel at what nature has wrought. This is truly a scenic land of ideal temperatures and happy smiling faces.
32-9341 35 min. $29.95

Video Trip Guide to Mexico's Beach Resorts

Joanna Cassidy reveals the most beautiful and exciting places south of the border.
32-2276 60 min. $19.95

VIDEO TITLES LISTED IN THIS GUIDE ARE AVAILABLE FOR PURCHASE OR RENTAL. CONTACT YOUR LOCAL VIDEO STORE OR TELEPHONE (800) 383-8811

Other United States & Canada

AAA TRAVEL VIDEO SERIES:
Through expert photography and informative narration, these videos will provide the perfect preview for your travels through these inspiring lands.

• **Appalachian Trail/Kentucky, Tennessee, Virginia and West Virginia**
32-9380 60 min. $24.95

• **California**
32-9373 60 min. $24.95

• **Eastern Great Lakes**
32-9382 60 min. $24.95

• **Florida**
32-9372 60 min. $24.95

• **Great Plains/Arkansas, Kansas, Missouri, Oklahoma, Nebraska and Iowa**
32-9374 60 min. $24.95

• **Gulf Coast/Texas, Louisiana, Mississippi and Alabama**
32-9377 60 min. $24.95

• **Mid Atlantic/Pennsylvania, Maryland, Delaware and District of Columbia**
32-9370 60 min. $24.95

• **New England**
32-9371 60 min. $24.95

• **New York and New Jersey**
32-9381 60 min. $24.95

• **North Central/North Dakota, South Dakota, Montana and Wyoming**
32-9376 60 min. $24.95

• **Pacific Northwest/Washington, Oregon and Idaho**
32-9379 60 min. $24.95

• **Quebec and the Atlantic Provinces**
32-9375 60 min. $24.95

• **Southeast/North Carolina, South Carolina and Georgia**
32-9378 60 min. $24.95

• **Southwest/Colorado, Utah, Nevada, Arizona and New Mexico**
32-9369 60 min. $24.95

• **Western Great Lakes**
32-9382 60 min. $24.95

America's Monumental Story
Tour our nation's capitol and learn how its statues and granite buildings tell the story of America's evolution into a center of democracy. Highlights: Mount Vernon, Washington Monument, Jefferson Memorial, Library of Congress Capitol Building, White House, Arlington Cemetery, Vietnam Memorial and the Smithsonian Institute.
32-8189 30 min. $24.95

Arizona Highways Presents the Grand Canyon with Lorne Greene
Join a mule ride from the mile-high rim down to the Colorado River. Ride thundering rapids in a small raft. Visit the Havasupai Indians and idyllic blue-green waterfalls. Explore the ruins of ancient civilizations that mysteriously vanished. Includes graphic demonstrations of how the vast chasm was formed.
32-9993 55 min. $29.95

Arizona Highways Presents Lake Powell & the Canyon Country
William Shatner hosts a visit to world-famed Lake Powell, where the majestic cliffs of Glen Canyon form the backdrop for 2,000 miles of shoreline. Spectacular scenery, water sports, fishing and unusual rock formations are highlighted. Also included are visits to the Grand Canyon's North Rim, Zion and Bryce Canyon National Parks, Monument Valley and the prehistoric Anasazi ruins at Navajo National Monument.
32-9994 60 min. $29.95

Atlantic City - America's First Resort
Join Video Visits and experience the full spectrum of leisure time activities and savor the richness and diversity of the surrounding area.
32-1747 26 min. $24.95

Bed & Breakfast/Country Inns Guide to Vermont
Come along with us to Vermont and get the feel of the charm and character it's Country Inns. Experience the various styles and atmospheres, from simple country to the elegance of yesteryear. Visit the quaint, scenic, and historic towns and nearby

attractions. Includes map & guide.
32-9033 90 min. $19.95

Big Bend: America's Last Primitive Frontier

Murmuring current of the Rio Grande, natural boundary between U.S. and Mexico; timelessness, solitude; ancient mountains, miracle of lowland desert, Green Gulch: the west as it was a century ago.
32-8270 60 min. $29.95

California Wine Country by Video Visits

Explore California's premium wine regions from Sonoma to Carmel Valley. Watch the harvest and learn how wine is made. Discover the history of early California while visiting Sonoma's Mission and town plaza and General Vallejo's barracks. See rare footage of Jack London at his ranch and most of all, partake in sweeping views of the Napa Valley in a hot-air balloon.
32-8037 53 min. $24.95

California's Wine Country

A tour through vineyards of the Napa Valley. Visit 14 of California's finest wineries, meet the winemakers, experience the harvest as the grapes are hand-picked, crushed, and readied for the casks, and eventual bottling. Explore the rich history of the Napa and Sonoma Valley's as you discover the enduring charm of the beautiful California wine country. Vineyards visited include Spring Mountain, Rutherford, Mondavi, Kenwood and others.
32-194 40 min. $29.95

Banff/Lake Louise

Marvel at the magnitude of the Canadian Rockies. Banff and Lake Louise have awed visitors since the first train loads arrived in the late 1800's. Ski with us on the luminous snow of Victoria Glacier; visit the Banff Springs Hotel and Chateau Lake Louise. Wintertime in Banff, a fun filled vacation with skiing, ice skating, sledding and many more activities. Also included is a reference guide to resorts and hotels plus travel tips by Berlitz travel guides.
32-040 60 min. $29.95

Boston With Laura McKenzie

Journey to the birthplace of the American Revolution, where thrilling moments from our nation's past come to life. Join Laura McKenzie on Boston's glorious Freedom Trail: View Paul Revere's house, the Old North Church and the Boston Tea Party Ship. This tour also includes the Boston Commons, Harvard University, Lexington, Concord, Plymouth Rock, Cape Cod and much more.
32-1516 55 min. $24.95

British Columbia - Rockies to the Pacific

Join Video Visits and explore the beauty and splendor of Canada's Province, enjoy its many scenic wonders.
32-1740 30 min. $24.95

Canada

Meet the igloo builders of Baffin Island, the "hot dog" skiers of Banff and the logging competitors of Sooke, British Columbia. Join Quebec Winter Carnival canoeists who scramble, slip, slide and paddle their crafts to victory on the icy St. Lawrence River. Dance with young Scots at Cape Breton's Festival of the Tartans. Rekindle the spirit of the Old West with buffalo riding, wild cow milking and thundering chuck wagon races of Alberta's Calgary Stampede. Experience Canada's diversity and enduring splendor from the changing of the guard on Ottawa's Parliament Hill to the technological amusements of Ontario's science Center.
32-307 30 min. $24.95

Canadian Rockies/Bannf, Lake Louise

Travel with Gay Lewis and Doug Clovechok as they share with you the excitement of the Calgary Stampede and the breathtaking splendor of mountains, glaciers and emerald lakes.
32-9002 40 min. $29.95

Cavaliers and Craftsmen of Jamestown

Welcome to the world of Virginia's first colonists, and enjoy a visit to an exploration of two of America's most important colonies - Williamsburg and Jamestown - with a pleasant side trip to the nearby Flowerdew Hundred windmill. Panoramic vistas provide the timeless backdrop for the rich details of colonial life: the clothes, the crafts, and the artifacts. An historically charged narration and period music help create a feeling for the life and times of this era.
32-261 30 min. $19.95

Challenge of Niagara Falls

Join Video Visits and experience the majestic views of North America's best-known scenic marvel, Niagara Falls, a name synonymous with mankind's urge to challenge the forces of nature.
32-219 25 min. $24.95

Chicago!

It's all here, 101 things to see and do in Chicago. From landmarks as familiar as the Water Tower and the Picasso to the little neighborhood festivals.
32-9579 30 min. $19.95

Chicago: One Magnificent City

Explore the treasures of the Chicago Art Institute, the Museum of Natural History and Shedd Aquarium. Discover the grandeur of Miracle Mile, a stylish boulevard of prestigious stores and

architectural marvels. With Chicago's multicultural neighborhoods enjoy the vast array of cultural celebrations. Spend a night on the town and feel the passionate beat of the Chicago Blues.
32-8016 55 min. $24.95

Columbia River Gorge: A Chasm of Beauty
History comes to life in the magnificently photographed, in-depth portrait of the Columbia River Gorge National Scenic Area and its special beauty--waterfalls, rivers, trails, parks and vistas. Come explore this biological and geological wonder.
32-9068 60 min. $29.95

Crater Lake: Relic of a Vanished Mountain
Nature's holocaust, a vanished mountain collapsed in a fiery caldera 6,000 years ago. Awesome volcanic cliffs, fascinating wildlife; human and natural history.
32-8264 45 min. $29.95

Easy Access: National Parks
This video opens the doors of national parks to people with disabilities and special needs, such as seniors and young children in strollers. Wendy Roth, a wheelchair user, experienced firsthand the trails, campgrounds and nature walks. Includes: Acadia, ME; Chaco Culture, NM; Everglades, FL; Mesa Verde, CO; Olympic, WA; Rocky Mountain, CO; Shenandoah, VA; Yellowstone and Yosemite.
32-8175 30 min. $19.95

Experience Utah
A trip through an incredibly beautiful land of snow-capped mountains, red rockdesert canyons, world famous ski resorts, historic sites and modern cities - the state of Utah. A glorious panorama of natural splendor like no other in the world.
32-252 60 min. $29.95

Explore Colorado
Capture the breathtaking scenery and pioneer spirit of Colorado, including her natural wonders, mining towns, scenic railroads and historic sites. Visit Mesa Verde, Rocky Mountain, and six other national park sites. Drive the Million Dollar Highway through Durango, Silverton and Ouray; plus visit Pikes Peak, Colorado Springs, Royal Gorge and much more. Includes visits to four of Colorado's famed scenic narrow gauge railroads.
32-1703 60 min. $29.95

Exploring Lake Powell
Come with Video Visits and explore this nine trillion gallon body of water formed by Glen Canyon Dam between Southern Utah and Northern Arizona.
32-1753 29 min. $24.95

Florida Keys
From Biscayne Bay to Dry Tortugos the diamond necklace of the Florida Keys stretches 200 miles into the Atlantic.
32-5009 30 min. $24.95

Florida Gulf Coast
Presents the unique character of the vacation opportunities and attractions in Pinellas and Lee Counties. From Clearwater to Fort Myers, the myriad of activities along that 128-mile stretch of glistening white beach make this area the ideal family vacation destination.
32-130 30 min. $19.95

Florida: America's Vacationland
From St. Augustine to the Florida Keys, from the Everglades to the Gulf Islands, enjoy Florida's natural splendor, unique wildlife, rich history, fascinating cities, and lots of exciting attractions. Experience the technology of Kennedy Space Center, then wander through centuries-old Castillo de San Marcos. Alligators, manitees, scuba diving, gorgeous beaches and more! Visit places like Miami Beach, Key West, Vizcaya, Silver Springs, Fort Jefferson and Cypress Gardens. It's a fun-filled and educational tour.
32-1704 60 min. $29.95

Florida-Playground in the Sun
Few tourists ever see the sides of the sunshine state that you'll see here! Travel to the Keys, islands made famous by Hemingway and Humphrey Bogart, to Disney World and Universal Studios, to the delicate ecosystem of the Everglades and St. Augustine, the oldest European settlement in North America.
32-8017 56 min. $24.95

Ghost Towns USA
Step back in time to relive the spirit of legends and lore! Survey once-booming towns gone bust after mining played out: California's Caloma, Calico and Bodie; Colorado's Tuckerville, Nevada's Famous Gold Point and Goldville plus Arizona's Jerome and Oatman.
32-8132 31 min. $16.95

Grand Canyon: A Journey Into Discovery
Thrill to the awesome grandeur. Breathtaking views of the canyon and its many treasures.
32-8255 90 min. $29.95

Grand Canyon: An Ariel Odyssey
Explore the magnitude and grandeur of the canyon.

Enjoy the spires and formations that make up this incredible world.
32-8267 60 min. $29.95

Great Smokies: A Wildlands Sanctuary
Breathtaking photography over the ridges, into coves and hollows; wonders of life at every turn.
32-8258 90 min. $29.95

Great Smokey Mountains
Discover the natural wonders, breathtaking scenery and pioneer spirit of three national park areas with this inspiring tour. From the rich wilderness of the Great Smokies, to the scenery and folklore of the Blue Ridge Parkway, to the gentle mountain beauty of Shenandoah, you'll learn the stories and secrets of each.
32-5043 60 min. $29.95

Guide To Northern Florida
Journey through North Florida, from Pensacola and the Gulf of Mexico, to the inland towns of Tallahassee and Gainesville, and on to the Atlantic seaboard communities. On this adventurous trip, you will encounter the inviting beauty of powdered sands, spraying surf, the thrill of world class sportfishing, unmatched golf, and exciting water sports. View the captivating emerald backwater lakes and lagoons, surrounded by lush, tropical forests and exotic wildlife.
32-6623 47 min. $19.95

Guide To Ohio
Ohio is fast becoming one of America's most popular getaway destinations. Northeast Ohio is highlighted by some of the largest amusement parks in the country, along with Pro Football's Hall of Fame. Enjoy riverboat rides on the mighty Ohio River, see mysterious monuments left by prehistoric Indians. You will see some of the best walleye fishing in the country... See why Ohio is called "the heart of it all!"
32-6624 50 min. $19.95

Guide To South Florida And The Keys
Take a trip from the sparkling, shell covered beaches, off Fort Meyers, to the enchanting Caribbean Gardens, at Naples. Travel from the haunting mystery and beauty of the Everglades to the mesmerizing seascapes of the Florida Keys.
32-6622 50 min. $19.95

Houston
Visit dynamic Houston, the newest big city in Texas.
32-300 80 min. $29.95

John Wesley Powell: Canyon Geologist
Relive parts of John Wesley Powell's pioneer exploration through the Grand Canyon in 1869, this film traces the expedition that opened a large unknown region of the west. Scenes are visited of Powell's early exploits showing the geologic features he observed. Excerpts from his diary are used to tell of the ordeals sustained during the exploration voyage.
32-8224 40 min. $24.95

LAKE POWELL/ADVENTURES IN GLEN CANYON
With 1,960 miles of undeveloped shoreline and literally thousands of spectacular inlets, canyons, caves and coves, plus Indian ruins, petroglyphs, pictographs and more.

Lake Powell: Heart of the Grand Circle
Lake Powell, with its 96 breath-taking canyons, 200 miles of crystal waters and 1,900 miles of sandy beaches and high cliffs, awaits you. Any season, any style-Lake Powell has it all.
32-318 27 min. $29.95

Las Vegas: The Glamour & the Glitter
A city enamored of neon where entertainment shines brightest: showgirls, casinos and the excitement of the "strip".
32-8273 90 min. $29.95

Las Vegas and Hoover Dam
Three exciting subjects in one. Experience fabulous Las Vegas - including gambling, hotels, the Strip, show girls, etc. Marvel at the incredible design and grandeur of mighty Hoover Dam, plus witness the great Colorado River flood of 1983. This unprecedented disaster overflowed Glen Canyon, Hoover and Davis Dams on the mighty Colorado.
32-166 25 min. $29.95

Las Vegas: Only in America
Join Video Visits and experience the neon night life of "Glitter Gulch". Thrill to the excitement of glamorous show- girls, international superstars and high-stakes casino gambling. Discover Hoover Dam, Lake Mead and unspoiled desert vistas. Uncover the city's cultural diversity and history.
32-8034 52 min. $24.95

Las Vegas and Surrounding Day Trips With Laura McKenzie
Hoover Dam, Lake Mead and Calico.
32-354 56 min. $24.95

Majestic National Parks
Visit ancient cliff dwellings. Walk through eerie monoliths. Watch wildlife in their natural homes. Discover Yellowstone, Acadia, Mount Rainier, Arches, Mesa Verde, Bryce Canyon and Grand Tetons national parks.
32-8133 40 min. $16.95

VIDEO TITLES LISTED IN THIS GUIDE ARE AVAILABLE FOR PURCHASE OR RENTAL. CONTACT YOUR LOCAL VIDEO STORE OR TELEPHONE (800) 383-8811

Mammoth Cave National Park, Kentucky

Descend into the mysterious world of Mammoth Cave - the longest cave on Earth! Discover Mammoth's fascinating features and explore its winding tunnels and passageways, rich with unique formations such as helictites, gypsum flowers, soda straws and flowstone. Learn the fascinating human history, including the Saltpeter mining during the War of 1812.

32-1779 30 min. $29.95

Mesa Verde: Where the Spirits Rise

Before the pioneers, before the Pilgrims, before Columbus, were the Anasazi--the Ancient Ones. A thrilling journey into the remains of a vanished civilization. Haunting, beautiful photography of the people who suddenly, mysteriously abandoned their homes 700 years ago.

32-8263 45 min. $29.95

Miami and the Beaches

Miami - the cruise ship capital of America's East Coast and gateway to Florida's Keys. This cassette takes you on a tour to see its racetracks, Tai Alai, deep sea fishing, sailing and art deco architecture. Visit Little Havana and follow us on a short trip into the Everglades. Also included is a Reference Guide to resorts and hotels plus travel tips by Berlitz travel guides.

32-050 60 min. $29.95

Mississippi

Explore America, along this storied river and steamboat territory. A photo/travel adventure with Audubon, sugar cane, steamboat whistles and Dixieland. Travel its 2,340 miles and 29 locks and dams to Vicksburg, Natchez and New Orleans. Meet a former pilot of the Delta Queen, the last authentic steamboat carrying overnight passengers on the Mississippi. Hop aboard for a Mississippi River ride complete with Creole cooking and calliope music.

32-313 30 min. $24.95

Monument Valley--Navajo Homeland

In this beautifully filmed video discover the majestic beauty of Monument Valley and the mystical bond between the Navajo and their ancient homeland.

32-8114 30 min. $29.95

Mount McKinley: Denali: A Subarctic Wonderland

Visit the highest mountain in North America and the last truly wild country.

32-8269 60 min. $29.95

Mount Rainier: Arctic Island in the Sky

Above a tidal wave of evergreen rises a shining vision. Discover a wondrous and alien world of mountain lakes, meadows, and dwarf flowers in bloom.

32-8260 60 min. $29.95

Mount St. Helens

Spectacular exploding volcano and the catastrophic devastation, explore the gaping crater atop the dome. Will it erupt again? Learn its violent history and wonder at its force.

32-8261 90 min. $29.95

Mount Washington Valley

Filmed in all four seasons. The beauty and wonder of the white mountains are featured in this picturesque program. Witness the beauty of Winter and the great skiing that takes place. Autumn explodes with its famous foliage and color. Spring and Summer are a hiker and campers delight. A perfect gift of a true vacation land.

32-8188 25 min. $29.95

Naturally Niagara Falls

Observe the changing seasons of Niagara Falls as summer changes to autumn and autumn transforms into winter. Visit Ontario Water Park, Goat Island and Three Sisters Islands. See the Whirlpool, trails into Devil's Hole and the Canadian and American Falls from a variety of spectacular viewpoints. Niagara Falls--a rare combination of beauty and power that only nature could perform.

32-8191 30 min. $24.95

NATURE/SCENE VIDEO SERIES:

Winner of the National Wildlife Federation Conservation Award

• Outer Banks of North Carolina & Padre Island

Travel through the raw beauty of the Outer Bank Barrier Island and see the astonishing wildlife off the Texas Coast.

32-8135 60 min. $16.95

• New England Autumn & New Jersey Pine Barrens

This award winning series continues with the dazzling array of fall foliage plus the teeming vast pinelands of New Jersey.

32-8136 60 min. $16.95

• Mount Rainier & Custer State Park

(The Black Hills of South Dakota)
See the great mountain created by fire and ice and the huge granite masses of the Black Hills. A rich variety for nature lovers.

32-8137 60 min. $16.95

• Everglades & Sanibel Island

Spend time in Florida with a close-up view of

tropical flora and fauna followed by the shell strewn beaches of Sanibel.
32-8138 60 min. $16.95

• **Okefenokee & Devil's Tower**
Discover the eerie mystery of the Swamp then head for the stunning Black Hills of Wyoming and the prairie wildlife.
32-8149 60 min. $16.95

• **Mountain Magic (Appalachian Mountain) & Natchez Trace**
Trace eons of erosion in the Appalachians then stroll though ceremonial grounds on one of America's oldest trails.
32-8140 60 min. $16.95

New Orleans
A city that charms you with its French and Spanish heritage, its music, food, historic sights, Bourbon Street and Mardi Gras. The sounds range from pop to blues to jazz. Savor the cuisine that makes New Orleans an epicurean fantasyland.
32-131 30 min. $19.95

New Orleans Style
Carriage through the French Quarter and navigate the Mississippi on a paddle wheel steamboat. Taste seafood gumbo and spicy jumbalaya and join festive crowds electrified by New Orleans Jazz. Visit the bayou where alligators stalk. Experience the celebration of Mardi Gras in a city with a style all its own.
32-8190 30 min. $24.95

New Orleans with Laura Mckenzie
Explore the French Quarter, jazz it up on Bourbon Street, Dine on Creole cuisine. Ride Mississippi River ferries and visit plantations. All before you go!
32-1867 60 min. $24.95

New York: A Really Great City
Visit the city that lovers love, artists paint the New York that you can experience over and over again in this video guide to America's greatest city.
32-9578 60 min. $24.95

New York - City of Cities
Join Video Visits and enjoy this fast-paced tour of one of the world's great cities and capture the flavor and excitement of the unique neighborhoods and famous landmarks.
32-1738 45 min. $24.95

New York City
See the best the Big Apple has to offer with Laura McKenzie as your guide. Visit the World Trade Center, Wall Street, the Brooklyn Bridge, the Statue of Liberty, Greenwich Village, Soho,

Chinatown, Little Italy, the Empire State Building, the United Nations, Broadway, Times Square, Central Park and more!
32-1518 60 min. $24.95

Niagara Scene
Springtime in Niagara - see the beautiful blossoms as well as the major attractions of this popular area. Take a look at the charm of historic Niagara-on-the-Lake, Fort George, and Brock's Monument overlooking the majestic lower Niagara River. Ride the Spanish Aerocar and see an overhead view of the thundering lower rapids and famous whirlpool. See the Canadian Horseshoe Falls and the American Falls. Take a boat ride on the Maid of the Mist to the base of the mighty falls. And see Niagara in winter. A spectacular scenic video.
32-198 42 min. $39.95

Northern Saskatchewan
Escape to the alluring majesty of Northern Saskatchewan, heart of Canada. Enjoy outdoor wilderness adventures in a land of unexcelled beauty.
32-053 60 min. $29.95

Old West Trail Country
Presented as a vacation destination area which features the best that America has to offer for outdoor recreation and family fun and education. Take a video visit to the nation's premiere showcase of mountain, prairies, badlands, waterfalls and western history.
32-132 30 min. $19.95

Olympic - A Wonderland of Shore, Mountain & Rain Forest
An abundance of three worlds including: wildlife, rain forests and mountain views.
32-8268 60 min. $29.95

Oregon: State of Wonder
The pounding surf, volcanic peaks, gushing waterfalls and green valleys welcome you to Oregon. Join Video Visits and relive the history of the land's formation and the hardy pioneers who trekked across the Oregon Trail.
32-8035 60 min. $24.95

OREGON TRAIL SERIES:
This series of programs tells the story of these great pioneers undertaking a great 2000 mile journey. Detailing the reasons and rigors they underwent in its course.

• **Across the Plains**
Topics include: Lewis and Clark, The Great Migration and the first emigrants. Covers the trail from Independence, Missouri to

Fort Laramie, in what is now Wyoming.
32-8278 60 min. $29.95

• **Through the Rockies & The Final Steps**
This tape covers the steps from Fort Laramie to Fort Hail, in modern-day Idaho. Includes dangers of disease (cholera), and trail overcrowding.
32-8279 60 min. $29.95

Orlando, Kissimmee & St. Cloud, Florida
The sunny center of the state offers Walt Disney World, EPCOT Center, Sea World, Circus World, and Medieval Times to fun-seeking vacationers. There are also the very real worlds of lakes, wildlife sanctuaries and gator farms.
32-133 30 min. $19.95

OUR NATIONAL HERITAGE SERIES:
This series is a unique collection of entertaining and educational programs on America's exceptional natural and cultural heritage. Whether you're planning a trip or sharing a past visit, these programs offer the very best of U.S. travel, culture and more!

• **Atlanta Cyclorama: Battle of Atlanta**
32-8146 30 min. $24.95

• **Canyon de Chelly/Hubbell Trading Post**
32-8143 30 min. $24.95

• **Indian & His Homeland: American Images: 1590-1876**
32-8141 30 min. $24.95

• **Las Vegas and The Enchanted Desert**
32-8148 45 min. $24.95

• **Luray Caverns**
32-8150 30 min. $24.95

• **Red Rock Canyon, Nevada**
32-8149 45 min. $24.95

• **Strawberry Banke: A New England Neighborhood**
32-8145 25 min. $24.95

• **Stones River National Battlefield**
32-8142 35 min. $24.95

• **Touring the Southwest's Grand Circle**
32-8147 60 min. $24.95

• **Virginia's Civil War Parks**
32-8144 56 min. $24.95

OUR NATIONAL PARK AND MONUMENT SERIES:

• **Olympic National Park: Wilderness Heritage**
32-8139 30 min. $24.95

• **Zion National Park: Towers of Stone**
32-8140 30 min. $24.95

Pikes Peak Country with Colorado Springs
Colorado's premiere vacation land! Explore the area's scenic wonders and visit over 40 of its finest attractions, including museums, historic sites and rustic towns where the pioneer spirit of true-to-life legends like Buffalo Bill lives on. See Garden of the Gods, Pikes Peak, Royal Gorge, the Air Force Academy and more.
32-169 50 min. $29.95

Purgatory, Colorado
Featuring southwest sunshine all year around, with fabulous skiing in the winter and spectacular hiking in the summer, this is a family resort for people who love the outdoors.
32-146 60 min. $29.95

READER'S DIGEST VIDEO SERIES:
Reader's Digest brings you this award winning series of videos that will allow you to explore some of our greatest natural wonders without leaving your home.

Double Features:

• **Bryce Canyon & Zion: Canyons of Wonder**
32-8038 64 min. $24.95

• **Grand Teton & Glacier: Land of Shining Mountains**
32-8040 71 min. $24.95

• **Mount Rainier & Olympic: Northwest Treasures**
32-8039 66 min. $24.95

Single Features:

• **Bryce Canyon**
32-8041 32 min. $16.95

VIDEO TITLES LISTED IN THIS GUIDE ARE AVAILABLE FOR PURCHASE OR RENTAL. CONTACT YOUR LOCAL VIDEO STORE OR TELEPHONE (800) 383-8811

- **Glacier**
32-8046 37 min. $16.95

- **Grand Teton**
32-8046 36 min. $16.95

- **Mount Ranier**
32-8043 34 min. $16.95

- **Olympic**
32-8044 32 min. $16.95

- **Zion**
32-8042 32 min. $16.95

River of the Red Ape
This is the true story of the first attempt to navigate the wild Atlas River on Indonesia's Equatorial island of Sumatra. Join host William Devane in an exploration of the magic and madness of a river that penetrates one of the last, great wildernesses on earth and into the heart of the last large population of orangutans. This is a region rich in wildlife and exotic cultures, and an area doomed to extinction. A high adventure through a dramatic and delicate land.
32-341 56 min. $39.95

Rocky Mountain National Park
Discover the Crown Jewel of Colorado - a land of towering peaks, where fully one-third of the park is above the tree line. The variety of landscapes is stunning - glacier-carved canyons, vast forests and arctic tundra. See some of the North America's most splendid mountain lakes and drive spectacular Trail Ridge Road - the highest continuous highway in the U.S. Includes great scenes of native wildlife, including the Bighorn Sheep, living symbol of the Rockies.
32-1706 30 min. $29.95

Salt Lake City, Utah
See Alpine mountains, shimmering lakes and river, carved sandstone formations, national parks and a clean, sophisticated city.
32-350 30 min. $29.95

Scenic Seattle
Seattle blends city life with a love for the outdoors - bustling metropolis intertwined with lakes, rivers and streams. Visit the Space Needle, Science Center, boat canals, waterfront, Snoqualimie Falls, Mt. Rainier and more.
32-287 30 min. $29.95

SCENIC WONDERS VIDEO SERIES:

- **American West**
Start where America's mighty Mississippi empties into the Gulf of Mexico. Voyage upriver and wonder at the majestic Great Lakes. Then west to visit the Parks of Yellowstone, Grand Teton, Bryce Canyon, Zion and the Grand Canyon. Take in the breath-taking landscapes of Devil's Tower in Wyoming, the Dakota Badlands and the sculptural elegance of Utah's Arches.
32-8047 60 min. $24.95

- **Atlantic Vistas**
From early morning sunlight on the shores of Maine's Acadia National Park to sunset over the Everglades, here's an unforgettable Niagara Falls and the primordial beauty of Georgia's Okefenokee Swamp.
32-8048 60 min. $24.95

- **Pacific Frontiers**
Your journey begins in the stark beauty of Death Valley National Monument and ends with enthralling closeups of rare nene birds nesting in the crater of a dormant volcano in Hawaii. In between, experience a dense rain forest, crashing waves and icy glaciers. Explore the ancient sequoias of California, the frozen landscapes of Alaska's Glacier Bay and Oregon's pristine Crater Lake.
32-8049 60 min. $24.95

Sequoia & Kings Canyon: Monarchs of the Forest
The largest and one of the rarest, oldest living things--the magnificent Giant Sequoias. Kings Canyon--rivers, waterfalls and meadows adorn a glacier-carved mountain wilderness.
32-8262 35 min. $29.95

Shenandoah
The sacrifice and struggle from mountaineers to presidents in presenting a new national park. Experience a feeling of Shenandoah's settlers and mountain people amid meadows and forests where wildlife are seen in natural habitats.
32-8259 55 min. $29.95

Ski Colorado
Guides the skiing holiday vacationer, not only to the thrill of downhill and cross-country skiing, but also exposes the skier and non-skier alike to the other recreational possibilities for the vacationer to the Colorado Ski Country USA, such as hot-air ballooning and ice skating.
32-134 30 min. $19.95

Ski New England
Sports enthusiasts and sightseers will marvel at U.S. Olympic Ski Coach Bob Beattie's trip to New England.
32-2277 60 min. $19.95

VIDEO TITLES LISTED IN THIS GUIDE ARE AVAILABLE FOR PURCHASE OR RENTAL. CONTACT YOUR LOCAL VIDEO STORE OR TELEPHONE (800) 383-8811

Ski Vermont

Vermont is epitomized by the six-mountain Killington Ski Area. Some of America's finest downhill and cross-country skiing is explored; as is the Alpine Ski School and its "Accelerated Ski Method". Lodging, dining and accessibility are discussed for your planning purposes.
32-135 30 min. $19.95

Sweet Land of Liberty

Look at America in this photographic spectacular saluting the Statue of Liberty. See her at birth in 1886 and in all her glory at the 100-year birthday celebration. Relive the excitement of out country's Fourth of July celebration with highlights from the laser light show, fireworks display, sporting events, tall ships' arrival and the opening/closing ceremonies.
32-317 30 min. $16.95

This is Toronto

Join Video Visits and experience Canada's largest city, with its showcase of culture, entertainment and beauty in this colorful video tour.
32-1746 30 min. $24.95

Travel Florida State and National Parks

A traveler's guide to the best State and National parks in Florida: camping, canoeing, swimming, fishing, boating, and more.
32-5007 30 min. $24.95

Vancouver - The World in a City

Join Video Visits and discover this young and vibrant city, explore its many wonderful attractions, sporting events, festivals and unmatched scenic beauty on this video tour.
32-1745 30 min. $24.95

Video Journey Through San Francisco

See the old and the new from the Bay to the Ocean, with excursions to Muir Woods, Sausalito and the wine country.
32-105 30 min. $29.95

Virginia Plantations: Mount Vernon, Monticello and Other Great Houses

Explore Virginia's old plantations, reminders of a unique society of early America. The homes are stunning and history-laden, and provide vivid evidence of their tremendous importance. The program focuses on two of the most famous, George Washington's Mt. Vernon and Thomas Jefferson's Monticello.
32-353 30 min. $16.95

Washington, D.C.

The Today Show's wacky weatherman Willard Scott is your personal guide to our nation's capital.
32-2274 60 min. $16.95

Washington, D.C.

In this inspiring tour, you will explore Washington's rich heritage, magnificent architecture, historic treasures, and honored memorials and monuments. Tour inside the Smithsonian Museums and the Library of Congress. Visit the White House, the Capitol, the Lincoln and Vietnam Memorials, and much more.
32-172 30 min. $29.95

Washington D.C.: A Capital Experience

Join Video Visits and enjoy this exciting adventure with its grand monuments and special historical sites.
32-1739 30 min. $24.95

Washington Monuments

This video captures the beauty and history of the Capital's major landmarks in a presentation that is informative, picturesque and entertaining. Featured are the U.S. Capitol, the Smithsonian Institute, the Washington Monument, The White House, the Jefferson Memorial, the Lincoln Memorial, the Vietnam Veterans Memorial and more.
32-1675 30 min. $16.95

Washington, D.C. and Surrounding Day Trips with Laura McKenzie

Highlights include visits to the Capitol, the White House and Lincoln, Jefferson, Washington and Vietnam War Memorials. Plus Georgetown, Alexandria, Mt. Vernon and Arlington.
32-256 56 min. $24.95

Wild Florida

Explore the Great Peninsula and discover its extraordinary wildlife. Manatees in the Crystal River, the Everglades, Alligators at Corkscrew Swamp and Silver Springs, Key Deer, Nesting Sea Turtles, then Pelican Island Bird Rookery, underwater life at John Pennekamp Coral Reef State Park and Wakulla Springs, Sturgeon in the Suwannee River, Otters at Fisheating Creek, Snail Kites at Lake Okeechobee, and more.
32-5006 42 min. $29.95

Wilderness Vacations

Coleman Guide to Camping with Bruce Jenner

One of America's foremost manufacturers of sporting goods, Coleman Industries, and one of

America's finest athletes, Bruce Jenner, have joined forces to bring you a videotape about camping. This program presents a complete look at the perfect camping vacation, from where to go, to how to enjoy camping thoroughly. You'll learn everything you'll need to know to make your camping trip a great experience.
32-431 60 min. $19.95

Yellowstone
Geysers in violent eruption, mudpots in turmoil: experience the thrill of discovery by historic expeditions through Yellowstone. Explore the massive citadels of the Grand Tetons.
32-8257 90 min. $29.95

Yosemite
Magnificent topographical sculpture. Rare views of granite peaks, rock climbing, wildlife and an incredible history.
32-8256 90 min. $29.95

Miscellaneous

10 Hottest South Pacific Resorts
32-8239 60 min. $16.95

10 Hottest Ski Resorts
32-8240 90 min. $16.95

10 Hottest Tours
32-8241 90 min. $16.95

America's Secret Places
A video for explorers who want to see where to go to escape civilization, to find their own fairylands and lands of Oz; places where, in some cases, you'll have to take your own food and provisions, since the nearest road is 40 miles away. You will find your secret refuge in places smooth and rough, dry and wet, high and low, barren and abundant; from Maine to Florida, up through the heartland to the northern coast of California.
32-1721 54 min. $29.95

Australia
The former home of the America's Cup, Australia is the oldest, flattest and driest continent. Yet it boasts more snow than Switzerland. This travel adventure takes you to the world's supply of opals, to wild camel country, a koala bear sanctuary and the mystical Olga mountains. Kangaroos and wallabees maintain a strong presence in the land "down under". An absolute paradise.
32-1716 60 min. $29.95

Consumer Report: Traveling - How to Spend Less and Enjoy It More
Picking a good agent, how to get health care, luggage, and best bets on vacations with kids are just some of the interesting things you will learn from this guide.
32-296 60 min. $19.95

Dive Pennekamp
Explore the secrets of the Coral Reef and meet the mysterious residents of America's first underwater park. Dive Pennakamp will take you on glassbottom boats, snorkeling, scuba diving and camping in the U.S.A.'s most visited state park.
32-5010 30 min. $24.95

Everglades, Big Cypress
Tour these four National parks: Everglades, Big Cypress, Biscayne, and Fort Jefferson. Discover the inspiring natural beauty of these four parks and learn about the amazing variety of plant and animal life that are found here. From the teeming waters of the Everglades to the underwater world of Biscayne, these are the natural treasures of Southern Florida.
32-5044 56 min. $29.95

G' Day From Australia
This video visits: Sydney, the Gold Coast, the Barrier Reef, Queensland, Melbourne, Tasmania, Adelaide, Perth, and Northern Territory
32-6180 45 min. $19.95

GREAT JOURNEY SERIES:
In the tradition of the award-winning series "River Journeys", this BBC series follows eight distinguished writers on modern day adventures along the highways of history.

• **Across the South Pacific**
32-8250 60 min. $99.95

• **Burma Road**
32-8253 60 min. $99.95

• **Ho Chi Minh Trail**
32-8249 60 min. $99.95

• **Pan-American Highway**
32-8247 60 min. $99.95

• **Russia's Road West**
32-8252 60 min. $99.95

• **Salt Road**
32-8248 60 min. $99.95

• **Silk Road**
32-8251 60 min. $99.95

VIDEO TITLES LISTED IN THIS GUIDE ARE AVAILABLE FOR PURCHASE OR RENTAL. CONTACT YOUR LOCAL VIDEO STORE OR TELEPHONE (800) 383-8811

- **Silver Tracts**
32-8254 60 min. $99.95

IF THESE WALLS COULD SPEAK:
In this series, Vincent Price visits the haunted palaces of the world.

- **Chapultepec Palace**
32-329 30 min. $19.95

- **Edinburgh Castle**
32-326 30 min. $19.95

- **Fushimi Castle**
32-325 30 min. $19.95

- **Hampton Court**
32-323 30 min. $19.95

- **Iolani Palace**
32-321 30 min. $19.95

- **Kilmainham Jail**
32-327 30 min. $19.95

- **Kronborg Castle**
32-320 30 min. $19.95

- **Mount Vernon**
32-370 30 min. $19.95

- **Palace of Versailles**
32-324 30 min. $19.95

- **Pompeii**
32-322 30 min. $19.95

- **Port Arthur Jail**
32-368 30 min. $19.95

- **San Juan Capistrano**
32-369 30 min. $19.95

- **Sutters Fort**
32-328 30 min. $19.95

- **Virginia City**
32-367 30 min. $19.95

Kremlin
The heart of Soviet Russia, the center of the Communist World is embodied in the Kremlin. From its early beginnings to its present base of power, this look at the Kremlin won the Emmy Award for outstanding programming.
32-1872 60 min. $24.95

Mount Vernon
Mount Vernon is more than a hand-some and historic estate, home of America's most famous hero. Washington's personality and interests are evident everywhere. Textbooks describe the General and the President, but Mount Vernon, as seen in this video program, tells us about the man. Washington's home is shown in its entirety, including the third floor, which is not usually viewed by the public. Finally, the nation's most celebrated fife and drum corps performs at Washington's Tomb.
32-5141 30 min. $29.95

New Zealand
A cross-section of the world. Placid lakes, Alpine peaks, totem poles, rocks as flat as pancakes, more wool than anyplace else in the world and tomatoes that grow on trees. This colorful tape which surveys the North and South Islands that comprise New Zealand does not neglect the famed flightless Kiwi bird. Comparable to a Japanese countryside with cities and cable cars reminiscent of San Francisco, it is also London with a climate similar to Florida. Everyman's land.
32-1717 56 min. $29.95

Passport Travel Guide: Arctic And Antarctica
Arctic...man has only slightly penetrated and certainly not yet conquered the polar regions at the top of the world. Gunther Less explores this adventure filled land of oceans and ice, wild mountains, deep blue lakes and serene but dangerous floating icebergs. Antarctica...still almost unknown, the "white continent" of Antarctica is the most remote of all the world's places. Gunther views some of the awesome wonders of the highest, coldest, windiest spots on earth: the mysterious yet beautiful polar land.
32-6428 35 min. $16.95

Puerto Rico and the U.S. Virgin Islands
Join Video Visits and travel to sunny Puerto Rico beginning at El Morro, the Spanish fortress that once protected the island from marauders and would-be conquerors. Then stroll through Old San Juan, with its 16th-century atmosphere of pastel walls and wooden balconies.
32-5030 45 min. $24.95

RAND McNALLY TRAVEL GUIDES:

- **Alaska**
32-5529 55 min. $29.95

- **Australia**
32-5533 55 min. $29.95

• **Austria**
32-5542 50 min. $29.95

• **Bermuda, The Bahamas & Jamaica**
32-5531 55 min. $29.95

• **Central Florida**
32-291 60 min. $29.95

• **Colorado Golf Resorts**
32-5536 50 min. $29.95

• **Colorado Ski Resorts**
32-293 60 min. $29.95

• **Great Honeymoon Resorts**
32-5535 50 min. $29.95

• **Hawaii**
32-292 60 min. $29.95

• **Mexico's Beach Resorts**
32-5530 46 min. $29.95

• **New York City**
32-289 60 min. $29.95

• **Rio De Janeiro**
32-5534 45 min. $29.95

• **San Francisco**
32-290 60 min. $29.95

• **Ski New England**
32-294 60 min. $29.95

• **South Seas**
32-5532 60 min. $29.95

• **Vienna**
32-5543 50 min. $29.95

RAND McNALLY - THE NATIONAL PARK SERIES:

• **Glacier**
32-5541 47 min. $29.95

• **Grand Canyon**
32-5538 47 min. $29.95

• **Grand Teton**
32-5540 47 min. $29.95

• **Yellowstone**
32-5537 47 min. $29.95

• **Yosemite**
32-5539 47 min. $29.95

Touring Australia
This video captures the uniqueness of this beautiful nation, its harbors, beaches, forests and red deserts, all transformed into a colorful adventure story.
32-2432 48 min. $29.95

Travel With Barry and Corrine: India's Palace on Wheels
Join Barry & Corrine in this earthly travel documentary as they ride the railroad famously known as India's Palace on Wheels.
32-8280 60 min. $16.95

SOUTHWEST TRAVEL SERIES:

• **Trail to Rainbow Bridge**
In this inspirational video, an unforgettable adventure unfolds as the trail to Rainbow Bridge crosses some of the most rugged and inaccessible country in the entire Southwest to culminate at the Rainbow Bridge itself.
32-8242 55 min. $24.95

• **Grand Gulch**
Explore the Anasazi cliff dwellings of one of southeastern Utah's most intriguing and inaccessible canyon systems.
32-8243 50 min. $24.95

• **Salt: Untamed and Unpredictable**
Join a group of rafters and kayakers on a 55 mile trip down one of the most beautiful and exciting rivers in America.
32-8244 80 min. $24.95

• **Hiking Lake Powell**
32-8245 63 min. $24.95

Travel Without Terror
Author of the bestseller "Five Minutes to Midnight", Dr. Sabi H. Shabtal is an internationally known authority on terrorism and political violence. In this program, he provides a comprehensive, step-by-step guide for travelers to avoid, prevent and handle hijacking. He tells you how to prepare for a trip, what to wear and how to act during the trip, and vital first hand information that may save your life in the midst of a terrorist attack.
32-253 30 min. $39.95

Video Visits: Australia - Secrets of the Land Down Under
Sample the delights of Sydney, take a trek to the Outback of New South Wales, visit the busy cosmopolitan city of Melbourne, and much more.
32-1744 30 min. $24.95

VIDEO TITLES LISTED IN THIS GUIDE ARE AVAILABLE FOR PURCHASE OR RENTAL. CONTACT YOUR LOCAL VIDEO STORE OR TELEPHONE (800) 383-8811

Video Visits: New Zealand Coast to Coast

Explore this spectacular southwest Pacific Island, discover its many scenic wonders, attractions and activities in this colorful video tour.

32-1742 30 min. $24.95

Vizcya Museum and Gardens

Come discover the magical grandeur and beauty of Vizcaya - a magnificent Italian Renaissance-style villa built by James Deering in Florida, and now a renowned museum of European decorative arts. Unmatched in the Western hemisphere, this grand mansion and surrounding gardens, has often been referred to as the finest private house ever built in America. Each room is filled with magnificent centuries-old art treasures. Outside, the Gardens come to life with water fountains and music. Fully narrated with classical music accompaniment.

32-1705 30 min. $29.95

Wild Rides

Matt Dillon rides the rails of the country's most thrilling roller coasters in this music video experience.

32-1923 29 min. $24.95

Perfect for the

Armchair Traveler:

A Trip Down the Nile…

A Rendezvous in the

French Alps…

Have An Exciting Adventure

Without Leaving Your VCR!

VIDEO TITLES LISTED IN THIS GUIDE ARE AVAILABLE FOR PURCHASE OR RENTAL. CONTACT YOUR LOCAL VIDEO STORE OR TELEPHONE **(800) 383-8811**

New
Special Interest Video Titles
Become Available
Often.

Please Inquire
If A Title Or Subject
You Are Looking For
Is Not Listed.

Index

ABC

DEF

GHIJ

KLM

NOP

QRS

TUV

WXYZ

A

A.D., 506
AAA TRAVEL VIDEO
  SERIES:, 601
  Appalachian Trail:
  Kentucky, Tennessee,
  Virginia and West
  Virginia, 601
  California, 601
  Eastern Great Lakes, 601
  Florida, 601
  Great Plains: Arkansas,
  Kansas, Missouri,
  Oklahoma, Nebraska,
  601
  Gulf Coast: Texas,
  Louisiana, Mississippi
  and Alabama, 601
  Mid Atlantic:
  Pennsylvania, Maryland,
  Delaware and District of
  Columbia, 601
  New England, 601
  New York and New
  Jersey, 601
  North Central: North
  Dakota, South Dakota,
  Montana and Wyoming,
  601
  Pacific Northwest:
  Washington, Oregon and
  Idaho, 601
  Quebec and the Atlantic
  Provinces, 601
  Southeast: North Carolina,
  South Carolina and
  Georgia, 601
  Southwest: Colorado,
  Utah, Nevada, Arizona
  and New Mexico, 601
  Western Great Lakes, 601
Abandon Ship, 57
ABC Funfit: The Mary Lou
  Retton Workout For
  Kids, 105
ABC's of Basic Dressage,
  332
Abduction from the Seraglio,
  440
Abduction of Figaro, 440
Above And Beyond The Call
  Of Duty, 222
Abraham Lincoln By James
  McPherson, 48
Abraham Lincoln:
  Emancipation
  Proclamation, 193
Abraham's Sacrifice, 506

Acadia National Park and
  Cape Cod National
  Seashore, 452
Acapulco, 598
Accident Hazards Of Nuclear
  Power Plants, 465
Accounting, 364
Aces of the I.A.F., 30
Achieving Excellence, 71
ACOG: Postnatal Exercise
  Program, 502
ACOG: Pregnancy Exercise
  Program, 502
ACT Math Review, 2
ACT Verbal Review, 13
Acting Careers, 364
Action Photography, 494
ACTOR'S VIDEO
  LIBRARY SERIES, 364
  Building a Character, 364
  Combat for the Stage, 364
  Creative Drama &
  Improvisation, 364
  Directing Process, 364
  Make-up Workshop, 364
  Mime over Matter, 364
Acupressure, 307
Acupressure Facelift, 307
Adam's Garden, 506
Admiral's Cup 1987, 60
Adolescence, 382
Adolf Hitler, 48
Adrian Belew Electronic
  Guitar, 406
Advanced Centerpieces,
  One-Sided and Layered
  "Mass" Designs, 169
Advanced Chipping, 543
Advanced Country and Blues
  Harmonica, 415
Advanced dBase II Plus
  Literacy, 134
Advanced dBase III Plus
  Literacy, 134
Advanced Golf Swing, 543
Advanced Rock and Roll
  Bass, 406
Advanced Tarot, 396
Advanced Trolling for
  Saltwater Fish, 277
Advanced Wordperfect for
  Windows Version 5.1,
  134
Adventurcize, 105
Adventures in Caves, 5
ADVENTURES IN
  CHARACTER
  BUILDING, 506
  Good Samaritan, 506
  Story of Joseph, 506
ADVENTURES OF
  BABAR, 84
Adventures of Gallant

Bess, 84
Adventures of Hunting
  Trophy Caribou, 349
Adventures of Kauai, 596
Advertising: Tricks Of The
  Trade, 364
Aerobic Dancing: Medicine,
  Health and Exercise, 240
Aerobic Self-Defense, 240
Aerobic Yoga, 254
Aerobicise: The Beautiful
  Workout, 240
Aerobicise: The Beginning
  Workout, 240
Aerobicise: The Ultimate
  Workout, 240
Aerobics on the Easy Side,
  240
Aerobics: Medicine, Health
  & Exercise, 240
Aerobics: The Winner's
  Edge, 240
Aesop and His Friends, 84
AFRICA ARMCHAIR
  SAFARI SERIES:, 457
  Masai Mara Lions/Virunga
  Gorillas, 457
  Serengeti
  Migration/Amboseli
  Elephants, 457
African Adventure Safari,
  349
After the Driving Range...
  Then What?, 543
AFTER THE WARMING
  SERIES:, 465
Age of Ballyhoo, Narrated
  by Gloria Swanson, 193
Age of Intelligent Machines,
  134
Agricultural Hall of Fame,
  222
AIDS, 302
AIDS: Everything You and
  Your Family Need to
  Know...But Were Afraid
  to Ask, 302
AIDS: Answers For
  Everyone, 302
AIDS: Profile of an
  Epidemic, 302
AIDS: What You Need to
  Know, 302
Ailey Dances, 428
Air Born, 558
Air Force Academy: A
  Commitment To
  Excellence, 35
Air Force Story Series, 44
Air Power, 30
Air Strike, 30
Air Transport: Flight
  Services, 364

VIDEO TITLES LISTED IN THIS GUIDE ARE AVAILABLE FOR PURCHASE OR RENTAL. CONTACT YOUR LOCAL VIDEO STORE OR TELEPHONE (800) 383-8811

**VIDEO TITLES LISTED IN THIS GUIDE ARE AVAILABLE FOR PURCHASE
OR RENTAL. CONTACT YOUR LOCAL VIDEO STORE OR TELEPHONE (800) 383-8811**

VIDEO TITLES LISTED IN THIS GUIDE ARE AVAILABLE FOR PURCHASE
OR RENTAL. CONTACT YOUR LOCAL VIDEO STORE OR TELEPHONE (800) 383-8811

VIDEO TITLES LISTED IN THIS GUIDE ARE AVAILABLE FOR PURCHASE OR RENTAL. CONTACT YOUR LOCAL VIDEO STORE OR TELEPHONE (800) 383-8811

VIDEO TITLES LISTED IN THIS GUIDE ARE AVAILABLE FOR PURCHASE OR RENTAL. CONTACT YOUR LOCAL VIDEO STORE OR TELEPHONE (800) 383-8811

VIDEO TITLES LISTED IN THIS GUIDE ARE AVAILABLE FOR PURCHASE OR RENTAL. CONTACT YOUR LOCAL VIDEO STORE OR TELEPHONE (800) 383-8811

VIDEO TITLES LISTED IN THIS GUIDE ARE AVAILABLE FOR PURCHASE
OR RENTAL. CONTACT YOUR LOCAL VIDEO STORE OR TELEPHONE (800) 383-8811

VIDEO TITLES LISTED IN THIS GUIDE ARE AVAILABLE FOR PURCHASE
OR RENTAL. CONTACT YOUR LOCAL VIDEO STORE OR TELEPHONE (800) 383-8811

VIDEO TITLES LISTED IN THIS GUIDE ARE AVAILABLE FOR PURCHASE
OR RENTAL. CONTACT YOUR LOCAL VIDEO STORE OR TELEPHONE (800) 383-8811

VIDEO TITLES LISTED IN THIS GUIDE ARE AVAILABLE FOR PURCHASE OR RENTAL. CONTACT YOUR LOCAL VIDEO STORE OR TELEPHONE (800) 383-8811

VIDEO TITLES LISTED IN THIS GUIDE ARE AVAILABLE FOR PURCHASE
OR RENTAL. CONTACT YOUR LOCAL VIDEO STORE OR TELEPHONE (800) 383-8811

E

VIDEO TITLES LISTED IN THIS GUIDE ARE AVAILABLE FOR PURCHASE
OR RENTAL. CONTACT YOUR LOCAL VIDEO STORE OR TELEPHONE (800) 383-8811

F

VIDEO TITLES LISTED IN THIS GUIDE ARE AVAILABLE FOR PURCHASE
OR RENTAL. CONTACT YOUR LOCAL VIDEO STORE OR TELEPHONE (800) 383-8811

VIDEO TITLES LISTED IN THIS GUIDE ARE AVAILABLE FOR PURCHASE OR RENTAL. CONTACT YOUR LOCAL VIDEO STORE OR TELEPHONE (800) 383-8811

VIDEO TITLES LISTED IN THIS GUIDE ARE AVAILABLE FOR PURCHASE OR RENTAL. CONTACT YOUR LOCAL VIDEO STORE OR TELEPHONE (800) 383-8811

G

VIDEO TITLES LISTED IN THIS GUIDE ARE AVAILABLE FOR PURCHASE
OR RENTAL. CONTACT YOUR LOCAL VIDEO STORE OR TELEPHONE (800) 383-8811

VIDEO TITLES LISTED IN THIS GUIDE ARE AVAILABLE FOR PURCHASE
OR RENTAL. CONTACT YOUR LOCAL VIDEO STORE OR TELEPHONE (800) 383-8811

VIDEO TITLES LISTED IN THIS GUIDE ARE AVAILABLE FOR PURCHASE OR RENTAL. CONTACT YOUR LOCAL VIDEO STORE OR TELEPHONE (800) 383-8811

H

Hagler vs. Hearns, 539
Hair Loss Connection, 479
Hair: Know it...Grow it, 478
Haircutting at Home, 479
Hairstyling At Home, 479
HAL REED SERIES, 262
HALF SLAVE, HALF FREE SERIES, 50
Halter Showmanship, Fitting, 340
Hamlet, 235
Hammered Dulcimer, 417
Handel's Messiah: Complete Performance, 434
Handgun Safety, 482
Handling and Anchoring Your Boat, 58
Hank Williams, "The Show He Never Gave", 436
Hank Williams, Jr.: A Star Spangled Country Party, 436
Hans Christian Andersen's Fairy Tales, 89
Hansel and Gretel by Engelbert Humperdinck, 434
Happy Birdy - Hey It's Your Birthday!, 103
Hard Day's Night, 445
Harmonic Convergence, 315
Harmony, 499
Harness Racing, 287
Harness Racing: The Horse In Sport, 338
Harp and Voice, 417
Harry S. Truman Library and Museum, 199
Harvesting Fall Turkeys, 349
Have Fun Learning to Read, 98
Having Your Baby, 502
Havoc 7, 27
Hawaii, 596, 597
Hawaii Adventure for Kids, 89
Hawaii: Islands of Relaxation, 597
Hawaii With Laura Mckenzie, 597
Hawaii: A Pacific Paradise, 597
Hawaii: Sights and Sounds of the Islands, 597
Hawaii's Magic: Prince Lot Hula Festival, 449
Hawaii's Underwater

Paradise: Adventure Beneath the Sea, 597
Hawaiian Islands, 597
Hawaiian Paradise: Reader's Digest, 597
Hazards Of Being A Therapist, 375
Hazel's People, 514
Head to Toe: Soccer for Little Leaguers, 552
HEADLINE STORIES OF THE CENTURY, 199
America in Sports, 200
America in the News, 200
American Nostalgia, 200
World War II, 200
Healing Massage for Lovers & Friends, 307
Healing Power of Herbs: The European Tradition for Natural Herbs, 321
Healing Way Song: Tuning Body Energy, 315
Healing with Crystals, 315
Health & Beauty, 479
Health and Beauty with Lillian Grant, 315
Health Through God's Pharmacy: A Plant for Every Illness, 316
Health, Maintenance, Grooming, 336
Healthier Cooking For Time-Pressed People, 161
Healthy Back - Healthy Mind, 253
Healthy Cooking By Melissa Ann Homann, 161
Healthy Heart: "Say Goodbye To High Blood Pressure", 304
HEALTHY MASSAGE, 307
Back, 307
Legs and Feet, 307
Scalp, Face, Neck and Chest, 307
Hearst Castle: The Enchanted Hill, 226
HEARST METRO-TONE VIDEO GAZETTE SERIES, 212
WWII Volume I, 212
WWII Volume II, 212
WWII Volume III, 212
Heartbar Shoe, 337
Heartland Reggae, 449
Hearts and Minds, 212
Hearty New England Dinners, 161
Heavensent, 518
Heavy Metal Primer with Jay Jay French of Twisted

Sister, 410
Heidi Miller's Body Sculpting, 245
Heifetz, 434
Heil Hitler: Confessions of a Hitler Youth, 189
Helen Keller: Separate Views, 50
Helicopter-Safe Pilot, 38
Helicopters, 38
Hell for Leathernecks, 213
Hell on the Western Front, 213
Hell Over Korea, 31
Hell's Aces High, 32
Hello PC, 137
Help Save Planet Earth, 467
HELP!, 445
Helping Hands: The Right Way to Choose a Nursing Home, 316
Herbie Hancock Trio with Billy Cobham & Ron Carter, 439
Here We Go: Volume 1, 89
Here We Go: Volume 2, 89
Heritage of Glory, 213
HERITAGE TRAVEL SERIES, 590
Ireland & Your Irish Ancestry, 591
Scotland & Your Scottish Ancestry, 591
Wales & Your Welsh Ancestry, 591
Hey, What About Me?, 109
HIGH IMPACT COMMUNICATION SKILLS, 80
HIGH IMPACT LEADERSHIP, 72
High Plains Mulies: Method for Stalking and Driving, 353
High-Tech Workout, 245
Hiking the West Coast Trail, 564
Hinkler: The Lone Eagle, 39
Hip Hop Dancing, 402
His Land, 580
History, 39
History & Collecting, 22
History & Traditions Of Golf In Scotland, 545
History of Aviation, 39
History of Baseball, 532
History of Flight, 39
History of Naval Aviation, 39
History of the Apollo Program, 41
Hit It Farther With Betsy Cullen, 545

VIDEO TITLES LISTED IN THIS GUIDE ARE AVAILABLE FOR PURCHASE OR RENTAL. CONTACT YOUR LOCAL VIDEO STORE OR TELEPHONE (800) 383-8811

VIDEO TITLES LISTED IN THIS GUIDE ARE AVAILABLE FOR PURCHASE OR RENTAL. CONTACT YOUR LOCAL VIDEO STORE OR TELEPHONE (800) 383-8811

VIDEO TITLES LISTED IN THIS GUIDE ARE AVAILABLE FOR PURCHASE OR RENTAL. CONTACT YOUR LOCAL VIDEO STORE OR TELEPHONE (800) 383-8811

VIDEO TITLES LISTED IN THIS GUIDE ARE AVAILABLE FOR PURCHASE OR RENTAL. CONTACT YOUR LOCAL VIDEO STORE OR TELEPHONE (800) 383-8811

VIDEO TITLES LISTED IN THIS GUIDE ARE AVAILABLE FOR PURCHASE
OR RENTAL. CONTACT YOUR LOCAL VIDEO STORE OR TELEPHONE (800) 383-8811

VIDEO TITLES LISTED IN THIS GUIDE ARE AVAILABLE FOR PURCHASE OR RENTAL. CONTACT YOUR LOCAL VIDEO STORE OR TELEPHONE (800) 383-8811

VIDEO TITLES LISTED IN THIS GUIDE ARE AVAILABLE FOR PURCHASE OR RENTAL. CONTACT YOUR LOCAL VIDEO STORE OR TELEPHONE (800) 383-8811

VIDEO TITLES LISTED IN THIS GUIDE ARE AVAILABLE FOR PURCHASE OR RENTAL. CONTACT YOUR LOCAL VIDEO STORE OR TELEPHONE (800) 383-8811

VIDEO TITLES LISTED IN THIS GUIDE ARE AVAILABLE FOR PURCHASE
OR RENTAL. CONTACT YOUR LOCAL VIDEO STORE OR TELEPHONE (800) 383-8811

VIDEO TITLES LISTED IN THIS GUIDE ARE AVAILABLE FOR PURCHASE OR RENTAL. CONTACT YOUR LOCAL VIDEO STORE OR TELEPHONE (800) 383-8811

M

VIDEO TITLES LISTED IN THIS GUIDE ARE AVAILABLE FOR PURCHASE OR RENTAL. CONTACT YOUR LOCAL VIDEO STORE OR TELEPHONE (800) 383-8811

VIDEO TITLES LISTED IN THIS GUIDE ARE AVAILABLE FOR PURCHASE OR RENTAL. CONTACT YOUR LOCAL VIDEO STORE OR TELEPHONE (800) 383-8811

VIDEO TITLES LISTED IN THIS GUIDE ARE AVAILABLE FOR PURCHASE OR RENTAL. CONTACT YOUR LOCAL VIDEO STORE OR TELEPHONE (800) 383-8811

VIDEO TITLES LISTED IN THIS GUIDE ARE AVAILABLE FOR PURCHASE OR RENTAL. CONTACT YOUR LOCAL VIDEO STORE OR TELEPHONE (800) 383-8811

VIDEO TITLES LISTED IN THIS GUIDE ARE AVAILABLE FOR PURCHASE OR RENTAL. CONTACT YOUR LOCAL VIDEO STORE OR TELEPHONE (800) 383-8811

O

VIDEO TITLES LISTED IN THIS GUIDE ARE AVAILABLE FOR PURCHASE OR RENTAL. CONTACT YOUR LOCAL VIDEO STORE OR TELEPHONE (800) 383-8811

P

VIDEO TITLES LISTED IN THIS GUIDE ARE AVAILABLE FOR PURCHASE
OR RENTAL. CONTACT YOUR LOCAL VIDEO STORE OR TELEPHONE (800) 383-8811

VIDEO TITLES LISTED IN THIS GUIDE ARE AVAILABLE FOR PURCHASE OR RENTAL. CONTACT YOUR LOCAL VIDEO STORE OR TELEPHONE (800) 383-8811

VIDEO TITLES LISTED IN THIS GUIDE ARE AVAILABLE FOR PURCHASE OR RENTAL. CONTACT YOUR LOCAL VIDEO STORE OR TELEPHONE (800) 383-8811

Q

R

VIDEO TITLES LISTED IN THIS GUIDE ARE AVAILABLE FOR PURCHASE
OR RENTAL. CONTACT YOUR LOCAL VIDEO STORE OR TELEPHONE (800) 383-8811

S

VIDEO TITLES LISTED IN THIS GUIDE ARE AVAILABLE FOR PURCHASE
OR RENTAL. CONTACT YOUR LOCAL VIDEO STORE OR TELEPHONE (800) 383-8811

VIDEO TITLES LISTED IN THIS GUIDE ARE AVAILABLE FOR PURCHASE OR RENTAL. CONTACT YOUR LOCAL VIDEO STORE OR TELEPHONE (800) 383-8811

VIDEO TITLES LISTED IN THIS GUIDE ARE AVAILABLE FOR PURCHASE OR RENTAL. CONTACT YOUR LOCAL VIDEO STORE OR TELEPHONE (800) 383-8811

VIDEO TITLES LISTED IN THIS GUIDE ARE AVAILABLE FOR PURCHASE
OR RENTAL. CONTACT YOUR LOCAL VIDEO STORE OR TELEPHONE (800) 383-8811

VIDEO TITLES LISTED IN THIS GUIDE ARE AVAILABLE FOR PURCHASE
OR RENTAL. CONTACT YOUR LOCAL VIDEO STORE OR TELEPHONE (800) 383-8811

T

VIDEO TITLES LISTED IN THIS GUIDE ARE AVAILABLE FOR PURCHASE
OR RENTAL. CONTACT YOUR LOCAL VIDEO STORE OR TELEPHONE (800) 383-8811

VIDEO TITLES LISTED IN THIS GUIDE ARE AVAILABLE FOR PURCHASE OR RENTAL. CONTACT YOUR LOCAL VIDEO STORE OR TELEPHONE (800) 383-8811

VIDEO TITLES LISTED IN THIS GUIDE ARE AVAILABLE FOR PURCHASE OR RENTAL. CONTACT YOUR LOCAL VIDEO STORE OR TELEPHONE (800) 383-8811

U

VIDEO TITLES LISTED IN THIS GUIDE ARE AVAILABLE FOR PURCHASE
OR RENTAL. CONTACT YOUR LOCAL VIDEO STORE OR TELEPHONE (800) 383-8811

VIDEO TITLES LISTED IN THIS GUIDE ARE AVAILABLE FOR PURCHASE OR RENTAL. CONTACT YOUR LOCAL VIDEO STORE OR TELEPHONE (800) 383-8811

Resorts, 600
Video Tutor: Decimals, 4
Video Tutor: Fractions, 4
Video Tutor: Percents, 4
Video Tutor: Pre-Algebra, 4
Video Visits: Australia -
Secrets of the Land
Down Under, 612
Video Visits: New Zealand
Coast to Coast, 613
Video Wine Guide with Dick
Cavett, 155
Videoano: Beginning
Keyboard for Real
People, 422
VIDEOCOACH SOCCER
SERIES, 552
Ball Control, 552
Dribbling & Feinting, 552
Kicking, 552
Soccer Tips, 552
Soccerobics, 552
Super Skills & Heading,
552
Vidisco: SAT - Math, 4
Vidisco: SAT-Verbal, 14
Viennese Waltz, 406
Vietnam Choppers, 39
Vietnam Experience, 217
Vietnam Requiem, 217
Vietnam: In the Year of the
Pig, 217
Vietnam: The Air War, 218
Vietnam: The Secret Agent,
218
Vietnam: Time of the
Locust, 218
Vietnam: War at Home, 207
Vietnam: A Mission, 32
Vietnam: Remember!, 218
Vietnam: The News Story,
217
Vietnamese Cuisine, 153
Viktoria Mullova and Maxim
Shostakovich in
Performance, 435
Vintage Racing in the
Rockies, 22
Vinyl Floors, 326
Virginia Plantations: Mount
Vernon, Monticello and
Other Great Houses, 609
Virginia Wade's Visual
Tennis, 556
Visual Arts, 371
Visual Dynamics, 500
VISUAL HISTORY OF
CARS SERIES, 23
VISUAL TALES, 95
Father, the Son and the
Donkey, American Sign
Language, 95
Father, the Son and the

Donkey, Open
captioned, 95
Father, the Son and the
Donkey, Signed English,
95
Greedy Cat, American
Sign Language, 95
Greedy Cat, Open
captioned, 96
Greedy Cat, Signed
English, 95
House that Jack Built,
American Sign
Language, 96
House that Jack Built,
Open Captioned, 96
House that Jack Built,
Signed English, 96
Magic Pot, American Sign
Language, 96
Magic Pot, Open
captioned, 96
Magic Pot, Signed English,
96
Village Stew, American
Sign Language, 96
Village Stew, Open
Captioned, 96
Village Stew, Signed
English, 96
Vitamins & Nutrition For A
Healthier Life, 311
VITSIE VIDEO SITTER
Dinosaurs, 105
Oceanlife, 105
Space, 105
Vizcya Museum and
Gardens, 613
Vocal Coach Public Speaker
Video, 79
Vocal Ease: Care and
Exercise for the Singing
Voice, 423
Vocal Workout Video With
Chris & Carole Beatty,
423
VOCATIONAL VISIONS
CAREER SERIES, 371
Auto Mechanic, 371
Band Director, 371
Chef, 371
Florist, 371
Insurance Agent, 371
Letter Carrier, 371
National Park Ranger, 371
Paralegal, 371
Physical Therapist, 371
Potter, 371
Voice, 422
Voices from the Ice,
Alaska, 582
Voices Of Peace, 476
Volcano, 231

VOLCANO SCAPES
SERIES, 12
Volcanoes of The United
States, 12

W

W.C. Fields: On Stage, On
Screen, On The Air, 54
Waiting for the Wind, 517
Waking Up from Dope, 305
Walk Aerobics, 252
Walk in the Forest, 456
Wall Hangings, 169
Wall In Jerusalem, 231
Wall: The Making And
Breaking Of The Berlin
Wall, 191
Walleye Fishing Basics, 282
Walleye Strategies, 282
Walls, 326
Walls/Framing and Removal,
326
WALLSTREET WEEK
WITH LOUIS
RUKIESER, 71
Mutual Funds, Options &
Commodities, 71
Stocks, Bonds & Gold, 71
Wally's Workshop: Alarms
& Safes, 327
Waltz Dancin' Texas Style,
406
Wapiti Creek: Story of
American Elk, 350
War & Military History, 214
War Aces, 32
War and Peace, 238
War Between the States,
1860's, 207
War Birds of Chino, 35
War by the Shore: 1991
Ryder Cup, 548
WAR CHRONICLES
SERIES, 218
Battle of Germany, 218
Battle of the Bulge, 218
Beachhead at Anzio, 218
Bomber Offensive, Air
War Europe, 218
Desert War, 218
Greatest Conflict, 218
Normandy Invasion, 218
Pursuit of the Rhine, 218
War Comes to America, 218
War Hawks, 32
War in the Pacific, 218
War of Weeds, 296
WAR STORIES SERIES, 218

VIDEO TITLES LISTED IN THIS GUIDE ARE AVAILABLE FOR PURCHASE OR RENTAL. CONTACT YOUR LOCAL VIDEO STORE OR TELEPHONE (800) 383-8811

VIDEO TITLES LISTED IN THIS GUIDE ARE AVAILABLE FOR PURCHASE OR RENTAL. CONTACT YOUR LOCAL VIDEO STORE OR TELEPHONE (800) 383-8811

VIDEO TITLES LISTED IN THIS GUIDE ARE AVAILABLE FOR PURCHASE
OR RENTAL. CONTACT YOUR LOCAL VIDEO STORE OR TELEPHONE (800) 383-8811

VIDEO TITLES LISTED IN THIS GUIDE ARE AVAILABLE FOR PURCHASE OR RENTAL. CONTACT YOUR LOCAL VIDEO STORE OR TELEPHONE (800) 383-8811

Note:
An **UPPERCASE** listing within this **Index** denotes a video series which includes multiple titles.

ORDER FORM

Name _____ Phone (___) _____

Company Name _____

Address _____

City _____ State _____ Zip _____

NOTE: All addresses must include street name for UPS delivery.

Please send me the following items:

ITEM	QTY	TITLE	PRICE
PC COMPATIBLE COMPUTER DISK		**The Complete Guide To Special Interest Videos** $69.95 + $4.00 Shipping. *Specify 3 1/2 or 5 1/4*	
CD-ROM		**The Complete Guide To Special Interest Videos** $69.95 + $4.00 Shipping.	
GUIDE		**The Complete Guide To Special Interest Videos** $19.95 + $2.50 Shipping.	

SHIPPING CHARGES
Purchases: $4.00 for first tape, plus $1.50 for each additional tape. Alaska and Hawaii residents, add $1.00 for each tape.

Please make your check or money order payable to: **Video Learning Library.**

SUBTOTAL	
(Sales Tax 6.7% AZ)	
SHIPPING	
TOTAL	

☐ Please send me the 110-page book entitled **Selling Special Interest Videos As A Profitable Home-Based Business** @ $39.95 + $4.00 shipping.

✔ **Telephone Orders:** Call 800-383-8811 toll-free. Visa, MasterCard, Discover, American Express

✔ **FAX:** (602) 596-9973

✔ **Mail Orders:** Video Learning Library, 15838 N. 62nd Street, Scottsdale, AZ 85254

✔ **Payment:** ☐ Check ☐ Visa ☐ MasterCard ☐ Discover ☐ AMEX

Credit Card #: _____ Expires _____

Signature: _____

Please allow 4-6 weeks for delivery

FOLD HERE

NO POSTAGE
NECESSARY
IF MAILED
IN THE
UNITED STATES

BUSINESS REPLY MAIL

FIRST CLASS MAIL   PERMIT NO. 8   ALTA LOMA, CA

POSTAGE WILL BE PAID BY ADDRESSEE

VIDEO LEARNING LIBRARY
15838 N 62ND ST STE 101
SCOTTSDALE AZ 85254-9888

ORDER FORM

Name _____ Phone (___) _____

Company Name _____

Address _____

City _____ State _____ Zip _____

NOTE: All addresses must include street name for UPS delivery.

Please send me the following items:

ITEM	QTY	TITLE	PRICE
PC COMPATIBLE COMPUTER DISK		**The Complete Guide To Special Interest Videos** $69.95 + $4.00 Shipping. *Specify 3 1/2 or 5 1/4*	
CD-ROM		**The Complete Guide To Special Interest Videos** $69.95 + $4.00 Shipping.	
GUIDE		**The Complete Guide To Special Interest Videos** $19.95 + $2.50 Shipping.	

SHIPPING CHARGES
Purchases: $4.00 for first tape, plus
$1.50 for each additional tape.
Alaska and Hawaii residents, add
$1.00 for each tape.

Please make your check or money order
payable to: **Video Learning Library.**

SUBTOTAL	
(Sales Tax 6.7% AZ)	
SHIPPING	
TOTAL	

☐ Please send me the 110-page book entitled **Selling Special Interest Videos As A Profitable Home-Based Business** @ $39.95 + $4.00 shipping.

✔ **Telephone Orders:** Call 800-383-8811 toll-free. Visa, MasterCard, Discover, American Express

✔ **FAX:** (602) 596-9973

✔ **Mail Orders:** Video Learning Library, 15838 N. 62nd Street, Scottsdale, AZ 85254

✔ **Payment:** ☐ **Check** ☐ **Visa** ☐ **MasterCard** ☐ **Discover** ☐ **AMEX**

Credit Card #: _____ Expires _____

Signature: _____

Please allow 4-6 weeks for delivery

FOLD HERE

NO POSTAGE
NECESSARY
IF MAILED
IN THE
UNITED STATES

BUSINESS REPLY MAIL

FIRST CLASS MAIL   PERMIT NO. 8   ALTA LOMA, CA

POSTAGE WILL BE PAID BY ADDRESSEE

VIDEO LEARNING LIBRARY
15838 N 62ND ST STE 101
SCOTTSDALE AZ 85254-9888

ORDER FORM

Name _____ Phone ( ) _____

Company Name _____

Address _____

City _____ State _____ Zip _____

NOTE: All addresses must include street name for UPS delivery.

Please send me the following items:

ITEM	QTY	TITLE	PRICE
PC COMPATIBLE COMPUTER DISK		**The Complete Guide To Special Interest Videos** $69.95 + $4.00 Shipping. *Specify 3 1/2 or 5 1/4*	
CD-ROM		**The Complete Guide To Special Interest Videos** $69.95 + $4.00 Shipping.	
GUIDE		**The Complete Guide To Special Interest Videos** $19.95 + $2.50 Shipping.	

SHIPPING CHARGES **Purchases:** $4.00 for first tape, plus $1.50 for each additional tape. Alaska and Hawaii residents, add $1.00 for each tape. Please make your check or money order payable to: **Video Learning Library.**	SUBTOTAL _____ (Sales Tax 6.7% AZ) _____ SHIPPING _____ **TOTAL** _____

☐ Please send me the 110-page book entitled **Selling Special Interest Videos As A Profitable Home-Based Business** @ $39.95 + $4.00 shipping.

✔ **Telephone Orders:** Call 800-383-8811 toll-free. Visa, MasterCard, Discover, American Express

✔ **FAX:** (602) 596-9973

✔ **Mail Orders:** Video Learning Library, 15838 N. 62nd Street, Scottsdale, AZ 85254

✔ **Payment:** ☐ **Check** ☐ **Visa** ☐ **MasterCard** ☐ **Discover** ☐ **AMEX**

Credit Card #: _____ Expires _____

Signature: _____

Please allow 4-6 weeks for delivery

FOLD HERE

NO POSTAGE
NECESSARY
IF MAILED
IN THE
UNITED STATES

BUSINESS REPLY MAIL

FIRST CLASS MAIL   PERMIT NO. 8   ALTA LOMA, CA

POSTAGE WILL BE PAID BY ADDRESSEE

VIDEO LEARNING LIBRARY
15838 N 62ND ST STE 101
SCOTTSDALE AZ 85254-9888

ORDER FORM

Name _____ Phone (___) _____

Company Name _____

Address _____

City _____ State _____ Zip _____

NOTE: *All addresses must include street name for UPS delivery.*

Please send me the following items:

ITEM	QTY	TITLE	PRICE
PC COMPATIBLE COMPUTER DISK		**The Complete Guide To Special Interest Videos** $69.95 + $4.00 Shipping. *Specify 3 1/2 or 5 1/4*	
CD-ROM		**The Complete Guide To Special Interest Videos** $69.95 + $4.00 Shipping.	
GUIDE		**The Complete Guide To Special Interest Videos** $19.95 + $2.50 Shipping.	

SHIPPING CHARGES		
Purchases: $4.00 for first tape, plus $1.50 for each additional tape. Alaska and Hawaii residents, add $1.00 for each tape.	SUBTOTAL	
	(Sales Tax 6.7% AZ)	
Please make your check or money order payable to: **Video Learning Library.**	SHIPPING	
	TOTAL	

☐ Please send me the 110-page book entitled **Selling Special Interest Videos As A Profitable Home-Based Business** @ $39.95 + $4.00 shipping.

✔ **Telephone Orders:**   Call 800-383-8811 toll-free. Visa, MasterCard, Discover, American Express

✔ **FAX:**   (602) 596-9973

✔ **Mail Orders:**   Video Learning Library, 15838 N. 62nd Street, Scottsdale, AZ 85254

✔ **Payment:**   ☐ **Check**   ☐ **Visa**   ☐ **MasterCard**   ☐ **Discover**   ☐ **AMEX**

Credit Card #: _____   Expires _____

Signature: _____

Please allow 4-6 weeks for delivery

FOLD HERE

NO POSTAGE
NECESSARY
IF MAILED
IN THE
UNITED STATES

BUSINESS REPLY MAIL

FIRST CLASS MAIL   PERMIT NO. 8   ALTA LOMA, CA

POSTAGE WILL BE PAID BY ADDRESSEE

VIDEO LEARNING LIBRARY
15838 N 62ND ST STE 101
SCOTTSDALE AZ 85254-9888